Organization of the Text

Each chapter in Units 1, 2, and 3 of *Canadian Jensen's Nursing Health Assessment* begins with specific learning objectives. Starting with Unit 2, the chapters follow a consistent organization to facilitate learning and highlight the key content needed for a full understanding of health assessment in nursing.

Case Study (woven throughout)

Presents a patient with a health concern corresponding to the chapter focus; ongoing related information, exercises to promote learning, and patient details continue throughout the chapter.

Anatomy and Physiology Overview

Reviews anatomy and physiology, with additional content on variations according to lifespan and culture or genetic background.

Acute Assessment

Summarizes emergency signs and symptoms to look for and immediate assessments and interventions.

Subjective Data Collection

Focuses on health history questions related to areas for health promotion and risk reduction, risk factors, risk assessment, important topics for health promotion, and focused assessments of common symptoms and signs. Questions to assess history, risk factors, and symptoms/signs are accompanied by rationale. Additional questions associated with lifespan and/or cultural variations are included, as well as examples of documentation.

Objective Data Collection

Covers equipment; promoting patient comfort, dignity, and safety; physical examination techniques; expected findings; unexpected findings; lifespan and cultural adaptations; and examples of documentation.

Evidence-Informed Critical Thinking

Discusses methods for organizing and prioritizing history and physical examination findings, key laboratory and diagnostic test results, and foundations for clinical reasoning.

Tables of Unexpected Findings

Clusters common alterations in health related to the assessment being explored, with compare-and-contrast information on key data points.

Brief Table of Contents

UNIT 1 Foundations of Nursing Health Assessment 1

1 The Nurse's Role in Health Assessment 3
2 The Interview and Therapeutic Dialogue 20
3 The Health History 37
4 Techniques of Physical Examination and Equipment 52
5 Documentation and Interprofessional Communication 69

UNIT 2 General Examinations 89

6 General Survey and Vital Signs Assessment 91
7 Pain Assessment 125
8 Nutrition Assessment 152
9 Assessment of Developmental Stages 185
10 Mental Health Assessment 204
11 Assessment of Social, Cultural, and Spiritual Health 231
12 Assessment of Human Violence 248

UNIT 3 Regional Examinations 265

13 Skin, Hair, and Nails Assessment 267
14 Head and Neck with Lymphatics Assessment 326
15 Eyes Assessment 351
16 Ears Assessment 387
17 Nose, Sinuses, Mouth, and Throat Assessment 414
18 Thorax and Lungs Assessment 452
19 Cardiovascular Assessment 493
20 Peripheral Vascular and Lymphatic Assessment 536
21 Breasts and Axillae Assessment 571
22 Abdominal Assessment 602
23 Musculoskeletal Assessment 645
24 Neurological Assessment 697
25 Male Genitalia and Rectal Assessment 755
26 Female Genitalia and Rectal Assessment 789

UNIT 4 Special Populations and Foci 831

27 Women Who Are Pregnant 833
28 Newborns and Infants 863
29 Children and Adolescents 899
30 Older Adults 925

UNIT 5 Putting It All Together 957

31 Head-to-Toe Assessment of the Adult 959

Answers to Review Questions 981
Illustration Credit List 983
Index 987

Canadian Jensen's Nursing Health Assessment

A BEST PRACTICE APPROACH

Tracey C. Stephen, MN, RN
D. Lynn Skillen, PhD, RN
Rene A. Day, PhD, RN
Faculty of Nursing
University of Alberta
Edmonton, Alberta, Canada

Sharon Jensen, MN, RN
School of Nursing
Seattle University
Seattle, Washington, United States

. Wolters Kluwer | Lippincott Williams & Wilkins
Health

Philadelphia · Baltimore · New York · London
Buenos Aires · Hong Kong · Sydney · Tokyo

Acquisitions Editor: Elizabeth Nieginski
Product Manager: Helene T. Caprari
Editorial Assistants: Jacalyn Clay & Zachary Shapiro
Design Coordinator: Joan Wendt
Manufacturing Coordinator: Karin Duffield
Prepress Vendor: SPi Global

Printed in the United States of America

Library of Congress Cataloging-in-Publication Data
Canadian Jensen's nursing health assessment : a best practice approach / Tracey C. Stephen ... [et al.].
    p. ; cm.
  Jensen's nursing health assessment
  Nursing health assessment
  Companion vol. to: Nursing health assessment / Sharon Jensen. c2011.
  Includes bibliographical references and index.
  ISBN 978-1-4511-4369-0
  1. Nursing assessment. I. Stephen, Tracey C. II. Jensen, Sharon, 1955- Nursing health assessment. III. Title: Jensen's nursing health assessment. IV. Title: Nursing health assessment.
  [DNLM: 1. Nursing Assessment—methods—Canada. 2. Medical History Taking—methods—Canada. 3. Physical Examination—methods—Canada. WY 100.4]
  RT48.C355 2011
  616.07′5—dc23
                                      2011026639

LWW.com

9 8 7 6 5 4 3 2 1

Acknowledgments

The Nursing Education staff at Wolters Kluwer Health are truly invested in nursing and on the frontlines of health care. We would like to thank several specific people:

- **Helene Caprari** has been a strong supporter and tireless Product Manager for a book that is based upon current pre-registration clinical experience, although advanced techniques for advanced practice nurses also are included. Helene supported the authors as they ensured that Canadian standards, guidelines, terminology, and practice were represented.
- **Jacalyn Clay & Zachary Shapiro** delivered the contracts and kept things organized during busy days.
- **Elizabeth Nieginski** attended to all the administrative details.

We truly hope that this text lays out real-life situations so that nursing students and registered nurses understand the importance of observation, with subjective and objective assessments as the essential processes on which all nursing is based.

Inspiration

"The most important practical advice that can be given to nurses is to teach them what to observe."

(Florence Nightingale, *Notes on nursing: What it is and what it is not*, 1860)

Dedication

Tracey Stephen
- To Andy, Jenelle, Taylir, and Mackenna for all that you are. There are not enough words to describe how much I love you.
- To my friends and colleagues for all your support and encouragement.
- To the nursing students and nurses I am so privileged to work with. Thank you.

D. Lynn Skillen
- To my students past and present who raised the questions that needed answering
- To my colleagues and friends who encouraged me at every step of the way.
- To Christie, Sofie, and JC for their trust, confidence, and unconditional support

Rene A. Day
- To nursing students and registered nurses, may you be successful in gaining the necessary knowledge and skills of health assessment and in applying them to clinical practice.
- To my husband Wayne, for his patient and unwavering support, and his technical expertise.
- To Jason and Mary, and Stephen, Cher and Victoria, for understanding why the dining room table was always covered with book chapters.

Sharon Jensen
- To my parents, who instilled in me my strong work ethic and understanding of community.
- To my husband, who has been my most loyal supporter.
- I appreciate the sacrifices of my children, Anna and Eric Jensen.
- To Kathy and Mark and my social network and all of the wonderful faculty and staff at Seattle University, a teaching university forming nursing leaders focused on vulnerable populations in the heart of Seattle.

Contributors: *Canadian Jensen's Nursing Health Assessment: A Best Practice Approach*

Seanna Chesney-Chauvet, MN, RN
Faculty Lecturer
Faculty of Nursing
University of Alberta
Edmonton, Alberta
Chapter 28: Newborns and Infants

Rene A. Day, PhD, RN
Professor Emerita
Faculty of Nursing
University of Alberta
Edmonton, Alberta
Chapter 7: Pain Assessment
Chapter 8: Nutrition Assessment
Chapter 9: Assessment of Developmental Stages
Chapter 18: Thorax and Lungs Assessment
Chapter 20: Peripheral Vascular and Lymphatic Assessment
Chapter 21: Breasts and Axillae Assessment
Chapter 26: Female Genitalia and Rectal Assessment
Chapter 27: Women Who Are Pregnant

Gerri C. Lasiuk, PhD, RN
Assistant Professor
Faculty of Nursing
University of Alberta
Edmonton, Alberta
Chapter 10: Mental Health Assessment

Stewart MacLennan, MN, NP, RN
Faculty Lecturer
Faculty of Nursing
University of Alberta
Edmonton, Alberta
Chapter 13: Skin, Hair, and Nails Assessment
Chapter 15: Eyes Assessment
Chapter 23: Musculoskeletal Assessment

Lori Pollard, MN, RN
Faculty Lecturer
Faculty of Nursing
University of Alberta
Edmonton, Alberta
Chapter 27: Women Who Are Pregnant

Sheri Roach, BComm, BJ, BScN, RN
MN/MHA Candidate
Dalhousie University
Halifax, Nova Scotia
Chapter 22: Abdominal Assessment

D. Lynn Skillen, PhD, RN
Professor Emerita
Faculty of Nursing
University of Alberta
Edmonton, Alberta
Chapter 1: The Nurse's Role in Health Assessment
Chapter 4: Techniques of Physical Examination and Equipment
Chapter 6: General Survey and Vital Signs Assessment
Chapter 11: Assessment of Social, Cutural, and Spiritual Health
Chapter 19: Cardiovascular Assessment
Chapter 23: Musculoskeletal Assessment
Chapter 24: Neurological Assessment
Chapter 25: Male Genitalia and Rectal Assessment
Chapter 30: Older Adults
Chapter 31: Head-to-Toe Assessment of the Adult

Tracey C. Stephen, MN, RN
Faculty Lecturer
Faculty of Nursing
University of Alberta
Edmonton, Alberta
Chapter 2: The Interview and Therapeutic Dialogue
Chapter 3: The Health History
Chapter 5: Documentation and Interprofessional Communication
Chapter 12: Assessment of Human Violence
Chapter 13: Skin, Hair, and Nails Assessment
Chapter 14: Head and Neck with Lymphatics Assessment
Chapter 15: Eyes Assessment
Chapter 16: Ears Assessment
Chapter 17: Nose, Sinuses, Mouth, and Throat Assessment
Chapter 29: Children and Adolescents
Chapter 31: Head-to-Toe Assessment of the Adult

Additional Contributors to *Canadian Jensen's Nursing Health Assessment: A Best Practice Approach*

Joan Anderson, PhD
Professor Emerita
School of Nursing
University of British Columbia
Vancouver, British Columbia

Judy A. Bornais, MSc, RN
Experiential Learning Specialist
Faculty of Nursing
University of Windsor
Windsor, Ontario

Angela Bowen, PhD, RN
Associate Professor
College of Nursing and Associate Member
Department of Psychiatry
College of Medicine
University of Saskatchewan
Saskatoon, Saskatchewan

Annette Browne, PhD, RN
Professor
School of Nursing
University of British Columbia
Vancouver, British Columbia

Kim Brunet-Wood, MSc, RD
Nutrition Services Director
Alberta Health Services
Capital Region
Edmonton, Alberta

William L. Diehl-Jones, PhD, RN
Associate Professor
Faculty of Nursing and Faculty of Science
University of Manitoba
Winnipeg, Manitoba

Dana S. Edge, PhD, RN
Associate Professor
School of Nursing
Queen's University
Kingston, Ontario

Nicole Harder, MPA, RN
Coordinator
Simulation Learning Centres
Faculty of Nursing
University of Manitoba
Winnipeg, Manitoba

Kathleen Hunter, PhD, RN
Assistant Professor
Faculty of Nursing
University of Alberta
Edmonton, Alberta

Kaysi Eastlick Kushner, PhD, RN
Associate Professor
Faculty of Nursing
University of Alberta
Edmonton, Alberta

Janice A. Lander, PhD, RN
Professor
Faculty of Nursing
University of Alberta
Edmonton, Alberta

Gerri C. Lasiuk, PhD RN
Assistant Professor
Faculty of Nursing
University of Alberta
Edmonton, Alberta

Diana Mager, PhD, RD
Assistant Professor
Clinical Nutrition
Agricultural, Life and Environmental Sciences
University of Alberta
Edmonton, Alberta

Linda Reutter, PhD, RN
Professor Emerita
Faculty of Nursing
University of Alberta
Edmonton, Alberta

Sheri Roach, BComm, BJ, BScN, RN
MN/MHA Student
Dalhousie University
Halifax, Nova Scotia

Pat Roddick, MHSA, RN
Instructor
School of Nursing
Grant MacEwan University
Edmonton, Alberta

Sarla Sethi, PhD, RN
Associate Professor (Retired)
Faculty of Nursing
University of Calgary
Calgary, Alberta

Colleen Varcoe, PhD, RN
Professor
School of Nursing
University of British Columbia
Vancouver, British Columbia

Contributors: *Nursing Health Assessment: A Best Practice Approach*

Yvonne D'Arcy, MS, CRNP, CNS
Pain Management and Palliative Care Nurse Practitioner
Suburban Hospital
Bethesda, Maryland
Chapter 7: Pain Assessment

Karen S. Feldt, PhD, ARNP, GNP
Associate Professor
College of Nursing, Seattle University
Seattle, Washington
Chapter 30: Older Adults

Cynthia Flynn, MSN, CNM, PhD, ARNP
General Director
Family Health and Birth Center
Washington, DC
Chapter 28: Newborns and Infants

Nan Gaylord, PhD, RN, CPNP
Associate Professor
University of Tennessee, College of Nursing
Knoxville, Tennessee
Chapter 29: Children and Adolescents

Nancy George, PhD, FNP-BC
Assistant Professor (Clinical)
Wayne State University
Detroit, Michigan
Chapter 15: Eyes Assessment

Constance Hirnle, MN, RN, BC
Sr. Lecturer, SON, and Education Specialist
University of Washington Virginia Mason Medical Center
Seattle, Washington
*Chapter 5: Documentation and Interdisciplinary
   Communication*

Kathy Kleefisch, RN
Instructor
Purdue University at Calumet
Calumet, Indiana
Chapter 25: Male Genitalia and Rectal Assessment

N. Jayne Klossner, MSN, RNC
Director, Patient Care Improvement
Baptist Health System
San Antonio, Texas
Chapter 27: Pregnant Women

Margaret Kramper, RN, FNP
Allergy Sinus Nurse Coordinator
Department of Otolaryngology/Head and Neck Surgery
Washington University
St. Louis, Missouri
Chapter 17: Nose, Sinuses, Mouth, and Throat Assessment

Sharon Kumm, RN, MN, MS, CCRN
Clinical Associate Professor
University of Kansas
Kansas City, Kansas
Chapter 23: Musculoskeletal Assessment

Janet Lohan, PhD, RN, CPN
Clinical Associate Professor
Washington State University
Spokane, Washington
Chapter 9: Assessment of Developmental Stages

Amy Metteer-Storer, RN, BSN, MSN
Assistant Professor of Nursing
Cedar Crest College
Bethlehem, Pennsylvania
Chapter 20: Peripheral Vascular and Lymphatic Assessment

Jennifer Mussman, RN, ARNP
Clinical Instructor
Seattle University
Seattle, Washington
Chapter 16: Ears Assessment

Michelle Pardee, MS, FNP-BC
Lecturer
University of Michigan, School of Nursing
Ann Arbor, Michigan
Chapter 15: Eyes Assessment

Debra A. Phillips, PhD, PMHNP
Associate Professor
Seattle University College of Nursing
Seattle, Washington
Chapter 12: Assessment of Human Violence

Margaret S. Pierce, DNP, FNP-BC
Assistant Professor
University of Tennessee College of Nursing
Knoxville, Tennessee
Chapter 14: Head and Neck with Lymphatics Assessment

Barbara Rideout, MSN
Nurse Practitioner
Drexel University College of Medicine
Department of Family, Community, and Preventive
   Medicine
Philadelphia, Pennsylvania
Chapter 22: Abdominal Assessment

Debra Lee Servello, RNP, MSN
Assistant Professor of Nursing
Rhode Island College School of Nursing
Providence, Rhode Island
Chapter 6: General Survey and Vital Signs Assessment

Ann St. Germain, MSN, ANP-BC, WHNP-BC
Assistant Clinical Professor
Texas Woman's University, College of Nursing
Houston, Texas
Chapter 26: Female Genitalia and Rectal Assessment

Karen Gahan Tarnow, RN, PhD
Clinical Associate Professor
University of Kansas School of Nursing
Kansas City, Kansas
Chapter 23: Musculoskeletal Assessment

Lisa Trigg, PhD, PMHNP-BC
Instructor
University of Kansas
Kansas City, Kansas
Chapter 23: Musculoskeletal Assessment

Joyce B. Vazzano, MS, APRN, BC, CRNP
Instructor
Johns Hopkins University School of Nursing
Baltimore, Maryland
Chapter 21: Breasts and Axillae Assessment

Deborah Webb, RN (Deceased)
Neurological Clinical Nurse Specialist
Harborview Medical Center
Seattle, Washington
Chapter 24: Neurological Assessment

Mary P. White, MSN, APRN, BC
Clinical Instructor
Director, Campus Health Center
Wayne State University College of Nursing
Detroit, Michigan
Chapter 13: Skin, Hair, and Nails Assessment

Danuta Wojnar, PhD, RN
Assistant Professor
Seattle University, College of Nursing
Seattle, Washington
*Chapter 11: Assessment of Social, Cultural, and Spiritual
   Health*

Reviewer: *Canadian Jensen's Nursing Health Assessment: A Best Practice Approach*

Kathleen Hunter, PhD, RN
Assistant Professor
Faculty of Nursing
University of Alberta
Edmonton, Alberta
Chapter 30: Older Adults

Reviewers: *Nursing Health Assessment: A Best Practice Approach*

Marianne Adam, MSN, CRNP
Assistant Professor
Moravian College
Bethlehem, Pennsylvania

Colleen Andreoni, MSN, APRN, BC-NP
Instructor, Marcella Niehoff School of Nursing
Loyola University Chicago
Chicago, Illinois

Terri J. Ashcroft, RN, MN
Instructor, Faculty of Nursing
University of Manitoba
Winnipeg, Manitoba

Debra L. Benbow, MSN, APRN, FNP-BC
Assistant Professor of Nursing
Winston Salem State University
Winston Salem, North Carolina

Adrienne Berarducci, PhD, ARNP, CS
Associate Professor
University of South Florida at Tampa
Tampa, Florida

Jayne Bielecki, RN, BSN, MPH&TM
Clinical Instructor
University of Wisconsin at Eau Claire
Eau Claire, Wisconsin

Judy Bornais, MSc, RN
Experiential Learning Specialist and Lecturer
University of Windsor
Windsor, Ontario

Judith Young Bradford, RN, DNS, FAEN
Associate Professor, School of Nursing
Southeastern Louisiana University
Hammond, Louisiana

Linda M. Caldwell, PhD, APRN
Professor of Nursing
Curry College
Milton, Massachusetts

Celestine Carter, APRN, DNS
Assistant Professor of Clinical Nursing
Louisiana State University Health Sciences Center
New Orleans, Louisiana

Pamella I. Chavis, MSN, RN
Clinical Assistant Professor
North Carolina Agricultural and Technical State University
School of Nursing
Greensboro, North Carolina

Janis Childs, PhD, RN
Professor and Director of Learning Resources and Simulation
Center
University of Southern Maine
Portland, Maine

Michael S. Congemi, ACNP-BC, MSN
Acute Care Nurse Practitioner, Research Scientist and
Clinical Instructor
University of Wisconsin, Milwaukee & Alverno College
Milwaukee, Wisconsin

Valorie Dearmon, RN, DNP, CNAA-BC
Assistant Clinical Professor
University of South Alabama College of Nursing
Mobile, Alabama

Joseph T. DeRanieri, MSN, RN, CPN, BCECR
Assistant Professor, Faculty of Nursing
Thomas Jefferson University
Philadelphia, Pennsylvania

Holly Diesel, PhD, RN
Assistant Professor
Goldfarb School of Nursing at Barnes Jewish College
St. Louis, Missouri

Martha A. Donagrandi, BSN, MSN
Faculty of Nursing
Madonna University
Livonia, Michigan

Kimberly N. Dunker, MSN, RN
Associate Professor of Nursing
Atlantic Union College
South Lancaster, Massachusetts

Mary Ann Fegan, RN, BNSc, MN
Lecturer, Faculty of Nursing
University of Toronto
Toronto, Ontario

Susan Hall, EdD(C), MSN, RNC, CCE, C-EFM
Instructor
Winston Salem State University
Winston Salem, North Carolina

Diana D. Hankes, APRN, BC, PhD
Clinical Associate Professor
Marquette University
Milwaukee, Wisconsin

Nicole Harder, MPA, RN
University of Manitoba
Faculty of Nursing
Winnipeg, Manitoba

Karen Ippolito, RN, MSN, FNP
Instructor
San Joaquin Delta College
Stockton, California

Kynthia James, RN-MSN
Instructor
Southwest Georgia Technical College
Thomasville, Georgia

Pat Keene, PhD
Instructor
Union University
Germantown, Tennessee

Fadi Khraim, RN, ACNP, PhD
Assistant Professor, Hahn School of Nursing and
Health Science
University of San Diego
San Diego, California

Shantia McCoy, MSN, CRNP
Assistant Professor of Nursing
LaSalle University
Philadelphia, Pennsylvania

John J. McNulty, MS, RN, BC
Instructor
University of Connecticut
Storrs, Connecticut

Anna P. Moore, MS
Associate Professor
J. Sargeant Reynolds Community College
Richmond, Virginia

Michelle Perkins, RN
Instructor
University of Akron
Akron, Ohio

Karen Piotrowski, RN, MS
Instructor
D'Youville College
Buffalo, New York

Nikki Pittman, MSN, RNC-OB
Instructor
University of Mississippi School of Nursing
Jackson, Mississippi

Chris Poitras, RN, BN, MHSA
Faculty
Saskatchewan Institute of Applied Science and Technology
Regina, Saskatchewan

Nancy A. Prince, MSN, RN, FNP
Assistant Professor
Eastern Michigan University
Ypsilanti, Michigan

Susan M. Randol, RN
Instructor
University of Louisiana at Lafayette
Lafayette, Louisiana

Stephanie A. Reagan, MSN, CNS
Assistant Professor of Nursing
Malone College
Canton, Ohio

Susan Reeves, RN
Assistant Professor of Nursing
Tennessee Technical University at Cookville
Cookville, Tennessee

John Silver, RN, PhDc, FINL
Assistant Professor of Nursing
NOVA Southeastern University
Ft. Lauderdale, Florida

John Stone, RN
Faculty of Nursing
Humber Polytechnic
Toronto, Ontario

Gloria Ann Jones Taylor, DSN, RNc
Professor of Nursing
Kennesaw State University
Kennesaw, Georgia

Jill Thornton, RN
Suffolk County Community College at Selden
Selden, New York

Nancy Whitman, PhD, RN
Faculty of Nursing
Lynchburg College
Lynchburg, Virginia

Mary Wilby, PhD (c), MSN, RN, CRNP
Assistant Professor, Nursing
LaSalle University
Philadelphia, Pennsylvania

Tamara Wright, RN, MSN
Clinical Instructor
The University of Texas at Arlington
Arlington, Texas

Alice B. Younce, DNP, RN
Associate Professor of Nursing
University of Mobile
Mobile, Alabama

Erica Teng-Yuan Yu, PhD
Assistant Professor, School of Nursing
The University of Texas Health Science Center at Houston
Houston, Texas

Preface

Canadian Jensen's Nursing Health Assessment: A Best Practice Approach reflects a progressive and modern view of nursing practice in the Canadian context. The text combines elements of traditional health assessment texts with innovative elements that facilitate understanding of how best to obtain accurate data from patients. It not only includes thorough and comprehensive examinations for each specific topic, but also presents strategies for adapting questions and techniques when communication is challenging, the patient's responses are unexpected, or the patient's condition changes over time. Unique features assist with application and analysis, enhancing critical thinking skills and better preparing all readers for active practice.

A real-life approach is introduced at the beginning of each chapter and continued throughout. This includes recurring features that provide related questions, additional data, and variations that challenge the nurse to modify responses. These cases encourage the progressive building and synthesis of knowledge. They require critical thinking and clinical reasoning to analyze data, document, plan for care, and communicate findings. Additionally, other features, ancillary material, and media related to the book build on the in-text cases to reinforce correct elements of subjective data collection, objective data collection, and variations necessary for different conditions, age groups, and cultures/genetic backgrounds in Canada.

In addition to the case studies, other distinctive aspects of this text include the following:

- **Emphasis on health promotion, risk reduction, evidence-informed critical thinking, and clinical reasoning.** The book's introductory units provide foundational explanations of these core threads. The emphasis on health promotion, risk factors, and prevention reflect the text's forward-thinking stance and underscores the key role of nurses as partners with and advocates for patients. Each chapter ends with a demonstration of how to use critical thinking and clinical reasoning to cluster data and to analyze findings.
- **Distinctions between common techniques and advanced practice skills.** Recurring features within the Subjective Data and Objective Data sections differentiate focused versus comprehensive assessments, indicating how to modify approaches based on circumstances. The Subjective Data section includes questions about risk factors, health history issues, and common symptoms/signs, with follow-up questions for positive responses. A recurring table in the Objective Data section explains which techniques are more commonly performed in routine examinations to distinguish basic from advanced practice. This structure helps users prepare for actual patient interactions, as well as to modify techniques for individual situations.
- **Distinctive two-column format emphasizes not just techniques and findings, but also ways to differentiate expected data, common variations, and unexpected findings.** Like many health assessment books, this text uses a two-column presentation to differentiate techniques and findings. This text goes another step, however, by differentiating expected responses and variations of unexpected findings.. Expected findings are italicized in the left column, and unexpected findings are in the right column. Pictures of unexpected findings are generally grouped together in tables at the very end of the chapters. This structure facilitates quick and easy comparing and contrasting of findings and conditions.
- **Emphasis on knowledge application and analysis.** End-of-chapter review sections contain questions and critical thinking challenges related to the previously established case

study. Additionally, the last section of each chapter focuses on prioritizing and modifying assessments to promote the best care possible and summarizing all findings to create an appropriate plan for the patient's health.

Organization of the Text

Unit 1, *Foundations of Nursing Health Assessment,* provides in-depth coverage of the basic components of nursing health assessment. The rest of the text builds on and expands the material in this first unit. Chapter 1 explicates the nurse's role in assessment. Chapter 2 reviews the importance of effective communication and interviewing. Chapter 3 explores history taking in subjective data collection, while Chapter 4 outlines the techniques, common equipment, approaches, and process of physical examination for objective data collection. With Chapter 5, the unit concludes with information on the important components of documenting findings and sharing them with the interprofessional team. Using the correct terminology, principles of recording, and accurate documenting are important, especially avoiding the words "good," "poor," and "normal." This factor is highlighted by italicizing the expected findings in the left column and describing the unexpected findings in the right column.

Unit 2, *General Examinations,* presents those assessments consistently applicable to all patients, regardless of age, gender, culture, health status, or circumstance. These topics reflect the holistic nature of nursing health assessment, as opposed to the traditional medical model that generally focuses on the physical domain and "body systems." Topics in Unit 2 include General Survey and Vital Signs (Chapter 6); Pain (Chapter 7); Nutrition including Medications and Supplements (Chapter 8); Developmental Stages (Chapter 9); Mental Health and Mental Status (Chapter 10); Social, Cultural, and Spiritual Health (Chapter 11); and Human Violence (Chapter 12).

Unit 3, *Regional Examinations,* presents individual chapters focusing on assessment of the key areas of the body, beginning with the integument and ending with the genital and rectal examinations. The material focuses primarily on adults; lifespan and cultural variations and considerations are highlighted throughout.

Unit 4, *Special Populations and Foci,* synthesizes previous discussions for different lifespan groups and presents summational content of assessments for women who are pregnant, newborns and infants, children and adolescents, and older adults. The content in Units 2 and 3 explicate what is different, unique, or in need of modification for specific age groups when approaching the various assessments discussed. The content in Unit 4 describes how to synthesize and apply these understandings to comprehensive assessments for maternal, pediatric, and geriatric populations.

Unit 5, *Pulling It All Together,* reinforces the book's earlier content by outlining how to complete a full, comprehensive, head-to-toe examination for an adult. This is a summary of the units previously studied in depth.

Chapter Organization and Features

Case Features

Progressive case study material is woven throughout every chapter. From the beginning to the end of the content presentation, readers follow a patient's story and are challenged to apply their reading to the unfolding scenario. A recurring structure serves as a mechanism for supplying more information but also for reinforcing the core assessment foundations of critical thinking, therapeutic communication, documentation, analysis of findings, interprofessional collaboration, and "pulling it all together."

- **Chapter Opener:** The case begins with a picture, reading, and bulleted list of three to five questions. These elements introduce the patient and generate beginning issues to consider.
- **Therapeutic Dialogue:** These displays provide examples of therapeutic communication with patients. "Critical Thinking Challenges" offer an opportunity for the reader to consider how the nurse might gather more information. These dialogues in Units 2 to 5 consistently end the sections on Subjective Data.

- **Analyzing Findings:** This feature focuses on documented summaries of findings related to the case in four areas: Subjective Data (S), Objective Data (O), Analysis (A), and Plan (P). This "SOAP" format follows the nursing process, with assessment as the first and most important step.
- **Documenting Unexpected Findings:** This feature summarizes unexpected findings relevant to the case study patient from the physical examination: Inspection, Palpation, Percussion, and Auscultation. These are the techniques used in objective health assessment.
- **Collaborating With the Interprofessional Team:** This unique feature describes scenarios in which the nurse in the case must coordinate referrals or other advocacy needs for the patient. The feature shows how to organize details using the SBAR framework: **S**ituation, **B**ackground, **A**nalysis (or **A**ssessment), and **R**ecommendations. A Critical Thinking Challenge ends the section, prompting the reader to consider how the nurse might better communicate findings and recommendations.
- **Pulling It All Together:** A table shows how to bring all the elements of assessment together when arriving at a nursing diagnosis based on current findings and includes beginning to develop goals, interventions, rationale, and evaluation criteria.
- **Applying Your Knowledge:** This last case-related feature in the chapters includes summary text and presents bulleted questions related to the six dimensions of critical thinking: Knowledge, Comprehension, Application, Analysis, Synthesis, and Evaluation. This feature shows how assessment generates intervention, evaluation, and collaboration based upon accurate and complete data to generate more effective care.

Other Features
- **Learning Objectives:** These objectives present the most important goals for learning by completion of the chapter.
- **Clinical Significance:** This feature highlights content critically related to a point of application. It may appear wherever appropriate in the chapter.
- **Safety Alert:** These recurring boxes present important areas of concern or results that require immediate intervention or adjustments. Safety Alert features are placed wherever applicable in the chapter. Not all acute features are labelled, but the most common ones are highlighted.
- **Equipment Needed:** This box reviews essential equipment relative to each assessment that the nurse will need to identify, gather, and clean, and gather before beginning the physical examination.
- **Key Points:** Key points are summarized at the end of each chapter to reinforce the most important information.
- **Review Questions:** Each chapter has 10 test questions. The case study and related critical thinking questions are a higher level of thinking. They should be discussed with an instructor.
- **Unexpected Findings:** Tables of unexpected findings are located at the end of the chapters. Art or tables of expected findings may be integrated into the chapter in the appropriate location, but comparative depictions of unexpected findings generally are found in groups at the end of the chapter.

Icons
 This designation is used to designate content specifically related to lifespan-oriented issues.

 This icon is found with material specifically related to culturally-oriented issues.

 This icon sets off Unexpected Findings Tables at the end of the chapter.

 This icon clues readers to visit thePoint or their accompanying DVD-ROM to review a corresponding video asset.

 This icon clues readers to visit thePoint or their accompanying DVD-ROM to review a corresponding animation.

 This icon clues readers to visit thePoint or their accompanying DVD-ROM to access an interactive media element.

A Comprehensive Package for Teaching and Learning

To further facilitate teaching and learning, a carefully designed ancillary package is available. In addition to the usual print resources, Wolters Kluwer Health is pleased to present multimedia tools that have been developed in conjunction with *Canadian Jensen's Nursing Health Assessment: A Best Practice Approach.*

thePoint (http://thepoint.lww.com/Stephen1E) provides every resource that instructors and students need in one easy-to-use site. Advanced technology and superior content combine at **thePoint** to allow instructors to design and deliver online and offline courses, maintain grades and class rosters, and communicate with students. Students can visit **thePoint** to access supplemental multimedia resources to enhance their learning experience, check the course syllabus, download content, upload assignments, and join an on-line study group. ThePoint … where teaching, learning, and technology click!

Resources for Students

thePoint Students can visit http//thepoint.lww.com/Stephen1E to access supplemental multimedia resources that enhance the learning experience:

- More than 500 self-study questions
- Concepts in Action™ Animations
- Watch and Learn™ Videos
- Journal Articles
- Clinical Simulations
- And more!

Canadian Jensen's Laboratory Manual for Nursing Health Assessment. Available at bookstores or at www.LWW.com, this student laboratory manual presents various exercises to reinforce textbook content and enhance learning. It is very helpful for students to complete these exercises before laboratory practice.

Resources for Instructors

thePoint Instructors can visit http//thepoint.lww.com/Stephen1E to access supplemental multimedia resources that enhance the teaching experience:

- A thoroughly revised and augmented test generator, containing more than 500 NCLEX-style questions
- Sample syllabi
- PowerPoint™ lectures with guided lecture notes
- Pre-lecture quizzes
- Image bank
- Discussion topics
- Assignments
- Case studies
- And more!

Contents

Acknowledgments/Inspiration/Dedication v

Contributors vii

Reviewers xi

Preface xv

UNIT 1 Foundations of Nursing Health Assessment 1

1 The Nurse's Role in Health Assessment 3
Role of the Professional Nurse 4
  Advocacy 5
  Scholarship and Research 5
  Registered Nurse and Advanced Practice Nurse
    Roles 5
Purposes of Health Assessment 5
Wellness and Health Promotion 6
  Health Promotion and Health Assessment 6
  Focused Health History Related to the Case
    Study 6
  Risk Assessment and Health Promotion 7
The Nursing Process 7
  Phases of the Nursing Process 7
    Assessment 8
    Diagnosis 8
    Planning Goals and Outcomes 8
    Planning Care 8
    Intervention/Implementation 8
    Evaluation 9
  Critical Thinking 9
  Clinical Reasoning 9
Types of Health Assessments 10
  Emergency Assessment 10
  Comprehensive Assessment 11
  Focused Assessment 11
Priority Setting 11
Frequency of Health Assessment 11
Lifespan Issues 12
Cultural and Environmental Considerations 12
Components of the Health Assessment 13
Documentation and Communication 14
**Organizing Frameworks for Health
  Assessment 15**
Evidence-Informed Critical Thinking 16

2 The Interview and Therapeutic Dialogue 20
Communication Process 21
  Nonverbal Communication Skills 22
  Verbal Communication Skills 23
    Active Listening 23
    Restatement 23
    Reflection 23
    Encouraging Elaboration (Facilitation) 24
    Silence 24
    Focusing 24
    Clarification 24
    Summarizing 24
  Nontherapeutic Responses 24
    False Reassurance 24
    Sympathy 25
    Unwanted Advice 25
    Biased Questions 26
    Changes of Subject 26
    Distractions 26
    Technical or Overwhelming Language 26
    Interrupting 26
Professional Expectations 27
Phases of the Interview Process 27
  Preinteraction Phase 27
  Beginning Phase 27
  Working Phase 28
  Closing Phase 28
Intercultural Communication 28
  Patients with Limited English 29
  Working with an Interpreter 30
  Gender and Sexual Orientation Issues 30
  Lifespan Issues 31
    Newborns and Infants 31
    Children and Adolescents 31
    Older Adults 32
Special Situations 32
  Patients with Hearing Impairment 32
  Patients with Altered Level of
    Consciousness 32
  Patients with Cognitive Impairment 33
  Patients with Mental Health Illness 33
  Patients with Anxiety 33
  Patients Who Are Crying 33
  Patients Who Are Angry 33
  Patients Under the Influence of Alcohol
    or Drugs 33
  Personal Questions 34
  Sexual Aggression 34

3 The Health History 37

Primary and Secondary Data Sources 38
Reliability of the Source 38
Components of the Health History 38
  Demographical Data or Identifying Data 39
  Reason for Seeking Care or Chief Concern 40
  Present Illness 40
    Pain Goal 40
    Functional Goal 40
  Past Health History 40
  Current Medications and Indications 40
  Family History 42
  Functional Health Assessment 43
  Growth and Development 43
  Review of Systems 44
Psychosocial and Lifestyle Factors 47
  Social, Cultural, and Spiritual Assessment 47
  Mental Health 47
  Human Violence 48
  Sexual History and Orientation 48
Lifespan Considerations 48
  Women Who Are Pregnant 48
  Newborns, Children, and Adolescents 48
  Older Adults 49
Cultural and Environmental Considerations 49

4 Techniques of Physical Examination and Equipment 52

Overview of Anatomical Terms 53
  Anatomical Position 53
  Anatomical Surfaces 53
  Anatomical Quadrants 53
  Anatomical Regions 53
  Anatomical Terms of Comparison and
    Movement 54
Routine Practices and Additional Precautions 55
  Hand Hygiene 55
  Routine Practices 56
  Additional Precautions 57
  Latex Allergy 57
  Skin Reactions 58
Subjective Data Collection 59
Objective Data Collection 59
  Promoting Patient Comfort, Dignity, and
    Safety 59
Inspection 59
Palpation 60
  Light Palpation 60
  Deep Palpation 61
**Characteristics of Sound and Sound
  Transmission 61**
Percussion 62
  Direct Percussion 62
  Indirect Percussion 62
Auscultation 63
Lifespan Considerations 65
  Women Who Are Pregnant 65
  Newborns and Infants 65
  Children and Adolescents 65
  Older Adults 65
Cultural Considerations 65
  Advanced Techniques 65

5 Documentation and Interprofessional Communication 69

Patient Health Record 70
  Purposes of the Patient Health Record 70
    Legal Document 70
    Communication and Care Planning 70
    Quality Assurance 70
    Education 71
    Research 71
  Components of the Patient Health Record 71
  Electronic Patient Health Record 71
  Principles Governing Documentation 71
    Confidential 72
    Accurate and Complete 72
    Organized 73
    Timely 73
    Concise 74
  Critical Thinking and Clinical Judgment 75
  Nursing Admission Assessment 75
  Flow Sheets 75
  Plan of Care/Clinical Pathway 75
  Progress Note 75
    Narrative Notes 80
    SOAP Notes 82
    PIE Notes 82
    Focus Note 82
  Charting by Exception 82
  Discharge Note 83
  Written Handoff Summary 83
Verbal Communication 83
  Verbal Handoff 83
  Reporting 83
    Qualities of Effective Reporting 84
    SBAR 84
    Reporting with other Health Care
      Professionals 84
  Telephone Communication 85
  Patient Rounds and Conferences 86
  Critical Thinking and Clinical Judgment 86

UNIT 2 General Examinations 89

6 General Survey and Vital Signs Assessment 91

Acute Assessment 92
Objective Data Collection 92
  Promoting Patient Comfort, Dignity, and
    Safety 92
  General Survey: General Inspection 92
    Physical Appearance 93
    Behaviour 93
    Mobility 94
    Height 95
    Weight 95
  Anthropometric Measurements 95
  Vital Signs 96
    Temperature 97
    Pulse 100
    Respirations 103
    Oxygen Saturation 104
    Blood Pressure 105

Risk Assessment and Health Promotion 111
Vital Signs Monitor 112
Doppler Technique 112
Lifespan Variations 112
Infants and Children 113
Older Adults 113
Infants and Children 113
Older Adults 117
Cultural Variations 118
Evidence-Informed Critical Thinking 118

7 Pain Assessment 125
Anatomy and Physiology Overview 126
Peripheral Nervous System 126
Central Nervous System 126
Gate Control Theory 127
Nociception 127
Pain Classification 128
Duration: Acute Pain 128
Duration: Chronic (Persistent) Pain 128
Frequency: Continuous or Intermittent/
Episodic Pain 129
Form: Nociceptive Pain 129
Form: Neuropathic Pain 129
Location 130
Etiology 130
Association with Cancer 130
Lifespan Considerations 130
Newborns, Infants, and Children 130
Older Adults 130
Cultural Considerations 131
Acute Assessment 131
Subjective Data Collection 131
Risk Assessment and Health Promotion 131
Location 132
Quality/(Description) 132
Quantity (Intensity) 132
Timing 132
Setting 132
Associated Symptoms 132
Alleviating Factors 132
Aggravating Factors 133
Environmental Factors 133
Significance to the Patient 133
Patient Perspective 133
Pain Management Goal 133
Functional Goal 133
Focused Health History Related to Common
Symptoms/Signs 134
Pain Measurement/Assessment Tools 134
One-Dimensional Pain Scales 134
Multidimensional Pain Scales 135
Objective Data Collection 139
Promoting Patient Comfort, Dignity, and
Safety 139
Comprehensive Physical Examination: Pain 140
Lifespan Considerations 141
Newborns, Infants, and Children 141
Older Adults 143
Special Situations 143
Patients Unable to Report Pain 143
Patients With Opioid Tolerance 143

Nursing Diagnoses, Outcomes, and
Interventions 144
Reassessing and Documenting Pain 144
Barriers to Pain Assessment 146
Evidence-Informed Critical Thinking 146

8 Nutrition Assessment 152
Nutritional Concepts 153
Primary Nutrients 153
Carbohydrates 153
Proteins 153
Lipids 153
Vitamins and Minerals 154
Supplements 154
Fluid and Electrolytes 154
Food Safety and Food Security 155
Nutritional Guidelines 156
Lifespan Considerations 156
Women Who Are Pregnant 156
Infants, Children, and Adolescents 157
Adults/Older Adults (Age 51 to 70+ years) 157
Cultural Considerations 158
Collecting Nutritional Data 159
Acute Assessment 160
Subjective Data Collection 160
Assessment of Risk Factors 160
Personal History 160
Medications and Supplements 161
Food and Fluid Intake Patterns 162
Psychosocial Profile 162
Family History 163
Risk Assessment and Health Promotion 163
Focused Health History Related to Common
Symptoms/Signs 163
Comprehensive Nutritional History 163
Changes in Body Weight 163
Change in Eating Habits 163
Symptoms of Malnutrition 163
Food Records 164
Direct Observation 165
Lifespan Considerations 165
Women Who Are Pregnant 165
Newborns, Infants, and Children 166
Adolescents 167
Older Adults 167
Objective Data Collection 169
Promoting Patient Comfort, Safety, and
Dignity 169
Physical Assessment 169
Body Type 169
General Appearance 169
Swallowing 170
Elimination 170
Body Mass Index 170
Weight Calculations 170
Percentage of Ideal Body Weight 170
Recent Weight Change 171
Percent Usual Body Weight 171
Waist Circumference 171
Waist-to-Hip Ratio 172
Skinfold Thickness 172
Mid Upper Arm Muscle Circumference 173

Derived Measures (Using MAMC and TSF) 173
Lifespan Considerations 175
Women Who Are Pregnant 175
Infants, Children, and Adolescents 175
Older Adults 176
Evidence-Informed Critical Thinking 176
Common Laboratory and Diagnostic
Testing 176
Serum Proteins 176
Hemoglobin and Hematocrit 176
Lymphocyte Count 176
Creatinine Excretion 176
Nitrogen Balance 176
Skin Testing 176
Lipid Measurements 176
Other Laboratory Tests 176
Clinical Reasoning 177
Nursing Diagnosis, Outcomes, and
Interventions 177

9 Assessment of Developmental Stages 185
Subjective Data Collection 186
Psychosocial Development 186
Infant: Trust Versus Mistrust 186
Toddler: Autonomy Versus Shame and
Doubt 186
Preschooler: Initiative Versus Guilt 186
School-age Child: Industry Versus
Inferiority 186
Adolescent: Identity Versus Role
Confusion 186
Early Adult: Intimacy Versus Isolation 188
Middle Adult: Generativity Versus Self-
Absorption 188
Late Adult: Ego Integrity Versus Despair 188
Cognitive Development 188
Infant: Sensorimotor 188
Toddler and Preschooler: Preoperational 188
School-Age Child: Concrete Operational 190
Adolescent: Formal Operations 191
Young Adult: Formal Operations 191
Middle Adult: Cognitive Expertise 192
Older Adult: Wisdom 192
Language Development 194
Cultural Considerations 194
Objective Data Collection 196
Physical Growth 196
Motor Development 196
Evidence-Informed Critical Thinking 198
Clinical Reasoning 201

10 Mental Health Assessment 204
**Role of the Nurse in Mental Health and Psychiatric
Assessment 205**
Acute Assessment 206
Subjective Data Collection 206
Risk Assessment and Health Promotion 206
Anxiety 206
Depression 207
Suicide 207
Dementia 207
Addiction 207

Canada's National Mental Health Strategy:
Toward Recovery and Well-Being 208
Assessment of Risk Factors 208
Identification/Biographical Data 208
Current Health Status 208
Past Health History 209
Medications 210
Psychological Trauma 210
Family History 210
Psychosocial 210
Cultural Background/Spirituality 212
Focused Health History Related to Common
Symptoms 213
Altered Mood and Affect 213
Suicidal Ideation 214
Homicidal Ideation and Aggressive
Behaviour 214
Auditory Hallucinations 215
Visual Hallucinations 215
Other Hallucinations 215
Lifespan Considerations 216
Women who Are Pregnant 216
Children and Adolescents 216
Older Adults 216
Cultural Considerations 217
Using an Interpreter for the Patient With a
Mental Health Condition 217
Objective Data Collection 218
A: Appearance 219
Overall Appearance 219
Posture 219
Movement 219
Hygiene and Grooming 219
Dress 219
B: Behaviour 220
Level of Consciousness 220
Eye Contact and Facial Expressions 220
Speech 220
C: Cognitive Function 221
Orientation 221
Attention Span 221
Memory 221
Judgment 221
T: Thought Processes and Perceptions 222
Mini-Mental Status/Mini-Cog 222
Set Test 222
Assessment of Dementia, Confusion, Delirium,
and Depression 223
Evidence-Informed Critical Thinking 223
Nursing Diagnoses 223
Patient Outcomes 223
Nursing Diagnosis, Outcomes, and
Interventions 225

**11 Assessment of Social, Cultural,
and Spiritual Health 231**
Models of Health 232
Social Assessment 233
Social Assessment of the Individual 233
Social Assessment of the Community 233
Social Assessment at the Societal Level 237
Cultural Assessment 237

Characteristics of Culture 237
Aims of Cultural Assessment 237
Cultural Health Beliefs and Practices 239
  Cultural Food and Nutrition Practices 239
  Cultural Beliefs and Practices of Pregnancy
    and Childbirth 239
  Cultural Beliefs and Expressions of Illness and
    Pain 240
Spiritual Assessment 240
Evidence-Informed Critical Thinking 242
Nursing Diagnoses, Outcomes,
  and Interventions 242

12 Assessment of Human Violence 248
Types of Human Violence 249
Family Violence 249
  Child Maltreatment 250
  Sibling Violence 250
  Intimate Partner Violence 250
  Elder Abuse 251
Violence Against Adults with Disabilities 251
"Youth" and School Violence 251
  Punking and Bullying 251
Sexual Violence 252
Hate Crimes 252
Human Trafficking 252
War-Related and Military Violence 252
Importance of Violence safety assessment 252
Subjective Data Collection 253
Interviewing Patients About Human Violence 253
Objective Data Collection 255
Documentation 256
Mandated Reporting 256
Lifespan Considerations 257
  Women Who Are Pregnant 257
  Infants, Children, and Adolescents 257
  Older Adults 258
Cultural Considerations 258
Evidence-Informed Critical Thinking 258
Nursing Diagnoses, Outcomes, and
  Interventions 258

UNIT 3 Regional Examinations 265

13 Skin, Hair, and Nails Assessment 267
Anatomy and Physiology Overview 268
Skin 268
  Epidermis 268
  Dermis 269
  Subcutaneous Layer 269
Hair 269
Nails 269
Glands 269
Lifespan Considerations 269
  Women Who Are Pregnant 269
  Newborns and Infants 270
  Children and Adolescents 270
  Older Adults 272
Cultural Considerations 272
Acute Assessment 273
Subjective Data Collection 273

Assessment of Risk Factors 273
  Personal History 274
  Medications 276
  Family History 277
  Lifestyle, Occupational History, and Personal
    Behaviours 277
Risk Assessment and Health Promotion 278
Focused Health History Related to Common
  Symptoms 280
  Pruritus (Itching) 281
  Rash 281
Lifespan Considerations 282
  Women Who Are Pregnant 282
  Newborns, Infants, and Children 282
  Adolescents 282
  Older Adults 283
Cultural Considerations 283
Objective Data Collection 284
Promoting Patient Comfort, Dignity, and Safety 284
Common and Specialty or Advanced
  Techniques 285
Comprehensive Skin Assessment 285
  Inspection: Skin 285
  Inspection: Nails 289
  Inspection: Hair 290
  Palpation: Skin 290
  Palpation: Nails 290
  Palpation: Hair 290
Lifespan Considerations 291
  Women Who are Pregnant 291
  Newborns, Infants, Children, and
    Adolescents 292
  Older Adults 293
Evidence-Informed Critical Thinking 293
Organizing and Prioritizing 293
Common Laboratory and Diagnostic Testing 293
Clinical Reasoning 293
  Nursing Diagnosis, Outcomes, and
    Interventions 293

**14 Head and Neck with Lymphatics
    Assessment 326**
Anatomy and Physiology Overview 327
The Head 327
The Neck 327
  Trachea 328
  Thyroid and Parathyroid Glands 329
Lymphatics 329
Lifespan Considerations 329
  Women Who Are Pregnant 329
  Newborns, Infants, and Children 330
  Older Adults 330
Cultural Considerations 330
Acute Assessment 330
Subjective Data Collection 331
Assessment of Risk Factors 331
  Personal History 332
  Medications 332
  Family History 332
Risk Assessment and Health Promotion 332
Focused Health History Related to Common
  Symptoms 333

Headache 333
Neck Pain 333
Limited Neck Movement 334
Facial Pain 334
Lumps or Masses 334
Symptoms/Signs of Hypothyroidism 334
Symptoms/Signs of Hyperthyroidism 334
Lifespan Considerations 335
Women Who Are Pregnant 335
Newborns and Infants 335
Children and Adolescents 335
Older Adult 335
Cultural Considerations 335
Objective Data Collection 335
Promoting Patient Comfort, Dignity, and
Safety 335
Common and Specialty or Advanced
Techniques 336
Comprehensive Physical Examination 337
Inspection 337
Palpation 338
Auscultation 340
Lifespan Considerations 341
Women Who Are Pregnant 341
Infants and Children 341
Older Adult 341
Evidence-Informed Critical Thinking 342
Common Laboratory and Diagnostic Testing 342
Clinical Reasoning 342
Nursing Diagnosis, Outcomes, and
Interventions 342

15 Eyes Assessment 351

Anatomy and Physiology Overview 352
Extraocular Structures 352
Extraocular Muscle Function 352
Intraocular Structures 353
Vision 354
Lifespan Considerations 354
Women Who Are Pregnant 354
Newborns and Infants 355
Children and Adolescents 355
Older Adults 355
Cultural Considerations 355
Acute Assessment 355
Subjective Data Collection 355
Assessment of Risk Factors 355
Current Concerns 356
Personal History 356
Medications 356
Family History 356
Risk Factors 356
Risk Assessment and Health Promotion 357
Focused Health History Related to Common
Symptoms 357
Pain 358
Trauma or Surgery 358
Visual Change 358
Blind Spots, Floaters, or Halos 358
Discharge 358
Change in Activities of Daily Living 358
Lifespan Considerations 359
Women Who Are Pregnant 359

Newborns, Infants, and Children 359
Older Adults 359
Objective Data Collection 360
Promoting Patient Comfort, Safety,
and Dignity 360
Common and Advanced Techniques 360
Assessment of Visual Acuity 361
Assessment of Visual Fields 361
Distance Vision 361
Near Vision 362
Colour Vision 362
Static Confrontation 363
Kinetic Confrontation 363
Assessment of Extraocular Muscle
Movements 364
Corneal Light Reflex 364
Cover Test 364
Cardinal Directions 365
Lacrimal Apparatus 366
Bulbar Conjunctiva 366
Sclera 367
Eversion of the Eyelid 367
Assessment of Exterior Ocular
Structures 368
Cornea and Lens 368
Iris 368
Pupils 368
Assessment of External Eyes 369
Assessment of Internal Ocular Structures 369
Lifespan Considerations 372
Infants, Children, and Adolescents 372
Older Adults 372
Cultural Considerations 373
Evidence-Informed Critical Thinking 373
Clinical Reasoning 373

16 Ears Assessment 387

Anatomy and Physiology Overview 388
External Ear 388
Middle Ear 388
Inner Ear 388
Hearing 390
Air and Bone Conduction 390
Hearing Disorders 391
Vestibular Function 391
Lifespan Considerations 391
Women Who Are Pregnant 391
Newborns, Infants, and Children 391
Adolescents 392
Older Adults 392
Cultural Considerations 393
Acute Assessment 393
Subjective Data Collection 393
Areas of Health Promotion 393
Assessment of Risk Factors 393
Personal History 394
Medications 394
Family History 394
Risk Factors 394
Risk Assessment and Health Promotion 395
Focused Health History Related to Common
Symptoms 395
Hearing Loss 396

Feeling Dizzy (Vertigo) 396
Ringing in Ears (Tinnitus) 396
Ear Pain (Otalgia) 396
Lifespan Considerations 397
Newborns, Infants, and Children 397
Objective Data Collection 398
Promoting Patient Comfort, Dignity, and
Safety 398
Inspection 398
Palpation 399
Whisper Test 399
Rinne Test 399
Weber Test 401
Otoscopic Evaluation 401
Auditory Acuity 403
Equilibrium 403
Lifespan Considerations 404
Infants and Children 404
Older Adults 405
Evidence-Informed Critical Thinking 406
Common Laboratory and Diagnostic Testing 406
Clinical Reasoning 406
Nursing Diagnosis, Outcomes, and
Interventions 406

17 Nose, Sinuses, Mouth, and Throat
Assessment 414
Anatomy and Physiology Overview 415
Nose 415
Nerve and Blood Supply 416
Lymph Drainage 416
Sinuses 416
Mouth 417
Tongue 417
Salivary Glands 418
Teeth and Gums 419
Throat 419
Lifespan Considerations 419
Women Who Are Pregnant 419
Infants and Children 419
Older Adults 420
Cultural Considerations 420
Acute Assessment 420
Subjective Data Collection 420
Assessment of Risk Factors 421
Personal History 422
Medications and Supplements 422
Dental Health 423
Psychosocial History 423
Family History 423
Environment Exposure 423
Risk Assessment and Health Promotion 424
Facial Pressure, Pain, and Headache 424
Snoring and Sleep Apnea 424
Focused Health History Related to Common
Symptoms/Signs 424
Obstructed Breathing 425
Nasal Congestion 425
Nosebleed (Epistaxis) 425
Bad breath (Halitosis) 425
Decreased Sense of Smell (Anosmia) 425
Cough 425

Sore Throat (Pharyngitis) 425
Difficulty Swallowing (Dysphagia) 425
Dental Pain 425
Voice Changes 425
Oral Lesions 425
Lifespan Considerations 426
Women Who are Pregnant 426
Infants and Children 426
Cultural Considerations 427
Objective Data Collection 428
Promoting Patient Comfort, Dignity, and
Safety 428
Common and Advanced Techniques 428
Comprehensive Physical Examination: Nose,
Sinuses, Mouth, and Throat 428
External Nose 428
Internal Nose 428
Sinuses 429
Mouth 430
Throat 433
Swallowing Evaluation 434
Lifespan Considerations 434
Women Who are Pregnant 434
Newborns, Infants, and Children 434
Older Adult 435
Cultural Considerations 436
Evidence-Informed Critical Thinking 437
Common Laboratory and Diagnostic
Testing 437
Clinical Reasoning 437
Nursing Diagnosis, Outcomes, and
Interventions 437

18 Thorax and Lungs Assessment 452
Anatomy and Physiology Overview 453
The Thorax 453
Anterior Thoracic Landmarks 453
Posterior Thoracic Landmarks 454
Reference Lines 455
Lobes of the Lungs 456
Lower Respiratory Tract 457
Upper Respiratory Tract 458
Mechanics of Respiration 458
Lifespan Considerations 458
Women Who Are Pregnant 458
Infants and Children 458
Older Adults 458
Cultural Considerations 459
Acute Assessment 459
Subjective Data Collection 459
Assessment of Risk Factors 459
Personal History 460
Medications 460
Family History 461
Lifestyle and Personal Habits 461
Occupational History 461
Environmental Exposures 462
Risk Assessment and Health Promotion 462
Smoking Cessation 462
Prevention of Occupational Exposure 463
Prevention of Asthma 463
Immunizations 463

Focused Health History Related to Common
  Symptoms 463
  Patient Perspective 464
  Chest Pain 464
  Dyspnea 464
  Orthopnea and Paroxysmal Nocturnal
    Dyspnea 464
  Cough 464
  Sputum 465
  Wheezing 465
  Functional Abilities 465
Lifespan Considerations 466
  Women Who Are Pregnant 466
  Newborns, Infants, and Children 466
  Older Adults 466
Cultural Considerations 467
Objective Data Collection 467
Promoting Patient Comfort, Dignity, and
  Safety 467
Common and Advanced Techniques 467
Initial Survey 468
Comprehensive Physical Examination 470
  Posterior Chest 470
  Anterior Chest 477
Lifespan Considerations 480
  Women Who Are Pregnant 480
  Newborns, Infants, and Children 480
  Older Adults 481
Evidence-Informed Critical Thinking 482
Organizing and Prioritizing 482
Laboratory and Diagnostic Testing 483
Clinical Reasoning 484
  Nursing Diagnoses, Outcomes, and
    Interventions 484

19 Cardiovascular Assessment 493
Anatomy and Physiology Overview 494
Anatomy 494
  Neck Vessels 494
  Heart Chambers 496
  Valves 496
  Heart Wall 496
  Coronary Arteries and Veins 496
Conduction System 497
Physiology 497
  Pulmonary and Systemic Circulation 497
  Cardiac Cycle 497
  Jugular Pulsations 499
Lifespan Considerations 499
  Women Who are Pregnant 499
  Newborns and Infants 500
  Children and Adolescents 500
  Older Adults 500
Cultural Considerations 501
Acute Assessment 502
Subjective Data Collection 502
Assessment of Risk Factors 502
  Past Medical History 503
  Medications 504
  Family History 504
  Lifestyle and Behavioural Issues 504
Risk Assessment and Health Promotion 505

Smoking Cessation 505
Control of Blood Pressure and Cholesterol
  Level 505
Control of Weight and Stress 505
Focused Health History Related to Common
  Symptoms/Signs 505
  Chest Pain 506
  Dyspnea 506
  Orthopnea and Paroxysmal Nocturnal
    Dyspnea 507
  Cough 507
  Diaphoresis 507
  Fatigue 507
  Edema 507
  Nocturia 507
  Palpitations 508
Lifespan Considerations 508
  Women Who are Pregnant 508
  Newborns and Infants 508
  Children and Adolescents 508
  Older Adults 509
Cultural Considerations 509
Objective Data Collection 510
Promoting Patient Comfort, Dignity, and
  Safety 510
Comprehensive Physical Examination:
  Cardiovascular System 510
  Jugular Venous Pulses Inspection 510
  Jugular Venous Pressures 511
  Hepatojugular Reflux Inspection and
    Palpation 512
  Carotid Arteries Inspection 512
  Auscultation 512
  Palpation 513
  Inspection of the Precordium 514
  Palpation of the Precordium 514
  Percussion of the Precordium 514
  Auscultation of the Precordium 515
Lifespan Considerations 519
  Women Who are Pregnant 519
  Newborns and Infants 519
  Children and Adolescents 520
  Older Adults 520
Evidence-Informed Critical Thinking 521
Common Laboratory and Diagnostic Testing 521
Clinical Reasoning 522
  Nursing Diagnoses, Outcomes, and
    Interventions 522

20 Peripheral Vascular and Lymphatic
    Assessment 536
Anatomy and Physiology Overview 537
Arterial System 537
Venous System 537
Capillaries 538
Lymphatic System 539
Fascia Compartment of Limbs 539
Lifespan Considerations 540
  Women Who Are Pregnant 540
  Newborns, Children, and Adolescents 540
  Older Adults 541
Cultural Considerations 541

Acute Assessment 541
Subjective Data Collection 542
Assessment of Risk Factors 542
Personal History 542
Medications 542
Family History 542
Risk Assessment and Health Promotion 543
Patients With Peripheral Arterial Disease 543
Patients With Venous Disease 544
Patients With Lymphatic Disorders 544
Focused Health History Related to Common
Symptoms/Signs 544
Pain 545
Numbness or Tingling 546
Cramping 546
Skin Changes 546
Edema 546
Functional Ability 546
Lifespan Considerations 546
Women Who Are Pregnant 546
Newborns, Children, and Adolescents 546
Older Adults 547
Cultural Considerations 547
Objective Data Collection 548
Promoting Patient Comfort, Dignity, and
Safety 548
Comprehensive Physical Examination: Peripheral
Vascular and Lymphatic Systems 548
Arms 548
Legs 551
Advanced Techniques 554
Lifespan Considerations 556
Women Who Are Pregnant 556
Newborns, Children, and Adolescents 556
Older Adults 556
Evidence-Informed Critical Thinking 557
Organizing and Prioritizing 557
Common Laboratory and Diagnostic
Testing 557
Clinical Reasoning 558
Nursing Diagnoses, Outcomes, and
Interventions 558

21 Breasts and Axillae Assessment 571
Anatomy and Physiology Overview 572
Landmarks 572
Breast Structures 572
Axillae and Lymph Nodes 573
Lifespan Considerations 574
Women Who Are Pregnant 574
Newborns and Infants 574
Children and Adolescents 574
Older Adults 576
Male Breasts 576
Cultural Considerations 576
Acute Assessment 576
Subjective Data Collection 576
Assessment of Risk Factors 577
Past Medical History 578
Medications 579
Family History 579
Lifestyle and Personal Habits 579

Breast Examination 580
Risk Assessment and Health
Promotion 580
Focused Health History Related to Common
Symptoms/Signs 580
Pain 581
Rash/Ulceration 582
Lumps 582
Swelling—Change in Breast Shape 582
Discharge—Nipples 582
Trauma 582
Lifespan Considerations 583
Women Who Are Pregnant 583
Adolescent Females 583
Objective Data Collection 584
Promoting Patient Comfort, Dignity, and
Safety 584
Comprehensive Physical Assessment 584
Inspection 584
Palpation 587
Transillumination 590
Examining the Patient Postmastectomy 590
Male Breasts 591
Expected Findings 591
Unexpected Findings 591
Teaching the Know Your Breasts
Approach 592
Lifespan Considerations 592
Women Who Are Pregnant/Lactating 592
Newborns and Infants 592
Children and Adolescents 592
Older Adults 592
Evidence-Informed Critical Thinking 592
Organizing and Prioritizing 592
Laboratory and Diagnostic Testing 592
Clinical Reasoning 594
Nursing Diagnoses, Outcomes, and
Interventions 594

22 Abdominal Assessment 602
Anatomy and Physiology Overview 603
Anatomical Landmarks 603
Reference Lines 603
Abdominal Organs 603
Gastrointestinal Organs 603
Genitourinary Organs 605
Blood Vessels, Peritoneum, and
Muscles 606
Ingestion and Digestion 607
Absorption of Nutrients 607
Elimination 607
Lifespan Considerations 607
Women Who are Pregnant 607
Newborns, Infants, and Children 607
Older Adults 607
Acute Assessment 607
Subjective Data Collection 607
Assessment of Risk Factors 608
Current Concerns 608
Medications 608
Personal History 608
Family History 610

Risk Factors 610
Occupation 610
Foreign Travel 610
Lifestyle 611
Risk Assessment and Health Promotion 611
Focused Health History Related to Common
Symptoms/Signs 612
Indigestion 612
Anorexia 613
Nausea, Vomiting, Hematemesis 613
Abdominal Pain 613
Dysphagia/Odynophagia 613
Change in Bowel Function 613
Jaundice/Icterus 613
Urinary/Renal Symptoms 614
Lifespan Considerations 615
Women Who are Pregnant 615
Newborns, Infants, and Children 615
Adolescents 616
Older Adults 616
Cultural Considerations 617
African Canadians 617
Asian Canadians 617
Canadians of Jewish Descent 617
Canadians of Mediterranean
Descent 617
Aboriginal Canadians 617
Objective Data Collection 618
Promoting Patient Comfort, Dignity, and
Safety 618
Comprehensive Physical Assessment: Abdominal
Assessment 619
Inspection 619
Auscultation 620
Percussion 622
Palpation 624
Assessing for Ascites 628
Eliciting the Abdominal Reflex 630
Lifespan Considerations 631
Women Who are Pregnant 631
Infants and Children 631
Older Adults 631
Cultural Considerations 631
Evidence-Informed Critical Thinking 632
Common Laboratory and Diagnostic
Testing 632
Esophagogastroduodenoscopy 632
Barium Enema 632
Colonoscopy 633
Endoscopic Retrograde
Cholangiopancreatography 633
Computerized Tomography Scan 633
Magnetic Resonance Imaging 633
Clinical Reasoning 633

23 Musculoskeletal Assessment 645
Anatomy and Physiology Overview 646
Bones 646
Muscles 646
Joints 647

Temporomandibular Joint 647
Shoulder 647
Elbow 649
Wrist and Hand 649
Hip 650
Knee 650
Ankle and Foot 651
Spine 651
Lifespan Considerations 651
Women Who are Pregnant 652
Infants and Children 652
Older Adults 652
Cultural Considerations 653
Acute Assessment 653
Subjective Data Collection 653
Assessment of Risk Factors 653
Demographic Data 654
Past Medical History 654
Nutrition and Medications 654
Family History 654
Occupation, Lifestyle, and Behaviours 654
Psychosocial History 655
Scoliosis Screening 655
Risk Assessment and Health Promotion 656
Bone Density 656
Focused Health History Related to Common
Symptoms/Signs 657
Pain or Discomfort 657
Weakness 658
Stiffness or Limited Movement 658
Deformity 658
Lack of Balance and Coordination 658
Lifespan Considerations 659
Women Who are Pregnant 659
Newborns, Infants, and Children 659
Older Adults 660
Cultural Considerations 660
Objective Data Collection 662
Promoting Patient Comfort, Dignity, and
Safety 662
Comprehensive Physical Examination:
The Musculoskeletal System 662
Initial Survey 662
Inspection 662
Posture 662
Gait and Mobility 663
Balance 663
Coordination 663
Inspection of Extremities 663
Palpation 664
Temporomandibular joint 666
Cervical Spine 667
Shoulder 668
Elbow 670
Wrist and Hand 672
Hip 673
Knee 674
Ankle and Foot 678
Thoracic and Lumbar Spine 680
Fall Risk 682
Lifespan Considerations 682

Women Who are Pregnant 682
Newborns, Infants, and Children 682
Older Adults 683
Lifestyle and Work-Related Considerations 683
Advanced Techniques 683
Evidence-Informed Critical Thinking 684
Organizing and Prioritizing 684
Laboratory and Diagnostic Testing 684
Clinical Reasoning 684
Nursing Diagnoses, Outcomes, and
Interventions 684

24 Neurological Assessment 697

Anatomy and Physiology Overview 698
Central Nervous System 698
Brain 698
Protective Structures of the CNS 702
Spinal Cord 702
Peripheral Nervous System 704
Cranial Nerves 705
Spinal Nerves 705
Autonomic Nervous System 705
Lifespan Considerations 706
Women Who Are Pregnant 706
Newborns and Infants 707
Children and Adolescents 707
Older Adults 707
Acute Assessment 707
Subjective Data Collection 708
Assessment of Risk Factors 708
Risk Assessment and Health Promotion 710
Stroke Prevention 710
Injury Prevention 710
Prevention of Meningeal Infections 711
Reduction of Risk for Seizure Activity 711
Focused Health History Related to Common
Symptoms/Signs 711
Headache or Other Pain 712
Limb or Unilateral Weakness 712
Generalized Weakness 712
Involuntary Movements or Tremors 712
Balance/Coordination Difficulties 712
Dizziness or Vertigo 713
Difficulty Swallowing 713
Intellectual Changes 713
Speech/Language Difficulties 713
Changes in Taste, Touch, Smell,
or Sensation 713
Lost or Blurred Vision 713
Hearing Loss or Tinnitus 713
Lifespan Considerations 714
Women Who Are Pregnant 714
Newborns and Infants 714
Children and Adolescents 714
Older Adults 714
Cultural Considerations 715
Objective Data Collection 716
Promoting Patient Comfort, Dignity, and
Safety 716
Level of Consciousness 716
Comprehensive Physical Examination:
Neurological System 716

Cognitive Function 718
Communication (Speech/Language) 718
Pupillary Response 719
Cranial Nerve Testing 719
Motor Function 723
Coordination (Cerebellar Function) 725
Sensory Function 726
Reflex Testing 730
Lifespan Considerations 734
Newborns, Infants, and Children 734
Older Adults 735
Neurological Assessment in Selected
Situations 736
Screening Examination of a Healthy
Patient 736
Serial Neurological Assessment and
Documentation 736
Assessment of Meningeal Signs 736
Assessing the Unconscious Patient 737
Brain Herniation Syndromes 738
Evidence-Informed Critical Thinking 738
Common Laboratory and Diagnostic
Testing 738
Clinical Reasoning 739

25 Male Genitalia and Rectal
Assessment 755

Anatomy and Physiology Overview 756
External Genitalia 756
Internal Genitalia 757
Testes 757
Ducts 757
Secretory Structures 757
Rectum and Anus 758
Rectum 758
Anal Canal and Anus 758
Lifespan Considerations 758
Infants and Children 758
Adolescents 759
Older Adult 760
Cultural Considerations 760
Acute Assessment 760
Subjective Data Collection 761
Assessment of Risk Factors 761
Personal History 761
Medical and Surgical History 761
Medications 762
Family History 762
Additional Risk Factors 762
Risk Assessment and Health Promotion 763
Testicular Self-Examination 763
Screening for Prostate Cancer 763
Focused Health History Related to Common
Symptoms/Signs 763
Pain 764
Difficulty With Urination 764
Male Sexual Dysfunction 765
Penile Lesions, Discharge, or Rash 765
Scrotal Enlargement 765
Lifespan Considerations 765
Newborns, Infants, and Children 765
Older Adults 766

Cultural Considerations 766
Objective Data Collection 767
  Promoting Patient Comfort, Dignity, and
    Safety 767
  Comprehensive Physical Assessment: Male
    Genitalia and Rectum Assessment 767
    Groin and Pubic Area 767
    Penis 767
    Scrotum 768
    Sacrococcygeal Areas 768
    Perineal Area 768
    Inguinal Region and Femoral Areas 769
  Special Circumstances or Advanced
    Techniques 769
    Testicles 769
    Vas Deferens 769
    Transillumination of the Scrotum 769
    Hernias 770
    Perianal and Rectal Examination 770
  Lifespan Considerations 773
    Infants and Children 773
    Older Adults 773
  Cultural Considerations 773
Evidence-Informed Critical Thinking 773
  Common Laboratory and Diagnostic Testing 773
  Clinical Reasoning 774
    Nursing Diagnosis, Outcomes, and
      Interventions 774

26 Female Genitalia and Rectal
  Assessment 789
  Anatomy and Physiology Overview 790
    External Genitalia 790
    Internal Genitalia 790
      Vagina 790
      Uterus 790
      Cervix 790
      Fallopian Tubes 790
      Ovaries 791
    Rectum, Anal Canal, and Anus 791
    Hormone Regulation 791
    Lifespan Considerations 792
      Women Who Are Pregnant 792
      Infants, Children, and Adolescents 792
      Older Adults 794
  Acute Assessment 794
    Excessive Vaginal Bleeding 794
    Abdominal Pain 794
    Bartholin Gland Infection 794
    Pelvic Inflammatory Disease 794
    Ruptured Tubal Pregnancy 794
  Subjective Data Collection 795
    Assessment of Risk Factors 795
      Personal History 795
      Medications and Supplements 797
      Family History 797
      Risk Factors 797
    Risk Assessment and Health Promotion 799
    Focused Health History Related to Common
      Symptoms/Signs 800
      Pelvic Pain 801
      Vaginal Burning, Discharge, Itching 802

Menstrual Disorders 802
Structural Conditions 802
Hemorrhoids 802
Lifespan Considerations 802
  Women Who Are Pregnant 802
  Newborns, Infants, and Children 803
  Older Adults 803
Cultural Considerations 804
Objective Data Collection 805
  Promoting Patient Comfort, Dignity, and
    Safety 805
  Comprehensive Physical Examination: Female
    Genitalia and Rectum 806
    External Genitalia 806
  Advanced Techniques 806
    Internal Genitalia 807
    Speculum Examination 808
    Bimanual Examination 812
    Rectovaginal Examination 814
  Lifespan Considerations 817
    Women Who Are Pregnant 817
    Child 817
    Adolescent 817
    Older Adult 817
Evidence-Informed Critical Thinking 817
  Common Laboratory and Diagnostic
    Testing 817
  Nursing Diagnosis, Outcomes, and
    Interventions 818

UNIT **4** Special Populations
  and Foci 831

27 Women Who Are Pregnant 833
  Anatomy and Physiology Overview 834
    Preconception 834
    First Trimester 835
    Second Trimester 835
    Third Trimester 836
  Determining Weeks of Gestation 836
  Role of the Nurse in the Outpatient Setting 837
  Acute Assessment 838
  Subjective Data Collection 838
    Cultural Considerations 838
    Assessment of Risk Factors 839
      Personal History 839
      Medications and Supplements 840
      Family History 841
      Additional Risk Factors 841
    Risk Assessment and Health Promotion 841
      Prevention of Gestational Diabetes 842
      Promotion of Nutrition and Oral Health 842
      Promotion of Healthy Lifestyle Habits 842
      Promotion of Mental Health and Safety 843
      Prenatal and breast-feeding classes 843
      Follow-Up Visits and Prenatal Monitoring 843
    Focused Health History Related to Common
      Symptoms/Signs in Pregnancy 843
      Morning Sickness 844
      Growing Pains 844

Increased Vaginal Discharge 845
Increased Urination 845
Breast Tenderness and Discharge 845
Periumbilical Pain 845
Fetal Hiccups and Other Spasms 845
Braxton Hicks Contractions 846
Objective Data Collection 847
Promoting Patient Comfort, Dignity, and Safety 847
Assessment During the Initial Visit 847
General Survey and Vital Signs 847
Nutrition 848
Skin 849
Abdomen 849
Breasts 850
Genitalia 850
Assessment During Routine Pregnancy Visits 850
General Survey and Vital Signs 850
Skin 851
Nose, Mouth, and Throat 851
Thorax and Lungs 851
Heart 851
Peripheral Vascular 852
Breasts 853
Abdomen 853
Musculoskeletal System 854
Genitalia 854
Evidence-Informed Critical Thinking 855
Common Laboratory and Diagnostic Testing 855
Nonstress Test 855
Leopold's Manoeuvres 855
Clinical Reasoning 858
Nursing Diagnosis, Outcomes, and Interventions 858

28 Newborns and Infants 863
Anatomy and Physiology Overview 864
Physical Growth 864
Motor Development 864
Language, Psychosocial, and Cognitive Development 864
Acute Assessment 864
Emergent Concerns 864
Subjective Data Collection 865
Assessment of Risk Factors 865
Personal History (Infant) 865
Medications and Supplements 865
Risk Factors 866
Risk Assessment and Health Promotion 866
Safe Sleep Habits 866
Choking 866
Immunization Schedules 867
Child Safety Car Seat 868
Cardiopulmonary Resuscitation Training for Parents 868
Poison Control 868
Breastfeeding/Iron-Rich Foods 868
Baby Bottle Tooth Decay 868
Focused Health History Related to Common Symptoms 869
Respiratory Concerns/Distress 869
Fever 869
Skin Conditions 869

Gastrointestinal Distress 870
Crying/Irritability 870
Cultural Considerations 870
Objective Data Collection 871
Promoting Patient Comfort, Dignity, and Safety 871
Comprehensive Physical Examination: Newborn and Infant 871
Newborn: Apgar Score 872
Newborn: Gestational Age 872
Reflexes 872
General Survey/Observation 872
Vital Signs 873
Pain 875
Measurements 875
Nutrition 877
Mental Status 878
Violence 878
Skin, Hair, and Nails 878
Head and Neck 879
Eyes 881
Ears 882
Nose, Mouth, and Throat 882
Thorax and Lungs 883
Heart and Neck Vessels 883
Peripheral Vascular 884
Breasts 884
Abdomen 884
Musculoskeletal 884
Neurological 886
Genitalia 886
Anus and Rectum 886
Documentation of Examination Findings 887
Cultural Considerations 887
Evidence-Informed Critical Thinking 887
Organizing and Prioritizing 887
Laboratory and Diagnostic Testing 887
Clinical Reasoning 887
Nursing Diagnosis, Outcomes, and Interventions 887

29 Children and Adolescents 899
Anatomy and Physiology Overview 900
Physical Growth 900
Motor Development 900
Language 900
Psychosocial and Cognitive Development 900
Acute Assessment 900
Subjective Data Collection 902
Assessment of Risk Factors 902
Reason for Seeking Care 902
Personal History 902
Prenatal History 902
Postnatal History 903
Developmental History (Depending on Current Age of Child) 903
Medications and Supplements 903
Family History 903
Risk Factors 903
Risk Assessment and Health Promotion 905
Immunization Schedules 905
Car Safety 905

Poison Control 906
Safety in the Home 906
Fire Safety 906
Water Safety 906
Outdoor Safety 906
Prevention of Drug and Alcohol Use 906
Nutrition and Prevention of Obesity 906
Mental Health Issues 907
Promotion of Contraception and STI
Prevention 907
Focused Health History Related to Common
Symptoms 907
Abdominal Pain 907
Headache 907
Leg Pain 907
Cultural Considerations 908
Objective Data Collection 909
Equipment 909
Preparation: Promoting Patient Comfort, Dignity,
and Safety 909
Developmental Assessment 909
Comprehensive Physical Examination 910
Vital Signs 910
General Survey 910
Skin, Hair, and Nails 911
Head and Neck 911
Eyes and Vision 911
Ears and Hearing 911
Nose, Mouth, and Throat 914
Thorax and Lungs 914
Heart and Neck Vessels 916
Peripheral Vascular 917
Breasts 917
Abdomen 917
Musculoskeletal 918
Neurological 918
Male and Female Genitalia 919
Evidence-Informed Critical Thinking 919
Common Laboratory and Diagnostic Testing 919
Clinical Reasoning 919

30 Older Adults 925
Anatomy and Physiology Overview 926
Skin, Hair, and Nails 926
Head and Neck 926
Eyes and Vision 926
Ears and Hearing 927
Nose, Mouth, and Throat 927
Thorax and Lungs 927
Heart and Neck Vessels 927
Peripheral Vascular and Lymphatics 927
Breasts and Lymphatics 927
Abdomen, Metabolism, and Elimination 928
Musculoskeletal 928
Neurological 928
Male and Female Genitourinary 928
Endocrine 928
Acute Assessment 929
Subjective Data Collection 929
Interviewing the Older Adult 929
Cultural Considerations 930

Assessment of Risk Factors 931
Current Concern 931
Personal History 931
Risk Assessment and Health Promotion 934
Focused Health History Related to Common
Symptoms/Signs 935
Incontinence 935
Sleep Deprivation 935
Pain 935
Cognitive Status 935
Depression 936
Abuse 936
Cultural Considerations 937
Objective Data Collection 938
Promoting Patient Comfort, Dignity, and
Safety 938
Comprehensive Physical Examination: The Older
Adult 938
Instruments 938
General Survey 939
Height and Weight 939
Vital Signs 940
Auscultation 940
Inspection 940
Skin, Hair, and Nails 941
Head and Neck 941
Eyes and Vision 942
Ears and Hearing 942
Nose, Mouth, and Throat 943
Spine, Thorax, and Lungs 944
Heart and Neck Vessels 944
Peripheral Vascular 945
Breasts and Axillae 945
Abdomen and Elimination 946
Musculoskeletal System 946
Neurological 946
Male and Female Genitourinary 947
Endocrine, Immunologic, and Hematologic
Systems 947
Cultural Considerations 947
Evidence-Informed Critical Thinking 949
Organizing and Prioritizing 949
Common Laboratory and Diagnostic Testing 949
Clinical Reasoning 950
Nursing Diagnosis, Outcomes, and
Interventions 950

UNIT Putting It All Together 957

31 Head-to-Toe Assessment of the Adult 959
Acute Assessment 960
Subjective Data Collection 960
Areas for Health Promotion 960
Assessment of Risk Factors 960
Demographic Data 961
History of Present Concern/Illness 961
Past Health History 962
Growth and Development 963
Review of Systems 963

Risk Assessment and Health Promotion 964
Focused Health History Related to Common
    Symptoms 964
Objective Data Collection 965
Promoting Patient Comfort, Dignity, and
    Safety 965
Comprehensive Physical Examination 965
    Vital Signs 966
    General Survey 966
    Skin 966
    Head 966
    Mouth and Throat 967
    Eyes 967
    Ears 968
    Nose and Sinuses 968
    Neck 968
    Neurological 969
    Upper Extremities 969
    Anterior Thorax 969
    Female Breasts 970
    Abdomen 970
    Lower Extremities 971

Posterior Thorax 971
Gait and Balance/Fall Risk 972
Musculoskeletal and Neurological 972
Skin Breakdown 972
Wounds, Drains, Devices 972
Male Genitalia 973
Female Genitalia 973
Rectum 973
Closure 974
Lifespan and Cultural Considerations 974
Hospital Assessment 975
Comprehensive Admitting Assessment 975
Screening Hospital Assessment 975
Focused Hospital Assessment 975
Evidence-Informed Critical Thinking 976
Common Laboratory and Diagnostic Testing 976
Clinical Reasoning 976

Answers to Review Questions 981
Illustration Credit List 983
Index 987

UNIT

1

Foundations
of Nursing
Health
Assessment

The Nurse's Role in Health Assessment

Learning Objectives

1 Describe the role of the professional nurse in health assessment.

2 Demonstrate knowledge of the purposes of health assessment.

3 Explain the relationship of health assessment to health promotion.

4 Explain the roles of the nursing process, critical thinking, and clinical reasoning in nursing care.

5 Demonstrate knowledge of the differences in the types and frequencies of assessments.

6 State the components of a comprehensive health assessment.

7 Describe organizing frameworks for collecting health assessment data.

*M*rs. *Rosa* Ortiz, a 52-year-old member of the Latino community, has a follow-up appointment at the outpatient diabetic clinic related to type 2 diabetes mellitus, which was diagnosed 2 weeks ago during an annual physical assessment. Her primary language is Spanish. Although her English language skills are good, she has difficulty understanding complex terminology related to health and illness. Mrs. Ortiz lives with her husband of 30 years. Her three adult children live nearby.

Mrs. Ortiz is 160 cm tall, weighs 75 kg (body mass index [BMI] 29), and eats a diet high in fats and starches. Her blood glucose levels at home have been elevated. She is otherwise healthy. Current vital signs are temperature 36.5°C tympanic, pulse 82 beats/min regular, respirations 16 breaths/min, and blood pressure (BP) right arm (sitting) 138/78 mm Hg. Medications include an oral hypoglycemic-glyburide-(DiaBeta) 2.5 mg daily (start-up dosage) and a daily multivitamin.

You will gain more information about Mrs. Ortiz throughout this chapter. As you study the content and features, consider the patient's case and its relationship to what you are learning. Begin thinking about the following points:

- What are potential health promotion topics for Mrs. Ortiz based on the above information?
- How should the nurse approach a discussion of the patient's diet with respect to her diabetes?
- How will the nurse individualize today's health assessment, considering the patient's gender, age, and cultural background?
- What is the role of the nurse in providing care for Mrs. Ortiz during this visit?

Nursing is a rewarding and challenging profession that requires extensive knowledge and skills. When performing health assessments, nurses integrate the art and science of nursing. Nurses assess health on many levels, including psychosocial, physical, emotional, mental, spiritual, cultural, and nutritional. They practise primary, secondary, and tertiary prevention (Skillen, Anderson, et al., 2010; Reutter & Kushner, 2010a). Wellness and health are concepts that are influenced by the health beliefs and practices of patients, their families, and their communities. Nurses explore factors related to such beliefs and behaviours in order to understand better how to promote health and care for their patients. They develop and apply skills in communication to provide therapeutic responses to patients' concerns. Accurate and complete health assessment data are the foundation for what is a collaborative process between nurses and their patients. Nurses apply the nursing process by assessing health status comprehensively, developing nursing diagnoses, planning goals and outcomes, creating plans for care, performing interventions, evaluating effectiveness, and revising interventions as needed.

Role of the Professional Nurse

Nurses provide direct care to help restore or maximize health for individuals in settings that include hospitals, ambulatory clinics, continuing care facilities, public health clinics, primary care networks, schools, forensic institutions, military sites, parishes, and workplaces (Fig. 1-1). They work in hospices, rehabilitation centres, and homes, to help patients and their families cope with compromised health, chronic illness, disability, and dying. When death is unavoidable, nurses facilitate the most comfortable and dignified death. This includes fostering comfort, mitigating suffering, advocating for pain relief, and supporting a peaceful death (Canadian

Nurses Association [CNA], 2008). Canadian nurses provide holistic health and illness care in urban, rural, remote, and international health care settings (Skillen, Anderson, et al., 2010). As clinicians, researchers, educators, policy analysts, and administrators, nurses' actions are ultimately directed to influencing patient care and best practices (CNA, 2007).

In addition to assessment and direct care, nurses also have roles as **planners, coordinators, and managers of care**. While practitioners of medicine focus on the anatomical, biological, and physiological aspects of diseases to determine the necessary medications and treatment modalities, nurses focus on how diseases affect patients' abilities to perform activities of daily living and what their coping mechanisms are for dealing with health issues and losses of function. They gather assessment information that takes into account how a condition influences the patient's functional ability and quality of life. Nurses collaborate with interprofessional health team members and also have an area of independent practice within which they function autonomously. Independent nursing actions include therapeutic communication, health teaching, taking comprehensive health histories, performing emergent, focused, or comprehensive physical examinations, and providing physical care procedures (eg, bathing, turning patients, monitoring response to treatment, or assisting with ambulation).

Nurses are constantly making treatment decisions to manage and coordinate care. They are in a position to be appreciated and respected by patients because of the time they often spend with patients and their families, and the opportunities they have to acquire knowledge of their health issues. Nurses document assessment data to share with other health team members and communicate findings opportunely. Being in close proximity and regular contact with their patients, they identify trends or changes in the patients' condition promptly. Their referral of patients to other health care providers (eg, dietitians, speech therapists, pharmacists, dentists) is

Figure 1-1 Nurses promote health and prevent illness in various ways. **A.** Family teaching during wellness visits reinforces positive habits and helps parents and children understand behaviours for optimal well-being. **B.** Promoting regular health screenings with patients, such as scheduled mammograms, is critical to reducing risks for disease. **C.** Assisting patients with long-term health challenges to restore or maintain optimal functioning is another essential nursing activity.

discussed in the SBAR (situation, background, assessment, recommendation), a feature found in later chapters.

Advocacy

Nurses are members of a profession and in this role, are advocates for the patient, health, environment, and the profession (College and Association of Registered Nurses of Alberta [CARNA], 2011; CNA, 2009a; Reutter & Kushner, 2010a; Registered Nurses Association of Ontario [RNAO], 2011). Nurses advocate for patients in many ways: keeping them safe, communicating their needs, identifying side effects of treatment and finding better options, and helping them to understand their diseases and treatments so that they can optimize self-care. Safety is defined as the minimization of "risk of harm to patients and providers through both system effectiveness and individual performance" (Cronenwett, Sherwood, et al., 2007, p. 128). In primary care settings, for example, registered nurses have a responsibility to look at system redesign and system processes (CARNA, 2011). Across the country, nurses are examining health services as a system so that real change can occur in improving access to care and reducing wait times (CNA, 2009b). In Canada, nurses are

- reducing adverse events by conducting skilled health assessments and detecting health issues promptly
- providing increased entry points to the health care system
- promoting better health
- maximizing application of their skills in new collaborative models of health care
- embracing information and communication technologies (CNA, 2009b)

More than all other health care professionals, nurses can recognize, interrupt, evaluate, and correct health care errors (Rothschild, Hurley, et al., 2006).

As advocates, nurses take responsibility to protect the legal and ethical rights of patients. They believe in health as a human right (CNA, 2009a), and are guided by professional values in their practice.

Values and ethical principles are beliefs or ideals to which a person is committed. In Canada, the seven primary nursing values in the *Code of Ethics for Registered Nurses* are

- providing safe, compassionate, competent and ethical care
- promoting health and well-being
- promoting and respecting informed decision-making
- preserving dignity
- maintaining privacy and confidentiality
- promoting justice
- being accountable (CNA, 2008)

Nurses are altruistic when they demonstrate a true concern for the welfare of others as reflected in the desire to understand the patient's perspective and health beliefs. They preserve human dignity when they show respect for patients such as by ensuring privacy and confidentiality. In their role as advocates, nurses provide accurate, nonbiased, and comprehensive information to patients and their families in order to promote patient autonomy (CARNA, 2011). Nurses act with integrity when providing honest information to patients, documenting care accurately, and reporting errors (Institute for Safe Medication Practices, 2007). When nurses safeguard human rights, and promote equitable treatment, fairness (access to quality health care and resources), and the public good, they support social justice (CNA, 2008).

The roles as a provider of care, manager of health services, researcher of care modalities, educator of nursing students, and member of a profession give nursing a unique advantage in understanding and acting on the patient's behalf in the most holistic way.

Scholarship and Research

Nurses demonstrate **scholarship and perform research** to provide evidence-informed care. Professional nursing practice is grounded in skilled questioning, critical inquiry, and best practice. Knowledge of patient care technologies and information systems is essential in the management of care. Nurses use systems to influence health care policy, finance, and regulatory agencies. Health promotion and disease prevention are necessary to improve health at both the individual and population levels (Reutter & Kushner, 2010a).

Registered Nurse and Advanced Practice Nurse Roles

Registered nurses (RNs) and advanced practice nurses fulfill the roles described above in the previous section. The RN is regulated and licensed by Canadian provinces or territories and practises independently within the scope of nursing practice and diagnosis. RNs practise wherever people need nursing care, including such common sites as hospitals, homes, schools, workplaces, and community health centres. In 2009, the majority of RNs in Canada (62.6%) worked in hospitals; 14.2% were working in the community health sector (Canadian Institute for Health Information, 2010).

Advanced practice nurses are RNs who meet advanced educational and clinical practice requirements, preferably at a Master's level beyond the basic nursing education and licensing required of all RNs. They provide at least some level of direct care to patient populations. Advanced practice nurses typically also perform more advanced assessments. See the advanced techniques in Unit 2 in the chapters on regional and system examinations. Advanced practice nurses include nurse practitioners, midwives, and clinical nurse specialists. Many opportunities exist for RNs in Canada to advance their education and careers in a way that capitalizes on their strengths, interests, and expertise.

Purposes of Health Assessment

Health assessment is the collection of subjective and objective data to develop a database about a patient's health status (past and present), health concerns, and usual coping mechanisms so that an individualized care plan can be created (Wood & Ross-Kerr, 2010). Health assessment encompasses a health history, physical examination, documentation of findings, and analysis of the data.

The health history includes skillful interviewing to collect the patient's current symptoms; history of the present concern(s); past medical, surgical, gynecological/obstetric, and psychiatric histories; and personal, social, and relevant family history. A comprehensive health history includes nutritional, developmental, mental, social, cultural, and spiritual dimensions (Stephen & Bickley, 2010). It also addresses safety issues, risk factors, and functional abilities. It provides the nurse with direction for the focus of the physical examination. Data that nurses collect during the physical assessment vary depending on the acuity of a patient's situation, health history, and current symptoms. In emergencies, nurses focus the collection of information in order to pinpoint the source of the challenging issues and treat the presenting conditions. For healthy patients seeking a wellness checkup, the assessment focuses on updating patient health information, ensuring laboratory and diagnostic screening tests are requested, assessing for risk factors (eg, overweight), and creating opportunities for teaching and health promotion (eg, exercise, dietary intake, and stress management).

Other purposes of health assessment are to gain further insight into the current condition and to establish or update a database that subsequent assessments can be measured against. Nurses identify patterns and trends in findings to determine if a patient's condition is improving or worsening. They incorporate focused history-taking and focused physical examination in their daily routine with their patients. By monitoring the health status of their patients, nurses detect early changes in condition and responses/nonresponses to treatment. Nurses think logically to analyze how the data they collect are related and what interventions may be indicated. Critical thinking is fundamental to analysis of the data (Wood & Ross-Kerr, 2010). Nurses apply the nursing process continuously, moving back and forth among the phases of this problem-solving approach.

The nursing process is used by nurses everywhere (American Nurses Association [ANA], 2009) The five phases of the nursing process are discussed below. A complete and accurate health assessment assists nurses to promote health at the highest level. *Because all future care is based upon the health assessment, it is extremely important that health assessment data be complete, accurate, and current.* Health assessment is an important and essential activity of professional nurses.

Wellness and Health Promotion

High-level **wellness** is a process to which people aspire. They want to maintain balance and direction in their environments. The role of nurses is to facilitate this achievement through health promotion and teaching. Nurses collaborate with individuals, families, groups, and communities to promote higher levels of wellness. People who tend toward high-level wellness focus on awareness, education, and growth. People who are more likely to develop illness or suffer premature death develop signs, symptoms, and disability, which, unfortunately, is when most treatment occurs in the current health care system (Satcher, 2006).

Health Promotion and Health Assessment

Nurses assess health promotion activities of patients, including nutritional intake, activity and fitness levels, mental health, safety and violence, and stress and coping measures. They start by using screening questions in the health history and ask follow-up questions in higher risk areas. Rather than addressing all areas associated with healthy behaviours and overwhelming patients, nurses collaborate with them to identify areas that the patients are considering or in which they are indicating willingness to make changes.

The Centers for Disease Control and Prevention (CDCP) have a Behavioral Risk Factor Surveillance System Survey to assess risk, lifestyle, and stress (2008). Specific tools for various body systems, age groups, and other factors are discussed in chapters throughout this book under the "Risk Assessment" sections.

Nurses consider how social determinants affect the health of their patients. They know that income, culture, education, age, gender, social support, work conditions and environments can influence individuals' coping mechanisms and health practices (Reutter & Kushner, 2010b). The Canadian Population Health Promotion Model was developed by Hamilton and Bhatti in 1996 and has been expanded. The model is aligned with nurses' understanding of the social determinants of health and how nurses can make a difference with patients to improve their health status (Reutter & Kushner, 2010b). The health history incorporates questioning about the broader social and physical environments that influence patients' health. Sometimes factors are beyond the control of patients and are determined by policies developed by governments. Knowing this has led some Canadian nurses into the realm of political action.

Focused Health History Related to the Case Study

As part of Mrs. Ortiz's assessment, the nurse assesses her risk factors for diabetes to identify elements in her lifestyle, environment, and genetic background that contribute to her condition. Following such identification, the nurse works with Mrs. Ortiz to modify the risk factors that can be altered to help her control the diabetes. The following questions are examples of how the nurse assesses risk factors.

Questions to Assess History and Risk Factors	Rationale
From the patient's chart, first obtain the following data: • Age • Height and weight • Ethnicity and genetic background • Blood Pressure (BP) • Recent cholesterol level • Any history of the following: gestational diabetes, polycystic ovarian syndrome, impaired glucose tolerance or impaired fasting glucose, cardiovascular disease • Family history	Older age and overweight or obesity increase the patient's risk of type 2 diabetes. Over 50% of First Nations and Inuit populations in Canada have type 2 diabetes or obesity (Brunet, Day, et al., 2010). Additional risk factors for diabetes include age 40 or over; a parent or sibling with type 2 diabetes; genetic background that is Aboriginal, Hispanic, Asian, South Asian, or African; a history of gestational diabetes or prediabetes; and heart disease, high blood pressure, or high cholesterol (Canadian Diabetes Association, 2011).
What is your typical daily diet?	A diet low in fat, calories, and sodium is recommended. Fresh fruits and vegetables should replace high-calorie foods (Brunet, Day, et al., 2010).
How often do you exercise?	Exercising less than three times a week increases the risk for diabetes. Thirty minutes of exercise 5 days a week is recommended (American Diabetes Association, 2009).
Considering your weight, diet, and exercise, which is the most important for you to work on right now?	It is important to identify the issues that the patient is willing to modify and prioritize as most important.

Risk Assessment and Health Promotion

Nurses collaborate with individuals, families, groups, and communities to implement health promotion, risk reduction, and disease prevention strategies. The three levels of interventions to promote healthy change are primary, secondary, and tertiary (Leavell & Clark, 1965).

- **Primary prevention** involves strategies aimed at preventing health concerns. Immunizations, health teaching, safety precautions, and nutrition counselling are examples.
- **Secondary prevention** includes the early diagnosis of health issues and prompt treatment to prevent complications. Vision screening, Pap smears, BP screening, hearing testing, scoliosis screening, and tuberculin skin testing are examples.
- **Tertiary prevention** focuses on preventing complications of an existing disease or condition and promoting health to the highest possible level. Diet teaching for patients with diabetes, inhaler teaching for patients with lung disease, and exercise programs for those who have had myocardial infarction are examples.

The Nursing Process

The **nursing process** is a systematic problem-solving approach to identifying and treating human responses to actual or potential health conditions (ANA, 2009). It serves as a framework for providing individualized care not only to individuals but also to families, groups, and communities. It is patient centered, focusing on enhancing strengths and resolving health issues. The nursing process is applicable to patients in all stages of the lifespan and in all settings.

Phases of the Nursing Process

The five phases of the nursing process are: **assessing** the patient, analyzing data and making **diagnoses**, determining patient outcomes or **planning** care, implementing or **intervening**, and then **evaluating** the patient's status to determine if interventions were effective (Fig. 1-2). Evaluation is an assessment of the degree to which planned outcomes are

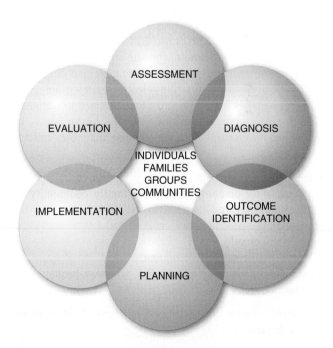

Figure 1-2 The phases of the nursing process are assessment, diagnosis, outcome, identification or planning, implementation, and evaluation. Nurses apply these activities to the care of individuals, families, groups, and communities.

observed in the patient. Nurses continually assess the patient's progress. From this evaluation, interventions may continue or be revised depending on whether the patient is progressing.

Assessment

The nursing process is not linear (progressing from one phase to another) (Wood & Ross-Kerr, 2010). It is interactive and involves interrelated, sometimes overlapping, phases. As nurses collect assessment data, they provide educational or emergency interventions simultaneously. Nurses also evaluate care during an assessment, such as checking patients for side effects of medications. Nurses set outcomes collaboratively with patients—established priorities guide not only the treatment plan but also the types of future assessments performed. For example, if a hospitalized patient's priority is sleep, the nurse may decide to eliminate taking vital signs every 4 hours during the night if the patient's condition is stable.

Diagnosis

Diagnosis is the clustering of data to make a judgment or statement about the patient's condition. The North American Nursing Diagnosis Association-International (NANDA-I) defines nursing diagnosis as "a clinical judgment about individual, family or community responses to actual or potential health problems/life processes. A nursing diagnosis provides the basis for selection of nursing interventions to achieve outcomes for which the nurse is accountable" (2009, p. 277). NANDA-I has developed some common nursing diagnoses and interventions to provide a specific language and way of thinking. They are helpful for nurses who are learning about the professional scope of practice. In clinical practice, nursing diagnoses are individualized to the patient or family, serving as a foundation for the labelling of health status. Nurses use critical thinking and clinical reasoning to formulate diagnostic statements. They use clustering of findings, cluster interpretation, and diagnostic validation to ensure accuracy in selecting or determining the correct diagnosis. Diagnoses may be orientated to wellness, risks for developing conditions, potential health issues, or actual health challenges. Each nursing diagnosis reflects seven axes:

- The diagnostic concept
- Subject of the diagnosis (individual, family, community)
- Judgment (impaired, ineffective)
- Location (bladder, auditory, cerebral)
- Age (infant, child, adult)
- Time (chronic, acute, intermittent)
- Status of the diagnosis (actual, risk, wellness, health promotion) (NANDA-1, 2007, p. 255)

Applicable nursing diagnoses are found throughout the chapters of this text.

Planning Goals and Outcomes

Outcome identification includes the formulation of measurable, realistic, patient-centered goals (ANA, 2009b). Goal identification provides for individualized care as nurses collaborate with patients. For example, when a patient in acute pain is given a pain medication, the nurse assesses the pain level. The nurse collaborates with the patient to identify the pain goal, determines what level of pain is acceptable, and discusses when the patient should take more pain medication. Goals are broader than outcomes, such as "Patient's pain is within realistic limits."

Patient outcomes are specific, measurable, attainable, realistic, and time-oriented (Alfaro-LeFevre, 2010). For example, it may not be realistic for a patient to be completely free of pain, but a level of 2 on a 0-to-10 scale (with 10 being the worst) might be acceptable to the patient. Because pain is subjective, the nurse gathers this information in addition to measurable objective pain indicators of acute pain such as facial grimaces, elevated pulse and BP, restlessness, or rubbing of the affected body part. An example of an outcome is "Pt states pain < 2 on a 0 to 10 scale, without facial grimacing, P < 80 beats/min and regular, BP right arm (supine) < 120/80 mm Hg and appears comfortable." Outcomes also assist in setting priorities for care, especially with complex issues (Johnson, Bulechek, et al., 2006). The most common nursing outcomes for each system are discussed in each specific chapter.

Planning Care

Care planning activities include determining resources, selecting nursing interventions, and writing the plan of care. In addition to the standard care and physician orders, the patient care plan requires an analysis about the individual patient and his or her needs. It promotes a higher level of individualized and holistic care in addition to that generally performed. The care plan is communicated verbally and is also documented in the patient's chart so that the next care provider is aware of the plan. Care planning may be documented as a care plan, care map, case note, clinical pathway, teaching plan, or discharge plan. Regardless of format, the care planning document incorporates the phases of the nursing process and the critical thinking that nurses incorporate into patient care.

Intervention/Implementation

Nursing interventions are "any treatment, based upon clinical judgment and knowledge that a nurse performs to enhance patient outcomes" (Bulechek, Butcher, et al., 2008, p. xix). Nursing interventions are used to monitor health status; prevent, resolve, or control a health condition; assist with activities of daily living; or promote optimum health and independence (Alfaro-LeFevre, 2010). It is important that nurses be aware of the standards of care within their employing agency because these standards define routine activities, such as taking vital signs every 8 hours. Nursing interventions include therapeutic communication, assessment, education, supervision, coordination, referral, support, and application of technical skills. Specific interventions for each system are covered in the appropriate chapters.

Evaluation

Evaluation of nursing care is the judgment of the effectiveness at meeting the patient's goals and outcomes based upon the patient's responses to the interventions (Craven & Hirnle, 2009). The purpose of evaluation is to make judgments about the patient's progress; analyze the effectiveness of nursing care, review potential areas for collaboration and referral to other health care professionals, and monitor the quality of nursing care and its effect on the patient (Alfaro-LeFevre, 2010). Nurses assess what facilitates and what hinders goal attainment. Goals may be completely met, partially met, or completely unmet; additionally, new issues and nursing diagnoses may be developed (Alfaro-LeFevre, 2010).

To evaluate effectively, nurses have knowledge of the standards of care, expected patient responses, and conceptual models and theories. They monitor the effectiveness of nursing interventions using interviewing skills for subjective data collection and physical examination skills for objective data collection. Nurses are also aware of the most current research and use this evidence to direct nursing care. They use critical thinking throughout the nursing process to assess, diagnose, plan, implement, and evaluate care.

Critical Thinking

Critical thinking in nursing is

- purposeful, outcome-directed/results-oriented thinking
- driven by patient, family group, and community needs
- based on the nursing process, evidence-informed thinking, and scientific method
- a result of specific knowledge, skills, and experience
- guided by professional standards and codes of ethics
- constant reevaluation, self-correction, and striving to improve (Alfaro-LeFevre, 2010)

Nurses frequently are involved in complex situations with multiple responsibilities. They analyze, develop alternatives, and implement the best interventions. Critical thinking is the key to resolving issues. Nurses who do not think things through critically deliver incomplete or misdirected care. Critical thinking is essential to passing the Canadian Registered Nurse Examination (CRNE). The CRNE incorporates questions related to six dimensions of critical thinking: knowledge, comprehension, application, analysis, synthesis, and evaluation. Accreditation visitors to schools and faculties of nursing, as well as to health care facilities, look for evidence of critical thinking ability. Critical thinking is a required component of health assessment and nursing care (Alfaro-LeFevre, 2010). Nurses use critical thinking to identify patterns and trends, consider missing or conflicting assessment information, and decide the type and frequency of future assessments.

Clinical Reasoning

The process of clinical reasoning is based on the nurse's critical thinking. It includes the collection and clustering of data to draw inferences and propose diagnoses. A seven-step process for clinical reasoning can be used in the context of health assessment (Weber & Kelley, 2010). Refer to Figure 1-3.

The first step is to gather assessment data to identify both patient strengths and health challenges. During history-taking and physical examination, nurses collect subjective and objective data. They then cluster data to establish themes, patterns, and common relationships. Additionally, nurses identify data that are inconsistent or missing.

After this clustering, nurses draw inferences or ideas about what the health issue is. A wellness diagnosis is appropriate when patients are healthy but would like an improved health state, such as "Readiness for enhanced knowledge" (NANDA-I, 2009). This is considered primary prevention. Patients may also be at risk for a condition, in which an at-risk-for-disease diagnosis is appropriate, such as "At risk for skin breakdown." This can be considered secondary prevention, and interventions are targeted to prevent complications. If patients have a cluster of signs and symptoms that indicate a current health condition, nurses determine the diagnoses that fit and compare assessment findings to the defining characteristics for the diagnosis. Nurses also review the suggested interventions for each diagnosis (tertiary prevention) to determine which diagnosis is most appropriate. The diagnoses are confirmed or ruled out based on these comparisons. Lastly, nurses document the assessment and diagnoses with the related factors. An example is "ineffective airway clearance related to secretions as evidenced by low pitched wheezes, cough, thick yellow sputum and oxygen saturation of 91%" (NANDA-I, 2009). No evidence is documented for the health-promotion or at-risk diagnosis, because patients do not yet have the diagnosis or supporting assessment findings.

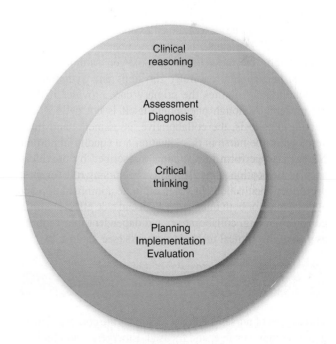

Figure 1-3 The clinical reasoning process.

Table 1-1 Common Nursing Diagnoses Associated with Health

Diagnosis and Related Factors	Point of Differentiation	Assessment Characteristics	Nursing Interventions
Health-seeking behaviour related to expressed desire for increased control of personal health	Actively seeking ways to move toward a higher level of health	Expressed desire to seek higher level of wellness, concern about current conditions on health status	Prioritize learner needs based on patient preferences. Emphasize the health benefits of positive lifestyle behaviours.
Ineffective health maintenance	Impaired abilities to select, implement, or look for assistance with healthy lifestyle behaviours	Lack of health-seeking behaviour, lack of resources, lack of adaptive behaviours to changes	Assess feelings, values, and reasons for not following plan of care. Assess family, economic, and cultural patterns that influence plan of care.
Ineffective management of therapeutic regimen	Not regulating and integrating a treatment for illness into daily life	Did not take action to reduce risk factors, difficulty with prescribed regimen for treatment or prevention of complications	Encourage active participation. Review actions that are not therapeutic. Identify the reasons for nontherapeutic actions.
Nonadherence	Behaviour that is nonadherent with a health treatment or management plan and may lead to ineffective or undesired outcomes	Failure to adhere to plan or keep appointments, evidence of complications, exacerbation of symptoms	Identify the cause of nonadherence. Monitor the ability to follow directions, solve issues, concentrate, and read. Identify cues that trigger healthy behaviours.

As part of the care planning for Mrs. Ortiz, who was recently diagnosed with diabetes, the nurse uses the clinical reasoning process to determine which nursing diagnoses best fit with her cluster of symptoms, including her teaching needs. Because she has shown effective management of her treatment thus far, the best diagnosis is health-seeking behaviour.

Health issues that require collaboration are monitored by nurses, but require the expertise of other health care professionals for interventions. In the above example, the collaborative health issue is written as a "potential complication: pneumonia." The nurse monitors temperature, respiratory rate, cough, shortness of breath, oxygen saturation, lung sounds, and sputum carefully for signs and symptoms of pneumonia and notifies the primary care provider if these are present. Although pneumonia itself is not defined as a nursing diagnosis, the collaborative assessments and interventions of the nurse in this situation are equally important. Nurses also perform interventions prescribed by providers, such as medication administration. The nursing role for these prescribed medications includes accurate administration and assessments for both intended effects and side effects. Nurses perform nursing, collaborative, and dependent interventions as part of the clinical reasoning process (see Table 1-1).

Types of Health Assessments

Three types of nurses' health assessments are common: emergency, comprehensive, and focused. Emergency and focused assessments address primarily health issues and conditions.

Comprehensive assessments are broad and wide-ranging. The amount and sort of information varies, however, for all types of assessment depending on the patient's needs, purpose of data collection, health care setting, and nurse's role.

Emergency Assessment

Emergency assessment is performed in a life-threatening or unstable situation, such as with a patient in an emergency department (ED) who has experienced a traumatic injury. Staff members in the ED use triage to determine the level of acuity by conducting assessments based upon the mnemonic A, B, C, and D:

- A—Airway (with cervical spine protection if an injury is suspected)
- B—Breathing—rate and depth, use of accessory muscles
- C—Circulation—pulse rate and rhythm, skin colour
- D—Disability—level of consciousness, pupils, movement

All life-threatening conditions identified during the initial assessment require the initiation of critical interventions. The nurse will

- open the patient's airway
- assist the patient's breathing

- provide assistance with circulation (cardiopulmonary resuscitation [CPR] if needed)
- protect the cervical spine if the patient is injured
- ensure that the disoriented or suicidal patient is safe
- provide pain management and sedation

Nurses perform assessments and critical interventions simultaneously to treat life-threatening conditions.

Comprehensive Assessment

A **comprehensive assessment** includes a complete health history and physical examination. It is done annually on an outpatient basis, following admission to a hospital or long-term care facility, or every 8 hours for patients in intensive care. In primary care, the history may be obtained by having the patient initially complete an in-depth form that includes a personal and family history of illness, medical treatment, and surgeries. Nurses discuss the information with patients and clarify any incomplete or unclear areas. Dates of diagnoses and treatments are important to note along with the rationale for taking medications (eg, if a beta-blocker is taken for high BP or for history of myocardial infarction). A comprehensive history also includes a patient's perception of health, strengths to build on, risk factors for illness, functional abilities, methods of coping, and support systems.

It is important to reconcile the medication list with what the patient is actually taking so that patients continue taking their prescribed medications (Institute for Healthcare Improvement [IHI], 2007a). Because patients may be unable to participate in data collection as a result of the high acuity of their situation, nurses may need to use secondary data sources for information, such as the history in the patient health record or the patient's family members.

Nurses assess the patient's health beliefs and discuss health-promotion measures. They conduct health screenings of patients according to national guidelines (eg, bowel cancer screening for a patient who has reached 50 years of age). Nurses answer questions and provide patient teaching in preparation for this diagnostic testing.

A complete physical examination includes all body systems and regions, usually in a head-to-toe format. This includes an assessment of the skin, hair and nails; head and neck; eyes; ears; nose, mouth, and throat; spine, thorax, and lungs; heart and great vessels; breasts and axillae; abdomen; musculoskeletal and neurological systems, and arms and legs. Rectal and genital assessments are completed when indicated. Comprehensive assessment is in depth when performed by a nurse practitioner.

Focused Assessment

A **focused assessment** is based on the patient's issues. This type of assessment can occur in all settings, including clinics, hospitals, and home health. It usually involves one or two body systems and is smaller in scope than a comprehensive assessment but more in depth on specific issue(s). An example is a patient who presents to a primary care network with a cough. The health history focuses on the location and quality of the cough, intensity, timing, associated symptoms such as wheezing or shortness of breath, factors that alleviate or worsen the cough, any relevant environmental factors, significance to the client, and the client's perspective on the cause. The physical examination includes a general survey, selected vital signs, an assessment of the ears, nose and throat, thorax, lungs, and heart, and inspection of sputum. The nurse gathers data to determine the etiology of the cough so that it may be appropriately treated.

Priority Setting

A priority issue assumes the most importance among several issues. **Priority setting** is an important skill in professional nursing practice. Its multidimensional nature and need for solid judgment make it challenging to learn. Priorities depend on the acuity of the situation. Nurses use knowledge, clinical experience, expertise, and professional judgment to determine priorities. Expert nurses sometimes prioritize in different ways based upon their experiences.

Guidelines to use when prioritizing are to first address life-threatening situations, an issue that needs immediate attention, a concern that is very important to a patient, or something on which the nurse is spending a lot of time. Life-threatening issues always take priority; airway, breathing, and circulation are considered before other factors such as elevated temperature. Often, priority setting is more subtle, such as deciding what to assess in a patient newly diagnosed with diabetes. In this situation, the issues that are more life threatening are assessed first, such as patient knowledge of signs and symptoms of hypoglycemia and what to do when it occurs. This assessment occurs before assessing the knowledge of dietary factors. A situation that requires immediate attention, for example, is a patient at risk for human violence or suicide. Although the patient may not currently have a life-threatening issue, the potential risk requires immediate attention.

An issue of top importance to a patient should also be considered high priority for the nurse. For example, a patient who is seen for an exacerbation of ulcerative colitis might prioritize a painful left knee as the highest priority. At times, the patient and nurse may disagree on the priority given to issues. For the postoperative patient, pain or discomfort may be the priority, while the nurse views immobility as the priority because of the potential complications of pneumonia and deep vein thrombosis. In this situation, the nurse works with the patient to control the pain and then implements interventions such as ambulating the patient or having the patient cough and do deep breathing exercises. Assessment information is used to direct care in all phases of the nursing process.

Frequency of Health Assessment

The frequency of assessment varies with the patient's needs, the purpose of data collection, and the health care

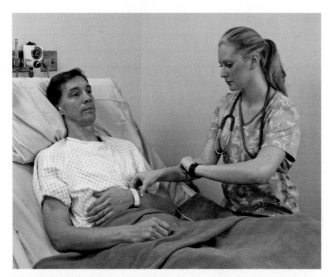

Figure 1-4 The frequency of assessment depends on the acuity of the patient's condition, which is also related to the setting for care. Hospitalized patients may undergo assessments whenever there is a change of shift.

setting. The patient in a long-term care setting may need a comprehensive assessment once a month, while the patient in an acute hospital setting may require an assessment once a shift (Fig. 1-4). Patients in intensive care settings have vital signs and a focused assessment hourly. A facility's standards of care often prescribe such time frames, so it is important for the nurse to identify those standards for the unit and facility in which he or she is working. Patients also have focused assessments following treatments to monitor their effectiveness. If a patient who is short of breath is given an inhaler, the nurse listens to lung sounds after the treatment to see if there has been an improvement in wheezing. The nurse also performs assessments to monitor for side effects from interventions, such as assessing for pedal pulses after a cardiac catheterization in which the femoral artery is punctured. Nurses use judgment to collect data at other times based upon changes in the patient's condition.

In the outpatient setting, the frequency of assessment depends upon the course of illness and whether the process is improving or worsening. Patients are assessed to evaluate the effectiveness of the treatment, such as follow-up for an infection, and for side effects of the treatment, such as immune suppression from chemotherapy.

Well visits are also an important component of health assessment. Periodic health assessment focuses on the most common screening and prevention services for four age groups: (1) birth to 10 years, (2) 11 to 24 years, (3) 25 to 64 years, and (4) 65 years and older. Patients are seen more frequently in the youngest years to monitor growth and development and in later years to promote health and longevity, and reduce the effects of acute or chronic illnesses.

Lifespan Issues

A comprehensive assessment includes cognitive and emotional development in addition to physical growth. Nurses identify expected growth and development patterns, expected variations, aberrations, and deviations. From infancy through adolescence, growth and development are marked by rapid spurts. From adolescence through 25 years, such growth and development proceed more slowly. Motor development occurs rapidly from birth through school age following maturation of the nervous system. Language skills develop rapidly in toddlers and preschool children as vocabulary increases and sentences become more grammatically complex.

Cognitive development follows Piaget's stages from sensorimotor to the age of magical thinking in preschool children to logical reasoning as a school-age child. Although memory may decline in older adults, wisdom remains. Psychosocial development is assessed using Erikson's stages from considering trust versus mistrust in an infant to generativity versus self-absorption in the older adult. The actual versus expected stage is compared. Differences are identified. For example, an older adult with addictions can have issues remaining from adolescence. Refer to Chapter 9 for more information.

Cultural and Environmental Considerations

Knowledge of cultural diversity is essential for nurses working in all practice settings. **Cultural competence** refers to the complex combination of knowledge, attitudes, and skills that a health care provider uses to deliver care that considers the total context of the patient's situation across cultural boundaries (Purnell, 2009). The term has been applied in different ways: addressing culture so that racism and inequity are considered; thinking about culture as shared values, beliefs, and practices of groups of people (Spector, 2009); or thinking about an evolving concept labelled cultural safety by Canadian nurse researchers (Varcoe, Browne, et al., 2010). The CNA incorporated the concept of cultural safety in its description of RN competencies for professional practice (2011). It is important to learn what the patient's specific beliefs or needs are within the patient's larger context. The nurse determines each patient's degree of assimilation into the dominant culture, and the extent to which he or she identifies with the ethnic community, considering such variables as dress, food, religion, customs, and interpretation of symptoms. An assessment for the effects of spirituality and religion on health is also important. "People create culture in relation to one another and their environments. Nurses need to understand how they are bearers of health care and other cultures and how they create culture even as they do health assessments" (Varcoe, Browne, et al., 2010, p. 30). Refer to Chapter 11 for more information.

Remember Mrs. Rosa Ortiz, introduced at the beginning of this chapter. She was seen in the clinic for newly diagnosed type 2 diabetes. Study the communication style of the nurse.

Nurse: Hello, Mrs. Ortiz. How are you doing today?

Mrs. Ortiz: Good.

Nurse: Tell me how things have been going for you.

Mrs. Ortiz: Well, 2 weeks ago, they told me that I had sugar diabetes. It runs in my family, so I shouldn't be too surprised. I just haven't gotten used to this new diet.

Nurse: Tell me more about your concerns.

Mrs. Ortiz: Well, my mother was diabetic and she couldn't eat sugar. But they said that I can have a little dessert, just a little though. The dietitian seemed to be more concerned about the cheese that I add to my refried beans.

Nurse: All food turns into sugar after you eat it, so having a little bit is OK. The dietitian is thinking about the long-term effects of the fat in the cheese, because it contains calories and cholesterol that can damage your blood vessels and lead to a heart attack, stroke, or kidney conditions over time. It's a different way of thinking about it than it used to be.

Mrs. Ortiz: Yes, it doesn't make sense to me. But things always change. Like this, I didn't think that I would end up with diabetes, too.

Nurse: Yes, it sounds like this might be a little overwhelming to you.

Critical Thinking Challenge

- What is the significance of Mrs. Ortiz saying "sugar diabetes" instead of diabetes mellitus?
- What is the role of the nurse related to health promotion and teaching?
- What would you identify as the priority issue at this time?

Components of the Health Assessment

During the interview, the nurse uses communication skills to gather data. Communication includes not only verbal communication but also nonverbal communication (body position, facial expression, and eye contact). Initially, the nurse introduces himself or herself and explains the purpose of the interview. Confidentiality is important, and the nurse must obtain permission from patients for other people to be present during the assessment or ask those people to step out for a few moments to allow some privacy. More information on the interview is found in Chapter 2.

The purpose of the health history is to collect personal and family histories of current health conditions, risk factors, and past issues. The personal history begins with biographical data on date of birth, primary language spoken, and allergies. A detailed history includes data on all systems, psychosocial and mental health, and functional status. The dates of health issues are documented along with treatments and treatment outcomes. More information on the health history is found in Chapter 3.

The primary source in subjective data collection is the patient. **Subjective data** are based on patient experiences and perceptions. The individual describes the feelings, sensations, or expectations to the nurse, who then documents them as subjective data or puts them in quotes. The nurse's role relative to subjective data collection is to gather information for the purpose of improving the patient's health status and helping to determine the cause of the patient's current symptoms.

The physical examination follows the history and focused interview and includes **objective data**, which are measurable.

The issues of Mrs. Rosa Ortiz have been outlined throughout this chapter. The initial subjective and objective data collection is complete, and the nurse has spent time reviewing findings and results. This information now needs to be documented. The following nursing note illustrates how subjective and objective data are analyzed and communicated in the form of a SOAPE note (subjective, objective, analysis, plan, evaluation) based on the nursing process.

Subjective: "I just haven't gotten used to this new diet."

Objective: Alert and oriented. Skin pink, warm, dry, and intact. Clean and groomed. Appears slightly overweight, appears stated age. BP right arm (sitting) 138/78 mm Hg, pulse 82 beats/min and regular, and respirations 16 breaths/min. Current medications include an oral hypoglycemic medication, glyburide (DiaBeta) on start-up dose of 2.5 mg and daily vitamin. Expressing concerns about diet and intake of sugar and fat. Typical diet is high in starch and fat and low in fresh fruits and vegetables.

Analysis: Health-seeking behaviours related to new diagnosis and medication.

Plan: Provide guidance on diet and safety related to potential hypoglycemia from oral hypoglycemic medication.

Evaluation: Patient stated signs and symptoms of hypoglycemia and treatment with 10–15 g of carbohydrate. Received written information on what to do if she becomes hypoglycemic in the future. Stated that she will try using low-fat cheese in her beans and check in at next visit. Will start reading labels for calorie and fat content. Made appointment for clinic visit in 2 weeks. Is enrolled in a diabetes-education class and will bring her questions to the next visit.

Critical Thinking Challenge

- What type of risk assessments will be performed at her next visit?
- What type of physical assessment might be performed at the next visit?
- How might the nurse consider Mrs. Ortiz's cultural background, language, and family in the assessment?

The nurse observes the patient's general appearance; assesses vital signs; examines the skin, listens to the heart, lungs, and abdomen; assesses sensation in the extremities, and assesses peripheral circulation. Chapters 13 to 26 include focused techniques specific to each body system. Because it is too overwhelming and time consuming to complete all focused techniques at once, only the most important screening assessments are included in the head-to-toe assessment (see Chapter 31). The nurse uses clinical judgment to decide which techniques to perform based upon the individual patient.

Documentation and Communication

Documentation of both subjective and objective findings is essential for legal purposes and also for communicating findings to others. Accurate documentation provides a baseline so that changes are noted between assessments. Documentation may be in the form of flow sheets, case notes, or care planning. Legislation regulates the security and privacy of information. One example is the Freedom of Information and Protection of Privacy Act (Government of Alberta, 2000). Confidentiality of documentation is essential, and only information that is pertinent to the care of the patient is shared. More information on documentation is found in Chapter 5. Samples of both expected and unexpected findings are also present in each system chapter.

Communication of assessment data may be shared verbally. Care of the patient is collaborative, and nurses use an organized method when communicating with other health care professionals. Commonly, nurses describe the situation, background, and assessment data to make recommendations about the treatment that is indicated—a system known as SBAR (IHI, 2007b). Nurses also use an organized method when giving a report between shifts or transferring (handing off) patients to other departments, such as when a patient is sent to the operating room (Joint Commission on Accreditation of Healthcare Organizations, 2007). Examples of SBAR are included in Chapter 5 and also in each individual system chapter.

Organizing Frameworks for Health Assessment

Three major frameworks for organizing assessment data are functional systems, head-to-toe system, and body systems. All these methods provide an organizing framework so that nurses do not inadvertently forget any of the important assessment data. Each approach begins with a general survey of the patient, vital signs, and level of distress. Developing a consistent and organized approach is more important than considering which system to use (Table 1-2).

A **functional assessment** focuses on the functional patterns that all humans share: health perception and health management, activity and exercise, nutrition and metabolism, elimination, sleep and rest, cognition and perception, self-perception and self-concept, roles and relationships, coping and stress tolerance, sexuality and reproduction, and values and beliefs (Gordon, 1987). Nurses incorporate functional patterns during the health history interview, but use a head-to-toe system for the physical assessment. Refer to Chapter 3 for more information.

A **head-to-toe assessment** is the most organized system for gathering comprehensive physical data. Because data in one functional area are collected from different parts of the body, it is very inefficient to collect physical data by functional status. For example, peripheral circulation is assessed in both the arms and the legs. Rather than assess the arms and legs and come back to listen to the heart and lungs, it is more organized to proceed from head to toe. When exposing the chest, both the heart and the lungs are auscultated. The chest is covered, then the abdomen is assessed and covered, and the legs and feet are assessed last. This method is more efficient and respects the modesty of patients. See Chapter 31 for more information.

A **body systems** approach is a logical tool for organizing data when documenting and communicating findings. This method promotes critical thinking and allows nurses to analyze findings as they cluster similar data. Data from the functional and head-to-toe assessments are reorganized. When reorganizing data related to the respiratory system, the nurse considers data from the general survey, such as posture, shortness of breath, and level of distress. The nurse also considers vital signs data including respiratory rate and oxygen saturation. He or she considers the patient's skin colour with lung sounds and any shortness of breath to determine the acuity of the issue and anticipate interventions. If the patient with shortness of breath is also cyanotic and wheezing, a respiratory issue is suspected. The condition is acute, and the nurse applies supplemental oxygen while contacting a primary care provider. Rather than identifying one piece of data in isolation, a systems approach allows nurses to cluster similar data together to identify issues.

Table 1-2 Comparison of Assessment Frameworks

Functional Health Pattern	Head to Toe	Body System
Nutrition and metabolism Cognitive perceptual	Head and neck	Neurological and cardiovascular
Cognitive perceptual	Eyes and ears	Neurological
Nutrition and metabolism	Nose, mouth, and throat	Gastrointestinal and respiratory
Activity exercise	Thorax and lungs	Respiratory
Activity exercise	Cardiac	Cardiovascular
Activity exercise	Peripheral vascular	Cardiovascular
Sexuality and reproductive	Breast	Reproductive
Nutrition and metabolism, sexuality and reproductive, elimination	Abdominal	Gastrointestinal, urinary, and reproductive
Activity exercise	Musculoskeletal	Musculoskeletal
Cognitive perceptual	Neurological	Neurological
Sexuality and reproductive	Male or female genitalia	Reproductive
Sexuality and reproductive, elimination	Anus, rectum, and prostate	Gastrointestinal and reproductive
Health perception, sleep, cognition, self-perception, roles, coping, sexuality, values	Functional health status	

Pulling It All Together: An Example of Reflection and Critical Thinking

The nurse uses assessment data to formulate a nursing care plan for Mrs. Rosa Ortiz. After these interventions are completed, the nurse will reevaluate the patient and document the findings in the chart to show critical thinking. This is often in the form of a care plan or case note similar to the one below.

Nursing Diagnosis	Patient Outcomes	Nursing Interventions	Rationale	Evaluation
Knowledge deficit related to new diagnosis and medication	The patient states what to do for symptoms of hypoglycemia.	Discuss signs and symptoms of hypoglycemia. Discuss what to do if hypoglycemic and provide a list of appropriate foods to increase blood glucose level.	Written information reinforces verbal information and can be used as a resource once at home.	Stated signs and symptoms of hypoglycemia. Stated four foods that contain 10 to 15 g of fast-acting carbohydrate. Will bring questions to next clinic visit.

Applying Your Knowledge

Think about Mrs. Ortiz, the 52-year-old patient who is being seen for a follow-up visit for her recently diagnosed type 2 diabetes. Consider responses to the questions introduced at the beginning of the chapter. Recognize how the knowledge gained in this chapter can be applied to her case using critical thinking.

- What are potential health-promotion and teaching needs for Mrs. Ortiz? (Analysis)
- How should the nurse approach a discussion of the patient's diet as related to her diabetes? (Comprehension)
- How will the nurse individualize today's health assessment, considering the patient's gender, age, and culture? (Synthesis)
- What type of health assessment will the nurse perform at the next visit? (Knowledge)
- What areas of the physical examination will the nurse concentrate on? (Application)
- How will the nurse evaluate the results of patient teaching with Mrs. Ortiz? (Evaluation)

Evidence-Informed Critical Thinking

Evidence-informed practice is an approach to patient care that minimizes intuition and personal experience and instead relies upon research findings and high-grade scientific support. **Evidence-informed thinking** helps nurses to solve common health issues through four steps:

1. Clearly identify the issue or condition based on an accurate analysis of current nursing knowledge and practice.

2. Search the literature for relevant research.
3. Evaluate the research evidence using established criteria regarding scientific merit.
4. Choose interventions and justify the selection with the most valid evidence (Evidence Based Practice, 2007).

Many ways are available for nurses to use research and evidence to provide holistic care to patients. McMaster University's Health Information Research Unit in Hamilton, Ontario has developed extensive resources in teaching and implementing evidence-based practice in nursing and other disciplines (2011). The International Honor Society for Nursing, Sigma Theta Tau, has also increased its capacity to support and disseminate nursing scholarships for nursing research (Sigma Theta Tau, 2009). In the USA, the National Institute for Nursing Research (http://www.nih.gov/ninr/), formed in 1986, greatly increased the visibility and funding opportunities for nursing research.

Some evidence is evaluated by performing randomized clinical trials, such as measuring the accuracy of a new oral thermometer against core temperature. If there are several clinical trials, a systematic review of the quality trials becomes the "gold standard." The Cochrane Database is considered the most complete and accurate collection of systematic reviews and is available in most libraries. The National Clearinghouse Guidelines also have recommendations based upon the clinical evidence. PubMed clinical inquiries are another site for obtaining the most current evidence. Many nursing facilities are implementing programs in which nurses develop a clinical question and find the best evidence to plan care. In this way, nurses base individual patient decisions upon the best existing evidence rather than upon their personal experience.

Key Points

- The role of the professional nurse is to promote health and well-being, prevent illness, treat human responses, and advocate for patients.
- Nurses are providers, planners, managers, and coordinators of care as well as advocates, researchers, and educators.
- Nursing values include accountability, justice, dignity, privacy, confidentiality, informed decision-making, health and well-being, and safe, compassionate, competent and ethical care.
- Primary, secondary, and tertiary prevention are used to promote health change.
- Phases of the nursing process include assessment, diagnosis, setting goals and outcomes, planning, intervening, and evaluating.
- Critical thinking is the key to resolving health issues.
- Clinical reasoning is a process by which nurses use critical thinking to cluster the assessment information and to draw inferences about the meaning of the data.
- Types of nursing health assessments include emergency, focused, and comprehensive.
- Subjective data are based on the patient's experiences and perceptions.
- Objective data are measurable and are collected as part of the physical examination.
- Organizing frameworks for assessment include functional, head-to-toe, and body systems.
- Evidence-informed nursing relies upon research findings and high-grade scientific support.

Review Questions

1. The patient is having side effects from a medication. The nurse calls the primary care provider to request a change to the medication order. The nurse is functioning as an/a
   A. educator
   B. advocate
   C. organizer
   D. counsellor

2. Nurses advocate for underserved populations to reduce health disparities. This promotes
   A. autonomy
   B. altruism
   C. social justice
   D. human dignity

3. Nurses belong to the Canadian Nurses Association as part of their
   A. ongoing professional responsibility
   B. role as manager of care
   C. wellness promotion for patients
   D. cultural education activities

4. The purpose of health assessment is to
   A. obtain subjective and objective data
   B. intervene to correct health conditions
   C. outline care that is appropriate
   D. determine if interventions are effective

5. The nurse documents the following information in a patient's chart: "cough and deep breathe every hour while awake." This is an example of
   A. evidence-informed nursing
   B. priority setting
   C. comprehensive assessment
   D. nursing interventions

6. The nurse provides teaching about smoking cessation to a 20-year-old man. The nurse assesses that the patient is concerned because his father died from lung cancer. Which approach would the nurse most likely use when providing teaching to this patient?
   A. Risk assessment model
   B. Clinical reasoning model
   C. Cultural competence model
   D. Body systems model

7. Which of the following processes is the most important when providing nursing care to an ill person?
   A. Writing outcomes
   B. Performing a focused assessment
   C. Collecting objective data
   D. Using critical thinking

8. A patient is admitted to a hospital for surgery for colon cancer. What type of assessment is the nurse most likely to perform on admission?

A. Emergency
B. Focused
C. Comprehensive
D. Illness

9. The nurse conducts the health history based on the patient's responses to the medical diagnosis. This type of framework is based on the

A. functional framework
B. objective framework
C. coordinator framework
D. collaborative framework

10. Which of the following are components of a comprehensive health assessment?

A. Nursing diagnoses
B. Goals and outcomes
C. Collaborative health conditions
D. Examination of body systems

References

Alfaro-LeFevre, R. (2010). *Applying nursing process: A tool for critical thinking* (7th ed.). Philadelphia, PA: Wolters Kluwer Health/Lippincott Williams & Wilkins.

American Diabetes Association. (2009). *Nutrition recommendations and interventions for diabetes.* Retrieved from http://care.diabetesjournals.org/cgi/content/full/30/suppl_1/S48

American Nurses Association. (2009). *The nursing process: A common thread amongst all nurses.* Retrieved from http://www.nursingworld.org/EspeciallyForYou/StudentNurses/Thenursingprocess.aspx

Brunet, K., Day, R. A., et al. (2010). Nutritional assessment. In T. C. Stephen, D. L. Skillen, R. A. Day, & L. S. Bickley (Eds.). *Canadian Bates' guide to health assessment for nurses* (1st ed., pp. 167–201). Philadelphia, PA: Wolters Kluwer Health/Lippincott Williams & Wilkins.

Bulechek, G. M., Butcher, H. K., et al. (2008). *Nursing Interventions Classification (NIC)* (5th ed.). St Louis, MO: Mosby.

Canadian Diabetes Association. (2011). *Are you at risk?* Retrieved from http://www.diabetes.ca/diabetes-and-you/what/at-risk

Canadian Institute for Health Information. (2010). *Regulated nurses: Canadian trends, 2005 to 2009.* Ottawa, ON: Author.

Canadian Nurses Association. (2007). *Framework for the practice of registered nurses in Canada.* Ottawa, ON: Author.

Canadian Nurses Association. (2008). *Code of ethics for registered nurses.* Ottawa, ON: Author.

Canadian Nurses Association. (2009a). *The NEXT decade: CNA's vision for nursing and health.* Ottawa, ON: Author.

Canadian Nurses Association. (2009b). *Registered nurses on the front lines of wait times.* Ottawa, ON: Author.

Canadian Nurses Association. (2011). *Canadian registered nurse examination: Competencies.* Retrieved from http://www.cnaaicc.ca/CNA/nursing/rnexam/competencies/default-e.aspx

Centers for Disease Control and Prevention. (2008). *About the BRFSS: Turning information into public health.* Retrieved from http://www.cdc.gov/brfss/about.htm

College and Association of Registered Nurses of Alberta. (2011). *Primary care: Vision, roles and opportunities.* Edmonton, AB: Author.

Craven, R. F., & Hirnle, C. J. (2009). *Fundamentals of nursing: Human health and function* (6th ed.). Philadelphia, PA: Lippincott.

Cronenwett, L., Sherwood, G., et al. (2007). Quality and safety education for nurses. *Nursing Outlook, 55*(3), 122–131.

Evidence-Based Practice. (2007). Retrieved from http://www.fhs.mcmaster.ca/ceb/acts/ebcp.htm

Gordon, M. (1987). *Nursing diagnosis: Process and application* (2nd ed.). New York, NY: McGraw Hill.

Government of Alberta. (2000). *F-25 RSA Freedom of information and protection of privacy act.* Edmonton, AB: Service Alberta.

Hamilton, H., & Bhatti, T. (1996). *Population health promotion: An integrated model of population health and health promotion.* Ottawa, ON: Health Promotion Development Division, Health Canada.

Health Information Research Unit. (2011). *Best evidence for nursing care.* Retrieved from http://plus.mcmaster.ca/np/Default.aspx.

Institute for Healthcare Information. (2007a). *Medication reconciliation review.* Retrieved from http://www.ihi.org/IHI/Topics/PatientSafety/MedicationSystems/Tools/Medication+Reconciliation+Review.htm

Institute for Healthcare Information. (2007b). *SBAR technique for communication: A situational briefing model.* Retrieved from http://www.ihi.org/IHI/Topics/PatientSafety/SafetyGeneral/Tools/SBARTechniqueforCommunicationASituationalBriefingModel.htm

Institute for Safe Medication Practices. (2007). *Medication tools and resources.* Retrieved from http://www.ismp.org/Tools/default.asp

Johnson, M., Bulechek, G. M., et al. (2006). *NANDA, NOC, and NIC linkages: Nursing diagnoses, outcomes, and interventions.* St. Louis, MO: Mosby.

Joint Commission on Accreditation of Healthcare Organizations. (2007). *National patient safety goals.* Retrieved from http://www.jointcommission.org/PatientSafety/NationalPatientSafetyGoals/.

Leavell, H. R., & Clark, E. G. (1965). *Preventive medicine for the doctor in his community: An epidemiologic approach.* New York, NY: McGraw-Hill.

North American Nursing Diagnosis Association-International. (2007). *Nursing diagnoses: Definitions and classifications 2007–2008* (7th ed.). Philadelphia, PA: Author.

North American Nursing Diagnosis Association-International. (2009). *Nursing diagnoses, 2009–2011 Edition: Definitions and classifications (NANDA NURSING DIAGNOSIS).* West Sussex, UK: John Wiley & Sons.

Purnell, L. D. (2009). *Guide to culturally competent health care* (2nd ed.). Philadelphia, PA: F. A. Davis, Co.

Registered Nurses Association of Ontario. (2011). *Mission statement.* Retrieved from http://www.rnao.org/Page.asp?pageID=122&ContentID=615&SiteNodeID=108&BL_Ex.

Reutter, L., & Kushner, K. E. (2010a). Health and wellness. In J. C. Ross-Kerr & M. J. Wood (Eds.). *Canadian fundamentals of nursing* (4th ed., pp. 1–13), Toronto, ON: Elsevier Canada.

Reutter, L., & Kushner, K. E. (2010b). The broad scope of health promotion in health assessment. In T. C. Stephen, D. L. Skillen, R. A. Day, & L. S. Bickley (Eds.). *Canadian Bates' guide to health assessment for nurses* (1st ed., pp. 3–25). Philadelphia, PA: Wolters Kluwer Health/Lippincott Williams & Wilkins.

Rothschild, J. M., Hurley, A. C., et al. (2006). Recovering from medical errors: The critical care nursing safety net. *Joint Commission Journal on Quality and Patient Safety, 32*(2), 63–72.

Satcher, D. (2006). The prevention challenge and opportunity. *Health Affiliations, 25*(4), 1009–1011.

Sigma Theta Tau. (2009). *Mission and vision*. Retrieved from http://www.nursingsociety.org/aboutus/mission/Pages/factsheet.aspx

Skillen, D. L., Anderson, M. C., et al. (2010). Health assessment and physical examination. In J. C. Ross-Kerr & M .J. Wood (Eds.). *Canadian fundamentals of nursing* (4th ed., pp. 540–634). Toronto, ON: Elsevier Canada.

Spector, R. E. (2009). *Cultural diversity in health and illness* (7th ed.). Upper Saddle River, NJ: Pearson Prentice Hall Health.

Stephen, T. C., & Bickley, L. S. (2010). The health history: Subjective data. In T. C. Stephen, D. L. Skillen, R. A. Day, & L. S. Bickley (Eds.). *Canadian Bates' guide to health assessment for nurses* (1st ed., pp. 51–90). Philadelphia, PA: Wolters Kluwer Health/Lippincott Williams & Wilkins.

Weber, J., & Kelley, J. (2010). *Health assessment in nursing* (4th ed.). Philadelphia, PA: Wolters Kluwer Health/Lippincott Williams & Wilkins.

Wood, M. J., & Ross-Kerr, J. C. (2010). Nursing assessment and diagnosis. In J. C. Ross-Kerr & M .J. Wood (Eds.). *Canadian fundamentals of nursing* (4th ed., pp. 158–177). Toronto, ON: Elsevier Canada.

The Canadian Jensen's Nursing Health Assessment suite offers these additional resources to enhance learning and facilitate understanding of this chapter:

- thePoint online resource, http//thepoint.lww.com/Stephen1E
- *Laboratory Manual for Canadian Jensen's Nursing Health Assessment: A Best Practice Approach*

The Interview and Therapeutic Dialogue

Learning Objectives

1 Identify the significance of verbal and nonverbal communication.

2 Describe how nurses use active listening, restatement, reflection, elaboration, silence, focusing, clarification, and summarizing in verbal communication.

3 Recognize the results of nontherapeutic responses.

4 Differentiate the preinteraction, beginning, working, and closing phases of the interview process.

5 Describe sensitivity to intercultural communication, including working with patients whose first language is not English, working with interpreters, and being sensitive to gender-related issues.

6 Recognize special communication techniques that nurses may use when working with newborns and infants, children, adolescents, and older adults.

7 Identify helpful techniques when working with patients in special situations: hearing impairment, low level of consciousness, cognitive impairment, psychiatric illness, anxiety, crying, anger, drug use, personal questions, and sexual innuendo.

8 Individualize health assessment interview techniques and therapeutic communication considering the condition, age, gender, and culture of the patient.

*M*r. Patrick O'Neill, a 36-year-old Caucasian man, resides in an assisted-living facility. He was diagnosed with AIDS 2 years ago. He has been nonadherent with his antiretroviral medication regimen, because he dislikes taking "artificial substances" and believes that natural methods (eg, nutrition) are more effective toward controlling his illness. He has been receiving meals and housekeeping as part of his services. The nurse has ongoing contact with him to encourage him to take his medications and to assess his condition and needs.

You will gain more information about Mr. O'Neill as you progress through this chapter. As you study the content and features, consider this patient's case and its relationship to what you are learning. Begin thinking about the following points:

- Is it important for the nurse to interview the patient about how he contracted AIDS?
- What is your perceived risk of exposure to HIV/AIDS?
- Which techniques of therapeutic communication might the nurse need to use when talking with Mr. O'Neill?
- How might the nurse's personal beliefs about AIDS and alternative therapies affect communication with Mr. O'Neill?
- How can the nurse communicate nonjudgmental care both verbally and nonverbally?
- What cultural, environmental, or developmental issues might you anticipate for Mr. O'Neill?

All nursing practice revolves around the **nurse–patient relationship**, which is built upon verbal and nonverbal communication within a specific setting. The nurse–patient relationship differs from personal and social relationships, because its foundation is the therapeutic use of self through verbal and nonverbal communication skills. The nurse has a privileged role as a respected health care professional. The relationships with patients are professionally intimate. For example, in some situations, patients disclose information to the nurse that they do not even share with family members. Within the nurse–patient relationship, the nurse learns wide-ranging things about patients—from minute physical details to feelings about spirituality, culture, and psychosocial concerns.

Communication Process

Communication is a complex, ongoing, interactive process that forms the basis for building interpersonal relationships (Adler & Proctor, 2007). It is a system of sending and receiving messages, forming a connection between sender and receiver (Fig. 2-1). This continuous and dynamic process is always subject to interpretation. The sender's purpose is translated into a code with verbal language, gestures, facial expressions, and body cues. The receiver decodes the message, making meaning of the verbal and nonverbal messages. Subjective understanding, perceptions, and other variables greatly influence the actual decoding, both correctly and incorrectly. For example, people from some cultures consider it respectful to shake hands gently; however, people from other cultures may incorrectly decode this nonverbal communication as cold or unfriendly.

Once messages are given and decoded, the receiver and sender give feedback and more messages to stimulate further dialogue. Communication ability, culture, and personal experience all influence the interpretation and decoding of messages. Communication ability means having the cognitive and physical faculties to communicate. People who

have experienced a cerebrovascular accident (stroke) may have permanent damage to the part of the brain that either elicits or interprets speech, making it difficult for them to understand (receptive aphasia) or speak (expressive aphasia). For patients with expressive aphasia, the nurse asks questions that facilitate yes or no answers or provides simple choices to ease communication and reduce frustration. For patients with receptive aphasia, the best approach is for the nurse to use short and simple words and sentences.

Additionally, culture can influence a person's understanding of communication. In many Asian cultures, mental health disorders carry great stigma, so patients may describe psychosocial problems instead as a lack of sleep or as feeling tired (Choi & Gi Park, 2006). There are many other situations where culture affects communication.

Both nurses and patients bring perceptions about the relationship with them. The patient who has had positive personal experiences with the health care system may be more open to developing a relationship with a nurse than the one who has had negative experiences. Perceptions of the health care system are important to assess.

Therapeutic communication is a basic tool that the nurse uses in the caring relationship with patients. In therapeutic communication, the interaction focuses on the patient and the patient's concerns. The nurse assists patients to work through feelings and explore options related to the situation, outcomes, and treatments. This skill takes practice but can be learned with attention and awareness. It takes time to learn to listen for messages that might otherwise be unheard, but this careful listening contributes greatly to a therapeutic relationship. Caring and empathy are useful when communicating therapeutically.

Caring encompasses the nurse's empathy for and connection with the patient. It also includes the ability to demonstrate emotional characteristics such as compassion, sensitivity, and patient-centered care (Canadian Nurses Association, 2010). The nurse shows warmth, caring, interest, and respect and values patients unconditionally and nonjudgmentally. Patients are more willing to discuss their health issues

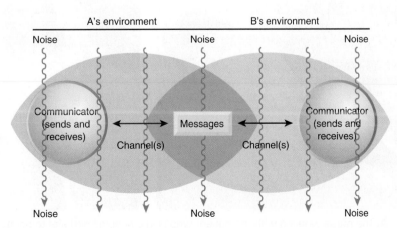

Figure 2-1 Communication is a system of sending and receiving messages, forming a connection between the sender and the receiver.

if they perceive the nurse as caring, understanding, and non-judgmental.

Empathy means the ability to perceive, reason, and communicate understanding of another person's feelings without criticism. It is being able to see and feel the situation from the patient's perspective, not the nurse's. When being empathetic, nurses ask questions that help patients express how they are feeling and what they are thinking. Nurses can communicate to patients that they accurately appreciate the thoughts, feelings, and experiences of patients. In some situations, such as death of a relative, the nurse may exhibit empathy simply by holding a person's hand or offering a tissue.

The nurse with a comfortable **self-concept** is aware of his or her own biases, values, personality, cultural background(s), and communication style. He or she builds such awareness through self-reflection and listening to and understanding feedback from others. Self-reflection increases the ability to be genuine, connect with patients, and meet their needs. Having a comfortable sense of self allows nurses to work with patients of different personalities, cultures, and socioeconomic backgrounds. "Self reflection is a continual part of professional development in clinical work. It brings a deepening personal awareness to our work with clients, which is one of the most rewarding aspects of client care." (Stephen, & Bickley, 2010, p. 54).

Nonverbal Communication Skills

Nonverbal communication is as important as, if not more important than, verbal communication. Communication that does not involve speech occurs continuously and provides important clues to feelings and emotions. The majority of human communication is nonverbal (Arnold & Boggs, 2007). Physical appearance, facial expression, posture and positioning in relation to the patient, gestures,

eye contact, voice, and use of touch are all important components. People tend to believe nonverbal communication over verbal communication when the two are inconsistent. For example, the nurse states that he or she is interested yet the nurse is yawning, looking around the room, and humming a melody. Patients tend to believe the message in the nonverbal behaviour. It is essential to be aware of nonverbal messages to help understand patients better and to ensure the correct messages are being sent. The nurse should not assume that touch is culturally acceptable. Permission to touch the patient is a courtesy by asking, "Is it OK if I feel your abdomen?"

The physical appearance of the nurse sends a message to the patient. Thus, it is important for nurses to ensure that their dress and appearance are professional. Facial expressions should be relaxed, caring, and interested. Some facial expressions (eg, rolling the eyes, looking bored, or disgusted) reduce trust. Use gestures intentionally to illustrate points, especially for patients who cannot communicate verbally. The nurse may point with a finger or gesture an action, such as pretending to drink or pointing to the bathroom. Gestures are purposeful rather than distracting from the communication.

To facilitate optimal eye contact, be at eye level with the patient. Those who stand while patients are in bed will be taller than patients, assuming a position of power. Some patients may interpret the nurse who sits on hospital beds or examining tables as too close or unprofessional, and possibly as infringing on personal space. Also, considering principles of infection control, beds or tables may contain microorganisms or body secretions that could be carried from one room to another (see Chapter 4). For these reasons, sit in chairs at eye level with patients who are in bed during interviews (Fig. 2-2A). For the patient seated on an examination table, the nurse will be near eye level when standing (Fig. 2-2B).

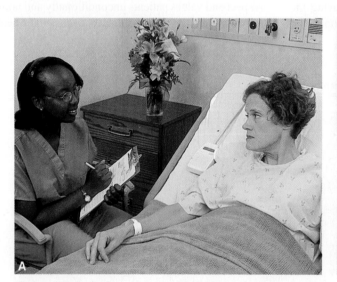

Figure 2-2 A. The nurse working with the patient who is in a hospital bed sits to be at eye level with the patient during the interview. **B.** The nurse stands to be at eye level with the patient on an examination table.

Touch is an essential and dominant component of the physical examination. During initial interviews, however, patients may misinterpret touch as being too casual. Use nonverbal skills to communicate messages to patients that facilitate a therapeutic relationship. If a nurse is positioned near the bed, speaks carefully, and maintains respectful eye contact, the patient feels that he or she is being heard.

Verbal Communication Skills

Effective interviewing skills are learned through practice and repetition. These skills encourage patients to further expand on their answers and also to redirect patients when they wander from the topic.

The nurse's speech is of moderate pace and volume, with clear articulation. A too soft voice might indicate embarrassment or discomfort, while a too loud voice may be powerful and controlling. Speech that is too fast indicates being rushed, while speech that is too slow might send a message that the patient is lacking in cognitive ability. For patients with a hearing impairment, the nurse may need to speak clearly and slowly into the better ear or be positioned so that patients can lip read (Fig. 2-3).

For patients whose first language is not English, use simple and clear language but do not speak louder. Instead of using complete sentences, speak in one or two words, such as "Pain?" Insert pauses in the conversation to allow patients an opportunity to speak; such pauses facilitate trust, respect, and sharing.

Active Listening

Active listening is the ability to focus on patients and their perspectives. It requires nurses to constantly decode messages including thoughts, words, opinions, and emotions. For example, if the patient is sad, it is appropriate for a nurse to place a hand over the patient's and to show a facial expression of compassion. If the patient is angry, the nurse listens to the reason for the anger, such as treatment failure. Rather than respond in turn with anger, the nurse attends to the patient's

feelings by pulling up a chair and taking the time to listen. He or she tries to uncover the hidden message and reflects appropriate body language.

Talking about difficult feelings helps patients to heal. The nurse is not expected to solve all the problems but instead to therapeutically use the self to assist patients to deal with them.

Restatement

Restatement relates to the content of the communication. The nurse makes a simple statement, usually using the words of the patient. The purpose is to encourage the patient to elaborate. Restatement provides an opportunity for the patient to further understand communication. For example, the nurse says, "You feel like there is a knot in your chest."

Reflection

Reflection is similar to restatement; however, instead of simply restating comments, the nurse identifies the main themes of communication and how the patient may be feeling. The conversation may be longer, in which the patient discusses several elements related to a topic. The nurse listens carefully to the different thoughts expressed and attempts to identify their relationship. With this technique, patients gain a better understanding of the issues that underlie their thoughts, which helps to identify their feelings. The following example illustrates how to use reflection.

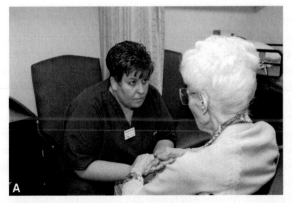
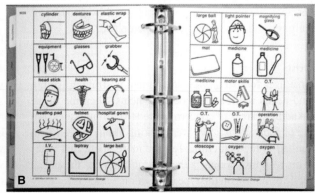

Figure 2-3 Nurses must be creative to communicate with patients who cannot fully interact verbally or who have sensory impairments. **A.** This nurse is making sure to sit directly in front of the patient and enunciate very clearly for the patient with hearing difficulties. **B.** Picture boards can be helpful for patients who cannot speak or who cannot communicate in the same language as the nurse.

Patient: I really hate getting shots. Do I really need to get the flu shot? My parents never had it and they stayed healthy during the winter.
Nurse: You sound a bit nervous about getting an injection. (Reflection)
Patient: The last shot that I had really hurt.

In this situation, the patient was not questioning the need for the injection but was expressing anxiety about it because of a previous experience. The nurse now knows to direct the conversation toward dealing with the anxiety rather than teaching about the risk for influenza.

Encouraging Elaboration (Facilitation)

Encouraging elaboration (facilitation) is a technique that assists patients to describe concerns more completely. These responses encourage patients to say more and continue the conversation. They show patients that the nurse is interested. The nurse may nod the head or say "Um hum," "Yes," or "Go on" to cue the patient to keep talking. Another technique is to let the patient know that his or her thoughts and feelings are common and give the patient permission to discuss them. The nurse might use a phrase such as, "Sometimes when patients are involved in a car accident, they have flashbacks or bad dreams."

Silence

Nurses use **silence** purposefully during the interview to allow patients time to gather their thoughts and provide accurate answers. Using silence therapeutically can communicate nonverbal concern. Silence also gives patients a chance to decide how much information to disclose. For example, patients may be embarrassed to discuss the events that led them to contract sexually transmitted infections. The use of silence sends a message that when the patient is ready, the nurse will be there to listen. Silence also provides the nurse with an opportunity to decide in which direction to take the conversation. He or she can attend to nonverbal language and note whether the patient seems like he or she does not want to continue talking or just needs time to gather thoughts and emotions. Be aware, however, that silence may not be appreciated by patients of some cultures and may be negatively perceived.

Focusing

The nurse uses **focusing** when the patient is straying from a topic and needs redirection. Focusing helps when the nurse needs to address areas of concern related to current issues. An example of focusing is, "We were talking about the reaction that you had to the penicillin. Tell me more about that reaction." This response connects the patient's story to the initial need for information on the type of reaction, which is a safety issue needing further discussion. It keeps the conversation on track without changing the subject and conveys the message that the nurse will assist the patient to provide important information.

Clarification

Clarification is important when the patient's word choice or ideas are unclear. For example, the nurse states, "Tell me what you mean by the evil eye." Another way to clarify is to ask, "What happens when you get low blood?" Such questions prompt the patient to identify other symptoms or give more information so that the nurse better understands. The nurse also can use clarification when the patient's history of illness is confusing. Putting data in chronological order or placing events in context can help make the story clearer. For example, a nurse might ask, "When you had chest pain, first you took three nitroglycerin tablets and then you called 911, is that right?"

Summarizing

Summarizing happens at the end of the interview, during the closure phase. The nurse reviews and condenses important information into two or three of the most important findings. Doing so helps ensure that the nurse has identified important information and lets the patient know that he or she has been heard accurately. It gives the nurse and patient future direction as they establish a therapeutic relationship. Summarizing includes the progress made toward problem solving and things to think about later. An example is, "It seems that you are most concerned about your child's appetite and lack of energy. We have talked about adding some low-cost and high-protein foods to her diet. When you come in for your next visit, we can talk about how that worked."

Nontherapeutic Responses

False Reassurance

Often in social situations, people use nontherapeutic casual responses. Probably the most common example is **false reassurance** to minimize uncomfortable feelings. In nurse–patient relationships, giving false reassurance also can minimize the amount of distressing information that the nurse has to handle. Nevertheless, such responses effectively close off communication from the perspective of patients. By providing false reassurance, the nurse unconsciously indicates to the patient that his or her concerns are not worth discussing. This situation enhances anxiety, which can increase the patient's urge to seek further reassurance, and diminishes his or her trust. Examples of false reassurance are, "It won't hurt." or "Don't worry. It will be all right." It would be better to say, "It will hurt a bit when I take off the bandage, but I'll do it carefully" or "It sounds like you're concerned that your cancer might have returned. I want you to know that I will be available to talk about the results when you get them." This type of reassurance validates the patient's concerns and reassures him or her that the nurse will be there to provide a therapeutic relationship.

The nurse's role related to interviewing is to gather information to assess the patient's health status and to provide therapeutic communication when indicated. A nursing student is visiting Mr. O'Neill, introduced at the beginning of this chapter, to remind him to take his antiretroviral medications and to assess his current needs.

Nursing Student: Hi, Mr. O'Neill. I'm Tom Fritz, a nursing student working with Betsy, your nurse. Betsy said to let you know that she's available if you would rather talk with her.

Mr O'Neill: You're working with Betsy?

Nursing Student: Yes, I'm a 3rd year nursing student. Betsy will be here in about 10 minutes. Is it okay if I come in?

Mr O'Neill: Yes, come on in. Would you like a glass of water?

Nursing Student: That would be great if it's not too inconvenient.

Mr O'Neill: (Gets water) You can sit down.

Nursing Student: Thank you. Tell me how you're doing today.

Mr O'Neill: I'm OK—you're here to make sure that I took my medication, aren't you? I already took it—you can count the pills if you want.

Nursing Student: We can do that in a minute. I'd just like to talk for a little bit to hear how you're feeling and if I can help in any way.

Mr O'Neill: Well, I'd rather be home, but I can't live by myself anymore. Every day I just seem to get weaker.

Critical Thinking Challenge

- What therapeutic communication techniques were used in the example?
- What interactions occurred in the dialogue that might influence the nursing student's ability to establish trust with Mr. O'Neill?

Sympathy

Sympathy is feeling what the patient feels from the viewpoint of the nurse. When the nurse is being sympathetic, he or she is not being therapeutic, because the nurse is interpreting the situation as he or she perceives it. By contrast, empathy is feeling what the patient feels from the patient's perspective. The nurse keeps the focus on the patient, allowing his or her complete self-expression.

Unwanted Advice

Giving unwanted advice happens frequently in social situations. It is nontherapeutic in professional relationships, because the advice is usually from the nurse's perspective, not the patient's. It is based on the experiences and opinions of the nurse, and it may not help patients. Giving advice differs from providing information. For example, if the patient asks, "How do I get rid of the lice in my son's hair?" the nurse answers using his or her knowledge base and current evidence. The patient who asks, "Do you think that I should have my knee replaced? I don't really know what to do" requires a different type of response. In this situation, when the nurse is using active listening, he or she understands that the patient is asking for an opportunity to discuss options, not what the nurse would want. Instead of responding to the request for an opinion, the nurse might state, "Tell me what you know about the surgery" or "You sound concerned about having knee surgery." Such responses give patients an opportunity to explore choices more fully, clarify any confusing points, and weigh risks versus benefits. They also incorporate the patient's perspective instead of adding potentially confusing or conflicting information or opinions. Nurses take time to focus on the concerns of patients and help them through decisions by using active listening, reflection, and restatement. In this way, patients reach their own conclusions.

Biased Questions

Using leading or **biased questions** is often an unintentional nontherapeutic response. Biased questions carry judgment and lead patients to respond in the most acceptable way. They also can cause patients to feel guilty or inferior because of unhealthy behaviours. An example of a biased question is, "You don't use drugs, do you?" To obtain a more honest response, the nurse asks objective questions such as, "It is important that we know what recreational drugs you are taking so that we avoid interactions with the medications that we are giving you. Do you use any recreational drugs?" In this way, the nurse places the need for information within the context of health care. Patients understand that the nurse wants to provide the best care, not to judge unhealthy behaviours.

Changes of Subject

Changing the subject may happen when a situation is uncomfortable for a nurse because of personal experiences or coping mechanisms. For example, if the nurse recently experienced the death of a parent, it may be challenging at this time for him or her to talk with a family about the patient who has terminal cancer. Although not therapeutic for the patient, the nurse is using coping mechanisms to protect against emotional distress. The nurse who uses self-reflection is aware when she or he is using less therapeutic communication strategies and seeks to improve them. Options are to control emotions with patients and seek support from others or to be honest with patients and families about the situation. If emotional control is too difficult for the nurse, she or he should refer patients to other health care professionals.

The nurse also might change the subject unconsciously when feeling rushed or stressed. In such cases, she or he may not take time to use active listening. As an example, on a busy day, the nurse wants to complete the intake and output record at the end of the shift. When the patient says, "I'm feeling a bit nauseous," the nurse may reply, "What did you have to drink?" instead of "How long have you been feeling nauseous?" Although the nurse constantly strives to use active listening, some situations dictate the type of communication used. The goal is to prioritize and block out times to use active listening when patients need to talk.

Distractions

Distractions in the environment contribute to nontherapeutic communication. Hectic and rushed work environments abound across settings, contributing to patient reports about depersonalized care (Hurst, 2007). Distractions come from several sources: equipment, other patients, colleagues, pagers, visitors, and overhead paging systems. When equipment poses a potential source of distraction, the nurse should silence any alarms and then resolve the issue before initiating a conversation. Equipment alarms indicate an immediate problem that usually takes priority over therapeutic communication. When the patient's roommate is asking for something, the nurse either decides to grant a simple request and then pull curtains and provide for privacy or asks the roommate to wait by saying, "I can get you some water in about 5 minutes." The nurse prioritizes the importance of answering pagers or calls depending on the type of page and the intensity of the conversation and point in the interview. Try to limit interruptions when talking with the patient. If an urgent request or situation arises, let the patient know and assure the patient that you will return to continue the discussion.

Technical or Overwhelming Language

Using too many technical terms or **providing too much information** is another nontherapeutic response. As she or he develops medical vocabulary and knowledge, the beginning nurse must practise translating from medical terminology to lay language. For example, the nurse documents "dysphagia" but asks the patient about "trouble swallowing." It also is important to conduct a conversation at the knowledge level of each patient. The nurse may use more technical descriptions with the patient who works in health care than with the patient who has limited medical knowledge. Complex concepts may best be presented through diagrams and pictures that illustrate points visually (Fig. 2-4). With a new diagnosis, the nurse prioritizes information and discusses the most important items first, pacing and spreading out teaching over several sessions. The nurse attends to nonverbal behaviours from patients, such as puzzled facial expressions, that may indicate a lack of understanding.

Interrupting

Talking too much and **interrupting** are two other nontherapeutic ways of communicating. Because of the nurse–patient relationship, the nurse in the professional role listens more than talks. Those who might be shy in social situations may exhibit excellent therapeutic communication not by talking but by communicating nonverbally through presence, facial expression, or touch. In health care settings, it is better to listen than to talk and to ask effective questions rather than have all the right answers.

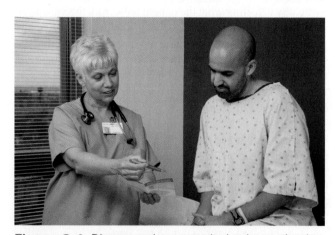

Figure 2-4 Diagrams, pictures, and other instructional materials can greatly assist with the processes of assessment and follow-up teaching related to findings.

Professional Expectations

Learning when to use the various techniques of therapeutic communication is part of both the science and the art of nursing. Because it is easy to overidentify with some patients, especially those who remind the nurse of someone he or she knows, it is important to establish clear professional boundaries. The nurse who becomes too involved with patients experiences burnout and decreased job satisfaction.

Nonprofessional involvement occurs when the nurse crosses the boundaries of professional relationships and establishes social, personal, or economic ties with patients (Holder & Schenthal, 2007). Although social chatting about the weather or current news may put patients at ease, too much personal conversation is unprofessional. Some disclosure may help establish a therapeutic relationship, but the nurse always presents such information with a focus on the patient. For example, the nurse is working with parents of a child who recently was diagnosed with asthma. Coincidentally, the nurse's son also has asthma. The nurse may use that information to say, "I have a child with asthma, too. I noticed that the cough would get worse at night. What was the first thing that you noticed?" The nurse uses personal information to quickly redirect a conversation to focus on patients and their families.

Sexual boundary violation is the clearest example of unprofessional involvement. Sexual contact is never acceptable within the therapeutic nurse–patient relationship. The Canadian Nurses Association (CNA, 2008) has established professional guidelines about behaviours such as dating or having outside contact with patients. Nurses always ensure their relationships are for the benefit of the persons in their care. They do not enter into romantic, sexual, or other personal relationships with people in their care (CNA).

Visiting patients beyond the role of the nurse or nursing student also breaks professional boundaries. The nurse recognizes that care continues with other health care professionals and trusts that the health care system exists to meet ongoing needs. Although many times the nurse remembers and becomes more attached to the first patients with whom she or he works, the nurse must not confuse the privileged intimacy associated with the nursing role with the intimacy involved in a social or personal relationship.

Phases of the Interview Process

The nurse–patient relationship differs from a social relationship because the nurse is in the role of a helper and the focus is on healing patients. In social relationships, the roles and power are closer to equal.

The nurse organizes interviews to use time efficiently and help patients to feel that their needs are met. The nurse is rewarded in the relationship by being able to help others.

It is important to consider the setting before beginning the interview. Ensuring privacy and confidentiality and trying to make the setting as comfortable as possible helps the interview. Using privacy curtains or a private room, ensuring the room is warm, and limiting the number of potential interruptions are some examples of adjusting the environment to encourage a more effective interview.

Preinteraction Phase

Before meeting with patients, the nurse collects data from the patient health record, including the previous history of illnesses or surgeries, current medication list, and list of concerns. She or he uses this information to conduct an interview, already knowing about some of the past illnesses and responses to treatments (Fig. 2-5). The nurse reviews the record chronologically to detect patterns of illness, such as declining functional status, and to identify how things fit together. For example, the patient who was diagnosed with breast cancer had a mastectomy, developed postoperative infection and lung injury, and now is on home oxygen. The record in this case assists in identifying why this patient with breast cancer has been placed on home oxygen.

Beginning Phase

The nurse initially introduces herself or himself by name and states the purpose of the interview. An example is, "Hello, my name is Sam Smith, and I am going to be your nurse this evening." At this time, it is appropriate to ask patients by what name they would like to be called. The nurse simply can say, "What name would you prefer me to use?" She or he listens

Figure 2-5 The nurse is reviewing data from the patient's health record before meeting with the patient to conduct the initial interview.

carefully for the correct pronunciation and may ask patients for confirmation that the pronunciation is correct. The nurse shakes hands if that seems comfortable for the patient and is appropriate for the setting.

To relax the patient, the beginning phase may continue with a discussion of some neutral areas, such as the weather, especially if anxiety is noted. The nurse moves through such discussion quickly, however, and introduces the purpose of the interview. For example, "Mrs. Lewis, I will need to ask you some questions about your personal and family history." The nurse also makes some overall remarks based on the observations, such as "You have been in the nurse's office for a cold three times in the last 3 weeks. It doesn't seem like your cold is going away."

Privacy is important. The nurse pulls drapes around patients if conducting interviews in hospital rooms or closes doors if working in examination rooms. In community settings where patients are disclosing personal information, the nurse identifies areas where others will not overhear conversations before beginning the interview.

Working Phase

During the working phase, the nurse collects data by asking specific questions. Two types of questions are closed-ended and open-ended questions. Each type has a purpose; the nurse chooses which type will help solicit the appropriate information.

Closed-ended or **direct questions** are best for specific information that yields yes or no answers, such as "Do you have a family history of heart disease?" In clinic settings, these questions commonly appear on forms that patients complete prior to meeting a nurse. During the interview, the nurse reviews completed forms with the patient, asking follow-up questions and clarifying information that the patient listed as problematic. The nurse also can use closed-ended questions, such as "Is your pain sharp? Or is it dull?" to help cue the patient who has had difficulty responding to an open-ended question such as "What does your pain feel like? Closed-ended questions are also helpful for patients with communication challenges, such as those with dementia or limited English knowledge.

Open-ended questions require patients to give more than yes or no answers. They are broad and permit responses in the patient's own words. Sometimes these answers are part of the subjective information and put in quotes. Examples of open-ended questions are, "Tell me about your chest pain." and "How are you doing with the low-salt diet?" Patients may find "Why" questions difficult to answer and view such inquiries as too interrogative or personal. They also may view such questions as accusatory, so it is helpful to avoid them. For example, "Why haven't you stopped smoking?" is more threatening than, "Tell me about how difficult it is to stop smoking."

During the working phase, the nurse also charts the patient's history and health issues. The goal is to achieve a balance between listening and documenting. Sometimes documentation is on paper; other times, on a computer. When using a computer, ideal positioning is for the nurse to be able

Figure 2-6 This nurse has situated herself so that she can talk and maintain eye contact with the patient while being able to record pertinent findings electronically.

to record data while maintaining eye contact with the patient and family members (Fig. 2-6). If using paper to document, the nurse may find that a clipboard placed in the lap allows him or her to record information without obstructing eye contact with the patient. Usually, the nurse records information during the interview and then returns to the form later to expand on and include any other descriptive information. This method allows the nurse to maintain better eye contact with the patient during the interview. It takes practice to achieve a comfortable blend of writing things down and listening.

Closing Phase

The nurse ends interviews by summarizing and stating what the two to three most important points might be. She or he might say, "It seems that you are most concerned about control of your pain. Would you agree?" Additionally, the nurse can close by letting the patient know the next steps, such as, "I'll make sure to put in your plan of care to ask about your pain level every 4 hours." The nurse also asks if the patient would like to mention or needs anything else. Doing so gives the patient a final opportunity to express any concerns and feel that he or she has been heard. If the nurse is using a checklist, the closing phase is a good time to review it for completeness and to make notes about future interventions.

The nurse thanks the patient and family members for taking the time to provide information. She or he acknowledges the commitment of patients to health promotion or disease management appropriately, such as by saying "It was good that you came in to the clinic now, so we can help sort out what is happening."

Intercultural Communication

During **intercultural communication**, the sender of an intended message belongs to one culture, while the receiver is from another. Cultural differences may exist related to a group or genetic background, region, age, degree of acculturation

After the initial interview, the nursing student assessed Mr. O'Neill. The assessment revealed the following subjective and objective data. Begin to think about how the data cluster together and what additional data the nurse might want to collect. The nurse also uses critical thinking to analyze health issues and anticipate nursing interventions. The following nursing note illustrates the use of clinical reasoning and the nursing process.

Subjective: "I'd rather be home, but I can't live by myself anymore. Every day I just seem to get weaker."

Objective: Appears slightly anxious and weak. Gait slow but steady. Can heat prepared meals in kitchen; housekeeping comes weekly for cleaning. Bathroom with grab bars by shower and toilet. No loose cords or rugs. Environment clean and without clutter. Pill count accurate. Dressing, grooming, and toileting independently.

Analysis: Risk for impaired home maintenance and increasing weakness with disease progression.

Plan: Continue with meal and housekeeping services. Continue to assess for needs related to dressing, grooming, toileting, and meals. Further discuss nutrition and supplements in addition to adherence to the medication regimen.

Critical Thinking Challenge

- What fears or concerns might a nurse have about visiting this setting or working with this patient?
- What elements should the nursing student include when closing the interview process with Mr. O'Neill?

---

into Western society, or a combination of these factors (see Chapter 11). Nonverbal differences in eye contact, facial expression, gestures, posture, timing, touch, and space needs are all culturally influenced. Language differences between the patient and the nurse can compound cultural differences and prevent the nurse from understanding the perspectives of the patient. Voice volume, vocal tone, inflections, pronunciation, and accents also influence meaning. More than simple language translation, the cultural meanings of health, illness, and treatment are important factors to consider (Murphy, 2007).

Communication etiquette refers to the code of conduct and good manners that show respect for others. Such etiquette varies between and within cultures. The nurse must assess the degree to which each patient identifies with cultural norms. Additionally, many patients identify with multiple cultures. It is important to avoid assuming that patients follow cultural beliefs and to assess the degree to which each individual perceives those beliefs. Nurses can bridge cultural differences by being sensitive to variations and using caring communication techniques. Refer to Chapter 11 for more information.

Patients with Limited English

Patients with limited English skills often identify language barriers as frustrating when navigating the health care system

(Dysart-Gale, 2007). When possible, an interpreter is used; however, interpreters cannot be involved continuously throughout the patient's care. Thus, the nurse must develop other communication tools. For example, the nurse covers one concept at a time instead of overwhelming the patient with several ideas at once. He or she uses simple words or phrases to facilitate understanding. At times, the nurse can pantomime questions, such as pretending to be in pain or having a questioning look on the face.

When communicating with patients with limited English proficiency, the nurse remembers the following principles:

- Limitations in English are not a reflection of intellectual functioning.
- Patients may be highly literate in another language but functionally illiterate in English.
- Patients tend to think in their native language and translate, delaying their responses.
- Patients interpret the message that reflects their cultural beliefs, often changing the intent.
- Written information in the native language supports verbal communication.

Nurses can use a sheet with common phrases (eg, "I am thirsty," "I need to use the bathroom") if patients are literate in their languages of origin. Resources with pictures are helpful if patients have good visual acuity but cannot read. It is also helpful for nurses to know a few key phrases in patients' languages to increase communication and trust.

Working with an Interpreter

The need for an interpreter should be established during the patient's first contact with the health care agency. Even when a patient's language skills are fluent, a trained medical interpreter may be necessary for discussing sensitive topics, such as end-of-life care or permission for consent to treatment. In inpatient settings, interpreters may check in with patients daily. In such situations, it is helpful to maintain a list of questions and areas for patient teaching to cluster the most important information during the time that the translator is available. Other occasions for using an interpreter are the admission assessment, complex treatments, patient education, informed consent, and discharge planning. Interpreters are chosen considering language (eg, Mandarin or Cantonese for a Chinese patient), dialect, gender for sensitive subjects, and social status if this is likely to be an issue.

Using children in the family, other relatives, or close friends as interpreters is not recommended because patients may not want to share personal information with others. Additionally, friends and family who are unfamiliar with medical terminology may misinterpret information. When possible, a trained medical interpreter is preferred. Not only are medical interpreters knowledgeable in terminology, but also they have a health care background. These interpreters also understand cultural health beliefs and practices and can help bridge the gap.

Interpreters are educated to remain neutral. Considering the natural communication process that involves the encoding and decoding of messages, however, interpreters still influence the content and context of communication. Issues can arise when interpreters add their opinion or bias communication. It is important to pay attention to and look at patients during interviews to keep the focus on them rather than on interpreters. Also being aware of nonverbal communication that seems inconsistent with the issues being discussed is essential. Tips for communicating through interpreters are in Box 2-1.

Gender and Sexual Orientation Issues

Communication styles vary between and within each gender group. Some believe that men commonly prefer more information and facts, whereas women prefer more social and emotional interactions (Seale, 2006). It may be helpful to provide more information and structure for male patients and ask questions that focus more on emotional response, role adjustment, and coping mechanisms for women.

Gender also influences family roles, defined as a "set of beliefs about or expectations of male and female behaviour and experiences within the family" (Wright & Leahey, 2009, pp. 71–72). Family roles can become involved in interviewing and history taking when cultural norms influence the nurse–patient relationship. For example, some cultures expect that the eldest male acts as the family leader and communicator. In others, patients may prefer that the husband is spoken with to represent the family. It is helpful to be aware of these cultural norms and ask patients about their preferences.

It is essential to be aware of societal biases about sexual preference when working with gay, transgender, lesbian, or bisexual patients. It is critical to treat all patients with respect and to provide pertinent information, such as safer-sex practices for all patients. Issues related to sexual orientation often become prominent when patients have life-threatening or chronic illnesses. In many cases, their life partners have no legal decision-making capacity. Sometimes, conflicts arise between partners and other family members of patients. Because many companies do not recognize relationships outside of legal marriage, gay and lesbian partners may have limited health care insurance benefits, family leave, or bereavement leave.

Additionally, subtle heterosexual assumptions arise in nursing communication. In many cases, it is assumed that a patient is heterosexual until the patient does or says something to disprove this assumption. Consider the simple intake questions, "Are you single?", "Married ?", or "Divorced?" and how a patient with an unmarried partner would respond. Gays and lesbians may choose to hide their orientations because of the heterosexual assumptions and fear of negative attitudes from health care providers or lack of confidentiality and family conflicts (Hutchinson, Thompson, et al., 2006). More inclusive, sensitive, and ultimately better questions are, "Do you live alone?" "Or with someone?" because this provides a more direct avenue for finding out about support at home.

Nurses may be afraid of behaving incorrectly when patients have a sexual orientation that differs from their own. This fear can lead to insecurity and cause misunderstandings (Rondahl, Innala et al., 2006). Emotions such as uncertainty may lead to incongruent or "double" messages in communication. As professionals, nurses must become educated about gay patients, same-sex families, and gay culture to learn to communicate naturally and to become aware of the assumptions communicated through language and behaviour.

BOX 2-1 GUIDELINES FOR INTERPRETER-DEPENDENT COMMUNICATION

- Take time to meet with the interpreter before meeting with the patient.
- Allow sufficient time—working with an interpreter may take twice as long as a meeting in which a common language is spoken.
- Speak directly to the patient.
- Speak in short sentences and allow the interpreter to interpret.
- Develop alternatives to direct questions.
- Avoid ambiguous language, abstractions, and technical jargon.
- Speak slowly and clearly; use repetition as needed.
- Be aware of nonverbal messages that may require interpretation just as verbal messages.
- Avoid using family members as interpreters.

Adapted from Kennedy, M. G. (1997). Cultural competency. In N. K. Worley (Ed.), *Mental health nursing in the community*. St. Louis, MO: Mosby.

▲ Lifespan Issues

Parents, legal guardians, or other adult representatives serve as primary interview sources of health care information when patients are children. As they age and become more independent, children can participate more fully in interviews.

It is helpful to refer to children by their first names and ask parents what name they prefer for being addressed. Avoid calling parents "mom" or "dad" to maintain professional communication. Also, be sure to validate the roles of people bringing children to the attention of the health care facility. For example, a mother may be accompanied by a boyfriend who is not the child's father; a stepparent may bring in a child; or a child of gay parents may have two mothers or fathers.

Begin by interviewing caregivers and children together. Provide toys for children to play with while interviewing parents and observe parent–child interactions. Also observe children in the environment for fine and gross motor skills, attention span, language, and development. If issues that need discussion require separation from parents (especially concerning violence or safety), ask parents to leave while the child is interviewed separately (Baren, 2006). Refer to Chapter 12 for more information.

Parents who work outside the home may bring ill children to health care facilities after a call from a day-care provider or babysitter or upon arriving home from work. Some parents may appear distracted or express guilt about not recognizing a symptom earlier.

Parents of children with developmental delays may be especially sensitive to achievements of developmental milestones. When collecting interview data, it may be helpful to compare a child's progress against past milestones instead of comparing against expected findings for the child's age group.

Nonverbal communication is very important with young children, who have limited verbal skills. Toddlers and preschoolers are quick to notice anxiety, pain, distress, or discomfort in either a caregiver or a nurse. Health care settings can be anxiety provoking for children, because many have had immunizations and tests that involved pain or discomfort. It is helpful to have "safe" zones for the interview and physical examination and other areas for drawing blood samples or administering injections. Instead of the formality found in other settings, pediatric and family practice settings usually are colourful, and many health care professionals there wear playful, bright clothing as well (Fig. 2-7).

Newborns and Infants

Families with newborns or infants are undergoing many changes that alter previous patterns and behaviours (see Chapter 28). Parents are often sleep deprived and learning how to feed, dress, and groom their babies while finding time to care for their own needs as well. The excitement of the birth of the infant may make rest difficult. Fatigue is common in the postpartum period from labour, cesarean birth, anemia, breast-feeding, and potentially depression and anxiety. Acknowledge these issues during the interview and allow time for discussion.

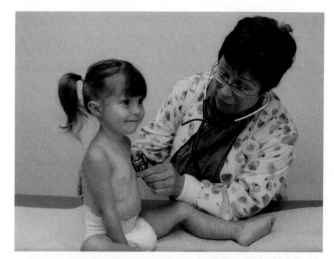

Figure 2-7 Family-practice and pediatric care settings often encourage a relaxed atmosphere and colourful, fun clothing for employees to help create a relaxed and inviting atmosphere for children and their caregivers.

Infants use primarily nonverbal language to communicate. When happy, they appear relaxed, smile, and maintain eye contact. Hungry, tired, or uncomfortable infants become tense, wrinkle the face, and cry. Observe parents as they speak to their infants for encouragement of happy behaviours and comfort for crying. Parental behaviour should be appropriate for the situation; a detached or irritable parent is cause for concern. Infants respond to the tone of voice and nonverbal communication, so speak softly and with caring. Observe a baby's nonverbal communication, including crooning or smiling.

Children and Adolescents

As children get older, they can begin to be more directly involved in aspects of care, including interviewing and history taking (see Chapter 29). During an interview, observe whether a child or parent does more of the talking and how the child and parent interact. If both parents are in attendance, one may be more dominant, answering for the child or other partner. Alternatively, a parent may encourage the child to answer questions and become more independent. With development, children can better verbalize symptoms and appreciate information and explanations.

Pose questions to children first and then encourage parents to fill in missing information. Verbal and social abilities vary widely in children of all ages, so nurses take cues from each specific child to appropriately direct the conversation. For example, one child may say "Hi" and start talking as soon as the nurse enters the room, while another may hide under the mother's chair. The nurse considers developmental level, personality, social and verbal skills, and parent–child interaction when interviewing the family. Preschoolers and school-age children have varying degrees of modesty and independence. Verbal communication becomes more important, and children can usually make choices.

Adolescents are sometimes capable of mature actions and other times return to a childlike, dependent role. Their developmental task is to achieve independence and separation from family. Increasing value is put on the peer group, which may place strain on family relationships. Adolescent concerns may involve sensitive issues such as sexuality, drugs, and alcohol. Privacy for these patients is especially important; adolescents need an opportunity to discuss health-related issues without parents present. Ask the parents for time alone with the patient and convey an attitude of respect toward teens by being honest and treating them maturely. Adolescents may appreciate some brief conversation about hobbies, activities, friends, or school. This establishes more of a relationship in which the nurse is interested in them as a person.

⚠ SAFETY ALERT 2-2

If an interview reveals confidential material, the nurse discloses those things required to be reported by law, such as suicidal thoughts, violence at home or school. The nurse informs the patient at the beginning of the interview that he or she must report harm to self or others to get needed assistance. The nurse should notify authorities only after ensuring the victim's safety (Sullivan, 2005).

Older Adults

Begin by introducing yourself and address the patient according to the patient's preference. Make sure that the room is free from distractions or interruptions (see Chapter 30). The interview may take longer with older patients who have more complex medical and surgical histories than younger patients. Although it lengthens the process, allow time for responses and redirect the conversation if the patient strays too far from a topic.

Avoid rushing the interview, which can frustrate patients and reduce their initiative to provide complete data. It may be necessary to prioritize questions. Ask the most important questions first. Additionally, the interview might be better accomplished over several visits rather than all at once. Touch, respectful eye contact, and clear speech are essential to optimal communication with this population. It is also important to pay particular attention to the temperature of the room, because some older people prefer warm temperatures.

Special Situations

Patients in health care settings may have emotional responses. Fears about illness, results from tests, interactions with health care professionals, and other factors may lead to crying, anxiety, or anger. Sometimes, issues arise related to sexual aggression or the crossing of professional boundaries. Other special situations that require altering the usual approach to to interviewing include patients with a hearing impairment, patients with an altered level of consciousness, and patients under the influence of drugs or alcohol. The nurse adapts

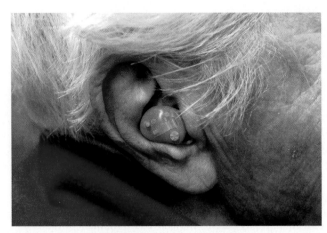

Figure 2-8 Before beginning a conversation with the patient who uses a hearing aid, the nurse should check to make sure the device is working and is turned on.

therapeutic techniques to complete the interview in these special cases.

Patients with Hearing Impairment

Approximately 33% of patients with hearing loss are older than 65 years (Hearing Foundation of Canada, 2009). Nurses who suspect that patients have new or previously unsubstantiated hearing loss can ask, "Just to be sure that you understand, please repeat what I said." For patients using hearing aids, make sure that such devices are turned on and working (Fig. 2-8). Gently touch or use visual signals with patients before speaking to them to verify that they are paying attention. Closing the door also may help to limit background noise. To ensure understanding from patients, give thorough explanations, provide diagrams and pictures, and supply written information. Ask patients to validate understanding by asking open-ended questions.

Many deaf patients communicate through a combination of methods, such as signing, writing, using speech, and moving the lips. They may sign with larger, quicker, and more forceful motions when expressing urgency, fear, or frustration. They may pantomime or use facial expressions to communicate. It is helpful to sit closer to patients who can lip read to facilitate a setting for lip reading. Use regular speech volume and lip movement but speak slightly more slowly. If the patient does not understand, use other wording because the sounds involved may be better decoded.

Patients with Altered Level of Consciousness

Patients with an altered level of consciousness may be unable to communicate to provide answers to interview questions. In this case, the nurse needs to rely on family members and previous documentation. Physical examination and circumstances surrounding the altered level of consciousness assume more importance until the nurse has obtained a complete history. Refer to Chapter 24 for more information.

Patients with Cognitive Impairment

Patients with cognitive impairment often have word-finding difficulties. They may often substitute sound-alike words and sounds, making conversations difficult to track (Acton, Yauk et al., 2007). It is important to allow these patients time to process as much as possible to avoid a one-sided conversation. Because it is easy to discount the communication as disordered or unreliable, many patients with cognitive impairment have unmet needs. Pain, hunger, thirst, and other basic needs that remain unaddressed may produce behaviours that others interpret as anxious or agitated (see Chapter 7). When these nonverbal behaviours are present, it is essential to perform assessments to help identify the source of the concern. Patients with closed-head injuries commonly have difficulties related to attention and social skills (Youse, 2005). They may need redirection and coaching on the organization and appropriateness of their communication.

Patients with Mental Health Illness

Patients with mental health illnesses often have difficulty attending to and sequencing communication (Docherty, Strauss et al., 2006). Observe patients for behaviours that indicate distraction, such as looking around the room or appearing to hear noises. Those with mental illness may process communication better if it contains clear, short phrases that require one step in thinking rather than complex directions. It also may be helpful to use restatement, reflection, or focusing to redirect conversation to the health topic being assessed (see Chapter 10).

Patients with Anxiety

Health care issues can cause great anxiety, which is an expected response to a threat to well-being. Behaviours that indicate anxiety are nail-biting, foot-tapping, sweating, and pacing. A voice may quiver, speech may be rapid, and language or tone may be defensive. These behaviours are an attempt to relieve anxious feelings. A mild level of anxiety heightens awareness of the surroundings and fosters learning and decision making. High levels of anxiety decrease perceptual ability and can progress to panic and immobilizing behaviour (Boyd, 2008).

Use active listening, honesty, and a calm and unhurried manner to reduce anxiety. If anxiety is severe, teach patients breathing and relaxation exercises, use therapeutic touch, and provide structure so that patients know that they will remain safe.

Patients Who Are Crying

Health issues are sensitive and sometimes pose sad situations for both patients and nurses. When sensitive issues arise, the nurse uses therapeutic communication techniques rather than progressing with additional interview questions. If a nurse notices that the patient is sad, he or she may say, "You look sad when talking about your prognosis" to show empathy

Figure 2-9 Nurses need to be prepared for emotional reactions to health concerns and challenges from patients and use their judgment about the best ways to offer support and caring presence.

for the patient. The nurse provides support through silence, acknowledging feelings, or offering a tissue (Fig. 2-9), and avoids giving false reassurance. Crying is therapeutic, and patients usually feel better after having a chance to express the associated emotions. Grief is an expected part of illness; it is therapeutic to express feelings of grief. At times, the nurse may also become emotional; in this case, it is acceptable to tear. However, sobbing or frank expression of emotion is not therapeutic.

Patients Who Are Angry

When the patient is angry, listen for the associated themes and avoid becoming defensive or personalizing the situation. The beginning nurse may think that she or he did something wrong and feel badly, but usually anger from the patient does not directly relate to one specific nurse. Such an emotion usually is a response to a situation in which the patient has lost control and feels anxious or helpless. Acknowledge the feelings by saying, "I understand that you are upset about being asked this question another time" or "I'm sorry that you're so angry." The nurse validates and encourages patients to express their feelings. The purpose of talking the emotion through is to help patients connect their emotions with related events.

Patients Under the Influence of Alcohol or Drugs

Patients with chemical impairment have difficulty answering complex questions, so the nurse uses direct and simple questions instead. Interview questions include the type of drug, amount ingested, and date and time of the last drink or use. It is helpful to explain that this information is important to provide accurate data regarding withdrawal. Patients who have used drugs or alcohol may also provide an unreliable history with a story that changes over time. Be aware that memory may be impaired and drug use and withdrawal can cause confusion. Similar to when working with patients who have reduced consciousness, the nurse will rely more on the circumstances and physical assessment data with patients who have substance use disorders. As patients become sober and family members are available, details about length of use, pattern of use, and related injuries or illnesses can be discussed.

Personal Questions

When interviewing patients, nurses ask questions within the nursing role. Some patients do not understand the boundaries that define the nurse–patient relationship and instead ask personal questions of the nurse. This situation can be uncomfortable, because the nurse must choose how much (if anything)

to disclose. The nurse may briefly provide a response or choose simply to redirect the conversation. The nurse might say, "My husband is a teacher. Tell me more about the occupational hazards that you have" or simply, "I would rather talk about the occupational hazards in your workplace."

Sexual Aggression

Sexual aggression includes inappropriate jokes, flirtatious comments, sexual suggestions, or sexual advances. Patients with low self-esteem may flaunt their sexual prowess as a way to increase feelings of self-worth. Listen for these themes in an attempt to understand why patients are acting this way and, most importantly, set limits on these behaviours. Although the nurse may be shocked, embarrassed, or angry, she or he needs to confront sexual innuendos and be clear that such behaviour is not acceptable. Say, "It makes me very uncomfortable when you tell that type of joke. I would prefer that we talk about other things" or, "Yes, I have a boyfriend. Tell me more about your support systems." If aggression is physical, it may be necessary to set limits, such as, "If you touch me there again, I will need to leave the room."

Applying Your Knowledge

Using the previous steps of clinical reasoning, organizing, and prioritizing, consider all the case study findings woven throughout this chapter. When answering the following questions, begin drawing conclusions and see how the pieces of assessment work together to create an environment for personalized, appropriate, and accurate care.

- What Canadian Nurses Association document guides professional nursing practice? (Knowledge)
- Compare nurse–patient relationships to personal and social relationships (Comprehension)
- Identify two possible nursing diagnoses for Mr. O'Neill? (Application)
- Identify the 7 axes for one of the nursing diagnoses for Mr. O'Neill? (Analysis)
- How can the nurse communicate nonjudgmental care both verbally and nonverbally? (Synthesis)
- How would you evaluate a successful interview and therapeutic dialogue? (Evaluation)

Key Points

- Nonverbal communication should be congruent with verbal communication.
- Active listening, restatement, reflection, elaboration, silence, focusing, clarification, and summarizing are techniques to facilitate therapeutic communication.
- Nontherapeutic responses include false reassurance, unwanted advice, leading or biased questions, changes of subject, distractions, too many technical terms, and talking too much.

- The phases of the interview process include preinteraction, beginning, working, and closing.
- Intercultural communication requires sensitivity to and knowledge of specific cultures, including language challenges, health beliefs, and gender issues.
- Assessment of newborns, infants, and children includes the care provider and his or her relationship to the patient.
- Privacy and respect are essential when assessing adolescents.
- The nurse may need to collect the health history of older adults over more than one visit because of the length and

amount of details involved as well as increased fatigue in these patients.

- Special techniques may be helpful when working with patients in special situations: hearing impairment, altered level of consciousness, cognitive impairment, mental health issues, anxiety, crying, anger, drug use, personal questions, and sexual innuendo.

Review Questions

1. Nonverbal communication skills include
   A. facial expression and body position
   B. speed of the voice and dress
   C. voice volume and gestures
   D. word choice and questions

2. The nurse talks with the patient and asks, "So tell me more about the chest pain that you had." This is an example of
   A. restatement
   B. reflection
   C. encouraging elaboration
   D. clarifying

3. When the patient says, "I'm so angry that I have to have surgery," the nurse says, "You sound very frustrated." This is an example of
   A. focusing
   B. summarizing
   C. silence
   D. reflection

4. The nurse is gathering the health history data before performing the physical assessment. This phase of the interview process is the
   A. preinteraction phase
   B. beginning phase
   C. working phase
   D. closing phase

5. When working with a medical interpreter, the nurse knows that it is best to
   A. look directly at the patient
   B. speak slightly louder than usual
   C. avoid using medical terms
   D. use closed-ended questions

6. When interviewing adolescents, the nurse recognizes that
   A. parents retain strict control
   B. health care professionals have the answers
   C. privacy may be especially important
   D. the peer group has little influence

7. The patient is crying after being given a diagnosis with a poor prognosis. The best response from the nurse is
   A. "Don't cry. It will be OK."
   B. "My mother has the same thing."
   C. "I think that you should have surgery."
   D. "I'll stay with you." (and gets a tissue)

8. An older adult says, "How come you're asking me so many questions?" The best response is
   A. "It's all a part of the health history."
   B. "We need a complete understanding of your concerns."
   C. "Are you getting tired? I can come back later."
   D. "Why are you asking me that?"

9. When the nurse asks the patient during a health history about mental health concerns, the patient responds by saying, "Don't you tell me I'm crazy!" The best response is
   A. "I didn't say that you were crazy."
   B. "Having mental health concerns is different from being crazy."
   C. "Tell me more about what you mean by that."
   D. "This sounds like a sensitive subject for you."

10. The mother of an infant with severe asthma is extremely anxious. The nurse is treating the patient in the emergency room. When collecting the history, the best response is
    A. "You must be extremely worried."
    B. "I'd be in worse shape than you are if it was my baby."
    C. "Is there anyone here that you can talk to?"
    D. "You seem worried, but I need to ask a few questions."

Canadian Nursing Research

Austin, W., Bergum, V., et al. (2006). A revisioning of boundaries in professional helping relationships: Exploring other metaphors. *Ethics & Behaviour, 16*(2), 77–94.

Chen, A. W., Kazanjian, A., et al. (2009). Why do Chinese Canadians not consult mental health services: Health status, language or culture? *Transcultural Psychiatry, 46*(4), 623–41.

Cossette, S., Cara, C., et al. (2005). Assessing nurse-patient interactions from a caring perspective: Report of the development and preliminary psychometric testing of the Caring Nurse-Patient Interactions Scale. *International Journal of Nursing Science, 42*(6), 673–686.

References

Acton, G. J., Yauk, S., et al. (2007). Increasing social communication in persons with dementia. *Research and Theory for Nursing Practice, 21*(1), 32–44.

Adler, R. B., & Proctor, R. F. (2007). *Looking out/looking in* (12th ed). Belmont, CA: Thomson/Wadsworth.

Arnold, E. C., & Boggs, K. U. (2007). *Interpersonal relationships: Professional communication skills for nurses.* St. Louis, MO: Saunders Elsevier.

Baren, J. M. (2006). Ethical dilemmas in the care of minors in the emergency department. *Emergency Medicine Clinics of North America, 24*(3), 619–631.

Boyd, M. A. (2008). *Psychiatric nursing: Contemporary practice* (4th ed.). Philadelphia, PA: Lippincott Williams & Wilkins.

Canadian Nurses Association. (2008). *Code of ethics for registered nurses.* Ottawa, ON: Author.

Canadian Nurses Association. (2010). *Becoming a registered nurse.* Ottawa, ON: Author.

Choi, H., & Gi Park, C. (2006). Understanding adolescent depression in ethnocultural context: Updated with empirical findings. *Advances in Nursing Science, 29*(4), E1–E12.

Docherty, N. M., Strauss, M. E., et al. (2006). The cognitive origins of specific types of schizophrenic speech disturbances. *American Journal of Psychiatry, 163*(12), 2111–2118.

Dysart-Gale, D. (2007). Clinicians and medical interpreters: Negotiating culturally appropriate care for patients with limited English ability. *Family & Community Health, 30*(3), 237–246.

Hearing Foundation of Canada. (2010). *Hearing aids & devices.* Retrieved from http://www.hearing foundation.ca/cms/en/ChildrenYouth/NewbornHearingScreening.aspx?menuid=106

Holder, K. V., & Schenthal, S. J. (2007). Watch your step: Nursing and professional boundaries. *Nursing Management, 38*(2), 24–29.

Hurst, K. (2007). Does workforce size and mix influence patient satisfaction? *Nursing Standard, 21*(46), 15.

Hutchinson, M. K., Thompson, A. C., et al. (2006). Multisystem factors contributing to disparities in preventive health care among lesbian women. *Journal of Obstetric, Gynecologic, and Neonatal Nursing, 35*(3), 393–402.

Kennedy, M. G. (1997). Cultural competency. In N. K. Worley (Ed.), *Mental health nursing in the community.* St. Louis, MO: Mosby.

Murphy, S. T. (2007). Improving cross-cultural communication in health professions education. *Journal of Nursing Education, 46*(8), 367–372.

Rondahl, G., Innala, S., et al. (2006). Heterosexual assumptions in verbal and non-verbal communication in nursing. *Journal of Advanced Nursing, 56*(4), 341–344.

Seale, C. (2006). Gender accommodation in online cancer support groups. *Health: An Interdisciplinary Journal for the Social Study of Health, Illness & Medicine, 10*(3), 345–360.

Stephen, T. C., & Bickley, L. S. (2010). The health history: Subjective data. In T. C. Stephen, D. L. Skillen, R. A. Day, & L. S. Bickley (Eds.). *Canadian Bates' guide to health assessment for nurses* (1st ed., pp. 51–90). Philadelphia, PA: Wolters Kluwer Health/Lippincott Williams & Wilkins.

Sullivan, C. M. (2005). Survivors' opinions about mandatory reporting of domestic violence and sexual assault by medical professionals. *Journal of Women & Social Work, 20*(3), 346–361.

Wright, L. M., & Leahey, M. (2009). *The nurse and families: A guide to family assessment and intervention* (4th ed.). Philadelphia, PA: F.A. Davis.

Youse, K. M. (2005). *Attentional deficits and conversational discourse in closed-head injury (includes abstract).* (p. 129). Doctoral dissertation—research, University of Connecticut.

The Canadian Jensen's Nursing Health Assessment suite offers these additional resources to enhance learning and facilitate understanding of this chapter:

• thePoint online resource, http//thepoint.lww.com/Stephen1E
• *Laboratory Manual for Canadian Jensen's Nursing Health Assessment: A Best Practice Approach*

The Health History

Learning Objectives

1 Differentiate primary from secondary data.

2 Differentiate between subjective and objective data

3 Compare and contrast emergency, focused, and comprehensive health histories.

4 Identify the components of the comprehensive health history.

5 Gather a complete history of present illness.

6 Complete a family history using a genogram to illustrate family patterns.

7 Perform a functional health assessment using Gordon's nursing framework.

8 Perform a complete review of systems.

9 Identify teaching opportunities for health promotion and risk reduction.

10 Use subjective data to analyze findings and plan interventions.

11 Document and communicate data using appropriate terminology.

12 Individualize health assessment considering the condition, age, gender, and culture of the patient.

*E*mma Anderson, a 17-year-old Canadian girl of African genetic background, was diagnosed with asthma when she was 3 years old. She has carried an inhaler with her for most of her life. She lives in an urban low-income housing area. Her house and school were both built in the 1940s. The house is known to have mold and dust. Emma's mother, a single parent, works two jobs. Three younger siblings also are in the household. The family is active in church and has faith that "someday there will be a better life." Today, Emma comes to the University health centre because her inhaler is empty.

You will gain more information about Emma as you progress through this chapter. As you study the content and features, consider this case and its relationship to what you are learning about the health history. Begin thinking about the following points:

- What perceptions do you hold about Emma's situation?
- What personal beliefs could affect communication with Emma?
- What areas of the health history are especially important to focus on with Emma?
- What age-related, cultural, environmental, or developmental issues might you anticipate for Emma?

The health history provides the foundation for the helping relationship and guides patient care. It is critical to obtain comprehensive, accurate information about the patient and his or her physical and mental health to develop a plan for care. The purposes of the health history are to establish a trusting and supportive relationship, gather information, and offer information (Bird & Cohen-Cole, 1990, Cohen-Cole, 1991, Lazare, Putnam et al., 1995). In the health history, nurses collect subjective data from patients.

Subjective data are the information that the patient reports. They include the data about signs and symptoms that the patient describes; they may not be perceived by observers (Thomas, 2007). Additionally, the nurse collects subjective data including demographic data, individual and family histories about past and current medical conditions, surgeries, personal and social history, review of systems, and risks for illnesses. Discussions also include information on health behaviours and activities that promote health. In many settings, patients complete comprehensive forms that the nurse reviews and then asks questions about to add detail during the interview. Subjective data differ from objective data in that subjective data are what the patient tells the nurse. **Objective data** are information gathered from the physical examination that can be seen, felt, heard, or smelled by an observer.

Most patients anticipate that the nurse may ask uncomfortable questions, such as those involving bowel habits or sexual practices and activities, because the nursing role focuses on health and screening for potential issues. The health history forms the foundation for care as patterns emerge and concerns are identified. It is important because it provides context for the current situation and a more complete picture of how issues are related. The nurse ensures that she or he gathers, records, and analyzes complete data. During history taking and interviewing, the nurse establishes a therapeutic relationship built on trust, and rapport with patients.

Through therapeutic communication, the patient and the nurse work together to resolve concerns by developing collaborative strategies and solutions (see Chapter 2). As they develop rapport with each other, the patient feels respected and understood. The nurse provides health teaching, based on each patient's needs and priorities, and weaves health promotion into care. For example, a nurse will teach a patient with a family history of breast cancer about breast health and the "Know Your Breasts (KYB)" approach (Fig. 3-1).

During a health history, nurses use special techniques and communication skills to gather complete and accurate data about the health state of patients. As nurses develop and refine their interviewing capabilities (see Chapter 2), conversations with patients become more comfortable, with smooth transitions from question to question. Each nurse develops a style of communication that suits his or her personality and values, blending together the professional and the personal.

Primary and Secondary Data Sources

The individual patient is considered the **primary data** source. Charts and family members are considered **secondary data** sources. When possible, patients provide subjective information regarding their health behaviours and concerns. Subjective data are collected from the perspective of the patient. Secondary data sources are all other sources of information.

Reliability of the Source

The nurse records the source of the information and considers the reliability of the source. A **reliable historian** provides information that is consistent with existing records and comprehensive in scope. If information differs from past descriptions, or if details change each time, the source may be unreliable or considered an **inaccurate historian**. The nurse notes any discrepancies and identifies other sources (such as previous records) to confirm the history.

Components of the Health History

Usually, demographical or identifying data are collected first and then followed by a complete description of the reason for seeking care. The amount of additional data collected depends on the reason for the visit, pertinence of the data,

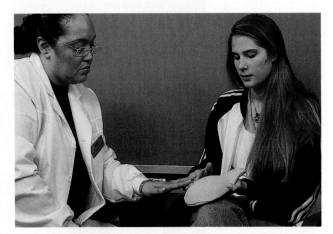

Figure 3-1 During a routine annual physical examination, this nurse uses a prosthetic model of a breast to instruct the patient about breast health.

COMPONENTS OF THE HEALTH HISTORY

- Demographical or identifying data (including reliability)
- Reason for seeking care or chief concern
- Present illness
- Past health history
- Medications
- Family history
- Personal and social history (includes growth and development for pediatric patients)
- Review of systems

Table 3-1 Types of Health Histories

Type	Purpose	Components
Emergency	Nurses collect the most important information and defer obtaining details until patients are stable. They elicit the reason for seeking care along with current health concerns, medications, and allergies.	Care focuses on gathering information so that interventions can resolve the immediate problem. Assessments and interventions are concurrent.
Focused	The focused health history involves questions that relate to the current situation.	An example is the patient visiting the primary care provider about a cough. In this case, the nurse asks about the length, severity, and timing of the cough and other related factors and completes a symptom/sign analysis of the cough. During focused health histories, nurses do not perform a complete review of systems (discussed later).
Comprehensive	The comprehensive health history takes place during an annual physical examination, sports participation screenings, preoperative examination, and a hospital admission.	It includes demographical data, a full description of the reason for seeking care, individual health history, family history, functional status, and a history in all physical and psychosocial areas.

and time restrictions within the setting. The nurse determines what data to collect beyond the minimum required. Data can be collected in an emergency, during a visit for a specific concern (eg, shoulder pain), or during a wellness visit. Refer to Table 3-1 to compare and contrast emergency, focused, and comprehensive health histories. The following sections explain the components of the comprehensive health history.

Demographical Data or Identifying Data

Depending on the health care setting, personnel at a front desk or admissions department often collect demographical data from patients, including name, address, and other contact information for patients and family members (see Fig. 3-2).

Demographical Data

Date of Interview: _____

Patient Name: _____

Date of Birth: _____ Age: _____ Gender: _____

Health Care Number: _____

Primary Language: _____

Marital Status: S M W D Other

Address: _____

_____

Phone Numbers: _____

Emergency Contact: _____ Phone Number: _____

_____

Information obtained from: Patient _____ Other_____

Patient accompanied: Yes _____ No _____

Religious preference: _____

Allergies: _____

Figure 3-2 An example of a demographical data form completed during arrival at or admission to a health care facility.

Other data including environmental data about exposure to contagious diseases, recent travel to high-risk areas, and concerns about exposure to pollution, hazards, and allergens are collected. For hospitalized patients, the nurse assesses living arrangements to identify the level of independence and support needed following discharge.

Reason for Seeking Care or Chief Concern

The reason for seeking care is a brief statement, usually in the patient's own words, about why he or she is making the visit. It is often referred to as the Chief Concern. Questions such as, "Tell me why you came to the clinic today" or "What happened that brought you to the hospital?" are helpful. This information is recorded in the subjective part of documentation. Putting the patient's statements in quotes ensures accurate documentation and reflection of what the patient is reporting. If the patient replies by giving a medical diagnosis such as "heart attack," the nurse encourages the patient to describe symptoms such as "shortness of breath and chest pain." When taking the health history, record the **symptoms**, or subjective sensations and reports of patients, versus the **signs**, or objective information, which are assessed during the physical examination.

Present Illness

The nurse collects information about the present illness by beginning with open-ended questions and having patients explain symptoms. A complete description of the present illness is essential to an accurate diagnosis. As well, the nurse completes a symptom or sign analysis to gather more specific and complete information. For example, if the patient states, "I've been having some abdominal pain," the nurse asks questions to try to find out its source and associated symptoms. Each symptom or sign has 10 attributes that must be clarified in order to understand what the patient is experiencing (see Table 3-2).

Some providers use a mnemonic to remember some of the elements that are important to assess for the presenting symptom (Johann, Shapourian et al., 2007). Some examples of the elements are as follows:

- OLDCARTS (onset, location, duration, character, associated or aggravating factors, relieving factors, timing, severity)
- PQRSTU (provoke/palliative, quality, region, severity, timing, understanding patient perception)

Regardless of the order of the data, the nurse guides the conversation following the cues of patients and uses a mental checklist to ensure that he or she has assessed all categories before the end of history taking.

Pain Goal

The nurse asks patients, "What is an acceptable level of pain?" or "What do you hope that we can get your pain down to?" This pain goal should be set to allow patients to perform the most important activities easily. Usually, a goal of zero to mild pain (1 to 3 on a 10-point scale) is acceptable.

Functional Goal

Some symptoms or signs can affect the ability to perform common movements and tasks. For example, shortness of breath or pain can decrease the patient's ability to move about at home. The nurse assesses the effects of the present illness on the functional ability by questioning patients about sitting, rising from a chair, standing for periods, climbing stairs, shopping, driving, and participating in sports.

Past Health History

The past health history includes an assessment of medical and surgical conditions along with the treatment and course. Some conditions are acute, some resolve, and others are chronic. Dates of initial diagnosis and surgeries are important to document. For example, the nurse writes, "Appendectomy 2003; testicular cancer 1/2006; orchidectomy 2/2006; chemotherapy with cisplatin, etoposide, and bleomycin 3/2006; currently in remission." He or she also notes any serious accidents and injuries. The nurse charts events chronologically when possible so that future readers can easily identify the sequence.

For female patients, note the last menstrual period (LMP) and whether the patient may be pregnant. The nurse notes the obstetric history, including number of pregnancies (gravida) and number of births (para). If any pregnancies are incomplete, the nurse documents the reason (eg, spontaneous abortion).

The record should include childhood illnesses with potentially lasting effects (eg, polio, varicella). Also, the nurse records the date of the most recent immunizations for tetanus; pertussis; polio; measles; rubella; mumps; influenza; hepatitis A and B; and pneumococcus. Refer to Appendix A for a table of recommended immunizations. The nurse also asks about screening tests and the results, such as tuberculin skin test, Pap smear, mammogram, colonoscopy, stool for occult blood, cholesterol, and blood pressure. The nurse documents the date of the last physical assessment.

Current Medications and Indications

The nurse asks patients about current medications including name, dose, route and purpose for each medication, because some drugs have more than one use. For example, one patient may take a beta-blocker for blood pressure control, while another may take the same drug to prevent a second

Table 3-2 The 10 Attributes of a Sign or Symptom

Attribute	Explanation	Considerations
1. Location	The anatomical area of the body that is affected. The location may be (a) localized—in one place; (b) generalized—over a large area or the entire body; or (c) radiating—moving to or from another area.	When possible, ask the patient to point to the affected area.
2. Quality or nature	What the symptom/sign is like, including consistency, colour, and type. For pain, descriptors such as crushing, aching, gnawing, and stabbing give more information about the type of pain the patient is experiencing. Thick sputum, dry cough, raised rash, purple spots, and tingling weakness are other examples of words that describe quality.	If the patient is having difficulty describing the quality of a symptom/sign, help him or her by suggesting several words that may be accurate descriptors.
3. Severity or quantity	How bad or how much the concern is. For pain, ask the patient to rate it on a scale of 0 to 10 (with 0 being no pain and 10 being the worst pain) or to compare it with a previous experience (eg, dental abscess, fracture). For bleeding, sputum, itchiness, and other symptoms/signs, ask the patient to describe the quantity. For example, how much blood have you noticed?	Ask the patient to describe the amount in quantifiable terms to improve understanding. For example, 100 mL of blood, two soaked hand towels, a blood clot the size of a toonie, or a lump the size of a golf ball enhance understanding of the amount.
4. Timing	Aspects about when the symptom/sign occurs: (a) onset—when the condition began and speed (slow or fast); (b) duration—the length of time; (c) constancy—whether the symptom/sign is intermittent or continuous; (d) time of day/month/year—patterns of when the condition occurs.	Assist the patient to recall when the concern happens. Using familiar days such as birthdays or holidays may help the patient remember when it began. Also, suggestions such as morning, night, or different seasons help the patient identify aspects of timing. Inquire about relationship of the symptom/sign with work.
5. Aggravating factors	Anything that makes the symptom/sign worse. Includes exposures and activities the patient has noticed that make the symptom/sign worse.	Temperature changes, altitude changes, different foods, amount of light, or chemicals are examples of exposures. Walking, sitting, reading, lifting, and bending are examples of activities.
6. Alleviating factors	Anything that makes the symptom/sign better. Includes exposures and activities the patient has noticed that improve the symptom/sign.	Ask about medications, over-the-counter remedies, herbal treatments, and changes in diet or temperature that have improved the symptom/sign. Inquire about position changes, acupuncture, or massages, for example.
7. Associated symptoms and signs	Other symptoms and signs that may be related to the symptom/sign.	If the patient is having difficulty recalling anything that may be related, ask about specific symptoms such as nausea, pain, weakness, or shortness of breath.
8. Environmental factors	Anything in the patient's surroundings, such as home, work, or hobbies, that may be related to the symptom/sign.	Consider exposures (thermal, chemical, infectious), psychosocial aspects (stress, loss of income), recent travel, or changes in surroundings (renovations).
9. Significance to patient	The effects on the patient's well-being and lifestyle.	Some symptoms/signs have minimal effects on some people but major influences on others. A painful finger may cause few changes for some people but can be career-threatening for a concert pianist.
10. Patient perspective	Thoughts and ideas from the patient about what may be happening or causing the symptom/sign and the associated feelings.	This gives the patient a chance to bring up any other information that may be related and provides insights that the nurse may not anticipate.

Adapted from Stephen, T. C., & Bickley, L. S. (2010). The health history: Subjective data. In T. C. Stephen, D. L. Skillen, R. A. Day, & L. S. Bickley (Eds.). *Canadian Bates' guide to health assessment for nurses.* Philadelphia, PA: Wolters Kluwer Health/Lippincott Williams & Wilkins.

The nurse's role relative to subjective data collection is to gather information to improve the patient's health status and to help determine the cause of current symptoms. Emma, introduced at the beginning of this chapter, has come to the university health clinic to see if her asthma inhaler is working. The following conversation gives an example of a therapeutic dialogue.

Nurse: Hi, Emma. How are you?

Emma: I'm okay. I think my inhaler is empty.

Nurse: Have you been using it more than usual?

Emma: Yes, I'm coughing and wheezing. I feel like I'm getting sick.

Nurse: Have you had any trouble breathing? Or chest tightness?

Emma: Just trouble breathing.

Nurse: How do you know when you need to use your inhaler?

Emma: I can't run and my chest gets tight. I've been using the inhaler a lot, too.

Nurse: How many times a day, Emma?

Emma: About two to three times.

Nurse: Is your chest tightness mild, medium, or really bad now?

Emma: Really bad. I knew that I needed a new inhaler, but I thought it was still okay.

Nurse: We'll see what we can do here.

Emma: Thanks.

Critical Thinking Challenge

- What type of assessment does this example represent?
- What components of the history of present illness are important to continue collecting?
- What techniques of therapeutic communication would you use when talking with Emma?

myocardial infarction. Additionally, the nurse queries the patient about any over-the-counter medications, supplements, or herbal remedies in use. If confusion about any medication exists, the nurse may ask patients or their family members to bring in the pill bottles to ensure accuracy (Fig. 3-3).

Allergies are verified with patients. When asking about allergies, note the type of response such as rash, throat swelling, difficulty breathing, or anaphylactic shock. Some patients may confuse a side effect or adverse reaction with an allergy; these should also be noted. For example, the patient may become nauseous when given opiates, but the nurse should note this response as an adverse reaction. He or she would chart a response that includes throat swelling and difficulty breathing as an allergic reaction. It is best to

document both the medication and the patient's reaction to it for future reference. Significant allergies must be appropriately noted in the chart and on a wrist band of a hospitalized patient.

Family History

The nurse asks the patient about the health of close family members (ie, parents, grandparents, siblings) to help identify those disorders for which patients may be at risk and to provide health education. Examples of important familial conditions to note include high blood pressure, coronary artery disease, high cholesterol, stroke, cancer, diabetes mellitus, tuberculosis, obesity, alcohol or drug addiction, and mental illness. Also, the nurse obtains the health history of children

Figure 3-3 It can be helpful for patients who are taking multiple medications, supplements, and over-the-counter drugs to bring the medications or a list of the medications with them to health assessment appointments.

and identifies patterns of disease that might be genetically transmitted. Ideally, the family history is recorded in a centralized area on a computer and all health care professionals can contribute.

A common tool used to understand family patterns is the genogram (Fig. 3-4). This graphic representation allows the nurse to map family structures and compile a large amount of information visually. Genograms make it easier for the nurse to identify the complexity of families and validate patterns pertinent to patients. A complete family history can take as little as 15 minutes or as long as 2 hours. Each family member is represented by a box (male) or circle (female). The patient is noted by using an arrow or doubling the line. Sometimes, the nuclear family is circled. Marriages are identified by lines between people, and divorces are indicated by placing a double slash through the line. Deaths are noted by the use of an X inside the box or circle. Children are linked to parents through a vertical line, beginning with the eldest on the left. The medical history is listed below the symbol. This graphic representation compiles information into a concise pattern of family history.

Functional Health Assessment

Functional health patterns are especially important to nursing because they focus on the effects of health or illness on the patient's quality of life. By using this approach, the strengths of patients as well as areas needing improvement can be assessed (Table 3-3) (Gordon, 1987). Some of the questions are personal and difficult to answer, so it is best to thread the questions throughout the history and address the more personal questions toward the end of the conversation. As the nurse performs care, she or he can integrate these questions into other activities, such as giving the bath or assisting with wound care, instead of sitting down and asking the questions in a structured and sequenced order. It is helpful to identify issues that may be potential concerns for patients and prioritize to ask those first.

As well, assessing the ability to perform self-care activities, or **activities of daily living (ADLs)** is useful. These include behaviours such as eating, dressing, and grooming. The nurse scores these items based on whether patients are totally independent, need assistance from a person or device such as a cane, or are dependent on others. See Box 3-1.

Additional considerations include number of stairs and concerns about structural barriers. The nurse collects occupational information to evaluate the ability of patients to work safely and return to work if an illness is present. She or he assesses any concerns about occupational hazards, personal protective equipment, access for people who are disabled, and adaptive devices.

Growth and Development

During the health history with pediatric populations, the nurse observes growth to determine how children compare to peers. It is important to consider genetic background when comparing growth. He or she assesses physical activities, fine and gross motor skills, and speech. Developmental assessment of infants, children, and adolescents is especially important to determine the achievement of developmental milestones and to gain awareness of deficits to facilitate early intervention and management.

Psychosocial development is part of assessment for all age groups, because even some adults have delays and do not progress as expected. For example, the patient may have challenges with drugs and alcohol that interfere with relationships, employment, and housing. This patient may not reach the generativity stage of Erikson's Psychosocial Theory of Development (Erikson, 1980) but instead remains self-absorbed. For all patients, the nurse also carefully evaluates the cognitive stage, which becomes especially pertinent for those at each end of the lifespan. The nurse assesses that younger patients are developing abstract thinking skills appropriately, while he or she evaluates older patients for any signs of memory decline. Refer to Chapter 9 for more complete information on the assessment of growth and development.

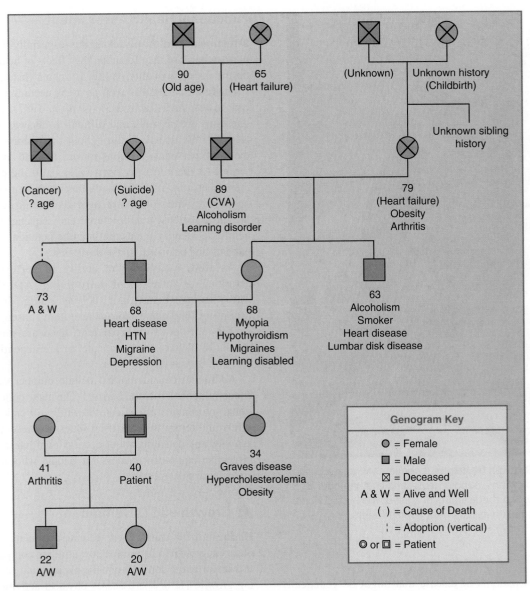

Genogram Key

O	= Female
■	= Male
⊠	= Deceased
A & W	= Alive and Well
( )	= Cause of Death
⦙	= Adoption (vertical)
◎ or ▣	= Patient

Figure 3-4 An example of a genogram.

Review of Systems

The **review of systems** is a series of questions about all body systems that helps to reveal concerns as part of a comprehensive health assessment. In clinic settings, patients usually fill out forms that give pertinent information, and then the nurse reviews answers with the patient to obtain a more complete and accurate history. The nurse may ask the patient about any symptoms related to each body system, such as a "cough" in discussion of the respiratory system. Other nurses integrate these questions during the physical examination of each region, such as chest pain when listening to the heart. However, this is not ideal practice. The sequence and format of this review vary with the setting, urgency of the issue, and style of the nurse.

In addition to the concerns covered in a review of systems, the nurse also obtains health-promotion practices and provides education about areas of interest or concern. Usually, the nurse begins with a general question, such as "How is your appetite?" and progresses more specifically, such as "Have you had any nausea?", "Food intolerances?", "Allergies?", or "Reflux?" For healthy behaviours, the nurse asks, "What types of foods do you eat to stay healthy?" In the review, the nurse documents not only the presence of findings but also the absence of symptoms or concerns, such as "Denies nausea, constipation, or diarrhea."

The nurse logically organizes his or her approach to the review. Most patients are unaware of the order, however, and also might remember other symptoms when talking about another topic. The conversation may be out of order from the usual body systems format. If the patient forgot to mention symptoms associated with the presenting concern until this review, the nurse documents those symptoms with the

Table 3-3 Gordon's Functional Health Patterns

Functional Health Pattern	Description	Sample Questions
Health perception/health management	Perceived health and well-being and how health is managed	How has your general health been? What things do you do to stay healthy?
Nutrition/metabolic	Food to metabolic need and indicators of local nutrient supply	How does your current nutritional status influence your health?
Elimination	Excretory function (bowel, bladder, and skin)	Do your patterns of bowel or bladder habits affect the types of activities that you do?
Activity/exercise	Exercise, activity, leisure, and recreation	Do you have sufficient energy for completing desired or required activities?
Cognition/perception	Sensory perceptions and thought patterns	Have you made any changes in your environment because of vision, hearing, or memory decrease?
Sleep/rest	Sleep, rest, and relaxation	Are you generally rested and ready for activities after sleeping?
Self-perception/self-concept	Self-concept, body comfort, body image, feeling state	How would you describe yourself? Are there any changes in the way that you feel about yourself or your body?
Role/relationship	Role engagements and relationships	Are there any family situations that you have difficulty handling? How has your illness affected your family?
Sexuality/reproductive	Satisfaction and dissatisfaction with sexuality, reproductive patterns	Have you had changes in sexual relations that you are concerned about? How has this illness affected your sexual relationship?
Coping/stress tolerance	General coping pattern and effectiveness in terms of handling stress	Have you had any major changes in the past year? How do you usually deal with stress? Is it effective?
Values/beliefs	Values, beliefs (including spiritual), or goals that guide choices or decisions	What are the most important things to you in life? What gives you hope when times are troubled?

BOX 3-1 ACTIVITIES OF DAILY LIVING

Self-care Activities

Eating
Bathing
Dressing
Grooming
Toileting

Mobility

Walking: miles, blocks, across a room
Climbing stairs, up or down
Balance
Grasping small objects, opening jars
Reaching out, down, or overhead
Use of devices

Home Maintenance

Heavy housekeeping: vacuuming, scrubbing floors, making beds
Light housekeeping: dusting, wiping surfaces, dishes
Washing laundry
Cooking
Shopping
Managing finances
Driving

presenting concern. If the patient forgets to mention major health events, the nurse documents them with the health history. When the nurse arrives at the section of the review that includes the presenting concern, she or he asks only those questions that have not yet been covered. The nurse explains to patients that although the review is lengthy, it is an opportunity to double check for completeness and accuracy of past and current conditions. When documenting findings, the nurse reorganizes the information to cluster data regarding a concern together. For example, if a patient is nauseous and vomiting, the nurse may cluster together findings from the nutrition–hydration, skin, and abdominal assessments.

The following information is part of the review of systems; note that the questions are not mutually exclusive. For example, weight gain or loss is part of the general health state, but it also provides information about fluid balance, edema, and appetite. The nurse adapts questions to the patient and directs conversation that is comfortable and logical, rather than asking a set of separate questions. The nurse omits questions that do not apply and adds questions that seem pertinent. Although the form below uses medical terminology, the nurse uses common lay language so that patients better understand the questions; these questions are further explored in each individual chapter.

- **General health state.** Weight gain or loss, fatigue, weakness, malaise, pain, usual activity, fever, chills.
- **Nutrition and hydration.** Nausea, vomiting. Usual daily intake, weight and weight change, dehydration, dry skin, fluid excess with shortness of breath, or edema in the feet and legs. Diet practices to promote health. Conditions that increase the risk of malnutrition or obesity.
- **Skin, hair, and nails.** Rash, itching, pigmentation or texture change, lesions, sweating, dry skin, hair loss or change in texture, brittle or thin nails, thick or yellow nails. Changes in moles. Skin, hair, or nail disease.
- **Head and neck.** Headaches, syncope, dizziness, sinus pain. High or low thyroid level.
- **Eyes.** Poor vision or vision concerns, glaucoma, cataracts. Use of contact lenses or glasses, change in vision, blurring, diplopia, light sensitivity, burning, redness, discharge. Date of last eye examination.
- **Ears.** Ear or hearing concerns. Ear pain, ear infection, change in hearing, tinnitus, vertigo. Date of last hearing evaluation, ear protection against noise.
- **Nose, mouth, and throat.** Colds, sore throat, nasal obstruction, nosebleeds, cold sores, bleeding or swollen gums, tooth pain, dental caries, ulcers, enlarged tonsils, dry mouth or lips. Difficulty chewing or swallowing, change in voice. Mouth or throat cancer. Date of last dental examination.
- **Thorax and lungs.** Emphysema, asthma, or lung cancer. Wheezing, cough, sputum, dyspnea, date of last chest x-ray and last tuberculin skin test.

- **Heart and neck vessels.** Congenital heart conditions, high blood pressure, myocardial infarction, heart surgery, heart failure, arrhythmia, murmur. Chest pain or discomfort, palpitations, exercise tolerance. Results of last screening for cholesterol and triglycerides, ECG results or other cardiac tests.
- **Peripheral vascular.** Peripheral vascular disease, thrombophlebitis. Peripheral edema, ulcers, circulation, claudication, redness, pain, tenderness, swelling in calves.
- **Breasts.** For adolescents, concerns about breast changes. Pain, tenderness, discharge, lumps, last mammogram, frequency and date of last self-examination. Breast cancer or cystic breast condition.
- **Abdominal–gastrointestinal.** Colon cancer, gastrointestinal bleeding, cholelithiasis, liver failure, hepatitis, pancreatitis, colitis, irritable bowel, celiac disease, ulcer, or gastric reflux. Appetite, nausea, vomiting, diarrhea. Food intolerance or allergy, constipation, diarrhea, change in stool colour, blood in stool. Dates of last sigmoidoscopy, colonoscopy, and stool for occult blood.
- **Abdominal–urinary.** Renal failure, polycystic kidney disease, urinary tract infection, nephrolithiasis. Pain, change in urine, dysuria, urgency, frequency, nocturia, incontinence. For children, toilet training, bed-wetting.
- **Musculoskeletal.** Injury, arthritis. Joint stiffness, pain, swelling, restricted movement, deformity, change in gait or coordination, strength. Pain, cramps, weakness.
- **Neurological.** Head or brain injury, stroke, seizures. Tremors, memory loss, numbness or tingling, loss of sensation or coordination, changes in mood, paralysis, headache, dizziness, fainting, blackouts, weakness.
- **Male genitalia.** Pain, burning, lesions, discharge, swelling. Change in penis or scrotum, protection against pregnancy and sexually transmitted infections. Undescended testicle, hernia, testicular cancer. Testicular self-examination.
- **Female genitalia.** Ovarian or uterine cancer, ovarian cyst, endometriosis, number of pregnancies, abortions, and children. Pain, burning, lesions, discharge, itching, rash. Menstrual and physical changes, protection against pregnancy and sexually transmitted infections. Date of last Pap smear.
- **Anus, rectum, and prostate.** Hemorrhoids; prostate cancer; benign prostatic hyperplasia; urinary incontinence, pain, burning, itching, blood in urine; for men, hesitancy, dribbling, loss in force of urine stream.
- **Endocrine and hematological system.** Diabetes mellitus, high or low thyroid levels, anemia. Polydipsia, polyuria, unexplained weight gain or loss, changes in body hair and body fat distribution, intolerance to heat or cold, excessive bruising, lymph node swelling. Result of last blood glucose. Hematologic: anemia, transfusions or reactions, bruising or bleeding.

The nurse completes the health history and physical examination of Emma, reviews findings, and develops a plan of care. She considers age-related, family, developmental, and cultural issues. The following nursing note illustrates how the nurse prioritizes, collects, and analyzes subjective and objective data and develops nursing interventions.

Subjective: "I'm coughing and wheezing. I feel like I'm getting sick. My inhaler doesn't make a sound when I puff it."

Objective: Respiratory rate 40 breaths/min and shallow. Skin colour pale. Lungs with moderate scattered wheezes. Intermittent dry, hacking, nonproductive cough. Peak flow measures 281 mL (70% of personal best). States that she has been using inhaler more frequently, up to two to three times daily with activity.

Analysis: Risk for impaired gas exchange with increased wheezing, most likely because of empty inhaler.

Plan: Provide an inhaler for self-carry as part of her asthma management plan. Assist Emma with counting doses so that she can recognize when she needs a new inhaler. Ask Emma to come back tomorrow to follow up. Include a review on proper inhaler use as part of the management plan.

Critical Thinking Challenge

- What is the nurse's role in health promotion and asthma control?
- What family history might be important to collect?
- How can the nurse assess how Emma's asthma has affected her functional status?
- Considering the elements of a complete health history, what information will be collected as a priority?

Psychosocial and Lifestyle Factors

The nurse may assess psychosocial and lifestyle factors at the end of the interview, because these issues may naturally arise during the review of systems. Because many of these questions are personal, the nurse asks them at the end after the relationship and rapport are established. Some examples of areas that involve sensitive questions are sexual orientation, risk for domestic violence (see Chapter 12), and drug use (see Chapter 10).

Social, Cultural, and Spiritual Assessment

The nurse assesses overall psychosocial well-being as part of the screening of the functional health patterns, including self-perception/self-concept, role/relationships, and coping/stress tolerance. The nurse obtains detailed information when patients have a history of psychosocial challenges or indicators of current distress (see Chapter 10). The nurse also assesses cultural beliefs and health practices that may influence care. More complete information on cultural assessment is in Chapter 11.

It is essential to assess spirituality and belief systems during the functional health screening questions related to values or beliefs. Additionally, assess specific spiritual beliefs, religious preferences, rituals, and practices that improve health status as needed. The nurse uses this information to support the patient during times when hope and guidance are needed. Ask about religious preference so that referrals to pastoral care can be initiated depending on the patient's preference (see Chapter 11).

Mental Health

If patients report feeling anxious, depressed, or illogical, or if an association exists between current physical status and psychiatric concerns, mental health requires a closer examination. Some potential screening questions that may be asked include "Describe any changes that you have had in your mood or feelings" and "Have you ever been treated for any conditions with your mood or behaviour?" The nurse notes medications during the initial history and asks follow-up questions regarding the purpose and effectiveness of any psychiatric drugs. As well, specific techniques for psychiatric screening, such as a depression screening tool or a full mental status examination may be used. When the primary concern is psychiatric, the nurse performs a complete mental health assessment (see Chapter 10).

The nurse assesses alcohol and drug use by direct questioning and also observation of behaviours that indicate impairment such as slurred speech, nodding off, and unstable gait. Although this may be an uncomfortable area for beginners to ask about, most patients recognize that the nurse needs information to avoid medication interactions, evaluate the effects of use on the current illness or injury, and refer to treatment programs to improve health. The nurse asks, "How many alcoholic drinks are usual for you in 1 week?" or "Do you use any recreational drugs?" To normalize the response, the nurse asks, "A lot of college students like to party. If you party, how much do you usually drink?" The nurse also assesses tobacco use directly by asking, "Have you ever smoked cigarettes?" "A pipe?", "Or a cigar?" "Or chewed tobacco?" For a complete assessment of drug and alcohol use, see Chapter 10.

Human Violence

Because of the prevalence of physical abuse in children and women, especially during pregnancy, many nurses routinely question patients about this (Public Health Agency of Canada, 2010). Because of the sensitive nature of the topic, the nurse poses questions so that the patient feels comfortable talking. Examples include, "Some women in your situation have experienced being hurt by someone. Within the past year, have you been hurt either physically or sexually by anyone?" and "Sometimes your mom or dad might get angry with you. What happens when your mom or dad gets mad?"

Abuse is suspected if injuries are inconsistent with explanations, the story changes over time, the patient has delayed getting treatment, there is a past history of injuries or accidents, there is associated drug or alcohol abuse, or there is a history of mental illness. Commonly, the patient's abuser is overly protective, may refuse to leave the room, or dominates the interview. Children who are abused may be overly attentive in an attempt to please the parent. Refer to Chapter 12 for more information.

⚠ *SAFETY ALERT 3-1*

When abuse is suspected, nurses are obligated to report it to a supervisor and obtain assistance from social work for further assessment. The nurse documents findings objectively in the patient health record and avoids judgment (see Chapter 12).

Sexual History and Orientation

The comprehensive history includes sexual history and sexual orientation to establish a baseline for health behaviours and identify the need for education. This may be another uncomfortable area for beginning nurses to ask about, but questions can provide information that allows for health teaching to prevent disease and illness. The nurse considers sexual history and pattern as a topic for health promotion, especially in high-risk patients such as those with multiple partners or having unprotected intercourse. These questions can be introduced during discussions of reproductive function or healthy behaviours or during the personal and social histories.

Examples of questions include, "As part of your physical examination, we like to provide information on healthy sexual practices. Would you like information about safer sex?" Some other questions are, "In the past year have you had intimate contact?", "Oral sex?", "Or intercourse?" "How many sexual partners have you had in the past year?" How many sexual partners all together?" "What measures do you take to protect yourself from sexually transmitted infections?" The nurse avoids bias about sexual orientation, culture, age, and marital status.

Many nurses provide opportunities for younger children to ask questions about sexuality in an attempt to increase patients' comfort level in discussing sexual topics with health care providers later in life. Refer to Chapters 25 and 26 for more information.

Lifespan Considerations

Women Who are Pregnant

The comprehensive health history is performed at the first prenatal visit. It is important to obtain information about the current pregnancy, previous pregnancies, obstetrical and gynecological history, the family, and psychosocial profile (see Chapter 27). Also, the nurse collects information on nutritional history, history of genetically inherited diseases, social and occupational histories, and history of abuse. Patients may be accompanied by family members or their partners. The nurse builds a relationship with support people as part of the process if patients give permission.

Newborns, Children, and Adolescents

The nurse collects the health history for infants and children from parents (Fig. 3-5). As children move into adolescence,

Figure 3-5 The nurse relies on parents and other caregivers to supply health history information for infants and children.

Although assessment can be viewed in isolation, it is important to realize the assessment data form the basis for planning and implementing care for patients. The reason for completing the assessment is to have data that are accurate and complete so that a plan can be developed with interventions that promote health. All pieces of the nursing process are interdependent and consider patients holistically.

Remember Emma, the 17-year-old girl with asthma. Using the previous steps of clinical reasoning, organizing, and prioritizing, consider the case study and its findings, which are woven throughout this chapter. When answering the following questions, begin drawing conclusions and see how the pieces of assessment must work together to create an environment for prioritized, appropriate, and holistic care.

- What type of data are colleted during the health history? (Knowledge)
- Describe the differences between subjective and objective data. (Comprehension)
- Identify a possible nursing diagnosis for Emma. (Application)
- What factors may contribute to the accuracy of a health history? (Analysis)
- What recommendations and screening for Emma would you suggest? (Synthesis)
- How would you evaluate a successful interview and completion of the health history? (Evaluation)

---

the nurse may interview both parents and adolescents. The relationship between the adolescent and the parent determines how the nurse collects data. It may be more comfortable and reliable to ask questions regarding sexual activity and drug use directly with the adolescent patient without the parent being present. The nurse may ask parents to step out of the room for a moment.

A health history that is especially relevant for children includes the pregnancy, birth, and perinatal histories. Immunizations and growth and development are also special areas of attention. Assessment of family structure, function, and home environment is important. Dietary intake and practices should be included because food choices change at each age (see Chapters 28 and 29).

Older Adults

When interviewing older adults, consider their increased risk for sensory deficits that might alter the history taking, such as loss of vision or hearing. However, do not assume that all older adults have sensory deficits. Older adults may have more complex histories. It is important to identify the pattern of the illnesses and recognize how they might be related. Lifestyle choices also begin to influence health later in life (see Chapter 30).

🌐 Cultural and Environmental Considerations

Cultural factors may influence the decisions patients make about their health status, lifestyle, dietary habits, and personal care. As previously discussed, consider religious and spiritual, social, political, economic, and educational factors

that influence beliefs and care decisions. Also, it is essential to be aware of illnesses that are more common among groups of patients, such as diabetes or genetically inherited diseases. Questions regarding the patient's environment might include safety in the home, transportation issues, or community involvement. The environmental assessment is necessary to evaluate the risk of exposure to hazardous substances. An exposure history includes the agent, length of exposure, and type of exposure. This information can be used to make a referral for further evaluation and follow-up if necessary.

Key Points

- Nurses collect primary data from patients. They collect secondary data from other sources such as the chart or family.
- An emergency assessment occurs when the patient's condition is unstable; a focused assessment is more narrow and specific to the presenting concern; a comprehensive assessment covers all body systems for screening and health promotion.
- Components of the comprehensive health history include the reason for seeking care, history of present illness, past health history, family history, functional assessment, growth and development, and review of systems.
- The history of present illness includes assessment of location (localized or generalized), quality or nature, intensity or severity, timing (onset, duration, constancy, time of day/month/year), aggravating and alleviating factors, associated symptoms and signs, environmental factors, significance to patient, patient perspective, functional impairment, and pain goal.
- A complete family history uses a genogram to illustrate family patterns.

- The functional health assessment includes health perception, nutrition, elimination, activity, sleep, cognition, self-perception, roles, sexuality, coping, and values.
- Nurses assess ADLs by asking about feeding, bathing, toileting, dressing, grooming, mobility, home maintenance, shopping, and cooking.
- A complete review of systems assesses the history of all body systems including nutrition/hydration, skin/hair/nails, head/neck, eyes/ears, heart, lungs, peripheral vascular, breasts, abdominal, musculoskeletal, neurological, genitalia, rectum, and endocrine/hematological.

Review Questions

1. The patient says that she is having throbbing pain that she rates as 6 on a 10-point scale. This is referred to as
   A. subjective primary data
   B. subjective secondary data
   C. objective primary data
   D. objective secondary data

2. The patient is having crushing chest pain that he rates as 8 on a 10-point scale. His blood pressure is 80/62. The nurse performs which type of assessment?
   A. Emergency
   B. Acute
   C. Focused
   D. Comprehensive

3. As part of the past health history, the nurse collects the following data:
   A. Mother had a history of thyroid disease at 50 years.
   B. Patient uses walker to ambulate at home.
   C. Patient had breast cancer in 2007; treated with chemotherapy.
   D. Child rolls onto stomach; reflexes intact.

4. When gathering the family history, the nurse draws a genogram, using
   A. circles for males and squares for females
   B. the patient on the left to show birth order
   C. lines between parents to show marriage
   D. health conditions listed above the symbol

5. The history of present illness includes an assessment of
   A. location, intensity, duration, description, aggravating and alleviating factors, functional impairment, and pain goal
   B. health perception, nutrition, elimination, activity, sleep, cognition, self-perception, roles, sexuality, coping, and values
   C. feeding, bathing, toileting, dressing, grooming, mobility, home maintenance, shopping, and cooking
   D. nutrition/hydration, skin/hair/nails, head/neck, eyes/ears, heart, peripheral vascular, breasts, abdominal, musculoskeletal, neurological, genitalia, rectum, and endocrine/hematological

6. The nurse asks, "What are the most important things to you in life?" to assess the functional pattern related to
   A. role
   B. self-perception
   C. coping
   D. values

7. To assess self-perception, the nurse asks
   A. How would you describe yourself?
   B. Are you having difficulty handling any family issues?
   C. What gives you hope when times are troubled?
   D. How do you usually deal with stress? Is it effective?

8. When the nurse asks about feeding, bathing, toileting, dressing, grooming, mobility, home maintenance, shopping, and cooking, he or she is assessing
   A. whether the patient is a reliable historian
   B. functional health patterns
   C. Activities of daily living (ADLs)
   D. review of systems

9. The nurse assessing the child focuses the health history on
   A. previous pregnancies, obstetrical history, psychosocial factors
   B. birth history, immunizations, growth and development
   C. sensory deficits, illness history, lifestyle factors
   D. religion, spirituality, culture, and values

10. Patient education is included after assessing that the nutritional history reveals the patient generally consumes a high-fat, high-calorie diet. This critical thinking
    A. uses subjective data to analyze findings and intervene
    B. documents and communicates data using appropriate medical terminologies
    C. individualizes health assessment considering the age, gender, and culture of the patient
    D. uses assessment findings to identify medical and nursing diagnoses

Canadian Nursing Research

Austin, W., Bergum, V., et al. (2006). A revisioning of boundaries in professional helping relationships: Exploring other metaphors. *Ethics & Behaviour, 16*(2), 77–94.

Kunyk, D., & Olson, J. (2001). Clarification of conceptualizations of empathy. *Journal of Advanced Nursing, 35*(3), 317–325.

Tilley, J. D., Gregor, F. M., et al. (1987).The nurse's role in patient education: Incongruent perceptions among nurses and patients. *Journal of Advanced Nursing, 12*(3), 291–301.

References

Bird, J., & Cohen-Cole, S. A. (1990). The three-function model of the medical interview. *Advanced Psychometric Medicine, 20,* 65–88.

Cohen-Cole, S. A. (1991). *The medical interview: The three-function approach.* St. Louis, MO: Mosby Year Book

Erikson, E. H. (1980). *Identity and the life cycle.* New York, NY: W. W. Norton.

Gordon, M. (1987). *Nursing diagnosis: Process and application* (2nd ed.). New York, NY: McGraw Hill.

Johann, D., Shapourian, B., et al. (2007). Screening for pain. *Nursing Management, 38*(6), 42–44, 46–47.

Lazare, A., Putnam, S. M., et al. (1995). Three functions of the medical interview. In M. Lipkin Jr, S. M. Putnam, et al. (Eds.). *The medical interview: Clinical care, education, and research* (pp. 3–19). New York, NY: Springer-Verlag.

Public Health Agency of Canada. (2010). *Canadian incidence study of reported child abuse and neglect.* Retrieved from www.phac-aspc.gc.ca/cm-vec/csca-ecve/2008/fs-am/index-eng.php

Stephen, T. C., & Bickley, L. S. (2010). The health history: Subjective data. In T. C. Stephen, D. L. Skillen, R. A. Day, & L. S. Bickley (Eds.). *Canadian Bates' guide to health assessment for nurses.* Philadelphia, PA: Wolters Kluwer Health/Lippincott Williams & Wilkins.

Thomas, C. L. (2007). *Taber's cyclopedic medical dictionary.* Philadelphia, PA: F.A. Davis.

> *The Canadian Jensen's Nursing Health Assessment suite offers these additional resources to enhance learning and facilitate understanding of this chapter:*
>
> - thePoint online resource, http//thepoint.lww.com/Stephen1E
> - *Laboratory Manual for Canadian Jensen's Nursing Health Assessment: A Best Practice Approach*

Techniques of Physical Examination and Equipment

Learning Objectives

1 Demonstrate knowledge of routine practices and additional precautions for infection control and safety.

2 Demonstrate knowledge of the anatomical position and anatomical terms.

3 Describe inspection and the specific characteristics to be assessed.

4 Describe palpation and the specific characteristics to be assessed.

5 Explain the physical properties of sound and sound conduction.

6 Describe percussion and the specific characteristics to be assessed.

7 Describe auscultation and the specific characteristics to be assessed.

8 Demonstrate knowledge of the equipment used during the physical examination.

9 Document findings from the four basic examination modes of inspection, palpation, percussion, and auscultation.

*C*hris Chow is a 6-year-old boy visiting the primary care network today with a fever and "stuffy nose." He came in with his mother who took the day off from work to stay home with him. His temperature is 38.6°C tympanic, pulse 110 beats/min and regular, respirations 20 breaths/min, and blood pressure right arm (sitting) 108/66 mm Hg. Chris is healthy and meeting developmental milestones, as indicated on the documentation from his well-child visit 2 months ago. He is being seen by a nurse practitioner.

You will gain more information about Chris as you progress through this chapter. As you study the content and features, consider Chris's case and its relationship to what you are learning. Begin thinking about the following points:

- How can the nurse facilitate comfort and reduce anxiety when performing the assessment?
- How does the nurse use infection control and safety principles during an assessment?
- What information does the nurse gain about patients during inspection, palpation, percussion, and auscultation?

Clinical examination is a tradition dating back 2,500 years (Orient & Sapira, 2005). Nurses combine subjective data from the health history (see Chapters 2 and 3) with objective data from the physical examination to form a more complete assessment database and develop an impression of the underlying etiology of any health concerns.

The four basic examination modes of inspection, palpation, percussion, and auscultation form the basis for the physical examination. They permit nurses to acquire first-hand objective data, function in environments without technology, and develop capacity for critical analysis. Each mode is used to identify specific characteristics of the body. *Inspection* is the use of the nurse's visual, auditory, and olfactory senses to make purposeful observations of the patient. *Palpation* is the use of the nurse's fingers and hands on body regions. *Percussion* is a tapping movement by the nurse that produces sounds to be interpreted about the body area being examined. *Auscultation* is the use of a stethoscope to detect sounds produced by movements of air or fluid in the body.

Overview of Anatomical Terms

Anatomical Position

To promote clear and accurate communication in both verbal and written documentation, the *anatomical position* has been adopted internationally to standardize descriptions of assessment findings for the health care providers on the interprofessional health team (Moore & Dalley, 2006). Whether the patient is prone, supine, side-lying, sitting, or standing for aspects of the physical examination, the nurse imagines that the patient is standing in the anatomical position when communicating findings (Fig. 4-1). This facilitates accurate comparisons of change in patients over a period of time, even when the health care providers are different. To use the anatomical position, the nurse imagines that the patient's

• posture is erect
• great toes and heels are touching one another
• palms are facing forward (anteriorly)
• arms are at the sides, and
• head, eyes, and toes are facing anteriorly.

Anatomical Surfaces

Nurses use anatomical surfaces to describe location (eg, medial, lateral), or direction (anteroposterior) of objective data. They avoid describing location as "over," "under," or "above" because these are not clear. Precise wording is essential for promoting patient safety. Nurses use the following words when communicating location or direction of findings during the physical examination:

• Anterior (ventral), eg, anterior thorax
• Posterior (dorsal), eg, dorsal surface of the hand
• Inferior (lower), eg, inferior to the patella

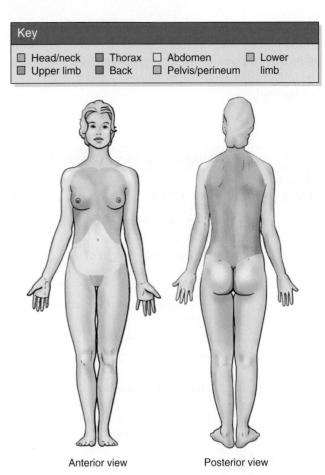

Key

☐ Head/neck ■ Thorax ☐ Abdomen ☐ Lower
☐ Upper limb ■ Back ☐ Pelvis/perineum limb

Anterior view   Posterior view

Figure 4-1 The anatomical position. **A.** Anterior view. **B.** Posterior view.

• Superior (upper), eg, superior to the patella
• Lateral, eg, lateral epicondyle of the arm
• Medial, eg, medial malleolus of the ankle
• Palmar, eg, palm of the hands
• Plantar, eg, plantar surface of the foot
• Flexor, eg, flexor surfaces of the arms
• Extensor, eg, extensor surfaces of the legs

Anatomical Quadrants

Usually, nurses observe for and communicate findings in the abdomen and in the breasts in terms of their quadrants (see Chapters 22 and 21, respectively). For the abdomen, they assess for objective data in the upper right quadrant, upper left quadrant, lower right quadrant, or lower left quadrant. For the breasts, they look for and communicate findings according to the upper outer quadrant, upper inner quadrant, lower outer quadrant, or inner lower quadrant. The breast also has the Tail of Spence (see Chapter 21).

Anatomical Regions

Nurses may also use anatomical regions to observe for and communicate findings more specifically in the abdomen.

They imagine two vertical lines and two horizontal lines creating nine imaginary abdominal regions: epigastric, umbilical, suprapubic, right hypochondriac, left hypochondriac, right lumbar, left lumbar, right inguinal, and left inguinal.

Anatomical Terms of Comparison and Movement

Nurses use terms of comparison to relate the position of one body structure to another (Table 4-1). For a discussion of terms of movement, see Chapter 23.

Table 4-1	Anatomical Terms of Comparison			
Term of Comparison	**Description**	**Opposite Term**	**Explanation/Example**	
Proximal	Nearest to the trunk of the body.	Distal	The upper arm is the proximal region of the arm. The elbow is proximal to the wrist.	
	Nearest to the origin of a structure.		When describing a nerve, muscle, or vessel, the term proximal refers to the point nearest to the origin of the structure.	
Distal	Farthest from the trunk of the body.	Proximal	The hand is the most distal part of the arm. The knee is distal to the hip.	
	Farthest from the origin of a structure.		When describing a nerve, muscle, or vessel, *distal* refers to the point farthest from the origin of the structure.	
Ipsilateral	The structure, surface, or function on the same side of the median plane as something else being described.	Contralateral	This term is used in neurological assessments. The right arm is ipsilateral to the right cerebral hemisphere.	
			Ipsilateral muscle strength (upper and lower extremities) is graded 2 on a scale of 5.	
Contralateral	The structure, surface, or function on the opposite side of the median plane as something else being described.	Ipsilateral	The term is used in neurological assessments.	
			The left arm is contralateral to the right cerebral hemisphere.	
			Contralateral sensation of upper body is intact.	
Superficial	Proximity to the surface of the body.	Deep	Lactiferous ducts in the breasts are in close proximity to the surface of the breasts.	
Deep	Distance from the surface of the body.	Superficial	The pectoralis major muscle is distant from the surface of the breast. The abdominal structures that are deep (>3 cm) to the surface skin are difficult to palpate.	
Interior	The location of a structure within another structure OR the location with respect to the body surface.	Exterior	The cochlea is internal to the ear and interior to the postauricular surface.	
Exterior	The location of a peripheral structure or the structure closer or nearer to the surface of the body.	Interior	The scrotum is exterior to the body. The epididymis is exterior to the testicle within the scrotum.	
Superior	Closer to the head than another structure.	Inferior	The superior vena cava carries blood to the heart from the upper regions of the body.	
Inferior	Closer to the feet than another structure.	Superior	The inferior vena cava carries blood to the heart from the lower regions of the body.	

Adapted from Skillen, D. L., & Bickley, L. S. (2010). The physical examination: Objective data. In T. C. Stephen, D. L. Skillen, R. A. Day, L. S. Bickley (Eds.). *Canadian Bates' guide to health assessment for nurses* (pp. 91-111). Philadelphia, PA: Wolters Kluwer Health/Lippincott Williams & Wilkins.

Routine Practices and Additional Precautions

During health assessments, the nurse comes into direct physical contact with patients. It is essential that they apply infection control principles at all times. Significant leadership regarding the principles and procedures is provided by Health Canada, the Public Health Agency of Canada and the Canadian Centre for Occupational Health and Safety. Links to these web sites are located on thePoint ✳. Infection control requires compliance with legislation, guidelines, and current information at federal, provincial, regional, or institutional levels. Nurses can access the Web sites for guidelines, a biweekly journal on communicable disease, recommendations, reports of outbreaks, and summaries related to infection control and prevention. Each health care organization develops policies and procedures within the context of relevant legislation. Competent nurses ensure that they are familiar with and compliant with those policies and procedures.

Health care environments contain a multitude of microorganisms that pose risks to health, especially for those patients with severe diseases, compromised host defenses from underlying conditions, history of recent surgery, or indwelling patient care devices (eg, urinary catheters, endotracheal tubes). Health care–associated (nosocomial) infections caused by pathogens such as methicillin-resistant *Staphylococcus aureus* (MRSA), vancomycin-resistant enterococci (VRE), and *Clostridium difficile* are prevalent. Treatment of MRSA and VRE is becoming increasingly difficult and Clostridium difficile is an antibiotic- and disinfectant-resistant spore (Siegel, Rhinehart, et al., 2006). Because of these risks, nurses take special measures to prevent the spread of infection before, during, and after performing each and every patient assessment.

⚜ Hand Hygiene

> ⚠ *SAFETY ALERT 4-1*
>
> *The single most important action to prevent an infection is hand hygiene. Contact transmission from the hands of all health care providers to patients is the most common mode of transmission, because microorganisms from one patient are then spread to others (Brunetti, Santoro, et al., 2006).*

Patient-to-patient transmission of pathogens depends on five sequential steps:

1. Organisms are present on the patient's skin or the patient's immediate environment.
2. Organisms are transferred from the patient to the nurse's hands or his or her environment.
3. Organisms survive on the nurse's hands for at least several minutes.

Figure 4-2 The nurse performs hand hygiene in preparation for conducting a physical examination.

4. The nurse omits or performs inadequate or inappropriate hand hygiene.
5. The contaminated hands of the nurse come into direct contact with another patient or the environment in direct contact with that patient (Pittet, Allegranzi, et al., 2006).

Hand hygiene helps prevent the transmission of pathogens and subsequent infections. It includes the use of alcohol-based hand rubs (sanitizers), handwashing with warm running water and soap, and use of gloves.

Proper technique for using alcohol-based hand rubs is necessary for effectiveness (Fig. 4-2). The nurse starts with dry hands, applies at least two pumps of the gel to the palm of one hand. He or she then rubs both hands together, making sure to cover all surfaces of the thumbs, fingers, and hands until they are dry (Health Canada, 2010; Widmer, Conzelmann, et al., 2007). See http://whglibdoc.who.int/publications/2009/9789241597906_eng.pdf for Figure 11.1 (page 156) for the technique of the entire procedure according to the World Health Organization (WHO). The WHO recommends that the process take 20 to 30 seconds.

Soap and warm running water are necessary for visibly soiled hands, hands contaminated with biological material, and when *C. difficile,* the spore-forming bacterium, is in the environment. Patients are cultured for *C. difficile* in cases of suspected infection, such as when a hospitalized patient has diarrhea. The nurse first removes jewellery, wets the hands with warm water, applies liquid soap, scrubs the hands together vigorously for 15 seconds (the length of time it takes to sing Happy Birthday), rinses the hands under warm running water with a rubbing motion, and then turns off the faucet with a paper towel (Health Canada, 2010). Nails must be trimmed to 0.6 cm or shorter; use of artificial nails is not acceptable (Centers for Disease Control and Prevention [CDCP], 2009).

CDCP (2009) recommended that nurses wear gloves to (1) reduce the risk of acquiring infections from their patients, (2) prevent the transmission of their flora to patients, and (3) reduce transient contamination of their hands by flora that can be transmitted from one patient to another. Nurses wear gloves when handling blood, body fluids, secretions, excretions, and contaminated items. They put on clean gloves just

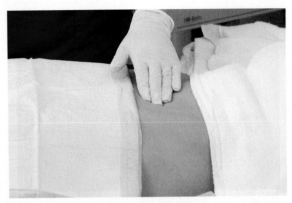

Figure 4-3 Use of gloves is important to protect against the spread of infection in cases in which the nurse could be exposed to the patient's body fluids. This nurse is wearing gloves while examining the patient who is experiencing urinary and fecal incontinence.

before touching the mucous membranes and nonintact skin of patients. They wear gloves when they anticipate general contact with any "wet" body secretion. For example, nurses do not need to wear gloves when taking an oral temperature, because only the thermometer probe cover comes in contact with the patient's oral secretions. In contrast, nurses need gloves while assessing the back of the patient with urinary incontinence in order to avoid contact with any of the patient's urine. Nurses wear gloves to avoid spreading micro organisms from one body area to another (Fig. 4-3).

The nurse changes gloves (1) between tasks and procedures on the same patient after contact with a material that contains a high concentration of microorganisms and (2) when going from a contaminated to a cleaner area. He or she removes gloves promptly after use, before touching noncontaminated items and environmental surfaces, and before going to another patient. Nurses remove gloves before touching the computer, supply drawers, and certain equipment. Nurses never wear gloves from the room out into the hallway. They wash their hands immediately after glove removal because gloves may have a small puncture and they must avoid transfering microorganisms to other patients or environments.

Hand hygiene is the single most important element of routine practices. See Box 4-1 for a summary of the indications for hand hygiene.

Routine Practices

Nurses use **routine practices** with all patients to reduce the transmission of pathogens in both diagnosed and unknown infections. The underlying assumption is that "all patients are colonized or infected with microorganisms, whether or not there are signs or symptoms" (Groeneveld, 2010, p. 2354). The intention of routine practices is to prevent disease transmission during contact with nonintact skin, mucous membranes, blood (eg, needle-stick injury), body fluids, and body substances (Box 4-2). Because many

---

BOX 4-1 INDICATIONS FOR HANDWASHING AND HAND HYGIENE

- When hands are visibly dirty or soiled, wash hands with either a nonantimicrobial soap and water or an antimicrobial soap and water.
- If hands are not visibly soiled, use an alcohol-based hand rub for routinely decontaminating hands in all other clinical situations.
- Decontaminate hands before having direct contact with patients and after contact with the patient's intact skin (eg., taking a pulse or blood pressure, lifting the patient).
- Decontaminate hands if moving from a contaminated body site to a clean body site during patient care.
- Decontaminate hands after contact with inanimate objects (including medical equipment) in the immediate vicinity of the patient.
- Decontaminate hands after removing gloves.
- Before eating and after using a restroom, wash hands with a nonantimicrobial soap and water or with an antimicrobial soap and water.
- Wash hands with nonantimicrobial soap and water or with antimicrobial soap and water if an exposure to Bacillus anthracis or Clostridium difficile is suspected or proven. The physical action of washing and rinsing hands under such circumstances is recommended, because alcohols, chlorhexidine, iodophors, and other antiseptic agents have poor activity against spores.

Adapted from CDCP. (2009). *Standard precautions excerpt from the guideline for isolation precautions: Preventing transmission of infectious agents in healthcare settings 2007*. Retrieved from http://www.cdc.gov/ncidod/dhqp/gl_isolation_standard.html

---

Box 4-2 BODY COMPONENTS THAT CONTRIBUTE TO TRANSMISSION OF INFECTIOUS AGENTS

Blood
- Whole blood
- Blood components
- Blood products

Body fluids
- Saliva
- Urine
- Semen
- Vaginal secretions
- Cerebrospinal fluid
- Synovial, pleural, peritoneal, amniotic, and pericardial fluids

Body substances
- Biopsy tissue
- Vomitus
- Feces
- Sputum
- Nasal secretions

Adapted from Skillen, D. L., & Bickley, L. S. (2010). The physical examination: Objective data. In T. C. Stephen, D. L. Skillen, R. A. Day, L. S. Bickley (Eds.). *Canadian Bates' guide to health assessment for nurses* (pp. 91–111). Philadelphia, PA: Wolters Kluwer Health/Lippincott Williams & Wilkins.

patients are unaware of being infected, routine practices help ensure that providers treat all patients equally and without stigma. In 1999, Health Canada adopted the term *routine practices* instead of *standard precautions* in order to emphasize that this level of care is essential for all patients in all health care settings.

Respiratory hygiene/cough etiquette is another important area. Patients, visitors, health care providers, and non-professional employees in health care facilities who have symptoms of a respiratory infection are asked to cough or sneeze into their sleeve or into tissues. They should dispose of tissues directly into receptacles and perform hand hygiene after hands have been in contact with respiratory secretions (CDCP, 2009).

The CDCP has developed transmission-based precautions for airborne, droplet, and contact routes of transmission. Health care providers combine the use of these specific precautions with routine practices. The general guideline is for health care providers to wear personal protective equipment whenever they are at risk for coming into contact with body secretions from patients, such as droplet exposure during coughing with tracheal suctioning. Nurses may require barriers (masks, safety glasses) to spray or splash exposures, in addition to gloves and gowns. Refer to Table 4-2 for a summary of routine practices.

Additional Precautions

Additional precautions may include avoidance of latex gloves due to a latex allergy, use of dedicated facilities or equipment that controls airflow or maintains negative air pressure, and use of N95 respirators to prevent exposure to airborne or droplet sources of infection. Direct contact (body surface to body surface) may be a source of infection and requires additional precautions. Indirect contact precautions are required to prevent a source of infection via an intermediate object (Health Canada, 1999). In addition to the resistant pathogens described above, other examples of infectious agents include hepatitis A to E viruses, Epstein-Barr virus, cytomegalovirus, and human immunodeficiency virus (HIV)

Latex Allergy

Latex allergy can result from repeated exposures through skin contact or inhalation to proteins in the natural rubber latex. Reactions usually begin within minutes of exposure to latex, but they can occur hours later and produce symptoms. Nurses are more likely to have latex allergy than the general population (8% to 12% compared to 1%) (Occupational Safety and Health Administration [OSHA], 2009). Nurses exposed

Table 4-2	Recommendations for Routine Practices
Device	**Routine Practices**
Mask, eye protection, face shield	Wear a mask and eye protection or a face shield to protect mucous membranes of the eyes, nose, and mouth during procedures and activities that are likely to generate splashes or sprays of blood, body fluids, secretions, and excretions.
Gown	Wear a gown (a clean, nonsterile gown is adequate) to protect skin and to prevent soiling of clothes during procedures and activities that are likely to generate splashes or sprays of blood, body fluids, secretions, or excretions. Remove a soiled gown as promptly as possible and wash hands to avoid transfer of microorganisms to other patients or environments.
Patient care equipment	Ensure that reusable equipment is not used for the care of another patient until it has been cleaned and reprocessed appropriately. Ensure the proper discarding of single-use items.
Environmental control	Ensure that the facility has adequate procedures for the routine care, cleaning, and disinfection of environmental surfaces, beds, bedrails, bedside equipment, and other frequently touched surfaces.
Linen	Handle, transport, and process used linen soiled with blood, body fluids, secretions, and excretions in a manner that prevents skin exposures and contamination of clothing and that avoids transfer of microorganisms to other patients and environments.
Occupational health and blood-borne pathogens	Never recap used needles. Do not remove used needles from disposable syringes by hand; do not bend, break, or otherwise manipulate used needles by hand. Place used disposable syringes and needles, scalpel blades, and other sharp items in appropriate puncture-resistant containers. Use mouthpieces, resuscitation bags, or other ventilation devices as an alternative to mouth-to-mouth resuscitation methods in areas where the need for resuscitation is predictable.
Patient placement	Place the patient who contaminates the environment or who does not (or cannot be expected to) assist in maintaining appropriate hygiene or environmental control in a private room.

Adapted from CDCP. (2009). *Standard precautions excerpt from the guideline for isolation precautions: preventing transmission of infectious agents in healthcare settings 2007*. Retrieved from http://www.cdc.gov/ncidod/dhqp/gl_isolation_standard.html

Remember Chris, the 6-year-old boy with a fever and "stuffy nose" who is visiting the the primary care network with his mother. He is anxious about coming to the ambulatory clinic, because he received an immunization during his previous appointment. The nurse uses professional communication that is appropriate for the child's developmental level to gather subjective data.

Nurse: Hi, Chris. I'm Lesley. How are you?

Chris: I feel sick. Am I going to have to get a shot today?

Nurse: No, you had your shots last time and they are good for a few years. Today, I want to listen to your lungs and look in your mouth and ears. Do you want me to listen or look first?

Chris: Mom, I don't want a shot.

Mother: You don't need one today. How about if you come and sit on my lap and Nurse Lesley can listen to your lungs?

Chris: OK. What does that thing do anyway? (points to the stethoscope)

Nurse: I can hear the air moving in your lungs and your heart beating. Would you like to listen first?

Chris: Sure. (The nurse positions the stethoscope for Chris, who smiles as he listens.)

Nurse: (to mother) So he's had a fever?

Mother: Yes, it's been up to 39.0°C.

Nurse: What else have you noticed?

Mother: A runny nose and a bit of a cough, too.

Nurse: (to Chris) That's the air moving in and out as you breathe (smiles). I want to ask your mother some more questions. Can I listen a little bit later?

Critical Thinking Challenge

- What questions does the nurse ask to gather a complete history (symptom/sign analysis) of the present illness?
- Why did the nurse allow Chris to sit on his mother's lap?
- How might the nurse facilitate comfort and reduce anxiety when performing inspection, palpation, percussion, and auscultation, using other equipment such as an otoscope and ophthalmoscope?

to latex show an increased risk of hand dermatitis, asthma, and rhinoconjunctivitis (Bousquet, Flahault, et al., 2006). As well, patients can develop allergies to latex, especially those who are admitted to hospital frequently.

The best preventive action is to avoid contact with latex. Health care facilities can establish latex-free zones for patients and staff. Nurses avoid carrying any latex substances into such zones, including stethoscopes, urinary catheters, and vials with rubber stoppers. To reduce exposure to latex and allergy rates, institutions are encouraged to substitute powder-free, low-allergen gloves and latex-free gloves (LaMontagne, Radi, et al., 2006).

Skin Reactions

Nurses have an increased rate of skin reactions because of the frequency of performing hand hygiene. To minimize the adverse effects, they select less irritating products purchased by institutions and use skin moisturizers after washing hands (Health Canada, 2010; Larson, Girard, et al., 2006). Other measures for reducing exposure to skin irritants include using hand gel instead of soap and water in disinfection procedures when the hands are not visibly dirty, and using gloves for "wet" activities (eg, bathing patients) to prevent the hands from becoming wet and visibly dirty.

Subjective Data Collection

The nurse's role in subjective data collection is to gather information to improve or maximize the patient's health status and to help determine the cause of the patient's current symptoms. An accurate health history provides direction to the nurse for the physical examination to follow. He or she will determine from the health history the extent to which the skills of inspection, palpation, percussion, and auscultation are to be applied.

⚠ SAFETY ALERT 4-2

It is imperative that nurses perform hand hygiene between patients. No compromised patients should be put at risk because of a nurse's neglect to use hand sanitizer, soap and water, or gloves according to the situation. Nurses use routine practices and additional precautions as outlined by Health Canada. They do not leave physical examination equipment where a mentally unstable patient might have access to it. They disinfect their stethoscopes and other equipment between patients.

Objective Data Collection

Promoting Patient Comfort, Dignity, and Safety

The nurse collects the equipment for a complete physical assessment (see Box 4-3), introduces himself or herself to the patient and gives an overview of what he or she is going to do. Nurses perform hand hygiene in front of patients, an action that will reassure patients that the nurses are protecting their welfare. The patient is draped to avoid unnecessary exposure. When performing inspection, palpation, percussion, and auscultation, the nurse uncovers only the body area or part being examined. Nurses use a logical sequence, minimizing repetitive patient position changes. They conduct those aspects of the examination that are possible with the patient seated or standing before asking the patient to lie down. Patients will be aware when the nurse is palpating, percussing, and auscultating, but they need to know what the nurse is inspecting.

Inspection

Nurses perform **general inspection** by intentionally observing patients for specific characteristics. Inspection is always the first technique of the overall general survey and for specific areas of the body, because it provides so much information. Inspection is the one technique that is performed for every body part and body system. Initially, the nurse observes the patient for overall characteristics that include apparent age, gender, level of alertness, body size and shape, skin colour, hygiene, posture, and level of discomfort or anxiety. General inspection is part of the general survey and is presented in more detail in Chapter 6. The nurse gathers data during this initial phase to determine an overall impression and the acuity of the situation (eg, indications of pain, shock). When using a planned approach during general inspection, the nurse minimizes the risk of failing to see or ignoring significant patient signs. Nurses use their sense of sight, hearing, and smell to focus on patient characteristics. Additionally, they observe cues that might indicate a condition that requires further assessment. Following general inspection, nurses proceed to perform **local inspection,** assessing specific body systems and areas.

Local inspection is a selective scrutiny of an anatomical region or body part with focus on specific characteristics (Box 4-4). Local inspection always follows general inspection. Adequate exposure of each body part is necessary at the same time that measures are taken to preserve the modesty of patients through appropriate draping, especially over the breasts in women and genitalia in both men and women (Fig. 4-4). Lighting is an important consideration and is either direct or oblique/tangential. Direct (perpendicular) lighting is

BOX 4-3	**EQUIPMENT FOR COMPLETE PHYSICAL ASSESSMENT**
Platform scale with height measure	Tongue depressors/blades
Thermometer	Snellen chart
Blood pressure cuff/machine	Tape measure
Watch with second hand	Reflex hammer
Stethoscope	Cotton swabs
Clean gloves	Tuning fork: 126 Hz OR 252 Hz
Penlight	Coin, paper clip, key, or safety pin (familiar objects)
Ophthalmoscope	Bivalve vaginal speculum
Otoscope	Materials for cytological study
Tuning fork: 1024 Hz OR 512 Hz	Lubricant
Nasal speculum	Culture media and test solutions
	Equipment wipes

BOX 4-4	**PATIENT CHARACTERISTICS TO ASSESS DURING LOCAL INSPECTION**

Alignment	Elevations	Movements	Secretions
Closure	Hygiene	Parasites	Shape
Colour	Integrity	Pigmentation	Size
Contraction	Integument	Pulsations	Sounds
Contour	Lesions	Range of motion	Spacing
Coordination	Lustre	Reaction to light	Symmetry
Curvature	Mass	Reflection	Vascularity
Depressions	Mobility	Reflexes	
Development	Moisture	Rhythm	

Adapted from Skillen, D. L., & Bickley, L. S. (2010). The physical examination: Objective data. In T. C. Stephen, D. L. Skillen, R. A. Day, & L. S. Bickley (Eds.). *Canadian Bates' guide to health assessment for nurses* (pp. 91–111). Philadelphia, PA: Wolters Kluwer Health/Lippincott Williams & Wilkins.

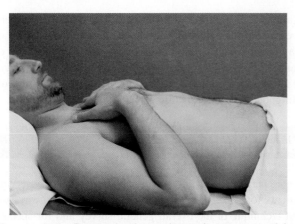

Figure 4-4 Proper draping and gowning are essential to preserving the patient's privacy and building his or her trust. The nurse is careful to expose only those areas pertinent to the immediate examination and to redrape or re-cover the patient upon completion.

used to examine the colour of the integumentary system and to assess skin lesions. Tangential lighting is used to cast shadows that permit nurses to detect movement, pulsations, and contour. The nurse informs the patient about what he or she is going to inspect. For example, "I need to look at your mastectomy incision to see how it is healing. Is it OK if I lift your gown?"

Sometimes devices limit visibility, such as a splint over a knee. When possible, such devices are loosened or removed to observe the skin adequately for any red, inflamed, or infected areas and also for intact circulation. When nurses are inspecting each region or body part, they use specific descriptions. For example, when inspecting the abdomen, the nurse notes the shape (whether it is flat, rounded, scaphoid, or distended), skin colour and texture, and any scars, bruising, pulsations, movements, and prominent veins. A common technique is to consider overall shape first and then compare the two sides for symmetry.

Paying attention to individual details of inspection, the nurse notes whether verbal, nonverbal, and inspection data are congruent and identifies any preliminary patterns or clusters. If patients appear anxious, the nurse notes facial expression, nervous gestures, body position or pacing, and voice characteristics. Inspection provides objective data regarding nonverbal communication and also physical data that can lead to an accurate diagnosis and appropriate treatment.

Inspection is assisted by the use of instruments such as the otoscope for the auditory canal and tympanic membrane (see Chapter 16), the ophthalmoscope for the lens and retina (see Chapter 15), and tuning forks for assessing hearing (512 or 1024 Hz) (see Chapter 16) and vibration sense (126 or 252 Hz) (see Chapter 24).

With experience, gathering data from inspection becomes automatic and this information is collected while performing other techniques or interventions. Inspection begins with the initial contact with each patient but continues through each individual body system and with every patient encounter.

Palpation

Palpation makes use of the sensory properties of the hand. When applied thoughtfully and appropriately, palpation yields a wealth of information. Light palpation is always part of the physical examination; deep palpation is used at the discretion of the nurse. Before performing this technique, the nurse informs the patient of the need to palpate the body part along with the rationale, and asks for permission to use touch. During abdominal assessment, he or she might say, "I know that you're having some abdominal pain, but I would like to gently feel your abdomen to see if a particular area is firm or tender. Would that be OK with you?" Beginning with a gentle and slow technique, the nurse inspects the patient's face for nonverbal indicators of discomfort such as frowning or grimacing.

Palpation requires the capacity of the nurse to identify tactile, kinesthetic, vibratory, and temperature sensations. Nurses use different parts of the hand depending on the data that they are gathering. The finger pads are sensitive to tactile discriminations and are used primarily to detect texture, moisture, contour, and consistency. Sensory nerve fibres are particularly abundant in the fingertips. The finger tips and pads help to determine the fluid content of tissues, elasticity, pulsatility, thickness, turgor, and vascularity of body structures. Some examples of the need for fine discrimination include locating the pulses, lymph nodes, or small lumps and assessing for skin texture and edema. The dorsum (back of the hand) and ulnar edge (along the little finger) of the hand are particularly sensitive to temperature variations because of thinner skin surfaces. The ulnar edge also is sensitive to vibrations. If the patient reports being hot, the nurse turns his or her hand over and uses this dorsal side to evaluate temperature. Vibratory tremors can be felt on the chest as the patient speaks and when the nurse is assessing for tactile fremitus (see Chapter 18). These are best felt with the ulnar edge or ball of the hand (palm).

Light Palpation

The nurse begins with light palpation to allow the patient to become accustomed to the touch. If pain is present, he or she might say, "Let me know if this hurts you" to gain trust and increase comfort. Tender areas are always palpated last. The nurse ensures correct draping and warms his or her hands before beginning. It may be necessary to warm them under running water or to gently rub them together. Short smooth nails are necessary for patient comfort. Palpation is difficult when patients' muscles are tense; a gentle, calm, and easy touch assists patients to relax.

Light palpation is appropriate for the assessment of skin surface characteristics, such as texture, surface lesions, lumps, inflamed areas of skin (eg, over an intravenous site) and structures that are at a depth of about 1 cm from the skin surface. The nurse places the finger pads of the dominant hand on the patient's skin (Fig. 4-5), slowly and gently moving the fingers in a circular motion. Intermittent

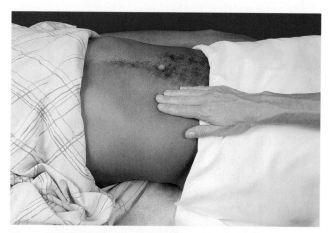

Figure 4-5 Technique for light palpation.

palpation using this technique is more effective than a single continuous palpation, because the fingers sense the movement of skin and tissue beneath the finger pads. Patients may perceive this gentle palpation as a light massage in the absence of pain. By starting with gentle palpation, the nurse facilitates continuation of the examination and collection of more data. The nurse communicates concern for patients verbally with conversation during the procedure and nonverbally through this caring touch. The patient who experiences tenderness to palpation may react by voluntarily increasing muscular resistance and that prevents detection of additional findings.

Deep Palpation

Deep palpation is used to detect information about structures that are 3 to 4 cm below the skin surface. The nurse uses firm, discontinuous pressure to avoid reducing tactile sensitivity. The same circular motion of light palpation is appropriate, but the extended fingers of the nondominant hand are placed over the dominant hand to provide the pressure. Pressure is firm enough to depress approximately 2 to 4 cm. The nurse observes the patient for any guarding, grimacing, or tension during deep palpation. With deep palpation, the nurse might say, "I'm going to touch you and push down more deeply than before. It might feel a little uncomfortable. Let me know if you feel pain or want me to stop." As palpation proceeds, the nurse continues conversation, asking patients about pain, presenting symptoms, or contributing factors while observing for nonverbal signs of tenderness or discomfort. A beginning nurse may initially be able to concentrate only on the technique. As he or she gains skill, it becomes possible to palpate, assess symptoms, and teach all at the same time.

⚠ *SAFETY ALERT 4-3*

Deep palpation should not be used over areas that pose a risk of injuring patients, such as over an enlarged spleen or inflamed appendix. Nursing students only do deep palpation under supervision.

Commonly used movements in palpation include circular (rotary), dipping, direct (perpendicular), gliding, and grasping (pincer) motions. Circular motions are used to roll skin surface over underlying structures so that characteristics of structures or masses may be detected. Dipping motions are used during abdominal palpation to detect contour, guarding, and mobility, for example. When the nurse uses direct pressure it detects much information that includes blanching, resistance, guarding, pulsations, and tenderness. To identify moisture, surface contour, and texture, the nurse uses gliding motions. A pincer motion (grasping) helps the nurse to assess turgor, characteristics of masses, and skin thickness. (Skillen & Bickley, 2010).

Characteristics of Sound and Sound Transmission

Sounds are perceived in terms of four characteristics:

- Pitch (frequency)—the measure in cycles per second, usually expressed in Hertz (Hz)
- Duration—the length of time in seconds, minutes, or hours that a sound is perceived by the human ear
- Quality (timbre)—the musical nature of the sound
- Intensity (loudness)—the perception of sound measured in decibels using an instrument calibrated to the human hearing curve.

A freely vibrating source of sound is capable of producing a loud sound, and its intensity varies according to the force applied to set the vibration in motion. For example, striking a drum produces a relatively loud sound because the drum has the capacity to vibrate freely. In contrast, striking the human forearm or thigh produces a sound of low intensity because the tissues are relatively dense and do not vibrate freely.

Example: Use of the Tuning Fork (see Fig. 4-6)

- When testing hearing, the nurse uses a tuning fork of 1024 Hz or 512 Hz. A 1024 Hz tuning fork has a high pitch, long duration, and a musical sound.
- When testing vibration, the nurse uses a tuning fork of 256 Hz or 128 Hz. A 256 Hz tuning fork has a low pitch, short duration, and a buzzing sound.

The sounds that are detected using percussion and auscultation depend not only on whether they pass through solid, fluid or gas, but also on the elasticity of body structures. Elasticity permits vibration of structures. Gases are poor transmitters of sound, fluids are better, and solids are best. The pitch, intensity, musical quality, and duration of sounds change as they are transmitted through solids, fluid, and air in tissues.

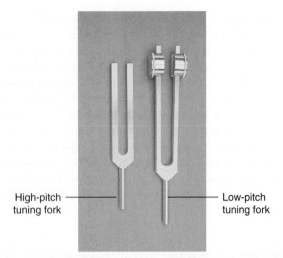

Figure 4-6 Tuning forks.

High-pitch tuning fork

Low-pitch tuning fork

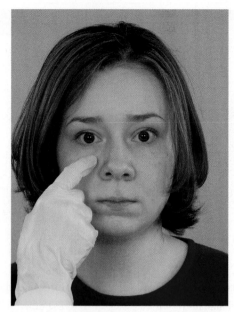

Figure 4-7 Direct percussion of the sinuses.

Percussion

Percussion notes are sounds produced in the body as a result of the percussing (tapping) on body surfaces. Percussion permits nurses to elicit tenderness and to infer from the type of percussion note the state of the underlying body tissues. Using a technique described below, the nurse taps his or her fingers on the patient, similar to the tap of a drumstick on a drum. The vibrations that the fingers produce create a percussion note for interpretation by the nurse. The five percussion notes are dullness, flatness, resonance, hyperresonance, and tympany. See Table 4-3 for a list of percussion notes and their characteristics. Each percussion note is characterized by pitch, intensity, quality, and duration. Vibrations of dense tissue produce quiet percussion notes; vibrations of air-filled tissue create louder percussion notes. The loudest percussion notes are over the lungs and gas-filled stomach and intestines; the quietest are over bones. Dullness is heard anterior to the liver, heart, or a distended urinary bladder. Flatness is percussed over the thigh or scapula. Resonance is heard when air-filled lung tissue is percussed. When lung tissue is hyper-inflated or when a child's chest is percussed, hyperresonance is heard. Tympany is a drumlike sound and is percussed over gas-filled tissues such as the stomach or intestine. (Skillen & Bickley, 2010). Two methods of percussion are direct and indirect.

Direct Percussion

In direct (nonmediated) percussion, the nurse taps with his or her finger directly on the patient's skin (Fig. 4-7). An example is percussion of the maxillary sinuses in patients with sinus infections, percussion of the skin over the clavicle to detect resonance in apical lung tissue, or percussion of the thorax in newborns to assess the air-filled lungs. Direct percussion is easier to learn than indirect percussion. For direct percussion of the maxillary sinuses with the finger, the nurse gently taps on the skin surface overlying the maxillary sinus to detect tenderness. It could indicate allergies, congestion, or infection. The lightest tap that will produce a response is used.

Indirect Percussion

Indirect (mediated) percussion is most commonly used. Rather than directly striking the skin surface of the patient, the nurse taps with the middle (plexor) finger of the dominant hand over the middle (pleximeter) finger of the nondominant hand, which is placed on a body surface (Fig. 4-8). Again, the lightest tap that will elicit a percussion note is used. The nurse also uses the ulnar surface of the fist to percuss the costovertebral angle for kidney tenderness (see Chapter 18 or 22).

Table 4-3	**Percussion Sounds**				
Note	**Intensity**	**Pitch**	**Duration**	**Quality**	**Location**
Hyperresonant	Very loud	Low	Long	Boomlike	Emphysematous lungs
Resonant	Loud	Low	Long	Hollow	Healthy lungs
Tympanic	Loud	High	Moderate	Drumlike	Gastric bubble (stomach)
Dull	Moderate	High	Moderate	Thud	Liver
Flat	Soft	High	Short	Dull	Bone

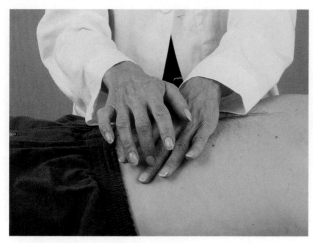

Figure 4-8 Indirect percussion.

This technique requires coordination of both hands. To perform indirect percussion, the nurse places the last joint (distal interphalangeal) or the last digit (phalanx) of a hyperextended middle finger of the nondominant hand firmly over the area to be percussed. The other fingers of that hand are lifted and spread slightly to avoid contact with the patient and dampening the sound created by the striking finger (plexor). The slightly flexed middle finger of the dominant hand is held approximately 2 to 3 cm above the distal interphalangeal joint that is in contact with the patient. Using only wrist action of the dominant hand, raise the dominant finger 4 to 5 cm and quickly strike the nondominant joint only twice, while listening for the elicited sound (Fig. 4-8). The nurse then moves the finger on the patient to a new area and strikes twice with the plexor finger. Beginners need to practise first to elicit a sound loud enough to hear. It helps to practise on a hard surface first such as a table or a wall. (Try to percuss the studs in a plastered wall). After perfecting the technique, listen carefully and compare sounds to identify the types of note heard.

Some helpful hints when learning percussion are as follows:

- The motion of the striking finger should be quick, forceful, and snappy, with only wrist action and not action at the elbow. Brisk action promotes a clear percussion note.
- Nails must be short and smooth to avoid tenderness and facilitate good contact. Using the pad of the finger dampens the sound.

- To avoid dampening the sound, the tapping finger is withdrawn immediately after striking the nondominant finger.
- A person with small hands and fingers needs to strike a bit more forcefully than a person with large hands.

It is also easier to hear the difference in percussion notes when percussing from resonance to dullness. For example, when percussing the liver span (see Chapter 22), the nurse percusses downward from resonance to dullness and upward from tympany over the intestine to dullness.

Auscultation

Auscultation using stethoscopes detects sounds created by vibration of underlying tissues transmitted to the skin surface and closure of heart valves. Auscultation requires a quiet environment with minimal distractions. Sometimes it is helpful for the nurse to close his or her eyes when auscultating to block out environmental stimuli.

Nurses perform auscultation commonly when assessing blood pressure, lung sounds, heart sounds, and the abdomen. The blood pressure produces Korotkoff sounds that correlate with the flowing of the pulse. Air moving in and out with each breath generates soft and rustling (vesicular) sounds in the lungs. The heart produces a lub–dub sound with the closure of the heart valves. Peristalsis in the abdomen produces typical gurgling, clicks, or growling sounds. Descriptors vary depending on the body part being auscultated and are found in individual chapters related to the body system being examined. Auscultated sounds are described in terms of intensity, pitch, duration, and quality (the same as percussion). Descriptors for quality are different with auscultation, however, such as knocking, gurgly, or rustling (see Table 4-4).

The stethoscope conducts sound from the patient's body to the listener and also blocks environmental noise to assist hearing. It does not amplify sounds, but an electronic stethoscope does. The binaural stethoscope is usually used. It has right and left ear pieces, single tubing, and two chestpieces, usually a bell and a diaphragm (Fig. 4-9). The ear pieces must fit snugly but comfortably in the ear canal. They are tilted slightly forward so that the point on the ear piece is forward in the same direction as the nose (Fig. 4-10). This position

Table 4-4	**Comparison of Auscultation Sounds**				
Focus	**Intensity**	**Pitch**	**Quality**	**Duration**	**Location**
Blood pressure	Soft to loud	High	Swooshing or knocking	60–100/min	Arm
Abdominal sounds	Soft to loud	High	Gurgly, intermittent	5–35/min	Abdomen
Heart sounds	Moderate	Low	Lub-dub, rhythmic	60–100/min	Anterior thorax
Lung sounds vesicular	Soft	Low	Rustling, wispy	Inspiration > expiration, 12–20/min	Anterior and posterior thorax

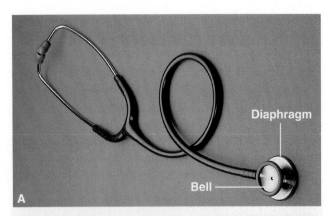

Figure 4-9 A. The stethoscope. **B.** Gently tap the bell or diaphragm after placing the stethoscope in the ears to check that the correct piece is turned on.

Figure 4-10 Correct positioning of the stethoscope to direct sound toward the tympanic membrane.

directs sound toward the nurse's tympanic membrane. Ear tips come in different sizes and firmness so nurses choose the type that is most comfortable. Tubing is thick to block environmental noise and is short (approximately 30 cm) to increase transmission of sound. Some pediatric nurses cover their stethoscopes with colourful fabric to distract children from touching the tubing during auscultation.

The chestpieces detect all four characteristics of sounds. The bell accentuates low-frequency sounds and is applied lightly to the skin. The diaphragm is used for high-pitched sounds (think "di-hi") and does not require a complete seal on the skin the way the bell does. If the bell is applied firmly, the skin functions as a diaphragm and high pitched sounds are accentuated instead of low-pitched sounds. It is practical for the nurse to place the earpieces in his or her ears and gently tap the diaphragm before auscultating to ensure that the preferred chestpiece is turned on.

The diaphragm is typically used for most sounds such as lung and heart sounds, although the bell works best for detecting low-pitched heart murmurs. For this reason, heart sounds are usually auscultated with both the diaphragm and the bell (see Chapter 19). See individual system chapters for variations. The appropriate-sized chestpiece facilitates good skin contact, so pediatric stethoscopes are best with small children The nurse holds the chestpiece by placing the end piece between

---

Documenting Findings

The nurse practitioner has just finished conducting a physical assessment of Chris, the 6-year-old boy with a fever, runny nose, sore throat, and cough. Review the following important findings that each of the steps of objective data collection for Chris revealed. Begin to think about how the data cluster together and what additional data the nurse might want to collect while thinking critically about the issues and anticipating nursing interventions

Inspection: Somewhat anxious boy, sitting on mother's lap. Face flushed, breathing effortlessly, no shortness of breath. Dry, hacking cough. Oropharynx red without lesions or drainage. Tonsils slightly red and enlarged, graded 1+. Nares red with some clear thin drainage bilaterally. Auditory canals are unobstructed. Tympanic membranes pearly gray without perforation. Light reflex and landmarks intact bilaterally. Gross hearing intact right and left.

Palpation: Nontender over maxillary and frontal sinuses bilaterally.

Percussion: Resonance throughout lung fields.

Auscultation: Vesicular sounds throughout lung fields; no adventitious sounds.

the index and middle fingers, not on top, which distorts the sounds. The tubing needs to be away from objects that might brush against it, producing extraneous noises. If the patient has a large amount of hair on the chest, it may help to moisten the hair to avoid the crackly noises caused when hair rubs against a stethoscope. For accuracy and hygiene, nurses use their own stethoscopes. They disinfect the stethoscope between patients with equipment wipes to avoid the spread of pathogens.

See Chapter 15 for the description and use of the ophthalmoscope. Chapter 16 contains the description and use of the otoscope.

Lifespan Considerations

Women Who Are Pregnant

Women who are pregnant usually provide a urine sample during each visit, so they can empty their bladder before undergoing the abdominal and vaginal examination. They may be uncomfortable while lying flat. The nurse can complete most components of the physical examination with the patient sitting. The lithotomy position is necessary for vaginal examination (see Chapter 27).

Newborns and Infants

Positioning of newborns and infants for a physical assessment can be either on an examination table or while held against a parent's chest. If the assessment is conducted on the examination table, the nurse is always in physical and visual contact with infants to maintain safety. Newborns and infants are comfortable without clothing in a warm environment; however, leaving their diapers on as long as possible is preferable, especially with boys, to avoid contamination of the nurse with urine or feces.

Warm hands and equipment to avoid startling babies. When infants are able to sit, the nurse performs most of the examination with the infant on a caregiver's lap. For sleeping infants, the nurse first listens to the heart, lung, and bowel sounds. The most uncomfortable assessments are performed at the end of the examination to prevent an infant's crying from compromising the quality of earlier assessment findings (see Chapter 28).

Children and Adolescents

Active toddlers may be afraid or shy. The nurse asks parents to assist with the physical examination by holding or positioning their children as needed. Young children may hesitate to have body parts exposed. An alternative is for a parent to partially undress a child and then cover each body part after it is examined. Many toddlers automatically say "no" to any question asked. To prevent negativism from prolonging the examination, nurses give specific choices, such as "Would you like to sit on the table or on your grandmother's lap while I listen to your heart?" Games also become prominent. Children may better participate if encouraged to "blow out" the ophthalmoscope light or listen to their own heart and lungs (see Chapter 29).

Figure 4-11 Slightly elevating the head of the bed or examination table may help facilitate breathing for older adults. Covering the patient to avoid chilling is another important consideration for patients in this age group.

When working with adolescents, nurses remain aware that their rapidly changing bodies may increase these patients' feelings of modesty or self-consciousness. Draping is especially important for patients of this age group. Additionally, adolescents appreciate explanations for the assessments, especially any related to body image or developmental stage. For example, the nurse can say "I would like to listen to your heart sounds and need to put the stethoscope on your chest, but I will be careful to keep you covered."

Older Adults

Older adults may chill more easily than younger patients, so the nurse considers offering them an additional blanket, flannel sheet or drape (see Chapter 30). These patients may also fatigue quickly, so it is important to perform the most important assessments in the beginning. When positioning older adults, slight elevation of the head of the bed or examination table may help facilitate breathing (Fig. 4-11).

Cultural Considerations

Each assessment must be individualized according to the patient's cultural, religious, and social beliefs. Many patients are anxious prior to a physical assessment. These feelings may be related to fear of disclosing private or uncomfortable information, embarrassment about being touched or looked at, or worry about potential findings. The nurse asks the patient about his or her preferences, such as having a family member in the room or having a same-gender examiner, before starting. Nurses perform less invasive assessments first, such as taking vital signs, and save the most personal assessments for the end (see Chapter 11).

Advanced Techniques

Each of the chapters on body system or body region assessments contains information on advanced techniques that nurses use during physical examination. Advanced techniques incorporate inspection, palpation, percussion, and auscultation.

Initial collection of subjective and objective data for Chris Chow is complete. The following nursing note documents the analysis of subjective and objective data and beginning development of nursing interventions.

Subjective: A 6-year-old seen for fever, cough, sore throat, and "runny nose." Mother states that patient has had a fever of 39.0°C for 2 days; symptoms and signs are not resolving.

Objective: Face flushed, breathing effortlessly, no shortness of breath. Dry, hacking cough. No tenderness or swelling over maxillary and frontal sinuses. Oropharynx red without lesions or drainage. Tonsils slightly red and enlarged, 1+. Nares red with clear thin drainage. Auditory canals unobstructed. Tympanic membranes pearly gray without perforation. Light reflex, landmarks, and hearing intact bilaterally. Lung fields resonant and vesicular sounds throughout; no adventitious sounds.

Analysis: Fever, viral rhinitis, and pharyngitis causing impaired comfort.

Plan: Encourage to drink at least 2 L of fluid a day. Frozen treats and jello may be included in fluid intake. Offer acetaminophen as needed for pain relief. Encourage frequent rest, including naps during the day. Teach measures for infection control including disposal of tissues, covering mouth with sleeve, and handwashing.

Critical Thinking Challenge

- How is the role of the nurse practitioner different from the role of the registered nurse?
- How does the nurse include mother and child in explanations?
- How can the nurse facilitate comfort and reduce anxiety when performing the assessment?

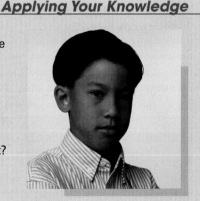

Using the previous steps of clinical reasoning, organizing, and prioritizing, consider all the case study findings woven throughout this chapter. When answering the following questions, begin drawing conclusions and see how the pieces of assessment must work together to create an environment for personalized, appropriate, and accurate care.

- What information does the nurse gain about patients during inspection, palpation, percussion, and auscultation? (Comprehension)
- How does the nurse use safety and infection-control principles during the assessment? (Application)
- What basic examination modes and equipment did the nurse practitioner use during the physical assessment? (Knowledge)
- How might the nurse organize the assessment sequentially to include the different body systems in this focused assessment for the child? (Synthesis)
- What factors might be contributing to Chris's illness? (Analysis)
- How will the nurse practitioner evaluate the outcome of her teaching? (Evaluation)

Key Points

- Hand hygiene is the most important action to prevent health-care acquired (nosocomial) infections.
- Nurses and other health care providers use routine practices and additional precautions with every patient because many infections are unknown.
- Latex allergies are more common in nurses and in patients who are frequently hospitalized.
- Nurses wear gloves during anticipated contact with body secretions and remove them when going from contaminated to cleaner areas.
- Inspection, percussion, palpation, and auscultation are the four basic examination modes of physical examination.
- Inspection relies on visual, auditory, and olfactory senses to assess general status as well as each body system.
- Nurses use light palpation to obtain an overall impression and deep palpation to assess pain, masses, or tumours.
- Percussion sounds vary based on tone, intensity, pitch, quality, duration, and location.
- Nurses commonly auscultate the heart, lungs, and abdomen with a stethoscope.
- During the complete assessment an ophthalmoscope, visual acuity chart, otoscope, tuning forks, percussion hammer, vaginal speculum, skin-fold calipers, tongue blades, familiar objects, cotton balls, culture media, test solutions, cytology materials, equipment wipes, penlight, and height/weight scales are equipment that are used. A goniometer may also be used.

Review Questions

1. Which of the following interventions is the most important to prevent health-care acquired infections?
   A. Proper glove use
   B. Hand hygiene
   C. Appropriate gowning
   D. Alcohol products

2. Routine practices are used
   A. on every patient, because many infections are unknown
   B. with hand gel for infection caused by *C. difficile*
   C. and include gloves and masks with all patients
   D. in recognition that transmission-based precautions are common

3. Latex allergies
   A. always result in anaphylactic reactions and shock
   B. diminish when moisturizers are used after the hands are washed
   C. increase because of equipment such as a stethoscope
   D. are more common in nurses and frequently hospitalized patients

4. Which of the following is an appropriate use of clean disposable gloves? They are
   A. required during anticipated contact with intact skin
   B. removed when going from clean to contaminated areas
   C. worn during anticipated contact with body secretions
   D. unnecesary when assessing the back of an incontinent patient

5. Which of the following is an example of documentation from inspection?
   A. Heart rate and rhythm regular
   B. Lungs clear in all fields
   C. Abdomen mixed tympany and dullness
   D. Skin pink and intact

6. The patient is reporting abdominal pain. In addition to inspection, what technique is used to form a preliminary impression?
   A. Auscultation
   B. Light palpation
   C. Direct percussion
   D. Deep palpation

7. Tympany is a percussion sound commonly heard in the
   A. apices of the lungs
   B. lower and lateral thorax
   C. upper quadrant of the abdomen
   D. thighs and popliteal space

8. The nurse auscultates which organs as part of an admitting assessment?
   A. Heart, lungs, and abdomen
   B. Kidneys, bladder, and ureters
   C. Abdomen, flank, and groin
   D. Neck, jaw, and clavicle

9. What technique facilitates accurate auscultation?
   A. Earpieces of the stethoscope are positioned to point toward the back.
   B. The tubing of the stethoscope is long and dark in colour.
   C. The bell chestpiece of the stethoscope is sealed lightly against the skin.
   D. The diaphragm of the stethoscope is used for low-frequency sounds.

10. When assessing the child, the nurse makes the following adaptation to the usual techniques:
   A. A pediatric stethoscope provides better contact.
   B. The child is seated away from the parent.
   C. The room is full of toys for play.
   D. The child is undressed, including the underwear.

References

Bousquet, J., Flahault, A., et al. (2006). Natural rubber latex allergy among health care workers: A systematic review of the evidence. *Allergy and Clinical Immunology, 118*(2), 447–454.

Brunetti, L., Santoro, E., et al. (2006). Surveillance of nosocomial infections: A preliminary study on hand hygiene compliance of healthcare workers. *Journal of Previews in Medical Hygiene, 47*(2), 64–68.

Centers for Disease Control and Prevention. (2009). *Standard precautions excerpt from the guideline for isolation precautions: Preventing transmission of infectious agents in healthcare settings 2007.* Retrieved from http://www.cdc.gov/ncidod/dhqp/gl_isolation_standard.html

Groeneveld, A. (2010). Management of patients with infectious diseases. In R. A. Day, P. Paul, et al. (Eds.). *Brunner & Suddarth's textbook of Canadian medical-surgical nursing* (2nd ed, pp. 2348–2381). Philadelphia, PA: Wolters Kluwer Health/Lippincott Williams & Wilkins.

Health Canada. (2010). *It's your health.* Retrieved from http://www.hc-sc.gc.ca/hlvs/iyh-vsv/dicasemaladies/hands-mains-eng.php

Health Canada. (1999). Routine practices and additional precautions for preventing the transmission of infection in health care. *Canada Communicable Disease Report,* 25S4.

LaMontagne, A. D., Radi, S., et al. (2006). Primary prevention of latex related sensitisation and occupational asthma: A systematic review. *Occupational and Environmental Medicine, 63*(5), 359–364.

Larson, E., Girard, R., et al. (2006). Skin reactions related to hand hygiene and selection of hand hygiene products. *American Journal of Infection Control, 34*(10), 627–635.

Moore, K. L., & Dalley, A. F. (2006). *Clinically oriented anatomy* (5th ed.). Philadelphia, PA: Lippincott Williams & Wilkins.

Orient, J. M., & Sapira, J. D. (Eds.). (2005). *Sapira's art & science of bedside diagnosis* (3rd ed.) Philadelphia, PA: Lippincott Williams & Wilkins.

Occupational Safety and Health Administration. (2009). *Latex allergy.* Retrieved from http://www.osha.gov/SLTC/latexallergy/index.html

Pittet, B., Allegranzi, H., et al. (2006). Evidence-based model for hand transmission during patient care and the role of improved practices. *The Lancet Infectious Diseases, 6*(10), 641D–652D.

Siegel, J. D., Rhinehart, E., et al., (2006). *Management of multidrug-resistant organisms in healthcare settings.* Washington, DC: CDC.

Skillen, D. L., & Bickley, L. S. (2010). In T. C. Stephen, D. L. Skillen, R. A. Day, & L. S. Bickley (Eds.). *Canadian Bates' guide to health assessment for nurses* (1st ed., pp. 91–111). Philadelphia, PA: Kluwer Wolters Health/Lippincott Williams & Wilkins.

Widmer, A. F., Conzelmann, M., et al. (2007). Introducing alcohol-based hand rub for hand hygiene: The critical need for training. *Infection and Control in Hospital Epidemiology, 28*(1), 50–54.

The Canadian Jensen's Nursing Health Assessment suite offers these additional resources to enhance learning and facilitate understanding of this chapter:

- thePoint online resource, http//thepoint.lww.com/Stephen1E
- *Laboratory Manual for Canadian Jensen's Nursing Health Assessment: A Best Practice Approach*

Documentation and Interprofessional Communication

Learning Objectives

1 Describe the multiple purposes of the patient health record.

2 Discuss the significance of accurate and timely documentation and the relationship between reporting patient assessment data and ensuring patient safety.

3 Compare and contrast various methods of documenting assessment data in the patient's health record.

4 Provide a concise, clear handoff report using a template such as SBAR (situation, background, assessment, and recommendation).

5 Discuss ethical and legal considerations when documenting and reporting assessment information into the patient health record.

*M*r. *Rafael* Chavez, 19 years old, was admitted to the hospital with a fractured humerus following a motor vehicle collision (MVC) in which he was a passenger wearing his seatbelt. His younger cousin, the driver, suffered a fractured tibia and fibula.

Mr. Chavez was born in Mexico; English is his second language, which he understands and speaks well. His temperature is 37.8°C orally, pulse 110 beats/min and regular, respirations 20 breaths/min, and blood pressure (BP) 122/66 mm Hg (lying, right arm). Current medications include patient-controlled analgesia (PCA) with morphine for pain, an antibiotic, ciprofloxacin (Cipro) 500 mg q 12 h, a multivitamin, a stool softener, and medications to be taken as needed for symptoms such as itching and nausea. Initial assessment was in the emergency department (ED); an admitting assessment occurred 4 hours ago upon transfer to acute care. The nurse caring for him is at the beginning of shift.

As you study the content and features, consider Mr. Chavez's case and its relationship to what you are learning. Begin thinking about the following points:

- What are the differences in the assessment data that nurses collect and document on the admitting assessment, flow sheets, SOAP notes, preoperative checklists, and postoperative assessments?
- How does the collection of data fluctuate between a comprehensive and a focused assessment?
- How do the patient situation and acuity influence the assessment, documentation, and communication of data?

Florence Nightingale is considered the founder of nursing documentation. In her 19th century publication *Notes on Nursing* she outlined the importance of recording patient information in a clear, concise, and organized manner (Stephen & Bickley, 2010, p. 113).

Prompt reporting and recording of patient assessment data are essential to ensuring safe and efficient delivery of care. Greater than 60% of all serious, often life-threatening, errors in health care **(sentinel events)** involved failures in communication as the root cause (Canadian Patient Safety Institute, 2008). Communication occurs both verbally and in writing. Documentation involves entering patient information into the written or computerized patient health record. The patient health record contains recorded information from all health care encounters.

All health team members document and retrieve information from the patient health record as they plan and provide care. In the last decade, many health care agencies have transitioned the patient record from paper to a computerized, electronic form. Whether the patient health record is paper or electronic, health care providers are responsible for always maintaining the confidentiality of all patient information.

Nurses use critical thinking and clinical judgment to determine when unexpected assessment data are significant, thus requiring verbal communication to other members of the health care team. Prompt, accurate documentation and reporting help ensure safe delivery and individualization of patient care.

Patient Health Record

Purposes of the Patient Health Record

The patient health record serves multiple purposes. In addition to being a legal document of patient care and nursing practice, the patient health record is used for communication among health team members, care planning, quality assurance, education, and research.

Legal Document

The patient health record serves as a legal document recording the patient's health status and any care he or she receives. The patient health record can be used in civil or criminal courts to provide evidence of wrongdoing. Health care agencies have policies and standards that govern documentation that staff members must follow. Documentation "demonstrates the visible and invisible work that RNs do for each of their clients" (College & Association of Registered Nurses of Alberta, 2007, p. 12).

⚠ *SAFETY ALERT 5-1*

The nurse must record assessment data, and the time of the assessment. In the legal world, a typical saying is "If it's not documented, it's not done." This reinforces the need to document not only unexpected findings but also expected findings. When listening to the lungs, it is important to note "lungs clear, no shortness of breath" to document that the assessments were performed and what the findings were. For significant unexpected

findings, it is also important to document the name of the physician who was notified, the time of notification, and any interventions. This provides evidence that the nurse communicated and acted on the assessment data to ensure patient safety.

Box 5-1 lists high-risk errors in documenting. Notice how many of these potential errors relate to the documentation of assessment data.

Communication and Care Planning

All members of the health care team access the assessment data documented in the patient's record to make care decisions. For example, a primary provider reviews documentation from the patient's pain assessment to determine whether to increase, maintain, or decrease the amount of pain medication prescribed. A social worker reviews the record for evidence of family support or a description of the home environment to plan for discharge. Assessment data provide the basis for the plan of care (POC) that identifies conditions, outcomes, and interventions for the patient. The POC helps caregivers coordinate and individualize care until discharge.

Quality Assurance

An **audit** occurs when an agency or outside group reviews the records of a health care facility to determine whether that facility is providing and documenting certain standards of care. During an *internal audit*, the goal is to evaluate the care provided for continual improvement. For example, an agency may audit the record to evaluate whether staff members are charting pain assessments in a timely manner on all patients. The audit might also include if nurses are administering PRN (as needed) pain medication for documented pain levels >4 (on a 0-to-10 scale). Such an audit helps target interventions or education to improve pain management.

Accrediting agencies such as Accreditation Canada (2011) can establish standards and audit patient health records to evaluate the quality of care provided. Accreditation Canada also requires each hospital to develop an ongoing objective review of patient health records for continuous quality improvement and to demonstrate correction of any deficiencies noted during

BOX 5-1 HIGH-RISK ERRORS IN DOCUMENTATION

- Falsifying patient health records
- Failing to record changes in the patient's condition
- Failing to document the notification of the primary provider when the patient's condition changes
- Performing an inadequate admission assessment
- Failing to document completely
- Failing to follow the agency's standards or policies on documentation
- Charting in advance

Adapted from Craven, R. C., & Hirnle, C. J. (2009). *Fundamentals of nursing: Human health and function* (6th ed.). Philadelphia, PA: Wolters Kluwer Health/Lippincott Williams & Wilkins.

the review. For example, if the standard of care is that postoperative patients have a surgical site check and assessment of vital signs every 15 minutes after surgery, the team conducting the audit will review records to identify if staff members are performing these assessments in a timely manner.

Education

Students in various health care disciplines review patient health records to enhance clinical learning and to better understand complex clinical situations. They can access and review records during care delivery. At times, students come to the clinical area before their assigned shift to read the patient health records and do the necessary research so that they can provide informed and individualized care. Nursing grand rounds or classroom discussions can use specific patient situations to educate nurses and students. For example, an audit of charts from patients who experienced oversedation or respiratory depression from opioid administration may be collected and presented to staff members to help educate nurses about safe pain management. Assessment data are used to identify trends in respiratory rates and to detect early warning signs of clinical deterioration.

Research

Health care professionals use patient health records to obtain data for nursing and medical research. If they obtain such data, they must follow strict policies to protect the privacy and rights of individual patients. They must obtain prior approval by the agency's Ethics and Review Boards before any research study. At times, professionals collect data without approval; however, these studies are limited to internal quality improvement, and data can never be reported to or used by any outside group. The assessments must be performed and documented accurately so that the research outcomes are valid and reliable.

Components of the Patient Health Record

The patient health record is not read like a book, from beginning to end. Instead, each nurse becomes skilled at finding pertinent information quickly. Each agency develops specific forms contained within the patient health record and policies governing documentation practice.

Assessment forms include an admitting assessment, flow sheets, and ongoing assessment forms. The patient health record usually contains the following components:

- Nursing admission assessment
- History and physical examination (H & P) by the primary health care provider
- Primary health care provider's orders
- POC or clinical pathway
- Flow sheets documenting vital signs, intake and output (I & O), and other routine assessments
- Focused assessment sheets (eg, neurological or postoperative reassessment)
- Medication administration record (MAR)
- Laboratory and diagnostic test results

- Progress notes by different members of the health care team
- Consultations
- Discharge or transfer summary

Electronic Patient Health Record

Many clinical agencies have computerized part or all of the patient's health record. Software programs allow nurses to enter assessment data quickly, usually by checking boxes and adding free text when appropriate. The electronic medication administration record (eMAR) interfaces medication orders with pharmacy dispensing and allows direct computer charting of medication administration (Fig. 5-1). Computerized provider order entry (**CPOE**) allows providers to enter all orders directly into the computer, electronically communicating orders to the laboratory, pharmacy, and nursing personnel. Appropriate staff members receive a computerized communication (task) when treatments and medications are due during their assigned shift. They also receive a message when the patient requires a reassessment (eg, with assessment of the effectiveness of the pain medication).

Although implementing a computerized system is expensive and requires much planning and education, such systems significantly increase patient safety (Moody, Slocumb, et al., 2004). They allow several health team members to view the patient health record simultaneously. For those with special clearance, they enable the off-site viewing of the electronic record to note changes in patient condition or to order necessary laboratory tests, diagnostic studies, or medications. Computerization ensures that all entries are legible and time dated. It enables the graphing of trends in vital signs or assessment data. It minimizes compliance issues because programs will not let nurses enter data until they have completed all required fields. This ensures a more complete assessment. Some programs create plans of care from entered assessment data.

Computerization of the patient health record also permits the use of automated clinical surveillance tools to scan in real time the health record of all patients to detect assessment data indicating issues. One such tool, the Risk Assessment Report, provides risk scores on sepsis, pressure ulcers, falls, unexpected laboratory reports, and other criteria of interest (Whittington, White, et al., 2007). This permits early intervention and saves lives. Frequently, patients show clinical signs of deterioration, but health care providers fail to respond for 24 hours before a critical adverse event (O'Neill & Miranda, 2006). A designated nurse can monitor warnings from the surveillance system for large groups of patients and ask the assigned nurse to assess patients to determine if an acute condition exists for those with a high-risk score. See Chapter 13 for a tool for identifying the risk for skin breakdown and Chapter 30 for a tool identifying the risk for falling.

Principles Governing Documentation

Quality documentation of assessment data remains confidential and is accurate, complete, organized, timely, and concise. The computerized patient health record has improved the quality of nursing documentation in some areas and posed challenges in others.

PowerChart Office - (Nsg Workflow) MAR

Task View Patient Chart Clinic Options Help

As Of: 10:43

| Jane Doe | MR # 123456789 |
| Room 4062B | Dr. W. Miller |

Time View	Medications	28MAR2011 0600	28MAR2011 0900	28MAR2011 1200	28MAR2011 1800	28MAR2011 2100	28MAR2011 2400	
☑ Scheduled	**Scheduled**							
☑ Unscheduled	Aspirin 325 mg P.O. daily							
☑ PRN	aspirin		325 mg					
☑ Continuous Infusions	Pain Intensity		0					
☑ Future	Pain Location		N/A					
☑ Discontinued Scheduled	Cefazolin 1 gram I.V. STAT and then 500 mg I.V. q 6 hours	STAT						
☑ Discontinued Unscheduled	cefazolin	1 gram I.V.		500 mg I.V	500 mg I.V		500 mg I.V	
☑ Discontinued PRN	Digoxin 0.125 mg P.O. daily							
☑ Discontinued Continuous Infusior	digoxin		0.125					
	Heart Rate		HR-78 reg					
	Docusate 100 mg P.O. at bedtime							
	docusate					100 mg		
	Furosemide 20 mg P.O. each morning							
	furosemide		20 mg					
	Systolic Blood Pressure		136/82 R arm					
Therapeutic Class View								

Ready

Figure 5-1 An eMAR.

Confidential

Nurses are required legally and ethically to keep all information in the patient health record confidential.

Confidentiality means keeping information private. This principle applies to computerized and written patient health records and any information pertaining to health status or care received (Fig. 5-2). All patient information is confidential and discussed only with other health care professionals directly involved in the patient's care. Nurses should never discuss patients (with or without names) and their situations in public places such as elevators, hallways, or the cafeteria. People who hear conversations can misinterpret information, leading to anxiety or fear. Additional methods of protecting confidentiality include never sharing computer passwords and never leaving a computer with patient information unattended. Forms from the agency should never be taken, even if the patient identification information is removed. Information from the patient's chart should be copied into a notebook without the patient's name.

Accurate and Complete

Assessment information that nurses enter into the patient's record must accurately reflect what they observed, heard, auscultated, palpated, percussed, or smelled. Nurses document subjective data using the patient's exact words whenever possible. Descriptions are as precise as possible. For example, nurses would document the size of a wound as "6 cm by 9 cm with a 1 cm depth" rather than as "large." Accuracy permits comparison of current findings with future data to detect changes in patient status. Thus, nurses avoid using the

Figure 5-2 Nurses must take all measures to keep patient information confidential and discuss such information only with other health care professionals directly involved in the patient's care.

Remember Mr. Chavez, introduced at the beginning of this chapter. The nurse uses professional communication techniques to gather subjective data from Mr. Chavez at the beginning of the shift. The following conversation gives an example of an interview. As you read the conversation, consider the purpose of this data collection.

Nurse: Hi, Mr. Chavez. How are you feeling? (Waits 10 s.) (Touches patient.) Mr. Chavez, I'm Shannon, your nurse.

Mr. Chavez: Oh, sorry. I was sleepy. Let me sleep.

Nurse: OK, but first I need to look at your arm.

Mr. Chavez: OK (turns over). My arm hurts.

Nurse: Is it OK if I look at it? (Patient nods.) (Nurse notes cool, pale right arm. Pulse is decreased. Capillary refill is slow.)

Nurse: Mr. Chavez, could you please wiggle your fingers? (Patient wiggles fingers.) Tell me what your pain is like.

Mr. Chavez: It's throbbing and kind of numb. Can I have something for the pain?

Nurse: Sure, go ahead and push the button (nods toward PCA apparatus). I'm concerned about your arm and will talk with the doctor about it. I'll be back in a minute. OK?

Critical Thinking Challenge

- Why did the nurse wake up Mr. Chavez instead of letting him sleep?
- What is the purpose of data collection? How will the nurse organize findings in this case?
- What information does the nurse need to document? Where?

words "normal" or "good"; instead, they use correct medical terminologies (eg, "heart rate and rhythm regular," not "normal."). See Table 5-1.

To avoid potential errors, the use of abbreviations is discouraged. It is important to be familiar with abbreviations and to use only those legally accepted. As nurses are learning health assessment techniques, they also should focus on learning the language, labelling the findings, and identifying abbreviations.

Computerization of the patient record has greatly increased the legibility of its information. Nevertheless, handwritten entries still occur; when they happen, they must be clear and legible. This is especially true when recording numbers that can easily be confused. Black ink is usually required for written documentation to provide clarity when faxing documentation from the patient health record.

Nurses need to correct errors in documentation so that the record is accurate. In the written record, they make corrections by drawing a line through the error and placing initials above the correction (Fig. 5-3). The computerized record permits electronic correction of errors, retaining both the original entry and the correction. Erasing, blacking out information, or using whiteout is not permitted.

Organized

Organized entry of assessment data demonstrates a logical and systematic grouping of information. Flow sheets and documentation systems often cue nurses to a specific organization structure. This encourages nurses to include all areas of assessment and provides an organized report so that other health team members can use the information to make sound clinical decisions. Nurses also should document entries of assessment chronologically so that a picture of the time certain assessments were made is clear. This is especially important if the patient health record is used as evidence during litigation.

Timely

Nurses must enter assessment data into the record in a timely manner. Most agencies have policies regarding the frequencies

Table 5-1	Accurate Documentation Using Medical Terminology
Ambiguous Documentation	**Accurate Documentation**
Expected vitals normal	T 37°C, P 80, regular, R 12 breaths/min, blood pressure (BP) 118/62 mm Hg (right arm, sitting)
Neuro status OK	Alert and oriented X 4, speech clear
Lung sounds good	Lung sounds clear
Heart sounds good	Heart rate and rhythm regular
Eating well	Ate 60% of regular diet
Voiding well	Voided 700 mL of clear yellow urine
No difficulty moving	Voluntary movement of all extremities with full range of motion and 5/5 strength
Skin colour good	Skin pink
Family was here	Family visiting with appropriate interactions

Figure 5-4 The nurse is using a portable computer to carry out point-of-care documentation.

of assessments. For example, on a medical–surgical unit, a complete assessment may occur every 8 hours; in the intensive care unit, it may be every hour; and in an extended care facility it might be weekly. Computerized charting automatically reflects the time the entry is made, but nurses can change the documented time to reflect the time of the assessment. Paper charting should also reflect the specific time (eg, 0204) rather than a shift designation (eg, 0000–0700).

Batch charting (waiting until the end of shift or until all patients have been assessed to document) contributes to many potential errors. Waiting to record may contribute to forgetting important information or charting assessment data on the wrong patient. **Point-of-care** documentation occurs when nurses document assessment information as they gather it, often using a portable computer (Fig. 5-4). This can be done during a home visit, a clinic visit, or in the patient's room during a hospital stay.

Prompt documentation allows health team members to use up-to-date assessment information to make clinical decisions. For example, a change in weight or vital signs might

prompt a primary provider to adjust a medication dosage. Computerized documentation systems allow other health team members to review the patient health record off-site so that they base decisions on the current record.

Clinical Significance 5-1

Clear documentation that reflects time sequencing is especially important for patients with unstable conditions. If the patient's condition deteriorates, or errors are made, documentation can be used to reconstruct the sequence of events, the time of interventions, and the time that providers were notified. In a code or emergency, the team should designate a single member to document so that entries are accurate and timely.

Concise

Charting is complete, yet concise. Unnecessary elaboration confuses important issues. Nurses record the findings, but not how they collected them. For example, the nurse would document "BP (Right arm, sitting) 124/78" instead of "BP was auscultated in the right arm at 124/78." Time is a precious health care resource, and long, rambling entries take more time to document and to read. In narrative notes, health care providers use sentence fragments (eg, "alert and oriented") and approved abbreviations instead of complete sentences.

Generally, health professionals chart information in one place and avoid "double charting." An exception is in the care plan or progress note, in which nurses synthesize the most important information to show critical thinking about a health issue.

Clinical Significance 5-2

Because assessment requires much critical thinking and clinical judgment and is a professional responsibility, nurses need to ensure it is documented accurately.

3/1/10	c/o SOB X 15 min. while ambulating.
3:15 pm	~~Denies chest pain. BP 126/84, P. 64, R. 16~~ *error–charted on wrong client S.N.*
	BP 134/90, P. 86 R. 24. Assisted to bed
	with hob elevated. Notified Dr. Smith.
	———————— Sally North RN

Figure 5-3 A sample of a corrected entry in a written patient health record.

The nurse has just finished a focused assessment of Mr. Chavez's fractured humerus. Review the following important findings that the relevant steps of objective data collection for Mr. Chavez revealed. Begin to think about how the data cluster together and what additional data the nurse might want to collect as he or she thinks critically and anticipates nursing interventions for the patient.

Inspection: Appears somewhat drowsy with facial grimace from pain. Guarding right humerus. Wiggles fingers, states some numbness and tingling. States 8/10 pain throbbing from above elbow to fingers. Increasing since injury; especially worse in the last 30 minutes. Movement increases pain. Given pain medication 2 hours ago for pain 4/10.

Palpation: Right radial artery 1+; limb pale and cool. Capillary refill 6 seconds. Sensation intact. Left arm pink, warm with 3+ pulse, no pain and intact sensation.

Critical Thinking and Clinical Judgment

Agency policy governs the precise documentation of assessment data in the patient's health record, but nurses continually use critical thinking and clinical judgment to determine the focus, depth, and frequency of assessment documentation. To provide safe individualized care in hospitals, nurses perform a complete nursing assessment for each assigned patient, evaluate the stability of the patient's condition, and determine what monitoring the patient requires during the shift. Nurses obtain assessments as soon as possible after handoff of the patient has occurred, such as after transfer from the ED to the patient care unit, so that a baseline can be determined. Nurses are responsible for interpreting assessment data to evaluate the patient's condition.

Based on knowledge and experience, nurses individualize assessments. For example, a middle-aged patient admitted for foot surgery may not require a comprehensive neurological assessment if he is alert and can answer questions appropriately. But an intoxicated patient with a head laceration who is admitted following an assault would definitely require a complete neurological assessment, including neurovital signs, to promptly detect increased intracranial pressure or alcohol withdrawal (see Chapter 24). Although a primary provider's order determines the minimum frequency of assessments, if the patient's condition appears unstable or deteriorating, nurses independently increase the frequency and documentation of assessments. They also use clinical judgment regarding when to notify the primary provider regarding unexpected findings. They need to document such reporting, including the time of notification and the primary provider's response.

Nursing Admission Assessment

Nurses conduct the *nursing admission assessment*, sometimes referred to as the *nursing history and physical*, to obtain patient history and baseline data so that they can individualize care. Agency policies direct how quickly these need to be completed and recorded. The agency usually provides separate forms to cue the assessment and standardize the documentation (Fig. 5-5).

The admission assessment provides all future care providers with comprehensive information about the patient's physical, psychological, functional, social, and spiritual abilities and forms the basis for an individualized POC. Care providers can refer to this initial assessment to obtain important baseline information and to detect changes in status.

Flow Sheets

Nurses usually document routine, scheduled assessments on flow sheets. Flow sheets are efficient and standardize the collected information, permitting easy comparison among assessment data to detect trends or a sudden change in status. Common flow sheets in the patient's record include vital signs, intake and output, routine assessments, and diabetic record. More complex flow sheets are used in critical care, where frequent, extensive physiological assessments are necessary to quickly detect and treat life-threatening situations.

Plan of Care/Clinical Pathway

An assessment of the patient allows for the development of a **POC** that individualizes his or her goals, outcomes, and interventions. The POC is part of the permanent patient health record, and nurses update it as the patient's condition changes. A **clinical pathway** is a multidisciplinary tool that identifies a standard plan for a specific patient population (eg, those undergoing total hip replacement). It includes patient conditions, expected outcomes, and interventions within an established timeframe. The POC or clinical pathway often provides the structure for shift report handoff.

Progress Note

Multiple health team members (physician, physical therapist, respiratory therapist, social workers, and nurses) document in

University Hospital

NURSING ADMISSION HISTORY

I. GENERAL INFORMATION

ARRIVAL: Date: _20MAR2011_   Time: _1400_

Transportation Method: ☐ Ambulatory ☐ Stretcher ☑ W/C

Admitted Via: ☑ ED ☐ Direct Admission ☐ PACU

☐ Other: _____

Accompanied By: ☐ Self ☐ Spouse ☑ Daughter ☐ Son

☐ Mother ☐ Father ☐ Friend ☐ Other: _____

Correct Name On Identiband?   ☑ YES ☐ NO

PATIENT/SIGNIFICANT OTHER ORIENTED TO:

Call Light at Bedside/in BR: ☑ YES ☐ NO ☐ N/A
Operation of Bed/Siderails: ☑ YES ☐ NO ☐ N/A
Phone/TV: ☑ YES ☐ NO ☐ N/A

PATIENT ADVISED HOSPITAL NOT RESPONSIBLE FOR VALUABLES: ☑ YES ☐ NO

Does Patient Have Any Valuables?   ☑ YES ☐ NO

If Yes, Disposition of Valuables?   ☐ Sent Home
☐ Security – Envelope # _____
☑ Patient Refused Security – Valuables kept with Patient

LIST & DESCRIBE PATIENT'S VALUABLES

eyeglasses @ bedside

yellow metal watch on patient

yellow metal wedding ring on patient

sent purse home with daughter

MEDICATION BROUGHT TO HOSPITAL: ☑ YES ☐ NO

If Yes, : ☐ Home ☐ Pharmacy

_____ Date: _____ Time: _____

INFORMATION GIVEN BY PATIENT: ☑ YES ☐ NO

If NO: Name: _____
Phone: _____
Relationship: _____
☐ Unable to obtain history – REASON

REASON FOR ADMISSION ACCORDING TO PATIENT:

I fell at home this a.m. Couldn't move left

leg for awhile; headaches.

ALLERGIES:

*****ALLERGY DOCUMENTATION MUST BE COMPLETED AT TIME OF ADMISSION ON THE ALLERGY FORM*****

CURRENT MEDICATIONS   ☐ NONE
(INCLUDE RX, INHALERS, OVER-THE-COUNTER)

NAME	DOSE	FREQUENCY	LAST DOSE	REASON
hydralazine	dose ?	Q day	yesterday a.m.	
			for high blood pressure	
aspirin	2 tabs	prn	< noon today for headache	
metamucil	15 ml	prn	this a.m. for constipation	

HOSPITALIZATIONS/SURGICAL HISTORY   ☐ NONE
DIAGNOSIS/REASON

gallbladder surgery 1985

hospitalized for increased BP 2002

FAMILY HISTORY: ☐ NONE

☐ Diabetes ☐ Pulmonary ☑ Heart Disease ☑ Cancer
☐ Anesthesia Complication ☐ Other: _____

II. PAST MEDICAL HISTORY

SKIN: ☑ NEGATIVE HISTORY

☐ Scars ☐ Eczema ☐ Psoriasis ☐ Cancer
☐ Other: _____

NEUROLOGICAL: ☐ NEGATIVE HISTORY

☐ TIA ? ☐ Anxiety ☐ Dementia ☐ Syncope
☑ H/A ☐ Tremors ☐ Parkinson's ☐ Depression

Figure 5-5 A sample admission record.

University Hospital

NURSING ADMISSION HISTORY

Date of LMP: __N/A__

Patient Name: SMITH, Dorothy Emily
Birthdate: 02JAN1937
Age: 74
Personal Health Care Number:
012345-678

FUNCTIONAL STATUS PRIOR TO ADMISSION

I – Independent   A – Assistance Required   D – Dependent

FEED SELF	☑ I	☐ A*	☐ D*
BATHE SELF	☑ I	☐ A*	☐ D*
DRESS SELF	☑ I	☐ A*	☐ D*
HOUSE CHORES	☑ I	☐ A*	☐ D*
AMBULATE	☑ I	☐ A*	☐ D*
CLIMB STAIRS	☑ I	☐ A*	☐ D*
CHAIR BOUND	☐ I	☐ A*	☐ D*
BED BOUND	☐ I	☐ A*	☐ D*

If * or ** checked, were changes made within past 6 months?
    ☐ YES*   ☐ NO
If YES*, Notify Coordinated Care

III. PSYCHO-SOCIAL ASSESSMENT

Occupation: __homemaker__   ☑ RETIRED

Marital Status: ☐ Married   ☐ Single   ☐ Separated
☐ Divorced   ☑ Widowed   ☐ Common Law   *husband died this year

Residential Information: ☐ Home   ☐ ECF   ☑ Other *just moved in with daughter
Usual Living Arrangement: ☐ Alone   ☐ Child   ☐ Spouse
☑ Other Family   ☐ Parent   ☐ Friend   ☐ S.O.   ☐ ECF
Contact Person #1: __Barbara Tembra__
    Relationship: __daughter__   H#: __215-634-5221__   W#: _____

PRIMARY LANGUAGE:

☑ English   ☐ French   ☐ Other _____

Does Patient understand English?   ☑ YES   ☐ NO*
    *Contact Person for Translation: _____
    Relationship: _____   H#: _____   W#: _____

ASSISTIVE DEVICES/DURABLE MEDICAL EQUIPMENT: ☑ NONE

☐ Cane ☐ w/pt   ☐ Crutches ☐ w/pt   ☐ Walker ☐ w/pt   ☐ Wheelchair ☐ w/pt
☐ Tub Seat   ☐ Commode   ☐ Grab Bars   ☐ Hospital Bed
☐ Stair Glide   ☐ Other: _____

SPIRITUAL/CULTURAL ASSESSMENT:

Does patient express any spiritual, cultural, or emotional concerns
which may impact on this hospitalization?   ☐ YES   ☑ NO
    Explain: _____
Does patient express a desire to meet with a Spiritual Care member?
her own minister
Priest? ☐ YES*   ☑ NO   If YES*, notify Spiritual Care.
Coping Mechanisms (How does patient deal with stress?)   ☐ NONE

    Type: __talk with friends, pray, misses husband__
Support Groups   ☑ NONE
    Type: _____

ETOH: ☐ YES ☑ NO
Substance Abuse: ☐ YES* ☐ NO   *Type _____
    Has patient been in treatment? ☐ YES   ☐ NO
Sleep: __8__ hrs/night   Up at night: __1-2__ times/night
Tobacco: ☐ YES ☑ NO **Amount/day:** _____ **How Long:** _____
Date Stopped: _____

IV. EDUCATIONAL ASSESSMENT

Patient Assessed: ☑ YES ☐ NO   Family Assessed: ☐ YES   ☐ NO
Patient Responsible for Learning Anticipated Needs: ☑ YES ☐ NO*
    *OTHER: _____   #: _____
Patient's Preferred Method of Learning: ☑ No Preference Stated
    ☐ Hearing   ☐ Seeing   ☐ Reading   ☐ Hands-on
What does patient want to learn about?   ☐ Unidentified At This Time
☑ Disease Process   ☐ Diet & Nutrition   ☐ Community Resources
☐ Medication   ☐ Assistive Equipment   ☑ Follow-up Care
☐ Pain Management   ☐ Rehab Techniques   ☐ Other: _____

ANTICIPATED EDUCATIONAL NEEDS IDENTIFIED BY STAFF:

☑ Disease Process   ☐ Diet & Nutrition   ☑ Community Resources
☑ Medication   ☐ Assistive Equipment   ☑ Follow-up Care
☐ Pain Management   ☐ Rehab Techniques   ☐ Other: _____

ASSESSMENT OF PATIENT'S BARRIERS TO LEARNING:

Motivation:	☑ Good	☐ Fair	☐ Poor
Learning Ability:	☑ Good	☐ Fair	☐ Poor
Emotional/Mental Factors:		☐ NONE	

☑ Anxious   ☐ Confused   ☐ Depressed
☐ Agitated   ☐ Combative   ☐ Does Not Follow Command
Physical Factors: ☐ NONE
☐ Pain   ☑ Age Related   ☐ Language Barrier
☐ Fatigue   ☐ Medical Equipment   ☐ Limitation of Illness

V. PERSONAL DIRECTIVE

Patient has a personal directive?   ☐ YES ☑ NO
Patient would like help to prepare a   ☑ YES ☐ NO
personal directive?

VI. DISCHARGE PLANNING

Return: ☐ Home ☑ Family ☐ Rehab ☐ ECF ☐ Unknown
Is Patient currently receiving Home Care Services? ☐ YES* ☑ NO
    *Agency: _____
Were any needs identified requiring notification of Home Care?
        ☐ YES ☑ NO

VII. PHYSICIAN NOTIFICATION

ATTENDING: __Dr. Skomar__

20MAR2011	1430	C Tayn RN
DATE	TIME	NOTIFIED BY

NURSING ASSESSMENT COMPLETED BY:

20MAR2011	1435	C Tayn RN
DATE	TIME	RN SIGNATURE

Figure 5-5 *(Continued)*

University Hospital

Patient Name: SMITH, Dorothy Emily
Birthdate: 02JAN1937
Age: 74
Personal Health Care Number:
012345-678

NURSING ADMISSION HISTORY

- ☐ Falls
- ☐ Seizures
- ☐ Alzheimer's
- ☐ Vertigo
- ☐ CVA
- ☐ Tumour
- ☐ Migraines
- ☐ Mood Changes
- ☐ R Hemiplegia
- ☐ Benign
- ☐ Vertigo
- ☐ L Hemiplegia
- ☐ Malignant
- ☐ Other: "slightly dizzy"

Memory Impairment: ☑ NONE
- ☐ Acute → ☐ Short Term ☐ Long Term
- ☐ Chronic → ☐ Short Term ☐ Long Term

MUSCULOSKELETAL: ☐ NEGATIVE HISTORY

- ☐ Fractures: _____
- ☐ Arthritis: _____
- ☐ Amputation: _____
- ☐ Prosthesis: **TYPE:** _____ ☐ R ☐ L ☐ WITH PATIENT
- ☑ Other: movement & strength left leg

If **with patient, remind patient hospital not responsible for article.
"pins & needles in left leg

MUSCULOSKELETAL

VISION: ☐ NEGATIVE HISTORY

- ☑ Glasses ☑ WITH PT ☐ Contacts ☐ WITH PT ☐ Prosthesis ☐ WITH PT
- ☐ Nearsighted ☐ R ☐ L ☐ R ☐ L
- ☐ Farsighted ☑ Blurred Vision ☐ Blind
- ☐ Glaucoma ☐ R ☐ L ☐ R ☐ L
- ☐ R ☐ L ☐ Double Vision ☐ Implants
- ☐ Cataract ☐ R ☐ L ☐ R ☐ L
- ☐ R ☐ L

HEARING: ☐ NEGATIVE HISTORY

- ☑ HOH ☐ Deaf ☐ Earache
- ☐ R ☑ L ☐ R ☐ L ☐ R ☐ L
- ☐ Tinnitis ☐ Hearing Aid ☐ WITH PT ☐ Cataract
- ☐ R ☐ L ☐ R ☐ L ☐ R ☐ L

If with patient, remind patient hospital not responsible for article.

THYROID: ☑ NEGATIVE HISTORY

- ☐ Hypothyroid ☐ Hyperthyroid ☐ Surgery
- ☐ Radiation → Have large doses of radioactive material been used within last week? ☐ YES* ☐ NO

Speech Impairment: ☐ NONE ☐ New* ☐ Old
If NEW, notify Speech Therapy.

CARDIOVASCULAR: ☐ NEGATIVE HISTORY

- ☐ MI ☐ PVD ☐ Anemia ☐ Rheumatic H D
- ☑ HTN ☐ CHF ☐ Phlebitis ☐ Syncope Fainting
- ☐ CP/Angina ☐ Palpitations ☐ Bleeding Problems
- ☐ Hypotension ☐ Murmur ☐ Arrhythmia
- ☐ Pacemaker ☐ Internal
- Date: _____ Defibrillator ☑ Other: _____
- Plutonium Operated Date: _____
- ☐ YES* ☐ NO

PULMONARY: ☑ NEGATIVE HISTORY

- ☐ TB ☐ Hemoptysis ☐ Cancer
- ☐ Asthma ☐ Emphysema
- ☐ Bronchitis ☐ Asbestos Exposure ☐ Other
- ☐ Pneumonia
- ☐ Trach ☐ Exposure to
- ☐ Old ☐ New Fumes/Smoke
- ☐ Closed

Dyspnea: ☑ NONE ☐ Activity ☐ Walking Stairs ☐ #pillows/sleep ____
Oxygen: ☑ NONE ☐ Activity ☐ Night ☐ Day ☐ PRN FlowRate ____

GASTROINTESTINAL: ☐ NEGATIVE HISTORY

- ☐ Colitis ☐ Hepatitis ☐ Diabetes
- ☐ Ulcers ☐ Heart Burn ☐ Diet
- ☐ Reflux ☐ Hiatal Hernia ☐ Insulin
- ☐ Jaundice ☑ Hemorrhoids ☐ PO Meds
- ☐ Nausea ☐ Hematemesis ☐ Vomiting within
- ☐ Cirrhosis ☐ Diverticulosis last 24–48 hrs
- ☐ Cancer _____ _____ /day
- ☐ Other: _____

Bowel Pattern:
Last BM: 19MAR2011 ☐ Daily ☑ Other: Q2-3 day
Bowel Concern: ☐ Daily ☑ Constipation ☐ Incontinence
☐ Diarrhea within last 24–48 hours _____ /day

NUTRITION:

- ☑ Regular Diet ☐ High Fibre ☐ _____ Calorine CDA
- ☐ Low Fat ☐ Bland ☐ Fluid Restriction
- ☐ Low Chol ☐ Gluten Free _____ cc
- ☐ Low Sodium ☐ Kosher
- ☐ Other

Food Intolerances: ☑ NONE ☐ Type: _____
Supplements: ☑ NONE ☐ Type: _____
Weight Change: ☑ NONE ☐ Gain ☐ Loss
Amount: _____ Time Period: _____ ☐ Intentional ☐ Unintentional*
Intake <50% in 3 Days: ☐ YES* ☑ NO
Chewing Difficulties: ☐ YES* ☑ NO
If any* above, notify Nutrition Services.

DENTURES: ☑ YES* ☐ NO *BROUGHT TO HOSPITAL:** ☑ YES* ☐ NO
- ☐ **Partial** ☐ Upper ☐ With Pt FIT: ☐ Loose ☐ Good ☐ Not Worn
-   ☐ Lower ☐ With Pt FIT: ☐ Loose ☐ Good ☐ Not Worn
- ☐ **Full** ☑ Upper ☐ With Pt FIT: ☐ Loose ☑ Good ☐ Not Worn
-   ☑ Lower ☐ With Pt FIT: ☐ Loose ☑ Good ☐ Not Worn

If with Patient, remind patient hospital not responsible for article

---

Swallowing Difficulties: ☑ NONE ☐ Recent* ☐ Long Term
☐ Solids ☐ Liquids
Coughing During Or After Meals: ☑ YES* ☐ NO
If any* above, notify Home Care.

GENITOURINARY: ☑ NEGATIVE HISTORY

- ☐ Renal Disease ☐ Kidney Stones ☐ Prostate Problems
- ☐ Cancer _____ ☐ Other: _____

PROBLEMS URINATING: ☑ NONE

- ☐ Anuria ☐ Nocturia ☐ Dialysis
- ☐ Hesitancy _____/night ☐ Peritoneal
- ☐ Dysuria ☐ Self ☐ Hemo
- ☐ Urgency Catheterization Site _____
- ☐ Incontinence Frequency _____ Schedule _____
- ☐ Frequency ☐ Hematuria ☐ Other: _____

GENITALIA PROBLEMS: ☑ NONE

- ☐ Discharge ☐ Burning ☐ Abnormal Bleeding ☐ STI
- ☐ Other: _____

Figure 5-5 (*Continued*)

University Hospital

Patient Name: SMITH, Dorothy Emily
Birthdate: 02JAN1937
Age: 74
Personal Health Care Number:
012345-678

NURSING ADMISSION PHYSICAL

V S
BP _184/120_ P _88_ R I R _18_ T _36.7_ O R A T
HT (_158 cm_) Estimated WT _63 kg_ Actual (Estimated)

P A I N
Current Pain Intensity (0-10): _3_
Scale Used: (Numeric Scale) Faces Scale FLACC Scale
Has Patient had pain in the last week? (Yes) No H/A
Unable to obtain information
Complete Initial Pain Assessment Form if Pain Intensity is >5 or if patient has had pain in the last week.

S K I N
Turgor: (Normal) Tenting
Colour: Pink (Pale) Flushed Mottled
　　　　Jaundiced Dusky Cyanotic
Temperature: (Cool) Warm Clammy Hot Wet
Integrity: (Intact)
　Abrasion _____ Burn _____
　Ecchymosis _____ Scar _____
　Laceration _____ Wound _____
　Rash → Macule _____ Papule _____
Are Multiple Alterations in Skin Integrity or Pressure Ulcers
Present? ☐ YES* ☑ NO
If YES*, Complete Skin Integrity Assessment

N E U R O M U S C U L A R
LOC: (Alert) Lethargic Unresponsive
Mental Status: Pleasant (Cooperative) (Anxious) Agitated
(Follows Command) Depressed Confused Combative
Oriented: (Person) (Place) (Time)
Pupils: Right (/mm) Left (/mm)
　Reaction: (Brisk) (Brisk)
　　　　　　Sluggish Sluggish
　　　　　　Non-reactive Non-reactive
　Appearance: (Normal) (Normal)
　　　　　　Dilated Dilated
　　　　　　Constricted Constricted
　　　　　　Fixed Fixed
Speech: (Clear) Slurred Garbled Stuttering
　　　　Aphasic Receptive Expressive
Gait: Steady (Unsteady) Shuffling Limping
Extremities: (Well Developed) Hypertrophied
　　　　　　Atrophied Contracted
Tone: (Normal) Rigid Flaccid Spastic
Strength: Strong (Weak) Left leg

E E N T
Eyes: Normal R: (Normal) Red Jaundiced Discharge
　　　　　L: (Normal) Red Jaundiced Discharge
Ears: Normal R: (Normal) Discharge Other: _____
　　　　　L: (Normal) Discharge Other: _____
Nose: Normal R: Nare: (Normal) Discharge/Drainage
　　　　　L: Nare: (Normal) Discharge/Drainage
Oral Cavity: (Normal) Bleeding Lesions Other: ___
Teeth: Normal (Missing) Dentures

C A R D I A C
Edema: None
　Arm: RU: +1 +2 +3 +4　LU: +1 +2 +3 +4
　　　　RL: +1 +2 +3 +4　LL: +1 +2 +3 +4
　Leg: RU: +1 +2 +3 +4　LU: +1 +2 +3 +4
　　　　RL: (+1) +2 +3 +4　LL: (+1) +2 +3 +4
　Sacral Anasarca Other: _____
Apical Rate: _90_ Regular Irregular
Radial Pulse: R: (Strong) Weak Absent Doppler
　　　　　　　L: Strong Weak Absent Doppler
Pedal Pulse: R: (Strong) Weak Absent Doppler
　　　　　　　L: (Strong) Weak Absent Doppler
Vascular Dialysis Access: None R L
Type: _____ Bruit: Present Absent N/A

P U L M O N A R Y
Cough: (None) Non-Productive Productive
　　　　Clear White Green Yellow Tan
　　　　Hemoptysis Thick Thin
Breathing Pattern: (Normal) Dyspnea Kussmaul
　　　　Laboured Periodic Apnea Cheyne-Stokes Agonal
Breath Sound: (Clear) **Right Lung** **Left Lung**
　Absent _____ _____
　Diminished _____ _____
　Rhonchi _____ _____
　Rales/Crackles _____ _____
　Insp. Wheeze _____ _____
　Exp. Wheeze _____ _____

G A S T R O
Bowel Sounds:
RUQ:	(Normal)	Increased	Decreased	Absent
LUQ:	Normal	Increased	Decreased	Absent
RLQ:	Normal	Increased	Decreased	Absent
LLQ:	Normal	Increased	Decreased	Absent

Abdomen: (Soft) Firm Tender Non-tender
Abdominal Tubes/Ostomies: (None) Peg Gastro
　Biliary Jejunostomy Colostomy Illeostomy
APPLIANCE: _____

G U
Urinary Device: ☑ NONE ☐ Catheter-TYPE _____
　　　　　　　　LAST CHANGED _____
Urostomy - APPLIANCE _____
Nephrostomy Tube: ☑ NONE Right Left
Flank Tenderness: ☑ NONE Right Left
Urine Appearance: ☑ Not Visualized
　Clear Cloudy Pale Straw
　Sediment Hematuria Concentrated
Genitalia Appearance: ☑ Not Visualized Normal
　Other: _____

Any of the physical assessment findings reflect suspected
elder, domestic or child abuse?
☐ YES* ☑ NO
If YES*, notify Social Worker by consult.
RN Signature: _Tayn, RN_

Date: _20MAR2011_ Time: _1435_

Figure 5-5 (*Continued*)

a **progress note** the patient's progress toward recovery. There has been a movement away from each team member documenting assessments in a discipline-specific section of the patient's health record. The current trend is for personnel from different disciplines to consolidate all entries in one place. This permits all team members to quickly locate and read how the patient is progressing and meeting (or not meeting) goals.

Many nurses use progress notes to summarize how the patient is doing, but formats for this type of documentation can vary. Narrative, SOAP, PIE, and Focus notes are common methods of recording assessments, interventions, and patient responses. See Table 5-2 comparing these formats of documentation.

Regardless of the format used, the progress note is an evaluative statement summarizing significant conditions or improvements. Flow sheets record all collected assessment data, whereas progress notes allow nurses to use critical thinking to document and communicate priority issues to other health team members.

Narrative Notes

Using narrative notes, nurses record, in an unstructured paragraph, relevant assessments and nursing activities during a shift or visit. Usually, the organizing structure is time rather than an identified issue. Historically, narrative notes

Table 5-2	Comparing Documentation Formats			
	Format	**Example**	**Advantages**	**Disadvantages**
Narrative	Information written in phases, usually time sequenced	18APR2011, 1500: 37.2C, 98 beats/min, regular, 22 breaths/min, 130/82 mmHg. Pt reports pain 8/10; states he is using his patient-controlled analgesia (PCA), but it doesn't help. Notified Dr. Cisco of pain level at 1430. Pain is throbbing from fingers to elbow; has worsened over last 30 min. Pain increases with movement. Fingers of left hand pink, warm, able to move with strong pulse and no c/o of pain with movement. Right hand cool and pale with capillary refill 6 s.	Easy to learn Easy to adjust length Can explain in detail	Time consuming Difficult to retrieve information May include irrelevant information Possibly unfocused and disorganized
SOAP(IE)	S—subjective data O—objective data A—analysis P—plan I—intervention E—evaluation	18APR2011 1500 S—States pain 8/10 from elbow to fingertips. Intensity increases with movement, especially over last 30 min. PCA does not seem to help. O—37.2C, 98 beats/min, regular, 22 breaths/min, 130/82 mmHg. Right radial artery 1+, limb pale and cool. Capillary refill 6 s. Sensation intact. Left arm pink, warm with 3+ pulse; no pain, intact sensation. A—Reduced tissue perfusion to right hand related to injury and inadequate pain control. P—Contact Dr. Cisco to evaluate patient. Saw patient at 1430 and indicated no change from baseline; left orders for increased morphine dose. I—PCA morphine increase at 1435, right hand elevated. E—Evaluate analgesic effectiveness in 30 min and increase circulation, sensation, and movement (CSM) checks to hourly.	All charting focuses on identified or new issues Interprofessional, so all team members chart on same progress note using same format Easy to track progress for identified conditions Similar to steps in the nursing process	Specific focus, which makes charting general information difficult without identifying an issue Lengthy and time consuming Repeats assessment data on flow sheets

| Table 5-2 | **Comparing Documentation Formats** (*continued*) |

	Format	Example	Advantages	Disadvantages
PIE	P—problem I—intervention E—evaluation	P—Inadequate tissue perfusion and inadequate pain control. I—Dr. Cisco contacted 1430 to report pain 8/10 and cool, pale right hand with capillary refill of 6 seconds. Saw patient and left orders for increased PCA morphine. Right hand elevated. E—Dr. Cisco reports circulation same as admission baseline. Continue hourly CSM checks; evaluate analgesic effectiveness after 30 minutes.	Incorporates POC Includes outcomes, which increases quality assurance Less redundancy Easily adapted to computerized charting	May need to read progress note to determine POC if not on separate document Not interprofessional
Focus	D—data A—action R—response	D—37.2C, 98 beats/min, regular, 22 breaths/min, 130/82 mm Hg. Right radial artery 1+, limb pale and cool. Capillary refill 6 s. Sensation intact. Left arm pink, warm with 3+ pulse, no pain, intact sensation. States pain 8/10 from elbow to fingertips. Intensity increases with movement; has increased especially over last 30 min; PCA does not seem to help. A—Dr. Cisco contacted at 1430 to report pain 8/10 and cool, pale right hand with capillary refill of 6 s. Saw patient and left orders for increased PCA morphine. Right hand elevated. R—Dr. Cisco reports circulation is same as admission baseline. Continue hourly CSM checks and evaluate analgesic effectiveness after 30 min.	Broad view, permitting charting on any significant area, not just conditions Works well in ambulatory and long-term care	Not interprofessional May be difficult to identify chronological order May not relate to POC
Charting by exception	Standards met—sign or check off Standards unmet—write narrative or SOAP note	Unexpected findings require a note rather than signing off. See above for different note formats.	Efficient No duplicate charting, because most assessments are charted on flow sheets Clearly outlines unexpected findings	Expensive to develop and educate staff regarding standards Not prevention focused Not useful for ambulatory or long-term care May pose legal challenges, because details are often missing

Adapted from Craven, R. C., & Hirnle, C. J. (2009). *Fundamentals of nursing: Human health and function* (6th ed., p. 212). Philadelphia, PA: Wolters Kluwer Health/Lippincott Williams & Wilkins.

Analyzing Findings

Remember Mr. Chavez, who was admitted to the hospital with a fractured right humerus. The nurse has gathered a more complete assessment, clustered findings, and contacted the physician about concerns over inadequate tissue perfusion to the patient's arm. The following nursing note illustrates how the nurse collects and analyzes subjective and objective data and begins to develop nursing interventions.

Subjective: States pain 8/10 from above elbow to fingertips. Characterized pain as numb and achy. Increased since admission, especially in the past 30 minutes. Morphine less effective now than earlier. Pain increased by movement.

Objective: Right radial artery 1+, limb pale and cool. Capillary refill 6 seconds. Sensation intact. Left arm pink, warm with 3+ pulse, no pain and intact sensation.

Analysis: Reduced tissue perfusion to right arm related to injury. Increasing pain.

Plan: Contacted Dr. Cisco to evaluate limb. Patient seen at 1930; physician indicated that there was no change from baseline. Patient is on call for surgery for open reduction internal fixation (ORIF) this evening. Orders written to assess circulation, sensation, and movement (CSM) every hour. Morphine PCA orders increased—see orders. Reevaluate the effectiveness of morphine in 30 minutes.

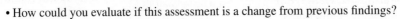

Critical Thinking Challenge

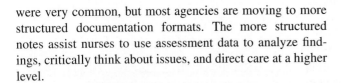

- How could you evaluate if this assessment is a change from previous findings?
- How should the nurse organize information before contacting the physician?
- What concepts of confidentiality should the nurse use if the patient asks about the status of his cousin or other people with injuries in the collision?
- What further assessments will be important for the nurse to perform and document? Where will the nurse document them?

---

were very common, but most agencies are moving to more structured documentation formats. The more structured notes assist nurses to use assessment data to analyze findings, critically think about issues, and direct care at a higher level.

SOAP Notes

The SOAP format focuses on a single condition and includes subjective (**S**) assessment findings, objective (**O**) assessment findings, analysis (**A**) of the assessment data to identify a condition or indicate whether the condition is improving or worsening, and plan (**P**) for treating or improving the condition. Some agencies expand SOAP to SOAPIE. In this case, the **I** represents interventions to treat the condition and the **E** represents evaluation of the condition. This text uses examples of the documentation of unexpected findings using the SOAP note format, both in the case below and throughout.

PIE Notes

The PIE format includes Problem (**P**), Interventions (**I**), and Evaluation (**E**). Its goal is to incorporate the POC into the progress note. Patient assessments are not part of the PIE note but are charted on flow sheets. Some agencies adapt the PIE note to an APIE note with (**A**) for Assessment, so

documentation reflects pertinent assessment data to support the problem (Craven & Hirnle, 2009).

Focus Note

The focus system of documentation organizes entries by DAR data (**D**), action (**A**), and response (**R**). Documentation can focus on areas of strengths as well as health issues, family concerns, or nursing diagnoses. Using this chapter's case study as an example, data could include the phone conversation the nurse has with Mr. Chavez's mother who is very worried and is trying to get to the hospital to see her son but has younger children who cannot be left alone and she has no transportation. The data portion contains subjective and objective findings that support the focus of the note. The action section presents interventions and treatments, while the response section reviews how the patient responded or met outcomes (Craven & Hirnle, 2009).

Charting by Exception

Charting by exception (CBE) uses predetermined standards and norms to record only significant assessment data. Clearly identifying the standards and norms and educating all users take time and significant commitment from the agency using CBE. For example, a group may develop the standard of what it considers expected parameters for each area of assessment (eg, respiratory, mobility, psychosocial). These norms structure the patient assessment. Norms for respiratory function might include respiratory rate 12 to 18 breaths/min, lungs clear to auscultation with no adventitious breath sounds, oxygen saturation above 93% on room air, and no dyspnea with activity. This cues nurses to assess respiratory rate, auscultate the lungs for adventitious sounds, assess oxygen saturation on room air, and assess whether an activity causes shortness of breath. If the patient's assessment matches the designated norms, the nurse checks a box. Any unexpected assessment findings require additional documentation.

Discharge Note

When the patient is discharged, the nurse enters a discharge note in the chart. The note can be a computer-generated form, paper form, or narrative note in the progress notes. Assessment of the patient should indicate that he or she is stable and has received teaching regarding medications and follow-up care. The discharge note also contains patient discharge teaching, discharge medications, when to contact the provider, condition at discharge, and time of discharge. The nurse gives a copy to the patient of the discharge summary with patient teaching and discharge medication. Assessment information is used to identify necessary resources and strategies for successful home management. This information is useful for social work, physical and occupational therapies, and follow-up care by the nurse and provider when the patient returns to the outpatient setting.

Written Handoff Summary

Handoff, or transfer of care for the patient from one health provider to another, significantly increases the risk of errors. Receiving staff must have up-to-date assessment data to safely care for the patient. Traditionally, nurses think of handoff occurring during shift change, but handoff also occurs when the patient is transferred from one area of the hospital to another. For example, handoff occurs when a postoperative patient moves from the postanesthesia recovery unit (PACU) to the surgical floor or back to the medical unit following dialysis or an invasive diagnostic procedure. Transfers also occur when the patient is transferred from one health care facility to another (eg, to an extended care facility or a rehabilitation unit).

To minimize potential errors from lack of information, agencies may provide specific assessments on a written transfer summary in addition to a verbal report. Some agencies have created specific forms for this transfer of information, while others require documentation in the progress notes.

Verbal Communication

Verbal Handoff

A **handoff** occurs anytime one provider transfers the responsibility for the care of a patient to another. Other industries such as aviation, power plants, and the NASA Space Center have studied and standardized handoffs to prevent errors, but only recently has the health care industry started paying attention to handoffs. Effective communication at handoff is critically important to create a shared mental model around the patient's condition, which creates situational awareness (Haig, Sutton, et al., 2006) and helps to minimize errors. The greater the number of handoffs and the more caregivers involved, the greater the risk for errors (Dracup & Morris, 2008).

The Canadian Patient Safety Institute encourages agencies to develop a standardized approach to handoff communications, including the opportunity to ask and respond to questions. Box 5-2 lists common handoff situations and strategies for effective handoff communication.

Reporting

To provide safe patient care, nurses continually communicate with all members of the health care team. Reporting occurs at handoffs, during patient rounds, during patient and family

---

BOX 5-2 HANDOFF REPORTING

Handoff
Occurs anytime the responsibility for care of a patient transfers from one provider to another. Standardized reporting at handoffs promotes continuity of care and prevents errors.

Common Situation Handoffs
- At change of shift, when an oncoming nurse is assigned to care for the patient
- When a nurse leaves for a meal or a break
- When a change in status requires transfer of the patient to another unit such as the intensive care unit (ICU)
- When the surgical patient is transferred from the operating room (OR) to the postanesthesia recovery unit (PACU) or from the PACU to the surgical floor
- When the patient is admitted from the emergency department (ED) to a medical-surgical unit or to the ICU
- When the patient moves to or from a procedural care area for a diagnostic procedure or treatment (eg, cath lab, gastrointestinal [GI] lab, dialysis unit)
- When hospitalists or medical staff members change coverage

Strategies for Effective Handoff Communication
- Use a standardized format such as SBAR for handoffs so that all important information is presented in a predictable, clear manner.
- Communicate with face-to-face verbal update of current status and historical data with interactive questioning.
- Ensure limited interruptions.
- Use "read back" policies to ensure that both parties agree and comprehend.
- Use written documentation to supplement the verbal handoff.
- Cross monitor the handoffs of others with written and verbal communication.

Adapted from Clancy, C. (2006). Care transitions: A threat and opportunity for patient safety. *American Journal of Medical Quality, 21*(6), 414–417.

care conferences, and when calling or text paging a provider to report a change in status or provide requested information. Baseline assessment data or significant changes in patient status are crucial elements of most reporting.

In theory, effective communication seems like a simple task. In reality, it is very complex and often suboptimal. Many barriers potentially contribute to issues in communication:

• Lack of structured format for communication
• Lack of standards and policies for communication
• Uncertainty about who is responsible and who should be contacted
• Hierarchy of relationships
• Differences in ethnocultural background
• Poor clinical decision making regarding what needs to be reported
• Different communication styles of nurses and physicians (Haig, Sutton et al., 2006)

Qualities of Effective Reporting

To effectively communicate with members of the health care team, verbal communication needs to be organized, complete, accurate, concise, and respectful. An organizing framework, especially a tool such as SBAR, helps ensure complete and organized reporting. This textbook uses examples of SBAR to illustrate how nurses use and communicate assessment information in clinical settings.

Reporting, because it involves face-to-face communication, is influenced by nonverbal communication as well as the actual spoken words. It is important for nurses to maintain eye contact and to give their undivided attention during any reporting situation (Fig. 5-6). Negative nonverbal cues such as lack of respect, inattention, or irritation might negatively affect the quality or completeness of the report. Differences in communication style also influence reporting. Nurses are often instructed to be very descriptive and detailed in their communication, whereas physicians tend

Figure 5-6 During reporting, health care professionals should maintain attention, eye contact, and other positive nonverbal indicators.

to be more concise and to focus on objective facts (Haig, Sutton et al., 2006). Physicians may become impatient and inattentive with nurses who provide a rambling report. If a nurse, especially a student or a new graduate, experiences a hostile or disrespectful response when giving a report, he or she might hesitate or delay reporting significant information in the future.

SBAR

SBAR, first developed by Kaiser Permanente in Denver and supported by the Canadian Patient Safety Institute (2008), is a shared mental model for improving communication between and among clinicians. This model organizes communication around **S**ituation, **B**ackground, **A**ssessment, and **R**ecommendations. Note that situation, background, and assessment are all based on the collection of complete and accurate assessment data. The last piece, recommendations, encompasses the nurse's suggestions for the next interventions.

• **S**ituation: State concisely why you are communicating.
• **B**ackground: Describe the circumstances leading up to the current situation.
• **A**ssessment: Give objective and subjective data pertinent to the situation.
• **R**ecommendation: Make suggestions for what needs to be done to manage the issue.

Nurses most commonly use this model when contacting a physician regarding a patient issue. SBAR also can serve as a method for structuring communication during handoffs, when delegating care to nursing assistants, or when expressing concern regarding a patient's condition to the head nurse or manager. Historically, nurses have always attempted to provide concise, organized verbal communication. The SBAR tool, however, gives a standardized format and provides clear articulation of what is desired. Refer to the example in the case study below and in other cases throughout this text.

Reporting with other Health Care Professionals

Reporting to other health care professionals can occur face to face, by telephone, by text messaging, or, in some settings (eg, long-term or home care), by fax. First, the nurse needs to identify the appropriate health care professional to notify by checking the chart to ascertain the primary physician, surgeon, or resident responsible for managing care. This becomes more complex in a teaching centre, where multiple providers are involved in care, or during nights or weekends when cross coverage occurs. In these situations, a call schedule helps to determine the appropriate person to contact. Valuable time can be lost if the process and schedule are unclear. Nurses can use an organized framework such as SBAR to ensure that communications are clear and concise. Beginners learning this skill will be more organized and accurate if they write a draft of what they want to say before contacting the provider.

A t the change of shift, nurses need to organize information to provide a report on the patient. In this case, Mr. Chavez is still awaiting surgery, so staff members on the evening shift need to report to staff members on the night shift. After a brief introduction, the nurse reviews systems briefly. The nurse should organize pertinent items, including changes, so that the report is efficient and complete. The following report illustrates how the nurse might organize the data and make recommendations about Mr. Chavez.

Situation: I've been Mr. Chavez's nurse for the past 8 hours.

Background: He was admitted with his cousin about 12 hours ago following a MVC. His cousin is in Room 222 with a fractured tibia and fibula. Mr. Chavez fractured his right humerus and is waiting an ORIF tonight.

Assessment: *Neuro:* He is drowsy from the pain medication but oriented. *CV:* His pulse is high at 122, R 20, blood pressure (BP) 138/78. I think the BP is elevated because he's in pain. *Pulmonary:* His lungs are clear and oxygen saturation is 96%. *GI/GU:* Abdomen is soft with bowel sounds. He's voiding in the urinal clear yellow urine, no stool. circulation, sensation, and movement (CSM) is as expected in both feet and left arm. However, his radial pulse is 1+ in his right hand, and it's cool and pale. His capillary refill is also slow at 6 seconds. I contacted the physician, Dr. Cisco who came and looked at the arm and said that there's no change, just to keep an eye on it. He's on hourly CSM checks now and there hasn't been a change. We also increased his dose of morphine, because he was at an 8/10 but now is down to a 3, which is within his goal. The IV is infusing well with D5NS at 125/hr. It's a new IV from the ER, and I just changed the bag, so you have 1,000 mL hanging. *Psych/soc:* His mother has called and is very worried about him.

Recommendations: He's been using the patient-controlled analgesia (PCA) more frequently, so encourage him to do that before his pain gets too bad. We're basically just waiting for him to go to the OR to get the repair. He's on call and I think that he's next in line. He's NPO (nothing by mouth) for surgery and his consent has been signed. Everything's in the chart and ready to go. His antibiotic is in the med room. Do you have any questions?

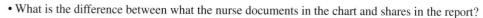

Critical Thinking Challenge

- What is the difference between what the nurse documents in the chart and shares in the report?
- What parts of the nursing process does the report include?
- How does the evening nurse use abbreviations to communicate and document data?

Telephone Communication

If a significant issue or situation occurs, the nurse may need to phone the primary provider to report this information. The nurse may call the physician's office or page the physician to call back. When talking to a physician over the phone, it is important to have the patient's record and important information available for reference. It is important to document the call, including the time, who was called, what information the nurse gave to the physician, and what information the nurse received. Most agencies now limit the use of telephone orders. For agencies that have CPOE, remote computer access allows physicians to enter orders when they are off-site. If a

nurse is taking a telephone order, it is important to write the order and then read it back to the provider to make sure it is correct. Students do not take telephone orders—only registered nurses can do so.

Nurses also communicate via the telephone with other departments to provide or to obtain information. When patients are transferring from one setting to another (eg, from ED or PACU), the nurse may give the handoff report by phone. Nurses often receive laboratory data, especially critical values, by telephone. For any critical values, all health personnel must read back values obtained over the telephone to ensure accuracy and avoid errors.

Figure 5-7 During a shift handoff in the patient's room, health care professionals can communicate with each other and directly with the patient to plan the day effectively and to ensure that the patient can participate as much as he or she is able to.

Patient Rounds and Conferences

Interprofessional rounds allow members of different professions to share assessment data in an effort to individualize and improve coordination of patient care. When rounds occur at the bedside and include the patient in the dialogue, the nurse facilitates active participation to set goals and plan care. During rounds, nurses present assessment data on nursing issues such as mobility, fluid balance, pain management, and emotional or family issues. Nurses can also help patients articulate questions or concerns. Shift handoffs are increasingly happening in the room with the patient to help communicate and plan the day (Fig. 5-7).

When working with patients with complex conditions (eg, end-of-life care), a nurse may request or help facilitate a family care conference. Family members and all members of the health care team meet to discuss how best to provide and coordinate care in challenging situations. Nurses need to plan these conferences in advance to coordinate schedules and to ensure that interpreters are present as needed.

Critical Thinking and Clinical Judgment

Nurses use critical thinking and clinical judgment to determine what assessment data to include in a verbal report, how quickly to report the assessment, the proper team member to receive the information, and what method of reporting (eg, face to face, telephone, text message) is most appropriate. Some reporting is scheduled at specific times, for example, shift change handoff. In other situations, the nurse decides whether an assessment finding or a change in the patient's status requires immediate or routine notification of the physician. For example, if a stable patient tells the nurse on night shift that he has not had a bowel movement in 2 days, the nurse waits until the patient rounds in the morning to report this and get an order for a laxative. Conversely, if the patient's BP is low and she is NPO for surgery, the nurse contacts the provider for an IV order to prevent severe dehydration. Refer to the Case Challenge toward the end of this chapter for an example of how this is prioritized. If the situation is acute and potentially life threatening, the nurse may activate and report to a Medical Emergency Team or Rapid Response Team. In this way, the nurse uses assessment information to take the next steps. Assessment information is never viewed in isolation from other parts of the nursing process.

Applying Your Knowledge

Consider Mr. Chavez's case and its relationship to what you are learning. Answer the following questions based on his initial injury, impaired tissue perfusion, pain, and the other changes that have occurred during the hours since admission.

- How do the patient situation and acuity influence the assessment, documentation, and communication of data?
- What is the importance of accurate and comprehensive documentation? (Knowledge)
- Describe the difference between recording and reporting? (Comprehension)
- What are important factors to consider when reporting? (Application)
- How does the collection of data fluctuate between a comprehensive and a focused assessment? (Analysis)
- Outline an example from the case study (Mr. Chavez) that incorporates SBAR. (Synthesis)
- How would you evaluate a successful handoff report? (Evaluation)

Key Points

- In addition to being a legal document, the patient health record serves many purposes, namely, communication, care planning, quality assurance, education, and research.
- The computerized patient health record helps ensure patient safety and enhances communication, because computerized documentation is legible and time dated, increases compliance, permits multiple simultaneous users, and permits surveillance of patient data to identify patients at risk.
- Critical thinking and clinical judgment are important in appropriately communicating and documenting assessment data to keep patients safe.
- Documentation should be accurate, objective, organized, concise, complete, and legible.
- Health care professionals must ensure confidentiality for all patient information, including what they document in the written or computerized record.
- Nurses can document assessment data in various forms (eg, nursing admission assessment, flow sheets, progress notes, transfer or discharge summaries) in the patient's record. Nurses working in home care and long-term care should follow the specific regulations governing documentation in those settings.
- Formats for nursing progress notes include narrative, SOAP, PIE, DAR, and CBE.
- Handoffs occur when one provider transfers the responsibility for patient care to another provider.
- SBAR (situation, background, assessment, and recommendation) is a mental model for organizing communication.
- Verbal communication of patient status occurs at handoff, over the telephone, via text message, or during rounds.
- Accurate and effective verbal communication and documentation are important to keeping patients safe.

Review Questions

1. Which of the following are advantages of the electronic patient health record? Select all that apply.
   A. Nurses can enter data by checking boxes and adding free full text.
   B. It is economical and easy to learn and implement.
   C. Physicians use CPOE to directly order into the computer.
   D. It cannot be used as a legal document in case of a lawsuit.

2. Which of the following are high-risk errors for documentation? Select all that apply.
   A. Failure to document completely
   B. Inadequate admission assessment
   C. Charting in advance
   D. Bunch charting at the end of shift

3. Which of the following is the purpose of auditing charting?
   A. To enhance nurses' learning and understanding of complex clinical situations
   B. To identify staff members who document completely and counsel those who do not
   C. To determine if staff members are providing and documenting standards of care
   D. To locate data in the chart the evening before a morning clinical

4. Which of the following are acceptable to maintain patient confidentiality? Select all that apply.
   A. Communicate report with the next nurse during change of shift.
   B. Communicate with the nurse practitioner about the patient's change in assessment.
   C. Consult in the hall with the instructor about the patient's assessment findings.
   D. Describe patient assessment findings to a colleague in the cafeteria.

5. Which of the following is the proper technique for correcting written documentation?
   A. Use whiteout and write over the error.
   B. Completely black out the error with a black marker.
   C. Write over the error in darker ink.
   D. Draw a single line through the error and initial.

6. What do the different formats of progress notes have in common?
   A. All use the nursing process in some form to show critical thinking.
   B. All identify the patient outcomes or goals to evaluate.
   C. All include head-to-toe assessment data for completeness.
   D. All have a section for evaluation of care so that nurses may revise interventions.

7. What are some strategies for effective handoffs during change-of-shift report?
   A. Tape record the report for efficiency.
   B. Vary the format to individualize to the patient.
   C. Allow an opportunity to ask and answer questions.
   D. Put report in writing so that the next shift provider can get right to work.

8. In the SBAR reporting format, which of the following would be an example of data found in the assessment?
   A. Mrs. Kelly's diagnosis is Stage II breast cancer.
   B. Mr. Imami's lungs sounds are decreased.
   C. Ms. Choi needs to have a social work consult.
   D. Mr. Jones was admitted at 1030 this morning.

9. Nursing assessment of trends in an unconscious patient's neurological status over time is best recorded on
A. an admission assessment
B. a plan of care (POC)
C. a progress note
D. a focused assessment flow sheet

10. Your patient with a fractured humerus is stating pain of 10 on a 10-point scale. His hand is pale, cool, and swollen. His pain medication is ineffective, and he is at risk for compartment syndrome. What action will the nurse take first?
A. Reassess the pain in 30 minutes and contact the provider if unresolved.
B. Give additional pain medication and reassess the pain in 30 minutes.
C. Document the findings and give an extra dose of pain medication now.
D. Contact the physician and document the findings now.

Canadian Nursing Research

Dubey, V., & Glazier, R. (2006). Preventive care checklist form: Evidence-based tool to improve preventive health care during complete health assessment of adults. *Canadian Family Physician, 52,* 48–55.

Hannah, K. (2005). Health informatics and nursing in Canada. *Healthcare Information Management and Communications, 19*(3), 45–51.

Howse, E., & Bailey, J. (1992). Resistance to documentation—A nursing research issue. *International Journal of Nursing Studies, 29*(4), 371–380.

Martin, A., Hinds, C., et al. (1999). Documentation practices of nurses in long-term care. *Journal of Clinical Nursing, 8*(4), 345–352.

References

Accreditation Canada. (2011). *Driving quality health services.* Retrieved from www.accreditation.ca/en/default.aspx

Canadian Patient Safety Institute. (2008). *Enhancing effective team communication for patient safety: An adapted SBAR communication tool for rehabilitation.* Retrieved from http://www.patientsafetyinstitute.ca/English/research/cpsiResearchCompetitions/2005/Documents/Velji/Deliverables/SBAR%20Communication%20Tool%20Presentation.pdf

College & Association of Registered Nurses of Alberta. (2007). Documentation guidelines. Alberta RN, *63*(1), 12–13. Edmonton, AB: Author.

Craven, R. C., & Hirnle, C. J. (2009). *Fundamentals of nursing: Human health and function* (6th ed.). Philadelphia, PA: Lippincott Williams & Wilkins.

Dracup, K., & Morris, P. (2008). Passing the torch: The challenge of handoffs. *American Journal of Critical Care, 17*(2), 95–97.

Haig, K., Sutton, S., et al. (2006). SBAR: A shared mental model for improving communication between clinicians. *Joint Commission Journal on Quality and Patient Safety, 32*(3), 167–175.

Moody, L., Slocumb, E., et al. (2004). Electronic health records documentation in nursing: Nurses' perceptions, attitudes, and preferences. *Computers Informatic Nursing, 22*(6), 337–344.

O'Neill, A., & Miranda, D. (2006). The right tools can help critical care nurses save more lives. *Critical Care Nursing Quarterly, 29*(4), 275–281.

Whittington, J., White, R., et al. (2007). Using an automated risk assessment report to identify patients at risk for clinical deterioration. *Joint Commission Journal on Quality and Patient Safety, 33*(9), 569.

The Canadian Jensen's Nursing Health Assessment suite offers these additional resources to enhance learning and facilitate understanding of this chapter:

- thePoint online resource, http//thepoint.lww.com/ Stephen1E
- *Laboratory Manual for Canadian Jensen's Nursing Health Assessment: A Best Practice Approach*

General Examinations

General Survey and Vital Signs Assessment

Learning Objectives

1 Describe the general survey in the comprehensive physical examination.

2 Demonstrate knowledge of the importance of taking vital signs.

3 Demonstrate critical thinking for accurately assessing vital signs.

4 Describe factors that cause variations in vital signs and their measurement.

5 Identify risk factors for alterations in vital signs.

6 Document and report vital sign measurements.

7 Identify age-related variations in vital signs.

8 Identify cultural variations in vital signs.

Mr. Boris Odynak is a 55-year-old man of East Ukrainian heritage who was transferred by ambulance from a walk-in clinic and was admitted to the intensive care unit (ICU) following an episode of rapid heart rate and dizziness. He was monitored in the ICU for 2 days because he had atrial fibrillation (a cardiac dysrhythmia that causes a fast and irregular heartbeat). He was placed on medication, digoxin (Lanoxin), loading dose 1.25 mg, to decrease his heart rate; he also is taking an antihypertensive drug, diltiazem hydrochloride (Apo-Diltiaz), 30 mg for high blood pressure. He was transferred in stable condition yesterday to the medical unit.

You will gain more information about Mr. Odynak as you progress through this chapter. As you study the content and features, consider Mr. Odynak's case and its relationship to what you are learning. Begin thinking about the following points:

- Is Mr. Odynak's condition stable, urgent, or an emergency?
- What immediate health promotion and teaching needs are evident?
- What are the relationships among the patient's pulse, respirations, and blood pressure?
- How will a comprehensive general survey and vital signs differ from a focused assessment for this patient?

This chapter explores the assessment techniques required to perform the general survey and take vital signs. The general survey begins during the interview phase of health assessment (see Chapter 2). While collecting subjective data, nurses observe patients, develop initial impressions, and formulate plans for collecting objective data from the physical examination. An accurate and thorough physical examination requires keen observational skills. During health assessments, nurses use the senses of vision, hearing, touch, and smell.

Vital signs encompass temperature, pulse, respirations, blood pressure (BP), and pain. Pain is covered in Chapter 7. A sixth vital sign, functional ability, is assessed in older adults (see Chapter 30). Vital signs are important indicators of the patient's physiological status and response to the environment. Nurses assess vital signs frequently and use findings as guidance for further physical assessment. Ability to differentiate between expected and unexpected results is crucial.

Acute Assessment

Indicators of an acute situation include extreme anxiety, acute distress, pallor, cyanosis, and a change in mental status. In cases of such acute or urgent findings, the nurse begins interventions while continuing the assessment. He or she will obtain vital signs including BP, pulse, respiratory rate, oxygen saturation, temperature, and pain, and will request help as needed. The nurse may call a rapid response team if he or she has an intuitive sense that something is going wrong with the patient or if the patient displays any of the following emergency concerns:

- An acute change
- Stridor
- Respirations <10 breaths/min or greater than 32 breaths/min
- Increased effort to breathe
- Oxygen saturation <92%
- Pulse <55 beats/min (bpm) or >120 bpm
- Systolic BP <100 or >170
- Temperature <35°C or >39.5°C
- New onset of chest pain
- Agitation or restlessness

Experienced nurses will assist beginners in determining the level of response needed.

Objective Data Collection

Equipment

• Weight scale	• Watch with second hand or
• Height bar	digital display
• Stethoscope	• Sphygmomanometer
• Thermometer	• Pulse oximeter
	• Tape measure (for infants)

Promoting Patient Comfort, Dignity, and Safety

The room needs to be warm, comfortable, and relaxing. A quiet, well-lit setting provides privacy. The nurse performs hand hygiene (see Chapter 4), preferably in the presence of the patient, and cleanses the stethoscope with equipment wipes to prevent the transmission of bacteria. All necessary equipment is within reach.

The general survey begins immediately upon meeting the patient and continues throughout the assessment. The patient removes shoes and heavy outer garments before being weighed and measured. Prior to assessment of vital signs, the patient must rest quietly for 5 minutes. The nurse establishes that the patient has not had anything to eat or drink and has not smoked for at least 30 minutes. The patient must remove constricting clothing on the upper arm to provide access to the brachial artery for measurement of BP. The patient may be sitting or supine for vital signs.

General Survey: General Inspection

The **general survey** begins with the first moment of the encounter with the patient and continues throughout the health history, during the physical examination, and with each subsequent interaction. It is the first component of the assessment, when the nurse makes mental notes of overall behaviour, physical appearance, and mobility. This helps to form a global impression of the individual. Physical appearance and mental status provide valuable clues to overall health. Assessment of these areas requires that nurses use their visual, auditory, and olfactory senses, and their observational skills to look, listen, and note any unexpected findings, including sounds and odours.

When nurses introduce themselves, they shake hands with the patient as appropriate to the situation. A handshake not only portrays caring but also allows assessment of the patient (eg, hand strength). The nurse notes if the patient makes eye contact, smiles, and speaks clearly. Some general things to note when first meeting the patient are as follows:

- What is the first impression of the patient? Are there any outstanding features?
- After stating the patient's name, does the patient respond immediately?
- Is the patient's hand moist? Did the patient extend the arm completely? What is the temperature and texture of the skin on the hand? In addition to muscle strength, there is the opportunity to assess for edema, clubbing, malformations, or enlarged joints.
- How does the patient interact with others? Can he or she participate in conversation? Does the patient look healthy or ill?

As the nurse proceeds through the assessment, he or she notes the patient's physical appearance, body structure, mobility (posture, gait, motor activity), and behaviour (insight, judgment, thought processes, cognitive functions) (Skillen & Bickley, 2010). Because these characteristics are general overall indicators of health, nurses consider how the data fit together with other systems. They think about what other data they will want to collect to identify patterns. Data collection begins as soon as the nurse enters the area where the patient is or just hears the patient talking, and continues until he or she leaves the area.

Technique and Expected Findings	Rationale/Unexpected Findings
Physical Appearance	
Overall Appearance. Is appearance consistent with stated chronological age? Are the face and body symmetrical? Are any deformities obvious? Does the patient look well, unhealthy, or in distress? *The patient appears stated age. Facial features, movements, and body are symmetrical.*	Deficiencies in growth hormones may cause patients to appear younger than they are. Severe illness, chronic disease, prolonged sun exposure, and various genetic syndromes may contribute to premature aging. Facial asymmetry may indicate Bell's palsy or cerebral vascular ischemia. Obvious deformities may indicate fractures or displacements.
Hygiene Grooming and Dress. Note hygiene by observing clothing, hair, nails, and skin. What is the patient wearing? Is it appropriate for age, gender, culture, context, and weather? Is clothing clean and neat or disheveled? Does it fit? Are any breath or body odours noted? Note the odour of alcohol or urine. Is the patient's skin clean and dry? Are nails and hair groomed, neat, and clean? *Dress is appropriate for age, gender, culture, and weather. The patient is clean and groomed. No odours present.*	Poorly fitting clothes may indicate weight loss or gain. Type or condition of footwear used can indicate painful foot conditions. Bad breath can result from poor hygiene, *allergic rhinitis*, or infection (*tonsillitis, sinusitis*). Sweet-smelling breath may indicate *diabetic ketoacidosis*. Body odour may be from poor hygiene or increased sweat-gland activity, which accompanies some hormonal disorders. Previously well-groomed patients who are now untidy may have *depression*. Eccentric makeup or dress may indicate *mania*. Worn or disheveled clothes may indicate inadequate finances or knowledge.
Skin Colour and Lesions. Observe for even skin tones and symmetry. Note any areas of increased redness, pallor, cyanosis, or jaundice. Observe for any lesions or variations in pigmentation. Note the amount, texture, quality, and distribution of hair. *Skin colour is even-toned, with pigmentation appropriate for genetic background and no obvious lesions or variations in colour. Hair is smooth, thick, and evenly distributed.*	Pallor, erythema, cyanosis, jaundice, and lesions can indicate disease states (see Chapter 13).
Body Structure and Development. Is the patient's physical and sexual development consistent with expected findings for stated age? Is the patient obese or lean? Is the height appropriate for age and genetic background? Are body parts symmetrical? What is the patient's build? Is the patient barrel chested? Note the fingertips. Are there any joint abnormalities? *Physical and sexual development is appropriate for age, culture, and gender. No joint abnormalities are noted.*	Delayed puberty may indicate a deficiency of growth hormones. Altered growth hormones may lead to markedly short or tall stature. Disproportionate height and weight, obesity, or emaciation can indicate *eating disorders* or hormonal dysfunction.
Behaviour	
Note the patient's behaviour. Is he or she cooperative or uncooperative? Is affect animated or flat? Does the patient appear anxious? *The patient is cooperative and interacts pleasantly.*	Uncooperative behaviour, flat affect, or unusual elation may indicate a psychiatric disorder (see Chapter 10). Note that mild anxiety is common in people seeking health care.
Facial Expressions. Assess the face for symmetry. Note expressions while the patient is at rest and during speech and whether he or she seems appropriate. Are movements symmetrical? Does the patient maintain eye contact appropriate to culture? *Facial expression is relaxed, symmetrical, and appropriate for the setting and circumstances. The patient maintains eye contact appropriate for age and culture.*	Inappropriate affect, inattentiveness, impaired memory, and inability to perform activities of daily living may indicate *dementia* (eg, Alzheimer's disease) or another cognitive disorder. A flat or masklike expression may indicate *Parkinson's disease* or *depression*. Drooping of one side of the face may indicate *transient ischemic attack* or *cerebral vascular accident*. Exophthalmos (protruding eyes) may indicate *hyperthyroidism*.

(text continues on page 94)

Level of Consciousness.

Continually assess the patient's mental status throughout all encounters, but pay particular attention to it when gathering the health history. Can the patient state his or her name and location, and the date, month, season, and time of day? Is the patient awake, alert, and oriented to person, place, and time? Look for the eyes to open spontaneously, a verbal response oriented to the questions, and a motor response to what you might request (Skillen & Bickley, 2010). Note any confusion, agitation, lethargy, or inattentiveness. Is there a change in mental status? If the patient appears confused, ask him or her to respond to the following:

• Tell me your full name.
• Where are you now?
• What is today's date?
• What time of the day is it?

The patient is awake, alert, and oriented to person, place, and time (abbreviated A&O × 3). He or she attends and responds to questions appropriately.

Confusion, agitation, drowsiness, or lethargy may indicate hypoxia, decreased cerebral perfusion, or a psychiatric disorder. Refer to Chapters 10 and 24.

⚠ **SAFETY ALERT 6-1**
Change in level of consciousness often is the first indication of hypoxia.

Speech.

Listen to the speech pattern. Is the patient speaking very rapidly or very slowly? Is speech clear and articulate? Does the patient use words appropriately? Vocabulary and sentence structure may offer clues to educational level. Also, assess for fluency in language and the need for an interpreter. *The patient responds to questions quickly and easily. Volume, pitch, and rate are appropriate to the situation. Speech is clear and articulate, flowing smoothly. Word choice is appropriate.*

Slow, slurred speech can indicate *alcohol intoxication* or *cerebral vascular ischemia*. Rapid speech may indicate *hyperthyroidism, anxiety*, or *mania*. Difficulty finding words or using words inappropriately may indicate *cerebral vascular ischemia* or a psychiatric disorder. Loud speech may indicate hearing difficulties.

Mobility

Posture.

Note how the patient sits and stands. Is the patient sitting upright? When standing, is the body straight and aligned? *Posture is upright while sitting, with the limbs and trunk proportional to the body height. The patient rises unaided from seat to stand erect with no signs of discomfort and the arms relaxed at the sides.*

Slumped or hunched posture may indicate *depression*, fatigue, pain, or *osteoporosis*. Long limbs may indicate *Marfan syndrome*. A tripod position when sitting can indicate respiratory disease (see Chapter 18). If the patient is in bed, note the position of the head of the bed or if the patient is lying on the left or right side.

Range of Motion.

Can the patient move all the limbs equally? Are there limitations? *The patient moves freely in the environment.*

Asymmetrical motion occurs in *stroke*; paralysis may accompany spinal cord injury. Limited range of motion might be present with injuries or degenerative disease.

Gait.

If the patient is ambulatory, observe his or her movement around the room. Note if movements are coordinated. Typically, an individual ambulates with arms swinging freely at the sides. Note any tremors or involuntary movements, as well as any body parts that do not move. Does the patient use assistive devices? *Gait is steady and balanced, with even heel-to-toe foot placement and smooth movements. Other movements are also smooth, purposeful, effortless, and symmetrical.*

Tics, paralysis, ataxia, tremors, or uncontrolled movements may indicate neurological disease. Patients with Parkinson's disease may display a shuffling gait. Arthritis may result in a slow, unsteady gait. For patients in bed, note their ability to move and reposition themselves in bed, turn side to side, and sit up. Further evaluate any unexpected findings when assessing the neurological and musculoskeletal systems during the comprehensive physical examination (see Chapters 23 and 24).

Anthropometric Measurements

Anthropometric measurements are the various measurements of the human body, including height and weight. Accurate measurements provide critical information about the adult's state of health and the child's growth pattern. They are important parameters for evaluating nutritional status, assessing fluid gain or loss, and calculating medication dosages.

Specific measurements can be compared against standardized charts. The first time a nurse meets a patient, he or she records height and weight as a baseline measurement. Afterward, the nurse takes measurements at regular intervals, depending on the patient's state of health and agency policy. A series of measurements provide more information than any single measurement. Taking baseline height and weight provides a reference point for weight changes and for assessing body mass index (BMI).

Technique and Expected Findings	Rationale/Unexpected Findings
Height Measure patients older than 2 years, with them standing. Ask the patient to place the heels up against a height bar. Feet should be together, with knees straight and the patient looking forward. Lower the horizontal bar until it touches the top of the patient's head. Read and record the measurement on the height bar (Fig. 6-1).	*Chronic malnutrition* may result in decreased height from lack of nutrients for proper growth. Decreased height also may result from *osteoporosis*. Hormonal aberrations may cause excessive growth, as seen in *gigantism* and *acromegaly*. Deficiency in growth hormone may be seen in *dwarfism*.

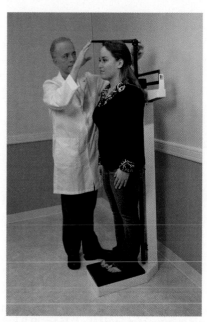

Figure 6-1 Measuring height in an adult.

Sometimes, patients cannot stand up straight for the measurement of height. In such cases, estimate the height by measuring "wingspan." Have the patient hold both arms straight from the sides of the body. Measure from the tip of one middle finger to the tip of the other middle finger. This distance is approximately the same as the patient's height.	The patient with muscle weakness, *scoliosis*, or neurological disorders may not be able to stand.
Weight Primary care facilities may use a calibrated balance-beam scale for obtaining weights. Prior to weighing a patient, the nurse must balance the scale by sliding both weight bars to zero. The balancing arm should balance in the center of the gauge. Follow the manufacturer's instructions to balance if needed. Lock the scale if it is	Excessive unexplained weight loss may result from nutritional deficiencies, decreased intake, decreased absorption, increased metabolic needs, or a combination. Other causes may be endocrine, neoplastic, gastrointestinal, psychiatric, infectious, or neurological. Chronic disease also may contribute to weight loss. Excessive weight

(text continues on page 96)

on wheels. Have the patient stand on the scale. Slide the lower weight bar to the right until the arm drops to the bottom of the gauge (Fig. 6-2).

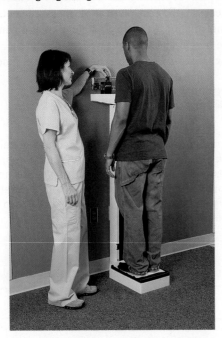

Figure 6-2   Measuring weight in an adult.

Slide the weight bar one notch back. Move the upper weight bar to the right until the arrow is balanced in the center of the gauge. The patient's weight is the total of these two readings. Record the weight. Many facilities use an electronic scale to weigh patients; hospitals may use a scale built into the bed. These scales must be calibrated, or "zeroed," prior to use.

To obtain the most accurate readings when a series of weights are required, weigh the patient at the same time of the day in similar clothing each time.

Calculate body mass index (BMI) by dividing the weight in kilograms by the height in metres squared (or the weight in pounds divided by the height in inches squared and then multiplied by 703). (See Health Canada website (2003) for an image of the BMI Nomogram.)

gain results when a person consumes more calories than his or her body requires. Overweight may result from endocrine disorders, genetics, or emotional factors such as stress, *anxiety, depression*, or guilt. Drug therapy, especially steroids, may contribute to weight gain.

According to Health Canada (2003) underweight is BMI < 18.5 kg/m^2; overweight is BMI of 25 to 29.9 kg/m^2; obese class I is BMI 30 to 34.9; obese class II is BMI 35 to 39.9, and obese class III is > 40 kg/m^2. The BMI nomogram is not to be used with patients under 18 years of age or women who are pregnant/lactating. Older adults may extend into the overweight range. See Chapter 8 for more information.

The BMI is considered a more reliable indicator of healthy weight than weight measurement alone (see Chapter 8). To obtain accurate height and weight, ask the patient to remove his or her shoes and heavy articles of clothing (eg, winter coat).

Vital Signs

Temperature, pulse, respirations, and BP make up four of the vital signs. Pain, considered the fifth vital sign, is covered in Chapter 7. Functional ability is considered to be the sixth

vital sign and is assessed in older adults (see Chapter 30). Oxygen saturation is also collected in hospitalized patients. Nurses interpret the significance of vital signs within the context of other data from the patient assessment.

Vital signs reflect health status, cardiopulmonary function, and overall body function. Vital signs are indicators of physiological state and response to physical, environmental, and psychological stressors. Changes in vital signs often indicate changes in health, but may also reflect recent exercise, response to pain, stress, or anxiety. Assessment of vital signs helps nurses to establish a baseline, monitor the patient's condition, evaluate responses to treatment, health issues, and assess risks for alterations in health.

Measurement of vital signs assists with the process of physical examination. Findings help the nurse determine specific body systems that need more thorough investigation. For example, if respiratory rate or rhythm is altered, the nurse assesses skin colour, respiratory effort, signs of accessory muscles use, oxygen saturation with pulse oximetry, and auscultates the patient's lung sounds.

Prior to taking vital signs, it is important to inquire about any medications the patient is currently taking. Nurses must be aware of the side effects of all medications administered, because many medications alter vital signs. In that event, the nurse assesses the effects and provides appropriate teaching to the patient.

The patient's physical condition, the situation, and agency policies determine how often to take vital signs (Box 6-1). Nurses are responsible for determining when more frequent assessment of vital signs is warranted.

The initial set of vital signs provides a baseline. A series of readings is more informative than a single value because the series provides information about trends over time. Many variables may affect vital signs, including pain, emotional state, and activity. It is imperative that nurses measure vital signs correctly and accurately, understand the data, and communicate appropriately.

Nurses observe patients for other findings to support or refute their assessments. When encountering an unexpected value, they obtain the vital sign(s) again to check for accuracy. They also look at the patient. Does he or she appear to be in distress? They document the colour of the skin, respiratory effort, and behaviour. Expected parameters for readings vary according to age. Furthermore, a usual value for one patient may be unusual for another. When assessing vital signs, nurses compare their results to standardized values for the patient's age and also to the patient's own baseline.

Occasionally, only one vital sign requires assessment. For example, before administering a cardiac medication, the nurse assesses heart rate, BP, or both, but not temperature. If fever is suspected, the nurse may take only the temperature. After administering an antipyretic for fever, the nurse reassesses the effect of the medication by measuring the temperature again.

Temperature

The hypothalamus is the body's thermostat; it functions to maintain a steady core temperature. This thermostat balances the heat produced from food digestion, exercise, and increased metabolism with the heat lost from evaporation of sweat and exposure to environmental elements. Cellular metabolism requires this steady state of temperature to function properly. In Canada, body temperature is measured in degrees **Celsius (C)**. Elsewhere temperature may be measured in degrees **Fahrenheit (F)** (Box 6-2).

The expected range for body temperature is 35.9°C to 37.5°C (96.7°F–100.5°F), depending on the route used for measurement. Rectal and temporal artery measurements are 0.4°C to 0.5°C (0.7°F–1°F) higher than oral measurements. Axillary temperatures average 0.5°C (1°F) lower than oral temperatures. No single temperature is constant for all adults. Body temperature fluctuates with diurnal cycle, physical activity, age, gender, and state of health. A low temperature usually occurs in the early morning, with temperature peaking in the late afternoon. Temperature may vary as much as 0.5°C (1°F). This variation is called the **diurnal** or **circadian cycle.** Variation according to time of day is somewhat more pronounced in infants and children.

Moderate to hard exercise increases body temperature. In women of childbearing age, increased progesterone secretion that accompanies ovulation causes temperature to rise 0.3°C to 0.5°C (0.5°F–1°F) and remain elevated until menses commence. Stress may elevate core (central) temperature as a result of increased production of epinephrine and norepinephrine. These increase both metabolic activity and heat production.

Factors such as age, level of consciousness, patient care equipment (eg, endotracheal tubes), availability of temperature equipment, and agency policies influence the choice of route. Each route has advantages and disadvantages. Although some routes or devices may be easier than others, they may not be the most accurate. Nurses determine the safest and most accurate site for assessment. They select and use alternative methods when warranted by the patient's condition. The same site should be used when follow-up measurements are needed for comparisons.

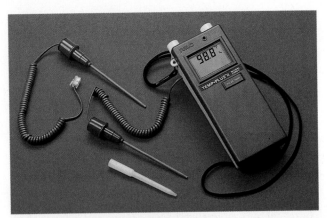

Figure 6-3 Electronic thermometer.

To ensure accuracy, temperatures must be measured correctly. *Electronic thermometers* are fast, safe, and convenient; they can accurately measure the oral, rectal, and axillary temperatures (Fig. 6-3). Temperature readings can be measured in as quickly as 2 to 60 seconds. Oral (blue-tip) and rectal (red-tip) probes are available; they come with disposable, single-use covers. Equipment must be fully charged and correctly calibrated to ensure accuracy. *Disposable, single-use thermometers* can be used for oral, rectal, and axillary temperature assessment. Readings are available within 1 minute. Disposable thermometers are an effective measure to decrease spread of infection.

Oral. The oral route is common and comfortable for many patients, but it may be contraindicated for others. The

sublingual pockets under the tongue are rich in blood supply that responds quickly to changes in the core temperature.

⚠ *SAFETY ALERT 6-2*

The oral route cannot be used to measure temperature in patients who are unconscious, orally intubated, or confused, or with those who have a history of seizures. Oral temperatures are also contraindicated in cases of postoperative oral surgery or oral trauma. Oral thermometers are not recommended for children younger than 6 years.

Axillary. The axillary route is less common than the oral route. It can be used with infants and young children. It may also be used with patients of other ages who cannot have oral temperature assessed. Electronic or disposable thermometers may be used to access axillary temperatures, which are lower than oral temperatures by 0.3°C to 0.5°C (0.5°F–1°F). One disadvantage to the axillary route is the need to wait 30 minutes after washing the axilla. The axillary temperature also measures skin surface temperature which varies and is less reliable than other methods (Lawson, Bridges, et al., 2007).

Tympanic Membrane. The tympanic thermometer uses infrared sensors to detect the heat that the tympanic membrane produces. The tympanic membrane thermometer is noninvasive, safe, efficient, and quick. Because the reading is so quick (2–3 s), it is commonly used in emergency departments, pediatric settings, and hospitals. The tympanic temperature should be avoided in patients with ear drainage, ear pain, suspected infection, or scarred tympanic membranes.

Table 6-1   Advantages and Disadvantages to Various Temperature Routes

Route	Expected Temperature Range	Appropriate Use	Advantages	Disadvantages
Oral	36.5°C–37.5°C (97.7°F–99.5°F)	Older children and adults who are awake, alert, and oriented	Easily accessible and comfortable; provides accurate readings	Do not use with people who have altered mental status. Values may vary because of mouth breathing, oral intake, and smoking. Risk for body fluid exposure is increased.
Axillary	35.9°C–37.2°C (96.7°F–98.5°F)	Infants, young children, and patients with impaired immune systems	Easy to obtain	The nurse must hold the thermometer in place for longer time. Readings reflect temperature of the skin surface, which may be variable. This method may be less accurate than oral or rectal.
Rectal	37.0°C–37.5°C (98.7°F–100.5°F)	Young children and confused or unconscious adults	Very accurate; more reflective of core temperature than other routes	This invasive method should not be used for people with rectal surgery, diarrhea, abscesses, or low white blood cell count. It is contraindicated for newborns and patients with cardiac disease. Risk is increased for exposure to body fluids.
Tympanic	36.0°C–37.5°C (98.2°F–100.5°F)	All patients except those with ear infection or ear pain	Easily accessible, quick, unaffected by oral intake or smoking	Studies have not proven accuracy. Thermometer is available only in one size. Positioning in children younger than 3 years is difficult.
Temporal	36.5.°C–37.5°C (98.7°F–100.5°F)	All patients	Quick and easy to obtain	Diaphoresis or sweat can impair reading.

One disadvantage of tympanic temperature is that reports of accuracy are conflicting. Studies have shown as much as 0.5°C (1°F) variation between tympanic and core pulmonary artery temperatures. The positioning of the probe in the ear canal is inconsistent among examiners, which may account for falsely low readings and missed fevers (Mackechnie & Simpson, 2006).

Temporal Artery. Temporal artery thermometers are quick, safe, and convenient, and they do not require contact with mucous membranes. An infrared sensor measures body temperature by capturing the heat emitted from the skin over the temporal artery. Measurement on either the right or left side of the forehead is equally effective. If a patient is in the lateral position, the nondependent side of the forehead should be used. Moving the device too quickly across the forehead or breaking contact with the skin can cause inconsistent results. To enhance accuracy, keep the thermometer's infrared lens clean and avoid interference because of buildup of skin oil (Lawson, Bridges, et al., 2007). Temporal artery thermometers are especially useful with confused or unconscious patients and with children.

Rectal. Rectal temperatures, considered one of the most accurate, are taken when other routes are not practical or an accurate core reading is necessary. Adults are usually uncomfortable having a rectal temperature taken.

Adults who cannot close their mouths because of intubation, surgery, change in mental status, or unresponsiveness may require rectal temperatures if tympanic or temporal thermometers are unavailable. Rectal temperatures accurately reflect core temperature changes but are inconvenient, disrupting usual activity, and cause discomfort to patients.

Rectal temperatures are 0.4°C to 0.5°C (0.7°F–1°F) higher than oral temperatures. Electronic and disposable thermometers may be used to measure rectal temperatures. Rectal thermometers are differentiated from oral thermometers by a red colour rather than the blue colour. The nurse uses critical thinking to select the correct route for taking the temperature. See Table 6-1 for a comparison of routes.

Technique and Expected Findings	Rationale/Unexpected Findings
Oral Temperature. To ensure accuracy, wait 15 to 30 minutes after a patient has had anything either hot or cold to eat or drink, smoked, or chewed gum. Turn the thermometer device on. Cover the tip of the probe with a protector. Gloves are unnecessary unless you expect contact with body secretions. Place the thermometer in the sublingual area at the base (back) of the tongue, which has a rich blood supply and corresponds with core temperature. Instruct the patient to keep the lips closed tightly and to breathe through the nose. Hold the probe until it beeps, then remove it.	Hypothermia is temperature <35°C (95°F). Prolonged exposure to cold may cause hypothermia. It may be induced purposefully during surgery to reduce the body's oxygen demands. Hyperthermia, also known as *pyrexia* or *fever*, is body temperature exceeding 38.0°C (100.5°F) orally. It occurs during infections caused by toxic bacterial secretions called pyrogens. Another cause is tissue breakdown, as seen in trauma, surgery, *myocardial infarction*, and *malignancy*. Certain neurological disorders, such as *cerebral vascular accident, cerebral tumour*, or cerebral trauma, can affect thermoregulation by the brain.
Note the reading and directly dispose of the cover into a wastebasket. Electronic or disposable thermometers have replaced old glass thermometers containing mercury because of toxicity of mercury in the environment. *Oral temperature ranges from 36.5°C to 37.5°C (96.4°F–99.1°F).*	
	⚠ SAFETY ALERT 6-4 *Fever above 39.5°C (103°F) in adults requires immediate assessment and rapid cooling measures. Monitor rectal temperature constantly during cooling measures to prevent a hypothermic response. Temperature below 35°C (95°F) may require rewarming, according to established protocols.*
Axillary Temperature. Follow the procedure above, except place the electronic thermometer in the axillary fold and have the patient lower the arm, keeping it close to the body. Hold it in place until it reads the temperature. Stay with the patient to ensure correct placement. *Axillary temperature ranges from 35.9°C to 37.2°C. It is approximately one degree lower than oral.*	Axillary temperature is the least accurate, so if there are discrepancies, recheck the temperature with another route.

(text continues on page 100)

Tympanic Temperature. Turn the unit on and wait for the ready signal. Place a disposable single-use cover on the probe tip. Then, place the tip gently in the patient's ear canal, angling the thermometer toward the patient's jaw. In an adult, pull the pinna (auricle) up, back, and slightly outward to straighten the curvature of the external auditory canal (Fig. 6-4). Take care not to force the probe or to occlude the ear canal. Push the trigger and note the reading. Dispose the cover directly into the wastebasket. Temperature readings are available in 2 to 3 seconds. *Tympanic temperature ranges from 36.0°C to 37.5°C. It is approximately equal to oral.*

Temporal Temperature. Position the probe directly on the skin above the eyebrow. Activate the thermometer by depressing and holding the scan bottom. Move the probe slowly from the forehead, across the temporal artery to level with the top of the ear (Fig. 6-5). Continue to hold the scan button while moving the probe to behind the earlobe. The process requires 5 to 7 seconds. *Temporal temperature ranges from 36.5°C to 37.5°C. It is approximately equal to oral.*

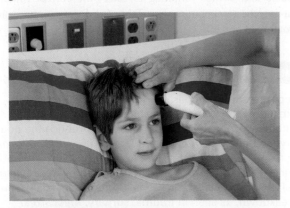

Figure 6-5 Temporal temperature assessment.

Rectal. To assess rectal temperature, ensure that the correct rectal tip is in place. Turn on the unit. Don gloves and cover the probe of the electronic thermometer with a protector. Lubricate the rectal thermometer, and insert the probe 2 to 3 cm into the adult rectum. Hold the thermometer in place and stay with the patient until the temperature is read. Directly dispose the cover into the wastebasket. Using tissue, wipe off any remaining lubricant. Cover the patient and ensure that he or she is comfortable. *Rectal temperature ranges from 37.0°C to 37.5°C. It is approximately 1°C warmer than oral.*

Pulse

Contraction of the heart causes blood to flow forward, which creates a pressure wave known as a **pulse**. The pulse is the throbbing sensation that can be palpated over a peripheral artery or auscultated over the apex of the heart. The pulse reflects the amount of blood ejected with each beat of the heart, which is the stroke volume. The number of pulsations occurring in 1 minute is the heart (pulse) rate.

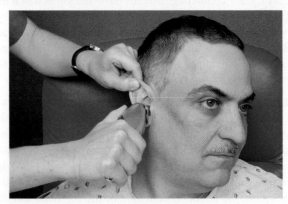

Figure 6-4 Tympanic temperature assessment. Note placement of the thermometer in the adult's ear.

Studies have shown that the temporal artery measurement using the forehead and behind the ear method is more accurate than temporal artery measurements using just the forehead and is comparable to oral temperature (Lawson, Bridges, et al., 2007).

Avoid placing the probe directly into stool, which may cause an inaccurate reading. The probe should be in contact with the rectal mucosa.

Table 6-2   Age-Related Variations in Vital Signs

Age	Heart Rate Average (bpm)	Heart Rate Expected Range (bpm)	Respiration (breaths/min)	Blood Pressure (mm Hg)
Newborn	120	70–190	30–40	73/55
Infant	120	80–160	20–40	85/37
Toddler	110	80–130	25–32	89/46
Child	95	70–115	20–26	95/57
Preteen	90	65–110	18–26	102/61
Teen	80	55–105	12–22	112/64
Adult	70–75	60–100	12–20	120/80
Well-conditioned athlete	May be 50–60	50–100	10–20	120/80

Technique and Expectetd Findings (continued)

To assess the pulse, palpate one of the patient's arterial pulse points (usually the radial artery), noting the rate, rhythm, and strength (amplitude) of the pulse. Also note the elasticity of the vessel.

Rate. Heart rates vary with age. Infants and children have a faster heart rate than adults. Gender, activity, pain, stimulants, emotional state, medications, and disease state also can affect heart rate. *The expected heart rate for an adult is 60 to 100 bpm (beats/min). Also see Table 6–2.*

Rhythm. Pulse rhythm refers to the interval between beats. Pulses are described as regular or irregular. A regular pulse occurs at evenly spaced intervals. An irregular pulse has a varied interval between beats. If a pulse is irregular in rhythm, auscultate an apical pulse for 1 full minute.

A **pulse deficit** provides an indirect evaluation of the ability of each heart contraction to eject enough blood into the peripheral circulation to create a pulse. The pulse deficit is the difference between the apical and radial pulse rates.

Pulse deficits are frequently associated with dysrhythmias. It is essential to recognize a pulse deficit, because it indicates the heart's ability to provide adequate blood flow to the body (perfusion). When cardiac contractions do not produce enough force or volume to perfuse, a difference exists between apical

Rationale/Unexpected Findings (continued)

Tachycardia is a heart rate >100 bpm in an adult. Trauma, *anemia*, blood loss, infection, fear, fever, pain, *hyperthyroidism*, shock, and anxiety can increase pulse rate as a result of increased metabolic demands or low blood volume. In patients with cardiac disease, tachycardia may indicate *congestive heart failure*, *myocardial ischemia*, or *dysrhythmia*. **Bradycardia** is a heart rate <60 bpm. Medications such as digoxin and beta-blockers decrease heart rate. *Myocardial infarction, hypothyroidism, increased intracranial pressure*, and eye surgery also can decrease heart rate. **Asystole** is the absence of a pulse. *Cardiac arrest, hypovolemia, pneumothorax, cardiac tamponade*, and *acidosis* can cause asystole.

Rhythm may vary with respirations, speeding up during inspiration and slowing with expiration. This is common in children and young adults and is called a **sinus dysrhythmia** or **sinus arrhythmia**.

Table 6-3   Scale for Measuring Pulse

Scale	Description
0	Nonpalpable or absent
1+	Weak, diminished, and barely palpable
2+	Strong
3+	Full, increased
4+	Bounding

(text continues on page 102)

and peripheral pulses. To assess for a pulse deficit, the beginner nurse and a colleague will at the same time assess the peripheral and the apical pulse rates and compare measurements (see Chapter 19). The more experienced nurse may be able to count the two simultaneously. The pulse deficit is the difference between the apical and radial pulse rates.

Amplitude. The strength of the pulse or *amplitude* indicates the volume of blood flowing through the vessel. It is described on a scale of 0–4 + (Table 6-3).

Usual strength is 2+.

Elasticity. The healthy artery feels smooth, straight, and resilient. This is known as elasticity of the pulse.

Any artery may be used to assess pulse rate, but the radial and apical are the most common sites because of their accessibility (Fig. 6-6).

Heart failure, hypovolemia, shock, and *dysrhythmias* can cause decreased pulse strength. Bounding pulses are noted with early stages of septic shock, exercise, fever, and anxiety.

Vessels become less elastic with increasing age.

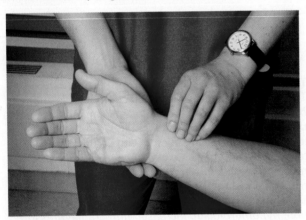

Figure 6-6 Taking a radial pulse.

In cardiac emergencies, the carotid and femoral pulses are assessed. These vessels are larger, closer to the heart, and more accurate in reflecting the heart's activity than are other pulse sites (Table 6-4).

Other sites used to assess circulation include the brachial, ulnar, popliteal, dorsalis pedis, and posterior tibial arteries (see Chapter 20).

The integrity of these peripheral pulses indicates the status of perfusion to the area distal to them.

Assessment. Use the pads of your index and middle fingers. The thumb has pulsations that may interfere with accuracy. You may use the thumb to palpate the carotid artery. Press the patient's artery gently against the underlying bone or muscle until you feel a pulsation. Do not press too hard, because you may obliterate the pulsation. If the pulse is regular in rhythm, count the beats for 30 seconds and then multiply by 2 to obtain the number of beats per minute. If the rhythm is irregular, auscultate the apical pulse for 1 full minute and assess for a pulse deficit (see Chapter 19). Assess the pulse for 1 full minute when obtaining a baseline on a patient. When counting, begin with "0" to avoid double counting beats at both beginning and end. *Right radial pulse is 60–100 beats/min, regular, and 2+/4+.*

⚠ *SAFETY ALERT 6-5*

Auscultate the carotid artery before palpating the artery. If a bruit is heard, the pulse should not be palpated and the primary care provider informed. The carotid pulse should be palpated only in the lower third of the neck to avoid stimulation of the carotid sinus. Never palpate both carotid pulses simultaneously. Palpating both together can significantly decrease cerebral blood flow and cause the patient to lose consciousness.

If a peripheral pulse is diminished or absent, the tissue below may have an inadequate blood supply. This finding indicates the need for further assessment (see Chapter 20).

⚠ *SAFETY ALERT 6-6*

Sudden changes in pulse rates or pulse rates that are >120 bpm or <55 bpm may indicate life-threatening emergencies requiring immediate attention.

⚠ *SAFETY ALERT 6-7*

Absent pulse indicates a need for immediate further assessment and intervention. In combination with pain, pallor, or paresthesia, the viability of a limb may be threatened.

Table 6-4   **Pulse Sites**

Site	Location	Use
Temporal	Superior and lateral to the eye, posterior to the ear, over the temporal bone	Routinely in infants
Carotid	Medial edge of sternocleidomastoid muscle lateral to trachea	With infants and during shock and cardiac arrest in adults
Apical	Fifth intercostal space, medial to left midclavicular line	To assess pulse deficit and auscultation of heart sounds
Brachial	Proximal to antecubital fossa, in the groove between the biceps and triceps muscles	With cardiac arrest in infants and to auscultate blood pressure (BP)
Radial	Thumb side of forearm, at wrist	Routinely to assess heart rate in adults
Ulnar	Ulnar side of forearm, at wrist	To assess ulnar circulation in hand and when performing Allen's test (see Chapter 20)
Femoral	Inferior to the inguinal ligament in the groin	To assess circulation in lower extremities and during cardiac arrest
Popliteal	Behind the knee in popliteal fossa, midline	To assess circulation in the lower extremities and to auscultate leg BP
Dorsalis pedis	Lateral to and parallel with the extensor tendon of the great toe	To assess circulation in the feet
Posterior tibial	Behind the medial malleolus	To assess circulation in the feet

Technique and Expected Findings (continued)

To assess apical pulse, place the diaphragm of a stethoscope at the left, fifth intercostal space, midclavicular line and auscultate for 1 full minute (see Chapter 19). On many patients, it may be easier to auscultate in the second or third intercostal space on the left. This avoids exposing the breast in women, and usually the first and second sounds are heard equally well. *Apical pulse is 60 to 100 bpm and regular.*

Respirations

Respiration is the act of breathing, which supplies oxygen to the body and vital organs and eliminates carbon dioxide. **Inspiration** occurs when the intercostal muscles and diaphragm contract and expand the pleural cavity, creating a negative pressure for air to flow actively into the lungs. During **expiration** the intercostal muscles and diaphragm relax, decreasing the space in the pleural cavity and passively pushing air out of the lungs.

Rate and depth of respiration change with the demands of the body. Nurses assess for factors that influence respirations. Examples include exercise, anxiety, pain, smoking, positioning, medications, neurological injury, and hemoglobin level.

Rationale/Unexpected Findings (continued)

> ### Clinical Significance 6-2
>
> Assess patients with dyspnea (difficulty breathing) in the position of greatest comfort to them. Repositioning may increase the work of breathing, which will alter the respiratory rate.

- **Exercise.** Respirations increase in rate and depth to meet additional oxygen demands.
- **Anxiety/pain.** Sympathetic nervous system stimulation increases respiratory rate and depth.
- **Smoking.** Chronic smoking alters pulmonary airways, increasing resting respiratory rate.
- **Positioning.** Slouching impedes the ability of the lungs to fully expand, while standing or sitting erect promotes full expansion.

(table continues on page 104)

- **Medications.** Narcotics, anesthesia, and sedatives decrease respiratory rate, while stimulants and bronchodilators increase it.
- **Neurological injury.** Damage to the brainstem inhibits respiratory rate and rhythm.
- **Hemoglobin levels.** Decreased levels of hemoglobin lower the oxygen-carrying capacity of the blood, which in turn increases respiratory rate to increase oxygen delivery.

⚠ *SAFETY ALERT 6-8*

Get help if the respiratory rate is <10 or >32 breaths/min. Such findings may indicate acute distress and prompt the need for a rapid response.

Observe both inspiration and expiration discretely. Most patients are not aware of their breathing. Do not make the patient aware that you are assessing respirations. Increased awareness of what the nurse is doing may alter the respiratory pattern. One way to assess respirations is to maintain the position of fingers on the radial artery as if continuing to assess the pulse, while counting respirations. *Respirations are relaxed, smooth, effortless, and silent.*

The respiratory rate is a count of each full inspiration and expiration cycle in 1 minute. Count for 30 seconds and multiply by 2 to obtain breaths/min. If anything unusual is noted, assess respiratory rate for 1 full minute. *Respiratory rates for adults < 65 years are 12 to 20 breaths/min and regular. Respiratory rates for adults 65 and over are 12 to 24 breaths/min and regular (see Chapter 30).*

Tachypnea is a rapid, persistent respiratory rate >20 breaths/min in an adult. It may occur with fever, exercise, **anemia**, or anxiety. Persistent respiratory rate <12 breaths/min is **bradypnea**. It accompanies **increased intracranial pressure**, neurological disease, and sedation. **Dyspnea** is a term used for difficult breathing. Resting respiration that is deeper and more rapid than usual is known as **hyperpnea**. **Apnea** is the absence of spontaneous respirations for more than 10 seconds.

In addition to rate, observe for the rhythm, depth, and quality of respiration. Is the rhythm regular? As with the pulse, the rhythm refers to the interval between breaths. Regular respiratory rhythm has even intervals. Note the depth of respirations. Is the patient's breath shallow, moderate, or deep? Depth of respirations is a reflection of tidal volume. Also note if the patient uses any accessory muscles while breathing. Usual respiratory effort uses the diaphragm and intercostal muscles. Note the presence of retractions. *Expected respiratory rate, rhythm, and effort are called* **eupnea**.

Hyperventilation is deep, rapid respiration, which may result from hypoxia, **anxiety**, exercise, or **metabolic acidosis**. **Hypoventilation** is shallow, slow respiration that may be related to sedation or *increased intracranial pressure*. Use of accessory muscles (eg, abdominal or neck muscles) may indicate *respiratory distress*. Also note any cyanosis, retractions, or audible sounds such as wheezing or congestion.

⚠ *SAFETY ALERT 6-9*

High-pitched crowing sounds from tracheal or laryngeal spasm, called stridor, may indicate a life-threatening emergency. Any periods of apnea, tachypnea, bradypnea, or irregular respiratory pattern are indications of underlying disease and warrant further assessment.

Accessory muscles include the sternomastoid, rectus abdominis, and internal intercostals. Retractions, or a pulling inward of the soft tissue, are noted in the supraclavicular, intercostal, and costal margin area.

Oxygen Saturation

Pulse oximetry is a noninvasive technique to measure **oxygen saturation** of arterial blood. Oxygen saturation is the percent to which hemoglobin is filled with oxygen. It does not replace measurement of arterial blood gases for assessment of aberrations, but it does indicate inadequate gas exchange.

⚠ *SAFETY ALERT 6-10*

Get a second opinion if the patient's oxygen saturation is <92%. This finding may require a rapid response. SpO₂ < 85% indicates inadequate oxygenation to the tissues and may be an emergency.

Assess capillary refill and strength of the pulse in the extremity to be used for measuring oxygen saturation. Typically, a finger is used to obtain a reading.

Nail polish may also affect the accuracy of pulse oximetry readings so it should be removed. If circulation is poor, consider using an earlobe or bridge of the nose. A newer oximeter sensor, which attaches to the forehead, has also been useful in patients with poor peripheral perfusion. When compared with arterial blood gases, the forehead sensor is more accurate than the finger probe (Schallom, Sona, et al., 2007).

Potential errors in oximetry measurements may result from hemoglobin value outside expected parameters, hypotension, hypothermia, patient movement, or skin breakdown. Falsely low measurements may be associated with cold extremities, hypothermia, and hypovolemia. Falsely high readings may be associated with carbon monoxide poisoning and anemia. *Expected measurement for pulse oximetry is SpO$_2$ from 92% to 100%. An SpO$_2$ of 85% to 89% may be acceptable for patients with certain chronic conditions such as emphysema.*

Conditions that decrease arterial blood flow may compromise the accuracy of readings, such as *peripheral vascular disease*, edema, and *hypotension*. Patients with *anemia* may have a falsely elevated pulse oximetry reading from circulating hemoglobin containing sufficient oxygen but inadequate hemoglobin to carry adequate oxygen.

Blood Pressure

Blood pressure (BP) is the measurement of the force exerted by the flow of blood against the arterial walls. The pressure in the arteries changes with contraction and relaxation of the heart. Maximum pressure is exerted on the walls of the arteries with contraction of the left ventricle at the beginning of systole. This is known as the **systolic blood pressure** (SBP). The lowest pressure, called the **diastolic blood pressure** (DBP), occurs when the left ventricle relaxes between beats.

Millimetres of mercury (mm Hg) is the standard unit for measuring BP, which is recorded as a fraction with the SBP as the numerator and the DBP as the denominator. According to the Canadian Hypertension Education Program (CHEP) (2011), the preferred BP for most adults is <140 mm Hg for SBP and <90 mm Hg for DBP; it is <130/80 mm Hg in individuals with chronic renal disease or diabetes. Variations occur naturally and are influenced by many factors, including age, gender, genetic background, weight, circadian cycle, position, exercise, emotions, stress, medications, and smoking.

- **Age.** BP increases gradually throughout childhood into the adult years.
- **Gender.** Prior to puberty, males and females show no discernable difference in BP. After puberty, males show a higher BP measurement than females, but this reverses after menopause, with BP tending to be higher in females than in males.
- **Genetic Heritage.** Individuals with African genetic background are 1.5 times and Aboriginals are 1.3 times more likely to have high BP than Caucasians (Wallace, Fullwood. et al., 2008) Using Canadian population health surveys from 1996 to 2007, it is recognized that ethnicity can determine cardiovascular risk factors. Blacks, South Asians, and Chinese demonstrated greater risk for hypertension than Caucasians (Institute for Clinical Evaluative Sciences [ICES], 2010).
- **Weight.** SBP elevates 2 to 3 mm Hg and DBP elevates 1 to 3 mm Hg for each 10 kg of extra weight (World Health Organization, 1996).

- **Circadian (diurnal) cycle.** A daily cycle of BP occurs, with it increasing late in the afternoon and decreasing in the early morning.
- **Position.** BP can drop as a patient moves from lying to sitting or standing.
- **Exercise.** Increased activity increases BP, with a return to baseline within 5 minutes of stopping activity.
- **Emotions.** Fear, anger, and pain momentarily increase BP due to stimulation of the sympathetic nervous system.
- **Stress.** Patients under continuous tension will experience elevated BP.
- **Medications.** Many medications can lower BP, including antihypertensives, diuretics, narcotics, and general anesthesia.
- **Smoking.** Smoking causes increased vasoconstriction. BP returns to baseline in approximately 15 minutes after cessation of smoking.

A series of BP measurements provides more information than a single measurement. The CHEP recommends the use of automated office blood pressure monitors These take a series of BP readings and calculate an average. The health care provider is not in the room, and "white coat syndrome" is avoided. In 2010, Hypertension Canada was formed (a combination of CHEP, the Canadian Hypertension Society, and Blood Pressure Canada). See www.hypertension.ca for CHEP information and recommendations about BP.

Elevated BP indicates a need for a series of follow-up readings to assess if BP is consistently elevated. Data from the Canada Health Measures Survey 2007–2009 provide evidence that high BP (hypertension) is about equal in men (19.7%) and women (19.0%) (Statistics Canada, 2010). Five factors contribute to the BP: (1) cardiac output, (2) peripheral vascular resistance, (3) circulating blood volume, (4) viscosity, and (5) elasticity of the vessel walls. See Table 6-5.

Traditionally and typically, nurses measure BP using a **sphygmomanometer** and stethoscope. The sphygmomanometer

Table 6-5 **Factors Contributing to Blood Pressure**

1. Cardiac Output. The more blood the heart pumps, the greater the pressure in the blood vessels. For example, blood pressure (BP) increases during exercise.

2. Peripheral Vascular Resistance. An increase in resistance in the peripheral vascular system, as happens with people who have circulatory disorders, will increase BP.

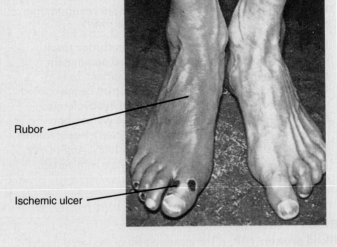

Rubor

Ischemic ulcer

3. Circulating Blood Volume. An increase in volume will increase BP. A sudden drop in BP may indicate a sudden blood loss, as with internal bleeding.

4. Viscosity. When the blood becomes thicker or more viscous (as with polycythemia), the pressure in the blood vessels will increase.

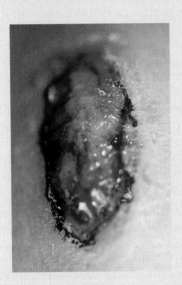

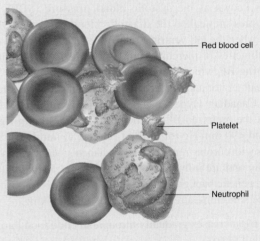

Red blood cell

Platelet

Neutrophil

Densely Packed Red Blood Cells

5. Elasticity of Vessel Walls. An increase in stiffness of the vessel walls (eg, atherosclerotic changes) will increase BP.

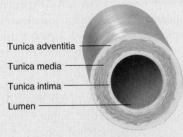

Tunica adventitia
Tunica media
Tunica intima
Lumen

Healthy coronary artery

Fatty streak

Fibrous plaque

Complicated plaque

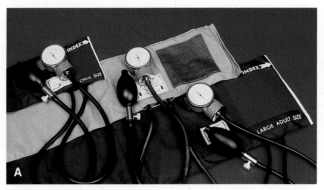 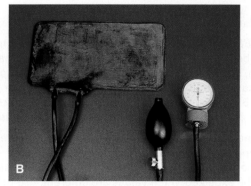

Figure 6-7 A. Three sizes of blood-pressure cuffs. **B.** Bladder is inside the cuff.

consists of an aneroid or mercury gauge and an inflatable rubber bladder in a cloth covering called the cuff. Many facilities have prohibited the use of mercury-containing devices and have changed to electronic or automatic BP cuffs. Cuffs are available in various sizes, ranging from very small for newborns to extra-large arm cuffs for adults and thigh cuffs (Fig. 6-7). It is important to choose the correct cuff size to obtain accurate readings (Table 6-6). The width of the cuff equals two thirds of the length of the patient's upper arm, 40% of the circumference of the upper arm, or is 20% more than the diameter of the upper arm (Castelein & Fetzer, 2010). If a large cuff is not available in a patient with morbid obesity, blood pressure can be measured on the forearm. The cuff can be placed midway between the elbow and the wrist (Rauen, Chulay, et al., 2008).

Table 6-6	Common Errors in Blood Pressure Measurement	
Error	**Contributing Factors**	**Nursing Action**
Falsely low reading	Noisy environment	Maintain a quiet environment during assessment.
	Too large cuff	Use a smaller cuff.
	Improper placement of earpieces of stethoscope	Place earpieces pointing forward.
	Stethoscope not directly over brachial artery	Palpate brachial artery for stethoscope placement.
	Hearing deficit	Use amplified stethoscope.
	Deflating cuff too quickly	Decrease rate of deflation.
	Deflating cuff too slowly (false high diastolic)	Increase rate of deflation.
	Failing to palpate radial artery for estimated systolic blood pressure (SBP)	Estimate SBP using palpation.
	Arm position above level of heart	Support patient's arm at the level of the heart.
Falsely high reading	Assessing blood pressure (BP) immediately after exercise	Wait 15 min after the patient has exercised to assess.
	Assessing anxious or angry patient	Wait until patient is calm.
	Cuff too small	Obtain larger cuff.
	Cuff wrapped too loosely	Wrap cuff snugly and smoothly.
	Reinflation of cuff during auscultation	Deflate cuff, wait 30 s, and reassess BP.
	Patient talking	Ask patient not to talk
	Arm position below level of heart	Support patient's arm at the level of the heart.
	Patient supporting own arm	Support the patient's arm.
	Legs crossed	Uncross legs.
Inaccurate readings	Examiner's eyes not at level of the meniscus	Maintain eye level parallel with meniscus.
	Examiner bias	Do not anticipate or predict what BP should be.
	Defective or inaccurately calibrated equipment	Calibrate equipment regularly.
Other errors	Inflation of cuff too high, causing patient pain	Estimate SBP by palpation.

Arm Blood Pressure (BP). Before assessing BP in the arm, be sure the patient is calm and relaxed and has not eaten, smoked, or exercised for 30 minutes prior to the measurement. It is best to allow the patient to rest for at least 5 minutes prior to assessing BP (Skillen & Bickley, 2010). Measure initial BP in both arms for comparison.

A difference of 10–15 mm Hg or more between the two arms may indicate arterial obstruction on the side with the lower value.

Ask the patient not to talk while the blood pressure is being taken. Measure initial BP in both arms for comparison. A variation of 5 to 10 mm Hg between arms may be expected. If the values are different, use the higher value but record both.

When patients talk, there is a significant rise in heart rate and blood pressure (Norris & Clark, 2010).

The patient may be supine or sitting. Support the bare arm at heart level, with palm upward (Adiyaman, Verhoeff, et al., 2006). When sitting, the patient's feet are flat on the floor. Crossed legs may falsely elevate BP (Adiyaman, Tosun, et al., 2007). The back should be supported.

Do not allow the patient to hold up the arm. Tension from muscle contraction can elevate SBP. Elevating the arm above the heart may result in a false low measurement (Eser, Khorshid, et al., 2006).

Assess the extremity to be used for BP assessment. Do not use an extremity with an arteriovenous shunt, on the same side as a mastectomy, trauma or burns, or with an intravenous infusion. Choose the correct size cuff.

⚠ SAFETY ALERT 6-11

Using a cuff that is too narrow causes a falsely high BP reading; using one that is too large causes a falsely low BP reading.

Estimate the Systolic Blood Pressure (SBP). Palpate the brachial artery above the antecubital fossa and medial to the biceps tendon. Center the deflated cuff approximately 2.5 cm above the antecubital crease. Line up the arrow on the cuff with the brachial artery. Tuck the Velcro end of the cuff under so that the cuff is snuggly fastened around the arm.

Estimate the SBP by palpating the radial artery and inflating the cuff until the pulsation disappears. Hold the bulb in your dominant hand. Close the valve on the bulb by turning it away from you but make sure that it will easily release. To control the bulb, it is easiest to brace your fingers against the metal of the valve. Squeeze the bulb to pump air into the bladder. Continue feeling the pulse, and identify when it disappears. Pump the cuff to 20 mm Hg above where the pulse stopped.

Estimating the SBP will prevent missing an **auscultatory gap**, a period in which there are no Korotkoff sounds during auscultation. Typically, the auscultatory gap occurs between the first and second Korotkoff sounds. Missing the gap may lead to an underestimation of the SBP or overestimation of the diastolic blood pressure (DBP) (Castelein & Fetzer, 2010).

Slowly open the valve by turning it toward you to deflate the cuff. Feel for the pulse, noting the number when the pulsation is palpable again and then quickly deflate the cuff completely. This is the estimated SBP. Wait 15 to 30 seconds before reinflating the cuff to allow trapped blood in the veins to dissipate.

Position the earpieces of the stethoscope in your ears and place the diaphragm or bell of the stethoscope over the brachial artery, using a light touch (Fig. 6-8A). Position yourself so that you can avoid bumping the tubing and can easily see the gauge. Note that you will not hear the tapping of the pulse until the cuff is inflated.

The bell is designed to pick up low-pitched sounds, such as the turbulent blood flow caused by the BP cuff partially occluding the brachial artery. Canadian Hypertension Education Program (CHEP) suggests that either the bell or diaphragm may be used.

Inflating the BP cuff around the extremity alters the flow of blood through the artery, which generates Korotkoff sounds (Fig. 6-8B). The sounds are audible with a stethoscope at a pulse site distal to the cuff.

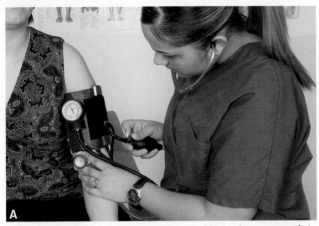
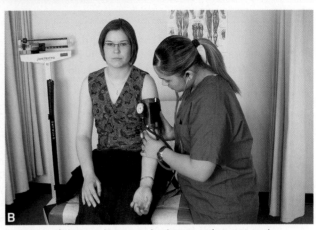

Figure 6-8 A. Arm blood pressure. Note placement of the earpieces of the stethoscope in the nurse's ears as she auscultates over the brachial artery. **B.** Inflating the BP cuff around the arm alters arterial blood flow.

As pressure against the artery wall decreases from completely occluded blood flow to free flow, nurses can auscultate five distinct sounds (Table 6-7). You will hear sounds only during the period of partial occlusion and not at the top or bottom.

Quickly inflate the cuff to 30 mm Hg above the estimated SBP. Then deflate the cuff slowly, approximately 2 mm Hg/heart beat, while listening for pulse sounds (Korotkoff sounds). Note the number when you hear the first Korotkoff sound (Korotkoff I), which coincides with the patient's SBP. Be aware of the tendency to round to zero and make sure to read the gauge accurately. Continue deflating the cuff, noting the point of the last pulse sound (Korotkoff IV) and when it disappears (Korotkoff V). Korotkoff V is used to define DPB (see Table 6-7).

Record BP in even numbers as a fraction, with SBP as the numerator and DBP as the denominator. Also record the patient's position, arm used, and cuff size if different from the standard cuff.

Slow or frequent cuff inflations can cause venous congestion. Be sure to deflate the cuff completely after each measurement and wait at least 2 minutes between measurements.

The **pulse pressure** is the difference between the SBP and the DBP and reflects the stroke volume. *Pulse pressure is approximately 40 mm Hg.* The **mean arterial pressure** is calculated by adding one third of the SBP and two thirds of the DBP. A mean pressure of 60 mm Hg is needed to perfuse the vital organs.

Guidelines from CHEP set the standards for diagnosis of high BP. See Table 6-10 at the end of this chapter. **Hypertension** is not diagnosed on one BP reading alone, but on an average of two or more readings taken on subsequent visits. Based on survey data from 2007 to 2009, 19% of Canadians from age 20 to 79 years have hypertension (Statistics Canada, 2010). Pre-hypertension is the diagnosis of SBP 120 to 139 mm Hg or DBP 80 to 89 mm Hg (Statistics Canada, 2010). **Hypotension** is SBP < 90 mm Hg (Castelein & Fetzer, 2010). In most adults, low BP indicates illness.

⚠ *SAFETY ALERT 6-12*

Any sudden change in BP may be an emergency. SBP < 90 or 30 mm Hg below the patient's baseline needs immediate attention. Sudden drop in BP can signify blood loss or a cardiovascular, respiratory, neurological, or metabolic disorder. Sudden, severe rise in BP (above 200/120 mm Hg) is a life-threatening hypertensive crisis.

Decreased elasticity of the arterial blood vessel walls, as well as increased intracranial pressure, can cause the difference between SBP and DBP to increase. This is called a *widened pulse pressure*. Patients with *hypovolemia, shock*, or *heart failure* may exhibit a narrowed pulse pressure. DBP is weighted more heavily because two thirds of the cardiac cycle is spent in diastole.

(text continues on page 110)

Table 6-7	Korotkoff Sounds	
Phase	Description	Illustration
I	Characterized by the first appearance of faint but clear tapping sounds that gradually increase in intensity; the first tapping sound is the systolic pressure	
II	Characterized by muffled or swishing sounds; these sounds may temporarily disappear, especially in people with hypertension; the disappearance of the sound during the latter part of phase I and during phase II is called the *auscultatory gap* and may cover a range of as much as 40 mm Hg; failing to recognize this gap may cause serious errors of underestimating systolic pressure or overestimating diastolic pressure	
III	Characterized by distinct, loud sounds as the blood flows relatively freely through an increasingly open artery	
IV	Characterized by a distinct, abrupt, muffling sound with a soft, blowing quality; in adults, onset of this phase is considered the first diastolic sound	
V	The last sound heard before a period of continuous silence; the pressure at which the last sound is heard is the second diastolic measurement	

Adapted from Taylor, C., Lillis, C., et al. (2011). *Fundamentals of nursing: The art and science of nursing care* (7th ed.). Philadelphia, PA: Wolters Kluwer Health/Lippincott Williams & Wilkins.

Technique and Expected Findings (continued)

Thigh Blood Pressure. Compare a thigh BP with an arm BP if the arm BP is extremely high, particularly in young adults and adolescents, to assess for coarctation of the aorta. Position the patient prone if possible. Place a large cuff around the lower third of the thigh, centered over the popliteal artery. Proceed as directed for the brachial artery (Fig. 6-9). *The thigh SBP is 10 to 40 mm Hg higher than the arm SBP, while the DBPs are approximately the same in both sites.*

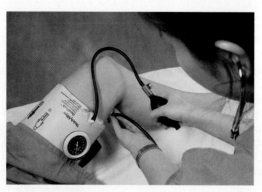

Figure 6-9 Thigh blood pressure.

Rationale/Unexpected Findings (continued)

A thigh or calf may also be used if the patient's arms are unavailable, such as in those with bilateral burns or IVs. *Coarctation of the aorta* (congenital narrowing of the aorta) will produce high arm BP and lower thigh BP as a result of restricted blood supply below the narrowing.

Orthostatic (Postural) Vital Signs. These are measured in patients to assess for a drop in BP and change in heart rate with position changes. When a healthy patient changes position, the peripheral blood vessels in the extremities constrict and the heart rate increases to maintain adequate BP for perfusion to the heart and brain. Orthostatic changes may indicate blood volume depletion. Some medications can have a side effect of orthostatic hypotension. Additionally, conditions that cause the arterial system to become less responsive, such as immobility or spinal cord injury, can cause orthostatic changes.

Assess BP and heart rate with the patient supine, sitting, and then standing. The patient should rest supine for at least 2 minutes prior to the assessment of the baseline reading. Repeat measurements with the patient sitting and standing, waiting 1 to 2 minutes after each position change to assess the readings (Lance, Link, et al., 2000). *A drop in SBP of <15 mm Hg may occur and is considered acceptable.*

Drop in SBP of 15 mm Hg or greater, drop in DBP of 10 mm Hg or greater, or increased heart rate indicates **orthostatic hypotension** and possibly intravascular volume depletion (Calkins & Zipes, 2007). Patients with orthostatic hypotension may exhibit dizziness, lightheadedness, or syncope. *Hypovolemia*, certain medications, and prolonged bed rest may cause orthostatic hypotension. Autonomic dysregulation, as in *Parkinson's disease*, interferes with the sympathetic response and may cause orthostasis.

⚠ *SAFETY ALERT 6-13*
Patients with orthostatic hypotension are at risk for falling from dizziness, lightheadedness, and syncope.

Documentation of Expected Findings

Parameters: Temperature and route; pulse rate, rhythm, strength, and site; respiratory rate, rhythm, quality, and depth; pulse oximetry; and BP are recorded on the vital sign flow sheet or other forms per agency policy. Measurements taken after administration of medications or other therapies are documented in the nurse's notes. Strength of peripheral pulses can be documented either as a chart or diagram. When there is a difference >10 mm Hg between the distinct muffling of Korotkoff IV and the disappearance of sound (Korotkoff V), record both readings (eg, 138/92/72) (Skillen & Bickley, 2010). Report unexpected findings to the primary care provider.
Expected Findings: T 37°C orally. R radial P 68 bpm, regular, elastic, 2+/4+. R—14 breaths/min, regular, no use of accessory muscles, no retractions. *SpO₂—98%. BP 118/64, right arm (supine).*

Risk Assessment and Health Promotion

Nurses teach patients to consistently weigh themselves at the same time of the day, wearing clothing of similar weight. They educate patients about risk factors for hypothermia (ie, frostbite; fatigue; malnutrition; hypoxemia; cold, wet clothing; alcohol intoxication) and hyperthermia (ie, exercising in poorly ventilated areas and hot humid climate, sudden exposures to hot climates, tight-fitting clothing in hot environments, and poor fluid intake before, during, and after exercise).

Patients taking cardiac medications, undergoing cardiac rehabilitation, or starting a new exercise regimen should learn how to take their own pulse rates. Monitoring carotid pulse rate is the most common technique taught to patients. It is important to teach patients to avoid palpating over the carotid sinus which is level with the superior border of the thyroid cartilage. Patients undergoing surgery and those with decreased ventilation are taught coughing and deep-breathing exercises.

The nurse educates patients about the risks of hypertension. Risk factors include obesity, cigarette smoking, heavy alcohol consumption, prolonged stress, high cholesterol and triglyceride levels, family history, and renal disease. Primary prevention includes lifestyle modifications such as weight loss, regular exercise, dietary modifications, cessation of smoking, reduction of stress, and reduction of saturated fats and sodium in diet.

Every interaction with a patient is a teaching opportunity. Even patients who are normotensive and have a body weight within recommended limits using the BMI can learn how to maintain a healthy body. According to the Heart and Stroke Foundation of Canada (2011a,b), patients can be taught the following recommendations to reduce risk factors for heart disease:

• If more than 10% above ideal body weight, lose weight.
• Limit alcohol to 1 to 2 drinks/d (weekly maximum 9 for women, 14 for men).
• Be physically active, at least 30 min/d, a majority of days in the week.
• Make time every day to relax.

The nurse has just finished conducting a physical examination of Mr. Odynak, the 55-year-old man admitted to the hospital with a dysrhythmia. Both expected and unexpected findings are documented, including the absence of positive findings. Review the following data that were collected during the general survey and vital signs. Begin to think about how the data cluster together and what additional data the nurse might want to collect while thinking critically about Mr. Odynak's health issues.

Inspection: 55-year-old man of East Ukrainian background without obvious deformities appears older than stated age; facial features and body structure symmetrical; wearing hospital gown, clean and groomed. Skin even tone, pink, without lesions. Physical and sexual development appropriate for age and gender. Cooperative and interacts pleasantly. Facial expression relaxed; maintains eye contact. A&O × 3; responds appropriately to questions. Speech is clear and articulate. Sitting upright, posture erect, arms relaxed at the side. Gait steady, well-balanced. Denies any discomfort. No signs of distress. T 36.8°C oral, R 14 breaths/min, regular, no use of accessory muscles, oxygen saturation 96%. Height 162 cm, weight 65 kg, body mass index (BMI) 26.

Palpation: Apical pulse 88 and irregular. Pulse deficit of 2 noted.

Auscultation: Blood pressure 142/66 mm Hg right arm (sitting).

- Limit sodium intake (see Chapter 8)
- Quit smoking.
- Use Canada's Food Guide.
- Reduce fat intake to 20 to 35% of calories in a day; limit saturated fat.

Vital Signs Monitor

Many agencies use a monitor for all vital signs (Fig. 6-10). This portable device usually is on a stand that nurses can wheel from one room to another. It is plugged in when not in use to charge the battery. When taking vital signs with this machine, first unplug it and roll it next to the patient. Attach the cuff. In some agencies, each patient has his or her own cuff; in others, patients share the cuff. Place the cuff on the patient's arm and press the inflate button. After the display, remove the cuff. The monitor will display the pulse sensed during the BP or SpO₂ reading. Attach the finger clip for the SpO₂. Note the reading that the monitor displays. Load the probe cover on the thermometer. Place the thermometer for the appropriate mode. Note the reading after it is displayed. Eject the probe cover into the wastebasket, using routine practices. Wash your hands and disinfect the machine according to agency precautions before allowing it to come into contact with the next patient.

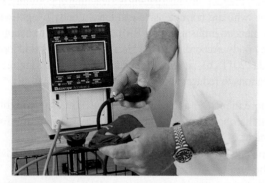

Figure 6-10 Vital signs monitoring device.

> ⚠️ *SAFETY ALERT 6-14*
>
> *When using automatic devices for serial readings, check the patient's cuffed limb frequently to ensure sufficient perfusion to areas distal to the cuff.*

Doppler Technique

In some cases, pulse and BP are difficult to auscultate or palpate, such as in patients with shock or poor peripheral circulation. Health care providers use a device called a *Doppler* in this case. This handheld transducer senses and amplifies changes in sound frequency. A whooshing sound similar to the Korotkoff sounds is audible. The procedure for the assessment of the pulse using Doppler is as follows:

- Apply gel that is specifically for the Doppler to the transducer probe.
- Turn the Doppler on.
- Adjust the volume.
- Touch the probe lightly to the skin at the expected pulse site.
- Hold the probe perpendicular to the skin and move it slowly where you anticipate that the pulse should be until it is located.
- Wipe off the gel and mark the location of the loudest sound with indelible ink.
- Attempt to palpate the pulse in this location.

If you are taking a patient's BP by Doppler, put on the cuff first. Once the pulse is located by Doppler, inflate the cuff until the sounds go away. Pump up the cuff another 20 to 30 mm Hg. Slowly deflate the cuff and note the reading for the SBP when the whooshing sounds return. Only the systolic pressure is recorded by documenting 88/Doppler.

🔍 Lifespan Variations

Infants, young children, and older adults are more sensitive to environmental temperature than younger adults. Infants and young children have a wider range of expected temperature related to less efficient mechanisms of heat control. Thermo-regulation in older adults is less efficient; they have a lower temperature than younger adults, with an average temperature of 36.2°C (97.2°F) (Clark & Baldwin, 2004). They are less likely to mount a fever with the immune response and are more likely to develop hypothermia. Temperature is a less valid indication of infection or inflammation in older adults.

Infants and Children

Although a physical examination consists of painless procedures, it can be scary to children. The use of probes in ears and mouths, a tight BP cuff, and a cold stethoscope can be intimidating. In most cases, allowing the parent of a young child to remain during the assessment is helpful. Young children may feel more secure with their parents present. If appropriate, ask parents to help. Older children and adolescents may prefer not to have parents present. Often it is helpful to allow the child to touch the equipment.

Older Adults

Older adults also have some special considerations related to the general survey and vital signs. The nurse does not rush the patient and allows enough time for him or her to ask or respond to questions. Do not assume that a patient has a deficit. For example, some but not all elderly patients have a decline in vision or hearing.

Technique and Expected Findings	Rationale/Unexpected Findings
Infants and Children	Note the facial expression and appearance, which may give clues to pain, fear, happiness, or acute illness.
General Survey. As with adults, the general survey begins when the nurse first encounters the child and continues throughout the interaction. What do you see, hear, or smell? Does the child appear well or ill? Never discount your first impression.	
Parent–Child Interaction. Observe the interaction between parent and child. Do they mutually respond? Are they warm and affectionate? Remember that children tend to regress developmentally with illness.	⚠ *SAFETY ALERT 6-15* *Indications of child abuse include the child avoiding eye contact, lack of separation anxiety when appropriate for age, and lack of physical or emotional care. See Chapter 12.*
Physical Appearance. Observe the same basic components as with an adult, while considering the child's age and developmental stage.	Physical appearance includes an overall impression of the child's state of nutrition, including overweight and wasting.
Note hygiene. Are clothes clean? Do they fit appropriately? Are fingernails, hair, and teeth well groomed? Observations provide clues to possible neglect, inadequate finances, or lack of knowledge.	These observations provide clues of neglect, inadequate finances, unstable housing, or lack of knowledge.
Behaviour. Observe the child's response to stimuli and level of alertness. Include personality, level of activity, and interaction with others (especially the primary caregivers) in the assessment.	
Mobility. Observe position, posture, and body movement. *A newborn's posture is flexed, with arms and legs tucked in. Toddlers may exhibit slight lordosis (exaggerated curve in the lower back). Preschoolers appear more erect and slender than toddlers. School-age children and adolescents have upright, straight, and well-balanced posture.*	Children with *hearing* or *vision loss* may have a characteristic tilt of the head to see or hear better. Children with low self-esteem may slump.
Anthropometric Measurements. Measurements of physical growth in children are essential to assess health status. They include height (length), weight, head circumference, and chest circumference. Values are plotted on growth charts and compared to same-age children.	
Length/Height. The term "length" is used when the child is measured in the supine position. Until approximately age 2 years, length should be measured. Because of the infant's typically flexed position, it is important to fully extend the body by holding the head midline, grasping	

(text continues on page 114)

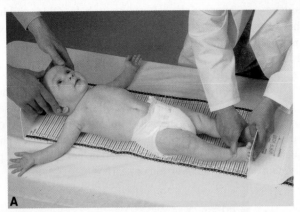
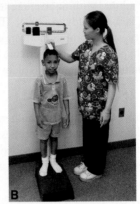

Figure 6-11 **A.** Measuring length of an infant. **B.** Measuring height of a school-age child.

the knees together, and gently pushing down on the knees to extend the legs until they are flat on the table. An assistant or the parent can hold the head while you extend the legs (Fig. 6-11A).

For children older than 2 years, have them stand against the height bar as with adults. Feet are together and heels touch the wall. Encourage the child to stand up straight, looking forward without tilting the head (Fig. 6-11B).

Weight. To weigh an infant, use a platform-style scale. Be careful to watch that the infant does not fall. Nurses may use upright scales starting with children 2 to 3 years old. Respect modesty by letting older children continue to wear lightweight clothing. See Figure 6-12.

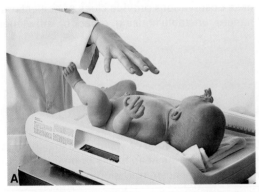

Figure 6-12 **A.** Weighing an infant. **B.** Weighing a toddler sitting up on the scale.

Head Circumference. Head circumference is measured at birth and at each well-child visit up to 2 to 3 years old. Place a tape measure around the head, encircling the frontal and occipital bones, measuring the largest point across the skull, not including the ears. Plot and compare measurements against expected findings on a standardized growth chart for the age of the infant. A series of measurements is more informative than a single measurement (Fig. 6-13).

Head circumference may be increased with *hydrocephalus*.

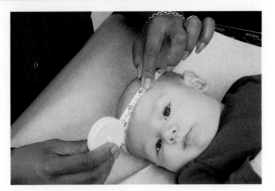

Figure 6-13 Measuring a newborn's head circumference.

Chest Circumference. Measurement of chest circumference is valuable as a comparison to the head circumference, but not by itself. At birth, the newborn's head is approximately 2 cm larger than the chest circumference. The chest grows faster than the cranium, and between 6 months and 2 years, the chest and head circumferences are equal. After 2 years, the chest circumference is greater than that of the head.

Vital Signs. When assessing vital signs in infants, obtain respiratory and pulse rates first. Taking a temperature, especially rectal, may cause a child to cry and alter the respiratory and pulse rates. Therefore, assess respiratory rate first, then pulse, and the temperature last (Kyle, 2008). Explain the procedure to school-age children and allow them to handle the equipment to promote cooperation. The approach for adolescents is similar to that for adults.

Respirations. Count the respiratory rate in the same manner as for adults, but with an infant, watch the abdomen for respiratory movement. Infant respiration is more diaphragmatic than thoracic in nature. Because infants have varying patterns of respirations, assess respiratory rate for 1 full minute. Infants and young children have a respiratory rate more rapid than that of adults (see Table 6-2).

Pulse. For infants and toddlers younger than 2 years, nurses assess the apical pulse because the radial pulse is difficult to palpate accurately. Assess the apical pulse at the point of maximum intensity (PMI), which for infants is located at the third to fourth intercostal space just above and lateral to the nipple. The PMI moves to a more medial and slightly lower area (fourth or fifth intercostal space, left midclavicular line) at approximately 7 years. In children older than 2 years, use a radial pulse for assessment.

Children often have a sinus dysrhythmia, an irregular heartbeat that increases with inspiration and decreases with expiration. Therefore, assess the pulse for 1 full minute to note any irregularities.

Pulse Oximetry. With infants, the great toe is the recommended site for placement of the pulse-oximetry probe. Cover the patient's foot with a sock to help secure the probe. For an older child, the index finger is the recommended placement.

⚠ *SAFETY ALERT 6-16*
Periods of apnea lasting 10 to 15 seconds are common for infants. Apnea longer than 15 seconds is cause for concern.

Heart rates in infants and children fluctuate more in response to activity, emotions, and illness than do those of adults.

(text continues on page 116)

Tympanic Temperature. The tympanic thermometer is useful with young children who tend to squirm when being restrained for rectal temperature and are not old enough to cooperate with an oral temperature. Measurement with a tympanic thermometer is quick and usually completed before the child is even aware of it. As noted earlier, research studies have not shown conclusively the accuracy of tympanic thermometers (Farnell, Maxwell, et al., 2005).

Inguinal Temperature. The inguinal route is safer than the rectal route. Because of the rich supply of blood vessels in the inguinal area and the ability to form a tight seal around the thermometer, results are closer to the core temperature than the axillary route.

To assess the inguinal temperature, abduct (open) the infant's leg and palpate for the femoral pulse. Place the tip of the thermometer lateral to the pulse site and adduct (close) the leg to create a seal.

Axillary Temperature. Axillary temperature assessments are safer than those of rectal temperatures, but accuracy in children has been questioned. Axillary temperature is commonly assessed in healthy newborns to avoid the risk of perforating the rectum with the thermometer. When the axillary route is used, place the thermometer well into the axilla and hold the child's arm close to the body.

Oral Temperature. Oral temperatures are contraindicated in children younger than 4 years, sometimes even older. Oral thermometers should be used only when a child can keep the mouth closed around and not bite the thermometer. When possible, use an electronic thermometer because it is less likely to break and yields faster readings.

Rectal Temperature. Rectal temperature is used in infants and other children when other routes are not practical. Position the child supine or sidelying with knees flexed. Insert the lubricated thermometer into the rectum no further than 2.5 cm and hold the thermometer securely to prevent rectal perforation.

⚠ *SAFETY ALERT 6-17*
Because of the risk of trauma to the rectal mucosa, rectal thermometers are contraindicated in newborns and infants.

Temporal Temperature. Like the tympanic method, temporal temperature assessment is quick and noninvasive. Allow the child to handle the equipment to decrease fear.

Blood Pressure. BP is assessed annually in healthy children 3 years or older; it is not part of routine assessment for children younger than 3 years. Although BP measurement is generally the same for children as for adults, accurate assessment of BP in children requires some modifications. Because unfamiliar procedures can easily upset children, explain to them what will occur. Tell them what the cuff will feel like. Let them play with the equipment.

If BP is above the 90th percentile, measurement should be repeated on two other occasions to assess for prehypertension (National Institute of Health, 2007).

Cuff width must cover two thirds of the upper arm, and the bladder must encompass the whole arm. Auscultate using a pediatric end piece on the stethoscope.

Crying may elevate BP; therefore, if possible, allow a crying child to relax for 5 to 10 minutes prior to assessing BP.

Children younger than 3 years have very small arms, making BP assessment difficult. Electronic BP devices are frequently used in this age group. Refer to Box 6-3 for average systolic blood pressures (SBPs) in children.

BOX 6-3 QUICK FORMULA (USING AUSCULTATION) FOR AVERAGE BLOOD PRESSURE IN CHILDREN

Systolic Blood Pressure	Diastolic Blood Pressure
1–7 years: Age in years +90	1–5 years: 56
8–18 years: (2 × age in years) +83	6–18 years: Age in years +52

Older Adults

General Survey. By the 8th or 9th decade, physical appearance changes, with sharper body contours and more angular facial features. Posture tends to have a general flexion, and gait tends to have a wider base of support to compensate for diminished balance. Steps tend to be shorter and uneven. Patients may need to use the arms to help aid in balance. Observe for expected changes of aging. Assess for any decreasing abilities to function and care for self. Functional assessment is the sixth vital sign in older adults. Note any changes in mental status.

Compromised hygiene and inappropriate dress may indicate decreased functional ability, medication reactions, infection, dehydration, malnutrition, or neglect/abuse by a caregiver. Inappropriate affect, inattentiveness, impaired memory, and inability to perform activities of daily living may indicate *dementia* (eg, *Alzheimer's disease*). Changes in mental status may be from poor nutrition, medications, dehydration, underlying infection, or hypoxia.

Height and Weight. People in their 80s and 90s may be shorter than they were in their 70s as a result of thinning of the vertebral discs and postural changes (eg, kyphosis) causing the spinal column to shorten. The proportions of the aging person tend to look different, because the long bones do not shorten but the trunk does. The aging person tends to lose body weight during the 8th and 9th decades from muscle shrinkage and fat distribution changes. Subcutaneous fat is lost from the face and periphery, even with adequate nutrition.

Kyphosis is an exaggerated posterior curvature of the thoracic spine associated with aging.

Vital Signs

Temperature. The temperature of older adults is at the lower end of the acceptable range. Because of changes in the body's temperature regulatory mechanism and decreased subcutaneous fat, aging adults are less likely to develop fevers but more likely to succumb to hypothermia. *Mean body temperature for the older adult is 36°C to 36.8°C (96.9°F–98.3°F).*

Temperatures accepted for younger adults may constitute fever in older adults.

Pulse. Aging adults have a range between 60 and 100 bpm. Variation in rhythm may develop. The radial artery may stiffen from peripheral vascular disease. A rigid artery does not indicate vascular disease elsewhere in the body.

The pulse rate of older adults takes longer to rise to meet sudden increases in demand; the pulse rate takes longer to return to resting state; and it tends to be lower than that of younger adults. Heart sounds may be more difficult to auscultate and PMI more difficult to palpate.

Respirations. Aging causes rigidity of the costal cartilage, decreasing chest expansion and vital capacity. Decreased vital capacity and inspiratory volume can cause respirations to be shallower and more rapid than that of younger adults, with a respiratory rate of 16 to 24 breaths/min. Decreased efficiency of respiratory muscles results in breathlessness at lower activity levels.

(text continues on page 118)

Technique and Expected Findings (continued)	Rationale/Unexpected Findings (continued)
Pulse Oximetry. Placement of the pulse oximetry probe can present a challenge in older adults. Peripheral vascular disease, decreased carbon dioxide levels, cold-induced vasoconstriction, and anemia may complicate assessment of oxygen saturation on the fingers. Consider using the ear lobe as the placement site. Sensors designed for the forehead or bridge of nose may be indicated.	
Blood Pressure. Special attention to correct cuff size is necessary when assessing BP in older adults because of loss of upper arm mass, obesity, and decreased arm size. BP tends to increase from atherosclerosis.	In older people, both SBP and DBP increase, but SBP more so, leading to a widened pulse pressure (Anderson, Hunter, et al., 2010). Elevated BP in older adults is not an expected aspect of aging. Remind older adults to change positions slowly to avoid orthostatic hypotension that increases the risk for falling.

Cultural Variations

During the general survey of every patient, note any ethnic influences on dress, grooming, speech, and nonverbal communication. Some common cultural differences may include the following:

- Patients with a Latino background may expect nurses to show warmth to them and their family members; interactions should not be strictly business. A nurse is attentive, takes some time, shows respect, and, if possible, communicates in Spanish.
- In many Asian cultures, the spoken and written order of the name is last name, then first name with no comma. This often creates confusion in the patient health record. Care must be taken to use a consistent format.
- Southeast Asian patients use "krun" to describe a wide range of symptoms including "feeling ill," "feeling hot and cold," or "having a warm body." It may be translated as a fever, although a fever may not be present.
- Patients from Arab cultures may not disclose personal or sexual information.
- Some patients (eg, from Muslim communities) apply skin decorations with henna. Black henna causes major errors in oxygen saturation readings, while red henna does not. Use of ear oximetry is recommended if patients have black henna applied to their fingertips (Ethnomed, 2008).

Height varies little among groups with different genetic backgrounds compared to other anthropometric measures. Height results from genetics, nutrition, and stressors. Mean height varies by gender. In men, Caucasians are tallest, followed by individuals with African genetic backgrounds, and then Latinos (Ogden, Carroll, et al., 2007). Women of African descent are tallest, followed by Caucasian women, and then Latino women. Height is generally not a health concern unless there is more than a 20% variance such as in gigantism or dwarfism (see Table 6-9 at the end of the chapter).

Weight varies considerably among individuals with different genetic heritage. In the past 25 years in Canada, a striking increase has occurred in obesity and now two out of three adults are obese or overweight. With the exception of preschool children, boys and girls across all age groups are now presenting with remarkably increased rates of obesity. Contributing factors have been dietary patterns, portion sizes, less physically demanding occupations, increased use of transportation instead of walking, and more passive leisure activities. Obesity contributes to heart disease, stroke, and type 2 diabetes (this affects 1.8 million Canadians) (Health Canada, 2006). Obesity has a five-fold increase in Blacks and Caucasians compared to Chinese Canadians. Black women have a greater prevalence of obesity than Black men. Approximately two thirds of the Caucasians, South Asians, Chinese, and Blacks in the study had <15 minutes of physical activity each day (ICES, 2010). Reduction in obesity is a focus of Canada's major health organizations and agencies.

Evidence-Informed Critical Thinking

Several nursing diagnoses can be addressed under vital sign assessment. Many are covered in the appropriate body systems chapters of this book, such as respiratory diagnoses in Chapter 18 "Thorax and Lung Assessment." Table 6-8 provides examples of nursing diagnoses commonly seen in relation to vital signs and general survey. These diagnoses are based on vital sign measurements and supporting data. They are used to label the health issues and plan care that is individualized to the patient.

Nurses learn the techniques for assessment of the general survey and vital signs, but use critical thinking to individualize assessments of the patient. The nurse collects these data for an initial database, monitors trends over time, and identifies patterns, such as a daily temperature spike in the late afternoon. Additionally, the nurse focuses the assessment on the patient situation and current symptoms/signs.

Table 6-8	Common Nursing Diagnoses Related to Vital Signs		
Diagnosis and Related Factors	**Point of Differentiation**	**Assessment Characteristics**	**Nursing Interventions**
Hypothermia related to prolonged exposure to cold climate	Core temperature < 95°F (35°C)	Tachycardia, peripheral vasoconstriction	Provide warming measures, including warming blankets and warmed IV fluids.*
Impaired gas exchange related to immobility	Changes in capillary refill and respiratory rate, rhythm, and effort	Decreased oxygen saturation, fatigue, confusion, tachypnea, tachycardia, and use of accessory muscles for breathing	Administer oxygen.* Teach coughing and deep breathing exercises. Instruct patient in use of incentive spirometer.

*Collaborative intervention.

Analyzing Findings

Consider the case of Mr. Boris Odynak, the 55-year-old man admitted to the hospital with a cardiac dysrhythmia. The initial collection of subjective and objective data is complete, and Mr. Odynak is stable. The plan of care includes patient teaching and planning for discharge tomorrow. Unfortunately, Mr. Odynak develops a new onset of symptoms. The following nursing note illustrates how the nurse focuses the assessment, analyzes subjective and objective data, and develops nursing interventions when he is having symptoms.

Subjective: "Every once in a while I can feel my heart racing. It doesn't happen very often but it feels like my heart's going to jump out of my chest. It's doing it right now." States no chest pain or pressure.

Objective: Skin colour even and pink. Sitting upright, holding chest. Tense facial expression, maintains appropriate eye contact. Talking to his wife in complete sentences. Right radial pulse 122 and irregular, strength 2+/4+, R 22 and regular, blood pressure (BP) 136/66 mm Hg right arm (sitting), and oxygen saturation 96%. Apical pulse 126 and irregular.

Analysis: Subjective feeling of heart racing may be related to new onset of cardiac dysrhythmia. Pulse deficit of 4 bpm indicates inadequate perfusion of some apical beats. BP lower than usual measured value may be related to decreased cardiac output with increased heart rate.

Plan: Contact primary care provider to inform of new onset of fast and irregular apical pulse. Reassess pulse and BP in 5 minutes. Take apical pulse for 1 full minute and assess for a pulse deficit. Stay with patient and his wife and assure them that the best care will be provided. Use touch and therapeutic communication to reduce anxiety. Primary care provider present and ordered stat 12-lead electrocardiogram that indicated atrial fibrillation with a rate of 126. Consult with provider on collaborative treatment.

Critical Thinking Challenge

- How is this focused assessment different from the previous documentation?
- Critique the objective data that the nurse documented. What patterns connect the general survey and vital signs with the focused findings?
- How are the nursing and medical issues similar or different?

The nurse observes information from the general survey upon each encounter. A complete set of vital signs are taken at the beginning of each shift to establish a baseline. Additionally, the nurse assesses pulse and blood pressure (BP) prior to administration of the medications to evaluate effectiveness and side effects, and holds the medications if the pulse or BP is too low. The nurse continually collects assessment data and incorporates it into the care. An accurate and complete general survey and vital signs are the foundation for further assessment and interventions.

You have been studying Mr. Odynak, who was initially admitted to the ICU following an episode of tachycardia and dizziness. He was started on antiarrhythmic medication, stabilized, and transferred to the cardiology unit. He developed a new onset of tachycardia and was reassessed by the nurse. The nurse obtained assistance and Mr. Odynak was successfully treated. He will need ongoing assessments related to his conditions including hypertension and dysrhythmia.

Using the previous steps of clinical reasoning, organizing, and prioritizing, consider all the case study findings woven throughout this chapter. When answering the following questions, begin drawing conclusions and see how the pieces of assessment must work together to create an environment for personalized, appropriate, and accurate care.

- Is Mr. Odynak's condition stable, urgent, or an emergency? (Analysis)
- What immediate health-promotion and teaching needs are evident? (Synthesis)
- What are the relationships among his pulse, respirations, and BP? (Knowledge)
- How will the general survey and vital signs differ from the focused assessment? (Comprehension)
- How did the nurse demonstrate application when Mr Odynak developed tachycardia? (Application)
- How will the nurse evaluate the effectiveness of using touch and therapeutic communication with Mr Odynak? (Evaluation)

Key Points

- The general survey begins with the first moments of the patient encounter, progresses through the history and physical examination, and continues with each subsequent interaction.
- Extreme anxiety, acute distress, pallor, cyanosis, changes in mental status, and changes in vital signs may indicate the need for assistance and a rapid response.
- The general survey includes overall appearance, hygiene and dress, skin colour, body structure and development, behaviour, facial expression, level of consciousness, speech, mobility, posture, range of motion, and gait.
- Anthropometric measurements include height and weight.
- Vital signs reflect patient health status, cardiopulmonary function, and overall function of the body.
- The nurse assesses the appropriate route of temperature including oral, axillary, tympanic, temporal artery, and rectal.
- The pulse is assessed for rate, rhythm, amplitude, and elasticity.
- Smoking, positioning, medication, neurological injury, and hemoglobin levels affect the respiratory rate.
- An oxygen saturation level <92% indicates inadequate oxygenation to the tissues.
- Age, gender, ethnicity, weight, circadian cycle, position, exercise, emotions, stress, medications, and smoking affect the BP.
- The brachial artery is commonly used to measure the BP.
- Width of the cuff size equals two thirds of the length of the upper arm, 40% of the circumference of the upper arm, or is 20% greater than the diameter of the upper arm.
- Postural vital signs are taken sitting, lying, and standing; they indicate intravascular volume depletion.
- A vital signs monitor is commonly used in the hospital setting.
- The Doppler is used if the pulse and BP are difficult to palpate or auscultate.
- In children add the length, head circumference, and variations in vital signs to the physical assessment.
- Vital signs alterations occurring in older adults result from physiological changes in the body.
- Height and weight variations are related to genetic background, nutrition, and activity.

Review Questions

1. Mr. Sean O'Neal has come to the ambulatory clinic for a well-patient visit. When assessing his vital signs, the nurse palpates an irregular heart rate. The nurse must then auscultate for a full minute at the apical pulse site. Locate the apical pulse on the image below.

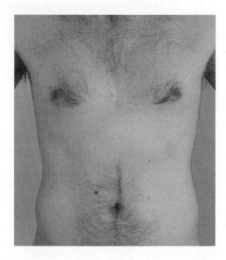

2. What are the four characteristics of a pulse?

3. An unconscious 20-year-old woman arrives at the emergency room after drinking large quantities of alcohol. Her vital signs are T 36.8°C, temporal; P 58 and regular; R 9; blood pressure (BP) 100/64 right arm (supine). What conclusion would the nurse make about this patient's respiratory status?
A. The patient is experiencing apnea.
B. The patient is experiencing bradycardia.
C. The patient is experiencing bradypnea.
D. The patient's respiratory status is within expected limits.

4. The patient's radial pulse is weak and thready. The nurse would document the finding as
A. 3+/ 4+
B. 2+/ 4+
C. 1+ /4+
D. Radial pulse absent

5. The nurse is preparing to assess the vital signs of a 62-year-old woman following hip surgery. When the nurse arrives, the patient is sitting in her chair having just finished breakfast. What is the appropriate nursing action?
A. Take vital signs as planned.
B. Wait 20 to 30 minutes and then take vital signs.
C. Ask the patient to lie down in bed to assess vital signs.
D. Take a rectal temperature.

6. The postoperative vital signs of a 47-year-old man with a ruptured appendix are BP 112/68 right arm (supine), pulse 56 and regular, R 8, T 37.6°C temporally. The patient is pale and confused, with minimal urine output. The nurse should
A. recheck the vital signs in 30 minutes
B. continue with care as planned
C. administer pain medication
D. notify the surgeon

7. The pulse pressure for a patient with a BP of 144/86 is
A. 58
B. 86
C. 144
D. 230

8. The nurse is caring for a patient who is elderly and confused. When assessing temperature, the nurse will obtain the reading using a/an
A. oral thermometer
B. rectal thermometer
C. tympanic thermometer
D. mercury thermometer

9. The nurse notes an irregular radial pulse in a patient. Further assessment includes assessing the
A. carotid pulse
B. apical pulse
C. femoral pulse
D. brachial pulse

10. Which actions will result in an accurate BP reading? Select all that apply.
A. Applying the centre of the bladder of the cuff directly over the brachial artery.
B. Raising the arm to the level of the heart.
C. Using the bell to assess the BP.
D. Pumping the cuff 60 mm Hg above the estimated BP.

Canadian Research

Alberta Heritage Foundation for Medical Research. (2008). The sixth vital sign. *Research News, Summer 2008,* 18–19.

Skjodt, N., & Hodgetts, B. (2008). *An MP3 recorder/player could replace the traditional stethoscope.* Paper presented September 17, 2008, at the Congress of the European Respiratory Society in Stockholm, Sweden.

References

Adiyaman, A., Tosun, N., et al. (2007). The effect of crossing legs on blood pressure. *Blood Pressure Monitoring, 12*(3), 189–193.

Adiyaman, A., Verhoeff, R., et al. (2006). The position of the arm during blood pressure measurement in sitting position. *Blood Pressure Monitoring, 11*(6), 309–313.

Anderson, M. C., Hunter, K., et al. (2010). The older adult. In T. C. Stephen, D. L. Skillen, R. A. Day, & L. S. Bickley (Eds.). *Canadian Bates' guide to health assessment for nurses* (1st ed., pp. 887–932). Philadelphia, PA: Wolters Kluwer Health/Lippincott Williams & Wilkins.

Calkins, H., & Zipes, D. P. (2007). Hypotension and syncope. In P. Libby, R. O. Bonow, et al., (Eds.). *Braunwald's heart disease: A textbook of cardiovascular medicine* (8th ed.). Philadelphia, PA: Elsevier.

Canadian Hypertension Education Program. (2011). *2011 Canadian hypertension education program one page update.* Retrieved from http/www.hypertension.ca/

Castelein, P., & Fetzer, S. J. (2010). Vital signs. In J. C. Ross-Kerr & M. J. Wood (Eds.). *Potter & Perry Canadian Fundamentals of nursing* (rev. 4th ed., pp. 493–539). Toronto, ON: Mosby Elsevier.

Clark, A. P., & Baldwin, K. (2004). Best practices for care of older adults. *Clinical Nurse Specialist, 18*(6), 288–299.

Eser, I., Khorshid, L., et al. (2006). The effect of different body positions on blood pressure. *Journal of Clinical Nursing, 16*, 137–140.

Ethnomed. (2008). *Clinical topics.* Retrieved from http://www.ethnomed.org/

Farnell, S., Maxwell, L., et al. (2005). Temperature measurement: Comparison of non-invasive methods used in adult critical care. *Journal of Clinical Nursing, 14*(5), 632.

Health Canada. (2006). *Obesity.* Retrieved from http://www.hc-sc.gc.ca/hl-vs/iyh-vsv/life-vie/obes-eng.php

Health Canada. (2003). *Food and nutrition: Body mass index (BMI) nomogram.* Retreived from http://www.hc-sc.gc.ca/fn-an/nutrition/weights-poids/guide-ld-adult/bmi_chart_java-grap

Heart and Stroke Foundation of Canada. (2011a). *Want to improve your heart health?* Retrieved from http://www.heartandstroke.com/site/c.ikIQLcMWJtE/b.3484027/k.8419/Heart_disease.

Heart and Stroke Foundation of Canada. (2011b). *High blood pressure: Here are some tips to get your blood pressure in check.* Retrieved from http://www.heartandstroke.com/site/c.ikIQLcMWJtE/b.3484023/k.2174/Heart_disease_

Institute for Clinical Evaluative Sciences. (2010). *Largest comparison of cardiovascular risk profiles of Canada's major ethnic groups.* Retrieved from http://www.ices.on.ca/webpage.cfm?site_id=1&org_id=117&morg_id=0&gsec_id=3089...

Kyle, T. (2008). *Essentials of pediatric nursing.* Philadelphia, PA: Wolters Kluwer Health/Lippincott Williams & Wilkins.

Lawson, L., Bridges, E., et al. (2007). Accuracy and precision of noninvasive temperature measurement in adult intensive care patients. *American Journal of Critical Care, 16*(5), 485–496.

Mackechnie, C., & Simpson, R. (2006). Traceable calibration for blood pressure and temperature monitoring. *Nursing Standard, 2*(11), 42–47.

National Institute of Health. (2007). *Age appropriate vital signs.* Retrieved from http://clinicalcenter.nih.gov/ccc/pedweb/pedsstaff/age.html

Norris, C. & Clark, A. M. (2010). Assessment of cardiovascular function. In R. A. Day, P. Paul., et al. (Eds.). *Brunner & Suddarth's textbook of Canadian medical-surgical nursing* (2nd ed., pp. 732–770). Philadelphia, PA: Wolters Kluwer Health/Lippincott Williams & Wilkins.

Ogden, C. L., Carroll, M. D., et al. (2007). *Obesity among adults in the United States—no statistically significant change since 2003–2004.* Retrieved from http://www.cdc.gov/nchs/data/databriefs/db01.pdf.

Rauen, C. A., Chulay, M., et al. (2008). Seven evidence-based practice habits: Putting some sacred cows out to pasture. *Critical Care Nurse, 28*(2), 98–124.

Schallom, L., Sona, C., et al. (2007). Comparison of forehead and digit oximetry in surgical/trauma patients at risk for decreased peripheral perfusion. *Heart & Lung, 36*(3), 188–194.

Skillen, D. L. & Bickley, L. S. (2010). General survey and vital signs. In T. C. Stephen, D. L. Skillen, R. A. Day, & L. S. Bickley (Eds.). *Canadian Bates' guide to health assessment for nurses* (1st ed., pp. 129–146). Philadelphia, PA: Wolters Kluwer Health/Lippincott Williams & Wilkins.

Statistics Canada. (2010). *The Daily Statistics Canada February 17, 2010.* Ottawa, ON: Author Catalogue 11-001-XIE.

Wallace, M. F., Fulwood, R., et al. (2008). NHLBI step-by-step approach to adapting cardiovascular training and education curricula for diverse audiences. *Previews in Chronic Disease, 5*(2), A61. Epub 2008 March 15.

World Health Organization. (1996). *Hypertension control.* Geneva, Switzerland: Author. Tech Rep Ser No 862.

> *The Canadian Jensen's Nursing Health Assessment suite offers these additional resources to enhance learning and facilitate understanding of this chapter:*
>
> - thePoint online resource, http//thepoint.lww.com/Stephen1E
> - *Laboratory Manual for Canadian Jensen's Nursing Health Assessment: A Best Practice Approach*

Tables of Unexpected Findings

Table 6-9 Unexpected Findings: Anthropometric Measurements

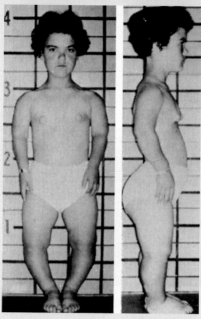

Achondroplastic Dwarfism. Characteristics of this genetic disorder include short stature, short limbs, and a relatively large head. Also note the thoracic kyphosis and lumbar lordosis.

Acromegaly. This condition results from excessive growth hormone secretion during adulthood, after body growth has stopped. Overgrowth of bone causes changes in the size of the head, face, hands, feet, and internal organs; height is not affected.

Gigantism. Excessive growth hormone secretion in childhood causes increased height and weight with delayed sexual development. Note the differences in these same-age individuals, one of whom has gigantism and the other whose anthropometric measurements are within expected limits.

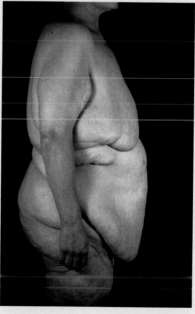

Obesity. Excessive body fat results when calories continually exceed body requirements. It can result from overeating, genetics, endocrine or hormonal disorders, lifestyle issues, or a combination of factors.

(table continues on page 124)

Table 6-9   Unexpected Findings: Anthropometric Measurements (*continued*)

Anorexia Nervosa. Severe restriction of caloric intake and disturbance in body image contribute to this psychiatric disorder. Affected patients are clearly emaciated and display other physical findings, such as brittle hair and nails, absent menstruation, delayed puberty, sunken eyes, dry skin, and other manifestations.

 Table 6-10   Unexpected Findings: Blood Pressure in Adults (mm Hg)

Category	Systolic	Diastolic
Hypotension	<90	<60
Normotension	<120 and	<80
Prehypertension	120–139 or	80–90
Hypertension	>140 or	>90

Source: Canadian Hypertension Education Program (2010).

Pain Assessment

Learning Objectives

1. Discuss the basic theories of pain.

2. Identify the elements of pain transmission.

3. Determine the different types of pain.

4. Differentiate musculoskeletal pain from neuropathic pain.

5. Examine the one-dimensional, multidimensional, and behavioural pain tools for newborns, children, adults, and older adults.

6. Identify important topics for health promotion and risk reduction related to pain.

7. Collect subjective data related to pain.

8. Collect objective data related to pain using physical examination techniques.

9. Identify issues in assessing pain in special populations such as patients with opioid tolerance or those with difficulty communicating about their pain.

10. Document and communicate data from the pain assessment using appropriate terminology and principles of recording.

11. Consider age, gender, condition, and culture of the patient to individualize the assessment of pain.

*M*rs. Seanna Bond, 42 years old, is visiting the clinic for follow-up care for musculoskeletal pain related to fibromyalgia. She was diagnosed 5 months ago and still has not been able to control her pain to a desirable goal. Her temperature is 37°C orally, pulse 112 beats/min and shallow, respirations 20 breaths/min, and blood pressure 142/88 mm Hg (right arm, sitting). Current medications include a selective serotonin reuptake inhibitor citalopram hydrobromide (Apo-Citalopram) 20 mg/d, and a prescription nonsteroidal anti-inflammatory drug naproxen (Naproxen EC) 750 mg/d, for pain. She had a comprehensive assessment documented 5 months ago and has been seen twice since for pain control.

You will gain more information about Mrs. Bond as you progress through this chapter. As you study the content and features, consider Mrs. Bond's case and its relationship to what you are learning. Begin thinking about the following points:

- What is the role of the nurse in assessing Mrs. Bond's pain?
- What subjective information will the nurse gather during the history and interview? What pain assessment tools would be most appropriate?
- What objective data will the nurse assess during today's assessment?
- How will the nurse assess the effectiveness of interventions?
- What other associated findings would the nurse assess when considering Mrs. Bond's pain?

urses are the health professionals who spend the most time with patients who are experiencing pain. Key nursing roles include assessing the pain and the patient's response to it, providing pain-relief strategies and assessing the patient's response, monitoring for adverse effects, being an advocate for the patient when pain-relieving strategies need changing, and teaching the patient and family how to manage pain following discharge. Nurses are aware that nonpharmaceutical modalities such as therapeutic touch, acupuncture, reflexology, transcutaneous electrical neural stimulation, Tai chi, and Qi gong can also relieve pain.

This chapter contains the measurement of pain using reliable and valid pain assessment scales. It presents the basic elements of pain assessment as well as background information on pain, pain transmission, and assessing pain in difficult-to-assess populations.

Pain is the primary reason that patients access health care in Canada (Lander & Adams, 2010) and is reported by 50% of hospitalized patients (Canadian Pain Society, 2005). Pain does not respect gender, age, or genetic background. It can occur at any time, to anyone. Pain can profoundly affect quality of life, interactions with family and friends, sense of well-being and self-esteem, and financial resources. For many patients, pain is the result of injury or surgery, but for others, pain has no identifiable cause.

Pain has three components:

1. *Sensory discriminative* (severity and location of pain) which receives the most attention within the health care professions
2. *Affective motivational* (emotional aspects) "how the pain makes us feel and what it makes us do" (Lander, 2010, p. 147)
3. *Cognitive evaluative* (meaning attributed to the pain)

Anatomy and Physiology Overview

Peripheral Nervous System

Several different types of nerve fibres that transmit pain are located in the peripheral nervous system. The two main types of nerve fibres are as follows:

1. **A delta fibres,** large nerve fibres covered with myelin; they conduct pain impulses rapidly. Patients often describe the type of pain impulse that A delta fibres conduct as sharp or stabbing (Purves, 2008) and well localized; these fibres stimulate motor responses such as withdrawal or flinching.
2. **C fibres,** smaller unmyelinated nerve fibres; they conduct pain impulses more diffusely and slowly. Patients often describe the pain conducted by C fibres as achy and ongoing, even after the pain stimulus is removed (Purves) and not well localized; these fibres stimulate a protective response such as guarding.

C fibres release a pain-facilitating substance from nerve endings called substance P. The function of substance P is to speed the transmission of the pain stimulus up the pain pathway. Bradykinin, another pain-facilitating substance, is released at the site of injury. It is a cellular chemical released from the damaged tissue. The function of bradykinin is to cause continued irritation at the injury site (D'Arcy, 2007a).

These specialized peripheral A- and C-nerve fibres are referred to as **nociceptors**. They carry the pain signal to the central nervous system.

Central Nervous System

Once the pain stimulus is transferred into the central nervous system via the dorsal root ganglion, it synapses in the substantia gelatinosa in the dorsal horn of the spinal cord and enters the central nervous system. Opening or closing the "gate" to nociception is controlled by the combined effect of both the sum of the pain-facilitating impulse and the facilitating substances and the sum of the pain-blocking impulses and substances as they are received in the substantia gelatinosa. Simplistically, if facilitator impulses predominate, the pain stimulus is passed on; if blocking impulses predominate, the pain stops (Cervero, 2005).

If the pain is allowed to continue, the pain stimulus passes through the spinal cord into the lateral spinothalamic tracts, which lead directly to the thalamus, and then into the limbic system. In the limbic system, the emotions that control pain are produced, and the stimulus is then passed to the cerebral cortex when the sensation is recognized as pain. The whole process takes milliseconds (D'Arcy, 2007a) (see Fig. 7-1).

Two substances are very important to pain transmission at this level. Some nerves use substance P to fire at synaptic junctions. Glutamate is the neurotransmitter responsible for the communication of the peripheral nervous system with the central nervous system (Rowbotham, 2006). An additional function of glutamate is thought to be activation of N-methyl D-aspartate receptors, which can help intensify and prolong persistent pain (Mersky, Loeser, et al., 2005).

Clinical Significance 7-1

To treat some chronic pain conditions such as fibromyalgia, health care providers may prescribe medications that increase serotonin, such as tricyclic antidepressants and selective serotonin reuptake inhibitors, to modulate incoming pain stimuli.

Descending nerve fibres from the locus ceraleus and periaqueductal grey matter transmit the response to the efferent nerve pathways. Substances that can modulate the pain response at this level include opiates, endorphins, and enkephalins. These substances can bind to the opiate receptors in the dorsal horn of the spine and block pain transmission. Gabapentin (GABA) blocks pain transmission by binding to GABA-specific receptors in the dorsal horn (Bennett, Attal, et al., 2007).

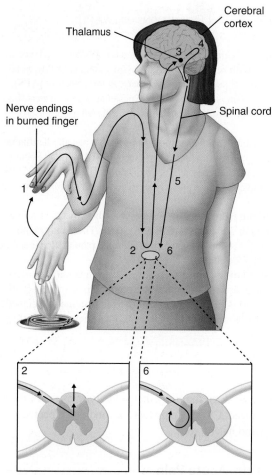

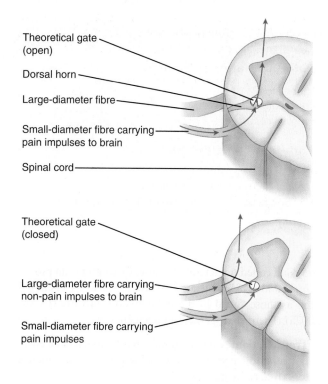

Figure 7-2 The gate control theory.

Figure 7-1 (1) Pain begins as a message received by nerve endings, such as in a burned finger. (2) The release of substance P, bradykinin, and prostaglandins sensitizes the nerve endings, helping to transmit the pain from the site of injury toward the brain. (3) The pain signal then travels as an electrochemical impulse along the length of the nerve to the dorsal horn on the spinal cord, a region that receives signals from all over the body. (4) The spinal cord then sends the message to the thalamus and then to the cortex. (5) Pain relief starts with signals from the brain that descend by way of the spinal cord, where (6) chemicals such as endorphins are released in the dorsal horn to diminish the pain message.

Clinical Significance 7-2

Opiates, antidepressants, and GABA agonists are pharmacological alternatives in the treatment of chronic pain.

Gate Control Theory

Currently, the theory of pain with the widest acceptance is the gate control theory developed by Ron Melzak (a Canadian psychologist) and Patrick Wall (Melzack & Wall, 1975). This theory posits that the body responds to a painful stimulus by either opening a neural gate to allow pain to be produced or

creating a blocking effect at the synaptic junction to stop the pain (Fig. 7-2). The steps for pain transmission in the gate control theory follow.

1. Continued painful stimulus on a peripheral neuron causes the "gate" to open through depolarization of the nerve fibre. This is accomplished by ion influx and outflow.
2. The pain stimulus then passes from the peripheral nervous system at a synaptic junction to the central nervous system up the afferent nerve pathways.
3. The pain stimulus passes up through and across the dorsal horn of the spine to the structures of the limbic system and the cerebral cortex.
4. In the cerebral cortex, the stimulus is identified as pain and a response is created. The response, once generated, passes down the efferent pathways where reaction to the pain is created (D'Arcy, 2007a).

Although this theory seems simple, proponents continue to expand and refine it. Recent data suggest that the degree of the stimulus can produce varied responses. Current research focuses on those elements that can affect pain inhibition and stop the pain stimulus. Additionally, pain-facilitating and pain-inhibiting substances that can either help or hinder pain processing have been discovered. Refer to Box 7-1.

Nociception

The most common clinical interpretation of pain transmission is a concept called **nociception**, which means the perception of pain by sensory receptors located throughout the body and called **nociceptors**. These nociceptors can produce pain resulting from heat, pressure, or noxious chemicals, such as those found in the inflammatory process (D'Arcy, 2007a). There are four steps in nociception:

1. **Transduction:** Noxious stimuli create enough of an energy potential to cause a nerve impulse perceived by nociceptors (free nerve endings).
2. **Transmission:** The neuronal signal moves from the periphery to the spinal cord and up to the brain.
3. **Perception:** The impulses being transmitted to the higher areas of the brain are identified as pain.
4. **Modulation:** Inhibitory and facilitating input from the brain modulates or influences the sensory transmission at the level of the spinal cord (Berry, Covington, et al., 2006).

Persistent or chronic pain can exist without any identifiable cause and cause the body to adapt or change how it transmits or perceives the pain signal. These changes in transmission (**neuronal plasticity**) can cause the pain to become more severe by activating additional structures for facilitating transmission.

Clinical Significance 7-3

The transmission of a pain stimulus uses two separate but continuous systems: the peripheral nervous system and the central nervous system. Continued input from the peripheral nervous system can create a centrally mediated pain syndrome, in which pain occurs without a pain stimulus.

Pain Classification

Pain can be classified based on duration (acute, chronic), frequency (intermittent, continuous), form (nociceptive, neuropathic), and association with cancer and treatment of cancer. Definitions of pain emphasize that it is an unpleasant experience (Box 7-2). Because pain is so damaging, it is important to understand just how this experience is created. Acute pain

is meant to warn the body that some type of insult or injury has occurred. Chronic pain lasts beyond the expected healing period and has no role.

Duration: Acute Pain

Acute pain results from tissue damage, whether through injury or surgery. Acute pain runs a finite course and then resolves. It is typically associated with specific events (such as trauma) or disease (such as appendicitis). Acute pain is very prevalent in hospital settings and primary care clinics. In one Canadian hospital, pain prevalence was 84%, and 25.8% of patients had severe pain in the previous 24 hours. In addition, only 50% of the patients had PRN (Pro Re Nata, or "as needed") orders for pain medication. The authors concluded "pain was not well controlled at our institution" (p. 45) (Sawyer, Haslam, et al., 2010).

Clinical Significance 7-4

Untreated or undertreated acute pain may lead to chronic pain syndromes, such as complex regional pain syndrome (CRPS), which are difficult to treat (D'Arcy, 2007b).

Duration: Chronic (Persistent) Pain

Chronic pain is also prevalent in Canadian adults and exceeds 38%; approximately 10% of the population has disabling chronic pain (Birse & Lander, 1998; Queen's News Centre, 2004). Estimates of the costs of chronic pain in Canada, combining lost income, health care costs, and worker nonproductivity, equal $6 billion annually (Canadian Pain Society,

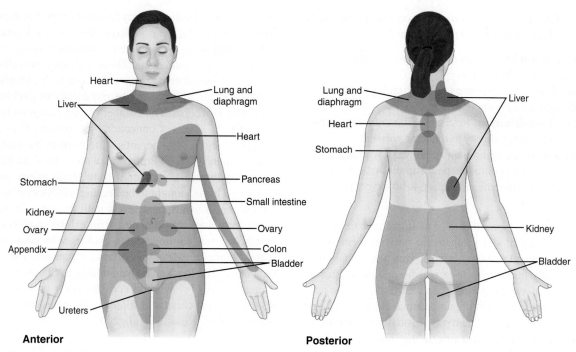

Figure 7-3 Common sites of referred pain.

2011). Because of the stigma associated with chronic pain and its treatment in the health care setting, it is also referred to as **persistent pain**. Pain becomes chronic when it lasts 3 months or longer. Signs of distress seen with acute pain are absent in chronic pain and the biological signs are also missing (Lander, 2010). Chronic pain "can disrupt a person's life, limiting ability to care for self, earn an income, and sustain personal relationships" (Lander, 2010, p. 151).

Frequency: Continuous or Intermittent/Episodic Pain

While some pain is mainly continuous, other pain is intermittent or episodic. Pain from arthritis can be continuous (but may vary in intensity). Pain from migraine headaches is episodic (associated with particular events or times such as related to the female menstrual cycles) (Lander, 2010).

Form: Nociceptive Pain

Pain nociception has various locations. **Visceral pain** originates from abdominal organs, and patients often describe this pain as crampy or gnawing. **Somatic pain** originates from skin, muscles, bones, and joints. Patients usually describe somatic pain as sharp (D'Arcy, 2007a). **Cutaneous pain** derives from the dermis, epidermis, and subcutaneous tissues. It is often burning or sharp, such as with a partial thickness burn. **Referred pain** originates from a specific site, but the person experiencing it feels the pain at another site along the innervating spinal nerve (Fig. 7-3). An example is cardiac pain that a person experiences as indigestion, neck, or arm pain. **Phantom pain** is pain in an extremity or body that is no longer there (eg, the patient who experiences pain in a leg that has been amputated). **Parietal pain** refers to pain located in the wall of a body cavity. It is also nociceptive.

Form: Neuropathic Pain

Neuropathic pain is described as "burning, tingling, numbness, stabbing, shooting, or electric," and different approaches to treating this type of pain are necessary (Lander, 2010, p. 151). Once pain becomes a more constant stimulus, the nervous system can modify its function (**neuronal plasticity**) (Rowbotham, 2006). In turn, this can lead to another phenomenon called **peripheral sensitization**, by which peripheral nociceptors are sensitized to pain stimuli. As an example, inflammation can cause peripheral sensitization related to the continued release of inflammatory mediators such as nitric oxide, bradykinin, serotonin (opposite of acute injury), histamine, and adenosine (D'Arcy, 2007a). This irritating process causes cytokines and growth factors to be recruited to the site of injury, prolonging the inflammatory response. Over time, this sensitization produces a condition in which nonpainful touch or pressure becomes painful.

Neuronal windup is produced when repeated assaults on the afferent neurons create enhanced response and increased activity in the central nervous system. Windup can cause tissues in the affected area to become extremely sensitive to pressure in areas not identified usually as painful. Examples of windup include rheumatoid arthritis and osteoarthritis (Rowbotham, 2006).

The following list includes some conditions resulting from physiologic responses to painful stimuli:

- **Neuronal plasticity:** Ability of the nervous system to change or alter its function
- **Windup:** Enhanced response to pain stimulus produced by prolonged pain production
- **Peripheral sensitization:** Result of inflammatory process that creates hypersensitivity to touch or pressure
- **Central sensitization:** Excitatory process involving spinal nerves produced by continued pain stimuli that can persist even after peripheral stimulation is no longer present (D'Arcy, 2007b)

Sympathetic pain, a special case of neuropathic pain, results from overactivity of the sympathetic nervous system and central or peripheral nervous systems. This type of pain may follow typically minor muscle or soft tissue injury. Characteristics include sweating of the affected tissues, poor temperature control in the area of pain, edema, changes in blood flow to the skin, and extreme hypersensitivity of skin in the affected area. The term used currently is complex regional pain syndrome (CRPS).

A mixed pain syndrome also has been reported. This type of pain has neuropathic and nociceptive features. Fibromyalgia, a chronic pain syndrome, is an example. People (like our patient, Mrs. Bond) with this syndrome have generalized musculoskeletal pain, tenderness (specific trigger points), stiffness, fatigue, and sleep disturbances (Gevirtz, 2007).

Location

Pain can be described by its location (eg, chest pain, pelvic pain, or headache). This categorization assists health care professionals in selecting necessary diagnostic tests and treatment (Lander, 2010)

Etiology

Pain can be classified by etiology or cause. Examples include burn pain and postmastectomy pain syndrome. Health care professionals can often predict the course of the pain and effectively treat the pain (Lander, 2010).

Association with Cancer

Pain can be classified as cancer pain or chronic cancer pain. Pain that arises from treatment of cancer is still classified as cancer pain.

🔍 Lifespan Considerations

Newborns, Infants, and Children

Unrecognized and undertreated pain is common in newborns, infants, and children despite the abundance of pain assessment tools. Preverbal newborns and infants are at risk for undertreatment because of myths that they do not experience pain. Additionally, they undergo many painful procedures such as heel sticks, venipuncture, immunizations, vitamin K injection, and circumcision. However, many providers have fears about the adverse effects associated with analgesic use.

Much of the research on the physiology of pain has been done with newborns. The number of pain receptors in babies is similar to adults. Connections are present between the peripheral and central nervous systems from 30 weeks' gestation (Anand, 2007). Preterm newborns have an increased sensitivity to pain, compared with full-term babies and older children. This is thought to be because inhibitory neurotransmitters are in insufficient levels until full-term birth. Compared with older children, newborns exhibit more hormonal, metabolic, and cardiovascular responses to pain and may require higher doses of analgesics for adequate pain control (Anand, 2007). Inadequate pain treatment can lead to a delay in healing and behavioural consequences, such as learning disabilities, psychiatric disorders, and neurodevelopmental issues (Astuto, Rosano, et al., 2007).

Older Adults

Pain is prevalent in older adults, with 80% of all patients in long-term care facilities and 25% to 50% of community-dwelling elders reporting chronic daily pain (American Geriatric Society [AGS], 2002). Pain is not an expected consequence of aging.

Chronic disease may affect accurate pain assessment, such as with osteoarthritis, peripheral vascular disease, or cancer. Patients who experience surgical or diagnostic procedures may experience acute pain. They may be unable to distinguish if their pain is surgically induced or chronic from preexisting painful conditions. Because the Canadian population is aging proportionately, understanding how to assess pain in older patients is a critical skill for nurses.

Little is known about the effect of increased age on pain perception. No evidence suggests that pain sensation is diminished in older adults, a common misperception. Transmission along the A delta and C fibres may become altered with aging, but it is not clear how this change affects the pain experience. Studies of sensitivity and pain tolerance have indicated that changes in pain perception are probably not clinically significant (AGS, 2002; McCleane, 2008; Reyes-Gibby, Aday, et al., 2007).

Care provider issues also may affect the treatment of pain in older populations. Because older people are likely to experience more side effects from analgesia, especially from opiates, health care providers may undertreat pain in older adults.

The nurse assesses if the older patient has any auditory impairment. If present, the nurse positions his or her face in the patient's view, speaks in a slow, usual tone of voice, reduces extraneous noises, and provides written instructions. If the patient has visual impairment, the nurse uses simple lettering, at least 14-point font, adequate line spacing, and nonglare paper. The patient should wear eyeglasses or a functioning hearing aid if these devices are in routine use and have adequate time to respond to questions (Herr, Coyne, et al., 2006). Because older adults may process information more slowly than younger patients, the nurse allows sufficient time for older adults to respond.

Cognitive impairment, dementia, and delirium are more common in older adults (Linton & Lach, 2007). Accurately assessing pain is more challenging when patients have these conditions. Nevertheless, no evidence shows that patients with cognitive impairment experience less pain. Nurses should not consider pain reports from these patients any less valid than those from other patients. Health care providers may use behavioural observations of acute pain in patients (eg, restlessness, guarding, pacing) to assess pain, but these observations are not pain specific and may represent responses to other conditions.

Cultural Considerations

Health care providers are more likely to rate pain scores lower in patients of different genetic backgrounds than in Caucasian patients (Green, Anderson, et al., 2003). In a study of wait times in an emergency department, African Canadian patients waited longer than Caucasian patients, and patient reports of pain by all study participants had little effect on waiting time (Wheeler, Hardie, et al., 2010). There are also differences in expectations for adequate pain treatment. People from different genetic backgrounds receive less pain medication compared to Caucasians across a range of conditions, including cancer pain, acute postoperative pain, chest pain, acute pain presenting in the emergency department, and chronic low back pain (Green, Anderson, et al.). This disparity may be the result of patient variables such as nociceptive differences, communication processes, or pain behaviours (Green, Anderson, et al.). In a study of chronic pain, being an African American male "was a direct predictor of greater pain, and through pain, was an indirect predictor of depression, affective distress, PTSD, and disability" (Green & Hart-Johnson, 2010a, p. 321). In a study of the adequacy of pain medication for patients with chronic pain, African Americans were prescribed fewer pain medications, women received less adequate medication strength, and younger women had a higher risk for inadequate pain management, while young men had better pain management (Green & Hart-Johnson, 2010b). In studies of experimentally induced pain, no direct evidence relates biopsychosocial factors to ethnic differences in pain (Reyes-Gibby, Aday, et al., 2007). Ethnicity-related differences may exist, however, in willingness to communicate about pain to avoid being stereotyped.

Gender differences in pain exist. Conditions such as fibromyalgia, irritable bowel syndrome, migraines, and temporomandibular joint pain are more prevalent in women than in men (APS, 2007). All patients with acute pain show an increased physiologic response to pain including heart rate and blood pressure increase. Conditions such as menstrual migraine, a women's pain syndrome, have demonstrated the estrogenic effect of pain (Brandes, 2006). Though considerable attention has been devoted to biological variables such as hormonal influences and genetics, psychological and social factors might also account for gender differences in reporting pain. It is unknown if fundamental, gender-specific differences in basic pain mechanisms exist. Stutts, McCulloch, et al. (2009) researched common pain experiences in men and women. Men experienced more concussions and women tended to rate minor surgery as more painful than men, but there was no evidence that overall pain experience differed between the sexes (p. 1226). A better understanding of the physiological, social, and psychological issues that influence pain is needed.

Nurses need to assess sociocultural variables such as genetic background, acculturation, and gender that influence pain behaviour and expression. They also identify social and contextual variables that may lead to pain disparities among people of genetic background minorities. For example, the nurse can work closely with the patient and his or her family to identify pain and functional goals that consider the patient's values, resources, and expectations (Green, Anderson, et al., 2003).

Acute Assessment

Patients in severe pain not relieved by over-the-counter analgesics need immediate attention to investigate the cause of the pain and to provide pain relief. Sudden onset of pain may indicate life-threatening conditions, such as aortic aneurysm, cardiac disease, pneumothorax, deep vein thrombosis, cerebrovascular accident, pulmonary embolus, or acute appendicitis. Immediate assessment and treatment are required. Patients with acute severe back pain and headache also require assessment and treatment to minimize the risk of severe disability (Lander, 2010). (See the Acute Assessment sections in other chapters for additional information).

Subjective Data Collection

Risk Assessment and Health Promotion

Important Topics for Health Promotion

- Prevention of loss of core strength and of muscle flexibility
- Prevention of development of secondary pain, such as from poor posture, change in gait
- Adequate treatment of acute pain to prevent chronic pain
- Correct self-administration of analgesics (issues of over- and underadministration)
- Reduction of risk associated with use of alcohol, over-the-counter drugs, and recreational drugs

Adapted from Lander, J. A. (2010). Pain assessment. In T. C. Stephen, D. L. Skillen, R. A. Day, & L. S. Bickley (Eds.). *Canadian Bates' guide to health assessment for nurses* (1st ed., p. 156). Philadelphia, PA: Wolters Kluwer Health/Lippincott Williams & Wilkins.

Examples of Questions to Assess Symptoms/Signs	Rationale/Unexpected Findings

Location

Where is your pain? Ask the patient to point to the painful area. If more than one area is painful, have the patient rate each one separately, and note which area is the most painful.

Note any pain that radiates from the affected area, for example, down the leg with a report of low back pain, because such radiation may affect treatment choices.

Quality/(Description)

What does your pain feel like?

• Describe the quality of the pain. (Allow the patient to describe the pain in his or her own words without any prompts. It is very important to record exactly how the patient describes the pain.)

• If the patient is having difficulty describing the pain, then ask: Is the pain sharp? Prickling? Burning? Shock-like? Dull? Aching? Cramping? Jabbing? Shooting? Squeezing? Rhythmic? Pulsating? Gnawing? Burning? Shooting? Sharp? or Dull?

A description of pain from the patient is more accurate than when the nurse suggests possible descriptors. Descriptors such as burning, painful numbness, or tingling from patients may alert the nurse to a neuropathic source for the pain.

Quantity (Intensity)

How much pain do you have on a 0–10 scale, with 0 being no pain and 10 being the worst possible that you can imagine, and how would you rate your pain? (A scale of 0–5 can also be used.)

• Does pain medication decrease the intensity?

The numbering scale assists in quantifying the pain from the patient's perspective. If the patient cannot use a numeric rating scale, ask the patient if the pain is mild, moderate, or severe.

Timing

When did you first notice the pain? What were you doing when you first noticed the pain? Did the pain start slowly? Or suddenly? Is there a time of day when the pain seems worse? Or a time of the night when the pain seems worse? Or a time of day when the pain seems better? Or a time at night when it seems better? Is the pain always present? Does it come and go? How often are you having the pain? Are there times when you are free of the pain? Have you had previous experience with pain?

This question helps identify onset and duration. Pain for more than 3 months is chronic or persistent.

Past experience with pain is a factor that influences the patient's present pain response (Lander, 2010).

Setting

Where were you when you first noticed the pain? What were you doing when the pain started?

The setting and activity can provide clues to the cause of the pain, for example, instant onset of lower back pain following lifting a heavy object.

Associated Symptoms

What other symptoms have you noticed besides the pain? [*Allow the patient to describe other symptoms first.*] *Then ask about other symptoms* such as Nausea? Vomiting? Coughing?" "Shortness of breath? Dizziness? Inadequate sleeping? Fatigue? Exhaustion? Do you feel anxious? Depressed? Do you have increased sensitivity to pain? How is your appetite? Do you have constipation? Diarrhea?

Associated symptoms provide additional information—for example, abdominal pain may be accompanied by nausea and vomiting.

Alleviating Factors

What makes the pain better?

• What methods have you used that relieved the pain? Does the application of heat have any effect?

• Does a cold pack help relieve any of the pain?

• Does any activity decrease the pain?

• Does sitting in a certain position make the pain better?

Most patients will try to treat their own pain before they seek health care.

Provides information the nurse can use to help relieve the patient's pain.

Examples of Questions to Assess Symptoms/Signs	Rationale/Unexpected Findings
• Use of prescribed medications? (names of medications, dose, amount used daily). Use of over-the-counter medications? (names of over-the-counter medications, dose, amount used daily) Use of herbal products? (names of herbal products, dose, amount used daily) Measures other than medications—Massage? Acupuncture? Other?	
Aggravating Factors • What makes the pain worse? Movement? Breathing?	Alerts the nurse to what may increase the patient's pain.
Environmental Factors • Are there things in your home environment that affect the pain? Does anyone in your family experience pain? Are there things in your work environment that affect the pain? How much stress is in your life right now?	Pain may be linked to something in the home or work environment. Stress may increase the pain.
Significance to the Patient How is this pain affecting your daily life? Work? Studies? Financial implications? The things you enjoy doing? How is the pain affecting your family? Or other interpersonal relationships?	Provides information on the effects of the pain on the patient's activities and relationships
Patient Perspective • What do you think is the meaning of your pain? What is happening with your pain? Are you concerned it might mean the presence of disease? Does it mean increasing disease? Presence of infection?	Some patients believe that pain is a punishment; or it could be a worsening of disease.
Pain Management Goal • What would be an acceptable level of pain for you? Setting a pain goal is helpful for all patients, especially for those with chronic pain.	Most patients do not expect to be pain free and are willing to tolerate some discomfort. Ask patients what pain level they think is acceptable, and then tailor interventions to achieve the patient's expectations.
Functional Goal What would you like to be able to do that you can't do because of the pain? (This question is most often used for patients with chronic or persistent pain.) Pain is dynamic and increases with activity (Falla, Farina, et al., 2007). • How does the pain interfere with your activities of daily living? • How far can you walk? • Can you care for yourself at home? Or do you require help?	Setting a pain functionality goal with the patient allows the nurse to measure the efficacy of pain interventions and adjust the treatment accordingly. Providing maximum pain relief and functionality is the goal of any pain-relief treatment for the patient with chronic pain (Ackley, Ladwig, et al., 2008; D'Arcy, 2007a).

Pain is not an experience without risk. It can cause both physical and emotional harm. For nurses caring for patients experiencing pain, adequate treatment is a crucial factor. Acute pain that is not adequately treated can impair pulmonary function, decrease the immune response, and prolong the length of stays in hospitals. Carlson (2010) noted that "over the past 30 years, postoperative pain relief has been shown to be inadequate" (p. 245). Nurses who were open to innovation, and read nursing journals, were the most likely to adopt true evidence-based postoperative pain assessment practices (Carlson). For patients with chronic pain, adequate pain management decreases stress and increases the patient's ability to function.

If acute pain is undertreated or untreated, patients are at risk for harder-to-treat neuropathic pain syndromes, such as CRPS. Continued painful assault on the peripheral nerves results in neuronal plasticity and transfer of the pain stimulus to the central system. Patients who have had surgery or a crush type of injury are at high risk for developing CRPS. Nurses should be aware that when the patient with such an injury continues to report high levels of pain and begins to experience a subsequent loss of function, temperature sensitivity, sweating, swelling, or other skin changes (eg, hair loss in the affected area), the patient may be developing CRPS. Nurses should also be alert for the common terms that patients use to report neuropathic pain such as burning, painful tingling, pins and needles, and painful numbness.

Teaching patients about the benefits of controlling pain may help correct misperceptions that some have about tolerating pain stoically rather than taking medication to relieve it. Pain has many negative consequences—it is important to help patients understand that reporting pain and treating pain are ways of maintaining a higher level of health and avoiding some chronic pain syndromes. If the patient continues to refuse pain medication, the nurse may consider asking these questions:

- Does the patient have negative biases about taking pain medication?
- Are unwanted side effects such as constipation, nausea, or dizzy feelings causing the patient to refuse pain medications?

In some cases, patients can be given antiemetics, laxatives, or dose adjustments that make it easier for them to tolerate pain medications. Above all, if the patient continues to refuse to take pain medication, it is extremely important to understand the root cause of this refusal so that appropriate treatment can take place.

Focused Health History Related to Common Symptoms/Signs

Pain is what the patient says it is, and it exists whenever the patient says it does (McAffery & Pasero, 1999). Pain assessment is always subjective. For verbal patients, self-report is the gold standard for assessing pain. Nurses also assess additional pain behaviours, such as grimacing, rocking, or guarding. Increased heart rate and blood pressure are indicators of the physiological response to acute pain. (See Box 7-3.)

Start with the sign or symptom reported by the patient. Always begin with open-ended questions. Then probe with specific questions (see Examples of Questions to Assess Symptoms/Signs, pp. 132–133). "Pain is *the* symptom that is often used to illustrate all aspects of a symptom analysis" (Lander, 2010, p. 153). Nurses select the specific questions relevant to each patient.

Once you have collected all the data described previously, the most important factor is to accept the patient's rating of the pain. It is incumbent on nurses to respect the reports of pain as patients present them and then act to help relieve the pain. While a nurse may not believe the patient's pain rating, he or she is obligated to accept the report of pain. Health care providers may have biases that influence decision making about pain but they have "minimal awareness of and/or lack of willingness to acknowledge this bias" (Hirsh, Jensen, et al., 2010, p. 454).

The use of in-depth questions to collect all the salient data from the pain assessment will be the biggest help in determining what types of interventions will be most beneficial for providing adequate pain relief to the patient. Using a reliable and valid pain assessment tool can help provide subjective criteria for pain measurement.

BOX 7-3 KEY SYMPTOMS AND SIGNS REPORTED BY PATIENTS

Acute Pain	Chronic Pain
• Sweating	• Sleep disturbances
• Rapid heart rate (tachycardia)	• Feeling apathetic
• Rapid breathing (tachypnea)	• Decreased concentration
• Feeling anxious	• Withdrawal from life
• Vomiting	• Decreased functional activities
• Feeling restless	• Feeling depressed
• Holding, supporting, protecting the pain site (guarding)	• Decreased interest in sex (decreased libido)
• Seeking help	• Suicidal thoughts
• Muscle spasms	• Feeling lethargic
	• Lack or loss of appetite (anorexia)
	• Wondering what is wrong and what will fix it (diagnosis/cure seeking)

Adapted from Lander, J. A. (2010). Pain assessment. In T. C. Stephen, D. L. Skillen, R. A. Day, & L. S. Bickley (Eds.). *Canadian Bates' guide to health assessment for nurses* (1st ed., p. 152). Philadelphia, PA: Wolters Kluwer Health/ Lippincott Williams & Wilkins.

Pain Measurement/Assessment Tools

Pain tools can be one-dimensional and rate only pain intensity, or multidimensional and include behavioural, affective, and functional domains. Some of the first multidimensional pain assessment tools were developed for assessing experimentally induced pain, chronic pain, and cancer pain and provide a more comprehensive pain assessment.

One-Dimensional Pain Scales

One-dimensional pain assessment tools measure one element of the pain experience—intensity. Although these tools seem simple and the data they allow examiners to gather are limited, single-item ratings of pain intensity are valid and reliable indicators of pain intensity (Victor, Jensen, et al., 2008). These scales also help health care providers identify the effects of administered medications on pain intensity. A two-point or 30% reduction in pain intensity on the Numeric Pain Intensity (NPI) scale is a clinically significant improvement in pain level (Farrar, Young, et al., 2001).

Visual Analog Scale (VAS). The VAS is a 100-mm line with "no pain" at one end and "worst possible pain" at the other end. When using this scale, the nurse asks the patient to mark on the line the intensity of the pain he or she is experiencing. If the patient marks the line at 70 mm, the nurse would note the pain level as 7/10.

This tool is one of the simplest and most basic one-dimensional pain scales. Limitations to the VAS include the observation that some older adults have difficulty marking on the line and place the mark above or below 100 mm (D'Arcy, 2003; Herr & Mobily, 1993).

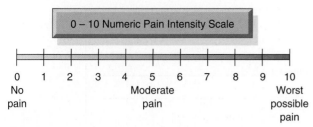

Figure 7-4 Numeric Pain Intensity (NPI) Scale.

Verbal Descriptor Scale (VDS). The VDS uses words such as "mild," "moderate," and "severe" to measure pain intensity. It asks patients to select the word or phrase that best describes their pain. Some patients prefer to use words rather than a number to rate their pain. Limitations to the VDS include the fact that the patient must be able to understand the meaning of the words.

Numeric Pain Intensity Scale (NPI). The NPI is the most commonly used one-dimensional pain scale (Fig. 7-4). In this 11-point Likert-type scale, 0 means "no pain" and 10 means "worst possible pain." The NPI asks patients to select the number that best fits their pain intensity—the higher the score, the more intense the pain.

In general:

- **Mild pain** is considered in the 1 to 3 range.
- **Moderate pain** is considered in the 4 to 6 range.
- **Severe pain** is considered in the 7 to 10 range.

> **Clinical Significance 7-5**
>
> There is no right or wrong number for patients to report. They are using a very objective tool to report a subjective experience. Believe the pain rating the patient reports. Patient self-report is considered the gold standard for pain assessment (APS, 2003).

Combined Thermometer Scale. The combined thermometer scale combines the VDS and the NPI (Fig. 7-5). Some patients respond well to this scale and like its vertical orientation, with numbers that increase from the bottom up.

Multidimensional Pain Scales

Multidimensional scales are also available for the assessment of chronic pain, cancer pain, or complex medical–surgical pain conditions. Figure 7-6 shows an example. Two other commonly used scales are the McGill Pain Questionnaire (MPQ) and the Brief Pain Inventory (BPI). Both have a combination of indices that measure pain intensity, mood, pain location (via body diagram), verbal descriptors, and questions about medication efficacy. They are most often used for research or with patients who are being actively treated for pain over an extended period.

McGill Pain Questionnaire (MPQ). The MPQ was developed to measure pain in experimentally induced circumstances, following procedures, and with several medical–surgical conditions. It consists of a set of verbal

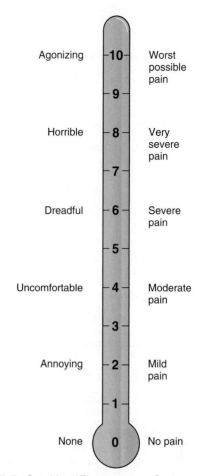

Figure 7-5 Combined Thermometer Scale.

descriptors used to capture the sensory aspect of pain, a VAS scale, and a present pain intensity rating made up of words and numbers. The tool has been found reliable and valid and has been translated into several languages (McDonald & Weiskopf, 2001; Melzack, 1975, 1987; Mystakidou, Cleeland, et al., 2004). Limitations include scoring and weighting the verbal descriptor section and difficulty translating the verbal descriptor section into words that indicate syndromes.

Brief Pain Inventory (BPI). The BPI was first developed to measure pain in patients with cancer; however, it also has reliability and validity for assessing acute pain (eg, postoperative) as well as chronic conditions (eg, osteoarthritis, low back pain) (Daut, Cleeland, et al., 1983; Raichle, Osborne, et al., 2006; Tan, Jensen, et al., 2004; Williams, Smith, et al., 2006). The BPI consists of a pain intensity scale; a body diagram to locate the pain; a functional assessment of the effects of pain on general activity, mood, walking, employment, housework, relationships, sleep, and enjoyment of life; and questions about the efficacy of pain medications (Fig. 7-7). Nurses can use the BPI either as an interview or as a patient self-report. The short form of the tool is recommended and can be completed in 5 minutes. An additional advantage of the BPI is that it has been validated in 25 languages (Hølen, Lydersen, et al., 2008; Mystakidou et al., 2004). Limitations

Date ____________

Patient's name ______________________ Age ______ Room ____________

Diagnosis ______________________ Physician ______________________

Nurse ______________________

1. LOCATION: Patient or nurse marks drawing.

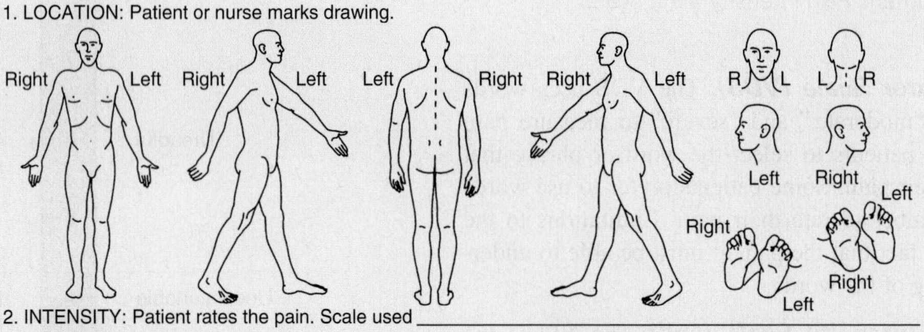

2. INTENSITY: Patient rates the pain. Scale used ______________________
   Present: ______________________
   Worst pain gets: ______________________
   Best pain gets: ______________________
   Acceptable level of pain: ______________________
3. QUALITY: (Use patient's own words, eg, prick, ache, burn, throb, pull, sharp)
4. ONSET, DURATION, VARIATION, RHYTHMS: ______________________
5. MANNER OF EXPRESSING PAIN: ______________________
6. WHAT RELIEVES THE PAIN? ______________________
7. WHAT CAUSES OR INCREASES THE PAIN? ______________________
8. EFFECTS OF PAIN: (Note decreased function, decreased quality of life.)
   Accompanying symptoms (e.g., nausea) ______________________
   Sleep ______________________
   Appetite ______________________
   Physical activity ______________________
   Relationship with others (e.g., irritability) ______________________
   Emotions (e.g., anger, suicidal, crying) ______________________
   Concentration ______________________
   Other ______________________
9. OTHER COMMENTS: ______________________
10. PLAN: ______________________

Figure 7-6 Sample multidimensional pain assessment tool.

of the BPI include that the patient must be able to correlate the questions to their individual pain experience using the various scales.

Brief Pain Impact Questionnaire (BPIQ). Another way to assess pain quickly in patients with chronic pain is to use a set of structured questions, such as those in the BPIQ:

- How strong is your pain, right now? What was the worst/average pain the past week?
- How many days over the past week have you been unable to do what you would like to do because of your pain?
- Over the past week, how often has pain interfered with your ability to take care of yourself, for example, with bathing, eating, dressing, and going to the toilet?
- Over the past week, how often has pain interfered with your ability to take care of your home-related chores such as grocery shopping, preparing meals, paying bills, and driving?
- How often do you participate in pleasurable activities such as hobbies, socializing with friends, and travel? Over the past week, how often has pain interfered with these activities?
- How often do you do some type of exercise? Over the past week, how often has pain interfered with your ability to exercise?
- Does pain interfere with your ability to think clearly?
- Does pain interfere with your appetite? Have you lost weight?
- Does pain interfere with your sleep? How often over the last week?

STUDY ID#_____   HOSPITAL ID#_____

_____
DO NOT WRITE ABOVE THIS LINE

Brief Pain Inventory (Short Form)

Date: _____ / _____ / _____   Time: _____

Name: _____ _____ _____
　　　　　　　Last　　　　　　　　　　　　First　　　　　　　Middle Initial

1. Throughout our lives, most of us have had pain from time to time (such as minor headaches, sprains, and toothaches). Have you had pain other than these everyday kinds of pain today?

1. Yes　　　　　　　　**2. No**

2. On the diagram, shade in the areas where you feel pain. Put an X on the area that hurts the most.

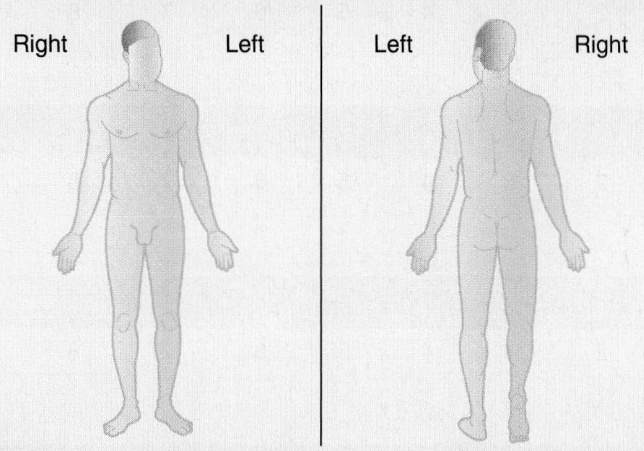

Right　　　Left　　　　　Left　　　Right

3. Please rate your pain by circling the one number that best describes your pain at its **worst** in the last 24 hours.

0　　1　　2　　3　　4　　5　　6　　7　　8　　9　　10

No pain　　　　　　　　　　　　　　　　　　Pain as bad as you can imagine

4. Please rate your pain by circling the one number that best describes your pain at its **least** in the last 24 hours.

0　　1　　2　　3　　4　　5　　6　　7　　8　　9　　10

No pain　　　　　　　　　　　　　　　　　　Pain as bad as you can imagine

5. Please rate your pain by circling the one number that best describes your pain on the **average.**

0　　1　　2　　3　　4　　5　　6　　7　　8　　9　　10

No pain　　　　　　　　　　　　　　　　　　Pain as bad as you can imagine

6. Please rate your pain by circling the one number that tells how much pain you have **right now.**

0　　1　　2　　3　　4　　5　　6　　7　　8　　9　　10

No pain　　　　　　　　　　　　　　　　　　Pain as bad as you can imagine

Figure 7-7 Brief Pain Inventory (BPI).

7. What treatments or medications are you receiving for your pain?

8. In the last 24 hours, how much relief have pain treatments or medications provided? Please circle the one percentage that most shows how much **relief** you have received.

0%	10%	20%	30%	40%	50%	60%	70%	80%	90%	100%
No relief										Complete relief

9. Circle the one number that describes how, during the past 24 hours, pain has interfered with your:

A. General Activity

0	1	2	3	4	5	6	7	8	9	10
Does not interfere										Completely interferes

B. Mood

0	1	2	3	4	5	6	7	8	9	10
Does not interfere										Completely interferes

C. Walking Ability

0	1	2	3	4	5	6	7	8	9	10
Does not interfere										Completely interferes

D. Normal Work (includes both work outside the home and housework)

0	1	2	3	4	5	6	7	8	9	10
Does not interfere										Completely interferes

E. Relations With Other People

0	1	2	3	4	5	6	7	8	9	10
Does not interfere										Completely interferes

F. Sleep

0	1	2	3	4	5	6	7	8	9	10
Does not interfere										Completely interferes

G. Enjoyment of Life

0	1	2	3	4	5	6	7	8	9	10
Does not interfere										Completely interferes

Figure 7-7 (*Continued*)

- Has pain interfered with your energy, mood, personality, or relationships with other people?
- Over the past week, have you taken pain medications?
- Has your use of alcohol or other drugs ever caused a concern for you or those close to you?
- How would you rate your health at the present time? (Weiner, Herr, et al., 2002)

These questions capture the major elements of pain assessment for patients with chronic pain and are easy to use in the clinical setting. They assist in identifying the effects of pain on the patient's functional abilities and daily life so that the nurse can fully appreciate a holistic perspective on the patient's pain experience.

Objective Data Collection

Equipment

- Tongue blade—broken
- Test tubes with stoppers (one for hot water, one for cold water)
- Cotton balls
- Tuning fork—128 Hz or 256 Hz
- Disposable gloves (for use if a rash or wound drainage is expected)

Promoting Patient Comfort, Dignity, and Safety

Since pain is the subjective outcome of a biological and psychological process, there are no clinical tests to directly measure pain. It is critical for nurses to accept that "pain is what the patient says it is" (Lander, 2010, p. 159). When a health professional tries to rate a patient's pain, the patient often is left feeling that she or he has not been believed and that the pain is "imagined." Patients want to know what is causing their pain and how it can be cured. They may appear

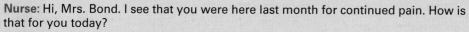

An Example of a Therapeutic Dialogue

The nurse's role relative to subjective data collection is to gather complete information about the symptoms and to help determine the effectiveness of treatments. Remember Mrs. Bond, who was introduced at the beginning of this chapter. She is 42 years old and was diagnosed with fibromyalgia 5 months ago. Her pain control is less than desired; because this concern is her priority, the nurse will perform a complete assessment. The following conversation gives an example of questions and an approach to pain assessment.

Nurse: Hi, Mrs. Bond. I see that you were here last month for continued pain. How is that for you today?

Mrs. Bond: It really seems like it's worse instead of better.

Nurse: That must be very frustrating for you. Let's talk a little bit about it. Can you show me where your pain is?

Mrs. Bond: (rubs lower back with her palm) It's here and then it goes down into my bottom and my legs.

Nurse: On a 0–10 scale with 10 being the worst and 0 no pain, how would you rate it?

Mrs. Bond: Probably about a 5.

Nurse: What level of pain would be acceptable to you?

Mrs. Bond: I would be happy with a 3.

Nurse: How would you describe your pain?

Mrs. Bond: It's an aching pain. In the morning, I'm so stiff that I can hardly get out of bed.

Nurse: Are there other things that you notice with it?

Mrs. Bond: I have trouble sleeping and I just feel tired all of the time.

Nurse: What do you notice makes it worse?

Mrs. Bond: When I'm tired or stressed, it's worse.

Nurse: What makes it better?

Mrs. Bond: If I can get a good night's sleep, it seems better the next day.

Nurse: It seems that being tired is a big part of your pain. How has it influenced your usual activities?

Mrs. Bond: I used to love doing yard work, and I haven't been outside to work for 3 months. I miss that—not the housework, though (laughs)!

Critical Thinking Challenge

- What is the advantage of having Mrs. Bond point to where it hurts first?
- Why is it important to evaluate each item separately rather than to combine them?
- How does the nurse use listening techniques to help Mrs. Bond to relax?

demanding or overly agreeable, defensive or apprehensive, desperate or needy. These behaviours can raise suspicions about the authenticity of the pain. "Patients with chronic pain have been ejected from emergency departments and physicians' offices, been told they are wasting health care dollars, and called drug addicts and other names" (Lander, 2010, p. 159–160). The effect of not being believed and being badly treated by health professionals is seen by patients as a breach of trust.

For some patients, the cause of their pain and a cure cannot be determined. However, "they need to know that everything that can be done will be done." (Lander, 2010, p. 160) As well, new diagnostic procedures and treatments may be developed in the future. This support can help the patient to move forward in life.

Pain has objective effects in other body systems. Acute pain may activate a fight-or-flight stress response in patients. In such an event, blood pressure, pulse, and respirations may increase and the patient will feel the urge to move away from the painful stimulus. These commonly observed responses may not happen with chronic pain, however, because patients have adapted to its ongoing continued stress. Therefore, nurses cannot view a rise in vital signs as an indication of pain level in the patient with chronic pain. They consider vital signs data in addition to other indicators, because there is no way to isolate the changes with other causes. For example, the patient may be experiencing anxiety for another reason such as fear of needles or a previous difficult experience in a health care facility. Assess joints, muscles, the abdomen, and other areas where patients commonly experience pain.

The stress response causes the release of epinephrine, norepinephrine, and cortisol. These hormones have neuroendocrine and metabolic responses. They use stored energy to facilitate the healing of injured tissues. Some effects of these hormones include increases in oxygen consumption, blood glucose and lactate levels, metabolism, and ketones.

Muscle tension may increase; the patient may respond by guarding, or protecting, the affected area. While increased muscle tension helps to protect patients against further pain, chronic tension can contribute to impaired muscle metabolism, muscle atrophy, and delayed return of function.

Inadequately treated pain may contribute to nausea, diaphoresis, and vomiting. Providing pain medication will help alleviate these unwanted effects. Refer to Table 7-1.

In addition to physiological responses, pain manifests with observable behavioural responses. Verbal reports are the most dependable. In patients who cannot verbalize, vocal responses may include moaning or crying. Six pain behaviours indicate pain in patients who cannot verbalize: (1) vocalizations, (2) facial grimacing, (3) bracing, (4) rubbing painful areas, (5) restlessness, and (6) vocalized concerns (Feldt, 2000; Feldt, Ryden, et al., 1998). Many pain assessment tools incorporate the evaluation of these pain behaviours and facilitate accurate detection of pain in various patient populations.

Comprehensive Physical Examination: Pain

A comprehensive assessment of pain follows.

Ask Mrs. Bond to point to her tender areas. Compare these areas with the nine symmetrical "trigger" or tender spots characteristic of fibromyalgia (front and back of neck, shoulders, elbows, chest, upper and lower back, hips, and knees) (Editors of Prevention Health Books for Women, 2002). Give close attention to these painful areas and those nearby. Inspect the skin, looking for changes such as absent or excessive sweating, atrophic skin, and ulcerations. Carefully test the areas for hypo- and hyperalgesia, paresthesia, and allodynia. Nurses can use the DN4 Questionnaire (Bouhassira, Attal, et al., 2005) to assess whether the pain has neuropathic features (see Box 7-4). Also inspect nearby joints for redness and edema. Assess the muscles for tone, strength, and signs of wasting.

The key principles in testing for pain, temperature, sensation, and vibratory sense are to always compare symmetrical areas (right and left side of the body) and, with the extremities, to move from the distal (farthest away) to the proximal areas (closest to the body [Lander, 2010]).

- Test for pain using a broken tongue blade for "sharp" and the rounded end for "dull")
- Test temperature sensation using two test tubes [one with hot water and one with cold])
- Test for light touch, using a wisp of cotton made from a cotton ball
- Test vibratory sensation using a tuning fork—128 Hz or 256 Hz

Assess the four sensations listed above by testing over most of the dermatomes (parts of the body innervated by afferent fibres from one spinal root) and major peripheral nerves (see Chapter 24). For example, include both shoulders (Cervical [C4]), inner and outer aspects of forearms (C6 and Thoracic [T1]), fronts of both thumbs and little fingers (C6 and C8), fronts of both thighs (Lumbar [L2]), medial and lateral aspects of both calves (L4 and L5), little toes (Sacral [S1]), and medial aspects of each buttock (S3). Test vibratory sense bilaterally with a tuning fork (128 or 256 Hz), beginning with finger joints and moving proximally to the wrists, elbows, and shoulders, stopping when sensation is noted.

BOX 7-4 DN4 (DOULEUR NEUROPATHIQUE EN 4 QUESTIONS)

Does your pain have one or more of the following characteristics?	Is your pain associated with one or more of the following symptoms in the same area?
• Burning	• Tingling
• Painful cold	• Pins and needles
• Electric shocks	• Numbness
	• Itching

Adapted from Bouhassira, D., Attal, N., et al. (2005). Comparison of pain syndromes associated with nervous or somatic lesions and development of a new neuropathic pain diagnostic questionnaire (DN4). *Pain, 114*(1–2), 29–36.

Table 7-1   Physiological and Behavioural Pain Indicators

Pain Indicators	Findings
Vocalization	Moaning, groaning, grunting, sighing, gasping, crying, screaming
Verbalization	Stated pain, praying, counting, swearing, repeated phrases
Facial expression	Grimacing, clenching teeth, tightly shutting lips, staring, facial mask (flat emotion), wrinkling forehead, tearing
Body actions	Thrashing, pounding, biting, rocking, rubbing, stretching, shrugging, rotating body part, shifting weight
Behaviours	Massaging, immobilizing, guarding, bracing, applying pressure/heat/cold, assuming special position or posture, crossing legs
Neurological	Agitation, restlessness, stillness, irritability, fear, anxiety, fatigue
Cardiac	Tachycardia, increased blood pressure, increased oxygen demand, increased cardiac output
Pulmonary	Hyperventilation with anxiety or hypoventilation with pain, shallow respirations, hypoxia, depressed cough, atelectasis
Gastrointestinal	Nausea, vomiting, decreased bowel sounds, stress ulcer
Genitourinary	Reduced urine output, urinary retention
Musculoskeletal	Muscle tension, spasm, joint stiffness, immobility
Skin	Pallor, diaphoresis
Metabolic	Increased catabolism, increased glucose, increased lactate and ketones, impaired immune function, impaired wound healing
Emotional	Depression, excessive sleeping, anxiety, fear, impaired individual or family coping
Social	Isolation, impaired role performance, impaired home maintenance, financial burden if unable to work

Then test the toe joints bilaterally, again moving proximally to ankles, knees, and hips, stopping when sensation is noted.

If an area of sensory loss or hypersensitivity is detected, map out the boundaries in detail, using a cotton wisp for light touch and a broken tongue blade for "sharp" and "dull." Start with the point of reduced sensation and move until the patient detects a change. Ask the patient, "Does this feel the same as this?" (Lander, 2010, p. 161). For infection control purposes, be sure to dispose of the cotton and tongue blade. (See Table 7-2 for sample documentation.)

Lifespan Considerations

In several patient populations, pain assessment poses significant challenges. Examples include children and older adults. These patients all have a need for adequate pain relief, yet the assessment process can be difficult.

Newborns, Infants, and Children

Assessment of pain in children is complex and challenging. The best practice is to consistently use a scale specific to the patient's age. Pain scales have been developed that are specific to infants and children. Infants in pain may exhibit brow bulge, eye squeeze, nasolabial fold, open lips, stretched mouth, lip purse, taut tongue, chin quiver, and tongue protrusion (Grunau, Oberlander, et al., 1998). The difficulty with these behavioural measures is that they do not discriminate between pain behaviours and reactions from other sources of discomfort, such as hunger. The nurse should assume that if a condition or procedure is painful for an adult, it is also painful for an infant or child.

Infants and children may exhibit physiological responses to pain including increased heart rate, respiratory rate, blood pressure, palmar sweating, cortisone levels, oxygen requirements, vagal tone, and endorphin levels. Because the preverbal infant cannot self-report pain, the nurse relies on these physiological and behavioural indicators.

The two most common tools used to assess pain in children are the Face, Legs, Activity, Cry, Consolability (FLACC) scale and the FACES pain scale. The FLACC scale was originally designed to measure acute postoperative pain in children 2 months to 7 years old. It uses the indicators of facial expression, leg movement, activity, cry, and ability to console the patient. Behaviours include frowning, kicking, arched back, crying, and difficulty consoling. The tool has established reliability and validity.

Children 2 years and older can identify pain and point to its location. Nurses can use a facial expression scale for children starting at approximately 3 years. The FACES scale (Fig. 7-8) uses six faces ranging from happy with a wide smile to sad with tears on the face. The nurse asks the child to pick the face that best represents the pain he or she is experiencing. FACE zero is very happy because there is "no hurt"; FACE five hurts "as bad as you can imagine." The nurse points to each face, explains the pain intensity, asks the child to choose the FACE that best describes his or her own

Table 7-2 **Documentation of Examination Findings**

Sample Documentation for Pain Assessment

Area	Expected Findings	Unexpected Findings
Temperature	37°C*	38°C
Blood Pressure	118/78 mm Hg (right arm, sitting)	142/88 mm Hg (right arm, sitting)*
Heart Rate	76 beats/min	112 beats/min*
Respirations	16 breaths/min	20 breaths/min, shallow breaths*
Pain	No pain reported with light palpation of hands, arms, elbows, shoulders, front and back of neck, upper and lower back, buttocks, hips, thighs knees, lower legs, or feet, bilaterally	No pain reported in hands, arms, lower legs, or feet bilaterally. Pain reported as 3/10 with light palpation over symmetrical areas of front and back of neck, chest, shoulders, upper back, elbows, and knees bilaterally. Pain reported as 5/10 with light palpation over symmetrical areas of lower back, buttocks, and hips bilaterally.*
Skin	White tones, moist—both arms and hands. Red hair evenly distributed over both arms. Warm skin temperature over both hands and arms. Warm skin temperature over both feet and legs. No hair on legs (shaved).*	Left hand—white tone, moist. Right hand—skin is red and the hand is edematous. Red hair over left arm; red hair from mid-right forearm to shoulder. Skin temperature over left hand and arm is slightly warm; right hand and wrist are hot to touch.
Muscles	Muscle mass symmetrical in size and contour bilaterally—hands, forearms, upper arms, and shoulder girdle, feet, calves, and thighs.*	Muscle mass of left hand, forearm, upper arms and shoulder girdle greater than on right side. Muscle mass of left and right feet, calves, and thighs is symmetrical.
Range of Motion (ROM)	Full ROM bilaterally of thumbs, fingers, wrists, elbows, and shoulders, toes, ankles, knees, and hips without discomfort.*	Full ROM on left (thumb, fingers, wrist), with more movement at elbow and shoulder. Limited ROM on right thumb, fingers, and wrist, with more movement at elbow and shoulder. Full ROM bilaterally of toes, ankles, knees, and hips without discomfort.
Muscle Tone	Slight resistance felt bilaterally with passive movement of upper and lower extremities.*	Slight resistance felt on left upper extremity with passive movement. Unable to test right extremity because of intense pain. Slight resistance felt bilaterally with passive movement of lower extremities.
Muscle Strength	Strong, 5/5; active motion against resistance for all muscle groups.*	Strong, 5/5; active motion against resistance for all muscle groups of left fingers, wrist, elbow, shoulder, hips, thighs, and ankles. Unable to test right fingers, wrist, elbow, and shoulder because of pain. Strong, 5/5; active motion against resistance for all muscle groups of lower extremities.
Sensation	Both superficial pain and light touch intact bilaterally over dermatomes C4 to C8 and T1. Vibratory sense and position sense intact bilaterally at fingers. Extinction, stereognosis, and graphesthesia intact bilaterally. Both superficial pain and light touch intact over dermatomes L2 to S1 bilaterally. Vibration sense at great toes and position sense at toes intact bilaterally.*	Superficial pain and light touch intact over dermatomes C4 to C8 and T1 on left side. On right side, light touch intact over dermatomes C4 to C8 and T1. Patient refused the test of superficial pain, vibratory sense, extinction, stereognosis, and graphesthesia on the left side because the tests would be too painful. Both superficial pain and light touch intact over dermatomes L2 to S1 bilaterally. Vibration sense at great toes and position sense at toes intact bilaterally.

*Indicates findings for Mrs. Bond.
Adapted from Lander, J. A. (2010). Pain assessment. In T. C. Stephen, D. L. Skillen, R. A. Day, & L. S. Bickley (Eds.). *Canadian Bates' guide to health assessment for nurses* (1st ed., pp. 161–162). Philadelphia, PA: Wolters Kluwer Health/Lippincott Williams & Wilkins.

pain, and records the appropriate number. The young child's thinking is concrete and egocentric, so it is important to use vocabulary such as "no hurt" or "biggest hurt" for the scale. The nurse can also talk with the caregiver to learn vocabulary that the child uses at home to describe pain, such as "owie" or "ouchie." The FACES scale has been evaluated with young children (Hunter, McDowell, et al., 2000). The scale has also been used to measure pain intensity with the elderly and

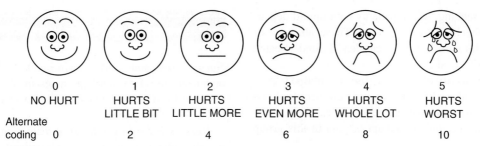

| 0 | 1 | 2 | 3 | 4 | 5 |
| NO HURT | HURTS LITTLE BIT | HURTS LITTLE MORE | HURTS EVEN MORE | HURTS WHOLE LOT | HURTS WORST |

Alternate coding 0 — 2 — 4 — 6 — 8 — 10

Figure 7-8 The FACES scale is used in children 3 years of age and older.

non-verbal older adults with dementia (Herr, Mobily, et al., 1998); (Herr, Bjoro, et al., 2006).

Starting between 7 and 10 years, children can use numeric rating scales used with adults. Use of a colour-coded scale, such as the combined thermometer, may be helpful (see Fig. 7-5). Additionally, with this scale the child can specify location and quality. He or she might describe the pain experience as horrible, terrible, terrifying, or stabbing.

Pain also affects children in the affective and sensory dimensions. Children may have reduced sleep, appetite, and fitness level, all of which can affect both school and play. Pain can disturb mood, leading to emotional distress, depression, and anxiety. It also can disrupt family functioning and make the child fearful for the future (Eccleston, Bruce, et al., 2006). An accurate assessment is essential for adequate treatment.

Older Adults

Older patients have some specific circumstances that can lead to concerns with pain assessment. Many older patients have chronic illnesses such as osteoarthritis or diabetes that cause pain. Although pain is prevalent in older patients, some of them see pain as just part of natural aging. They may be reluctant to report pain, because they want their providers to consider them "good patients," or they may fear that reports of pain may lead to more tests, or expensive medications that they cannot afford. The older person may hide expressions of pain and be stoic. Although experiencing pain, their outward reaction to it may hide their discomfort.

When assessing pain in older adults, nurses reassure patients of their interest in the pain and their desire to help manage it. Older patients may fear uncontrolled pain, because it could result in hospitalization or affect their long-term ability to maintain independent living. They also may fear dependency on others and thus avoid reporting or treating pain.

When assessing pain in older adults, the nurse should be sure to also review the following:

• Question about the effects of pain on diet, sleep, and mood. Unrelieved pain may lead to insomnia or depression and seriously affect the patient's quality of life.
• Ask about any comorbidities such as osteoarthritis that may cause pain or have an influence on medication choices.
• Review all medications that the patient is taking, including vitamins and herbal supplements. Older patients may not take medications as ordered or refuse to take drugs that cause side effects such as sedation or constipation.

Assessment of pain leading to effective treatment can improve the quality of life for older adults. Providing adequate pain management for them can occur through care and reassurance and by taking the time to assess pain accurately.

Special Situations

Patients Unable to Report Pain

Nurses are required to regularly assess patients for pain. While self-report is the most reliable indicator of pain, many patients cannot verbally communicate this information. The development of behavioural tools for assessing pain in non-verbal patients is the newest area of pain assessment and a developing science. For example, the Payen Behavioural Pain Scale (BPS), the Critical-Care Pain Observation Tool, and the Non-Verbal Pain Scale have been used with intubated and/or unconscious patients (American Society for Pain Management Nursing [ASPMN], 2006). The FLACC (Fowler, 2010) tool continues to be used although it is not valid and reliable with older adults who are cognitively impaired and has not been tested with critically ill patients (Marmo & Fowler, 2010)

When attempting to perform a pain assessment on the patient who cannot self-report pain:

• Try one of the tools listed above.
• Try to identify any potential causes for pain.
• Observe patient behaviours.
• Ask the family or other caregivers if they have noticed any changes in behaviour.
• Attempt an analgesic trial (Herr, Bjoro, et al., 2006).

Patients With Opioid Tolerance

"Fear of engendering addiction is frequently reported as both a provider barrier and a patient barrier to effective pain management" (Goebel, Sherbourne, et al., 2010, p. 92). Nurses need to address patients' concerns about addiction. Patients with a history of opioid tolerance pose difficult challenges to nurses for pain assessment (Jage, 2005). They have an altered physiologic response to the pain stimulus, and the repeated use of opioids causes their bodies to become more sensitive to pain. This sensitivity is called **opioid hyperalgesia** and can occur as soon as 1 month after opioid use begins.

Not only are patients with opioid tolerance more sensitive to pain, they experience considerable bias from health care providers because they often report high levels of pain with little relief from usual doses of opioids. They are often labelled as drug seeking. Many patients with opioid dependence mistrust the health care system. These attitudes of patients and health care providers can lead to undertreated pain (Grant, Cordts, et al., 2007).

Patients with a history of substance use are entitled to pain relief. Using a standard reliable pain measurement tool and setting a reasonable pain management goal can help avoid misunderstanding and undertreatment of pain in this group of patients.

⚠ SAFETY ALERT 7-1

Some patients are at high risk when receiving pain medication. Be aware of common aberrant behaviours when reassessing patients, especially when opioids have been prescribed to treat pain: purposeful oversedation, negative mood changes, appearing intoxicated, increasingly unkempt or impaired appearance, involvement in car or other accidents, increased doses without authorization, reports of lost or stolen prescriptions, use of pain medication to ease situational stressors, abuse of alcohol or illicit drugs, or record of arrests.

Nursing Diagnoses, Outcomes, and Interventions

The nurse assesses the patient's pain level in the initial pain assessment and uses specialized pain tools if indicated. Using the assessment data, the nurse incorporates critical thinking to establish a nursing diagnosis list. Table 7-3 compares two sets of nursing diagnoses, unexpected findings, and interventions commonly related to pain (Bulechek, Butcher, et al., 2008). The assessment data are the basis for the care provided to relieve acute or chronic pain.

Reassessing and Documenting Pain

Nurses assess and reassess pain regularly. Most health care organizations set standards for assessment such as every shift or every 4 or 6 hours depending on the specific practice area and needs of the patient.

Reassessing pain is similar to reassessing the patient taking blood pressure medication or a patient with diabetes who needs regular blood glucose level testing. For patients taking pain medication, reassessment provides a measure of the drug's efficacy. It allows the nurse to see if pain intensity has decreased since administration—much as blood pressure should be lower once the patient takes blood pressure medication. Most hospitals have a standard time frame for reassessment, such as 1 hour for oral medication and 30 minutes for pain medication given intravenously. They base these time frames on the time it takes a pain medication to provide a noticeable decrease in pain intensity.

⚠ SAFETY ALERT 7-2

Health care providers often write orders on an "as needed" (PRN) basis for hospitalized patients. Nurses must use critical thinking and nursing judgment about administration, dose, route, and frequency. It is essential to accurately assess, document, and reassess the pain level and response to treatment.

Health care facilities are shifting from paper documentation to computerized systems to enter nursing data (see Chapter 5). Figure 7-9 shows examples of documentation of pain intensity for (A) shift assessment and (B) medication administration reassessment. Nurses are legally accountable for the quality of their pain management, including assessment, treatment, and reassessment (Camp & O'Sullivan, 1987).

Table 7-3	Common Nursing Diagnoses Associated With Pain		
Diagnosis and Related Factors	**Point of Differentiation**	**Assessment Characteristics**	**Nursing Interventions**
Acute pain related to actual or potential tissue injury	Sudden and/or severe pain lasting from 1 s to 3 mo	Self-report of pain; increased P, BP, R; diaphoresis; guarded position; crying; moaning; nausea; facial grimace	Administer ordered pain medication on time* Assess effectiveness of medication Promote factors that increase pain tolerance (music [Good & Sukhee, 2008], distraction) Utilize relaxation strategies, breathing, and distraction to decrease pain intensity
Chronic pain	Pain that lasts more than 3 mo	Self-report of pain, discomfort, facial mask, weight loss, depression, insomnia, frequent position changes	Assess pain experience and effect on life Evaluate depression Consider methods to reduce pain intensity: muscle relaxation, and cutaneous stimulation (heat/ice, TENS—Transcutaneous Nerve Stimulation)* Evaluate side effects of medications

*Collaborative interventions.

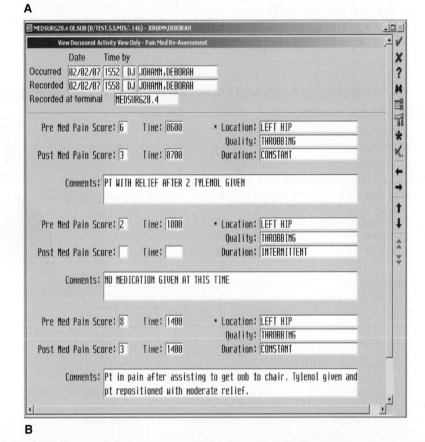

A

B

Key:
- Questions with (→) indicate a group reponse is available.
- (→ →) indicates group response with option to write in.
- Questions without an arrow are free text.
- If pain score at rest is elevated, a consult is sent to the Pain Nurse and a care plan is Query linked
- A second page of this intervention is the same as the first, just allowing the RN to document to a site.

Figure 7-9 **A.** Example of an electronic pain shift assessment (done every shift). **B.** Example of a post pain medication assessment, completed after medication is given; can have multiple entries.

Barriers to Pain Assessment

Prejudices and bias related to educational, family, or cultural values can affect how nurses perceive the patient's self-report of pain. Studies have shown that nurses have difficulty accepting the patient's report of pain as valid and credible (Berry, Covington, et al., 2006; D'Arcy, 2008). It is important to recognize the issues surrounding bias and prejudice and work to minimize their effect on pain management.

When a pain assessment is inaccurate or incomplete, patients suffer because of incorrect medication and treatment choices. Fear of respiratory depression and addiction affect pain assessment and management (Lander & Adams, 2010). Focusing on pain relief as the primary end to the assessment process and treatment selection will help control fears and bias that can negatively affect patient care.

Evidence-Informed Critical Thinking

The nurse is responsible for assessing pain and negotiating pain and functional goals with the patient. Based upon those goals, the nurse implements pharmacologic and nonpharmacological interventions. He or she documents the assessment, analysis, interventions, and reassessment in the patient health record. Additionally, the nurse may identify pain as a priority concern and consider its broader effects on sleep, activities, and mood. The nurse can analyze and document this information in a SOAP (subjective, objective, analysis, plan) note that shows this critical thinking.

R*emember* Mrs. Bond — *Analyzing Findings From Health History and Physical Examination*

Remember Mrs. Bond, who was recently diagnosed with fibromyalgia. The nurse has completed the initial data collection, set goals with her, and established a plan of care. The following nursing note illustrates the documentation of subjective and objective data.

Subjective: States that the pain is getting worse instead of better. "It's all over, but especially in my lower back." The pain radiates into her buttocks and legs bilaterally. Rates it 5 on a 0 to 10 scale. Has been present for 5 months since her diagnosis. Described as an achy pain with increased stiffness in the morning. Being tired or stressed aggravates it. Reports feeling "exhausted" even after 10 hours of sleep. Able to perform functional activities with more effort except that she has not done any yard work. Pain goal stated at 3/10.

Objective: Appears older than her age. Facial expression fatigued with dark circles under her eyes. Posture slightly slouched in chair, shifting from side to side frequently. Affect flat. Dress appropriate to weather and well groomed. T 37°C, P 112 beats/min, R 20 breaths/min and shallow, BP 142/88 mm Hg (right arm, sitting).

Analysis: Chronic pain related to fibromyalgia; impaired sleep related to fibromyalgia.

Plan: Communicate findings to health care provider. Provide patient education on medications and side effects. Discuss ways that patient can get some mild exercise (such as yoga, stretching, warm water aerobics, walking), working up to three to five times weekly. Help Mrs. Bond to understand that even though she is in pain, activity will help to decrease the pain. Evaluate sleep hygiene and recommend routines that promote sleep. Suggest massages with long gentle stroking rather than those with deep muscle tissue massage. Discuss ways that she can make household tasks more efficient to save energy for enjoyable activities, possibly including some light gardening. Provide information about support group for patients with fibromyalgia.

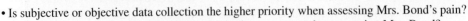

Critical Thinking Challenge

- Is subjective or objective data collection the higher priority when assessing Mrs. Bond's pain?
- What techniques of physical assessment might the nurse use when assessing Mrs. Bond?
- How do assessments from the general survey cluster with the pain assessment?

In many facilities, nurses initiate referrals based on assessment findings. In this case, the health care provider ordered a referral to the pain team because Mrs. Bond's pain is not responsive to her current medical treatment. The nurse communicates the reason for the consult using the following SBAR (Situation, Background, Assessment, Recommendations) format. Other results that might trigger a pain consult include history of chronic pain, regular use of opioids for more than 3 months, substance abuse, difficult pain management, patient dissatisfaction with pain relief, high dose requirements, or significant side effects related to pain management.

The following conversation illustrates how the nurse organizes the information to provide necessary details about Mrs. Bond to the pain team.

Situation: Hi, this is Belinda and I've been talking with Mrs. Bond about her pain management in the clinic today.

Background: She's 42 years old and was diagnosed with fibromyalgia about 5 months ago. We've been seeing her to help manage her pain. She currently is taking a selective serotonin reuptake inhibitor and a prescription nonsteroidal anti-inflammatory (NSAID) for pain.

Assessment: She's reporting a pain level of 5/10 and really would like to be down to about a 3/10. Mostly, it's an achy pain all over but especially is in her lower back and radiates into her buttocks and legs, bilaterally. She appears to be fatigued and a little depressed and is having difficulty sleeping. She reports feeling "exhausted," even after 10 hours of sleep.

Recommendations: We have discussed gentle exercises, massage, stretching, and walking. We would like you to see her to see if you have any suggestions about a different medication dose or combination—perhaps something to improve her sleep such as amitriptyline (Elavil) and something else for pain such as pregabalin (Lyrica). She's been very patient in working with us on this, and we would like to get something that works for her. She said that she could wait about an hour now or come back to see you for another appointment.

As well, I think that she would benefit from seeing other members of the pain team. The physical therapist could teach her some stretching exercises and assist her in developing a plan of graduated exercises. Seeing the massage therapist for regular gentle massages may help her pain. At some point, Mrs. Bond could see the clinical psychologist regarding cognitive therapy.

Critical Thinking Challenge

- At what point would you decide to contact other health care providers for more pain medication?
- What is the role of the nurse in working with the pain team?
- What parts of the pain treatment are within the nursing domain? Which are within collaborative practice?

Pain is a complex syndrome that involves an accurate and complete assessment. Pain is often a subjective symptom, although with acute pain there are objective signs of its presence. Many pain tools have been developed for different populations. Pain assessment and its treatment are primarily within the role of nursing practice.

Now that you have completed the reading and case features for this chapter, consider Mrs. Bond's case and its relationship to what you are learning. Answer the following questions.

- Describe the mechanisms of pain. *(Knowledge)*
- Differentiate between neuropathic and nociceptive pain. *(Comprehension)*
- How would you assess pain if Mrs. Bond were a mentally challenged young adult or a cognitively impaired older adult? *(Application)*
- What factors might contribute to observations made during the pain assessment? *(Analysis)*
- What data would you use to plan patient education for the reduction of pain? *(Synthesis)*
- How would you assess the effectiveness of health promotion strategies for the patient who experiences chronic pain? *(Evaluation)*

Key Points

- Pain can result from various stimuli transmitted via the peripheral nervous system to the central nervous system for processing.
- Pain can be musculoskeletal or neuropathic, depending on the source of the pain stimulus.
- Verbal descriptors that patients use include burning and tingling. Painful numbness or tingling is associated with neuropathic pain.
- A decrease of three points on the Numeric Pain Intensity (NPI) Scale is considered clinically significant.
- When assessing pain, nurses use scales designed for the specific population to which the patient belongs (eg, children).
- Patients with chronic pain need more than just a pain intensity rating and require use of a multidimensional scale such as the Brief Pain Inventory (BPI).
- Nurses believe the patient's report of pain.
- Avoidance of labelling and stigmatization is important for patients who are dependent on pain medications to control their pain.
- Nurses always assess the patient's pain. If the patient is nonverbal, the nurse can use a behavioural pain scale designed to identify pain in that particular population.
- Nurses are aware of the legal implications of pain assessment. Not documenting an assessment means it has not been done.
- Reassessing pain can provide a means of determining the efficacy of an administered pain medication.

Review Questions

1. The patient has pain of a short duration with an identifiable cause. This is referred to as
   A. acute pain
   B. chronic pain
   C. neuropathic pain
   D. complex pain

2. To identify the location of pain, the nurse asks the patient
   A. how long he or she has had the pain
   B. to rate the intensity of the pain on a scale from 0 to 10
   C. to point to the painful area
   D. to describe the quality of pain

3. A patient says that his pain worsens with weight-bearing activity. The nurse would consider this
   A. an alleviating factor
   B. a functional pain goal
   C. quality/description
   D. an aggravating factor

4. Which of the following tools would a nurse use to perform a multidimensional pain assessment?
   A. Visual Analog Scale (VAS)
   B. Brief Pain Impact Questionnaire (BPIQ)
   C. Numeric Pain Intensity Scale (NPI)
   D. Verbal Descriptor Scale (VDS)

5. For what circumstance would the nurse be most likely to assess pain using the McGill Pain Questionnaire (MPQ)?
   A. Verbal description
   B. Alleviating factors
   C. Functional status goal
   D. Pain goal

6. Which of the following indicators would be most likely to signify to the nurse that the patient is having pain?
   A. Falling asleep
   B. Rubbing a body part
   C. Relaxed body position
   D. Facial relaxation

7. The patient reports pain, depression, and insomnia. The nurse observes a masklike facial expression and frequent position changes. Which of the following is the nurse most likely to use to describe the patient's findings?
   A. Acute pain
   B. Chronic pain
   C. Neuropathic pain
   D. Complex Regional Pain Syndrome (CRPS)

8. The nurse is most likely to use the FACES pain scale with
   A. children
   B. patients with dementia
   C. older adults
   D. unconscious patients

9. Which of the following is the rationale for the nurse to reassess the patient's pain after treatment?
   A. To pinpoint the pain's location
   B. To measure the pain's duration
   C. To establish the efficacy of medication
   D. To make changes to the patient's pain goal

10. Barriers to pain assessment include that nurses
   A. believe that patients suffer if undermedicated
   B. focus on pain relief as a primary end to the assessment process
   C. choose treatment that will positively affect the patient care
   D. have difficulty accepting the patient's self-report as valid

Canadian Nursing Research

Allen, M., Oberle, K., et al. (2008). A randomized clinical trial of elk velvet antler in rheumatoid arthritis. *Biological Research for Nursing, 9*(3), 254–261.

Morse, J. M., Beres, M. A., et al. (2003). Identifying signals of suffering by linking verbal and facial cues. *Qualitative Health Research, 13*(8), 1063–1077.

Sawyer, J, Haslam, L., et al. (2010). Pain prevalence study in a large Canadian teaching hospital. Round 2: Lessons learned? *Pain Management Nursing, 11*(1), 45–55.

International Nursing Research

Carlson, C. L. (2010). Prior conditions influencing nurses' decisions to adopt evidence-based postoperative pain assessment practices. *Pain Management Nursing, 11*(4), 245–258.

Kindler, L. L. Bennett, R. M., et al. (2011). Central sensitivity syndromes: Mounting pathophysioloic evidence to link fibromyalgia with other common chronic pain disorders. *Pain Management Nursing, 12*(1), 15–24.

Shaw, S. M. (2007). Responding appropriately to patients with chronic illnesses. *Nursing Standard, 21*(24), 35–39.

Shaw, S., & Lee, A. (2010). Student nurses' misconceptions of adults with chronic nonmalignant pain. *Pain Management Nursing, 11*(1), 2–14.

Ware, L. J., Bruckenthal, P., et al. (2011). Factors that influence patient advocacy by pain management nurses: Results of the American Society for Pain Management Nursing survey. *Pain Management Nursing, 12*(1), 25–32.

Wheeler, E., Hardie, T., et al. (2010). Level of pain and waiting time in the emergency department. *Pain Management Nursing, 11*(2), 108–114.

References

Ackley, B., Ladwig, G., et al. (2008). *Evidence-based nursing care guidelines*. St. Louis, MO: Mosby Elsevier.

American Geriatric Society. (2002). The management of persistent pain in older persons—The American Geriatric Society Panel on Persistent Pain in Older Persons. *Journal of the American Geriatrics Society, 50*(6), 205–224.

American Pain Society. (2003). *Principles of analgesic use in the treatment of acute and cancer pain* (5th ed.). Glenview, IL: Author.

American Pain Society. (2007). *Are basic pain mechanisms different in women than in men?* Retrieved from http://www.ampainsoc.org/enews/sept07/

American Society for Pain Management Nursing. (2006). *Position statement. Pain assessment in the nonverbal patient*. Retrieved from http://www.aspmn.org/Organization/documents/Nonverbal0306FINAL_003.pdf

Anand, K. J. (2007). Pain assessment in preterm neonates. *Pediatrics, 119*(3), 605–607.

Astuto, M., Rosano, G., et al. (2007). Methodologies for the treatment of acute and chronic nononcologic pain in children. *Edizioni Minerva Anestesiologica, 73*(9), 459–465.

Bennett, M., Attal, N., et al. (2007). Using screening tools to identify neuropathic pain. *Pain, 127*(3), 199–203.

Berry, P. H., Covington, E., et al. (2006). *Pain: Current understanding of assessment, management, and treatments*. Reston, VA: National Pharmaceutical Council, Inc and the Joint Commission on Accreditation of Healthcare Organizations.

Birse, T. M., & Lander, J. A. (1998). Prevalence of chronic pain. *Canadian Journal of Public Health, 89*, 129–131.

Bouhassira, D., Attal, N., et al. (2005). Comparison of pain syndromes associated with nervous or somatic lesions and development of a new neuropathic pain diagnostic questionnaire (DN4). *Pain, 114*(1–2), 29–36.

Brandes, J. L. (2006). The influence of estrogen on migraine. *Journal of the American Medical Society, 295*(15), 1824–1830.

Bulechek, G. M., Butcher, H. K., et al. (Eds.). (2008). *Nursing intervention classification (NIC)* (5th ed.). St. Louis, MO: Mosby Elsevier.

Camp, L. D., & O'Sullivan, P. (1987). Comparison of medical, surgical, and oncology patients' descriptions of pain and nurses' documentation of pain assessments. *Journal of Advanced Nursing, 12,* 593–598.

Canadian Pain Society. (2005). *Accreditation pain standard: Making it happen!* Retrieved from http://www.canadianpainsociety.ca/accreditation_manual.pdf

Canadian Pain Society. (2011). Pain is costing Canada big-time in dollars,' doctor says. *Edmonton Journal,* Monday, March 21, 2011, A5.

Carlson, C. L. (2010). Prior conditions influencing nurses' decisions to adopt evidence-based postoperative pain assessment practices. *Pain Management Nursing, 11*(4), 245–258.

Cervero, F. (2005). The gate control theory, then and now in the paths of pain. In H. Mersky, J. Loeser, et al. (Eds.). *The paths of pain.* Seattle, WA: IASP Press.

D'Arcy, Y. M. (2003). Pain assessment. In P. Iyer (Ed.). *Medical-legal aspects of pain and suffering.* Tucson, AZ: Lawyers and Judges Publishing Company.

D'Arcy, Y. (2007a). *Pain management: Evidence-based tools and techniques for nursing professionals.* Marblehead, MA: HcPro.

D'Arcy, Y. (2007b). What's the diagnosis? *The American Nurse Today, 1*(4), 29–30.

D'Arcy, Y. (2008). Pain management survey report. *Nursing, 38*(6), 42–49; quiz 49–51.

Daut, R. L., Cleeland, C. S., et al. (1983). Development of the Wisconsin Brief Pain Questionnaire to assess pain in cancer or other diseases. *Pain, 17,* 197–210.

Eccleston, C., Bruce, E., et al. (2006). Chronic pain in children and adolescents. *Paediatric Nursing, 18*(10), 30–33.

Editors of Prevention Health Books for Women. (2002). *Prevention's ultimate guide to women's health and wellness: Action plans for more than 100 women's health problems* (pp. 378–382). Emmaus, PA: Rodale Inc.

Falla, D., Farina, D., et al. (2007). Muscle pain induces task-dependent changes in cervical agonist/antagonist activity. *Journal of Applied Physiology, 102*(2), 601–609.

Farrar, J. T., Young, J. P., et al. (2001). Clinical importance of changes in chronic pain intensity measured on an 11 point numerical pain rating scale. *Pain, 94,* 149–158.

Feldt, K. S. (2000). The checklist of non-verbal pain indicators (CNPI). *Pain Management Nursing, 1*(1), 13–21.

Feldt, K. S., Ryden, M. B., et al. (1998). Treatment of pain in cognitively impaired compared with cognitively intact older patients with hip fractures. *Journal of the American Geriatrics Society, 46,* 1079–1085.

Gevirtz, C. (2007). Treating sleep disturbances in patients with chronic pain. *Nursing, 37*(4), 26–27.

Goebel, J. R., & Sherbourne, C. D., et al. (2010). Addressing patients' concerns about pain management and addiction risks. *Pain management nursing, 11*(2), 92–98.

Good, M., & Sukhee, A. (2008). Korean and American music reduces pain in Korean women after gynecologic surgery. *Pain Management in Nursing, 9*(3), 96–103.

Grant, M. S., Cordts, G. A., et al. (2007). Acute pain management in hospitalized patients with current opioid abuse. *Topics in Advanced Practice Nursing.* Retrieved from http://www.medscape.com/viewarticle/557043

Green, C. R., Anderson, K. O., et al. (2003). The unequal burden of pain: Confronting racial and ethnic disparities in pain. *Pain Medicine, 4*(3), 277–294.

Green, C. R., & Hart-Johnson, T. (2010a). The impact of chronic pain on the health of black and white men. *Journal of the National Medical Association, 102*(4), 321–331.

Green, C. R., & Hart-Johnson, T. (2010b). The adequacy of chronic pain management prior to presenting at a tertiary care pain center: The role of patient socio-demographic characteristics. *Journal of Pain, 11*(8), 746–754.

Grunau, R. V. E., Oberlander, T. F., et al. (1998). Bedside application of the Neonatal Facial Coding System in pain assessment of premature neonates. *Pain, 76,* 277–286.

Herr, K., Bjoro, K., et al. (2006). Tools for assessment of pain in nonverbal older adults with dementia: A state-of-the-science review. *Journal of Pain and Symptom Management, 31*(2), 170–192.

Herr, K., Coyne, P., et al. (2006). Pain assessment in the nonverbal patient: Position statement with clinical practice recommendations. *Pain Management Nursing, 7*(2), 44–52.

Herr, K., Mobily, P., et al. (1998). Evaluation of the faces pain scale for use with the elderly. *Clinical Journal of Pain, 14,* 29–38.

Hirsh, A. T., Jensen, M. P., et al. (2010). Evaluation of nurses' self-insight into their pain assessment and treatment decisions. *Journal of pain, 11*(5), 454–461.

Hφlen, J. C., Lydersen, S., et al. (2008). The Brief Pain Inventory: Pain's interference with functions is different in cancer pain compared with noncancer chronic pain. *Clinical Journal of Pain, 24*(3), 219–225.

Hunter, M., McDowell, L., et al. (2000). An evaluation of the faces pain scale with young children. *Journal of Pain and Symptom Management, 20*(2), 122–129.

Jage, J. (2005). Opioid tolerance and dependence—do they matter? *European Journal of Pain, 9*(2), 157–162.

Lander, J. A. (2010). Pain assessment. In T. C. Stephen, D. L. Skillen, R. A. Day, & L. S. Bickley (Eds.). *Canadian Bates' guide to health assessment for nurses* (1st ed., pp.147–166). Philadelphia, PA: Wolters Kluwer Health/Lippincott Williams & Wilkins.

Lander, J. A., & Adams, N. (2010). Pain. In R. A. Day, P. Paul, et al. (Eds.). *Brunner & Suddarth's textbook of Canadian medical-surgical nursing* (2nd ed., pp. 252–292). Philadelphia, PA: Wolters Kluwer Health/Lippincott Williams & Wilkins.

Linton, A., & Lach, H. (2007). *Matteson & McConnells' gerontological nursing concepts and practice* (3rd ed.). St. Louis, MO: Saunders, Elsevier.

Marmo, L. & Fowler, S. (2010). Pain assessment tool in the critically ill post-open heart surgery patient population. *Pain Management Nursing, 11*(3), 134–140.

McAffery, M., & Pasero, C. (1999). *Pain: Clinical manual* (2nd ed.). St. Louis, MO: Mosby.

McCleane, G. (2008). Pain perception in the elderly patient. *Clinics in Geriatric Medicine, 24*(2), 203–211.

McDonald, D. D., & Weiskopf, C. S. A. (2001). Adult patients' postoperative pain descriptions and responses to the Short Form McGill Pain Questionnaire. *Clinical Nursing Research, 10*(4), 442–452.

Melzack, R. (1987). The short form McGill Pain Questionnaire. *Pain, 30,* 191–197.

Melzack, R. (1975). The McGill Pain Questionnaire: Major properties and scoring methods. *Pain, 1,* 277–299.

Melzack, R., & Wall, P. (1975). Pain mechanisms: A new theory. *Science, 150*(699), 971–979.

Mersky, H., Loeser, J., et al. (Eds.). (2005). *The paths of pain.* Seattle, WA: IASP Press.

Mystakidou, K., Cleeland, C., et al. (2004). Greek M.D. Anderson Symptom Inventory: Validation and utility in cancer patients. *Oncology, 57*(3–4), 203–210.

Purves, D. (2008). *Neuroscience* (4th ed.). Sunderland, MA: Sinauer Associates, Inc.

Queen's News Centre. (2004). *Chronic pain incidence in S.E. Ontario higher than average.* Retrieved from http://qnc. queensu.ca/story_loader.php?id=40bf31d155807

Raichle, K. A., Osborne, T. L., et al. (2006). The reliability and validity of pain interference measures in persons with spinal cord injury. *Journal of Pain, 7*(3), 179–186.

Reyes-Gibby, C. C., Aday, L. A., et al. (2007). Pain in aging community-dwelling adults in the United States: Non-Hispanic Whites, Non-Hispanic Blacks, and Hispanics. *Journal of Pain, 8*(1), 75–84.

Rowbotham, M. (2006). Pharmacologic management of complex regional pain syndrome. *Clinical Journal of Pain, 22*(5), 425–429.

Sawyer, J, Haslam, L., et al. (2010). Pain prevalence study in a large Canadian teaching hospital. Round 2: Lessons learned? *Pain Management Nursing, 11*(1), 45–55.

Staats, P. S., Argoff, C., et al. (2004). Neuropathic pain: Incorporating new consensus guidelines into the reality of clinical practice. *Advanced Studies in Medicine, 4*(7B), S542–S582.

Stephen, T. C., Skillen, D. L., et al. (Eds.). (2010). *Canadian Bates' guide to health assessment for nurses* (1st ed.). Philadelphia, PA: Wolters Kluwer Health/Lippincott Williams & Wilkins.

Stutts, L. A., McCulloch, R. C., et al. (2009). Sex differences in prior pain experience. *Journal of Pain, 10*(12), 1226–1230.

Tan, G., Jensen, M. P., et al. (2004) Validation of the Brief Pain Inventory for chronic nonmalignant pain. *Journal of Pain, 5*(2), 133–137.

Victor, T. W., Jensen, M. P., et al. (2008). The dimensions of pain quality: Factor analysis of the Pain Quality Assessment Scale. *Clinical Journal of Pain, 24*(6), 550–555.

Weiner, D. K., Herr, K., et al. (2002). *Persistent pain in older adults: An interdisciplinary guide for treatment.* New York, NY: Springer Publishing Company.

Wheeler, E., Hardie, T. et al. (2010). Level of pain and waiting time in the emergency department. *Pain Management Nursing, 11*(2), 108–114.

Williams, V. S., Smith, M. Y., et al. (2006). The validity and utility of the BPI interference measures for evaluating the impact of osteoarthritic pain. *Journal of Pain Symptom Management, 31*(1), 48–57.

The Canadian Jensen's Nursing Health Assessment suite offers these additional resources to enhance learning and facilitate understanding of this chapter:

- the Point online resource, http//thepoint.lww.com/Stephen1E
- *Laboratory Manual for Canadian Jensen's Nursing Health Assessment: A Best Practice Approach*

Nutrition Assessment

Learning Objectives

1 Discuss the role of primary nutrients in maintaining health.

2 Outline dietary guidelines based on the Canada's Food Guide.

3 Discuss developmental, social, cultural, and religious factors affecting the nutritional status of patients.

4 Describe the nurse's role in nutritional assessment.

5 Evaluate the potential effects of medications and nutritional supplements on nutrient intake, absorption, utilization, and excretion.

6 Identify physical signs and symptoms of malnutrition.

7 Differentiate expected from unexpected findings in patients based on the calculation of body mass index (BMI) and ideal body weight, in addition to the consideration of muscle mass and fat distribution.

8 Consider age, condition, gender, and culture to individualize nutritional assessments for infants, children, adolescents, women who are pregnant and lactating, and older adults.

9 Document and communicate data from nutritional assessments using appropriate terminology and principles of recording.

10 Use nutritional assessment findings to identify nursing diagnoses and initiate a plan of care.

*M*iss Heidi Schneider, 15 years old (weight is 40 kg, height is 1.64 m), was recently discharged from the hospital with a diagnosis of anorexia nervosa. This hospital stay was the most recent of three in the past year. Her mother, a full-time homemaker, is very involved in Heidi's school and social activities.

The family is being visited today by a home care nurse for a follow-up assessment. The role of the home care nurse is to assess Heidi's nutritional status and ability to care for herself at home.

You will gain more information about Heidi as you progress through this chapter. As you study the content and features, consider her case and its relationship to what you are learning. Begin thinking about the following points:

- How might the nurse's previous experiences with patients who have eating disorders influence the assessment of Heidi?
- What subjective and psychosocial data will the nurse collect?
- How will the nurse assess Heidi's current nutritional status using objective data?
- What adaptations will the nurse make to the assessment based on Heidi's condition?

As frontline providers of health care, nurses are involved intimately in all aspects of assessing nutritional status of patients. Determining adequate and appropriate caloric and nutrient intake occurs by analyzing data to identify actual and potential nutritional concerns. Because foods rather than nutrients make up the building blocks of a wholesome diet, nurses must be aware of nutrients in whole foods to accurately complete nutritional assessments.

When completing a nutritional assessment, the nurse considers a broad range of influences on the patient's food choices. A complete nutritional assessment includes a history of food intake, weight; height, waist and waist to hip measurements; calculation of Body Mass Index (BMI) and ideal weight; blood pressure; exercise; laboratory data; and the use of specific nutritional tools when indicated.

Nutritional Concepts

Primary Nutrients

Primary nutrients, essential for optimal body function, include carbohydrates, proteins, fats, vitamins, minerals, water, and major electrolytes. Nutrients are the building blocks for tissue maintenance and repair. Furthermore, carbohydrates, proteins, and fats are sources of energy for the body. Fats yield 9 cal/g, while proteins and carbohydrates yield 4 cal/g. Vitamins and minerals also play key roles in cellular function. Water makes up more than half of adult body weight, serves many vital functions within the body, and is essential to support life.

Carbohydrates

Carbohydrates provide the body's main source of energy. Simple sugars consist of glucose or dextrose, fructose, galactose, sucrose, maltose, or lactose. These simple sugars are absorbed as basic units without undergoing digestion, hence forming a "quick" source of energy. Complex carbohydrates, on the other hand, known as *polysaccharides*, consist of starch, glycogen, and fibre.

Primary sources of carbohydrates are natural and added sugars, starch, fibre, grains, fruits, and vegetables. The recommended daily allowance for carbohydrates varies depending on the activity level; however, the distribution range in a usual healthy diet is 45% to 65% of calories for all age groups (Health Canada, 2007a).

Proteins

Proteins serve important functions in cell structure and tissue maintenance. Amino acids are the building blocks of all proteins. Amino acids and proteins are involved in many essential body functions such as regulating fluid and electrolyte balance and transporting molecules and other substances through the blood. Body tissues such as muscles, bones, teeth, skin, and hair primarily consist of protein. While the body can synthesize most amino acids from nonprotein dietary sources, eight essential amino acids must be obtained through dietary sources. Recommended daily allowances are 5% to 20% (ages 1 to 3 years), 10% to 30% (4 to 18 years), and 10% to 35% (19 years and over) (Health Canada, 2007a).

Lipids

Lipids or **fats** include triglycerides (fats and oils), sterols (eg, cholesterol), and phospholipids (eg, lecithin). Fats in food are made up of varying kinds of fatty acids such as polyunsaturated, monosaturated, saturated, and trans. Fats help to maintain body functions by providing essential fatty acids (linoleic and linolenic acids) and promoting the absorption of fat-soluble vitamins A, D, E, and K.

Triglycerides. Saturated fats (solid at room temperature) and hydrogenated fats (liquid oils made into semi-solid fats such as shortening and hard margarine) raise levels of low-density lipoprotein (LDL) cholesterol. Saturated fats include those found in animal products such as butter, cheese, and fatty meats. Health Canada (2007a) recommends limiting the amount of saturated fats in the diet. Hydrogenation refers to the chemical processing of animal fats used by food manufacturers to extend the shelf life of products susceptible to rancidity, such as cookies and crackers.

Clinical Significance 8-1

Foods made with hydrogenated fats are particularly harmful to the diet because they are the largest contributors of trans fats. Empirical evidence suggests that trans fats are as damaging to the heart and blood vessels as saturated fats (Mente, de Koning, et al., 2009). In late 2005, Canada became the first country to regulate mandatory labelling of trans fats on pre-packaged foods.

Unsaturated fats (liquid at room temperature) are known to reduce LDL levels as well as triglycerides (high levels of which are a major cause of coronary heart disease). Unsaturated fats come in two forms. They are either *omega-3 oils*, found primarily in fish oils and some plant oils such as canola, flaxseed, walnut, and hazelnut, or *omega-6 oils*, found in plant oils such as safflower, sunflower, corn, soybean, and cottonseed (Tangney, Rosenson, et al., 2009). Health Canada recommends 30 to 45 mL of unsaturated fat every day to ensure that Canadians obtain enough essential fats (2007a). Monounsaturated fats such as canola and olive oils may lower cholesterol if consumed in place of saturated fats.

Cholesterol. Cholesterol is essential to cellular maintenance and repair; however, the body can synthesize sufficient cholesterol to meet its daily requirements. In the typical Canadian diet, cholesterol primarily comes from meat and egg yolks. Cholesterol ingested in excess of daily requirements contributes to atherosclerosis, stroke, and myocardial infarction (heart attack).

Because of the substantial rise in obesity throughout Canada and subsequent increases in incidences of diabetes and heart disease directly attributable to dietary triglycerides and cholesterol, Health Canada (2007a) recommends that daily fat intake for adults should not exceed 20% to 35% of total calories. In addition, because saturated fats contribute heavily to elevated serum triglyceride and cholesterol levels, they should not exceed 10% of daily calories.

Phospholipids. Phospholipids are emulsifiers that occur naturally in many foods and are used extensively by the food industry. They serve many vital functions such as transporting fat-soluble substances across cell membranes. Lecithin, the best-known phospholipid, is a popular food supplement. Powdered soy lecithin lowers cholesterol absorption and LDL levels when consumed in fat-free foods (Spilburg, Goldberg, et al., 2003).

Vitamins and Minerals

Vitamins play a key role in the metabolism of most nutrients. Light-skinned people obtain vitamin D, also known as the "sunshine vitamin," through exposure to sunlight. People living more than 37° south or north of the equator (all of Canada) cannot make adequate vitamin D from sun exposure from October to April even with sun exposure on the face, hands, and arms (Hemmelgarn, 2009). Additionally, people who use sunscreens in sunny climates and dark-skinned people may require a dietary source to meet daily requirements. Older adults and those who smoke also need added vitamin D, because aging and smoking tend to impair vitamin D synthesis.

⚠ SAFETY ALERT 8-1

Low levels of vitamin D may contribute to falls and fractures; cardiovascular, autoimmune, and infectious diseases; some cancers; type 1 and type 2 diabetes; and reduced muscle strength. Conversely, excessive intake of fat-soluble vitamins may result in toxicity because vitamins A, E, D, and K are stored in adipose tissue (Hemmelgarn, 2009).

Another important vitamin is folate, a B vitamin considered essential to metabolism and cell synthesis. Dietary sources of folate include leafy greens, peas, beans, lentils, broccoli, asparagus, seeds, liver, orange juice, grains, and cereals. Mandatory food fortification with folic acid in Canada (eg, breads fortified with folic acid) resulted in decreased neural tube defects (NTD) by 46% in newborns (Society of Obstetricians and Gynaecologists of Canada [SOGC], 2003). Other groups at risk for folate deficiency include people with alcoholism, older adults, those who follow "fad" diets, and people of low socioeconomic status.

⚠ SAFETY ALERT 8-2

Adequate maternal intake of folate (from food), fortification of foods with folic acid, and supplementation with a multivitamin with 0.4 mg of folic acid is recommended for all women of childbearing age before conception and during pregnancy to reduce the incidence of neural tube defects (eg, spina bifida). (Health Canada, 2007a; SOGC, 2003).

Vitamin B_{12} and folate need each other to be activated (Dudek, 2010). Vitamin B_{12} is the only water-soluble vitamin not found in plants. In addition to being involved in DNA synthesis and maintaining red blood cells, vitamin B_{12} plays an important role in maintaining the myelin sheath around nerves. Sources of vitamin B_{12} include beef, lamb, organ meats, shellfish, sardines, salmon, canned tuna, catfish, pike, whiting, milk, and dairy products such as yogurt and cheese.

Three **minerals** deserve special consideration in a healthy diet, particularly for vegetarians: iron, zinc (trace element), and calcium (Craig, 2009). Iron and zinc are best absorbed from animal sources; therefore, vegetarians may need to increase their intake of iron, zinc, and vitamin B_{12} by eating meat alternatives such as lentils, beans, tofu, eggs, soy-based meat substitutes, nuts, nut butters, and seeds. Calcium, vitamin B_{12}, vitamin D, and protein can be obtained from milk and fortified soy beverages. (Health Canada, 2007a).Vitamin C is required for proper absorption of iron.

Supplements

Patients may not consider food supplements, such as vitamins and herbal remedies, when questioned during a nutritional assessment. Certain drug–herb interactions may be serious and life threatening (Woo, 2008).

Herbs beginning with the letter "g" (eg, garlic, ginger, ginkgo, and grapefruit) are most commonly involved in herb–drug interactions. Drugs prescribed for anticoagulant/antiplatelet activity (eg, warfarin, aspirin) are frequently involved in herb–drug interactions, causing excessive bleeding. Because many herbs adversely affect the liver, there is a potential for interaction with hepatotoxic medications (eg, acetaminophen). St. John's wort reduces the effectiveness of many medications prescribed for heart disease, depression, seizures, some cancers, organ transplant rejection, and oral contraceptives.

Fluid and Electrolytes

Water is essential for life. The adult body loses 1,500 to 2,800 mL/d of water through perspiration, exhalation, and excretion of urine and feces. The body requires a minimum fluid intake of 1,500 mL/d to maintain the excretion of metabolic wastes through urine and feces. However, extreme environmental temperatures, high altitude, low humidity, fever, and exercise increase water loss. Therefore, the recommended **adequate intake** (AI) of water varies depending on gender, age, air temperature, activity level, and state of health. Careful consideration of intake and output is warranted in infants and older adults, particularly when vomiting, diarrhea, or fever is present. Other conditions characterized by high water losses include burns, fistulas, hemorrhage, uncontrolled diabetes, and some renal disorders (Dudek, 2010). Nurses caring for anyone requiring fluid and electrolyte adjustments such as those mentioned above are advised to seek additional evidence-informed information to guide practice.

Sodium and potassium are major **electrolytes**. Sodium regulates fluid balance and cell permeability, hence the movement of fluid, electrolytes, glucose, insulin, and amino acids across cellular membranes. It serves to regulate acid–base balance, nerve transmission, and muscular irritability (Dudek, 2010). The National Academy of Science (2004) reported that an adequate intake of sodium is:

- 9 to 50 years: 1,500 mg
- 50 to 70 years: 1,300 mg
- >70 years: 1,200 mg

Most Canadians consume more than triple these amount daily (4,000 to 6,000 mg/d, depending on food choices. Excess sodium intake kills about 15,000 Canadians yearly (Canadian Nurses Association, 2011). Patients are educated to reduce the consumption of sodium and sodium-containing foods, addition of salt at the table, and in cooking. Reading food labels is strongly encouraged for everyone as 75% of Canadians' sodium intake is from processed foods (Canadian Nurses Association). Note the specific information about sodium found on labels:

- Sodium-free products have 5 mg or less of sodium in each serving.
- Low sodium products have 140 mg or less of sodium in a 100 g serving.
- Reduced or less sodium is at least 25% less sodium than the regular version.
- Lightly salted is at least 50% less sodium than the regular version
- If sodium, salt, or soda is listed near the beginning of the ingredient list, the product is likely high in salt. After comparing the sodium content of similar products (eg, different brands of canned vegetables, canned soup), select items with less sodium (Brunet, Day, et al. 2010).

As people age, they become more "salt sensitive," and their risk of developing high blood pressure, coronary heart disease, and renal failure increases. This may be problematic to control because approximately 75% of sodium consumed in the average diet comes from salt added by food manufacturers (Dudek, 2010).

Potassium is also implicated in regulating fluid and acid–base balance. In addition, it serves functions in nerve impulse transmission, carbohydrate metabolism, protein synthesis, and skeletal muscle contractility. The AI for potassium is 4.7 g/d; however, on average, North Americans consume only 2.1 to 3.2 g/d (Dudek, 2010). African Canadians have a lower than average potassium intake,

high salt sensitivity, and increased rate of hypertension. A rule of thumb is that sodium and potassium contents are inversely related; that is, processed foods typically low in potassium tend to be high in sodium, and fresh wholesome foods typically high in potassium are low in sodium.

⚠ SAFETY ALERT 8-3
Potassium levels must be maintained in a very narrow range. A potassium level outside of the expected range of 3.5 to 5.5 mmol/L requires immediate correction. Too high or too low potassium level may cause potentially fatal cardiac dysrhythmias.

Many drugs commonly prescribed for people with chronic illnesses such as cardiovascular disease or renal failure interfere with electrolyte balance. In particular, low-sodium or high-potassium foods (or the opposite) may be desirable under such circumstances. Nurses are well advised to consult reliable sources of information on food and drug interactions.

Food Safety and Food Security

Food safety has gained importance in the past decade. Several outbreaks of **food pathogens**, such as salmonella in peanuts and listeriosis in cheeses and processed meats, are contemporary examples of food-borne pathogens affecting the health of large segments of the population. Food pathogens sometimes travel huge distances, making them difficult to trace and thus compromising the health and safety of many people over a matter of days. Despite the best efforts of regulatory bodies and food inspection agencies striving to maintain food safety, food-borne pathogens are becoming increasingly problematic.

Amidst a growing body of evidence showing the link between herbicide and pesticide use in agriculture and certain cancers, many people are seeking organic food sources. Further, the public has also questioned the use of antibiotics and hormones in raising cattle, pork, and poultry. Increased production of genetically modified foods has contributed to a move toward consuming organically grown foods from plant sources (Magana-Gomez & Calderon de la Barca, 2008).

Similarly, public awareness of food security is increasing. Food sources have become highly centralized. Modern urban lifestyles are contrary to people growing and processing their own food. Food sources are sometimes continents away from where foods are consumed, occasionally resulting in sudden, unexpected food shortages. Global climactic and catastrophic events may interfere with water and food production and distribution. Under such circumstances, nurses may be called on to assist in reestablishing food security within communities. They are sometimes also engaged in triage and advocacy to ensure that the most vulnerable segments of society are not forgotten.

Nutritional Guidelines

Health Canada publishes Canada's Food Guide (Health Canada, 2007b) which is designed to provide Canadians with guidelines for choosing and eating healthy foods that will meet standards for nutrients (dietary reference intakes or DRIs). "The DRIs summarize research findings about the amount of each nutrient and calories (energy) needed for good health and the prevention of chronic disease, while avoiding the negative effects of consuming too much of any individual nutrient" (Health Canada, 2007a, p. 4). Consuming foods from all four food groups (vegetables and fruit, grains, milk and alternates, and meat and alternates), as well as some added fats and oils will meet the DRIs. The emphasis is on reducing fats, sugars, and sodium, while encouraging more variety; increased intake of vegetables, fruits, lentils, and grains, particularly from plant sources; and meeting individual nutritional needs while avoiding either deficiencies or excesses in nutrient intake. The overall aim is to gradually promote healthier eating habits among Canadians of all ages, lifestyles, and genetic backgrounds. Individuals who eliminate food groups or who do not eat the appropriate number of servings require additional analysis and education by nurses and dietitians (see Table 8-1 and Box 8-1).

Canada's Food Guide (Health Canada, 2007b) is available online in multiple languages (including French) at http://www.hc-sc.gc.ca/fn-an/food-guide-aliment/index_e. html and for First Nations, Inuit, and Metis at http://www. hc-sc.gc.ca/fn-an/pub/fnim-pnim/index_e.html.

Lifespan Considerations

Women Who Are Pregnant

Women who are pregnant or lactating require special nutritional considerations for healthy outcomes. They need an additional 350 calories/day in the second trimester and 450 extra calories in the third trimester, which should be met by adding two to three Food Guide servings (Health Canada, 2007a). While whole foods offer the best bioavailable sources of vitamins and minerals and should always be the first choice, a multivitamin with iron and 0.4 mg of folic acid is always required (Health Canada, 2007a; SOGC, 2003).

⚠ *SAFETY ALERT 8-4*

Women who do not meet nutritional requirements of pregnancy are at risk for having premature, low–birth-weight, or small-for-gestational-age infants. Their infants are also at higher risk for disabilities and congenital anomalies including anencephaly, myelomeningocele, meningocele, spina bifida, oral facial cleft, structural heart disease, limb defect, urinary tract anomaly, and hydrocephalus (SOGC, 2003; Wilson, 2007).

Table 8-1 Recommended Numbers of Food Guide Servings per Day

Age in Years	Teens(14–18 Y)		Adults(19–50 Y)		Older Adults(51 + Y)	
Gender	*Females*	*Males*	*Females*	*Males*	*Females*	*Males*
Vegetables and fruits	7	8	7–8	8–10	7	7
Grain products	6	7	6–7	8	6	7
Milk and alternatives	3–4	3–4	2	2	3	3
Meat and alternatives	2	3	2	3	2	3

Adapted from Health Canada (2007a). *Eating well with Canada's food guide. A resource to educators and communicators.* Ottawa, ON: Minister of Health Canada.

Table 8-2	Recommended Numbers of Food Guide Servings per Day for Children 2–13 Years		
Age in Y	Children 2–3 y, Boys and Girls	Children 4–8 y Boys and Girls	Children 9–13 y Boys and Girls
Vegetables and fruits	4	5	6
Grain products	3	4	6
Milk and alternatives	2	2	3–4
Meat and alternatives	1	1	1–2

Adapted from Health Canada (2007a). *Eating well with Canada's food guide. A resource to educators and communicators.* Ottawa, ON: Minister of Health Canada.

Infants, Children, and Adolescents

More protein is needed for tissue building in periods of rapid growth such as adolescence. Ensuring dietary sources of essential amino acids from protein is critical for children because of their rapid growth (Pencharz, 2010). This is also the case when tissue damage occurs or during prolonged illness.

Infants, children, and adolescents require different nutrients based on developmental and growth factors. For example, fat intake is crucial to brain development in infants and young children, and adolescents require different nutrients based on developmental and growth factors. Therefore, whole milk is recommended for children younger than 2 years. Tables 8-2 and 8-3 provide age-related developmental and growth considerations in the diet.

Adults/Older Adults (Age 51 to 70+ years)

Older adults also require special consideration during assessments of dietary requirements. They may compensate for diminished taste of sweet and salty foods by adding sugar and salt to their diet at a time when they are at increased risk for diabetes, hypertension, and heart disease. Their basal metabolic rate is declining concurrently with reductions in physical activity. When this occurs, caloric needs are significantly reduced. Older adults are also at increased risk for malnutrition as a result of social isolation.

In addition, adults and older adults need vitamin D supplementation because of changes in nutrient metabolism, particularly when exposure to sunlight is reduced, and between October and April in Canada. They are advised to increase the AI of vitamin D to 2,000 IU through dietary sources such as fortified milk (500 mL = 200 IU and dairy products, fatty fish, and fortified cereals and a supplement if necessary) (Alberta Health Services, 2008). Other nutrients not likely to be consumed in adequate amounts by older adults include calcium, folate, vitamin B_{12}, and riboflavin (Dudek, 2010). Adults and older adults need 1,200 mg of calcium (Alberta Health Services, 2008).

Older adults may also experience a reduced sense of thirst, thereby increasing their risk for dehydration. They are also at

Table 8-3 Recommended Dietary Reference Intakes* for Some Macronutrients						
Category	Age or Time Frame (y)	Protein (g/kg)	Energy (kcal/kg)	Calcium (mg/kg)	Phosphorus (mg/kg)	Magnesium (mg/kg)
Infants	0.0–0.5	2.2	108.3	66.7	50.0	6.7
	0.5–1.0	1.6	94.4	66.7	55.6	6.7
Children	1–3	1.2	100.0	61.5	61.5	6.2
	4–6	1.2	90.0	40.0	40.0	6.0
	7–10	1.0	71.4	28.6	28.6	6.1
Males	11–14	1.0	55.6	26.7	26.7	6.0
	15–18	0.9	45.5	18.2	18.2	6.1
	19–24	0.8	40.3	16.7	16.7	4.9
	25–50	0.8	36.7	10.1	10.1	4.4
	51+	0.8	29.9	10.4	10.4	4.5
Females	11–14	1.0	47.8	26.1	26.1	6.1
	15–18	0.8	40.0	21.8	21.8	5.5
	19–24	0.8	37.9	20.7	20.7	4.8
	25–50	0.8	34.9	12.7	12.7	4.4
	51+	0.8	29.2	12.3	12.3	4.3
Pregnant		0.9	4.6	18.5	18.5	4.9
Breastfeeding	First year	1.0	7.9	19.0	19.0	5.4

*These amounts, expressed as average daily intakes over time, are intended to provide for individual variations among most healthy people living in the United States under usual environmental stresses.

Adapted from Food and Nutrition Board, Institute of Medicine of the National Academies. (2005). *Dietary Reference Intakes for energy, carbohydrate, fiber, fat, fatty acids, cholesterol, protein, and amino acids.* Washington, DC: National Academies Press and Food and Nutrition Board, Institute of Medicine of the National Academies. (1997). *DRI Dietary Reference Intakes for calcium, phosphorus, magnesium, vitamin D, and fluoride.* Washington, DC: National Academies Press.

BOX 8-2 FACTORS THAT AFFECT NUTRITION IN THE OLDER ADULT

- Illness or chronic disease, including depression or dementia, which may alter nutrient needs or intake
- Excessive or inadequate intake of a limited variety of foods, with missing food groups or compromised by alcohol
- Dental concerns (eg, missing or decayed teeth, ill-fitting dentures), which may lead to the avoidance of foods that are difficult to chew (eg, fruits, vegetables, whole grains)
- Low economic status, which can compromise a food budget
- Social isolation—older adults living alone are more likely to experience hunger than households with more than one older adult member

- Use of three or more prescribed or over-the-counter daily medications. Drugs may affect nutritional status by altering appetite; ability to taste and smell; or digestion, absorption, metabolism, and excretion of nutrients. Also, if a large percentage of a fixed income is spent on medications/supplements, less money is available for food.
- Significant unintentional weight loss (defined as 5% or more in 30 days, 10% or more in 180 days)
- Self-care deficits that may complicate food purchasing, food preparation, and eating
- Age older than 80 years

Adapted from Dudek, S. G. (2010). *Nutrition essentials for nursing practice* (6th ed.). Philadelphia, PA: Wolters Kluwer Health/Lippincott Williams & Wilkins.

increased risk for osteoarthritis, osteoporosis, dementias, and obesity. This presents unique challenges and increases their susceptibility to dubious claims made by manufacturers of pharmaceutical and nutritional supplements. Social isolation may further compound nutritional issues associated with aging.

Eating alone is particularly problematic for people with reduced mobility, receiving social assistance, or both. They may lack the resources required to maintain a nutritious and appealing diet. Poor dentition may also be an issue. Missing teeth, gum disease, and poor-fitting dentures can all detract from enjoying meals. Community programs such as Meals on Wheels offer food services to people with disabilities or chronic illnesses who live in social isolation.

Malnutrition and dehydration are also common among residents of long-term care facilities (Simmons, Bertrand, et al., 2007). Commercial supplements aimed at providing added proteins and calories are not advisable over the long term (Dudek, 2010). Rather, nurses should strive to make meal times as enjoyable as possible by encouraging both independent eating and family involvement. It is also advisable to adhere to food preferences as much as possible and to maintain adequate hydration. Other recommendations for maintaining adequate nutrition among long-term care residents include providing clean, comfortable, pleasant surroundings; offering water; providing small, frequent meals; and minimizing distractions during meals. Refer to Box 8-2.

Cultural Considerations

Several factors influence nutritional health including medications, lifestyle choices, socioeconomic status, geographical location, education, and cultural and religious influences. Athletes may require additional protein for muscle building and maintenance. Animal sources of protein include meat, fish, poultry, eggs, milk, and dairy products. Vegetarian diets containing soy protein may also contain essential amino acids if food intake is varied, calories are sufficient, and whole grains, legumes, vegetables, seeds, and nuts are included.

Some cultural groups believe in the healing properties of foods, while others follow food restrictions during illness. It is important for nurses working with patients from different cultures to assess dietary habits. Box 8-3 outlines items to consider.

The nurse who recognizes that each culture has its own food standards, determining what is edible and what is not, how foods are prepared and when they are eaten, as well as what role foods play in treating illness, is not likely to be ethnocentric when assessing nutritional status. Food preferences are learned, yet they vary depending on tradition, geography, education, income, and employment outside the home. In the 2006 census, 200 ethnic origins were identified in Canada. About 41.4% of the population come from multiple genetic backgrounds, with 16.2% of the population being visible minorities (Statistics Canada, 2008).

Additionally, food practices may be based on religious beliefs, such as fasting or abstaining from eating certain foods. Some common restrictions include the following (Dudek, 2010):

- Catholicism: Avoid meat on Fridays, mainly during Lent (6 weeks preceding Easter).
- Hinduism: Avoid beef, pork, and alcohol. Many are vegetarians.
- Mormon: Avoid coffee, tea, alcohol, and tobacco.
- Seventh Day Adventist: Many are lacto-ovo-vegetarians. Food is primarily of vegetable origin but does include milk and cheese (lacto) and eggs (ova), but no meat, fish, or poultry (Health Canada, 2007a).

BOX 8-3 CULTURAL INFLUENCES ON NUTRITION

- What foods are eaten during stress, trauma, or illness? To prevent illness?
- What are the common food preferences? Likes or dislikes?
- In what context is the food purchased, prepared, served, and eaten?
- What are the food nutrients, and what are acceptable versus prohibited foods?
- What are the accepted food combinations (eg, hot and cold or milk and meat together)?
- How do foods facilitate communication and relationships within cultures?
- What geographic or environmental influences exist?

Adapted from Leininger, M. M., & McFarland, M. R. (2002). *Transcultural nursing: Concepts, theories, research, and practice* (3rd ed.). New York, NY: McGraw-Hill Professional.

- Judaism: Eat only Kosher meat and no crustaceans; avoid consuming milk and meat in the same meal.
- Islam: Avoid pork and birds of prey. Fast during the day during Ramadan.
- Buddhism: Many are lacto-ovo-vegetarians.

Collecting Nutritional Data

Collecting nutritional data is an ongoing process, partly because nutritional intake is an everyday activity. The patient may be seen in the primary care centre or may enter hospital care with short- or long-term nutritional deficiencies (eg, a person experiencing complications from liver cirrhosis). At least some malnutrition is expected in hospitalized adults. Additionally, nutritional status does not improve during hospitalization. Malnutrition can be generalized, targeted to specific nutrients, or exist in combination with obesity, cachexia, trauma, or aging.

The responsibility for screening patients to assess their level of nutritional risk and reinforcing dietary counseling is often delegated to the nurse. The nurse's role in the nutritional assessment of patients is complex because of developmental, social, economic, and cultural factors. Nevertheless, nutrition screening is noninvasive, inexpensive, and easy to perform. An example of a simple nutrition screening tool is found in Figure 8-1 below.

Nutrition History

1. How many meals and snacks do you eat each day?

   Meals _____ Snacks _____

2. How many times a week do you eat the following meals away from home?

   Breakfast _____ Lunch _____ Dinner _____

   What types of eating places do you frequently visit? (Check all that apply)

   Fast-food _____ Restaurant _____ Diner/cafeteria _____

   Other _____

3. On average, how many pieces of fruit or how much juice do you eat or drink each day?

   Fresh fruit _____ Juice (250 mL = 1 cup) _____

4. On average, how many servings of vegetables do you eat each day? _____

5. On average, how many times a week do you eat a high-fibre breakfast cereal? _____

6. How many times a week do you eat red meat (beef, lamb, veal) or pork? _____

7. How many times a week do you eat chicken or turkey? _____

8. How many times a week do you eat fish or shellfish? _____

9. How many hours of television do you watch every day? _____

   Do you usually snack while watching television?

   Yes _____ No _____

10. How many times a week do you eat desserts and sweets? _____

11. What types of beverages do you usually drink? How many servings of each do you drink a day?

    Water _____

    Juice _____

    Soft drink _____

    Diet soft drink _____

    Sports drink _____

    Energy drink iced tea _____

    Iced tea with sugar _____

    Milk:

        Whole milk _____

        2% milk _____

        1% milk _____

        Skim milk _____

    Alcohol:

        Beer _____

        Wine _____

        Hard liquor _____

Figure 8-1 Nutrition Screening Tool.

Parameters for a complete nutrition screening assessment include a risk assessment, focused history of common symptoms, comprehensive nutritional history, physical examination, calculated measurements, and serial laboratory values (especially during times of high metabolic demand, such as fever, pain, or infection, or during limited nutritional intake).

Acute Assessment

Nutritional deficits are rarely acute—most of them develop over time. During trauma or stress, calorie needs increase. Stress factors that increase the risk for nutritional deficit include surgery, trauma, infection, head injury, and burns. Additionally, the patient may have reduced consciousness or injuries that make it difficult to take in nutrients. In acute illnesses, nutrition assessment and appropriate interventions should be addressed within days of the diagnosis.

Subjective Data Collection

Assessment of Risk Factors

An assessment of risk factors includes questions about past medical and surgical histories, medication and supplement use, past history, family history, food and fluid intake patterns, and the patient's psychosocial profile (Dudek, 2010). If indicated, the nurse may follow up with a tested and valid tool for screening a specific population for risk factors.

Questions to Assess History and Risk Factors	Rationale
Personal History	
Do you have a medical condition, such as diabetes? Or hypertension?	Medical conditions, increased metabolic demand, and malabsorption increase the risk for nutritional deficits. Patients with diabetes or hypertension may benefit from nutrition therapy.
Do you have, or have you recently had, fever? An infection? Sepsis? Burn injuries? Skin breakdown? Cancer? AIDS? Major surgery? Or trauma?	These conditions increase nutritional needs.
Do you have, or have you recently had, malabsorption? Or renal diseases?	These conditions lead to loss of nutrients; special attention to increased nutritional requirements is necessary.
Appetite and Taste Changes	
Do you have a history of any concerns related to nutrition? Or weight?	Being underweight, overweight, or obese influences self-perception of health. Such a perception may be distorted or inaccurate, but it is important to know it to address it. Asking how the patient perceives self can be challenging, particularly when the body is visibly outside expected limits (eg, anorexia, obesity).
	Main causes of malnutrition in Canada are poverty, alcoholism, hospitalization, aging, and eating disorders. Other risk factors are poor dentition, chronic illness, multiple medications, social isolation, severe burns, and lack of knowledge.
	Risk factors commonly associated with overweight and obesity include excessive intake of high-calorie foods, typically high in fat and sugar; not enough exercise; alcohol abuse; and lack of knowledge.
Appetite and Taste Changes • Have you noticed any changes in your ability to smell odours? In the taste of food? If so, what are the changes? • How would you rate your appetite? • How does food taste to you?	Senses of taste and smell decrease with aging. Additionally, some medications alter taste and smell. For example, amiodarone, a medication to regulate the heart rhythm, causes food to taste like garlic.
Gastrointestinal Symptoms. Have you ever been diagnosed with a gastrointestinal concern or other disease that affects your nutrition? Anorexia? Heartburn? Nausea? Diarrhea? Vomiting? Or pain?	Gastrointestinal diseases may impair appetite and also reduce the absorption of nutrients.

Questions to Assess History and Risk Factors	Rationale

Food Allergy or Intolerance. Have you ever been diagnosed with a food intolerance? Or allergy?

Note differences between intolerances (nausea, bloating, and flatulence) and allergies (hives, wheezing, and anaphylaxis). Food allergies and intolerances must also be considered when evaluating risk factors for malnutrition because they affect food choices. Patients intolerant to lactose, for example, need sources other than dairy products for calcium. Common food allergens include milk, eggs, soy, peanuts, nuts (eg, cashews, almonds), wheat, fish, and shellfish (Dudek, 2010).

Medications and Supplements

Medication Schedule

- What system or systems have you developed to ensure an accurate schedule for your medications?
- Are there particular reminders or methods that are helpful for you? If so, please describe.

Barriers to Accuracy. Have you experienced any difficulty in getting your medicines? Or your medicines as they have been prescribed? If so, please describe.

A medication history is included because diet and food intake affect medications. For example, dark green leafy foods can decrease the effect of some anticoagulants.

Remembering to take medications requires intact memory and cognitive skills. If there is any difficulty, the nurse may suggest a medi-set with small compartments for medications for each time of the day. Pharmacists can organize medications in dosettes according to when to take the medications—there is a cost involved.

Adverse Effects. When do you tend to report any adverse effects of your medicines? For example, as soon as you notice? When things get really bad for you? Only when they interfere with what you need to do? Never?

Patterns of health-seeking behaviour vary widely, from patients who visit the provider for health promotion to those patients who defer care until emergently or critically ill.

Resources for Medication-Related Information

- From whom have you received most of your medication information? TV? Relatives? Neighbours? Books? Magazines? Pharmacist? Health store personnel? Doctor? Nurse? Nurse practitioner? Others?
- Do you ask questions about your medicines? Do you expect that people helping you with medicines will give you needed information?

Nurses can provide patients with resources for answers. It is important to teach patients to inform providers of side effects, financial concerns, or other health beliefs that affect the ability to take medications as prescribed. An alternative plan can then be developed collaboratively with patients.

Supplements. Do you take any vitamins? Minerals? Or other nutritional supplements? If so, describe the substance, amount, and frequency.

Approximately one third of patients use some type of supplement, and it is important to monitor for side effects and drug–supplement interactions.

Alcohol and Drug Use

- How much alcohol do you drink in a day? Or a week?
- Do you feel that you are a "average" drinker? (By "average," I mean that you drink less than other people? Or as much as other people? Or more than most other people?)

Alcohol can adversely affect the liver and its multiple functions, including protein synthesis. In addition, chronic alcohol exposure can injure the stomach and pancreas. Lack of the digestive enzymes produced by the pancreas can impair the absorption of nutrients including fat.

- (If the person does drink): How much did you drink yesterday? Is that about usual for you? When did you take your last drink (date and hour)? What is your usual pattern for alcohol intake? If you do not have a drink for a few days, how do you feel? Have you ever gone through alcohol withdrawal? If so, when, and describe the circumstances. Do you go into a DT (delirium tremors) if you do not drink for a few days? See Chapter 10 for the CAGE questionnaire.
- Could you tell me about your drug use? **(Ask about the substance and quantity after each question.)** Do you smoke marijuana? Have you ever used another person's prescription. Do you use sleeping pills? Downers? Uppers? Speed? Ritalin? Cocaine? Meth? Do you use, or have you ever "tripped"? Or used hallucinogens?

Alcohol intake can affect the metabolism of nutrients as well as alter the overall nutrient density of the diet. It is common for patients with a high alcohol intake to be deficient in the B vitamins and vitamin K.

(text continues on page 162)

Food and Fluid Intake Patterns

Eating Patterns. Describe a typical day's eating (include content and amount of meals, meal times, and snacking patterns).
- Are you on a special diet? If so, please describe.
- Are there times of the day when you feel hungry? If so, when? What is satisfying? Are there particular foods that you like? Dislike? If so, please describe.
- Are any foods or food habits important to you? If so, please describe.
- Who shares your mealtimes?

Food habits and intake patterns may vary according to culture, religion, and region. Because variation is wide, it is important to obtain a history for the individual patient.

Fluid Intake Patterns
- How much fluid do you drink each day? How many cups? Approximate size of a cup (usually 250 mL)
- Are there particular fluids that you like? Dislike?
- Are there certain times of the day when you drink fluids? Or refrain from drinking fluids?
- How much of each of the following (in cups or mLs) do you usually drink in a day? Water? Tea? Hot chocolate? Sports drinks? Soft drinks? Energy drinks? Coffee? How much caffeine? If you do not have any caffeine for a few days, how do you feel (eg, Headache? Nausea? Other sensations?)

Fluid intake may be in excess of needs, causing fluid volume excess. Low fluid intake may cause a fluid volume deficit, or dehydration.

Large consumption of unfiltered coffee such as through a French press may increase low-density lipoprotein (LDL) levels and the risk for miscarriage (van Dam, 2008).

Concerns are being raised about children consuming energy drinks which have high levels of caffeine.

Psychosocial Profile

Habits
- Does stress affect your eating habits? Or drinking habits? If so, please describe.
- Do you smoke? If so, does smoking affect your appetite? If so, describe.

Some patients gain weight with stress, while others lose weight.
Smoking impairs both senses of smell and taste.

Cooking Habits
- Who does your food shopping?
- Do you have a food budget? If so, could you describe it?
- How often do you eat out? Who prepares your food?
- Does food preparation provide a source of enjoyment for you?
- Could you describe your food preparation facilities?

Functional limitations influence the ability to obtain or prepare food. The nutrition-metabolic pattern does not involve only nutrients ingested each day. It encompasses aspects such as culture, religion, and geography; food and fluid preferences and dislikes; patterns of eating, allergies, digestion, shopping resources, and skills; kitchen facilities; food preparation and eating; meaning of food and feeding; social patterns at meals; and gastrointestinal structures, including dentition. Such information aids in individualizing actions, assisting patients to modify current eating practices, and adopting new eating patterns into everyday life. Knowing what roles the patient plays in groups can aid in prioritizing health concerns that relate to the gastrointestinal system. For example, if the patient has primary food preparation responsibilities, he or she may need to relinquish them temporarily or permanently. Should major roles change, the patient will need to be able to assume other roles deemed equally important to maintain a contributing role with the group.

Dietary Lifestyle Changes
- Do environmental factors affect your ability to make dietary changes? Or do social factors?
- Do you feel that you have sufficient resources to support healthy food intake?

Many social functions revolve around food. If signs, symptoms, or treatments disrupt such functions, social isolation can be a consequence. Asking about such possibilities can be important when assessing the patient's overall health.

Questions to Assess History and Risk Factors	Rationale

Family History

Do you have a family history of gastrointestinal or other diseases that influence your nutrition?
- Who had the illness?
- What was the illness?
- When did the person have it?
- How was the illness treated?
- What were the outcomes?

A family history of conditions such as Crohn's disease, ulcerative colitis, celiac, type 2 diabetes, cystic fibrosis, or anemia should be included. Consideration must be given to respecting cultural food patterns and preferences. Gathering information on the patient's family history of obesity, cancer, heart disease, and atherosclerosis may also be useful in developing a nutrition plan.

Risk Assessment and Health Promotion

Nurses promote healthy nutrition in all settings including health fairs, schools, clinics, and hospitals. People often are interested in nutrition as a way to improve their health. Nurses can teach about Canada's Food Guide, increasing the intake of fruits and vegetables, and decreasing the intake of foods with low nutrient density. Nurses play a key role in identifying and assessing individuals at risk (under weight and over weight), and providing education. Everyone should be taught to read food labels, but especially when the intake of a nutrient is limited because of dietary restrictions, such as a low-salt diet. When patients are placed on restricted diets, teaching must be provided. Many organizations, such as the Canadian Diabetes Association, have helpful written materials to reinforce such teaching.

Focused Health History Related to Common Symptoms/Signs

Common Symptoms/Signs of Altered Nutrition

- Sudden or gradual changes in body weight (see Box 8-4)
- Changes in eating habits
- Changes in skin, hair, or nails
- Decreased energy level (see also Box 8-4)

Comprehensive Nutritional History

If, after assessing risk factors and common symptoms, data reveal the patient to be at risk for altered nutrition, the nurse takes a comprehensive nutritional history. Commonly used tools include food records, food frequency questionnaires, and direct observations.

Examples of Questions to Assess Symptoms/Signs	Rationale/Unexpected Findings

Changes in Body Weight

What is your present height? Weight? How do these compare with your height and weight 5 years ago? Have there been any changes in your weight over the past year? If so, please describe. How do you feel about your present weight?

Weight can change or remain stable with illness. The patient taking steroids may gain weight, while the patient undergoing cancer treatment may lose weight if nauseous or anorexic. Eating disorders, such as anorexia nervosa and bulimia nervosa, can profoundly affect nutritional health. Typically, patients with anorexia are preoccupied with distorted perceptions of themselves as fat when they actually are emaciated. They feel "fat" despite being underweight.

Change in Eating Habits

Have you experienced a change in a regular diet pattern (Number of meals? Size of meals? Content of meals?)

If yes, investigate potential causes (eg, change in appetite, mental status, or mood; ability to prepare meals; ability to chew or swallow; nausea or vomiting). Patients with eating disorders reduce the size and content of meals or may binge and then purge.

Symptoms of Malnutrition

- Have you noticed any changes in your hair? Nails? Skin? If so, describe.
- Would you say that you heal well? Poorly? Other? Do you have any difficulty tolerating hot weather? Or cold weather?
- How much energy would you say that you have?
- Has your energy level changed recently, say during the past year? If so, describe.

See Box 8-5 for other symptoms of malnutrition, and Box 8-4 for examples of questions for symptom analysis.

Skin, hair, and nails are indicators of nutritional status because those cells turn over rapidly. Thin or brittle hair, thin skin, skin that bruises easily or flakes, and weak or brittle nails are typical symptoms/signs. A malnourished person lacks energy.

Food Records

Food records are integral to nutritional assessment. To ensure accurate and complete data collection, records ought to include all food supplements and drinks consumed over a specified period, including the amount and times they were consumed.

24-Hour Recall. A 24-hour recall consists of asking the patient what he or she had to eat and drink within a 24-hour period. The nurse collects information from patients and their families without appearing judgmental (Fig. 8-2). He or she uses open-ended questions such as "Tell me the first thing that you ate yesterday" or "When was the first time you ate anything yesterday? Or drank anything yesterday?" The nurse continues by asking, "Did you have anything else to eat

Figure 8-2 The nurse is reviewing a patient's food intake using the 24-hour recall method.

or drink at the time?" and then "What was the next thing you had to eat or drink?"

In this method, the patient tends to overestimate low intakes and underestimate high intakes. To control this tendency, it is important for the nurse to use prompts such as "golf-ball size" or "the size of your fist or thumb." Life-size models and digital images of various foods can also be useful in eliciting accurate portion estimates. Also, the nurse cues the patient to include beverages or condiments (eg, "Did you have anything on the toast?"). It is important for the nurse to remember to ask about fortified foods, such as fruit juices and cereals fortified with calcium, other food supplements, and alcohol.

The 24-hour recall is reliable only if the patient or family can recall the type and amount of food eaten. Additionally, the intake over the past 24 hours may not be typical—foods eaten on a weekend may differ from those eaten during the week. Therefore, the 24-hour recall is usually the most complete and accurate when the nurse obtains a recall for a weekday and weekend day.

Three-Day Food Diary. To increase accuracy, the nurse may repeat diet recalls, stagger them through several health assessments, or have the patient keep a 3-day food diary. The diary shifts most of the responsibility for data collection from the nurse to the patient. It is best for the patient to write down the intake immediately after eating. This record is not reliant on memory, but the patient may consciously alter the diet during recording. It also is time consuming. For at-risk patients, an analysis of dietary intake is carried out in combination with weight, observation of signs and symptoms of poor nutrition, and consideration of laboratory values that reflect malnutrition.

Food-Frequency Questionnaires. Food-frequency questionnaires help assess the intake of certain required foods for special situations (eg, calcium or folate/folic acid in pregnancy). Nurses use these questionnaires to track the frequency of intake of a certain food or foods over time, such as each day, week, or month. Food-frequency questionnaires are quick and often combined with the 24-hour recall. They require accurate reporting and intact memory (see Fig. 8-3).

Nutrition Questionnaire

During the past 4 weeks, how often did you
eat a serving of the foods listed here?

Mark only one ✗ for each food

	Last 4 weeks		Each week			Each day			
Number of times	0	1–3	1	2–4	5–6	1	2–3	4–5	6+
Milk						✗			
Hot chocolate	✗								
Cheese, plain or in sandwiches				✗					
Yogurt	✗								
Ice cream		✗							
	0	1	2	3	4	5	6	7	8

Figure 8-3 An example of a food-frequency questionnaire.

Direct Observation

With hospitalized patients, it is possible to directly observe the amount and types of food they eat. Commonly, nurses describe intake as a percentage of the meal eaten, such as 50% of breakfast or 75% of dinner. When inadequate intake is suspected, the nurse can count the calories. The nurse records the percentage of each food eaten, and the dietitian performs a calorie count based on what is consumed. If intake is inadequate, the patient may need supplements such as high-calorie shakes.

Additionally, the nurse monitors the fluid intake and output for patients receiving intravenous fluids or at risk for fluid volume excess or deficit. The nurse totals the fluids taken in, including orally and intravenously. He or she totals the output by measuring urine output, drainage from tubes or drains, and emesis (vomiting).

🏔 Lifespan Considerations

Additional Questions	Rationale/Unexpected Findings
Women Who are Pregnant	
Preconception: How many servings do you eat daily of each of the following high sources of folate? Peas? Beans? Lentils? Broccoli? Spinach? Breakfast cereal? Or wheat germ? Do you take a vitamin supplement with folic acid?	Neural tube defects are more common in infants of women with low folate intake from foods or folic acid (from fortified foods and supplements).
Do you avoid any foods? Are you on a special diet? Do you skip meals?	Any of these practices may lead to nutritional deficiencies.
Do you smoke cigarettes? Drink alcohol? Or use any recreational drugs?	Stimulants may increase energy requirements and cause inadequate weight gain. The use of alcohol and recreational substances can cause addiction and injury to the fetus.
Do you use any mineral substances? Or herbal products?	Such supplements, including excessive vitamin A, may harm the fetus and should be avoided. Evidence about the safety of herbal remedies is lacking, so a careful history of their use is important when the patient is considering pregnancy, or is pregnant, or lactating.
Pregnancy: How much weight have you gained during the first trimester? Any vomiting? How often? Are you taking an iron supplement?	Average total weight gain is a maximum of 1–2.5 kg. No weight gain often occurs, especially with vomiting.
	Beginning with the pregnancy, an iron supplement is necessary. A health care professional should recommend the amount.

(text continues on page 166)

How much weight have you gained during the second trimester? And third trimester?

Nutritional requirements to produce a healthy baby and associated weight gain include increasing intake by about 350 cal/d in the second trimester, and 450 cal/d in the third trimester (two or three more Food Guide servings per day); increasing elemental iron intake and vitamin intake may be appropriate, especially for women who have multiple fetuses, smoke, or use alcohol or drugs.

⚠ SAFETY ALERT 8-5

Women who fail to meet these requirements risk low–birth-weight or intrauterine growth-restricted infants and increased difficulties with breastfeeding.

What is your usual intake of dairy products? Do you take a calcium supplement?

If the diet is low in calcium-rich foods, a supplement with 600 mg of calcium may be needed.

How many servings of fish do you eat weekly?

⚠ SAFETY ALERT 8-6

Women who may become or are pregnant or nursing should avoid predator fish that may be high in mercury, such as shark, fresh and canned tuna, and swordfish. High mercury levels can harm the fetal or neonatal nervous system. Refer to www.healthcanada.gc.ca for Health Canada's most recent advisory on safe fish consumption for those at high risk–women who are pregnant and young children.

For the breastfeeding mother: Are you getting adequate calories to produce milk for your baby? Enough fluids?

The recommended intake is an increase of 350 to 400 additional cal/d for the first year of breastfeeding. The mother can use her thirst as a guide for adequate fluids (Lowdermilk & Perry, 2007).

Newborns, Infants, and Children

Are you breast feeding your newborn? Or bottle feeding? How is your baby tolerating the feedings? And you?

Breast fed babies require 400 IU of Vitamin D until they are drinking whole milk. The healthy term infant who is formula fed usually requires no supplements before 6 months of age.

⚠ SAFETY ALERT 8-7

Whole cow's milk should not be introduced to infants younger than 1 year of age because of allergies and intolerances.

What solid foods have you added to your baby's diet? Has tooth eruption begun? Can your baby pick up finger foods and feed himself or herself?

⚠ SAFETY ALERT 8-8

When solid foods are introduced, beans, grains, and vegetables should be cooked and mashed to avoid choking and aspiration.

How much milk is your preschooler drinking per day (250 mL =1 cup)? How much cheese per day? Amount of yogurt per day? How many servings of the following is your preschooler eating: Vegetables? Fruits? Grains?

Milk and dairy products provide major sources of calcium. Preschoolers may change to low-fat or nonfat milk (500 mL/d). For this age group, adequate dietary fibre intake is achieved with four to five Food Guide servings of vegetables and fruits and, three to four servings of grains each day (Health Canada, 2007a).

How much fruit juice does your preschooler drink each day?

An increased intake of fruit juices has been associated with dental caries, gastrointestinal symptoms, and obesity. Drinking more water is encouraged (Health Canada, 2007a).

Additional Questions	Rationale/Unexpected Findings
Do you eat family meals together?	Maintaining healthy eating for families with busy lifestyles means providing balanced meals at designated times with few distractions such as television. Evidence suggests that people eating in a vehicle, or within hearing distance of a television, tend to make unhealthier food choices than those who share meals in more traditional family surroundings.
Adolescents	
What have you eaten in the past 24 hours? Is this intake typical? What did you drink in the past 24 hours?	Discuss body mass index (BMI) according to the adolescent's gender and age. Intervene with nutritional and activity information early if BMI is ≥85th percentile. Provide nutrition information with Canada's Food Guide (Health Canada, 2007a).
What is your typical meal pattern of eating?	Adolescents may have irregular meal patterns or skip meals such as breakfast.
Are you concerned about your weight? Do you think that you are too fat? Too skinny?	Provide information about Food Guide servings for adolescents. Ask about food choices at school and assist with wise choices based on the Food Guide.
Do you ever use diet supplements? Or take laxatives? Limit calories?	Screen for risk factors for anorexia and bulimia.
Have you ever used any supplements to boost your physical performance?	The use of anabolic steroids or other supplements usually begins in adolescence. Side effects include suppression of testicular function, gynecomastia, hepatotoxicity, mood disorders, elevated blood lipids, and cardiac disease (Snyder, Matsumoto, et al., 2009).
What type of physical activity do you get each day? For how long each day? In a week?	A healthy diet should be balanced with adequate physical activity. For children aged 5 to 11 years and youth (12 to 17 years) a total of at least 60 minutes daily of moderate to vigorous physical activity is needed (Public Health Agency of Canada [PHAC], 2011).
Do you suspect that you might be pregnant?	A teen who is pregnant has greater nutritional requirements than adult women, because she is still growing herself. Also, her pelvis may not be fully developed. Teens are at greater risk for pregnancy complications, especially preeclampsia, probably because of inadequate nutrient intake (Lowdermilk & Perry, 2007).
Older Adults	
What medications are you taking?	Those taking medications or with diseases that create less saliva or xerostomia are more likely to have issues with taste (Boyce & Shone, 2006).
Use a screening tool to evaluate the risk of malnutrition in the older adult (see Table 8-4).	Financial and transportation issues can limit access to nutritional foods. Functional abilities or sensory losses can affect the ability to physically prepare nutritious foods. Early cognitive losses that impair judgment, planning, foresight, or sequencing of complex tasks may reduce the ability to follow recipes or prepare complete meals. Recent weight loss can cause dentures to fit poorly and interfere with chewing.

Table 8-4 **Tools to Evaluate Risk of Malnutrition in the Older Adult**

Tool	Description	Validity and Reliability
Mini-nutritional Assessment	Perception of health, global assessment, questions about diet, and anthropometric measurements	Widely validated, predictive of poor outcomes
Simplified Nutrition Assessment Questionnaire	Four-item screening tool	Highly sensitive and specific for those at risk for >10% weight loss
Screen II	Seventeen-item tool that evaluates food intake, chewing, swallowing, weight change, and social or functional barriers	High sensitivity and specificity, inter-rater reliability, and test–retest reliability
Malnutrition Universal Screening Tool	Includes anorexia, disease, body mass index (BMI), and percentage of weight loss	Particularly sensitive for undernutrition in hospitalized patients
DETERMINE	Ten-item checklist to increase the awareness of nutritional risk	Commonly used, but criticized for lack of validity; more useful to promote nutrition awareness than to detect malnutrition

Adapted from Ritchie, C., Schmader, et al. (2009). *Geriatric nutrition: Nutritional issues in older adults.* Retrieved from http://www. uptodateonline.com.proxy.seattleu.edu/online/content/topic.do?topicKey=geri_med/8473&selected Title=1~150&source=search_result

An Example of a Therapeutic Dialogue

Remember Heidi Schneider, the 15-year-old girl receiving home care following hospitalization for anorexia nervosa. The home care nurse is collecting data to assess Heidi's health. The nurse uses professional communication techniques to gather subjective data from Heidi. The nurse is interviewing Heidi to obtain a 24-hour diet recall.

Nurse: So, Heidi, tell me the first thing that you ate yesterday.

Heidi: Some fruit.

Nurse: What kind of fruit was it?

Heidi: A grapefruit.

Nurse: How much of the grapefruit did you eat? And did you have anything else with the grapefruit?

Heidi: I had a yogurt.

Nurse: And was it regular yogurt? Or light?

Heidi: No, light.

Nurse: How much of the yogurt did you eat?

Heidi: (Silent, looks at her mother)

Mrs. Schneider: She only ate half of it.

Nurse: And did you have anything to drink with it?

Heidi: Some water.

Nurse: What else did you eat yesterday?

Heidi: Half a chicken sandwich, with a pickle, celery, carrots, salad, and a diet soft drink.

Nurse: Did you exercise yesterday? What did you do? How long did you exercise?

Heidi: I just ran on the treadmill for about 90 minutes.

Critical Thinking Challenge

- Who should the nurse be communicating with—Heidi, her mother, or both?
- Who should the nurse be assessing? Heidi, her mother, or both?
- What additional assessment information might the nurse collect in addition to the diet recall?

Objective Data Collection

Collecting objective data for a mini-nutritional assessment includes calculating the BMI and percentage of weight change. Findings will determine the need for further anthropometric measurements and laboratory tests.

Equipment Needed

- Scale with a height measure
- Measuring tape
- Growth charts (for children)
- Skin calipers

Promoting Patient Comfort, Safety, and Dignity

Completing a physical assessment in a hospital, nursing home, or community setting may be embarrassing, especially for patients who are overweight or underweight patients. The nurse should reassure the patient of confidentiality and proceed with the examination in a straightforward, nonjudgmental manner while ensuring patient privacy and dignity.

Technique and Expected Findings	Unexpected Findings

Physical Assessment

Body Type

Observe body type, which is noted as small build, average build, or large build. *A wide variety of body types fall within the expected range; however, note that muscle tone and mass decrease with age. Aging also causes fat distribution to change. Fat is lost from the face and neck, while it tends to increase in the arms, abdomen, and hips.*

Major causes of morbidity and mortality are linked to poor diet and sedentary lifestyle with associated *obesity*. Obesity is a growing concern. Katzmarzyk (2007) reported that 36% of Canadians were overweight and 23% were obese. Lack of subcutaneous fat with prominent bones, abdominal ascites, and pitting edema are other unexpected findings. Amenorrhea is a cardinal symptom of eating disorders; other physical consequences of eating disorders, such as cardiac failure or muscle wasting, can be fatal.

Cachexia means a highly catabolic state with accelerated muscle loss and a chronic inflammatory response. It is a distinct syndrome separate from anorexia with the production of proinflammatory cytokines that contribute to the breakdown of fat and muscle protein, causing loss of both muscle mass and fat stores (Jatoi, Loprinzi, et al., 2009). These inflammatory mediators accelerate inflammation, increase the production of C-reactive protein, and reduce albumin levels. Cachexia is common with *cancer*, *hyperthyroidism*, and *AIDS* and is difficult to treat.

General Appearance

Observe general appearance. *A healthy adult appears energetic, alert, and erect. Skin is smooth, warm, moist and is of uniform colour. Hair appears shiny, lustrous, with minimal loss., Nails are pink and firm.*

Clinical findings of malnutrition can occur in many places throughout the body (see Table 8-8 at the end of the chapter). Visible signs include muscle wasting, particularly in the temporal area, and muscle weakness; tongue atrophy; and bleeding or changes in the integrity or hydration status of the skin, hair, teeth, gums, lips, tongue, eyes, and, in men, genitalia (Bellini, Parsons, et al., 2009). See Box 8-5.

Malnutrition is less common in developed countries than obesity but can lead to several poor health outcomes including protein-calorie malnutrition, growth retardation, compromised immunity, poor wound healing and muscle loss, and physical and functional decline.

(text continues on page 170)

Swallowing

Observe the patient's ability to swallow. *Swallowing is smooth, with no difficulty with the ingestion of food.*

Difficulty swallowing, known as *dysphagia*, is common in *stroke* and *neuromuscular diseases.*

Elimination

Inspect urine, emesis, and stool. See Chapter 22.

Emesis refers to vomited contents from the gastrointestinal tract. Emesis should be described and measured.

Body Mass Index

BMI is a guide for maintaining ideal weight for height. It is also used as a benchmark for obesity or protein-caloric malnutrition. Body mass index (BMI) calculation is nonthreatening, noninvasive, and inexpensive. It has one major limitation—BMI can be elevated from large muscles or edema rather than from excess fat.

Calculate BMI as follows: BMI = weight in kg ÷ height in m^2

See the Point for a website for calculating BMI.

A BMI of 18.5 to 24.9 for adults ages 18 to 65 years suggests the lowest risk of developing health challenges. For adults 65 years and older, "normal weight" or "low risk" BMI range may be 22 to 29 with no added risks. However, a "low normal" BMI of 18.5 to 20 may actually indicate increased risk of morbidity.

BMI <18.5 or >24.9 is an unexpected finding and a health risk for conditions such as type 2 diabetes, hypertension, coronary artery disease, stroke, osteoarthritis, and some cancers (Douketis, Paradis, et al., 2005) (Table 8-5). Adults with a BMI <17.5 or children and adolescents with a BMI less than the 5th percentile is associated with malnutrition and osteoporosis and meets the criteria for an eating disorder (Katzmaryz, Craig, et al., 2001).

While it was thought that the BMI would apply to people of all genetic backgrounds, that now appears to be untrue. In a study with an Asian population, it was determined that a BMI of 23 would indicate 'overweight,' while a BMI of 27 would indicate 'obesity' (World Health Organization Expert Consultation, 2004).

Weight Calculations

Reference standards for height and weight are published, with the most common being the Metropolitan Life Insurance Tables (see Chapter 6). These were made available in 1959 and were revised in 1999. Refer to Table 8-6 for calculations of weight for height based on frame size.

In theory, elbow width or wrist width correlates fairly well with muscle and bone mass. But in practice, frame size is too difficult to use, so instead patients subjectively choose their own categories.

Percentage of Ideal Body Weight

The percentage of ideal body weight is based on the ideal and current weight:

Percentage of ideal body weight = current weight/ideal weight × 100.

Mild malnutrition: 80% to 90% of ideal weight
Moderate malnutrition: 70% to 80% of ideal weight
Severe malnutrition: <70% of ideal weight

Table 8-5 **Classification of Overweight and Obesity by body mass index (BMI), Waist Circumference, and Associated Disease Risks**

	BMI (kg/m^2)	Obesity Class	Disease Risk* Relative to Normal Weight and Waist Circumference[†]	
			Men 102 cm (40 in) or Less Women 88 cm (35 in) or Less	Men > 102 cm (40 in) Women > 88 cm (35 in)
Underweight	<18.5		—	—
Normal	18.5–24.9		—	—
Overweight	25.0–29.9		Increased	High
Obesity	30.0–34.9	I	High	Very high
	35.0–39.9	II	Very high	Very high
Extreme obesity	40.0+	III	Extremely high	Extremely high

*Disease risk for type 2 diabetes, hypertension, and cardiovascular disease.
[†]Increased waist circumference can also be a marker for increased risk even in persons of normal weight.
Source: National Heart Lungs and Blood Institute. (2009). *Classification of overweight and obesity by BMI, waist circumference, and associated disease risks.* Retrieved from http://www.nhlbi.nih.gov/health/public/heart/obesity/lose_wt/bmi_dis.htm

Table 8-6   Calculations and Analysis of Weight for Height

1. "Ideal" weight based on height:

Men: 48.1 kg (106 lb) for the first 1.5 m (5 ft) of height and 2.7 kg (6 lb) for each additional 2.5 cm (inch)

Women: 45.4 kg (100 lb) for the first 1.5 m (5 ft) of height and 2.3 kg (5 lb) for each additional 2.5 cm (inch)

Add or subtract 10%, depending on body frame size

2. Use current weight and "ideal" weight to determine the percent ideal body weight:

$$\text{Percentage of ideal body weight} = \frac{\text{Current weight}}{\text{Ideal weight}} \times 100$$

>200%	Morbid obesity
120%–199%	Obese
110%–119%	Overweight
90%–110%	Within expected range
89%–90%	Mild malnutrition
70%–79%	Moderate malnutrition
<69%	Severe malnutrition

Adapted from Dudek, S. G. (2010). *Nutrition essentials for nursing practice* (6th ed.). Philadelphia, PA: Wolters Kluwer Health/ Lippincott Williams & Wilkins.

Technique and Expected Findings (continued)	Unexpected Findings (continued)
Recent Weight Change Carefully assess the circumstances surrounding any change in weight to determine causes. Cluster weight and weight change with other data to analyze if the change is from fluid, muscle mass, or fat stores. After collecting the usual weight from the history and current weight on a scale (see Chapter 4), calculate the percent weight change (percentage loss of usual weight) as follows: (usual weight − present weight) ÷ usual weight × 100	The following guidelines indicate significant weight loss: • 1% to 2% in 1 week • 5% in 1 month • 7.5% in 3 months • 10% in 6 months (Dudek, 2010) Unintentional weight gain or loss is a significant finding. This may occur from a change in fluid volume, such as in *heart* or kidney failure, pathology, or from a change in nutritional status. Weight gain may result from metabolic issues, such as *hypothyroidism*.
Percent Usual Body Weight Another calculation can be made based on the current and usual weight. The percentage of usual weight is calculated as follows: Percentage of usual body weight = current weight/usual weight × 100.	*Mild malnutrition*: 85% to 95% of usual body weight *Moderate malnutrition*: 75% to 84% of usual body weight *Severe malnutrition*: <75% of usual body weight
Waist Circumference Where fat is deposited on the body is a more reliable indicator of disease risk than the amount of fat deposited in the body. Use waist circumference to evaluate the amount of abdominal fat in men and women. The patient should stand straight with the feet about 25 to 30 cm apart and arms hanging at the sides. Place the tape measure around the trunk midway between the lower costal margin and the top of the iliac crest. Fit the tape measure snugly around the abdomen but do not	Waist circumference >102 cm in men and >88 cm in women increases the risk for chronic illness associated with adiposity (National Heart Lungs and Blood Institute [NHLBI], 2009). See Table 8-5. The accumulation of abdominal body fat significantly increases the risk for *type 2 diabetes, hypertension*, and cardiovascular disease. Waist measurement provides information about morbidity and relative risk of disease (NHLBI, 2009).

(text continues on page 172)

compress the underlying soft tissue. Have the patient take a breath and record the measure at the end of a usual expiration. The waist circumference is recorded to the nearest 0.5 cm (Canadian Medical Association, 2005) (Fig. 8-4).

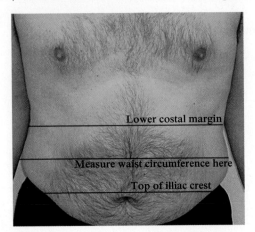

Lower costal margin

Measure waist circumference here

Top of illiac crest

Figure 8-4 Measuring the waist circumference.

Waist-to-Hip Ratio

Assess waist-to-hip ratio to determine body fat distribution as an indicator of risk to health. The waist-to-hip ratio is calculated as follows:

Waist-to-hip ratio = waist circumference ÷ hip circumference (largest part of the buttocks).

Note: *Waist circumference measurement has largely replaced waist-to-hip ratio because it is easier and more accurate to measure* (Bray, Xavier Pi-Sunyer, et al., 2009).

A waist-to-hip ratio ≥1.0 in men or >0.8 in women indicates upper body (android) obesity, which puts the patient at risk for increased mortality and heart attack (NHLBI, 2009).

Skinfold Thickness

Skinfold thickness is a measure used to indicate subcutaneous fat reserves. It requires an experienced person using a reliable caliper at the correct standardized locations on the body. If this measure is inaccurate, data will be misleading. Measurements of skinfold thickness are much less accurate than measurements of height or

Patients above the 95th or below the 5th percentile are at risk for altered nutritional status.

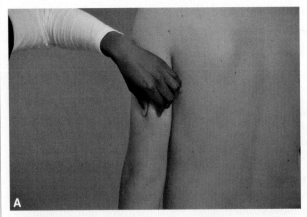
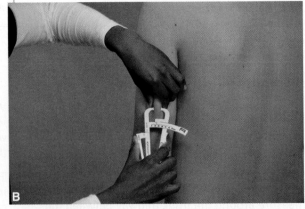

Figure 8-5 Measuring the skinfold thickness. **A.** Gently grasp and pull away a vertical fold of the skin from the muscle. **B.** With the calipers at a right angle to midpoint, apply pressure on the calipers until the spring-loaded level is depressed completely.

weight, especially in patients who are obese. Thus, it has little practical clinical value unless performed by the same person over a period of time to evaluate trends (Bray, Xavier Pi-Sunyer, et al., 2009). If performed, a dietitian usually takes this measurement.

Measure the skinfold thickness at the triceps, subscapular, biceps, and suprailiac areas. Although the triceps is the most commonly used, it does not accurately represent the adipose tissue of the entire body. For the triceps skinfold (TSF) measurement

- locate the mid upper arm point with the arm at 90°
- use the fingers to gently grasp and pull away a vertical fold of the skin from the muscle (Fig. 8-5A)
- apply the calipers at a right angle to the midpoint
- apply pressure on the calipers until the spring-loaded level is depressed completely (Fig. 8-5B)
- take three readings 3 seconds apart and average the values

Expected findings are according to standardized tables that adjust for age and gender.

Mid Upper Arm Muscle Circumference

The **mid upper arm muscle circumference (MAMC)** is an indirect measure of bone, muscle area, and fat reserves. Measure around the arm, midway between the elbow and the shoulder (Fig. 8-6).

A higher number on the arm circumference indicates both fat and muscle stores. Findings below the 10th percentile are unexpected, indicating loss of muscle. Trends that decrease over time are also significant.

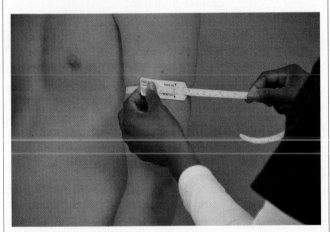

Figure 8-6 Measuring the MAMC around the arm, midway between the elbow and the shoulder.

Derived Measures (Using MAMC and TSF)

The **MAMC and the mid upper arm muscle area (MAMA)** are indicators of muscle and body protein reserves.

MAMC = Mid arm circumference (MAC) − ($\pi \times$ TSF)

MAMA = (MAC − MAMC)² ÷ 4π

A higher number indicates more muscle. These findings are compared to charts with expected values.

Findings below the 10th percentile are unexpected, indicating loss of muscle. Trends that decrease over time are also significant.

Documentation of Examination Findings

Areas of Assessment	Expected Findings	Unexpected Findings
Height	170 cm (1.7 m) at age 35 years	162 cm (1.62 m) at age 60 years
Weight	59 kg at age 35 years	89 kg at age 60 years
Body mass index	20.4 at age 35 years	34.0 at age 60 years
Waist circumference	71 cm at age 35 years	90 cm at age 60 years
Blood pressure	118/76	150/100
Inspection of oral cavity	Own teeth, in good repair Gums: pink, no bleeding Lips: moist, no lesions in corners of mouth	Dentures: poorly fitting Gums: bleed easily Lips: dry, cracks in corners of mouth
24-Hour food recall (using Canada's Food Guide for number of servings per day)	Vegetables and fruits: 7–8 Grain Products: 6–7 (particularly whole grain) Milk and alternates: 2 Meat and alternates: 2 Fats: 30–45 mL of unsaturated fat Snacks: apple, peapods	Vegetables and fruits: 3 Grain Products: 9 (mainly white bread, pasta) Milk and alternates: 0 Meat and alternates: 4 Fats: 45 mL of butter Snacks: Two pieces of chocolate cake, potato chips
Comfort foods	Fruits, milk, raw vegetables	Bread and butter, chocolate bars, donuts
Dietary restrictions	None	Allergic to eggs, all nuts, and sesame seeds Lactose intolerant
Caffeine intake	1 cup of coffee daily	1400 mL of diet cola daily
Alcohol intake	1 glass of red wine daily	12 beers every weekend
Exercise	Treadmill × 30 minutes, 5 days per week	Walking very restricted due to osteoarthritis in both knees. Uses walker outside of house. No other exercise
Ability to shop for food	Has transportation to grocery store	A family member shops for groceries
Resources for food	Has resources to purchase all types of food: fruits, vegetables, grain products, and milk and meat alternatives	Has food insecurity because of limited resources. Purchases few fruits, some vegetables such as carrots and potatoes, day-old white bread, macaroni and other pasta, and occasional meat, and cheese
Physical ability to prepare food	Can prepare all types of foods	Limited ability to stand and prepare food—uses mostly canned and packaged foods

Adapted from: Brunet, K., Day, R. A., et al. (2010). Nutritional assessment. In T. C. Stephen, D. L. Skillen, R. A. Day, & L. S. Bickley (Eds.). *Canadian Bates' guide to health assessment for nurses.* (1st ed., p. 192). Philadelphia, PA: Wolters Kluwer Health/Lippincott Williams & Wilkins.

The home care nurse has just completed the physical examination of Heidi Schneider, a 15-year-old girl with anorexia. Review the following important findings revealed in each of the steps of data collection for Heidi. Consider the techniques of subjective and objective data collection during the assessment. Notice that the objective data include findings from several body systems.

Subjective: "I'm still fat. I don't want to eat because I won't fit into my clothes anymore." 24-hour diet recall: one serving fruit, half a low fat yogurt, half a chicken sandwich with pickle, celery, carrots, salad, and a diet soft drink. Exercise: "I just ran on the treadmill for about 90 minutes."

Objective: The 15-year-old female is thin and appears older than her age. Temperature 36°C oral, Pulse 88 beats/min regular, Respiration 20 breaths/min, BP 108/66 mm Hg (sitting, right arm). Taking fewer than 500 cal/day orally. Weight increased 0.5 kg, since discharge from hospital. BMI 14.8, which is classed as "underweight". Ideal weight is 56.8 kg, weighs 71% of ideal weight, "moderate malnutrition". Skin pale and dry with some flaking. Appears distressed about eating. No edema, peripheral pulses strong. Nails brittle, skin very thin and dull. Wearing bandana, hair appears dull and thin. Eyes sunken with dark circles. Upper and lower extremities with full range of motion, muscle strength 3/5. Abdomen soft, concave, nondistended, nontender. Heart rate and rhythm regular. Lung sounds clear bilaterally.

Analysis: Nutrition, less than body requirements related to low calorie intake.

Plan: Continue to encourage nutritious foods with adequate calories and protein. Schedule a visit next week to evaluate weight. Refer to a dietitian for further counselling on food choices.

🔺 Lifespan Considerations

Women Who are Pregnant

Vitamin deficiency is rare in developed countries and uncommon among healthy women who are pregnant (Health Canada, 2007a). Women who skip several meals each week, have a high intake of soft drinks, snack foods, and fast foods, or both can benefit from nutritional counselling by a dietitian. Because of financial concerns, some women may require assistance from social services, or specific programs for women who are pregnant.

The main measure of nutritional health in a woman who is pregnant is prepregnancy BMI. Prepregnancy body weight and weight gain are associated with both the infant's birth weight and the length of term. Women who are underweight with low weight gain during pregnancy are at higher risk of having a low-birth-weight infant and preterm birth. Women who are obese are at increased risk of having a larger than expected infant and late birth.

Recommendations for weight gain during pregnancy are as follows:

- 12.5 to 18 kg for women who are underweight—BMI < 19.8 kg/m²
- 11.5 to 16 kg for women of expected weight —BMI 19.9 to 26.0 kg/m²
- 7 to 11.5 kg for women who are overweight—BMI 26.0 to 29.0 kg/m²
- At least 6.8 kg for women who are obese—BMI > 29.0 kg/m² (Mayo Clinic Staff, 2010).

Infants, Children, and Adolescents

Growth charts are commonly used to indicate nutritional status. One set of charts commonly used from birth to 36 months includes length, weight, and head circumference. See Chapter 6 for measurement techniques. Another set of charts includes height and weight and is used for children 2 to 18 years. Children who should be followed up closely and need a more complete nutritional assessment include those whose height for age is less than the 10th percentile, weight for height is less than the 15th percentile, or BMI is greater than the 85th percentile (Phillips, Jensen, et al., 2009).

Of particular concern is the prevalence of obesity in children. The percentage of Canadian children who are obese has increased over the past 25 years (1978/1979 to 2004) as follows:

- 2 to 5 years: 0% to 6%
- 6 to 11 years: 0% to 8%
- 12 to 17 years: 3% to 9% (Shields, 2005)

Children and adolescents who are obese are more likely to have risk factors associated with cardiovascular diseases (ie, high blood pressure, high cholesterol, type 2 diabetes) than are other children and adolescents (CDCP, 2009). Finally, it is important to remember that obesity and malnutrition are not mutually exclusive. Children with high-fat, high-carbohydrate diets may lack sufficient fruits and vegetables to meet daily requirements for other nutrients such as vitamins.

The physical assessment includes observing for signs of genetic disorders or medical diseases contributing to malnutrition (eg, lack of feeding or vitamin deficiencies) and child abuse or neglect (Kirkland, Drutz, et al., 2009). The nurse also observes the relationship of the parent to the child and, when able, the parent feeding the child.

Older Adults

In older adults, BMI and weight change are the simplest screening measures. Weight loss in older adults, especially unintentional, is associated with an increased risk of death. It may be difficult to obtain an accurate weight in an older adult. A chair or bed scale that is regularly calibrated may be needed for patients who cannot stand on a scale. Low body weight is defined as <80% of ideal body weight (Ritchie, Schmader, et al., 2009). Interestingly, loss of as little as 5% of weight over a 3-year period is associated with increased mortality among older adults living in the community. Residents who live in nursing homes have meaningful weight loss if they have lost 5% of usual body weight in 30 days, or 10% in 6 months. Valid and reliable tools have been developed for older adults (see Table 8-4).

Evidence-Informed Critical Thinking

Nurses usually complete nutritional assessments in collaboration with dietitians. Often, however, nurses are the first providers to identify patients at nutritional risk. Nutritional issues can affect all body systems, fluid balance, and electrolytes. Patients who are undernourished may have electrolyte imbalances, delayed healing, and slowed recovery from illness.

Common Laboratory and Diagnostic Testing

No single laboratory test is nutritionally specific. Health-related conditions or treatments can affect each measure. For example, with protracted illness or hospitalization, circulating and nutrient storage pools shift, depending on resources and demands, and body stores of macronutrients and micronutrients may decline to dangerously low levels. Most biochemical measures detect only circulating levels of nutrients; thus, reported values can lead to an incomplete nutritional picture because there is no indication of how much of a measured nutrient is still stored in the body. Therefore, the use of serial tests rather than a single value is suggested to achieve greater accuracy and to discover nutritional trends. Additionally, it is useful to cluster a group of tests and data together to analyze nutritional status.

Serum Proteins

The liver synthesizes several serum proteins. *Albumin* is a prime ingredient of blood oncotic pressure and a carrier protein for many body and pharmacologic substances. The serum protein albumin level is low with liver cell damage, malnutrition, and renal disease. With a low albumin level, interstitial fluid is not drawn back into the vascular system,

causing fluid to accumulate in the tissues. Because of the long half-life (18 to 30 days) of albumin, this value is not the best indicator of current nutritional status, although it is often used. Another circulating protein, *prealbumin*, has a half-life of 2 days. Though less commonly ordered than albumin, prealbumin level is a better indicator of current nutritional status because of its shorter half-life. *Transferrin* has a half-life of 9 days, putting it between prealbumin and albumin. Another serum protein is *creatinine*; however, because the kidneys excrete creatinine, it is more reflective of renal function. Total protein levels measure all circulating body proteins and provide an overview of protein stores.

Hemoglobin and Hematocrit

Low hemoglobin and hematocrit counts may indicate poor iron intake or absorption. Other factors such as bleeding, fluid excess, or low intake of vitamin B_{12} and folate may also decrease these values.

Lymphocyte Count

Severe malnutrition may compromise inflammatory response. An indicator of the ability to mount an immune response is the total lymphocyte (white blood cell) count.

Creatinine Excretion

Creatinine excretion reflects muscle mass, but individual variations are wide. This is a measure of excretion of creatinine in the urine according to the patient's height. A 24-hour urine collection is needed, and there are many sources of error.

Nitrogen Balance

Nitrogen balance reflects total protein mass, but laboratory testing of it is expensive and time consuming. Three consecutive 24-hour measurements of urine are needed because of large variations; there are many potential sources of error.

Skin Testing

Delayed-type hypersensitivity testing is performed by skin testing with common irritants. Theoretically, the immune response will be reduced in the patient who is malnourished. Skin testing is not commonly performed because it is uncomfortable, and the immune response can be depressed during an acute illness even in the absence of malnutrition (Olendzki, Lipman, et al., 2009).

Lipid Measurements

Lipid measurements are used to assess the status of cardiovascular health, including total cholesterol, high-density lipoprotein, LDL, and triglyceride levels. Findings are associated with risks for atherosclerosis, heart attack, and stroke.

Other Laboratory Tests

Anemias are associated with iron, vitamin B_{12}, and folate deficiencies. Sodium, potassium, magnesium, calcium, and phosphate are serum electrolytes associated with nutritional status. Because of other factors that can influence these values, they must be considered within a cluster of data rather than independently as a reflection of nutritional status (Olendzki, Lipman, et al., 2009).

Clinical Reasoning

Nursing Diagnosis, Outcomes, and Interventions

Patients may be at risk for fluid volume or nutritional imbalance as listed in the North American Nursing Diagnosis Association-International (NANDA-I) nursing diagnoses. North Americans are at most risk for "imbalanced nutrition: more than body requirements," given that more than two thirds of the population is overweight or obese. The World Health Organization (WHO) states that obesity is a much neglected public health issue and that the world's population is becoming either obese or undernourished (Murray, Zentner, et al., 2009). North Americans with a lower socioeconomic background, minimal education, or eating disorders are at greatest risk for malnutrition today.

The risk of excess fluid volume is rare. Nevertheless, patients on intravenous therapy may experience fluid overload if fluid replacement is not closely monitored, particularly in cases of cardiac or renal failure. Older adults in care homes run the highest risk of deficient fluid volume. Other possible nursing diagnoses pertaining to nutrition include adult failure to thrive, risk for delayed development, and deficient

knowledge. Adult failure to thrive may be linked to an endocrine or metabolic imbalance, whereas delayed development may be related to nutritional deficiencies in pregnancy.

Deficient knowledge is the most pervasive cause of nutritional imbalances. Hence, nurses have a significant role in patient education and follow-up regarding optimal nutrition for people from all sectors and age groups of society. The ongoing proliferation of nutrition information means that nurses must access evidence-informed sources of nutrition information regularly to maintain a credible body of knowledge. Table 8-7 compares and contrasts nursing diagnoses, unexpected findings, and interventions related to nutritional care (NANDA-I, 2009).

Nurses use assessment information to identify patient outcomes. Some outcomes related to nutrition include the following:

- Less than body requirements: The patient will show progressive weight gain toward the desired goal.
- More than body requirements: The patient will state pertinent factors contributing to weight gain (Moorhead, Johnson, et al., 2007).

After outcomes are established, nurses implement care to improve the patient's status. The nurse uses critical thinking and evidence-informed practice to develop interventions. He or she evaluates the patient to determine the effectiveness of those interventions and revises the plan as needed.

Table 8-7	Common Nursing Diagnoses Associated with Nutrition		
Diagnosis and Related Factors	**Point of Differentiation**	**Assessment Characteristics**	**Nursing Interventions**
Imbalanced nutrition, less than body requirements	Nutrient intake that fails to meet metabolic needs	Body weight 20% or more below ideal, body mass index (BMI) < 20, lack of interest in food, nausea, vomiting, diarrhea	Weigh the patient daily. Monitor the intake. Provide nutritional supplements. Offer food frequently.
Imbalanced nutrition, more than body requirements	Nutrient intake that exceeds metabolic needs	Body weight more than 20% above ideal, BMI > 30, eating in response to cues other than hunger, triceps skinfold >25 mm in women or >15 mm in men	Keep a food diary and record every food and drink. Teach reading of food labels. Weigh twice a week. Teach an increased intake of vegetables and fruits.
Fluid volume excess	Increased retention of isotonic fluid	Altered electrolytes, elevated creatinine, decreased hematocrit and hemoglobin, weight gain	Monitor the intake and output. Weigh daily at the same time of the day. Evaluate serum sodium, creatinine, and hematocrit.
Deficient fluid volume	Decreased intravascular, interstitial, or intracellular fluid; dehydration	Decreased BP, increased pulse, orthostatic BP changes, thirst, dry skin, sunken eyeballs	Monitor the intake and output. Weigh daily. Provide fluids every 2 h. Treat causes including nausea, vomiting, or diarrhea.*

*Collaborative interventions.

In addition to completing a nutritional assessment, the nurse facilitates the patient's nutritional care by serving as a liaison between the primary provider and the dietitian. The nurse also confers with colleagues in social work and physical or occupational therapy during discharge planning to ensure that patients benefit from community programs to provide easy-to-prepare food (Box 8-6).

Patients with eating disorders respond best to a highly individualized, interprofessional approach to outpatient treatment consisting of nutrition counselling, psychotherapy, and family or group counselling. Treatment plans are designed to foster slow, gradual behavioural changes aimed at maintaining appropriate eating patterns and promoting long-term maintenance of ideal weight. This can be achieved only by involving the patient in establishing an individualized plan with realistic goals. Patients with eating disorders must be reassessed over time because they often experience chronic issues with eating and exercise as well as weight maintenance.

BOX 8-6 NURSE'S ROLE IN FACILITATING NUTRITIONAL CARE

- Communicate with the Registered Dietitian.
- Serve as a liaison between the physician and the dietitian.
- Identify patients who may benefit from programs such as Meals on Wheels.
- Request a referral to a speech therapist to evaluate gag reflex and ability to swallow.
- Confer with the discharge planner, social services worker, and physical and occupational therapist.

From Dudek, S. G. (2010). *Nutrition essentials for nursing practice* (6th ed.). Philadelphia, PA: Wolters Kluwer Health/Lippincott Williams & Wilkins.

In many facilities, nurses initiate referrals for nutritional issues. Assessments that might trigger a nutrition consult include patients who are food or housing insecure, have not eaten in several days, or have wasting syndrome. Additionally, patients with more than three nutritional risk factors or diagnoses that could improve with counselling can be referred to a dietitian.

Karen has more than three nutritional risk factors and her health state would improve if she ate more protein and calories. The following conversation illustrates how the nurse might organize data and make recommendations to the dietitian.

Situation: Hello, I'm Frances Welly, a home care nurse working with Heidi Schneider, a 15-year-old female. She was recently hospitalized for anorexia. I saw her at home today.

Background: She is eating only about 500 cal/d, and I think that she would benefit from a nutrition consult. Although her weight has increased 0.5 kg since discharge from hospital, her BMI is 14.8 and she weighs 71% of ideal weight. She gets distressed about eating and increasing her calorie intake. Heidi reported about 90 minutes of running on treadmill yesterday.

Assessment: I am hoping that you might be able to negotiate some food choices that would be good for her.

Recommendations: Would you be able to see her in the next week? Her mother may also want to participate, but I think that you might want to ask Heidi for her permission. Thanks so much.

Critical Thinking Challenge

- Why did the nurse leave out most of the physical assessment data?
- How does the nurse use assessment data to make the recommendations?
- How does the assessment performed by the nurse compare to that performed by the dietitian?

The nurse uses assessment data to formulate a nursing care plan for Heidi Schneider. After completing the interventions, the nurse will reevaluate Heidi and document the findings in the chart to show critical thinking. This is often in the form of a care plan or case note similar to the one below.

Nursing Diagnosis	Patient Outcomes	Nursing Interventions	Rationale	Evaluation
Imbalanced nutrition, less than body requirements	Gain 10% of body weight, or 4 kg, in next 2 months.	Continue to complete home visits. Assess weight at each weekly visit. Discuss the use of 30 mL of nutritional shake each hour.	Develop a relationship with family. Follow trends of weight over time. Small amounts of intake may be more acceptable.	The patient talks more about anorexia. Weight increased by 4 kg. The patient declines the use of a supplement and will continue to increase her intake.

Using the previous steps of clinical reasoning, organizing, and prioritizing, consider all the case study findings woven throughout this chapter. When answering the following questions, begin drawing conclusions and see how the pieces of assessment must work together to create an environment for personalized, appropriate, and accurate care.

- What subjective and psychosocial data will the nurse collect frrom Heidi and her mother? (Knowledge)
- How might the nurse's previous experiences with patients who have eating disorders influence the assessment of Heidi? (Comprehension)
- What adaptations will the nurse make to the assessment based on Heidi's condition? (Application)
- What factors are contributing to Heidi's current nutritional status? (Analysis)
- What recommendations for further assessment of Heidi by the interprofessional team would the nurse suggest? (Synthesis)
- How will the nurse evaluate the success of the interventions of the interprofessional team with Heidi? (Evaluation)

Key Points

- Primary nutrients essential for optimal body function include carbohydrates, proteins, fats, vitamins, minerals, water, and major electrolytes.
- Vitamin D, folate, folic acid and B vitamins have important health implications.
- Drug–herb interactions may be serious—even life threatening.
- Three important minerals in a healthy diet are iron, zinc, and calcium.
- Water, sodium, and potassium need to be kept in balance for proper fluid and electrolyte functions.

- Inadequate intake of folate (from foods) and folic acid (from fortified foods and supplements) during pregnancy is linked to neural tube defects in newborns.
- Newborns and infants have a higher need for proteins and other nutrients than do other age groups.
- Canada's Food Guide emphasizes the need to select foods from each of the four food groups, while reducing fats, sugars, and sodium.
- Risk factors to review in a nutritional assessment include medical history, unexpected weight history (gains or losses), appetite or taste changes, gastrointestinal symptoms, food allergies or intolerances, changes in eating or

fluid patterns, poor food habits, inability to cook, multiple medications, inappropriate or lack of supplements, and alcohol or drug use.

- Common symptoms that indicate potential nutritional concerns include sudden or gradual changes in body weight, eating habits, skin, hair, nails, and energy level.
- Older adults at risk for malnutrition are those who take multiple medications, are socially isolated, or cannot shop, cook, or eat independently.
- Nurses recognize that each culture has its own food standards, determining what is edible, how foods are prepared, and special foods to eat when ill.
- Comprehensive nutritional screening tools include 24-hour recall, 3-day diet history, and food-frequency questionnaire.
- BMI is calculated as weight in kg divided by height in m^2. BMI of 18.5 to 24.9 is healthy, <18.5 is underweight, 25 to 29.9 is overweight, and ≥30 is obesity. For adults 65 years and older, a BMI <30 may not increase risk; however, a BMI of 18.5 to 20 may increase risk.
- Waist circumference is an indicator of accumulated body fat in the abdomen; a high circumference places people at increased risk of obesity-related diseases and early mortality.
- Children who should be followed up closely and need a more complete nutritional assessment include those whose height for age is less than the 10th percentile, weight for height is less than the 15th percentile, or BMI is greater than the 85th percentile (Phillips, Jensen, et al., 2009).
- Laboratory values related to nutrition include serum albumin, prealbumin, transferrin, total protein, creatinine, sodium, potassium, hemoglobin, hematocrit, total lymphocyte count, and hypersensitivity reaction.
- Nursing diagnoses related to nutrition include imbalanced nutrition, less than body requirements; imbalanced nutrition, more than body requirements; fluid volume excess; and deficient fluid volume.

Review Questions

1. The patient has serum values that are unexpected for sodium and potassium. The nurse recognizes that these values are important to maintain an expected range for proper
   A. tissue oxygenation
   B. tensile strength in the hair
   C. oil production in the skin
   D. fluid and electrolyte function

2. Primary nutrients essential for optimal body function include
   A. carbohydrates, proteins, and fats
   B. folate, vitamin B_{12}, and iron
   C. vitamins A, D, E, and K
   D. iron, zinc, and calcium

3. The patient reports taking St. John's wort along with a medication prescribed for heart disease. Which of the following is the most appropriate response from the nurse?
   A. Never take supplements in addition to prescribed medications.
   B. Supplements act in a very different way from prescribed medications.
   C. Sometimes there might be supplements that interact with your medications.
   D. It is known that St. John's wort interacts with medications for heart disease.

4. The patient who is pregnant is being screened for AI of calcium and vitamin D. Which of the following tools is most appropriate for the nurse to administer?
   A. 24-hour recall
   B. 3-day diet history
   C. Food-frequency questionnaire
   D. Comprehensive nutritional assessment

5. Which of the following patients has the healthiest eating plans? A plan that
   A. excludes lean meats, poultry, and fish
   B. allows for moderate intake of salt and sugars
   C. emphasizes low-fat milk and dairy products
   D. emphasizes fruits, vegetables, and whole grains

6. The patient has a body mass index (BMI) of 14. Which nursing intervention is indicated?
   A. Provide additional high protein and calorie shakes.
   B. Reduce total fat and calorie intake.
   C. Increase the intake of green leafy vegetables.
   D. Eat complete meals twice a day.

7. The nurse is caring for a child who is at the 95th percentile for weight. Which nursing diagnosis is most appropriate?
   A. Imbalanced nutrition, less than body requirements
   B. Imbalanced nutrition, more than body requirements
   C. Fluid volume excess and deficient fluid volume
   D. Fluid volume deficit and deficient fluid volume

8. From the list below, select the older adult at greatest risk for malnutrition.
   A. A 67-year-old married man with poor dentition
   B. A 73-year-old woman in a nursing home
   C. An 80-year-old widow who lives alone
   D. A 78-year-old widower who receives Meals on Wheels

9. The patient hospitalized 3 days ago has an expected albumin level. The patient is most likely to be
   A. well nourished because albumin is the main protein
   B. moderately nourished because total protein is a better indicator
   C. poorly nourished because hospitalization causes albumin to increase
   D. well nourished 1 month ago but prealbumin is a more current indicator

10. Which of the following patients is at highest risk for complications related to folate deficiency?
 A. A 3-year-old boy who is developmentally delayed
 B. A 15-year-old girl who just started her menses
 C. A 24-year-old woman who is attempting pregnancy
 D. An 82-year-old man living in a nursing home

Canadian Nursing Research

Chang, C.C., & Roberts, B. L. (2008). Cultural perspectives in feeding difficulty in Taiwanese elderly with dementia. *Journal of Nursing Scholarship, 40*(3), 235–240.

Johnson, R. L., Williams, S. M., et al. (2006). Genomics, nutrition, obesity, and diabetes. *Journal of Nursing Scholarship, 38*(1), 11–18.

Kara, B., Caglar, K., et al. (2007). Nonadherence with diet and fluid restrictions and perceived social support in patients receiving hemodialysis. *Journal of Nursing Scholarship, 39*(3), 243–248.

References

Alberta Health Services. (2008). *Calciium and vitamin D for prevention and treatment of osterporosis.* Edmonton, AB: Author.

Bellini, L. M., Parsons, P. E., et al. (2009). *Assessment of nutrition in the critically ill.* Retrieved from http://www.uptodateonline.com.proxy.seattleu.edu/online/content/topic.do?topicKey=cc_medi/17912 &selectedTitle=6~150&source=search_result

Boyce, J. M., & Shone, G. R. (2006). Effects of aging on smell and taste. *Postgraduate Medicine, 82,* 249–251.

Bray, G. A., Xavier Pi-Sunyer, F., et al. (2009). *Determining body composition in adults.* Retrieved from http://www.uptodateonline.com.proxy.seattleu.edu/online/content/topic.do?topicKey=obesity/7584&selectedTitle=2~150&source=search_result

Brunet, K., Day, R. A., et al. (2010). Nutritional assessment. In T. C. Stephen, D. L. Skillen, R. A. Day, & L. S. Bickley (Eds.). *Canadian Bates' guide to health assessment for nurses* (1st ed., pp. 167–201). Philadelphia, PA: Wolters Kluwer Health/Lippincott Williams & Wilkins.

Canadian Medical Association. (2005). Canadian guidelines for body weight classification in adults: Application in clinical practice to screen for overweight and obesity and to assess disease risk. *Canadian Medical Association Journal, 172*(8), 995–998.

Canadian Nurse Association. (2011). Helping people shake the habit. *Canadian Nurse, 107*(3), p. 15.

Centers for Disease Control and Prevention. (2009). *Overweight and obesity.* Retrieved from http://www.cdc.gov/nccdphp/dnpa/obesity/index.htm

Craig, W. J. (2009). Health effects of vegan diets. *American Journal of Clinical Nutrition, 89*(5), 1627S–1633S.

Dudek, S. G. (2010). *Nutrition essentials for nursing practice* (6th ed.). Philadelphia, PA: Wolters Kluwer Health/Lippincott Williams & Wilkins.

Douketis, J. D., Paradis, G., et al. (2005). Canadian guidelines for body weight classification in adults: Application in clinical practice to screen for overweight and obesity and to assess disease risk. *Canadian Medical Association Journal, 172*(8), 995–998.

Health Canada. (2007a). *Eating well with Canada's food guide: A resource to educators and communicators.* Ottawa, ON: Minister of Health Canada.

Health Canada (2007b). *Eating well with Canada's food guide.* Ottawa: ON: Minister of Health Canada. Retrieved from http://www.hc-sc.gc.ca/fn-an/alt_formats/hpfb-dgpsa/pdf/food-guide-aliment/print_eatwell_beinmang-eng.pdf

Hemmelgarn, M. (2009). Shedding light on vitamin D. *American Journal of Nursing, 109*(4), 19–20.

Jatoi, A., Loprinzi, C. L., et al. (2009). *Clinical features and pathogenesis of cancer cachexia.* Retrieved from http://www.uptodateonline.com.proxy.seattleu.edu/online/content/topic.do?topicKey=genl_onc/4404&selectedTitle=1~77&source=search_result

Katzmarzyk, P. T. (2007). The metabolic syndrome: An introduction. *Applied Physiology, Nutrition & Metabolism, 32*(1), 1–3.

Katzmarzyk, P. T., Craig, C. L., et al. (2001). Underweight, overweight and obesity: Relationships with mortality in the 13-year follow-up of the Canada Fitness Survey. *Journal of Clinical Epidemiology, 54,* 916–920.

Kirkland, R. T., Drutz, J. E., et al. (2009). *Etiology and evaluation of failure to thrive (undernutrition) in children younger than two years.* Retrieved from http://www.uptodateonline.com.proxy.seattleu.edu/online/content/topic.do?topicKey=gen_pedi/2884&linkTitle=EVALUATION&source=preview&selectedTitle=10~150&anchor=14#14

Lowdermilk, D. L., & Perry, S. E. (2007). *Maternity & women's health care* (9th ed.). St. Louis, MO: Elsevier.

Magana-Gomez, J. A., & Calderon de la Barca, A. M. (2008). Risk assessment of genetically modified crops for nutrition and health. *Nutrition Reviews, 67*(1), 1–16.

Mayo Clinic Staff. (2010). *Prenatal vitamins: Give your baby the best start.* Retrieved from http://www.mayoclinic.com/health/prenatal-vitamins/pr00160

Mente, A., de Koning, L., et al. (2009). A systematic review of the evidence supporting a causal link between dietary factors and coronary heart disease. *Archives of Internal Medicine, 169*(7), 659–669.

Moorhead, S., Johnson, M., et al. (2007). *Nursing outcomes classification (NOC)* (4th ed.). Philadelphia, PA: Mosby.

Murray, R. B., Zentner, J. P., et al. (2009). *Health promotion strategies through the lifespan* (2nd Canadian ed.). Toronto: Prentice Hall.

National Academy of Science. (2004). *Dietary Reference Intakes for water, potassium, sodium, chloride and sulfate.* Retrieved from http://books.nap.edu/catalog.php?record_id=10925

National Academy of Science. (2005). *Dietary Reference Intakes for energy, carbohydrates, fiber, fat, fatty acids, protein and amino acids (macronutrients).* Retrieved from http://books.nap.edu/catalog.php?record_id=10490

National Heart Lungs and Blood Institute (2009). *Classification of overweight and obesity by BMI, waist circumference, and associated disease risks.* Retrieved from http://www.nhlbi.nih.gov/health/public/heart/obesity/lose_wt/bmi_dis.htm

North American Nursing Diagnoses Association-International (NANDA-I). (2009). *Nursing diagnoses, 2009–2011 Edition: Definitions and classifications.* West Sussex, UK: John Wiley & Sons.

Olendzki, B., Lipman, T. O., et al. (2009). *Dietary and nutritional assessment in adults.* Retrieved from http://www.uptodateonline. com.proxy.seattleu.edu/online/content/topic.do?topicKey=nutriti o/4489&selectedTitle=8~150&source=search_result

Pencharz, P. B. (2010). Protein and energy requirements for optimal catch-up growth. *European Journal of Clinical Nutrition, 64*, 55–57.

Phillips, S. M., Jensen, C., et al. (2009). *Indications for nutritional assessment in childhood.* Retrieved from http://www. uptodateonline.com.proxy.seattleu.edu/online/content/topic. do?topicKey=nutri_ch/5413&selectedTitle=10~150&source=s earch_result

Public Health Agency of Canada. (2011). *Physical activity. Information and tips for parents, teachers, and caregivers of children (5–11 years) and youth (12–17 years).* Retrieved from http://phac-aspc.gc.ca/hl-mvs/p-ap/eng.php

Ritchie, C., Schmader, K. E, et al. (2009). *Geriatric nutrition: Nutritional issues in older adults.* Retrieved from http://www. uptodateonline.com.proxy.seattleu.edu/online/content/topic. do?topicKey=geri_med/8473&selectedTitle=1~150&source=s earch_result

Shields, M. (2005). Measured obesity, overweight Canadian children and adolescents. *Nutrition: Findings from the Canadian Community Health Survey. Issue 1.* Ottawa, ON: Statistics Canada. Cat No 82–620-MWE2005001.

Simmons, S. F., Bertrand, R., et al. (2007). A preliminary evaluation of the paid feeding assistant regulation. Impact on feeding assistance care process quality in nursing homes. *The Gerontologist, 47*(2), 184–192.

Society of Obstetricians and Gynaecologists of Canada. (2003). Clinical practice guideline: The use of folic acid for prevention of neural tube defects and other congenital abnormalities. *Journal of Obstetrics and Gynaecology Canada, 25*(11), 959–965.

Snyder, P. J., Matsumoto, A. M, et al. (2009). *Use of androgens and other drugs by athletes.* Retrieved from http://www. uptodateonline.com.proxy.seattleu.edu/online/content/topic. do?topicKey=r_endo_m/9455&selectedTitle=4~150&source= search_result

Spilburg, C. A., Goldberg, A. C., et al. (2003). Fat-free foods supplemented with soy stanol-lecithin powder reduce cholesterol absorption and LDL cholesterol. *Journal of American Dietetic Association, 103*(5), 577–581.

Statistics Canada (2008). *Canada's ethnocultural mosaic; 2006 census.* Retrieved from http://www.12.statcan.ca/english/census06/release

Tangney, C. C., Rosenson, R. S., et al. (2009). *Lipid lowering with diet or dietary supplements.* Retrieved from http://www. uptodateonline.com.proxy.seattleu.edu/online/content/topic. do?topicKey=lipiddis/6831&selectedTitle=17~51&source=search_result.

Tjepkema, M. (2005). Adult obesity in Canada: Measured height and weight. *Nutrition: Findings from the Canadian Community Health Survey. Issue 1.* Ottawa, ON: Statistics Canada. Cat No 82-620-MWE2005001.

van Dam, R. M. (2008). Coffee consumption and risk of type 2 diabetes, cardiovascular diseases, and cancer. *Applied Physiology of Nutrition and Metabolism, 33*(6), 1269–1283.

Wilson, M. M. G. (2007). *Nutrition: General considerations.* Retrieved from http://www.merck.com/mmpe/sec01/ch001/ch001a.html#BABFCEFH

Wilson, R. D., Johnson, J. A., et al. (2007). Pre-conceptional vitamin/folic acid supplementation 2007: The use of folic acid in combination with a multivitamin supplement for the prevention of neural tube defects and other congenital anomalies. *Journal of Obstetrics and Gynaecology Canada, 12*, 1003–1026.

Woo, T. M. (2008).When nature and pharmacy collide: Drug interactions with commonly used herbs. *Advanced Nurse Practitioner, 16*(7), 69–72.

World Health Organization Expert Consultation. (2004). Appropriate body-mass index for Asian populations and its implications for policy and intervention strategies. *The Lancet, 363*(9414), 1077.

The Canadian Jensen's Nursing Health Assessment suite offers these additional resources to enhance learning and facilitate understanding of this chapter:

- thePoint online resource, http//thepoint.lww.com/Stephen1E
- *Laboratory Manual for Canadian Jensen's Nursing Health Assessment: A Best Practice Approach*

Table 8-8 Physical Signs of Nutritional Deficiency

	Signs	Deficiencies
Hair	Alopecia	Protein-calorie malnutrition
	Brittle	Biotin
	Colour change	Zinc
	Dryness	Vitamins E and A
	Easy to pluck	

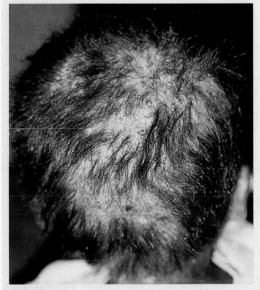

Alopecia (hair loss)

	Signs	Deficiencies
Skin	Acneiform lesions	Vitamin A
	Follicular keratosis	
	Xerosis (dry skin)	
	Ecchymosis	
	Intradermal petechia	
	Erythema	
	Scrotal dermatitis	
	Angular palpebritis	

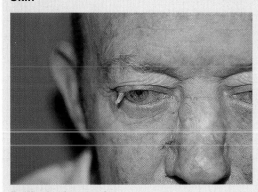

Follicular keratosis

	Signs	Deficiencies
Eyes	Bitot's spots	Vitamin A
	Conjunctival xerosis	Vitamin A

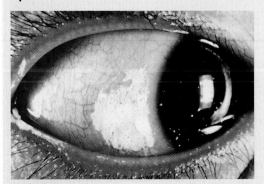

Bitot's spots

(table continues on page 184)

Table 8-8   **Physical Signs of Nutritional Deficiency** (continued)

	Signs	Deficiencies
Mouth	Angular stomatitis	Vitamin B$_{12}$
	Atrophic papillae	Niacin
	Bleeding gums	Vitamin C
	Cheilosis	Vitamin B$_2$
	Glossitis	Niacin, folate, vitamin B$_{12}$
	Magenta tongue	Vitamin B$_2$

Magenta tongue

	Signs	Deficiencies
Extremities	Genu valgum or varum	Vitamin D
	Loss of deep tendon reflexes of the lower extremities	Vitamins B$_1$ and B$_{12}$

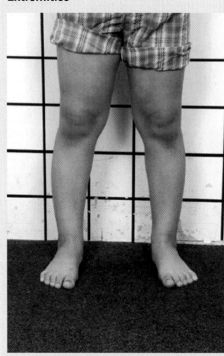

Genu varum

Source: Bernard, M. A., Jacobs, D. O., & Rombeau, J. L. (1986). *Nutrition and metabolic support of hospitalized patients.* Philadelphia, PA: W. B. Saunders.

Assessment of Developmental Stages

Learning Objectives

1. Demonstrate knowledge of physical, psychosocial, and cognitive changes across the life span.

2. Describe both individual and family developmental tasks across the life span.

3. Identify important topics for health promotion and risk reduction across the lifespan.

4. Consider the patient's age, condition, gender, and culture to individualize health promotion interventions.

5. Collect subjective and objective data about the patient's adaptation to expected developmental tasks and their relationship to health and wellness.

6. Collect subjective and objective data about alterations in the patient's adaptation to developmental tasks and the wellness risks of those alterations.

7. Analyze subjective and objective data and plan interventions to promote health and wellness across the life span.

8. Document and communicate data from the assessment of growth and development, using appropriate terminology and principles of recording.

9. Identify nursing diagnoses and initiate a plan of care based on assessment findings.

*M*r. and Mrs Carr (Amber and Michael) have just become first-time adoptive parents to three biological siblings: Emily, 2 months; Jacob, 2 years; and Madeline, 5 years. Amber, a 31-year-old real-estate broker, will be leaving her job to care for the children. Michael, a 35-year-old tax accountant, is enthusiastic about fatherhood but worries about providing for the family's needs with only one income. Both Amber's and Michael's parents, who are in their late 50s and early 60s, are thrilled. They look forward to spending time with their grandchildren and teaching them about outdoor activities, such as camping and hiking. The Carrs are attending a well-child clinic today to have the children weighed and measured and to learn more about growth and development milestones.

You will gain more information about the Carrs as you progress through this chapter. As you study the content, consider this family's case and its relationship to what you are learning. Begin thinking about the following points:

- In what stage of psychosocial development are members of the Carr family?
- In what stage of Piaget's cognitive thought are members of the Carr family?
- What nursing diagnoses might be appropriate for members of the Carr family?

Each human being experiences physical growth, psychosocial development, and cognitive development as he or she progresses from infancy through old age. Furthermore, each particular life journey varies in unique ways, depending on the person's environmental context and interaction with the world. Understanding the processes of growth and development is essential for nurses. It enables them to provide developmentally appropriate care (Thies & Travers, 2009) and support as patients make inevitable transitions from one life stage to another, become more complex in their thinking and interactivity, and seek to maintain their health.

This chapter contains important information about growth and development across the life span. The content serves as a foundational context to support nurses when assessing patients of all age groups and their families. Nurses provide information, anticipatory guidance, role modelling, and protection to individuals, families, groups, and communities to enable optimal, healthy growth and development for children and adults.

Subjective Data Collection

Psychosocial, cognitive, and language **developments** involve qualitative changes in an individual over time. Language acquisition and relationships with others are examples of development. Developmental changes are not easily measured with universal tools. Therefore, this chapter covers such material within this section on "Subjective Data Collection."

Psychosocial Development

Uri Bronfenbrenner proposed a frequently cited systems model of development, which describes the individual's development in interaction with the immediate environment (Bronfenbrenner, 1979). In this approach, development is continuous, important at all ages, and an active rather than a passive process.

Erik Erikson (1963, 1980) provided another valuable model for viewing individual development over time. His model divides the life span into eight stages, with different psychosocial tasks to complete at each stage (Fig. 9-1). Even if the person does not complete the task, according to Erikson, he or she still must move on to the next stage (which will, in turn, be more difficult because the basis for the new stage has not been established during a previous one).

Infant: Trust Versus Mistrust

The first task for the infant is **trust versus mistrust**. The infant learns that physiologic regulation is linked to a caregiver's provision of comfort. This task depends on consistency, continuity, and sameness of experience; the infant learns that when he or she is uncomfortable, the caregiver comes and provides the appropriate soothing measure. Erikson (1963, 1980) also says that, by learning to cope with discomfort, the infant learns to trust himself or herself as well.

Toddler: Autonomy Versus Shame and Doubt

The task for the toddler is **autonomy versus shame and doubt**. The toddler learns about "two simultaneous sets of social modalities: holding on and letting go" (Erikson, 1963, p. 251). He or she cannot discriminate between appropriate circumstances that require the choice of retaining or eliminating objects. Caregivers must help toddlers learn how to discriminate and manipulate appropriately. Otherwise, toddlers will overmanipulate themselves and work to repossess the environment in a repetitive fashion.

Preschooler: Initiative Versus Guilt

The preschooler's task is **initiative versus guilt**. According to Erikson (1963), this task has "the quality of undertaking, planning, and 'attacking' a task for the sake of being active and on the move" (p. 255). The preschooler is actively engaged in making plans, setting goals, and accomplishing them. Erikson describes the preschooler as "eager and able to make things cooperatively, to combine with other children for the purpose of constructing and planning" (p. 258). The child learns to work with others and can share ideas and plans with peers.

School-age Child: Industry Versus Inferiority

The life of the school age child is, for Erikson (1963), naturally centered on school. His or her task is **industry versus inferiority**. School prepares the child to become "a worker and potential provider" (pp. 258–259). The child must learn to use the tools that adults commonly use within the specific society or environment. At the same time, the school in a literate society has its own culture "with its own goals and limits, its achievements and disappointments" (p. 259). As the child spends more time in the school culture, prepared by teachers for the literate world, the influence of other adults dilutes the role of parents in the child's life. The danger in this stage is that the child will not be able to learn to use the adult tools and will feel a sense of inferiority and inadequacy. It is difficult for the child to be admitted to an adult role in society without the tools to deal with the technology and economy of the culture. If the family has not prepared the child for school, or school does not support the promises of earlier stages of development, the child suffers.

Adolescent: Identity Versus Role Confusion

In Erikson's (1963) model, puberty signals the end of childhood. The task for the adolescent becomes **identity versus role confusion**. With the somatic growth and genital

Figure 9-1 Erikson's psychosocial model involves the attainment of different qualities in each of eight life stages. **A.** Infants gain **trust** when caregivers consistently meet their needs. **B.** Toddlers develop **autonomy** as they make simple choices and exert some independent control. **C.** Preschoolers learn **initiative** by engaging in cooperative projects with others. **D.** School-age children develop **industry** by acquiring skills that will assist them in adult roles and responsibilities. **E.** Adolescents achieve **identity** by establishing their own opinions, views, and ideas apart from parents, peers, and other influences. **F.** Young adults achieve **intimacy** by fusing their identity with others. **G.** Middle adults attain **generativity** by sharing their knowledge with younger generations. **H.** Older adults achieve **ego integrity** through acceptance and pride in their life histories.

maturity that accompany adolescence, the teen revisits some battles from earlier stages. Adult tasks and roles are now close at hand, and adolescents are "concerned with what they appear to be in the eyes of others as compared with what they feel they are, and with the question of how to connect the roles and skills cultivated earlier with the occupational prototypes" (p. 261) available. The question "What do you want to be when you grow up?" is more complex for the adolescent than for the child. It is now a question not only about a potential career but also about the sort of person the teen wishes to become and his or her social values.

Role confusion in this stage may involve sexual identity but more often involves the teen's struggle to choose an occupational identity. This confusion partially explains why adolescents cling together in cliques and crowds. Doing so helps to protect against the loss of identity through the assumption of a group identity that temporarily defines for the adolescent how to dress, act, and belong. Erikson explained that this behaviour will eventually fall away as the individual defines his or her own identity.

Early Adult: Intimacy Versus Isolation

The sixth psychosocial task, occurring in early adulthood, is **intimacy versus isolation**. After the person has navigated the search for personal identity, he or she is willing to fuse with the identity of others. As Erikson (1963) expressed it, the person is "ready for intimacy, that is, the capacity to commit himself [sic] to concrete affiliations and partnerships and to develop the ethical strength to abide by such commitments, even though they may call for significant sacrifices and compromises" (p. 263). By intimate relationships, Erikson meant not only sexual unions but also close friendships and physical expressions. The danger of this developmental task is isolation, in which the person separates himself or herself from others to avoid commitment to intimacy.

Middle Adult: Generativity Versus Self-Absorption

The seventh stage in Erikson's model is **generativity versus self-absorption**, which he described as a central issue in adulthood (Erikson, 1980). Generativity "encompasses the evolutionary development which has made man the teaching, instituting, and learning animal" (Erickson, 1963, p. 266). Erikson argued that when adults focus too exclusively on the dependence of their children, they may forget about the importance of their own dependence on the next generation. The essence of generativity is that "mature man [sic] needs to be needed, and maturity needs guidance as well as encouragement from what has been produced and must be taken care of. Generativity, then, is primarily the concern in establishing and guiding the next generation" (pp. 266–267).

Generativity also involves and includes productivity and creativity. Simply having children does not make an adult generative. In fact, adults who seem to think of themselves as their own "spoiled child" or who demonstrate physical or psychological invalidism have, in Erikson's model, fallen into the trap of self-absorption (Erikson, 1980). They have nothing to offer the next generation, even if they wished to contribute something.

Late Adult: Ego Integrity Versus Despair

Erikson's (1963) eighth and last stage applies to late adulthood. The task for the older adult is **ego integrity versus despair**. Ego integrity is difficult to achieve:

Only in him who in some way has taken care of things and people and has adapted himself [sic] to the triumphs and disappointments adherent to being, the originator of others or the generator of products and ideas—only in him [sic] may gradually ripen the fruit of these seven stages (p. 268).

The older adult with ego integrity has come to terms with his or her life choices. He or she comes to recognize that the life that has been lived was the only possible one. If successfully completed, the person is ready to defend against physical or economic threats. If unsuccessful, the person will not come to this understanding of "the one and only life cycle" (Erikson, 1963, p. 269) and will then fear death, which results in despair. "Despair expresses the feeling that the time is now short, too short for the attempt to start another life and to try out alternate roads to integrity" (p. 269). By late adulthood, there is no way to go back and try different paths; choices that were made in life are permanent now.

Erikson (1963) finished his developmental stage model by relating the circular fashion of the stages. "Trust (the first of our ego values) is here defined as 'the assured reliance on another's integrity,' the last of our values" (p. 269). Erikson further linked the circularity of the relationship between childhood and adulthood in the statement "healthy children will not fear life if their elders have integrity enough not to fear death" (p. 269).

Cognitive Development

Jean Piaget (1952) formulated a theory of cognitive development that begins at birth and continues until adulthood. Like Erikson's model, Piaget's theory is in stages, and Piaget claimed that the person uses experience to move from stage to stage as thinking becomes more sophisticated and complex in interaction with his or her environment.

Infant: Sensorimotor

The first stage of cognition, the **sensorimotor** stage, is divided into six substages (see Table 9-1).

Toddler and Preschooler: Preoperational

The second stage of Piaget's (1952) cognitive model is **preoperational**, which lasts from approximately ages 2

- Emily, 2 months old, is in the trust versus mistrust developmental stage. She must learn to trust that Amber and Michael will care for her.
- Jacob, 2 years old, is in the stage of autonomy versus shame and doubt. His task is to learn to be autonomous.
- Madeline, 5 years old, is in the initiative versus guilt stage; she should be able to plan an activity such as painting a picture and carry out that plan.
- Amber and Michael are in early adulthood. Certainly, the addition of three children to their household will call for significant sacrifices and compromises in their marital relationship.
- Amber's and Michael's parents are committing themselves to being grandparents to Madeline, Jacob, and Emily. They want to demonstrate their generativity by teaching the new generation the things they previously taught their children.

to 7 years. The preoperational child is forming stable concepts. Mental reasoning begins, and the child constructs magical beliefs (Santrock, 2006). The child is highly egocentric at the beginning of the preoperational stage but begins, by the end, to be able to consider the perspectives of others. The preoperational child cannot yet think in a well-organized way, but during this period, the child moves from using primitive to more sophisticated symbols (Piaget, 1952).

Piaget divided the preoperational stage into two substages: (1) symbolic function and (2) intuitive thought. The child in the symbolic function substage, which lasts roughly from ages 2 to 4 years of age, can now mentally represent an absent object. For example, he or she can talk about a grandparent's house for many days after a visit. Scribbled designs represent people, houses, cars, clouds, and other objects (Santrock, 2006). Using language and pretend play (Fig. 9-2) are other characteristics of this substage (Santrock).

Table 9-1	Piaget's Sensorimotor Substages	
Age	**Substage**	**Description and Examples**
Birth to 1 mo	Simple reflexes	Behaviours coordinate sensation and action; newborns suck reflexively when a nipple is placed in their mouths; focus is on infant's body
1–4 mo	Primary circular reactions	Coordination of sensation and two types of schemes: reflexes and primary circular reactions (reproducing an event that initially happened by chance); main focus is still infant's body; infant sucks on hand differently than on a nipple
4–8 mo	Secondary circular reactions	Infant becomes more object oriented, moving beyond being preoccupied with the body; repeats actions that make interesting things happen, such as infant kicks and sees a mobile move and then kicks again to make the mobile move again
8–12 mo	Coordination of secondary circular reactions	Infant is beginning to coordinate vision and touch as eye–hand coordination; coordination of schemes and intentionality, such as using one toy to reach another
12–18 mo	Tertiary circular reactions	Infant experiments with new behaviour; learning about the properties of objects and what they can do; toys can be dropped, pushed, pulled, and used to hit other toys
18–24 mo	Internalization of schemes	Infants develop the ability to use simple symbols and form enduring mental representations; the infant sees another child have a tantrum and has one himself or herself the next day

Adapted from Santrock, J. (2006). *Life-span development* (10th ed.). New York, NY: McGraw-Hill.

Figure 9-2 Children in the preoperational symbolic function substage rely on pretend play with imagination and creative toys as part of their cognitive development.

While the ability to use symbols greatly increases the child's cognitive abilities, this substage is largely limited because of egocentrism and animism. *Egocentrism* is the inability to distinguish one's own perspective from another person's (Santrock, 2006). The child sees his or her view of the world only. For example, he or she expects that a parent who is away on a business trip still can see what the child sees and know what the child knows, and the child is very confused when the parent does not know what went on at home during the day. *Animism* is the belief that inanimate objects are capable of action and have life-like qualities (Santrock). Dead leaves blowing down the street are still alive for the child, and objects that cause the child to trip and fall have bad intentions. Imagination and invention are characteristic of children in this substage, and they are as comfortable in the world of make-believe as they are in the world of reality (Santrock).

The intuitive thought substage occurs from ages 4 to 7 years (Piaget, 1952). These children begin to use reasoning, though it is still very crude. They ask questions constantly and want to know the answers (Santrock, 2006). Piaget referred to this substage as intuitive because these children seem very sure about *what* they know but cannot tell *how* they know it. They have not used rational thinking to reach conclusions. An important characteristic of this stage is *centration*, which Piaget defined as the child centering attention on one aspect of a situation and failing to consider other dimensions. It is obvious to an adult that pouring water from a wide and short container to a long and narrow one has no effect on the volume of water. The child in the intuitive substage, however, can see only that the water level is higher in the new container. The child cannot reason that, if the adult poured the water back into the original container, it would be the same volume. This inability to understand conservation lasts until approximately age 7 or 8 years (Piaget).

School-Age Child: Concrete Operational

Piaget's (1952) next stage of cognitive development is the **concrete operational** stage, which lasts approximately from ages 7 to 11 years. Piaget defined *operations* as internalized sets of actions that permit children to do mentally what they once did physically. Concrete operations are reversible mental actions; children now understand conservation and can tell the adult who pours water from one container to another that the volume remains the same and that to prove it, one could just pour the water back into the original container. These children recognize that the original container was short and wide, whereas the new container is tall and thin.

Concrete operational thinkers are also much better able to categorize objects (Fig. 9-3). For example, a school-age child may have a collection of baseball cards carefully organized by team and by each player's position on the team. The child understands that a player can be both a pitcher and a team member at the same time. In addition, children at this stage can reason about relationships between classes, which Piaget called *seriation*. To continue the baseball-card example, the child understands that one team has better players than another team and might organize the cards according to league standings. He or she might then rearrange the cards as teams win or lose during a season. Seriation also refers to the ability to arrange objects by quantitative dimensions.

Piaget's concept of *transitivity* refers to the child's ability to consider such statements as if A is greater than B, and B is greater than C, then it must be true that A is greater than C. So the child understands that if John is taller than Jordan, and Jordan is taller than Justin, then John must also be taller than Justin as well.

Figure 9-3 A characteristic of concrete operational cognition involves the ability to characterize and sort objects in complex ways. For example, children may have closely catalogued collections of action figures, science specimens, sports materials, or books and spend much time attending to and enhancing such collections.

Adolescent: Formal Operations

The last stage in Piaget's (1952) cognitive theory is **formal operations**. The formal operator uses abstract reasoning far better than the concrete operator and can discuss theoretical concepts that escape younger children. Piaget contended that adolescence is the beginning of formal operations. The adolescent can now talk about "what if…" statements and think logically about abstract solutions. Formal operations also include verbal problem-solving skills. The adolescent who uses formal operations can be presented verbally with "A = B, B = C, A ? C" and substitute the "=" for the question mark without having to see the written problem.

For the first time, those in the formal operations stage can use metacognition (Piaget, 1952), or the ability to "think about thinking." The adolescent also can now think idealistically and consider new possibilities. These abilities lead adolescents to wonder how they could become ideal, and how they compare with role models and heroes. Such insights, however, may have drawbacks. The adolescent who can view world issues in a new light may wonder why those issues have not been solved. Additionally, the teen may find that he or she falls short of the qualities of role models and may then feel inadequate and hopeless about the self.

Formal operations also encompass scientific thinking. The adolescent can now engage in what Piaget referred to as hypothetical-deductive reasoning. He or she can develop hypotheses about issues and deduce the best way to solve them. The concrete operational child uses much less efficient trial-and-error methods of problem solving. Hypothetical-deductive reasoning enables the person to reject some solutions as impractical or inefficient without having to test them and to use logic to arrive at the most likely and feasible solutions (Piaget, 1952).

Adolescent thinking, however, has fundamental shortcomings that result from physiologic changes in the brain. Magnetic resonance imagery studies have shown two main changes before and after puberty. One is the development of myelin in the frontal cortex, and the other is the development of additional synapses (Blakemore & Choudhury, 2006). Because the prefrontal cortex is involved in planning, setting priorities, suppressing impulses, and weighing behavioural consequences (Santrock, 2006), a natural outcome is that adolescents might struggle with these cognitive tasks as the brain undergoes changes in this region. In addition, the amygdala (part of the brain involved in processing emotional information) matures sooner than the prefrontal cortex (Santrock). This finding may partially explain why teens frequently react emotionally before weighing the consequences of such behaviour.

Young Adult: Formal Operations

As the individual moves into young adulthood, Piaget (1952) contended that the person becomes more quantitatively advanced in formal operations. He also believed that the young adult increased knowledge in a specific area (eg, skills regularly used in his or her career). Other developmental theorists have challenged this view.

It may be that the idealism that Piaget considered part of formal operational thinking decreases in early adulthood, because the person moves into the professional world and must face the constraints of reality (Labouvie-Vie, 1986). It is not likely that adults go beyond the scientific thinking methods that accompany formal operational thinking, but that adults surpass adolescents in their *use* of intellect (Schaie & Willis, 2000). While adolescents are more concerned with acquiring knowledge (because they are usually engaged in educational settings or perhaps vocational training), adults move beyond acquisition to application. Pursuing long-term career goals and beginning to achieve professional success (eg, as the person moves from an entry-level to a supervisory position) require much more application than acquisition of knowledge, although certainly the person never stops learning new things.

William Perry (1970, 1999) describes another perspective about changes in adult thinking. His view is that adolescents tend to look at the world in terms of polarities. Things are either right or wrong, people fall into the categories of we and they, and decisions are either bad or good. Such thinking often proves less useful to adults who move into a broader environment and encounter diverse opinions, multiple perspectives, and cultural differences among the people they meet and situations they face. Over time, the reflective, relativistic thinking of adulthood replaces the absolute, dualistic thinking of adolescence. Perry's theory assumes that the individual encounters diverse opinions and values in his or her environment; however, it is possible that a person who isolates himself or herself from new people, situations, and value systems might not move from dualistic to relativistic thinking. Or, the person may simply choose not to accept others' viewpoints, rejecting their belief systems as simply untrue or misguided. The person may even find different ideas threatening instead of evaluating why another person from a certain group or belief system might value the things that are important to that group.

It may be that the changes in thinking that occur as the person moves into young adulthood are qualitatively different than Piaget's (1952) stage of formal operations. Such cognitive development has been termed *postformal thought*. Santrock (2006) explained postformal thought as

> …*understanding that the correct answer to a problem can require reflective thinking, that the correct answer can vary from one situation to another, and that the search for truth is often an ongoing, never-ending process. It also involves the belief that solutions to problems need to be realistic and that emotion and subjective factors can influence thinking* (p. 452).

Middle Adult: Cognitive Expertise

Some people believe that cognitive abilities peak in adolescence or early adulthood and then begin to decline. Research with middle adults, however, shows that this pattern is not at all true. It is important to examine the kinds of intelligence that middle adults use to solve challenges at work and in daily living to appreciate what happens with cognition. There are two types of intellectual skills (Craig & Dunn, 2007). The first is *crystallized intelligence*, which is "accumulated knowledge and skills based on education and life

experiences" (p. 450) and can also be referred to as *cognitive pragmatics*; this intelligence is learned and influenced by the individual person's culture. The second type is *fluid intelligence*, which means "abilities involved in acquiring new knowledge and skills" (p. 450) and can also be referred to as *cognitive mechanics*; this intelligence is a reflection of neurological functioning and more likely to be affected negatively by brain damage (Craig & Dunn, 2007). It appears that declines in memory actually do not appear until the last part of middle adulthood or into late adulthood (Santrock, 2006). What may look like memory declines may be attributable to using ineffective memory strategies. When middle adults use organization and imagery to remember things, they can improve their memories.

Another important aspect of intelligence is *expertise*, described by Santrock (2006) as "having an extensive, highly organized knowledge and understanding of a particular domain" (p. 515). Because expertise requires years of experience, learning, and work, middle adults are far more likely to have it compared to young adults. When solving issues, expertise allows the person to rely on past experience, to use automatic processing of information and efficient analysis, to use better strategies and shortcuts, and to be more creative and flexible (Fig. 9-4). The novice must work much harder and less quickly than the expert, because he or she is unfamiliar with the kinds of situations often encountered in a given area.

Figure 9-4 Expertise allows middle adults to automatically apply their experience to current situations, which facilitates efficiency and creativity.

Older Adult: Wisdom

Cognition is multifaceted, and aging affects some dimensions of intellectual functioning more than others (Craig & Dunn, 2007). Therefore, it is a myth to believe that all older adults are cognitively impaired.

Numerous studies have examined the speed of cognition in older adults, and the results have shown that older adults take about 50% longer than younger adults to do a simple comparison task (Craig & Dunn, 2007). With more complex tasks, older adults take even longer. These differences may partly result from neurological changes that occur with aging, but they may also be linked to the older adult's decreased use of different strategies to perform cognitive tasks (Craig & Dunn). Older adults may make fewer guesses and try harder to answer items correctly. If older adults are compared with college students, who are more accustomed to doing tests

Table 9-2 Memory Functions

Type	Description	Aging Effect
Sensory memory	Retention of a sensory image for a very brief time	Slight or no decrease
Short-term memory	Memory for things the person is presently and actively thinking about	Slight or no decrease
Working memory	Active processing of information while it is held in short-term memory; active thinking	Decreases, but may use better strategies to limit decrease
Episodic long-term memory	Recollection of past events and personally relevant information	Decreases, but may be from slower processing speed
Semantic long-term memory	Retrieval of facts, vocabulary, and general knowledge	Decreases minimally

Adapted from Craig, G. J., & Dunn, W. L. (2007). *Understanding human development.* Upper Saddle River, NJ: Pearson Education.

of recall, the older adults will appear less adept at such a test. Older adults may be able to learn new strategies to compensate for their lack of processing speed (Craig & Dunn, 2007).

Memory has been studied by numerous researchers. Table 9-2 shows different memory functions and the effects of aging on those functions.

Despite the small declines in memory in older adults, older adults are wiser comparatively (Craig & Dunn, 2007). *Wisdom* refers to an expert knowledge system comprised of several characteristics:

• Wisdom appears to focus on important and difficult matters often associated with the meaning of life and the human condition.

• The level of knowledge, judgment, and advice reflected in wisdom is superior.
• The knowledge associated with wisdom has extraordinary scope, depth, and balance and is applicable to specific situations.
• Wisdom combines mind and virtue (character) and is employed for personal well-being as well as for the benefit of humankind.
• Although difficult to achieve, wisdom is easily recognized by most people, and it represents the capstone of human intelligence (p. 511).

Although some older adults do not attain wisdom, it is only in older adulthood that the accumulation of life experience results in the acquisition of wisdom.

Cognitive Development for the Carr Family

• Emily Carr, 2 months, is in the primary circular reactions stage.
• Jacob Carr is likely to be in the preoperational stage/symbolic function substage. At 2 years, his thinking is still very primitive, and he cannot see the perspectives of his parents or siblings.
• Madeline Carr is in the intuitive thought substage; her thinking is much more sophisticated than is Jacob's. Although she may be very confident about the things she knows, she will not be able to tell her parents how her thought process worked to enable her to know things.
• The stage of postformal thought is still controversial among developmental theorists (Santrock, 2006), but considering some practical problems for the Carr family may demonstrate the challenges a young adult couple faces. Amber and Michael need to learn how to make decisions for their newly adopted children, and they need to recognize that they make better decisions when they are not stressed, angry, or upset.
• Amber and Michael's parents, who are in the later years of middle adulthood, will have cognitive expertise. They should be able to expect that their numerical abilities and perceptual speed may have declined somewhat, but their superior abilities to solve practical issues may offset this decline.

Table 9-3	Language Development in Childhood
Age	**Language Skill**
Birth	Crying
1–2 mo	Cooing
Middle of first year	Babbling
8–12 mo	Gestures such as showing and pointing
10–15 mo	Uses first word; has receptive vocabulary of 50 words
18 mo	Has expressive vocabulary of 50 words
18–24 mo	Uses two-word utterances (telegraphic speech) such as "more milk"
2 y	Expressive vocabulary of 200 words
3–6 y	Learns 5–8 new words a day; works on syntax and meaning
6 y	Expressive vocabulary of 8,000–14,000 words; learns 22 new words per day
7 y	Begins to categorize words by parts of speech; learns comparatives (bigger, longer, etc.) and subjectives ("If you were the school principal...")
6–12 y	Understands and uses more complex grammar; must be able to do this orally in order to read

Adapted from Santrock, J. (2006). *Life-span development* (10th ed.). New York, NY: McGraw-Hill.

Language Development

All human societies use language as a means to communicate with one another. Language development consists of two parts. *Receptive language* is the understanding of spoken or written words and sentences, and *productive language* is the individual's use of spoken or written words (Craig & Dunn, 2007). Receptive language leads productive language, and throughout the life span, receptive vocabulary tends to be larger than productive vocabulary (Craig & Dunn). A student who comes across an unfamiliar word while reading a book can relate to this phenomenon. One could stop reading to look up the meaning of the new word, figure out its meaning from the context of the sentence, or simply skip the new word and continue reading. Of course, the choice of options depends on whether the student really wants to understand the meaning of the word,

incorporate the new word into productive vocabulary, or not bother to learn it at all. Using the new word in conversation is risky, however, if the student does not realize its cultural or social connotations before using it in conversation.

Table 9-3 shows the range of ages for the development of language skills in infants and young children.

Cultural Considerations

Culture profoundly affects individual development. Jean Piaget, Erik Erikson, and Uri Bronfenbrenner all came from Western European backgrounds, and their theoretical frameworks clearly reflect the value their cultures placed on such characteristics as independence, self-motivation, and primacy of the individual. The Western viewpoint, however, is not universally supported. Some cultures value dependence and interdependence over independence.

Language Development for the Carr Family

- The Carr family can expect that Emily will make cooing sounds and listen to the language of the people around her.
- Jacob should have a vocabulary of some 50 words, though he may be frustrated when he cannot express all his emotions in words.
- Madeline should be easy for Amber and Michael to understand, and she may be able to translate some of Jacob's words, because she knows Jacob better than his parents do early in the adoption process. Madeline needs to work on her skills with oral language to prepare her for school entry and the development of reading skills.

Through their choices about feeding, carrying, and dressing infants and by sending messages about which temperamental qualities are desirable, parents, families, groups, and communities convey to children which behaviours they consider positive and which they deem as negative or unacceptable (Santrock, 2006). The toddler learns quickly whether independence is more valued than dependence on a caregiver for decision making and exploration. The preschooler may or may not get formal early childhood education, depending on whether his or her parents place value on such preparation for school. Erikson's (1963) emphasis on the school-age child's acquisition of adult tools might mean, for some cultures, learning to read in a classroom, but for others, it might involve following older children to learn livestock herding skills, hunting strategies, or how to care for younger siblings and other domestic skills. Adolescents may be required to stay in school until they are 14 years old, as in Brazil, or until they are 17 years old, as in Russia (Santrock). What a given culture views as a basic education to acquire the tools needed to enter adulthood clearly varies greatly; the curricula in secondary schools depend on what cultures value as important topics and the time it takes to teach those topics (Santrock).

In addition, some cultures have rites of passage that mark the transition from childhood to adulthood. Santrock defines a rite of passage as "the avenue through which adolescents gain access to sacred adult practices, to knowledge, and to sexuality" (pp. 415–416). Examples include the Jewish ritual of bar mitzvah for boys and bat mitzvah for girls,

Catholic confirmation, and the Hispanic girl's quinceanera (Fig. 9-5). In Canada, these rites do not necessarily give adolescents status as adults in the community outside their faith or cultural communities. Graduation from high school may or may not lead to adulthood; the graduate may go on to a vocational school, college, university, or the world of work but may continue to live with or be economically dependent on parents for some years after (Santrock, 2006). The transition to adulthood is a long process for some cultures (particularly those with higher education opportunities) and a very short one in others.

Culture affects intimate relationships in adulthood as well. Desired characteristics in a long-term partner vary across cultures—for example, there are differences in how much people seek out attributes such as chastity, domesticity, spirituality, and age (Santrock, 2006). The ideal age at which to marry is also culturally determined, as is whether it is acceptable to live with a potential spouse before marrying (Santrock).

By middle adulthood, culture still exerts a large influence on the developing person. Cultures that emphasize parenting as a key role in adulthood may leave the middle adult in an awkward position in a society where the expectation is that children will grow up and leave home; what is the adult's role when parenting is no longer central in his or her life (Santrock, 2006)? Grandparenting may vary greatly depending on cultural expectations for providing childcare, advice, and support to their children and grandchildren (Santrock).

Figure 9-5 Culturally associated rites of passage in Western countries are often symbolic. Often, such occasions are accompanied by large parties with gatherings of family and friends to celebrate. **A.** The bar mitzvah marks mastery by a boy of the concepts of Judaism and is ready to worship with adults. **B.** The Hispanic quinceanera marks the occasion of a girl's 15th birthday.

Table 9-4	Physical Growth in Childhood and Adolescence
Developmental Stage	Expected Growth
Infant	Double birth weight by 6 months; 1½ times birth length and triple birth weight by age 1 year; head circumference of 33.0–35.5 cm at birth to 46.5 cm at age 1 year
Toddler	½ adult height and quadruple birth weight by age 2 years
Preschooler	6.4–7.6 cm and 2.3–3.2 kg/y; birth height doubled by age 4 years
School-age child	5.1 cm and 2.3–3.2 kg/y
Adolescent	Girls: Growth spurt of 6.4–12.7 cm and 3.6–4.6 kg
Boys: Growth spurt 7.6–15.2 cm and 5.5–6.4 kg

Sources: Murray, R. B., & Zentner, J. P. (2008). *Health promotion strategies through the life span* (8th ed.). Upper Saddle River, NJ: Prentice Hall; Thies, K. M., & Travers, J. F. (2009). *Quick look nursing: Growth and development through the lifespan* (2nd ed.). *Sudbury, MA: Jones & Bartlett.*

For the older adult, cultural expectations are important in determining whether or not the individual engages in work and leisure activities. A society's acceptance of older adults may be very limited by ageism and sexism (Santrock, 2006) so that the older adult finds no place in the social order even if he or she has wisdom and experience to share with younger generations. If a woman's role is limited to family maintenance and a man's role to financial productivity, when the older persons are no longer able to fill those roles, they may be defined as no longer useful once their children are grown or they retire from work (Santrock, 2006).

Objective Data Collection

Physical **growth** refers to quantitative changes in a person over time. Increases in height and weight are examples. The ways in which nurses measure these changes involve universal tools and metrics (eg, centimetres and kilograms). In addition, nurses can assess motor development more easily through physical examination and use of screening tools. Therefore, this chapter designates physical growth and motor development under the heading "Objective Data Collection."

Physical Growth

Physical growth takes place in an expected pattern, but at a variable pace over time in childhood (Leifer & Hartston, 2004). Table 9-4 shows expected growth patterns in childhood and adolescence. It is important to assess children who are growing more slowly or more rapidly than usual for any potential underlying conditions.

There are formulas for estimating potential adult height for children (Leifer & Hartston, 2004). For boys, the formula is

$$\frac{\text{Father's height (cm) + mother's height (cm) + 12.7 cm}}{2}$$

For girls, the formula is

$$\frac{\text{Father's height (cm) + mother's height (cm) − 12.7 cm}}{2}$$

Motor Development

Motor development also follows a pattern, but individuals develop at variable rates. Table 9-5 shows gross motor

Expected Growth for the Carr Family

Amber and Michael will need to monitor the growth and nutrition patterns of their three newly adopted children. They need to monitor intake of all the children to ensure that each child consumes high-quality calories and sufficient protein, carbohydrates, and fats to sustain growth (Murray & Zentner, 2008).

- Two-month-old Emily should grow about 2.54 cm/month and gain 18.7 g/day.
- Jacob, 2 years old, should have quadrupled his birth weight by now. His growth will slow in the next year; however, over the next 12 months, his height should increase by 6.4 to 7.6 cm, and he should gain about 2.3 to 3.2 kg.
- Madeline, 5 years old, should grow 6.4 to 7.6 cm in the next year and gain 2.3 to 3.2 kg.

Table 9-5	Gross and Fine Motor Development: Infancy to Early Childhood	
Age	**Gross Motor Skills**	**Fine Motor Skills**
0–1 mo	Lifts head up off of the bed when prone	Ruled by newborn reflexes
2–4 mo	Lifts head and chest up off of the bed when prone, using arms for support	Begins to reach using shoulders and arms
2–4.5 mo	Rolls over	Tracks moving objects well
3–6 mo	Supports some weight with legs	Begins using hand–eye coordination to reach
5–8 mo	Sits without support; some creeping/crawling	Uses visually guided reach; passes object hand to hand
5–10 mo	Stands with support	Rolls a ball back and forth to an adult
6–10 mo	Pulls self to stand	Looks for a partially hidden object
7–13 mo	Walks using furniture for support	Uses pincer grasp to pick up objects
10–14 mo	Stands alone easily	Feeds self using spoon and cup, though not neatly
11–14 mo	Walks alone easily	
13–18 mo	May be able to climb stairs	Stacks 2–4 cubes or blocks, scribbles
19–24 mo	Can pedal a tricycle, jumps on both feet, throws a ball	Pours water, molds clay, partially dresses self
2 y	Climbs, pushes, pulls, runs, hangs by both hands	Partially dresses self; stacks 6–8 cubes or blocks
3 y	Runs and moves smoothly	Builds high block towers, assembles large jigsaw puzzles but often forces pieces into place
4 y	Skips awkwardly, jumps; changes speed while running	Much more precise building and assembling skills
5 y	Skips smoothly, stands on one foot	Draws rectangle, circle, square, and triangle; ties own shoes

Sources: Craig, G. J., & Dunn, W. L. (2007). *Understanding human development.* Upper Saddle River, NJ: Pearson Education; Santrock, J. (2006). *Life-span development* (10th ed.). New York, NY: McGraw-Hill.

developmental milestones and activities for infants, toddlers, and young children. It is important to recognize that there is a range of ages at which children acquire new skills. Parents concerned about a child's development may need education about the expected range of skill acquisition. Nevertheless, nurses always take parental concerns about a child seriously so that health care providers can assess delays and intervene quickly, if needed.

Motor Development for the Carr Family

All the Carr family adults should monitor the children's motor development as well as the physical growth.

- Baby Emily will soon be lifting her head off the mattress, although she will not yet be able to reach for objects.
- Toddler Jacob should be very active, learning to pedal a tricycle, jump with both feet, and throw a ball. He may be able to remove clothing and partially dress himself. However, Amber and Michael should not expect Jacob to completely dress himself without help. They will have to closely monitor Jacob, because his ability to climb and run may get him into dangerous situations. Blocks and push or pull toys (eg, wagon, toy lawnmower) are age-appropriate toys.
- Five-year-old Madeline should be able to dress herself independently and will run and jump much more easily than Jacob. She should be learning to tie shoes and will be able to draw figures beyond her brother's abilities. Toys could include those that encourage gross and fine motor development (eg, riding toys, toys that she can assemble into shapes).

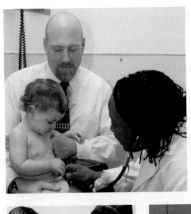

Figure 9-6 Nurses interact with patients at all stages of the life span. **A.** Infants and their caregivers. **B.** Older children. **C.** Young adults. **D.** Older adults.

Evidence-Informed Critical Thinking

When making decisions about how the patient is progressing along a developmental trajectory, the nurse needs to use evidence-informed knowledge and critical thinking during assessments. Refer to Unit III for more information on women who are pregnant, infants, children, adolescents, and older adults.

Nurses are concerned with promoting health and wellness in individuals and families across the life span (Fig. 9-6). Healthy children are much more likely to grow into healthy adults, and they need a great deal of support to make healthy and safe choices. Parents also need a great deal of support

Evidence-Informed Critical Thinking for the Carr Family

Amber and Michael require assistance to help them navigate the major life changes they are facing. They want information that can help them meet the needs of a preschooler, toddler, and infant. Specific concerns include caring for baby Emily, toilet training Jacob, and preparing Madeline for school.

In assessing and intervening with the Carr family, the nurse relies on evidence-informed information about childhood growth and development to advise the parents about the best ways to care for their children. It is also important to use accurate information to advise Amber and Michael about how they can make the healthiest choices for themselves. Doing so will help them maintain their relationship and personal wellness so that they are healthy and able to support their children effectively.

Amber and Michael's parents need careful, evidence-informed information to guide them as they move through middle adulthood. Health promotion in middle adulthood is important as it sets the stage for health and wellness in older adulthood (Santrock, 2006).

Physical safety of Emily, Jacob, and Madelaine is the initial primary focus, and child-proofing the home is essential. Examples include the following.

1. Removing all small objects such as coins, toys, and deflated balloons to prevent choking.
2. Gates are needed at all stairs to prevent falls.
3. Cleaning products are stored in locked cupboards to prevent poisoning.
4. All medications should be in child-proof containers and locked in high cupboards.
5. Pots on stove with handles turned to back of stove to prevent scalds/burns.
6. Supervision of Jacob and Madelaine is needed in the kitchen and the bathroom.
7. For Emily, sleeping on her back on a firm mattress with no toys, pillows, or loose blankets is necessary to prevent suffocation and Sudden Infant Death Syndrome (SIDS). For Jacob and Madelaine, also consider a comfortable and safe environment to promote sleep; control factors such as light, noise, temperature, and bedding (Wilkinson & Ahern, 2009).
8. Age appropriate car seats for Emily, Jacob, and Madelaine.

Emotional safety of Emily, but especially Jacob and Madelaine is important. The work of Wallerstein (Wallerstein, Lewis, et al., 2000) with children of divorce can be used to understand that when children's life circumstances change they may be overwhelmed by what has happened to them. Depending on their previous family situation, Jacob and Madelaine may experience either a lack of or an increased sense of security. Their emotional feelings are of loss and having to reconcile themselves to the change to new parents. The children may react with aggression, withdrawal, irritability, or even illness (Thies & Travers, 2009).

The nurse should teach Amber and Michael that Emily needs environmental stimuli (auditory, visual, tactile, vestibular, and gustatory) to stimulate brain development, each day in short periods when she is awake, and that she must have a parent respond to her vocalization.

Amber and Michael are likely experiencing a knowledge deficit in terms of how to care for Emily, Jacob and Madelaine. As new parents, Amber and Michael are faced with the challenges of being responsible for managing age-appropriate food, clothing, activities, and rest for the children. By keeping their focus on the childrens' needs, Amber and Michael can help the children to feel safe and cared for (Thies & Travers, 2009). Encourage Amber and Michael to seek out assistance from public health nurses (well-child clinic), the two sets of grandparents, friends and relatives with children, reading material, and websites such as the Canadian Paediatrics Society, Safe Kids Canada, Canadian Coalition for the Rights of Children, and the Canadian Institute of Child Health.

Amber and Michael are likely experiencing the stress of now having three children. Amber is experiencing a major change in her life as she has exchanged her career as a real estate broker for caring for three children. Michael is concerned with managing the new family with only one salary. Both are experiencing interrupted sleep patterns and a decrease in amount of sleep. The public health nurse can help the couple explore their feelings, discuss possible strategies, and identify people in their lives who could assist them, such as their parents.

Developmental assessment should be done for each of the Carr children to help identify any developmental delays quickly and begin intervention as early as possible. The nurse can work to decrease the risk for developmental delay in the children by encouraging Amber and Michael to become attached to all of them (especially Emily), and by teaching the parents about nutrition and social skills Jacob should be acquiring.

Assessment of each child's immunization status needs to be completed.

Table 9-6 Common Nursing Diagnoses Associated with Development

Diagnosis and Related Factors	Point of Differentiation	Assessment Characteristics	Nursing Interventions
Risk for delayed child development	At risk for delay in social, cognitive, language, gross motor, or fine motor skills	*Prenatal:* Endocrine or genetic disorders, substance abuse *Child:* Adoption, brain damage, chronic illness, congenital disorder, prematurity	*Prenatal:* Avoid exposure to toxins, alcohol, and substances. *Child:* Provide adequate nutrition. *Caregivers:* Teach appropriate interventions for developmental stages.
Readiness for enhanced family processes	Family patterns that support overall family unity and the well-being of its members	Activities promote balance between family cohesion and member autonomy. Boundaries are clear and respected. Communication is appropriate. Family adapts to change	Assess the family stress level and coping abilities. Use family-centered care and role modelling. Identify resources. Provide parenting classes. Encourage family meals.
Risk for impaired attachment	Risk for disruption in the usual interactive process that fosters a nurturing relationship	Anxiety, inability to initiate contact, or meet personal needs	Encourage mothers to breast-feed. Identify postpartum depression. Offer parents the opportunity to describe their childhood experiences.

Pulling It All Together: An Example of Reflection and Critical Thinking

After completing evidence-informed interventions, the nurse reevaluates the Carrs and documents findings in the chart to show progress toward outcomes. The nurse uses critical thinking and judgment to continue or revise the diagnosis, outcomes, or interventions. This is often in the form of a care plan or case note similar to the one below.

Nursing Diagnosis	Patient Outcomes	Nursing Interventions	Rationale	Evaluation
Risk for delayed child development related to recent adoption	Children will be within 25% of expected limits for growth, motor, and language development.	Teach that Emily needs environmental stimuli each day, in short periods when she is awake. Teach parents to respond to her vocalizations. Consider public health nurse visit to the home to assess the environment for safety and comfort.	Interventions appropriate to developmental stages improve neurodevelopmental outcomes.	Performed screening on all children. Growth, motor, and language development are within expected limits. Continue regular well visits with the family. Allow time for the family members to ask questions as they adjust to the changes.

Understanding expected developmental processes is crucial for nurses, so that they can recognize patients who are developing appropriately and also those who are differing in some way from a usual developmental trajectory. Using the previous steps of the nursing process and clinical reasoning, consider all the case study findings about the Carr family woven throughout this chapter. When answering the following questions, begin drawing conclusions and see how the pieces of assessment must work together to create an environment for personalized, appropriate, and accurate care.

- How much weight should 2-year old Jacob have gained since his birth weight? (Knowledge)
- Why do Madelaine and Jacob require supervision in the kitchen and bathroom? (Comprehension)
- In what stage of psychosocial development are members of the Carr family? (Application)
- In what stage of Piaget's cognitive thought are members of the Carr family? (Application)
- What nursing diagnoses might be appropriate for members of the Carr family? (Analysis)
- How will the nurse individualize assessments of Emily, Jacob and Madelaine, considering their ages and being newly adopted? (Synthesis)
- How will the nurse evaluate the success of health teaching with Amber and Michael about home hazards? (Evaluation)

so that they can choose the healthiest possible lifestyles for themselves and their children. As adults move through the different stages of adulthood, they also need to make healthy and safe choices for themselves to lead productive, satisfying lives well into old age.

Clinical Reasoning

Nurses use the nursing process to assess, diagnose, plan, implement, and evaluate care. Some examples of nursing diagnoses commonly related to growth and development are included in Table 9-6.

Some outcomes that are related to growth and development concerns include the following:

- The child will achieve developmental milestones without a delay of 25% or more in one or more areas of social or self-regulatory behaviour or cognitive, language, or gross or fine motor skills (Moorhead, Johnson, et al., 2007; Wilkinson & Ahearn, 2009).
- The family members will report improvement in their communication, processes, and daily functioning.

Key Points

- Each human experiences physical growth, psychosocial development, and cognitive development.
- Growth refers to changes in height and weight.
- Development refers to changes in motor, language, psychosocial, and cognitive developments.
- Erickson's stages of psychosocial development include (1) trust versus mistrust, (2) autonomy versus shame and doubt, (3) initiative versus guilt, (4) industry versus inferiority, (5) identity versus role confusion, (6) intimacy versus isolation, (7) generativity versus self-absorption, and (8) ego integrity versus despair.

- Cognitive development includes sensorimotor, preoperational, concrete operational, and formal operations stages.
- Language development involves receptive and productive language.
- Physical growth takes place in an expected pattern, but at a variable pace.
- Motor development follows a pattern, but individuals develop at variable rates.

Review Questions

1. Caitlyn was 51 cm long at birth and weighed 3.4 kg. At her 1-year well-child checkup, the nurse determines that Caitlyn is 66 cm and weighs 7.25 kg. The nurse's reaction to these assessment findings is to be
   A. concerned; Caitlyn should have quadrupled her birth weight by now.
   B. unconcerned; Caitlyn is growing in height and weight at an expected pace.
   C. concerned, because Caitlyn should have tripled her birth weight by now.
   D. unconcerned, because she has slightly more than doubled her birth weight.

2. The nurse's response to Emily's length, which is 66 cm now at 2 months and was 51 cm at birth, is to be
   A. concerned, because Emily should have grown 25.4 to 30.5 cm by now.
   B. unconcerned, because Emily should have grown 15 cm by now.
   C. concerned, because Emily should have doubled her birth length by now.
   D. unconcerned, because Emily should have grown 7.6 to 10.2 cm by now.

3. Jasmyn, who has just had her second birthday, comes to the well-child clinic for an assessment. The nurse reviews her records and discovers that Jasmyn weighed 3.2 kg at birth. Today the nurse expects that Jasmyn's weight should be
   A. 9.5 kg
   B. 12.7 kg
   C. 15.9 kg
   D. 19.1 kg

4. Tamika is often in a hurry with her toddler daughter, Samantha, and usually does things for her that Samantha could do herself if given more time. Erikson would say that Tamika's daughter
   A. will develop a healthy sense of autonomy because of her mother's help.
   B. will not develop shame and doubt because of these interactions with her mother.
   C. will develop a sense of autonomy no matter what her mother does.
   D. is at risk of developing a sense of shame and doubt because of her mother's behaviour.

5. Oscar, 6 years old, has come to the well-child clinic for a visit. He is 117 cm tall today. Assuming that he grows at an expected pace, how tall would the nurse expect Oscar to be at 10 years?
   A. 127 cm
   B. 132 cm
   C. 137 cm
   D. 158 cm

6. Mallory, 16 years old, is having difficulty in school and with her friends. She has not decided what she wants to do with the rest of her life after high school. Erik Erikson would say that Mallory is at risk for
   A. industry
   B. inferiority
   C. identity
   D. role confusion

7. At 27 years, Steve is considering purchasing his first house. How might the nurse characterize Steve's cognitive processes now that he has entered into early adulthood?
   A. He will be very optimistic about the purchase regardless of the housing market.
   B. He will use only logical analysis to systematically consider all the pros and cons of the purchase.
   C. He will be less optimistic and more practical, considering the complexities of the situation.
   D. He will be more logical and more optimistic than he would have been a little earlier in development.

8. Nell, 50 years old, is worried about whether her intelligence will change as she continues to advance through middle age. What can the nurse tell Nell about what might happen to her cognitive skills in middle age?
   A. Nell can expect her vocabulary to gradually decrease over time.
   B. Nell can expect to be slightly slower as she does cognitive tasks.
   C. Nell will have great difficulty learning new skills.
   D. Nell will find that her life experience is unhelpful in problem solving.

9. Earl is healthy and vigorous at 68 years. Which of the following will NOT be true of his cognition as he ages?
   A. His long-term memory will definitely be impaired.
   B. His speed of processing information will slow down.
   C. His short-term memory should not be impaired.
   D. His sensory threshold will increase.

10. Amber and Michael Carr need to be taught that 2-month-old Emily
   A. needs stimuli each day, in short periods when she is awake.
   B. will benefit from as much attention as possible.
   C. needs to have stimuli limited to basic needs.
   D. will benefit from long periods of attention with rest.

References

Blakemore, S.-J., & Choudhury, S. (2006). Brain development during puberty: State of the science. *Developmental Science, 9*(1), 11–14.

Bronfenbrenner, U. (1979). *The ecology of human development.* Cambridge, MA: Harvard University Press.

Craig, G. J., & Dunn, W. L. (2007). *Understanding human development.* Upper Saddle River, NJ: Pearson Education.

Erikson, E. H. (1963). *Childhood and society* (2nd ed.). New York, NY: W.W. Norton & Co.

Erikson, E. H. (1980). *Identity and the life cycle.* New York, NY: W. W. Norton.

Labouvie-Vief, G. (1986, August). *Modes of knowing and life-span cognition.* Paper presented at the meeting of the American Psychological Association, Washington, DC.

Leifer, G., & Hartston, H. (2004). *Growth and development across the lifespan: A health promotion focus.* St. Louis, MO: Saunders.

Moorhead, S., Johnson, M., et al. (2007). *Nursing outcomes classification (NOC)* (4th ed.). Philadelphia, PA: Mosby.

Murray, R. B., & Zentner, J. P. (2008). *Health promotion strategies through the life span* (8th ed.). Upper Saddle River, NJ: Prentice Hall.

Perry, W. G. (1970). *Forms of intellectual and ethical development in the college years.* New York, NY: Holt, Rinehart & Winston.

Perry, W. G. (1999). *Forms of ethical and intellectual development in the college years: A scheme.* San Francisco, CA: Jossey Bass.

Piaget, J. (1952). *The origins of intelligence in children.* New York, NY: International Universities Press.

Santrock, J. (2006). *Life-span development* (10th ed.). New York, NY: McGraw-Hill.

Schaie, K. W., & Willis, S. (2000). A stage theory model of adult development revisited. In R. Rubinstein, M. Moss, et al. (Eds.). *The many dimensions of aging: Essays in honor of M. Powell Lawton*. New York, NY: Springer.

Thies, K. M., & Travers, J. F. (2009). *Quick look nursing: Growth and development through the lifespan* (2nd ed.). Sudbury, MA: Jones & Bartlett.

Wallerstein, J., Lewis, J., et al. (2000). *The unexpected legacy of divorce*. New York, NY: Hyperion.

Wilkinson, J. M., & Ahern, N. R. (2009). *Nursing diagnosis handbook* (9th ed.). Upper Saddle River, NJ: Pearson Prentice Hall.

Mental Health Assessment

Learning Objectives

1 Compare characteristics of mental health and mental illness.

2 Identify important topics for health promotion and risk reduction related to mental health.

3 Differentiate among comprehensive, psychosocial, and focused assessments related to mental health.

4 Collect subjective data related to psychosocial and mental health.

5 Collect objective data related to psychosocial and mental health, using physical examination techniques.

6 Identify expected and unexpected findings related to assessment of mental health.

7 Analyze subjective and objective data from the mental health assessment and consider initial interventions.

8 Document and communicate data from the mental health assessment using appropriate terminology and principles of recording.

9 Consider age, condition, gender, and culture of the patient to individualize the mental health assessment.

10 Identify nursing diagnoses and initiate a plan of care based on findings from the mental health assessment.

Mr. Jari Shytowski, a 75-year-old Caucasian man, arrives at a primary health care centre and asks to have his blood pressure checked. He has been to the clinic several times in the last few weeks for the same purpose. His vital signs are as follows: temperature is 37°C orally, pulse 86 beats/min and regular, respirations 16 breaths/ min, and blood pressure 146/82 mm Hg (Left arm, sitting). Current medications include a multivitamin, an antihypertensive, nadolol (Apo-Nadol) 80 mg/d, and an antidepressant, citalopram (Co Citalopram) 40 mg/d.

You will learn more about Mr. Shytowski and his situation as you progress through this chapter. As you study the content and features, consider Mr. Shytowski's case and its relationship to what you are learning. Begin thinking about the following points:

- How do the various elements of the health history and mental status assessment contribute to a comprehensive understanding of the patient's health–illness status?
- What attitudes, behaviours, and communication techniques convey respect and facilitate trust?
- How might the nurse effectively approach sensitive topics such as suicide/self-harm, homicidal ideation, and perceptual disturbances?
- What are your own attitudes, beliefs, and experiences about persons

Good mental health is essential to well-being and a high quality of life. It is associated with good physical health, educational and vocational achievement, economic success, and satisfying relationships (Friedli & Parsonage, 2007). In fact, good health is not possible without good mental health.

In a 1999 report titled *Mental Health,* the U.S. Surgeon General presented mental health and mental illness, not as polar opposites, but as two points on a continuum. Later in the same report, mental health was described as

> *a state of successful performance of mental function, resulting in productive activities, fulfilling relationships with other people, and the ability to adapt to change and to cope with adversity (U.S. Department of Health and Human Services [USDHHS], 1999, Chapter 1).*

Similarly, the World Health Organization (WHO) (2007a) characterizes mental health as

> *a state of wellbeing in which the individual realizes his or her own abilities, can cope with the usual stresses of life, can work productively and fruitfully, and is able to make a contribution to his or her community... mental health is the foundation for wellbeing and effective functioning for an individual and for a community.*

Mental illnesses/disorders are "clinically significant patterns of behaviour or emotions that are associated with some level of distress, suffering or impairment in one or more areas such as school, work, social and social and family interactions or the ability to live independently" (Mental Health Commission of Canada, 2009, p. 5). The *Diagnostic and Statistical Manual of Mental Disorders* (DSM-IV-TR) (American Psychiatric Association, 2001) and the *International Classification of Diseases* (ICD-10) (WHO, 2007b) outline specific diagnostic criteria for the various types of mental illnesses/disorders.

Individuals can have varying degrees of mental health without being mentally ill. Mental health and mental illness influence each other but are not mutually exclusive; the absence of mental health does not necessarily mean the presence of mental illness, and more than the presence of mental illness implies a complete absence of mental wellness. As the Mental Health Commission of Canada (2009) explains, an individual may not be diagnosed with a mental illness/disorder and yet may experience day-to-day life as a struggle, be easily set back by life's challenges, and have limited prospects. In contrast, individuals diagnosed with a mental illness/disorder may have a sense of coherence that enables them to function well despite challenges and the resiliency to bounce back from setbacks.

Based on these definitions, mental health is an integral part of the patient's well-being; thus, the assessment of mental health status is essential. A nurse is often the first health care professional whom the patient sees in any health care setting. The patient may be seeking care for a physical concern, and a thorough assessment by the nurse uncovers an underlying mental health issue. It is not uncommon for the patient to have lived with a mental health condition for a long time, even since childhood, and not realize that he or she has a health issue. People with a mental health concern are at high risk for a number of physical conditions and are less likely to regularly seek out medical care (Maj, 2009). The patient may be self-medicating with alcohol or other substances to feel better.

Nursing assessment of mental health consists of screening for preexisting, as well as current, mental health conditions for all age groups. This chapter includes the techniques that nurses can use to identify risk factors, assess psychosocial, mental status and mental health, and guide patients in planning care.

Role of the Nurse in Mental Health and Psychiatric Assessment

Assessment is a purposeful and systematic activity that involves the ongoing collection, validation, analysis, synthesis, and documentation of information related to the patient's health–illness status. An assessment may be comprehensive or focused. A **comprehensive assessment** is a collaborative activity involving all members of the interprofessional health care team. Its purpose is to establish a baseline understanding of the patient's concerns and needs, as well as his or her strengths and resources. It includes a health history and physical and mental status examinations. Team members seek information from a variety of sources (eg, the patient and his or her family, existing health records, and other service providers) and then collaborate with the patient to establish a diagnosis, identify treatment goals, and develop a plan of care. Because of its broad scope and the time it takes to establish rapport, a comprehensive assessment may take days or even weeks to complete (Lasiuk, 2010).

A **psychosocial assessment** is one component of the comprehensive assessment and is typically performed by nurses. By its nature, a psychosocial assessment is holistic and attends to the biological, psychological, developmental, emotional, and spiritual dimensions of the patient in the context of his or her physical and social environments. The overarching goal is to determine how these things interact to influence well-being and function. At each encounter, nurses synthesize new information with existing information to re-evaluate the patient's responses to treatments and interventions, nursing diagnoses, and the plan of care (Lasiuk, 2010).

A **focused assessment** is the collection of specific information about a particular need, concern, or situation (eg, medication effects, risk for self-harm, risk to harm others, knowledge deficits, or the adequacy of supports and resources). As the name suggests, focused assessments are briefer, narrower in scope, present oriented, and may be used to screen for particular issues or disorders. In these instances, nurses often employ standardized assessment tools (Lasiuk, 2010).

Acute Assessment

The nurse decides which type of assessment is most appropriate in a given situation based on the immediate needs of the patient. It is important for the nurse to ask the safety questions first and leave the presenting concern for last. An acute mental health assessment includes questions about harm to self or others. Acute situations include a risk for injury with psychotic states, depression, dementia, and delirium. Attempting to perform a comprehensive assessment during a psychiatric emergency (eg, when the patient is floridly psychotic or actively suicidal) may be both futile and dangerous. The quality and trustworthiness of information collected in these circumstances is influenced by the patient's symptoms and the high emotionality of the situation. The priority in acute situations is to deal with the safety issues first and then to perform a focused assessment to provide the treatment team with sufficient information to treat the patient's symptoms and to ensure the safety of all involved.

Subjective Data Collection

Subjective data are what the patient reports, is overheard telling someone else, or what family and friends have said. The best way to obtain subjective data during an interview is to ask open-ended questions. Doing so encourages the patient to elaborate when answering. It also allows the nurse to assess the patient's cognition processes and understanding of the question. Common practice is to obtain information from family or friends to elaborate and/or validate information that the patient provides.

Assessing mental health is an art as well as a science. The art lies in the nurse's ability to communicate and accurately assess the patient, listening for not only what is said but also what is unsaid. The nurse needs be comfortable asking questions about psychosis, suicide, history of abuse, and sexuality. If the nurse is uncomfortable, the patient will sense it and be reluctant to respond. Nurses may even avoid asking relevant questions because of emotions evoked within themselves. It is important for nursing students to practise asking these types of questions during laboratory and clinical experiences to increase their skill and comfort level. The science lies in the knowledge base that the nurse incorporates in the examination, including the accurate labelling of findings and the precise use of reliable and valid tools that screen for mental health issues.

When assessing a new patient, the nurse establishes rapport first. If there is not much time to establish rapport or the patient is guarded or suspicious, the nurse can say, "The questions I am about to ask you I ask all of my patients" and then proceed. Questions in a mental health assessment are designed to elicit information about various mental health risks and concerns.

Patients may use divergent tactics to avoid answering questions. Examples include laughing spontaneously, giving responses that do not follow a logical order, asking the nurse personal questions, or being insulting toward the nurse. These tactics will likely disrupt the flow of communication and the nurse's thought processes. Assessing the reasons for such tactics is important. Patients may try to avoid answering questions because they are embarrassed, the topic is too emotionally overwhelming, or they cannot remember and do not want the nurse to realize that. They might also fear being judged or have difficulty concentrating. Being focused on what the patient is saying helps the nurse identify when divergent tactics are being used as well as what is being left unsaid.

Risk Assessment and Health Promotion

Important Topics for Health Promotion

- Alterations in interest in life, motivation, energy, sleep patterns, appetite, and sexual desire/behaviour
- Current stressors and coping abilities
- Past or current physical, sexual, or psychological abuse/assault
- Pervasive or prolonged worry or anxiety
- Alterations in affect or mood
- Thoughts or behaviours of self-harm or suicide
- Alcohol or drug use
- Memory, concentration, and problem-solving abilities

From: Lasiuk, G. C., & Bickley, L. S. (2010). Psychosocial and mental status assessment. In T. C Stephen, D. S. Skillen, R. A. Day, & L. S. Bickley (Eds.). *Canadian Bates' guide to health assessment for nurses.* (1st ed., pp. 220). Philadelphia, PA: Wolters Kluwer Health/Lippincott Williams & Williams.

For the general population, health promotion should be focused on four important conditions that are often overlooked: anxiety, depression, suicidality, and dementia. Routinely screening for addiction to alcohol or drugs is also required (Lasiuk & Bickley, 2010).

Anxiety

Regardless of their presenting concern, many people seeking primary care have mental health concerns. For example, generalized anxiety disorder (GAD) is higher in patients in primary care settings than in the general population (Toft, Fink, et al., 2005). In a study of 965 primary care patients, 19.5% had at least one anxiety disorder, 8.6% met the criteria for posttraumatic stress disorder (PTST), 7.6% for GAD, 6.8% for panic disorder, and 6.2% for social anxiety disorder (Kroenke, Spitzer, et al., 2007). Patients who had more than one disorder showed substantial impairment. Of particular concern was the result that 41% of the patients with anxiety were not currently receiving any medications, counselling, or psychotherapy.

People with PTST report "waves of anxiety, anger, aggression, and suspicion that threaten sense of self and interfere with daily functioning" (Day, Paul, et al., 2010, p. 119). People at risk include individuals who have been sexually assaulted, who have experienced family violence, been caught in terrorist attacks and disasters such as fire and earthquakes, and military personnel who served in combat in places like Afghanistan.

Depression

Data from the 2003 Joint Canada/U.S. Survey of Health (Vasiliadis, Lesage, et al., 2007) found similar rates of depression for both countries at 8.5%. Worldwide, major depressive disorder (MDD) occurs twice as often in women as in men (Lopez, Mathers, et al., 2006). While the cause of depression is not known, it does involve an interaction of genetic, biological, social, and psychological factors (Lasiuk & Bickley, 2010). According to Parikh and Lam (2001), those at higher risk for depression are patients who have:

- A history of depression
- Female gender
- A family history of depression and/or suicide
- Major life stress (eg, relationship conflict, interpersonal violence, death of a loved one, economic strain)
- Serious or chronic disease/illness (eg, hypertension, type 2 diabetes, arthritis, chronic pain)
- Particular personality traits (eg, poor self-esteem, dependent, self-critical, or pessimistic)
- Recently given birth

Primary care providers often fail to diagnose depression (Seelig & Katon, 2008). Use of the following two questions (Safety Alert 10-1) would be helpful.

> ⚠ SAFETY ALERT 10-1
>
> In a primary care setting, asking the following two questions regarding mood and anhedonia (inability to experience pleasure)—*Over the past 2 weeks, have you felt down? Depressed? Or hopeless?* and *Over the past 2 weeks, have you felt little interest or pleasure in doing things?*—may be as effective as longer instruments for detecting depressive symptoms (MacMillan, Patterson, et al., 2005).

Suicide

Worldwide trends suggest that the rate of suicide increases with age. Rates for people aged 60 years and older are around three times higher than for those aged 15 to 29 years (Statistics Canada, 2005). As age increases, suicide as a cause of death decreases, indicating an increase in deaths from cancers, heart disease, etc. (Murray, 2010). Suicide rates for men are higher than for women for the following age categories: 15 to 24 years and 70 to 74 years, with the highest rates for men 80 years and older (Public Health Agency of Canada, 2002). See table below.

The most common causes of suicides were hanging (39%), poisoning (26%), and firearms (22%) (Statistics Canada, 2006). Suicide is strongly connected to depression (O'Connell, Chin, et al., 2004) and the best predictor for suicide is a previous attempt (Nemeroff, Compton, et al., 2001), while being married with dependent children is a protective factor (Tondo & Baldessarini, 2001).

For persons of aboriginal origin (First Nations, Inuit, & Métis), suicide rates are three to six times that of the general population, with teens and young adults having the highest rates of all. The aftermath of abuse and loss of aboriginal languages and ways in connection with residential schools, sexual abuse, family violence, gangs, substance abuse, and access to firearms all contribute to higher rates of suicide (Health Canada, 2002).

Dementia

Dementia is an "irreversible syndrome that is characterized by ongoing decline in intellectual functioning sufficient to disrupt social and/or occupational functioning" (Haase, 2010, p. 759). There are four main types of dementia: Alzheimer's disease, vascular dementia, dementia with Lewy bodies, and frontotemporal dementia.

- Alzheimer's disease (AD). Risk factors for AD according to the Alzheimer Society of Canada (2009) include age, family history and genetics, diabetes, Down's syndrome, mild cognitive impairment (MCI), female gender, head trauma, and having a low level of formal education.
- Vascular dementia (occurs in 20% of dementia cases, occurs between ages 60 and 75 years, and affects slightly more men than women).
- Dementia with Lewy bodies (DLB) (occurs in 20% patients with dementia, usually occurs between 75 and 80 years, may be associated with Parkinson's disease, and affects more men).
- Frontotemporal dementia (FTD) (affects personality, behaviour, and speech, with changes in mood and anxiety).

As more Canadians (the baby boomers) enter their 60s, they are among the group with the highest risk for dementia (Forbes & Neufeld, 2008).

Addiction

Addiction is considered a real, chronic, relapsing, and treatable medical condition, which is the leading preventable cause of death and disease in Canada (Kunyk & Els, 2010). "Repeated exposure to alcohol, tobacco, and/or other drugs (ATOD) over time may alter brain structure, chemistry, and function in susceptible individuals, leading to a potential loss of control over their use of ATOD, and continued use despite harm" (Kunyk & Els, 2010, p. 534). Alcohol, tobacco, and

Suicide Deaths in Canada, 2005						
Age Group	<15 y	15–24 y	25–44 y	46–65 y	>65 y	
Number of Deaths	43	509	1387	1343	460	Total = 3742

Adapted from Day, R. A., & Paul, P. (2010). Individual and family considerations related to illness. In R. A. Day, P. Paul, et al. *Brunner & Suddarth's textbook of Canadian medical-surgical nursing.* (2nd ed., p. 121). Philadelphia, PA: Wolters Kluwer Health/Lippincott Williams & Williams

other drugs take a great toll on individuals and their communities. In Canada, addiction is the leading cause of morbidity and mortality, and accounts for 21% of total mortality, 23% of total potential years of life lost, 8% of all hospitalizations, and 10% of hospitalization days due to any cause (Single, Robson, et al., 1997). Total costs to Canadian society in 2002 was about $40 billion when health care, workplace, transfer payments (social welfare and workers' compensation), crime and law enforcement, and lost productivity are all considered (Rehm, Ballunas, et al., 2006).Other issues include perinatal and childhood exposure to ATOD. Being impaired when carrying out duties of significant responsibility such as at work, school, or caring for children is a common experience of adults (26%) who are dependent on alcohol. As well, the sale and distribution of drugs in schools and neighbourhoods leads to increasing community violence (Kunyk & Els, 2010).

Canada's National Mental Health Strategy: Toward Recovery and Well-Being

The Mental Health Commission of Canada is a nonprofit corporation created by the Federal Government to promote mental health. In 2009, after an extensive national consultation process, the commission declared the following goals to help all Canadians achieve the highest level of mental health and well-being possible:

1. People of all ages living with mental health problems and illnesses are actively engaged and supported in their journey of recovery and well-being.
2. Mental health is promoted, and mental health problems and illnesses are prevented wherever possible.
3. The mental health system responds to the diverse needs of all people in Canada.
4. The role of families in promoting well-being and providing care is recognized, and their needs are supported.

5. People have equitable and timely access to appropriate and effective programs, treatments, services, and supports that are seamlessly integrated around their needs.
6. Actions are informed by the best evidence based on multiple sources of knowledge, outcomes are measured, and research is advanced.
7. People living with mental health problems and illnesses are fully included as valued members of society.

Assessment of Risk Factors

During the Mini Mental Status Examination (MMSE), the nurse is aware that certain situations are considered risk factors for contributing to, or exacerbating, a mental health condition. Factors that cannot be changed include family history, age, and gender.

Pregnancy may also exacerbate an existing mental health condition or precipitate postpartum depression.

⚠ SAFETY ALERT 10-2
Women with postpartum depression with psychotic features may harm their infants. The nurse needs to ask specifically if the mother has thoughts of harming her baby.

Environmental factors that may influence mental health include support systems, housing, health care accessibility, and literacy. The nurse also considers metabolic issues and associated physiological processes such as Parkinson's disease, cancer, HIV/AIDS, and other chronic conditions. Identification of the exact risk factors and causes for illness is often complex and interrelated. Nevertheless, identification of these risks helps identify topics for health-promotion teaching.

Questions to Assess History and Risk Factors	Rationale
Identification/Biographical Data What is your legal name? Nicknames? Aliases? Birth date? Gender? Genetic background? Address? Telephone numbers? Next of kin? Employer? School? Health Insurance Number? Band name and treaty number (if applicable)?	As this information is relatively nonthreatening, it is a safe place to begin an interview and provides insight into the patient's current living situation. If the patient has provided this information elsewhere, review it and ask for missing data. It can be annoying to be asked the same questions repeatedly; it may seem like no one is actually tracking responses. Diagnoses early in life may indicate more concerns with developmental, cognitive, social, and coping skills. Children are at risk for abuse. Adolescence is a risk because of hormonal changes as well as growth and developmental stage. Older adults are at increased risk for *depression*. Females are more prone to *depression,* and males are more apt to commit *suicide* or *violence*.
Current Health Status How are you feeling today?	This generic question opens a conversation about mental health concerns.

Questions to Assess History and Risk Factors	Rationale
Do you have any health concerns? • Pain? Can you point to where it is? • Thyroid imbalance? Diabetes? • Hepatitis? Kidney disease? • Stroke (Brain attack)? Breathing concerns? Asthma? COPD?	Record the patient's words verbatim. This provides information on the patient's perception of the situation, their insight and judgment, and goals for treatment. Does the patient's account match information from other informants? Physiological changes with or without emotional responses to illness can affect mental status. Also consider how the medical condition might affect any psychiatric medications, such as causing poor absorption or impaired elimination.
• Stomach concerns? (Vomiting? Heartburn?) Bowel concerns? (Diarrhea? Irritable bowel syndrome? Crohn's disease? Ulcerative colitis? Celiac disease?) • Potentially terminal illnesses: Do you have HIV/AIDS? Cancer? • Surgery that has resulted or may result in disfiguring or incapacitating alteration of ability to function	
When did you first notice this mental health concern? • Why do you think it started when it did? • How often does it occur?	Response indicates how long the patient has had a concern. It also can be compared to family perceptions. Identify any possible contributing factors. Response indicates how it might be affecting functioning.
• What changes have you noticed?	Changes include frequency, intensity, or effects on functioning or well-being.
• Have you ever felt this way before?	This is to assess for any previous episodes, especially if untreated.
• What do you think is causing the concern?	Assess the patient's understanding of the situation and whether it is logical.
• How is this affecting your life now?	Assess implications of how this illness is affecting the patient's life. Assess feelings of self-worth from the patient's responses to the above questions and statements the patient might make about himself or herself or the illness, such as "I don't like feeling this way. I can't be a good mom when I'm feeling depressed."
Describe your typical day.	This helps to identify the ability to perform activities of daily living.
Have you experienced recent weight loss? Or gain?	Some medications cause weight gain and metabolic issues. Weight changes also may be related to *anxiety*, early *dementia*, *depression*, or *eating disorders*. Physical concerns can manifest with mental health issues.
Have you noticed any change in your sleeping habits?	Sleep disorders may be associated with *anxiety, depression, bipolar disorder*, or *substance abuse*.
Past Health History Have you had any surgeries? If so, please list when and why.	Some patients with mental health conditions present with multiple surgeries and psychosomatic symptoms.
Have you ever been told that you have a mental health condition? • Have you ever received treatment for a mental health condition? • Have you ever been hospitalized for a mental health condition?	Assess for the patient's history of mental health conditions. Treatment could be outpatient, inpatient, from a general practitioner, or from another health care practitioner. Hospitalization indicates the severity of the condition. It is helpful to get the names of facilities and dates when admitted.
Have you ever been abused? Physically? Sexually? Or emotionally? If so, did this occur when you were a child? Or when you were older?	Assess for situational stressors such as bullying at school, family violence, or war violence (see Chapter 12). People maltreated in childhood are more likely to develop depression or posttraumatic stress disorder and to attempt suicide. Also, abused children develop riskier behaviours (eg, substance use, unprotected sexual activity) as adolescents (Felitti, Andra, et al., 1998).

(text continues on page 210)

Questions to Assess History and Risk Factors	Rationale

Medications

What psychiatric medications are you taking? Are you taking them as prescribed?

Consider interactions between medications taken for psychiatric and medical conditions. For example, if the patient has a medical condition such as prolonged QT wave interval (a cardiac issue), the patient should not take or be prescribed some classes of antidepressants. Identify any psychiatric drugs taken, drug interactions, herb–drug interactions, and alternative treatments that might cause psychiatric side effects.

Do you use, or have you ever used, any alternative treatments, herbs, or other substances? If yes, list the specific treatments or substances.

Patients may be taking substances to self-medicate. Keep in mind that some patients consider marijuana a natural herb or alternative medical treatment, not a recreational drug.

Psychological Trauma

Have you ever experienced or witnessed an event that threatened your life or safety or those of a loved one? If yes, can you describe the details?

Psychological trauma associated with natural disasters, motor vehicle crashes, combat, abuse/assault (physical or sexual), and childhood neglect is a risk factor for a number of adult health conditions (eg, posttraumatic stress disorder [PTSD], other anxiety disorders, and depression)

Family History

Has anyone in your family been diagnosed with a mental health condition?
• If so, which family member(s)?
• What was the diagnosis and treatment plan for each family member diagnosed with a mental health condition?

Many diseases/disorders are genetically linked; a family health history provides information about the patient's risk factors.

A genogram is a useful tool for recording the name, age, and current health status of first- and second-degree relatives (spouse/partner, children, parents, siblings, grandparents, and aunts/uncles). If a family member is deceased, note the date and cause of death and indications of unresolved grief/loss.

Inquire specifically about diseases/disorders that "run in the family," including psychiatric illnesses/disorders and addictions. Answers may help direct the line of treatment or medication options for the patient.

How is the treatment plan working for the particular family member?

Psychosocial

Support Network. Do you have a support system?
• Whom do you consider as part of your support system?
• How well does your support system meet your needs?

Assess the patient's coping skills and resources.
Assess members and their effectiveness. Some patients with chronic mental conditions have only their health care providers as a support system.

Do you have a significant other in your life? Such as a spouse? Partner? Or close friend?
• How do you get along?
• How often do you get together with people with whom you do not live?

Assess the stability and effectiveness of the patient's relationships. Patients with high demands often move among relationships as family members, partners, or friends become fatigued.

Stressors. What are some stresses that you have been experiencing?
• Have you experienced a loss recently? Death of a family member? Or friend? Or loss of job? Or income?
• How do you cope with stress?
• How is that working for you now?

Assess for the degree or amount of current stress.

Coping skills are used to deal with stress.
Evaluate their effectiveness.

Are there any other factors in your life that may be contributing to your stress level?
• What are your living arrangements?
• Do you work? How many hours a week do you work?
• Is this affecting your work?
• Is this affecting your level of functioning? Or thinking?

Factors that contribute to mental health issues include the following:
• Isolation: lives alone or is withdrawn
• Finances: lower socioeconomic status
• Poor or diminished cognitive abilities
• Housing: homeless or unsafe environment

	• Health care accessibility: has difficulties with cost, transportation, or ability to cognitively and safely use public transportation
	• Language: cannot speak or understand the predominant language
	• Literacy: cannot read or write
Do you have any legal concerns? Or have you had any legal concerns in the past? If so, please specify what happened? Were you sent to jail/prison for them? When?	Patients with issues of judgment, substance abuse, or anger management may become involved with the legal system.
Substance Use. Do you drink alcohol? Or use recreational substances? (If you suspect that alcohol use might be a concern, the CAGE is a quick first-step questionnaire to use as an assessment tool. The acronyms are easy for the nurse to remember and use at any time (see Box 10-1).	Whenever the patient comes in for treatment of substance use, it is important to be aware of the possibility of an underlying mental health issue. Also, it is very important to know the effects that alcohol and other substances can have on mental health (Table 10-1). When screening for substance abuse, the patient may deny a concern. The CAGE tool is valuable because it addresses this denial.

BOX 10-1 CAGE QUESTIONNAIRE FOR SUBSTANCE USE

• Have you ever felt the need to **C**ut down on drinking?
• Have you ever felt **A**nnoyed by criticism of drinking?
• Have you ever had **G**uilty feelings about drinking?
• Have you ever taken a drink first thing in the morning (**E**ye-opener) to steady your nerves or get rid of a hangover?

Adapted from Ewing, J. A. (1984). Detecting alcoholism: The CAGE questionnaire. *Journal of the American Medical Association, 252,* 1905–1907.

Table 10-1 Substances That Can Affect Mental Health

Substance Used	Effect on Health
Injectable drugs	Abscesses, sepsis, endocarditis, pulmonary fibrosis, renal disease
Narcotics	Dependence, addiction, drowsiness, respiratory arrest, overdose
Central nervous system stimulants	Possible dependence, weight loss, tooth decay
Club drugs	Possible loss of memory and subsequent sexual assault
Recreational drugs (specify)	Sherm—formaldehyde-laced marijuana that causes irreversible brain damage
Herbs (specify)	Salvia—a psychedelic that, when misused, can cause errors in judgment, headaches, and vomiting
	Peyote/mescaline hallucinogenic herbs—used in native
	American rituals under the guidance of a Shaman; often misused by individuals; visual hallucinations may persist
Misused prescription medicines	
• Taking too much? (sleeping pills, diet pills, painkillers)	Sleeping pills and painkillers to ease emotional distress
• Using prescribed medicine for other purposes?	Patient experiences a "buzz" with no cognitive impairment
• Experimenting with other people's medications (common with teens)?	
• Intentionally taking other people's medications (eg, parent taking a child's Ritalin)?	
• Taking cogentin?	
• Sniffing household chemicals, glue, or car exhaust fumes?	
• Misusing cold medicine or other over-the-counter drugs?	Contain chemical solvents that can cause fatal cardiac arrhythmias, rapid loss of consciousness, and respiratory arrest

Questions to Assess History and Risk Factors	Rationale

- What do you use? (ie, Beer? Wine? Hard liquor? And/or recreational substances? Marijuana? Cocaine ("crack")? Methampetamine—MDMA ("meth", "crystal")? Or club drugs such as LSD? Ecstasy?
PCP ("angel dust"?)

Ketamine ("Special—K")

Inhalants: Volatile solvents (eg, glue, lighter fluid)? Aerosols or spray cans? Gases (eg, propane, ether)? Or nitrites?
- How often do you use each substance?
- How is the use of alcohol affecting your life? Or recreational substances?

MDMA can cause hallucinations, depression, confusion, severe anxiety, and malignant hyperthermia, which can cause death (Kunyk & Els, 2010).

PCP causes delusions and mental turmoil, which mimic symptoms of schizophrenia. (Kunyk & Els, 2010) Ketamine is often used as a "date rape" drug.

Inhalants cause "euphoria, sedation, emotional lability and/or impaired judgment" (Kunyk & Els, 2010, p. 550). Respiratory depression, stupor, and coma can occur, as well as hearing loss, damage to kidneys, liver, heart, and lungs. Nitrate use is connected with unsafe sexual practices (increased risk of HIV and hepatitis (Kunyk & Els, 2010).

Cultural Background/Spirituality

Should one be aware of any cultural beliefs while caring for you? Are there any cultural beliefs that would be helpful for us to be aware of?

Information about the patients' self-identified cultural background provides some insight into their social history, meaning systems, social roles, and lifestyle choices and practices.

Do you have any religious beliefs regarding your illness?

Asking how the patient views the mental health condition in the context of religion and beliefs allows the nurse to provide culturally sensitive patient care.

Do you have a sense of hope for your future?
- What provides you with your emotional support? Or sense of faith?
- What is your religious affiliation?
- What are your spiritual beliefs?
- What spiritual practices are important to you?

No sense of hope for the future may be an indicator of risk for suicide. Refer to Box 10-2 for further assessment of spiritual beliefs using the HOPE Assessment of Spiritual Beliefs.

BOX 10-2   HOPE ASSESSMENT OF SPIRITUAL BELIEFS

H: Sources of Hope, Meaning, Comfort, Strength, Peace, Love, and Connection

- We have been discussing your support systems. I was wondering, what is there in your life that gives you internal support?
- What are your sources of hope? Strength? Comfort? And peace?
- What do you hold on to during difficult times?
- What sustains you and keeps you going?
- For some people, religious or spiritual beliefs act as a source of comfort and strength in dealing with life's ups and downs; is this true for you? (If the answer is "Yes," go on to O and P questions. If the answer is "No," consider asking "Was it ever?" If the answer is "Yes," ask "What changed?")

O: Organized Religion

- Do you consider yourself part of an organized religion?
- How important is this to you?
- What aspects of your religion are helpful? Not so helpful?
- Are you part of a religious or spiritual community? Does it help you? How?

P: Personal Spirituality/Practices

- Do you have personal spiritual beliefs that are independent of organized religion? What are they?

- Do you believe in God? What kind of relationship do you have with God?
- What aspects of your spirituality or spiritual practices do you find most helpful to you personally? (eg, prayer, meditation, reading scripture, attending religious services, listening to music, hiking, communing with nature)

E: Effects on Medical Care and End-of-Life Issues

- Has being sick (or your current situation) affected your ability to do the things that usually help you spiritually? (Or affected your relationship with God?)
- What can I do to help you access the resources that usually help you?
- Are you worried about any conflicts between your beliefs and your medical/mental situation/care/decisions?
- Would it be helpful for you to speak to a clinical chaplain/community spiritual leader?
- What specific practices or restrictions should I know about in providing your care? (eg, dietary restrictions, use of blood products)
- If the patient is dying: How do your beliefs affect the kind of medical care you would like me to provide over the next few days/weeks/months?

Adapted from Anandarajah, G., & Hight, E. (2001). Spirituality and medical practice: Using the HOPE questions as a practical tool for spiritual assessment. *American Family Physician, 63*, 81–89.

Focused Health History Related to Common Symptoms

Common Symptoms and Signs of Altered Mental Health

- Changes in mood and affect (see also Box 10-3)
- Suicide ideation
- Homicide ideation and aggressive behaviour

- Auditory hallucinations
- Visual hallucinations
- Other hallucinations

BOX 10-3 EXAMPLES OF QUESTIONS FOR SYMPTOM ANALYSIS- "STRESSED OUT, NERVOUS, OR ANXIOUS"

- "Think about a time when you felt particularly 'stressed out,' nervous, or anxious—where do you feel it in your body?" "Do these sensations or feelings move or are they always in the same place(s)?" *(Location/radiation)*
- "Describe what being 'stressed-out,' nervous, or anxious is like for you." "Complete this phrase—being 'stressed-out,' nervous, or anxious is like…" (The intent is to invite the client to offer a metaphor or compare these sensations to something else [eg, "having a big knot in my gut" or "like I am vibrating all of the time"].) (Quality)
- "On a scale of 0–10 with 0 being no stress, nervousness, or anxiety and 10 being the most you have ever experienced, where would you rate yourself right now?" "Using this same scale, where are you on an average day?" *(Intensity/Severity/Quantity)*
- "When did this stress, nervousness, or anxiety begin?" *(Onset)* "Did it start suddenly?" "Or did it start gradually?" "Are there times when you feel 'stressed-out,' nervous, or anxious?" "How long do those feelings last?" *(Duration).* "How often do they come?" *(Frequency).* "Is there a time of day that it seems worse?" "Or better?" "Has this stress, nervousness, or anxiety ever gone completely away?" *(Timing)*
- "Where were you when you first noticed being 'stressed-out,' nervous, or anxious?" *(Setting)*
- "What other symptoms have you noticed?" *(Associated symptoms)*
- "What makes it (stress, nervousness, or anxiety) worse?" *(Aggravating factors)*
- "What makes it (stress, nervousness, or anxiety) better?" *(Alleviating factors)*
- "What was going on in your life when this stress, nervousness, or anxiety began? [Probe for details about developmental, relationship, health, or career changes; use of prescribed medications or other substances; and traumatic or extremely distressing events.]" Do things in your home environment make you feel stressed, nervous, or anxious? "Do things in your work environment make you feel stressed, nervous, or anxious?" *(Environmental/situational factors)*
- "Tell me how this stress, nervousness, or anxiety is affecting your daily life." "Your work?" "Are there financial implications?" "How is it affecting your family?" "Or other interpersonal relationships?" *(Significance to patient)*
- "What do you think is happening?" *(Patient perspective)*

Adapted from Lasiuk, G. C., & Bickley, L. S. (2010). Psychosocial and mental status assessment. In T. C Stephen, D. S. Skillen, R. A. Day, & L. S. Bickley (Eds.). *Canadian Bates' guide to health assessment for nurses.* (1st ed., pp. 208). Philadelphia, PA: Wolters Kluwer Health/Lippincott Williams & Wilkins.

Examples of Questions to Assess Symptoms/Signs	Rationale
Altered Mood and Affect What has your mood been like? *Usual mood is pleasant.*	Mood is a sustained emotion. Assess the intensity, depth, and duration of altered mood.
On a scale of 0 to 10, with 10 being most intense, how depressed do you feel now?	Patients may use descriptors to describe mood, such as sad, tearful, depressed, angry, anxious, grandiose, or fearful. Mood inappropriate to the situation is unexpected.
Assess the patient's affect. Affect is an objective observation of how the patient expresses his or her feelings and mood. Assess whether affect matches what the patient says. *Expected affect is congruent with the situation.*	Affect may be temporary and changing compared with mood. Bland, apathetic, dramatic, bizarre, constricted, blunted, flat, labile, and euphoric are descriptors of altered affect. See Table 10-4 at the end of the chapter.

(text continues on page 214)

Suicidal Ideation

Do you have any thoughts of wanting to harm yourself? Or kill yourself? Use the SAD PERSONAS mnemonic to assess for risk of suicide (Box 10.4). This scale facilitates the systematic gathering of patient data and relevant psychosocial history.

Box 10-4   SAD PERSONAS SUICIDE RISK ASSESSMENT

- Sex
- Age
- Depression
- Previous attempt
- Ethanol abuse
- Rational thought loss
- Social supports lacking
- Organized plan
- No spouse
- Access to lethal means
- Sickness

The presence of each factor is given a point value of one. Total scores range from 0 to 10. Higher scores indicate greater patient suicide risk.

Adapted from Patterson, W. M., Dohn, H. H., et al. (1983). Evaluation of suicidal patients: The SAD PERSON Scale. *Psychosomatics, 24*(A), 343–349.

Clinical Significance 10-1

Medical students who received training in SAD PERSO-NAS showed a greater ability to evaluate suicide risk and make appropriate clinical interventions (Juhnke, 1994). Shea (1999) concludes that the strength of the scale is not as a precise risk predictor but as a way to alert the clinician that the patient may be at higher risk.

Homicidal Ideation and Aggressive Behaviour

Do you have any thoughts of wanting to harm anyone? Or kill anyone?

⚠ *SAFETY ALERT 10-3*

The nurse assesses for safety of others. If the patient replies "yes," then ask if he or she wants to harm a specific person, and if so, how. Notify the attending primary care provider who will determine if there is a "duty to warn" the other person. The exact nature of the plan for harm and ability to carry it out are important parts of the assessment.

Suicide happens in all ages, social classes, and cultures. Worldwide, 815,000 people killed themselves in 2000 (WHO, 2002). This works out to one death due to suicide every 40 seconds. The number of suicide attempts are 10 to 20 times the actual completed suicides. It may accompany any psychiatric illness or occur without a psychiatric diagnosis. In 2004, there were 11.3 deaths per 100,000 in Canada due to suicide and suicide accounted for 22% of all deaths in Canada (Statistics Canada, 2008). It is the leading cause of death for men 25–29 years and 40–49 years, and for women aged 30–34. It is the second leading cause of death for both sexes for those aged 10–24 years. Men are more than four times more likely to complete suicide than are women (Centers for Disease Control and Prevention & National Center for Injury Prevention and Control, 2008). Patients who are suicidal may present in any health care setting with various concerns, not necessarily sad mood or suicidal thoughts. They may hint or joke about suicide or wanting to die to test the nurse's comfort with discussing the subject. In many cases, patients do not want to talk, but despondent behaviours indicate that they are suicidal. Failure to ask if these patients have had suicidal thoughts would be a lost opportunity to assist them.

The patient is considered to have very "lethal" suicidal ideation if he or she has a history of suicide attempts, a specific plan, and access to the means (eg, owns a gun, has medications).

⚠ *SAFETY ALERT 10-4*

The nurse assesses for safety. Some patients are not suicidal but perform self-mutilation, often to release pain. Asking about suicidal thoughts covers both suicidal and parasuicidal gestures. Identifying parasuicidal thoughts is important because patients can accidentally kill themselves while releasing pain.

Risk factors for aggressive behaviour include male gender, history of violence, and substance abuse. Ethnicity, diagnosis, age, marital status, and education do not reliably identify this behaviour (Moore & Pfaff, 2008). Patients with a history of violence are more likely to inflict serious injuries. Typically, the patient becomes angry, resists authority, and finally becomes confrontational. Violent behaviour may occur without warning, however, especially when caused by medical issues or dementia. The nurse should always trust his or her "gut feeling" about the potential for violence. The nurse considers an obviously angry patient potentially violent. It is important to take actions to avoid injury.

Examples of Questions to Assess Symptoms/Signs	Rationale
	Signs of violence include the following: • Provocative behaviour • Angry demeanour • Loud, aggressive speech • Tense posturing (eg, gripping side rails tightly, clenching fists) • Frequently changing body position, pacing • Aggressive acts (eg, pounding walls, throwing objects, hitting oneself) (Moore & Pfaff, 2008)
Auditory Hallucinations Do you hear voices that others do not hear? (Ask this question while closely observing the patient.)	The patient may answer "no" even though he or she is actually experiencing auditory hallucinations. The patient may not realize that others do not hear voices or not want to tell the nurse for fear of ramifications, such as continued hospitalization or starting medications. If the answer is "yes," alert the primary provider; the patient may need more supervision if it seems that he or she cannot resist "command" hallucinations.
Assess the nature of auditory hallucinations. • Does the voice tell you what to do? • Must you listen or do what the voice says or does?	⚠ *SAFETY ALERT 10-5* *If the patient confirms auditory hallucinations, it is important to ask about their nature. Are they hostile or critical? Do they "command" or tell the patient to do things such as harm self or others?*
Visual Hallucinations Do you see things that other people do not see?	Common causes of visual hallucinations include side effects from medications, alcohol withdrawal, and *Parkinson's disease.*
Other Hallucinations If there is a history of hallucinations or assessment indicates otherwise, continue to ask questions about other types of hallucinations such as olfactory and tactile.	Some patients with *psychotic disorders* smell smoke or feel someone touching them.
Do you smell things that other people do not smell?	*Brain tumours,* toxins, and hallucinogens are common causes of olfactory hallucinations.
Do you have any unusual sensations on your skin such as bugs crawling?	Hallucinogen and methamphetamine use is associated with tactile hallucinations.

Documentation of Expected Findings

Reports no suicidal or homicidal thoughts. Mood pleasant; affect appropriate to situation. Denies visual, auditory, olfactory, or tactile hallucinations.

Compare these expected findings with the assessment of Mr. Shytowski, the 75-year-old man at the clinic who has come to have his blood pressure checked.

Documentation: Making some inappropriate comments such as asking personal information. Denies thoughts of harming self or others. Mood is anxious; affect is labile. Hearing mumbling conversations with several people talking. The voices are telling him to run away and they frighten him. He states that he can tell the difference between what the voices are saying and what is real. He knows that running away would not be good and that he needs to be here to get better. Talking to others usually makes the voices go away. Reports no visual, olfactory, or tactile hallucinations.

Additional Questions	Rationale/Unexpected Findings

Women who are Pregnant

Are you feeling blue? Risk factors include prior psychopathology, poor marital relationship, lack of social support, and stressful life events in the past 12 months (O'Hara & Swain, 1996).

Pregnancy is associated with relapse in psychotic disorders, and women with a history of depression are at highest risk for an episode during pregnancy or postpartum (Cohen, Altshuler, et al., 2006). Women who are pregnant experience hormonal changes and also may need to stop psychiatric medications because of side effects in the fetus.

Have you used alcohol during this pregnancy? Have you used other drugs during this pregnancy?

Substance abuse during pregnancy is a concern for the mother and the fetus.

Children and Adolescents

How are you adjusting to the changes in your body?

Adolescence may be difficult because of hormonal changes as well as growth and developmental stage. The onset of menarche and puberty can contribute to *depression*.

Have you ever thought of harming yourself?

△ SAFETY ALERT 10-6

Previous history of suicide attempt is an indicator for future possible suicide completion.

Suicide is rare in children under 10 years of age but this may be an underestimation. By grade 3, children "have a comprehensive understanding of suicide, and younger children understand what is means to kill themselves" (Mishara, 1999, p. 947). For children ages 10 to14 years, 35 (10.5% of all deaths in that age group) died from suicide (Statistics Canada, 2008).

Do you feel like you "belong" or are part of your school? How are you getting along with your friends?

Social stress and isolation can contribute to *depression* leading to suicide.

Are there firearms in your home? Other weapons? Prescription drugs?

The chances of risky behaviour leading to accidental death is increased in adolescents.

△ SAFETY ALERT 10-7

Be aware of firearms in the home.

Have you used alcohol? Or other drugs? Do any of your friends use alcohol? Or other drugs?

Adolescents may experiment with substance use, causing impaired judgment.

Older Adults

Have you felt sad lately? Risk factors to assess include the following:
- Female gender
- African Canadian or Latino background
- Social isolation
- Widowed, divorced, or separated marital status
- Lower socioeconomic status
- Comorbid medical conditions
- Uncontrolled pain
- Insomnia
- Functional impairment
- Cognitive impairment (Hirsch, Duberstein, et al., 2009)

Females are at higher overall risk for *depression*. Older men and older African Canadian and Latino adults are at higher risk for unrecognized *depression*. Assess for poor cognitive performance, sleep issues, and lack of initiative (Craven & Hirnle, 2009). Older adults may also have physical health changes or end-of-life issues (Randall, Espinoza, et al., 2008). People who lose interest in work or hobbies, sleep too much, or live alone may be at risk for social isolation. Those experiencing financial pressure may have increased stress and potential depression.

"Of all suicides in Canada in 2001, 11.8% were by people older than 65 years of age" (Murray, 2010, p. 948). Although older adults have a higher rate of completing suicide, they have the lowest rate of suicide except for children 5–14 years. However, elderly widowed men are at the highest risk for suicide (Tondo & Baldessarini, 2001).

Use the Geriatric Depression Scale to assess for the risk of depression in older adults (Box 10-5).

The more "yes" answers the patient gives, the more depression is likely.

To family: have you noticed any memory lapses or confusion?

Delirium, dementia, and depression are more common in older adults (Wasynski, 2007).

Box 10-5 GERIATRIC DEPRESSION SCALE: SHORT FORM

Choose the best answer for how you have felt over the past week:

1. Are you basically satisfied with your life? YES/**NO**
2. Have you dropped many of your activities and interests? **YES**/NO
3. Do you feel that your life is empty? **YES**/NO
4. Do you often get bored? **YES**/NO
5. Are you in good spirits most of the time? YES/**NO**
6. Are you afraid that something bad is going to happen to you? **YES**/NO
7. Do you feel happy most of the time? YES/**NO**
8. Do you often feel helpless? **YES**/NO
9. Do you prefer to stay at home, rather than going out and doing new things? **YES**/NO

10. Do you feel you have more problems with memory than most? **YES**/NO
11. Do you think it is wonderful to be alive now? YES/**NO**
12. Do you feel pretty worthless the way you are now? **YES**/NO
13. Do you feel full of energy? YES/**NO**
14. Do you feel that your situation is hopeless? **YES**/NO
15. Do you think that most people are better off than you are? **YES**/NO

Answers in **bold** indicate depression. Score 1 point for each bold-faced answer.

A score >5 points is suggestive of depression. A score >10 points is almost always indicative of depression. A score >5 points should warrant a follow-up comprehensive assessment.

Adapted from Yesavage, J. A., Brink, T. L., et al. (1982). Development and validation of a geriatric depression screening scale: A preliminary report. *Journal of Psychiatric Research, 17,* 37–49.

 Cultural Considerations

Using an Interpreter for the Patient With a Mental Health Condition

When using an interpreter, the nurse greets him or her first without the patient being present. If an interpreter has not been trained to work with psychiatric patients, the nurse will need to address a few preliminary points. First is confidentiality. The interpreter cannot discuss any part of the communication with anyone other than the health care professionals working with the patient. Even if the interpreter translated for that patient at another time, the interpreter cannot share information about how the patient is currently doing with primary providers or nursing staff members who previously cared for the patient.

Also, the interpreter can tell no one that the patient has some mental health issues. This can be a very difficult concept for patients from very community-oriented cultures in which people band together to assist one another in times of need. If the interpreter has interpreted for other family members or friends in the community, he or she should not divulge that information to the patient. The interpreter may think such disclosure is a way of connecting and establishing rapport, when in reality it could cause the patient to feel uncomfortable or worry that the interpreter will share information with others. Be aware if the interpreter seems to not be providing

Additional Questions	Rationale/Unexpected Findings
With what cultural or genetic background group do you identify?	Patients from different groups tend to selectively express or present symptoms in culturally acceptable ways. For example, Asian patients may be more likely to report physical (eg, dizziness) but not emotional symptoms (USDHHS, 2009). Attitudes and beliefs that a culture holds influence whether the patient considers an illness "real" or "imagined" and if it is of the body or mind (or both). Cultural meanings of illness have real implications for whether people are motivated to seek treatment, how they cope with symptoms, how supportive families and communities are, and where they seek help (mental health specialist, primary care provider, clergy, and/or traditional healer).
Do you have an inherited family pattern of mental concerns?	The prevalence of *bipolar disorder and panic disorder* is higher in parts of Asia, Europe, and North America (USDHHS, 2009). Poverty, violence, and other stressful social environments increase risks for *depression*.
Are you concerned about seeking health care because of issues related to your living situation? Have you experienced traumatic situations in your life?	Traumatic experiences are common for combat veterans, inner-city residents, and immigrants from countries at war, placing them at risk for posttraumatic stress disorder.

The nurse's role relative to subjective data collection is to gather information to improve the patient's health status and to help determine the cause of the patient's current symptoms. Remember Mr. Shytowski, introduced at the beginning of this chapter. This 75-year-old man has come to the health care walk-in clinic to have his blood pressure checked on several occasions. He is currently taking a prescription antidepressant.

The nurse uses professional communication techniques to gather subjective data from Mr. Shytowski. It is important to assess for suicidal ideations. The following conversation provides an example of a therapeutic dialogue.

Nurse: Hi, Mr. Shytowski (pauses and smiles).

Mr. Shytowski: You're cute. Are you married?

Nurse: I'm sorry but the hospital policy is not to disclose personal information. I would like to talk to you today.

Mr. Shytowski: Where do you live?

Nurse: I'm sorry but I can't tell you that. How is that book that you're reading?

Mr. Shytowski: It's good. I like to read novels that have some mystery in them.

Nurse: (nods head and smiles) Reading is a good way to relax.

Mr. Shytowski: I don't have much time for relaxing. They keep us all busy with therapy and groups. I wish that I could rest more.

Nurse: You're here so that you can be safe. Do you have any thoughts of wanting to harm or kill yourself?

Mr. Shytowski: No. I did when I came here but not now.

Critical Thinking Challenge

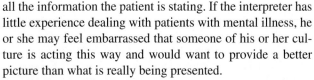

- Did any elements in the conversation make you feel uncomfortable?
- How can the nurse provide an environment so that Mr. Shytowski will feel comfortable and safe talking about feelings?
- What are some other ways that the nurse can ask either directly or indirectly about suicidal ideation?

all the information the patient is stating. If the interpreter has little experience dealing with patients with mental illness, he or she may feel embarrassed that someone of his or her culture is acting this way and would want to provide a better picture than what is really being presented.

After the interview, walk out of sight of the patient and, in a private area, ask the interpreter about the communication style and context. Did the patient make sense? Were sentences structured properly and completely? Did the patient have difficulty expressing himself or herself? Was the patient oriented to reality? Are there any cultural practices or beliefs to be aware of? Be sure to include the interpreter's name in the nursing documentation of the interview.

Objective Data Collection

The nurse obtains objective data by observing the patient and the patient's behaviour, which includes not only how the patient communicates and responds to questions but also physical presentation. The patient's physical presentation may be the first indication of toxicity, an underlying medical issue, or psychosis. Collecting objective data is an ongoing process throughout the time the nurse spends with the patient. Data for the objective assessment are usually organized by **A** (appearance), **B** (behaviour), **C** (cognitive function), and **T** (thought process), plus the MMSE.

Technique and Expected Findings	Unexpected Findings

A: Appearance

Overall Appearance
Observe the overall physical appearance including noticeable physical deformities, weight, and asymmetrical movements. *The patient appears stated age, is appropriate weight, and shows symmetrical movements without obvious deformity.*

There may be evidence of cutting or self-harm. Physical concerns such as stroke or dementia may exacerbate some mental health conditions. Cradle cap around the face of adults indicates long-term lack of care and is often seen in patients with schizophrenia.

Posture
Assess the posture. *Posture is erect but relaxed.*

Unexpected postures are rigid (indicates *anxiety*) or slouching (indicates *withdrawal*). A rigid posture might indicate that the patient is trying to hide, either from a real person or from his or her thoughts.

Movement
Assess baseline and additional movements. Observe their pace, range, and character. *Movements are voluntary, deliberate, coordinated, smooth, and even.*

Immobility (or tremor) might indicate *Parkinson's disease* or *schizophrenia.* The patient may walk a lot to distract from "voices." He or she may feel the need to keep physically occupied to avoid having to deal with emotional thoughts. The patient might have a tic or tardive dyskinesia.

Assess the gait for steadiness and rhythm. *Gait is steady and even.*

Unexpected gaits include limping, fast or slow speed, pacing, shuffling, and stiff. The gait is altered in some patients who take antipsychotic medications. Arm movements are lost with some gait deviations and in patients who have taken antipsychotic medications.

Observe the activity level. Is it under voluntary control? Do posture and motor activity change with topics under discussion or with activities or people around the patient? *Activity is moderately paced and relaxed.*

The activity level may be altered from *hypomania* or *ADHD,* side effects of medications, or internal *anxiety.* Activity may be hypoactive, hyperactive, rigid, restless, agitated, gesturing, posturing, with inappropriate mannerisms, hostile or combative, or unusual. See Table 10-5 at the end of the chapter.

Hygiene and Grooming
Note hair, nails, teeth, skin, and, if present, beard. Observe hygiene and grooming, including body odour and hair. If the patient is unwashed or unkempt, estimate for how long. Note a change in appearance in a previously well-groomed patient. Compare one side of the body with the other. *Patient is well groomed and has no unusual body odours.*

Poor hygiene may be from *paranoia* of water, homelessness, severe *depression,* or incapacitation as a result of mental illness. Risk of lice increases with poor grooming. Excessive fastidiousness may accompany *obsessive–compulsive disorder* (OCD). One-sided neglect may result from *stroke,* brain trauma, or physical injury. An unkempt state might indicate *depression* or *psychosis.*

Observe for makeup and how it is worn. *Makeup is appropriate to age, gender, culture, and social situation.*

Garish makeup with bold colours and outside the lines may indicate *mania.* Inappropriate makeup may also indicate a decline in mental status.

Observe the hands for colouration, cleanliness, tremors, pill rolling, or clubbing of the nail bed. Look for any signs of itching or scratching.

Hands may provide indicators of health issues, smoking status, drug withdrawal, low blood glucose level, or side effects of medications. Clubbing is seen in patients with emphysema or patients who use recreational drugs with talc in them; poor oxygenation affects cognition. Itching or scratching may be related to hallucinations, crystal methamphetamine use, or self-harm.

Dress
Observe how the patient is dressed. Is clothing clean, pressed, and fastened properly? How does it compare with clothing worn by people of comparable age and social group?

Clothing style and colour may indicate an identified social group (eg, gangs, Goth).

(text continues on page 220)

Is clothing worn correctly such as right side out, not backward, shirt buttoned in alignment? How many layers is the patient wearing? *Clothing is clean and appropriate for culture and weather.*

B: Behaviour
Level of Consciousness
Is the patient awake and alert? To assess if the patient is arousable, gently shake the bed or chair that the patient is in; do not directly shake the patient.

- Note if the patient is aware of surroundings and environmental situations.
- Is the patient aware of self?
- Does the patient respond appropriately to stimuli? *The patient is awake and alert, responding appropriately to voice cues.*

⚠ *SAFETY ALERT 10-8*
The patient's ability to correctly interpret the environmental cues and respond accordingly addresses safety.

Eye Contact and Facial Expressions
Assess eye contact. *The patient converses with eyes open and maintains eye contact.*

Observe facial expressions at rest and when the patient is interacting with others. Watch for variations in facial expression with topics under discussion. Are they congruent? Is the face relatively immobile throughout? *The patient is calm, alert, and expressive. Facial expressions are congruent with subjects.*

Speech
Assess speech for

- Rate. *The rate is moderately paced.*

- Rhythm. *The rhythm has appropriate fluctuations.*

- Loudness. *Speech is audible with moderate loudness.*

- Fluency. *Speech is fluent.*

- Quantity. Does the patient respond only to direct questions? Assess for voluminous speech, poverty of speech, talkativeness, silence, or spontaneity. *There is usually a flow of conversation with pauses.*

Unfastened or incorrectly worn clothes might indicate physical difficulty, cognitive deficits, or altered mental status. Clothing may be slovenly, unkempt, overly meticulous, disheveled, inappropriate, provocative, unusual, inappropriate for weather, or with multiple layers. The patient wearing five shirts and three pairs of pants at once may be cold, homeless (and wearing so many clothes because there is nowhere to store them), or irrational.

Unexpected findings include drowsy, hyperalert, somnolent, intermittent alertness, or stupor. If the patient is not arousable, assess for breathing, stupor, or psychosis. This addresses the patient's ability to remain safe.

Unexpected findings are a lack of awareness of own physical needs and emotional responses. Refer to Chapter 24 for more information on neurological assessment and the Glasgow coma scale.

Unexpected findings are eyes closed, avoiding eye contact, staring, looking vacantly ahead, or twitching to side when discussing a traumatic event. The patient who looks away may be responding to voices or is easily distracted by the environment. Poor eye contact may indicate low self-esteem, shame, embarrassment, *depression,* or a cultural trait.

Facial expressions indicate the emotional state. Unexpected expressions are perplexed, stressed, tense, dazed, grimacing, and lacking in expression. Facial expressions may give clues to *depression, anxiety,* hallucinations, physical injury, *mania,* side effects of medications, or possible symptoms from medial and lateral nerve track alterations.

Slow, fast, latent, pressured, monotone, or disturbed rates are unexpected. Determine if causes are anxiety, depression, or auditory hallucinations.

Rhyming, slurring, mumbling, or unusual rhythm is unexpected. Determine if the cause is a hearing issue, anger or agitation, or *mania.*

Note if barely audible or too loud. Determine if the cause is a hearing issue, auditory hallucination, or speech alteration.

Note any lengthy pauses, hesitancy, or stuttering (specify the frequency). Determine if these are from difficulty speaking (aphasia) or hallucinations.

Too much speech may be covering feelings of discomfort, embarrassment, not knowing answers, or avoiding questions. Too much or too little speech may indicate auditory hallucinations. Too little speech may indicate poverty of thought or developmental delay.

- **Articulation.** *Speech is articulate with words clear and distinct.*

- **Content.** *Content is organized and congruent with behaviour or nonverbal communication.*

- **Pattern.** *There is a pattern of exchange in conversation*

Note difficulty expressing self or finding words. See also Chapter 24.

Disorganized, nonsensical, judgmental, religiously preoccupied, or sexually preoccupied speech may indicate impaired judgment and illogical thinking.

Note if the patient uses fragmented sentences, circuitous speech (talks in circles and cannot answer questions), confabulation (makes up answers to cover for loss of memory), or intellectualization (uses intellectual analysis to avoid dealing with emotions). Frequent or inappropriate laughter may indicate hallucinations or disordered perception. See also Table 10-6 at the end of this chapter.

C: Cognitive Function

Orientation

Assess orientation through the following questions.

- Tell me what day of the week it is now? Month? And year? (time)
- Where are you right now? (place)
- What is your name (first and surname)? (name)
- Why are you here right now? (aware of current situation)

The patient is alert and oriented, which is commonly written as A&O × 3—alert and oriented times 3. It is also written as A&O × 4 indicating the additional information that the patient is aware of current situation (eg, why hospitalized).

Note any inconsistencies regarding orientation.

Determine if the patient is new to the area and might not know the place. If a woman provides her maiden versus her married surname when questioned, determine if she retained her maiden surname or is confused. A confused patient will lose time first, then place, and lastly name. As confusion clears, the patient will regain knowledge in the reverse order (name, place, and time). If the patient is aware of person and time but not place (out of appropriate sequencing order), it is indicative of an organic process for the confusion. Refer to Chapter 24 for more information.

Attention Span

Can the patient follow the conversation? Is the patient easily distractible? *The patient can follow conversation and events.*

Attention span indicates the current level of cognitive functioning. Note if altered attention span is from restlessness, poor focus, ADHD, or hallucinations.

Memory

Assess memory using the MMSE or Mini-Cog (Box 10-6).

- Does the patient have short-term memory?
- Does the patient have long-term memory?

Short- and long-term memories are intact.

Short- and long-term memories indicate the current level of cognitive functioning. Altered memory may be from *dementia, Alzheimer's disease,* or other processes. Refer to Chapter 24 for more information on the assessment of memory.

Judgment

Assess judgment by noting the patient's responses to family situations, employment, interpersonal conflict, and use of money. Ask direct questions such as

- How will you get home if you have no money?

Assess the patient's ability to solve problems.

- What will you do if you feel the urge to use alcohol again (in patients with alcoholism)? (They might respond with answers such as seek help, call my AA sponsor, or talk myself out of it.)

Assess the patient's ability to choose among alternatives based on reality.

- What will happen if you hit someone you love? A neighbour? Or someone else?

Assess the patient's ability to understand the consequences of behaviour and take responsibility for actions.

- What is your part in this conflict? Or how might you have contributed to this situation?

Note if the patient lacks insight, judgment, or impulse control and what these findings might indicate.

The patient makes appropriate judgments and takes responsibility for own actions.

(text continues on page 222)

Box 10-6 THE MINI-COG

Administration

The test is administered as follows:

1. Instruct the patient to listen carefully to and remember three unrelated words and then to repeat the words.

2. Instruct the patient to draw the face of a clock, either on a blank sheet of paper or on a sheet with the clock circle already drawn on the page. After the patient puts the numbers on the clock face, ask him or her to draw the hands of the clock to read a specific time.

3. Ask the patient to repeat the three previously stated words.

Scoring

Give 1 point for each recalled word after the clock-drawing test (CDT) distractor.

Patients recalling none of the three words are classified as demented (Score = 0).

Patients recalling all three words are classified as nondemented (Score = 3).

Patients with intermediate word recall of 1–2 words are classified based on the CDT (Unexpected = demented; Expected = nondemented)

Note: The CDT is considered expected if all numbers are present in the correct sequence and position, and the hands readably display the requested time. Adapted from Borson, S., Scanlan, J., et al. (2000). The Mini-Cog: A cognitive 'vital signs' measure for dementia screening in multi-lingual elderly. *International Journal of Geriatric Psychiatry, 15*(11), 1021–1027. Copyright John Wiley & Sons Limited. Reproduced with permission.

Technique and Expected Findings (continued)	Unexpected Findings (continued)
T: Thought Processes and Perceptions Assess thought processes. *Thought processes are easy to follow, logical, coherent, relevant, goal directed, consistent, and abstract.*	Illogical, incoherent, irrelevant, wandering, inconsistent, or concrete thought processes are unexpected indications that the patient is thinking less efficiently. Refer to Table 10-7 at the end of the chapter.
Mini-Mental Status/Mini-Cog Assess cognitive function by using the MMSE or Mini-Cog (Box 10-6). The self-explanatory MMSE has 11 questions about time and place orientation, serial 7s (subtract 7 from 100 and continue to subtract 7 from each subsequent remainder), naming objects (eg, pencil), repeating phrases (eg, "No ifs, ands, or buts"), following a 3-step direction, reading and responding, writing a sentence, and drawing intersecting pentagons (Folstein, Folstein, et al., 1975). It takes 10 to 15 minutes to administer. The Mini-Cog takes about 3 minutes to administer and is perceived as less stressful. It includes recall and the clock drawing test. Registration is the ability to immediately state three words; recall is the ability to state them 3 minutes later. Recall is tested in both.	The MMSE and Mini-Cog are both scored tests. A score of 23 or lower on the MMSE indicates cognitive impairment (Folstein, Folstein, et al., 1975). For more information on this copyrighted tool, contact Psychological Assessment Resources, Inc., 16204 North Florida Avenue, Lutz, Florida 33549. Unsuccessful recall of three items or an unusual clock drawing test indicates dementia on the Mini-Cog.
Set Test Set Test is designed to test for dementia in patients 65 years and older. Do not use if patient has hearing loss or aphasia. Ask the patient to name 10 items in each of four categories: fruits, animals, colours, and towns/cities. Score each correct answer as 1 point for a total possible score of 40. There is no time limit. *Patient was easily able to name 10 fruits, 10 animals, 9 colours, and 10 towns/cities for a score of 39/40.*	The Set Test requires the patient to categorize, name, remember, and count items. The examiner is "assessing the patient's alertness, motivation, concentration, short-term memory, and problem-solving ability." (Jarvis, 2004, p. 114). Responses such as "*apples...oranges,*" and then the patient's voice trails off or "*apples, oranges...Oh I could tell you lots more if I wanted to!*" indicate the patient is struggling with the test. A score of 24 or less suggests dementia.

Documentation of Expected Findings

Appears stated age and expected weight, no obvious deformity. Posture is erect and relaxed. Movements are symmetrical, voluntary, deliberate, coordinated, smooth, and even. Gait is steady and even. Activity is moderate and relaxed. Patient is groomed with no unusual body odours. Makeup is appropriate to culture and social situation. Clothing is clean and appropriate for gender, age, culture, and weather. Patient is awake, alert, calm, and expressive, responding appropriately to voice cues. Patient converses with eyes open and maintains eye contact. Facial expressions are congruent with subjects. Speech is of moderate pace and volume, fluent with expected fluctuations, and articulate with clear and distinct words. Speech is organized and congruent with behaviour and nonverbal communication. A&O × 3. Patient follows conversation and events; attention span is appropriate. Short- and long-term memory intact. MMSE completed with no deficits. Score on Set Test is 39/40. Patient makes appropriate judgments and takes responsibility for actions. Thought processes are easy to follow, logical, coherent, relevant, goal directed, consistent, and abstract.

Assessment of Dementia, Confusion, Delirium, and Depression

Dementia is more common in older adults. It is usually a gradual process over months to years. Delirium generally has an underlying health issue that, once treated, results in the delirium resolving.

Some cues that the patient may have dementia include the following:

- Seems disoriented
- Is a "poor historian"
- Defers to a family member to answer questions directed to the patient
- Repeatedly and apparently unintentionally fails to follow instructions
- Has difficulty finding the right words or uses inappropriate or incomprehensible words
- Has difficulty following conversations (Waszynski, 2007)
- Scores 23/40 on the Set Test

Delirium, dementia, and depression can also be acute situations. Delirium usually has an acute onset, and the disorganized thoughts can place the patient at risk for injury. The risk of suicide increases with depression. Refer to Table 10-2 for a comparison of findings.

Evidence-Informed Critical Thinking

Nursing Diagnoses

When formulating nursing diagnoses, it is important to use critical thinking to cluster data and identify patterns that fit together. Table 10-3 compares and contrasts nursing diagnoses, unexpected findings, and interventions commonly related to mental health assessment (Bulechek, Butcher, et al., 2008). Note that altered thought processes and sensory perceptions are also related to the neurological system (see Chapter 24). Some coping behaviours are also relevant to other body systems and how patients cope with the effects of physical concerns.

Patient Outcomes

Nurses use assessment information to identify patient outcomes. Some outcomes related to mental health issues include the following:

- The patient does not harm self.
- The patient demonstrates appropriate social interactions.
- The patient identifies personal strengths (Bulechek, Butcher, et al., 2008).

Table 10-2	Comparison of Delirium, Dementia, and Depression		
	Delirium	**Dementia**	**Depression**
Onset	Acute over a few hours, lasting hours to weeks. Occurs in the context of physical illness, substance abuse or withdrawal	Slow, lasting months to years	Slow
Description	Impaired recent and remote memory	Impaired remote memory	Impaired memory
	Fluctuating attention	Attention preserved	Attention intact
	Thoughts disorganized	Thoughts impoverished	Impaired concentration
	Change in cognition	Global impairment of intellect	If psychosis is present, it is usually systematized and with expected emotional response
	Clouding of consciousness	Alert	
	Perceptual disturbances—usually disorganized	Aware	Perceptual disturbances
	Does not usually present with mood components		Sad affect or mood

Sources: Sadock, B. J., Sadock; V. A., et al. (2004). *Kaplan & Sadock's comprehensive textbook of psychiatry* (8th ed.). Philadelphia, PA: Lippincott Williams & Wilkins; Edwards, N. (2003). Differentiating the three D's: Delirium, Dementia, and Depression. *MEDSURG Nursing, 12*, 347–358.

Table 10-3 Common Nursing Diagnoses Associated with Mental Health

Diagnosis and Related Factors	Point of Differentiation	Assessment Characteristics	Nursing Interventions
Risk for suicide	At risk for potentially fatal, purposefully self-inflicted injury	States desire to die; hopelessness, impulsiveness, loneliness	Establish a relationship. Assess for suicide risk. Refer for counselling. Remove lethal medications and weapons from the environment.
Risk for self-mutilation	At risk for deliberately injuring self to relieve stress and tension, but not to end his or her life	Cuts or scratches on body, picking at wounds, self-inflicted burns, insertion of objects into body orifices	Establish trust. Provide medical treatment for injuries.* Assess for depression, anxiety, impulsivity, and suicide. Secure a contract to notify staff when experiencing a desire to mutilate.
Altered thought processes	Alterations or disruption in cognition, thinking, and associated activities	Perceiving or interpreting surroundings incorrectly, nonreality-based thinking	Reorient as needed. Use concrete, nontechnical words and short phrases. Assess for hallucinations. Convey that you would like to understand what the patient is trying to say, but make sure that the patient does not follow through on harmful processes.
Sensory-perceptual alterations	Disturbances in and inappropriate responses to incoming stimuli	Poor concentration, auditory or visual hallucinations, irritability, agitation, change in behaviour	Validate that the patient is the only person hearing or seeing the hallucination. Provide a safe environment. Encourage expression of responses to hallucinations. Encourage the use of alternate coping strategies, such as singing or wearing headphones.
Ineffective individual coping	Impairments in the way appraises, responds to, or uses resources to deal with stressors	Substance abuse, ignoring issues, lack of concentration, sleep disturbances	Assess for causes. Build on the patient's strengths. Set realistic goals. Listen and avoid false reassurance.
Self-esteem disturbance	Negative self-evaluation; long-term view of self or self-capabilities that is focused on negative aspects	Does not believe or trust positive feedback from other people, exaggerates or fixates on negative feedback, displays shame or guilt	Listen to and respect the patient. Assess strengths and coping abilities. Reframe difficulties as learning opportunities.
Impaired social interaction	Engagement with others that is insufficient in frequency, lacking in quality, or both	Feeling ill at ease during social situations; interactions with peers, family, or others that are limited or result in negative consequences (eg, arguments, poor communication)	Assess the social support system. List behaviours associated with being disconnected and alternative responses. Role play social interactions and appropriate responses.

*Collaborative interventions.

Nursing Diagnosis, Outcomes, and Interventions

Once outcomes are established, the nurse implements care to improve the patient's status. The nurse uses critical thinking and evidence-informed practice to develop interventions. Some examples of nursing interventions for mental health challenges are as follows:

- Assess for risk of harm to self or others.
- Provide a safe environment by removing items that might cause harm.
- Identify support systems and involve them in care (Bulechek, Butcher, et al., 2008).

Analyzing Findings

Remember Mr. Shytowski, whose concerns have been outlined throughout this chapter. Initial subjective and objective data collection is complete, and the nurse has spent time reviewing findings and other results. The following nursing note illustrates how subjective and objective data are collected and analyzed and nursing interventions are developed.

Subjective: "I'm scared when the voices tell me to run away. I know that I should stay here to stay safe."

Objective: A&O × 3. Some inappropriate comments, such as asking personal information. Denies thoughts of harming self or others. Hearing mumbling conversations with several people talking. He states that he can tell the difference between what the voices are saying and what is real. Talking to others usually makes the voices go away. Denies visual, olfactory, and tactile hallucinations. Somewhat distracted during initial conversation but attends more as conversation progresses.

Analysis: Altered auditory sensory perception. Risk for suicide.

Plan: Continue involuntary treatment hold. Monitor for effectiveness and side effects of medications. Encourage participation in both individual and group therapies. Assess for suicide and hallucinations every shift and as needed. Avoid asking questions about the past and focus on teaching skills to remain safe. Allow time to build a trusting relationship. Assist with problem solving. Avoid disclosing personal information.

Critical Thinking Challenge

- What will the nurse observe during the assessment of Mr. Shytowski?
- What other assessments might be indicated?
- What other nursing diagnoses might be considered?

Applying Your Knowledge

Using the previous steps of the nursing process, consider all of the case study findings woven throughout this chapter. When answering the following questions, begin drawing conclusions and see how the pieces of assessment must work together to create an environment for personalized, appropriate, and accurate care.

- List three techniques of mental health assessment the nurse could use to gain Mr. Shytowski's trust? (Knowledge)
- How are the mental status assessment and mental health history integrated? (Comprehension)
- How will the nurse assess for suicidal ideation, homicidal ideation, and hallucinations? (Application)
- What developmental, behavioural, and life choices may contribute to Mr. Shytowsi's symptoms? (Analysis)
- What recommendations for followup would the nurse suggest for Mr. Shytowski? (Synthesis)
- How would the nurse evaluate the effectiveness of teaching for Mr. Shytowski? (Evaluation)

Key Points

- During a mental health assessment, the nurse assesses the patient and family history, including gender, age, genetic background, current health status, history of mental health concerns, functional status, weight gain or loss, sleeping difficulties, and medications.
- Risk factors for mental health conditions include abuse, family history, poor support network, stressors, substance abuse, and loss of hope.
- The nurse assesses for alcohol or substance abuse using the CAGE tool.
- The nurse assesses spirituality and sense of meaning using the HOPE tool.
- Suicidal ideation is assessed by asking, "Do you have any thoughts of wanting to harm or kill yourself?"
- Homicidal ideation is assessed by asking, "Do you have any thoughts of wanting to harm or kill anyone?"
- Altered moods include sad, tearful, depressed, angry, anxious, grandiose, and fearful.
- Altered sensory perceptions include auditory, visual, tactile, and olfactory hallucinations.
- Depression may be assessed using the SAD PERSONAS scale.
- Assessment of mental status includes **A**ppearance (posture, movement, hygiene, and dress), **B**ehaviour (level of consciousness, eye contact, facial expressions, speech), **C**ognitive function (orientation, attention span, memory, judgment), and **T**hought processes.
- The MMSE tool measures cognitive function and includes orientation, registration, attention and calculation, recall, and language to determine mental status.
- Common nursing diagnoses include risk for suicide, risk for self-mutilation, altered thought processes, sensory-perceptual alterations, ineffective individual coping, self-esteem disturbance, and impaired social interaction.

Review Questions

1. A nurse is working with a new patient. To establish rapport, the nurse would use which of the following statements?
   A. "These are questions that I ask all my patients."
   B. "Don't worry because we are working with crazy patients."
   C. "We're here because we want to help psych people."
   D. "These questions are silly, but I have to ask them."

2. The patient's family should not be present during the interview with the patient requiring a translator because
   A. the patient may feel uncomfortable speaking openly with a relative present, especially if that person is contributing to the patient's stress
   B. the translator may not ask questions related to the family member and could be perceived as insensitive or inappropriate

   C. the family member may be ashamed or embarrassed by the patient's actions or statements and try to withhold or change the facts
   D. all of the above

3. "Do you have any thoughts of wanting to kill or harm yourself?" is a common question to assess for suicidal ideation because it
   A. is blunt and patients cannot refuse to answer
   B. will cover both suicidal and parasuicidal thoughts
   C. is subtle and patients will not know how to answer
   D. will encourage patients who perform self-harm to stop cutting

4. When charting general appearance and behaviour, documentation may include
   A. alert and oriented × 3
   B. thought logical
   C. judgment intact
   D. clothes disheveled

5. Unexpected movements resulting from medications might be described as
   A. voluntary
   B. deliberate
   C. uncoordinated
   D. smooth and even

6. 'Speech is audible' is an expected finding describing which quality of speech?
   A. Fluency
   B. Quality
   C. Loudness
   D. Articulation

7. A 90-year-old patient has a drooped body position, appears sad, and says that she has seasonal affective disorder. What tool would the nurse use to assess her?
   A. Mini Mental Status Examination (MMSE)
   B. CAGE
   C. HOPE Assessment of Spiritual Beliefs
   D. Geriatric Depression Scale

8. Which of the following represents the nurse's documentation of the patient with expected mood?
   A. Pleasant or appropriate to situation
   B. Grandiose or strongly confident
   C. Fearful but mildly humble and meek
   D. Sad and tearful during conversation

9. Patients may laugh spontaneously, provide inappropriate responses, ask the nurse personal questions, or insult the nurse. These are examples of
   A. perseveration
   B. auditory hallucinations
   C. divergent tactics
   D. altered mood

10. The Mini Mental Status Examination (MMSE) is used to assess for severity in orientation, registration, attention and calculation, recall, and language. For which of the following patients would the MMSE be most appropriate?
A. Women during the postpartum period
B. Adolescents struggling with sexual orientation
C. Various cultural groups not tested by other tools
D. Adults to assess for cognitive impairment and the severity

Canadian Nursing Research

Austin, W., Goble, E., et al. (2009). Compassion fatigue: The experience of nurses. *Ethics & Social Welfare, 3*(2), 195–214.

Forbes, D. A., & Neufeld, A. (2008). Looming dementia care crisis: Canada needs an integrated model of continuing care now! *Canadian Journal of Nursing Research, 40*(1), 9–16.

Forbes, D. A., Markle-Read, M., et al. (2009). Formal care providers' perceptions of home – and community-based services: Informing demential care quality. *Home Health Care Services Quarterly, 28,* 1–23.

Lasiuk, G. C., & Hegadorn, K. (2006a). Posttraumatic stress disorder. Part 1: Historical development of the concept. *Perspectives in Psychiatric Care, 42*(1), 13–20.

Lasiuk, G. C., & Hegadorn, K. (2006b). Posttraumatic stress disorder. Part 2: Development of the construct within the North American Psychiatric Taxonomy. *Perspectives in Psychiatric Care, 42*(2), 72–81.

References

Alzheimer Society of Canada. (2009). *Alzheimer's disease and risk factors*. Retrieved from www.alzheimer.ca/english/disease/causes-riskfac.htm

American Psychiatric Association. (2001). *Diagnostic and statistical manual of mental disorders* (4th ed.; text revision). Washington, DC: Author.

Anandarajah, G., & Hight, E. (2001). Spirituality and medical practice: Using the HOPE questions as a practical tool for spiritual assessment. *American Family Physician, 63*(1), 81–89.

Borson, S., Scanlan, J., et al (2000). The Mini-Cog: A cognitive "vital signs" measure for dementia screening in multi-lingual elderly. *International Journal of Geriatric Psychiatry, 15*(11), 1021–1027.

Bulechek, G. M., Butcher, H. K., et al (2008). *Nursing interventions classification (NIC)* (5th ed.). St. Louis, MO: Mosby.

Canadian Federation of Mental Health Nurses. (2006). *Standards of practice: Canadian standards for psychiatric-mental health nursing* (2nd ed.). Retrieved from http://cfmhn.ca/sites/cfmhn.ca/files/CFMHN%20standards%201.pdf

Centers for Disease Control and Prevention & National Center for Injury Prevention and Control. (2008). *WISQARS leading causes of death reports, 1999–2005*. Retrieved from http://webappa.cdc.gov/sasweb/ncipc/leadcaus10.html

Cohen, L. S., Altshuler, L. L., et al. (2006). Relapse of major depression during pregnancy in women who maintain or discontinue antidepressant treatment. *Journal of the American Medical Association, 295*(5), 499.

Craven, R. C., & Hirnle, C. J. (2009). *Fundamentals of nursing: Human health and function* (6th ed.). Philadelphia, PA: Wolters Kluwer Health/Lippincott Williams & Wilkins.

Day, R. A., & Paul, P. (2010). Individual and family considerations related to illness. In R. A. Day, P. Paul, et al. (Eds.). *Brunner & Suddarth's textbook of Canadian medical-surgical nursing.* (2nd ed., pp. 112–126). Philadelphia, PA: Wolters Kluwer Health/Lippincott Williams & Wilkins.

Edwards, N. (2003). Differentiating the three D's: Delirium, Dementia, and Depression. *MEDSURG Nursing, 12,* 347–358.

Ewing, J. A. (1984). Detecting alcoholism: The CAGE questionnaire. *Journal of the American Medical Association, 252*(14), 1905–1907.

Felitti, V. J., Anda, R. F., et al. (1998). Relationship of childhood abuse and household dysfunction to many of the leading causes of death in adults: The adverse childhood experiences (ACE) study. *American Journal of Preventive Medicine, 14*(4), 245–258.

Folstein, M. F., Folstein, S. E., et al (1975). "Minimental state." A practical method for grading the cognitive state of patients for the clinician. *Journal of Psychiatric Research, 12*(3), 189–198.

Forbes, D. A., & Neufeld, A. (2008). Looming dementia care crisis: Canada needs an integrated model of continuing care now! *Canadian Journal of Nursing Research, 40*(1), 9–16.

Friedli, L., & Parsonage, M. (2007). *Mental health promotion: Building an economic case*. Northern Ireland Association for Mental Health. Retrieved from http://www.chex.org.uk/uploads/mhpeconomiccase.pdf?sess_scdc=ee4428ebde41914abac0e0535f55861c

Haase, M. (2010). Delirium, dementias, and other related disorders. In W. Austin, & M. A. Boyd. (Eds.). *Psychiatric & mental health nursing for Canadian practice* (2nd ed., pp. 750–789). Philadelphia, PA: Wolters Kluwer Health/Lippincott Williams & Wilkins.

Hirsch, J. K., Duberstein, P. R., et al (2009). Chronic medical problems and distressful thoughts of suicide in primary care patients: Mitigating role of happiness. *International Journal of Geriatric Psychiatry, 24*(7), 671–679.

Jarvis, C. (2004). *Physical examination and health assessment.* (4th ed., p. 114). St. Louis, MO: Elsevier Science

Juhnke, G. (1994). SAD PERSONS Scale review. *Measurement and Evaluation in Counseling and Development, 27*(1), 325–327.

Kroenke, K., Spitzer, R. L., et al. (2007). Anxiety disorders in primary care: Prevalence, impairment, comorbidity, and detection. *Annals of Internal Medicine, 146*(5), 317–325.

Kunyk, D., & Els, C. (2010). Substance-related disorders. In W. Austin, & M. A. Boyd. (Eds.). *Psychiatric & mental health nursing for Canadian practice.* (2nd ed., pp. 534–575). Philadelphia, PA: Wolters Kluwer Health/Lippincott Williams & Wilkins.

Lasiuk, G. C., (2010). The assessment process. In W. Austin, & M. A. Boyd. (Eds.). *Psychiatric & mental health nursing for Canadian practice* (2nd ed., pp. 173–190). Philadelphia, PA: Wolters Kluwer Health/Lippincott Williams & Wilkins.

Lasiuk, G. C., & Bickley, L. S. (2010). Psychosocial and mental status assessment. In T. C. Stephen, D. L. Skillen, R. A. Day, & L. S. Bickley (Eds.). *Canadian Bates' guide to health assessment for nurses.* (1st ed., pp. 203– 237). Philadelphia, PA: Wolters Kluwer Health/Lippincott Williams & Wilkins.

Lopez, A. D., Mathers, C. D., et al. (2006). Global and regional burden of disease and risk factors, 2001: Systematic analysis of population health data. *The Lancet, 367*(9524), 1747–1757.

MacMillan, H. L., Patterson, C., et al. (2005). Screening for depression in primary care: Recommendation statement from the Canadian Task Force on Preventive Health Care. *Canadian Medical Association Journal, 172*(1), 765–776.

Maj, M. (2009). Physical health care in persons with severe mental illness: A public health and ethical priority. *World Psychiatry, 8*(1), 1–2.

Mental Health Commission of Canada. (2009). *Toward recovery & well-being: A framework for a mental health strategy for Canada.* Retrieved from http://www.mentalhealthcommission.ca/SiteCollectionDocuments/boarddocs/15507_MHCC_EN_final.pdf

Mishara, B. L. (1999). Comceptions of death and suicide in children ages 6–12 and their implications for suicide prevention. *Suicide and Life-Threatening Behaviour, 29,* 105–119.

Moore, G., & Pfaff, J. A. (2008). *Assessment and management of the acutely agitated or violent patient.* Retrieved from http://www.uptodateonline.com.proxy.seattleu.edu/ online/content/topic.do?topicKey=ad_symp/6273&selectedTitle=2~6&source=search_result

Murray, B. L.(2010). Care for self-harm and suicidal behaviour: Children, adolescents, and adults. In W. Austin, & M. A. Boyd (Eds.). *Psychiatric & mental health nursing for Canadian practice.* (2nd ed., pp. 945–970). Philadelphia, PA: Wolters Kluwer Health/Lippincott Williams & Wilkins.

National Scientific Council on the Developing Child. (2007). *The science of early childhood development.* Retrieved from http://developingchild.harvard.edu/index.php/library/reports_and_working_papers/foundations-of-lifelong-health/

Nemeroff, C. B., Compton, M. T., et al. (2001). The depressed suicidal patient: Assessment and treatment. *Annnals of American Academy of Sciences, 932,*1–23.

O'Connell, H., Chin, A., et al. (2004). Recent developments: Suicide in older people. *British Medical Journal, 329,* 895–899.

O'Hara, M. W., & Swain, M. (1996). Rates and risk of postpartum depression: A meta-analysis. *International Review Psychiatry, 8*(1), 37.

Parikh, S. V., & Lam, R. L. (2001). The CANMAT Depression Work Group. Clinical giuidelines for the treatment of depressive disorders. 1. Definitions, prevalence, and health burden. *Canadian Journal of Psychiatry, 46*(Suppl. 1), 13S–20S.

Patterson, W. M., Dohn, H. H., et al. (1983). Evaluation of suicidal patients: The SAD PERSON Scale. *Psychosomatics, 24*(4), 343–349.

Public Health Agency of Canada. (2002). *Suicidal behaviour. In A report on mental illnesses in Canada.* Ottawa, ON: Author. Retrieved from http://www.phac-aspc.gc.ca/publicat/miic-mmac/index-eng.php

Randall, T., Espinoza, R. T., et al. (2008). Diagnosis and management of late-life depression. Retrieved from http://www.uptodateonline.com.proxy.seattleu.edu/online/content/topic.do?topicKey=psychiat/12560&selectedTitle=1~150&source=search_result

Rehm, J., Ballunas, D., et al. (2006). *The costs of substance abuse in Canada.* Ottawa, ON: Canadian Centre for Substance Abuse.

Sadock, B. J., Sadock, V. A.,et al. (2004). *Kaplan & Sadock's comprehensive textbook of psychiatry* (8th ed.). Philadelphia, PA: Lippincott Williams & Wilkins.

Seelig, M. D., & Katon, W. (2008). Gaps in depression care: Why primary care physicians should hone their depression screening, diagnosis, and management skills. *Journal of Occupational and Environmental Medicine, 50*(4), 451–458.

Shea, S. C. (1999). *The practical art of suicide assessment: A guide for mental health professionals and substance abuse counselors.* Hoboken, NJ: John Wiley and Sons, Inc.

Single, E., Robson, L., et al. (1997). *Morbidity and mortality related to alcohol, tobacco, and illicit drug use among indigenous people in Canada.* Ottawa, ON: Canadian Centre on Substance Abuse.

Statistics Canada. (2005). *Chapter XX: External causes of morbidity and mortality (V01-V89), by age group and sex.* Retrieved from http://www.statcan.gc.ca/pub/84-208-x/2002/t/4152749-eng.htm

Statistics Canada. (2006). *Causes of death, 2003.* Ottawa, ON: Author.

Statistics Canada. (2008). *Suicides and suicide rate, by sex and by age group.* Ottawa, ON: Author. Retrieved from htrtp://www40.statcan.gc.ca/101/cst01/perhlth66a-eng.htm

Toft, T., Fink, P., et al. (2005). Mental disorders in primary care: Prevalence and co-morbidity among disorders. Results from the functional illness in primary care (FIP) study. *Psychological Medicine, 35*(8), 1175–1184.

Tondo, L., & Baldessarini, R. J. (2001). *Suicide: Historical, descriptive, and epidemiological considerations.* Retrieved from http://yenoh93.medceu.com/index/courses/suicide.htm

U.S. Department of Health and Human Services. (1999). Mental health: A report of the surgeon general. Rockville, MD: U.S. Department of Health and Human Services, Substance Abuse and Mental Health Services Administration, Center for Mental Health Services, National Institutes of Health, National Institute of Mental Health.

U.S. Department of Health and Human Services. (2009). Culture counts: The influence of culture and society on mental health, mental illness. Retrieved from http://mentalhealth.samhsa.gov/cre/ch2_culture_of_the_patient.asp

Vasiliadis, H. M., Lesage, A., et al. (2007). Do Canada and the United States differ in prevalence of depression and utilization of services, *Psychiatric Services, 58*(1), 63–71.

Waszynski, C. M. (2007). How to try this: Detecting delirium. *American Journal of Nursing, 107*(12), 50–59.

World Health Organization. (2002). *Self directed violence.* Retrieved from http://www.who.int/violence_injury_prevention/violence/world_report/factsheets/en/selfdirectedviolfacts.pdf

World Health Organization. (2007a). *Mental health: Strengthening our response.* Fact Sheet # 220 Retrieved from http://www.who.int/mediacentre/factsheets/fs220/en/

World Health Organization. (2007b). *International statistical classification of diseases and related health problems* (10th Revision). Retrieved from http://apps.who.int/classification/apps/icd/icd10online/

Yesavage, J. A., Brink, T. L., et al. (1982). Development and validation of a geriatric depression screening scale: A preliminary report. *Journal of Psychiatric Research, 17*(1), 37–49.

> *The Canadian Jensen Nursing Health Assessment suite offers these additional resources to enhance learning and facilitate understanding of this chapter:*
>
> • thePoint online resource, http//thepoint.lww.com/Stephen1E
> • *Laboratory Manual for Canadian Jensen's Nursing Health Assessment: A Best Practice Approach*

Tables of Unexpected Findings

Table 10-4 Unexpected Findings: Mood Disorders

Euphoria	Excessive sense of emotional and physical well-being inappropriate to the actual situation or environmental stimuli
Flat affect	No emotional tone or reaction
Blunted affect	Severe reduction in emotional expressiveness (often confused with fiat affect)
Elation	High degree of confidence, boastfulness, uncritical optimism, and joy accompanied by increased motor activity
Exultation	Reaction extending beyond elation and accompanied by feelings of grandeur
Ecstasy	Overpowering feeling of joy and rapture
Anxiety	A feeling of apprehension or worry, especially about the future
Fear	An emotional reaction to an environmental threat
Ambivalence	Having two opposing feelings or emotions at the same time
Depersonalization	Feeling that the self or its environment is unreal
Irritability	Feeling of impatience, annoyance, and easy provocation to anger
Rage	Furious, uncontrolled anger
Lability	Quick change of expression of mood or feelings
Depression	Feeling characterized by sadness, dejection, helplessness, hopelessness, worthlessness, and gloom

Adapted from Department of Health. (2008). *Psychiatry*. Retrieved from http://www.doh.gov.ph/zcmc/index.php?option=com_content&task=view&id=101&Itemid=26

Table 10-5 Unexpected Findings: Motor Movements

Akathisia	Motor restlessness, inability to remain still; can also be a subjective feeling
Akinesia	No movement or difficulty with movement
Dystonia	Muscle spasms, spastic movements of the neck and back, can be painful or frightening
Parkinsonism	Slow, shuffling gait; masklike facial expression; tremors; pill-rolling movements of the hands; stooping posture; rigidity
Tardive dyskinesia	Involuntary and unexpected movements of the mouth, tongue, face, and jaw, may progress to the limbs; irreversible condition; may occur months after antipsychotic medication use
Neuroleptic malignant syndrome	Develops as a potentially lethal side effect of antipsychotic medications, with muscle rigidity, tremors, altered consciousness, and incontinence; first warning signs are usually hyperthermia and hypertension, tachycardia. May be referred to as "lead-pipe" rigidity
Choreiform movements	Irregular, involuntary actions of muscles of face and extremities
Waxy flexibility	Holding body posture that is imposed by another person for a long time
Hyperkinesias	Excessive movement; destructive or aggressive activity
Compulsive	Unwanted repetitive actions
Automatism	Not consciously controlled, automatic, undirected motor activity
Cataplexy	Temporary loss of muscle tone precipitated by strong emotions
Catalepsy	Trancelike state with loss of voluntary motion
Stereotypy	Repetitive imitation of another person's movements
Psychomotor retardation	Decreased, slowed activity
Catatonic stupor	Extreme underactivity
Catatonic excitement	Extreme overactivity
Impulsiveness	Outbursts of unpredictable and sudden activity
Tics and spasms	Involuntary twitching and jerking of muscles, usually above the shoulders

Adapted from Department of Health. (2008). *Psychiatry*. Retrieved from http://www.doh.gov.ph/zcmc/index.php?option=com_content&task=view&id=101&Itemid=26

Table 10-6 Unexpected Findings: Speech Patterns

Verbigeration	Repetitive, meaningless expression of sentences, phrases, or words
Rhyming	Interjecting into conversation regular, recurring, corresponding sounds at the ends of phrases or sentences, as in poetry
Punning	Interjecting clever and humourous uses of a word or words
Mutism	No expression of words or lack of communication over a period of time
Selectively mute	Mostly mute with intermittent periods of verbal expression
Aphasia	Partial or total loss of the ability to express self through language or to understand the verbal communication of another person
Neologisms	Words created by the patient that are either not easily understood by others or unintelligible
Spontaneous	Communication initiated by the patient with others
Circumlocutions	Phrases or sentences substituted for a word that the person cannot think of (eg, "what you write with" for a pen)
Paraphasias	Malformed, wrong, or invented words

Adapted from Department of Health. (2008). *Psychiatry*. Retrieved from http://www.doh.gov.ph/zcmc/index.php?option=com_content &task=view&id=101&Itemid=26

Table 10-7 Unexpected Findings: Thought Processes

Thought blocking	Sudden cessation of flow of thought and speech related to strong emotions
Flight of ideas	Rapid conversation with logically unconnected shifting of topics
Word salad	Disconnected and incoherent combination of phrases, words, and sentences
Perseveration phenomena	Repetitive behaviours such as lip licking, finger tapping, pacing, or echolalia
Circumstantiality	Interjection of great detail and incidental material with no primary significance to the central idea of the conversation
Tangential	Deviation from the central theme of conversation
Echolalia	Repetitive imitation of another person's speech
Delusion	False belief kept despite nonsupportive evidence
Phobia	Strong, persistent, unexpected fear of an object or situation
Obsession	Persistent, unwanted, recurring thoughts
Compulsions	Repetitive mental act or physical behaviour that the patient feels driven to perform to reduce distress, prevent a dreaded event or situation, or respond to an obsession
Hypochondriasis	Morbid concern for one's health and feeling ill without any actual medical basis
Psychosis	Disorderly mental state in which the patient has difficulty distinguishing reality from internal perceptions
Thought broadcasting	Delusion that others can hear one's thoughts
Thought control	Delusion that others can control a person's thoughts against one's will
Thought insertion	Delusion that others have the ability to put thoughts in a person's mind against one's will
Neologisms	Creating and using new words
Loose associations	Changes of conversation in an unrelated, fragmented manner
Incoherent	Not making any sense
Confabulation	Making up answers to cover for not knowing. Demonstrates the ability to think and reason with only short-term memory present. Symptom of Korsakoff syndrome
Ideas of reference	Perception that others or the media are talking to or about the patient
Ruminating	Getting "stuck" on, worrying, or thinking about an idea repetitively

Adapted from Department of Health. (2008). *Psychiatry*. Retrieved from http://www.doh.gov.ph/zcmc/index.php?option=com_content& task=view&id=101&Itemid=26

Assessment of Social, Cultural, and Spiritual Health

Learning Objectives

1 Identify "models of health" and how they relate to social, cultural, and spiritual assessment.

2 Identify the components of social assessment for individuals, communities, and societies.

3 Describe the components of the core community assessment.

4 Identify the components of the McGill Model and the Community as Partner Assessment Model.

5 Describe the elements and use of *cultural safety*.

6 Demonstrate knowledge of the attributes and behaviours of a nurse practising effective care within the nurse–patient cultural context.

7 Define *spirituality* and how it influences patient care in health care settings.

8 Discuss why it is important to be aware of the roles of religions and places of worship in sustaining patient development, national identity, and survival.

9 Discuss how spirituality often takes central position during life transitions, such as loss of loved ones, accidents, or serious illnesses.

10 Identify nursing diagnoses related to social, cultural, and spiritual nursing assessments.

*M*r. Ahmed El-Kebbi, a 54-year-old Somalian Muslim immigrant, is being seen in a hospital diabetes clinic for follow-up care. He works in maintenance at another hospital during the day and also has a part-time job selling used goods at auction in the evening. He takes an oral hypoglycemic, metformin hydrochloride (Fortamet) 500 mg, and is otherwise healthy. A focused assessment was documented during his last clinic visit 6 months ago.

You will gain more information about Mr. El-Kebbi as you progress through this chapter. As you study the content and features, consider Mr. El-Kebbi's case and its relationship to what you are learning. Begin thinking about the following issues:

- How might Mr. El-Kebbi's social network influence his healthy lifestyle?
- How will the nurse assess this patient's ethnic and cultural needs?
- What effect might religion have on Mr. El-Kebbi's diabetes management?

Canadian society is increasingly a cultural mosaic. In the 2006 census, over 200 ethnic origins were identified and some Canadians reported multiple ethnicity (Statistics Canada, 2010a). Given the country's multicultural composition and the steady influx of new and diverse immigrants, nurses' sensitivity to patients' social and cultural backgrounds and their spiritual beliefs becomes imperative. Nurses acknowledge and address the biopsychosocial, spiritual, and cultural needs of patients. In Canada, cultural competence is considered to be an entry-to-practice competency of registered nurses (Canadian Nurses Association [CNA], 2010). Nurses are expected to demonstrate cultural competence with their patients and their co-workers. Furthermore, CNA is committed to social justice as a central tenet for nursing. It recognizes a more comprehensive concept, that of *cultural safety* which encompasses not only cultural competence, but also cultural awareness and cultural sensitivity. Cultural awareness is a beginning understanding of difference between the nurse, the patient, and the health care agency. Cultural sensitivity legitimizes the difference. Cultural safety is safe patient care as defined by the patient (Astle, Barton, et al., 2010).

This chapter presents basic principles for conducting social, cultural, and spiritual assessments and ways to incorporate subjective findings into plans of care for patients.

Models of Health

Across times and cultures, the concept of *health* has been defined from various perspectives. In the Western world, several models of health emerged in the 20th century. The most prominent, the **biomedical model**, views health as the absence of disease (Wade, 2004). From the biomedical standpoint, health is restored by prompt diagnosis of illness, prevention of complications, and elimination of pathology. Nurses incorporate the biomedical model when they inquire about medications during a health history, and collect objective data, observing for expected and unexpected findings (Reutter & Kushner, 2010). Social, cultural, and spiritual dimensions of health are not central to the biomedical perspective which continued to serve as the philosophical basis for Western medical care. In recent years, however, a trend in the biomedical community has emerged to consider the social, cultural, and spiritual aspects of health during decision making about treatment regimens (Wade, 2009).

The **complementary and alternative medicine (CAM) model** of health, which emerged in the later 20th century, has been defined largely in relation to the biomedical perspective. When CAM therapies are used instead of conventional treatments to restore health they are often termed *alternative*, while CAM therapies used with conventional medicine are often labelled *complementary* (Barrett, Marchand, et al., 2003). The evolving process of integration between the two perspectives evokes a new conceptual framework, which considers the complex interplay of mind, body, and spirit and offers opportunities to explore ways to facilitate healing (Berman, 2006).

This notion of wholeness is not a new concept to nursing. Florence Nightingale, the matriarch of modern nursing, described the nurse's duty as putting the patient in the best condition for nature to act upon him or her (Nightingale, 1860/1992). She maintained that healing can occur only in an environment equipped with proper ventilation, adequate temperature, pure air and water, efficient drainage, cleanliness, light, and diminished noise. Environmental features are as important to health and healing today as they were to Nightingale in the 19th century. That focus away from disease to one of a health-promoting environment differentiates nursing from medicine (Thorne, 2010). Evidence that care embracing the patient's biopsychosocial and spiritual dimensions is important to health is also growing, because it puts the patient's life context and perceived needs first and offers healing for both body and spirit (Burkhardt, 2009). This holistic approach to care results in more favourable outcomes than conventional treatments alone (Bradwell, 2009; Burkhardt, 2009; Kerwin, 2009; Liu, Hsiung, et al., 2008; McCaffrey, 2008; Morad, 2008; Palmer & Ward, 2007; Vance, Struzick, et al., 2008). Nursing considers the wholeness of individuals to properly manage the resources and constraints in their internal (biological, mental, and spiritual) and external (social and cultural) environments (Leininger & McFarland, 2005).

In Canada, the health promotion approach began with the groundbreaking Lalonde Report (1974) that introduced four determinants of health (biology, lifestyle, environment, and health care organizations). During the health history, nurses collect subjective data about lifestyle practices such as exercise, diet, smoking, alcohol intake, use of safety helmets, and dental care (Reutter & Kushner, 2010). They inquire about occupational, recreational, and community environments. For many years, the health promotion perspective focused primarily on lifestyle change and health education (Pinder, 2007). The Canadian Population Health Model drastically changed the national approach to health promotion by considering all conditions, factors, and interactions that affect population health (Health Canada, 1998). When nurses comprehend the relationships among determinants of health, they appreciate the complexity of patients' health states (Reutter & Kushner).

Several models of health emerged in nursing. A systems theory, **Roy's Adaptation Model**, linked the biopsychosocial being with an ever changing environment and was one of the earliest conceptualizations (Roy & Andrews, 1999). Roy refers to health as the patient's ability to adapt, compensate, manage, and adjust to physiologic–physical health-related setbacks (Hobfoll, 2001). The Adaptation Model holds that a person is a set of connected parts which function as a whole. The goal of nursing care is to assist the patient to attain an optimal level of

- *physical health*: also described as physiological processes involved in the proper functioning of a living organism
- *self-concept*: mental health
- *role function*: ability to adequately perform in roles occupied in society
- *Interdependence*: satisfying interpersonal relationships (Roy & Andrews, 1999)

A healing environment addresses symptoms of disease, supports bodily functioning, and sustains life by infection control, adequate oxygenation and nutrition, a balance between activity and rest, and protection of the individual from harm (Roy & Andrews, 1999). This Adaptation Model maintains that the optimal level of adaptation is accomplished by educating the patient about the management of illness, and health promotion activities (Swanson & Wojnar, 2004).

Another broadly used nursing model is **Gordon's functional health model** (Gordon, 2006). Gordon posits that people are considered healthy if they can fulfill their social roles by contributing to family and society in meaningful ways. She emphasizes the importance of personal role fulfillment. The primary focus of the functional health model is the use of the person's skills and talents to their full potential and avoidance of the risks associated with losing independence.

Gordon identified 11 categories of **functional health patterns**, which she refers to as behaviours that occur sequentially across time: (1) health perception–health management; (2) nutrition–metabolic; (3) elimination; (4) activity–exercise; (5) sleep–rest; (6) cognitive–perceptual; (7) self–perception–self–concept; (8) role–relationship; (9) sexuality–reproductive; (10) coping–stress tolerance; and (11) value–belief. Chapter 3 addresses these patterns within the context of the patient's health history. From the functional health perspective, an optimal healing environment sustains life to a level expected for and desired by the patient, using various treatment modalities (Swanson & Wojnar, 2004).

A practice-based theory, the widely-valued **McGill Model**, was conceived and developed in Canada at McGill University (Gottlieb & Rowat, 1987). It views nursing as a complementary balance to medicine and focuses on health promotion, building on patient/family goals, strengths, resources, and potentials (Feeley & Gottlieb, 2000; Thorne, 2010). A central tenet of the model is the belief that a nation's health is its most valuable resource (Gottlieb & Rowat). The model develops the nurse's role as a partner with families to engage them in optimizing health goals (Cohen, 2005). The nurse's goal is to have the family become an active learner in the process of achieving health goals (Patrick & Edmunds, 2005). His or her role is to collaborate with the family and facilitate development of a learning environment. One example of the application of this strength-based model is its use by faith community nurses who work in settings where professional and social boundaries are blended. The McGill Model guides their practice and reduces the potential strain on those boundaries (Olson & Anderson, 2005).

Social Assessment

Social assessment recognizes the determinants of health and illness for individuals, groups, communities, and populations. During health assessments, nurses consider individuals' factors and their social, physical, and economic environments, in addition to the quality and accessibility of their health services. Variables of social assessment include gender, age, ethnicity, culture, marital status, social support systems, lifestyle, occupation, housing, income, employment status, education level, and exposure to human violence—it is important to understand how these variables interact with the broader sociocultural environment. Knowledge obtained from social assessment helps nurses promote health, and address issues related to equity, social justice, and the common good (Canadian Public Health Association, 1996). It helps providers create new ways to improve patients' access to resources (Anderson & McFarlane, 2011; Kaplan, 2006; Marmot & Wilkinson, 2006; Reutter & Kushner, 2010).

Social assessment is integral to effective nursing practice at every level. It emphasizes the interconnectedness of physical, psychosocial, and spiritual dimensions of health for individuals, communities, and populations. It helps health care professionals and health policy makers refrain from making sweeping generalizations not grounded in data about three levels of social assessment: individual, community, and societal. Nurses who apply the McGill model in their practice include a fourth level of social assessment: family. Though on the surface social assessment might appear simple, it is a daunting task that requires knowledge, creativity, and skill to make the connections among the assessment variables and to interpret data accurately before incorporating them into plans of care.

Social Assessment of the Individual

Social assessment of the individual is intended primarily to inform nurses about the patient's physical and mental health as related to the patient's existing resources, constraints, and demands. Resources might include education, income, housing, and support systems; constraints might be unemployment, single-parent family, minority status, unsafe neighbourhood, and lack of social support; demands might involve struggling to live on a fixed income or caring for aging parents (Seid, 2008). Although information obtained from an individual's social assessment may not be necessary to diagnose illness or initiate treatment, it is essential for planning long-term management of illness as well as evidence-informed health promotion activities for that patient (Melnyk & Fineout-Overholt, 2004).

Methods for individual social assessment predominantly entail personal interviews. Depending on assessment goals, interview questions vary from open- to close-ended, often guided by agency-designed assessment forms. Examples of questions in a comprehensive nursing assessment that attends to both social and cultural dimensions are in Figure 11-1. Nurses cannot conduct a complete assessment on admission to inpatient or outpatient care for every patient. Instead, they determine which questions are most relevant based on the patient's symptoms and learning needs. They also consider any potential effects of culturally based practices on health and recovery.

Social Assessment of the Community

At the community level, the scope of social assessment is broader and more complex than at the individual level.

Affiliations
- With what culture(s) does the patient self-identify?
- To what degree does the patient identify with the cited cultural group(s)?
- What is the patient's place of birth?
- Where has the patient lived? When? (If the patient is a recent immigrant, ask about or research prevalent diseases in the country of origin and the genetic background.)
- What is the patient's current residence?
- What is the patient's occupation?

Values
- How does the patient view birth and death?
- What is the patient's view of health versus illness?
- How does the patient regard health care providers?
- How do culture and ethnicity affect the patient's body image and any changes resulting from illness or treatment? For example, what emphasis does the patient's culture or ethnic community place on appearance, beauty, and strength?
- Is stigma associated with any of the patient's illnesses or conditions?
- How does the patient view work?
- What is the patient's perspective on leisure?
- What are the patient's views on education?
- How does the patient feel about/perceive change?
- What effects on lifestyle do health, illness, treatments, and surgery pose for the patient?
- What is the patient's perspective on privacy? Courtesy? Touch? Age? Class? Gender?
- What perspective does the patient have regarding biomedical/scientific health care?
- How does the patient relate to those not from his or her culture?

Cultural Sanctions/Restrictions
- How do members of the patient's culture or ethnic community typically express emotion and feelings?
- How do they view dying, death, and grieving?
- How do men and women show modesty? Does the cultural community place expectations on male–female relationships? The nurse–patient relationship?
- Does the patient have restrictions related to sexuality, body exposure, or type of surgery?
- Are there restrictions about discussing the dead or fears related to the unknown?

Communication
- What is the patient's primary language? What other languages does the patient speak or read? In what language would the patient prefer to communicate with the nurse?
- What is the patient's level of fluency in English (written and spoken)?
- Does the patient need an interpreter?
- How does the patient prefer to be addressed?
- How does the patient's cultural background influence expectations about tempo of conversation, eye contact, topical taboos, confidentiality, and explanations?
- How does the patient's nonverbal communication compare with those from other cultural backgrounds? How does it affect the health care relationship?
- How does the patient view health care providers from different cultural, ethnic, or genetic backgrounds?
- Does the patient prefer to receive care from a nurse of the same cultural or ethnic background, gender, or age group?
- What are overall cultural characteristics of the patient's language and communication?

Health-Related Beliefs/Practices
- To what cause(s) does the patient attribute illness and disease (eg, punishment from God, imbalance in hot/cold or yin/yang)?
- What are the patient's beliefs about ideal body size and shape?
- What name does the patient give to his or her health-related conditions?
- What does the patient believe promotes health (eg, certain foods, amulets)?
- What is the patient's religious background (if any)?
- Does the patient rely on indigenous healers (eg, curandero, shaman, spiritualist, priest)?
- Who influences the patient's choice/type of healer and treatment?
- In what types of healing practices does the patient engage (eg, herbal remedies, potions, massage, talismans, healing rituals, incantations, prayers)?
- How does the patient perceive biomedical/scientific health care providers? Nurses? Nursing care?
- What comprises appropriate "sick " behaviour? Who determines what constitutes symptoms? How are symptoms interpreted in the patient's ethnic or cultural community? Who decides when the patient is no longer sick? Who cares for the patient?
- How does the patient's culture view mental disorders? Are there differences in acceptable behaviours for physical versus psychological illnesses?

Nutrition
- How does the culture influence the patient's nutritional factors?
- What is the meaning of food and eating for the patient?
- With whom does the patient usually eat? What is the timing and sequencing of meals?

Figure 11-1 Examples of questions in a comprehensive health assessment related to ethnicity, genetics, and culture.

- What does the patient define as food? What is "healthy" versus "unhealthy" eating?
- Who shops for food? Where are groceries purchased? Who prepares the meals? How are foods prepared at home?
- Has the patient chosen a specific practice (eg, vegetarianism, abstinence from alcohol)?
- Do religious beliefs/practices influence the patient's diet? Does the patient abstain from certain foods regularly, on specific dates determined by the religion, or at other times?
- If the patient's religion mandates or encourages fasting, what does "fast" mean (eg, refraining from certain types or quantities of foods, eating only during certain times)? For how long does the patient fast?
- While fasting, does the patient refrain from liquid? Does the religion allow exemption from fasting during illness? Does the patient believe the exemption applies to him or her?

Socioeconomic Considerations
- Who comprises the patient's social network (family, friends, peers, and cultural healers)? How do they influence health or illness status?
- How do members of the patient's social support network define caring (eg, being continuously present, doing things for the patient, providing material support, looking after family)?
- What is the role of various family members during health and illness?
- How does the patient's family participate in health promotion (eg, dietary modifications, exercise) and care (eg, bathing, feeding, touching) of the patient?
- Does the family structure influence the patient's response to health or illness? Does one key family member especially influence health-related decisions?
- Who is the principal wage earner in the family? To what extent is the total annual income meeting their needs? (Note: This is a potentially sensitive question.) Is there more than one wage earner? Are there other sources of financial support?
- What effects does economic status have on lifestyle, residence, and living conditions? How does the home environment influence nursing care?

Organizations Providing Cultural Support
- What influences do ethnic/cultural organizations have on the patient?

Educational Background
- What is the patient's highest educational level obtained?
- Does the patient's educational background affect his or her knowledge of the health care delivery system, how to obtain needed care, teaching–learning, and any written material that he or she receives from health care providers?
- Can the patient read and write English, or is another language preferred? Are materials available in the other language?
- What learning style is most comfortable/familiar? Does the patient prefer to learn through written materials, oral explanation, or demonstration?

Religious Affiliation
- How does the patient's religious affiliation affect health and illness?
- What is the role of religious beliefs and practices during health and illness? Are there special rites or blessings for those with serious or terminal illnesses?
- Does the patient believe that any healing rituals or practices can promote well-being or hasten recovery from illness? If so, who performs these?
- What is the role of significant religious representatives during health and illness? Are there recognized religious healers?

Cultural Aspects of Disease
- Are there any genetic or acquired conditions more prevalent for the patient's cultural group (eg, hypertension, sickle-cell anemia, Tay Sachs)?
- Are socioenvironmental diseases more prevalent among a specific genetic background (eg, lead poisoning, alcoholism, HIV/AIDS, ear infections)?

Biocultural Variations
- Does the patient have distinctive physical features characteristic of a particular ethnic or genetic background?
- Does the patient have any anatomical variations of a particular genetic background (eg, body structure, height, weight, facial shape and structure)?
- How do anatomic, genetic, and ethnic variations affect the physical examination?

Developmental Considerations
- Do any developmental characteristics vary based on the patient's genetic background (eg, bone density)?
- What developmental factors are genetically influenced (eg, expected growth, age for toilet training, feeding practices, gender expectations, methods of discipline)?
- What is the cultural perception of youthfulness?
- How does the cultural community view older adults?
- What are culturally acceptable roles for older adults?
- Are older adults isolated from culturally relevant supportive people?

Figure 11-1 (*Continued*)

Community social assessment involves gathering data to identify community resources, constraints, and high-priority health concerns (Anderson & McFarlane, 2011).

Ideally, the process begins with the assessment of various social, economic, environmental, and quality-of-life health indicators and their relationship with the community's health concerns. Examples of findings from a community social assessment include the relationship between social determinants of health (eg, family income, level of education, social support, and living conditions) with family violence (Bonomi, Anderson, et al., 2009; Romito, Turan, et al., 2009), chronic illness (Lipstein, Perrin, et al., 2009; Seid, 2008), and teen pregnancy (Crittenden, Boris, et al., 2009). This knowledge is invaluable for planning community-based health promotion campaigns while keeping in mind that every community is unique with different strengths, challenges, and concerns. Ongoing community assessments are fundamental for tailoring interventions to each community's unique needs (Basara & Yuan, 2008; Reutter & Kushner, 2010).

Community-level social assessment techniques range from interviewing key informants through focus groups and mailed surveys to analyzing global housing situations, environmental concerns, and general access to health services. Core community assessment variables include the gender, age, ethnicity, culture, marital status, housing, employment status, and education of members.

One example of a community assessment framework is Anderson and McFarlane's (2011) **Community as Partner Assessment Model** (Fig. 11-2). It has been designed to help nurses thoroughly assess the demographics of a given

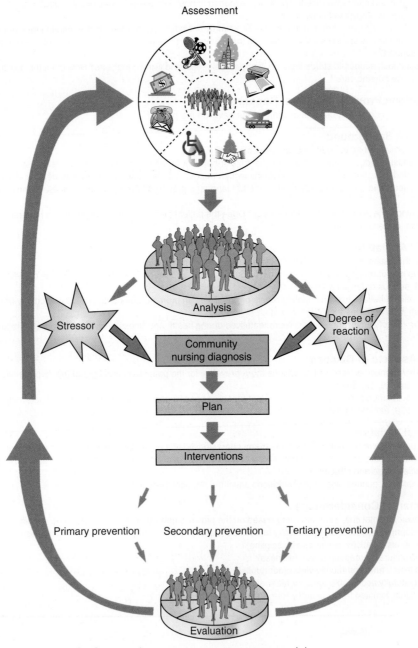

Figure 11-2 Community as partner assessment model.

community, including its values, beliefs, and history. It also assesses how resources (ie, recreation, physical environment, education, safety and transportation, politics and government, health and social services, communications, and economics) affect and influence the community. This information is used to define community nursing diagnoses and to plan and implement interventions in collaboration with community members. Anderson and McFarlane's model mandates that every community assessment and intervention include systematic evaluation to identify the effects of interventions.

Social Assessment at the Societal Level

At the societal level, social assessment is intended to generate information about population trends and relationships among the social variables and prevalent health concerns. Data collected through national assessments are used to inform healthy public policy and broad health promotion initiatives. One example is the National Population Health Survey conducted on a regular basis in Canada by Statistics Canada. In 1992, Statistics Canada obtained funding to develop the first National Population Health Survey and it collects data on three components: households, health institutions, and Canada's North. Starting in 2000, the survey of households began a longitudinal study, collecting data from the same individuals every 2 years (the cycle). The longitudinal sample has over 17,000 individuals in its interview schedule. The data are used by Health Canada, the Public Health Agency of Canada (PHAC) and ministries of health in the provinces and territories to evaluate health policies and programs for the improvement of health services (Statistics Canada, 2010b).

Collecting data and analyzing findings at the societal level are very complex. Social assessments are conducted to identify human and material assets, social networks, and the norms and sanctions that govern character, which, in turn, influences health behaviour and values. Societal-level social assessment can also be used to identify, for example, ecological risks, disaster preparedness, or posttraumatic stress. Social assessment at the society level can be conducted using diverse research methods including mailed surveys, telephone interviews, internet-based questionnaires, opinion polls, and focus groups in multiple locations. Data analyses include summary statistics from complex samples, population stratification, associations between variables, and predictions.

Cultural Assessment

Cultural health assessments and related care are known to promote health and healing. Nurses have an ethical, moral, and professional responsibility to conduct cultural assessments and create safe, culturally congruent physical and emotional environments in which patients and their families feel cared for and well supported (CNA, 2010).

Characteristics of Culture

From a culturalist point of view, **culture** refers to shared, learned, and symbolic systems of values, beliefs, and attitudes that shape and influence how people see and behave in the world (Varcoe, Browne, et al., 2010). But culture as a dynamic, lived process is more than values, practices, and beliefs (Aboriginal Nurses Association of Canada, 2009). Culture is a complex, shifting relational process (Varcoe, Browne, et al., 2010). Major influences that shape worldview, and the extent to which people identify with their culture of origin, are called *primary and secondary characteristics* of culture (Purnell & Paulanka, 2005). Primary characteristics include age, gender, nationality, and ethnicity. Secondary characteristics include cultural values, religious beliefs, morals, occupation, socioeconomic status, immigration status, reasons for migration, and beliefs about health held as important to life and healthy living. All people's cultural beliefs about health are important and often powerfully influence health practices. Health professionals, like their patients, add a unique dimension to the complexity of culturally based care (Purnell & Paulanka, 2005). They bring their health care culture to their interactions with patients in addition to their own cultural identities (Varcoe, Browne, et al.).

Aims of Cultural Assessment

From a holistic perspective, all patients have the right to receive **cultural assessment.** It means more than having their health beliefs, values, and practices acknowledged and incorporated into plans of care with consideration for safety concerns. Nurses remember that within the same ethnic or social group, cultural characteristics can vary because of gender, age, political affiliations, religion, and other factors (Aboriginal Nurses Association of Canada, 2009). The specific aim of cultural assessment is to provide an all-inclusive picture of the patient's culture-related health care needs by:

1. gaining knowledge about the patient's beliefs and practices, including food and eating rituals, daily and nightly personal hygiene rituals, and sleeping habits
2. comparing culture care needs of the specific person with the general themes of their self-identified cultural background
3. identifying similarities and differences among the cultural beliefs of the patient, health care agency, and nurse (Varcoe, Browne, et al., 2010)
4. generating a holistic picture of the patient's care needs, upon which a culturally congruent patient care plan is developed and implemented (Leininger & McFarland, 2005).

Based on the comprehensive body of knowledge drawn from anthropology and nursing, Madeline Leininger developed the Theory of Culture Care Diversity and Universality (Leininger & McFarland, 2005). She proposed essential areas of assessment to better understand the relationship between individuals' culture and health. Leininger's theory identifies the relationships among cultural variables (ie, cultural values and beliefs, religion and personal philosophy of life and spiritual beliefs, educational and economic background, relationship with family and friends, views on and use of technology, politics, and the patient's legal status) and health, and highlights the nursing behaviours and skills necessary to carry out effective cultural assessment. Leininger's research was critical to the development of concepts related to culture and health care in nursing. At the same time, nurses in Canada need to be aware of the model's tendency to incorporate American values, and to consider the patient as culturally different from themselves without recognizing themselves as different from their patients (Aboriginal Nurses Association of Canada, 2009; Varcoe, Browne, et al., 2010). Even more importantly, the concept of culture applies to everyone and individuals' personal characteristics need to be considered in light of the social determinants of health and power relationships in society (Varcoe, Browne, et al.).

Leininger suggests that the attributes and behaviours of a nurse practising effective care within the patient's cultural context include the following:

- genuine interest in a patient's cultural identity and personal life experiences
- active listening, and awareness of meanings behind the patient's verbal communication (story telling)
- nonverbal communication (body language, eye contact, facial expressions, interpersonal space, and preferences regarding touch)
- acknowledgement that the nurse's own beliefs and prejudices might create barriers to providing culturally sensitive care.

Nurses need to listen to patients' explanations of their health condition so that they can plan care within the context of the patient's life (Varcoe, Browne, et al., 2010) (see Fig. 11-3).

Figure 11-3 A. Patients benefit when nurses discuss with them cultural or spiritual practices they follow that may influence their health. Examples include **(B)** Chinese medicine, **(C)** meditation/relaxation, and **(D)** participation in religious services.

Cultural Health Beliefs and Practices

At the core of culturally based care is the assessment of the patient's health beliefs and practices (Box 11-1) and, when no safety concerns arise, incorporation of the patient's beliefs and practices into the plan of care. Seeking an understanding of patients' culturally related health care practices is essential to nursing because of traditional values and beliefs about health and illness that may affect individuals' acceptance of treatments. For example, health care services may not be culturally relevant for some individuals, especially when dietary habits and preferences are not taken into consideration when treatments are ordered. Others, because of the unequal distribution and underrepresentation of ethnic minorities in health care, may reluctantly decide to seek conventional care from a provider who is not from a culture with which they self-identify after traditional healing remedies prove unsuccessful.

Cultural Food and Nutrition Practices

Food and nutrition are an important part of cultural nursing assessment because they represent an expression of peoples' culture and ethnicity, and their consumption may affect individuals' physical health. People all over the world use food to celebrate special events or religious holidays. In some cultures, food represents wealth and health; others use food as an offering to gods or a special gift to guests. All cultures relish ethnic dishes as symbols of identity or cultural expression that they often pass from generation to generation. Nurses are sensitive to the meaning of food to people.

They are careful about refusing food that accompanies special events such as childbirth or infant circumcision performed in hospitals for religious reasons, because patients might perceive such refusal as personal rejection (Purnell & Paulanka, 2005).

In many cultures, ideal body weight is higher than recommended according to Canadian guidelines. Such cultures may not consider "dieting" healthy. People may prefer to consume foods high in fat, salt, and cholesterol, and low in fruit and vegetables because they believe it is best for their health (Purnell & Paulanka, 2005). Others may have awareness that the ideal diet is well balanced and rich in different nutrients, but cannot afford it. Similarly, new immigrants may have difficulty finding ethnic food stores that carry healthy foods with which they are familiar and unknowingly select unhealthy foods in nearby supermarkets based on affordability. It is very important that nurses provide facts about the nutritional value of various foods and help patients make choices that promote health yet are congruent with their cultural background and personal preferences.

Cultural Beliefs and Practices of Pregnancy and Childbirth

Cultural beliefs and practices surrounding pregnancy care and childbirth are powerful and cannot be ignored. Many culture-specific taboos are believed to promote well-being and prevent bad outcomes for mother and child (Enang, Wojnar, et al., 2002). For example, some women claim that the fetus signals what he or she wants them to consume via cravings and that if they do not eat the foods they are craving, the child will be birth-marked for that particular food.

> △ SAFETY ALERT 11-1
>
> *Certain cravings in women who are pregnant may be unhealthy. Nurses need to provide evidence-informed information about the benefits of a well-balanced diet and **avoidance of substances** that might harm mother and fetus.*

Women in many cultures believe that buying infant clothing before birth is bad luck and may contribute to a stillbirth. As a result, they might arrive at the hospital for childbirth without infant clothing. In these situations, nurses seek information about beliefs regarding pregnancy and childbirth rather than make assumptions that the baby is unwanted (Purnell & Paulanka, 2005).

Across cultures, childbirth is a time of celebration. Relatives and friends might congregate in a hospital or house where childbirth is occurring. While some cultures permit their presence in birthing rooms, others might forbid even the father to visit the mother until after the baby is born. Understanding and accepting cultural differences and preferences surrounding childbirth help to alleviate interpersonal barriers between nurses and patients, make families feel more at ease to discuss their beliefs and needs, and enhance the experience (Enang, Wojnar, et al., 2002).

Culturally based postpartum practices are also diverse. Generally, most cultures recognize that, after childbirth, women must rest, take care of the baby, and "eat for two" when breastfeeding. In some cultures, people may believe that a fat baby is a healthy baby and new parents might be advised to offer their baby a bottle after breastfeeding to ensure that the infant is not hungry and gains weight quickly. In these situations, nurses provide facts about infants' nutritional needs and weight-gain patterns, as well as health risks associated with infant formula consumption and overfeeding (Riordan & Auerbach, 2005).

In some situations, adhering to culture-based postpartum practices is difficult. For example, women who are practising Muslims are expected to rest, eat well, take care of the baby, and stay at home for 40 days. Traditionally, they are cared for by other women in the community and not expected to have demands put on them during this time. This may be difficult, if not impossible, when they arrive as new immigrants and give birth before they make new friends or have a community network. In such cases, nurses might help by making arrangements for visitations of volunteer women in the community (Purnell & Paulanka, 2005).

Cultural Beliefs and Expressions of Illness and Pain

In some cultures, the roles of men and women, young and old, can vary greatly. Also, it is important to consider differences in culture and religion—for example, a Canadian-born Muslim may have a different kind of cultural orientation than a Muslim who has immigrated to Canada. While many immigrants transition to Western medicine, some maintain their roots in traditional healing practices, and others mix traditional and Western therapies to restore health. When a nurse conducts a cultural health assessment, he or she might find that an African Canadian patient mentions already consulting the *Farmers' Almanac* with limited success. Patients of Latino background may mention that they have already turned for help to a "*curandero(a)*" spiritualist, herbalist, or traditional healer. Asian patients may report that they received care from a herbalist, acupuncturist, or bone setter (Andrews & Boyle, 2003; Purnell & Paulanka, 2005).

Pain assessment is an integral feature of culturally based health assessment. The nurse remembers that pain interpretation is also an individual experience, but one that may be influenced by a cultural community. For many people, pain is a sign of disease. In the absence of pain, they may decide to not take prescribed medications or take them only when they feel discomfort, which could have grave consequences. Others believe that pain is an inevitable part of being human and endure pain in silence. This belief might contribute to a high pain tolerance or complete refusal of pain medication. Therefore, nurses rely on patients' verbal and nonverbal manifestations when assessing and treating pain (Purnell & Paulanka, 2005).

Some cultures believe that praying and laying on of hands or using holy water and religious symbols will free the person of all pain and suffering. Under some circumstances, sick patients who still report pain may be considered to have little faith. In contrast, other cultural communities expect sick patients to be pampered and to express pain freely. Whatever the situation, nurses display a nonjudgmental attitude, provide facts, and use a culturally specific approach when administering prescribed treatments. They do not interpret patients' inactivity and dependence as apathy, depression, or being difficult without first conducting a cultural assessment and gaining insight into the patient's medical diagnosis and behaviour.

Spiritual Assessment

Spirituality, in the most fundamental sense, pertains to matters of the human soul, be it a state of mind, a state of being in the world, a journey of self-discovery, or a place outside the five senses (Holt, Lewellyn, et al., 2005). In general, spirituality emphasizes a notion of a path to achieve better understanding and connectedness with nature, inner harmony, other people, or an improved relationship with the divine (Fig. 11-4).

Figure 11-4 A sense of spirituality can be manifested through a relationship with **(A)** oneself, **(B)** other people, or **(C)** transcendent forces, such as God or nature.

Assess the cultural background of Mr. El-Kebbi, who is mentioned at the beginning of this chapter, in relation to his concerns about diabetes care during the Muslim religious holiday of Ramadan. Using therapeutic dialogue, the nurse seeks to incorporate the patient's social, cultural, and spiritual dimensions of health.

Nurse: Hello, Mr. El-Kebbi. How are you doing today? (smiles)

Mr. El-Kebbi: Very well, thank you.

Nurse: How are you doing with managing your diabetes?

Mr. El-Kebbi: I think, well. I am going to fast during Ramadan and want to know if I should do anything special with my diabetes management.

Nurse: I am glad that you came in to talk to us about it. We may need to make some changes in your medication and diet regimen. (smiles)

Mr. El-Kebbi: Allah will take care of me.

Nurse: When do you usually take your Fortamet? We may need to adjust the timing.

Mr. El-Kebbi: In the morning.

Nurse: How do you usually break your daily fast?

Mr. El-Kebbi: We have a big meal together after sunset.

Nurse: You might want to have a few small meals after sunset instead. And what is your typical daily exercise?

Mr. El-Kebbi: I go for a 30-minute brisk walk after work on most days.

Nurse: During Ramadan, you may want to exercise a few hours after eating so that you don't get hypoglycemia. We can talk with your doctor about making adjustments so that your diet, exercise, and medication management all fit together during Ramadan.

Mr. El-Kebbi: Thank you so much.

Critical Thinking Challenge

- What might be the social, cultural, or spiritual influences on Mr. El-Kebbi's decision to fast?
- What communication skills did the nurse use with Mr. El-Kebbi?
- What is the role of a nurse when counselling a patient making this decision?

Spirituality is also considered an integral part of one's religion or self-directed path modelled after several different religions. In all cases, spirituality is concerned with matters of the soul rather than the world of senses and material things (Borysenko, 2005). Similar to social and cultural assessments, spiritual assessment involves understanding the relationship between spirituality and health (Borg, Andree, et al., 2003).

To be meaningful, spiritual care within the health care context must be congruent with the patient's spiritual beliefs (Thomas-McLean, 2004). Just as with social and cultural assessment, making assumptions or generalizations about a patient's spiritual needs based on ethnic or religious affiliation is almost certain to be an oversimplification. Nevertheless, it is important to be aware that for people of many cultures, church, and religion play important roles in sustaining their

development, national identity, and survival and are treated as such. For example, patients of Polish descent may identify the Catholic Church, as a symbol of their national identity and sustainability, because it helped the nation to survive and maintain native language and culture for more than 150 years of foreign occupation (Pease, 1991). Similarly, Black churches played a major role in the development and survival of a self-identified Black culture. Many people of African heritage make no distinction between the Black church and the Black community (Pinn, 2002). These specific examples are not isolated. Having faith in God and participating in organized religious life are important to people of diverse cultures and ethnicities and are often seen as a source of inner strength and spirituality. It is therefore important to assess the meaning of the church and

BOX 11-2 SPIRITUAL ASSESSMENT

1. Do you consider yourself deeply religious?
2. Are there times in the day that you wish to pray?
3. What do you need in order to say your prayers?
4. Do you meditate?
5. What gives strength and meaning to your life?
6. In what spiritual practices do you engage for your physical and emotional pain?
7. How do faith, spirituality, or religion play a part in what is happening to you? In how your community chooses to act?
8. Who are the story tellers in your faith community?

Adapted from Clancy, C. (2006). Care transitions: A threat and opportunity for patient safety. *American Journal of Medical Quality, 21(6),* 414–417 with additions from Clark, M. B., & Olson, J. K. (2000). *Nursing within a faith community: Promoting health in times of transition.* Thousand Oaks, CA: Sage Publications, Inc.

organized religion in the patient's life and how it might best be incorporated in the plan of care to promote health and healing. See questions related to a spiritual assessment in Box 11-2.

During spiritual assessment, a nurse might learn that a practising Muslim wishes to combine conventional biomedical treatments with spiritual nourishment consisting of daily prayers and reading or listening to the Qur'an. He or she may request to have a hospital bed turned to face Mecca and have a hospital gown changed and a basin of water placed near the bed for ritualistic washing of hands before praying. By making simple accommodations, nurses can create environments in which Muslim patients may have their spiritual needs met and experience a general sense of respect and understanding (Purnell & Paulanka, 2005).

For practising Jews, observance of Jewish Holidays and participating in religious rituals are also important to health and healing. Some Jews may want to pray three times a day and bring their prayer items such as Yarmulke or kippah, tallit, tzitzit, and tefillin to the hospital. They may refuse medical or surgical procedures on the Sabbath or other holidays unless the situation is life threatening. A nurse may also find many visitors in the patient's room because visiting the sick is a social obligation for Jews. It is important that nurses and others accommodate and respect the patient's wishes and create an environment in which the physical and spiritual healing of the patient occurs concurrently (Robinson, 2000).

For many practising Hindus, spirituality and religion are also closely related. Those who live far away from temples often pray, sing, recite scriptures, and repeat the names of deities at home or other places. Shrines that represent symbols of one or more deities may therefore be set up in the back of the house or even by the sick person's bedside in the hospital. It is important that nurses assess the extent to which the patient who discloses Hinduism as his or her religion practises it and how beliefs relate to health and illness and to daily religious prayer. Assessing the spiritual needs of these patients may assist nurses in accommodating their need for prayer in privacy (Jambunathan, 2003).

Even when daily prayers or other religious practices are not a routine part of a patient's life, they often take central position during life transitions, such as loss of a loved one, accident, or serious illness (Hudson & Rumbold, 2003; Rumbold, 2003). Assessment of spiritual needs might reveal that the use of blood products or modern technologies to sustain life may not be congruent with their beliefs. On the other hand, another patient's spirituality allows aggressive medical treatments until the end of life. In each instance, imposing the values of the health care professional may be stress provoking and counterproductive (Holt, Lewellyn, et al., 2005). To promote acceptance and spiritual well-being of individuals across the lifespan, it is essential to incorporate individual patient assessment and spiritual assessment findings into plans of care.

Evidence-Informed Critical Thinking

Nursing Diagnoses, Outcomes, and Interventions

Table 11-1 compares and contrasts nursing diagnoses, unexpected findings, and interventions commonly related to social, cultural, and spiritual assessments (North American Nursing Diagnosis Association-International, 2009). Note the differences between the diagnoses arising from spiritual and social assessments.

Nurses use assessment information to identify patient outcomes. Some outcomes related to social, cultural, and spiritual issues include the following:

- the patient will express a sense of connectedness with self, others, arts, music, or power greater than oneself.
- the patient will express meaning and purpose in life.
- the patient will initiate interactions with others (Moorhead, Johnson, et al., 2007).

When the outcomes are established, patient care is implemented to improve the patient's status. The nurse uses critical thinking and evidence-informed practice to develop the interventions. Some examples of nursing interventions for the social, cultural, and spiritual domains are as follows:

- monitor and promote supportive social contact.
- integrate family into spiritual practices as appropriate.
- offer visits with spiritual or religious advisors (Bulecheck, Butcher, et al., 2008).

The nurse then evaluates care according to the patient outcomes that were developed, reassessing the patient and continuing or modifying the interventions as appropriate. An accurate and complete nursing assessment is an essential foundation for holistic patient care. Even as a beginner, the nursing student can use the patient assessment to implement new interventions, evaluate their effectiveness, and make a difference in the quality of patient care.

Table 11-1   Common Nursing Diagnoses Associated with Social and Spiritual Domains

Diagnosis and Related Factors	Point of Differentiation	Assessment Characteristics	Nursing Interventions
Social interaction impaired related to knowledge/skill deficit, isolation, sociocultural misfit, physical or communication barriers, altered thought processes	Engagement with others that is insufficient in frequency, lacking in quality, or both	Failure to maintain eye contact (as culturally appropriate); minimal verbal communication; decreased interaction with friends, neighbours, family, work, and groups	Assess cause of discomfort. Use listening skills. Encourage feelings. Role play situations. Use humour as appropriate.
Readiness for enhanced spiritual well-being	Developing of inner strengths to understand life's purpose and harmony with all	Expresses feelings of hope; recognizes inner strength; states purpose of life; feels at peace with self, others, and higher power	Assess spiritual or religious preferences. Make referrals when indicated. Promote support from friends and family. Allow time for praying, talking, or journalling. Provide music.

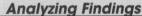

Analyzing Findings

Remember Mr. Ahmed El-Kebbi, the patient with diabetes who was planning on fasting for Ramadan. Initial subjective and objective data collection is complete, and the nurse has spent time reviewing findings with the primary care provider. The following nursing note illustrates how subjective and objective data are collected and analyzed and nursing interventions are developed.

Subjective: Mr. El-Kebbi, a 54-year-old Somali immigrant man seen in clinic for 6-month follow-up appointment related to type 2 diabetes. Plans on fasting for Ramadan next month. Asks for advice on how to best manage diabetes during this time. Usually, takes Fortamet in the morning and exercises on a treadmill after work in the evening. States that he has a large family with seven children and that some of his children live away from home. During Ramadan, his entire family gathers together at his home to break the fast each night. Prays to Allah five times daily and attends mosque weekly and on holidays. Allah is a source of strength for him and he reads the Qur'an daily. He is involved in a community of Somali immigrants in the Somali Community Services Agency. He is also very much involved in a Sunni mosque in the central district of town. He feels well supported and connected to others.

Objective: Wearing Western clothing, groomed, and clean. Conversing appropriately, maintaining distance because of gender roles. Affect responsive, interested, and animated. Temperature 36.8°C tympanic, Pulse 78 beats/min and regular, Respiration 16 breaths/min, Blood Pressure (BP) right arm (sitting) 112/68 mm Hg. Height 157 cm, weight 66 kg, BMI 26.8. Skin with red undertones, erect posture, and breathing easily.

Analysis: Health-seeking behaviours related to anticipated fast for Ramadan.

Plan: Consult with physician to establish risk for fasting and modifications to usual routine. May need adjustments in medication, diet, and activity, to prevent glycemic complications and dehydration. Further assess types of food eaten and nutritional content to promote a healthy diabetic diet. Assess knowledge of symptoms of hypoglycemia and hyperglycemia and the actions that should be taken.

Critical Thinking Challenge

- What are your beliefs about a diabetic fasting? How might such beliefs influence care provided?
- What information on the social, cultural, and spiritual practices of Mr. El-Kebbi is needed to provide culturally competent care?
- How will Mr. El-Kebbi recognize that his fasting has been successful?

In many facilities, nurses initiate referrals to social or spiritual care based on assessment findings. Results that might trigger a consult include patients and families expressing social concerns, cultural concerns, or spiritual concerns; death; receiving a terminal diagnosis; comfort care; family conferences; and families in crisis (Interdisciplinary Plan, 2007). It is important to assess if the patient or family is interested in receiving social or spiritual care. Because of the personal nature of religion and the meaning of spirituality, an open-ended question such as, "How would you feel about talking to someone about your spiritual needs?" or "Tell me about whether you want someone to talk or pray with you?" can offer support. Follow-up questions, such as "Do you have a religious preference?" or "Would you like to have someone important from your church or faith community visit with you?" can help identify the most appropriate person to contact. Many patients appreciate spiritual guidance, especially during challenging times. Social issues may be referred to social workers who have knowledge of resources that can be gathered during times of need. Cultural understandings can be learned through dialogue with the patient and his or her family. It is especially important to interpret issues within the context of the individual patient, family, groups, and community.

Using the previous steps of clinical reasoning, organizing, and prioritizing, consider all the case study findings woven throughout this chapter. When answering the following questions, begin drawing conclusions and see how the pieces of assessment must work together to create an environment for personalized, culturally safe, and accurate care.

- What is the physiological effect of adjusting exercise, meal size, and timing of medication? (Knowledge)
- How might Mr. El-Kebbi's social network influence his healthy lifestyle? (Comprehension)
- How will the nurse assess this patient's cultural needs? (Application)
- What effect might religion have on Mr. El-Kebbi's diabetes management? (Analysis)
- Why did the nurse consider a combination of approaches to the patient's concern about Ramadan? (Synthesis)
- How will the nurse assess this patient's understanding of the recommendations related to fasting during Ramadan? (Evaluation)

Key Points

- CAM therapies used instead of conventional treatments to restore health are often termed alternative, while CAM therapies used with conventional medicine are often labelled complementary.
- Social assessment refers to identifying the social context influencing the patterns of health and illness for individuals, communities, and societies.
- During cultural assessment, the nurse determines which questions to ask based on the patient's symptoms, learning needs, and potential effects of the patient's self-identified cultural practices on health.

- Core community assessment variables include gender, age, ethnicity, cultural heritage, marital status, housing, employment status, and education of community members.
- The McGill Model focuses on family strengths, resources, potentials, and health promotion using a collaborative approach with the family to create a learning environment for meeting family health goals.
- The Community as Partner Assessment Model was designed to help nurses thoroughly assess the demographics of a given community and its values, beliefs, and history, and to determine how the community is affected by resources (recreation, physical environment, education, safety and transportation, politics and

government, health and social services, communications, and economics).

- A culturalist perspective defines culture as a shared, learned, and symbolic system of values, beliefs, and attitudes that shape and influence the way people see and behave in the world.
- Cultural safety incorporates cultural awareness, cultural sensitivity, and cultural competence. It reflects dialogue with individuals and their families; this is the source of their cultural information.
- The goal of cultural assessment is to provide a picture of the patient's culture-related health care needs by (1) gaining knowledge about the patient's ethnocultural beliefs and practices including food and eating rituals, daily and nightly personal hygiene rituals and sleeping habits; (2) comparing culture care needs of the individual with general themes of the individual's self-identified cultural background; (3) identifying similarities and differences between the cultural beliefs of the patient, health care agency, and the nurse; and (4) generating a holistic picture of the patient's care needs, upon which culture congruent patient care plan is developed and implemented.
- The attributes and behaviours of a nurse practising effective care within the patient's cultural context include genuine interest in culture and personal life experiences, active listening, and effective nonverbal communication.
- Seeking understanding of patients' culturally related health care practices is essential to nursing because traditional values, beliefs, and practices that influence health and illness may affect patients' acceptance of treatments.
- Spirituality pertains to the matters of human soul—be it a state of mind, state of being in the world, journey of self-discovery, or place outside of our five senses.
- For many people, church and religion play important roles in sustaining their development, national identity, and survival.
- Even when daily prayer or other religious practices are not part of a patient's life routine, they often take central position during life transitions, such as loss of a loved one, accident, or serious illness.
- Common nursing diagnoses related to social, cultural, and spiritual assessments include impaired social interaction, and readiness for enhanced spiritual well-being.

Review Questions

1. The Canadian Nurses Association includes competency in cultural safety
   A. only in private offices
   B. in publicly-funded settings
   C. only in hospitals
   D. in every health care setting

2. CAM therapies used instead of conventional treatments to restore health are often termed
   A. alternative
   B. advantaged
   C. complementary
   D. conventional

3. The social context influences the patterns of health and illness for individuals, communities, and societies. An example is
   A. assessment of the patient's health beliefs and practices
   B. assessment of focus groups in multiple locations
   C. assessment of culturally based postpartum practices
   D. assessment of the religious practices of the patient

4. The purpose of considering culture care needs of the individual who self-identifies with a cultural background is to
   A. identify the dietary needs of a specific religious preference
   B. determine if the patient needs a spiritual consultation
   C. provide a picture of the individual's culture-related health care needs
   D. consider how closely the patient follows his or her religion

5. During cultural assessment, the nurse
   A. asks all the questions for completeness
   B. determines which questions to ask
   C. includes all the questions as part of an admitting assessment
   D. waits until the relationship is established to ask questions

6. A shared, learned, and symbolic system of values, beliefs, and attitudes that shapes and influences the way people see and behave in the world has been defined as
   A. society
   B. community
   C. culture
   D. spirituality

7. Even when daily prayers or other religious practices are not a part of a patient's life routine, they often take central position during life transitions, such as loss of a loved one, accident, or serious illness. A related nursing diagnosis might be
   A. spiritual distress
   B. impaired social interaction
   C. readiness for enhanced spiritual well-being
   D. social isolation

8. It is important to identify similarities and differences among the cultural beliefs of the patient, health care agency, and the nurse to
   A. get the proper diet
   B. perform a spiritual consult
   C. communicate with family
   D. avoid making assumptions

9. Seeking understanding of culturally related health care practices is essential to nursing because traditional values and beliefs about health and illness
   A. have practices that need to be avoided
   B. affect the body image and overweight habits
   C. may affect patients' acceptance of treatments
   D. use various health practices that might be harmful

10. What is the nurse's best response when a Muslim patient has a basin of water on his bedside stand that he does not want emptied?
   A. Educate him that the water can be a hazard to his health.
   B. Empty it because it could spill and get the bed wet.
   C. Talk with him about why he should not have it there.
   D. Support and accommodate his preference.

Canadian Nursing Research

Anderson, J. M., Tang, S. et al. (2007). Health care reform and the paradox of efficiency: "Writing in" culture. *International Journal of Health Services, 37*(2), 291–320.

Browne, A. J. (2007). Clinical encounters between nurses and First Nations women in a Western Canadian hospital. *Social Science & Medicine, 64*(10), 2165–2176.

Guruge, S., & Collins, E. (2008). *Working with immigrant women: Issues and strategies for mental health professionals.* Toronto, ON: Canadian Centre for Addictions and Mental Health.

Srivastava, R. (2007). *The healthcare professional's guide to clinical cultural competence.* Toronto, ON: Elsevier Canada.

References

Aboriginal Nurses Association of Canada/Canadian Association of Schools of Nursing/Canadian Nurses Association. (2009). *Cultural competence and cultural safety in nursing: A framework for First Nations, Inuit, and Métis nursing.* Ottawa, ON: Aboriginal Nurses Association of Canada.

Anderson, E. T., & McFarlane, J. (2011). *Community as partner: Theory and practice in nursing* (6th ed.). Philadelphia, PA: Lippincott Williams & Wilkins.

Andrews, M. M., & Boyle, J. S. (2003). *Transcultural concepts in nursing care* (4th ed.). Philadelphia, PA: Lippincott Williams & Wilkins.

Astle, B. J., Barton, S., et al. (2010). Culture and ethnicity. In J. C. Ross-Kerr & M. J. Wood (Canadian Eds)., *Potter & Perry Canadian fundamentals of nursing* (Rev. 4th ed., pp.114–131). Toronto, ON: Elsevier Canada.

Barrett, B., Marchand, L., et al. (2003). Themes of holism, empowerment, access and legitimacy define complementary, alternative and integrative medicine in relation to conventional biomedicine. *Journal of Alternative and Complementary Medicine, 9*(6), 937–948.

Basara, H. G., & Yuan, M. (2008). Community self assessment using self organizing maps and geographic information systems. *International Journal of Health Geography, 7*(1), 67.

Berman, B. M. (2006). Cochrane complementary medicine field. About the Cochrane collaboration (Fields), Issue 1. Art. No.: CE000052.

Bonomi, A. E., Anderson, M. L. et al. (2009). Intimate partner violence in Latina and non-Latina women. *American Journal of Preventive Medicine, 36*(1), 43–48.

Borg, J., Andree, B., et al. (2003). The serotonin system and spiritual experience. *American Journal of Psychiatry, 11*, 965–969.

Borysenko, J. (2005). *Healing and spirituality: The sacred quest for transformation of body and soul.* Carlsbad, CA: Hay House Audio.

Bradwell, M. (2009). Survivors of childhood cancer. *Pediatric Nursing, 21*(4), 21–24.

Bulecheck, G. M., Butcher, H. K., et al. (2008). *Nursing interventions classification (NIC)* (5th ed.) St Louis, MO: Mosby.

Burkhardt, M. A. (2009). Commentary on "Existential and spiritual needs in mental health care: An ethical issue. *Journal of Holistic Nursing, 27*, 43–44.

Canadian Nurses Association. (2010). *Canadian registered nurse examination: Competencies.* Retrieved from: http://www.cna-aiic.ca/CNA/nursing/rnexam/competencies/default_e.aspx.

Canadian Public Health Association. (2006). *Action statement for health promotion in Canada.* Ottawa, ON: Author.

Clark, M. B., & Olson, J. K. (2000). *Nursing within a faith community: Promoting health in times of transition.* Thousand Oaks, CA: Sage Publications, Inc.

Cohen, B. (2005). Health promotion. In L. L. Stamler & L. Yiu (Eds.). *Community health nursing: A Canadian perspective* (pp. 117-136). Toronto, ON: Pearson.

Crittenden, C. P., Boris, N. W., et al. (2009). The role of mental health factors, behavioral factors, and past experiences in the prediction of rapid repeat pregnancy in adolescence. *Journal of Adolescent Health, 44*(1), 25–32.

Enang, J., Wojnar, D., et al. (2002). Childbearing among diverse populations: How one hospital is providing multicultural care. *Lifelines, 6*(2), 153–158.

Feeley, N., & Gottlieb, L. N. (2000). Nursing approaches for working with family strengths and resources. *Journal of Family Nursing, 6*(1), 9–24.

Gordon, M. (2006). *Manual of nursing diagnosis* (11th ed.). Boston, MA: Barnes & Noble.

Gottlieb, L., & Rowat, K. (1987). The McGill model of nursing: A practice-derived model. *Advances in Nursing Science, 9*(4), 51–61.

Health Canada. (1998). *Taking action on population health: A position paper for Health Promotion and Programs Branch staff.* Ottawa, ON: Author.

Hobfoll, S. E. (2001). Social and psychological resources and adaptation. *Review of General Psychology, 6*, 307–324.

Holt, C. L., Lewellyn, L. A., et al. (2005). Exploring religion-health mediators among African American parishioners. *Journal of Health Psychology, 10*(4), 511–527.

Hudson, R., & Rumbold, B. (2003). Spiritual care. In M. O'Connor & S. Aranda (Eds.). *Palliative care nursing* (2nd ed., pp. 69–86). Melbourne: Ausmed Publications.

Interdisciplinary Plan. (2007). *Interdisciplinary plan for assessment/reassessment and care planning.* Retrieved from https://hmcweb.washington.edu/ADMIN/APOP/Administration/5.20.htm

Jambunathan, J. (2003). People of Hindu heritage. In L. Purnell & B. Paulanka (Eds.). *Transcultural care: A culturally competent approach* (2nd ed., chapter on CD). Philadelphia, PA: F. A. Davis.

Kaplan, G. (2006). Book review: *Social determinants of health* (2nd ed.). In M. Marmot & R. Wilkinson (Eds.). Oxford. *International Journal of Epidemiology, 35*(4), 1111–1112.

Kerwin, R. (2009). Connecting patient needs with treatment management. *Acta Psychiatrica Scandinavica, 438*, 33–39.

Lalonde, M. (1974). *A new perspective on the health of Canadians.* Ottawa, ON: Minister of Supply and Services.

Leininger, M. M., & McFarland, M. (2005). *Culture care diversity and universality: A worldwide nursing theory* (2nd ed.). Boston, MA: Jones & Bartlett.

Lipstein, E. A., Perrin, J. M., & et al. (2009). School absenteeism, health status, and health care utilization among children with asthma: Associations with parental chronic disease. *Pediatrics, 123*(1), e60–e66.

Liu, C. J., Hsiung, P. C., et al. (2008). A study on the efficacy of body-mind-spirit group therapy for patients with breast cancer. *Journal of Clinical Nursing, 17*(19), 2539–2549.

Marmot, M. G., & Wilkinson R. G. (2006). *Social determinants of health* (2nd ed.). Oxford: Oxford University Press.

McCaffrey, R. (2008). Music listening: Its effects in creating a healing environment. *Journal of Psychosocial Nursing and Mental Health Services, 46*(10), 39–44.

Melnyk, B., & Fineout-Overholt, E. (2004). *Evidence-based practice in nursing and healthcare: A guide to best practice.* New York, NY: Lippincott Williams & Wilkins.

Moorhead, S., Johnson, M., et al. (2007). *Nursing outcomes classification (NOC)* (4th ed.). Philadelphia, PA: Mosby.

Morad, M. (2008). Focus on holistic care for children and adolescents with diabetes. *International Journal of Adolescent Med Health, 20*(4), 387–388.

North American Nursing Diagnosis Association-International. (2009). *Nursing diagnoses, 2009–2011 Edition: Definitions and classifications (NANDA-I NURSING DIAGNOSIS).* West Sussex, UK: John Wiley & Sons.

Nightingale, F. (1860/1992). *Notes on nursing: What nursing is, what nursing is not.* New York, NY: Lippincott Williams & Wilkins.

Olson, J. K., & Anderson, L. J. (2005). Faith community health nursing. In L. L. Stamler & L. Yiu (Eds.) *Community health nursing: A Canadian perspective* (pp. 342–345). Toronto, ON: Pearson.

Palmer, D., & Ward, K. (2007). 'Lost': Listening to the voices and mental health needs of forced migrants in London. *Medicine, Conflict, and Survival, 23*(3), 198–212.

Patrick, L., & Edmunds, K. (2005). Family care. In L. L. Stamler & L. Yiu (Eds.). *Community health nursing: A Canadian perspective* (pp. 137–152). Toronto, ON: Pearson Prentice Hall.

Pease, N. (1991). Poland and the Holy Sea, 1918–1939. *Slavic Review, 50*(3), 521–530.

Pinder, L. (2007). The federal role in health promotion. In M. O'Neill, A. Pederson, et al. (Eds.). *Health promotion in Canada* (2nd ed., pp. 92-105). Toronto, ON: Canadian Scholars' Press.

Pinn, A. H. (2002). *Fortress introduction to Black Church history.* Minneapolis, MN: Augsburg Fortress.

Purnell, L. D., & Paulanka, B. J. (2005). *Guide to culturally competent health care.* Philadelphia, PA: F. A. Davis.

Reutter, L., & Kushner, K. E. (2010). The broad scope of health promotion in health assessment. In T. C. Stephen, D. L. Skillen, R. A. Day, & L. S. Bickley (Eds). *Canadian Bates' guide to health assessment for nurses* (1st ed., pp. 3–25). Philadelphia, PA: Wolters Kluwer Health/Lippincott Williams & Wilkins.

Riordan, J., & Auerbach, K. (2005). *Breastfeeding and human lactation.* Boston, MA: Jones & Bartlett.

Robinson, G. (2000). *Essential Judaism: A complete guide to beliefs, customs, and rituals.* New York, NY: Pocket Books.

Romito, P., Turan, J. M., et al. (2009). Violence and women's psychological distress after birth: An exploratory study in Italy. *Health Care for Women International, 30*(1–2), 160–180.

Roy, C., & Andrews, H. (1999). *The Roy adaptation model* (2nd ed.). Stamford, CT: Appleton & Lange.

Rumbold, B. (2003). Caring for the spirit: Lessons from working with the dying. *Australian Medical Journal, 179*(6 Suppl), S11–S13.

Seid, M. (2008). Barriers to care and primary care for vulnerable children with asthma. *Pediatrics, 122*(5), 994–1002.

Statistics Canada. (2010a). *Canada's ethnocultural mosaic, 2006 census: National picture.* Retrieved from http://www12.statcan.ca/census-recensement/2006/as-sa/97-562/p8-eng.cfm

Statistics Canada. (2010b). *National Population Health Survey-Household component-longitudinal (NPHS).* Retrieved from http://www.statcan.gc.ca/cgi-bin/imdb/p2SV.pl?Function=getSurvey&SDDS=3225%lang

Swanson, K. M., & Wojnar, D. M. (2004). Optimal healing environments in nursing. *Journal of Alternative and Complementary Medicine, 10*(1), 43–48.

Thomas-MacLean, R. (2004). Understanding breast cancer stories via Frank's narrative types. *Social Science and Medicine, 58*(9), 1647–1657.

Thorne, S. (2010). Theoretical foundations of nursing practice. In J. C. Ross-Kerr & M. J. Wood (Canadian Eds.) *Potter & Perry Canadian fundamentals of nursing* (Rev. 4th ed.; pp. 63–73). Toronto, ON: Elsevier Canada.

Vance, D. E., Struzick, T. C., et al. (2008). Biopsychosocial benefits of spirituality in adults aging with HIV: Implications for nursing practice and research. *Journal of Holistic Nursing, 26*(2), 119–125.

Varcoe, C., Browne, A., et al. (2010). Cultural considerations in health assessment. In T. C. Stephen, D. L. Skillen, R. A. Day, & L. S. Bickley (Eds.). *Canadian Bates' guide to health assessment for nurses* (1st ed., pp. 27–49). Philadelphia, PA: Wolters Kluwer Health/Lippincott Williams, & Wilkins.

Wade, D. T. (2004). Education and debate: Do biomedical models of illness make for good healthcare systems? *British Medical Journal, 329*, 1398–1401.

Wade, D. T. (2009). Goal setting in rehabilitation: An overview of what, why and how. *Clinical Rehabilitation, 23*, 291–295.

The Canadian Jensen's Nursing Health Assessment suite offers these additional resources to enhance learning and facilitate understanding of this chapter:

- thePoint online resource, http//thepoint.lww.com/Stephen1E
- *Laboratory Manual for Canadian Jensen's Nursing Health Assessment: A Best Practice Approach*

Assessment of Human Violence

Learning Objectives

1 Describe the different types of human violence.

2 Recognize the scope of the human violence problem.

3 Identify physical, mental, psychosocial, and environmental health effects of human violence.

4 Collect subjective and objective data on violence.

5 Analyze subjective and objective findings from assessment of patients victimized by human violence to plan effective interventions.

6 Document assessment findings related to human violence and safety concerns.

7 Identify the basics of a safety plan.

8 Identify key differences among various forms of human violence and how these differences affect assessment and intervention.

*S*ue Brown is a 24-year-old, middle-class Caucasian woman being interviewed by a psychiatric nurse practitioner at a day treatment substance-abuse program. Sue, who tells the nurse that she prefers to be called by her first name, is dependent on opiates to treat chronic back pain from a car accident. When Sue was a child, her father traveled for work frequently; her mother stayed at home. Sue was an athlete in high school and attended 1 year of college. She has seen health care professionals throughout her life for routine examinations, injuries, sexually transmitted infections (STIs), and dental care. Sue lives with her parents and brother and works part time as a grocery checker.

Across the various forms of human violence are commonalities in signs and symptoms (red flags), effects, appropriate assessment techniques, interview strategies, documentation, and resources for nurses and patients. As you study the content and features of this chapter, consider Sue's case and its relationship to what you are learning. Begin thinking about the following points:

- Based on Sue's history, what red flags might prompt health care providers to perform a complete safety assessment?
- How do Sue's symptoms and behaviours cluster together?
- What is the role of the nurse in assessing safety?

Men, women, and children perpetrate violence against others, the effects of which ripple through the lives of individuals, families, communities, and societies. Because of the high prevalence of human violence, nurses come into contact with victims and perpetrators daily. A health care visit may be the first time that a patient discusses a violent experience. Conversely, many people, including nurses, are unaware of or are in conscious or unconscious denial about the prevalence, types, and effects of human violence. Appropriate, compassionate, and sincere awareness and assessment are crucial to stopping violence and to assisting those victimized by it toward safety and recovery, thereby preventing ongoing consequences.

This chapter includes basic information on human violence related to assessment, safety, prevention, and recovery. It describes many different types of violence, their prevalence rates, and physical and psychological effects. The chapter explores important screening and assessment techniques, such as observation for signs and symptoms of violence and interview strategies, both of which are used to collect subjective and objective data. The last part of the chapter provides information on nursing interventions related to safety, recovery, and healing.

Types of Human Violence

Almost half of all people (44%) report experiencing human violence (Plichta & Falik, 2001). The following paragraphs discuss various forms of violence in detail; Table 12-1 summarizes and defines them.

Family Violence

A crime is considered **family violence** if the victim is biologically related to the offender or is related to him or her

Table 12-1	Types of Human Violence
Type	**Definition**
Family violence	All types of violent crime committed by an offender who is related to the victim either biologically or legally through marriage or adoption
Child maltreatment	Covers a wide range of abusive and neglectful behaviours toward children; figures are based primarily on reported cases of child abuse and neglect investigated by child welfare and protection services
Polyvictimization	Experiences of more than one type of violence
Sibling violence	Not frequently taken seriously in Canada; it often comes under the rubric of sibling rivalry or roughhousing
Intimate partner violence (IPV)	Between spouses or nonmarital partners, threatened or actual physical or sexual violence or psychological/emotional abuse, coercive tactics, or both when there has been prior physical and/or sexual violence
IPV in pregnancy	Violence between spouses or nonmarital partners during the prenatal, intrapartum, or postpartum period
Punking and bullying	Aggression in which (1) the behaviour is intended to harm, (2) the behaviour occurs repeatedly over time, and (3) there is an imbalance of power, with a more powerful person or group attacking a less powerful one
School violence	Crimes at school including theft, simple assault, and serious violent crime
Sexual violence	Forced sex in dating and marital relationships, gang rape, sexual harassment, inappropriate touching or molestation, sex with a patient, and forced prostitution and/or exposure to sexually explicit behaviour
Violence against older adults	Intentional or unintentional acts such as physical, sexual, psychological, and financial abuse and neglect against older adults
Violence against adults with developmental disabilities	Intentional or unintentional acts such as physical, sexual, psychological, and financial abuse and neglect against adults with developmental disabilities
Hate crimes	Crime in which a victim is selected based on a characteristic such as genetic background, ethnicity, sexual orientation, age, and the like and for which the perpetrator provides evidence that hate prompted him or her to commit the crime
Human trafficking	The recruitment, transportation, transfer, harbouring, or receipt of people by threats, force, coercion, or deception
War and violence victimization	Witnessing the killing of human beings including friends and fellow service people, intentionally killing and injuring other humans, and being intentionally injured or potentially killed by another human

through marriage, adoption, or legal guardianship. The term family violence often is used interchangeably with *domestic violence, intimate partner violence (IPV)*, and *male violence against women*. It is best to ask the patient for clarification and specifics if he or she uses any of these terms.

Types of family violence include child maltreatment, sibling violence, IPV, and elder abuse. The nurse may encounter all these types during patient assessments. Some patients never disclose that they have been hurt or seek assistance from police, health care professionals, counsellors, or lawyers.

Child Maltreatment

Child maltreatment covers a wide range of violent behaviours against children. Prevalence rates, however, have focused primarily on abuse of children by parents and are based mainly on reported cases of abuse investigated by Child Welfare Authorities. In 2009, approximately 55,000 cases of physical and/or sexual violence toward children (214 cases per 100,000 people) were reported in Canada (Statistics Canada, 2011). Of these cases, over half were committed by a family member. Violent practices rarely occur as isolated incidents; often, children have more than one victimization experience (Finkelhor, Ormrod, et al., 2005, 2007). Polyvictimization is the highest in children who report rape and dating violence (Finkelhor, Ormrod, et al., 2007). About 25% of children experience four or more different kinds of victimization (Finkelhor, Ormrod, et al., 2007). Trauma symptoms such as anxiety, depression, anger, and aggression are "red flags" of polyvictimization.

Sibling Violence

Historically, violence between and among siblings has not been taken seriously. It often has been considered within the realm of typical sibling relationships and represented by such terms as *sibling rivalry, roughhousing*, and *sibling competition* (Phillips, Phillips, et al., 2009). Nevertheless, sibling violence is among the most common type that children experience (Finkelhor, Turner, et al., 2006).

Intimate Partner Violence

IPV has been defined as behaviours between spouses or nonmarital partners involving threatened or actual physical or sexual violence, psychological/emotional abuse, and/or coercive tactics when there has been prior physical or sexual violence (Saltzman, Fanslow, et al., 1999). Nonmarital partners include those in adolescent and adult dating relationships and in long-term, committed, intimate, heterosexual or homosexual relationships. In Canada, 3.8% of married people reported spousal abuse with 83% being female and 17% being male (Statistics Canada, 2011).

No group is immune to IPV—it occurs in all cultures and populations and across all ages, genetic backgrounds, ethnicities, education levels, and socioeconomic statuses (Moracco, Runyam, et al., 2007). Perpetrators of IPV are most often male. Of women who report being raped, physically assaulted, or stalked since age 18 years, approximately two thirds are victimized by a current or former husband, cohabiting male partner, boyfriend, or date (Rape, Abuse & Incest National Network [RAINN], 2008). Abusive and controlling behaviours and practices by perpetrators of IPV are described in Table 12-2.

Table 12-2	Methods of Power and Control in Intimate Partner Violence (IPV)
IPV Behaviours and Practices by Perpetrators	**Descriptions**
Intimidation	Making victims afraid by using looks, actions, gestures; smashing things; destroying property; abusing pets; displaying weapons
Coercion and threats	Making and/or carrying out threats to do something to hurt victims; threatening to leave, commit suicide, report victims to welfare; making victims drop charges or do illegal things (ie, take drugs)
Emotional abuse	Putting down victims or making them feel bad about themselves; calling victims names; making victims think they are crazy; playing mind games; humiliating or making victims feel guilty
Isolation	Controlling what victims do or read, whom they see or talk to, or where they go; limiting their involvement outside the home; using jealousy to justify actions
Minimizing, denying, and blaming	Making light of abuse and not taking concerns of victims seriously; saying abuse did not happen; shifting responsibility for abusive behaviour; saying victims caused it
Using children	Making victims feel guilty about children; having children relay messages; using visitation to harass victims; threatening to take children away; using children as spies
Privilege	Treating victims like servants; making all big decisions; acting like the "master of the castle"; being the one who defines men's and women's roles
Economic abuse	Preventing victims from getting or keeping a job; making victims ask for money or giving them an allowance; taking money; not letting victims know about or have access to family income

Adapted from Domestic Abuse Intervention Project. (2008). *The power and control wheel.* Retrieved from http://theduluthmodel.org/pdf/PhysVio.pdf

IPV among immigrants and refugees. Female immigrants and refugees, particularly those who do not speak English or have legal documents, are especially vulnerable to IPV (Papp, 2010). Rates of IPV may be higher in female immigrants than in female citizens for several reasons. Some cultures more visibly accept violence against women than does the Canadian culture. In addition, immigrants who attempt to escape IPV face significant barriers. For example, they may not have access to bilingual safety shelters, financial assistance, food, or other support services. It is also unlikely that they have assistance from certified interpreters during court proceedings, when reporting complaints to police, or even when acquiring information about their rights and the legal system. Lastly, perpetrators of IPV may use their partners' immigration status as a tool of control and force women to remain in the relationship, making it difficult for victims to escape the violence.

⚠ *SAFETY ALERT 12.1*

Murder, homicide, or femicide (murder of a female) is IPV when perpetrated by a current or ex-intimate partner. Most femicides are preceded by a history of IPV before the woman's death (Campbell, 1992; Campbell, Sharps, et al., 2000).

IPV in pregnancy. IPV in pregnancy is a serious and widespread problem. Of women abused during pregnancy, more than half also experienced IPV before pregnancy. Between 4% and 32% of women from nonindustrialized countries are abused during pregnancy, a much greater percentage than in industrialized countries (Campbell, Garcia-Moreno, et al., 2004). For nurses working with Canadian citizens, immigrants, and refugees, the high rates of abuse demonstrate that an assessment for violence in the prenatal, intrapartum, and postpartum periods is essential. Approximately 6% of new mothers in 2006 reported experiencing IPV during and after pregnancy (Canada Centre for Justice Statistics, 2008). See also Chapter 27.

Elder Abuse

Maltreatment of older adults can be in the form of abuse, neglect, financial exploitation, or abandonment. In 2009, approximately 7900 seniors (over 65 years) reported experiencing violence (Statistics Canada, 2011). Of these, 70% of these attacks were committed by a family member, friend, or acquaintance. Abuse includes intentional actions that cause harm or create a serious risk to a vulnerable elder, by a caregiver or other person who stands in a trust relationship with the elder (Fulmer, 2008). Examples include kicking, punching, slapping, or burning. Factors that put older adults at risk include dependency, cognitive decline, strained mental or physical health of caregivers, and financial issues. A commonly used tool to screen for maltreatment in older adults is the Elder Assessment Inventory (Fulmer, 2008).

Violence Against Adults with Disabilities

Violence against vulnerable adults, such as those with physical and mental disabilities, includes harmful acts of commission (abuse) or omission (neglect). Physical, sexual, psychological, and financial abuse and neglect may be intentional or unintentional (National Center for Elder Abuse, 1998; Sengstock, Ulrick et al., 2004). Adults with disabilities are more likely to experience severe and long-term abuse, be victims of multiple violent episodes, and be abused by many perpetrators. In addition, sexual assault is exceptionally high in women with developmental disabilities—they are 4 to 11 times more likely to be sexually assaulted than women without disabilities (Schaller & Lagergren Fieberg, 1998; Stromsness, 1993).

⚠ *SAFETY ALERT 12.2*

Statistics Canada (2011) reported that senior women are almost equally likely to be abused by their spouse as by their grown children. Findings showed that older women are far more likely than older men to suffer from abuse or neglect. Two of every three victims of elder abuse were women; more than two in five victims were 80 years or older.

"Youth" and School Violence

Many young people witness, perpetrate, and are victimized by violence in and around their schools and neighbourhoods. This includes daily nonfatal crimes, such as theft and simple assault, as well as serious violent crime (National Center for Education Statistics, 2007). Violent practices include being slapped, hit, or punched at school; beaten or mugged in neighbourhoods. and being shot, shot at, or stabbed. Rates of recent witnessing of violence range widely from 5% to 72% (Singer, Anglin, et al., 1995).

Punking and Bullying

Punking and bullying are common among middle- and high-school males, usually resulting in shame, humiliation, and anger. Similar to bullying and sometimes used interchangeably, *punking* is a practice of verbal and physical violence, humiliation, and shaming, usually done in public or with an audience (Phillips, 2007). Bullying in the form of verbal violence is common among middle- and high-school girls (Beaty & Alexeyev, 2008; O'Moore & Hillery, 1989).

Sexual Violence

Sexual violence includes forced sex in dating and marital relationships, gang rape, sexual harassment, inappropriate touching, molestation, sex with the patient, forced prostitution, and forced exposure to sexually explicit behaviour. Child sexual abuse and adult rape are two relatively common types. Marital rape is not a crime in all countries; in fact, it has been illegal in Canada only for 28 years. Strongly patriarchal societies, cultures, and religions are strictly organized around the supremacy of the father as head of the family or clan, with wives and children dependent (legally and otherwise) on him. Many women in some countries do not have the right or a voice to say "no" to sex in such patriarchal relationships.

Hate Crimes

Statistics Canada (2011) defines a **hate crime** as one in which a perpetrator chooses a victim because of a characteristic such as genetic background, ethnicity, gender, sexuality, or religion and provides evidence that hate motivated the crime. Psychological and emotional violence are the most common forms of hate crimes, which include practices such as racism, homophobia, and discrimination. Nurses and other health professionals often meet people who have experienced hate crimes; however, such violence may never be disclosed by patients or asked about by professionals.

⚠ SAFETY ALERT 12.3

Genetic background "motivates" approximately 50% of all hate crimes, while ethnicity is the reason in 25% of cases. In Canada, the most targeted religious group is Jewish while African Canadians are the most targeted group for their genetic background (Statistics Canada, 2011).

Human Trafficking

The United Nations (2008) defines **human trafficking** as the recruitment, transportation, transfer, harbouring, or receipt of people through threats, force, coercion, or deception. Misleading or false advertising (eg, offers of good wages and "legitimate" work abroad) may entice women attempting to escape unemployment in their home countries. After responding to such advertising, these women may be abducted, bonded, or sold into indentured servitude. Reasons people are trafficked include sexual exploitation, forced marriage, and cheap labour for domestic or commercial purposes. Those who own and manage commercial "sex trade" businesses (ie, forced prostitution, stripping, pornography, live-sex shows) are the major perpetrators of human trafficking (U.S. Department of Health & Human Services, 2006).

Labour exploitation includes domestic servitude, sweatshop factories, and migrant agricultural work.

War-Related and Military Violence

A relatively common form of violence is related to military combat. War-related fighting can involve witnessing killing, including of friends and fellow service people; intentionally killing and injuring other humans; and being intentionally injured or potentially killed. People who have experienced war violence include veterans of all ages, families of veterans who are traumatized vicariously by living with them, and people of all ages who witness war and its violence. This group also includes those who escaped war, spent time in a "camp" before immigrating. The escape or camp experience may have been traumatic and included actual or witnessed violence. Rates of IPV perpetration are increased in veterans with posttraumatic stress disorder (PTSD) related to combat exposure (Gerlock, 2004; Prigerson, Maciejewski et al., 2002).

Importance of Violence/Safety Assessment

Many of those who receive care for violence-related trauma do not disclose the cause of their injuries. When the patient presents with any injury, screening and assessing for violence as the cause are parts of a complete nursing assessment.

Clinical Significance 12-2

Like Sue, nearly all child and adult victims of violence have contact with health care professionals throughout their lives. Although violence frequently is undetected, patients often seek care for many different related reasons. Victims of violence often have increased health conditions, health care visits, and financial burdens (Dube, Anda, et al., 2005; Felitti, 2002; Felitti, Anda, et al., 1998).

Routine assessment for violence and safety is important during every encounter with patients because of the high prevalence of human violence and its short- and long-term effects on health, relationships, and well-being. Community-based entry points for such screening and assessment include home visits and immunization, school, and Woman/Infant/Children (WIC) clinics. Other entry points are nursing homes, primary care offices and clinics, mental health services, substance-abuse services, and medical emergency services. Any health care or community setting with a nursing presence is an appropriate point for such assessment, however.

Violence assessment can range from brief screening questions for all patients to a thorough history and head-to-toe physical examination for those who disclose violence or present with violent injuries. See Box 12-1.

BOX 12-1 ABUSE ASSESSMENT SCREEN

1. **Within the last year**, have you been hit, slapped, kicked, or otherwise physically hurt by someone? YES NO
   If YES, by whom? _____
   Total number of times ____
2. **Since you've been pregnant**, have you been hit, slapped, kicked, or otherwise physically hurt by someone? YES NO
   If YES, by whom? _____
   Total number of times ____
3. **Within the last year**, has anyone forced you to have sexual activities? YES NO
   If YES, by whom? _____
   Total number of times ____

Score each of the following incidents according to the following scale. If any of the descriptions for the higher number apply, use the higher number.

1 = Threats of abuse including use of a weapon
2 = Slapping, pushing; no injuries and/or lasting pain
3 = Punching, kicking, bruises, cuts, and/or continuing pain
4 = Beating up, severe contusions, burns, broken bones
5 = Head injury, internal injury, permanent injury
6 = Use of weapon; wound from weapon

Developed by the Nursing Research Consortium on Violence and Abuse. Readers are encouraged to reproduce and use this assessment tool.

Subjective Data Collection

The pace and extent of safety assessment should be geared to the patient's needs. The nurse provides the safe opportunity and environment for disclosure as well as the skills and attitude needed to support the patient through what can be a difficult process. Sometimes a nurse is the first person to "bear witness" to the truth of the patient's story of violence victimization. Validating the importance and difficulty of disclosure is essential. Conversely, some patients deny the seriousness of violence or consider it "normal." They may feel this way because many people in their family have also experienced violence or because most women or men or a specific group in their culture commonly experience it.

When a nurse asks about violence, some patients decide that the time, setting, or health care professional is not a comfortable fit for them to disclose their story. In such cases, violence-screening questions provide an opportunity for the nurse to let patients know about the high prevalence of human violence so that they do not feel singled out or alone. During these encounters, the nurse also can teach about the health effects of violence, review safety and resources, and connect and establish rapport.

Most women, regardless of victimization status, are comfortable being screened for IPV; in fact, approximately 80% of female victims disclose IPV when asked (Plichta, 2007). They are unlikely to disclose abuse, however, without being asked (Plichta).

Some health professionals are inhibited from asking about, screening for, or assessing for violence (Fahey, 2007; Plichta, 2007). There are many reasons why health professionals, including nurses, do not ask about violent experiences. Examples include a lack of education about such assessment, deficient knowledge about resources to provide to patients who disclose violence, and discomfort with this discussion. Health professionals need to ask questions and be prepared for patients who disclose childhood or adult experiences of violence. This statement has several implications. Being prepared to hear that "Yes, my partner raped me" or "My father molested me"

requires that nurses hear what patients are saying and not deny, discount, ignore, disconnect, judge, or be overly solicitous.

Largely as a result of work of the Nursing Network on Violence Against Women International and the Nursing Research Consortium, screening and assessment of violence against women have become more common practices (Harley, 2006; Hindin, 2006; Plichta, 2007). Nevertheless, bearing witness to disclosures of violence can be particularly difficult for nurses and other health care professionals who have experienced and/or witnessed human violence themselves. In such cases, nurses need to recognize unresolved aspects of their lives and move forward on recognition, healing, and resolution so that they can do their professional work and uphold standards of care.

Similar to other sensitive or difficult topics (eg, constipation, flatulence, disfigurement), asking about violence breeches social taboos and may seem to some nurses as "too personal" or "none of my business." While this may be true in nonprofessional relationships, nurses remember that they are in professional, therapeutic relationships with patients. Their assessments need to include questions about intimate body functions, intimate relationships, and negative life experiences—including human violence—that cause physical and mental health consequences.

Interviewing Patients About Human Violence

Asking patients about personal experiences of violence is a key aspect of assessment. Of utmost importance is how such assessment is conducted. First and foremost in every nurse's mind should be the patient's physical and emotional safety. A universal rule is that patient interviews are done in private—including without significant others or anyone who may be or could represent the perpetrator (eg, friend, mother-in-law). Nurses should not assume who may or may not be a perpetrator or have power over the patient and who may prevent her or him from talking freely and safely.

Asking about violent experiences works best when it is a routine part of nursing assessment, similar to asking about sleep or activity concerns or dietary or sexual concerns. It is important to try to establish a connection with the patient first. In general, nurses listen to patients more than they talk, using an 80% to 20% guideline (80% patient, 20% nurse). The possible exception is during patient education.

Nurses can also encourage rapport, connection, and patient participation by using a narrative approach in their interactions. In the narrative approach, the patient of any age tells her or his story, whether it involves abdominal pain, sore throat, headache, or experiences of bullying or other violence. As the patient provides the account, the nurse collects data and listens for aspects of the story that need clarification, elaboration, or both. Taking time to listen in a nonjudgmental, nondirective way and to ensure confidentiality helps create a safe, supportive atmosphere (Plichta, 2007).

Basics for nurses to review when assessing for violence include the following:

• Perform assessment and screening only when the patient is alone in a safe, private environment.
• Establish rapport and connection by showing interest in the patient and by listening.
• Be very patient as the patient talks.
• Move from general, open-ended questions to specific questions.
• Demonstrate compassion, not judgment.
• Use interpreters if there is any question about understanding on the patient's or nurse's part. Clarify and reflect back to the patient what he or she says and what you understand.
• Maintain comfortable and neutral body language.
• Remain close to and at eye level with the patient, but not in her or his "personal" space.
• Use a relaxed and calm tone of voice at medium volume, with pacing appropriate to the patient's developmental level and level needed for clear understanding.
• Do not ask the patient if he or she wants to press charges against the perpetrator. This decision is up to a prosecutor and is not part of a violence assessment.
• Often, the best way to ask a patient about violence is simple and direct.

These above points are generalizations. It is essential to always ask the patient if she or he is comfortable with the approach taken and the physicality of the interview space. Open-ended questions, such as "What would you like to know?" "How can I help you understand?" or "What would you like me to know?" are especially helpful if the patient appears uncomfortable.

Nurses can prepare patients for sensitive or difficult questions about violence by prefacing comments with statements such as, "Now is the point in the interview where I ask patients about relationships in their family. Who lives in your home with you? How do you feel in that relationship?" It is also common to ask, "Because violence is so common for so many people, I routinely ask all patients about violent experiences—in the past and currently. I wonder if you have experienced or are experiencing violence?" See Box 12-2 for other ways to phrase questions about violence.

Another way to begin assessment about controlling behaviours or emotional and psychological abuse is to assess daily routines. Examples of questions include, "Tell me what you did today from the time you got up until the time you got here" or "Describe your last 3 days." Sometimes asking patients about their daily lives and routines reveals detailed information about victimizing behaviours and isolation, even when abuse is by a sibling, peer, or parent. In addition, this approach gives the patient a chance to share her or his story, connect with the nurse, and display strengths. It also provides the nurse opportunities for teaching, providing resources, affirming strengths, and giving support.

Include questions about adverse childhood and family events and about current living context; these questions may elicit information about adverse experiences. Psychosocial histories often include violence assessment, but they can be very sensitive areas for patients to discuss (see Chapter 10). Moving into this area of assessment toward the end of the patient history allows time to build rapport and to ask less sensitive questions first.

Nurses should be patient and not pressure patients to disclose, leave their partners, or otherwise make decisions that patients are not ready for, all of which can cause disconnection in the nurse–patient relationship. This outcome may lead a

---

BOX 12-2   ASSESSMENT QUESTIONS: VIOLENCE VICTIMIZATION AND PERPETRATION

Assessing Violence Victimization Sample Questions (See Also Box 12-1)

• "Because violence is so common in many people's lives, I ask all patients about it routinely."
• "Are you in a relationship with a person who physically or sexually hurts or threatens you?"
• "Did someone cause those injuries? Who?"
• "Injuries like yours could have been caused by someone hurting you. Did someone hurt you?"
• "Sometimes when people feel the way you do, it's because they have been hurt or abused at home. Is that happening to you?"

• "Many of the adults (children, teens) I work with have experienced violence in their past, and some are experiencing it in their current lives. I wonder if you have any experiences of violence."

Assessing Violence Perpetration

• "Some people think that under certain circumstances it's OK to hit a person you love. What are your thoughts about that?"
• "If you were faced with overwhelming stress (eg, losing your job, spouse/partner leaving you), what behaviours might you display?"
• "Have you ever physically hurt someone in your family?" (Ask for specifics and think safety first.)
• "Have you ever physically hurt someone?"

Until her current interview sessions, Sue never told anyone about her experiences of sibling violence or IPV by former boyfriends. Growing up, she assumed that violence was normal, despite being asked about it in other health care encounters. The following conversation occurs near the end of the fifth session.

Nurse: You've had other injuries—ruptured eardrum, broken arm, bruises, and black eyes.

Sue: Yeah, I'm accident prone.

Nurse: I know that I asked you before, but I routinely ask all patients about past and current violent experiences. I wonder if you have experienced or are experiencing violence?

Sue: (hesitates) Well, my brother and I are close, but sometimes we get a little rough.

Nurse: What would you like me to know?

Sue: I'm beginning to think that my relationships aren't healthy. My brother and I are very physical, and he has thrown me against walls and punched me.

Nurse: (Silent, nonverbal active listening)

Sue: It's hard to talk about (pause). I just assumed that getting hit was normal. My brother has ADHD. He's been kicked out of school for being so aggressive.

Nurse: (Silent, nonverbal active listening)

Sue: I just got used to being hit and learned to fight back. Maybe that's why I get involved in relationships where I get hurt.

Critical Thinking Challenge

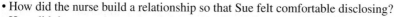
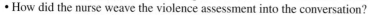

- How did the nurse build a relationship so that Sue felt comfortable disclosing?
- How did the nurse weave the violence assessment into the conversation?
- What other questions can the nurse ask before ending the interview?

patient not to return for follow-up care and, thereby, possibly be less safe and with fewer resources. The nurse's responsibility is to screen for and identify controlling and abusive behaviours, provide information about safety and resources, and report when mandatory reporting is required (see later discussion). Normally, patient information is confidential, which remains true when patients report violence, but with some exceptions.

Objective Data Collection

While performing physical assessments, a nurse may find signs of violence in patients. The nurse assesses nonverbal behaviours, such as the patient's eyes scanning the environment or the patient jumping or startling when a door slams. A nurse may notice that a child is very clingy to the person accompanying him or her, has a flat affect, or does not establish eye contact.

The following signs are indicators of possible abuse or neglect:

- Injuries not consistent with the story of their cause
- Sexual activity in a child younger than 14 years
- Inadequate supervision
- Serious injury
- Failure to seek timely medical care
- Multiple hospital or clinic visits for injuries
- Multiple previous fractures
- Bruises in multiple stages of healing

If any of the above occurs, the nurse should perform a complete physical assessment to evaluate for other manifestations of violence.

Many additional indications, or "red flags," alert nurses to the possibility of past or current human violence (Edwards, Anda, et al., 2007; Felitti, 2002) (Fig. 12-1). Common psychological red flags are unusual mood and behaviour changes for

Child Abuse Assessment Red Flags

✓ Mood changes, anger, isolating, sullenness
✓ Critical of self and/or others
✓ Risky behaviours
✓ Behaviour changes
✓ Friend changes
✓ School troubles
✓ Short temper, difficulty getting along with others
✓ Verbal and physical violence with siblings, parents, peers
✓ Weight gain or loss
✓ Quitting teams and activities

General Assessment Red Flags

✓ New-onset behaviours or change in behaviour
✓ Withdrawal, depression
✓ Agitation, hyperarousal
✓ New displays of anger, noncompliance
✓ Sexualized behaviour
✓ Bowel or bladder concerns
✓ Sleep problems
✓ Unexplained and/or "curious" injuries

Abuse/Neglect Assessment Red Flags

✓ Bruises, welts, cuts, scratches, restraint marks
✓ Open wounds, punctures, untreated sores, maggots
✓ Sprains, dislocations, internal injuries
✓ Victim changes in behaviour
✓ Caregiver refuses to allow visitors to see the victim
✓ Victim reports being hit and/or maltreated
✓ Soiled clothing or linens
✓ Overall bad hygiene, poor oral hygiene
✓ Dehydration, malnutrition, extreme weight loss

IPV Assessment Red Flags

✓ Physical injury (facial fractures, dental, neurological, soft tissue, internal, "falls")
✓ Chronic pain (back, abdomen, chest, head)
✓ Fibromyalgia, chronic irritable bowel
✓ Hypertension, smoking
✓ Unintended pregnancy, adolescent pregnancy
✓ Abortion
✓ Anal and vaginal tearing, painful intercourse
✓ Depression

Elder/Vulnerable Adult Violence Assessment Red Flags

✓ Frailty, cognitive impairment
✓ Psychiatric disorder, depression, anxiety
✓ Alcohol abuse
✓ Decreased social network
✓ Shared living arrangements
✓ External stressors on family
✓ Vague excuses for missing activities, therapy
✓ Untrimmed, dirty nails
✓ Inadequate or absent assistive devices
✓ History of family violence
✓ Unexplained injuries
✓ Explanation not consistent with findings
✓ Recurrent UTIs or other infections
✓ Poor hygiene, poor oral hygiene, dirty clothes
✓ Weight loss/lack of interest in meals
✓ Recurrent or worsening pressure ulcers, dehydration

Violence in Pregnancy Assessment Red Flags

✓ Late or inconsistent prenatal care
✓ Preterm bleeding and/or labour
✓ Abruption placentae–especially more than one time/with more than one pregnancy
✓ Low birth weight
✓ Unexplained fetal death
✓ Suicide attempts during pregnancy
✓ Postpartum depression
✓ Injuries during pregnancy
✓ Poor weight gain during pregnancy
✓ Partner unwilling to leave woman's side during prenatal visits, labour and delivery, and/or postpartum
✓ Partner speaks for woman and/or condescending to woman
✓ Partner makes negative comments about woman's appearance
✓ Woman speaks less or is very quiet especially when partner around, poor eye contact
✓ Partner oversolicitous with care providers

Sexual Abuse Assessment Red Flags

✓ Bruising or scratching around breasts, genitals
✓ Unexplained venereal or genital infections (children should not have STIs)
✓ Unexplained vaginal or anal bleeding
✓ Torn, stained, bloody underclothes
✓ Victim reports being sexually assaulted
✓ Victim withdrawn, personality changes, behaviour changes

Figure 12-1 General assessment of violence.

the specific patient. Depression and anxiety can manifest as a flat, quiet, and sullen affect (emotional dullness), withdrawal, or irritability and impulsive anger (see Chapter 10), which can further manifest as acting-out behaviours (eg, impulsive aggression toward others, risky and dangerous behaviours). Some violence victims use substances such as alcohol, marijuana, methamphetamines, cocaine, and narcotics to feel better while simultaneously numbing feelings of anxiety, low self-worth, sadness, and fear. Nevertheless, a link between human violence and mental health issues is usually hidden, and health care providers may frequently overlook opportunities for healing interventions.

Mental health effects associated with human violence that can be assessed during patient visits include depression, PTSD, panic disorders, dissociative symptoms, relationship and marital problems, acting out violently, and sexual and substance abuse (Basile, Arias, et al., 2004; Chu & Dill, 1990; Dube Anda et al., 2005; Stein, Lang, et al., 2004; Steel, Sanna, et al., 2004; Winfield, George, et al., 1990). Symptoms and signs common during assessment are: easily triggered anxiety and panic episodes, isolation and social withdrawal, numbing or shutting down feelings, spacing out and forgetfulness, and difficulty focusing.

Assessment findings are similar and different among violence survivors. Differences in how each person experiences and is affected by violence depend on the type and severity and the lived experiences of a person in her or his family, community, and society. Age, ethnicity, socioeconomic status, education, sexual orientation, religion, urban or rural living, culture, and relationships can be highly influential on outcomes. Thus, it is very important not to make assumptions but to use open-ended questions such as, "How are you coping?" and "What has your experience been?"

Documentation

Documentation is an important aspect of violence assessment. Close listening and keen observation skills are necessary to capture key details. It is important to reassure adults that their patient health records are available only with their consent and may be useful someday if needed for legal action. Nurses document subjective data in quotes as much as possible (eg, "pt states…").

When documenting objective data, it is important to be detailed, be descriptive, and note findings without bias. Box 12-3 outlines basic information about forensic evidence and documentation.

Mandated Reporting

Nurses and other health care professionals are "mandated reporters" when child, elder, or vulnerable-adult abuse or neglect is disclosed, assessed, or suspected (Sheridan, 2004). Mandated reporters must call protective services when they suspect abuse or neglect including child pornography. Provided the report is done in good faith and without malice, the nurse and other professionals mandated by the province/territory to report are protected by the province/territory.

BOX 12-3 FORENSIC EVIDENCE AND DOCUMENTATION

Written Documentation: Use Verbatim Subjective Data (ie, "pt states…")

Photographs: "Rule of Thirds" for each injury

- Take photos before the patient is cleaned or clothes are changed.
- Take an overall image of the patient plus three photographs of each injury.
  - First: Several feet away, injury clear, in context of patient
  - Second: Distance cut by one third, photo more focused on injury
  - Third: Distance cut by another one third, 2 ft from actual injury

Injury Maps: Locations, Measurements of Bruises, Incisions, Lacerations, Punctures, Hematomas

- Assess mouth and teeth.
- Do not throw away evidence even if badly soiled or ruined.
- Do not cut through clothing, undergarments, or bedding where evidence is visible.
- Store items, such as clothes, in paper bag (not plastic).
- Label evidence: patient's name, ID number, date of birth, date and time of documentation/photo.

Clinical Significance 12-3

Nurses need to be aware of the mandatory reporting laws in the province/territory where they practice. They also need to be aware of their institution or agency's policies and procedures regarding disclosure of violence perpetration and/or victimization and its appropriate documentation.

In addition to documenting findings from the patient assessment on forms approved by the clinical agency, the nurse should document the call to the protective services hotline in the patient's file, including the reason for the call, time of the call, full name of the person who took the call, and response of the worker. Provincial and territorial laws on reporting domestic violence in adults or IPV vary and it is essential to be aware of the appropriate laws and agency policies for reporting abuse or neglect.

Lifespan Considerations

Women Who Are Pregnant

Women who are pregnant constitute a population group at particularly high risk for IPV. Some of these patients also may have experienced adverse childhood experiences (Felitti, Parker, McFarlane et al., 1994). In addition to assessing for human violence, nurses need to assess for physical and mental health effects and specific effects related to pregnancy. Potential effects against pregnant women include increased chance of low birth weight infants, decreased maternal weight gain, and late prenatal care. Women who are pregnant who have or are experiencing IPV are also at increased risk for alcohol, tobacco, and street drug use throughout pregnancy when compared to women who have not experienced IPV in pregnancy (Hindin, 2006).

Infants, Children, and Adolescents

Of all age groups, infants are the most likely to be abused. Too often, health care providers do not suspect or report suspected abuse. Long-term psychological and emotional sequelae from abuse are cumulative. When a nurse reports suspected abuse and, thereby, prevents future violent episodes, he or she has made a significant difference in the health of a child for the rest of his or her life.

In addition to the common red flags (see Fig. 12-1), red flags for infants, children, and adolescents include the following:

- The story keeps changing or is inconsistent between partners or over time.
- No history of trauma is given, but signs of trauma are present.
- Parent changes physicians, health care facilities, or both frequently.

Documenting Unexpected Findings

The nurse has finished a physical assessment of Sue Brown. Note the following unexpected findings.

Inspection: Appears anxious, scanning environment visually. Fearful when touched. Multiple bruises in various stages of healing, including two 5 × 7.5 purple ecchymoses on buttocks, one yellow 2.5-cm ecchymosis on forearm, and three 3 × 3 blue and yellow ecchymoses on legs. See attached photographic documentation. 2 × 3 scar present on left forearm from previous repair of fracture.

Palpation: Area over buttocks is tender, painful. Lesions on legs and arms are nontender, nonraised. Full range of motion and strength in left arm.

- Infants have bruises before they are walking.
- Injuries resemble objects, such as cigarette burns, burns in the shape of an iron, loop marks, etc.
- Grab, slap, or human-bite marks are evident.
- There is evidence of immersion burns, which are usually well demarcated and bilateral (eg, both hands or feet) or occur on the buttocks and feet.

Any fracture in an infant who is not walking should raise the index of suspicion for abuse, unless there is a verifiable cause (eg, motor vehicle collision, documented bone disorder predisposing to bone fragility) (Kemp, Dunstan, et al., 2009). Bleeding, bruising, or redness in the genital area, anus, or both is cause to suspect sexual abuse. In the general survey and vital measures, symptoms and signs include poor hygiene, infant dressed in clothing inappropriate for the weather, evidence of tissue wasting, signs of poor nutrition, failure to gain weight, or an untreated illness (see Chapter 6). Symptoms of shaken baby syndrome include subdural hematoma, retinal hemorrhages, rib fractures, and bilateral bruising in the rib cage area. See also Chapter 28.

Older Adults

Many older adults are vulnerable to abuse by family members. Continued abuse may be compounded because of nondetection by professionals, in part because elderly patients often do not report violence. Many victims are isolated; some have shame, guilt, embarrassment, and self-blame. In addition, some elders experience fear of reprisal, retribution from caregivers, or losing their home or independence. Others are pressured by relatives not to report.

 ## Cultural Considerations

Cultural differences between patients and caregivers may lead to an erroneous suspicion of abuse. For example, a nurse might observe a patient and caregiver having an aggressive conversation that includes shouting. Some cultures consider such behaviour acceptable, whereas others consider it verbal abuse. Views on financial or personal autonomy of patients, their right to make decisions independently, or the amount of respect they deserve may also differ among cultural or socioeconomic groups (Fulmer, 2008). More information is needed about the influence of culture on disclosure of abuse and fear of retribution (Montalvo-Liendo, 2009). The social stigma attached to human violence may vary among cultures. For example, the patient from a neighbourhood with a high rate of violent crime may feel less stigmatized because it is a common occurrence.

Evidence-Informed Critical Thinking

Nursing Diagnoses, Outcomes, and Interventions

After the nurse assesses for violence, he or she can establish one or more nursing diagnoses. A nursing diagnosis labels the findings and suggests potential interventions. Table 12-3 compares nursing diagnoses, unexpected findings, and interventions commonly related to human violence (North American Nursing Diagnosis Association-International, 2009).

The nurse establishes and develops realistic and measurable outcomes with the patient. These outcomes must be

Table 12-3	Common Nursing Diagnoses Associated with Human Violence		
Diagnosis and Related Factors	**Point of Differentiation**	**Assessment Characteristics**	**Nursing Interventions**
Impaired parenting related to abuse	Failure of a parent or guardian to establish, enforce, or sustain an environment that nurtures and protects children	Abandonment, abuse, neglect of attachment or health care, harsh punishments, hostility between spouses or other relatives	Examine the characteristics of parenting style and behaviours. Institute abuse/neglect projection measures.* Assess maternal depression. Appraise the parent's resources and support systems.
Rape-trauma syndrome	Long-term psychological, emotional, and physical consequences following one or more episodes of sexual abuse, sexual assault, or both	Use of drugs or alcohol, anger, aggression, anxiety, difficulties in relationships, confusion, embarrassment, fear, guilt, humiliation, loss of self-esteem	Stay with the patient. Explain the rationale for interventions. Warn in advance before touching the patient. Observe for signs of physical injury. Document according to forensic standards.
Risk for posttrauma syndrome	Potential to experience long-term maladaptive consequences following one or more traumatic, overwhelming events	Risk factors include poor self-esteem, chronic duration, minimal or ineffective social support	Assess history; question about sleep, bad dreams, and reexperiencing the event.

Nursing assessment at each point includes assessing verbal and nonverbal behaviours. These include what the patient says (responses to questions and spontaneous comments or silence), how he or she appears (physical signs and symptoms), and his or her behaviours. The following note describes important information from Sue Brown's interview and physical assessment.

Subjective: "I'm beginning to think that the relationships that I have aren't very healthy. My brother and I are very physical, and he has thrown me against walls and punched me. It's hard to talk about. (pause) I just assumed that getting hit was normal. My brother has ADHD. He's been kicked out of school for being so aggressive and impulsive. I just got used to being hit and learned to fight back. I think that might be part of why I'm getting involved in relationships where I get hurt."

Objective: Appears anxious, scanning environment visually. Withdraws when touched. Multiple bruises in various stages of healing, including two 5 × 7.5 purple ecchymoses on buttocks, one yellow 2.5-cm ecchymosis on forearm, and three 3 × 3 blue and yellow ecchymoses on legs. See attached photographic documentation. Area over buttocks is tender, painful. Lesions on legs and arms are nontender.

Analysis: **Risk for posttrauma syndrome** related to sibling abuse

Plan: Needs abuse protection support to prevent infliction of physical and emotional harm. Call in report to get assistance in analyzing how to proceed with this case.

Critical Thinking Challenge

- What challenges are involved with this case?
- What strengths does Sue bring? How will the nurse assess these?
- What dilemmas does the nurse face when working with Sue?

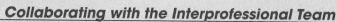
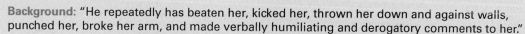

Sue has been seeing the nurse practitioner for five sessions. She has disclosed some reportable information. The following conversation illustrates how the nurse might organize data and make recommendations about Sue's situation.

Situation: "I've been seeing Sue Brown for five sessions now. Over the course of several interviews, she has disclosed abuse by her older brother throughout her childhood and adolescence, and it is continuing at this time."

Background: "He repeatedly has beaten her, kicked her, thrown her down and against walls, punched her, broke her arm, and made verbally humiliating and derogatory comments to her."

Assessment: "Sue's brother was diagnosed with ADHD and conduct disorder. She reports that her brother's signs and symptoms include acting out aggressively; severe physical, verbal, and psychological violence against her; and repeated expulsions from schools because of violence toward peers, teachers, and property. He has also been treated for self-injury (Phillips, unpublished data, 2009). Sue reports that her parents, neighbours, and friends witnessed her brother's violence, and the police did not assess for this violence when contacted (Phillips, Phillips, et al., 2009). In addition to disclosing this information to me, Sue has physical signs of injury including bruising in multiple stages of healing."

Recommendations: "I am calling to report this situation to you. I want to get help with protecting Sue."

Critical Thinking Challenge

- What are your reactions to Sue's situation?
- How might your reactions influence your assessment of her situation?
- Describe the issues related to the victimization. What type of violence is described?

Table 12-4   **Part of the Solution**

Advocacy Practices	Descriptions
Respect confidentiality.	Discussions must be private with no other family members present; this is essential to building trust and ensuring the patient's safety.
Believe and validate his or her experiences.	Listen to the patient and believe; acknowledge her or his feelings and let the patient know that she or he is not alone; many other people have similar experiences.
Acknowledge the injustice.	Violence perpetrated against the patient is not her or his fault; no one deserves to be abused.
Respect her or his autonomy.	Respect the patient's right to make decisions when ready; she or he is the expert at her or his life.
Help the patient plan for future safety.	What has the patient tried in the past to stay safe? Is it working? Does she or he have a place to go if escape is necessary?
Promote access to community services.	Know resources in your community; is there a hotline and shelter for victims of violence?

Adapted from "The Medical Power & Control Wheel," developed by the Domestic Violence Project in Kenosha, WI 53143. Based on the "Power & Control and Equality Wheel" developed by the Domestic Abuse Intervention Project, Duluth, MN 55306.

based on respect for autonomy and recognition of patient safety. Some outcomes related to human violence include the following:

- The patient maintains social safety.
- The patient demonstrates personal safety behaviours.
- The patient avoids injury.
- Abuse ceases.
- The patient exerts abusive-behaviour self-control (Moorhead, Johnson et al., 2007).

Nurses need to ask about adverse childhood experiences, especially violence (Felitti, 2002). This type of assessment and subsequent interventions can assist the patient to find treatment for "root" causes of physical and mental health issues and prevent years of treating symptoms while underlying causes go undetected. Nurses are on the frontlines to assess for adverse health consequences and to intervene in ways that decrease suffering and promote healing. Figure 12-1 shows many specific physical and mental health red flags for which nurses can intervene. Table 12-4 describes even more basic ways to begin providing support and advocacy for all victims.

Patient needs following violent experiences can be categorized as immediate, transitional, and long term (Box 12-4). Safety planning is key to intervention. If the patient is in an unsafe or potentially unsafe situation, nurses suggest and encourage a safety plan. The first step is to ask the patient what he or she has done in the past to be safe and then build on this.

Basic components of safety plans usually include the following:

- Charged cell phone with preprogrammed emergency phone numbers (or these numbers readily available but not necessarily identifiable to the perpetrator) for police, support people, and safe housing

- Copies of important or difficult-to-replace documents such as birth certificate or insurance papers stored in a safe place (possibly with support person)
- Change of clothes for self (and children) packed and hidden
- Extra set of house and car keys
- Transportation plan
- Extra money hidden in a safe location
- Escape plan from potential house or apartment exits
- Escape locations/safe places

BOX 12-4   PATIENT SAFETY NEEDS

Immediate

- Safety and support
- Medical stabilization
- Psychological and emotional stabilization
- Collect forensic evidence

Transitional

- Safety and support
- Connect to resources: financial, parenting, health, housing, immigration, legal
- Teaching: safe and healthy coping skills, social skills, positive relationships
- Promote sense of mastery

Long Term

- Safety and support
- Healing: trauma psychotherapy
- Support systems/resource building
- Physical rehabilitation/physical therapy
- Long-term health needs

Each patient will have individualized safety needs. It is very important for the nurse to explain to the patient that research shows that danger of violence is particularly high when victims leave or have left a relationship with a perpetrator (Campbell, Koziol-McLain, et al., 2006). This fact makes patient teaching and safety planning even more essential aspects of nursing interventions.

Sometimes nurses and other health professionals contribute to victims failing to ask for and receive assistance or perpetuate attitudes that reinforce violent practices. Six methods of "medical power and control" should be avoided: (1) violating confidentiality, (2) trivializing and minimizing violence and abuse, (3) blaming the victim, (4) not respecting autonomy, (5) ignoring the victim's safety, and (6) normalizing victimization. Each of these can cause victims to feel an increased sense of entrapment and could potentially escalate the danger of a current violent situation.

It is important to be especially careful not to pressure patients to make decisions about the violence, perpetrator, relationship, or particular interventions. Contrary to experiences of violence involving power and control in which victims have few, if any, choices, patient decisions about their care, interventions, and future are just that: patient decisions. Nurses need to be explicit and patient about this— because making decisions and having choices may be new experiences for those who experienced violence in the past or present.

A Pulling It All Together: An Example of Reflection and Critical Thinking

ssessment data help nurses to formulate nursing care plans. Outcomes are specific to the patient are realistic, are measurable, and have a time frame for completion. The nurse performs interventions based on evidence and practice guidelines. He or she also charts progress toward patient outcomes. See a sample care plan related to Sue Brown below.

Nursing Diagnosis	Patient Outcomes	Nursing Interventions	Rationale	Evaluation
Risk for posttrauma syndrome related to sibling abuse	The patient discloses abuse. The patient states that she is not to blame for the events.	Provide support person to stay with the patient; explain protocols; determine any cuts, bruises, bleeding, lacerations, or other signs of injury. Assess for past experiences and symptoms.	Evidence must be collected as soon as possible, although it may be difficult for the patient. Dissociation, avoidant behaviour, hypervigilance, and reexperiencing are ongoing symptoms.	Photos are taken of bruises in multiple stages of injury. No bleeding, lacerations, or other signs of acute injury are evident. Will interview about mood and behaviour changes.

U Applying Your Knowledge

sing the previous steps of clinical reasoning, organizing, and prioritizing, consider all case study findings throughout this chapter. When answering the questions, begin drawing conclusions and see how the pieces of assessment must work together to create an environment for personalized, appropriate, and accurate care.

- What are the types of human violence? (knowledge)
- How do Sue's symptoms and behaviours cluster together? (Comprehension)
- Based on Sue's history, what red flags should prompt health care professionals to conduct a complete safety assessment? (Application)
- What is the role of the nurse in assessing safety? (Analysis)
- What recommendations for follow up for Sue would you make? (Synthesis)
- How would you evaluate Sue's understanding of a safety plan? (Evaluation)

Key Points

- Types of human violence include family violence (which encompasses child maltreatment, sibling violence, IPV, and elder abuse), violence against vulnerable populations, youth and school violence, sexual violence, hate crimes, human trafficking, and war/combat violence.
- IPV in pregnancy is a serious and widespread problem.
- Elders are vulnerable to continued abuse, partly as a result of nondetection by professionals.
- The patient's physical and emotional safety is a key aspect of assessment.
- The nurse moves from general to specific questions about violence.
- Open-ended versus closed questions about violence are best.
- Phrasing to normalize questions about the experience of violence is "Because violence is common in so many people's lives, I ask all patients about it routinely."
- One safety assessment question is "Tell me what you did today from the time you got up until the time you got here."
- Red flags of violence victimization include mood and behaviour changes.
- Nurses are mandated reporters when child, elder, or vulnerable adult abuse or neglect is disclosed, assessed, or suspected.
- Documentation is an important aspect of nursing assessment and intervention.
- Human violence has psychological, mental, physical, emotional, and social consequences.
- Nursing diagnoses associated with violence experiences include risk for other-directed violence, impaired parenting, dysfunctional family processes, and rape–trauma syndrome.

Review Questions

1. Child maltreatment, sibling violence, bullying, elder abuse, hate crimes, and war/combat violence are types of
   A. punking
   B. sexual violence
   C. intimate partner violence
   D. human violence

2. Intimate partner violence in pregnancy is
   A. a serious and widespread problem
   B. associated with unwanted pregnancy
   C. a serious but uncommon situation
   D. usually the fault of the mother

3. Older adult abuse
   A. usually occurs when the caregiver is tired
   B. is usually not detected by health care providers
   C. usually occurs once and then stops
   D. is usually detected by social work

4. When questioning the patient about violence, it is best to
   A. ask to get the police involved to collect evidence
   B. have the perpetrator present to assess behaviours
   C. move from general to specific questions
   D. ask the patient what he or she did to provoke the violence

5. When child, elder, or vulnerable adult abuse or neglect is disclosed, nurses
   A. must contact a physician
   B. may get family involved
   C. might consider referral
   D. are mandated reporters

6. Red flags of signs and symptoms of violence include which of the following?
   A. Stating that everything is just fine
   B. Displaying mood and behaviour changes
   C. Expressing sadness over loss
   D. Wanting to have family involved

7. The patient is seen in the emergency department for a fracture that is inconsistent with the description of the cause of it. Which question would be best in this situation?
   A. "Because violence is so common for so many people, I routinely ask all patients about experiences of violence—in the past or currently. I wonder if you have experienced or are experiencing violence?"
   B. "Sometimes people fall because someone hurt them. Your injury looks like someone might have done this to you on purpose. Do you have a violent boyfriend?"
   C. "Your injury doesn't look like what you described. It looks to me like someone might have intentionally done this to you. With whom do you live?"
   D. "It's common for women to get shoved, kicked, or beaten. You seem like you might be in this situation. Who would do this to you?"

8. The patient's physical and emotional safety is
   A. a key aspect of assessment
   B. discussed in the interventions section
   C. considered during outcomes
   D. written up in interventions

9. It is best to ask questions about violence that are
   A. reflective
   B. focused
   C. closed ended
   D. open ended

10. Interventions that might be appropriate for victims of violence include which of the following?
    A. Maximizing protective influences
    B. Involving police and pressing charges
    C. Getting placement in a shelter and telling them to leave home
    D. Calling parents of victims to provide support

Canadian Nursing Research

Berman, H., Alvernaz Mulcahy, G., et al. (2009). Uprooted and displaced: A critical narrative study of homeless, Aboriginal, and newcomer girls in Canada. *Issues in Mental Health Nursing, 30*(7), 418–430.

Berman, H., Irias Giron, E. R., et al. (2006). A narrative study of refugee women who have experienced violence in the context of war. *Canadian Journal of Nursing Research, 38*(4), 32–53.

Campbell, M., Neil, J. A., et al. (2010). Engaging abusive men in seeking community intervention: A critical research & practice priority. *Journal of Family Violence, 25*(4), 413–422.

Normandeau, S., Harper, E., et al. (2005). *Evaluation of the implementation process of intersecting sites of violence in the lives of girls: A national participatory action project with girls and young women and the organizations that work with them.* Montreal, Quebec: Le centre de recherche interdisciplinaire sur la violence familiale et la violence faite aux femmes.

References

Basile, K. C., Arias, I., et al. (2004). The differential association of intimate partner physical, sexual, psychological, and stalking violence and posttraumatic stress symptoms in a national representative sample of women. *Journal of Trauma and Stress, 17*(5), 413–421.

Beaty, L. A., & Alexeyev, E. B. (2008). The problem of school bullies: What the research tells us. *Adolescence, 48*(169), 1–11.

Campbell, J. C. (1992). "If I can't have you, no one can": Power and control in homicide of female partners. In J. Radford & D. E. H. Russell (Eds.). *Femicide: The politics of woman killing* (pp. 99–113). New York, NY: Twayne.

Campbell, J. C., Garcia-Moreno, A., et al. (2004). Abuse during pregnancy in industrialized and developing countries. *Violence Against Women, 10*(7), 770–789.

Campbell, J. C., Koziol-McLain, J., et al. (2006). *Validation of the danger assessment: Results from the 12 city femicide study.* National Institute of Justice Briefs.

Campbell, J. C., Sharps, P. W., et al. (2000). Risk assessment for intimate partner homicide. In G. F. Pinard & L. Pigani (Eds.). *Clinical assessments of dangerousness: Empirical contributions* (pp. 136–157). New York, NY: Cambridge University Press.

Canada Centre for Justice Statistics. (2008). *Family violence in Canada: A statistical profile 2008.* Retrieved from www.statcan.gc.ca/pub/85-224-x/85-224-x2008000-eng.pdf

Chu, J. A., & Dill, D. L. (1990). Dissociative symptoms in relation to childhood physical and sexual abuse. *American Journal of Psychiatry, 147*(7), 887–892.

Domestic Abuse Intervention Project. (DAIP). (2008). *The power and control wheel.* Retrieved from http://www.theduluthmodel.org/pdf/PhyVio.pdf

Dube, S. R., Anda, R. F., et al. (2005). Long-term consequences of childhood sexual abuse by gender of victim. *American Journal of Preventitive Medicine, 28*(5), 430–438.

Edwards, V. J., Anda, R. F., et al. (2007). Adverse childhood experiences and smoking persistence in adults with smoking-related symptoms and illness. *Permanente Journal, 11*, 5–7.

Fahey, J. (2007). Unpublished research. Seattle, WA: Seattle University College of Nursing.

Felitti, V. J. (2002). The relation between adverse childhood experiences and adult health: Turning gold into lead. *Permanente Journal, 6*(1), 44–51.

Felitti, V. J., Anda, R. F., et al. (1998). Relationship of childhood abuse and household dysfunction to many of the leading causes of death in adults: The adverse childhood experiences (ACE) study. *American Journal of Preventive Medicine, 14*(4), 245–258.

Finkelhor, D., Ormrod, R. K., et al. (2005). The victimization of children and youth: A comprehensive, national survey. *Child Maltreatment, 10*(1), 5–25.

Finkelhor, D., Ormrod, R. K., et al. (2007). Poly-victimization: A neglected component in child victimization. *Child Abuse & Neglect, 31*, 7–26.

Finkelhor, D., Turner, H., et al. (2006). Kid's stuff: The nature and impact of peer and sibling violence on younger and older children. *Child Abuse & Neglect, 30*, 1401–1421.

Fulmer, T. (2008) Screening for mistreatment of older adults. *American Journal of Nursing, 108*(12), 52–60.

Gerlock, A. A. (2004). Domestic violence and post-traumatic stress disorder severity for participants of a domestic violence rehabilitation program. *Military Medicine, 169*(6), 470–474.

Harley, A. M. (2006). Domestic violence screening: Implications for surgical nurses. *Plastic Surgery Nursing, 26*(1), 24–28.

Hindin, P. K. (2006). Intimate partner violence screening practices of certified nurse-midwives. *Journal of Midwifery and Women's Health, 51*(3), 216–221.

Kemp, A. M., Dunstan, F., et al. (2008). Patterns of skeletal fractures in child abuse: Systematic review. *British Journal of Medicine, 337*, a1518.

Montalvo-Liendo, N. (2009). Cross-cultural factors in disclosure of intimate partner violence: An integrated review. *Journal of Advanced Nursing, 65*(1), 20–34.

Moorhead, S., Johnson, M., et al. (2007). *Nursing outcomes classification (NOC)* (4th ed.). Philadelphia, PA: Mosby.

Moracco, K. E., Runyan, C. W., et al. (2007). Women's experiences with violence: A national study. *Women's Health Issues, 17*(1), 3–12.

National Center for Education Statistics. (2007). *Indicators of school crime & safety: 2007.* Retrieved from http://www.ojp.usdoj.gov/bjs/pub/pdf/iscs07.pdf

National Center on Elder Abuse. (1998). *The national elder abuse incidence study: Final report.* Madison, WI: Publisher.

National Center on Elder Abuse. (2004). *Abuse of adults aged 60+: 2004 Survey of adult protective services.* Retrieved from http://www.ncea.aoa.gov/NCEAroot/Main_Site/pdf/2-14-06%2060FACT%20SHEET.pdf

North American Nursing Diagnosis Association-International. (2009). *Nursing diagnoses, 2009–2011 edition: Definitions and classifications (NANDA-I NURSING DIAGNOSIS).* West Sussex UK: John Wiley & Sons.

O'Moore, A. M. & Hillery, B. (1989). Bullying in Dublin schools. *Irish Journal of Psychology, 10*, 426–441.

Papp, A. (2010). *Culturally-driven violence amongst women: A growing problem in Canada's immigrant communities.* Retrieved from www.fcpp.org/publicaion.php/3351

Parker, B., McFarlane, J., et al. (1994). Abuse during pregnancy: Effects on maternal complications and birthweight in adult and teenage women. *Obstetrics and Gynecology, 84*(3), 323–328.

Phillips, D. A. (2007). Punking and bullying: Strategies in middle school, high school, and beyond. *Journal of Interpersonal Violence, 22*(2), 158–178.

Phillips, D. A., Phillips, K. H., et al. (2009). Sibling violence silenced: Rivalry, competition, wrestling, playin', roughhousing, benign. *Advances in Nursing Science, 32*(2), E1–E16.

Plichta, S. B. (2007). Interactions between victims of intimate partner violence against women and the health care system: Policy and practice implications. *Trauma Violence Abuse, 8*(2), 226–239.

Plichta, S. B., & Falik, M. F. (2001). Prevalence of violence and its implications for women's health. *Women's Health Issues, 11*(3), 244–258.

Prigerson, H. G., Maciejewski, P. K., et al. (2002). Population attributable fractions of psychiatric disorders and behavioral outcomes associated with combat exposure among US men. *American Journal of Public Health, 92*(1), 59–63.

Rape, Abuse & Incest National Network. (2008). *Who are the victims?* Retrieved from http://www.rainn.com/get-information/statistics/sexual-assault-victims

Saltzman, L. E., Fanslow, J. L., et al. (1999). *Intimate partner violence surveillance: Uniform definitions and recommended data elements, version 1.0.* Atlanta, GA: National Center for Injury Prevention and Control, Centers for Disease Prevention.

Schaller, J., & Lagergren Frieberg, J. (1998). Issues of abuse for women with disabilities and implications for rehabilitation counseling. *Journal of Applied Rehabilitation Counseling, 29*(2), 9–17.

Sengstock, M.C., Ulrick, Y. C., et al. (2004). Abuse and neglect of elderly in family settings. In J. Humphreys & J. C. Campbell (Eds.). *Family violence and nursing practice* (pp. 97–149). Philadelphia, PA: Lippincott Williams & Wilkins.

Sheridan, D. J. (2004). Legal and forensic nursing responses to family violence. In J. Humphreys & J. C. Campbell (Eds.). *Family violence and nursing practice* (pp. 385–406). Philadelphia, PA: Lippincott Williams & Wilkins.

Singer, M. I., Anglin, T. M., et al. (1995). Adolescents' exposure to violence and associated symptoms of psychological trauma. *JAMA, 273*(6), 477–482.

Statistics Canada. (2011). *Family violence in Canada: A statistical profile.* Retrieved from www.publications.gc.ca/collections/collection_20111/statcan/85-224-x/85-224-x2010000-eng.pdf

Steel, J., Sanna, L., Hammond, B., et al. (2004). Psychological sequelae of childhood sexual abuse: Abuse-related characteristics, coping strategies, and attributional style. *Child Abuse Neglect, 28*(7), 785–801.

Stein, M. B., Lang, A. J., et al. (2004). Relationship of sexual assault history to somatic symptoms and health anxiety in women. *General Hospital Psychiatry, 26*(3), 178–183.

Stromsness, M. M. (1993). Sexually abused women with mental retardation: Hidden victims, absent resources. *Women & Therapy, 14*(3–4), 139–152.

United Nations. (2008). *What is human trafficking?* Retrieved from http://www.ungift.org/ungift/en/humantrafficking/index.html

U.S. Department of Health & Human Services. (2006). *HHS fights to stem human trafficking.* Retrieved from http://www.hhs.gov/news/factsheet/humantrafficking.html

U.S. Department of Justice, Bureau Justice of Statistics. (2005a). *Human trafficking.* Retrieved from http://www.ojp.usdoj.gov/ovc/ncvrw/2005/pg5l.html

U.S. Department of Justice, Bureau Justice of Statistics. (2005b). *Family violence statistics: Including statistics on strangers & acquaintances.* Retrieved from http://www.ojp.usdoj.gov/bjs/pub/pdf/fvs.pdf

U.S. Department of Justice, Bureau Justice of Statistics. (2005c). *Hate crime reported by victims and police.* Retrieved from http://www.ojp.usdoj.gov/bjs/pub/pdf/hcrvp.pdf

U.S. Department of Justice, Bureau Justice of Statistics. (2006). *Criminal victimization, 2006.* Retrieved from http://www.ojp.usdoj.gov/bjs/pub/pdf/cv06.pdf

Winfield, I., George, L. K., et al. (1990). Sexual assault and psychiatric disorders among a community sample of women. *American Journal of Psychiatry, 147*(3), 335–341.

The Canadian Jensen's Nursing Health Assessment suite offers these additional resources to enhance learning and facilitate understanding of this chapter:

• thePoint online resource, http//thepoint.lww.com/Stephen1E
• *Laboratory Manual for Canadian Jensen's Nursing Health Assessment: A Best Practice Approach*

Regional Examinations

Skin, Hair, and Nails Assessment

Learning Objectives

1 Demonstrate knowledge of anatomy and physiology of the integumentary system.

2 Identify important topics for health promotion and risk reduction related to the integumentary system.

3 Collect subjective data related to the integumentary system.

4 Collect objective data related to the integumentary system using physical examination techniques.

5 Identify expected and unexpected findings related to the integumentary system.

6 Analyze subjective and objective data from assessment of the integumentary system and consider initial interventions.

7 Document and communicate data from the integumentary assessment using appropriate terminology and principles of recording.

8 Consider age, condition, gender, and culture of the patient to individualize the integumentary assessment.

9 Identify nursing diagnoses and initiate a plan of care based on findings from the integumentary assessment.

Mr. Nuryev Stoli, a 65-year-old Russian immigrant, has been on an acute care medical unit since yesterday for a venous stasis ulcer of his lower leg. He is scheduled to have a wound vacuum applied later today. Current medications include a thiazide diuretic, chlorothiazide (Diuril) for high blood pressure, platelet inhibitor, anagrelide hydrochloride (Agrylin) for peripheral vascular disease, and insulin for type 2 diabetes mellitus. The nurse notes Mr. Stoli's most recent vital signs to be temperature 37.4°C orally, pulse 92 beats/min and regular, respirations 16 breaths/min, and blood pressure 142/78 mm Hg (left arm, lying).

You will gain more information about Mr. Stoli as you progress through this chapter. As you study the content and features, consider the patient's case and its relationship to what you are learning. Begin thinking about the following points:

- How will the nurse assess and document Mr. Stoli's wound and peripheral circulation?
- What information will the nurse collect to assess risk for skin breakdown related to hospitalization?
- In what circumstances would the nurse refer Mr. Stoli to a wound care nurse? How would the nurse communicate information to the wound care nurse?
- Following discharge, what data would a homecare nurse need to collect to evaluate wound healing?

The integumentary system—skin, hair, nails, sebaceous, and sweat glands—provides vital information about the patient's health status and provides data indicating potential concerns related to the thermoregulatory, endocrine, respiratory, cardiovascular, gastrointestinal, neurological, urinary, and immune systems. Integumentary findings also reflect the patient's hydration, nutrition, and emotional status and help direct the nurse to other systems or organs that may be compromised. For example, cyanosis in the patient's lips may prompt the nurse to further evaluate the respiratory and circulatory systems. Skin assessment is ongoing and integrated in the examination of all other body systems.

This chapter includes a review of the anatomy and physiology of the integumentary system and presents common variations within expected examination findings, as well as findings associated with systemic illnesses. Data collection strategies related to common skin lesions, alterations in skin integrity, risk factors for skin cancer (ie, excessive sun exposure, inadequate skin protection), health promotion practices, and wound assessment are included. A systematic approach for the comprehensive assessment of the integumentary system and strategies for incorporating the assessment of skin, hair, and nails during the examination of other body systems is provided. This chapter includes approaches for accurately documenting examination findings and presents information relating to health promotion, such as skin self-assessment, dry skin care, pressure ulcer prevention, and skin protection.

Anatomy and Physiology Overview

Skin

The skin offers the human body protection from ongoing environmental damage (harmful substances, radiation) and a barrier to infectious organisms. In addition to its role as the body's primary immune defence system, the skin is elemental in thermoregulation and the synthesis of vitamin D. As an organ, the skin accounts for approximately 16% of an individual's body weight and its appendages include the hair, nails, and glands (sebaceous and sweat). The skin is comprised of three layers with distinct and separate functions: the epidermis, dermis, and subcutaneous layer (Fig. 13-1).

Epidermis

As the outermost skin layer, the **epidermis** serves as both the location for vitamin D synthesis and the body's first line of defense against pathogens, chemical irritants, temperature fluctuations, and fluid balance (Amirlak, Shahabi, et al., 2008). The epidermis contains no blood vessels and relies entirely on the underlying dermis for both delivery of nutrients and expulsion of waste products. The five layers of the epidermis are (1) *stratum corneum,* (2) *stratum lucidum,* (3) *stratum granulosum,* (4) *stratum spinosum,* and (5) *stratum germinativum.* The stratum germinativum, the inner most layer of the epidermis contains keratinocytes and melanocytes. *Keratinocytes* are composed chiefly of keratin, a tough protein providing resistance against friction and trauma. Keratinocytes differentiate over time and move through the more superficial strata, become anuclear, and eventually are shed from the stratum corneum. *Melanocytes* produce two types of melanin, *eumelanin* and *pheomelanin,* which contribute to integumentary variations based on their amounts and proportions in each person. Larger amounts of eumelanin produce darker skin and hair, whereas larger amounts of pheomelanin are responsible for lighter skin and hair (Ortonne, 2002). The absolute number of melanocytes, however, is consistent in all people (Barsh, 2003).

The epidermis contains specialized cells responsible for perception of pain, light touch, vibration, and temperature, as well as detection of foreign antigens (Kamel, 1998). In other

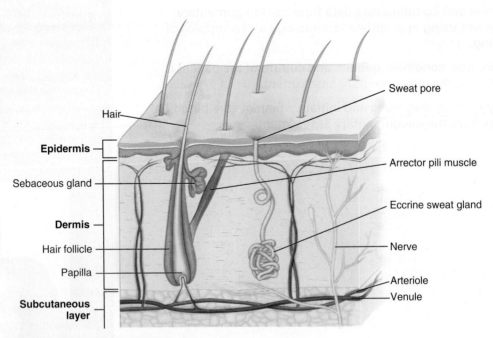

Hair

Epidermis

Sebaceous gland

Dermis

Hair follicle

Papilla

Subcutaneous layer

Sweat pore

Arrector pili muscle

Eccrine sweat gland

Nerve

Arteriole

Venule

Figure 13-1 Anatomy of the skin.

words, the epidermis is the first part of the body to initiate the immune response. Thickness of the epidermis remains constant throughout the lifespan and in both genders.

Dermis

The second layer, the **dermis,** supports the epidermis. The dermis contains blood vessels, nerves, sebaceous glands, lymphatic vessels, hair follicles, and sweat glands, which support the nutritional needs and protective function of the epidermis (Amirlak, Shahabi, et al., 2008). The two layers of the dermis are papillary and reticular. The *papillary dermis,* composed primarily of loose connective tissue and elastin, contains capillaries, smaller blood vessels, and nerve endings. It connects directly to the epidermis, facilitating the exchange of oxygen, nutrients, and waste products. The deeper *reticular dermis,* composed of collagen and elastin, provides the resilience, distensibility, elasticity, and turgor of the skin.

Variations in skin thickness result from changes in dermal thickness, with the thinnest being the eyelids and the thickest being located on the palms and soles. Dermal thickness varies across the lifespan and with gender. Skin is thinnest at birth but gradually increases until the 4th or 5th decade of life, when thickness begins to decline. Men have consistently thicker skin than women as a result of their greater number of androgens (Zouboulis, Chen, et al., 2007).

Subcutaneous Layer

The **subcutaneous layer** provides insulation, storage of caloric reserves, and cushioning against external forces. Composed mainly of fat and loose connective tissue, it also contributes to the skin's mobility.

Clinical Significance 13-1

The integumentary system is a window to other body systems. Changes in skin, hair, or nails may be the first clue to other health issues. See Table 13-7 at the end of this chapter.

Hair

Hair is an appendage of skin. It protects various body areas from debris and invasion, provides insulation, enables the conduit of sensory stimulation to the nervous system, and contributes to gender identification.

Vellus hair is fine, short, hypopigmented, and located all over the body. **Terminal hair** is darker and coarser than vellus hair. It varies in length and is generally found on the scalp, brows, and eyelids. In postpubertal people, terminal hair also is found on the axillae, perineum, and legs; in postpubertal males, it appears on the chest and abdomen.

Hair, composed of keratin, is produced by hair follicles located deep in the dermis. Hair follicles are present in all body areas except the palms and soles. Follicular activity is cyclical, with approximately 30% of follicles in a resting state at any given time (Brannon, 2006).

Shape of the hair shaft determines the curliness of hair, with oval shape producing curlier hair than rounded shape. The amount and proportion of eumelanin and pheomelanin produced by melanocytes in the hair bulb influences the colouration of an individual's hair. Arrector pili muscles attached to each hair follicle contract in response to environmental and nervous stimuli, causing erection of the hair and follicle. Sebaceous glands supporting each follicle secrete sebum, maintaining hair moisture and condition. Sebum production declines with increasing age (Fig. 13-2).

Nails

Another epidermal appendage, the **nails** arise from a nail matrix in the epidermal layer, near the distal portions of each finger and toe. The nail plate, comprised of hardened keratin, grows at varying rates, with fingernails growing faster than toenails. The highly vascular nail bed is visible as a pink colour through the transparent nail plate. There are lateral folds of skin on each side and a proximal fold of skin at the base border of each nail plate (Fig. 13-3).

Some systemic illnesses and infectious processes affect the growth rate and thickness of nails (Fawcett, Linford, et al., 2005). Changes caused by illness or infection generally are not visible for some time after the incident. See Table 13-22 at the end of this chapter for more information.

Glands

Sweat (cutaneous) glands function to maintain body temperature by controlling the evaporation and reabsorption of water. The two types of sweat glands are eccrine and apocrine (Amirlak, Shahabi, et al., 2008).

Eccrine glands cover most of the body, with the exception of the nailbeds, lip margins, glans penis, and labia minora. They are most numerous on the palms and soles. Eccrine glands open directly onto the skin surface and secrete *sweat* in response to environmental or psychological stimuli. Sweat assists in thermoregulation.

Apocrine glands, located in the axillae and genital areas, open into hair follicles and become active during puberty. Apocrine glands secrete a thicker, milky sweat into the hair follicle that, once mixed with bacterial flora on the skin, produces a characteristic musky odour (adult body odour). Apocrine glandular activity decreases with age.

Sebaceous glands are located throughout the body, except the palms and soles, and open into hair follicles. These glands secrete sebum, an oil-like substance that assists the skin with moisture retention and friction protection (Fig. 13-4).

Lifespan Considerations

Women Who Are Pregnant

During pregnancy, increased levels of progesterone, estrogen, and melanocyte-stimulating hormone cause increased pigmentation in body areas that typicallly have higher pigmentation

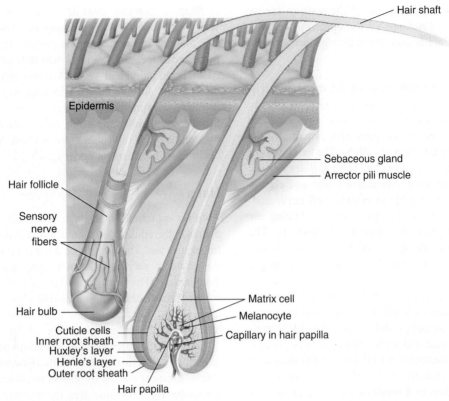

Figure 13-2 Anatomy of hair.

Labels for Figure 13-2:
Hair shaft
Epidermis
Sebaceous gland
Arrector pili muscle
Hair follicle
Sensory nerve fibers
Matrix cell
Melanocyte
Capillary in hair papilla
Hair bulb
Cuticle cells
Inner root sheath
Huxley's layer
Henle's layer
Outer root sheath
Hair papilla

(ie, areolae, nipples, axillae, vulva, and inner thighs). *Melasma,* increased pigmentation of the face in response to the hormonal changes of pregnancy, occurs mainly on the chin, cheeks, and upper lip. Integumentary changes generally resolve after delivery; however, in a minority of cases, the changes may be permanent. *Linea nigra* is a darkened line extending from the umbilicus to the pubic area. See also Chapter 27.

Both sweat and sebaceous glands may become hyperactive during pregnancy, causing worsened acne and increased sweating. Hair loss usually decreases, because increased hormonal levels influence the retention of hair at the resting phase of growth. After childbirth, retained hairs as well as those just entering the resting phase fall out quickly, giving the appearance of accelerated hair loss.

Newborns and Infants

At birth, an infant's skin can be red or flushed. It is usually smooth and may be covered with *vernix,* which is a cheese-like substance comprised of epithelial cells and sebum. Vernix protects the infant's skin from the effects of prolonged exposure to amniotic fluid. Postterm infants have little if any vernix. Fine hair called *lanugo* may cover the newborn. Vellus hair replaces lanugo over the first few months after birth, and terminal hair begins to grow on the scalp and eyebrows. Physiologic jaundice may occur within the first 48 hours following delivery, giving the skin, mucous membranes, and conjunctiva a yellowish hue.

The skin of a preterm infant may be translucent or gelatinous. In contrast to a full-term newborn, the preterm baby has less dermal collagen and elastin, increased visibility of vascular structures (contributing to a ruddy appearance), thinner subcutaneous fat, more lanugo (dependent on gestational age), and increased risk for inadequate thermoregulation, skin injury, and edema (Lowdermilk & Perry, 2007). See also Chapter 28.

Children and Adolescents

Skin thickness continues to develop throughout childhood. During childhood, eccrine glands produce sweat in much lower quantities than in adults. Apocrine glands are generally inactive until puberty when these glands enlarge due

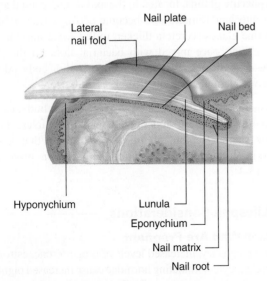

Labels for Figure 13-3:
Nail plate
Lateral nail fold
Nail bed
Hyponychium
Lunula
Eponychium
Nail matrix
Nail root

Figure 13-3 Anatomy of nails.

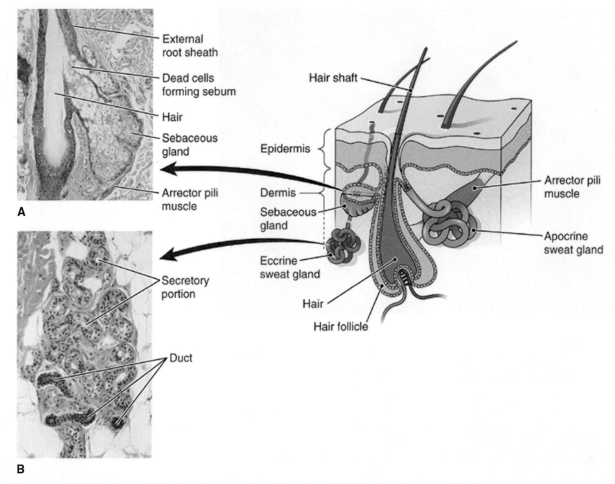

Figure 13-4 Portion of skin showing associated glands and hair. **A.** A sebaceous gland and its associated hair follicle. **B.** An eccrine (temperature-regulating) sweat gland.

to hormonal changes. At puberty, increased sebaceous activity results in the secretion of large amounts of sebum into the hair follicles of the face, neck, chest, and back. Anything impeding sebum secretion onto the skin surface may result in the formation of closed comedones and eventually acne (Fig. 13-5). As adolescents move through puberty, increased terminal type hair growth occurs in the pubic, axillary, and navel regions. Adolescent males, in particular, begin to have increased hair on the face, chest, and back.

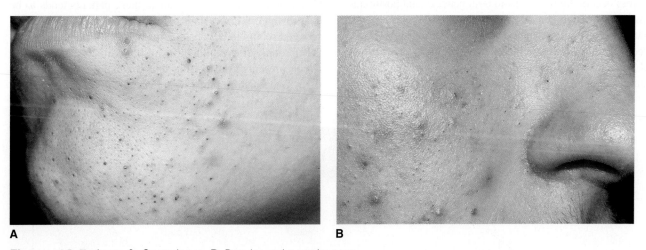

Figure 13-5 Acne. **A.** Comedones. **B.** Papular and pustular acne.

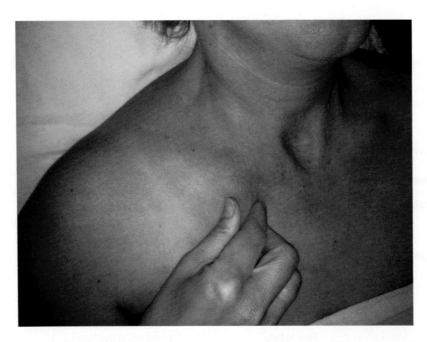

Figure 13-6 Assessing skin turgor.

Older Adults

As skin ages, it gradually loses elastin, collagen, and subcutaneous fat, resulting in overall thinner skin (Amirlak, Shahabi, et al., 2008). Effects of these changes include decreased resilience, sagging and wrinkling of skin structures, and increased visibility and fragility of superficial vascular structures. Elders are prone to increased bruising and shearing injury.

Turgor, a measure of skin elasticity, decreases as a result of thinning of the dermis and reduced elastin production. The patient's hydration status also can affect skin turgor (Fig. 13-6). Replacement of the epidermal layer decreases with aging, resulting in rougher skin texture and prolonged time for wound healing. These changes affect thermoregulation, resulting in increased risk for hypothermia and heat stroke. Function of the eccrine and apocrine glands is reduced, causing increased skin dryness. Decreased melanin production in the hair matrix and epidermis results in gray or white hair and increased risk for the damaging effects of ultraviolet (UV) radiation (Ortonne, 2002). Hair follicles atrophy, and resultant hair loss occurs. Influences from both genetics and hormones may result in androgenic hair loss (Fig. 13-7). Nail growth slows, with resulting thinning and increased brittleness. Effects of sun damage are more apparent among older adults and evidenced by increased wrinkling, yellowing, leathery texture, and uneven pigmentation of sun-exposed areas.

🌐 Cultural Considerations

Culturally sensitive assessment includes consideration of the patient's cultural beliefs and practices. Based on a variety of cultural practices, some people may not remove their head coverings during an assessment, while others may request that the examination be completed by a clinician of the same sex. Some cultures prohibit directly touching the patient, requiring a nurse to wear gloves to avoid skin-to-skin contact. Becoming familiar with such cultural practices facilitates communication, accurate assessment, and necessary patient education. When the nurse is unfamiliar with the patient's cultural practices, inquiring about cultural practices and expectations of patient care is indicated prior to beginning.

Individuals of African descent are more likely to experience keloids, traction alopecia, pseudofolliculitis, folliculitis barbarae, and perineal follicularis (Juckett, 2005). African Canadian women have increased incidence of melasma in pregnancy; Mongolian spots are fairly common in African Canadian newborns. Curly hair in these patients tends to be coarser than in Caucasians because of a decreased ability of secreted sebum to travel along the hair shaft to the skin. Skin is commonly dry, resulting in ashy dermatitis. Pityriasis rosea, which presents as a macular hyperpigmented viral dermatitis in Caucasians, commonly presents with papular, maroon

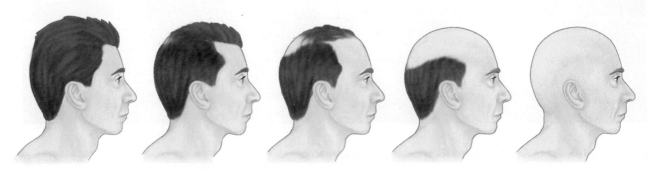

Figure 13-7 Common hair loss patterns in men.

or purple lesions in African Canadians. Skin cancers are more common on the palms, soles, and nail beds in African Canadians than in other groups (Hemenway, 2006). Patients of Asian and First Nations genetic backgrounds have less body and facial hair than patients of other genetic backgrounds.

Tattoos, body piercings, and other skin adornments are common in various Asian cultures (Ethnomed, 2008). Skin discolourations from cupping or coining may be found. Pigmentary disorders such as vitiligo or melasma in darker-skinned Asian populations carry a higher degree of psychosocial and emotional distress than in Caucasian patients (Parsad & Kumarasinge, 2006). Other lesions rarely found outside Asian populations include Hori's nevus and nevus of Ota. Other common lesions include solar lentigo, dark eye circles, postinflammatory hyper- or hypopigmentation, ashy dermatoses, and melanocytic nevi. Many Asian men request removal of nevi from body parts for cultural rather than cosmetic reasons (Ethnomed).

Henna tattoos are common in Arabic and Indian females. Newborns of Arabic descent commonly have Mongolian spots, café au lait spots, and congenital nevi (Kahana, Feldman, et al., 1995). Individuals with darker skin pigmentation and women who are pregnant are reported to experience greater vitamin D deficiency (Schwalfenberg, Genuis, et al., 2010). Although it is not clear as to the reasons for this finding, routine supplementation of vitamin D among these population groups may be indicated.

Acute Assessment

Pressure ulcers are areas of tissue necrosis due to the prolonged compression of body tissue between a firm surface and bony prominences. In Canada, the prevalence of pressure ulcers occurring in the healthcare setting is 26%, with the highest occurring in hospitalized subpopulations such as older adults with femoral fractures (66%) and persons with quadriplegia (60%) (Davis & Caseby, 2001; Woodbury & Houghton, 2005). Prevention of pressure ulcers within acute care environments is crucial. The Braden scale is one of the most common tools used in hospitals and community settings to assess an individual's risk of developing pressure ulcers (Fig. 13-7). Early identification of pressure ulcers is crucial in order to promptly prevent a worsening of the degree of tissue damage, begin wound management, and take measures to prevent infection. Routine monitoring of vital signs and direct inspection of the wound will provide the nurse with valuable data. Fever, increased heart rate, and inflammation and pain of the wound may indicate wound sepsis. A delay in treating wound sepsis with intravenous fluids and antibiotics may result in a fatal outcome.

Skin findings indicating dehydration, cyanosis, or impaired skin integrity (acute lacerations) require prompt evaluation and intervention with fluids, oxygen administration, skin repair, or a combination. Most skin findings are nonemergent but require nurses to report them to other health care providers for further evaluation and management.

The patient may present with infections or infestations that necessitate use of gloves or, in the case of measles, isolation. Rash and fever in the patient should raise suspicion of an infectious process (McKinnon & Howard, 2000). The patient should avoid contact with others to avoid infecting them.

Patients with acute trauma and burns may require immediate attention, depending on severity (Hettiarachi & Papini, 2004). With large lacerations, the nurse must control bleeding and then work with colleagues to manage the wound. Individuals with burns can lose large amounts of fluid through their wounds, so rapid fluid replacement may be necessary. Both large wounds and burns are acute and potentially life-threatening situations that require considerable interventions and prolonged patient care.

Subjective Data Collection

During subjective data collection, nurses have the opportunity to integrate health teaching with history taking. For the integumentary system, a major focus of such teaching relates to prevention of skin cancers, including melanoma.

Assessment of Risk Factors

The presence of risk factors increases the probability that the patient will experience health concerns. Nurses have a critical role in teaching patients about self-examination techniques and the reduction of risk factors for skin cancers and other skin-related illnesses. Clinicians also help patients understand the significance for the early detection of suspicious lesions, the use of protective skin products, and avoiding excessive quantities of sun exposure. Exposure of patients to knowledge of such risk factors can help the nurse identify areas of potential understanding and self-care deficits. Identifying concerns directs the implementation of therapeutic interventions, education for prevention, management of related issues, and documentation of status in the patient health record.

When assessing general skin condition in patients without an identified concern, the nurse gathers information about general health, including nutritional status, which may identify any potential causes for skin disorders. In patients at high risk for skin alterations, such as immobile or bed-bound patients, additional information related to potential alterations in skin integrity is necessary.

Clinical Significance 13-2

If the patient has a specific concern about his or her skin, inspect the area/lesion first and ask other questions second. Often, once the nurse has identified the type of lesion (inflammatory, infectious, tumour, or altered integrity), he or she can focus questions to address the specific type of lesion. For instance, if the patient is scratching a deep pink scaly lesion on his elbow, the nurse may want to inquire about atopic illness or contact irritants instead of about melanoma.

Questions to Assess History and Risk Factors	Rationale

Personal History

How frequently do you examine your skin for any new or changing lesions? When was the last time a nurse or physician examined your skin?

About 53% of skin cancers are discovered by the patient, another 17% are discovered by family members (Canadian Dermatology Association [CDA], 2011a). A 90% cure rate exists for patients who regularly examine their skin and discover a cancerous skin lesion. Provide the patient with information related to identifying potentially serious skin lesions by teaching what changes warrant evaluation by a nurse practitioner or allied health professional. A simple method is to use the *ABCDEs* for screening moles for possible melanoma:

* **A**symmetry
* **B**order irregularity
* **C**olour
* **D**iameter of more than 6 mm
* **E**volution of lesion over time

See Table 13-1 for more information.

Table 13-1   ABCDEs for Screening Moles for Possible Melanoma

A: Asymmetry

Does one half look like the other half?

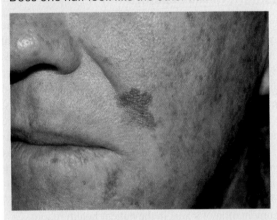

B: Border irregularity

Is the border ragged or notched?

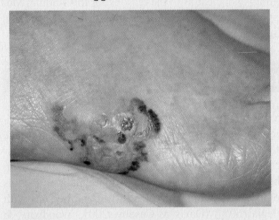

C: Colour

Does the mole have a variety of shades or different colours?

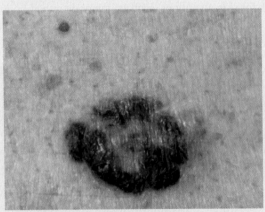

D: Diameter

Is the diameter >6 mm (pencil eraser)?

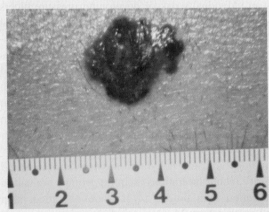

Table 13.1   ABCDEs for Screening Moles for Possible Melanoma (*Continued*)

E: Evolution
Has the lesion evolved or changed over time?

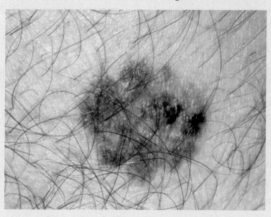

Questions to Assess History and Risk Factors

Do you have any pigmented skin lesions?
- How many lesions?
- Where are they located?
- Are any larger than a pencil eraser?
- Have any lesions changed? (itching, bleeding, nonhealing, colour change, size change, change in borders)

Did you ever have severe sunburn, particularly during childhood or adolescence?

Have you ever had skin cancer?
- When did you have skin cancer?
- Where was it located?
- How deep was it?
- How was it treated?

Rationale

Any **dysplastic nevi** (Fig. 13-8) or more than 50 moles increases risk for melanoma. These moles can be in sun-exposed or sun-protected skin areas. Melanomas are most common on the face, shoulder, and upper arms for both genders, back for men, and legs for women, most likely related to sun exposure (Bulliard, De Weck, et al., 2007). Evolving changes in moles that warrant further evaluation are changes in size, colour, texture, or shape, onset of itching or bleeding, and nonhealing wounds.

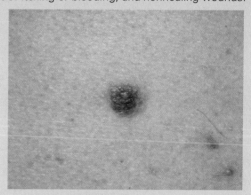

Figure 13-8 Dysplastic nevus.

Melanoma on the trunk, arms, or legs is associated with severe (blistering) sunburn during childhood or adolescence. Fair-skinned people who turn red after minimal exposure to sunlight have less melanin, with less protection from the sun's harmful ultraviolet (UV) rays, and are at increased risk for melanoma (CDA, 2011a).

Prior history of any skin cancer (squamous cell, basal cell, or melanoma) significantly increases the risk of developing additional cancerous skin lesions by 5%, especially during the first year following treatment (CDA, 2011a). Deeper melanoma lesions indicate advanced staging and increased risk for metastases. Prior treatment may have caused additional skin issues, such as burns from radiation or extensive scarring or disfigurement from surgical excision.

(text continues on page 276)

Questions to Assess History and Risk Factors	Rationale
Medications Are you taking any medications? Herbal products? Nutritional supplements? Vitamins? Over-the-counter medications? • Have you recently begun a new prescription or nonprescription medication/supplement? Which one(s)?	Certain medications (Table 13-2), sunscreens, perfumes, cosmetics, and topical skin creams can cause ***photosensitivity*** reactions (Barrett, 2008; Guthrie Ambulatory Health Care Clinic Pharmacy, 2008), which usually present

Table 13-2 Medications That Cause Photoreactions

Antimicrobials	Psychotropics and Other Psychiatric Agents	Cardiovascular Agents	Herbals and Topicals
Azithromycin	Alprazolam	Amiloride	Bergamot
Chloroquine	Amitriptyline	Amiodarone	Bitter orange peel
Ciprofloxacin	Clomipramine	Captopril	Cedar
Doxycycline	Chlordiazepoxide	Chlorothiazide	Celery
Griseofulvin	Desipramine	Digitoxin	Citron
Mefloquine	Doxepin	Diltiazem	Dong quai
Minocycline	Haloperidol	Enalapril	Lavender
Naldixic acid	Imipramine	Fosinopril	Motherwort
Ofloxacin	Isocarboxazid	Furosemide	Musk
Oxytetracycline	Maprotiline	Hydrochlorothiazide	PABA esters
Pyrvinium pamoate	Nortriptyline	Methyldopa	Parsley
Quinine	Prochlorperazine	Metolazone	Peppermint oil
Sulfonamides	Risperidone	Nifedipine	St. John's wort
Sulfasalazine	Sertraline	Quinapril	Sandalwood
Tetracyclines	Thiothixine		Wormwood
Trimethoprim	Thioridazine		
	Trazodone		
	Venlafaxine		

Antihistamines	Disease-Modifying Agents	Chemotherapeutic Agents	Hypoglycemics
Cetirizine	Dapsone	Dacarbazine	Chlorpropamide
Cyproheptadine	Gold	Fluorouracil	Glimepiride
Dimenhydrinate	Hydroxychloroquine	Methotrexate	Glipizide
Diphenhydramine	Methotrexate	Procarbazine	Glyburide
Hydroxyzine	Sulfasalazine	Vinblastine	Tolbutamide
Loratadine			Tolazamide
Promethazine			

Other Agents	Topical Agents	NSAIDs	
Carbamazepine	Benzocaine	Diclofenac	
Gabapentin	Benzoyl Peroxide	Etodolac	
Interferon beta	Bithionol	Ibuprofen	
Oral contraceptives	Coal tar	Ketoprofen	
Zolpidem	Hexachlorophene	Nabumetone	
	Isotretinoin	Naproxen	
	Psoralen	Oxaprozin	
	Tretinoin	Piroxicam	

Questions to Assess History and Risk Factors	Rationale

- Do you use topical medicated creams or ointments?
- Do you have allergies to medications? Foods? Environments? Any other allergies? What happened during your allergic reaction?
- Have you ever had an allergic reaction to sunscreen?

with rash following sun exposure. Other medications stimulate **phototoxicity,** a reaction caused by a drug's molecules absorbing energy from a particular UV wavelength and then damaging surrounding tissues. The result is marked and severely tender sunburn (Eustice & Eustice, 2007). Phototoxicity usually develops immediately (within 24 h of initial ingestion of the photoreactive medication) and resolves soon after discontinuation of the medication, UV exposure, or both. **Photoallergy** manifests with blisters and redness on exposed skin, occurs only after repeated exposure to the drug, and persists for some time after discontinuation of the drug, UV exposure, or both.

Family History

Do you have any first degree family members (parent, sibling, and child) with a history of any skin conditions such as cancer? Psoriasis? Or eczema?
- Do any first-degree relatives have multiple dark, irregular moles?

Having one or more first-degree relatives with a history of **melanoma** increases the patient's risk (CDA, 2011a). Two or more first-degree relatives with a history of melanoma and a personal history of one or more dysplastic nevi increase risk for melanoma by 50% (Canadian Cancer Society, 2009). Approximately 10% of all patients with melanoma have a family member with melanoma.

Lifestyle, Occupational History, and Personal Behaviours

What is your occupation? Your hobbies?
- Are you exposed to excessive sunlight? Other sources of radiation?
- What do you do to protect yourself from excessive sun exposure?

- How often do you shower or bathe?
- What is the water temperature?
- How often do you apply moisturizer after you bathe?

Work or hobbies involving excessive exposure to sunlight, especially during intensive midday hours, increases risk for melanoma. Determining what protection the patient uses (ie, gloves, hats, long-sleeved shirts, pants, shoes, socks, sunscreens, sunblock) helps the nurse to ascertain the patient's risk level for melanoma.

Excessively dry skin may result from frequent bathing and inadequate moisturizing. Showering or bathing more than once daily in the healthy adult causes excessive loss of skin oils. Elderly patients need to bathe less often, usually every 2–3 days. Using hot water to bathe increases loss of skin oils. Bathing should be with warm water only and for the shortest time necessary to cleanse all body areas. Use of moisturizing creams (not lotions) immediately after towelling dry decreases the effect of loss of skin oils from bathing.

Determine risk for skin breakdown.
- Are you confined to bed?
- Do you have a cast, brace, or other immobilizing device on any body part?
- Can you change your body position or position of the immobilized body part?
- How often are you changing position or shifting weight from one part of your body to another?
- Do you have any loss of sensation or position sense to any part of your body?
- Do you have diabetes mellitus? Peripheral vascular disease? Or any known sensory loss?
- How is your nutritional intake?
- What is your age?
- What is your weight?

Immobility of the body or a body part increases risk for pressure ulcers. The National Pressure Ulcer Advisory Panel (2007, p. 1) defines a **pressure ulcer** as a "localized injury to the skin and/or underlying tissue usually over a bony prominence, as a result of pressure or pressure in combination with shear and/or friction." Casts, splints, or other immobilizing devices may exert pressure on bony prominences of an immobilized extremity or part and increase risk for pressure ulcer. This risk is amplified in patients with decreased sensory perception of the immobilized extremity or body part (eg, in diabetic neuropathy, venous insufficiency, other sensory deficits), because they cannot sense discomfort associated with decreased circulation to an area caused by prolonged pressure. The adult who is older is at increased risk for pressure ulcers from age-related loss of subcutaneous fat and decreased cushioning. Thin patients have less subcutaneous fat to cushion the skin against pressures exerted on it (see Table 13-18 at the end of the chapter).

Risk Assessment and Health Promotion

Topics for Health Promotion

- Risk factors for skin cancer
- Skin self-examination
- Sun safety
- Tanning booths
- Vitamin D deficiency

As mentioned previously, risk assessment identifies areas of concern and provides direction for patient education. Excessive UV radiation is the most important focus area for the integumentary system, because exposure to it has been shown to cause skin cancers, particularly melanoma.

Skin self-examination (SSE) assists patients with identifying potentially problematic lesions through the detection of moles (Fig. 13-9). The nurse educates the patient that a benign mole has the following features (CDA, 2011a):

- A solid tan, brown, black, or skin-toned colour
- Size smaller than 6 mm in diameter (approximately the size of a pencil eraser)
- Well-defined edges
- Usually round or oval shape with a flat or domelike surface
- Emergence before 30 years of age

The nurse emphasizes to the patient the following steps of the SSE:

1. Get fully undressed and stand in front of a full-length mirror.
2. Carefully scan the entire body, using a hand-held mirror to look at areas difficult to see (eg, soles of feet).
3. When examining the scalp, use a comb or blowdryer to part the hair and examine the scalp section by section.
4. Report any suspicious lesion to a health care provider.

Both natural and artificial forms of UV light are carcinogenic, and exposure to UV light directly increases risk for skin cancer (Canadian Cancer Society, 2008). Short ultraviolet B (UVB) waves are more likely than ultraviolet A (UVA) waves to cause sunburn. UVB waves are directly linked with skin cancers, especially basal cell and squamous cell cancers. Longer UVA waves have deeper skin penetration than UVB (Environmental Protection Agency, 2008). UVA waves are responsible for some melanomas, but are chiefly responsible for the effects of photoaging, specifically wrinkling and leathering of the skin. Intensity of UV waves is greatest during midday, and exposure between 10 AM and 4 PM increases potential damaging effects. Reflection of UV waves off sand, concrete, snow, and water doubles UV exposure and its damaging effects.

Nurses can simplify the education of patients about decreasing UV light exposure by teaching the phrase "Seek, Slip!! Slap!... and Slop!" Coined by the CDA (20011b), it reminds people to Seek out shade, Slip on a shirt, Slap on a hat and sunglasses, and Slop on sunscreen, to increase protection against UV exposure. Sunburn protection from clothing depends on how much skin is covered, fabric colour, and fabric weave. Dark colours reflect UV rays better than light colours, and tightly woven fabrics afford less penetration by harmful UV rays. Some fabrics provide less protection than sunscreen with sun-protective factor (SPF) of 15 or higher. Wearing a hat with a wide all-around brim protects the face, neck, and ears—common sites for skin cancer (Canadian Cancer Society, 2008).

The SPF is defined as the amount of time a product protects the skin from reddening, as compared to the amount of time for unprotected skin to redden (CDA, 2011b). If it usually takes 10 minutes for unprotected skin to redden, use of a product with SPF 15 would protect the skin from reddening for 150 minutes. Applying sunscreen 15 to 30 minutes prior to exposure enhances absorption of the sunscreen into the skin and increases protection. Sunscreen application needs to happen every 2 hours for maximum benefit. **Sunscreens** absorb harmful UV rays; **sunblocks** deflect rays from absorption. People also should apply lip balm with SPF repeatedly during sun exposure to protect the lips. To be effective when extended sun exposure is anticipated, sunglasses should have at least 99% UVA and UVB protection.

Another helpful reminder to limit excessive UV exposure is "short shadow seek shade" (Canadian Cancer Society, 2008). Sun that is overhead casts a shadow shorter than the actual person and should serve as an alert to seek more shade for protection. As a shadow lengthens, it signifies decreased UV intensity and thus a need for less protection. Changes in the weather, seasons, and ozone layer affect the intensity of UV rays (WHO, n.d.). The **UV Index** (Table 13-3), published daily, uses a scale from 0 to 11 or higher to indicate the degree of predicted UV radiation based on weather, season, and ozone layer changes. The higher the number, the greater the risk, and the greater degree of protection required.

The use of tanning booths is discouraged for persons under the age of 16 and some provinces, such as British Columbia, Nova Scotia, and New Brunswick, have introduced or are in the process of introducing legislation to prevent minors from using tanning salons. Health Canada (2010) overviews strict guidelines for the use of tanning booths. The World Health Organization (WHO, 2009) has moved tanning beds into the highest risk category for skin cancer meaning tanning beds definitely cause cancer.

Vitamin D deficiency is another topic of concern for Canadians especially between the months of October and April. See Chapter 8 for more information on vitamin D deficiency.

Melanoma is a less common but most dangerous form of skin cancer since it can spread in the body.

MELANOMA SKIN CANCER
KNOW THE SIGNS, SAVE A LIFE

ABCDEs of Melanoma

A ASYMMETRY
The shape on one side is different than the other side.

B BORDER
The border or visible edge is irregular, ragged and imprecise.

C COLOUR
There is a colour variation with brown, black, red, grey or white within the lesion.

D DIAMETER
Growth is typical of melanoma. It is usually more than 6 mm although it can be less.

E EVOLUTION
Look for change in colour, size, shape or symptom such as itching, tenderness or bleeding.

Photos provided by Dr Joël Claveau

5 steps to SKIN CANCER SELF-EXAM

1 Using a mirror in a well lit room, check the front of your body - face, neck, shoulders, arms, chest, abdomen, thighs and lower legs.

2 Turn sideways, raise your arms and look carefully at the right and left sides of your body, including the underarm area.

3 With a hand-held mirror, check your upper back, neck and scalp. Next, examine your lower back, buttocks, backs of thighs and calves.

4 Examine your forearms, palms, back of the hands, fingernails and in between each finger.

5 Finally, check your feet - the tops, soles, toenails, toes and spaces in between.

PROTECT YOURSELF!
The best ways to protect yourself are to:
- Find out your risk factors
- Learn the early signs, the ABCDEs of melanoma
- Protect yourself from the sun from spring to fall and avoid sunbeds
- Check your skin once a month
- Take action if you see any suspicious spots

Dermatologists
Your **SKINexperts**
Canadian Dermatology Association
Association canadienne de dermatologie

For further information, visit www.dermatology.ca

Figure 13-9 Skin self-examination.

Table 13-3   Ultraviolet Light (UV) Index and Skin Protection Recommendations

| UV Index | Level | Minutes to Reddened Skin | | | Recommended Skin Protection |
		Fair Skin	Medium Skin	Dark Skin	
0–2	Low	44–120+	74–120+	120+	Wear sunglasses when it is bright outside.
					Wear sunscreen, especially fair-skinned patients and those who burn easily.
3–5	Moderate	26–43	44–71	77–120	Wear sun-protective clothing. Follow "Short Shadow Seek Shade."
6–7	High	18–26	31–43	55–76	Unprotected skin can burn quickly.
					Wear sun-protective factor (SPF) ≥ 15 sunscreen or sunblock, protective clothing, sunglasses, shade, hat.
					Reduce exposure between 10 AM and 4 PM.
8–10	Very high	13–18	22–31	38–54	Risk of harm from unprotected sun exposure is high.
					Wear SPF ≥ 15 sunscreen or sunblock, protective clothing, sunglasses, shade, and hat.
					Reduce exposure between 10 AM and 4 PM.
11+	Extreme	9–13	14–21	25–38	Avoid UV exposure if possible.
					Use liberal application of SPF ≥ 15 sunscreen or sunblock.
					Wear protective clothing, sunglasses, shade, and hat.
					Reduce exposure between 10 AM and 4 PM.

Adapted from Environmental Protection Agency. (2008). *UV index*. Retrieved from http://epa.gov/sunwise/uvindex.html

Focused Health History Related to Common Symptoms

Common Integumentary Symptoms and Signs

- Itchiness
- Rash
- Moles
- Lesions
- Hair loss
- Dry skin or winter skin

Obtaining an accurate and detailed sign or symptom analysis is instrumental in determining the exact nature of skin conditions. For example, for the patient presenting with a generalized body rash, the symptom analysis may lead the nurse to consider a benign condition or one requiring immediate attention. The nurse caring for the patient with a generalized rash may identify the rash as an allergic reaction. On the other hand, the patient presenting with a similar rash, headache, fever, and lethargy may have meningococcemia, a bacterial infection carrying high rates of mortality. (See Box 13-1.)

BOX 13-1   EXAMPLES OF QUESTIONS FOR SIGN/SYMPTOM ANALYSIS—RASH

- "Where is the rash?" "Where did the rash start?" "Has the rash spread?" "Is it all over your legs?" *(Location, Radiation)*
- "Describe what the rash is like." "Is it raised?" "Scaly?" "Itchy?" "Painful?" *(Quality)*
- "Describe how itchy (or painful) the rash is." *(Severity)*
- "When did the rash start?" "Did it start suddenly?" "Did you notice it starting over time?" *(Onset)*
- "Has the rash stayed the same since you first noticed it?" *(Duration)*
- "Have there been times when it got better?" "Or worse?" *(Constancy)*
- "Is there a time of day that it (rash) seems worse? Or better?" *(Time of day/month/year)*
- "What makes the rash worse?" *(Aggravating factors)*
- "What makes the rash better?" *(Alleviating factors)*
- "What other symptoms have you noticed?" *(Associated symptoms)*
- "Have you been exposed to any chemicals?" "Or other substances?" "Have you recently changed anything in your house or office such as laundry detergent or soap?" "Have you been experiencing more stress than usual?" *(Environmental factors)*
- "Describe how this is affecting your life." *(Significance to patient)*
- "What do you think may be happening?" *(Patient perspective)*

Adapted from Stephen, T. C., & Bickley, L. S. (2010). The skin, hair, and nails. In T. C. Stephen, D. L. Skillen, R. A. Day, & Bickley, L. S. (Eds.). *Canadian Bates' guide to health assessment for nurses* (p. 248). Philadelphia, PA: Wolters Kluwer Health/Lippincott Williams & Wilkins.

Tell me about your skin concern.

Pruritus (Itching)

Do you have concerns with itching?
- How long have you had the itchiness?
- Where do you itch?
- (If there are signs of a rash) Did you first have itching followed by the rash?
- What makes the itching worse? Better?
- Does itching disrupt rest and sleep?
- Have you tried any remedies for the itching? What was the result?
- What do you think is happening?

Rash

Where is/are the lesion(s) located?
- Do you have a single lesion? Or are there several?
- Is the rash all over? Or just in one area?
- Does the rash appear to have a pattern?

Has the rash changed since you first noticed it?

Have you been exposed to anything that would cause itching or the rash?
- Have you been exposed to any chemicals, either at work or play?
- Do you have pets or frequent contact with animals?
- Is anyone close to you with a similar skin issue?
- Have you recently started any new medications? Vitamins? Herbal product? Over the Counter drug or supplement?
- Have you eaten unusual foods recently?
- Any recent travel? When? Where?
- Have you shared clothing, equipment or bedding recently?
- Do you live in a communal dwelling?

How would you describe your rash?
- Flat?
- Raised?
- Blister like?
- Pus-filled?
- Looks like thickened skin?

Do you have any other symptoms?
- Any recent illness?
- Any fever? Chills? Or headache?

This question encourages the patient to present his or her view and perceptions of the issue.

Skin lesions or conditions are pruritic, occasionally pruritic, or never pruritic. Pruritus frequently precedes atopic lesions but follows inflammatory lesions. Recent pruritus may indicate toxic exposure, insect bites, parasite infestations, or viral xanthems. Localized pruritus may indicate infestation, insect bite, allergic reaction, or toxic exposure. Generalized pruritus is common in medication or food allergies. Severe pruritus interfering with sleep is common in bedbug and *scabies* infections. *Psoriasis* is occasionally pruritic. Moles usually do not itch. Noting what, if any, remedies the patient tried and their effectiveness may help identify the cause.

Lesions from *contact or allergic dermatitis* are usually on the body part exposed to an irritant or allergen (Hogan, 2007). Lesions over the entire body, including palms and soles, may be linked to *syphilis*. *Seborrheic dermatitis* is often found on the face, head, and hair-covered body areas. *Herpes zoster* follows a dermatome and is often found on the chest, back, abdomen, and face and rarely on the extremities. Genital lesions are commonly from sexually transmitted infections.

Varicella begins with macular lesions, progresses to papular, then vesicular, and ultimately to superficial ulcers. *Pityriasis rosea* begins as a single large macular lesion (Herald patch) on the trunk and progresses to multiple smaller scaling lesions distributed predominately over the chest and back. *Contact dermatitis* spreads from initial point of contact; in severe cases, lesions appear in unexposed areas.

Skin exposure to an allergen releases histamine from mast cells, resulting in pruritus. Scratching causes additional histamine release, thus further pruritus. This prompts further scratching, and develops into a persistent cycle of itching and scratching. Determining recent occupational and leisure activities, animal or plant contacts, and outdoor activities may identify exposures to poison ivy, insects, microbes such as fungus or bacteria, chemicals, and pesticides. Medications, vitamin or herbal supplements, and foods new to the patient may be causes for *allergic dermatitis*. Insect bites or contact with foods or other products not found in the patient's home country may cause lesions that present during or shortly after travel. Wearing another person's clothes, sleeping in someone else's bed, or living in communal dwellings may expose the patient to *scabies* or *lice*.

Macular lesions could be ecchymosis, pressure point, or *tinea versicolour*. **Papular** lesions may indicate *acne, warts*, nevi, insect bites, or early *varicella*. **Pustular** lesions include *acne*, furuncles, and carbuncles. **Vesicular** lesions may be *herpes simplex, varicella*, or *impetigo*. **Plaque** lesions are commonly *psoriasis* or *lichen simplex*. (See Table 13-8 at the end of the chapter.)

Fevers and chills often accompany infectious skin disorders such as *measles, rubella*, and *varicella* (McKinnon & Howard, 2000). Headache often accompanies *mumps* and *meningitis*.

Lifespan Considerations

Additional Health History Questions	Rationale/Unexpected Findings

Women Who Are Pregnant

What skin changes have you noticed since becoming pregnant?

Hormonal changes in pregnancy produce multiple effects on the skin. Striae ("stretch marks") appear as the skin stretches to accommodate the growing fetus and do not completely disappear after pregnancy but may fade to a light silvery colour. Fingernails may grow at an accelerated rate.

Do you have any acne?

Women with a history of acne before pregnancy may experience a resurgence of acne lesions during pregnancy.

Any itchy skin?

Itchiness is common in the second and third trimesters and results from stretching of the skin, particularly on the abdomen and breasts, to accommodate the growing fetus and milk production. Severe itchiness may indicate *intrahepatic cholestasis of pregnancy;* it may be associated with nausea, vomiting, fatigue, jaundice, and decreased appetite.

Do you have excessively oily skin?

Hormonal changes increase the oil secretion of sebaceous glands, contributing to the "glow of pregnancy."

Any colour changes to your face or body?

Pigmentary changes of pregnancy include **linea nigra** (darkened line from umbilicus to pubis) and **melasma** (blotchy facial discolouration known as the "mask of pregnancy").

Have you had concerns regarding skin tags?

Hormonal changes potentiate small growths of skin that extend from the epidermis. Skin tags do not resolve spontaneously after pregnancy. The patient's Nurse Practitioner may surgically remove cutaneous growths if desired by the patient.

Newborns, Infants, and Children

Any frequent or persistent bruising?
• What safety precautions do you use at home? In the car?
• Has your child been ill recently?

Petechiae often indicate decreased clotting ability as a result of a profound or disseminated infection, hematologic conditions, or cancers. Bruising or **ecchymosis** may indicate hematological issues, child abuse, or improper safety precautions (stair gates, age inappropriate toys). Bruises in various stages of healing require careful questioning to determine if nonaccidental trauma has caused them. Nurses have a legal and professional obligation to report any **suspicion** of child abuse to local authorities (ie, police, department of social services)

Does your child have a rash?
• Any fever? Nausea? Vomiting?
• Any recent medication use?
• Do you have any pets in your home?
• Does your child attend daycare?

Many bacterial, fungal, and viral infections cause *dermatoses.* The papulovesicular lesions and honey-coloured crusting of *impetigo* result from staphylococcal or streptococcal infection. *Tinea pedis, capitis, cruris,* or *corporis* are caused by fungal elements. Childhood xanthems as seen in *roseola, varicella,* and *herpes* are often of a viral origin. Generalized burn-like blistering following antibiotics (penicillin, sulfa, ciprofloxacin) or some antiseizure medications may potentiate *Stevens-Johnson syndrome,* a serious and even lethal syndrome (Parrillo, 2008).

Adolescents

Tell me about your acne?
• What makes your acne worse? Food? Activity?
• Have you tried any products to clear your acne?
• (In females) Do you tend to break out before or during menstruation?

Diet generally does not influence acne, but in some people certain foods or a high glycemic load tend to be associated with an increased number or severity of acne lesions (Smith, Mann et al., 2007). Sporting equipment (such as hockey helmets) may cause a worsening of acne. Hormonal influences can increase acne lesions. Identifying what remedies the patient has tried will help determine what other therapeutic regimens may help resolve the acne.

Additional Health History Questions	Rationale/Unexpected Findings
Do you intentionally cut or harm any part of your body?	"Cutting" or "self-mutilation" is a form of self-harm behaviour often associated with psychiatric or mental health disorders such as depression, or evolving personality disorder. It is the self-inflicted act of using a razor, knife, or other sharp instrument to make "cut marks" on the extremities. This manifestation of mental health issues often begins in late childhood or adolescence, and is frequently associated with depression.
Do you have any piercings or tattoos? • Where are your piercings? Ear? Chest? Genitals? • Where did you have this piercing or tattoo done? • Any swelling? Redness? Tenderness? • How are you keeping the area clean? • Did your tattooist use sterile, single-use needles and dyes?	Tattooing and piercings of various body parts frequently begin in adolescence and coincide with increased risk taking among this population (Mayer & Chiffrieller, 2008). The reuse or improper sterilization of tattooing and piercing equipment places individuals at high risk for hepatitis C infection. Education regarding the selection of tattooing parlours or piercing shops should include verifying that the business adheres to regulations and is regularly inspected by public health officials. Swelling, redness, or tenderness at a piercing site may indicate infection or allergic reaction to the inserted metal stud, ring, or rod. Dyes used in tattooing may cause an allergic reaction and result in swelling, redness, and tenderness at the tattoo site (Health Canada, 2008).

Older Adults

Do you bruise easily? Does your skin tear or split easily?	Multiple ecchymosis may be from repeated trauma (falls), clotting disorder, or physical abuse. Aging causes the junction between the dermis and epidermis to flatten, increasing the tendency of the skin to tear. Decreased eccrine gland function results in a decreased sweat response. Nerve endings in skin decrease with age, causing decreased sensation to 2-point discrimination, touch, and vibration.
Are your nails brittle or splitting?	Nail growth decreases with aging, leading to the formation of concave, flat, or dry and brittle nails. Pigmented nail bands present earlier in life are more pronounced in aging patients.

Cultural Considerations

• What are some treatments you use at home for this skin condition? • Is it common in your culture to apply any health or beauty products or adornments directly to the skin? • What do you think caused this issue? • Do you engage in any activities or cultural practices that leave marks on the body?	More than half of all patients are likely to self-treat a skin lesion or dermatitis prior to seeking advice from a health care professional. Inquiring about cultural practices and home remedies provides insight into the patient's specific approaches to treating common skin conditions.

A common practice among Southeast Asians is *coining,* in which they rub a coin or other object across the skin in a specific manner to treat various health concerns (Fig. 13-10). Coining frequently results in bruising and abrasions and is often mistaken as a sign of physical abuse. Cupping involves placement of cups on the skin surface, applying heat to form a vacuum. This practice often leaves circular bruises on the skin. The patient's perception of the cause, reason for onset, type of treatment needed, and fears related to any illness will affect the approach and effectiveness in treating the patient's skin condition. Another common cultural practice is the application of henna tattoos in an array of patterns and at specific locations to represent a particular occasion in the patient's life and culture (Ethnomed, 2008).

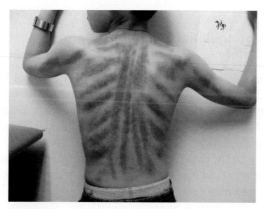

Figure 13-10 Effects of coining.

Remember Mr. Stoli, the patient described at the beginning of this chapter, who was admitted to the hospital with a venous stasis ulcer. The nurse uses professional communication techniques to gather subjective data from Mr. Stoli. The following conversation provides an example of a therapeutic dialogue.

Nurse: Hello, Mr. Stoli. My name is Lilin Cho. I'll be your nurse for today. (smiles, pauses) How are you?

Mr. Stoli: Fine.

Nurse: I understand that you are in the hospital for the treatment of your lower leg wound. Is that right?

Mr. Stoli: Yeah, I was doing fine at home, you know, but the home care nurse wanted me to come here.

Nurse: What changes to your wound prompted the home care nurse to recommend that you be admitted to the hospital?

Mr. Stoli: My wife said it was looking worse. My wife told me I should be resting more so it would get better. I didn't do that.

Nurse: It sounds like you really like to be active.

Mr. Stoli: I don't like being here. I can take care of my leg myself, you know.

Nurse: You sound like you like being independent. It must be hard for you to be in the hospital.

Mr. Stoli: (silent)

Nurse: Let's look at your leg. It would be really helpful if you could tell me how the wound has changed since being at home. I know that it's difficult to have us help you, but we really want to help you to get better (smiles). Perhaps we can talk about other things you can do at home to help your leg improve and prevent further issues requiring hospitalization.

Critical Thinking Challenge

- How might the nurse's nonverbal communication promote a therapeutic relationship?
- How might the patient's Russian heritage influence his perceptions, values, and beliefs about his diagnosis and healing?

Objective Data Collection

Equipment Needed

- Examination gown
- Tape measure
- Adequate light source
- Magnifying glass
- Disposable non latex gloves

Promoting Patient Comfort, Dignity, and Safety

Ensure a comfortable room temperature. Wash your hands thoroughly. Apply clean gloves if you anticipate contact with a skin lesion and during inspection of the scalp. Examination of the skin involves inspection and palpation. Inspect the entire skin surface using good lighting. Expose only areas being directly examined to facilitate privacy, decrease the patient's anxiety, and show consideration for possible cultural concerns.

Common and Specialty or Advanced Techniques

Objective assessment of the skin is performed in a head-to-toe format if the patient is seeking a complete skin assessment. More commonly, the nurse assesses skin with inspection of each body area, such as abdominal skin when inspecting the abdomen. General skin assessment includes colour, texture, moisture, turgor, and temperature. Additionally, the nurse might assess a specific issue, such as a rash on the thorax. The nurse assesses and describes wounds, lesions, rashes, and hematomas separately during the focused assessment.

Comprehensive Skin Assessment

First, the nurse assesses the overall skin appearance and inspects the face and exposed skin surfaces for colour and pigmentation. The nurse needs to turn patients confined to bed to visualize all body surfaces. If the patient cannot help with the movement, additional help may be necessary to position the patient safely.

Patients confined to bed require frequent detailed inspection of dependent areas, especially bony prominences, to detect early evidence of skin breakdown. As well, it is important to evaluate skin folds for infection or irritation, especially under the breasts, in the groin, and under the abdominal pannus.

Individual lesions may be categorized generally as primary or secondary. *Primary lesions* arise from previously intact skin and include maculae, papules, nodules, tumours, polyps, wheals, vesicles, cysts, pustules, and abscesses. Primary lesions may be further described as nonelevated, elevated-solid, or fluid-filled. *Secondary lesions* follow primary lesions (eg, scar tissue, crusts from dried burns). Review Tables 13-8 and 13-9 at the end of this chapter for more details.

The language of the integumentary system can be very complex and intimidating. Remember it is best to describe lesions if you are unsure about how to label them. A complete and accurate description can be used to identify if the patient is healing.

Technique and Expected Findings	Unexpected Findings
Inspection: Skin If performing a complete skin assessment, inspect all body areas, beginning at the crown of the head, parting the hair to visualize the scalp, and progressing towards the feet. Make sure to assess the undersides of the feet and between the toes. Note general skin colour. *Pigmentation is consistent throughout the body. Patients with darker skin pigmentation may have hypopigmented skin on the palms and soles.*	Note variations in pigmentation in any areas. *Vitiligo* is characterized by areas of no pigmentation. Other unexpected colour changes include *flushing, erythema* (redness), *cyanosis* (bluish discolouration), *pallor* (paleness), *rubor* (dependent redness), *brawny* (dark leathery appearance), and *jaundice* (yellow discolouration of skin and sclera). The tongue, lips, nail beds, and buccal mucosa are less pigmented areas and may be the best indicators of pallor or cyanosis. *Uremic frost* is a whitish coating caused by urea and nitrogen skin excretion in the presence of severe and prolonged kidney failure. See Table 13-7 at the end of this chapter.
Inspect for any lesions. If observed, identify the configuration, pattern, morphology, size, distribution, and body location. *Common benign lesions include freckles, birth marks, skin tags, moles, and cherry angiomas.*	A lesion's primary morphology or the configurations may be characterized as being annular, arciform, iris, linear, polymorphous, punctuate, serpiginous, nummular/discoid, umbilicated, filiform, or verrucaform. Secondary morphology includes shape, size, arrangement, and distribution. Such patterns include asymmetric, confluent, diffuse, discrete, generalized, grouped, localized, satellite, symmetric, or zosteriform. Lesion morphology is a key determinant in identifying a skin disorder. Primary morphology is the type. Secondary morphology includes shape, size, arrangement, and distribution, which further defines the underlying lesion (or variant). *Vitiligo*, a miscellaneous lesion, causes skin depigmentation. See Tables 13-8 and 13-11 at the end of this chapter.
Differentiate infectious versus inflammatory lesions. Be sure to use infection control principles if infection is suspected.	Infections include *acne, cellulitis, impetigo,* German *measles* (rubella), *herpes simplex* (cold sores), *measles* (rubeola), *pityriasis rosea, roseola, warts, candida, tinea corporis,* and *tinea versicolour.* See Table 13-12.

(text continues on page 286)

Observe for growths, tumours, or vascular and other miscellaneous lesions.

These include *psoriasis, eczema, urticaria, contact dermatitis,* allergic drug reaction, insect bites, or seborrhea. See Table 13-13.

Lice *(pediculosis),* scabies, or ticks may infest the skin and produce lesions. See Table 13-14.

Growths and tumours include *moles or nevi,* skin tags, *lipoma, lentigo, actinic keratosis, basal or squamous cell carcinoma, malignant melanoma,* and *Kaposi's sarcoma.* Vascular lesions include *hemangiomas, nevus flammeus* (port-wine stain), *spider or star angiomas,* and *venous lakes.* See Table 13-15.

Inspect any wounds or incisions. If observed, note the shape and measure the length, width, and depth with a ruler. If a wound is deep or tunnelled, insert a probe to measure its depth. Wounds can be intentional (surgical) or unintentional (trauma); open or closed; acute or chronic; superficial or deep; and clean, contaminated, or infected. Determine the phase of wound healing and wound classification (Table 13-4). Wound assessment involves some knowledge of the healing process, which is divided into inflammatory, proliferative, and remodelling phases (Mercandetti & Cohen, 2008).

Partial-thickness wounds involve the epidermis; *full-thickness wounds* involve the dermis and subcutaneous tissue.

Table 13-4	**Wound Classification**
Wound Healing Phase	**Description**
Inflammatory Phase: Begins within 30 min of injury; lasts 2–3 d	Upon injury, vasoconstriction, platelet aggregation, and release of thromboplastin promotes *hemostasis.* An *inflammatory* reaction follows, initially through polymorphonuclear cells to cleanse the wound of debris and kill bacteria. Mononuclear cells follow and become macrophages to further cleanse the wound of debris, dead bacteria, and spent neutrophils.
Proliferative Phase: Begins at the end of inflammatory phase; may last up to 4 wk	Fibroblasts migrate into the wound bed to deposit collagen and secrete growth factors. Macrophages now produce enzymes to stimulate tissue growth and generate blood vessels. The wound bed has the appearance of *granulation.* As the wound bed continues to regenerate, the wound edges begin to *contract* and move centrally to close the defect. Finally, *epithelial regrowth* closes the defect.
Remodelling Phase: Begins at end of proliferative phase; may last as long as 2 y	Once deposition of new collagen is maximized (at ~ 3 wk), macrophages stimulate a gradual replacement of the new, rapidly replaced collagen with mature collagen, which greatly increases the tensile strength of the wound.
Wound Classification	**Description**
Clean	Made under sterile conditions and not at risk for infection. Usually skin or vascular incisions
Clean-contaminated	Made under sterile conditions but involving the respiratory, gastrointestinal, genital, or urinary tracts without unusual contamination. Includes appendectomies, hysterectomies, cholecystectomies, and oropharyngeal surgeries.
Contaminated	Exposed to contents of the gastrointestinal tract or infected fluids from the genitourinary systems. Also includes open, traumatic wounds such as lacerations, puncture wounds, and open fractures.
Infected	Exposed to contaminants or exhibiting evidence of infection prior to surgery. Includes any traumatic wound because of the high risk for foreign body, bacteria, and chemical or other organic contaminant.

Necrotic tissue (eschar) may be yellow, white, brown, or black. Pale tissue may indicate poor circulation and wounds to that area may be slow to heal. The surrounding area may be inflamed and red or pale with poor circulation. See Table 13-16.

Describe any wounds related to trauma. Assess status of the blood supply to the skin, making note of any bleeding or ecchymosis (bruising).

Trauma associated lesions include *ecchymosis, hematomas, lacerations, abrasions, puncture wounds,* or *avulsions.* See Table 13-17.

Identify risk for skin breakdown, which is especially important in hospitalized or inactive patients. Many health care facilities use the Braden scale (Table 13-5) to assess risk in patients, with interventions based on the total score (Bergstrom, Braden, et al., 1987). Alternatively, the similar Norton scale includes incontinence and other variables (Norton, 1989).

The Braden scale rates patients from 1 to 4 in each of six subscales: sensory perception, moisture, activity, mobility, nutrition, and friction (Braden & Bergstrom, 1989). The Norton scale rates patients from 1 to 4 in each of five subscales: physical condition, mental condition, activity, mobility, and incontinence. A score <14 on the Norton scale or from 14–18 on the Braden scale indicates a high-risk of pressure ulcer development.

Classify the wound as partial or full thickness; if a pressure ulcer is present, identify the stage. When assessing any ulcer, it is important to observe and document the depth and diameter, margins, condition of surrounding tissues, degree of tissue granulation, and any drainage, odour, or necrotic tissue. Describe the colour and texture of the tissue. Identify the amount, colour, consistency, and odour of exudate (drainage). Describe the location using appropriate landmarks. Use an appropriate tool to measure associated pain (see Chapter 7).

Pressure ulcers may be deep tissue, Stage I, Stage II, Stage III, Stage IV, or unstageable (Black, Baharestani, et al. 2007). Stages I and II are partial thickness into the dermis. Stages III and IV are full thickness.

(text continues on page 289)

Table 13-5 The Braden Scale for Predicting Pressure Sore Risk

Patient Name: _____ Room Number: _____ Date: _____

Sensory Perception	1. Completely Limited	2. Very Limited	3. Slightly Limited	4. No Impairment	Indicate Appropriate Numbers Below
Ability to respond meaningfully to pressure-related discomfort	Unresponsive (does not moan, flinch, or grasp) to painful stimuli, due to diminished level of consciousness or sedation. OR limited ability to feel pain over most of body surface.	Responds only to painful stimuli. Cannot communicate discomfort except by moaning or restlessness. OR has a sensory impairment that limits the ability to feel pain or discomfort over half of the body.	Responds to verbal commands, but cannot always communicate discomfort or need to be turned. OR has some sensory impairment that limits ability to feel pain or discomfort in one or two extremities.	Responds to verbal commands. Has no sensory deficit that would limit ability to feel or voice pain or discomfort.	
Moisture	**1. Constantly Moist**	**2. Very Moist**	**3. Occasionally Moist**	**4. Rarely Moist**	
Degree to which skin is exposed to moisture	Skin is kept moist almost constantly by perspiration, urine, etc. Dampness is detected every time patient is moved or turned.	Skin is often, but not always, moist. Linen must be changed at least once a shift.	Skin is occasionally moist, requiring an extra linen change approximately once a day.	Skin is usually dry. Linen only requires changing at routine intervals.	

(table continues on page 288)

Activity	1. Bedfast	2. Chairfast	3. Walks Occasionally	4. Walks Frequently
Degree of physical activity	Confined to bed.	Ability to walk severely limited or nonexistent. Cannot bear own weight and/or must be assisted into chair or wheelchair	Walks occasionally during day, but for very short distances, with or without assistance. Spends majority of each shift in bed or chair	Walks outside the room at least twice a day and inside room at least once every 2 h during waking hours.

Mobility	1. Completely Immobile	2. Very Limited	3. Slightly Limited	4. No Limitations
Ability to change and control body position	Does not make even slight changes in body or extremity position without assistance.	Makes occasional slight changes in body or extremity position but unable to make frequent or significant changes independently	Makes frequent though slight changes in body or extremity position independently	Makes major and frequent changes in position without assistance

Nutrition	1. Very Poor	2. Probably Inadequate	3. Adequate	4. Excellent
Usual food intake pattern	Never eats a complete meal. Rarely eats more than one third of any food offered. Eats two servings or less of protein (meat or dairy products) per day. Takes fluids poorly. Does not take a liquid dietary supplement. OR is NPO and/or maintained on clear liquids or IVs for more than 5 days.	Rarely eats a complete meal and generally eats only about a half of any food offered. Protein intake includes only three servings of meat or dairy products per day. Occasionally will take a dietary supplement. OR receives less than optimum amount of liquid diet or tube feeding.	Eats over half of most meals. Eats a total of four servings of protein (meat, dairy products) each day. Occasionally will refuse a meal, but will usually take a supplement if offered. OR is on a tube feeding or TPN regimen which probably meets most of nutritional needs.	Eats most of every meal. Never refuses a meal. Usually eats a total of four or more servings of meat and dairy products. Occasionally eats between meals. Does not require supplementation.

Friction and Shear	1. Problem	2. Potential Problem	3. No Apparent Problem	
	Requires moderate to maximum assistance in moving. Complete lifting without sliding against sheets is impossible. Frequently slides down in bed or chair, requiring frequent repositioning with maximum assistance. Spasticity, contractures or agitation lead to almost constant friction.	Moves feebly or requires minimum assistance. During a move, skin probably slides to some extent against sheets, chair restraints, or other devices. Maintains relatively good position in chair or bed most of the time, but occasionally slides down.	Moves in bed and in chair independently and has sufficient muscle strength to lift up completely during move. Maintains good position in bed or chair at all times.	

Note: 1. Bed and chairbound individuals or those with impaired ability to reposition should be assessed upon admission for their risk of developing pressure uclers. Patients with established pressure ulcers should be reassessed periodically. 2. Patients with a total score of 16 or less are considered to be at risk of developing pressure ulcers (15 or 16 = low risk; 13 or 14 = moderate risk; 12 or less = high risk). TPN, total parenternal nutrition; NPO, nothing by mouth.

Total Score:

Assess for nonpressure ulcers; note the characteristics of the wound.

Burns are classified based on depth of tissue destruction and percentage of total body surface area (TBSA) affected (Table 13-21). Depth involves assessing vascular and sensory status and appearance and blanching of the burn. Assess blanching by applying pressure with a sterile cotton-tipped applicator and observing capillary refill time. Calculate the percentage of TBSA affected using the Wallace Rule of Nines (Fig. 13-11) or the Lund and Browder chart (Fig. 13-12).

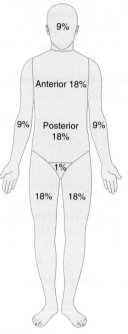

Figure 13-11 Wallace Rule of Nines to estimate percentage of TBSA burned in adults. Different areas are sectioned into numerical values related to nine (9). Note that the anterior and posterior head equate to 9% each.

Inspection: Nails

Inspect each fingernail and toenail. Assess for colour, thickness, and consistency. *Nails are smooth, translucent, and consistent in colour and thickness. Longitudinal ridging is common in aging patients. Longitudinal pigmentation in dark-skinned patients is an expected variant.*

Have the patient place the fingernails of both index fingers together to assess the nail angle. *A diamond-shaped opening is visible between the two fingernails, indicating a nail angle of at least 160°.*

Wound drainage is classified as serous (clear), sanguineous (bloody), serosanguineous (mixed), fibrinous (sticky yellow), or purulent (pus). Note any signs or symptoms of infection. See Table 13-18.

Examples include neuropathic, venous (vascular), and arterial (vascular) ulcers. See Tables 13-19 and 13-20 at the end of this chapter.

Superficial burns involve the epidermal layers, superficial dermal burns involve the epidermis and part of the dermis, deep dermal burns involve the epidermis and all of the dermis, and total thickness burns involve all layers of the skin and may extend into the supportive fascia below (Hettiarachi & Papini, 2004). See also Table 13-21.

Relative percentage of body surface areas affected by growth

	0 y	1 y	5 y	10 y	15 y
A—½ of head	9½	8½	6½	5½	4½
B—½ of thigh	2¾	3¼	4	4¼	4½
C—½ of lower leg	2½	2½	2½	3	3¼

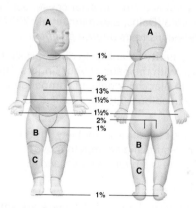

Figure 13-12 The Lund & Browder burn estimation chart. This chart and method for assigning percentage of burns are commonly used in pediatric populations.

Dietary deficiencies lead to splitting of nail tips (Fawcett, Linford, et al., 2005). Thickened nails may be due to fungal infection. Discolouration of the nailbed may indicate trauma, fungal infection, or melanoma.

Clubbing of the nails indicates chronic hypoxia. Clubbing is identified when the angle of the nail to the finger is more than 160° (see Table 13-7). Also see Table 13-22 at the end of the chapter for common nail variations.

(text continues on page 290)

Inspection: Hair

Inspect the hair, noting colour, consistency, distribution, areas of hair loss, and condition of the hair shaft. *Hair is equally and symmetrically distributed across the scalp. Hair shafts are smooth, shiny, of even consistency, and without evidence of breakage.*

In female patients, ovarian dysfunction may be characterized by hair on the beard area, abdomen, upper back, shoulders, sternum, and inner upper thighs.

Note areas of decreased or absent hair (alopecia). Parting the hair enables visualization of the scalp skin. Note any lesions or colour changes there. *Scalp skin is of consistent colour with the rest of the body.* Observe hair shafts near the root for lice or nits.

Brittle or broken hair shafts may indicate endocrine or metabolic dysfunction. Lice or their nits (eggs) may be on the hair shaft. Excessive dryness and scaling of the scalp is often present in *seborrheic dermatitis*. See Table 13-23.

Palpation: Skin

Using the dorsal surface of the hands, assess skin temperature. *Skin temperature is consistently warm or cool and appropriate, considering the environmental temperature.*

Further assess any areas of increased temperature for lesions, swelling, and colour changes.

Using the palmar surface of the fingers and hands, assess for skin moisture and texture. *Moisture is consistent throughout, with evenly smooth skin texture.*

Excessive dryness may be from frequent bathing or *hypothyroidism*. Excessive moisture may signify an issue with temperature regulation. Cracked or fissured skin may indicate hydration disorders, infections, or chemical injuries.

Assess skin turgor. Gently grasp a fold of the patient's skin between your fingers and pull up. Then, release. This is easiest performed on the dorsal surface of the patient's hand or lower arm, but the most accurate reflection of turgor in the adult is on the anterior chest, just below the midclavicular area (Dains, Baumann, et al., 2007). *The skin promptly recoils to its neutral position.*

A persistent **tenting** of the skin when assessing skin turgor indicates dehydration.

Assess for vascularity by applying direct pressure to the nail surface with the pads of your fingers. This will cause the nail to blanch, or pale, in comparison with surrounding skin colour, *Capillary refill is <3 s.*

Decreased vascular supply is marked by a capillary refill time of > 3 s. This is a tool used to evaluate underlying vascular deficiencies. Delayed return of skin colour after direct pressure indicates decreased circulation. Altered circulation can result in pallor or rubor of an extremity.

Palpate lesions for tenderness, mobility, and consistency. Apply gentle pressure and attempt to move the skin under your finger. *Lesion is smooth, mobile, and non-tender.*

Tenderness of a lesion or dermatitis may indicate infection. Mobile nodes are often benign, while stationary lesions may be cancerous.

Palpation: Nails

Palpate each fingernail and toenail. *Nails are smooth, and nontender. Lateral and proximal folds are nontender.*

Swelling, redness, or tenderness in the lateral or proximal folds may indicate *paronychia*. Sponginess of the nail bed may indicate clubbing.

Palpation: Hair

Palpate the hair. *Hair is smooth.* Grasp 10–12 hairs and gently pull. *Just a few hairs are in your hand.*

Note excessive hair loss and then assess for presence or absence of the hair bulb. Absent hair bulb may indicate chemical damage to the hair shaft (excessive colouration). Presence of the hair bulb may indicate endocrine dysfunction. Note quantity, texture, distribution. *Alopecia* is a term used to describe hair loss.

Documentation of Expected Findings

Skin evenly coloured, smooth, soft, consistently warm, with intact turgor. No suspicious lesions. Nails smooth and translucent, lateral and proximal folds without swelling or erythema. Hair smooth texture, symmetrically distributed on the scape, consistent colouration and hydration, without evidence of excessive breakage or loss. Scape with consistent pigmentation, no lesions.

Documentation of integumentary findings is crucial to ensure proper continuity of care from clinician to clinician and to monitor the progression (healing) of skin conditions (ie, wound).

Examples of Documentation for Skin, Hair, and Nails

Area of Assessment	Expected Findings	Unexpected Findings
Skin colour	Pink, uniform colour bilaterally	Pale, bluish tinge around lips
Moisture	Moist, dry areas noted to elbows bilaterally	Excessive sweating noted to forehead and bilateral axillary areas
Temperature	Hands, forearms, shoulders warm bilaterally	Right hand, forearm, and shoulder warm. Left forearm and hand cool
Texture	Uniformly smooth, rough areas on elbows bilaterally	3-cm diameter rough area noted on dorsal surface of left hand
Mobility and turgor	Fold of skin returns to original position <1 s	Fold of skin remains tented for >5 s
Lesions	Smooth, uniform, no lesions noted bilaterally. Freckles on nose and cheeks bilaterally	1 cm × 2 cm bicoloured, irregularly shaped lesion on right upper cheek
Hair	Uniformly distributed over scalp (coarse, black, curly)	Patches of alopecia on left side of scalp
Nails	Intact, white with pinkish undertones, angle < 180° bilaterally	Thickened, yellow with ragged edges, angle >180° bilaterally

Adapted from Stephen, T. C., & Bickley, L. S. (2010). The skin, hair, and nails. In T. C. Stephen, D. L Skillen, R. A. Day, & L. S. Bickley (Eds.). *Canadian Bates' guide to health assessment* (p. 256). Philadelphia, PA: Wolters Kluwer Health/Lippincott Williams & Wilkins.

Documenting Unexpected Findings

The nurse has just finished a physical examination of Mr. Stoli, the 65-year-old male with a venous ulcer secondary to peripheral vascular disease. Mr. Stoli has unexpected findings. Review the following important findings revealed in each step of objective data collection for Mr. Stoli. Consider how these results compare with the expected findings. Note that inspection is the major technique used in wound assessment.

Inspection: A 6 × 8 cm wound on left lateral leg above the malleolus. Irregular wound margins with pallor to the edges. Wound is partial thickness with 80% beefy red and 20% yellow. Large quantity of fibrinous exudate on dressing. Left leg skin hyperpigmented and ruddy. Minimal flaking is present, no hair on lower legs. 3+ pitting edema, capillary refill 5 seconds.

Palpation: Leg is cool, sensation decreased.

 Lifespan Considerations

Women Who Are Pregnant

Common skin findings in women who are pregnant include *melasma, striae gravidarum* (stretch marks), *spider telangiectasias, and hyperpigmentation.* Others include enlargement of preexisting keloids; edema of the face, legs, and hands; rapid nail growth; and increased nail brittleness (March of Dimes, 2008). During pregnancy, women may report rapid hair growth; during the postpartum period, they may experience excessive hair loss (March of Dimes).

Unexpected skin findings in pregnancy include *pyogenic granuloma, erythema nodosum,* and *pruritic urticarial papules and plaques of pregnancy* (PUPPP) (Hebel, 2006) (Fig. 13-13). Pyogenic granuloma commonly arises during the late second or third trimester and develops rapidly over a few weeks (Pierson & Pierson, 2006). In pregnancy, it usually appears on the oral mucosa or lips as a glistening

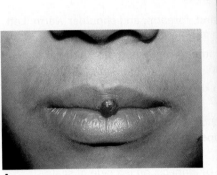

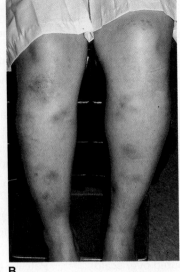

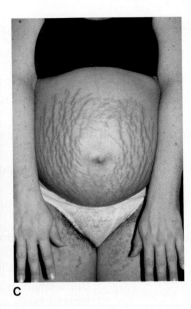

A **B** **C**

Figure 13-13 A. Pyogenic granuloma. **B.** Erythema nodosum. **C.** PUPPP

red papule or nodule that bleeds easily if traumatized. *Erythema nodosum* presents as a 2- to 6-cm tender, red, painful nodule usually on the extensor surfaces of the lower extremities. The lesions usually resolve postpartum. *PUPPP* is a benign disorder of the third trimester, usually in first or multiple-gestation pregnancies, and is characterized by intensely pruritic reddish papules and plaques within striae gravidarum.

Newborns, Infants, Children, and Adolescents

Evaluation for cyanosis, a cutaneous manifestation of hypoxemia, is part of the Apgar scoring done at 1 and 5 minutes after birth (see Chapter 6). The more cyanotic the appearance, the lower is the score and thus the greater indication of compromised circulation. Cyanosis on the hands and feet that persists for several days after birth can be an expected response to cool temperatures. Bluish mottling of the skin, known as *cutis marmorata,* is from chilling or stress. Some newborns exhibit a harlequin colour change, usually seen when lying on the side, with the dependent half of the body a darker pink colour while the upper half is paler. Jaundice may be evident within 24 hours of birth due to the liver's initial inability to metabolize and excrete bilirubin. Jaundice disappears once the liver can process bilirubin more effectively (usually 5 to 10 days after birth) (Lowdermilk & Perry, 2007). To verify jaundice, apply light pressure to the skin to cause blanching. Jaundice does not blanch, while yellowish skin tones from other causes turn white. *Physiologic jaundice* occurs after 24 hours and persists approximately 72 hours. Jaundice is always considered pathologic if it appears in the first 24 hours of birth (Fig. 13-14).

Pigmented lesions (eg, *nevus flammeus, cavernous hemangioma, strawberry hemangioma, capillary hemangioma*) are common in newborns. Greater than 6 café au lait spots or a single lesion larger than 3 cm has been associated with severe

illness. Careful monitoring is indicated. See Chapter 28 for a more complete discussion.

At birth, a newborn's skin is flushed and appears deep red. By the 2nd day of life, the skin becomes pink, flaky, and dry. Skin is usually thin and almost transparent, especially in premature newborns. Vernix or lanugo may appear, depending on gestational age. *Milia* are tiny white papules on the cheeks, chin, and nose of newborns. They result from distended sebaceous glands, and generally resolve spontaneously in a few weeks or months. *Erythema toxicum* is a pink papular, vesicular, and occasionally pustular rash on the trunk and extending outward. Lesions of erythema toxicum are surrounded by an erythematous, blotchy halo and usually resolve spontaneously. Ecchymosis and scratching may be from birth trauma. It is common to observe edema of the eyes,

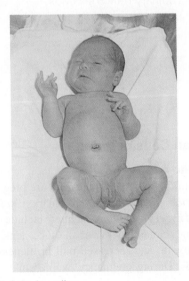

Figure 13-14 Jaundice.

scrotum, and labia in neonates. See Chapter 28 for a more complete discussion.

The evaluation of an infant's hydration is best assessed using capillary refill, skin turgor, and respiratory assessment. Turgor in newborns, infants, and young children is best evaluated by gently pinching a fold of abdominal skin and watching the skin recoil to its expected state (Steiner, DeWalt, et al., 2004). Turgor in the older child or adolescent can be assessed on the medial aspect of the lower forearm. Capillary refill is assessed by applying just enough pressure to the nail bed to cause blanching. Complete capillary refill in healthy individuals occurs in less than 3 seconds.

Infants and young children with yellowish palms, soles, and face, but not sclera, may have carotenemia from excessive ingestion of yellow or orange vegetables or chronic renal disease. Skin findings in children are commonly the result of an infectious process, such as varicella, roseola, rubella, measles, or erythema infectiosum. All these conditions present with systemic symptoms (fever, malaise) in addition to their characteristic skin lesions (O'Connor, McLaughlin, et al., 2008). See Table 13-7 for commonly observed lesions related to viral, bacterial, or fungal infections.

Pubertal adolescents will have maturation of the apocrine glands in the axillae and genitalia areas with production of malodorous sweat. Sebaceous gland secretion increases, as does the predisposition to acne lesions.

Older Adults

As discussed earlier, common skin assessment findings for older adults include decreased elasticity, thinness, excessive dryness, and lesions associated with aging such as seborrheic *keratosis, actinic keratosis,* and *lentigines.* In addition, they are at increased risk for skin cancer, ecchymosis, purpuric lesions, and trauma.

Evidence-Informed Critical Thinking

Organizing and Prioritizing

Integumentary findings often reflect the status of other systems (see Table 13-7). Nurses constantly observe the skin while assessing other systems and interpret skin findings in conjunction with other systemic findings to determine underlying function. Interpreting these findings assists in planning appropriate interventions and making necessary referrals.

Common Laboratory and Diagnostic Testing

Once a dermatologic concern has been identified, inspected, and palpated, one of several laboratory tests may be indicated to determine the most effective treatment. A superficial scraping or punch biopsy of affected skin may help to identify a lesion through histological analysis. Excisional biopsies remove larger segments of affected tissue or entire lesions to evaluate for conditions such as vasculitis (inflammation of distal blood vessels) and cancer (melanoma).

If infection is suspected, a sample may be collected and cultured in a laboratory for identification. Further analysis reveals specific antimicrobial sensitivity of the organism. These cultures are beneficial and are often collected as a mode of ensuring appropriate antibiotic therapy. For suspected fungal infections, a culture using a preparation of potassium hydroxide (KOH) may confirm the presence of fungal elements.

Clinical Reasoning

Nursing Diagnosis, Outcomes, and Interventions

When formulating a nursing diagnosis, it is important to use critical thinking to cluster data together and identify patterns. The nurse compares these clusters of data with health history and physical examination findings to ensure accuracy in the diagnosis and appropriateness of nursing interventions. See Table 13-6 (North American Nursing Diagnosis Association-International, 2009).

Nurses use assessment information to identify patient outcomes. Some outcomes related to integumentary concerns include the following:

- Skin and mucous membranes are intact.
- Patient reports no altered sensation or pain at site.
- Patient demonstrates measures to protect and heal the skin (Moorhead, Johnson, et al., 2007).

Once outcomes are established, interventions are enacted to improve the patient's status. The nurse uses critical thinking and evidence-based practice to develop them. Some examples for integumentary care are as follows:

- Assess skin and risk for skin breakdown.
- Change dressing as ordered with topical agent that promotes a moist healing environment.
- Evaluate for specialty mattress (Bulechek, Butcher, et al., 2007).

Table 13-6　Common Nursing Diagnoses Associated With the Integumentary System

Diagnosis and Related Factors	Point of Differentiation	Assessment Characteristics	Nursing Interventions
Impaired skin integrity	Alterations in or damage to one or more layers of the skin	Wound, surgical incision, break in skin integrity	Classify wound as partial or full thickness (Stage I–IV). Document wound assessment. Assess for risk of skin breakdown. Apply appropriate dressing. Evaluate for use of specialty mattress. Avoid positioning over bony prominences. Reposition patient frequently (every 1–2 h).
Risk for infection	At risk for pathogenic organisms from break in the skin or tissue, the body's primary defense	Break in skin integrity, tubes and procedures, exposure to pathogens, malnutrition, inadequate immunity, chronic disease	Practice frequent handwashing (routine practices) and additional precautions in infection control. Protect wound with dressing. Monitor for fever, increased heart rate, elevated WBCs, wound drainage, increasing pain, or erythema. Encourage adequate nutrition.

*Collaborative interventions.

Analyzing Findings

Mr. Stoli's concerns have been outlined throughout this chapter. Initial subjective and objective data collection is complete, and the nurse has spent time reviewing findings. The following nursing note illustrates how the nurse analyzes subjective and objective data to plan nursing interventions, including additional monitoring.

Subjective: Throbbing 4/10 pain that increases when legs are dependent and with ambulation, decreases when lying in bed. Declined medication for pain. States "Those pills make me sleepy, and I don't like that."

Objective: Grimacing with movement. Ambulates in room to bathroom, sits in chair for meals with legs elevated. A 6 × 8 cm wound on left lateral leg above the malleolus. Irregular wound margins with pallor to the edges. Wound is partial thickness with 80% beefy red and 20% yellow. Large quantity of fibrinous exudate on dressing. Left leg skin hyperpigmented and ruddy. Minimal flaking is present, no hair on lower legs. 3+ pitting edema, capillary refill 5 seconds.

Analysis: Impaired skin integrity related to venous impairment as evidenced by ulcer on left lateral leg above ankle. Pain related to ulcer.

Plan: Hydrocolloid dressing changes. Consult with wound care nurse about placement of wound vacuum. Elevate legs when awake. Monitor wound for signs of infection by measuring temperature every 4 hours, evaluating drainage, assessing pain, and other wound changes (ie, erythema). Encourage fluid intake.

Critical Thinking Challenge

- What type of ongoing assessments are indicated?
- How should the nurse address Mr. Stoli's pain management concern?
- What teaching should the nurse provide related to venous stasis and its treatment?

In many facilities, nurses initiate referrals based on assessment data. Findings that might increase urgency of a referral include decreased vascularity, new infection, and increased pressure/shearing forces (Gorst, Bagg, et al., 2008). Wound and ostomy nurses are available for consultation for complex wounds, ostomy management, and monitoring of pressure ulcers.

A wound care consult is indicated for placement of the wound vacuum. The following conversation illustrates how the nurse might organize data and make recommendations about Mr. Stoli when the wound care nurse arrives.

Situation: Hello. I'm taking care of Mr. Stoli. He's 65 years old admitted yesterday for the placement of a wound vacuum because his left leg ulcer isn't healing.

Background: He has a history of peripheral vascular disease, high blood pressure, and diabetes. Blood pressure and diabetes have been under fairly good control. He's had the ulcer for about 3 months, and the Nurse Practitioner would like a wound vacuum applied. Mr. Stoli can potentially go home as he has a home care nurse to assist with the wound vacuum as needed.

Assessment: The wound doesn't look infected. It's fairly clean and about 6 × 8 cm just above his left lateral malleolus. He's fairly independent and eager to go home. He doesn't like taking pain medications because they make him drowsy.

Recommendations: When you place his wound vacuum, I think that you might discuss how he can manage with it at home. His wife should be there, so that will be a good teaching opportunity. He's really anxious to get back home, so if you can work with him to get prepared, he'll appreciate it. He prefers to be as independent as possible.

Critical Thinking Challenge

- What other assessments might be performed related to the patient's history?
- What further assessment information might need collection before discharge?

Pulling It All Together: An Example of Reflection and Critical Thinking

The nurse uses assessment data to formulate a nursing care plan with patient outcomes and interventions for Mr. Stoli. After interventions are completed, the nurse reevaluates Mr. Stoli and documents findings in the chart to show progress. The nurse uses critical thinking and judgment to diagnose or revise diagnoses, outcomes, or interventions.

Nursing Diagnosis	Patient Outcomes	Nursing Interventions	Rationale	Evaluation
Impaired skin integrity related to venous stasis as evidenced by ulcer on left lateral leg above the malleolus	Patient demonstrates understanding of the plan to heal skin and prevent re-injury.	Teach care for wound vacuum. Notify home care of patient's return to home. Teach patient signs of healing, infection, and complications. Involve wife in care.	Knowledge of the function and purpose of the wound vacuum promotes patient autonomy. He should know when to call the NP if the wound is worsening.	Patient and wife asked multiple questions about wound vacuum at home; especially related to mobility. Wife appreciates home health visit and looks forward to patient returning home.

Using the previous steps of clinical reasoning, organizing, and prioritizing, consider all the case findings woven through this chapter. When answering the following questions, see how pieces of assessment work together to create an environment for personalized, appropriate, and accurate care.

- What are the major functions of the skin? (Knowledge)
- What other assessments are indicated given Mr. Stoli's history? (Comprehension)
- What information would you teach Mr. Stoli about managing his wound care at home? (Application)
- What factors in the patient's home might aggravate Mr. Stoli's wound? (Analysis)
- What precautions at home and during leisure would benefit Mr. Stoli? (Synthesis)
- How would you evaluate Mr. Stoli's understanding of the teaching you have done? (Evaluation)

Key Points

- Skin assessment findings reflect overall health, hydration, and nutritional status.
- Skin colour variations largely result from the amounts and proportions of eumelanin and pheomelanin produced by the melanocytes.
- Skin changes during pregnancy include melasma, linea nigra, increased sebaceous and cutaneous gland function, and hair loss postpartum.
- Loss of elastin, collagen, and subcutaneous fat result in decreased resilience, wrinkling, and increased fragility of the skin in the older adult.
- The ABCDEs of melanoma detection include Asymmetry, irregular Border, Colour, Diameter of more than 6 mm, and Evolution of the lesion over time.
- Skin self-examination assists patients to identify suspicious lesions.
- Common integumentary symptoms include pruritus, rash, and lesions or wounds.
- Coining and cupping are treatments performed as cultural home remedies or by acupuncturists.
- Skin assessment involves inspection of general colour, texture, moisture, turgor, and temperature and focused inspection and palpation of rashes, lesions, or wounds.
- When assessing a lesion, identify configuration, pattern, morphology, size, distribution, and exact body location.
- Assess a wound for location, size, colour, texture, drainage, margins, surrounding skin, and healing status.
- Depth of a burn can be superficial, superficial–dermal, dermal, or full thickness.
- Assessment of the nails and hair is performed as a part of the integument assessment.
- Unexpected skin findings include infection, inflammation, infestation, growths and tumours, trauma, and ulcers.

Review Questions

1. The nurse is admitting a 75-year-old man with a 50 pack-year smoking history to a medical unit due to shortness of breath. One nail finding that demonstrates chronic hypoxia is
   A. pitting
   B. thickening and discolouration of the nailbed
   C. clubbing
   D. brittleness and cracking of the nails

2. All of the following skin lesions are papular except
   A. warts
   B. acne
   C. moles
   D. herpes zoster

3. The ABCDEs of melanoma identification include all of the following except
   A. A (asymmetry): one half does not match the other half
   B. B (birthmark): recently changed in appearance
   C. C (colour): pigmentation is not uniform; there may be shades of tan, brown, and black as well as red, white, and blue
   D. D (diameter): >6 mm

4. A nurse observes a skin lesion with well-defined borders on the upper left thigh. It is 1.5 cm in diameter, flat, hypopigmented, and nonpalpable. What is the correct terminology for this lesion?
   A. Patch
   B. Plaque
   C. Papule
   D. Macule

5. When assessing hydration in an infant, the nurse would
A. pinch a fold of skin on the medial aspect of the forearm and observe for recoil to original position
B. pinch a fold of skin on the abdomen and observe for recoil to original position
C. pinch a fold of skin just below the midpoint of one of the clavicles and allow the skin to recoil to original position
D. pinch a fold of skin on the head and allow for skin to recoil to original position

6. A fair-skinned, blonde, 18-year-old woman is at a clinic for a skin examination. She reports that she always turns red within 10 minutes of going outside. She is planning a trip to Mexico and wants to avoid getting sunburned. What would the nurse teach the patient?
A. Excessive exposure to ultraviolet A (UVA) and ultraviolet B (UVB) rays increases risk of sunburn and skin cancer.
B. Apply a sunscreen or sunblock at least 15 to 30 minutes prior to sun exposure.
C. Avoid sun exposure between 10 AM and 4 PM to reduce UVA and UVB exposure.
D. All of the above.

7. An 8-year-old patient presents to the clinic with erythematous vesicles on the face and chest. Some vesicles have broken open, revealing a moist, shallow ulcerated surface; some have scabbed over. The nurse suspects which of the following infectious illnesses?
A. Varicella
B. Measles
C. Roseola
D. Herpes simplex

8. A 24-year-old patient reports an itchy red rash under her breasts. Examination reveals large, reddened, moist patches under both breasts in the skin folds. Several smaller, raised, red lesions surround the edges of the larger patch. What is the correct terminology for the distribution pattern of these smaller lesions?
A. Satellite
B. Discrete
C. Confluent
D. Zosteriform

9. A 22-year-old patient presents to the clinic with a large firm mass on her left earlobe. She had her ears pierced approximately 3 weeks ago. The mass began as a small bump and progressively enlarged to its current size of approximately 2.5 cm in diameter. It is not tender, reddened, or seeping any drainage. What is the term used to describe this secondary skin lesion?
A. Crust
B. Lichenification
C. Keloid
D. Scale

10. An 83-year-old woman is undergoing a routine physical examination. Which of the following assessment findings would the nurse consider an expected age-related variation?
A. Thinning of the skin
B. Increased skin turgor
C. Hypopigmented, flat macules and patches over sun-exposed areas
D. Multiple purplish bruises on the arms and legs

11. The patient has several red, inflamed, superficial, palpable lesions containing a thickened yellowish substance. How would the nurse document this lesion?
A. Papule
B. Pustule
C. Cyst
D. Vesicle

Canadian Nursing Research

Humphrey, S., Bergman J. N., et al. (2006). Practical management strategies for diaper dermatitis. *Skin Therapy Letter, 11*(7), 1–6.

Provost, N., Landells, I., et al. (2006). Sunscreens—Past, present, and future. *Journal of Cutaneous Medicine and Surgery,* (Suppl. 1), S14–S21.

Yu, M., Finner, A., et al. (2006). Hair follicles and their role in skin health. *Expert Review of Dermatology, 1*(6), 855–871.

References

Amirlak B., Shahabi, L., et al. (2008). *Skin anatomy*. Retrieved from http://emedicine.medscape.com/article/1294744-overview

Barrett, S. (2008). *A sensitive subject: Defining photosensitivity*. Retrieved from http://www.sun-wellness.com/articles/251 column1.html

Bergstrom, N., Braden, B. J., et al. (1987). The Braden Scale for predicting pressure sore risk. *Nursing Research, 36*, 205.

Black, J., Baharestani, M., et al. (2007). National Pressure Ulcer Advisory Panel's updated pressure ulcer staging system. *Dermatological Nursing, 19*(4), 343–349.

Braden, B., & Bergstrom, N. (1989). Clinical utility of the Braden scale for predicting pressure sore risk. *Decubitus, 2*(3), 44–51.

Brannon, H. (2006). *The biology of Hair: Your guide to skin & beauty*. Retrieved from http://dermatology.about.com/cs/hairanatomy/a/hairbiology.htm

Bulechek, G. M., Butcher, H. K., et al. (2008). *Nursing interventions classification (NIC)* (5th ed.). St. Louis, MO: Mosby.

Bulliard, J.-L., De Weck, D., et al. (2007). Detailed site distribution of melanoma and sunlight exposure: Aetiological patterns from a Swiss series. *Annals of Oncology, 18*(4), 789–794.

Canadian Cancer Society. (2008). *What is non-melanoma skin cancer?* Retrieved from www.cancer.ca/ccs/internet/standard/0,2939,3278_10175_87619_langID-en,00.html

Canadian Cancer Society. (2009). *What is melanoma?* Retrieved from: http://www.cancer.ca/Canada-wide/About%20cancer/Types%20of%20cancer/What%20is%20melanoma.aspx

Canadian Dermatology Association. (2011a). *Melanoma*. Retrieved from http://www.dermatology.ca/programs/melanomainfo/index.html

Canadian Dermatology Association. (2011b). *Sun protection for children and teenagers*. Retrieved from www.dermatology.ca/sap/safety_resources/cancer/melanoma.html

Dains, J., Baumann, L., et al. (2007). *Advanced health assessment and clinical diagnosis in primary care* (3rd ed.). St. Louis, MO: Mosby.

Davis, C. M., & Caseby, N. G. (2001). Prevalence and incidence studies of pressuire ulcers in two long-term care facilities in Canada. *Ostomy Wound Management. 47*(11), 28–34. Retrieved from: http://www.o-wm.com/article/1091

Environmental Protection Agency. (2008). *UV Index*. Retrieved from http://epa.gov/sunwise/uvindex/html

Ethnomed. (2008). *Self teaching module for the influence of culture on skin conditions in children*. Retrieved from http://ethnomed.org/ethnomed/clin_topics/dermatology/pigmented_main.html

Eustice, C., & Eustice, R. (2007). *Sun sensitivity can be side effect of some medications*. Retrieved from http://arthritis.about.com

Fawcett, R., Linford, S., et al. (2005). Nail abnormalities: Clues to systemic disease. *American Family Physician, 69*(6), 1417–1424.

Gorst, R., Bagg, G., et al. (2008). *The interdisciplinary urgency tool – A comprehensive wound-care referral form*. Retrieved from http://www.cawc.net/open/wcc/1-1/gorst.html

Guthrie Ambulatory Health Care Clinic Pharmacy. (2008). *Sunless sunburn*. Retrieved from http://www.drum.amedd.army.mil/CLINIC/Pharmacy/sunless_sunburn.htm

Health Canada. (2010). *Guidelines for tanning salon owners, operators, and users*. Retrieved from http://www.hc-sc.gc.ca/ewh-semt/pubs/radiation/tan-bronzage/index-eng.php

Health Canada. (2008). *It's your health: Tattooing and piercing*. Retrieved from www.hc-sc.gc.ca/iyh-vsv/life-vie/tat_e.html

Hebel, J. (2006). Erythema nodosum. *eMedicine*. Retrieved from http://www.emedicine.com/derm/topic138.htm

Hettiarachi, S., & Papini, R. (2004). Initial management of a major burn: II-assessment and resuscitation. *British Medical Journal, 329*, 101–103.

Hogan, D. J. (2007). *Contact dermatitis, irritant*. Retrieved from http://www.emedicine.com/DERM/topic85.htm

Juckett, G. (2005). Cross-cultural medicine. *American Family Physician, 72*(11), 2267–2274.

Kahana, M., Feldman, M., et al. (1995). The incidence of birthmarks in Israeli neonates. *International Journal of Dermatology, 34*(10), 704–706.

Kamel, M. (1998). Anatomy of the skin. In *The electronic textbook of dermatology*. Retrieved from http://www.telemedicine.org/anatomy/anatomy.htm

Lowdermilk, D. L., & Perry, S. E. (2007). *Maternity & women's health care* (9th ed.). St. Louis, MO: Elsevier.

March of Dimes. (2008). *Pregnancy & newborn health education center: Skin changes*. Retrieved from www.marchofdimes.com/pnhec/159_15294.asp

Mayers, L. B., & Chiffrieller, S. H. (2008). Body art (body piercing and tattooing) among undergraduate university students: Then and Now. *Journal of Adolescent Health, 42*(2), 201–203.

McKinnon, H., & Howard, T. (2000). Evaluating the febrile patient with a rash. *American Family Physician, 62*(4), 804–816.

Mercandetti, M., & Cohen, A. (2008). Wound healing, healing and repair. *eMedicine*. Retrieved from www.emedicine.com/plastic/TOPIC411.HTM.

Moorhead, S., Johnson, M., et al. (2007). *Nursing outcomes classification (NOC)* (4th ed.). St. Louis, MO: Mosby.

National Pressure Ulcer Advisory Panel. (2007). *Updated staging system*. Retrieved from http://www.npuap.org/pr2.htm

North American Nursing Diagnosis Association-International. (2009). *Nursing diagnoses, 2009–2011 Edition: Definitions and classifications (NANDA-I NURSING DIAGNOSIS)*. West Sussex, UK: John Wiley & Sons.

Norton, D. (1989). Calculating the risk: Reflections on the Norton scale. *Decubitus, 2,* 24.

O'Connor, N., McLaughlin, M., et al. (2008). Newborn skin: Part 1. Common rashes. Retrieved from http://www.aafp.org/afp/20080101/47.html

Ortonne, J. (2002). Photoprotective properties of skin melanin. *British Journal of Dermatology, 146*(Suppl. 61), 7–10.

Parrillo, S. (2008). *Steven-Johnson syndrome*. Retrieved from www.emedicine.com/emerg/topic555.htm

Pierson, J., & Pierson, D. (2006). *Pyogenic granuloma (lobar capillary hemangioma)*. Retrieved from www.emedicine.com/derm/topic368.htm

Parsad, D., & Kumarasinge, S. (2006). *Psychosocial implications of pigmentary disorders in Asia*. Retrieved from wwwpasper.med.umn.edu/Commentary/Parsad_Kumarasingecommentary.pdf

Schwalfenberg, G. K., Genius, S. J., et al. (2010) Addressing vitamin D deficiency in Canada: A public health innovation whose time has come. *Public Health, 126*(6), 350–353.

Smith, R. N., Mann, N. J., et al. (2007). A low-glycemic-load diet improves symptoms in acne vulgaris patients: A randomized controlled trial. *American Journal of Clinical Nutrition, 86*(1), 107–115.

Steiner, M., DeWalt, D., et al. (2004). Is this child dehydrated? *Journal of the American Medical Association, 291*(22), 2746–2754.

Stephen, T. C., & Bickley, L. S. (2010). The skin, hair, and nails. In T. C. Stephen, D. L. Skillen, R. A. Day, & L. S. Bickley (Eds.). *Canadian Bates' guide to health assessment for nurses* (pp. 245–278). Philadelphia: Wolters Kluwer Health/Lippincott Williams & Wilkins.

Woodbury, G. M., & Houghton, P. E. (2005). The extent of chronic wounds in Canada: What we know and what we don't know. *Wound Care Canada, 3*(1), 18–21. Retrieved from http://www.cawc.net/os/open/wcc/3-1/woodbury-houghton.pdf

World Health Organization. (2009). *Tanning beds cause cancer: WHO*. Retrieved from www.cbc.ca/news/health/story/2009/07/28/tanning-beds-cancer.html

World Health Organization. (n.d.). *Ultraviolet radiation and the INTERSUN Programme*. Retrieved from http://www.who.int/uv/intersunprogramme

Zouboulis, C. C., Chen, W. C., et al. (2007). Sexual hormones in human skin. *Hormone and Metabolic Research, 39*(2), 85–95.

The Canadian Jensen Nursing Health Assesemnt suite offers these additional resources to enhance learning and facilitate understanding of this chapter:

- thePoint on line resource, http//thepoint.lww.com/Stephen1E
- *Laboratory Manual for Canadian Jensen's Nursing Health Assessment: A Best Practice Approach.*

Tables of Unexpected Findings

Table 13-7 **Manifestations in Integument of Systemic Disorders**

Integument Finding	Associated Disorder	Other Considerations/Depictions
Cardiovascular		
Flushing	Increased permeability of the peripheral capillaries, as with *fever*	May be expected depending on activity (ie, flushing with exercise)
Pallor (shown)	Decreased arterial blood flow of *arterial insufficiency*	
Rubor and brawny skin	Decreased venous return in *venous insufficiency*	Skin is cool or cold over areas of decreased circulation.
Cyanosis	*Circumoral cyanosis* in *congestive heart failure* or *chronic obstructive pulmonary disease (COPD)* *Peripheral cyanosis* in areas of impaired circulation with oxygenated blood	Bluish skin discolouration occurs in areas of decreased blood flow or poor blood oxygenation.
Fingernail clubbing	Illness with prolonged hypoxia (eg, *COPD)*	
Gastrointestinal		
Thinning of the skin, hair, and nails and hair loss	Nutritional deficiencies, inadequate absorption of vitamins A, B_6 (riboflavin), and C	

(table continues on page 300)

Integument Finding	Associated Disorder	Other Considerations/Depictions
Jaundice (yellow discolouration of the skin, sclera, or buccal mucosa)	Liver disease	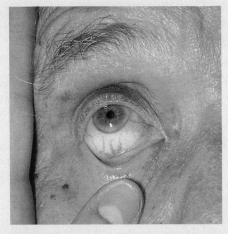
Pigmented macules	Peutz-Jeghers disease	Pigmented areas may be on hands, lips, or buccal mucosa. 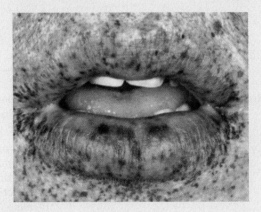
Facial flushing	Gastrointestinal cancers	
Genitourinary		
Uremic frost	Marked renal failure	Results from precipitation of renal urea and nitrogen waste products through sweat onto skin
Hirsutism	Polycystic ovarian syndrome	Affected women show male-pattern hair distribution, usually on face, chest, abdomen, or genital area 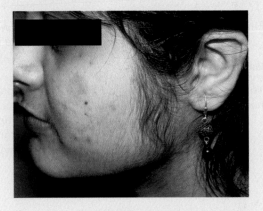

Table 13-7   Manifestations in Integument of Systemic Disorders *(continued)*

Integument Finding	Associated Disorder	Other Considerations/Depictions
Endocrine		
Thick, coarse hair, dry skin, and cool skin temperature	Hypothyroidism	See Chapter 6
Smooth skin, thin, silky hair, and brittle nails	Hyperthyroidism	See Chapter 6
Excessive hair growth or thinning; development of or worsening of acne	Androgen disorders	
Striae	Cushing's syndrome	
Hyperpigmentation of skin and mucous membranes; nevi	Addison's disease	
Flushing	Pheochromocytoma	
Thickened skin	Pituitary tumour	
Decreased sweating (hypohidrosis), frequent cutaneous yeast infections, and hair loss on distal extremities	Diabetes mellitus	
Acanthosis nigricans (hyperpigmentation)	Diabetes mellitus and many other endocrine disorders	
Neurological		
Neuropathic ulcers on distal extremities	Peripheral neuropathy in diabetes	Decreased sensation of any body area increases risk for injury, including burns and pressure ulcers.
Café au lait macules	Neurofibromatosis	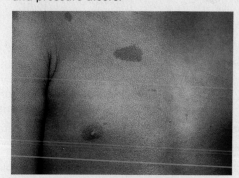
Musculoskeletal		
Photosensitivity, ***malar rash*** (red macular lesions distributed over forehead, cheeks, and chin, resembling a butterfly, as shown), coin-shaped lesions on trunk and extremities, and apthous ulcers on buccal mucosa	Systemic lupus erythematosus	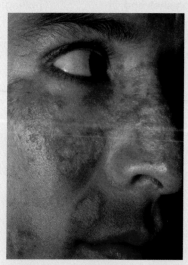

(table continues on page 302)

Integument Finding	Associated Disorder	Other Considerations/Depictions
Annular erythema (shown)	Sjögren's syndrome	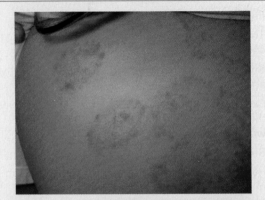
Pallor of fingers and toes in response to cold (shown)	Raynaud's phenomenon	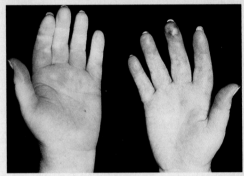
Erythema and increased temperature over a joint	Sepsis or acute inflammation of the joint	
Heme/Lymph		
Generalized pallor	Anemia	
Pruritus	Polycythemia, mastocytosis, lymphoma, or leukemia	
Spooning of nails	Iron deficiency states	
Psychiatric		
Patchy alopecia on the scalp or body, as well as missing or sparse eyelashes and eyebrows	Trichotillomania (compulsive hair pulling)	
Small linear cuts on patient's arms, legs, or anterior torso	"Cutting"	This self-injury coping method occurs in patients with borderline personality disorder, depression, and other psychiatric states.

Table 13-8   **Primary Skin Lesions**

Macule

Flat, circumscribed, colour/discoloured, <1 cm diameter. *Examples:* Freckles (shown), tattoo, stork bite

Patch

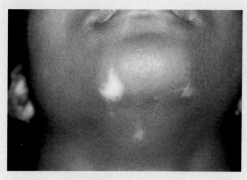

Flat, circumscribed, colour/discoloured, >1 cm diameter. *Examples:* Vitiligo (shown), melasma, tinea versicolour

Papule

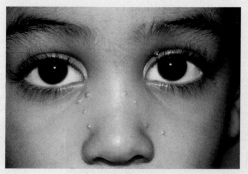

Raised, defined, any colour, <1 cm diameter

Examples: Wart, insect bite, molluscum contagiosum

Plaque

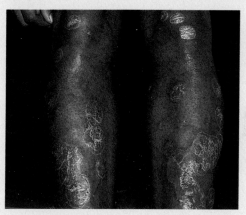

Raised, defined, any colour, >1 cm diameter *Examples:* Psoriasis (shown), lichen sclerosus

Wheal

Raised, flesh-coloured or red edematous papules or plaques, vary in size and shape

Example: Urticaria (shown)

Nodule

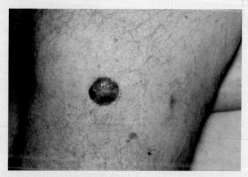

Solid, palpable >1 cm diameter, often with some depth

Example: Basal cell carcinoma (shown)

(table continues on page 304)

Table 13-8 **Primary Skin Lesions** *(continued)*

Tumour

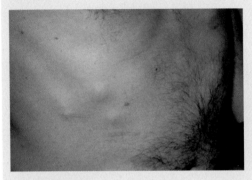

Large nodule

Examples: Large nevus, basal cell carcinoma, lipoma (shown)

Vesicle

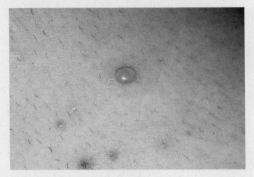

Fluid-filled, <1 cm diameter

Examples: Herpes simplex, chicken pox (shown)

Bulla

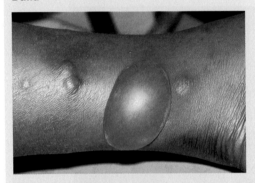

Fluid-filled, >1 cm diameter

Examples: Second-degree burns, bullous impetigo (shown)

Pustule

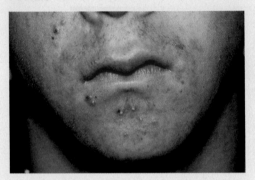

Purulent, fluid-filled, raised of any size

Examples: Pustular acne (shown), folliculitis

Cyst

Distinct and walled-off, containing fluid or semisolid material, varied in size

Examples: Epidermal cysts (shown), cystic acne

Table 13-9   Secondary Skin Lesions

Atrophy

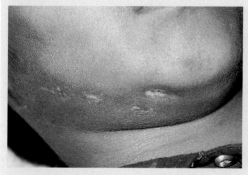

Thinning of skin from loss of skin structures

Examples: Steroid-induced atrophy, scleroderma (shown)

Keloid

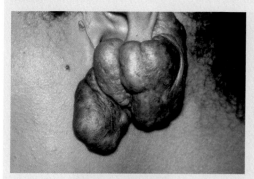

Excessive fibrous tissue replacement resulting in enlarged scar and deformity

Scale

Rapid turnover of epidermal layer resulting in accumulation of and delayed shedding of outermost epidermis

Examples: Psoriasis (shown), tinea corporis

Scar

Fibrous replacement of lost skin structure

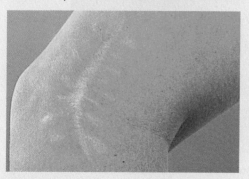

Example: Surgical scar (shown)

Crust

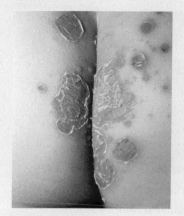

Dried secretions from primary lesion

Example: Impetigo (shown)

Lichenification

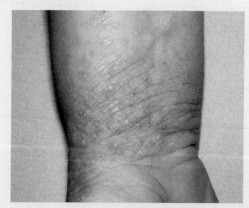

Accentuation of skin lines resembling tree bark, commonly caused by excessive scratching

Examples: Lichen simplex chronicus (shown), psoriasis, chronic contact dermatitis

(table continues on page 306)

Table 13-9 **Secondary Skin Lesions** (*continued*)

Excoriation

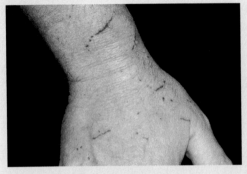

Lesion resulting from scratching or excessive rubbing of skin

Example: Cat scratches (shown)

Erosion

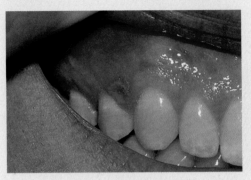

Loss of epidermal layer, usually not extending into dermis or subcutaneous layer

Examples: Apthous stomatitis (shown), varicella

Fissure

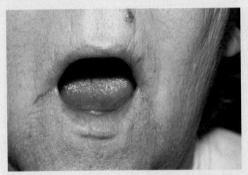

Linear break in skin surface, not related to trauma

Examples: Cheilitis, angular stomatitis (shown)

Ulcer

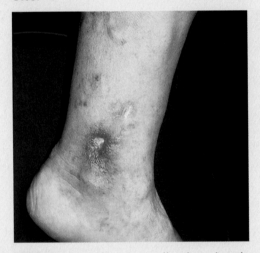

Loss of skin surface, extending into dermis, subcutaneous, fascia, muscle, bone, or all

Examples: Pressure ulcers, vascular ulcers, neuropathic ulcers (shown)

Table 13-10   Primary Morphology of Lesions

Annular

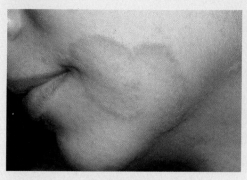

Ring-like, circular

Example: Tinea corporis (shown)

Linear

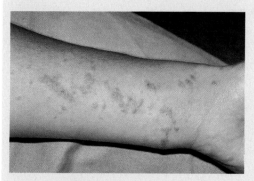

Line shape

Example: Contact dermatitis (shown)

Punctate

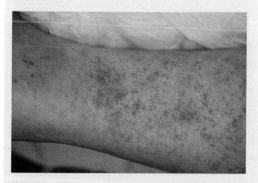

Small, marked with points or dots

Examples: Petechiae, Rocky Mountain spotted fever (shown), meningococcemia, vasculitis

Iris

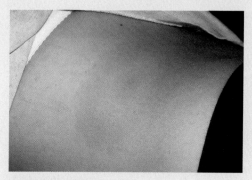

Bull's eye

Examples: Lyme disease (shown), erythema nodosum

Polymorphous

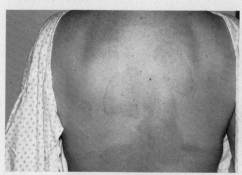

Several different shapes

Examples: Urticaria, tinea corporis (shown)

Serpiginous

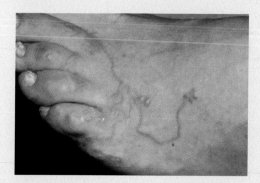

Curving, snake-like

Examples: Cutaneous larva migrans (shown), scabies

(table continues on page 308)

Table 13-10   **Primary Morphology of Lesions** (*continued*)

Nummular/Discoid

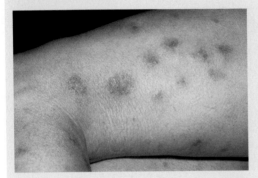

Coin-shaped

Examples: Nummular psoriasis, nummular eczema (shown)

Umbilicated

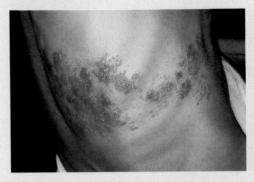

Central depression

Examples: Herpes zoster (shown), basal cell carcinoma

Filiform

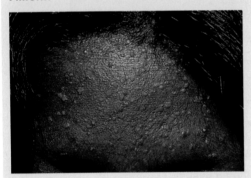

Papilla-like or finger-like projections (similar to tongue papillae)

Example: Warts

Verrucaform

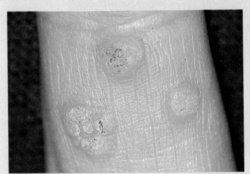

Circumscribed, papular with rough surface

Example: Warts

Table 13-11 **Secondary Morphology of Lesions**

Asymmetric

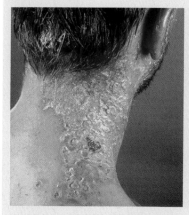

Distributed solely on one side of body

Examples: Contact dermatitis (shown), herpes zoster

Confluent

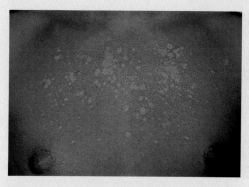

With enlargement or multiplication, begin to coalesce to form larger lesion

Examples: Urticaria, tinea versicolour (shown)

Diffuse

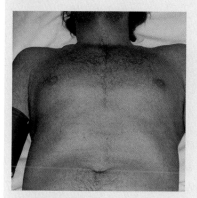

Distributed widely across affected area without any pattern

Examples: Drug reaction (shown), rubella, rubeola

Discrete

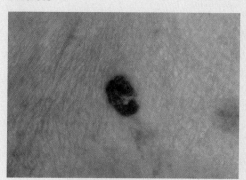

Single, separated, well-defined borders

Examples: Malignant melanoma (shown), wart

Generalized

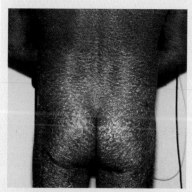

Distributed over large body area

Examples: Psoriasis (shown), acne vulgaris, exfoliative dermatitis

Grouped

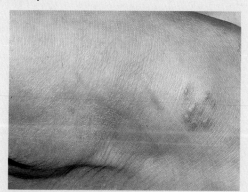

Clustered

Examples: Herpes simplex (shown)

(table continues on page 310)

Table 13-11 **Secondary Morphology of Lesions** (*continued*)

Localized

Located on distinct area

Examples: Giant nevus (shown), contact dermatitis, vitiligo

Satellite

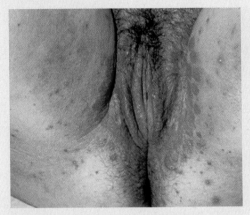

Single lesion(s) in close proximity to larger lesion, as if "orbiting"

Example: Cutaneous candidiasis (shown)

Symmetric

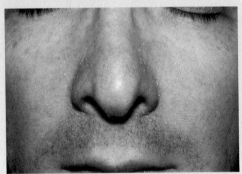

Distributed equally on both sides of body

Examples: Pityriasis rosea, freckles, seborrheic dermatitis (shown)

Zosteriform

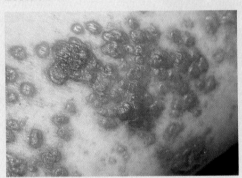

Distributed along dermatome

Example: Herpes zoster (shown)

Table 13-12   **Common Skin Infections**

Acne

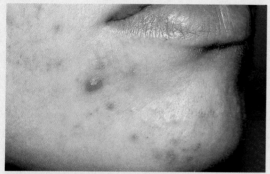

Pustular acne

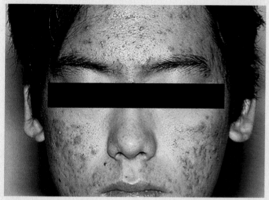

Cystic acne

Acne presents as an inflammatory and noninflammatory skin disorder characterized by one or a combination of the following lesions: comedone, papule, pustule, or cyst. Distribution of acne is frequently on the face, neck, torso, upper arms, and legs, although lesions may occur in other areas.

Warts

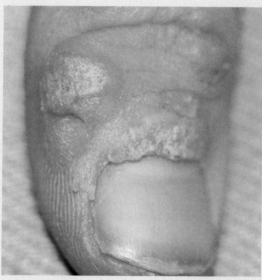

Warts are flesh-coloured papules commonly caused by viruses. Their surface is usually rough and textured without scale.

Cellulitis

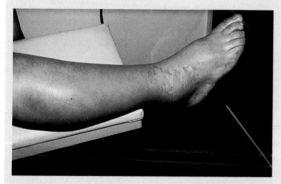

Cellulitis is a bacterial infection of deep skin tissues, often preceded by a minor wound to the area allowing bacteria to invade the tissue. Cellulitis can occur anywhere and is characterized by swelling, redness, warmth, and tenderness or pain.

Impetigo

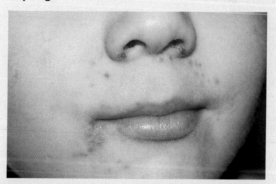

This highly contagious superficial skin infection commonly results from *Staphylococcus aureus* or group A β-hemolytic streptococci. It is characterized by vesicles or bullae that eventually rupture and ooze serous fluid that forms the classic honey-coloured crust.

(table continues on page 312)

Table 13-12   **Common Skin Infections** (*continued*)

Herpes Simplex

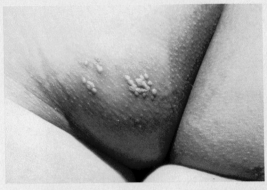

The herpes simplex virus is characterized by grouped vesicles on an erythematous base. These lesions can appear anywhere. Generally lesions on or around the mouth are *herpes labialis,* lesions in the genital regions are *herpes genitalis,* and lesions elsewhere are *cutaneous herpes*.

Pityriasis Rosea

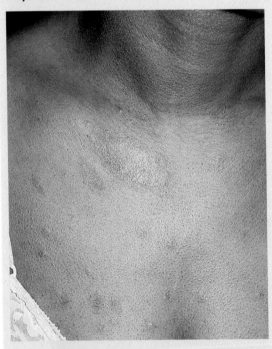

This viral infection is initially characterized by a "herald patch"—a large oval hyperpigmented lesion with a fine scale, usually on the chest or back. Over subsequent days, additional similar but smaller lesions develop and are distributed generally over the torso and extremities, with the face usually spared.

Measles (Rubeola)

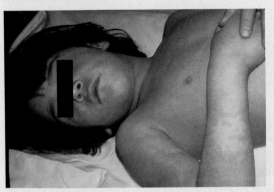

Commonly called the hard measles, rubeola is a virus characterized by pinkish, erythematous macules and papules initially on the face, with progressive caudal spread. In 3–4 d, the rash becomes brownish with a fine desquamation.

German Measles (Rubella)

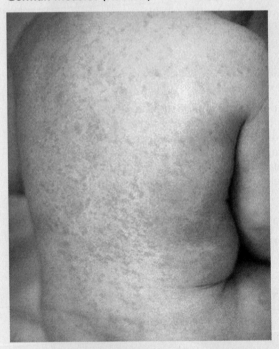

Commonly called the 3-d measles and largely vaccine preventable, this viral illness presents as a pinkish discrete macular and papular rash covering the entire body. It usually resolves in 3 d.

Table 13-12 **Common Skin Infections** (*continued*)

Roseola

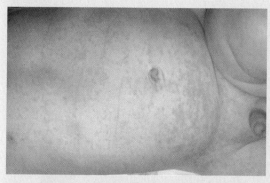

Roseola is a viral illness whose rash appears as the fever resolves. The rash of roseola is described as discrete macules and papules, usually no more than 1–5 mm in diameter, with an area of pallor surrounding each lesion.

Candida

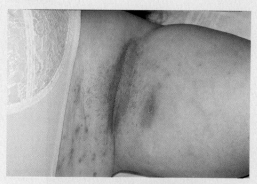

Candida is a fungus commonly found in skin folds or generally warm and moist areas. Commonly affected sites are the axillae, inframammary areas, and groin. Satellite pustules commonly surround the erythematous macules.

Tinea Corporis

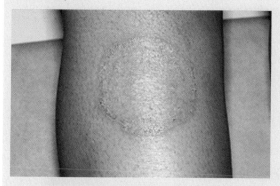

Commonly called *ringworm,* this dermatophyte skin infection results in an erythematous, commonly pruritic, annular lesion with a raised border and central clearing.

Tinea Versicolour

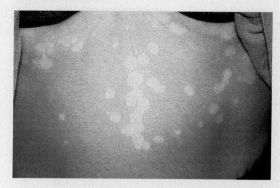

This dermatophyte infection caused by skin flora results in hypopigmented patchy lesions generally distributed on the upper chest, upper back, and proximal extremities. It rarely occurs on the face and legs.

Table 13-13 **Inflammatory Skin Lesions**

Psoriasis

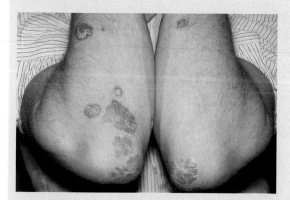

This chronic skin disorder is commonly characterized by reddish-pink lesions covered with silvery scales. It occurs on extensor surfaces (eg, elbows and knees), but can appear anywhere on the body.

(table continues on page 314)

Table 13-13   Inflammatory Skin Lesions (*continued*)

Eczema

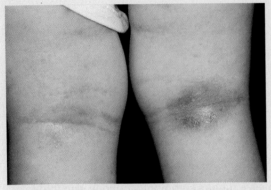

Also known as *atopic dermatitis,* eczema is characterized by itchy, pink macules or papules, commonly on intertriginous areas (eg, inner elbows and posterior knees). Eczema can occur anywhere on the body.

Urticaria

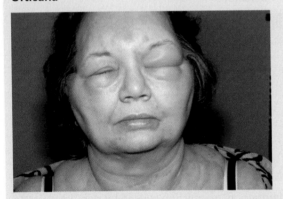

Commonly called *hives,* urticaria is the accumulation of fluid in the dermal layer of the skin as a direct result of histamine release.

Insect Bites

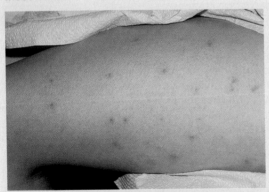

Insect bites usually cause an inflammatory and pruritic response at the site. Lesions are usually erythematous and papular with a visible puncta at the central part.

Contact Dermatitis

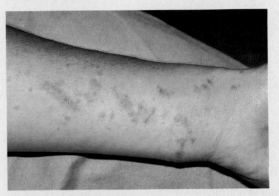

This inflammatory response to an antigen that has contact with exposed skin initially causes stimulation of the histamine receptors, which results in the classic erythematous and pruritic lesions.

Allergic Drug Reaction

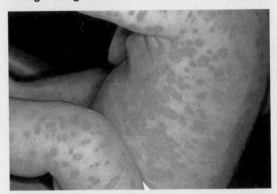

Drug allergies can occur immediately or have a delayed response after exposure to the agent.

Seborrhea

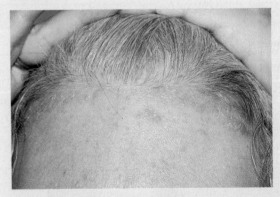

Seborrhea (seborrheic dermatitis) is an inflammatory skin disorder characterized by macular pink, red, or orange-yellow lesions that may or may not have a fine scale. Distribution is usually on the face, scalp, and ears.

Table 13-14 Skin Lesions From Infestations

Lesion	Description
Lice (Pediculosis) 	Infestations on the head *(pediculosis capitis)*, body *(pediculosis corporis)*, or genitals *(phthirus pubis)* are frequently characterized by the secondary lesions resulting from scratching. Visualization of the louse is common, and eggs on the hair shaft also indicate infestation in the absence of visualization.
Scabies 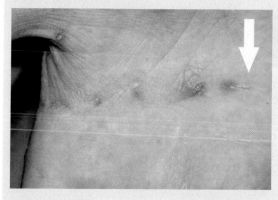	Scabies is caused by a mite that burrows into the epidermis and deposits eggs and waste materials as it progresses, resulting in a hypersensitivity reaction of erythema and pruritus.
Ticks 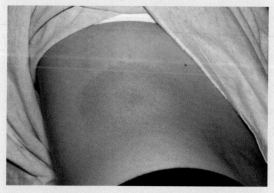	Tick bites frequently resemble simple insect bites. Nevertheless, certain ticks cause systemic illness, with a characteristic erythematous target lesion that appears at the site of the bite, and requires prompt medical evaluation.

Table 13-15 Skin Tumours and Growths

Moles or Nevi

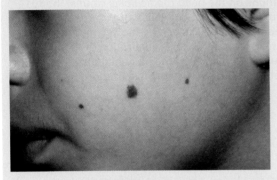

Nevi (moles) are typical variants. They can be macular or papular and distributed anywhere. They are congenital or acquired. *Congenital nevi* exist from birth and are commonly referred to as "birth marks." *Acquired nevi* occur most commonly in childhood and adolescence.

Skin Tags

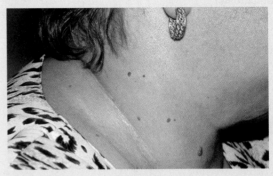

These papules are generally <1 cm and commonly distributed on the neck, axillae, inframammary area, and groin. Skin tags are common in pregnancy and in aging skin.

Lipoma

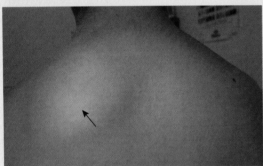

Lipomas are tumours comprised of fat cells and commonly located on the back of the neck, torso, arms, and legs. Though benign, some varieties are painful. Lipomas occur singly and multiply, ranging in size.

Lentigo

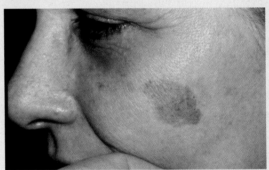

Lentigines are benign, acquired, circumscribed, pigmented macules found generally on sun-exposed skin.

Actinic Keratosis

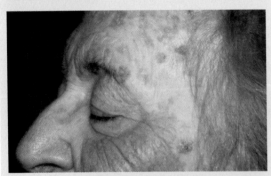

Also commonly called solar keratosis, they usually are found on sun-exposed skin, and are thought to result from UV damage. These macular or papular lesions are discrete, with a rough or scaly surface.

Basal Cell Carcinoma

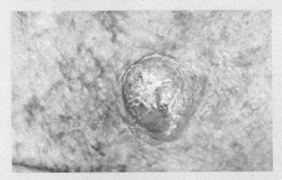

This nodular or papular lesion appears shiny with a rolled pearly border, and typically has telangiectases (small spider veins) on its surface. This skin cancer grows slowly and rarely metastasizes.

Table 13-15   **Skin Tumours and Growths** *(continued)*

Squamous Cell Carcinoma

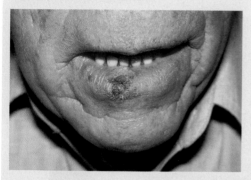

The second most frequently found skin cancer is related to actinic keratosis and sun exposure. Lesions are typically papular, nodular, or plaques located on sun-exposed skin surfaces.

Malignant Melanoma

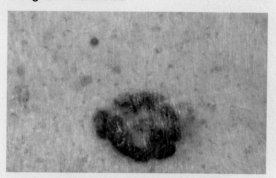

Malignant melanoma is identified by the ABCDEs of skin cancer detection (see Table 13-2).

Kaposi's Sarcoma

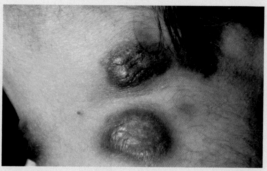

This opportunistic skin infection is a consequence of impaired immune status, as with AIDS. Lesions generally occur on the nose, penis, and extremities, though with advanced HIV, distribution may be more generalized. Improved immune status may cause resolution.

Table 13-16 Common Vascular Lesions

Hemangioma

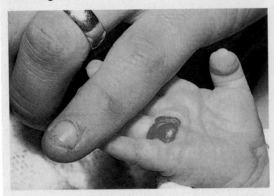

These vascular lesions, present at birth, rapidly develop and grow, but spontaneously resolve by age 9 years. Comprised of endothelial cells that form caverns and fill with blood, they blanch with applied pressure.

Spider or Star Angioma

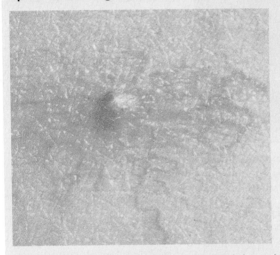

This vascular lesion arises from a central dermal arteriole with multiple extensions forming the appearance of spider legs. Distribution can be anywhere, but is commonly found on the face, arms, and torso.

Nevus Flammeus (Port Wine Stain)

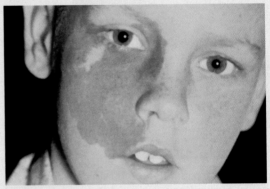

Malformation of superficial dermal blood vessels is present at birth. The lesion grows with the child and never resolves on its own.

Venous Lake

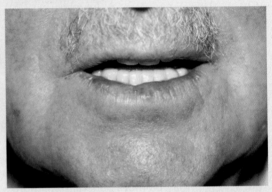

This papular bluish to purple lesion blanches on pressure, and is generally found on the face, especially on the lips or ears. It is benign, and often associated with sun exposure.

Table 13-17   Acute Wounds and Lesions From Trauma

Petechiae

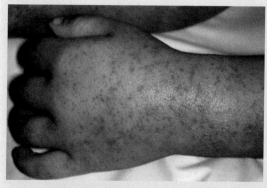

These small reddish to purple macules or papules can develop anywhere on the body in response to hematological issues or regional trauma.

Purpura

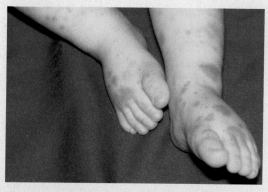

Purplish macules or papules result from bleeding under the skin secondary to inadequate clotting mechanisms.

Ecchymosis

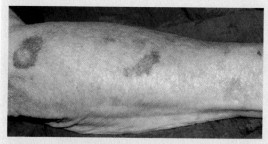

Physical trauma to the skin damages capillaries and allows blood to seep into surrounding tissues. As blood is gradually resorbed, colour of ecchymosis changes and can be purple, blue, green, yellow, or brown.

Hematoma

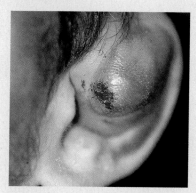

Collection of blood under the skin usually results from blunt-force trauma. Hematomas are palpable lesions, and colouration mimics that of ecchymosis.

Laceration

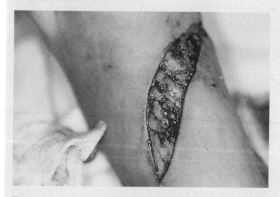

Tears in the skin can be superficial or deep, short or long and frequently require suturing to heal correctly.

Abrasions

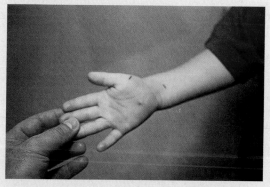

Abrasions are caused by shear force or friction against the skin, removing several layers and exposing the dermis.

(table continues on page 320)

Puncture Wound

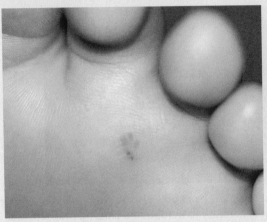

A sharp object pierces the skin, causing a wound with greater depth than width.

Avulsion

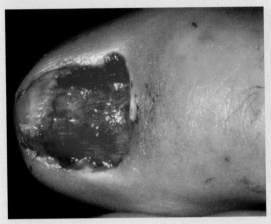

Trauma forces the skin to separate from underlying structures, leaving an open ragged wound.

⚠ Table 13-18   **Pressure Ulcers**

Suspected Deep Tissue Injury

Purple or maroon localized area of colour/discoloured intact skin or blood-filled blister from damage to underlying soft tissue as a result of pressure, shearing, or both. The area may be preceded by tissue that is painful, firm, mushy, boggy, warmer, or cooler as compared to adjacent tissue. Evolution may include a thin blister over a dark wound bed. The wound may further evolve and become covered by thin eschar. Evolution may be rapid, exposing additional layers even with optimal treatment.

Stage I

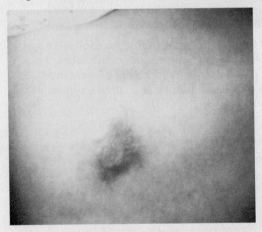

Intact skin with nonblanchable redness of a localized area, usually over a bony prominence. Darkly pigmented skin may not have visible blanching; its colour may differ from the surrounding area. The area may be painful, firm, soft, warmer, or cooler as compared to adjacent tissue.

Table 13-18 Pressure Ulcers (continued)

Stage II

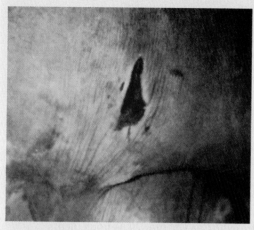

Partial thickness loss of dermis presenting as a shallow open ulcer with a red pink wound bed, without slough. May also present as an intact or open/ruptured serum-filled blister. Presents as a shiny or dry shallow ulcer without slough or bruising (indicates suspected deep tissue injury). This stage should not be used to describe skin tears, tape burns, perineal dermatitis, maceration, or excoriation.

Stage III

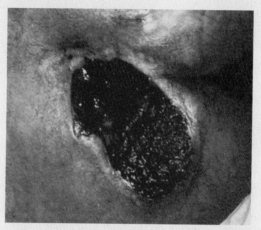

Full thickness tissue loss. Subcutaneous fat may be visible, but bone, tendon, or muscle is not exposed. Slough may be present but does not obscure the depth of tissue loss. May include undermining and tunnelling. The depth of a stage III pressure ulcer varies by anatomical location. The bridge of the nose, ear, occiput, and malleolus do not have subcutaneous tissue, and stage III ulcers can be shallow. In contrast, areas of significant adiposity can develop extremely deep stage III pressure ulcers. Bone/tendon is not visible or directly palpable.

Stage IV

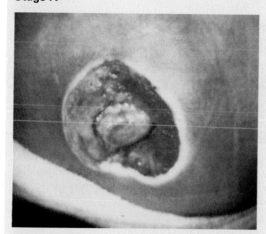

Full thickness tissue loss with exposed bone, tendon, or muscle. Slough or eschar may be present on some parts of the wound bed. Often include undermining and tunnelling. Depth of a stage IV pressure ulcer varies by anatomical location. The bridge of the nose, ear, occiput, and malleolus do not have subcutaneous tissue and these ulcers can be shallow. Stage IV ulcers can extend into muscle, supporting structures (eg, fascia, tendon, joint capsule), or both, making osteomyelitis possible. Exposed bone/tendon is visible or directly palpable.

Unstageable

Full thickness tissue loss in which the base of the ulcer is covered by slough (yellow, tan, gray, green, or brown), eschar (tan, brown, or black), or both. Until enough slough or eschar is removed to expose the base of the wound, true depth, and therefore stage, cannot be determined. Stable (dry, adherent, intact without erythema or fluctuance) eschar on the heels serves as "the body's natural (biological) cover" and should not be removed.

Source: National Pressure Ulcer Advisory Panel. (2007). *Updated staging system.*
Retrieved from http://www.npuap.org/pr2.htm

Table 13-19   Nonpressure Ulcers

Neuropathic Ulcer

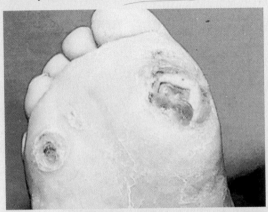

Loss of sensation in an extremity impairs the patient's ability to detect pressure on the feet. Sustained pressure or friction results in lost skin surface, which often remains unnoticed because the patient is not detecting pain. Diabetes is a common cause of this type of ulcer. Use the Wagner's classification to determine grade (severity) (see Table 13-20).

Venous Ulcers (Vascular)

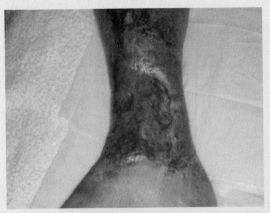

Venous ulcers develop from chronic pooling of blood in the extremity. See Chapter 20. Venous ulcers usually occur between ankle and knee in a "gaiter" distribution. Wound edges are ragged and irregular; the base is beefy red with evident granulation tissue. There is much exudate. Some ulcers can be deep. These ulcers are generally painless. The surrounding tissue commonly is hyperpigmented.

Arterial Ulcer (Vascular)

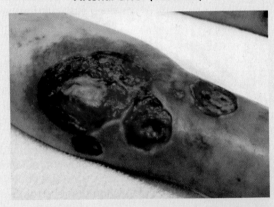

Arterial ulcers result from chronic ischemia as a consequence of impaired arterial circulation to an extremity. See Chapter 20. Arterial ulcers are usually located distally, such as at the ends of the toes or fingers. Wound edges are sharply defined; the base is pale when elevated and appears ruddy when dependent. These ulcers may be deep, frequently infected, and painful; they exhibit minimal granulation tissue.

Table 13-20   Wagner's Classification of Ulcers

Grade	Classification
0	Preulcerative lesion, healed ulcers, presence of bony deformity
1	Superficial ulcer without subcutaneous tissue involvement
2	Penetration through the subcutaneous tissue (may expose bone, tendon, ligament, or joint capsule)
3	Osteitis, abscess, or osteomyelitis
4	Gangrene of the forefoot
5	Gangrene of the entire foot

Table 13-21 **Burn Classification**

Depth of Burn	Bleeding	Sensation	Appearance	Blanching
Superficial	Brisk	Pain	Rapid capillary refill	Moist, red
Superficial–dermal	Brisk	Pain	Slowed capillary refill	Dry, pale pink
Dermal	Delayed	No pain	No capillary refill	Mottled cherry red colour
Full thickness	None	No pain	No blanching	Dry, leathery or waxy hard wound surface

Table 13-22 **Nail Findings**

Longitudinal Ridging

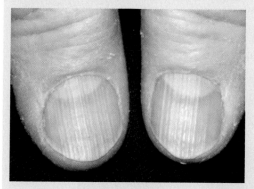

Expected variation, especially in the older adult.

Onycholysis

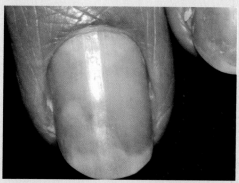

Separation of a portion of the nail plate from the nail bed; results in opaqueness to the affected part of the nail, appearing white to yellow to green. Common causes include trauma, fungal infections, topical irritants, psoriasis, and subungual neoplasms or warts.

Koilonychia (Spoon Nails)

Transverse and longitudinal concavity of the nail, giving the appearance of a spoon. May be observed in infants (usually resolves in few months). Other causes include trauma, iron deficiency anemia, and hemochromatosis.

Pitted Nails

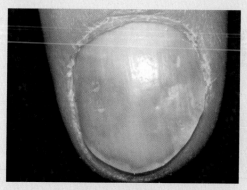

Lesions from psoriasis; arise from nail matrix that cause pitting on the nail plate as it grows.

(table continues on page 324)

Table 13-22 **Nail Findings** *(continued)*

Beau's Lines

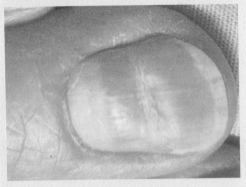

Results from slowed or halted nail growth in response to illness, physical trauma, or poisoning.

Yellow Nails

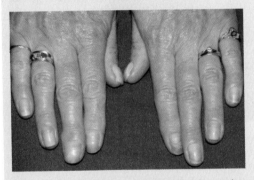

Slowly growing nail, without cuticle, and onycholysis resulting in thickening of nail and yellowish appearance. Causes include lung disorders and lymphedema.

Dark Longitudinal Streaks

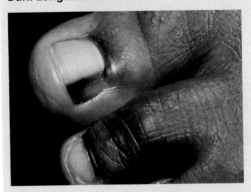

Often an expected variant in dark-skinned patients. Suspicious for malignancy if the streaks blur, spread, or are not solid the full length of the nail.

Clubbing

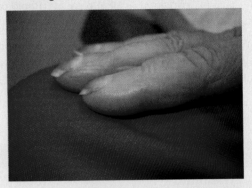

Results from chronic hypoxia to distal phalanges, such as with emphysema or congestive heart failure.

Half-and-half Nails

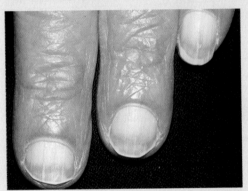

Colour changes associated with chronic renal failure; proximal portion of nail is white, distal portion is pink or brown.

Splinter Hemorrhages

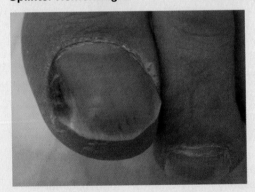

Brownish red longitudinal lines in the direction of nail growth that result from damage to capillaries (eg, endocarditis, vasculitis, antiphospholipid syndrome) supplying the nail matrix caused by microemboli.

Table 13-23   **Hair Findings**

Alopecia Areata

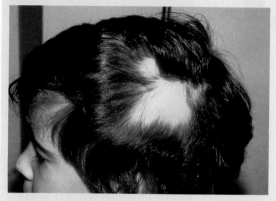

This autoimmune disorder results in noninflammatory loss of hair in a circumscribed distribution.

Hirsutism

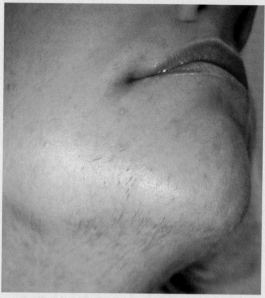

Excessive androgenic hormones in a female patient can cause masculine changes including hair in male distribution patterns (beard, chest, back, upper thighs).

Traction Alopecia

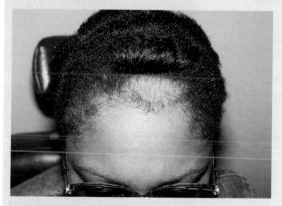

Tight hair braiding practices exert traction force on the hair bulb with subsequent hair loss.

Trichotillomania

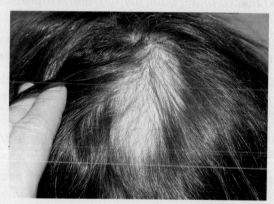

Compulsive hair pulling causes breakage of hair and thinned or balding areas on scalp, although some hair remains present and visible in the affected area.

Head and Neck with Lymphatics Assessment

Learning Objectives

1 Demonstrate knowledge of anatomy and physiology of the head, neck, and associated lymphatics.

2 Identify important topics for health promotion and risk reduction related to the skull, thyroid, and lymphatics of the head and neck.

3 Collect subjective data related to headache, head trauma, neck pain, neck masses, and thyroid dysfunction.

4 Collect objective data related to the scalp, cranium, facial structures, neck, including lymphatics, and thyroid using physical examination techniques.

5 Identify expected and unexpected findings from inspection and palpation of the head and neck.

6 Analyze subjective and objective data from assessment of the head and neck to plan initial interventions.

7 Document and communicate findings from the head and neck assessment using appropriate terminology and principles of recording.

8 Consider age, condition, gender, genetic background, and culture of the patient to individualize the head and neck assessment.

9 Identify nursing diagnoses and initiate a plan of care based on findings from the head and neck assessment.

*F*aye Davis-Pierce, 21 years old, is visiting her college clinic for the first time with reports of fatigue and weight gain of 10 kg over the past 3 months. She is also concerned because her hair has been falling out. Her temperature is 36.8°C orally, pulse 64 beats/min and regular, respirations 12 breaths/min, oxygen saturation is 97% and blood pressure 98/66 mm Hg (right arm, sitting). Her height is 173 cm, weight is 95 kg, and BMI is 31.6 (obese). Current medications include an oral contraceptive, norgestrel (Ovrette) 0.075 mg, and a multivitamin.

You will gain more information about Faye as you progress through this chapter. As you study the content and features, consider Faye's case and its relationship to what you are learning. Begin thinking about the following points:

- How might Faye's physical issues relate to her psychosocial health, including potential issues related to her age and status as a college student?
- What other physical findings might be present, and what other body systems might be involved?
- What type of follow-up care and reassessment might the patient need at subsequent visits?

The focus of this chapter is assessment of the head and neck regions, which include the scalp, cranium, lymphatics, parathyroid, and thyroid gland. It includes pertinent anatomy the physiology, as well as variations based on age, gender, genetic background, and culture. Methods for collecting subjective and objective data related to skull or scalp injury, lymphatic function, and thyroid function are included. Other key components of the chapter include the signs and symptoms of headache, lymphadenopathy, and parathyroid and thyroid imbalances; correct techniques for inspection and palpation of the structures of the head and neck; and descriptions of common expected and unexpected findings.

Anatomy and Physiology Overview

Structures of the head and neck interact with multiple body systems—integumentary, neurologic, musculoskeletal, respiratory, vascular, gastrointestinal, lymphatic, and endocrine. Knowledge of important information for accurate determination of expected and unexpected function is included.

The Head

The head includes the cranium and facial skeleton, which together encompass 22 bones that support and contain soft-tissue organs, including the eyes (see Chapter 15), ears (see Chapter 16), and brain (see Chapter 24; Ellis, 2002). The bones of the cranium are the *frontal, parietal, occipital*, and *temporal* (Fig. 14-1). **Sutures** join these bones together. The major sutures are the *coronal*, which crosses the top of the scalp from ear to ear, *sagittal*, which crosses the skull from anterior to posterior, and *lambdoidal*, which separates the parietal and occipital bones (see Fig. 14-1). Fetal sutures are not tightly joined, which allows the skull to mold and pass through the maternal birth canal more easily. The sutures remain somewhat loose during childhood to facilitate

growth of the head and brain, but eventually knit together by approximately 12 to 18 months. When documenting assessments, the location of scalp or skull findings is described according to the bones and sutures.

The largest facial bones are the *maxilla, mandible, nasal, lacrimal, palatine,* and *vomer* (Fig. 14-2). The mastoid process, part of the temporal bone, has particular relevance during assessment of the ear, which is discussed in Chapter 16.

Clinical Significance 14-1

The major facial muscles are the *frontalis, temporalis, zygomaticus, masseter, buccinators, orbicularis oculi,* and *orbicularis oris.* These and other smaller muscles enable chewing, speaking, smiling, and frowning (Fig. 14-3).

Blood supply to the head is through the carotid artery, which then splits into the internal and external branches. The veins are the external and internal jugular. See Chapter 19. The temporal artery is a branch of the external carotid artery that supplies the face. The trigeminal nerve (cranial nerve V) supplies both motor and sensory innervations to the forehead, cheeks, and chin. See Chapter 24. The major neck muscles are the sternomastoid (sternocleidomastoid) and trapezius. The sternomastoid muscle arises from the sternum and medial clavicle and extends to behind the ear. The trapezius arises from the occipital bone and vertebra and fans out to the clavicle and scapula.

Clinical Significance 14-2

These muscles are major accessory muscles used when the patient has difficulty breathing.

Three pairs of salivary glands are present. The parotid glands are in the cheek anterior to the bottom half of the ear. The submandibular glands are at the angle of the jaw below the mandible. The sublingual glands are in the mouth and under the tongue. See Chapter 17.

The Neck

The neck is supported by the cervical vertebrae, C1 to C7. A useful neck landmark is the *vertebral prominence*, which is the spinous process of C7, the longest cervical vertebrae (Ellis, 2002). Of the vertebrae of the neck, C7 and T1 are usually the most easily palpable, and the one that protrudes the furthest is C7 (Fig. 14-4). Locating C7 during assessment of the head, neck, and posterior thorax facilitates more accurate description of findings.

⚠ *SAFETY ALERT 14-1*

Falls or sudden jerking of the head and neck (whiplash) are particularly likely to result in dislocation of the cervical vertebrae. Fractures also may occur with head-first falls. Any history of falls or sudden jerks of the neck requires careful investigation.

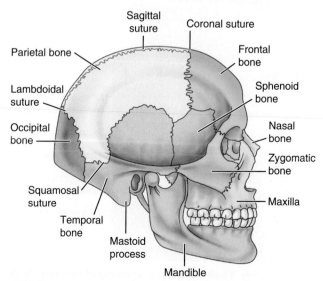

Figure 14-1 Bones and sutures of the cranium.

Sagittal suture
Coronal suture
Parietal bone
Frontal bone
Lambdoidal suture
Sphenoid bone
Occipital bone
Nasal bone
Zygomatic bone
Squamosal suture
Maxilla
Temporal bone
Mastoid process
Mandible

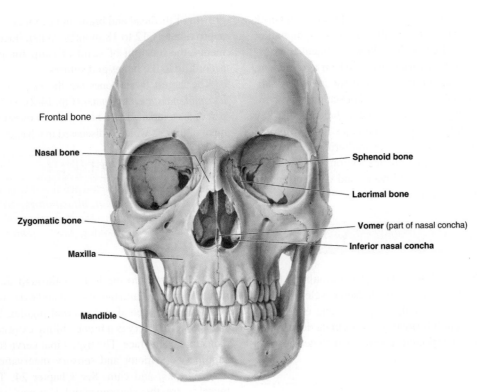

Figure 14-2 The facial bones.

Frontal bone

Nasal bone

Zygomatic bone

Maxilla

Mandible

Sphenoid bone

Lacrimal bone

Vomer (part of nasal concha)

Inferior nasal concha

Trachea

The trachea passes down the midline of the neck and is part of the upper respiratory system (see Chapter 18). Important landmarks for the head and neck region also are in the tracheal area (Fig. 14-5). The usually palpable U-shaped *hyoid bone* is located midline just beneath the mandible. The large *thyroid cartilage* consists of two flat, plate-like structures joined together at an angle and with a small, sometimes palpable notch at the superior edge. This structure, usually more prominent in males, is also called the "Adam's apple."

The palpable *cricoid cartilage* is a ringed structure just inferior to the thyroid cartilage.

Clinical Significance 14-3

Palpation of the thyroid gland reveals important landmarks of the trachea. Such landmarks are noted when assessing for tracheal deviation, which accompanies a potentially life-threatening condition called *tension pneumothorax* (see Chapter 18).

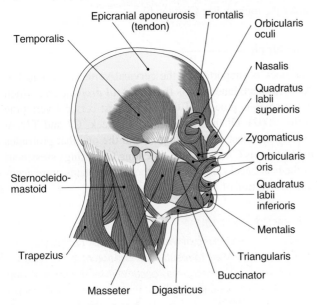

Temporalis

Epicranial aponeurosis (tendon)   Frontalis

Orbicularis oculi

Nasalis

Quadratus labii superioris

Zygomaticus

Orbicularis oris

Quadratus labii inferioris

Mentalis

Triangularis

Buccinator

Sternocleido-mastoid

Trapezius

Masseter   Digastricus

Figure 14-3 The facial muscles.

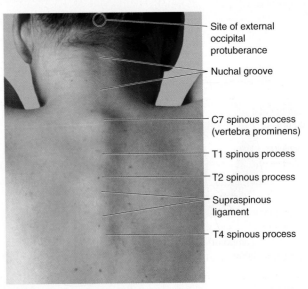

Site of external occipital protuberance

Nuchal groove

C7 spinous process (vertebra prominens)

T1 spinous process

T2 spinous process

Supraspinous ligament

T4 spinous process

Figure 14-4 Posterior surface anatomy of the neck. Note the location of C7.

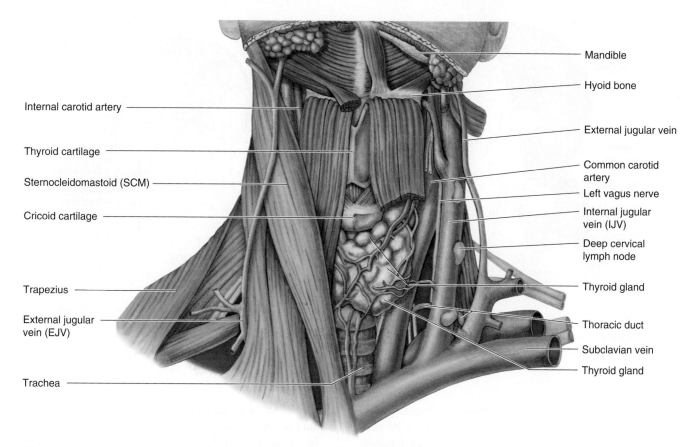

Internal carotid artery

Thyroid cartilage

Sternocleidomastoid (SCM)

Cricoid cartilage

Trapezius

External jugular vein (EJV)

Trachea

Mandible

Hyoid bone

External jugular vein

Common carotid artery

Left vagus nerve

Internal jugular vein (IJV)

Deep cervical lymph node

Thyroid gland

Thoracic duct

Subclavian vein

Thyroid gland

Figure 14-5 Key head and neck landmarks in the region of the trachea.

Thyroid and Parathyroid Glands

The butterfly-shaped *thyroid gland* consists of a band (the isthmus) that crosses the trachea and two symmetrical 3 to 4 cm lobes that lie on each side of the trachea. The *sternomastoid muscle* largely covers the thyroid lobes (see Fig. 14-5). The thyroid gland produces thyroid hormones, the most frequently measured being T3 and T4, which control metabolic rates and affect almost every body system. In all patients, the thyroid should be symmetrical without discrete masses, nodularity, or tenderness. Inspection of the patient's neck while he or she swallows can frequently reveal up and down movement of the thyroid gland. The thyroid gland is usually not palpable. If only the posterior portion of the gland is enlarged, it also may not be palpable. Therefore, it is essential to gather thorough data in history taking that may identify symptoms of hypothyroid or hyperthyroid function (Haddow, McClain, et al., 2007).

Two pairs of parathyroid glands are imbedded in the thyroid lobes and produce calcitonin, which helps move calcium into bones. The parathyroids are usually not palpable.

Lymphatics

The major chains of lymph nodes in the neck are the *preauricular, posterior auricular, occipital, superficial cervical* (extending from the tonsillar to supraclavicular nodes),

deep cervical, posterior cervical, submental, tonsillar, and *submandibular* (Fig. 14-6). Approximately 80 lymph nodes are in the head and neck region, serving as part of the immune system. These vessels filter potential pathogens from the body. They also drain fluid that has moved outside of the circulation back into the vessels. There are many other than those listed, and some are difficult to palpate (Drake, Vogl, et al., 2005). The lymph nodes are named for their anatomical location. They drain fluid along a path in a chain and have a particular direction of flow (Fig. 14-6B). An enlarged node indicates inflammation that is "upstream" from it.

Clinical Significance 14-4

It is important to understand the drainage patterns of the lymphatics, because enlargement of a node may be a sign of pathology that is not directly adjacent to that node.

⛰ Lifespan Considerations

Women Who Are Pregnant

Slight enlargement of the thyroid is common in approximately 5% to 10% of women postpartum (Burman, Ross, et al., 2009). In a condition called *silent thyroiditis*, women

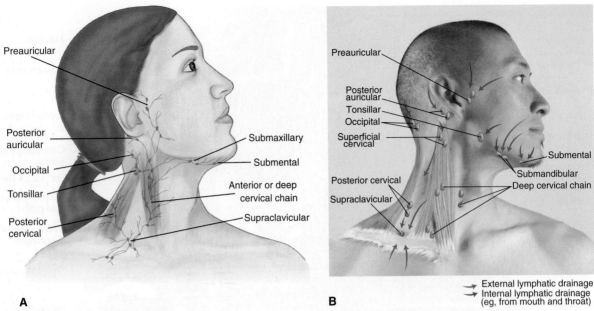

Figure 14-6 Lymphatics of the head and neck. **A.** Major chains of lymph nodes in the neck. **B.** Direction of lymphatic flow and drainage. See also Chapters 20 and 21.

may present with signs and symptoms of hyperthyroidism, followed by hypothyroid symptoms. It may be several months before returning to expected thyroid function (Uphold & Graham, 2003). Even though slight enlargement of the thyroid gland in pregnant or postpartum women may be usual, it still requires further investigation. A thrill may be palpable over the thyroid and a bruit may be auscultated; this is an unexpected condition.

Newborns, Infants, and Children

At birth, the newborn's head may be slightly asymmetrical, elongated, or both as a result of molding of the skull during passage through the birth canal. Head shape moves to normocephalic usually within a few days or weeks after. Newborns have two *fontanels*, areas of the skull with a soft and nonossified matrix. Fontanels enable the head and underlying structures to grow as the child develops. Assessing the size of the anterior and posterior fontanels at each evaluation of the infant is important to determine if ossification is happening at the appropriate time (Fig. 14-7). The posterior fontanel closes by 3 months of age, while the anterior fontanel closes by 18 months of age (Ellis, 2002).

Fontanels should be flat—neither bulging nor retracted. A bulging fontanel may be expected when an infant cries but otherwise needs further evaluation as a sign of possible increased intracranial pressure. A depressed fontanel may indicate dehydration. An unusual head shape may be noted if fontanels close prematurely but may also be from prolonged positioning of the infant in one way. Parents are encouraged to change their infant's position regularly throughout the day while babies are awake to enhance normal physical development. Infants who spend nearly all

their time on their backs may develop significant flattening of the posterior skull.

In children 1 to 5 years, nurses may palpate small (<10 mm), nontender, movable nodes in the head and neck region (Kliegman, Behrman, et al., 2007). These expected findings are sometimes referred to as "shotty," because they feel like BB gun pellets or shots. The thyroid gland and lymph nodes are usually nonpalpable in school-age children.

Older Adults

With aging, facial subcutaneous fat decreases, making the skeleton more pronounced. Skin may sag and wrinkle across the forehead, surrounding the eyes, at the tip of the nose, and on the cheeks, altering facial appearance. Skin lesions are more likely, and careful assessment for possible cancers, especially in commonly sun-exposed areas, is important (Ellis, 2002). See Chapter 13.

Cultural Considerations

The most noticeable variation among people from different genetic backgrounds is skin colour. Shape of the eyes, nose, and lips also varies based on background and genetics. Variations in skull or neck shape or size relate more to height and weight than to specific genetic backgrounds.

Acute Assessment

Patients with acute head injuries and neurologic changes (see Chapter 24) must be quickly and accurately assessed by the health care team. Stabilization of the head and neck is

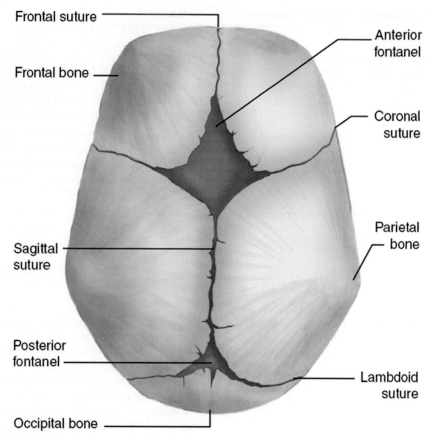

Figure 14-7 Anterior and posterior fontanels.

essential to avoid further neurologic injury. Any history of trauma to the head, neck, or both warrants a careful assessment of these structures for bleeding, swelling, loss of mobility or pain. Identifying the mechanism of injury helps the nurse to determine which anatomic regions require attention. It is essential to keep the spine immobilized to prevent spinal cord injury, and immobilization devices should not be removed until the spine is cleared of injury. Patients with severe headaches may be unable to provide a complete history, but a focused history and physical examination looking for neurologic changes are critical nursing actions.

Neck pain, a common symptom, is most often related to muscle tension or spasm. Neck pain associated with fever and headache may signify serious illness such as meningitis and should be carefully evaluated (see Chapter 24 for meningeal signs). Patients experiencing a myocardial infarction may present with neck pain—so any patient with sudden onset of neck or jaw pain should be evaluated for possible cardiac etiologies (Swartz, 2006).

Other conditions requiring emergency assessment and intervention include facial paralysis or unilateral drooping, sudden numbness or tingling, loss of consciousness, and sudden decrease in orientation. Lacerations to the face and head bleen profusely because these areas are highly vascular. Lacerations to these areas may require emergency assessment and treatment to ensure cessation of blood loss and also for cosmetic considerations (Roach, Roddick, et al., 2010).

Lymphatics larger than 1 cm, fixed, irregular, hard, or rubbery require prompt investigation. Such signs raise the possibility of cancer.

Hyperthyroidism may present as an emergency, with symptoms of hypermetabolism in all systems. The most common sign is tachycardia, but other possibilities include diarrhea, anxiety, fever, weakness, and even psychosis, coma, or death. It is essential to recognize patients at greatest risk for this emergency state. Such patients include those with thyroid tumours and those who have undergone thyroid surgery (Nayak & Hodak, 2007).

Subjective Data Collection

Assessment of Risk Factors

When assessing for risk factors associated with head and neck disorders, nurses remember that multiple systems may influence the structure or function of these regions.

Questions to Assess History and Risk Factors	Rationale
Personal History Have you ever had an accident that resulted in a loss of consciousness? Or head injury? Do you wear a seat belt? Bicycle helmet? Refer to Chapter 24 for more information.	Head injuries are a major cause of disability, which can be permanent. They may be preventable with appropriate use of protective gear, such as a helmet. Nurses can promote use of appropriate safety equipment for patients across the lifespan.
Were you ever treated with radiation to the neck, chest, or back?	Previously, acne on the neck and upper thorax was sometimes treated with radiation therapy. Patients who received such treatment are at significantly increased risk for thyroid and salivary gland malignancies (Smith, 2008).
Have you had any surgeries involving your head or neck?	Because the head and neck have multiple structures, surgeries may result in dysfunction of nerves, muscles, or vascular flow, or in endocrine changes. It is important to understand the specific procedure and assess for any functional changes that could occur.
Medications Do you take any regular medications? How much alcohol do you drink? Do you take any herbal products?	Many medications (eg, bronchodilators, oral contraceptives) and alcohol can precipitate headaches. Some studies have found herbal remedies and aromatherapy effective in relieving headaches (Evans & Taylor, 2006). While patients may use herbal products for relief of symptoms such as headaches, these potentially potent chemicals could actually cause headache and other neurologic side effects.
Family History Do you have a family history of thyroid disorders? • Who had the illness? • Was it hypothyroidism or hyperthyroidism? • When did the person have it? • How was it treated? • What were the outcomes?	*Graves' disease*, the most common type of *hyperthyroidism*, is autoimmune and may also be genetic. Some evidence supports that *medullary thyroid cancer* is genetically linked (Kim & Hatton, 2008).

Risk Assessment and Health Promotion

> *Important Topics for Health Promotion*
>
> • Injury prevention
> • Thyroid health

Education related to the head and neck involves reducing risk of injury to these areas, preventing complications from thyroid disorders, and promoting early detection of masses or lymph nodes that may be malignant. Between 1994 and 2004, several provinces introduced mandatory use of bike helmets for people under the age of 18. This resulted in 50% fewer children and youths admitted to hospitals for traumatic brain injuries (Canadian Institute for Health Information, 2006). Falls and motor vehicle collisions are responsible for the vast majority of traumatic brain injuries in Canadian adults (Canadian Institute for Health Information, 2009). Education for high-risk groups about not driving while under the influence of alcohol or drugs or when sleepy is critical. Another important education area, especially for older adults, is falls prevention.

Spinal cord injuries affect approximately 900 Canadians each year (Canadian Paraplegic Association [CPA], 2007). Motor vehicle collisions (35%), falls (16.5%), medical conditions (10.8%), sports (6.7%), diving (5.3%), work-related injuries (5.3%), and other (14.2%) are the major causes of spinal cord injury in Canadians. Health promotion related to head and neck injuries includes the following (Roach, Roddick, et al., 2010):

• Wear seatbelts in vehicles (mandatory in all provinces).
• Never drive under the influence of alcohol or drugs.
• Avoid distractions such as cell phones, loud music, eating, drinking, and personal hygiene while driving (legislation enacted or pending in most provinces).
• Wear appropriate helmets and protective gear for cycling, skiing, skating, and other sports. Replace equipment at regular intervals.
• Use harnesses and protective gear at work sites.
• Attend safety training in work and recreational settings.
• Assess environment and implement safety measures to prevents falls in the older adult population.
• Never dive into water of unknown depth.

Risk factors for cancers of the neck include male gender, age older than 50 years, tobacco use, and alcohol consumption (National Cancer Institute, 2008). For patients with such risk factors, nurses especially emphasize teaching related to smoking prevention or cessation (see Chapter 18).

A focus area for women who are pregnant is the need for regular examinations that include thyroid screening. Such prenatal care helps to ensure that thyroid levels remain within expected limits, protecting both mother and fetus.

Focused Health History Related to Common Symptoms

Common Head and Neck Symptoms

- Headache
- Neck pain
- Limited neck movement
- Facial pain
- Lumps or masses
- Symptoms/signs related to hypothyroidism
- Symptoms/signs related to hyperthyroidism

Examples of Questions to Assess Symptoms/Signs	Rationale/Unexpected Findings
Headache Have you had any unusually frequent or severe headaches? • Where is the headache? Does it radiate? Is it on one or both sides? • Describe the headache. What does it feel like? • How bad is it on a scale from 0 to 10, with 10 being the worst? • When did it start? How long has it lasted? How often do you get headaches? Do you ever have milder headaches? Is a pattern evident? • What makes it worse? What makes it better? What brings it on? Is there a relationship with food or alcohol? With activity? With menstrual cycle? • Do any other symptoms accompany the pain such as nausea, visual changes, or an aura? • Have you tried any treatments? How often do you take headache relievers or pain pills? Is it difficult to function without treatment? • Has there been any recent change in your headaches? (See also Box 14-1.)	When taking a history, pay attention to characteristics such as pain worse in the morning on awakening, precipitated or made worse by straining or sneezing (potentially *elevated intracranial pressure*) versus worse as the day progresses (more likely *tension*). A throbbing, severe, unilateral headache that lasts 6 to 24 hours and is associated with photophobia, nausea, and vomiting suggests *migraine*, while a constant, unremitting, general headache that is described as a feeling of a tight band around the head and lasts for days, weeks, or even months is usually characteristic of a *tension muscle contraction headache*. Headaches may be categorized as primary or secondary. *Primary headaches* are benign, often recurring, and not associated with underlying pathology. *Secondary headaches* are associated with underlying pathology that ranges from mild (eg, common cold) to severe (eg, subarachnoid hemorrhage, brain tumour, meningitis). See Box 14-2 for concerning red flags.
Neck Pain • Where exactly is the pain? • How long have you had it? • On a scale of 0 to 10 how would you rate your pain? • Describe the pain. • What makes it better? Worse? • What is your pain goal?	Neck pain can be from musculoskeletal injury, tension, or pathologic changes (Piatt, 2005). Common causes include *trauma* at any age, muscle tension in adolescents or adults, and *arthritis* in older clients.

BOX 14-1 EXAMPLE OF QUESTIONS FOR SYMPTOM/SIGN ANALYSIS—HEADACHE

- "Where is the headache located?" "Is it in one place?" "Does it change places?" (*Location, Radiating*)
- "Describe your headache." "Is the pain throbbing?" "Steady?" "Sharp?" "Dull?" (*Quality*)
- "Rate your pain on a scale of 0 to 10, with 0 being no pain and 10 being the worst pain." "Have you ever had a headache this painful before?" (*Severity*)
- "When did your headache start?" "Did it start gradually or suddenly?" (*Onset*)
- "How long do the headaches usually last?" "How long have you been having headaches?" (*Duration*)
- "How often do you have them?" (*Frequency*)
- "Have your headaches stayed the same?" "Do they get better then worse?" (*Constancy*)

- "Do your headaches occur at a particular time of day?" (*Time of day/month/year*)
- "What makes your headache worse?" "Does anything trigger your headaches?" (*Aggravating factors*)
- "What makes it (headache) better?" (*Alleviating factors*)
- "Do you have any other symptoms, such as nausea? Vomiting? Dizziness? Vision changes with your headache?" (*Associated symptoms*)
- "Have you recently changed anything in your home or office?" "Have you had any recent head injuries?" "How much stress is in your life right now?" (*Environmental factors*)
- "How do your headaches affect your life?" (*Significance to patient*)
- "Do you know what might be causing your headache?" (*Patient perspective*)

Adapted from Roach, S., Roddick, P., et al. (2010). The head and neck. In T. C. Stephen, D. L. Skillen, R. A. Day, & L. S. Bickley (Eds.). *Canadian Bates' guide to health assessment for nurses* (pp. 270–298). Philadelphia, PA: Wolters Kluwer Health/Lippincott Williams & Wilkins

BOX 14-2 LIST OF RED FLAGS FOR HEADACHES

- Onset of new or different headache
- Nausea or vomiting
- Worst headache ever experienced
- Progressive visual or neurological changes
- Paralysis
- Weakness, ataxia, or loss of coordination
- Drowsiness, confusion, memory impairment, or loss of consciousness
- Onset of headache after age of 50 years
- Papilledema
- Stiff neck
- Onset of headache with exertion, sexual activity, or coughing
- Systemic illness
- Numbness
- Asymmetry of pupillary response
- Sensory loss
- Signs of meningeal irritation

Adapted from Sobri, M. S., Lamont, A. C., et al. (2003). Red flags in patients presenting with headache: Clinical indications for neuroimaging. *British Journal of Radiololgy, 76*(908), 532–535.

Examples of Questions to Assess Symptoms/Signs	Rationale/Unexpected Findings
Limited Neck Movement Are you having any difficulty turning or flexing/extending your neck?	Limitation of neck mobility may be from muscle tension/strain or cervical vertebral joint dysfunction.
Facial Pain • Where exactly is the pain? • How long have you had it? • On a scale of 0 to 10 how would you rate your pain? • Describe the pain. • What makes it better? Worse? • What is your pain goal?	Trauma, infection, and neurologic disorders may result in facial pain, which also can be referred from another organ or system. Common causes of facial pain include the following: • Muscle over-use • Mouth/tooth infections • Sinusitis • Herpes zoster • Trauma • Migraine or cluster headaches • Jaw pain, especially if associated with shoulder or arm pain (could be cardiac); this medical emergency requires immediate evaluation and treatment • Skull pain, which may be related to tension headaches or tension of the neck muscles. Also consider skin lesions, trauma, and infection as possible causes.
Lumps or Masses Have you noted any lumps or masses in your head or neck? • How long have you had this? • How many are there? • How large are any? • Are they changing? • Are they tender or painful?	Nurses differentiate the many structures in the neck by careful questioning of the characteristics of any neck lump, followed by careful physical examination grounded in knowledge of the anatomy of this region.
Symptoms/Signs of Hypothyroidism Do you have any of these symptoms: fatigue; anorexia; cold intolerance; dry skin; brittle, coarse hair; menstrual irregularities; weight gain or difficulty losing weight; decreased libido?	Signs and symptoms of thyroid dysfunction are often nonspecific (Herrick, 2008). Nurses consider that the patient has a thyroid problem when several symptoms are "clustered together." Metabolism is low.
Symptoms/Signs of Hyperthyroidism Do you have any of these symptoms: fatigue; weight loss; anxiety; palpitations; rapid pulse; heat intolerance; fine, limp hair; sweating (diaphoresis); muscle weakness?	Similarly, hyperthyroidism usually presents with several of these signs or symptoms (Siraj, 2008). An overactive thyroid gland increases the metabolic rate.

Documentation of Subjective Findings

Patient reports no unusual, severe, or frequent headaches. Denies loss of neck mobility or neck pain. Denies any lumps or masses in the neck. Reports no concerns with fatigue, weight change, temperature discomfort, skin changes, sweating, or other unusual findings.

Lifespan Considerations

Additional Questions	Rationale/Unexpected Findings
Women Who Are Pregnant Have you noticed any changes or swelling in your neck?	The thyroid gland enlarges slightly and symmetrically in pregnancy. Marked or unilateral enlargement is unexpected and requires further evaluation. *Migraines* are more common, possibly from increased hormones.
Do you have a headache or any sensory, motor, or visual changes?	
Newborns and Infants To caregiver, "Is the infant properly secured in an approved car seat every time he or she is in an automobile?"	Because infants' heads are disproportionately large, they are likely to sustain severe head injuries or death even in minor traffic accidents or sudden stops, if not positioned properly in a securely fastened rear facing, 5 point harness car seat. Maternal use of alcohol or drugs can cause deformities of the fetal head and face, as well as other serious physical and mental disabilities. Thus, it is important to determine any and all in utero exposures.
Was there any possible exposure of the infant to alcohol or drugs while the mother was pregnant?	
Children and Adolescents Does the child wear a helmet for such actions as bicycling, skating, skiing, scooter riding, or skateboarding?	Properly used helmets can reduce risk of significant head injury. Headache should be suspected in young children who hold or bang their heads but cannot describe their symptoms. In children older than 3 years, headache is significant, requiring thorough evaluation to rule out conditions related to increasing intracranial pressure.
Does the child hold or bang his or her head?	
Older Adult • Have you noticed any lumps/masses in your neck? • Do you have a new type of headache? • Do you have any pain in your neck? • Any weakness, numbness or tingling in your arms? • Do you feel that you have a neck injury that has not been treated	Cervical lymph nodes are usually *not* palpable, but submandibular glands may be more prominent from less subcutaneous fat. New headache in a patient older than 50 years requires thorough investigation to determine etiology. Arthritic changes in the cervical spine may present as neck pain or loss of sensation or strength in the upper extremities. Diagnosis of a cervical spine injury is challenging and may go undiagnosed (Rubenstein & van Tulder, 2008). Patients at risk include those following a fall or collision, and patients with osteoporosis, advanced arthritis, cancer, or degenerative bone disease (Harris, Blackmore, et al., 2008).
Cultural Considerations • Do you use iodized salt?	Water and food intake provide the body with iodine. Some geographical areas have iodine deficiencies, for example, the Great Lakes areas of Canada and the United States. Although iodized salt is commonly used throughout North America, lack of dietary iodine may lead to increased incidence of thyroid disease in immigrant populations. Also, hypothyroidism is more prevalent in Caucasians than in African Canadians (Roach, Roddick, et al., 2010).

Objective Data Collection

Equipment

- Ambient lighting
- Penlight or flashlight for tangential lighting
- Disposable nonlatex gloves, if any lesions of the scalp or skin of head and neck are suspected
- Small cup of water

Promoting Patient Comfort, Dignity, and Safety

The patient can sit comfortably on the edge of the examination table with the patient's head at the nurse's eye level. If the patient is wearing a wig or hairpiece, ask him or her to remove it. Wash your hands. The patient is usually seated, facing the examiner. Instruct the patient that the head and neck will be inspected, palpated, and manipulated, but that the procedures should not be painful. Instruct the patient to tell you if any part of the head and neck examination causes discomfort (see Box 14.3).

BOX 14-3 CULTURAL CONSIDERATIONS

"Muslim women from parts of the Persian Gulf, North Africa, Southeast Asia, and India may wear veils or head scarves that cover a part or most of their faces. These patients regard this apparel as a symbol of modesty and piety. Wearing such clothing is often a personal choice of Canadian immigrants from these regions. The veil and head coverings may be removed for the purposes of examination, when required. Consideration must be given to the relationship of any male who is present when the patient's head is not covered.

Patients from some cultures, such as those of Southeast Asian descent, may prohibit others from touching their heads. Remember to consider the cultural norms for touch when assessing the head and neck." (Roach, Roddick, et al., 2010, p. 286)

Adapted from Roach, S., Roddick, P., et al. (2010). The head and neck. In T. C. Stephen, D. L. Skillen, R. A. Day, & L. S. Bickley (Eds.). *Canadian Bates' guide to health assessment for nurses* (pp. 270–298). Philadelphia, PA: Wolters Kluwer Health/Lippincott Williams & Wilkins

An Example of a Therapeutic Dialogue

Remember Faye Davis-Pierce, introduced at the beginning of this chapter. This 21-year-old college student has presented to the campus clinic with fatigue and weight gain. Professional communication techniques are used to gather subjective data from the patient. The following conversation gives an example of an interview.

Nurse: Hi, I'm Brenda. What name do you prefer to be called?

Faye: Faye is fine. Thanks for asking.

Nurse: Sure. So, how are you doing today?

Faye: I've just been feeling really tired.

Nurse: Tell me more about that.

Faye: Well, I've been really stressed out and having trouble sleeping. It's hard to get out of bed sometimes in the morning.

Nurse: I see that you're in college, which can be stressful.

Faye: Yes, it really can be.

Nurse: Have you noticed any other symptoms with your fatigue?

Faye: Yeah, I've gained 10 kg. I think that it's the dorm food.

Nurse: We can talk about some strategies for your nutrition later if you would like.

Faye: Yes, I would.

Nurse: Have you noticed anything else, such as loss of appetite, dry skin, or hair?

Faye: Well, yes, my skin and hair have been dry. You know my mother has been saying that she had a low thyroid when she was around my age. Could it be related?

Nurse: It's possible. I'll make sure to report this information to the nurse practitioner when she sees you.

Critical Thinking Challenge

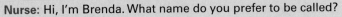

- What did the nurse do to establish a therapeutic relationship?
- How did the nurse use interviewing skills to collect pertinent data?

Common and Specialty or Advanced Techniques

The routine head-to-toe assessment includes the most important and common assessment techniques. Nurses may add specialty or advanced steps if concerns exist over a specific finding. Additional techniques may be added if the clinical situation warrants them.

Comprehensive Physical Examination

Inspection

Inspect the head (Fig. 14-8). Inspect scalp and skull. *The head is centered, proportional to the body (1/7), erect, and without tremors, tics, or unusual movements. The skull is round without obvious deformities. The neck muscles are symmetrical.*

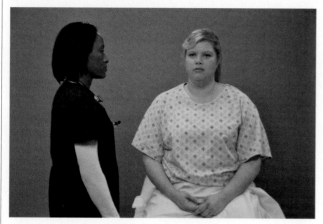

Figure 14-8 Inspecting the head.

Inspect facial features for symmetry and size. *Nasolabial folds are symmetrical.*

Inspect the hair (Fig. 14-9) for
- Distribution and quantity
- Texture
- Cleanliness

Hair is evenly distributed across the scalp, extending from the superior aspect of the forehead to the base of the cranium and to the top of the ears bilaterally.

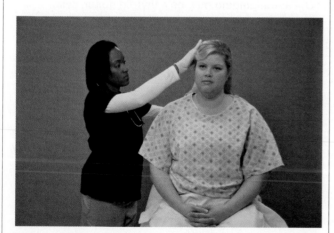

Figure 14-9 Examining the hair and scalp. The nurse wears gloves if there is any possibility of contact with an open sore or lesion.

Unexpected Findings

Facial asymmetry may indicate damage to the facial nerve (cranial nerve [CN] VII) or a serious condition such as a *stroke*. Enlarged bones or tissues are associated with *acromegaly*. A puffy "moon" face is associated with *Cushing's syndrome*. Increased facial hair in females may be a sign of *Cushing's syndrome* or *endocrinopathy*. Periorbital edema is seen with *congestive heart failure* and *hypothyroidism (myxedema)*. See Tables 14-2 and 14-3 at the end of this chapter for visual examples.

If asymmetrical, look for signs of trauma. Carefully assess any lesions for infection.

Testosterone stimulates hair growth on the face, pubis, axilla, and chest but diminishes scalp hair growth. Male-pattern baldness occurs when there is both a genetic predisposition and increased testosterone or other male hormones (Kaufman, Girman, et al., 2008). Adult men may present with male-pattern baldness in either an "M" pattern on the scalp or, as hair loss continues, a "U" pattern with hair growth around the skull at the level of the temples.

Such hair loss can occur any time after puberty but is usually more noticeable in middle and older adults (Guyton & Hall, 2006). Unusual distribution or patterns of hair growth on the face or skull are associated with endocrine conditions. Any nits (white to brown small 1 mm specks) attached to hair shafts are signs of *pediculosis* (head lice). Usually, intense itching accompanies infestation. Traction alopecia may occur with tight braiding (Khumalo, Jessop, et al., 2008) (see also Chapter 13).

(text continues on page 338)

Inspect the neck (Fig. 14-10). Look at the neck muscles, sternomastoid, thyroid, and isthmus (may be visualized with tangential light and asking the patient to tilt his or her head back a bit and swallow a sip of water). Use tangential lighting directed downward from the patient's chin. *Trachea is midline. A slight symmetrical elevation may be observed in the mid-neck. The neck muscles are symmetrical.*

Thyroid enlargement or masses can be seen more easily when the patient swallows and while illuminating the neck from the chin with a tangential light.

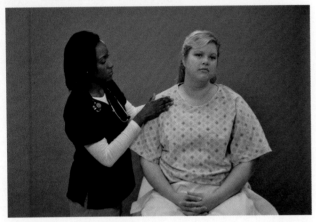

Figure 14-10 Inspecting the neck.

Palpation

Palpate the temporal artery in the space above the cheek bone near the scalp line.

The temporal artery pulse is 2 to 3 on a 4-point scale.

Temporal arthritis is a painful inflammation of the temporal artery. A biopsy is necessary for diagnosis.

Palpate the scalp. Refer to Chapter 13. *The scalp is symmetrical, intact without tenderness, masses, lesions, or differences in firmness.*

Bulging or depression of the bony structure of the scalp may result from trauma or tumour growth. Bulging fontanels in infants may be a clinical sign of *hydrocephalus*, or simply the result of lusty crying (see Table 14-2). Depressed fontanels are most often associated with dehydration.

Palpate the thyroid, either from the anterior or posterior approach.
- For the *anterior approach*, have the patient initially tilt the head slightly back to locate the thyroid and cricoid cartilages. The thyroid cartilage is larger, shield-shaped, and in the midneck, sometimes referred to as the "Adam's apple" in males.

- Unilateral bulging may be a thyroid goiter, cyst, or tumour.
- Neck masses may also originate from a lymph node or cyst.

Below is the ringed cricoid cartilage. Just below the cricoid cartilage the isthmus of the thyroid should be palpable as a smooth rubbery band that rises and falls with swallowing. With the pads of the fingers of one hand gently palpate the thyroid isthmus. Ask the patient to lower the head slightly and turn it slightly to one side. The sternomastoid muscle will relax on the side to which the patient turns. Palpate behind the sternomastoid muscle (Fig. 14-11).

- Any new neck mass in a patient older than 35 years should be carefully evaluated to rule out cancer. It could be a lymph node enlarged by metastatic cancer, a primary lymphoma, or a tumour of structures of the neck.
- Unusual hardness is a dangerous finding, possibly associated with cancer (Kim & Hatton, 2008).
- A toxic goiter may feel softer than healthy thyroid tissue.

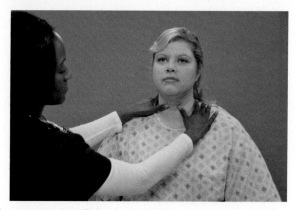

Figure 14-11 Palpating behind the sternomastoid muscle for the anterior thyroid.

- For the posterior approach, locate the thyroid and cricoid cartilages and the thyroid isthmus by palpation while standing behind the patient. Have the patient bend the head slightly forward and toward one side. Use your index finger to slightly retract the sternomastoid muscle on the side toward which the patient has tilted the head. Use the middle two or three fingers to locate the lobe of the thyroid. The fingers of the other hand should gently displace the trachea and thyroid cartilage on the opposite side, which helps to move the thyroid gland slightly forward and prominent and allows for easier palpation. It is, however, not unusual for the thyroid lobes to also be nonpalpable with this approach (Fig. 14-12).

If palpable, the thyroid is smooth, rubbery, nontender, symmetrical, and barely palpable beneath the sternomastoid.

Palpate for discernable lymph nodes in the head and neck following a systematic pattern (Fig. 14-13). The order of examination is usually preauricular, posterior auricular, occipital, submental, submandibular, tonsillar, anterior cervical chain, posterior cervical chain, and supraclavicular. Using the pads of the second, third, and fourth fingers, gently palpate with small circles, varying the amount of

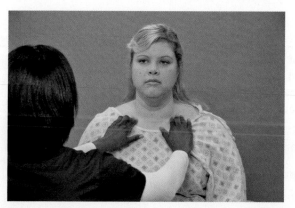

Figure 14-13 Palpating for any discernable lymph nodes.

- Tenderness is common with subacute infections, traumatic injury, and radiation thyroiditis (Burman, Ross, et al., 2009).
- The parathyroid gland is not independently palpated but may be noted when attempting to palpate the thyroid gland. Parathyroid carcinoma is a rare form of cancer. The tumours usually secrete parathyroid hormone, producing hyperparathyroidism, and increased calcium levels. Parathyroid carcinoma may be suspected, but it usually cannot be confirmed prior to surgery.

Figure 14-12 Palpating the thyroid from the posterior approach.

Palpable, tender, and warm lymph nodes usually indicate an infection in the area from which the lymph vessels drain to that node (Ellis, 2002):

- Anterior cervical nodes: *pharyngitis*
- Posterior cervical nodes: *mononucleosis*
- Posterior auricular nodes: *otitis media*
- Supraclavicular nodes: must be carefully evaluated as a possible sign of metastatic cancer. Virchow's node, the left supraclavicular, is associated with *lung and abdominal cancers*.

Hard, rubbery, irregular, fixed, and nontender lymph nodes are a possible sign of *lymphoma*.

(text continues on page 340)

pressure over each lymphatic region. *Usually no lymph nodes are palpable in the adult.* If a node is palpable, it is important to describe the following characteristics:
- Location—which lymphatic chain and where along that chain is the node
- Size—in mm or cm
- Consistency—how hard or soft is the node? It should be smooth, slightly soft, and nontender.
- Mobility—it should be freely movable
- Delimitation—there should not be any matting together of lymph nodes

Auscultation

If the thyroid is enlarged, either unilaterally or bilaterally, auscultate over each lobe for a bruit using the bell of the stethoscope (Fig. 14-14). *No bruit or vascular sounds are audible.*

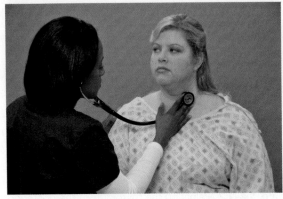

Figure 14-14 Auscultating the thyroid.

Bruits are most often found with a *toxic goiter, hyperthyroidism,* or *thyrotoxicosis.*

Documentation of Expected Findings

Thyroid gland palpable with swallow, symmetric, smooth, rubbery, and nontender. No bruit.

Documenting Unexpected Findings

The nurse reports and documents her findings and history of Faye Davis-Pierce, the 21 year old with fatigue and weight gain. Unlike the samples of documentation previously charted, Faye Davis-Pierce has unexpected findings. Review the following important findings revealed in each of the steps of objective data collection. Consider how the interprofessional team will collaborate related to these findings.

Inspection: Skull is normocephalic, atraumatic. Hair blondish and slightly dry. Skin dry and intact. Trachea midline. Skin colour slightly pale, appears puffy.

Palpation: Thyroid gland palpable and enlarged, rises symmetrically with swallow, smooth, rubbery, and nontender. No nodules or masses.

Auscultation: No bruit over thyroid.

Area of Assessment	Expected Findings	Unexpected Findings
Hair	Evenly distributed, clean, brown	Thinning and patchy, lice visualized
Scalp	Even colouration, skin intact	Soft lump superior to right mastoid process that is painful to touch
Skull	Size proportional to body, symmetrical	Depressed, tender area on left temporal bone
Face	Symmetrical movement of facial muscles	Involuntary muscle spasms inferior to left eye
Skin	Smooth, consistent colour, intact	Excessive facial hair (hirsutism), acne on face and anterior neck
Neck	Full range of motion, symmetrical	Limited forward flexion of neck, enlargement on left side of trachea
Lymph nodes and salivary glands	Nonpalpable, nontender	Tonsillar lymph nodes palpable and tender to touch
Trachea and thyroid	Trachea midline, thyroid isthmus midline with palpable, nontender lobes	Trachea deviates to right; enlarged, visible thyroid gland with nodular tissue palpated on left side

 Lifespan Considerations

Women Who Are Pregnant

Melasma, also known as chloasma may be present on the face. This blotchy and hyperpigmented patch appears on the cheeks and fades in the postpartum period. Detection of maternal (and fetal) hypothyroidism is of major importance because of potential damage to fetal neural development, an increased incidence of miscarriage, and preterm birth (Abalovich, Amino, et al., 2007). Autoimmune thyroid disease is associated with both increased rates of miscarriage and postpartum thyroiditis.

Infants and Children

Measure the infant's head circumference (see Chapter 6). Observe the head for shape and symmetry. Infants in one position for prolonged periods may have a flattening of one part of the head. Asymmetry may also result from premature closure of the sutures.

Note head control. The infant should be able to hold up the head by 4 months of age. Palpate the skull for patent sutures, fontanels, edema, fractures, or masses. Typically the posterior fontanel closes by 1 to 3 months; the anterior fontanel closes by 7 to 19 months. A caput succedaneum is a swollen and ecchymotic area caused from the birth process as the head is squeezed. It usually resolves in the first few days. A cephalohematoma is a hemorrhage defined over one cranial bone. It appears shortly after birth and increases in size. It also resolves on its own but the infant is more likely to develop jaundice because of the breakdown of the red blood cells.

Note any limitations in neck range of motion. If the child holds the head to one side with the chin pointing toward the opposite side, the sternomastoid muscle may be injured. The neck is typically short in an infant. Skinfolds are present between head and shoulders in infancy.

To palpate the lymph nodes, tilt the child's head upward slightly but without tensing the sternomastoid or trapezius muscles. Lymph nodes are not usually present in an infant but a child's may be palpable.

Observe the face or symmetry, movement and general appearance. Ask the child to make a face to assess for any paralysis. Note any unusual facial proportions that may be present with fetal alcohol syndrome or Down's syndrome.

Congenital hypothyroidism is rare, but if not identified early, it will result in cognitive delays (Lafranchi, 2008). All provinces screen all infants by measuring thyroid-stimulating hormone (TSH) levels shortly after birth (Public Health Agency of Canada, 2006). Early recognition and treatment (within 1 month of birth) can significantly mitigate associated developmental delays. Hypothyroidism is more common in infants with Down's syndrome (Kliegman, Behrman, et al., 2007).

Older Adult

The facial skin may appear more wrinkled and less elastic. Thinning of the hair is also an expected aging process. The neck may have reduced range of motion with chronic conditions such as arthritis. Additionally, there is an exaggerated concave curve of the spine.

Hypothyroidism in the older adult often lacks the classic symptoms seen in younger patients (Peeters, 2008). This is from a more subtle onset, chronic diseases, and the idea that typical signs and symptoms (fatigue, cold intolerance, constipation, or depression) may be attributed to aging. Additionally, the older adult is more prone to hyperthyroidism (Brunk, 2008). Unexplained weight loss, diarrhea or constipation, nausea, and vomiting may be presenting symptoms. Depression and mania can be presenting symptoms of hyperthyroidism in the elderly.

Evidence-Informed Critical Thinking

Common Laboratory and Diagnostic Testing

Evaluation of headaches may indicate the need for several diagnostic tests. Examples of such tests include computed tomography (CT), magnetic resonance imaging (MRI), or lumbar puncture.

Musculoskeletal injury or disease can be confirmed with an x-ray, CT, or MRI (see Chapter 23). If test results are negative, the nurse should assess for complete range of motion of the neck, looking for any muscle tension, loss of mobility, or pain. The nurse should recall that cardiac disease may present with referred pain to the neck or jaw, making it important to assess for signs of cardiovascular disease.

Tests of thyroid function are commonly performed for patients at any age presenting with signs or symptoms of hyperthyroidism or hypothyroidism. Usually TSH, T3, and T4 are measured.

Clinical Reasoning

Nursing Diagnosis, Outcomes, and Interventions

Table 14-1 compares nursing diagnoses, assessment findings, and interventions commonly related to assessment of the head and neck (North American Nursing Diagnosis Association-International, 2009). Nurses use assessment information to identify patient outcomes. Some outcomes related to head and neck issues include the following:

- Patient participates in physical activity with appropriate changes in vital signs.
- Patient verbalizes increased energy and well-being.
- Pain goals are met (Moorhead, Johnson, et al., 2007).

Once the outcomes area is established, nursing care is implemented to improve the status of the patient. The nurse uses critical thinking and evidence-informed practice to develop the interventions. Some examples of nursing interventions for the head and neck are as follows:

- Allow for periods of rest before planned activities.
- Set small, achievable short-term goals for activity that can be motivational.
- Treat pain before it becomes severe (Bulechek, Butcher, et al., 2008).

Table 14-1	Common Nursing Diagnoses Associated with the Head and Neck		
Diagnosis and Related Factors	**Point of Differentiation**	**Assessment Characteristics**	**Nursing Interventions**
Activity intolerance related to hypothyroidism	Inability to complete or continue daily activities as a result of a lack of physical or mental energy, which is symptomatic of the thyroid disorder	Verbal report of weakness, unusual Pressure or blood pressure (BP) during activity, dyspnea, ECG changes	Determine cause.* If appropriate gradually increase activity. Monitor response to activity. Refer patient to physical therapy.
Chronic pain related to cervical spine injury	Pain lasting more than 6 months. Use pain scale to describe.	Report of pain, facial grimace, muscle tension, increased P, (respiration) R, or BP, shifting or guarding	Assess characteristics. Work with pain team to determine appropriate medical treatment. Use nonpharmacologic interventions.

*Collaborative interventions.

Analyzing Findings from Health History and Physical Exmaination

Remember Faye Davis-Pierce, whose issues have been outlined throughout this chapter. Initial subjective and objective data collection is complete. Tests of Faye's thyroid levels reveal an elevated TSH and low T3 and T4, indicating hypothyroidism. The following nursing note illustrates how the assessment data are analyzed and nursing interventions are developed.

Subjective: I've just been feeling really tired. I've had some weight gain and I've been really cold.

Objective: Hair blondish, slightly dry. Skin dry and intact. Skin colour slightly pale, appears puffy and tired. Loss of lateral eyebrows (Matfin, 2010). TSH high and T3 and T4 are low. Skull is normocephalic, atraumatic. Trachea midline. Thyroid gland palpable and enlarged, symmetrical, smooth, rubbery, and nontender. No lumps or masses. No bruit over thyroid.

Analysis: Symptoms are related to low thyroid function. Need for teaching about new prescription for thyroid replacement.

Plan: Provide teaching about new thyroid replacement medication. Provide materials on nutrition for healthy food choices. Assess college stressors at next visit.

Critical Thinking Challenge

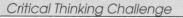

- What role and responsibility does the nurse have for assessment of the laboratory values?
- How will the nurse approach teaching about diet and exercise given sensitivity in many patients about weight gain?
- Why did the nurse decide to defer assessment of college stressors until the next visit?

Collaborating with the Interprofessional Team

In many facilities, nurses initiate referrals based on needs related to teaching or interventions. Results that might trigger a pharmacy consult include questions about the drug dose, route, or time; drug interactions; appropriate therapies; discharge teaching; and patient education (Interdisciplinary Plan, 2007). Read the following dialogue below to see how the nurse discusses with pharmacy personnel the new prescription for Faye Davis-Pierce.

Situation: Hi, I'm Patricia, a nurse who saw Faye Davis-Pierce in the clinic today. She has been diagnosed with hypothyroidism. She has a prescription for thyroid replacement with her.

Background: She has some questions regarding her medication and changes in how she will feel once she begins taking the medication.

Assessment: We want to make sure that the patient understands any overall changes in how she feels and possible side effects that need to be reported. We want to support her so she will take the medication correctly.

Recommendations: We have an information package on the medication that outlines when, how, with or without food, possible side effects, and other information that would be helpful for her to know. We can go over this pamphlet with her.

Critical Thinking Challenge

- What teaching will the nurse provide compared to the pharmacist?
- What is the role of the nurse in assessing for both the intended effects and also side effects of the new medication?

Pulling It All Together: An Example of Reflection and Critical Thinking

The nurse uses assessment data to formulate a nursing care plan with patient outcomes and interventions for Faye Davis-Pierce. After completion of interventions, the nurse reevaluates Ms. Davis-Pierce and documents findings in the chart to show progress toward goals. The nurse uses critical thinking and judgment to continue or revise the diagnosis, outcomes, or interventions. This is often in the form of a care plan or case note similar to below.

Nursing Diagnosis	Patient Outcomes	Nursing Interventions	Rationale	Evaluation
Knowledge deficit related to new diagnosis of hypothyroidism as evidenced by no knowledge of new medication	Patient will state intended effect and side effects of medication.	Teach patient not to take medication with food. Review effects and side effects of medication, including that it may take several weeks to notice a change. Provide written information. Give a phone number in case she has questions or experiences side effects.	Written instructions are a resource that the patient can access after leaving the clinic. Questions may not arise until the patient is home.	The patient stated the intended effect of resolution of her symptoms. She also stated the side effects of too high a level, including weight loss, anxiety, palpitations, rapid pulse, heat intolerance fine limp hair, and diaphoresis. The patient scheduled a follow-up appointment in 3 weeks.

Applying Your Knowledge

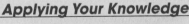

Using the previous steps of clinical reasoning, organizing, and prioritizing, consider all the case study findings woven throughout this chapter. When answering the following questions, begin drawing conclusions and see how the pieces of assessment must work together to create an environment for personalized, appropriate, and accurate care.

- What are the signs and symptoms of hypothyroidism? (Knowledge)
- How do hypothyroidism and hyperthyroidism differ? How are these differences manifested in client symptoms? (Comprehension)
- What other physical findings might be present, and what other body systems might be involved? (Application)
- How might Faye's physical issues relate to her psychosocial health, including potential issues related to her age and status as a college student? (Analysis)
- What type of follow-up care and reassessment might the patient need at subsequent visits? (Synthesis)
- How would you evaluate Faye's understanding of her diagnosis and determine any additional needed teaching? (Evaluation)

Key Points

- Structures of the head and neck also include the trachea, thyroid, and lymphatics.
- The anterior fontanel closes by 19 months of age, while the posterior fontanel closes by 3 months.
- Fontanels in the newborn should be flat, not bulging or retracted.
- Acute situations that need emergency assessment and intervention include head or neck injuries, neck pain (may be cardiac or thyrotoxicosis.
- Enlarged, hard, palpable lymph nodes or masses (which may indicate cancer) require prompt attention.
- Common symptoms of the head and neck include pain, limited neck movement, lumps or masses, hypothyroidism, and hyperthyroidism.
- The neck muscles, sternomastoid muscle, thyroid, and isthmus are inspected in the neck.
- The thyroid is smooth, rubbery, and moveable. It is also common for the thyroid to be nonpalpable.
- A bruit may be present with hyperthyroidism or thyrotoxicosis.
- Common nursing diagnoses for the head and neck include activity intolerance, fatigue, chronic pain, and knowledge deficit.

Review Questions

1. While examining the patient's neck, the nurse finds the trachea midline but has difficulty palpating the thyroid. What action would the nurse take next?
   A. Document this finding.
   B. Tell the patient that this finding is concerning.
   C. Report to the physician a suspicion of a slow growing goiter.
   D. Look for signs of hypothyroidism.

2. The lymph nodes that lie superficial to the mastoid bone are the
   A. preauricular nodes
   B. posterior auricular nodes
   C. superficial cervical nodes
   D. supraclavicular nodes

3. Which of the following descriptions is most consistent with the patient who has hypothyroidism?
   A. Slightly obese, perspiring female, who reports feeling cold all the time and having diarrhea
   B. Slightly obese female with periorbital edema and a flat facial expression, who reports constipation, decreased appetite, and fatigue
   C. Thin, anxious-appearing female with exophthalmos and a rapid pulse, and who reports diarrhea
   D. Thin, perspiring male with a deep hoarse voice, facial edema, a thick tongue, and reports of diarrhea

4. Physical examination of the patient reveals an enlarged tonsillar lymph node. Acutely infected nodes would be
   A. hard but smooth and nontender
   B. fixed and soft
   C. firm but movable and tender
   D. irregular and hard

5. While assessing the skin of a 24-year-old patient, the nurse notes decreased skin turgor. The nurse should further assess for signs and symptoms of
   A. hyperthyroidism
   B. hypothyroidism
   C. malnutrition
   D. dehydration

6. The nurse can best evaluate the strength of the sternomastoid muscle by having the patient
   A. clench his or her teeth during muscle palpation
   B. bring his or her head to the chest
   C. turn his or her head against resistance
   D. extend his or her arms against resistance

7. Which of the following best describes the instructions the nurse gives the patient when assessing the thyroid from the posterior approach?
   A. Please tilt your head back as far as possible.
   B. Please turn your head as far to the right as you can.
   C. Please bring your chin down toward your neck.
   D. Please look straight ahead and tilt your head slightly down and to one side.

8. While assessing a patient, the nurse finds a palpable lymph node in the left supraclavicular region. Which of the following should be the next action?
   A. Recognize that it is common to palpate lymph nodes in this region and they are usually not pathologic.
   B. Recognize that a palpable node in this region is a dangerous indication of metastatic cancer that requires further evaluation.
   C. Recognize that this is a common area for lymph nodes to be enlarged with minor infections.
   D. Recognize that a palpable lymph node in this region is always indicative of malignancy.

9. While reviewing laboratory values for thyroid function on an adult patient, the nurse sees that the thyroid-stimulating hormone (TSH) is elevated, and the T3 and T4 are decreased. The nurse recognizes that these findings are indicative of
   A. healthy thyroid function
   B. hypothyroidism
   C. hyperthyroidism
   D. thyroid cancer

10. The patient presents with a concern about of drooping of his eyes, cheeks, and mouth on one side. This finding is most likely associated with pathology of which cranial nerve?
   A. Cranial nerve III
   B. Cranial nerve VI
   C. Cranial nerve VII
   D. Cranial nerve IX

Canadian Nursing Research

Dooley, J. M., Gordon K. E., et al. (2005). Self-reported headache frequency in Canadian adolescents: Validation and follow-up headache. *The Journal of Head and Face Pain, 45*(2), 127–131.

Penner, J. (2008). Experiences of family caregivers of patients with advanced head and neck cancer receiving enteral tube feeding. *Journal of Palliative Care, 24*(3), 218–219.

References

Abalovich, M., Amino, N., et al. (2007). Management of thyroid dysfunction during pregnancy and postpartum: An endocrine society clinical practice guideline. *Thyroid, 17*(11), 1159–1167.

Brunk, B. (2008). Elders are at risk for thyroid dysfunction. *Caring for the Ages, 9*(5), 23.

Bulechek, G. M., Butcher, H. K., et al. (2008). *Nursing interventions classification (NIC)* (5th ed.) St. Louis, MO: Mosby.

Burman, K. D., Ross, D. S., et al. (2009). *Overview of thyroiditis.* Retrieved from http://www.uptodateonline.com.proxy.seattleu. edu/online/content/topic.do?topicKey=thyroid/12274&selected Title=2%7E20&source= search_result

Canadian Institute for Health Information. (2006). *Hospitalizations due to traumatic head injuries down 35% over a decade.* Retrieved from www.secure.cihi.ca/cihiweb/dispPage.jsp?cw_ page=media_30aug2006_e

Canadian Institute for Health Information. (2009). *Head injuries in Canada: A decade of change.* Retrieved from https://secure. cihi.ca/estore/productFamily.htm?locale=en&pf=PFC1360&la ng=en&media=0

Drake, R. L., Vogl, W., et al. (2005). *Gray's anatomy for students.* Philadelphia, PA: Elsevier.

Ellis, H. (2002). *Clinical anatomy: A revision and applied anatomy for clinical students* (10th ed.). Oxford, UK: Blackwell Science.

Evans, R. W., & Taylor, F. R. (2006). Natural or alternative medications for migraine prevention. *Headache, 46*(6), 1012–1018.

Guyton, A. C., & Hall, J. E. (2006). *Textbook of medical physiology* (11th ed.). Philadelphia, PA: Elsevier Saunders.

Haddow, J. E., McClain, M. R., et al. (2007). Urine iodine measurements, creatinine adjustment, and thyroid deficiency in an adult United States population. *Clinical Endocrinology and Metabolism, 92*(3), 1019–1022.

Harris, B. A., Blackmore, C. C., et al. (2008). Clearing the cervical spine in obtunded patients. *Spine, 33*(14), 1547–1553.

Herrick, B. (2008). Cochrane for clinicians: Subclinical hypothyroidism. *American Family Physician, 77*(7), 953–955.

Interdisciplinary Plan. (2007). *Interdisciplinary plan for assessment/reassessment and care planning.* Retrieved from https://hmcweb.washington.edu/ADMIN/APOP/ Administration/5.20.htm

Kaufman, K. D., Girman, C. J., et al. (2008). Progression of hair loss in men with androgenetic alopecia (male pattern hair loss): Long-term (5-year) controlled observational data in placebo-treated patients. *European Journal of Dermatology, 18*(4), 407–411.

Khumalo, N. P., Jessop, S., et al. (2008). Determinants of marginal traction alopecia in African girls and women. *Journal of the American Academy of Dermatology, 59*(3), 432–438.

Kim, N., & Hatton, M. P. (2008). The role of genetics in Graves disease and thyroid orbitopathy. *Seminars in Ophthalmology, 23*(1), 67–72.

Kliegman, R. M, Behrman, R. E., et al. (2007). *Nelson's textbook of pediatrics* (18th ed.). Philadelphia, PA: Elsevier Saunders.

Lafranchi, S. (2008). *Clinical features and detection of congenital hypothyroidism.* Retrieved from http://www.uptodateonline.com. proxy.seattleu.edu/online/content/topic.do? topicKey=pediendo/283 2&selectedTitle=4~150&source= search result

Matfin, G. (2010). Disorders of endocrine control of growth and metabolism. In R. A. Hannon, C. Pooler, et al. (Eds.). *Porth pathophysiology: Concepts of altered health states* (pp. 980–1004). Philadelphia, PA: Wolters Kluwer Health/ Lippincott Williams & Wilkins.

Moorhead, S., Johnson, M., et al. (2007). *Nursing outcomes classification (NOC)* (4th ed.). Philadelphia, PA: Mosby.

Mosby's medical nursing, and allied health dictionary (6th ed.). (2002). St. Louis, MO: Mosby.

National Cancer Institute. (2008). *Head and Neck Cancers: Questions and Answers.* Retrieved from http://www.cancer.gov/cancertopics/ factsheet/Sites-Types/head-and-neck

Nayak, P., & Hodak, S. P. (2007). Hyperthyroidism. *Endocrinology and Metabolism Clinics of North America, 36*(3), 617–656.

North American Nursing Diagnosis Association-International. (2009). *Nursing diagnoses, 2009–2011 edition: Definitions and classifications (NANDA-I NURSING DIAGNOSIS).* West Sussex, UK: John Wiley & Sons.

Public Health Agency of Canada. (2006). *Screening for congenital hypthyroidism.* Retrieved from www.phac-aspc.gc.ca/publicat/ clinic-clinique/pdf/s2c18e.pdf

Peeters, R. P. (2008). Thyroid hormones and aging. *Hormones, 7*(1), 28–35.

Piatt, J. H. (2005). Detected and overlooked cervical spine injury among comatose trauma patients: From the Pennsylvania Trauma Outcomes Study. *Neurosurgery Focus, 19*(4), E6.

Roach, S. Roddick, P., et al. (2010). The head and neck. In T. C. Stephen, D. L. Skillen, R. A. Day, & L. S., Bickley (Eds.). *Canadian Bates' guide to health assessment for nurses* (1st ed., pp. 279–298). Philadephia, PA: Wolters Kluwer Health/ Lippincott, Williams, & Wilkins

Rubenstein, S. M., & van Tulder, M. (2008). A best-evidence review of diagnostic procedures for neck and low-back pain. *Best Practice and Research: Clinical Rheumatolology, 22*(3), 471–482.

Siraj, E. S. (2008). Update on the diagnosis and treatment of hyperthyroidism. *Journal of Clinical Outcomes Management, 15*(6), 298–307.

Smith, R.V. (2008). *Tumors of the head and neck.* Retrieved from http://www.merck.com/mmpe/sec08/ch093/ch093a.htm

Sobri, M. S., Lamont, A. C., et al. (2003). Red flags in patients presenting with headache: Clinical indications for neuroimaging. *British Journal of Radiololgy, 76*(908), 532–535.

Swartz, M. H. (2006). *Textbook of physical diagnosis: History and examination* (5th ed.). Philadelphia, PA: Elsevier Saunders.

Uphold, C. R., & Graham, M. V. (2003). *Clinical guidelines in family practice* (4th ed.). Gainesville, FL: Barmarrae Books.

> *The Canadian Jensen's Nursing Health Assessment suite offers these additional resources to enhance learning and facilitate understanding of this chapter:*
>
> - thePoint on line resource, http//thepoint.lww.com/Stephen1E
> - *Laboratory Manual for Canadian Jensen's Nursing Health Assessment: A Best Practice Approach*

> ⚠ **Table 14-2   Head and Neck Conditions More Common in Childhood**

Hydrocephalus

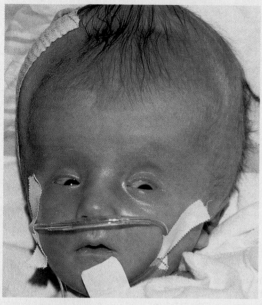

An increased collection of cerebrospinal fluid in the ventricles of the brain causes enlargement of the cranium. Infants with hydrocephalus may have separation of the cranial sutures, bulging fontanels, and dilated veins across the scalp.

Fetal Alcohol Syndrome (FAS)

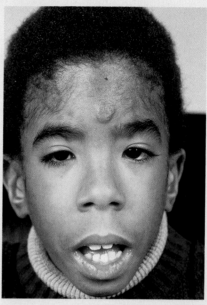

Developmental delays and congenital abnormalities are associated with maternal intake of alcohol during pregnancy. Physical manifestations include microcephaly, flattened cheekbones, small eyes, and a flattened upper lip. Children with FAS have multiple developmental and learning disabilities.

Down's Syndrome (Trisomy 21)

This congenital condition results from either an extra chromosome 21 or translocation of chromosome 14 or 15 with 21 or 22. Manifestations in the head and neck region include microcephaly, a flattened occipital bone, slanted small eyes, a depressed nasal bridge, low-set ears, and a protruding tongue.

Cretinism (Congenital Hypothyroidism)

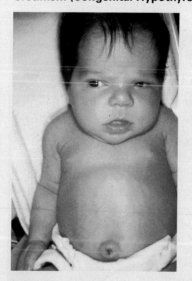

Affected infants have puffy facial features and often a larger tongue. This syndrome is more common in parts of the world where diets are deficient in iodine.

(table continues on page 348)

Craniocytosis

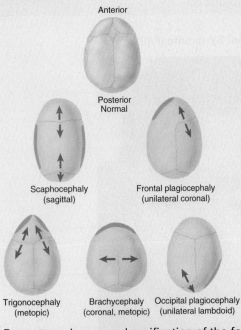

Premature closure and ossification of the fontanels results in skull deformities and microcephaly. Early diagnosis and surgical correction minimize malformations.

Torticollis

Congenital or acquired contraction of the sternomastoid muscle causes the patient to incline the head to one side. Range of motion of the head and neck is decreased.

Table 14-3   **Head and Neck Conditions More Common in Adults**

Acromegaly

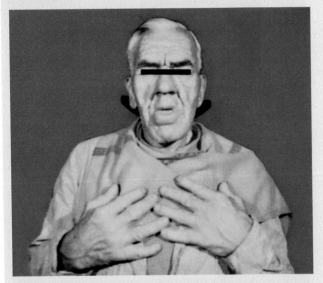

Overproduction of growth hormone in adults results in thickening of the skin, subcutaneous tissue, and facial bones and coarsening of facial features (see also Chapter 6).

Bell's Palsy

Paralysis, usually unilateral, of the facial nerve (CN VII) can be transient or permanent. Causes include trauma, compression, and infection.

Cushing's Syndrome

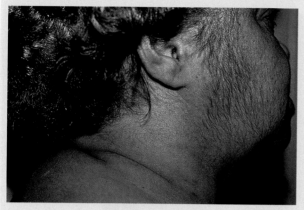

Excessive production of exogenous ACTH results in a round "moon" facies, fat deposits at the nape of the neck, "buffalo hump," and sometimes a velvety discolouration around the neck (*acanthosis nigra*).

Parkinson's Disease

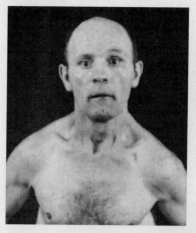

With this degenerative neurologic disease, patients present with a mask-like facial appearance, rigid muscles, diminished reflexes, and a shuffling gait.

Cerebral Vascular Accident (CVA/Stroke)

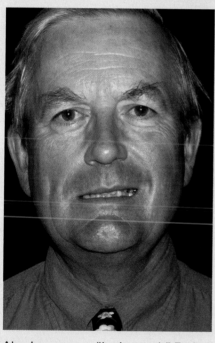

Also known as a "brain attack." Embolism, hemorrhage, or vasospasm in the brain results in ischemia of surrounding tissue and neurologic damage. Symptoms depend on the part of the brain affected.

Scleroderma

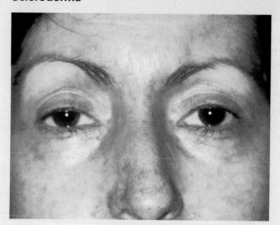

Hardening of the skin usually is noted first in the hands and face. Skin becomes firm and loses mobility, seemingly fixed to underlying tissues. Facial scleroderma presents with shiny taut immobile skin, which may make it difficult for patients to speak, chew, or even swallow. It can affect other organs and tissues.

(table continues on page 350)

Goiter

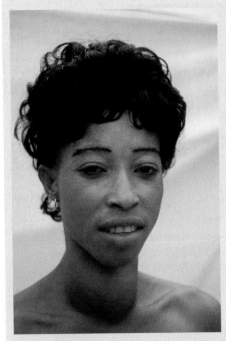

Enlarged thyroid gland can be associated with hyperthyroidism, hypothyroidism, or healthy thyroid function. Enlargement can compress other structures in the neck, making surgical removal necessary. After thyroidectomy patients must be treated with exogenous thyroid hormone for the rest of their lives.

Myxedema

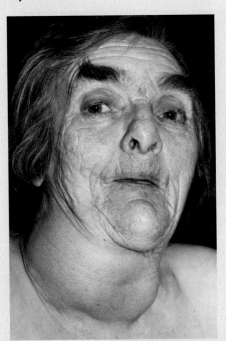

With severe hypothyroidism, patients present with periorbital swelling and edema of the face, hands, and feet. These patients must be identified and treated quickly and chronically with exogenous thyroid hormone.

Eyes Assessment

Learning Objectives

1 Identify common landmarks of the eye. Relate periorbital landmarks to eye structures.

2 Demonstrate knowledge of anatomy and physiology of the eye.

3 Identify important topics for health promotion and risk reduction related to the eye.

4 Collect subjective data related to the eye.

5 Collect objective data related to the eye using physical examination techniques.

6 Identify expected and unexpected findings related to the eye.

7 Analyze subjective and objective data from assessment of the eye and consider initial interventions.

8 Document and communicate data from the eye assessment using appropriate terminology and principles of recording.

9 Consider age, condition, gender, and culture of the patient to individualize the eye assessment.

10 Identify nursing diagnoses and initiate a plan of care based on findings from the eye assessment.

*M*r. Ed Harris, a 61-year-old African Canadian man, is in an adult medicine clinic for a routine physical examination. His temperature is 37°C, pulse 86 beats/min and regular, respirations 16 breaths/min, and blood pressure 118/68 (right arm, sitting). Upon reviewing documentation from his last annual assessment, the nurse notes that Mr. Harris takes captopril (Apo-Capto), 50 mg twice/d for his blood pressure and rosuvastin calcium (Crestor), 20 mg/d to lower his cholesterol. The patient previously worked as a janitor for the school system and now is a school bus driver. He has a 5-year history of glaucoma, for which he uses travoprost (Travatan Z), 0.004% eye drops, 1 drop in each eye at bedtime. Today, he states that his vision seems worse than usual.

You will gain more information about Mr. Harris as you progress through this chapter. As you study the content and features, consider Mr. Harris's case and the importance of patients seeking care for primary prevention. Begin thinking about the following points:

- What routine assessments should the nurse make related to the patient's eye health?
- What additional assessments should the nurse make based on the patient's reports of decreased vision?

This chapter includes a review of the anatomy and physiology pertinent to ocular and visual function, along with key variations in eye assessment across lifespan and among different ethnic groups. It explores subjective data collection for eye health, including assessment of risk factors and focused history related to common symptoms. Content on objective data collection includes correct techniques for assessing vision, ocular movements, the external eye, and exterior and interior ocular structures; expected and unexpected visual and ocular findings; and appropriate documentation. Tests of visual acuity are part of screening during the complete physical examination and ongoing assessments for patients with identified ocular and visual concerns or diseases. Although challenging, ocular and retinal assessments provide information that can assist with accurate diagnosis and early interventions leading to better patient outcomes.

Anatomy and Physiology Overview

The *eye* is the sensory organ for sight. The orbital socket of the skull protects the complex internal structures of the eye (see Chapter 14); only the anterior portion of the eye is visible.

The eye is small, with an approximate diameter of 2.5 cm. It takes in information in the form of light, which internal structures then analyze and interpret to produce shapes, colours, and objects.

Extraocular Structures

The external (extraocular) structures of the eye provide support and protection (Fig. 15-1). The **eyelids** are loose mobile folds of skin that cover the eye, protect it from foreign bodies, regulate light entrance, and distribute tears. The **palpebral fissure** is the almond-shaped open space between the eyelids. The lid margins approximate completely when the palpebral fissure is closed and the upper eyelid covers the upper portion of the iris. The lower eyelid's margin is at the **limbus**, which is the border between the cornea and sclera.

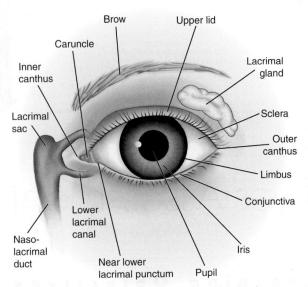

Figure 15-2 Structures of the eye and lacrimal apparatus.

The **conjunctiva** is a thin mucous membrane that lines the inner eyelids (palpebral conjunctivae) and also covers the sclera (bulbar conjunctivae). The **lacrimal apparatus**, which consists of the lacrimal gland, punctum, lacramal sac, and nasolacrimal duct, protects and lubricates the cornea and conjunctiva by producing and draining tears (Fig. 15-2).

Extraocular Muscle Function

The six extraocular muscles control eye movement and hold the eye in place in the socket. These muscles coordinate their actions to produce vision within both eyes (Fig. 15-3). Proper functioning of these muscles determines expected alignment or position of the eye. The muscles and their functions are as follows:

- **Superior rectus:** elevates the eye upward and adducts (toward the nose) and rotates the eye medially (inward)
- **Inferior rectus:** rotates the eye downward and adducts and rotates the eye medially

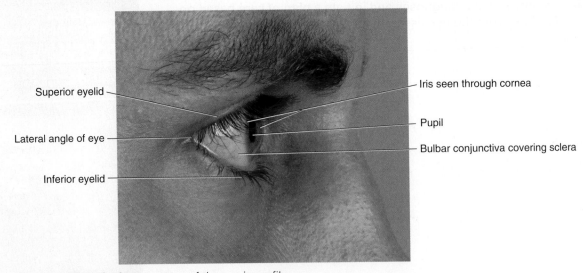

Figure 15-1 Surface anatomy of the eye in profile.

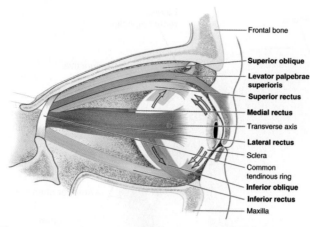

Figure 15-3 The extraocular muscles.

Frontal bone
Superior oblique
Levator palpebrae superioris
Superior rectus
Medial rectus
Transverse axis
Lateral rectus
Sclera
Common tendinous ring
Inferior oblique
Inferior rectus
Maxilla

- **Lateral rectus:** moves the eye laterally (toward the temple)
- **Medial rectus:** moves the eye medially
- **Superior oblique:** turns the eye downward and abducts (toward the temple) and rotates the eye laterally
- **Inferior oblique:** turns the eye upward and abducts and turns the eye laterally.

The oculomotor (CN III), trochlear (CN IV), and abducens (CN VI) nerves innervate and control the motor nerve activities of the eye (Table 15-1).

The extraocular muscles oppose one another, much like the muscles surrounding joints of the skeleton. One muscle's contraction causes the relaxation of the corresponding muscle.

Intraocular Structures

The internal (intraocular) structures are directly involved with vision. The eye itself contains three layers of tissue:

1. An outer fibrous layer contains the sclera and cornea.

2. A vascular middle layer is composed of the iris, ciliary body, and choroids.

3. An inner neural layer is the retina.

The white **sclera** helps to maintain the size and shape of the eye. The transparent and avascular **cornea** allows light rays to enter the eye. It is highly sensitive to touch. The **iris** regulates the amount of light that enters the **pupil**. The colour of the eye depends on the type and amount of pigment in the smooth muscles of the iris. The **pupil** dilates and constricts to permit light to enter the eye. Pupil size can range from 2 to 5 mm. The **lens**, which sits directly behind the pupil, refracts and focuses light on the retina. The **ciliary body** produces aqueous humor and contains the muscle that controls the shape of the lens. The **choroids**, which cover the recessed portion of the eye, are a network of blood vessels to the eye (Fig. 15-4).

The interior eye has three chambers: anterior, posterior, and vitreous. The **anterior chamber**, the space between the cornea and the anterior portions of the iris and lens, contains a clear liquid called aqueous humor. The aqueous humor is produced by the ciliary body and circulates from the posterior chamber through the pupil to the anterior chamber and drains through the **canal of Schlemm** via the trabecular meshwork. The circulatory pattern maintains a relatively constant pressure in the eye. The **posterior chamber** is a small loculated region between the posterior iris muscle and the ligament of the lens and ciliary processes. The largest chamber, the **vitreous chamber**, is adjacent to the inner retinal layer and lens. This chamber is filled with vitreous humor, a gel-like substance that holds the retina in place and maintains the shape of the eye.

The **retina**, which is the innermost layer of the eye, receives and transmits visual stimuli to the brain for processing. The retinal structures, the posterior part of the eye often referred to as the fundus, are best viewed using an ophthalmoscope. The retina contains photoreceptors (rods and cones) that make vision possible. The rods on the outer edge of the retina are primarily responsible for vision in low light and produce

Muscle	Cranial Nerve Innervation	Insertion	Action	
			Medial (Toward Nose)	Lateral (Toward Temple)
Superior rectus	CN III	Anterior, superior surface	Elevation, adduction	
Inferior rectus	CN III	Anterior, inferior surface	Depression, abduction	
Medial rectus	CN III	Anterior, medial surface	Adduction	
Lateral rectus	CN VI	Anterior, lateral surface		Abduction
Superior oblique	CN IV	Posterior, superior, lateral surface		Depression, abduction
Inferior oblique	CN III	Posterior, inferior, lateral surface		Elevation, abduction

Table 15-1   **Eye Muscles**

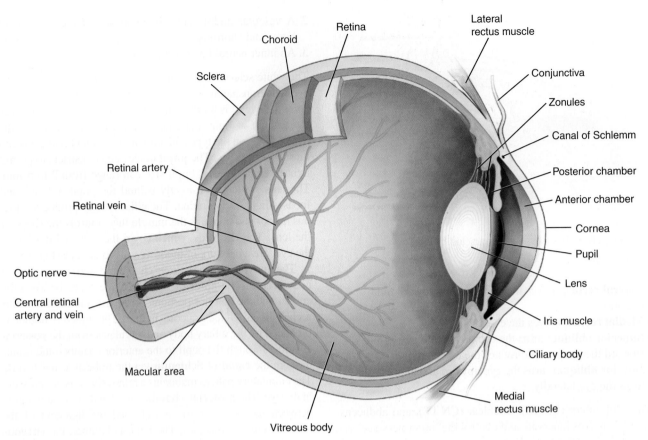

Figure 15-4 Intraocular structures.

images of varying shades of black and white. The cones, concentrated centrally, are adapted to bright light and produce colour images with sharp, fine details.

The **optic disc**, a well-defined round or oval area, is the location where the optic nerve innervates the eye. The **macula**, lateral to the optic disc, is the area with the greatest concentration of cones.

Vision

The light rays from a viewed object enter the cornea and are refracted on to the central fovea (an area on the macula). The stimulus is then inverted, reversed, and focused on the retina, which sends the stimulus through the visual pathway to the brain where the image is interpreted in its original form. The **neural pathway** consists of the optic nerves, optic chiasm, and optic tracts that continue into the optic region of the cerebral cortex. The neural pathway is part of the central nervous system (Fig. 15-5).

🔺 Lifespan Considerations

Women Who Are Pregnant

The most common eye condition during pregnancy is dry eyes, which result from decreased circulation within the conjuctival capillaries. The cornea may thicken, making use of contact lenses uncomfortable. The corneal curvature also increases in some women, with subsequent loss of accommodation. The curvature of the cornea increases, affecting

visual accommodation among some women. Visual field changes may occur, possibly related to the pituitary gland affecting the optic nerve. The increased blood viscosity due to gestational diabetes has the capacity to alter the visual acuity by damaging the microvascular structures within the eye.

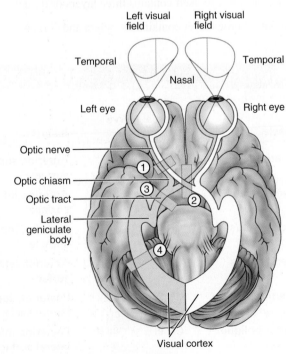

Figure 15-5 The neural pathway.

Decreased intraocular pressure is significant if the woman has glaucoma; adjustment of medications may be necessary. Melasma (Chloasma), or increased pigmentation around the eyes, is often present due to increased prenatal progesterone levels (Somami, Bhatti, et al., 2008).

Newborns and Infants

At birth, the visual system is the least mature compared to other sensory systems. Development progresses rapidly over the first 6 months and reaches adult level by 4 to 5 years. Newborns are sensitive to light and often keep their eyes closed for long periods. They have a limited ability to focus, but by 3 months of age they can follow objects. It is thought that visual acuity is sharpest at the distance from the infant to the mother's face. The pupils are reactive to light, the blink reflex is intact, and the corneal reflex is easily stimulated. Reflex tearing is present at birth, while emotional tearing develops by 3 months (Lowdermilk & Perry, 2007).

Children and Adolescents

It is estimated that in Canada 60% of children with reading difficulties have undetected or uncorrected vision problems (National Coalition for Vision Health, 2011). Visual acuity in toddlers ranges from 20/20 to 20/40. Depth perception develops throughout childhood. Vision changes, such as near-sightedness, are common in adolescents (Hockenberry & Wilson, 2007).

Older Adults

Older adults have changes both in eye structure and vision. Eyelids may droop and become wrinkled from loss of skin elasticity, and the eyes sit deeper in the orbits due to the loss of subcutaneous fat. Eyebrows become thinner, and the outer thirds of the brows may be absent. Conjunctivae are thinner and may appear yellowish from decreased perfusion. The iris may have an irregular pigmentation. Tearing decreases as a result of loss of fatty tissue in the lacrimal apparatus. Vision may decline because the pupil is smaller, there is loss of accommodation, decreased night vision, and decreased depth perception. The lens enlarges and transparency decreases, making vision less acute (Mackin, Mangin, et al., 2003).

🌐 Cultural Considerations

Eye colour differs among people of various genetic backgrounds, with lighter eyes more prevalent in more Northern countries. Genetic background also influences the diameters of eyelids and eyebrows (Price, Gupta, et al., 2009).

Acute Assessment

Two hundred Canadian workers suffer an eye injury each day (National Coalition for Vision Health, 2011). Acute assessment of the eye first involves identifying the concern and then determining if that concern requires immediate medical attention. In the case of emergent eye trauma or injury, time delay is potentially threatening to eye function. All sudden changes in vision such as blurring, double vision, or loss of vision require emergency assessment and intervention.

Visual acuity is often described as being the "vital sign" for the eye. All person with an eye injury or eye concern should have their visual acuity assessed as a primary mode for determining urgency for specialized eye care. In addition to determining visual acuity, a gradual vision loss, while significant, does not usually require an emergent referral. Further, ascertaining the source of the trauma/injury (eg, mechanical, thermal, radiant, chemical, electrical, or kinetic) helps determine whether the condition is emergent (immediate medical attention), urgent (medical attention within few hours), or nonurgent (appointment as soon as possible). Rapid assessment of the eye involves assessing for foreign bodies, lacerations, or hyphema (blood in the eye), testing extraocular movements, and examining the optic disc.

> ⚠ SAFETY ALERT 15-1
> Trauma that involves a penetrating injury or suspected fracture of the orbital bone requires an emergent referral. If the patient describes loss of vision, it is critical to ascertain a timeline of vision loss. Sudden loss of vision requires an emergent referral to an eye care specialist.

Subjective Data Collection

Subjective data collection begins with the health history, continues with questions about specific eye conditions, and ends with detailed collection of information concerning topics for health promotion. Health promotion focuses on prevention of age-related eye conditions and minimizing occupational or recreational risk factors contributing to eye injury.

Assessment of Risk Factors

Eye and vision conditions are common; 57% of Canadian adults report vision issues requiring the use of corrective lenses (Perruccio, Badley, et al., 2010). Some facts about eye concerns include the following:

- The prevalence of absolute vision loss in Canada is expected to increase from 2.5% in 2007 to 4.0% in 2032 (Canadian National Institute for the Blind, 2007 & The Canadian Ophthalmological Society, 2007).
- Leading causes of new cases of blindness are age-related macular degeneration (AMD), glaucoma, diabetic retinopathy, cataracts, and optic nerve atrophy.
- Eighty-eight percent of all computer users develop eye issues during, and related to, computer use.
- One in four children has an undetected vision concern that can interfere with learning.

The nurse needs to assess for risk factors related to eye issues, including family history, trauma, illnesses, and occupational hazards.

Questions to Assess History and Risk Factors	Rationale

Current Concerns
Tell me about any concerns you have with your eyes?

This general question opens discussion.

Personal History
Eye conditions
- Do you have a history of cataracts? Glaucoma? High blood pressure? Diabetes? Thyroid conditions?
- Have you ever injured your eye?

The focus is conditions that could affect vision and eye function.

Eye surgery
- Have you ever had any surgery on your eye(s)?
- Have you ever had any facial surgery?
- Have you ever had a cataract removed, lens implant, or LASIK?

The focus is eye or facial surgeries, which can change the landscape of eye structures.

Medications
Do you use artificial tears? Decongestants? Corticosteroids? Antihistamines? Prescribed eye drops?

Certain medications affect the eye and its functioning. Careful assessment is necessary.

Family History
Do any family members have eye conditions such as myopia, hyperopia, strabismus, colour blindness, cataracts, glaucoma, retinitis pigmentosa, or retinoblastoma?

Certain conditions and diseases that affect vision have a genetic link, which increases risk for patients. *Glaucoma* in a first-degree relative increases the patient's risk for the same condition two to three times (Jacobs, Trobe, et al., 2009).

Risk Factors
Allergies
- Do you have any allergies?
- Are they seasonal?
- Are you sensitive to pollen? Or animal dander? These allergies can cause watery and itchy eyes?
- Have you ever had an allergic reaction with any swelling around the eyes?

The body's response to allergens affects not only the respiratory system, but also the eyes through excessive tearing, allergic conjunctivitis, and itching.
Previous occurrences increase risk of an angioedema-type allergic response with repeat exposure.

Exposure to viruses.
- Were you exposed to rubella in the womb? Were you diagnosed with congenital syphilis?

Fetal exposure to rubella can cause neonatal blindness secondary to cataracts. Congenital syphilis can also cause neonatal blindness.

Environmental exposure
- At work, are you exposed to any toxins? Chemicals? Infections? Or allergens?
- How would you rate your current stress level: Low? Moderate? High?

Many activities can increase risk for eye injury, infections, or trauma. Stress has been linked with decreased vision.

Eye health
- When was your last eye examination?
- Were you screened for glaucoma?

The nurse needs to determine how the patient cares for the health of the eyes.

Corrective prescriptions
- Do you wear glasses? And/or contacts?
- Do you wear contacts only for the recommended time frame?
- How do you care for your contacts?
- How often do you change your contacts?

These questions address behaviours to reduce the number of people with uncorrected refractive errors. The nurse can discuss the reason for not wearing prescribed glasses or contacts and care of contacts to prevent injuries to the eye.

Questions to Assess History and Risk	Rationale
Eye protection • Are you exposed to any hazards that could affect your eyes? • Do you wear goggles or a face shield when you play sports? Do home projects? Mow the lawn? • Do you wear your protective eyewear 100% of the time?	Questions address activities to reduce injuries to the eyes of people whose occupation or leisure activities put them at risk.
Nutritional status. Do you generally eat a well-balanced diet?	Assess the diet for any vitamin deficiencies that could affect the eyes.

Risk Assessment and Health Promotion

Topics for Health Promotion

- Diabetes mellitus
- Prevention of eye injury
- Reduction of risk factors
- Changes in vision

Diabetes mellitus increases risks for eye conditions, including diabetic retinopathy, cataracts, and glaucoma. Sunlight exposure also increases risks, so use of sunglasses is important, especially if the patient lives in a sunny climate. Poor diet has been linked to eye disorders. Foods that promote eye health include deep-water fish, fruits, and vegetables (eg, carrots, spinach). Because the lens of the eye has no blood supply, staying well hydrated keeps the lens supple and moist.

Focused Health History Related to Common Symptoms

In assessing the patient's health history, it is important to immediately determine if an eye concern results from trauma, is related to changes in vision, or involves vision symptoms (see Box 15-1). Failure to obtain an accurate and complete history can lead to loss of sight.

Common Symptoms

- Eye pain
- Trauma or surgery
- Vision change
- Blind spots, floaters, or halos
- Discharge, redness, or inflammation
- Sensitivity to light
- Change in activities of daily living (ADLs)

BOX 15-1 EXAMPLE OF QUESTIONS FOR SYMPTOM/SIGN ANALYSIS— BLURRED VISION

- "When you look at something, what areas are blurry?" "Is the blurred vision in both eyes?" "Is the blurred vision in your entire field of vision?" "Is one part of your vision blurry?" "Is the same part of your vision blurry or does it change?" *(Location/radiating)*
- "Describe what the blurred vision is like." *(Quality)*
- "Describe how much blurriness you have." "Can you see large objects?" "Can you see large printed letters?" *(Severity)*
- "When did your blurred vision start?" "Did it start suddenly or gradually?" *(Onset)*
- "Has your vision been consistently blurry ever since the problem started?" *(Duration)*
- "Have there been times when your vision seemed more blurry? Or less blurry?" *(Constancy)*
- "Is there a time of day that it (blurred vision) seems worse? Or better?" *(Time of day/month/year)*
- "What makes it (blurred vision) worse?" *(Aggravating factors)*
- "What makes it (blurred vision) better?" *(Alleviating factors)*
- "What other symptoms have you noticed?" *(Associated symptoms)*
- "Have you recently changed anything in your home or office?" "Have you had any recent injuries to your eyes or head?" "Have your eyes been exposed to any chemicals or other substances?" "How much stress is in your life right now?" *(Environmental factors)*
- "Tell me how this is affecting your life." *(Significance to patient)*
- "What do you think is happening?" *(Patient perspective)*

Adapted from Stephen, T. C., & Bickley, L. S. (2010). The eyes. In T. C. Stephen, D. L. Skillen, R. A. Day, & L. S. Bickley (Eds.). *Canadian Bates' guide to health assessment for nurses.* (p. 299). Philadelphia, PA: Wolters Kluwer Health/Lippincott Williams & Wilkins.

Examples of Questions to Assess Symptoms/Signs	Rationale/Unexpected Findings
Pain Do you have any eye pain or discomfort?(Further characterize pain using the 10 characteristics of a sign/symptom located in Chapter 3.)	Pain in the eye is never expected and should always be further explored. See Chapter 7.
Trauma or Surgery Is your eye concern related to trauma or injury? If so • How was the injury/trauma sustained? • Was this a high-velocity injury? • Was this a blunt force trauma?	High-velocity injuries are typically penetrating. Blunt-force trauma often results in fracture of the orbit.
Visual Change Have you noticed any recent changes in your vision? • Describe the visual change • When did the change begin? • Was onset sudden? Or gradual? • Have you noticed any double vision?	If the patient describes loss of vision, it is critical to ascertain a timeline. Sudden vision loss requires an emergent referral.
Blind Spots, Floaters, or Halos • Have you noticed any blind spots in your vision? • Any difficulty seeing at night? • Do you see any spots (floaters)? • Do you have any associated symptoms (eg, flashing lights? Halos/rainbows around lights)?	Loss of night vision is associated with *optic atrophy, glaucoma*, and *vitamin A deficiency*. Floaters (translucent specks that drift across the visual field) are common in people older than 40 years and near-sighted patients. No additional follow-up is needed. Halos/rainbows around lights suggests possible glaucoma.
Discharge • Are you having any eye discharge? • Is there any pain? Grittiness? Redness? Or discharge associated? • Are one or both eyes affected? • Have you noticed any excessive tearing? Dryness? Or itching?	Discharge is associated with inflammation or infection.
Change in Activities of Daily Living How has your eye condition (eg, diplopia, dry eyes) affected your ability to perform activities of daily living (ADLs)?	Assess functional limitations.

Documentation of Expected Findings

Denies pain, trauma, visual changes, blind spots, floaters, halos, and discharge. No changes in ability to perform activities of daily living (ADLs).

Lifespan Considerations

Additional Questions	Rationale/Unexpected Findings
Women Who Are Pregnant	
Have you noticed any changes in your visual acuity?	Hormonal fluctuations can cause refractive changes, which are typically minor, but should be discussed with a health professional.
Have you had any eye dryness?	Dry eyes during pregnancy are usually temporary and resolve after childbirth.
Newborns, Infants, and Children	
Have you noticed tears when your baby cries?	Infants begin making tears at approximately 2 weeks old. Lack of tear production is a sign of blockages in the lacrimal apparatus.
Does your baby have red, dry, or irritated eyes?	Such findings may indicate lacrimal apparatus blockage or *conjunctivitis* (ophthalmia neonatorum).
Are you concerned your child may have vision issues? What worries you?	Parents and immediate family members often notice things that do not seem to fit within expected parameters.
Have you noticed any concerns or changes in the white of the eye? Pupils? Iris? Or lashes?	Parents and immediate family often notice things that do not seem to fit the range of expected appearance.
Have you noticed that your child is sensitive to light? If yes, is it accompanied by nausea/vomiting, dizziness, or signs/reports of headache?	These may be symptoms of other visual or eye issues.
Have you noticed your child exhibiting any of the following: • Poking at eyes? Rubbing frequently? • Poor eye contact? • Turning of one eye? • Inaccuracy in reaching for an item of interest?	These could be symptoms of allergies, *blepharitis*, dry eyes, or visual field issues. Visual impairment could cause poor eye contact (eg, amblyopia, strabismus). This may indicate a visual refractive error.
Has your child been diagnosed with hearing difficulty?	Infants with hearing issues are at increased risk for visual impairments.
Older Adults	
Do you have a history of diabetes? Glaucoma? High blood pressure?	Aging increases risks for visual complications related to other chronic diseases that affect blood vessels in the retina and fluid in the eye (Miller, 2008).
Have you noticed any tunnelling of your visual field?	This is a symptom of *macular degeneration*.
When was the last time you had your eyes checked?	This provides the nurse with an opportunity to promote eye health.
Do you have any trouble managing your usual activities because of vision changes? Have you stopped doing any activities because of vision changes?	It is important to focus on any visual impairment and how the patient functions with any visual changes.
When did you last have a test for glaucoma (tonometry)?	Older adults are at increased risk; glaucoma screening should be done every year (CNIB, 2007).
Have you ever tripped or fallen because of changes in your vision?	This question assesses awareness and presence of visual impairments.

Mr. Harris, introduced at the beginning of this chapter, is in the clinic for follow-up care related to high blood pressure, high cholesterol, and glaucoma. The following conversation provides an example of a therapeutic dialogue.

Nurse: I'm glad that you came back for your visit today. It's good to see you.

Mr. Harris: Thanks. I am really trying to take better care of myself.

Nurse: I noticed that your blood pressure is under good control.

Mr. Harris: Yes, I'm really trying to make sure to eat right, get some exercise, and take my medicine. I have two beautiful grandkids that I'm helping to raise. (pauses) I'm worried about my eyesight. I have glaucoma, and I can't see as well as I used to. I'm worried that I'll go blind and won't be able to help with my grandkids.

Nurse: You've had glaucoma for about 5 years now, is that correct?

Mr. Harris: Yes. The Nurse Practitioner gave me some drops for it.

Nurse: Can you take them as prescribed?

Mr. Harris: Well, I ran out a bit ago and had to wait a few days until the first of the month, but I have them now.

Critical Thinking Challenge

- How might nonverbal communication influence this therapeutic relationship?
- Within a culturally competent framework, how might the nurse address Mr. Harris's concern regarding being unable to help with his grandchildren?
- How might the nurse respond to Mr. Harris's not from taking his eye drops as prescribed?

Objective Data Collection

A comprehensive physical examination of the eye involves assessment of visual acuity, the external eye, eye muscle function, external ocular structures (including pupil reflexes), and internal ocular structures. The external eyes and external ocular structures are examined through inspection and palpation. The interior ocular structures are inspected with an instrument called an *ophthalmoscope*. Assessment of visual acuity, visual fields, and the retina helps you evaluate not only the function of the eye itself, but also part of the central nervous system. As you proceed with inspection and palpation of the eye you will assess for function of the sensory and motor function of four cranial nerves (Table 15-3). As you progress through the assessment, remember not only the sensory aspects of vision but also the motor function of the eyes. Identifying anatomical landmarks of the external eye assists nurses to accurately document findings.

Promoting Patient Comfort, Safety, and Dignity

Before the examination begins, perform hand hygiene. If you are using hand gel, be sure that your hands are completely dry

Equipment

Assemble the following equipment:

- Penlight
- Cotton wisps and cotton-tipped applicators
- Ophthalmoscope

- Snellen, Allen, or Jaeger eye charts
- Disposable gloves
- Eye covers or opaque cards for individual eye testing
- Ishihara plates (optional for testing colour vision)

before touching the patient's eye. If there is a possibility of an infection, make sure to avoid cross-contamination by wearing gloves, washing your hands, and cleaning all equipment before examining each eye. Always examine the infected eye last. (See Table 15-2.)

Common and Advanced Techniques

Routine eye assessment includes the most important and common assessment techniques performed to screen for disorders. Nurses may add specialty or advanced assessment techniques if concerns exist over a specific finding.

Table 15-2	Cranial Nerves Associated with the Eyes	
Cranial Nerve	**Name of Cranial Nerve**	**Assessment of Cranial Nerve**
II	Optic nerve	• Visual acuity • Visual fields • Funduscopic examination
III	Oculomotor	• Cardinal directions • Eyelid inspection • Pupil reaction (direct/consensual/accommodation)
IV	Trochlear	• Cardinal directions
VI	Abducens	• Cardinal directions

Assessment of Visual Acuity

Visual acuity tests include testing for distance vision, near vision, peripheral vision, and colour vision. This first step in an eye assessment is important to perform before any type of solution is used to dilate the pupil.

Assessment of Visual Fields

The *visual field* refers to what in the environment is visible when the eye fixates on a stationary object. Visual injury or illness may cause defects in the expected full visual field. The confrontation test is used to screen for visual field dysfunction, which may not be apparent to the nurse. When evaluating for visual field dysfunction, the visual field is divided into four quadrants—inferior, superior, left, and right.

Visual field testing in the clinic setting can be performed without computerized automated perimetry; it is a gross screening test of peripheral vision. The nurse can use either static or kinetic techniques.

The static test can help the nurse detect gross differences in all four quadrants of the visual field. The nurse does not move the fingers but presents one to four fingers in each quadrant.

Technique and Expected Findings

Distance Vision

Assess visual acuity by having the patient read the Snellen or Allen Chart (based on developmental age and/or reading ability). With the Snellen's test, measure and place a mark or piece of masking tape on the floor 20 ft (6.1 m) from the chart (Fig. 15-6). With the Allen test, place the mark or piece of masking tape on the floor 15 ft (4.5 m) from the chart. The area should be well lit, and the test should be at the patient's eye level.

A   **B**

Figure 15-6 Assessing distance vision. **A.** The Snellen chart. **B.** The patient reads the letters of the Snellen chart from 20 ft (6.1 m) away.

Give the patient an opaque card or eye cover to cover one eye at a time during the assessment. Stand by the chart and request that the patient read from the largest to the smallest letters (pictures if using the Allen chart) possible, occluding one eye at a time. If the patient wears glasses/contacts they should remain on; only reading glasses should be removed for this assessment.

Unexpected Findings

Unexpected findings include leaning forward, squinting, hesitation, misidentification of more than three of seven numbers, or more than a two-line difference between eyes. In Canada, an individual is considered legally blind when the vision in the better eye, corrected by glasses, is 20/200 or less. Refer to Table 15-6.

(text continues on page 362)

Acuity for distance vision is documented in two numbers, with reference to what a person with ideal vision sees 20 ft from the test. Someone with "20/20" (ideal) vision can read at 20 ft what one can expect to read at 20 ft. On top, mark the distance in feet the patient was from the test (eg, 20). On bottom, document the number under the smallest line of letters the patient correctly identified (eg, 40, 200). Also document the number of letters missed and if the patient wore corrective lenses (eg., right eye: 20/30 −2, with glasses). *Index of Refraction (emmetropia) of the eye is 20/20 bilaterally.*

A larger number on the bottom (eg, 20/60) indicates diminished distance vision.

⚠️ *SAFETY ALERT 15-2*

The abbreviations OD (oculus dexter-right eye), OS (oculus sinster-left eye), and OU (oculus uterque-each eye) are no longer used to document eye findings because of the potential for medical-order and medication errors. Instead it is recommended to use right eye, left eye, or both eyes to document findings.

Near Vision

Near vision is usually assessed in patients older than 40 years or younger patients who report difficulty reading. When no Jaeger test (pocket screener) is available, ask the patient to read newsprint (eg, newspaper, magazine).

Instruct the patient to hold the Jaeger chart 14 in (35 cm) from the eye. Request that the person read through the chart to the smallest letters possible, occluding one eye at a time (with corrective lenses on) (Fig. 15-7). *Visual acuity for near vision is 14/14 bilaterally.*

Patients older than 40 years often have a decreased ability to accommodate; therefore, they move the card further away to read it.

Figure 15-7 Assessing near vision with the Jaeger chart.

Colour Vision

Colour vision is assessed using Ishihara cards (Fig. 15-8) or by having the patient identify colour bars on the Snellen chart. *The patient correctly identifies the embedded figures in the Ishihara cards or the colour bars on the Snellen chart.*

The patient who incorrectly identifies the embedded figures or colour bars may have colour blindness.

Figure 15-8 Testing colour vision.

Static Confrontation

Stand approximately 60 to 90 cm (an arm's length) directly in front of the patient. Your eyes and the patient's eyes should be on the same level. Ask the patient to cover the left eye with the palm of the left hand (without putting pressure on the eye). Close your right eye and instruct the patient to look only at your open eye at all times. Present one to four fingers midway between yourself and the patient in each of the four quadrants of the visual field (Fig. 15-9). Ask the patient to report the number of fingers, without looking directly at them. Repeat the test with the other eye. *Patient accurately reports the number of fingers presented in all four quadrants.*

This screening test assumes that the nurse's visual field is intact and serves as the comparison for the patient's test. Reports of an incorrect number of fingers indicate a visual field defect.

Figure 15-9 Performing the static confrontation test.

Kinetic Confrontation

As with static confrontation, your eyes and the patient's eyes must be on the same level. Instruct the patient to say "now" when the fingers first come into view. Wiggle your fingers from a far distal point and move them toward the center of each quadrant (Fig. 15-10). Your fingers should not be immediately visible (except in the inferotemporal quadrant). *Patient sees the fingers at about the same time as the nurse if the peripheral visual field is as expected in that quadrant.*

The patient who sees fingers presented on either side or only on one side may have a hemianopic defect. If the patient sees only from an inferior or superior position, an attitudinal defect is suspected.

⚠ *SAFETY ALERT 15-3*

Defects in any quadrant in either the static or kinetic confrontation test require referral to an optometrist or ophthalmologist for more precise testing.

Figure 15-10 Performing the kinetic confrontation test.

Documentation of Expected Findings

Visual acuity 20/20 bilaterally. Accurately reads newsprint. Identifies colour bars on Snellen chart correctly. Patient sees finger at about 50° superior, 90° temporal, 90° inferior, and 60° nasal.

The static test effectively screens for differences from side-to-side (hemianopias) and inferior and superior (attitudinal).

The kinetic test assesses the gross peripheral boundaries of the patient's visual field. Kinetic technique is performed when the nurse moves an object or fingers from the periphery toward fixation at the point that the patient first becomes aware of the target (Dubois, 2005).

Assessment of Extraocular Muscle Movements

Three basic tests allow examiners to assess the movement of the extraocular muscles: (1) the corneal light reflex (Hirschberg) test, (2) the cover test, and (3) the cardinal directions. They assess movements of the eye in several planes: up

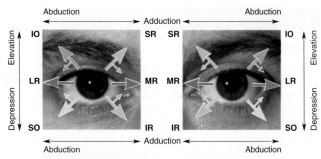

Figure 15-11 Extraocular movements.

and down, side-to-side, and diagonally from right superior to left inferior, and diagonally from left superior to right inferior (Fig. 15-11). The **corneal light reflex** tests for strabismus.

Technique and Expected Findings	Unexpected Findings
Corneal Light Reflex Instruct the patient to stare straight ahead at the bridge of your nose. Stand in front of the patient and shine a penlight at the bridge of the patient's nose. Note where the light reflects on the cornea of each eye (Fig. 15-12). *Light reflection is in exactly the same spot in both eyes.* 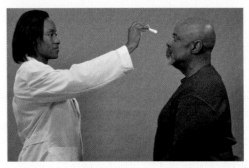 **Figure 15-12** Testing the corneal light reflex.	Unexpected findings indicate improper alignment and appear as asymmetric reflections. Documentation of unexpected findings is facilitated by using the face of the clock as a guide.
Cover Test The cover test, most typically performed on children, assesses ocular alignment. Stand in front of the patient and ask the patient to focus on a near object (bridge of your nose). Place an opaque card or eye cover over one eye; inspect for any movement of the uncovered eye that may indicate refixation of the gaze (Fig. 15-13). Remove the cover and observe the previously covered eye for refixation. Repeat the procedure for the other eye. *Gaze is steady and fixed.*  **Figure 15-13** Performing the cover test.	Any refixation is due to muscle weakness in the covered eye (ie, while covered, the eye drifted into a relaxed position).

Cardinal Directions

Further testing of the extraocular muscles assesses for symmetrical movements of the eyes in all six cardinal directions. Instruct the patient to hold the head steady and to follow the movement of your finger or pen with the eyes. Hold your finger or pen approximately 20 cm from the patient's face. Move slowly through positions 2–6, stopping momentarily in each position, then returning to the center (Fig. 15-14). Proceed clockwise. *Patient's eyes move smoothly and symmetrically in all six cardinal directions.*

Document a deficit by noting which field contains the unexpected finding. Mild nystagmus at the extreme lateral angles is expected; in any other position it is not. See Table 15-7.

Figure 15-14 Assessing the cardinal directions.

Documentation of Expected Response

Alignment symmetrical/corneal light reflex. Gaze fixed and steady. Extraocular movements intact (EOMI).

Stand facing the patient (who is sitting on the examination table or bed). Inspect eyebrows, lashes, and eyelids; note eye shape and symmetry. *Eyebrows vary based on genetic background but show no unexplained hair loss. Lashes curve outward away from the eyes and are distributed evenly along the lid margins. Eyelids open and close completely, with spontaneous blinking every few seconds. Eye shape varies from round to almond but is symmetrical.*

Note general appearance of the eyes. *Eyes are in parallel alignment.*

Eyebrows: unexplained hair loss; with aging, the outer third of the eyebrow thins
Eyelashes: curved inward toward the eye, distributed unevenly along lid margin, or both
Eyelids: incomplete opening or closing; no spontaneous blinking; improper positioning with respect to iris and limbus
Eye shape: asymmetry

Eyes not in parallel alignment require further assessment. **Ptosis**, drooping of the eyelids, is a common finding associated with *stroke* (Fig. 15-15).

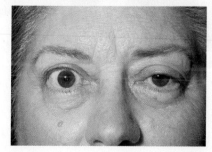

Figure 15-15 Ptosis in a patient following stroke.

(text continues on page 366)

Lacrimal Apparatus

Inspect and palpate the lacrimal apparatus. Identify the puncta, the opening of the lacrimal apparatus at the inner canthus. Gently retract the bottom eyelids to better expose the puncta. Gently press your index finger against the patient's nasolacrimal sac just inside the orbital ring (Fig. 15-16). *Lacrimal apparatus is not enlarged or tender.*

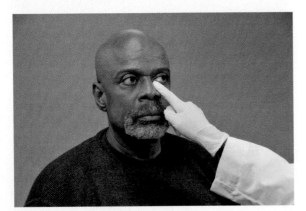

Figure 15-16 Palpating the lacrimal apparatus.

An enlarged lacrimal apparatus is rare. If you palpate an enlarged lacrimal apparatus, evert the eyelid and inspect the gland. Suspect conditions such as *sarcoid disease* and *Sjögren's syndrome* (Fig. 15-17).

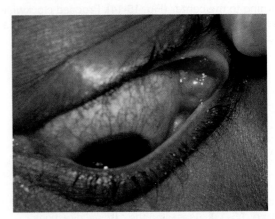

Figure 15-17 Sjögren's syndrome.

Bulbar Conjunctiva

Gently lift the upper eyelid. Instruct the patient to look down and then to the right and left. Note the surface for colour, injection (redness), swelling, exudates, or foreign bodies. Gently retract the lower lid (Fig. 15-18). Instruct the patient to look up and to the right and left. Again note the surface for colour, injection (redness), swelling, exudates, or foreign bodies. *Bulbar conjunctiva is usually transparent with small blood vessels visible.*

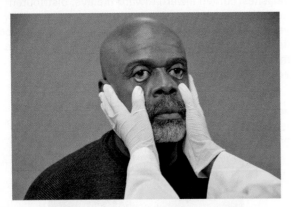

Figure 15-18 Inspecting the bulbar conjunctiva.

Erythema, cobblestone appearance, or both may indicate allergy or infection. Sharply defined bright red blood indicates a *subconjunctival hemorrhage* (Fig. 15-19).

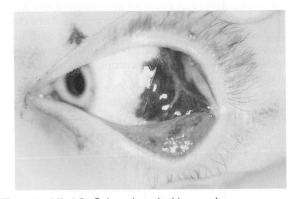

Figure 15-19 Subconjunctival hemorrhage.

A thickening of the conjunctiva from the limbus over the cornea is known as a *pterygium*. Pterygium is most common on the nasal side and occurs most commonly among people exposed to heavy ultraviolet light such as in equatorial regions. If pterygium advances over the pupil, it may interfere with vision (Fig. 15-20)

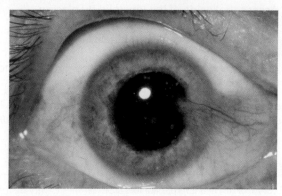

Figure 15-20 Pterygium.

Sclera

During inspection of the bulbar conjunctiva you can also inspect the sclera for colour, exudates, lesions, and foreign bodies. *Sclera is clear, smooth, white, and without exudate, lesions, or foreign bodies.*

Eversion of the Eyelid

Eversion of the eyelid is used in specialized situations. It is used only by advanced clinicians.

1. Grasp the lashes and lid margin gently between your thumb and forefinger.
2. Ask the patient to look down.
3. Pull the eyelid gently down and away from the eye.
4. Place a cotton tip applicator in the indentation between orbit and globe (Fig. 15-21).

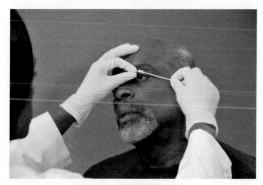

Figure 15-21 Placement of the applicator during eyelid eversion.

5. Pull the lashes and lid margin out and upward.
6. Fold the lid back over the cotton-tipped applicator, exposing the underside of the upper eyelid.
7. Hold the eyelid in this position while you remove the applicator.
8. Assess the underside of the eyelid, inspecting for any foreign bodies, chalazions, and so on.
9. Ask the patient to blink. The eyelid will return to its position.

Unexpected findings include jaundice, bluing, and drainage. Refer to Table 15-7 for further unexpected findings of the external eye.

(text continues on page 368)

10. Assess the inside of the lower lid by placing your thumb or a cotton-tipped applicator on the skin below the lower lid and pressing downward gently.
11. Ask the patient to look upward, to the right, and then to the left.

There are no foreign bodies, chalazions, redness, or injuries bilaterally. Tissue is pink and smooth bilaterally.

When examining the eye for a foreign body, it is important to examine the cornea, sclera, and palpebral conjunctiva. Eversion of the eyelid is essential during an assessment of an injured or red eye. Everting the upper eyelid allows for easy identification of foreign bodies.

⚠ *SAFETY ALERT 15-4*

Eversion of the eyelid should never be performed if a penetrating eye injury is suspected.

Documentation of Expected Findings

Eyebrows full and appropriate to age. Eyelashes evenly distributed. Blinking every 2 to 3 seconds. Eyes are symmetrical, and in parallel alignment. Lacrimal apparatus not enlarged or tender. Conjunctiva with small vessels visible. Sclera clear and white.

Assessment of Exterior Ocular Structures

Cornea and Lens

Stand in front of the patient. Use a penlight or ophthalmoscope split light to inspect the cornea. Shine the light directly on the cornea. Move the light laterally toward the bridge of the nose. Repeat on the other eye. Observe the angle of the anterior space and the clarity and translucence of the lens. *A wide angle allows full illumination of the iris. Lens is transparent.*

A narrow angle indicates *glaucoma*.

Cloudiness of the lens may indicate a *cataract*, which is associated with increased age, smoking, alcohol intake, and sunlight exposure. Risk factors for cataracts are primarily environmental. See also Table 15-6.

Fluorescein examination of cornea. The advanced practitioner uses this technique to determine any abrasions or lacerations to the cornea. Fluorescein is a dye taken up by the damaged corneal epithelium. Under blue ultraviolet light it fluoresces, allowing assessment of the nature and extent of corneal injury.

Corneal fluorescence reveals the extent of the injury to the corneal epithelium.

⚠ *SAFETY ALERT 15-5*

Fluorescein is never used if a penetrating eye injury is suspected.

Remove a fluorescein strip, wet it with a drop of normal saline, and apply it to the lower conjunctival sac (fluorescein drops are also available). Ask the patient to blink several times to distribute the fluorescein over the cornea. Remove excess fluorescein with a gentle irrigation of normal saline. Darken the room and expose the eye to blue filtered, cobalt, or "black" light.

Iris

Inspect the iris for colour, nodules, and vascularity. Brown is the most common eye colour in the world. *Colour is evenly distributed, smooth, and without apparent vascularity. An expected variation is mosaic variant.*

See Table 15-6.

Pupils

Examine the pupil using a direct method. Stand in front of the patient and use your light to observe the shape and size (mm) of the pupil. *Pupil is black, round, and equal with a diameter of 2 to 5 mm.* Gently place your open hand along the patient's nose. Shine the light into

See Table 15-7 at the end of the chapter for alterations in pupils. Also see Chapter 24 for more information on neurological findings related to altered pupils.

the right eyes as you observe the pupillary constriction (direct) (CN III) (Fig. 15-22). Repeat, except observe the left eye for pupillary constriction (consensual) (CN III). Repeat these two procedures in the left eye. *Pupils constrict directly and consensually.*

Figure 15-22 Pupillary constriction.

To test for accommodation (CN III), instruct the patient to stare at a distant object for 30 seconds. Hold an index finger, penlight, or other safe object (eg, pencil) about 30 cm in front of the nose. Ask the patient to focus on the pencil as you move it toward the patient's nose (Fig. 15-23). *Pupils constrict (accommodation) and eyes cross (converge). Accommodation is necessary for far-to-near focus. Documentation of this sequence of assessments is easily accomplished with the following acronym: PERRLA, which stands for Pupils Equal, Round, Reactive to Light, and Accommodation.*

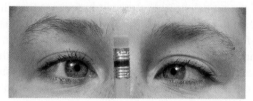

Figure 15-23 Accommodation.

Several unexpected findings can be seen in the pupil during assessment. See Table 15-7.

The **cover test** assesses for the presence and amount of ocular deviation. A low light level with no direct light sources shining in the patient's eyes is ideal. At rest, the extraocular muscles have very little activity. The assessment referred to as **cardinal directions** allows nurses to detect muscles causing misalignment or uncoordinated eye movements.

Assessment of External Eyes

Ensure good lighting. Wash your hands before touching the eyelids or face of the patient.

Assessment of Internal Ocular Structures

The ophthalmoscope has some basic features that make inspecting the interior ocular structures easier: (1) a light source; (2) viewing aperture; and (3) a lens refraction adjustment (Fig. 15-24). These features allow nurses to direct the light source toward the pupil by looking through the viewing aperture.

The *aperture*, which has a lens selector wheel, allows for adjustment of refraction to bring the internal ocular structures

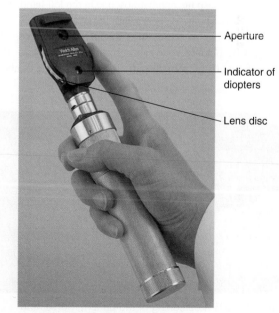

Aperture

Indicator of diopters

Lens disc

Figure 15-24 The ophthalmoscope.

into sharp focus, compensating for refractive errors of the patient or nurse. The aperture is set on large for the dilated pupil or small for the constricted pupil. The slit aperture is used to examine the anterior portion of the eye and evaluate lesions at the fundal level. The grid feature is used to locate and describe fundal-level lesions. The green beam (red-free filter) is often used to evaluate retinal hemorrhages (which appears black with this filter) or melanin spots (which appear gray).

Proper inspection of the posterior ocular structures with an ophthalmoscope requires that the pupils be slightly dilated. The optometrist or ophthalmologist will often use mydriatic eye drops, which are short-acting ciliary muscle paralytics to dilate the pupil. However, accommodation reflexes may be lost with the use of eye drops. Mydriatic drops are not used if a neurological assessment is necessary, because they may obscure pupil size and reactivity parameters used to determine neurological status.

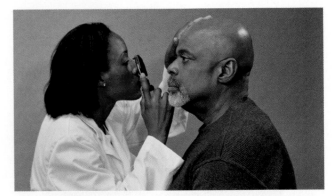

Figure 15-26 Using the ophthalmoscope to inspect the anterior ocular structures.

△ *SAFETY ALERT 15-6*

Midriatic drops may precipitate acute angle closure glaucoma. Those at risk include patients with a history of glaucoma and extremely farsighted patients. Additionally, the patient should be warned about blurring of vision and sensitivity to light. The patient should not drive for 1 to 2 hours following pupil dilation.

In the nonophthalmic setting, partial dilation of the pupil is accomplished by darkening the room. The skill of assessing the fundus of the eye requires much practice. For the nurse to be able to assess the fundus through a partially dilated pupil, he or she must become proficient in his or her technique.

Examination of the fundus is conducted in a darkened room to increase pupillary dilation without medications. First set the ophthalmoscope on the 0 lens and aperture on small round light. When examining the right eye, grasp the ophthalmoscope in your right hand and then turn on the light source. When examining the left eye, grasp the ophthalmoscope in the left hand. This helps you to avoid bumping noses with the patient.

Ask the patient to focus on a distant object across the room. Start by placing your hand on the patient's head; this puts you about 60 cm from the patient. From an angle of about

15° lateral to the patient's line of vision, shine the ophthalmoscope toward the pupil of the right eye (Fig. 15-25).

Look through the ophthalmoscope's viewing hole. Note the red reflex. Continue to look through the viewing hole and focus on the red reflex. Now, move toward the patient until you are about 10 cm away from the patient's forehead. Move the lens selector from 0 to the + or black numbers to focus on the anterior ocular structures. Inspect the anterior structures for transparency (Fig. 15-26). Now move the lens selector from the + black numbers to the − or red numbers to focus on structures progressively more posterior.

If the retinal structures are not in focus, adjust the focus with an index finger on the lens focus until the retina comes into focus. Look toward the nasal side of the retina. If you are having difficulty, ask the patient to look toward the right. Inspect the optic disc, which is the most prominent structure. The direct ophthalmoscope technique is difficult to master, and takes months of practice. The easiest way to find the optic disc is to find a blood vessel and then follow this vessel back to its origin at the optic disc. Inspect the shape (round or oval), colour (creamy yellow-orange to pink), disc margins (distinct and sharply demarcated), and size of the disc cupping (brighter yellow-white than rest of disc) (Fig. 15-27). Cup–disc ratio is genetically determined and usually equal in both eyes. You may be able to pick up AV nicking from high blood pressure and retinal hemorrhages in the form of dot-blot spots or flame hemorrhages (Fig. 15-28).

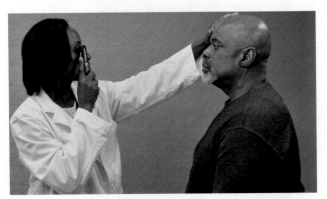

Figure 15-25 Positioning of the patient, nurse, and ophthalmoscope.

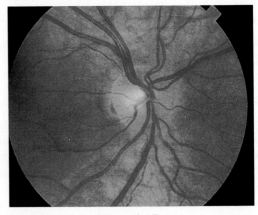

Figure 15-27 A healthy optic disc.

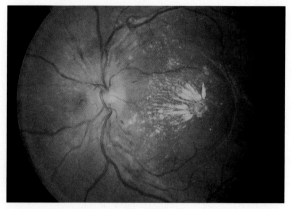

Figure 15-28 Flame hemorrhage in a patient with hypertensive retinopathy.

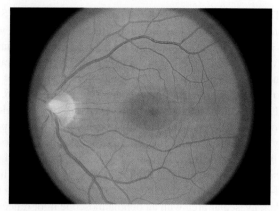

Figure 15-29 The macula.

Examples of Documentation for Eyes

Area of Assessment	Expected Findings	Unexpected Findings
Visual acuity	20/20 bilaterally	20/200 in left eye, 20/20 in right eye.
Fields of confrontation	Visual fields full bilaterally	Vision absent in right superotemporal field
Position and alignment of the eyes	Symmetrical, equally spaced from nose. Outer canthus of eye aligned with superior aspect of helix.	Left eye slightly lower than right eye. Left eye deviates medially.
Eyebrows	Symmetrical hair distribution	Patchy, asymmetrical hair distribution
Eyelids	Full closure, colour same as complexion, symmetrical blinking, overlie pupils slightly and symmetrically	Left lateral upper eyelid swollen with yellowish exudate along border, asymmetrical blinking
Eyelashes	Full, curl outward from upper and lower eyelids bilaterally	Right lateral eyelashes on upper eyelid curl inward, lashes missing from medial aspect of left lower eyelid
Lacrimal glands/sacs	No redness or inflammation bilaterally	Tender upon palpation bilaterally, excessive tearing in right eye
Conjunctiva	Clear, transparent bilaterally	Reddened area on lower medial margin of left eye
Sclera	White, clear bilaterally	Greyish, dull bilaterally
Cornea/lens	Shiny, clear bilaterally	Cloudy yellow opacity on right medial, superior left eye
Iris	Green/brown/blue; circular with regular border; symmetrical in size, colour, and shape	Right iris blue, left iris green; irregular border on superior lateral aspect of left iris
Pupils	Round and equal at 2 mm, direct and consensual reactions brisk bilaterally	Right pupil at 2 mm, left pupil at 4 mm
Pupillary reaction to light	PERRLA (pupils equal, round, reactive to light and accommodation)	Pupils unequal, left pupil fixed, right pupil sluggish
Accommodation (near reaction)	Pupils constrict with near gaze, dilate with far gaze	Pupils remain constricted with near and far gaze
Convergence	Gaze maintained to 4 cm	Gaze maintained to 10 cm
Extraocular muscles	Conjugate tracking in six cardinal directions, no eye movement noted in cover test, corneal light symmetrically reflected	Nystagmus present in left eye in all directions, left eye movement in cover test
Ophthalmoscopic (lens, vessels, optic discs)	Lens clear, bilateral red reflex, arterioles 2/3 size of veins with smooth crossings, optic discs round, yellowish pink	Absent red reflex in left eye, A/V nicking present bilaterally, optic disc round with irregular border in right eye

Adapted from Stephen, T. C., & Bickley, L. S. (2010). The eyes. In T. C. Stephen, D. L. Skillen, R. A. Day, & L. S. Bickley. (Eds.). *Canadian Bates' guide to health assessment for nurses* (p. 322). Philadelphia, PA: Wolters Kluwer Health/ Lippincott Williams & Wilkins.

The blood vessels can be directly observed in the retina. Systemic diseases of the body are often reflected in the blood vessels and can be directly observed in the eye. When examining the vascularity of the eye make note of the artery-to-vein ratio, tortuousity, and arteriovenous crossing. Also make note of the ratio of arteries to veins width, which is typically 2:3 or 4:5.

The final retinal structure to be assessed is the macula. Move the ophthalmoscope approximately two disc diameters temporally to view the macula. You can also ask the patient to look at the light. It can be difficult to find because the macula is light-sensitive. You may find that turning the aperture to green light (red-light filter) may make it easier to assess. The macula is a darker, avascular area with an ophthalmoscope light reflective center known as the fovea centralis. The colour of the macula varies with ethnicity and age (Fig. 15-29).

Review the structures and what you are looking for:

- **Disc:** What is the cup-to-disc ratio? Do the rims look pink and healthy? Is there any cupping? Edema?
- **Vessels:** Any signs of AV nicking?
- **Macula:** Does it look flat? Is there a good light reflex off the surface?
- **Periphery:** Any lattice or tears?

See Table 15-8 at the end of the chapter.

⚠ *SAFETY ALERT 15-7*

*A lack of **red reflex** may need urgent follow-up. If a white pupil reflex (leukokoria) is elicited, then an urgent ophthalmologic referral is required. Disease or trauma (eg. retinoblastoma, hyphema, toxocariasis, retinal detachment) often causes a white pupil reflex.*

🔺 Lifespan Considerations

Infants, Children, and Adolescents
Usually the iris has little colour at birth, taking approximately 3 months to take on any permanent eye colour. Ability to follow objects is usually present by 3 months. Binocular vision develops between 3 and 7 months (Coats, Paysse, et al, 2009).

Assess distance vision in children using a screening test based on developmental stage. Assess vision in infants through testing for pupillary light reflex and observing behaviour. Assess a toddler's visual acuity using the Allen

Lighthouse flash-card vision test. This test may be obtained from the New York Association for the Blind, 111 East 59th Street, New York, New York 10022.

Figure 15-30 Picture cards similar to those used in the Allen test.

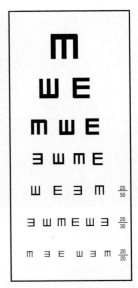

Figure 15-31 The Snellen E chart.

test, which uses picture cards of common objects for the toddler to identify (Fig. 15-30). Toddlers have bilateral visual acuity of approximately 20/200. In preschool children (3 to 5 years old), assess visual acuity with the Snellen E chart (Fig. 15-31). Preschool children are expected to have visual acuity approximately 20/40, improving to 20/30 or better by 4 years. The Snellen E chart is used to assess visual acuity in school-age children until the child develops reading skills. By 5 to 6 years of age, visual acuity should approximate that of adults or 20/20 in both eyes. Screening for colour blindness should occur between 4 and 8 years old.

Older Adults
Age-related visual changes and negative functional consequences occur slowly over time and are often overlooked. Visual impairments can begin to affect the older adult's functional capacity, decreasing ability to drive and perform usual activities. It is important to assess visual changes and how they affect lifestyle and activities of daily living (ADLs). Lens accommodation decreases with age, thus near vision is limited necessitating reading glasses among older adults. Presbyopia is considered an expected part of aging.

Cataracts and AMD are the two leading causes of vision loss and blindness in Canada (CNIB, 2007). Glaucoma is also more common with increased age.

Loss of acuity of central vision may decrease, especially after 70 years of age. Loss of visual acuity puts the older adult at increased risk for falls and associated hip fractures (Friedman, Munoz, et al., 2002). Additional findings related to aging include loss of adipose tissue in the orbit, decreased tear production, and decreased papillary response. Diabetic retinopathy is also increased in the elderly. Arcus senilis, a gray/white circle that circumscribes the limbus resulting from a deposition of lipids, is a common finding presenting as cloudiness around the corneas (Fig. 15-32).

Keep in mind that testing visual acuity in the older adult with dementia can be challenging. Provide simple, one-step directions for these patients.

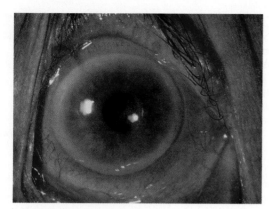

Figure 15-32 Arcus senilis.

Cultural Considerations

The Snellen E chart can be used for people who cannot read or speak English (see Fig. 15-31). Ethnic variations are found in the ocular sclera, depending on skin tone. In light-skinned people, the sclera appears white with some superficial vessels. In dark-skinned people, the sclera often has tiny brown patches (patches of melanin) or is grayish-blue.

People of African descent are four-to-five times more likely to develop glaucoma than any other ethnicity and its onset is on average 10 years earlier (Jacobs, Trobe, et al., 2009).

Evidence-Informed Critical Thinking

Clinical Reasoning

When formulating a nursing diagnosis, it is important to use critical thinking to cluster data together and identify patterns.

The nurse compares these clusters of data with health history and physical examination findings to ensure accuracy in the diagnosis, an appropriateness of nursing interventions. When formulating nursing diagnoses, nurses use critical thinking to cluster data and identify patterns that fit together. The nurse compares these data clusters with defining characteristics (unexpected findings) for the diagnosis to ensure the most accurate labelling and appropriate interventions. A nursing diagnosis is a clinical judgment about responses to health issues or life processes. Table 15-3 provides a comparison of nursing diagnoses, unexpected findings, and interventions commonly related to the eye assessment (North American Nursing Diagnosis Association-International, 2009).

Nurses use assessment information to identify patient outcomes. Some outcomes related to eye issues include the following:

• Patient will plan to modify lifestyle to accommodate vision disturbance.
• Patient will remain safe in home environment.
• Patient will state measures to reduce risk of visual loss (Bulechek, Butcher, et al., 2008).

Once outcomes are established, nursing care is implemented to improve the status of the patient. The nurse uses critical thinking and evidence-informed practice to develop nursing interventions. Some examples of nursing interventions for the eye are as follows:

• Identify name and purpose of visit when entering patient's personal space.
• Keep furniture out of pathways and keep cords against walls.
• Ensure access to eyeglasses or magnifiers as needed (Moorhead, Johnson, et al., 2007).

Documenting Unexpected Findings

The nurse has just finished conducting a beginning assessment of Mr. Harris, the patient who reports worsening vision and has a history of glaucoma. Review the following important findings revealed in each of the steps of objective data collection for Mr. Harris. Consider how these results compare with the expected findings presented in the samples of documentation. Note that inspection is the major technique used in eye assessment.

Inspection: External eyes symmetrical, no ptosis. PERRLA (pupils equal, round, reactive to light and accomodation). Extraocular movements intact (EOMI). Conjunctiva clear, sclera white. Distance vision: right 20/30, left 20/50. Visual fields reduced by approximately 20% by confrontation.

Palpation: External eye lacrimal apparatus without swelling or redness, nontender.

Table 15-3 Common Nursing Diagnoses Associated with the Eyes

Diagnosis and Related Factors	Point of Differentiation	Assessment Characteristics	Nursing Interventions
Altered sensory perception related to vision disturbance	Alterations in the way the patient takes in, processes, uses, or otherwise deals with sensory (especially visual) stimuli	Wears eyeglasses, uses contacts, uses computer assistive devices	Converse with and touch patient frequently. Use lighting for reading. Use a magnifying glass for shaving or to apply makeup.
Risk for injury related to impaired vision	At risk for physical harm and damage as a result of environmental limitations imposed by impaired vision	Near or far vision impaired, difficulty seeing in low lighting, difficulty seeing at night	Refer to optometrist for corrective lenses. Ensure that patient wears lenses and that eyeglasses are clean. Make sure that objects are out of the path. Remove hazards from room, such as razors and matches.

Analyzing Findings

Mr. Harris's eye concerns have been highlighted throughout this chapter. The following nursing note illustrates how the nurse analyzes subjective and objective data to plan nursing interventions including additional monitoring.

The following nursing note illustrates how subjective and objective data are collected and analyzed and nursing interventions are developed.

Subjective: "I'm here for my checkup to make sure that my eye medicines are doing what they're supposed to." Past history of high blood pressure, high cholesterol, and glaucoma.

Objective: A 61-year-old African Canadian, external eyes symmetrical, no ptosis. Conjunctiva clear, sclera white. Distance vision: right 20/30 left 20/50. Reads newsprint but states it is somewhat blurred compared to 1 year ago. Visual fields reduced by approximately 20% by confrontation.

Analysis: Disturbed visual sensory perception related to loss of visual field and visual acuity.

Plan: Make referral to ophthalmologist for further testing. Additionally refer to social work to assist with getting funding for new eyeglasses and to ensure no interruptions of medication regimes. Teach about safety issues related to vision loss, especially fall risk. Encourage him to use magnifying devices for reading until he can get his new glasses.

Critical Thinking Challenge

- What other assessment data might the nurse collect?
- What other nursing diagnoses might be appropriate for Mr. Harris?

Because of Mr. Harris's unexpected findings a referral to an optometrist and/or ophthalmologist is indicated. In addition to the expertise, eye specialists use specialized equipment for more precise measurements and diagnostics. For instance, tonometry is used to measure intra-ocular pressure, and visual fields may be more accurately defined. The following conversation illustrates how the nurse might organize data and make recommendations about the patient's situation to an eye care specialist.

Situation: Hi, I'm Bev Ryan, a nurse referring the patient for a consult.

Background: His name is Mr. Edward Harris. Date of birth is 31-OCT-1949. He's a 61-year-old man with a history of high blood pressure, high cholesterol, and glaucoma. We saw him for his annual visit and found some unexpected findings on his eye examination. Both his near and far vision have worsened, and he says that his vision is blurrier compared to 1 year ago. His visual fields are also reduced by about 20%.

Assessment: Because he has symptoms of worsening glaucoma, he'll need further evaluation.

Recommendations: If possible, would you have time to work him into your schedule in the next week? He also will most likely need new glasses.

Critical Thinking Challenge

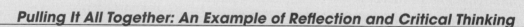

- What additional information might the eye care specialist request?
- How will the team collaborate to benefit Mr. Harris' health?

Pulling It All Together: An Example of Reflection and Critical Thinking

The nurse uses assessment data to establish a nursing diagnosis and formulate a nursing care plan outlining patient outcomes and interventions. Outcomes are specific to the patient, realistic to achieve, measurable, and have a time frame for meeting the outcome. The interventions are actions that the nurse performs, based on evidence and practice guidelines. After these interventions are completed, the nurse reevaluates and documents findings. The nurse uses critical thinking and judgment for diagnosis and/or the revision of a diagnosis to guide further interventions. This is often in the form of a care plan or case note similar to the one below.

Nursing Diagnosis	Patient Outcomes	Nursing Interventions	Rationale	Evaluation
Altered visual sensory perception	Patient will remain free from harm resulting from a loss of vision.	Refer to eye specialist for further testing. Teach patient to clear cords and furniture from pathways, and use good lighting.	Referral to the eye specialist will correct vision loss. Furniture and cords are environmental hazards that increase risk of falling. Adequate lighting increases visibility.	Patient will be seen by eye specialist in 2 days. Patient states that his home environment is uncluttered and all furniture and cords are out of the way. He plans to get lamp for the hallway at night.

Using the previous steps of clinical reasoning, organizing, and prioritizing, consider all of the case study findings woven throughout this chapter. When answering the following questions, see how the pieces of assessment work together to create an environment for personalized, appropriate, and accurate care. As you study the content and features, consider Mr. Harris's case and how it is important to seek care for primary prevention. Begin thinking about the following points:

- What pathological processes characterize glaucoma? (Knowledge)
- How can examination findings distinguish glaucoma from other eye conditions such as macular degeneration? (Comprehension)
- How would you teach Mr. Harris about preventing falls associated with vision loss? (Application)
- What factors may have contributed to Mr. Harris's glaucoma? (Analysis)
- What recommendation for additional screening and follow-up would you recommend for Mr. Harris? (Synthesis)
- How would you evaluate Mr. Harris's understanding of what you taught him about preventing vision loss related falls at home? (Evaluation)

Key Points

- Cranial nerves involved with the eyes include CN II (optic nerve), III (oculomotor), IV (trochlear), and VI (abducens).
- The use of protective eyewear for contact sports and occupational exposure minimizes eye-related trauma.
- Sudden vision loss is an emergency.
- Common symptoms related to the eye and vision include pain, trauma, visual change, blind spots, floaters, halos, discharge, and a related change in activities of daily living (ADLs).
- The Snellen chart is used to assess far vision; the Jaeger test is used for near vision. The patient with 20/20 vision can read at 20 ft (6.1 m) what the average person can read at 20 ft (6.1 m).
- Patients older than 40 years often have a decreased ability to accommodate, moving the objects further away to read.
- Static and kinetic confrontation tests measure peripheral vision.
- The cardinal directions allow the nurse to detect muscle defects that cause misalignment or uncoordinated movement of the eyes.
- PERRLA is documented when the pupils are equal, round, reactive to light, and accommodation.
- Cloudiness in the lens may indicate a cataract.
- Cataracts, glaucoma, and macular degeneration are more common in older adults.

Review Questions

1. Which of the following patients would require the most emergent nursing care?
   A. An 8-year-old girl with pink conjunctiva and drainage
   B. A 20-year-old man with sudden visual loss after playing football
   C. A 52-year-old woman with clouding of vision
   D. A 77-year-old man with loss of vision in his peripheral fields

2. Which of the following teaching points would the nurse emphasize related to eye health?
   A. Always wear eye protection for occupational exposures.
   B. Eat a diet high in animal protein and dairy.
   C. Exercise five times a week for at least 20 minutes.
   D. Get at least 7 hours of sleep each night.

3. Which of the following symptoms would the nurse expect the patient to report as translucent specks that drift across the visual field?
   A. Blind spot
   B. Ptosis
   C. Halo
   D. Floater

4. When working with an older adult, what would the nurse emphasize as increased risks for the patient?
   A. Myopia and strabismus
   B. Blepharitis and chalazion
   C. Glaucoma and cataracts
   D. Exophthalmos and presbyopia

5. A school nurse is performing annual vision screening for seventh grade students. Which of the following charts would the nurse most likely be using?
   A. Allen chart
   B. Snellen chart
   C. Ishihara cards
   D. Confrontation cards

6. Which of the following scores for distance vision indicates the patient with the poorest vision?
   A. 20/200
   B. 18/20
   C. 24/20
   D. 20/100

7. The nurse recognizes that the 60-year-old patient may have difficulty reading fine print because of the loss in the ability of the eye to
A. accommodate
B. aniscoria
C. amblyopia
D. asthenopia

8. Peripheral vision is evaluated by the nurse using
A. corneal light test
B. cover test
C. confrontation test
D. cardinal directions

9. The cranial nerves involved with eye movement include
A. II, V, and VII
B. III, IV, and VI
C. IV, V, and VIII
D. V, VI, and VII

10. The nurse assesses the response of the eye to light and documents expected findings as
A. PEERLA
B. PERRLA
C. PERLLA
D. PERLAA

Canadian Nursing Research

Dhillon, S., Shapiro, C. M., et al. (2007). Sleep-disordered breathing and effects on ocular health. *Canadian Journal of Ophthalmology, 42*(2), 238–243.

Perruccio, A. V., Badley, E. M., et al. (2007). Self-reported glaucoma in Canada: Findings from population-based surveys 1994–2003. *Canadian Journal of Ophthalmology, 42*(2), 219–226.

Russell-Minda, E., Jutai, J., et al. (2006). *An evidence-based review of the research on typeface legibility for readers with low vision.* Toronto, ON: Vision Rehabilitation Evidence-Based Review and Canadian National Institute for the Blind Research Unit.

References

Bulechek, G. M., Butcher, H. K., et al. (2008). *Nursing interventions classification (NIC)* (5th ed.) St. Louis, MO: Mosby.

Canadian National Institute for the Blind. (2007). *Vision loss: Fast facts about vision loss.* Retrieved from www.cnib.ca/vision-health/vision-loss/fast-facts.htm

Canadian National Institute for the Blind & The Canadian Ophthalmological Society. (2007). *The cost of vision loss in Canada.* Retrieved from www.cnib.ca/eng/cnib%20 document%20library/.../covl_full_report.doc

Coats, D. K., Paysse, E. A., et al. (2009). *Visual development and vision assessment in infants and children.* Retrieved from http://www.uptodateonline.com.proxy. seattleu.edu/online/content/topic.do?topicKey=ped_opth/4522&selectedTitle=1~150&source=search_result

Dubois, L. (2005). Informal visual fields. In L. Dubois (Ed.). *Clinical skills for ophthalmic examination: Basic procedures* (2nd ed., pp. 37–45). Thorofare, NJ: Slack Inc.

Friedman, D. S., Munoz, B., et al. (2002). Grading visual acuity using the preferential-looking method in elderly nursing home residents. *Investigative Ophthalmology and Visual Science, 43*(8), 2572–2578.

Hockenberry, M. J., & Wilson, D. (2007). *Wong's nursing care of infants and children* (8th ed.) St. Louis, MO: Mosby Elsevier.

Jacobs, D. S., Trobe, J., et al. (2009). *Primary open-angle glaucoma.* Retrieved from http://www.uptodateonline.com. proxy.seattleu.edu/online/content/topic.do? topicKey=priophth/7711&linkTitle=Risk%20factors&source=preview&selectedTitle=1~150&anchor=3#3

Javitt, J. C., Wang, F., et al. (1996). Blindness due to cataract: Epidemiology and prevention. *Annual Review of Public Health, 17,* 159–177.

Knowing, D., & Kester, K. (2007). Keep an eye out for glaucoma. *Nurse Practitioner, 32*(7), 18–23.

Lowdermilk, D., & Perry, S. (2007). *Maternity & women's health care* (9th ed.). St. Louis, MO: Mosby Elsevier.

Mackin, L. A., Mangin, E. J., et al. (2003). *Handbook of geriatric nursing care* (2nd ed.). Philadelphia, PA: Lippincott.

Miller, C. A. (2008). *Nursing for wellness in older adults* (5th ed.). Philadelphia, PA: Lippincott Williams & Wilkins.

Moorhead, S., Johnson, M., et al. (2007). *Nursing outcomes classification (NOC)* (4th ed.). St. Louis, MO: Mosby.

Mozaffariehm, M., Greishaber, M. C., et al. (2008). Oxygen and blood flow players in the pathogenesis of glaucoma. *Molecular Vision, 14*(Jan), 224–233.

National Coalition for Vision Health. (2011). *Vision loss in Canada 2011.* Retrieved from http://www.visionhealth.ca/news/Vision%20Loss%20in%20Canada%20-%20Final.pdf

North American Nursing Diagnosis Association-International. (2009). *Nursing diagnoses, 2009–2011 edition: Definitions and classifications (NANDA-I NURSING DIAGNOSIS).* West Sussex, UK: John Wiley & Sons.

Perruccio, A. V., Badley, E. M., et al. (2010). A Canadian population-based study of vision problems: Assessing the significance of socioeconomic status. *Canadian Journal of Ophthalmology. 45*(5), 477-83. Retrieved from http://www. ncbi.nlm.nih.gov/pubmed/20729934

Price, K. M., Gupta, P. K., et al. (2009). Eyebrow and eyelid dimensions: An anthropometric analysis of African Americans and Caucasians. *Plastic and Reconstructive Surgery, 124*(2), 615–623.

Somami, S., Bhatti, A., et al. (2008). *Pregnancy, special Considerations.* Retrieved from http://emedicine.medscape.com/article/1229740-overview

Sperduto, R. D., Clemons, T. E., et al. (2008). Age-related eye disease study research group: Cataract classification using serial examinations in the age-related eye disease study: AREDS Report No. 24. *Archives in Ophthalmology, 145,* 504–508.

Stephen, T. C., & Bickley, L. S. (2010). The eyes. In T. C. Stephen, D. L. Skillen, et al. (Eds.). *Canadian Bates' guide to health assessment for nurses* (pp. 299–340). Philadelphia, PA: Wolters Kluwer Health/Lippincott Williams & Wilkins.

> *The Canadian Jensen's Nursing Health Assessment suite offers these additional resources to enhance learning and facilitate understanding of this chapter:*
>
> • thePoint on line resource, http//thepoint.lww.com/Stephen1E
> • *Laboratory Manual for Canadian Jensen's Nursing Health Assessment: A Best Practice Approach*

⚠ Table 15-4 Refractive Errors

Finding	Description
Asthenopia (eye strain)	Eye strain develops after reading, computer work, or other visually tedious tasks from tightening of the eye muscles after maintaining a constant focal distance. Symptoms include fatigue, red eyes, eyestrain, pain in or around the eyes, blurred vision, headaches, and, rarely, double vision.
Astigmatism 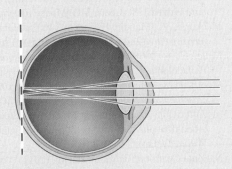 **Focal point of light rays:** multiple areas of the retina	Football-shaped curvature of the cornea prevents light from focusing on the retina. Images appear blurred because not all optical planes are focused. This condition is corrected with a cylindrical lens that has more focusing power in one axis than the other.
Myopia (nearsightedness) 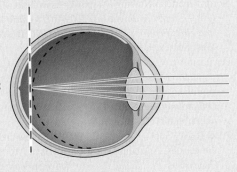 **Focal point of light rays:** in front of the retina	Images of distant objects focus in front of, instead of on the retina from an imperfection in the shape of the eye or lens. People with myopia can see clearly objects up close, but have difficulty seeing distant objects. Myopia is corrected with a concave lens that moves the focus back to the retina.
Hyperopia (farsightedness) 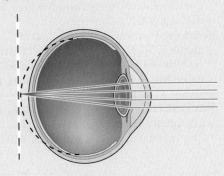 **Focal point of light rays:** behind the retina	Images of near objects focus behind, instead of on the retina from an imperfection in the shape of the eye or lens. People with it can see distant objects clearly but have difficulty seeing objects up close. A convex lens is used to treat hyperopia, moving the focus forward onto the retina.

Finding	Description

Presbyopia

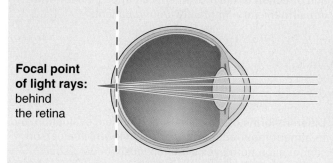

Focal point of light rays: behind the retina

This symptom, considered a natural part of aging, is believed to result from loss of elasticity of the crystalline lens. As this happens, the ciliary muscles that bend and straighten the lens lose their power to accommodate. This condition affects near vision and therefore is corrected with a convex lens in front of the eye in the form of half-glass or as bottom of a bifocal or multifocal lens if other correction is needed for distance viewing.

Colour blindness

Colour blindness (inability to distinguish colours) has a genetic component. It occurs in 2%–8% of males and 0.5% of females of European descent. The cones of the eye, located in the macula, contain blue, green, and red pigments that allow colour sight. Colour blindness results with damage to the cones or a cone that is missing pigment. The most common form is the red/green. No effective treatment for colour blindness exists. Many with it learn to compensate for the deficit and at times can discern details that a "normal"-sighted person would miss. Most people are not totally colour blind but have deficiencies that cause some challenges, such as with discerning traffic lights, weather forecasts, and light-emitting diodes; purchasing clothes; selecting crayons; cooking; and applying makeup.

Blindness

Blindness means loss of vision or visual acuity that cannot be corrected with glasses or contact lenses. Partial blindness refers to those with very limited vision; complete blindness means an inability to see anything, including light. People with vision worse than 20/200 are classified as legally blind in Canada. Numerous causes of blindness include congenital anomalies, diabetes complications, glaucoma, macular degeneration, and trauma. Worldwide, the leading causes of blindness are cataracts, river blindness (onchocerciasis), trachoma, leprosy, and vitamin A deficiency.

Table 15-5   Unexpected Findings in Eye Movement

Finding	Description
Nystagmus 	Involuntary rhythmic wobbling of the eyes; degree and direction of the movement can impair vision, with impairment varying greatly among patients
Strabismus (cross- or wall-eyed) 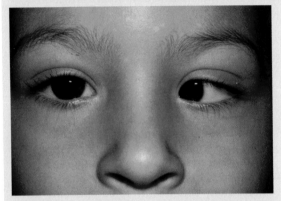 Crossed eye (esotropia) 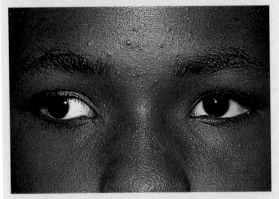 Wall eye (exotropia) 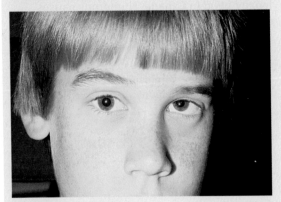 One eye pointing upward or downward (vertical deviation)	Different forms of strabismus; appropriate evaluation and treatment required for this condition in which a person cannot align both eyes simultaneously under usual conditions. To a certain degree strabismus occurs in 5% of all children. Strabismus is not the same as amblyopia. Children do not outgrow strabismus. Strabismus can be constant (eye turns out all the time) or intermittent (turning out only some of the time).

Table 15-6   **External Eye Conditions**

Jaundice

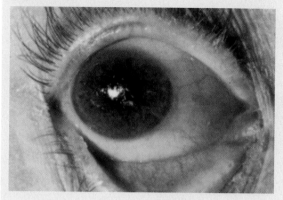

Yellowing of the sclera, which indicates liver disease

Hyphema

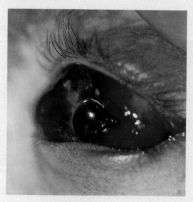

Blood in the anterior chamber of the eye, usually caused by blunt trauma

Chalazion

A cyst (meibomian gland lipogranuloma) in the eyelid resulting from inflammation of the meibomian gland. Most often on the upper eyelid and are sometimes confused with a hordeolum (sty); they can be differentiated because they are usually painless and tend to be larger. Rarely resolves spontaneously; usually requires treatment

Iris Nevus

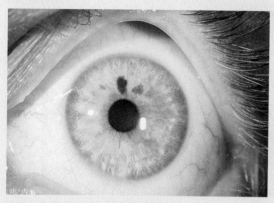

Rare condition affecting one eye, with deviations in appearance of the iris, pain, and decreased vision; patients may also have glaucoma on the same side

Blepharitis

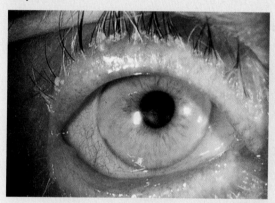

Inflammation of the margin of the eyelid; two types are anterior and posterior. Most common type is seborrheic, followed by staphylococcal, and then rosacea-associated

Viral Conjunctivitis

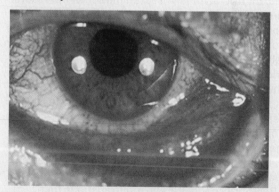

Most often associated with a watery discharge from the eye that may be accompanied by sinus congestion and rhinorrhea (runny nose), slightly injected (diffusely pink), and numerous follicles on the inferior conjunctiva

(table continues on page 382)

Table 15-6 **External Eye Conditions** (*continued*)

Bacterial Conjunctivitis

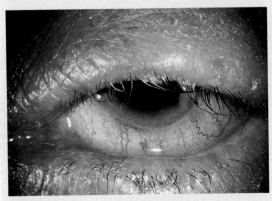

Should be suspected if there is purulent discharge (yellow or green), injected (red), and numerous follicles. Occasional blurring is common; should not be painful, constant blurring, or photophobia

Allergic Conjunctivitis

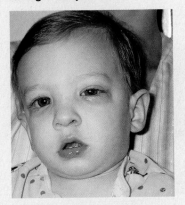

Usually bilateral and common in people with ectopic (allergic) conditions; associated with slight watery discharge and itching of the eyes

Glaucoma

The leading cause of irreversible blindness and most common chronic optic neuropathy. Disease of the optic nerve that involves loss of retinal ganglion cells. A significant risk factor is increased intraocular pressure. Impaired flow of aqueous humor leads to increased intraocular pressure. In open-angle glaucoma, aqueous humor flows in the trabecular meshwork (Mozaffariehm, Greishaber, et al., 2008). In closed-angle glaucoma, the anteriorly displaced iris pushes against the trabecular meshwork, blocking fluid flow. Glaucoma has three main types: primary (primary open-angle or closed-angle) secondary (inflammatory, phacogenic, related to intraocular hemorrhage) and developmental (primary congenital, infantile). The most common type is primary open-angle glaucoma (POAG), affecting 2.2 million US citizens (Knowing & Kester, 2007). POAG has a genetic link. Rarer are congenital eye malformations that develop in the third trimester of gestation, which cause early-angle closure and ocular hypertension, leading to optic neuropathies. Those at risk for glaucoma need an annual dilated eye examination (CNIB, 2007).

Amblyopia (Lazy Eye)

Condition in which the vision in one eye is reduced because the eye and brain are not working together. It is the most common cause of visual impairment in children (2–3 per 100). The eye upon examination looks normal, but vision is not as expected because the brain is favouring the other eye. If amblyopia is not properly treated, it persists into adulthood, leading to monocular visual impairment. Amblyopia can be caused by strabismus, visual field discrepancies, and occasionally cataracts. The direction that the lazy eye moves is described as esotropia (medial), exotropia (lateral), hypertropia (superior), or hypotropia (inferior).

Table 15-6   **External Eye Conditions** (*continued*)

Exophthalmos

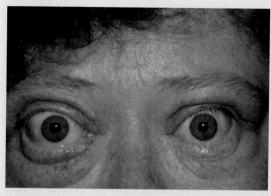

Protrusion of the eyeball anteriorly out of the socket. The most common cause is a thyroid disorder known as Graves disease. Untreated exophthalmos can impair the ability of the eyelid to close properly, especially during sleep, which increases dryness of the corneal epithelium. The process and displacement of the eye can lead to compression of the optic nerve or artery, leading to blindness.

Cataracts

Opacity of the crystalline lens of the eye, which obstructs the passage of light. The most common causes are long-term exposure to ultraviolet light, radiation, diabetes, hypertension, and advanced age (Sperduto, Clemons, et al., 2008). Opacity develops from a change in the lens protein (denatured). Genetics plays a role in congenital cataracts; positive family history of cataracts seems to increase risk. Wearing ultraviolet light blocking sunglasses is believed to slow the development of cataracts (Javitt, Wang, et al., 1996).

Hordeolum (Sty)

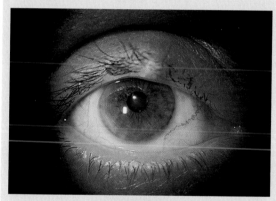

Caused by a blockage and infection of the sebaceous gland at the base of the eyelashes. While painful and unsightly, there is generally no lasting damage.

Osteogenesis Imperfecta

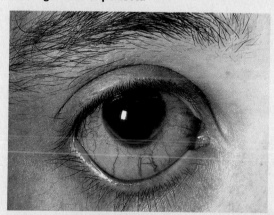

A blue sclera is due to a thinning of the sclera and is indicative of osteogenesis imperfecta.

Table 15-7 **Unexpected Findings in the Pupil**

Anisocoria (Unequal Pupils)

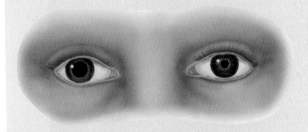

These usually result from a defect in the efferent nervous pathways controlling the oculomotor nerve. Deformities of the iris or eye must be ruled out.

Argyle Robertson

Bilateral pupils accommodate with distance but do not dilate when exposed to bright light. Direct and consensual pupil reflexes are absent.

Key Hole Pupil (Coloboma)

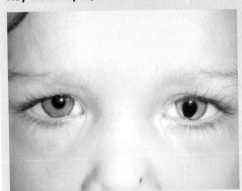

A gap appears in the iris. It can be congenital or caused during cataract or glaucoma surgery.

Horner's Syndrome

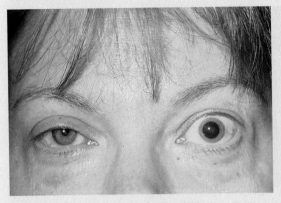

Pupillary miosis (constricted pupil) and dilation lag on the affected side. Also often present is ptosis.

Adie's Pupil

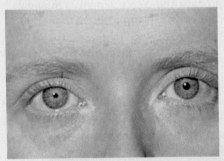

Pupils are fixed, dilated, and tonic. Direct and consensual pupil reactions are weak or absent.

Miosis (Small Fixed Pupil)

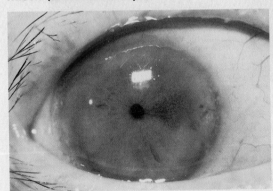

Pupils are constricted and fixed. Miosis occurs with eye drops for glaucoma, iritis, brain damage to pons, and narcotic drug use.

Mydriasis (Dilated Fixed Pupil)

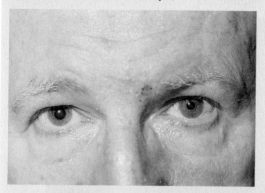

Pupils are dilated and fixed, usually from stimulation of sympathetic nerves as a consequence of CNS injury, circulatory arrest, deep anesthesia, acute glaucoma, or recent trauma. This may also follow administration of sympathomimetic eye drops.

Oculomotor (CN III) Nerve Damage

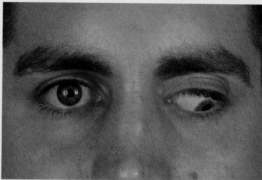

(A) Oculomotor paralysis

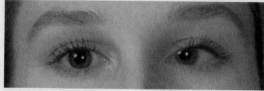

(B) Abducent paralysis

A unilateral dilated pupil has no reaction to light or accommodation.

! Table 15-8   **Retinal Conditions**

Age-Related Macular Degeneration (AMD)

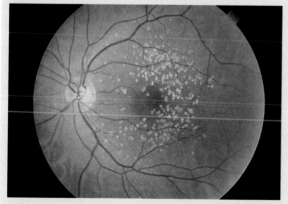

AMD gradually causes loss of sharp central vision, needed for common daily tasks (eg, driving, reading). The macula degenerates (dry) or abnormal blood vessels behind the retina grow under the macula (wet). The more common dry AMD occurs slowly in stages: early, intermediate, and advanced. Wet AMD develops quickly without stages. The main risk factor for AMD is age, with those older than 60 years mostly affected. Other risks are smoking, obesity, European ancestry, family history, and female gender. Health education for at-risk patients includes review of a healthy diet high in leafy green vegetables and fish, smoking cessation, blood-pressure and weight control, and exercise. Management options include ocular injections, laser surgery, and photodynamic therapy. None of these cure AMD, but they may slow vision loss.

Retinopathy

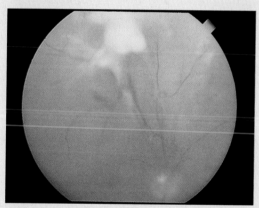

Retinopathy occurs from damage to retinal blood vessels. The two most common causes are diabetes and hypertension. *Diabetic retinopathy* is the most common cause of US blindness. Its stages are (1) mild nonprolifereative; (2) moderate nonproliferative; (3) severe nonproliferative; and (4) proliferative (most advanced). *Hypertensive retinopathy* presents with a dry retina (few hemorrhages, rare edema or exudate, multiple cotton wool spots), while diabetic retinopathy presents with a wet retina (multiple hemorrhages and exudate, extensive edema, few cotton wool spots).

(table continues on page 386)

Copper Wiring

Notching of vein by artery

Retinal artery with "copper wire" effect

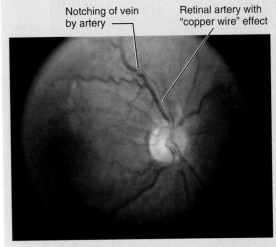

Chronic hypertension causes the retinal arterioles to thicken. The name *copper wiring* comes from the initial bronze appearance of the retina light reflection. As uncontrolled hypertension continues, the retina takes on a silvery or whitish appearance. The change comes from thickening of the retinal arterioles.

Retinitis Pigmentosa

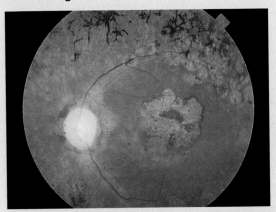

In this genetically transmitted disease, the retinas in both eyes progressively degenerate. It starts with loss of night vision, then loss of peripheral vision, progressing to tunnel vision, and finally no vision.

Ears Assessment

Learning Objectives

1 Demonstrate knowledge of anatomy and physiology of the ears.

2 Identify the common landmarks of the tympanic membrane.

3 Identify important topics for health promotion and risk reduction related to the ears and hearing.

4 Collect subjective data related to the ears and hearing.

5 Collect objective data related to the ears and hearing using physical examination techniques.

6 Identify expected and unexpected findings in the inspection and palpation of the ears.

7 Identify proper techniques for otoscope use.

8 Analyze subjective and objective data for assessment of the ears and consider initial interventions.

9 Document and communicate data from the ear assessment using appropriate terminology and principles of recording.

10 Consider age, condition, gender, and culture of the patient to individualize the ear assessment.

11 Identify nursing diagnoses and initiate a plan of care based on findings from the ear assessment.

*M*rs. Rosetta Bossio is a 25-year-old immigrant from Italy. She comes to the clinic today with concerns of ear pain, "buzzing" in her ears, and hearing loss. She has been to the clinic five times in the last 4 months for ear concerns. She was treated once for bilateral otitis media. She currently works in a clothing factory as a line custodian. Her immunizations are current. Temperature is 37.4°C orally, pulse 86 beats/min, regular, respirations 16 breaths/min, oxygen saturations 98%, and blood pressure 126/78 mm Hg (left arm, sitting). Current medications include 500 mg acetaminophen (Tylenol) taken 2 hours ago.

You will gain more information about Mrs. Bossio as you progress through this chapter. As you study the content and features, consider Mrs. Bossio's case and its relationship to what you are learning. Begin thinking about the following points:

- How will the nurse assess and document the patient's pain?
- How will the nurse assess and document the patient's hearing loss?
- What information will the nurse need to collect to assess the patient's risk for hearing loss?
- When will the nurse make a referral to the audiologist?

The focus of this chapter is ear assessment and includes anatomy and physiology related to the ear, hearing, and equilibrium, and key variations associated with lifespan, culture, and the environment. The section on subjective data collection covers personal history, medications, allergies, family history, and risk factors contributing to otitis media, loss of hearing, and vertigo. Information on collecting objective data describes methods for assessing anatomy, auditory perception, and equilibrium. A hearing screen is an essential portion of a complete physical examination. Early intervention for hearing deficit helps patients interact socially and decreases risk of injury.

Anatomy and Physiology Overview

The *ear* is divided into three distinct portions: (1) the *external ear*, most of which is visualized easily without instruments; (2) the *middle ear*, a small space behind the tympanic membrane (TM) extending to the eustachian tube; and (3) the *inner ear*, the vestibular portion. All three portions contribute to the process of hearing. An important additional structure is the *mastoid process*, a bony protrusion of the skull present behind the lobule (see Fig. 16-1). The eustachian tube, though not part of the ear, affects its function. This small tube connects the anterior middle ear to the nasopharynx. The ear has two separate functions: hearing and sustaining equilibrium.

External Ear

The external ear (also called the *auricle* or *pinna*) starts to develop in the 6th week of gestation and is identifiable by the 12th week of gestation (Isaacson, 2009). It is made up of flexible cartilage and skin (Fig. 16-1). Its design guides sound waves into the meatus of the *external auditory canal*, which is a chamber that transitions from firm cartilage to bone and ends at the TM. Development of the ears and kidneys in the embryo occurs at the same time. It is important to note that deviations in development of the ears may indicate underlying kidney conditions.

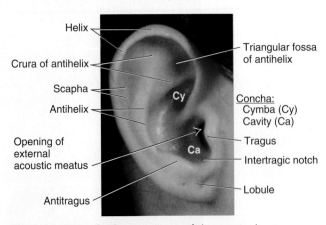

Helix
Crura of antihelix
Scapha
Antihelix
Opening of external acoustic meatus
Antitragus
Triangular fossa of antihelix
Cy
Concha: Cymba (Cy) Cavity (Ca)
Ca
Tragus
Intertragic notch
Lobule

Figure 16-1 Surface anatomy of the external ear.

In adults, a thin, sensitive layer of skin covers the external auditory canal, which is shaped similar to an S. Lining the canal are hairs and glands that secrete **cerumen**, a waxy substance. The slight S curve, hair, and cerumen help protect the canal and TM from foreign objects (see Fig. 16-2).

The TM is the oblique, multilayered, translucent, and pearly grey barrier between the external auditory canal and the middle ear. There is a first layer of epidermis uninterrupted from the external auditory canal, a center layer, and a final mucosal layer consistent with the mucosa of the middle ear (Cummings, Fredrickson, et al., 1998). The TM adheres through its concave shape to the malleus near the center. Some auditory ossicles in the middle ear can be distinguished on visualization of the translucent TM, as can portions of the malleus, umbo, manubrium, and short process (Fig. 16-3). A well-aerated middle ear allows visualization of part of the incus as well.

In the anterior quadrant of the TM, a distinct cone of light is visible, which is caused by the light of the otoscope reflecting off the oblique slant of the TM. The outer rim of the TM, the *annulus*, is thicker and more fibrous than the rest. Most of the TM, *pars tensa*, is stretched tightly and easy to see through. *Pars flaccida*, a small portion of the TM above the short process of the malleus, is more relaxed and opaque.

Middle Ear

The air-filled space behind the TM contains the **malleus, incus**, and **stapes**—tiny bones (ossicles) responsible for conducting sound waves to the inner ear. The middle ear acts as a volume dampener to protect the inner ear. There are four openings to the middle ear chamber:

1. The TM, the largest, which leads to the external ear
2. The *cochlear window*, also known as the round window, which connects the middle and inner ear
3. The *oval window*, on which the stapes rests to complete connection to the cochlea
4. The *eustachian tube*, a conduit that connects the middle ear to the nasopharynx and allows for pressure regulation of the middle ear (see Figs. 16-2 and 16-6).

> ### Clinical Significance 16-1
>
> Ability to equalize pressure keeps the TM intact with atmospheric variances. The eustachian tube opens briefly with swallowing and yawning; otherwise, this conduit remains closed.

Inner Ear

The inner ear is responsible for the translation of sound to the cranial nerve VIII (auditory nerve; see Chapter 24), which transmits it to the brainstem. While the external ear, middle ear, and inner ear all play roles in hearing, the inner ear is the only section responsible for vestibular function. The conduits of the inner ear are known collectively as the *bony labyrinth*, which consists of the **semicircular canals, vestibule,** and

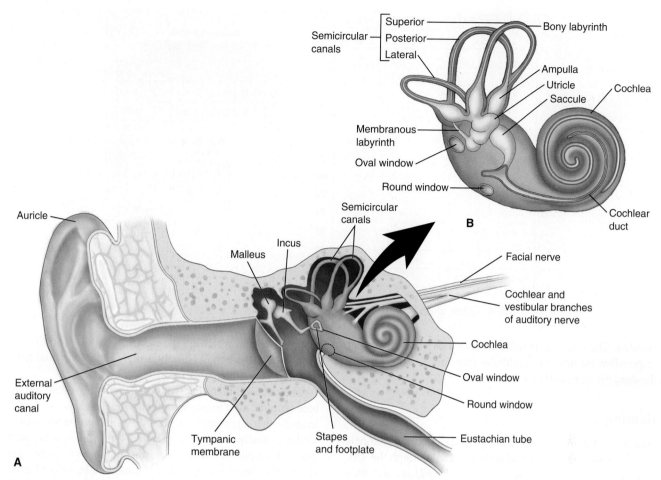

Figure 16-2 A. Anatomy of the external and middle ear. **B.** Anatomy of the inner ear.

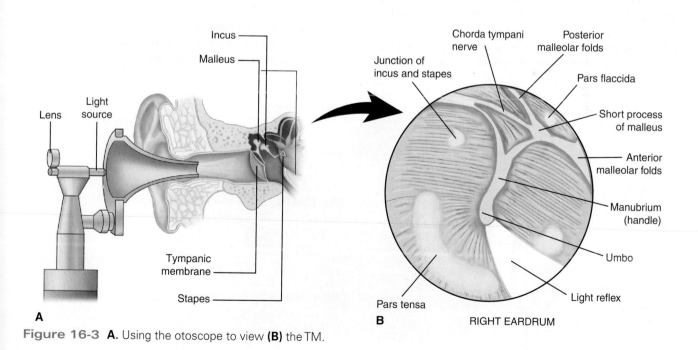

Figure 16-3 A. Using the otoscope to view **(B)** the TM.

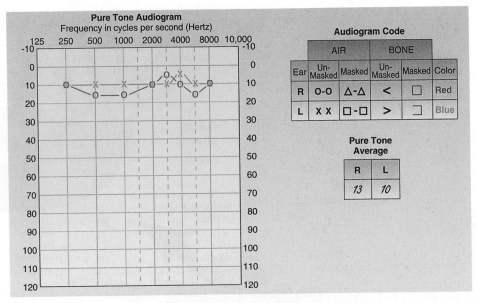

Figure 16-4 Graph of audiogram.

Hearing

cochlea. The cochlea includes the portions of the inner ear responsible for hearing. Vestibular function is maintained in the semicircular canals and vestibule.

Hearing is a complex experience. The external ear channels sound waves into the external auditory canal through the TM, to ossicles in the inner ear via the oval window, and then to the cochlea. The basal membrane in the cochlea vibrates the receptor hair cells of the **organ of Corti**, which transfer the signal into electrical impulses for the auditory nerve. The auditory nerve then delivers those impulses to the auditory cortex in the temporal lobe of the brain (see Chapter 24), which interprets them as and assigns meaning to the sound. The brainstem detects origination of the sound and can distinguish from which ear the electrical impulses originated, even though there may be only a slight delay of sound from one ear to the other.

The cochlea interprets two components of sound: amplitude (volume) and frequency (pitch). *Amplitude* is the change in atmospheric pressure against the TM and is directly related to the intensity of a sound. Decibels are the measurement units of amplitude. *Frequency*, the number of cycles per second the sound waves make, is measured in units of hertz (Hz). Ordinary conversation occurs between 10 to 60 decibels (dB) and 200 to 5,000 Hz. A jet engine is approximately 140 dB and a whisper is approximately 30 dB (Fig. 16-4).

Air and Bone Conduction

Sound is perceived two ways: air conduction (AC) and bone conduction (BC) (Fig. 16-5). AC, the most efficient method,

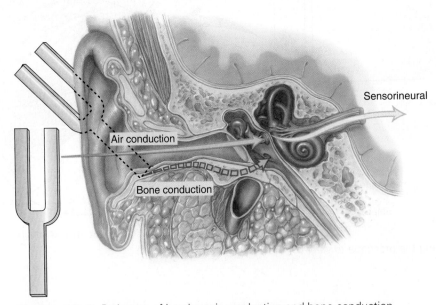

Figure 16-5 Pathways of hearing: air conduction and bone conduction.

is the usual pathway for sounds to travel to the inner ear. BC uses a different pathway, bypassing the external ear and delivering sound waves/vibrations directly to the inner ear via the skull. A compromise in either pathway causes hearing loss.

Hearing Disorders

Conductive hearing loss occurs when sound wave transmission through the external or middle ear is disrupted. It may result with either blockage of the external auditory canal by cerumen or fluid in the middle ear. The health care provider can easily remedy external auditory blockage by clearing the obstruction. Fluid in the middle ear requires further investigation for pathology. Increasing the amplitude of sound will overcome conductive hearing loss.

> ⚠ *SAFETY ALERT 16-1*
>
> *The most common cause of conductive hearing loss in adults is auditory trauma related to excessive noise exposure. This problem is increasing among younger people as well. Ninety-nine percent of cases of hearing loss caused by noise exposure are preventable (Canadian Association of Speech-Language Pathologists and Audiologists, 2000). Because of occupational risk of noise-induced hearing loss, Canadian provinces legislate 80 to 90 dB as the maximum exposure for an 8-hour period.*

Sensorineural hearing loss results from a problem somewhere beyond the middle ear, from inner ear to auditory cortex. Sites of dysfunction include the cochlea, organ of Corti, auditory nerve, or auditory cortex. **Presbycusis**, a common form of sensorineural loss, results from gradual degeneration of nerves and sensory hair cells of the organ of Corti. Such degeneration may be related to aging, use of ototoxic drugs (eg, gentamicin), and occupational or recreational noise exposure.

Tinnitus is a perception of buzzing or ringing in one ear or both ears that does not correspond with an external sound. Fifty different sounds have been reported from people who have tinnitus (Tinnitus Association of Canada, n.d.). The perceived sound of tinnitus may be quiet and a minor annoyance or so loud that it makes hearing regular conversation or enjoying restful sleep impossible. Little is known about what causes tinnitus in some people, though some degree of hearing loss often accompanies it. It is associated with extensive scarring of the TM from earlier ear infections, medications (excessive aspirin use, some antibiotics), trauma to the ear, and exposure to loud noises. Tinnitus may be the perception of natural sounds in the body that external noise usually blocks out. Currently, very few treatments for tinnitus are available (Davis, Paki, et al., 2007), but sufferers of tinnitus can obtain advice about coping mechanisms such as noise habituation, using hearing aids, practising relaxation techniques such as Tai Chi, or using a sound generator by the bedside that produces sounds such as birds or rain to help the individual fall asleep.

> **Clinical Significance 16-2**
>
> People with hearing loss are at increased risk for depression, dissatisfaction with life, reduced functional health, and withdrawal from social activities.

Vestibular Function

The semicircular canals and vestibule (utricle and saccule) provide the body with proprioception and equilibrium. Each organ contains specialized epithelium for sensing position. With illness the labyrinth can become inflamed and cause loss of equilibrium, which leads to a sense of vertigo. Symptoms of Meniere's disease include vertigo along with severe nausea and vomiting. This illness has a pattern of exacerbations that often last for 24 hours followed by periods of remission (Rubin & Strayer, 2008).

🔺 Lifespan Considerations

Women Who Are Pregnant

During pregnancy, estrogen levels stimulate the expansion of blood flow throughout the body. Increased blood flow and subsequent vessel changes in the middle ear may cause a sensation of fullness in the ear or intermittent otalgia. Vertigo in women who are pregnant can result from increased vascularity and edema.

Newborns, Infants, and Children

Infants and children are susceptible to otitis media, middle ear infection, largely because of the size and shape of their eustachian tubes, which are shorter, wider, and more horizontal compared to those of adults (Fig. 16-6). Infants with trisomy 21 or cleft palate have increased incidence of otitis media. Because of the frequent number of upper respiratory infections that infants and children have and their immature anatomy, bacteria and viruses have more opportunity to reflux into the middle ear via the eustachian tube. The middle ear also acts as a perfect reservoir for pathogens because it is dark, warm, and moist. Both bacteria and viruses thrive in this environment.

> **Clinical Significance 16-3**
>
> Enlarged adenoids related to nasal allergies often obstruct the outlets for the eustachian tube to drain in children (see Chapter 17).

While otitis media can cause severe discomfort, including difficulty feeding, sleeping, and general fussiness, it rarely causes permanent hearing loss. Following an episode, it is typical for fluid to remain in the middle ear for up to 3 months.

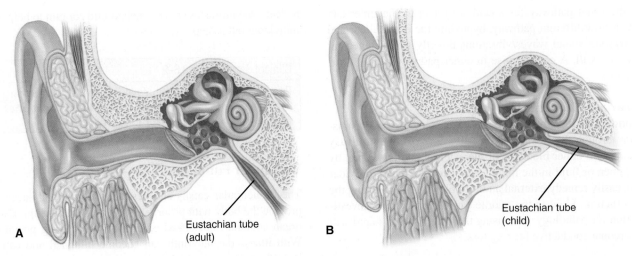

Figure 16-6 Differences in the eustachian tube between **(A)** adult and **(B)** child.

Repeated infections or persistent middle ear effusion (fluid) does cause temporary conductive hearing loss, which may delay onset or advancement of speech (because the child cannot hear the full range of spoken sounds). Hearing will return once the effusion is gone. Otitis media may also contribute to temporary attention difficulty from conductive hearing loss accompanied by persistent middle ear fluid.

The surgical placement of small tympanostomy tubes, myringotomy, through the TM to treat otitis media is used to reduce the overall number of cases of otitis media. Any otitis media can now be treated with topical antibiotic drops instead of oral antibiotics. Drops have the advantage of treating bacteria directly without side effects associated with oral antibiotics, such as diarrhea.

Adolescents

Recreational exposure to loud tones or noises may cause temporary or permanent hearing loss. With increased use of portable MP3 players and headphones designed to fit into the external ear canal, hearing loss in school-age and adolescent populations has escalated dramatically. For this reason, Apple (manufacturer of the iPod) has created software that limits the maximum volume possible. Unfortunately, this option exists on newer electronics and may not be available on all electronic devices. Attendance at sporting events, movies, concerts, or dance clubs is also a factor contributing to noise-induced hearing loss. Car and home stereo systems and crowd noise are other factors.

Older Adults

Cartilage formation continues over the lifespan, which may make ears seem more prominent in older adults. Though it may seem that extra cartilage would help to funnel sound to the external auditory meatus, it does not. In fact, it can lead to loss of rigidity and potential collapse of the external auditory canal. In addition, fine hairs lining the ear canal become coarser and stiffer, often protruding from the external auditory meatus. The coarse hair can interfere with sound waves as they move toward the TM, decreasing hearing. With decreased hair mobility, cerumen accumulates more readily in the ear canal. This is compounded by cerumen itself becoming drier. This combination of factors can lead to impaction and decreased hearing in older adults. Removing mechanical blockage can restore hearing and enhance socialization. It also helps to prevent injury by preserving the sense of hearing.

Otosclerosis is another common conductive hearing loss in this age group, resulting from the slow fusion of any combination of the ossicles in the middle ear. The fusion leads to obstruction of the transmission of sound waves from the TM to the oval window and inner ear (Manohar, 2007).

> #### Clinical Significance 16-4
>
> While hearing aids can help many people with hearing loss, 80% of those who would benefit do not use them. Many factors limit use such as cost, ill-fitting devices, and failure to follow-up.

Over time some people experience a natural sensorineural loss called *presbycusis*. It happens regardless of exposure to excessive noise. Just as the hair in the external auditory canal becomes less flexible, so do the hair cells in the cochlea. Difficulty distinguishing sounds increases, especially in noisy environments. Presbycusis includes loss of higher pitched sounds such as the spoken "s" or "th." Garbled or mumbled speech is a symptom. Amplification of sound, such as with simple hearing aids, does little to alleviate presbycusis. Some hearing aids are designed with noise cancellation to help manage this problem.

Adults older than 70 years face greater delays in the electrical responses in the brain; thus, it takes longer for the brain to interpret input. This is one factor that contributes to the increased auditory reaction time for those in the oldest age groups.

Cultural Considerations

Caucasian men older than 70 years have the highest incidence of hearing loss; the next highest prevalence is in Caucasian women (Pratt, Kuller, et al., 2009), followed by African Canadian men and women. Incidence of hearing loss declines with increases in socioeconomic status, regardless of ethnicity.

Incidence rates of otitis media are highest among First Nations, Alaskan and Canadian Inuit, and indigenous Australian children, compared to children of Caucasian genetic background (Klein, Pelton, et al., 2009). Forty percent of these high-risk populations may have chronic perforation by 18 months of age. Socioeconomic status and environmental exposure are also indicators of risk for otitis media. Lower socioeconomic status corresponds to higher rates of otitis media (Klein, Pelton, et al.). Exposure to cigarette smoke, propping bottles for babies to feed, and bottle feeding in a supine position are all environmental factors that increase risk for otitis media.

Colour and consistency of cerumen differs according to genetic background. Most commonly, cerumen is yellow to dark brown, varying from liquid to firm paste (known as *wet cerumen*). Wet cerumen is most common in Caucasians and people with African genetic backgrounds (Hosford-Dunn, Roeser, et al., 2008). Grey to white cerumen is often flaky and misdiagnosed as eczema. This type of cerumen, called *dry cerumen*, is most prevalent in peoples of Asian and First Nations genetic background (Pawson & Milan, 2005).

Acute Assessment

If inspection of the outer ear canal reveals a foreign object, it is best to refer the patient to an otolaryngologist for removal of the object. If the object appears to be a button battery, the patient must be referred to the emergency department for immediate object removal. Button batteries can quickly erode the ear canal and extensively damage the tissues and middle ear.

Foul-smelling drainage from the ear demands immediate attention. When possible wick the fluid from the external ear canal with either a wisp of cotton or cotton wick. Sending a culture of the fluid removed will identify the pathogen and help determine the proper antibiotic treatment. The patient with a chronically draining ear that is unresponsive to treatment requires referral to an otolaryngologist. The greatest concern with chronically draining ears is *cholesteatoma*, an increased accumulation of squamous epithelium within the middle ear. The growth can erode the auditory ossicles and cause great damage to the patient's hearing.

Patients with ear trauma also need evaluation for injury to nearby structures, including brain injury, basilar skull fracture, and neck injury. Hemotympanum, otorrhea, or TM rupture may indicate barotrauma from pressure changes or a basilar skull fracture. Sudden hearing loss also can be an acute situation; the cause must be found so that appropriate treatment can be initiated.

Subjective Data Collection

Subjective data are gathered by performing a complete and thorough health history, which begins by obtaining general information regarding the ear and its function. During the interview process it is important for the nurse to observe for any signs that the patient is having difficulty hearing. Some nonverbal cues of hearing loss include leaning forward, positioning the head or "good ear" to hear better, concentrating on lip or face movement instead of making eye contact, mumbling answers or giving answers not congruent with the question asked, asking the nurse to repeat questions frequently, responding with a loud voice, or using a monotone conversational voice. If any of these signs is present, the nurse needs to adjust the interview and environment to facilitate communication and gather accurate data.

Areas of Health Promotion

While gathering the patient's health history, the nurse needs to think critically about the data being gathered. The patient will reveal information about level of knowledge, health, and lifestyle. It is the nurse's role and responsibility to analyze these data for an overall sense of the patient's wellness and to give feedback about how the patient is meeting current evidence-based health guidelines. The nurse also needs to follow up on any deficits with patient teaching.

Assessment of Risk Factors

Risk factors play an important part in determining the patient's health status and degree of wellness related to the ear and its functions. Risk factors that cannot be controlled include age, gender, heredity, and family history. Risk factors that can be influenced are lifestyle choices and environmental risks. For example, as people age, so do the ears—like the rest of the body, the ears change with time. Nevertheless, people can influence the extent to which hearing changes or loss occurs by taking precautions to guard ears from loud noises. It is the nurse's role and responsibility to assess for risk factors such as listening to loud music or working with construction equipment. Once these factors have been thoroughly assessed, patient education can take place during the conversational interview. The nurse can give educational materials on how to prevent hearing loss to the patient to reinforce content covered.

| Questions to Assess History and Risk Factors | Rationale |

Personal History

How do you protect your skin from the sun?
- How often do you wear a hat?
- How often do you apply sunscreen?
- What Sun Protection Factor (SPF) is the sunscreen you use?
- When are you usually in the sun?
- How long do you usually stay in the sun?

The ear is commonly forgotten when it comes to sun protection. For this reason, 20% of all melanomas are found in the head and neck region. Of melanomas in this area, 7% to 15% affect the external ear, most commonly the helix (Mondin, Rinaldo, et al., 2005).

What ear concerns have you been diagnosed with—ear infections, hearing loss, tinnitus, or vertigo?
- What was the illness?
- When did you have it?
- How was the illness treated?
- What were the outcomes?

In children, ear infections are extremely prevalent. As many as 75% of children have at least one episode by their third birthday; 50% of these have three or more episodes in their first 3 years (National Institute on Deafness and Other Communication Disorders, 2009). These children are at risk for TM rupture, scarring, and hearing loss.

What ear surgeries have you had?
- What was the surgery?
- When did you have it?
- What were the outcomes?
- What complications or lasting effects (sequela) did you encounter?

Surgeries may be performed for artificial eustachian tube placement, TM repair, and cochlear implants. Cochlear implants for the hearing impaired are performed frequently (Watson, Hardie, et al., 2007). Ear surgery increases the likelihood of being exposed to ototoxic medications (eg, aminoglycoside antibiotics).

Medications

What prescription and over-the-counter medications are you currently taking?
- How often do you take them?
- What dosage?
- What route?

Several drugs have possible adverse effects (eg, hearing loss, tinnitus, vertigo) on the ears. Examples of ototoxic agents include all aminoglycosides, anti-inflammatory agents (eg, ibuprofen), antimalarials (eg, quinine), diuretics (eg, furosemide), nonnarcotic analgesics containing salicylates, antipyretics containing salicylates, erythromycin, quinidine sulfate, and antineoplastic drugs.

What immunizations have you received?
- What was the date of your last vaccinations?
- Have you received all required doses?

Mumps (a vaccine-preventable disease and part of the measles, mumps, rubella [MMR] shot) can cause sensorineural deafness in those who have not been vaccinated, did not develop immunity with vaccination, or had decreased immunity over time. Maternal exposure to rubella (a vaccine-preventable disease and part of the MMR shot) causes deafness in almost 90% of affected fetuses (Banatvala & Brown, 2004).

Family History

Tell me about your family's history of ear or hearing concerns, if any.
- Who had the illness?
- What was the illness?
- When did the person have it?
- How was the illness treated?
- What were the outcomes?

Identifying a family history of possible inherited and chronic disorders (eg, *Meniere's disease, otosclerosis*) is important in determining the patient's risk and providing anticipatory guidance (American Hearing Research Foundation, 2008).

Risk Factors

What type of loud noises have you been exposed to over your lifetime?
- When were you exposed to them?
- How long were you exposed to them?
- What protective ear equipment did you use?
- How did you monitor your exposure?

Hearing loss from loud noises is a major worldwide health issue (Hong & Samo, 2007). Workers at high risk for harmful noise exposure are farmers, firefighters, police, emergency medical technicians, heavy-machinery operators (eg, construction workers), military personnel, and members of the music industry.

What exposure to cigarette, pipe, or cigar smoke have you had over your lifetime?
- When were you exposed to it?
- How long were you exposed to it?

Those exposed to smoke show an increased prevalence of early onset hearing loss (Agrawal, Platz, et al., 2008).

Questions to Assess History and Risk Factors	Rationale
What allergies have you had? • To what are you allergic? • What were the symptoms? • How were these treated? • What were the outcomes?	Allergy symptoms such as runny nose and stuffy sinuses may lead to eustachian tube dysfunction in some patients.
How often do you travel by airplane? What related ear problems have you experienced, if any?	Air pressure changes with altitude. Those who travel by plane commonly experience some middle ear discomfort during the aircraft's descent. The eustachian tubes help equalize pressure on either side of the TM. Those whose eustachian tubes may malfunction include those with colds, sinus infections, other upper respiratory infections, and other ear conditions. If the eustachian tubes cannot equalize pressure, intense middle ear and sinus pain can occur. In severe cases the TM may rupture (Keystone, Kozarsky, et al., 2004).
What experience with diving do you have? • How often do you dive? • What ear concerns have you experienced, if any?	Air pressure changes with altitude; those who dive are at risk for middle ear trauma. Those at highest risk suffer from eustachian tube malfunction (as discussed under "Air Travel").
How do you clean your ears?	Inserting cotton-tipped applicators into the external ear canal may irritate the thin skin of the inner auditory canal and lead to impaction of cerumen, which can contribute to hearing loss.

Risk Assessment and Health Promotion

Important Topics for Health Promotion

> • Hearing loss
> • Sun exposure

The most significant topic for patient teaching based on thorough risk assessment of the ears is general hearing loss. Although ability to hear decreases somewhat with age, much hearing loss is preventable. Patients need to be asked about their exposure to noise and what protective equipment they use. Educating patients on the types, effectiveness, and instructions for use of protective ear equipment allows them to make decisions based on their needs. Education becomes even more important if the patient cannot make changes to the environment. For example, a construction worker who works daily surrounded by large, loud equipment may not be able to change the amount of machinery in close proximity to the work site, but he or she can be sure to wear adequate ear protection.

Another important topic to address is skin cancer prevention. Many melanomas are found near or on the helix of the ear. Teaching patients how to protect themselves from unnecessary sun exposure increases the likelihood of preventative behaviours (see Chapter 13).

In addition, it is important to address how the patient cleans the ears. Many people associate cerumen in the ear canal with lack of hygiene and therefore clean their ears routinely. Often patients think cotton-tipped applicators are for this purpose. This self-care behaviour is unsafe, placing patients at risk for cerumen impaction. It is important to reinforce proper cleaning techniques.

Focused Health History Related to Common Symptoms

While taking the health history it is essential for the nurse to ask about common symptoms of the ear. Questions about common symptoms will aid in identifying any concerns and possible problem areas related to the chief concern or a chronic diagnosis.

Common Ear Symptoms/Signs

> • Hearing loss
> • Feeling dizzy (vertigo)
> • Ringing or noises in the ears (tinnitus)
> • Ear pain (otalgia)
> • Discharge from the ears

Examples of Questions to Assess Symptoms/Signs	Rationale/Unexpected Findings

Hearing Loss

Describe your hearing. What changes, if any, have you noticed?

- When did this start?
- Did it start suddenly or gradually?
- In what situations do you find it hardest to hear?
- What have you done for it?
- What were the outcomes?
- Do you have a family history of hearing loss?
- Have you been exposed to loud noises such as machinery or loud music?

Determining onset of hearing loss may help uncover cause and if it can be reversed, such as with a cerumen or foreign-body obstruction. Sudden hearing loss indicates trauma or obstruction. Family history of hearing loss indicates *presbycusis*. Environmental damage to hearing may involve consistent or one-time exposure to loud noise.

Feeling Dizzy (Vertigo)

Have you ever felt dizzy or had difficulty with balance?

- Under what circumstances has this happened?
- How long does this continue?
- Does it feel like you are, or the room is, spinning?
- How have you treated this?
- What were the outcomes?

Transient vertigo and persistent vertigo have different etiologies and thus necessitate different treatments. *Vertigo*, the sensation of the room spinning, indicates dysfunction of the bony labyrinth in the inner ear.

Ringing or Noises in Ears (Tinnitus)

Do you ever have a sensation of a buzzing or ringing that no one else can hear?

- Is there any time that this seems louder?
- Are you currently taking any medications, vitamins, or herbal supplements?

Tinnitus is thought to be an inability to filter internal noise from the external input of sound. Ototoxic agents can cause tinnitus. Stopping their use may resolve tinnitus, although some ototoxic agents cause lasting damage.

Ear Pain (Otalgia)

Do you experience pain in either ear?

- Is it in both ears? One ear?
- Have you ever had this pain before?
- If so, what was the cause?
- Do you feel the pain deep inside or more on the outside of the ear?
- Does it hurt to touch your ear?
- Describe the pain—is it persistent or intermittent?
- What makes the pain better or worse?
- Have you had any drainage from your ears?
- What colour was the drainage?
- Did it have an odour?
- Have you had any surgeries or illnesses recently?
- How do you clean your ears?

Otalgia usually indicates ear dysfunction, most commonly *otitis media* or *otitis externa*. Pain in the ear can be referred from the pharynx. It is not uncommon for the patient recovering from tonsil surgery to complain of ear pain. Pain in the ear can also be referred from a dental issue in the *lower* jaw or from inflammation of the eustachian tube. Severe pain followed by relief and drainage indicates a *ruptured TM*. External ear sensitivity indicates *otitis externa*, which may result from self-induced trauma, such as inserting bobby pins, keys, or fingernails into the external ear canal.

EXAMPLE OF QUESTIONS FOR SYMPTOM/SIGN ANALYSIS—HEARING LOSS

- "Does your hearing loss involve both ears?" (Location)
- "Describe your hearing." "What types of sounds do you hear?" (Quality)
- "Do you have difficulty hearing people when they talk?" "What difference does a noisy environment make?" (Severity)
- "When did you start to notice the hearing loss?" "Did it happen suddenly or gradually?" (Onset)
- "Has your hearing loss continued since it started?" (Duration)
- "Do you feel like it is getting better or worse over time?" (Constancy)
- "Is your hearing better at different times of the day? "Or worse?" (Time of day/month/year)

- "Does anything make it more difficult for you to hear?" (Aggravating factors)
- "What makes it easier for you to hear?" (Alleviating factors)
- "Do you have any pain in your ears?" "Do you feel dizzy?" "Nauseated?" (Associated symptoms)
- "Have you had any exposure to loud noises?" "At work?" "Do you have any hobbies that have resulted in loud noise?" "Have you had any head injuries?" (Environmental factors)
- "How does your hearing loss affect your life?" (Significance to patient)
- "Tell me what you think is happening." (Patient perspective)

Adapted from Roach, S., Roddick, P., et al. (2010). The ear, nose, mouth, and throat. In T. C. Stephen, D. L. Skillen, R. A. Day, & L. S. Bickley (Eds.). *Canadian Bates' guide to health assessment for nurses* (pp. 341–380). Philadelphia, PA: Wolters Kluwer Health/Lippincott Williams & Wilkins.

Documentation of Expected Findings

Patient alert and following conversation with no evidence of hearing loss. Denies hearing difficulty, vertigo, tinnitus, and pain.

▲ Lifespan Considerations

Additional Questions	Rationale/Unexpected Findings
Newborns, Infants, and Children **Otitis media** • When was the last case of an ear infection? • How was it treated? • How many ear infections has your child had? • Did your child have middle ear infections over the summer months? • Has your child ever had surgery for ear infections? • Is your child exposed to cigarette smoke? • Does your child attend daycare?	Repeat or persistent infections may require surgery if conductive hearing loss causes great discomfort or speech delays. Incidence of otitis media is highest in winter months (Klein, Pelton, et al., 2009). Exposures to passive smoke or cigarette residue on clothes are risk factors for otitis media. Daycare attendance is also a risk factor and increases the risk of antibiotic-resistant otitis media.
Hearing • Did your child pass his or her newborn hearing screen? • Do you have concerns regarding your child's hearing? • Do you have concerns about your child's speech development? • Was your child born full term? • How long did your child stay in the hospital following birth?	Routine newborn hearing screening enhances early intervention for hearing loss. Speech development is delayed in children with a hearing deficit. Premature infants are at increased risk for hearing deficits. Incidence of hearing deficits increases greatly with prolonged hospital stays and exposure to ototoxic drugs.

An Example of a Therapeutic Dialogue

Remember Mrs. Bossio, introduced at the beginning of this chapter. She was admitted to the clinic today with concerns of ear pain. The nurse uses professional communication techniques to gather subjective data. The following conversation gives an example of an interview.

Nurse: Hello, Mrs. Bossio. I'm going to be your nurse today. My name is Lee (smiles, pauses). How are you feeling?

Mrs. Bossio: Fine.

Nurse: Your chart says that you came in because of your ears. Is that right?

Mrs. Bossio: Yes, I have had trouble with pain. But the pain gets better with medicine and a warm cloth.

Nurse: Are you having other concerns with your ears?

Mrs. Bossio: Yes, I have a buzzing noise in my ears. My husband says I can't hear well. My kids say I am yelling when I'm just talking. I can't understand them anymore.

Nurse: It sounds like your family is noticing the changes in your hearing (pauses).

Mrs. Bossio: My mom had problems hearing when she was my age, and it was hard for the family.

Nurse: This must bring back some of those memories for you. Let's talk about how your hearing has changed (smiles).

Critical Thinking Challenge

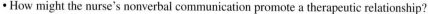

• How might the nurse's nonverbal communication promote a therapeutic relationship?
• How might the patient's experience and culture influence her perceptions, values, and beliefs about her diagnosis and healing?
• What is the role of the nurse in giving advice versus listening to the patient's perspective?

Equipment

- Otoscope with disposable speculum tips
- High-pitched tuning fork (512 or 1024 Hz)

Promoting Patient Comfort, Dignity, and Safety

To obtain objective data about the ears, it is best to make sure the patient is comfortable and the room is quiet. It is ideal for the patient's ears to be at the nurse's eye level to be able to inspect them without discomfort to the patient. For adults and older children, the examination can be performed with the patient sitting on the examination table.

Begin the examination by first washing your hands in warm water. Hand sanitizer is effective for bacteria control but leaves the hands cold and may cause discomfort for the patient.

When meeting with patients you will be able to move forward with the examination and intervention when you address the concern that is most important to them first. Often this may not be the issue of greatest clinical significance. Once you address this you will find your patient is more receptive to issues of greater significance such as hearing loss or cholesteatoma. Patient education is the primary tool to engage your patient in improved self-care practices and address issues that unaddressed may cause the patient harm or impair quality of life.

Routine head-to-toe assessment includes the most important and common assessment techniques. The nurse may add advanced steps if concerns exist over a specific finding. Additional techniques may be added if indicated by the clinical situation.

Techniques and Expected Findings	Unexpected Findings

Inspection

Inspect the ears (Fig. 16-7). *Ears are symmetrical, equal size, and fully formed.*

Figure 16-7 Surface anatomy of the ears.

Inspect the face. *Facial tone is uniform with the ears. Skin is intact. Small painless nodules on the helix are a variation of anatomy known as a darwinian tubercle* (Fig. 16-8).

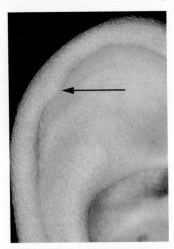

Figure 16-8 A common anatomical variation, the darwinian tubercle.

Microtia, macrotia, edematous ears, cartilage *Pseudomonas* infection, carcinoma on auricle, cyst, and frostbite are unexpected findings (see Table 16-2 at the end of this chapter).

Palpation

Palpate the auricle, tragus, and mastoid process. *Ears are firm without lumps, lymph tissue is not palpable, ears are nontender, and no pain is elicited with palpation or manipulation of the auricle. No pain occurs with palpation of the mastoid process.*

Enlarged lymph nodes indicate pathology or infection. Pain with auricle movement or tragus palpation indicates otitis externa or furuncle.

Whisper Test

The **whisper test** evaluates for loss of high-frequency sounds. Instruct the patient to plug (or plug for the patient) the ear opposite to the one you are testing. With your head approximately 30 to 40 cm from the patient's ear and your mouth not visible to the patient, whisper a two-syllable word (Fig. 16-9). Have the patient repeat what you have said. Repeat on the opposite side. *Patient repeats the entire word to you without errors.*

Not being able to repeat the word clearly or missing components may indicate hearing loss of higher frequencies and requires follow-up with formal testing.

Figure 16-9 The whisper test.

Rinne Test

A tuning fork is a U-shaped piece of metal with a handle attached at the apex of the U. When struck lightly against an object, it will vibrate at a specific frequency. Use of a tuning fork helps the nurse determine if hearing is equal in both ears and if there is either a conductive or sensorineural hearing loss by allowing the nurse to compare the difference in BC and AC. Remember AC has less resistance than BC.

The Rinne test examines the differentiation between BC and AC.

BC that is longer or the same as AC is evidence of conductive hearing loss. Conductive hearing loss on one side may indicate external or middle ear disease. Patients with conductive hearing loss should have an assessment of the auricle and external auditory canal to look for blockage. The TM should be assessed to ensure that there is no middle ear finding, such as fluid or a TM perforation.

(text continues on page 400)

1. To begin, grasp the base and tap the U of the tuning fork (512 or 1024 Hz) against the back or heel of your hand (Fig. 16-10).

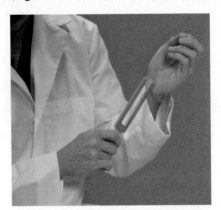

Figure 16-10 Striking the tuning fork against the back of the hand.

2. Place the base of the handle on the patient's mastoid process (Fig. 16-11). Note the time on the second hand of your watch.

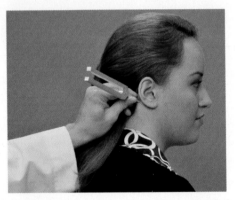

Figure 16-11 Rinne test: placing the tuning fork on the mastoid process.

3. Instruct the patient to tell you when he or she no longer hears the sound of the fork. Note the number of seconds.

4. Once the patient no longer hears the sound through the mastoid process, move the tip of the tuning fork to the front of the external auditory meatus (Fig. 16-12). Again note the time on the second hand of your watch.

Figure 16-12 Rinne test: moving the tip of the tuning fork to the front of the external auditory meatus.

5. Instruct the patient to inform you when he or she no longer hears the sound. *AC is twice as long as BC.*

Weber Test

The Weber test helps to differentiate the cause of unilateral hearing loss. After activating the fork, place its handle on the midline of the parietal bone in line with both ears (Fig. 16-13). *The patient hears the sound in both ears or in the midline, and at equal intensity.*

Unilateral identification of the sound indicates sensorineural loss in the ear that the patient did not hear or had reduced perception of the sound. Sensorineural hearing loss on one side may be related to an inner ear disorder such as *Meniere's disease* or a *vestibular schwannoma* (acoustic neuroma).

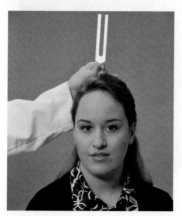

Figure 16-13 Weber test: placing the tuning fork on the midline of the parietal bone.

Otoscopic Evaluation

Inspect the external meatus and canal. Several sizes of speculum can be used for the otoscope. Choose one that fits into the external canal without discomfort, but large enough for you to see through. *The canal has fine hairs; some cerumen lining the wall skin is intact, with no discharge.*

Redness, swelling of the external auditory canal, and discharge are signs of external otitis. Either a foreign body or cerumen can obstruct the canal.

Hold the otoscope so that your thumb is by the window and you are bracing the shaft with your fingers along the patient's cheek. This allows you to stabilize the otoscope and decreases risk of scraping the external auditory canal with the speculum. Hold the patient's ear at the helix and lift up and back to align the canal for best visualization of the TM (Fig. 16-14). After visualization of the canal, rotate the otoscope slightly to be able to visualize the entire TM. Visualize portions of the malleus, umbo, manubrium, and short process through the translucent membrane (Fig. 16-15).

Swelling or bulging of the TM indicates acute otitis media (see Table 16-3 at the end of this chapter). A diffuse cone of light indicates *otitis media with effusion*. Air bubbles caused by a functioning eustachian tube allow drainage of effusion and aeration of the middle ear. A perforated TM may allow for direct visualization into the middle ear.

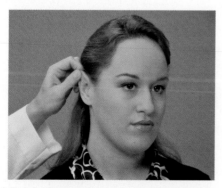

Figure 16-14 Otoscopi examination: holding the patient's ear at the helix and lifting up and back to align the canal for best visualization of the TM.

(text continues on page 402)

A

B

Figure 16-15 Correct placement of the otoscope.

A well-aerated middle ear allows visualization of part of the incus as well (Fig. 16-16). *TM is intact, pearly grey, and translucent, and allows visualization of the short process of the malleus. The cone of light is visible in the anterior inferior quadrant (5 o'clock in right ear, 7 o'clock in left).*

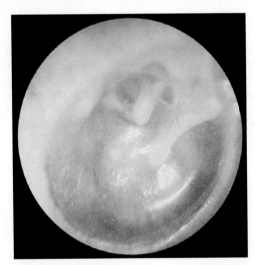

Figure 16-16 Right TM.

A variation is a TM with white areas (sclerosis). These white areas are visible scars from repeated ear infections. This scarring may make the TM less flexible (Fig. 16-17).

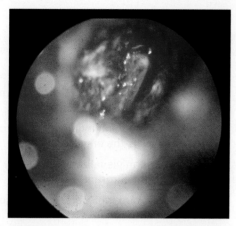

Figure 16-17 TM with tympanosclerosis.

Once the TM is visualized you may use the bulb insufflator attached to the head of the otoscope (Fig. 16-18) to observe TM movement. First, perform positive pressure that forces air into the external auditory canal and pushes down the TM. Then, release pressure and note the negative pressure pulling the TM outward. *The TM moves inward when inflated and outward with release.*

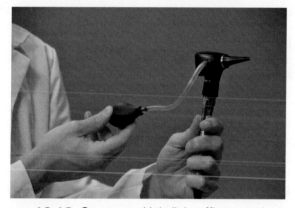

Figure 16-18 Otoscope with bulb insufflator attached.

Auditory Acuity

The most accurate way to evaluate hearing is by an audiologist or occupational health nurse performing an **audiogram** in a soundproof room. An audiogram gives exact information about absent or diminished frequencies for the patient. It also distinguishes sensorineural from conductive loss. Including tympanometry with the audiogram will show the compliance of the TM and if there is a pinhole rupture by providing the volume of the external ear canal. The primary provider in an advanced practice role orders this test. Though an audiogram is the most accurate test, most clinics are not supplied with it.

Equilibrium

Equilibrium can be assessed by using the Romberg's test as described in Chapter 24.

Failure of the Romberg's test may indicate dysfunction in the vestibular portion of the inner ear, semicircular canals, and vestibule.

Right pinna intact, canal well aerated, TM translucent with visible bony prominence of the malleus and sharp cone of light. Left pinna intact, canal well aerated, TM translucent with visible bony prominence of the malleus and sharp cone of light. Hearing intact bilaterally with whisper test. Rinne test AC > BC in both ears. Weber test heard equally in both ears.

Examples of Documentation for Ears

Area of Assessment	Expected Findings	Unexpected Findings
External ear	Aligned horizontally and vertically with eyes, symmetrical bilaterally	Lower than eyes, 0.5 cm × 0.25 cm fixed mass present on upper right helix
Ear canal	Pink, minimal cerumen visible bilaterally	Left canal reddened and inflamed; soft brown cerumen obstructs the entire right canal
Eardrum (tympanic membrane)	Pearly-grey, intact, cone of light visualized bilaterally	Central perforation visualized with yellow exudates on right eardrum
Hearing acuity	Accurately identifies low-whispered two-syllable words bilaterally	Identified three loud-whispered words accurately bilaterally
Conduction	AC > BC bilaterally	BC > AC left ear; AC = BC right ear

Adapted from Roach, S., Roddick, P., et al. (2010). The ear, nose, mouth, and throat. In T. C. Stephen, D. L. Skillen, R. A. Day, & L. S. Bickley (Eds.). *Canadian Bates' guide to health assessment for nurses* (pp. 341–380). Philadelphia, PA: Wolters Kluwer Health/ Lippincott Williams & Wilkins.

 ## Lifespan Considerations

Infants and Children

Assessing ears for children can be challenging and fun. When working with them, addressing parents' concerns helps you gain their trust and will encourage them to assist with examination. Ensure that you approach children in a playful manner and involve them in conversation as developmentally appropriate. They will often be more compliant with examination once they are involved in the process (eg, holding the otoscope, helping explain their history).

While you are introducing and acclimatizing a child to the equipment, note the placement of the external ear on the skull. The superior portion of the pinna should be congruent with the outer canthus of the eye. There should be no more than a 10° deviation from the medial fold of the lobe to the attachment of the superior portion of the helix. More than 10° deviation requires further investigation—it can signify a genetic defect in the renal system. It can also indicate neurodevelopmental challenges.

Older children can sit for the examination on the examination table. Children tend to be active, and you need to be creative with gaining cooperation for the otoscopic examination. Have them touch the light to see that it does not hurt or help you place the speculum on the head of the otoscope. Ask questions such as "What do you think I will find in here?" Some children are distracted by coming up with answers. Younger children and infants may need to be held safely to reduce the risk of injury to the external auditory canal during the otoscopic examination. Parents may use one arm to hold infants firmly against the chest while using the other arm to stabilize the baby's head (Fig. 16-19). For the right ear, have the parent hold the child on the left side and position the head so the infant faces away from the parent. Reverse for the left side.

Toddlers are best examined by sitting on the parent's lap facing forward while the parent "hugs" them with one arm and holds the head steady with the opposite arm. Preschoolers often need to be held down on an examination table. It is best to have the older children to be supine with the head turned toward the parent (Fig. 16-20). Once you examine the exposed ear, trade sides of the table with the parent and examine the opposite ear.

To insert the otoscope tip into a child's ear canal, the pinna must be manipulated differently than with an adult. Gently grasp the child's lobe and pull downward. A child's ear canal

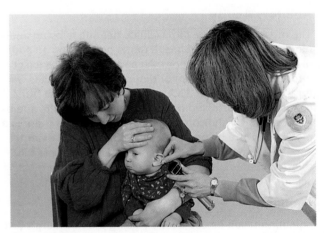

Figure 16-19 Adult holding infant for ear examination.

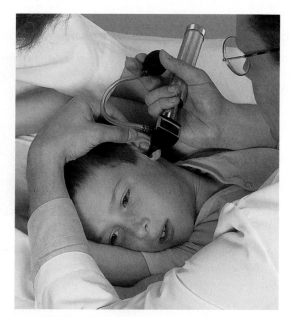

Figure 16-20 Older child on the examination table to facilitate ear examination.

is narrower and positioned in a more posterior angle than an adult's (see Fig. 16-6).

If a child has had a myringotomy with placement of tympanostomy tubes because of recurrent or persistent otitis media, the tube should be in the inferior portion of the TM, with the lumen of the tube patent.

Screening for hearing acuity in infants and young children includes evaluation of developmental milestones, such as the Moro reflex in neonates. If there is a developmental lag or concern by caregivers, a pediatric audiologist should perform a formal pediatric evaluation. Unexpected findings include absent Moro reflex, inability to localize sound, or lack of understandable language by 24 months.

Older Adults

The cartilage and skin around the external ear may be less pliable in older adults. The stiff hairs in the canal may require a smaller otoscope tip to separate them and increase visualization of the TM. The membrane itself may seem more opaque and less mobile.

Documenting Expected and Unexpected Findings

The nurse has just finished a beginning ear examination of Mrs. Bossio, who has unexpected findings. Review the following important findings revealed in each of the steps of objective data collection for Mrs. Bossio. Consider how these results compare with the expected findings. Note that inspection is the major technique used in ear assessment.

Inspection: Right ear is pink, skin is intact, external auditory canal appears clear. Left ear is pink, skin is intact, purulent drainage is noted in the external auditory canal.

Palpation: Right ear warm, no pain with palpation. Left ear is warm, painful with manipulation of the external ear and pain with pressure on the tragus.

Analyzing Findings

Mrs. Bossio is diagnosed with an ear infection. The following nursing note illustrates how subjective and objective data are collected and analyzed and nursing interventions are developed.

Subjective: States 5/10 pain that is constant. Increased to 8/10 when she touches her left ear.

Objective: Withdrawing from touch applied to left ear during assessment. Purulent drainage noted at the meatus of the external ear canal.

Analysis: Pain related to otitis externa of left ear.

Plan: Apply heat or cold for comfort. Encourage administration of ordered oral pain medication and adherence to antibiotic schedule to promote healing. Work with the patient's family and encourage them to speak more clearly and make eye contact.

Critical Thinking Challenge

• What type of ongoing assessment would you predict?
• How would you address the issue of pain assessment and management?
• What teaching should be performed related to Mrs. Bossio's otitis externa, loss of hearing, and treatment plan?

An audiology consult is indicated for evaluation of hearing loss. Audiologists are available in many specialty clinics to ensure proper evaluation. The following conversation illustrates how the nurse might organize data and make recommendations about Mrs. Bossio to the audiologist.

Situation: Hello. I'm taking care of Mrs. Bossio in the clinic today. She's a 25-year-old woman with ear pain, tinnitus, and possible hearing loss.

Background: Her mother had hearing loss at a young age. Mrs. Bossio also works in a clothing factory with many loud noises and uses ear protection. Her hearing was stable until 6 months ago when she noticed a buzzing sound in her ears. Around that time she also required the television to be turned up to hear it clearly.

Assessment: Her right ear is clear. She is having some drainage from her left ear and needs to have an audiogram to evaluate her hearing loss.

Recommendations: When you perform your audiogram would you please perform a tympanogram as well to check for a ruptured TM? What times do you have available for her? Thanks you.

Critical Thinking Challenge

- What assessments might be performed on other body systems related to the patient's findings?
- What health promotion and teaching needs would be related to the patient's history and risk factors?
- What further assessment information might the nurse want to collect in preparation for the end of the appointment?

Clinical Significance 16-5

For patients who wear hearing aids, accumulated cerumen and otitis externa can be ongoing challenges. It is important for this population to have frequent examination of their ear canals to ensure patency and health and to receive maximum benefits from their hearing aids.

Evidence-Informed Critical Thinking

Common Laboratory and Diagnostic Testing

Most common hearing tests in primary-care offices and schools are done with a device called an *audiometer*. This simple screening device consists of headphones and a box that delivers tones to each ear at variable frequencies and volumes. The purpose is to identify those patients who require further testing and examination by an audiologist. Audiologists perform various hearing tests, such as an *audiogram*, which is conducted in a sound-proof booth. This test differentiates conductive from sensorineural hearing loss. Audiologists also use tympanograms and tests to reveal otoacoustic emissions, which provide information about the function of the outer hair cells of the cochlea. The otoacoustic emissions test helps determine suspected hearing loss from ototoxic drugs. If the patient reports pain and drainage is present in the ear canal, this fluid may be cultured to determine the best topical treatment for either otitis externa or otitis media with TM perforation.

Clinical Reasoning

Nursing Diagnosis, Outcomes, and Interventions

When formulating a nursing diagnosis, it is important to use critical thinking to cluster data and identify patterns that fit together. The nurse compares these clusters of data with the defining characteristics (unexpected findings) for the diagnosis to ensure the most accurate labelling and appropriate interventions. Table 16-1 compares nursing diagnoses, unexpected findings, and interventions commonly related to the ear assessment (North American Nursing Diagnosis Association-International, 2009).

Table 16-1 Common Nursing Diagnoses Associated With the Ear

Diagnosis and Related Factors	Point of Differentiation	Assessment Characteristics	Nursing Interventions
Altered auditory sensory perception related to hearing loss	Alterations in the way the person interprets, uses, or organizes sensory (especially hearing-related) stimuli	Change in responses to environment, impaired communication, difficulty with concentration	Minimize background noise. Sit directly in front of the patient. Allow the patient to see your face. Do not overenunciate or shout at patient.
Pain related to inflammation of ear canal	Unpleasant sensory and emotional experience from skin or tissue damage	Self-report of pain is subjective. Expressions are variable and include facial grimace, guarding, muscle tension, tachycardia, tachypnea, and nausea.	Use pain scale to identify current pain intensity and effectiveness of medication. Develop pain goal collaboratively with the patient. Provide pain medications as ordered.* Provide alternatives such as distraction, breathing, and relaxation. Monitor for fever, white blood cells, wound drainage, or erythema Encourage adequate nutrition.

*Collaborative interventions.

Pulling It All Together: An Example of Reflection and Critical Thinking

The nurse uses assessment data to formulate a patient care plan with patient outcomes and interventions. This is often in the form of a care plan or case note similar to the one below.

Nursing Diagnosis	Patient Outcomes	Nursing Interventions	Rationales	Evaluation
Pain related to ear infection as evidenced by stating pain 5/10 scale	Patient rates ear pain at zero.	Provide warm or cool pack for comfort. Provide analgesics as prescribed.	Pain is subjective and treatment is aimed at controlling the symptoms until the cause can be resolved.	Patient states that ear pain is now 2/10 scale. Continue to provide analgesic every 4 h.*

*Collaborative interventions.

Nurses use assessment information to identify patient outcomes. Some outcomes related to ear concerns include the following:

• Patient is free from ear pain.
• Patient demonstrates understanding with a verbal response.
• Patient explains plan to accommodate hearing impairment (Moorhead, Johnson, et al., 2007).

Once the outcomes area is established, patient care is implemented to improve the status of the patient. The nurse uses critical thinking and evidence-based practice to develop the interventions. Some examples of nursing interventions for the ear and hearing are as follows:

• Turn off television and radio when communicating.
• Close the door if hallway noise is loud.
• Provide a communication board and visual aids for detailed discussions (Bulechek, Butcher, et al., 2008).

The nurse then evaluates the care according to the patient outcomes that were developed, therefore reassessing the patient and continuing or modifying the interventions as appropriate.

Applying Your Knowledge

Using the previous steps of clinical reasoning, organizing, and prioritizing, consider all the case study findings woven throughout this chapter. When answering the following questions, begin drawing conclusions and see how the pieces of assessment must work together to create an environment for personalized, appropriate, and accurate care.

• What are some of the possible causes of Mrs. Bossio's hearing loss? (Knowledge)
• How will the nurse assess and document the patient's pain?
• How will the nurse assess and document her hearing loss? (Comprehension)
• What information will need to be collected to assess the patient's risk for hearing loss? (Application)
• What lifestyle factors might be contributing to Mrs. Bossio's hearing loss? (Analysis)
• What recommendations for follow-up will the patient need? (Synthesis)
• How would you evaluate Mrs. Bossio's understanding of her condition, treatment, and follow-up? (Evaluation)

Key Points

• The ear consists of the external ear, middle ear, and inner ear.
• The TM is the barrier between the external auditory canal and the middle ear.
• The middle ear contains the malleus, incus, and stapes that conduct sound waves to the inner ear.
• The inner ear translates sound to the nerves and brainstem.
• The semicircular canals and vestibule provide the body with proprioception and equilibrium.
• The functions of the ear are hearing and equilibrium.
• Clues of hearing loss include leaning forward to hear, positioning the head with the "good ear" forward, concentrating on lip movement, asking to repeat questions, and using a loud or monotone voice.
• Risk factors for hearing loss include family history, frequent ear infections, use of some medications, lack of immunizations, exposure to loud noises, exposure to smoke, allergies, airplane travel, diving, inappropriate cleaning of ears, and increased age.
• Common disorders of the ear include hearing loss, vertigo, tinnitus, and otalgia.
• Otitis media is more common in children.
• Routine screening of newborn hearing leads to early intervention for hearing loss.
• The assessment includes inspection and palpation of the external ear.
• The otoscopic examination includes assessing the auditory meatus, canal, and TM.
• The most accurate evaluation of hearing is with an audiogram.
• The whisper test evaluates loss of high-frequency sounds.
• During the Rinne test, AC should be twice as long as BC. If BC is equal to or greater than AC, this is evidence of conductive hearing loss.
• The Weber test differentiates unilateral hearing loss.
• A child's ear canal is narrower and more posterior than an adult's.

Review Questions

1. The function of the ear is for
   A. hearing and equilibrium
   B. equilibrium and perforations
   C. perforations and balance
   D. balance and equilibrium

2. The inner ear
   A. contains the malleus, incus, and stapes
   B. conducts sound waves to the external ear
   C. translates sound to the nerves and brainstem
   D. provides the body with proprioception

3. Cues of hearing loss include which of the following? Choose all that are correct.
   A. Using a loud or monotonous voice
   B. Asking to repeat questions
   C. Concentrating on lip movement
   D. Leaning forward to hear

4. Risk factors for hearing loss include which of the following? Choose all that are correct.
   A. Frequent ear infections
   B. Being current on immunizations
   C. Exposure to smoke
   D. Decreased age

5. Tinnitus is described as
   A. inability to hear well
   B. dizziness
   C. ringing in the ear
   D. ear pain

6. Which of the following patients is most likely to have hearing loss?
   A. Caucasian man older than 70 years
   B. Hispanic woman older than 50 years
   C. Asian man younger than 30 years
   D. African girl younger than 10 years

7. Which of the following differentiates the nurse assessment from the audiologist assessment?
   A. History and risk factors
   B. Symptom analysis
   C. Inspection and palpation
   D. audiogram

8. A nursing diagnosis appropriate for the patient with ear concerns includes
   A. kinesthetic altered perception
   B. altered sensory perception
   C. sensory perception, gustatory
   D. olfactory sensory perception

9. An outcome that is appropriate for the patient with hearing impairment is
   A. Provide a communication board or picture to assist teaching.
   B. Minimize background noise and close door.
   C. Stand in front of the patient and explain procedure.
   D. The patient explains plan to accommodate hearing impairment.

10. Which of the following are appropriate interventions for the patient who is at risk for ear infection? Select all that apply.
    A. Be current on immunizations.
    B. Avoid secondhand smoke.
    C. Clean only external ear.
    D. Have audiogram yearly.

Canadian Nursing Research

Ayukawa, H., Lejeune, P. L., & Proulx, J. F. (2002). Hearing screening outcomes in Inuit children in Nunavik, Quebec, Canada. *International Journal of Circumpolar Health, 63*(Suppl 2), 309–311.

Davies, H., Marion, S., & Teschke, K. (2008). The impact of hearing conservation programs on incidence of noise-induced hearing loss in Canadian workers. *American Journal of Industrial Medicine, 51*(12), 923–931.

References

Agrawal, Y., Platz, E. A., et al. (2008). Prevalence of hearing loss and differences by demographic characteristics among US adults. *Archives of Internal Medicine, 168*(14), 1522–1530.

American Hearing Research Foundation. (2008). *Meniere's Disease.* Retrieved from http://www.american-hearing.org/disorders/menieres/menieres.html

Banatvala, J. E., & Brown, D. W. G. (2004). Rubella. *The Lancet, 363*(9415), 1127–1137.

Bulechek, G. M., & Butcher, H. K., et al. (2008). *Nursing Interventions Classification (NIC)* (5th ed.) St. Louis, MO: Mosby.

Canadian Association of Speech-Language Pathologists and Audiologists. (2000). *Adult Hearing Disorders: Fact sheet.* Retrieved from www.caslpa.ca/PDF/fact%20sheets/adult%20hearing%20disorders.pdf

Cummings, C., Fredrickson, J., et al. (1998). *Otolaryngology in head and neck surgery.* St. Louis, MO: Mosby.

Davis, P. B., Paki, B., et al. (2007). On tinnitus neuromonics tinnitus treatment: Third clinical trial. *Ear Hear, 2,* 242–259.

Hong, H. K. B., & Samo, J. (2007). Hazardous decibels: Hearing health of firefighters. *American Association of Occupational Health Nurses, 55*(8), 313–319.

Hosford-Dunn, H., Roeser, R. J., et al. (2008). *Cerumen management in audiology: Practice management* (2nd ed.). New York, NY: Thieme Medical Publishers Inc.

Isaacson, G. (2009). *Congenital anomalies of the ear.* Retrieved from UpToDate database.

Keystone, J. S., Kozarsky, P. E., et al. (2004). *Travel medicine.* Toronto, ON: Expert Consult Elsevier.

Klein, J. O., Pelton, S., et al. (2009). *Acute otitis media in children: Epidemiology, pathogenesis, clinical manifestations, and complications.* Retrieved from http://www.uptodateonline.com. proxy.seattleu.edu/online/content/topic.do?topicKey=pedi_id/2870&selectedTitle=2 150& source=search_result

Manohar, B. (2007). Hearing and aging. *Canadian Medical Association Journal, 176*(7), 925.

Mondin, A., Rinaldo, A., et al. (2005). Malignant melanoma of the auricle. *Acta Otolaryngology, 125*(11), 1140–1144.

Moorhead, S., Johnson, M., et al. (2007). *Nursing outcomes classification (NOC)* (4th ed.). Philadelphia, PA: Mosby.

National Institution on Deafness and Other Communication Disorders. (2009). *Otitis Media (Ear Infection).* Retrieved from http://www.nidcd.nih.gov/health/hearing/otitism.asp

North American Nursing Diagnosis Association-International. (2009). *Nursing diagnoses, 2009–2011 edition: Definitions and classifications (NANDA-I NURSING DIAGNOSIS).* West Sussex, UK: John Wiley & Sons.

Pawson, S., & Milan, F. A. (2005). Cerumen types in two Eskimo communities. *American Journal of Physical Anthropology, 41*(3), 431–432.

Pratt, S. R., Kuller, L., et al. (2009). Prevalence of hearing loss in black and white elders: Results of the cardiovascular health study. *Journal of Speech Language and Hearing Research, 52*(4), 973–989.

Rubin, R., & Strayer, D. S. (2008). *Rubin's pathology: Clinicopathologic foundations of medicine.* Philadelphia, PA: Wolters Kluwer Health/Lippincott Williams & Wilkins.

Tinnitus Association of Canada. (n.d.). *Questions and answers.* Retrieved from http://www.kadis.com/ta/tinnitus.htm

Watson, L. M., Hardie, T., et al. (2007). Oxford journals parents' views on changing communication after cochlear implantation. Retrieved from http://jdsde.oxfordjournals.org/cgi/content/full/enm036v1

The Canadian Jensen's Nursing Health Assessment suite offers these additional resources to enhance learning and facilitate understanding of this chapter:

- thePoint on line resource, http//thepoint.lww.com/Stephen1E
- *Laboratory Manual for Canadian Jensen's Nursing Health Assessment: A Best Practice Approach*

Tables of Unexpected Findings

Table 16-2   **Variations of the External Ear**

Microtia

Small or deformed auricle that may be associated with a blind or absent auditory canal

Macrotia

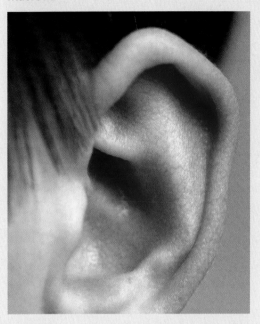

Excessive enlargement of the auricle; usually congenital

Edematous Ears

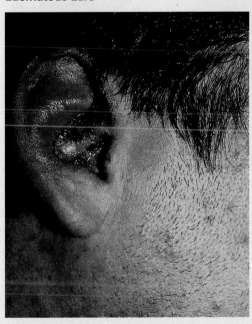

An external ear canal that is swollen with inflammation or infection

Cartilage *Staphylococcus or Pseudomonas* Infection

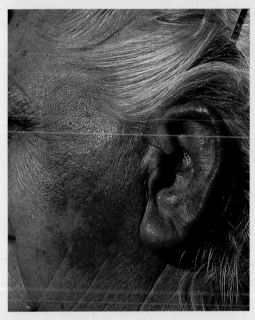

Painful, reddened ear usually surrounding incisions, ear piercing, or an area of traumatic injury

(table continues on page 412)

Table 16-2 **Variations of the External Ear** (*continued*)

Carcinoma on Auricle

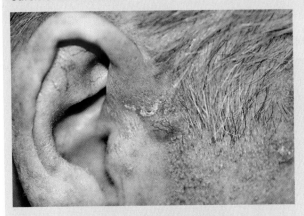

Common site of carcinoma related to sun exposure; either basal cell or squamous cell tumours may be present

Cyst

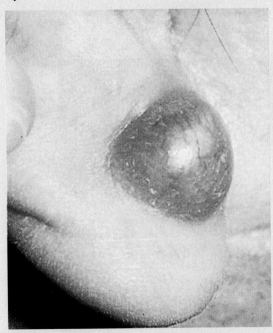

A sac or pouch with a membranous lining filled with fluid or solid material

Tophi

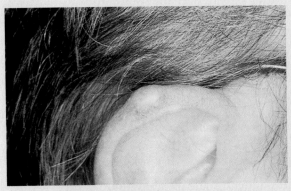

Uric acid crystals associated with gout; may appear as hard nodules on the ear surface

External Otitis

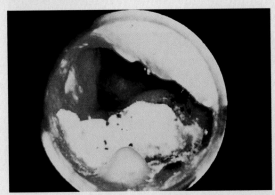

Inflammatory and infectious discharge in the external canal; associated with pain, itching, fullness, and reduced hearing

Table 16-3   **Unexpected Findings in the Internal Ear**

Tympanic membrane (TM) Rupture

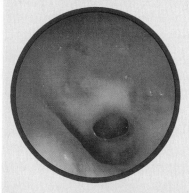

A nonintact TM; associated symptoms include clear, purulent, or bloody discharge; hearing loss in the affected ear; buzzing in the ear; and ear pain

Otitis Media With Effusion

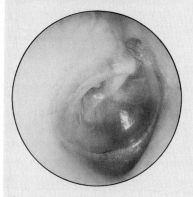

Purulent discharge associated with a bacterial infection. Redness and bulging on the eardrum. Onset can be sudden or gradual with increasing pain, fever, and hearing loss.

Foreign Body

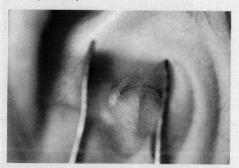

Most commonly these are found in the canal of a child who puts a bean or bead in the ear. If the object has been in the ear for several days, the patient may present with purulent discharge, pain, or hearing loss. If an insect is in the ear, the patient may hear a bug flying around in the ear.

Acute Otitis Media

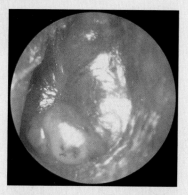

Acute infection in the middle ear. Onset is usually sudden and sometimes accompanied by fever and pain. Fluid may be in the middle ear, with signs or symptoms of middle ear inflammation. Causes may be viral or bacterial

Scarred TM

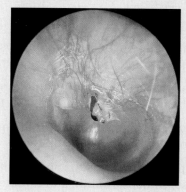

Caused by frequent ear infections with perforation of the TM. Scars are seen as dense white patches on the TM.

Tympanostomy Tube

Tympanostomy tubes are indicated for chronic otitis media and its complications, recurrent acute otitis media, and antibiotic failure in children. The tubes are usually made of plastics such as silicone or Teflon. After 2–5 y, the tubes spontaneously fall out and the membrane most often closes.

Nose, Sinuses, Mouth, and Throat Assessment

Learning Objectives

1 Demonstrate knowledge of anatomy and physiology of the nose, sinuses, mouth, and throat.

2 Identify important topics for health promotion and risk reduction related to the nose, sinuses, mouth, and throat.

3 Collect subjective and objective data for the nose, sinuses, mouth, and throat.

4 Differentiate expected from unexpected findings in the assessment of the nose, sinuses, mouth, and throat.

5 Analyze subjective and objective data for assessment of the nose, sinuses, mouth, and throat and consider initial interventions.

6 Document and communicate data for the nose, sinuses, mouth, and throat assessment using appropriate terminology and principles of recording.

7 Consider age, condition, gender, and culture of the patient to individualize the nose, sinuses, mouth, and throat assessment.

8 Use assessment findings of the nose, sinuses, mouth, and throat to identify pertinent nursing diagnoses and initiate a patient care plan.

Mrs. Ethel Wilson, an 89-year-old Caucasian woman, was admitted to the hospital 13 days ago with pneumonia. She is now on the rehabilitation unit in preparation for her return home. Her temperature is 37°C orally, pulse 88 beats/min and regular, respirations 20 breaths/min, and blood pressure 138/72 mm Hg (left arm, sitting). Current medications include a mild diuretic, amiloride hydrochloride (Midamor) and beta-blocker, atenolol (Apo-Atenolol) for blood pressure, an inhaler, albuterol sulfate (Salbutamol) to open her airways, and an antibiotic, amoxicillin trihydrate (Amoxil) for the pneumonia. Her assessment was documented on the previous shift.

You will gain more information about Mrs. Wilson as you progress through this chapter. As you study the content and features, consider Mrs. Wilson's case and its relationship to what you are learning. Begin thinking about the following points:

- The mucous membranes reflect the health of other body systems. What body systems are affecting the health of Mrs. Wilson's oral mucous membranes?
- Why is it especially important for nurses to inspect the mouths of hospitalized patients?
- How might improvement in the patient's mouth affect her rehabilitation and functional abilities?

The focus of this chapter is assessment of the nose, sinuses, mouth, and throat. It includes a review of anatomy and physiology and common variations from expected findings, with relevant lifespan, cultural, and environmental considerations. This chapter serves as a guide to the collection of subjective data related to upper respiratory and mouth issues, which can result from occupational exposures, recreational activities (eg, smoking), family history of allergic rhinitis, systemic disorders, and head and neck cancer. A review of common signs and symptoms such as nasal discharge, congestion, and obstruction; snoring; sore throat; and facial pain and pressure is included. Presentation of objective data collection includes examination techniques and correct documentation of expected and unexpected findings. The emphasis is on a systematic, uncomplicated approach to this rather complex anatomical area.

Anatomy and Physiology Overview

The upper respiratory system and mouth function as the entry point for air and food into the body. These organs serve as a common channel until air reaches the lungs and food reaches the esophagus. The upper respiratory tract warms, filters, humidifies, and transports air to the lower respiratory tract (see Chapter 18). The nose is the sensory organ for smell, while the mouth is the sensory organ for taste. An explanation of the anatomy of organs along this transport passageway promotes understanding of why structural deviations may interfere with function.

Nose

The external nose allows air to enter the respiratory tract (Fig. 17-1). The anterior slope of the nose is the *dorsum*, which ends inferiorly at the tip and laterally at the *ala*. Bone in the upper third and cartilage in the lower two thirds of the nose support its triangular shape. The nasal bone attaches superiorly at the bridge to the frontal bone and laterally to the lacrimal and maxillary bones. The floor of the nose rests on the superior portion of the hard palate, separating it from the mouth. The ethmoid bone forms and separates the roof of the

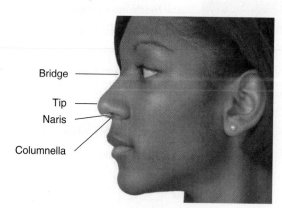

Bridge ———
Tip ———
Naris ———
Columnella ———

Figure 17-1 The external nose.

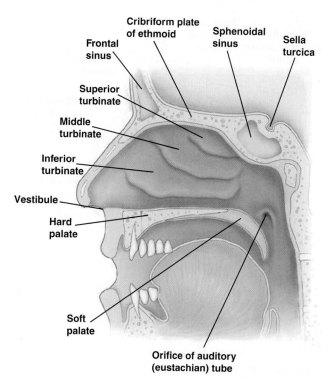

Figure 17-2 The nasal septum, left lateral wall.

nose from the brain. The midline **columella** divides the oval nares (nostrils), which are openings that lead into the internal nose and are lined with skin and ciliated mucosa. That space is known as the **vestibule**.

Clinical Significance 17-1

The ciliated mucosa inside the nose warm, filter, and humidify inspired air at nearly 100% and expend >1 L/d of water (Andresen, Hickey, et al., 2008).

The nasal septum is the center wall of bone and cartilage covered with mucosal membrane that divides the right and left nasal cavities (Fig. 17-2). Projecting from the lateral walls of the nose are three scroll-like bones covered with erectile mucous membranes: the inferior, middle, and superior turbinates. The inferior turbinates, which are most anterior, are usually the first internal structures seen on nasal examination. Lateral to each turbinate is an air space: the inferior meatus, middle meatus, and superior meatus. Cilia that trap particulates and sweep them posterior to the nasopharynx promote mucous drainage. The nasolacrimal duct drains into the inferior meatus (see Chapter 15). The middle turbinate and middle meatus areas are known collectively as the **osteomeatal complex**.

Clinical Significance 17-2

The osteomeatal complex is the most anatomically significant area involved in chronic sinusitis (Yian, 2003).

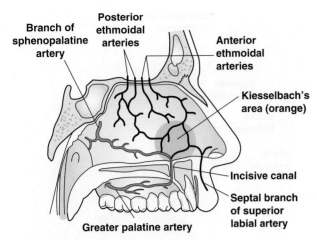

Figure 17-3 Kiesselbach's plexus.

The nose is the primary organ for smell. Air within the nasal roof stimulates the receptors of the olfactory nerve (CN I). Mucosal swelling from upper respiratory infections (colds) may obstruct olfactory sensory preceptors, compromising the sense of smell.

⚠ *SAFETY ALERT 17-1*

Patients with diminished smell are at risk for decreased detection of spoiled food, smoke, or gas fumes.

Nerve and Blood Supply

The maxillary and ophthalmic divisions of the trigeminal nerve (CN V) produce pain sensations. External movement of the nose, vasodilatation, and mucous production arise from the facial nerve (CN VII). The rhino-sino-brachial (sneeze) reflex results from the complex relationship of the medulla of the brain with the trigeminal (CN V), facial (CN VII), glossopharyngeal (CN IX), and vagus (CN X) nerves.

Branches of the internal and external carotid arteries supply blood to the nose. The anterior portion of the nasal septum has a rich vascular supply known as *Kiesselbach's plexus* (Fig. 17-3).

Clinical Significance 17-3
Kiesselbach's plexus is the most common site of nosebleeds (Andresen, Hickey, et al., 2008).

Lymph Drainage

Lymphatic drainage from the anterior nose leads to the preauricular and submandibular nodes. The deep cervical and retropharyngeal nodes drain the posterior nasal cavity.

Sinuses

The sinuses are hollow, bony, air-filled cavities within the forehead and facial cavities (Fig. 17-4). They lighten the

Anterior view

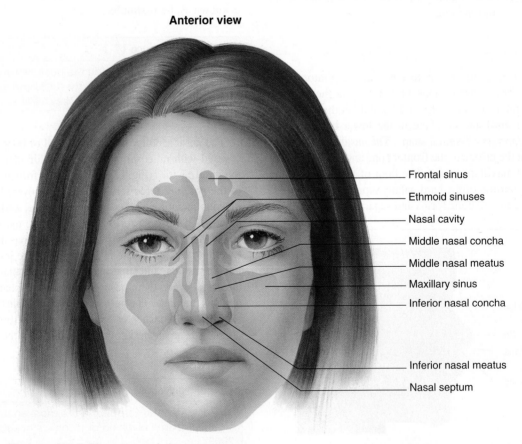

Figure 17-4 The paranasal sinuses.

weight of the skull and provide timbre and resonance to the voice. The sinuses also produce mucus that empties into the nasal cavity. Three major factors are related to the functions of the nose and sinuses: patency of the sinus ostia, cilia function, and quality and quantity of mucus.

The *frontal sinus* is above the eyebrows, the *ethmoid sinuses* are between the eyes, and the *maxillary sinuses* are below the eyes and above the teeth in each cheek. Sensory innervation of the sinuses is from the trigeminal (CN V) nerve. Lymphatic drainage from the sinuses is to the lateral and retropharyngeal nodes.

The nasopharynx contributes to nasal resonance and assists with equilibration of middle ear pressure (see Chapter 16). Air and nasal-sinus mucus passes through the posterior **choana** (opening) of the nose into the nasopharynx. The nasal end of the eustachian tube communicates with the middle ear by opening during swallowing and yawning. Just posterior to the eustachian tube opening is a mound of tissue known as the *torus tubarius.*

Clinical Significance 17-4

Posterior to the torus region is the pharyngeal recess or *Rosenmüller fossa*, which is a common site of occult nasopharyngeal malignancies (Andresen, Hickey, et al., 2008).

The *adenoids* are lymphoid tissue located in the roof of the nasopharynx and laterally in the eustachian tube orifice. They have a rich blood supply from branches of the facial and internal maxillary arteries.

Mouth

The *mouth* (oral cavity) is the structure for taste, mastication, and speech articulation. It extends from the lips to the anterior pillars of the tonsils (Fig. 17-5). Anteriorly, the cavity begins at the vermillion border, or junction of the lip and facial skin. The cheeks and palatine arches form the lateral border overlying the buccinator muscle of the cheek. The superior border includes the hard palate, palatine, and maxillary bone. The inferior border is the base of the tongue and muscular floor of the mouth.

Clinical Significance 17-5

The floor of the mouth is highly vascular, with the largest percentage in the area at the base of the tongue. This vascularity allows rapid absorption of sublingual medication.

The roof of the mouth contains the hard and soft palates. The anterior *hard palate* comprises two thirds of the total palate. The adjacent, posterior *soft palate* forms the uvula and separates the mouth from the pharynx. The *uvula* is midline at the inferior border of the soft palate.

Tongue

The tongue is muscle tissue that covers the floor of the mouth, with posterior–inferior extension into the pharynx. The median fold, also known as the **lingual frenulum**, connects the base of the tongue to the floor of the mouth (Fig. 17-6). The tongue manipulates solids and liquids in mastication and deglutition. It is also involved in speech production and taste. The anterior two thirds of the tongue surface contain taste buds known as *vallate papillae*, which identify sweet, sour, salty, and bitter (Fig. 17-7).

The tongue is one of the body's most vascular muscles; its blood supply includes the lingual, exterior maxillary, and ascending pharyngeal arteries. Innervation of the tongue includes lingual nerve fibres from the trigeminal (CN V),

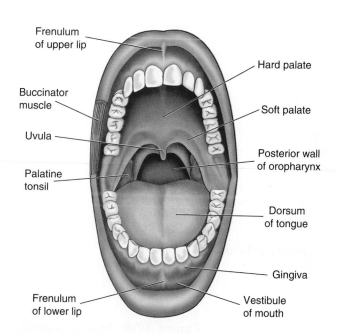

Figure 17-5 The oral cavity.

Frenulum of upper lip
Buccinator muscle
Uvula
Palatine tonsil
Frenulum of lower lip
Hard palate
Soft palate
Posterior wall of oropharynx
Dorsum of tongue
Gingiva
Vestibule of mouth

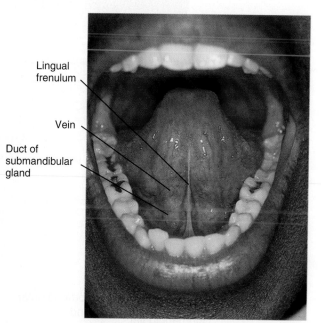

Figure 17-6 Underside of the tongue. Note the lingual frenulum.

Lingual frenulum
Vein
Duct of submandibular gland

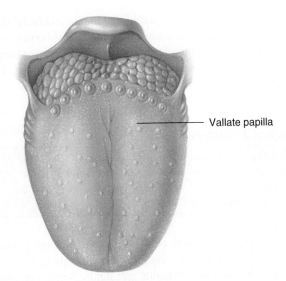

Figure 17-7 Vallate papillae.

facial (CN VII), glossopharyngeal (CN IX), vagus (CN X), and hypoglossal (CN XII) nerves.

Salivary Glands

The mouth also contains drainage ducts from three major salivary glands (Fig. 17-8). The largest, the *parotid gland*, is within the cheek anterior to the ear and extends from the zygomatic arch inferior to the angle of the jaw. The *parotid (Stensen's) ducts* open into the mouth in the buccal mucosa just opposite the upper second molar. The *submandibular gland* is beneath the body of the mandible. *Wharton's ducts*

run deep to the floor of the mouth and open on both sides of the frenulum. The small *sublingual salivary gland* lies within the floor of the mouth under the tongue with many openings along the submandibular duct. Many microscopic minor salivary glands are scattered throughout the oral mucosa.

Clinical Significance 17-6

The major salivary glands produce 1,500 to 4,000 mL/d of saliva (Andresen, Hickey, et al., 2008).

Saliva begins the digestive process by releasing enzymes upon contact with food. It protects the oral mucosa from heat, chemicals, and irritants. It also transmits taste information, rinses the oral cavity to maintain pH, and provides lubrication for the movement of food. Salivary production increases with smelling and seeing food, tasting, chewing, swallowing, and cigarette smoking. Decreased salivary flow, **xerostomia**, is related to emotional response, aging, disorders such as Sjögren's syndrome, and damage to the glands (eg, radiation therapy, obstruction, infection).

Clinical Significance 17-7

Blockage of the parotid duct increases the potential for periodontal disease as a result of pH imbalance and precipitation of calcium (Andresen, Hickey, et al., 2008).

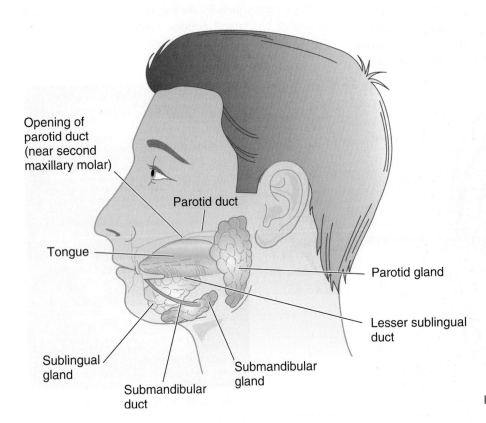

Opening of parotid duct (near second maxillary molar)

Parotid duct

Tongue

Parotid gland

Lesser sublingual duct

Sublingual gland

Submandibular duct

Submandibular gland

Figure 17-8 The salivary glands.

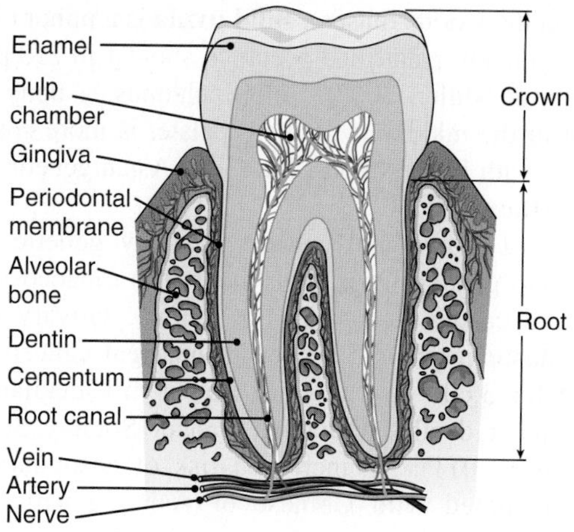
Enamel
Pulp chamber
Gingiva
Periodontal membrane
Alveolar bone
Dentin
Cementum
Root canal
Vein
Artery
Nerve
Crown
Root

Figure 17-9 Anatomy of the tooth.

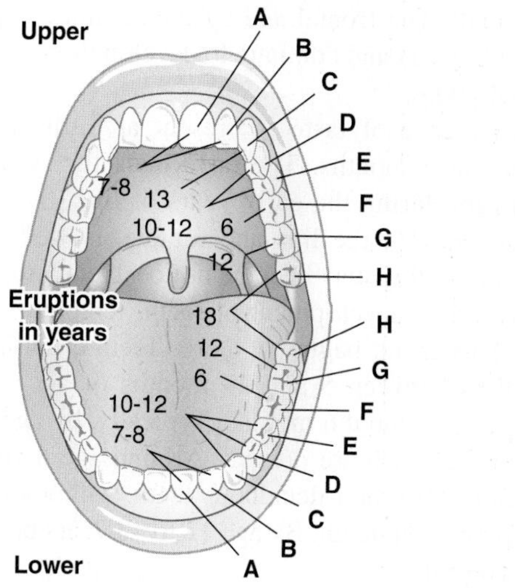
Upper
Lower
Eruptions in years
A
B
C
D
E
F
G
H
7-8
13
10-12
6
12
18
12
6
10-12
7-8

Key

A Central incisor	**D** First premolar	**G** Second molar
B Lateral incisor	**E** Second premolar	**H** Third molar
C Canine	**F** First molar	

Figure 17-10 Numbers and position of the adult teeth.

The autonomic nervous system and the facial (CN VII) and glossopharyngeal (CN IX) nerves innervate secretions of the major and minor salivary ducts. The hypoglossal (CN XII) nerve innervates the submandibular glands.

Teeth and Gums

The teeth contribute to the grinding and mastication of food to prepare for swallowing. They are composed of three layers: *crown, neck*, and *root* (Fig. 17-9). The crown, visible within the oral cavity, is the superior surface and also consists of three layers: enamel, dentin, and pulp. The outer *enamel* is an avascular surface with no pain receptors. It needs saliva to maintain its hard surface. Erosion of enamel may occur without pain. Regular dental follow-up is important in detecting early dental caries. The second layer, *dentin*, has tubules that connect to nerve fibres. Pain is experienced if damage to the dentin occurs by trauma or erosion. The innermost layer is the *pulp*, which has blood vessels and lymphatics, nerve tissue, and odontoblasts (dentin-forming cells). Increased pressure secondary to inflammation within the pulp may cause necrosis of the tooth.

There are 32 permanent teeth (Fig. 17-10; Andresen, Hickey, et al., 2008). The eight anterior incisors have flat surfaces for biting food. The most posterior teeth, the 12 molars, perform the grinding and final chewing process before swallowing. The maxillary bone supports the tissues of the upper jaw, while the mandibular bones support the tissues of the lower jaw. The periodontium is the gingival or gum tissue that supports the teeth.

Throat

The *throat* (oropharynx) is the common channel for the respiratory and digestive systems. It begins at the inferior border of the soft palate and uvula (see Fig. 17-5). The throat includes the base of the tongue, pharyngoepiglottic and glossoepiglottic folds, anterior and posterior pillars, and palatine tonsils. The *tonsils* are in the back of the throat between the anterior and posterior pillars. The tissue appears more granular and less smooth than the surrounding mucous membranes. Lymphatic tissue of the tonsils and adenoids provides immunologic defense. With chronic infections they may hypertrophy and produce chronic airway obstruction. **Tonsillitis** is inflammation of the tonsils. Hypertrophy of the tonsils and adenoids may develop secondary to sinusitis or otitis media (middle ear infection).

> **Clinical Significance 17-8**
>
> Removal of tonsils and adenoids does not increase risks of infection (Andresen, Hickey, et al., 2008).

Lifespan Considerations

Women Who Are Pregnant

Rhinitis during pregnancy results from the increased vascularity of the respiratory tract as well as hormonal effects on the mucosal lining. Increased reports of nasal congestion or obstruction are common in women who are pregnant. Increased sinus infections, epistaxis (nosebleeds), or both may occur. The gums also may become hyperemic and softened, leading to bleeding with toothbrushing.

Infants and Children

Infants are obligatory nose breathers. Ability to smell is fully developed at birth, but the cilia that line the adult nose are lacking. Odours reach the olfactory receptor cells readily and provide a clear sense of smell in newborns. This heightened olfactory ability is key to infant–parent bonding. The maxillary and ethmoid sinuses are present at birth but small. The frontal and sphenoid sinuses appear by the age of 3 years and continue to develop through adolescence (Yian, 2003).

The sense of taste is present at birth, and salivation begins at 3 months. The taste buds for sweets are more abundant during the early years of life. Tactile sensation, particularly of the lips and tongue, is well developed at birth. Drooling may become noticeable at around 4 months of age. The development of teeth, temporary (deciduous) and permanent, begins in utero. Teeth erupt in infants and toddlers between 5 and 27 months of age, with primary dentition at about 6 months. Typically, by age 2.5 years all deciduous teeth are present. Around age 6 years, children begin to lose their deciduous teeth, which are replaced by the permanent teeth. By age 12 to 13 years permanent teeth are present.

Older Adults

Gustatory rhinitis, clear rhinorrhea stimulated by the smell and taste of food, occurs most frequently in older adults. A decrease in olfactory sensory fibres occurs after age 60 years. In the oral cavity a thinning of the soft tissue of the cheeks and tongue results in an increased risk of ulcerations, infections, and oral cancers.

With advancing age, production of saliva and number of taste buds decrease. Resorption occurs in gum tissue, surrounding teeth, and the mandible bone. Natural tooth loss accompanies the breakdown of the tooth surface and receding gums. Malocclusion may occur with tooth loss and aggravate temporomandibular joint function (see Chapter 23). Although the number of older adults without teeth is declining because of more reconstructive dental practices, 6% of adult Canadians no longer have any natural teeth (Health Canada, 2010). Nevertheless, incidence of dental caries is rising related to retention of the teeth (Mungia, Cano, et al., 2008).

Cultural Considerations

Incidence of dental caries varies with sociodemographic groups. Sixty-two percent of Canadians have private dental insurance and 32% have no dental insurance (Health Canada, 2010). In a recent survey, 33% of the participants reported that they avoided seeing a dentist because of the costs (Health Canada). It is unknown how many untreated dental concerns exist in Canadians due to the costs associated with dental care.

Gingivitis, or inflammation with bleeding of the gums, is high among people of Latino and First Nations genetic heritage, and in adults of low socioeconomic classes. It may progress to periodontal disease with a loss of connective tissue and bone.

Cleft lip and cleft palate occur in approximately 1 in 1,000 births affecting between 400 and 500 newborns each year (Batsos, 2009). Prevalence of cleft lip and cleft palate in First Nations newborns in British Columbia is among the highest in the world (Batsos). **Bifid uvula** is a minor cleft of the posterior soft palate and occurs in about 1 in 250 people (Langlais & Miller, 2002). Torus palatinus, a bony ridge running in the middle of the hard palate, is more common in people with First Nations, Inuit, and Asian genetic backgrounds (Barnes, 2000).

Oral and pharyngeal cancers vary by genetic background and gender, most likely related to tobacco use. In 2011, oral cancer (including lip, tongue, salivary gland, mouth, nasopharyngeal, and oropharyngeal cancers) will account for 3,600 new cases of cancer in Canadians and 1,150 cancer deaths (Canadian Cancer Society Steering Committee, 2011). An increased risk of nasopharyngeal cancer is noted with Chinese or Asian genetic backgrounds.

Acute Assessment

Severe nosebleeds and trauma to the teeth, mouth, nose, tongue, and throat need to be treated immediately. Difficulty swallowing, swelling in the throat, or jaw pain also require immediate attention since these are symptoms of stroke, cardiac conditions, or anaphylactic shock. Infection in the floor of the mouth may produce *Ludwig's angina*, which is swelling that pushes the tongue up and back and results in eventual airway obstruction. Assessing risk for aspiration begins in the upper respiratory tract, focusing on laryngeal airway competency as well as the presence of dental prostheses or loose teeth, which may be accidentally swallowed or aspirated.

> ⚠ *SAFETY ALERT 17-2*
> *Acute airway obstruction such as in anaphylaxis, Ludwig's angina, and epiglottis may limit the opportunity for data collection other than specifics related to presentation of the patient.*

Abrupt loss of smell may indicate a brain tumour and warrants further evaluation with a magnetic resonance imaging (MRI) scan of the brain. Hard fixed nodes should be further evaluated by biopsy or radiological films for cancer.

Subjective Data Collection

Subjective data collection for this body region involves taking a detailed health history. Investigation creates an environment in which the nurse can suggest strategies to manage symptoms, avoid exposures that may exacerbate symptoms, and suggest health promotion measures. Examples include discussions of allergen/irritant exposure and smoking, which cause upper respiratory inflammation. Further education includes teaching patients to avoid environmental exposures

Table 17-1	Controlling Allergens in the Home Setting
Allergens	**Precautions in the Home**
House dust mites: Mites (microscopic bugs) live and feed in carpets, upholstery, and bedding. They produce droppings, which in humans cause allergic symptoms. Concentrate cleaning efforts in the bedroom to control dust mite allergies.	• Damp dust and vacuum weekly. • Change or clean furnace filter monthly. • Avoid feather pillows and down comforters. • Wash sheets and blankets weekly in hot water. • Avoid "dust catchers" (eg, stuffed animals). • Consider using high-efficiency particulate air filters in the bedroom and vacuum cleaner. • Use hardwood floors in the bedroom.
Mold spores: They are found in damp, dark areas of the home.	Discourage and eliminate mold growth by • Repairing leaks • Using dehumidifiers in damp basements • Cleaning shower grouting weekly • Decreasing houseplants, removing them from bedrooms, placing fungicide in soil • Cleaning refrigerator drip pan • Meticulously cleaning or avoiding portable humidifiers • Adjusting whole house humidity to 40% or less • Avoiding wool fabrics • Avoiding foods that contain mold: fermented beverages, especially wine and beer; vinegar; cheese; foods with yeast; breads and bakery products; canned tomato products; pizza; canned, smoked, and pickled meats; mushrooms
Foods: Any food can trigger an allergic reaction.	Eliminate forever foods suspected of producing acute life-threatening symptoms. Common culprits are shellfish and peanuts. Eliminate for 6 months foods that cause or contribute to chronic allergies, despite cravings for them. Then reintroduce the foods in a rotating manner. Common culprits are milk, egg, wheat, corn, soy, and yeast
Pet dander: Cat dander is light and highly allergenic; dog dander is heavier.	Decrease pet dander by • Having only outdoor pets • Removing pets from the bedroom • Grooming or bathing pets regularly (not by the allergic person) • Washing hands after touching pets
Pollens: Airborne pollens, present during blooming seasons, trigger allergic symptoms.	Decrease exposure to pollens by • Keeping windows closed • Grooming pets, which can carry pollens into the home • Avoiding attic fans

Adapted from Kramper, M. A. (2005). Patient education: Allergy precautions in the home. *ORL Head Neck Nurs, 23*(1), 27–28.

to irritants and chemicals and suggesting the use of personal protective equipment when exposures may be toxic. Opportunities for education about allergy exposure and smoking cessation fall well within the scope of nursing practice (Table 17-1). Such health education may help the patient to avoid upper respiratory disease and exacerbation of current illnesses.

Assessment of Risk Factors

When exploring risk factors the intention is to determine how likely a person is to develop upper respiratory disease. Questions open discussion for educational opportunities as well as for identifying areas that may require emphasis and follow-up. Teaching and interviewing can be blended.

Questions to Assess History and Risk	Rationale

Personal History

Have you ever been diagnosed with a mouth or upper respiratory condition?
• What was the specific condition?
• When did it occur?
• How was the condition treated?
• What were the outcomes?

Did you have a history of chronic upper respiratory infections as a child?

Positive history of frequent *upper respiratory infections* suggests underlying allergy, chronic hypertrophy of the adenoids and tonsils, or *chronic sinusitis*.

Frequent upper respiratory infections in childhood raise suspicion of *allergy*. Chronic inflammation of the respiratory tract may lead to mucosal damage with resultant chronic infections (eg, *sinusitis*).

Medications and Supplements

What medications are you currently taking?
• What are the names of all your current medications?
• What dose and how frequently do you take them?

It is helpful to know the patient's complete medication list, because all medications have potential side effects, which may affect the mouth, nose, and sinuses. Blood pressure drugs (eg, angiotensin-converting enzyme [ACE] inhibitors) may produce cough (Table 17-2). Anticoagulants may predispose patients to nosebleeds or exacerbate bleeding. Medications that dry the mouth may affect tooth and gum health.

Are you taking any over-the-counter (OTC) products? Natural or herbal supplements?
• What specific products?
• How frequently are you taking them?

Patients sometimes have a false sense of safety with OTC medications. Potentially unsafe OTC medications include topical decongestant sprays. Used appropriately for a short time, they provide effective nasal decongestion. These sprays also facilitate quick vasoconstriction and are beneficial in treating nosebleeds. With persistent use, however, they produce rebound congestion and are addictive. Natural agents (eg, *Ginkgo biloba,* garlic) may have undesirable effects on the respiratory lining, causing increased clotting times. They are thus contraindicated in patients with frequent nosebleeds (Bent, 2008). Other herbs may cross-react with pollen and stimulate *allergic rhinitis*. For example, *Echinacea* taken to strengthen the immune system can cross-react with ragweed, increasing symptoms in sensitive patients (National Center for Complementary and Alternative Medicine, 2008).

Table 17-2   Medications That May Produce Symptoms in the Nose, Sinus, Mouth, and Throat

Drug Class	Possible Adverse Reaction
Antihypertensives	Cough, nasal congestion
Hormones	Nasal congestion
Anticoagulants	Epistaxis
Antihistamines	Dry mucous membranes, epistaxis
Herbal supplements	Epistaxis
Analgesics	Nasal congestion
Central nervous system agents	Nasal congestion
Topical decongestants	Rebound nasal congestion
Antidepressants	Dry mucous membranes

Adapted from Lloyd, K. B., & Naclerio, R. M. (2008). Strategies for managing nasal congestion. *Post graduate healthcare education, LLC.* Philadelphia, PA: GlaxoSmith Kline.

Questions to Assess History and Risk	Rationale

Do you have any known sensitivities to inhalant allergens such as dust mites? Molds? Pollens? Or animal dander? Have you had specific allergy testing?
- What were the test results?
- What were your symptoms?
- When did you experience symptoms?
- What treatment measures were taken?
- What was the outcome of treatment?

Allergy can affect any target organ in the body. The nose and respiratory mucosa are the entry port for inhalant allergens. Thus, the nose and respiratory tract are common targets for inflammatory responses from allergen exposure.

Dental Health
- How regularly do you brush and floss?
- When were your teeth last cleaned?
- Do you have any concerns with your teeth or gums?

Regular dental cleanings are important to keeping teeth and gums healthy and identifying issues early.

Psychosocial History
Do you currently smoke cigarettes? Pipes or cigars?
- How many packs per day do you smoke?
- How many years have you smoked?
- Have you ever tried to stop smoking?
- Are you currently interested in stopping smoking?
- Do you currently or have you ever chewed tobacco?

Smoking increases respiratory inflammation, exacerbating *allergic rhinitis* and *chronic sinusitis*. It also increases risks for *head and neck carcinoma* (*in addition to lung cancer*). Chewing tobacco increases risk for *oral cancer* (Mayo Clinic, 2007) (see Chapter 18 for risks to the lower respiratory system related to smoking and tobacco use).

Are you frequently around others who smoke? What avoidance measures do you take to avoid smoke exposure?

Secondhand smoke increases risks for *head* and *neck cancer* and exacerbates *allergic rhinitis, pharyngitis,* and *sinusitis.* Researchers have identified >4,000 chemicals in tobacco smoke; of these at least 43 cause cancer in humans and animals (*Healthy People,* 2010, n.d.).

Do you inhale or have you ever inhaled marijuana, cocaine, methamphetamine, heroin, glue, or spray paint? If yes, are you interested in information to reduce associated risks or to help you quit?

Inhaling these substances can irritate the lining of the upper airway. Regular marijuana use may damage the cilia, leading to airway injury and potential infection, and increases the risk of **head and neck cancer**. Use of cocaine may permanently damage the nasal mucosa, resulting in nasal septal perforations. Use of methamphetamines may severely damage the teeth (Padilla & Ritter, 2008).

Family History
Do you have a family history of mouth or upper respiratory illness?
- What family member had the illness?
- What was the specific illness?
- What management was implemented?
- What was the outcome?

Atopy (allergic disease) occurs in 20% to 25% of the Canadian population (Allergy, Asthma Information Association, 2009). Hereditary prevalence is strong: if one parent has allergies, a child also has a 50% chance of developing them (Lloyd & Naclerio, 2008). Family history of *cancer* increases the patient's risk. Positive family history of genetic disorders such as *cystic fibrosis,* autoimmune diseases such as *Wegener's granulomatosis, Churg-Strauss syndrome,* and *Sjögren's syndrome* increases risk.

Environment Exposure
Are you currently or have you ever been exposed to chemical substances or irritants at work?
- Do you wear a mask or take other precautions to protect the respiratory tract?
- Do you monitor your exposures to chemicals?

Irritating chemicals may cause inflammation of the upper airway, which predisposes patients to chronic infections. Chemical exposures may damage the cilia, affecting the natural self-cleaning ability of the mucosal lining. Repeat exposures may produce allergic reactions in atopic patients. Chemicals may also be toxic.

Do you have hobbies that increase risk for upper respiratory symptoms? (eg, farming; care of or frequent exposure to animals; exposure to paint; chemical fumes; wood dust; airplane flying; scuba diving; or swimming).

Farming may expose patients to excessive pollens, animal dander, molds, or grain smuts. Atopic patients may experience adverse reactions with persistent allergen exposure. Chemical fumes from paints and solvents may irritate or damage the respiratory mucosa. Scuba diving and flying may produce negative pressure in the ear or sinuses, leading to barotrauma. Swimming may produce or aggravate *sinusitis* from chronic chlorine exposure. Chlorine may act as an allergen or irritant.

Example of Questions for Symptom/Sign Analysis—Nasal Congestion

- "Does your nasal congestion involve both sides of your nose?" (Location)
- "Describe your congestion." (Quality)
- "Do you have difficulty breathing when you talk?" "When you are active?" (Severity)
- "When did you start to notice the congestion?" "Did it happen suddenly or gradually?" (Onset)
- "Has your nasal congestion been about the same since it started?" (Duration)
- "Do you feel like it is getting better or worse over time?" (Constancy)
- "Is your congestion better at different times of the day? "Or worse?" (Time of day/month/year)
- "Does anything make it more difficult for you to breathe?" (Aggravating factors)
- "What makes it easier for you to breathe?" (Alleviating factors)
- "Do you have any pain in your nose?" "Do you feel dizzy?" "Nauseated?" (Associated symptoms)
- "Have you had any exposure to dust?" "Smoke?" Exposures at work?" "Do you have any hobbies that have resulted in dust?" "Or smoke?" (Environmental factors)
- "How does your nasal congestion affect your life?" (Significance to patient)
- "Tell me what you think is happening." (Patient perspective)

Risk Assessment and Health Promotion

Important Topics for Health Promotion

- Smoking cessation
- Oral health and hygiene

In assessing for risk factors, nurses can identify areas to focus efforts for patient teaching and related behaviour changes. As discussed in Chapter 18, smoking is a major risk to the respiratory tract and the leading cause of preventable death (*Risk factors and use of preventative services, United States, 2005*). At every encounter, patients should be questioned about smoking and their interest in stopping. Nurses document this discussion each visit. Offering multiple choices for discontinuing smoking as well as providing resources, such as support groups or individual counselling, are helpful. Clinician interest can be an effective motivator in stimulating clients to quit smoking.

Visits to dental care providers are an excellent opportunity to improve oral health. Reduction of dental caries through daily oral hygiene, good dietary nutrition, community water fluoridation, and application of dental sealants after the eruption of permanent teeth are all examples of opportunities to improve oral health. Daily toothbrushing and flossing are essential to decreasing dental carries as well as reducing gingivitis and periodontal disease.

Focused Health History Related to Common Symptoms/Signs

Common Mouth and Upper Respiratory Symptoms/Signs

- Facial pressure/pain/headache
- Snoring/sleep apnea
- Obstructed breathing
- Nasal congestion
- Epistaxis (nosebleeds)
- Halitosis (bad breath)
- Anosmia (decreased smell)
- Cough
- Pharyngitis/sore throat
- Dysphagia (difficulty swallowing)
- Dental aching/pain
- Hoarseness/voice changes
- Oral lesions

Examples of Questions to Assess Symptoms/Signs	Rationale
Describe your breathing and sinuses.	This question is an initial opportunity for patients to offer unbiased descriptions of how they feel their upper airway performs.
Facial Pressure, Pain, and Headache Do you have any pain? Pressure? Or headache?	Sinus pain or pressure is common with *colds, influenza,* and *sinusitis* (see also Chapters 14 and 24).
Snoring and Sleep Apnea • Do you snore? • Are you a restless sleeper? • Does anyone observe your sleep? • Do you stop breathing during sleep? • Are you rested in the morning? Do you experience daytime drowsiness? • Do you drool at night?	Snoring can be a nuisance or complicated by sleep apnea. All patients with *sleep apnea* snore, but not all who snore have sleep apnea. Patients with sleep apnea are typically unaware of night-time arousals and are at increased risk for hypertension, stroke, heart attack, and motor vehicle accidents. Hypertrophy of the tonsils or adenoids may cause airway obstruction or sleep apnea. Children with large tonsils and adenoids may be at risk.

Examples of Questions to Assess Symptoms/Signs	Rationale

Obstructed Breathing

Do you experience difficulty breathing through your nose?

• Is this one side? Or both?

• Have you had any injuries to your face or nose?

• Does the congestion alternate from side to side?

• Does anything aggravate or improve your nasal breathing?

Inflammation of the nose and sinuses from allergen or irritant exposure may decrease nasal breathing. Structural deviations such as a *deviated nasal septum, nasal polyp,* or tumour may cause nasal obstruction. Trauma may result in a *deviated nasal septum or hematoma,* obstructing the nasal airway. The typical diurnal nasal cycle involves a cyclical alternating pattern of congestion and decongestion from side to side (Derebery & Berliner, 2002). With inflammation, this cycle may become exaggerated.

Nasal Congestion

Do you have any nasal discharge?

• Is the discharge clear or cloudy?

• What colour is it?

• Is it bilateral, from both sides? Or unilateral, from one nostril?

Excessive clear rhinorrhea may represent *allergic* or *nonallergic rhinitis.* Unilateral clear discharge unresponsive to treatment may represent a rare *cerebrospinal fluid leak.* It can be determined by collection and laboratory examination of fluid for beta-2-transferrin (Nandapalan, Watson, et al., 1996). Cloudy or discoloured discharge indicates inflammation. Persistent inflammation may result in infection.

Nosebleed (Epistaxis)

Do you get nosebleeds? Do you pick or remove crusts from the nose?

Nasal inflammation causes dilatation of its blood vessels. The most common site of nasal bleeding is Kiesselbach's plexus on the anterior septum (Andresen, Hickey, et al., 2008). Digital manipulation or nose picking may aggravate nasal bleeding.

Bad breath (Halitosis)

Have you ever been told that your breath smells bad?

Foul breath suggests infection.

Decreased Sense of Smell (Anosmia)

Do you have a decreased sense of smell? Is this a long-term or sudden change?

Anosmia (decreased smell) may accompany chronic inflammation of the nose and sinus. A computerized tomography (CT) scan may reveal obstruction of one or more paranasal sinuses.

Cough

Do you have a cough?

• Does it feel like the cough comes from your chest or upper airway?

• Is your cough wet or dry?

• Is the cough productive or nonproductive?

• What makes the cough worse?

• What makes the cough better?

Sinus drainage, allergen or irritant exposure, or *chronic sinusitis* may produce cough. Persistent productive cough warrants a chest x-ray to determine lung pathology (see Chapter 18). Reactive airways in *asthma* may produce cough. Cough may be secondary to *gastroesophageal reflux disease* (GERD).

Sore Throat (Pharyngitis)

Do you have a sore throat?

Chronic hypertrophy or enlargement of the tonsils may produce sore throats. Typically hypertrophy of the tonsils is also associated with hypertrophy of the adenoids. Recurrent strep infections may occur with *chronic tonsillitis.*

Difficulty Swallowing (Dysphagia)

Do you have difficulty swallowing?

Dysphagia (difficulty swallowing) may accompany a growth or lesion in the respiratory tract or result from inflammation of the upper respiratory tract secondary to *GERD.*

Dental Pain

Do you experience aching or pain in your teeth? Or gums? Are your teeth sensitive to cold or heat?

Sinusitis may produce dental aching, particularly of the upper teeth. *Dental carries* or *abscess* may produce tooth pain.

Voice Changes

Have you experienced hoarseness or voice changes?

Common causes include sinus postnasal drainage, inflammation of the upper respiratory tract secondary to *GERD,* lesions of the upper respiratory tract, and inflammation from allergen or irritant exposure (eg, chemicals, cigarette smoke).

Oral Lesions

Do you have any sores in your mouth? If so, has there been any change in the size or appearance of the sore?

Smoking or chewing tobacco increases risk for *oral cancer.* Persistent or changing lesions may indicate *oral cancer.* Biopsy is warranted for persistent lesions.

Focused Health History Related to Common Symptoms/Signs

Common Mouth and Upper Respiratory Symptoms/Signs

- Facial pressure/pain/ headache
- Snoring/sleep apnea
- Obstructed breathing
- Nasal congestion
- Nosebleeds (epistaxis)
- Bad breath (halitosis)
- Decreased smell (anosmia)
- Cough
- Sore throat (pharyngitis)
- Difficulty swallowing (dysphagia)
- Dental aching/pain
- Hoarseness/voice changes
- Oral lesions

Documentation of Expected Findings

The patient states breathing is comfortable and quiet. Denies facial pressure, pain, headache, snoring, sleep apnea, obstructive breathing, or nasal congestion. Reports no nosebleeds, bad breath, decreased smell, or cough. States no sore throat, difficulty swallowing, dental pain, hoarseness, or oral lesions.

Lifespan Considerations

Additional Questions	Rationale/Unexpected Findings
Women Who Are Pregnant Have you experienced increased nasal congestion or nosebleeds with pregnancy?	Hormonal fluctuations often result in increased nasal congestion and may exacerbate allergies. Epistaxis may be secondary to engorged nasal vessels.
Infants and Children How many upper respiratory infections has your child had in the past year?	Recurrent infections suggest underlying *allergy*. They may result in enlarged tonsils and adenoids, which in turn may be responsible for frequent *sinus infections*. Recurrent strep infections are an indication for consideration of removal of the tonsils and adenoids because of the risk of rheumatic fever with resultant heart or kidney disease.
Does your child have an obstruction in his or her nose? Is the obstruction on one side or both? Is your child a good eater? Does your child snore?	Decreased nasal breathing may be secondary to hypertrophy of the adenoids, which may result in mouth breathing. Mouth breathers are typically poor eaters because eating interferes with breathing. Hypertrophy of tonsils and adenoids may produce sleep apnea in children. Unilateral nasal obstruction in children may represent **choanal atresia** (restriction of the bucconasal membrane).
Does your child have persistent nasal discharge? Is it clear or cloudy? Is the discharge from one side? Or both?	Clear rhinorrhea suggests allergic disease. Thick, discoloured discharge may represent chronic infection. With unilateral purulent discharge in children, a foreign body of the nose should be suspected.
Is your child exposed to cigarette smoke in the home? Or in a vehicle?	Secondhand cigarette smoke causes breathing disorders, sudden infant death syndrom (SIDS), ear infections, and serious diseases in children (Canadian Lung Association, 2011). Children also need to be protected from thirdhand smoke (smoke trapped in carpet, fabric, furniture).
Does your child get nosebleeds? Is the bleeding from one side? Or both?	Suspicion for **hemangioma** or a benign mass of blood vessels should be considered. They are present at birth and may expand with crying (Newland, 2003). **Angiofibroma** of the nasopharynx should be suspected with epistaxis and nasal obstruction in adolescent boys (Woodson, 2001).
Does your child suck his or her thumb? Does the child use a bottle for feeding?	Thumb-sucking past 6 to 7 years may cause malocclusion of the teeth. Prolonged use of baby bottles increases risk for dental decay.
Older Adults Do you experience decreased smell? Taste? Do you experience increased nasal drainage at meal time?	Diminished smell and taste may result in decreased nutrition and safety risks. Gustatory rhinitis may occur in older adults with increased clear rhinorrhea at meal time.

Additional Questions	Rationale/Unexpected Findings
Have you recently immigrated to Canada?	
What type of heat do you use at home? Are you aware of any mold in your home?	Recent immigrants may use wood or kerosene heat, which may exacerbate allergies or produce inflammation of the upper respiratory tract, leading to secondary infections. Mold may exacerbate allergies or, in the case of black mold, act as a toxin.
Note the patient's self-identified genetic background and gender in relationship to known congenital and assessed health risks.	As discussed earlier, the prevalence of cleft lip and palate is very high among First Nations people in British Columbia. The incidence of oral cancer in Canadians may increase due to immigration to Canada from high-risk areas for oral cancer, such as India, Pakistan, and Taiwan (Laronde & Hislop, 2008). The 5-year survival rate for oral cancer (62%) continues to improve.

An Example of a Therapeutic Dialogue

Remember Mrs. Wilson, introduced at the beginning of this chapter. This elderly woman has been in the hospital 13 days with pneumonia and now is on the rehabilitation unit preparing to go home. The nurse uses professional communication techniques to gather subjective data from Mrs. Wilson. The following conversation gives an example of an interview.

Nurse: Hi, Mrs. Wilson. I'm Jen and I'm going to be your nurse today.

Mrs. Wilson: Nice to meet you.

Nurse: And you, too. How are you feeling?

Mrs. Wilson: (swallows with difficulty). Just fine.

Nurse: It looks like you're having a little trouble swallowing … (pauses).

Mrs. Wilson: Well, my mouth seems so dry.

Nurse: I can see that. Let's wash your mouth out a little. Has it been awhile since you've brushed your teeth? (checks to see that there are no swallowing restrictions)

Mrs. Wilson: It was yesterday. That would be so nice of you, honey.

Nurse: That's what I'm here for. I'll get out your toothbrush and then we can clean things up and put on some lubricant to keep things moist. You'll feel a lot better.

Mrs. Wilson: You're such a good nurse.

Critical Thinking Challenge

- Why did the nurse discuss the dry mouth instead of the pneumonia?
- Why did the nurse check for swallowing restrictions?
- How did the assessment lead to an effective intervention?

Objective Data Collection

Much of the physical examination of the nose, sinuses, mouth, and oropharynx is performed by inspecting the area. Palpation for masses or tenderness is also performed. It is common to perform assessments in this region as focused examinations for symptoms, such as with nasal stuffiness or a sore throat.

Equipment

- Handheld otoscope with disposable covers
- Nasal speculum
- Tongue blades
- Cotton gauze 4 × 4
- Disposable nonlatex gloves
- Penlight
- Scratch or sniff test card or pungent odours (eg, spices, alcohol)
- Nasopharyngeal-laryngeal mirror

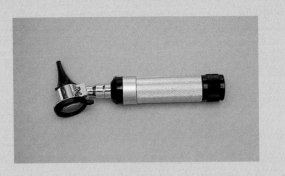

Promoting Patient Comfort, Dignity, and Safety

Preparation involves routine handwashing technique before beginning the examination. Gloves are used for the oral examination or with anticipated contact with mucous membranes. The patient is seated comfortably with the head at the examiner's eye level. If the patient wears dentures, offer a 4 × 4 gauze and ask the patient to remove them.

Common and Advanced Techniques

Common and specialized techniques are used to assess the nose, sinuses, mouth, and throat. Nurses primarily perform inspection of these organs. Inspection of the mouth is especially important in patients taking antibiotics who are at risk for oral candidiasis. The nurse also assesses the patient's nares for patency when inserting a tube through the nose for feeding. A deviated septum or obstructed nares may make insertion difficult.

Comprehensive Physical Examination: Nose, Sinuses, Mouth, and Throat

Technique and Expected Findings	Unexpected Findings
External Nose	
Inspection. Inspect the nose from anterior and profile perspectives. *It appears symmetrical, midline, and proportionally shaped to facial features. Skin surface is smooth without lesions; colouration is consistent with facial complexion.*	Asymmetry, swelling, or bruising may result from *trauma* or accompany lesions or growths.
Palpation. Gently palpate with the thumb and forefinger. *There is no pain, tenderness, or break in contour.*	Tenderness on palpation and crepitus suggest *fracture*.
Internal Nose The nurse generally inspects the internal nose with an otoscope, nasal speculum, or both (Fig. 17-11). Insert a wide-tipped speculum gently into the nasal vestibule or naris and open vertically while gently lifting up on the tip of the nose. The nasal speculum may be inserted horizontally, but should never be opened horizontally, because this puts uncomfortable pressure on the septum. Observe the colour of the mucous membranes. Inspect any mucus. Note the colour and character of the nose. The inferior turbinate is the first structure visualized. The middle	Infection and inflammation of nasal mucosa may be present with viral, bacterial, or allergic rhinitis. Excessive clear watery drainage suggests allergic rhinitis. Thick, discoloured mucus or gross pus may accompany infection. Absence of typical structures, such as the turbinates, suggests previous surgery. Deviation of the nasal septum may be congenital or acquired in trauma. Note any crusting or prominence of nasal vessels with special attention to the anterior septum. A septal perforation is a hole in the midline septum. It may be secondary to trauma,

turbinate can be noted superior and lateral. Assess nasal airflow by asking the patient to breathe in while holding the mouth closed. Gently manipulate the external nose to assess how these changes affect airflow. *Septum is midline; its mucosa is pink and moist with no prominent blood vessels or crusts. A small amount of drainage is clear. Airflow around the nasal structures is adequate.*

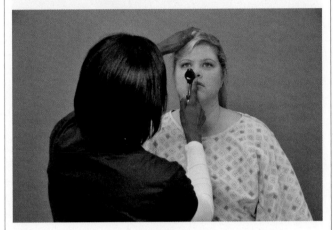

Figure 17-11 Inspecting the nasal mucosa.

If the patient notices a loss of smell, ask him or her to identify common scents. To do this, occlude one nostril and ask the patient to smell a sniff test card or pungent odour with eyes closed. Test both sides. *The patient correctly identifies scents.*

Sinuses

Inspection. Inspect the sinus areas (forehead, between the eyes, and both cheeks) for redness or swelling. *Findings are symmetrical with no redness or swelling.*

A method to assess sinus cavities is transillumination (Fig. 17-12). This method has limited clinical significance and provides inconsistent results. The gold-standard diagnostic technique in evaluating sinus disease is a CT scan.

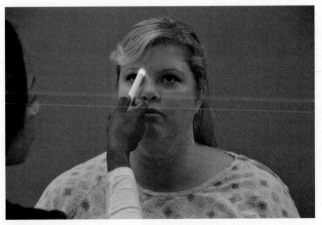

Figure 17-12 Transillumination of the sinuses.

surgery, or illicit drug use. **Polyps**, grapelike swollen nasal membranes, may appear white and glistening (see Table 17-5 at the end of this chapter).

Anosmia may occur with *trauma*, congestion, *polyps*, or *sinus infection*. Sudden loss of smell warrants consideration of radiological testing to rule out *intracranial masses*.

Redness and swelling over the sinuses may represent acute *infection, abscess*, or *mucocele*.

Positive findings in inspection of the sinuses warrant radiological imaging to assess involvement.

(text continues on page 430)

Palpation and Percussion. Palpate and percuss the maxillary and frontal sinus areas (Fig. 17-13). *No tenderness or fullness is present.*

Tenderness or fullness on palpation suggests infection. Positive findings on palpation may warrant radiological imaging.

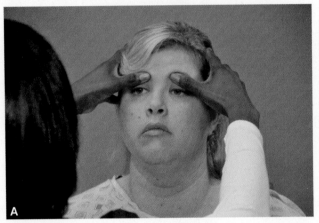
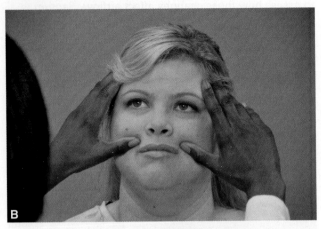

Figure 17-13 Palpating the sinus area. **A.** Palpate the frontal sinus. **B.** Palpate the maxillary sinus.

Mouth

External Inspection. Inspect lips, noting colour, moisture, lesions, and oral competence. *Lips are pink and moist with no lesions.*

Dryness or cracking may indicate inadequate hydration. Lesions or aphthous ulcers may represent a *viral infection.* Swelling or edema of lips suggests *allergy.* Oral incompetence may occur in cleft lip or with inadequate repair (see Table 17-6 at the end of this chapter).

Internal Inspection

Buccal mucosa. Holding a light in the nondominant hand and a tongue blade in the dominant one, gently separate areas to fully inspect the buccal mucosa, noting colour and pigmentation (Fig. 17-14). Inspect the entire U-shaped area in the floor of the mouth. Note the parotid (Stensen's) ducts appearing as a small dimple just opposite the second upper molars (Fig. 17-15). Small, isolated white or yellow papules (**Fordyce granules**) may be noted on the cheeks, tongue, and lips. These sebaceous cysts or salivary tissues are insignificant.

Poor oral hygiene has been linked to *pneumonia* and *heart disorders.* Inflamed buccal mucosa suggests *infection.* White patches (leukoplakia) may suggest a growth or lesion. Ulceration may represent viral infection or tumour. Petechiae or small red spots resulting from blood, which escapes the capillaries, may occur with trauma, infection, or decreased platelet counts (Fig. 17-16). Redness or swelling of Stensen's ducts may represent infection or blockage of the parotid gland.

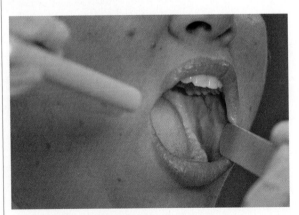

Figure 17-14 Inspecting the buccal mucosa.

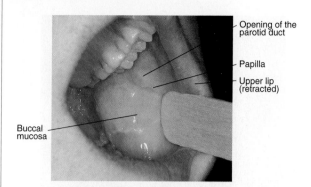

Figure 17-15 Examination of the parotid (Stensen's) ducts.

Teeth and gums. Inspect the teeth and gums. Note numbers and position of teeth. Note general appearance and signs of decay. Note alignment. Note the odour of the patient's breath.

Uvula. Note the position of the uvula (Fig. 17-17). Have the patient say "ah," noting the rise of the uvula and function of the vagus nerve (CN X).

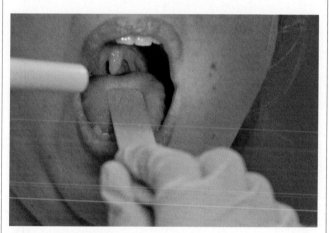

Figure 17-17 Observing the uvula.

Hard and soft palates. Inspect the colour and surface of the hard and soft palate.

Tongue. Inspect the tongue, including the dorsum (top surface), sides, and underneath. Note papillae on the dorsum, small on anterior, and large on posterior. Ask the patient to stick out the tongue (Fig. 17-18). Although generally not done during a screening assessment, the gag reflex may be tested. Gently place a tongue blade on the posterior dorsum bilaterally to produce the gag reflex, which ensures function of the hypoglossal nerve (CN XII).

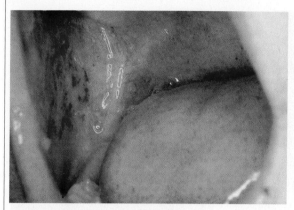

Figure 17-16 Oral petechiae.

Teeth may be stained or have *decay*. Swollen or red gums with bleeding may indicate *gingivitis*. Foul breath may suggest infection (see Table 17-7 at the end of this chapter).

Uvula may be swollen with allergic reactions. It may be bifid or have a notch or cleft.

With *cleft palate*, nasopharyngeal incompetence may be present along with resultant nasal air leak during speech.

Tongue may have lesions or ulcers. *Geographic tongue* (Fig. 17-19) tends to occur in people with allergic disease, but has no significant pathology. A white coating of the tongue may be oral candidiasis. This condition is very common in patients taking antibiotics (see Table 17-8 at the end of this chapter).

(text continues on page 432)

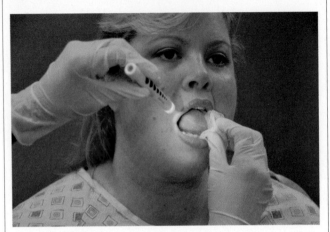

Figure 17-18 Sticking out the tongue.

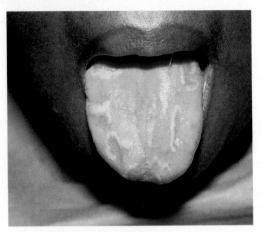

Figure 17-19 Geographic tongue.

Wharton's ducts and salivary flow. Inspect Wharton's ducts in the floor of the mouth. Evaluate salivary flow from the submandibular salivary gland. *Buccal mucosa and soft and hard palates are pink with no lesions. Gingiva is pink and moist without inflammation. Breath has no foul odour. Tongue is smooth and midline. Teeth are well aligned with no evidence of decay. Uvula rises symmetrically with "ah." Ducts are smooth without inflammation.*

Swelling or redness of Wharton's ducts suggests inflammation of the submandibular gland (Fig. 17-20). No upward movement of the uvula when the patient says "ah" indicates dysfunction of the vagus nerve (CN X). Infection in the floor of the mouth may produce *Ludwig's angina* (Wax, Myers, et al., 2004).

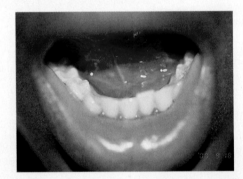

Figure 17-20 Swollen and red Wharton's ducts.

Palpation. Palpate the parotid, submandibular, and sublingual glands for swelling or tenderness (see Chapter 14). *There is no swelling or tenderness.*

Palpation of the mouth is usually completed as part of a specialty assessment. If performed, place a gloved hand inside the cheek to assess Stensen's ducts in the buccal mucosa opposite the second molars and Wharton's ducts. Assess these areas for a stone or growth. Palpate for any lesions. *Ducts are soft and nontender without lesions.*

Swelling may occur with mumps, blockage of a duct, abscess, or tumour. Duct obstruction can occur as a result of aging, dehydration, or use of anticholinergics.

A firm area at either Stensen's or Wharton's ducts may represent a stone or growth. Lesions of oral mucosa may indicate a growth. Examination with biopsy or radiological films may be recommended for oral lesions. When palpating masses, hard, fixed lesions have a higher incidence of cancer. Soft, mobile lesions are more often cysts or benign disease.

Throat

Inspection. Pressing down slightly with the tongue blade on the midpoint of the tongue, visualize the pharynx, tonsils, soft palate, and anterior and posterior tonsillar pillars. Note colour, symmetry, enlargement, and any lesions. The tonsils are in the back of the oropharynx between the anterior and posterior pillars. The tissue appears more granular and less smooth than the surrounding mucous membranes. *Tissue is pink and moist with symmetrical margins. No enlargement or lesions are noted. Grade the tonsils using the scale in Box 17-1. Tonsils are absent or 1+.*

BOX 17-1 TONSILLAR GRADING SCALE

- 1+ tonsil obstructs 0%–25% to midline
- 2+ tonsil obstructs 25%–50% to midline
- 3+ tonsil obstructs 50%–75% to midline
- 4+ tonsil obstructs 75%–100% to midline

Adapted from Newland, D. (2003). Pediatric otolaryngology. In M. Layland & T. Lin (Eds.). *The Washington manual survival guide series: Otolaryngology survival guide* (pp. 153–166). Philadelphia, PA: Wolters Kluwer Health/Lippincott Williams & Wilkins.

Mucosal inflammation may indicate *infection* or allergy. Hypertrophy of tonsils occurs with persistent recurrent infection. Frequent infections may leave superficial scars or crypts (Fig. 17-21). These crypts may collect food and oral debris, appearing as white curd-like material embedded in the tonsil mucosa. Generally, with chronic tonsillitis and hypertrophy, findings are symmetrical. Asymmetrical tonsillar enlargement raises suspicion of *neoplasia*. Peritonsillar abscess, *quinsy*, may occur with collection of fluid in the anterior tonsillar pillar (Fig. 17-22). This presents as a sore throat with increasing unilateral pain, deviated uvula, hot potato voice, dysphagia, and trismus (inability to open jaw) (Wax, Myers, et al., 2004). Sleep apnea should be suspected with a squeezed appearance of the general proportion of the throat. Strep throat presents with red and white patches in the throat, difficulty swallowing, tender or swollen glands (lymph nodes) in the neck, or red and enlarged tonsils.

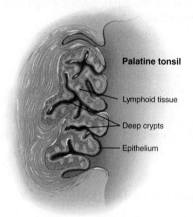

Palatine tonsil
Lymphoid tissue
Deep crypts
Epithelium

Figure 17-21 Tonsillar crypts with debris.

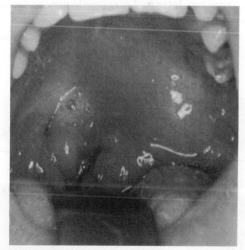

Figure 17-22 Peritonsillar abscess.

(text continues on page 434)

Palpation. Palpation of the neck is helpful to assess inflammatory and other changes that may occur in the throat. Anterior and posterior cervical chain lymph nodes and submental areas are palpated as part of a neck examination (see Chapter 14). *Nodes are symmetrical, soft, and nontender.*

Swallowing Evaluation

Evaluation of swallowing is a technique typically performed by speech therapists. Assess ability to swallow by positioning the thumbs and index finger on the patient's laryngeal protuberance. Ask the patient to swallow; feel the larynx elevate. Ask the patient to cough. Patients can aspirate even if they have an intact gag reflex (Nettina, 2006). Observe for signs associated with difficulty swallowing: coughing; choking; spitting of food; drooling; difficulty handling oral secretions; double or major delay in swallowing; watering eyes; nasal discharge; wet or gurgly voice; decreased ability to move tongue and lips, chew food, or move food to the back of the mouth; pocketing of food; and slow or scanning speech (Nettina). *Swallowing takes <1 second with no sign of aspiration.*

Lymph nodes are quick to respond to inflammation and slow to resolve. Inflammation causes enlargement of the anterior, posterior, or submental lymph nodes of the neck. Soft and tender enlargement may accompany minor inflammation. Hard, fixed nodes should be further evaluated by biopsy or radiological films for cancer.

Patients with *stroke, head injury*, or other neuromuscular disorders are at risk for dysphagia. Swallowing difficulties are common in hospitalized patients and may prolong length of stay because of an inability to obtain adequate nutrition for healing. Dysphagia may be from a growth in the airway or enlargement of surrounding glands or tissue. Dysphagia may be secondary to *GERD*, which should be suspected when inflammation of the larynx is visualized on indirect or direct view. Aspiration into the larynx may be observed with incomplete closure of vocal cords or impeded movement of the epiglottis.

Documentation of Expected Findings

Nose appears symmetrical, midline, and proportionally shaped to facial features. Skin surface is smooth without lesions; colouration is consistent with facial complexion. Sinus areas are symmetrical with no redness or swelling. Lips are pink and moist with no lesions. Buccal mucosa and soft and hard palates are pink with no lesions. Gingiva is pink and moist without inflammation. Breath has no foul odour. Tongue is smooth and midline. Teeth are well aligned with no evidence of decay. Uvula rises symmetrically with "ah." Ducts are smooth without inflammation. Mouth is pink and moist with symmetrical margins. Tonsils are absent.

🔺 Lifespan Considerations

Women Who Are Pregnant

Increased nasal congestion may occur in response to hormonal fluctuations. Increased nosebleeds may be secondary to increased congestion. Gum hypertrophy may also occur. Localized gingival enlargement may lead to a tumour-like mass known as **epulis** forming on the gums (Fig. 17-23).

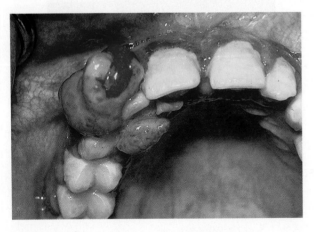

Figure 17-23 Epulis in pregnancy.

Newborns, Infants, and Children

The nasal and oral examination in infants and young children can be difficult. Many children will open their mouths for examination. If this is not the case, having the parent hold the child may calm him or her. Coaching the parent to hold the child's head and restrain the arms can be helpful and less threatening to the child. With the child sitting on the parent's lap facing the examiner, the parent uses one hand to hold the child's head, while using the other arm to restrain the child's arms and one leg to secure the child's legs (see Chapter 14). If the child is unwilling to open the mouth, gently closing the nostrils will result in an open mouth for air within seconds. Use of flavoured tongue blades may encourage small children to cooperate with the examination. Examiners can encourage children to growl "like a lion" to afford a thorough view of the oral cavity and throat.

Special pediatric considerations include checking for competency of the palate, which may be congenitally incompetent in the case of a cleft palate. Infants may have small white bumps or **milia** across the bridge of the nose (Fig. 17-24). These self-limiting superficial cysts contain keratinous material and exfoliate on their own. Older children with allergies may develop a traverse ridge across the bridge of the nose from habitually performing the "**allergic salute**" (Fig. 17-25), an upward rubbing of the external nose induced by itching.

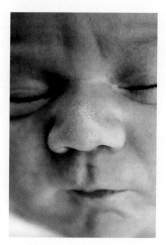

Figure 17-24 Milia.

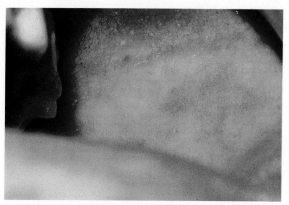

Figure 17-26 Koplik spots.

Examining the nose of children is best accomplished by gently pressing upward on the tip of the nose and visualizing the interior nares with the bright light from an otoscope. Assessing nasal breathing should include feeling for symmetrical airflow from each nostril. Holding a laryngeal mirror beneath the nose should demonstrate fogging from both nostrils. Congenital **choanal atresia** may be present when one nostril is not patent. This condition can present early in infancy as an emergency or may go undetected into adolescence. When suspected, a small red rubber catheter can be passed through each nostril. Inability to pass the catheter suggests choanal atresia. Nasal flaring or narrowing of the nose with inspiration is an indicator of respiratory distress. Foul odour or unilateral, thick nasal mucus suggests a foreign body in the nose. An expected finding in infants is the formation of a small pad of tissue in the middle of the upper lip known as the **sucking tubercle**.

Note age-appropriate eruption of teeth. For children younger than 2 years, the child's age in months minus the number 6 should equal the number of deciduous teeth (Hockenberry & Wilson, 2007). After 2.5 years, all 20 deciduous teeth should be present. Tetracycline ingestion

by the child or maternal ingestion in the last trimester of pregnancy may result in discolouration of an infant's teeth. Ingestion of excessive iron may cause a green or black discolouration of the teeth (Newland, 2003). Discolouration of the tooth enamel with plaque is a sign of poor dental hygiene. Brown spots in the crevices of the tooth may be caries (cavities).

Mobility of the tongue should extend to the alveolar ridge. **Ankyloglossia** (short lingual frenulum) may be congenital, restricting movement of the tongue and subsequently speech. An extremely narrow, flat roof or a high-arched palate affects placement of the tongue and can cause speech and feeding challenges (Hockenberry & Wilson, 2007). A high arch may also develop in chronic mouth breathers with hypertrophy of adenoids or allergic disorders.

Bednar's aphthae are ulcerative abrasions on the posterior hard palate that result from hard sucking. **Epstein's pearls**, appearing as small, white, glistening, pearly papules along the median border of the hard palate and gums, are a common finding in newborns. They represent small retention cysts that dissipate in the first few weeks of life. A maculopapular rash on the buccal mucosa that occurs within 24 hours of fever, inflammation of the nasal mucous membrane accompanied by nasal discharge (coryza), and cough are signs of **rubeola (measles)**. The rash, known as **Koplik spots**, appears as grains of salt on an erythematous base on the buccal mucosa opposite the first and second molars (Fig. 17-26) (Bickley, 2009).

Tonsils are not visible in newborns but gradually enlarge in toddlers. They remain proportionally large in young children and decrease in size as they mature. After puberty the tonsils proportionally decrease in size and are typically small in adults (see Box 17-1).

Chromosomal disorders may result in major multisystem disorders, some affecting the mouth, nose, and throat. Trisomy 21, **Down syndrome**, occurs in 1 in 800 to 1,000 live births with multiple system involvement (Burns, 2000). Mouth, nose, and throat involvement in Down syndrome includes a protruding tongue and flat nasal bridge.

Older Adult

Loss of subcutaneous fat may cause the nose to appear more prominent in older adults. **Edentulous** (without any teeth)

Figure 17-25 Allergic salute.

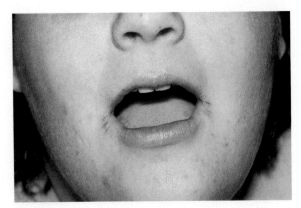

Figure 17-27 Angular cheilitis.

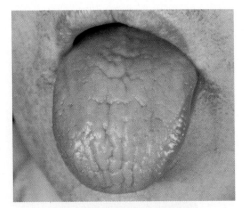

Figure 17-28 Smooth glossy tongue.

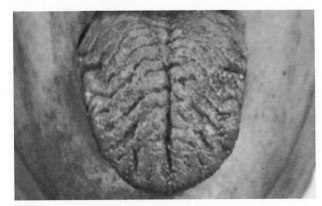

Figure 17-29 Scrotal tongue.

older adults may develop a pursed-lip appearance as mouth and cheeks fold inward. Overclosure of the mouth may lead to maceration of the skin at the corners of the mouth; this condition is called **angular cheilitis** (Fig. 17-27) (Bickley, 2009). Teeth may appear yellow as worn enamel reveals the dentin layer. They may also appear larger as the gums recede. Teeth may loosen with bone resorption and move with palpation.

The tongue and buccal mucosa may appear smoother and shiny from papillary atrophy and thinning of the buccal mucosa. This condition is called **smooth, glossy tongue** (Fig. 17-28) and may result from deficiencies of riboflavin, folic acid, and vitamin B_{12} (Bickley, 2009). **Fissures** may appear in the tongue with increasing age. This condition, called **scrotal tongue** (Fig. 17-29), can become inflamed with the accumulation of food or debris in the fissures. An oral health screening tool is available that includes assessment of the lymph nodes, tissue inside the cheek, floor, and roof of the mouth, gums between the teeth or under dentures, saliva, condition of teeth, and oral cleanliness (Chalmers, King, et al., 2005).

🌐 Cultural Considerations

The nasal bridge may be flat in African Canadians and Asians. In dark-skinned patients the gums are more deeply coloured and a brownish ridge is often found along the gumline (Hockenberry & Wilson, 2007). An increased risk of nasopharyngeal cancer is noted with Chinese or Asian genetic backgrounds.

Documenting Unexpected Findings

The nurse has just finished conducting a physical examination of Mrs. Wilson, the 89-year-old woman admitted with pneumonia 13 days ago. Unlike the examples of expected documentation previously charted, Mrs. Wilson has unexpected findings. Review the following important findings revealed in each of the steps of objective data collection for her. Consider how these results compare with the findings presented in the examples of documentation.

Inspection: Lips pale and dry with large amounts of crusting. No ulcers or lesions. Teeth yellowed and slightly crusted. Correct occlusion. Gums pale and intact. Tongue and buccal mucosa with cheesy white coating that scrapes off. Area under tongue is dry but smooth without lesions. Posterior palate also has white cheesy coating. Tonsils pink and smooth but not enlarged at 1+/4+ scale.

Palpation: No masses, lesions, or tenderness.

Area of Assessment	Expected Findings	Unexpected Findings
Nose	Mucosa dark pink, septum midline, nontender, intact	Septum appears eroded, purulent discharge noted from left nare
Turbinates	Mucosa pink, moist, no lesions bilaterally	Mucosa swollen and reddened bilaterally
Smell	Correctly identifies coffee (left nare) and soap odours (right nare)	Unable to distinguish odours bilaterally
Paranasal sinuses (frontal and maxillary)	Nontender on palpation bilaterally	Tenderness over right maxillary sinus
Lips	Pink, moist, and intact	Circumoral pallor, cracking at corners
Mouth (oral mucosa)	Buccal mucosa pink and moist, no lesions	Mucosa grey; red, open, 0.5 cm × 0.5 cm lesion on right buccal mucosa
Gums and hard palate	Gingiva pink and firm, upper and lower	Bleeding from lower gums, palate rough, painful to touch
Teeth	White, 32, intact, no debris	Mottled yellow, broken left lower molar, plaque evident
Tongue	Midline, no tremors, no lesions	Thick white coating, nodules noted on upper surface
Uvula	Midline, gag reflex intact bilaterally	Deviates right, no gag reflex noted on left
Pharynx	Pink, no exudates bilaterally	White patches on pharynx, tonsils red and swollen to 2 cm × 2 cm bilaterally

Adapted from Roach, S., & Roddick, P., et al. (2010). The ear, nose, mouth, and throat. In T. C. Stephen, D. L. Skillen, R. A. Day, & L. S. Bickley (Eds.). *Canadian Bates' guide to health assessment for nurses* (pp. 341–380). Philadelphia, PA: Wolters Kluwer Health/Lippincott, William, & Wilkins.

Evidence-Informed Critical Thinking

Common Laboratory and Diagnostic Testing

Laboratory studies of blood or other body fluids can give measures that are helpful in constructing a diagnosis. An elevated white blood count suggests infection, such as sinusitis. Nasal sinus cultures can help with identification of bacteria type. Biopsies provide tissue to determine if cancer is present. Examination of clear nasal discharge for beta-2-transferrin can identify cerebrospinal fluid in the nose. Throat culture can identify the type of bacteria producing tonsillitis or pharyngitis. Nasal and oral findings also may be evidence of systemic disease (Table 17-3).

Diagnostic testing for allergic sensitivity is helpful in managing persistent upper respiratory inflammation. Allergy testing may be performed via skin or blood. Various approaches to allergy skin testing include percutaneous or prick testing and intradermal testing. A blending of both types of skin testing is performed typically when evaluating upper respiratory conditions. Radioallergosorbent testing is a blood test that measures allergen-specific IgE antibody, which is elevated in reaction to allergens to which the patient is sensitive (Emanuel, 2002).

Radiographic studies are helpful in diagnosing chronic sinusitis. Plain-film x-rays may be used in acute sinusitis. The gold-standard radiological film in evaluating chronic sinusitis is CT scan. Note the detail provided by the sinus CT scan over plain x-ray views. CT scans or MRI films are helpful in evaluating masses and lesions of the upper respiratory tract. Routine dental x-rays improve early detection of dental carries.

Biopsy is performed on lesions of uncertain behaviour for tissue diagnosis. This can be accomplished by fine-needle aspiration in some situations. Other lesions may warrant an incisional biopsy.

Sleep studies are available to assess sleep apnea. Patients spend the night in a sleep laboratory and are monitored for breathing, heart function, oxygen saturation, and excessive leg movements.

Clinical Reasoning

Nursing Diagnosis, Outcomes, and Interventions

When formulating a nursing diagnosis, it is important to use critical thinking to cluster data and identify patterns that fit together. The nurse compares these data clusters with defining characteristics (unexpected findings) for the diagnosis to ensure the most accurate labelling and appropriate interventions. Table 17-4 provides a comparison of nursing diagnoses, unexpected findings, and interventions commonly related to nose, mouth, sinus, and throat assessment (North American Nursing Diagnosis Association, 2009).

Some outcomes commonly related to nose, mouth, sinus, and throat conditions include the following:

- The patient's oral mucous membranes are pink and intact.
- The patient swallows with no evidence of aspiration.
- The patient states that breathing is more comfortable and less congested (Moorhead, Johnson, et al., 2007).

Table 17-3 Nasal and Oral Findings in Systemic Disease

Disease	Etiology	Nasal Findings
Churg-Strauss syndrome	Vasculitis	Nasal crusting and polyps
Sjögren's syndrome	Chronic inflammatory disorder characterized by decreased lacrimal and salivary gland secretion	Atrophy and drying of oral and nasal mucosa; may lead to epistaxis
Pemphigus—pemphigoid	Autoimmune disorder	Blister formation on external nose or anterior septum
Scleroderma	Systemic sclerosis from increased collagen synthesis	**Telangiectasias** of nasal mucosa with no cilia
Bechet's disease	Chronic inflammatory disorder	Oral ulceration, rhinorrhea, rhinalgia, apthous ulceration of nose or nasopharynx that heals without scarring
Sarcoidosis	Noncaseating inflammatory disorder	Engorgement of turbinates with papules or nodules on septum
Wegener's granulomatosis	Necrotizing granulomatous vasculitis affecting respiratory tract, kidneys, and peripheral vessels	Nasal crusting, ulcerations, epistaxis, chronic rhinosinusitis, septal perforations
Syphilis	Sexually transmitted infection	Primary 3–4 wk after contact, ulceration in vestibule of nose or septum; secondary lesions after primary fades; tertiary nasal septal swelling may develop into perforation
Tuberculosis	Mycobacterial infection	Nasal crusting, mucosal ulcerations
Cystic fibrosis	Inherited absence of exocrine glands	Copious, thick, viscous mucus that blocks airways; chronic rhinosinusitis; nasal polyps
AIDS	HIV	Nasal ulcerations, lesions, Kaposi's sarcoma

Adapted from Higgins, T., LeGrand, M., et al. (2008). Nasal cavity, paranasal sinuses and nasopharynx. In L. Harris & M. Huntoon (Eds.). *Core curriculum for otorhinolaryngology and head-neck nursing* (2nd ed., p. 183). New Smyrna Beach, FL: Society of Otorhinolaryngology and Head-Neck Nurses, Inc.

Once outcomes are established, nursing care is implemented to improve the status of the patient. The nurse uses critical thinking and evidence-informed practice to develop the interventions. Some examples of nursing interventions for the nose, mouth, sinuses, and throat are as follows:

- Provide oral hygiene every 8 hours.
- Consult with a speech therapist to evaluate swallowing.
- Push fluids to 2 L to liquefy secretions (Bulechek, Butcher, et al., 2008).

Table 17-4 Common Nursing Diagnoses Associated With the Nose, Sinuses, Mouth, and Throat

Diagnosis and Related Factors	Point of Differentiation	Assessment Characteristics	Nursing Interventions
Impaired dentition	Disease, disruption, trauma, or other factors that cause changes in development, eruption, or structural integrity of teeth	Malocclusion, tooth pain, caries, plaque, halitosis, premature loss of teeth, tooth fracture	Teach toothbrushing and flossing. Provide assistance as needed. Perform mouth care if the patient is unable to do so independently.
Impaired swallowing	Associated with oral, pharyngeal, or esophageal structure or function	Delayed swallowing, gurgly voice, frequent coughing, choking or gagging, inability to clear oral cavity, food falling from mouth	Evaluate swallowing ability. Provide sips of fluids before giving dry foods. Elevate head of bed. Thicken liquids if needed.

Remember Mrs. Wilson, whose situation has been outlined throughout this chapter. Initial subjective and objective data collection is complete, and the nurse has spent time reviewing the findings and other results. The following nursing note illustrates how subjective and objective data are collected and analyzed and nursing interventions are developed.

Subjective: "My mouth is dry."

Objective: Lips pale and dry with large amounts of crusting. No ulcers or lesions. Teeth yellowed and slightly crusted. Correct occlusion. Gums pale and intact. Tongue and buccal mucosa with cheesy white coating that scrapes off. Area under tongue is dry, but smooth without lesions. Posterior palate also has white cheesy coating. Tonsils pink and smooth, but not enlarged at 1+/4+ scale. No masses, lesions, or tenderness palpated.

Analysis: Altered oral mucous membranes related to xerostomia, infrequent oral care, and possible infection.

Plan: Performed oral hygiene with positive results. Large reduction in crusting and mucous membranes now pink. White coating remains on tongue and buccal mucosa. Contact primary health care provider to evaluate for a possible infection. Continue oral hygiene every shift.

Critical Thinking Challenge

- Why did the nurse decide to focus the SOAP (subjective, objective, analysis, plan) on the status of the patient's mucous membranes rather than on the patient's diagnosis of pneumonia?
- What other effects might poor oral hygiene have on the patient's body systems?
- What data made the nurse suspect that there might be an associated infection?

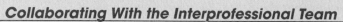

Collaborating With the Interprofessional Team

The nurse suspects that Mrs. Wilson has a yeast infection (*Candida albicans*) in her mouth. Treatment requires a prescription medication. Therefore, the nurse will need to notify the primary care provider. The following conversation illustrates how the nurse might organize the data and make recommendations about the patient's situation to the provider.

Situation: I'm Jen Tsang, and I've been caring for Mrs. Wilson today. She is an 89-year-old woman admitted 13 days ago with pneumonia.

Background: She's been on antibiotics for most of her stay here, which has been complicated.

Assessment: When I performed oral care on her today, I noticed a white coating on her tongue. I was able to clean off most of the crusts and moisturize her lips, but the white coating remains. She doesn't have any lesions, but she said that her tongue is quite tender and it got quite red when I tried to scrape off the coating.

Recommendations: I was thinking that she might have a fungal infection from the antibiotics and wonder if you could order a medication to swish in her mouth and swallow. Thank you.

Critical Thinking Challenge

- What information did the nurse decide not to include in the conversation and why?
- What risk factors does Mrs. Wilson have for *C. albicans*?
- How can the nurse ensure that oral hygiene becomes one of the priorities in care?

Pulling It All Together: An Example of Reflection and Critical Thinking

The nurse uses assessment data to formulate a nursing care plan with patient outcomes and interventions for Mrs. Wilson. The nurse uses critical thinking and judgment to continue or revise the diagnosis, outcomes, or interventions. This is often in the form of a care plan or case note similar to the one below.

Nursing Diagnosis	Patient Outcomes	Nursing Interventions	Rationale	Evaluation
Altered oral mucous membrane	Oral mucous membranes pink, moist, and without coating, lesions, or masses	Encourage fluids. Provide oral care every shift. Obtain order for medication. After oral care, have the patient swish and swallow medication.	Fluids will keep the membranes moist. Provide fluids, then oral care, and then medication last to allow the medication time in the oral cavity to work.	Patient with no crusts or dryness in mouth. States oral cavity and lips are more comfortable. Approximately half of coating on tongue is present. Continue with care.

Applying Your Knowledge

Using the previous steps of clinical reasoning, organizing, and prioritizing, consider all the case study findings woven throughout this chapter. When answering the following questions, begin drawing conclusions and see how the pieces of assessment must work together to create an environment for personalized, appropriate, and accurate care.

- What are some possible causes of Mrs. Wilson's altered oral mucosa? (Knowledge)

- Why is it especially important for nurses to inspect the mouths of hospitalized patients? (Comprehension)

- The mucous membranes reflect the health of other body systems. What body systems are affecting the health of Mrs. Wilson's oral mucous membranes? (Application)

- How might improvement in the patient's mouth affect her rehabilitation and functional abilities? (Analysis)

- What recommendations for follow-up would you make to Mrs. Wilson? (Synthesis)

- Once a diagnosis has been established for Mrs. Wilson, how would you evaluate her understanding of it and determine any additional needed teaching for discharge home? (Evaluation)

Key Points

- The nose, sinuses, and throat are parts of the upper respiratory tract.
- The mouth and throat are parts of the upper gastrointestinal tract.
- The nose is the primary organ of smell.
- The mouth is the primary organ of taste.
- Kiesselbach's plexus is the most common site of epistaxis.
- The pharyngeal fossa is the most common site of oral cancer.
- The highly vascular floor of the mouth is a good location for absorption of sublingual medications.
- Tonsillitis is inflammation of the tonsils; their removal does not increase risk for infection.
- Dental care is lacking in vulnerable groups.
- Acute airway obstruction requires immediate intervention.

- Risk factors for nose, mouth, sinus, and throat concerns include topical decongestant use, smoking, inhaling substances and chemicals, allergies, and dust exposure.
- Common symptoms in the nose, sinuses, mouth, and throat include facial pain, sleep apnea, obstructive breathing, nasal congestion, epistaxis, halitosis, anosmia, cough, pharyngitis, dental pain, dysphagia, hoarseness, and oral lesions.
- The nose is symmetrical, midline, and proportional to facial features.
- The sinuses may be tender when infection is present.
- Fordyce granules are insignificant sebaceous cysts or salivary tissue.
- A white coating of the tongue may be oral candidiasis and is common in patients taking antibiotics.
- Patients can aspirate even if they have an intact gag reflex.
- Milia are small white bumps across the bridge of the nose in infants.
- After age 2.5 years, all 20 deciduous teeth should be present.
- Epstein's pearls are small white glistening pearly papules commonly found in newborns.
- Fissures may appear in the tongue with increased age.

Review Questions

1. Which of the following is part of the upper gastrointestinal tract?
   A. Nasal septum
   B. Sinuses
   C. Throat
   D. Adenoids

2. The nurse is assessing the nares to evaluate the site of epistaxis. The most common site of bleeding is which of the following?
   A. Osteomeatal complex
   B. Nasal septum
   C. Kiesselbach's plexus
   D. Woodruff's plexus

3. The nurse knows that the floor of the mouth is highly vascular, so it is a good location for which of the following?
   A. Absorption of sublingual medications
   B. Identification of malignancy in the pharyngeal fossa
   C. Considering an infection with streptococcus
   D. Aspiration even if the gag reflex is present

4. Acute airway obstruction is a situation that should be
   A. reassessed during the next visit
   B. evaluated within 8 hours
   C. further assessed thoroughly
   D. quickly assessed and treated

5. Risk factors for nose, sinus, mouth, and throat disorders include
   A. topical decongestant use, smoking, and allergies
   B. smoking, allergies, and high blood cholesterol
   C. allergies, high blood cholesterol, and topical decongestant use
   D. high blood cholesterol, topical decongestant use, and smoking

6. The nurse has assessed the nose and documents expected findings as
   A. nose asymmetrical with clear drainage
   B. nose symmetrical and midline
   C. nose asymmetrical and proportional to facial features
   D. nose symmetrical with yellow drainage

7. The nurse is assessing the patient who has been taking antibiotics for 10 days. Oral assessment is important because of the increased risk for which of the following?
   A. Fordyce granules
   B. Pharyngitis
   C. Anosmia
   D. *Candida albicans*

8. An adolescent male presents with reports of nosebleeds. The nurse would further assess for
   A. hemangioma
   B. nasal trauma
   C. angiofibroma
   D. cystic fibrosis

9. The nurse assesses the child with purulent unilateral nasal discharge. The nurse knows that the most likely causative factor is
   A. allergic rhinitis
   B. choanal atresia
   C. foreign body in nose
   D. cystic fibrosis

10. During routine physical examination of a 20-year-old woman, the nurse notes a septal perforation. This finding may be significant for which of the following causes?
    A. Illicit drug use
    B. Nose picking
    C. Nasal trauma
    D. Bifid uvula

Canadian Nursing Research

Houk, S., & Macdonald, M. (2008). A pharyngitis-delegated medical function in the emergency department: The preimplementation process. *Advanced Emergency Nursing Journal, 30*(4), 357–368.

Yoon, M. N., Steele, C. M., et al. (2007). The oral care imperative: The link between oral hygiene and aspiration pneumonia. *Topics in Geriatric Rehabilitation, 23*(3), 280–288.

References

Allergy, Asthma Information Association. (2009). *Statistics.* Retrieved from www.aaia.ca/en/media_statistics.htm

Andresen, H., Hickey, M., et al. (2008). Normal anatomy and physiology. In L. Harris & M. Huntoon (Eds.). *Core curriculum for otorhinolaryngology and head-neck nursing* (2nd ed., pp. 41–77). New Smyrna Beach, FL: Society of Otorhinolaryngology and Head-Neck Nurses, Inc.

Barnes, L. (2000). *Surgical pathology of the head and neck* (2nd ed.). London, UK: Informa Healthcare.

Batsos, C. (2009). *An environmental scan of cleft lip or palate clinics and dental benefits programs in Canada.* Retrieved from www.fptdwg.ca/assets/PDF/CleftPalate/1008-CleftLipAndPalateScan.pdf

Bent, S. (2008). Herbal medicine in the United States: Review of efficacy, safety, and regulation: Grand rounds at University of California, San Francisco Medical Center. *Journal of General Internal Medicine, 23*(6), 854–859.

Bickley, L. S. (2009). *Bates' guide to physical examination and history taking* (10th ed.). Philadelphia, PA: Wolters Kluwer Health/Lippincott Williams & Wilkins.

Bulechek, G. M. Butcher, H. K., et al. (2008). *Nursing interventions classification (NIC)* (5th ed.). St. Louis, MO: Mosby.

Burns, C. (2000). Genetic disorders. In C. Burns, M. Brady, et al. (Eds.). *Pediatric primary care: A handbook for nurse practitioners* (2nd ed., pp. 1260–1282). Philadelphia, AP: W.B. Saunders.

Canadian Cancer Society Steering Committee. (2011). *Canadian cancer statistics: 2011.* Ottawa, ON: Canadian Cancer Society.

Canadian Lung Association. (2011). *Children & second-hand smoke.* Retrieved from http://www.lung.ca/protect-protegez/tobacco-tabagisme/second-secondaire/children-enfants_e.php

Chalmers, J. M., King, P. L., et al. (2005). The oral health assessment tool—Validity and reliability. *Australian Dental Journal, 50*(3), 191–199.

Derebery, J., & Berliner, K. (2002). Allergic disease and the middle ear. In J. Krouse, S. Chadwick, et al. (Eds.). *Allergy and immunology: An otolaryngic approach.* Philadelphia, PA: Wolters Kluwer Health/Lippincott Williams & Wilkins.

Emanuel, I. (2002). In vitro testing for allergens. In J. Krouse, S. Chadwick, et al. (Eds.). *Allergy and immunology: An otolaryngic approach* (pp. 124–133). Philadelphia, PA: Wolters Kluwer Health/Lippincott Williams & Wilkins.

Epstein, J. (2007–2008). *Oral malignancies associated with HIV.* Retrieved from www.cda-adc.ca/jcda/2007/73/10

Health Canada. (2010). *Canadian health measures survey: Oral health statistics.* Retrieved from www.hc-sc.gc.ca/hl-vs/pubs/oral-bucco/fact-fiche-oral-bucco-stat-eng.php

Healthy People 2010: What are its goals? (n.d.). Retrieved from http://www.healthypeople.gov/About goals.htm

Higgins, T., LeGrand, M., et al. (2008). Nasal cavity, paranasal sinuses and nasopharynx. In L. Harris & M. Huntoon (Eds.). *Core curriculum for otorhinolaryngology and head-neck nursing* (2nd ed., p. 183). New Smyrna Beach, FL: Society of Otorhinolaryngology and Head-Neck Nurses, Inc.

Hockenberry, M. J., & Wilson, D. (2007). *Wong's nursing care of infants and children.* St. Louis, MO: Elsevier.

Kramper, M. A. (2005). Patient education: Allergy precautions in the home. *ORL Head Neck Nurs, 23*(1), 27–28.

Langlais, R. P., & Miller, C. S. (2002). *Color atlas of common oral diseases.* Philadelphia, PA: Wolters Kluwer Health/Lippincott Williams & Wilkins.

Laronde, D., & Hislop, G. (2008). *Oral cancer: Just the facts.* Retrieved from www.cda-adc.ca/jcda/vol-74/issue3/269.pdf

Lloyd, K. B., & Naclerio, R. M. (2008). Strategies for managing nasal congestion. *Post graduate healthcare education, LLC.* Philadelphia, PA: GlaxoSmith Kline.

Mayo Clinic. (2007). *Chewing tobacco: Not a risk-free alternative to cigarettes.* Retrieved from http://www.nim.nih.gov/medicineplus/smokelesstobacco.hmtl

Moorhead, S., Johnson, M., et al. (2007). *Nursing outcomes classification (NOC)* (4th ed.). Philadelphia, PA: Mosby.

Mungia, R., Cano, S. M., et al. (2008). Interaction of age and specific saliva component output on caries. *Aging Clinical and Experimental Research, 20*(6), 503–508.

Nandapalan, V., Watson, I. D., et al. (1996). Beta-2-transferrin and cerebrospinal fluid rhinorrhea. *Clinical Otolaryngology Allied Science, 3,* 259–264.

National Center for Complementary and Alternative Medicine. (2008). *Herbs at a glance.* Washington, DC: National Institute of Health.

Nettina, S. M. (2006). *Lippincott manual of nursing practice* (8th ed.). Philadelphia, PA: Wolters Kluwer Health/Lippincott Williams & Wilkins.

Newland, D. (2003). Pediatric otolaryngology. In M. Layland & T. Lin (Eds.). *The Washington manual survival guide series. Otolaryngology survival guide* (pp. 153–166). Philadelphia, PA: Wolters Kluwer Health/Lippincott Williams & Wilkins.

North American Nursing Diagnosis Association. (2009). *Nursing diagnoses, 2009–2011 Edition: Definitions and classifications (NANDA NURSING DIAGNOSIS).* West Sussex, UK: John Wiley & Sons.

Padilla, R., & Ritter, A. (2008). *Talking with patients about meth mouth: Methamphetamine and oral health.* Chapel Hill, NC: Department of Diagnostic Services & General Dentistry, University of North Carolina at Chapel Hill School of Dentistry.

Risk factors and use of preventative services, United States. (2005). Retrieved from www.cdc.gov

Roach, S., Roddick, P., et al. (2010). The ear, nose, mouth, and throat. In T. C. Stephen, D. L. Skillen, R. A. Day, & L. S. Bickley (Eds.). *Canadian Bates' guide to health assessment for nurses* (1st ed., pp. 341—380). Philadelphia, PA: Wolters Kluwer Health/Lippincott Williams & Wilkins.

Wax, M., Myers, L. L., et al. (2004). *Primary care otolaryngology* (2nd ed.). Washington, DC: American Academy of Otolaryngology—Head and Neck Surgery Foundation.

Woodson, G. (2001). *Ear, nose and throat disorders in primary care.* Philadelphia, PA: W.B. Saunders.

Yian, C. (2003). Rhinosinusitis. In M. Layland & T. Lin (Eds.). *The Washington manual survival guide series. Otolaryngology survival guide.* Philadelphia, PA: Wolters Kluwer Health/Lippincott Williams & Wilkins.

The Canadian Jensen's Nursing Health Assessment suite offers these additional resources to enhance learning and facilitate understanding of this chapter:

* thePoint on line resource, http//thepoint.lww.com/Stephem1E
* *Laboratory Manual for Canadian Jenson's Nursing Health Assessment: A Best Practice Approach*

Tables of Unexpected Findings

Table 17-5 Common Assessment Findings: Nose and Sinuses

Condition	Description and Risk Factors	Findings and Diagnostic Testing
Epistaxis (nosebleed) 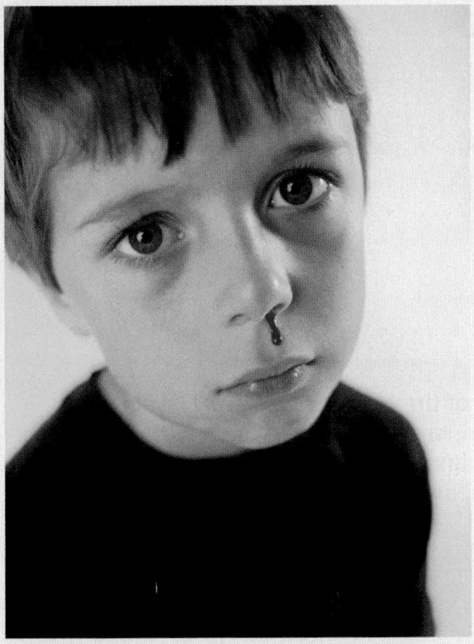 Most commonly involves Kiesselbach's plexus in the anterior septum (little area), which is vulnerable to trauma; also Woodruff's plexus under the posterior portion of the inferior turbinate	Increased nasal congestion; dry mucosa; digital manipulation or nose picking; trauma; anticoagulants; foreign bodies; tumours; infection; inflammation; blood or coagulation disorders	*Subjective:* Dry sensation or crusting in the nose *Objective:* Prominent vessels, scabs, or crusts on anterior septum; blood in nasal vestibule *Testing:* Consider hemoglobin and hematocrit levels with recurrent nosebleeds. Balloon angiography may locate posterior bleeds; intravascular embolization can occlude vessels.
Rhinitis 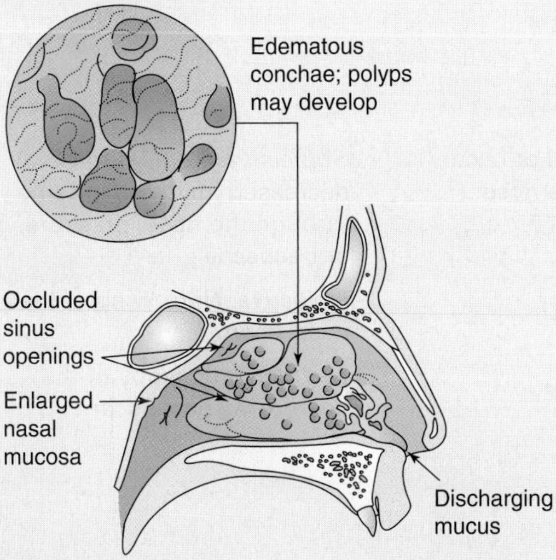 Edematous conchae; polyps may develop Occluded sinus openings Enlarged nasal mucosa Discharging mucus Inflammation of the nasal mucosa; may be subdivided as allergic and nonallergic	Familial or personal atopic disease; exposure to allergens (eg, pollens, dust, molds, animal dander, food) or chemical irritants (eg, smoke); use of illicit drugs; overuse of topical decongestant sprays	*Subjective:* Watery, itchy nose with frequent sneezing and congestion *Objective:* Excessive clear, watery nasal drainage; pale blue, boggy, mucosa, or redness and inflammation *Testing:* Specific skin or blood testing known as radioallergosorbent testing measures IgE antibody, which is elevated in atopic disease (Emanuel, 2002).

(table continues on page 444)

Condition	Description and Risk Factors	Findings and Diagnostic Testing
Sinusitis 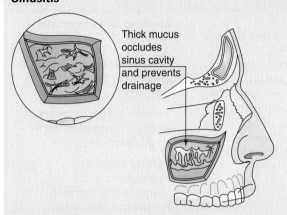 Thick mucus occludes sinus cavity and prevents drainage Infection of one or more paranasal sinuses; may be acute or chronic; chronic sinusitis may result in fungal pathology	Chronic mucosal swelling from allergy, irritants, or chemicals; inflammation secondary to gastroesophageal reflux disease (GERD)	*Subjective:* Facial pain or pressure, thick nasal discharge, fever, cough, halitosis *Objective:* Redness and inflammation of nasal mucosa; thick purulent drainage *Testing:* Endoscopic examination of nose; computerized tomography (CT) scan (gold-standard radiographic tool)
Nasal Polyps 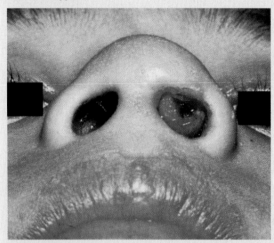 Grapelike swelling of the nasal and sinus mucosa leading to nasal obstruction; often associated with other inflammatory conditions of the nasal mucosa	Chronic inflammation of the nose and paranasal sinuses, allergic or chronic rhinitis, asthma, cystic fibrosis, and chronic sinusitis	*Subjective:* Nasal obstruction and congestion, facial pain and pressure *Objective:* White glistening grapelike structures in the nose that may also fill the sinus cavities *Testing:* Nasal/sinus endoscopy; CT scan
Deviated Septum 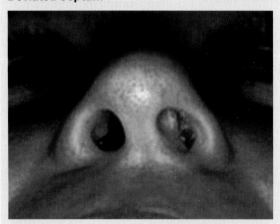 Deflection of the center wall of the nose (septum)	May be congenital or occur with trauma to the nose	*Subjective:* A unilateral decreased ability to breathe through the nose, pressure, or headache *Objective:* Narrowing of the nasal chamber *Testing:* Endoscopy of the nose; x-ray or CT scan

Table 17-5   **Common Assessment Findings: Nose and Sinuses** (*continued*)

Condition	Description and Risk Factors	Findings and Diagnostic Testing
Perforated Septum 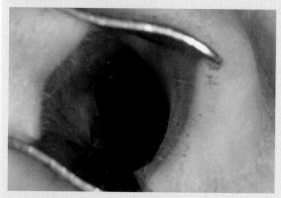 A hole in the nasal septum	Illicit drug use (eg, snorting cocaine); nasal trauma; nasal septal surgery; digital manipulation or nose picking; chronic epistaxis	*Subjective:* Foul odour, whistling sound, recurrent crusting or bleeding from the nose *Objective:* A hole in the septum, which may have crusting or purulent drainage *Testing:* Endoscopy, direct visualization, or CT scan
Foreign Body 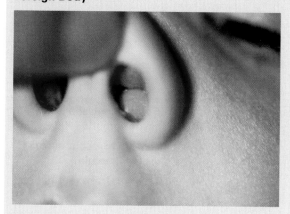 Any object not commonly found in the upper aerodigestive tract	Nasal piercing; deliberately placed objects in nose (as with young children); postsurgical remnant of cotton or gauze	*Subjective:* Unilateral nasal congestion or obstruction *Objective:* Unilateral purulence or thick nasal drainage *Testing:* Endoscopic examination; x-ray of the nose—in small children examination under anesthesia is typically performed with removal of the foreign body

Table 17-6 Common Assessment Findings: Palate and Throat

Condition	Risk Factors	Findings and Diagnostic Testing
Cleft lip/Cleft Palate 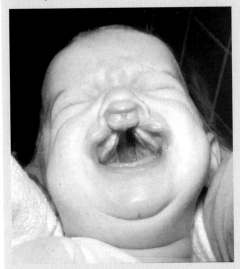 Most common congenital malformation of oral cavity (1 in 1,000 births); an opening or fissure of the lip/alveolus and palate; represents a fusion deviation of the midfacial skeleton and soft tissues	First Nations and Asian genetic background; maternal exposure to phenytoin, methotrexate, cigarette smoke, and alcohol abuse	*Subjective:* Recurrent middle ear and sinus infections; feeding difficulties *Objective:* Lip cleft apparent at birth; notch or full opening on hard palate, soft palate, or both *Testing:* Oral/facial examination
Bifid Uvula 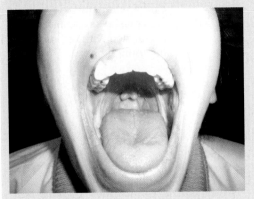 Congenital complete or partial split of uvula; adenoidectomy may be contraindicated	Submucosal cleft palate	*Subjective:* Usually asymptomatic *Objective:* A split or fork visible in uvula *Testing:* Oral examination
Kaposi's Sarcoma 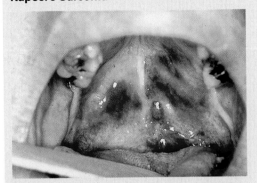 Rapidly proliferating malignancy of the skin or mucous membranes; oral involvement includes the tongue, gingiva, and palate	HIV; 5–10 times greater in male homosexuals infected with HIV than others with the illness (Epstein, 2007–2008)	*Subjective:* Nonhealing oral lesions; may report facial lymphedema *Objective:* Bruise-like lesions that form plaques and progress into nodular, red-purple, nonblanching firm lesions *Testing:* Endoscopic examination of nose; chest x-ray, computerized tomography (CT) scan, or magnetic resonance imaging (MRI) for disease surveillance

Table 17-6   **Common Assessment Findings: Palate and Throat** (*continued*)

Condition	Risk Factors	Findings and Diagnostic Testing
Acute Tonsillitis or Pharyngitis 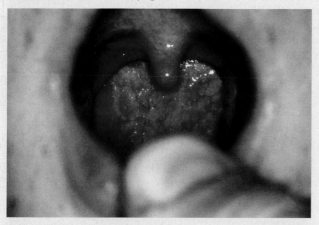 *Pharyngitis:* Inflammation of the pharyngeal walls—may include tonsils, palate, uvula *Tonsillitis:* Inflammation in lymphoid tissue of oropharynx including Waldeyer's ring, palatine or lingual tonsils, pharyngeal bands, nasopharynx, adenoids	Beta-hemolytic streptococcus; may be viral; smoking; mouth breathing	*Subjective:* Sore throat, malaise, anorexia, headache, dysphagia, increased postnasal secretions *Objective:* Infection, redness of pharyngeal walls, exudate, fever, rash; in severe cases, airway obstruction *Testing:* Throat culture; complete blood count (CBC) with differential to determine viral or bacterial
Strep Throat 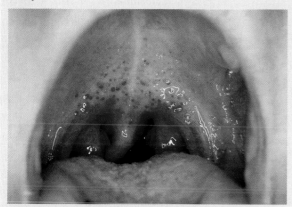 Infection of the tonsils involving streptococcus bacterium	Exposure to infected individuals; smoking	*Subjective:* Sore throat, chills, difficult painful swallowing, headache, laryngitis *Objective:* Infection and enlargement of tonsils; enlargement of jaw and neck lymph nodes *Testing:* Rapid strep swab, throat culture, monospot test, CBC with differential to determine viral or bacterial
Torus Palatinus 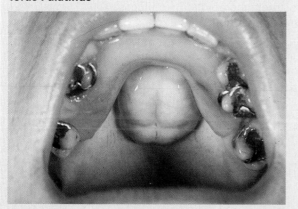 A bony prominence in the middle of the hard palate	Congenital; no clinical significance	*Subjective:* Patient reports feeling a lump on the roof of his or her mouth *Objective:* A bony growth midline in the hard palate *Testing:* Direct visualization

Table 17-7   Common Assessment Findings: Lips and Tongue

Condition	Risk Factors	Findings and Diagnostic Testing
Herpes Simplex Virus 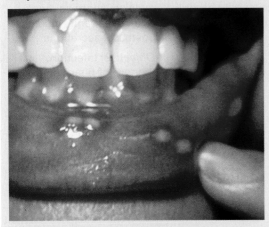 Clear vesicular lesions with indurated base caused by herpes simplex 1 virus	Direct contact with infected person, fever, colds, allergies; may be precipitated by sunlight exposure	*Subjective:* Painful oral lesions; frequently appears at lip–skin juncture *Objective:* Lesions evolve into pustules that rupture, weep, and crust; typical course is 4–10 d *Testing:* Typically none recommended, but may culture with persistent lesions
Aphthous Ulcers (Canker Sores) 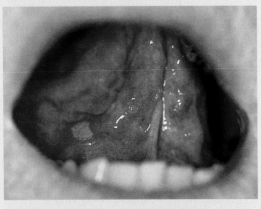 Vesicular oral lesion that evolves into a white ulceration with a red margin	Stress, fatigue, allergies, autoimmune disorders	*Subjective:* Pain at and around site *Objective:* Visible oral lesion(s) *Testing:* Typically not recommended, but may culture in persistent lesions
Candidiasis 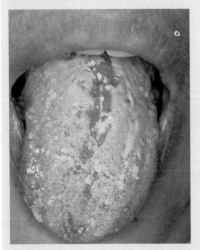 Opportunistic yeast infection of the buccal mucosa and tongue	May occur in newborns; antibiotic or corticosteroid therapy; immunosuppression	*Subjective:* White sticky mucus on tongue or oral mucosa *Objective:* White, cheesy mucus on tongue or buccal mucosa; may scrape mucus off yet tissue is raw and vascular beneath *Testing:* No specific recommendation; consider immune compromise work-up in recurrent infections

Table 17-7   Common Assessment Findings: Lips and Tongue (continued)

Condition	Risk Factors	Findings and Diagnostic Testing
Leukoplakia 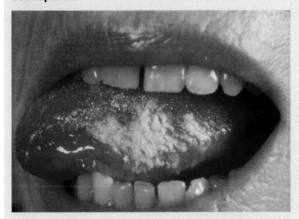 White patchy lesions with well-defined borders	Chronic irritation, smoking, excessive alcohol use	*Subjective:* Persistent oral lesion *Objective:* White lesion firmly attached to mucosal surface; does not scrape off *Testing:* May require biopsy
Black Hairy Tongue 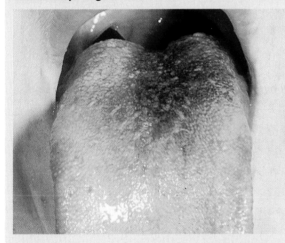 Fungal infection of the tongue involving elongation of the papillae	May follow antibiotic therapy; immunocompromised status	*Subjective:* Brown/black hairy coating on tongue *Objective:* Black/brown hairy appearance from elongation of papillae with a painless overgrowth of fungus *Testing:* None recommended
Carcinoma 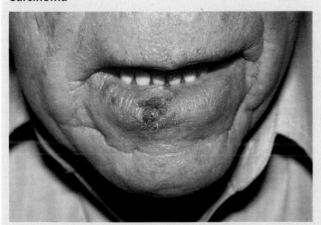 An initially indurated lesion with rolled irregular edges; later may crust or scab but does not heal	Tobacco use, heavy alcohol consumption, chemical exposure	*Subjective:* A lesion that may be painful or limit mobility of the tongue *Objective:* Initially indurated lesion with rolled irregular edges; later appears crusty; possible swelling in adjacent lymph nodes *Testing:* Biopsy

Table 17-8   Common Assessment Findings: Gums and Teeth

Condition	Risk Factors	Findings and Diagnostic Testing
Baby Bottle Tooth Decay 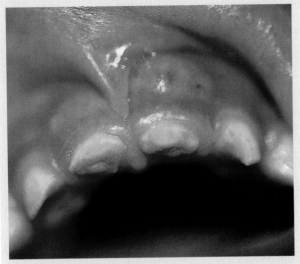 Decay of deciduous teeth in older infants and toddlers from pooling of liquid carbohydrate around front teeth; as mouth bacteria act on the carbohydrate, liquid metabolic acid forms that breaks down tooth enamel	Infants taking milk or sweet juice to bed; bottle-feeding past 1 y of age	Decay and destruction of upper front teeth *Testing:* Dental x-ray with extensive involvement
Dental Caries 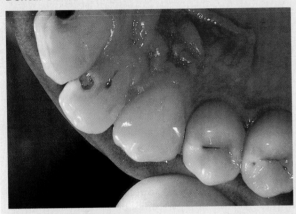 Progressive destruction of tooth	Poor oral hygiene	*Subjective:* No pain in early stages; pain with further destruction and with hot and cold substances *Objective:* Early stages may appear chalky white; later becomes brown or black and forms a cavity *Testing:* Dental x-ray
Gingival Hyperplasia 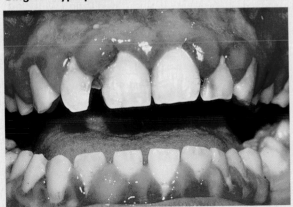 Painless enlargement of the gums	May accompany states of hormonal fluctuation (eg, puberty, pregnancy); leukemia; side effect of drugs (eg, phenytoin [Dilantin])	*Subjective:* Swelling of gums *Objective:* Enlargement of gum tissue; may overreach the teeth *Testing:* Dental x-ray

Condition	Risk Factors	Findings and Diagnostic Testing
Gingivitis 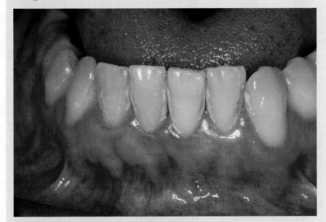 Painful, red, swollen gums	Poor oral hygiene; hormonal fluctuations; vitamin B deficiency	*Subjective:* Sore, bleeding gums *Objective:* Red, swollen, possibly bleeding gums; may involve desquamation of gingival tissue *Testing:* Dental x-ray
Ankyloglossia (Tongue Tie)  A shortened lingual frenulum	Congenital defect	*Subjective:* Limited movement of tongue; speech disruption, particularly with a, d, and n sounds *Objective:* A tight frenulum fixing the tongue to the floor of the mouth *Testing:* None recommended

Thorax and Lungs Assessment

Learning Objectives

1 Demonstrate knowledge of the anatomy and physiology of the respiratory system.

2 Identify important topics for health promotion and risk reduction related to the thorax and lungs.

3 Collect subjective data related to the respiratory system.

4 Collect objective data related to the respiratory system, using physical examination techniques.

5 Identify expected and unexpected findings related to the respiratory system.

6 Identify expected breath sounds and unexpected sounds including crackles, wheezes, gurgles, and stridor.

7 Analyze subjective and objective data from assessment of the respiratory system and consider initial interventions.

8 Document and communicate data from the respiratory system assessment using appropriate terminology and principles of recording.

9 Consider age, condition, gender, and culture of the patient to individualize the respiratory assessment.

10 Identify nursing diagnoses and initiate a plan of care based on findings from the respiratory assessment.

*M*r. Ken Jin, a 65-year-old Chinese man, has come to the clinic today reporting shortness of breath and fatigue. Mandarin is his first language, and he speaks English with a slight accent, well-developed vocabulary, and fluent pacing. He has smoked cigarettes for 49 years. Mr. Jin has a history of congestive heart failure (CHF) and high blood pressure, for which he takes a hydroclorothiazide (Apo-Hydro), 50 mg/d. He states that he uses albuterol (Ventolin), 2 puffs every 6 hours, and ipratropium (Apo-Ipravent), 2 puffs, 4 times/d to improve his breathing.

You will gain more information about Mr. Jin as you progress through this chapter. As you study the content and features, consider Mr. Jin's case and its relationship to what you are learning. Begin thinking about the following points:

- Is Mr. Jin's condition stable, urgent, or an emergency?
- What health promotion and teaching needs are identified? Which two areas are the highest priorities?
- How will the nurse focus, organize, and prioritize subjective and objective data collection?
- What nursing diagnosis is the highest priority? Provide rationale.
- How will the nurse individualize assessment to Mr. Jin's specific needs, considering his condition, age, and culture?

The focus of this chapter is the assessment of the thorax and lungs. It includes a review of pertinent anatomy and physiology related to respiratory and pulmonary function, as well as key variations based on lifespan, culture, and environment. The chapter includes methods for collecting subjective data about risks for pulmonary disease, such as smoking and family history of similar concerns. It reviews specific respiratory signs and symptoms, such as shortness of breath and coughing. Content about objective data explains the correct techniques for assessing respiratory patterns, identifying expected and unexpected breath sounds, and labelling findings. Lung auscultation is performed as a screening during the complete physical examination, as well as in ongoing assessments for patients with identified pulmonary disease or diseases. Although challenging, lung auscultation provides information that can assist with accurate diagnosis and related early interventions.

Anatomy and Physiology Overview

The respiratory system is separated into the upper and lower tracts. The upper airway warms, moisturizes, and transports air to the lower airway, where oxygenation and ventilation occur.

Understanding the anatomy of the thoracic cage and how to use its landmarks to reference underlying structures when conducting examinations and reporting findings is essential. Knowledge of the placement and divisions of the lungs, other vital organs within the respiratory system, and physiology of respiration enhances the potential for accurate assessments of the thoracic and lung regions.

The Thorax

The thorax is one of the most dynamic regions of the body because it is constantly moving (Moore & Agur, 2011). See Figure 18-1 for the surface anatomy of the thorax in men and women.

The bony **thoracic cage** includes the sternum and clavicle anteriorly, scapulae and 12 vertebrae posteriorly, and 12 pairs of ribs. The **thoracic cavity** contains the heart, lungs, thymus, distal part of the trachea, and most of the esophagus. The thoracic nerves in the chest (T1 to T12) supply a surrounding area of skin horizontally, following the dermatomes (areas of skin supplied with afferent nerve fibres by a single posterior spinal root) (see Chapter 24). The phrenic nerve innervates the diaphragm, and the intercostal nerves innervate the intercostal muscles. The thoracic muscles include the intercostals, transverse thoracic, subcostal, levator costarum, and serratus posterior (Moore & Agur, 2011). Arterial blood supply to the chest is through the thoracic aorta, subclavian artery, brachial artery, and axillary artery; numerous veins return blood to the heart. Each lung has a pulmonary artery that supplies deoxygenated blood for gas exchange, while two pulmonary veins return oxygenated blood to the left side of the heart for circulation to the rest of the body.

To label findings on the thorax, locations must be identified both vertically (up and down) and horizontally (side to side). The ribs provide vertical reference points, while a series of lines provide horizontal reference marks.

Anterior Thoracic Landmarks

The anterior vertical landmarks involve the ribs and their associated interspaces. The easiest place to start is at the **suprasternal (jugular) notch** (Fig. 18-2). This U-shaped depression lies just above the **sternum** and between the clavicles. Place your fingers on your sternum and walk them up to the notch; alternatively, you can lightly feel the trachea and move your fingers down. From the suprasternal notch, walk your fingers down approximately 5 cm to the bony ridge that joins the **manubrium** to the sternum. This ridge, called the

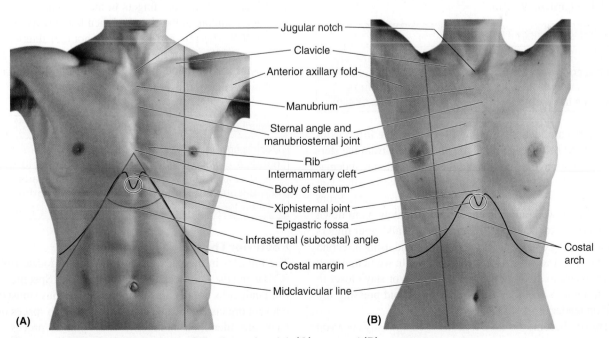

Jugular notch
Clavicle
Anterior axillary fold
Manubrium
Sternal angle and manubriosternal joint
Rib
Intermammary cleft
Body of sternum
Xiphisternal joint
Epigastric fossa
Infrasternal (subcostal) angle
Costal margin
Midclavicular line
Costal arch

(A)   **(B)**

Figure 18-1 Surface anatomy of the thorax in adult **(A)** men and **(B)** women.

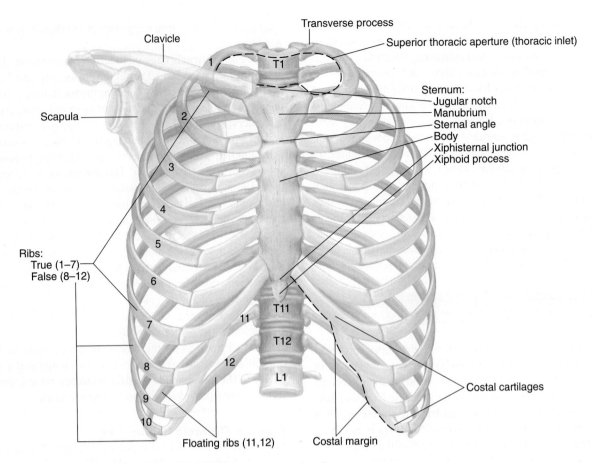

Figure 18-2 Landmarks of the thoracic cage, anterior view.

sternal angle (also known as the **angle of Louis** or **manubriosternal angle**), varies in prominence and is usually easier to locate in thinner people. The sternal angle is continuous with the second rib (Moore & Agur, 2011). It also marks the site of the apex of the heart and the bifurcation of the right and left mainstem bronchi.

Clinical Significance 18-1

The carina, found at the sternal angle, is also the site of the cough reflex. Patients who need nasotracheal suctioning will cough when the nasotracheal tube reaches the carina (approximately the 2nd rib space).

Landmarks are identified on the rib cage by the **intercostal space** (ICS) below each rib. Slide your fingers from the sternal angle over to the 2nd rib, and then down into the indentation that is the 2nd ICS. Take a moment to make sure that you can identify the bony raised rib and sunken rib space. From the 2nd ICS, walk another finger approximately 3 cm down the chest wall to the 3rd ICS. Continue to "walk" your fingers down, keeping one finger in the rib space and using a second to locate the next rib space (see Fig. 18-2). In women, it may be necessary to displace the breast laterally or stay closer to the sternum to avoid breast tissue. Also, avoid pressing too hard on tender breast tissue.

The ribs become too close together to count easily once you reach the 6th rib, which is usually at the bottom of the breast

tissue (where underwire in a bra would lie). Also, the costal cartilages of the 8th, 9th, and 10th ribs articulate with the ribs above them, not the sternum. Thus, if you palpate more laterally in the locations, shown in Figure 18-2, you can palpate more easily down to the 10th rib anteriorly. From the 6th to 7th rib space, walk your fingers in the rib space to approximately the middle of the chest and then laterally and down to the 9th ICS. The 11th and 12th ribs do not join anteriorly.

The angle between the ribs at the costal margins forms the **costal angle**, found at the bottom of the sternum at the **xyphoid process**. It is usually 90° or less.

Clinical Significance 18-2

During cardiopulmonary resuscitation (CPR), hands are placed above the xyphoid process to avoid breaking it off from the sternum and causing complications such as pneumothorax, hemothorax, or liver laceration.

Posterior Thoracic Landmarks

The muscles in the back make it difficult to locate ribs and ICSs using the same technique as on the front. Specific posterior landmarks usually are less important, because most of the relevant organs are located anteriorly. Thus, rib spaces on the back are identified indirectly, and spinous processes of the vertebrae are used to identify rib location.

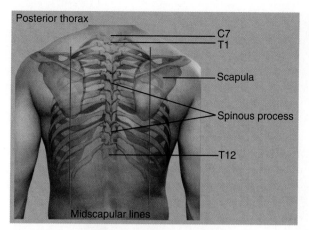

Figure 18-3 Posterior thoracic landmarks.

Flex your neck forward and feel the vertebral processes, the most protruding of which is usually C7 (Fig. 18-3; see also Chapter 14). If two are protruding, the upper one is C7, and the lower one is T1 (Moore & Agur, 2011). The spinous process of T1 usually correlates with the 1st rib. Posteriorly, the spinous processes correlate down to T4 only, because they start to angle down and overlie the vertebral body and underlying rib. A second method for identifying the ribs posteriorly is to locate the lower tip of the scapula; it is at the 7th to 8th rib (Moore & Agur). The tip of the 11th floating rib can be palpated laterally; the tip of the 12th floating rib can be palpated posteriorly.

Reference Lines

To label findings horizontally on the chest, a series of reference lines is used. On the anterior chest are the midsternal, midclavicular, and anterior axillary lines, named for the structures that they describe (Fig. 18-4). The **midsternal line** is in the center of the sternum. The **midclavicular line** (MCL) extends down from the clavicle halfway between the

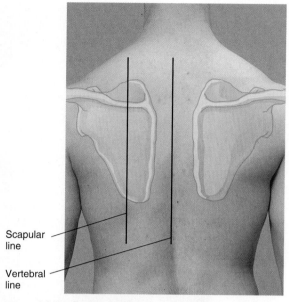

Figure 18-5 Reference lines of the chest, posterior view.

sternoclavicular and acromioclavicular joints. The **anterior axillary line** extends from the top of the anterior axillary fold when the arms are at the sides.

The posterior chest wall lines are vertebral and scapular (Fig. 18-5). The **vertebral line** lies over the center of the spinous processes of the vertebrae. The **scapular line** originates from the inferior angle of the scapula and is parallel to the vertebral line.

In addition to the previously mentioned anterior axillary line, other lines from a side view are based on their relation to the axilla. The **posterior axillary line** drops from the posterior axillary fold (Moore & Agur, 2011). The **midaxillary line** drops from the apex of the axilla and is parallel to the anterior axillary line (see Fig. 18-6).

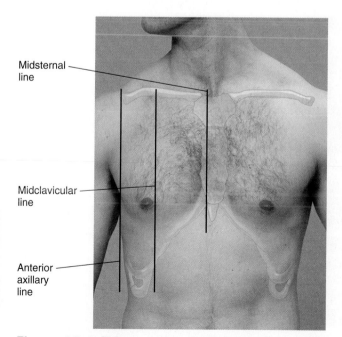

Figure 18-4 Reference lines of the chest, anterior view.

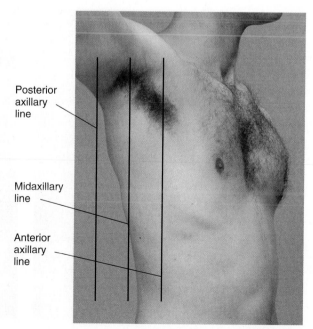

Figure 18-6 Reference lines of the chest, side view.

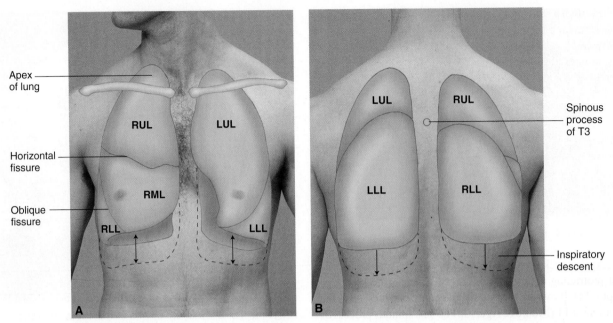

Figure 18-7 Views of the lungs. **A.** Anterior. **B.** Posterior.

Other areas that may be referenced when identifying findings include supraclavicular (above the clavicle), infra-clavicular (below the clavicle), interscapular (between the scapula), infrascapular (below the scapula), or medial or lateral to the reference lines.

Lobes of the Lungs

The previously described landmarks help pinpoint the approximate location of the lobes of the lungs on the chest wall. Each lung is divided almost in half by an **oblique fissure** that runs from the 6th rib MCL anteriorly to the T3 spinous process posteriorly (Figs. 18-7 A, B). The left lung has two lobes,

while the right lung has three. The **horizontal (minor) fissure** divides the right upper and middle lobes of the lung. The right upper lobe and right middle lobe (RML) are approximately the size of the left upper lobe. The RML extends from the 4th rib at the sternal border to the 5th rib at the midaxillary line (Fig. 18-8) (Moore & Agur, 2011). The right lower lobe and left lower lobe are approximately the same size.

> **Clinical Significance 18-3**
>
> The RML can only be auscultated anteriorly. It is often found under the breast, making it challenging to hear in women.

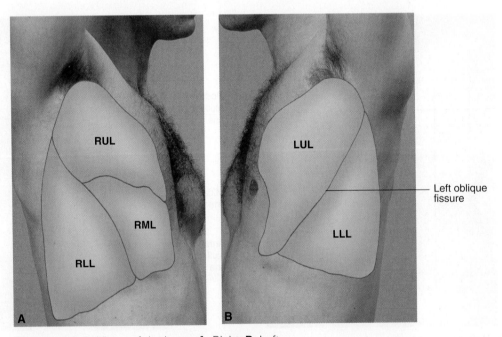

Figure 18-8 Views of the lungs. **A.** Right. **B.** Left.

The right lung is approximately 2.5 cm higher than the left because the liver displaces the lung tissue upward. The left lung is narrower than the right because the location of the heart on the left displaces the lung tissue. Note that the anterior chest is almost all middle and upper lobes, while the posterior chest is almost all lower lobes. These landmarks only approximate the lung lobes, so it is more accurate to label findings using chest wall landmarks instead of the lung lobes.

Upper, middle, and lower lung fields are divided into approximately equal thirds. The **base** refers to the very bottom of the lung fields; the **apex** is the very top (opposite of the labelling of the heart). Lungs should be auscultated from apex to base. Anteriorly, the apex of the lung extends approximately 2 to 4 cm above the inner third of the clavicle. The base rests on the diaphragm at the 6th rib MCL and the 8th rib at the midaxillary line. Posteriorly, the apex of the lung is near C7, while the base is near T10 (three rib spaces below the inferior tip of the scapula). With deep inspiration, the base may extend another two rib spaces to T12 (Moore & Agur, 2011).

Clinical Significance 18-4

The apex of the lung extends above the clavicle, where lung sounds may be audible. When primary health practitioners place a central line into the chest, they may accidentally nick the lung apex, causing a pneumothorax. The apex must be carefully auscultated following this procedure.

Lower Respiratory Tract

The trachea bifurcates into the right main and left main bronchi at the sternal angle anteriorly and the T4 spinous process posteriorly, and then further branches into terminal bronchioles and then alveoli (Fig. 18-9). The right main bronchus is shorter, wider, and more vertical than the left. The trachea and bronchi contain approximately 150 mL of dead space, or areas that transport gas but do not exchange oxygen and carbon dioxide (Moore & Agur, 2011).

Clinical Significance 18-5

The structure of the right bronchus makes it more susceptible to aspiration and intubation if an endotracheal tube is inserted too far. If the right bronchus is intubated, breath sounds will be auscultated only on the right because the tube will block the left main bronchus.

Narrowed **bronchioles** may lead to wheezing. If the goblet cells in the bronchi produce excessive mucus or if the cilia that transport mucus are slowed, crackling or gurgling breath sounds may result. Breath sounds differ in the trachea and bronchi because the trachea is much larger and thus has wider airways. As the airways narrow, sounds become softer, finer, and more difficult to auscultate.

The **alveoli** are the primary units in the lungs that absorb oxygen and excrete carbon dioxide. When fluid fills the

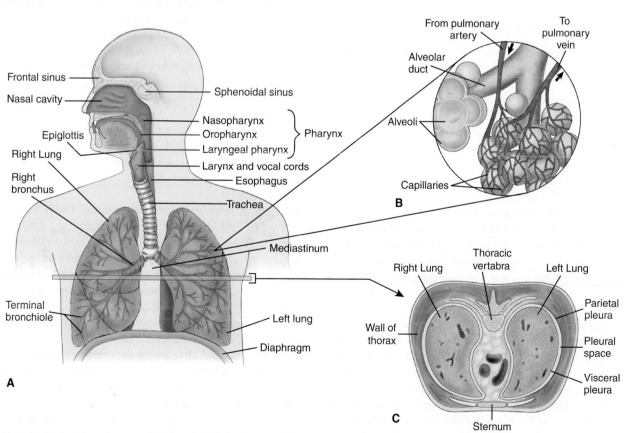

Figure 18-9 A. Structures of the upper and lower respiratory tracts. **B.** Alveoli. **C.** Horizontal cross-section of the lungs.

alveoli, fine crackles may be audible on auscultation. Excessive fluid in the alveoli may lead to airway collapse and decreased breath sounds. Pulmonary arterioles take oxygen from the alveoli to the cells, while pulmonary veins return carbon dioxide to the alveoli for excretion. Obstruction of a pulmonary artery by a blood clot or pulmonary embolus can lead to decreased blood oxygenation.

The pleurae are double-layered serous membranes. The **visceral pleura** encases the lungs and their surfaces, while the **parietal pleura** lines the thoracic wall, mediastinum, and diaphragm. "A thin film of serous fluid separates the two pleural layers allowing the two layers to glide over each other; and yet hold together" (Pooler, 2010, p. 622). Thus there is no separation between chest wall and the lungs. Trauma to the chest wall may lead to separation of the visceral pleura and, subsequently, a collapsed lung (pneumothorax).

The **mediastinum** extends from sternum to vertebrae, containing the organs and tissues between the right and left lungs. These structures include the trachea, pulmonary vasculature, heart, great vessels, esophagus, and lymph vessels. The other two cavities in the thorax are the pulmonary cavities which contain the lungs.

Upper Respiratory Tract

The upper respiratory tract is responsible for moisturizing inhaled air and filtering noxious particles. It is covered in depth in Chapter 17.

Mechanics of Respiration

Respiration is primarily an automatic process triggered in the respiratory center of the brainstem (pons and medulla) based on cellular demands (Benditt, 2006). The main trigger for breathing is increased carbon dioxide in the blood. Decreased oxygen or increased acidity also may trigger breathing. Some medications (eg, opiates) or an overdose of drugs may reduce the ability of the brain to trigger breathing, causing hypoventilation (slow breathing). Anxiety or brain injury may stimulate breathing, causing hyperventilation (fast breathing).

When breathing is triggered, the **diaphragm** contracts and flattens, pulling the lungs down. The thorax and lungs elongate, increasing the vertical diameter. The external intercostal muscles open the ribs and lift the sternum, and the anteroposterior (AP) diameter of the thorax increases. With increased thoracic size, pressure in the lungs is less than pressure in the atmosphere. As a result, approximately 500 to 800 mL of air enters the lungs with each breath in adults (Moore & Agur, 2011).

Expiration is primarily passive. As the diaphragm, internal intercostal muscles, and abdominal muscles relax, pressure in the lungs is greater than in the atmosphere. Subsequently, air is pushed out, and the chest and abdomen return to their relaxed position.

Sufficient innervation, muscle excursion, and strength are needed for effective breathing. Patients with disorders or conditions of the spinal cord, especially injuries above C3 to C5, may require ventilatory support. Extreme obesity can limit chest wall expansion (and thus compromise breathing), and progressive loss of muscle function (eg, muscular dystrophy) can limit ability to ventilate and cough (Benditt, 2006).

Lifespan Considerations

Women Who Are Pregnant
In late pregnancy, the lower ribs flare as the fetus and uterus grow. The costal angle increases, and the diaphragm rises approximately 4 cm above its usual position. Tidal volume increases because the diaphragm moves more, although respiratory rate remains approximately the same. Increased tidal volume meets the increased demands that the growing fetus places on the woman.

Infants and Children
The respiratory system does not function until birth. The fetus depends on the placenta for exchange of oxygen. Prenatal lungs contain no air, and the alveoli are collapsed. Passive air movements prepare the fetus to respond to chemical and neurological stimuli that will trigger breathing after birth. Surfactant production begins at 32 weeks of gestation to keep the alveoli open.

After the umbilical cord is cut at birth, the newborn's lungs fill with air as he or she takes the first breath. Blood perfuses the lungs quickly. The pulmonary arteries offer less resistance than the systemic circulation, so the lungs get more of the blood supply. The foramen ovale closes between the right and left atria of the heart. The ductus arteriosus, which shunts blood from the pulmonary artery to the aorta, closes; right to left blood flow in the heart is established (Woods, Sivarajan Froelicher, et al., 2005).

The chest in the newborn is round and consistent with the size of the head until approximately 2 years of age. The thin chest wall makes the ribs more prominent in newborns. Increased cartilage makes the chest wall also more compliant and flexible than in adults. Respiratory function continues to develop throughout childhood with increases in the size of the airways and in the size and number of alveoli.

Older Adults
With aging, respiratory strength declines. Lungs lose elasticity, cartilage in the ribs loses flexibility, and bones lose density. These changes result in smaller breaths (decreased inspiratory volumes) and more air remaining in the lungs after exhalation (increased residual volume) (Hankinson, Crapo, et al., 2003). The anterior to posterior depth of the chest widens, causing the thorax to become more rounded or barrel shaped. When the thorax is rounded, it is harder to inhale deeply. Costal cartilages are calcified, creating a less flexible thorax and more use of the upper lung fields, which are less efficient than the bases. As breathing becomes shallower, older adults inhale less air and may need to increase rate of breathing to maintain oxygenation.

More significantly, the alveoli are less elastic and more rigid, and the lungs may become "stiff." It takes more work to ventilate stiff lungs. Loss of alveoli renders less surface area available for gas exchange. Older adults are at increased risk for chronic obstructive pulmonary disease (COPD) (Crapo, Glassroth, et al., 2004). Their decreased reserves make it difficult to maintain ventilation during stress, such as exercise or illness. Additionally, decreased function of the cilia leads to the pooling of secretions in the lungs. Weaker chest muscles also decrease the older person's ability to cough up secretions. Thick, pooled secretions increase risks for pneumonia.

🌐 Cultural Considerations

Chest size influences how much a person can inhale and exhale. There is no significant difference in the chest volumes of Caucasians, Africans, or Latinos. Reference values for Caucasian adults are 5% to 19% higher than for Asian adults (Ip, Ko, et al., 2006). Variability is more closely linked to body size versus ethnicity. Women have a lower forced expiratory capacity than men (Hankinson, Crapo, et al., 2003), and older adults have a lower forced expiratory capacity than do younger adults (Ip, Ko, et al.).

Genetic patterns of inheritance increase risks for respiratory conditions such as cystic fibrosis (CF) and alpha-1 antitrypsin deficiency (associated with COPD). CF is characterized by high sodium and chloride levels in sweat, COPD, and pancreatic insufficiency. The Canadian Cystic Fibrosis Foundation (2010) reports that 1 out of every 3,600 babies will be diagnosed with CF. The mean age at death for people with CF has increased from 18 years in 1983 to 32.3 years in 2008 (Cystic Fibrosis Canada, 2011). The current success with lung transplants has benefited some individuals with CF. However, 90% of people with CF will die from pulmonary complications (Crapo, Glassroth, et al., 2004).

Before birth, the lecithin/sphigomyelin ratio can be calculated to help determine a preterm newborn's risk of fetal respiratory distress. Infants of African descent have a higher ratio and better outcomes than Caucasian infants because of accelerated lung maturation (Berman, Tanasijevic, et al., 1996).

Acute Assessment

Accurately prioritizing assessments and interventions in urgent or emergency respiratory situations is absolutely critical. If the patient has acute shortness of breath, immediate assessments include respiratory rate, pulse, blood pressure, and oxygen saturation. The lungs are auscultated. Simultaneously, oxygen is administered, and inhalers may be given. If the patient is in bed, the head of the bed is elevated to reduce the effect of gravity. Because anxiety increases the work of breathing, the nurse's role is to stay with and to calm the patient. Conversations should be limited while the nurse implements interventions to improve oxygenation. As oxygen levels drop, patients become more dyspneic and cyanotic; they also may become confused. If the situation does not resolve, an emergency response team or personnel from respiratory therapy may be necessary for assistance.

Patients at risk for pulmonary complications such as pneumonia following surgery include those who: currently smoke or have smoked in the 8 weeks prior to surgery, are in poor general health, have COPD, are having upper abdominal or thoracic surgery, or are having surgery that will last more than 3 hours. It is critical that nurses closely monitor patients for changes in pulmonary status in order to pick up early changes and deteriorating status (Duff, Gardiner, et al., 2007). Patients at risk for a pulmonary embolus include those with prolonged immobility, trauma, fractures, recent travel, pregnancy or post partum status, or a history of deep vein thrombosis (Edge & Bickley, 2010).

In some cases, patients are stable, but fatigue limits the collection of assessment data. In such instances, listen to the bases of the lungs first and to the posterior lungs before the anterior lungs. Consider clustering care. Auscultate the lungs when turning the patient or getting the patient up in a chair. Positioning with the head of the bed at a 30° to 45° angle may be more comfortable than lying flat. Prioritize the subjective data collected; ask only those questions important to current care. Questions relating to the future can be deferred. Simple daily tasks such as eating may consume much energy, so it is important to cluster interventions and time assessments for when the patient is more rested.

Subjective Data Collection

Subjective data collection begins with the health history, continues with questions about specific respiratory conditions, and ends with detailed collection of information involving areas of concern. If patients are short of breath, the interview will need to be shortened. In such instances, ask only those questions pertinent to the current condition and necessary for current care.

⚠ SAFETY ALERT 18-1

If the patient is having extreme difficulty breathing, stop the assessment and get help. A decreased level of consciousness, respiratory rate above 30 breaths/min, oxygen saturation <92%, cyanosis, retractions, and use of accessory muscles may indicate hypoxia (a medical emergency).

Assessment of Risk Factors

When questioning patients about risk factors, the intent is to identify how likely they are to develop or to already be experiencing consequences of respiratory disorders. Such investigation creates an environment in which health care providers can implement necessary interventions to control symptoms, direct education to prevent new or complications, and establish within the patient health record areas needing ongoing follow-up and emphasis. For example, smoking contributes to COPD. Thus, the smoking history requires a thorough assessment so that health care providers can give educational materials to patients willing to begin a smoking-cessation program. Teaching and questioning can be woven together.

Questions to Assess History and Risk Factors	Rationale

Personal History

Have you ever been diagnosed with a respiratory condition such as asthma? Bronchitis? Emphysema? Or pneumonia?
- When was the illness?
- How was the illness treated?
- What were the outcomes?

History of respiratory disease increases risk for recurrence. Chronic diseases such as chronic obstructive pulmonary disease *(COPD)* often have long-term effects that result in a slow but progressive decline in function. COPD is usually diagnosed by age 55 years, but chronic bronchitis and emphysema, the common underlying disease processes, occur earlier (Canadian Lung Association, 2008). An estimated 1.5 million Canadians have COPD and another 1.6 million are undiagnosed (Canadian Lung Association). Women who started smoking in the 1960s are now being diagnosed with COPD (Ross, 2010). By 2020, it is estimated that COPD will be the third leading cause of death in Canada and the world (Canadian Lung Association). *Asthma* symptoms may occur at any age and improve or worsen over time. *Pneumonia* usually has an acute course that improves with treatment.

As a child did you have frequent colds? Any chest infections?

Frequent childhood infections may lead to concerns later in life (Stick, 2000).

Do you now or have you ever had allergies?
- What are the allergens?
- When did you have allergies?
- What were the symptoms?
- How were the allergies treated?
- What were the outcomes?
- What are the allergens?

Allergies to foods or medications may precipitate bronchoconstriction. Common allergens include pollens, dust mites, grasses, molds, animal dander, latex, and food (eggs, peanuts and other nuts, dairy products, wheat, and fish). Exercise also induces allergies in some people.

When was your last tuberculosis (TB) skin test? Or chest x-ray?
- What was the result?
- Do you receive any treatment?

Risk factors include close contact with an infected person, being foreign-born, low income, substance abuse, and infection with HIV (Taylor, Nolan, et al., 2005). The Public Health Agency of Canada (PHAC) (2011a) reported more than 4 million new cases of TB and about 2 million deaths worldwide in 2009. In Canada, new TB cases are diagnosed every 6 hours, and a TB-related death occurs every 2 weeks. About 70% of TB cases in Canada originate from outside the country (Canadian Lung Association, 2011a). Those at the highest risk include Canadian-born First Nations and especially the Inuit who live in areas such as Nunavut (PHAC, 2011b).

When did you receive your last influenza (flu) vaccine? Are you interested in being immunized this year?

Influenza vaccine is recommended annually for people 65 years and older, all health care staff, and younger Canadians who are at high risk for influenza-related complications (eg, asthma) or who are immunocompromised (National Advisory Committee on Immunization [NACI], 2006).

Have you ever received the pneumococcal vaccine to prevent pneumonia?

Conjugate pneumococcal vaccine is given to all children older than 23 months, and a booster is given 3 to 5 years later. Pneumococcal vaccine is recommended for people 65 years or older, those younger than 65 years with respiratory conditions, and those who are immunocompromised (eg, people with AIDS) (NACI).

Medications

Are you taking any medications for breathing concerns?
- What are they?
- How often are you taking them?
- How well are you following your prescribed medication regimen?

Many respiratory medications, such as inhalers, are used as needed. Trends of increased use may indicate a worsening condition. Steroids also may be used during times of increased inflammation, such as an *acute asthma attack*.

Questions to Assess History and Risk Factors	Rationale

Are you taking any natural supplements? Or over-the-counter medications?
- What are they?
- How often are you taking them?

Over-the-counter medications that block beta-2 receptors may exacerbate bronchoconstriction. Sensitivity to non-steroidal anti-inflammatory agents (eg, Motrin, Indocin) may cause wheezing in patients with asthma.

Family History
Do you have any family history of respiratory (breathing) concerns?
- Who had the illness?
- What was the illness?
- When did the person have it?
- How was the illness treated?
- What were the outcomes?

A positive family history, especially of genetic concerns such as *cystic fibrosis (CF)*, increases the patient's risk for respiratory illness. Note any contagious diseases (eg, *TB*) and the possibility for familial transmission. Also consider whether the condition is chronic (eg, *COPD*) or transient (eg, *common cold*). Family history of *lung cancer* increases risk by two to three times (Crapo, Glassroth, et al., 2004). In Canada, 25,300 new cases of lung cancer and 20,600 deaths are expected in 2011. Lung cancer is the leading cause of cancer death for men (11,300 deaths expected in 2011) and for women (9,300 deaths expected in 2011) (Canadian Cancer Society's Steering Committee for Cancer Statistics, 2011).

Lifestyle and Personal Habits
Do you smoke? Or have you ever smoked cigarettes? Pipes? Or cigars?
- How many packs per day do you smoke?
- How many years have you smoked?
- Have you ever tried to stop smoking?
- Are you interested in quitting?

Smoking is described by the number of **pack years** (number of years × number of packs per day). For example, the patient who has smoked half pack per day for 30 years has a 15-pack-year history. Increased pack years increase the risk for respiratory disorders, including *lung cancer* and *COPD* (Tessier, Nejjari, et al., 2000).

Are you frequently around people who smoke in the home? Or car? At work? What measures do you take to control this exposure?

Second-hand smoke contains >4,000 chemicals. Regular exposure increases risks for COPD (emphysema and chronic bronchitis), asthma, and lung cancer by 25% and heart disease by 10% (Canadian Lung Association, 2010).

Have you ever inhaled recreational drugs such as marijuana? Cocaine? Methamphetamine? Glue? Or spray paint? Are you currently using any of these drugs? Are you interested in information about how to quit or reduce your risk?

These inhaled substances can irritate the linings of the upper or lower airway. People with injection substance-use disorders are at risk for *infectious pulmonary disease*, as well as *HIV* and its pulmonary manifestations (Wolff & O'Donnell, 2004). Regular marijuana use can lead to extensive airway injury, potentially causing pulmonary infection and respiratory cancer. Crack cocaine use can lead to exacerbations of asthma and an acute lung injury syndrome ("*crack lung*"). Heroin inhalation can induce severe and sometimes fatal exacerbations of asthma (Tashkin, 2001).

Do you have any hobbies that might increase your risk for respiratory conditions, such as exposure to paint fumes? Or wood dust? Bird breeding? Mushroom growing? Scuba diving? Swimming? And high-altitude activities?

Such hobbies may cause lung injury. Exposure over time to bird droppings or feathers may cause *hypersensitivity pneumonitis* and *pulmonary fibrosis*. Risk of drowning is increased for those younger than 18 years, especially toddlers. Being male and ingesting alcohol also increases risk (Crapo, Glassroth, et al., 2004). With rapid ascent to high elevation, *acute mountain sickness* may develop, causing fluid retention, hypoventilation, and mechanical dysfunction (Crapo, Glassroth, et al.).

Occupational History
Have you ever been exposed to substances or irritants at work? Are you currently exposed to substances at work?
- Do you wear a mask? Or do you take other precautions to protect your lungs?
- What steps do you take to monitor your exposure?

Coal miners have an increased risk of *pneumoconiosis*, or black lung disease (McPhee, Papadakis, et al., 2007). *Silicosis* is increased in glassmakers, stonecutters, miners, cement workers, and semiconductor manufacturers (Singh, Chowdhary, et al., 2006). *Occupational asthma* may develop in 2% to 5% of workers exposed to grain dust, wood dust, soldering flux, and dyes (McPhee, Papadakis, et al.). *Industrial bronchitis* is found in textile workers. Shipyard and construction workers, pipefitters, and insulators may develop *asbestosis* (McPhee, Papadakis, et al.).

(text continues on page 462)

Questions to Assess History and Risk Factors	Rationale

Environmental Exposures

Have you ever been exposed to substances or irritants at home such as pollen? Dust? Pet dander? Cockroaches? Or cooking smoke particles? Are you currently exposed to any of the above substances?

Is there any history of exposure to radon? Or asbestos from heating/cooling systems?

Have you recently travelled to any high-risk areas for respiratory conditions, such as Asia? Southern Africa? Indonesia? Or Turkey?
• Where?
• How long were you there?
• Were you exposed to people with a cough? Cold? Or the regular flu? Or the pandemic H1N1 2009 flu?

Common household irritants can contribute to *asthma*, as well as itchy eyes, sneezing, and runny nose. Radon and tobacco smoke can cause even more dangerous health effects, including *lung cancer* (American Lung Association, 2004).

Avian flu can be contracted through exposure to dead or infected birds in China, Indonesia, or Turkey (World Health Organization [WHO], 2006a). High-risk areas for TB include Asia and southern Africa (WHO, 2006b). Quick identification and treatment of these contagions is essential.

The WHO (2010) reported laboratory confirmed deaths from pandemic H1N1 2009 flu as of MAR2010: fewest deaths occurred in Africa (168), while Europe had at least 4,783 and the Americas had the most (8,309), for a total of at least 17,853 deaths. From 29AUG2010, to 12MAR2011, a total of 832 cases occurred in Canada, with the majority being people younger than 65 years. Of note is the 110 cases in children younger than 5 years old. Pandemic H1N1 2009 flu is still occurring in Canada: 66 cases in MAR2011.

Risk Assessment and Health Promotion

Important Topics for Health Promotion

• Smoking cessation
• Prevention of occupational exposure
• Prevention of asthma
• Immunizations

In 2010, six serious respiratory diseases—asthma, COPD, lung cancer, TB, sleep apnea, and CF—affected more than 6 million Canadians (Canadian Lung Association, 2011b). This statistic does not include people with influenza or pneumonia, which are the leading respiratory causes of hospitalization. Respiratory diseases accounted for nearly 9% of all deaths among Canadians in 2004, and the total health care cost for respiratory diseases was $8.63 billion in 2000 (PHAC, 2007). One Canadian dies from lung disease every 20 minutes and all Canadians have at least one risk factor for developing respiratory diseases: air quality, environmental factors, smoking, obesity, and lack of physical activity (Canadian Lung Association).

As mentioned, risk assessment helps identify potential concerns so that health care providers can give patients information to influence behavioural choices. The most important focus area for the respiratory system involves smoking.

Smoking Cessation

More than 70% of smokers indicate an interest in quitting, although <10% are successful (Centers for Disease Control and Prevention, 2008). Nurses need a nonjudgemental approach when asking people who smoke about quitting. Targeted groups include teenagers and women who are pregnant. Adopt the five "*A's*" (Agency for Healthcare Research and Quality, 2005; U.S. Public Health Service, 2009):

• *Ask* about smoking at each visit.
• *Advise* patients regularly to stop smoking, using a clear personalized message.
• *Assess* patient readiness to quit.
• *Assist* patients to set stop dates and provide educational materials for self-help.
• *Arrange* for follow-up visits to monitor and support patient progress.

All patients who smoke should be asked at every appointment about their readiness to stop. Smoking has been linked to *lung cancer, emphysema, bronchitis, cardiovascular disease*, and *oral cancer*; it is considered the leading cause of preventable death (Canadian Lung Association, 2011b). Studies have shown that when health care providers ask patients about their willingness to quit, smoking cessation is more likely (Smoking Cessation Leadership Center, n.d.). Patients can be given choices to assist with quitting, such as individual or group counselling, medical treatment, or nicotine replacement.

The Canadian Council for Tobacco Control (2011) cites documents for nurses on the need to integrate smoking cessation into daily nursing practice, role in reducing use of tobacco products, and a U.S. program to help nursing students and nurses to stop smoking.

Prevention of Occupational Exposure

Another focal point is modification of the work environment to limit exposure to irritants. In some cases, consultation with employees at the work site may be recommended. Occupational health and safety guidelines should be followed. For example, people exposed to dust should be wearing respirator masks.

Prevention of Asthma

About 3 million Canadians have asthma, and about 500 die each year. Of concern is the fact that only 4 out of 10 people with asthma have their condition under control (Asthma Society of Canada, 2011).

Asthma triggers include tobacco smoke, dust, dust mites, molds, furred and feathered animals, and cockroaches and other pests. For patients with allergies, modification of the home environment is recommended. Examples include covering the bed and pillows and ensuring that pets sleep separately (eg, outside the bedroom) from owners.

Immunizations

All adults (65 years and older); children and adults with respiratory or cardiac conditions, diabetes, or who are immunocompromised; and women who are pregnant and have health issues should be counselled to obtain the influenza vaccine annually (NACI, 2006). This consideration is especially important for health care providers. In addition to being at increased risk for contracting influenza from patients, providers also need to consider that they may infect others at risk, including those with suppressed immune systems and older adults. "In the absence of contraindications, refusal of Health Care Workers who have direct patient contact to be immunized against influenza implies failure in their duty of care to patients" (NACI, p. 213).

Focused Health History Related to Common Symptoms

Some common symptoms should be assessed in all patients to screen for the early presence of respiratory disease. Nurses can use any special concerns from patients about respiratory issues to identify focal areas. A thorough history of symptoms assists with identifying a current issue or condition.

Common Respiratory Symptoms and Signs

- Chest pain or discomfort
- Dyspnea
- Orthopnea or paroxysmal noctural dyspnea
- Cough
- Sputum
- Wheezing or tightness in chest
- Change in functional ability

Example of Questions for Symptom/Sign Analysis—Cough

- "In what part of your chest do you feel the cough?" (Location)
- "How would you describe the cough?" "What does the cough sound like?" "Would you describe the cough as dry? Or moist?" (Quality)
- "Describe how much coughing you have." "Is the coughing disrupting your sleep?" (Severity)
- "Describe when you first noticed the cough." "How did the cough start?" "Suddenly?" "Or gradually?" (Onset)
- "How long have you had the cough?" (Duration)
- "Is the cough becoming more frequent?" "Or is it getting worse?" (Constancy)
- "When is the cough at its worst?" "Daytime? Night time?" "Are there certain times of the year when your cough is worse?" (Time of day/month/year)
- "What have you tried to relieve the cough?" "What makes it better?" *(Alleviating factors)*
- "What makes the cough worse?" "Do you smoke?" "Does eating affect your cough?" "Do you take ACE-inhibitor pills (a type of antihypertensive medication) to manage your blood pressure?" (Aggravating factors)
- "What other symptoms have you noticed?" "Do you cough up sputum?" [If the client does cough up sputum, inquire about: Colour? Amount? Odour?] "Have you had a fever in the past week?" "Do you have a fever now?" "Have you had any difficulty breathing? If yes, please describe." "Any headache?" "Sore throat?" "Any sinus pain above the eyebrows?" "Below the eyes?" "Do you have the sensation that fluid/discharge is running down the back of your throat?" "Are you coughing to clear your throat?" (Associated symptoms)
- "What type of work do you do?" "Have you ever been exposed to any chemicals?" "Dust?" "Other substances?" "At work?" "Are you exposed to cigarette smoke on a regular basis?" "How does exercise affect your cough?" "What type of heating does your residence have?" "How does cold air outside affect your cough?" "What other weather conditions affect your cough?" (Environmental factors)
- "How is the coughing affecting your daily activities?" (Significance to the patient)
- "What do you think is causing the cough?" (Patient perspective)

Adapted from Edge, D. S., & Bickley, L. S. (2010). The thorax and lungs. In T. C. Stephen, D. L. Skillen, R. A. Day, & L. S. Bickley (Eds.). *Canadian Bates' guide to health assessment for nurses* (1st ed., p. 390). Philadelphia, PA: Wolters Kluwer Health/Lippincott Williams & Wilkins.

Examples of Questions to Assess Symptoms/Signs	Rationale/Unexpected Findings

Patient Perspective

Describe your breathing.

This question allows patients to share an unbiased perspective.

Chest Pain

Do you have chest pain? Or discomfort?
- Where is it? Can you point to where it hurts? Does the pain go anywhere else? Describe the discomfort.
- When did it start? How long has it lasted? What brought it on?
- How bad is it on a scale from 0 to 10, with 0 being no pain and 10 being the worst pain ever? Do any other symptoms accompany the pain?
- What does it feel like?
- What makes it better? Have you tried any treatments? Did they help? What makes it worse? What brings it on?
- What is your goal for the pain? What would you like to be able to do that you can't because of the pain?

> ⚠ *SAFETY ALERT 18-2*
>
> *Health care providers assume that chest pain is heart pain from cardiac ischemia until proven otherwise. Chest pain is an emergency requiring immediate assistance (see Chapter 19).*

Lung tissue has no pain fibres. Pleuritic chest pain (*pleurisy*) can follow inflammation of the parietal pleura. Patients usually describe such pain as sharp or stabbing, worsening with deep breathing or coughing, and often lateral or posterior in the lung. Anti-inflammatory agents often relieve pleuritic pain. *Tracheobronchitis* can cause pain starting in the trachea and large bronchi. Patients usually describe this as burning and in the upper sternum. It is associated with a cough. Chest wall pain can be muscle strain secondary to frequent coughing. Patients may describe it as achy; muscles may be tender to palpation. Coughing can cause pain at the junction of the ribs and sternum, resulting in severe pain with movement (costochondriasis).

Dyspnea

Have you had any difficulty breathing?
- How bad is it on a scale from 0 to 10, with 0 being no difficulty and 10 being the worst difficulty ever?
- When did it start? How long has it lasted?
- What activities make it worse? What makes it better?
- Do you have other symptoms?
- How has this limited your activities?
- Is the breathing difficulty associated with anxiety?

Dyspnea is a subjective term used when patients report laboured breathing and breathlessness. This response to exercise or heavy activity is expected if it rapidly disappears upon return to rest (Hannon, Pooler, et al., 2010). Patients with *lung disease*, however, may experience dyspnea with usual activities or even at rest. Note what causes dyspnea, such as climbing two stairs, walking one block, or walking uphill. Also note if onset was gradual (eg, chronic obstructive pulmonary disease [*COPD*]) or sudden (eg, *pneumonia*). Anxiety can precipitate dyspnea and hyperventilation. Anxious patients may describe dyspnea as smothering; they also may report tingling around the lips from a low carbon dioxide level. Patients with *COPD* or *CHF* (congestive heart failure) may describe dyspnea as scary, hard to breathe, shortness of breath, cannot get enough air, or gasping (Caroci & Lareau, 2004).

Orthopnea and Paroxysmal Nocturnal Dyspnea
- Do you have difficulty breathing when you sleep?
- How many pillows do you use for sleeping?
- Do you have difficulty breathing when lying flat?
- Do you wake up suddenly at night short of breath?
- Do you snore? Or stop breathing when you sleep?
- Do you have night sweats?

Gravity increases work of breathing when lying flat. Patients with **orthopnea** (difficulty breathing when lying flat) often sleep using two or more pillows or sleep in recliners. People who waken at night with sudden shortness of breath have **paroxysmal nocturnal dyspnea**. The cause is fluid overload from elevation of the legs, which shifts fluid from there to the body's core. The excess fluid cannot be pumped through the heart and suddenly accumulates in the lungs, causing dyspnea. *Sleep apnea* commonly interrupts sleep and can lead to pulmonary complications over time. Night sweats are associated with *tuberculosis (TB)*.

Cough
- Do you have a cough?
- Where does the cough come from—Sinuses? Throat? Or lungs?
- What does it feel like? What does it sound like?

Cough can originate in the upper or lower airway. With *sinus congestion*, mucus can drip into the throat and cause coughing. A tickle in the throat also can trigger coughing. A cough that accompanies laryngeal irritation is

Examples of Questions to Assess Symptoms/Signs	**Rationale/Unexpected Findings**

Examples of Questions to Assess Symptoms/Signs

- How bad is the cough?
- How often do you cough? When is it worse?
- When did it start? How long has it lasted?
- Is it worse in any particular setting?
- What makes it worse? What makes it better?
- Do you have other accompanying symptoms?
- What do you think has caused the cough?

Sputum

Do you cough up any mucus? Or phlegm? How much? Has the amount increased? Or decreased?
- What colour is it?
- Is it thin? Or thick?
- Do you notice an odour?
- Has the amount changed? Consistency changed? Or colour changed?

Wheezing

Do you have any wheezing? Or chest tightness?
- How severe is the wheezing compared to your usual functioning?
- Do you use a peak flow meter? What are your usual/current values?
- When did the wheezing start? How long has it lasted?
- Is wheezing associated with allergies? If so, what are they? Do you notice that the wheezing is worse in a particular environment?
- What makes it worse? What makes it better? How often do you use your inhalers?
- Do you have other symptoms?
- What do you think is causing this? What will make it better?

Functional Abilities

Have breathing difficulties changed any of your usual activities? How do you plan the day and pace activities?
(In addition to eating, grooming, and dressing, also consider the patient's ability to perform home maintenance, such as vacuuming, bed making, cooking, cleaning, and buying groceries.)

Rationale/Unexpected Findings

croupy, barking, or brassy. Alternatively, lung irritation can trigger coughing, such as with a *cold, early heart failure, viral infection,* or *bronchitis.* These coughs are usually dry and hacking. With *pneumonia* or the *common cold,* mucus in the lungs may trigger coughing. Such coughs usually are productive (wet or moist). Coughs upon waking are associated with pooled secretions secondary to smoking or *bronchitis.* Coughs at night may be from *sinus drainage, heart failure,* or *asthma.* Coughs following a meal may be related to a *gastroesophageal reflux disease (GERD)* or a *hernia* (Hancox, Poulto, et al., 2006). Treatment for conditions underlying coughs are different, so accurate detection of the cause is important.

Quantifying the amount of sputum (eg, teaspoon (5 mL), tablespoon (15 mL), quarter cup (62 mL), half cup (125 mL), or a cup (250 mL) may provide clues about the severity of the health concern. Sputum colour may differentiate the cause. The **mucoid** sputum of *bronchitis* is clear, white, or grey. **Purulent** yellow or green sputum indicates the presence of white blood cells and *bacterial infection.* Rust-coloured sputum is found with *TB* and *pneumococcal pneumonia.* **Tenacious sputum** may be thick with *dehydration* or *cystic fibrosis (CF)*; sputum from *heart failure* is thin and frothy and may be slightly pink. Sputum may be bloody with *lung cancer* or *TB* (Crapo, Glassroth, et al., 2004). Examine such sputum carefully to see if blood is integrated or just coats the outside. An irritated throat or sinus may bleed and contact the sputum during expectoration. **Hemoptysis** is the term for frankly bloody sputum. Some patients may expectorate from the mouth; this is not considered sputum but instead is oral secretions.

Wheezing is associated with *asthma, CHF,* and *bronchitis.* It occurs in response to narrowed bronchioles. Wheezing with asthma is worse in response to offending allergens, at night, and in the early morning (Crapo, Grassroth, et al., 2004). Patients with asthma are taught to use a peak flow meter to provide objective data about how much they can inhale with each breath. If airways are greatly constricted, breaths will be small, and patients may need to use their inhalers.

⚠ *SAFETY ALERT 18-3*

In an acute asthma attack, observe for wheezing that progresses to decreased lung sounds, which may indicate worsening status.

Patients with respiratory concerns commonly have more energy in the morning but need frequent rest during the day. Some are short of breath even at rest, needing to pause after a few words. Others become breathless when eating, grooming, or dressing. Patients with declining health may need plans for assistance. Ask what they like to do and if they can do these things. Patients with respiratory concerns may be able to engage in sexual activity and exercise if they plan to do so during higher-energy times.

Documentation of Expected Findings

Patient reports no chest pain or discomfort, dyspnea, orthopnea, paroxysmal noctural dyspnea, cough, mucus, wheezing or tightness in chest, or decrease in functional ability.

Lifespan Considerations

Additional Questions	Rationale/Unexpected Findings
Women Who Are Pregnant How is your breathing? Are you having any difficulty sleeping because of your breathing issues?	Dyspnea is common in late pregnancy as the uterus begins to compress the diaphragm. Assess the woman for sleep disturbances; teach that side lying may be more comfortable. Multiple fetuses contribute to increased size and associated maternal discomfort.
Newborns, Infants, and Children How many colds has your child had over the past year? How serious were they?	Poor and limited independent hygiene places infants and children at risk for *respiratory infections;* thus, emphasize infection-reduction measures such as handwashing and proper use of tissues. Frequent childhood infections are linked to later chronic obstructive pulmonary disease (COPD) and asthma (Crapo, Grassroth, et al., 2004).
What measures are you taking to avoid allergies in your child? Is your baby breast fed? Or bottle fed? How are you introducing new foods?	Teach parents of young babies about the proper introduction of solid foods (one at a time for 1 week at a time) to help determine new possible allergens. High body mass index is associated with increased risk of *asthma* in childhood, while regular intake of seafood, fresh fruits, and vegetables is associated with a decreased risk (Hong, Lee, et al., 2006).
How have you safety-proofed your home? And yard? Have you learned emergency techniques, such as first aid? Or cardiopulmonary resuscitation (CPR)?	Accidental aspiration of toys, foods, and poisons is a risk for young children. Evaluate the family's knowledge about common problematic items; teach prevention measures.
Is your baby experiencing any episodes of stopping breathing? Is there any family history of sudden infant death syndrome (SIDS)?	Teach parents the importance of placing all infants on their backs to sleep to help prevent *SIDS*.
Did your child have any health concerns related to birth?	For low-birth-weight or premature infants, review the duration of ventilator support and any complications or chronic issues. Meconium aspiration may cause *pneumonia* in newborns.
Has your child had frequent spitting up? Or difficulty swallowing?	Be aware of the risk of pulmonary complications related to *GERD*. Teach parents measures to prevent aspiration in children at high risk for GERD, such as elevating the head after meals. GERD in childhood is a risk factor for asthma in adulthood (Hancox, Poulto, et al., 2006).
Older Adults Have you noticed any shortness of breath? Or fatigue with your activities of daily living (ADLs)?	Older adults may have less tolerance for ADLs than younger patients. Assess how any respiratory conditions are affecting ability to function. Assess energy level and activities that cause patients to tire more easily. Consider recommendations for pacing activities, allowing for rest, and performing higher energy tasks earlier in the day when well rested.
Have you had any recent pulmonary infections? Or worsening of your current condition?	Counsel high-risk patients to avoid exposure to infections and to plan modifications for weather variations, such as walking in a shopping mall instead of outside on a cold day. Educate about lifestyle changes to increase health and prevent chronic disease (eg, not smoking).

Cultural Considerations

Additional Questions	Rationale/Unexpected Findings
Have you recently immigrated to Canada? Have you been immunized with the BCG vaccine?	Incidence of *tuberculosis (TB)* is approximately nine times higher among North American immigrants (Taylor, Nolan, et al., 2005).
Do you have concerns about exposure to environmental pollution?	Children in urban environments are more likely to have *asthma* (Lee, Brugge, et al., 2003). Air pollution contributes to *chronic obstructive pulmonary disease (COPD)* and *lung cancer* (Crapo, Grassroth, et al., 2004). Owning a home, a mark of socioeconomic status, is linked to less susceptibility to childhood *colds* (Cohen, Doyle, et al., 2004).
Are there any concerns about exposure to dust? Fumes? Or mold in your home?	Make sure that there is proper ventilation to avoid *carbon monoxide poisoning*. Also consider quality of housing, including density of residents, ventilation systems, and black mold (Crapo, Grassroth, et al., 2004).
Note the patient's self-identified ethnic group and gender.	Pacific Islanders, Filipinos, Cubans, and Puerto Ricans are at risk for *asthma* (Davis, Kreutzer, et al., 2006). Hispanics, Blacks, and Asians have *TB* rates 7 to 19 times higher than Caucasians (Taylor, Nolan, et al., 2005). Cigarette smokers, African Canadians, and First Nations are more susceptible to *lung cancer* than are Caucasians (Haiman, Stram, et al., 2006). Women who smoke also have increased susceptibility to adverse effects from tobacco and greater risk for *lung cancer* and *COPD* (Crapo, Grassroth, et al., 2004; Henschke, Yip, et al., 2006).

Objective Data Collection

Equipment

- Examination gown and sheet
- Stethoscope and equipment wipes
- Marking pen and small ruler to mark diaphragmatic excursion

Promoting Patient Comfort, Dignity, and Safety

Make sure that the room has a comfortable temperature. Take measures to facilitate a private and quiet setting. Wash and warm your hands to avoid spreading infection and to facilitate patient comfort. Studies have shown that a stethoscope can be a source of bacterial transmission across patients (Marinella, Pierson, et al., 1997). Thus, be sure to use an equipment wipe to clean the diaphragm and tubing of the stethoscope before bringing it into contact with the patient. You also may warm the diaphragm of the stethoscope with your clean hands prior to placing it on the patient's chest.

Explain that during the examination the nurse needs to able to see and compare both sides of the chest, front and back. Providing the rationale for the need to expose the chest may ease the patient's anxiety. For the nurse, it is helpful to visualize the underlying lobes of the lungs throughout the examination.

For inspection, expose only the area of the chest that you will be examining, especially for women. When visualization of the anterior chest is required for a female patient, switch the gown around so the back opening and ties are at the front. Reverse the gown to cover the anterior chest when inspecting posteriorly (Edge & Bickley, 2010).

Lung auscultation is easiest to perform with the patient sitting. If sitting is not possible, the anterior lungs can be auscultated when the patient is lying down. (This position works well for women as the breasts are more easily displaced.) The posterior lungs can be heard when the patient is turned from side to side. Alternatively, a second person may be able to assist the patient to sit.

Common and Advanced Techniques

Routine assessment includes the most important and common techniques. Examiners may add advanced steps if concerns exist over a specific finding.

The nurse's role relative to subjective data collection is to gather information to improve the patient's health status and to help determine the cause of current symptoms. Remember Mr. Jin, who was introduced at the beginning of this chapter. He has had chronic obstructive pulmonary disease (COPD) for 15 years. Today, he is visiting the clinic because of increasing dyspnea and fatigue. Because Mr. Jin is fatigued, efficient questioning is essential. Thus, questions must be prioritized, with the most important issues addressed first.

Note the following example of an interview style used by the nurse.

Nurse: (Before beginning, he reads the patient health record and notes that Mr. Jin has a 98 pack-year history of smoking and COPD for 15 years. The record states that Mr. Jin is allergic to pollen, with symptoms of red teary eyes and sinus congestion.) It looks like your last visit was 2 weeks ago, Mr. Jin. How do you feel now?

Mr. Jin: I'm still not feeling well. When I came in last time, they said I had bronchitis, but it feels like it's getting worse.

Nurse: It feels like it's getting worse ... (pause)

Mr. Jin: Last time I felt wheezy. This time I'm coughing more.

Nurse: Are you coughing anything up?

Mr. Jin: Yes.

Nurse: What does it look like?

Mr. Jin: It's yellow.

Nurse: And is it thin? Or thick?

Mr. Jin: It's quite thick.

Nurse: How much would you say you're coughing up—a tablespoon (15 mL)? A half cup (125 mL)? Or a cup (250 mL)?

Mr. Jin: I probably cough something up three to four times an hour. Maybe a half cup (125 mL).

Critical Thinking Challenge

- What makes the dialogue effective?
- Could the nurse have done anything differently to further improve data collection and communication with Mr. Jin?
- Does Mr. Jin's childhood and family history require further exploration? Provide rationale.
- Is this an appropriate time to discuss risk factor modification and smoking cessation? Provide rationale.

Initial Survey

Techniques and Expected Findings	Unexpected Findings
Closely assess the position that the patient is using to breathe. *Posture is relaxed and upright with the arms at the sides.*	Patients in respiratory distress may assume a **tripod** position, leaning forward on a stationary object such as a table or with their elbows on their knees (Fig. 18-10). This relaxes their abdominal, intercostals, and neck muscles and allows for less work in breathing.

Figure 18-10 The patient with COPD assuming the tripod position.

Always assess for any signs of respiratory distress. Observe for **pursed lips** and **nasal flaring**. *Facial expression is relaxed.*

Patients in *respiratory distress* may have an anxious expression. Patients with *COPD* may have pursed lips when exhaling, providing some positive pressure in the bronchial tree to prevent airway collapse. As well, It increases the amount of air expelled, which then allows more air in with inhalation. Nasal flaring may accompany *respiratory distress*, especially in children.

Evaluate level of consciousness. *Patient is alert, cooperative, and oriented to time, place, and person.*

The patient with *hypoxemia* may be irritable, somnolent, restless, confused, combative, or disoriented.

Inspect skin colour. Document the absence of cyanosis or pallor. *Skin colour is an appropriate tone for the patient's genetic background. Observe the undertone of the skin rather than the amount of melanin. Expected skin colour in Caucasians is pink.*

With hypoxemia, **cyanosis** (bluish discolouration) may occur either centrally or around the mouth (circumoral). **Pallor** (pale whitish colour) and greyish tones indicate poor oxygenation or *anemia*. Chronic respiratory disease may lead to **rubor** (reddish-purple colour) or **erythema** (flushed appearance).

Observe respiratory movements. Note if the patient uses the upper or lower chest to breathe. *Usually expiration is twice as long as inspiration (inspiration/expiration = 1:2).*

Patients with disease that impedes outflow (eg, *COPD*) may have **forced expiration**. **Guarding** may accompany pleuritic or postoperative pain. **Work of breathing** is less efficient with use of upper chest muscles.

As you observe the patient's respiratory movements, also count the rate. Do not tell the patient that you are assessing rate, because he or she may subconsciously alter it. If it is difficult to see the chest moving, gently rest your hand on the patient's shoulder to feel the rate. *Rate of a usual respiratory pattern is 12 to 20 breaths/min for adults. Rhythm is regular, and breathing appears easy and quiet. This is labelled eupnea. An occasional sigh is expected.*

Wheezing may be audible in severe asthma or bronchitis. **Tachypnea** is breathing >24 breaths/min; **bradypnea** is <10 breaths/min. See Table 18-6 at the end of this chapter for other unexpected respiratory patterns.

⚠ *SAFETY ALERT 18-4*
Stridor, a high-pitched crowing sound from the upper airway, results from tracheal or laryngeal spasm. In severe laryngospasm the larynx may completely close off. This life-threatening emergency requires immediate medical assistance.

(text continues on page 470)

Assess oxygen saturation level (see Chapter 6). *Expected is 95% to 100%.*

Assess the muscles used for breathing. *The diaphragm and external intercostals do most of the work.*

Note any retractions. *Retractions are absent.*

Observe fingers for clubbing. *No clubbing is present.*

Pulmonary embolism produces hypoxemia because of shunting of blood to areas of atelectasis in the lung.

> △ SAFETY ALERT 18-5
> *Oxygen saturation <92% may require immediate intervention.*

Patients with *respiratory distress* may use accessory muscles. **Sternocleidomastoid, scalene, trapezius, latissimus dorsi,** and occasionally **pectoralis major and minor** and **platysma** muscles are used in severe breathing difficulties (Benditt, 2006). The rectus abdominis and internal intercostals are used to facilitate expiration, such as in *COPD*.

Supraclavicular or intercostal retractions accompany resistance to airflow such as in *severe asthma*. Retractions appear as an indentation in the spaces in an effort to "suck in" more air.

Clubbing of the fingers is noted with chronic lung disease (see Chapter 13).

Documentation of Expected Findings

Patient lying in bed with head of bed flat. Relaxed breathing, posture, and facial expression. Respirations 16 breaths/min without accessory muscle use or retractions. Skin pink without cyanosis or pallor.

Comprehensive Physical Examination

Posterior Chest
Inspection. Note the shape and configuration of the thoracic cage. Observe spontaneous chest expansion.

Spinous processes of the vertebrae are midline; scapulae are symmetrical in each hemithorax. Chest wall is cone-shaped (narrower at the bottom than the top), symmetrical, and oval (narrower from front to back than from side to side). The transverse (side to side)/AP ratio is between 1:2 and 5:7. Although ribs are not visible in most people, those that are slope at approximately 45°. Chest expansion is symmetrical.

Palpation. Palpate the posterior chest for tender areas. Using the fingerpads, start above the scapula over the lung apex and progress from side to side to compare findings bilaterally, ending at the base of the lung and moving laterally to the midaxillary line (Fig. 18-11). Note any lesions, lumps, or masses; use gloves if there are lesions or open areas. Palpate for crepitus if the patient has had rib fractures, recent chest surgery, or chest tubes. *Thorax is nontender without any lesions, lumps, masses, or crepitus.*

Skeletal **scoliosis** and **kyphosis** can limit respiratory excursion. In **barrel chest**, which can accompany *chronic obstructive pulmonary disease (COPD)*, the transverse/AP ratio approximates 1:1, giving the chest a round appearance. Also with COPD, the expanded ribs slope more horizontally, inverting the chest's usual cone shape. **Pectus excavatum** and **pectus carinatum** are sternal deviations that limit respiratory excursion. Asymmetry and paradoxical respirations occur in flail chest. See Table 18-7 at the end of the chapter.

Tender areas may indicate *muscle strain, rib fracture,* or *soft tissue damage.* In chest trauma, air can enter the lungs to escape into subcutaneous tissue. This free air creates a crackling sensation similar to bubble wrap or crispy rice cereal under the skin **(crepitus)**. Because air floats, *subcutaneous emphysema* migrates, so it may be found in the head and neck. If there is a large amount, mark the borders with a pen so that changes can be noted.

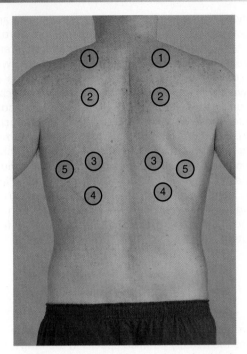

Figure 18-11 Sites for and sequence of palpation of the posterior thorax.

Test for symmetrical chest expansion when there are concerns about reduced lung volumes. With the thumbs at T9 to T10, wrap the palmar surface of the hands laterally and parallel to the rib cage (Fig. 18-12). Slide the thumbs and hands medially to raise a loose fold of skin between the thumbs and vertebra. Ask the patient to inhale deeply, while the nurse observes the thumbs and feels the extent of symmetrical chest movement. *The thumbs move apart symmetrically, approximately 5 to 10 cm. Chest expansion is symmetrical.*

Asymmetrical movements indicate collapse or blockage of a significant portion of the lung such as with *pneumothorax, rib fracture, severe pneumonia, pleural effusion,* or *atelectasis.* Patients with muscle weakness, respiratory disease, recent surgery, chest wall deviations, or obesity may have reduced chest expansion (Jones & Nzekwu, 2006).

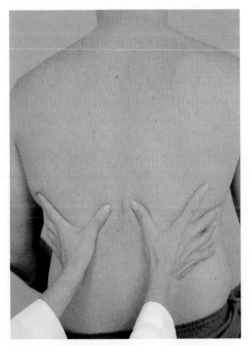

Figure 18-12 Testing for chest expansion.

(text continues on page 472)

Tactile fremitus is tested when concern exists about obstruction or consolidation of lung tissue. Following the sequence for palpation but avoiding the scapula, place the palmar base or ulnar surface of the hand on the patient's chest above the scapula. Ask the patient to say "ninety-nine." Vibrations of air in the bronchial tree are transmitted to the chest wall when the patient speaks. Assess for intensity and symmetry of fremitus. If fremitus is difficult to palpate, ask the patient to speak louder. As the technique is learned, fremitus may be palpated with a hand on each side simultaneously to further assess symmetry and gain efficiency. Because of the wide variation in findings, fremitus is usually interpreted in combination with other data. *Expected variations are wide-ranging, depending on voice intensity and pitch, position of the bronchi in relation to the chest wall, and chest size. Fremitus is usually more intense between the scapulae, where the bronchi bifurcate, and less intense at the bases, where more porous tissue reduces the transmission of vibrations.*

Percussion. Percussion is used when obstruction or consolidation of lung tissue is suspected (similar to testing of fremitus). This technique can help establish if underlying tissues contain air or fluid or are solid. Use the percussion technique covered in Chapter 4. On the posterior chest, begin at the apex of the lungs (C7 bilaterally) and percuss from side to side to compare symmetry (Fig. 18-13). Working toward the bases side to side in the intercostal spaces (ICSs), move fingers approximately 5 cm apart. When the fingers are below the level of lung tissue, the sound changes

Conditions that may obstruct lung tissue include an obstructed bronchus, *COPD, pleural effusion, fibrosis, tumour,* or *pneumothorax.* In these conditions, fremitus is decreased or absent. Fremitus also is reduced with increased distance between the lung parenchyma and chest wall, as with obesity or an extremely large chest. Fremitus is increased in conditions of increased consolidation close to the chest wall, in which a bronchus is open. Examples include severe localized *pneumonia* or *lung tumour.* **Rhonchal fremitus** is a coarse vibration produced by passage of air through or around thick exudates in the airways, such as in *pneumonia.* **Pleural friction fremitus** results from inflamed pleural surfaces rubbing together and causing a grating sensation synchronous with respirations and more commonly felt on inspiration.

Percussion may be dull when fluid or solid tissue replaces the usually air-filled spaces in the lungs, such as with lobar pneumonia, hemothorax, or tumour. If fluid is in the pleural space (eg, empyema, pleural effusion), the sound may also be dull. Generalized hyperresonance may be heard over the hyperinflated lungs found with COPD or emphysema. Unilateral hyperresonance may be found with a large pneumothorax.

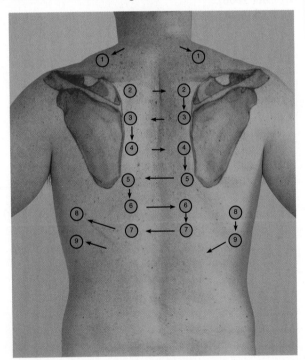

Figure 18-13 Sites and sequence for posterior chest percussion.

from resonant to dull (around T10); from this point move laterally to percuss near the anterior axillary line and the 7th and 8th ICSs. Avoid the area over the ribs and scapulae, because percussing over bone gives a flat percussion note. Percussion penetrates only 5 to 7 cm into the thorax, so deviations must be close to the surface and large enough (at least 2 to 3 cm) to be detected. Thus, percussion usually is combined with other tests (eg, chest x-ray). *Healthy lung tissue sounds resonant. In patients with extremely large chests, percussion sounds may become dull secondary to the increased tissue mass.*

Test **diaphragmatic excursion** in cases of concern about chest expansion (eg, spinal cord injury). Diaphragmatic excursion helps estimate how much the diaphragm moves between inhalation and exhalation. Ask the patient to deeply exhale and hold it; then, percuss in the ICSs down the scapular line (Fig. 18-14). A helpful strategy is for the nurse to hold his or her breath at the same time as the patient to remember to let the patient breathe after a short time. When the sound changes from resonant to dull, go back to the previous resonant rib space. This marks the location of lung tissue on deep expiration (it may also be marked with a pen) (Fig 18-15). Allow the patient to breathe if needed or ask the patient to take in and hold a deep breath. Percuss in the previously resonant spot; *it should remain resonant.*

Diaphragmatic excursion may be reduced in *emphysema* (in which the diaphragm is already flat) or *atelectasis* (in which lung tissue is collapsed at the base). Extreme *ascites,* advanced pregnancy, and extreme obesity also limit diaphragmatic excursion. Neuromuscular paralysis or weakening of the diaphragm in *spinal cord injury, stroke, Guillain-Barré syndrome,* or *muscular dystrophy* can also inhibit respiratory excursion. Lag in expansion may occur with *atelectasis, pneumonia,* or postoperative pain.

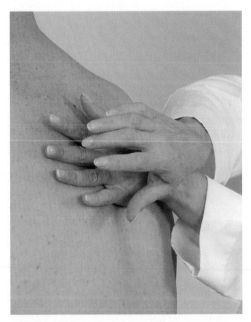

Figure 18-14 Assessing diaphragmatic excursion: percussing in the ICSs.

(text continues on page 474)

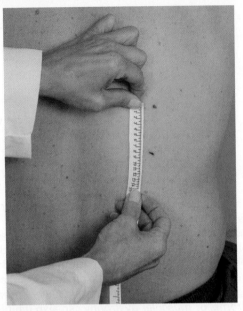

Figure 18-15 Assessing diaphragmatic excursion: marking the location of lung tissue.

Move down into the previously dull ICS; *it should now be resonant at deep inspiration because the lungs should have moved down with the diaphragm.* Move down one or two more rib spaces until the sound is dull again; *the difference should be one or two rib spaces, or 3 to 5 cm and 7 to 8 cm in well-conditioned adults (it may also be marked with a pen).* This estimates the amount of diaphragmatic movement between maximum inspiration and expiration, although this estimate does not correlate well with radiographic findings (Kleinman, Frey, et al., 2002). As always, interpret these data within the context of other findings, such as strength of cough.

Auscultation of Breath Sounds. Auscultation of the lung fields is the most important physical examination technique for assessing air flow through the respiratory passages and alveoli. In the larger airways, sounds are louder and coarser, while sounds in the smaller airways are softer and finer. Auscultate by listening from the top down alternating between left and right sides. It is very important to make sure that the stethoscope is in direct contact with the skin. If the patient is wearing a gown or clothing, the stethoscope can be placed underneath either from the top or bottom. Avoid listening through the gown, which can generate additional sounds that mimic adventitious sounds or that muffle existing sounds. Avoid allowing the tubing to rub against bed rails, patient, or nurse, which can create additional noise. Be careful not to interpret chest hair sounds as crackles; press more firmly or moisten the chest hair. Be sure to listen to the most important areas instead of only auscultating in convenient places. Additionally, listen for extra unexpected sounds of breathing such as wheezes. Ask the patient to breathe through the mouth a bit deeper than usual. Place the flat side of the stethoscope diaphragm on the chest wall firmly to block extraneous noise. Listen to one full breath in each location, moving from side to side to compare symmetry.

⚠ *SAFETY ALERT 18-6*

Deep breathing can be especially exhausting for patients with respiratory disease; it also can cause some patients to hyperventilate and become dizzy. Instruct patients to tell you if they need a break.

Stand behind and beside the patient and listen from the lung apices to the bases and then laterally in the same sequence as percussion (see Fig. 18-11). If breath sounds are too soft, ask the patient to breathe deeper.

Identify the breath sounds by listening for their intensity, quality, pitch, and duration of inspiration versus expiration:

- *Vesicular sounds are soft, low-pitched, and found over fine airways near the site of air exchange.*
- *Bronchovesicular sounds are found over major bronchi that have fewer alveoli.*
- *Bronchial sounds are loud, high-pitched, and found over the trachea and larynx.*

Expiration is longer than inspiration, similar to usual breathing. As auscultation progresses down to the smaller airways, it takes time for air to move in, so inspiration is longer than expiration in vesicular sounds. See Table 18-1 for more complete descriptions of the sounds.

Careful auscultation of the bases is important, because they often are the first area to collapse with atelectasis secondary to immobility. They are also often the first place to collect fluid in congestive heart failure (CHF) or fluid overload.

Breath sounds are considered unexpected when heard outside their usual location, such as bronchial breath sounds in the bases. Bronchial or bronchovesicular sounds in the usual vesicular location indicate airway thickening. Decreased lung sounds are very common, especially in patients with *atelectasis* or *pleural effusion* (Greco, 2004). Auscultating sounds in patients with large chests may be difficult, because the lungs are at a greater distance from the chest wall. The breath sounds may be very soft, so a quiet room and a good seal with the skin are especially important. Absent lung sounds may be noted over areas where air transmission through the bronchioles is completely blocked, as with dense areas of atelectasis.

⚠ *SAFETY ALERT 18-7*
Absent sounds over a large portion of the lung, such as with a large mucus plug, may be an emergency. Get help immediately.

Breath sounds can increase when expected sounds are transmitted more easily over areas of consolidation or compression, such as in *lobar pneumonia or pleural effusion.*

(text continues on page 476)

Table 18-1	**Characteristics of Expected Breath Sounds**			
	Intensity and Pitch	**Quality**	**Duration**	**Locations**
Tracheal	Very loud and harsh	Harsh	Inspiration = expiration	Over the trachea in the neck
Bronchial	Loud and high	Coarse or tubular	Inspiration < expiration	Over the manubrium, if heard at all
Bronchovesicular	Intermediate and intermediate	Intermediate	Inspiration = expiration	Anteriorly between first and second interspaces; between scapula
Vesicular	Soft and low	Whispering undertones	Inspiration > expiration	Over most of the lung fields

Usual breath sounds are vesicular without crackles, wheezes, or rhonchi. In some people, audible crackles with the first deep breath or before coughing are expected. These crackles are the sound of collapsed alveoli opening, which is a common consequence of immobility. It is important to note the absence of adventitious sounds when documenting.

Adventitious (added) sounds are not usually heard. These extra sounds are layered on top of underlying breath sounds. If extra sounds are heard, listen for their loudness, pitch, duration, number, timing in the respiratory cycle (inspiration versus expiration), location on the chest wall, any variation from breath to breath, and any change after a cough or deep breath. It may be necessary to listen in the same area for a few cycles of breathing to differentiate the timing in the respiratory cycle and note changes that occur with breathing. If crackles or wheezes are audible, ask the patient to cough to hear if they clear.

• Crackles can result from fluid in the airways or alveoli or from the opening of a series of collapsed airways and alveoli that reinflate during deep breaths. They sound like hairs rubbing together near the ear or Velcro opening.
• Wheezes sound more musical, and are caused by the fluttering of narrowed airway walls (as with asthma or bronchitis). Note if wheezes occur on inspiration, expiration, or both.
• Rhonchi (also called coarse wheezes or gurgles) are lower pitched and louder sounds resulting from secretions moving around during inhalation or exhalation. They commonly accompany pneumonia.

See Table 18-2 for a more complete comparison.

Table 18-2   Adventitious Breath Sounds

Unexpected Sound	Description	Mechanism	Associated Conditions
Fine crackles (rales)	High-pitched, soft, brief crackling sounds that can be simulated by rolling a strand of hair near the ear or stethoscope	Deflated small airways and alveoli will pop open during inspiration. In early congestive heart failure (CHF), small amounts of fluid in the alveoli may cause fine crackles.	Late inspiratory crackles are associated with restrictive disease (eg, fibrosis and heart failure). Early inspiratory crackles occur with obstructive diseases (eg, asthma and chronic obstructive pulmonary disease [COPD]).
Coarse crackles (rales)	Low-pitched, moist, longer sounds that are similar to Velcro slowly separating	Small air bubbles flow through secretions or narrowed airways.	Pulmonary fibrosis, pulmonary edema, COPD
Wheeze (high-pitched or sibilant)	High-pitched musical sounds heard primarily during inspiration	Air passes though narrowed airways and creates sound, similar to that of a vibrating reed. Note if inspiratory or expiratory.	Asthma, bronchitis, emphysema
Rhonchi (gurgle, low-pitched wheeze, sonorous wheeze)	Low-pitched snoring or gurgling sound that may clear with coughing	Airflow passes around or through secretions or narrowed passages.	Pneumonia
Pleural friction rub	Loud, coarse, and low-pitched grating or creaking sound similar to a squeaky door during inspiration and expiration; more common in the lower anterolateral thorax	Inflamed pleural surfaces lose their usual lubrication and rub together during breathing	Pleurisy
Stridor	Loud high-pitched crowing or honking sound louder in upper airway	Laryngeal or tracheal inflammation or spasm can cause stridor, as can aspiration of a foreign object.	Epiglottitis, croup, partially obstructed airway; can indicate an emergency requiring immediate attention

Auscultate voice sounds when an area of consolidation or compression is suspected. They may be assessed if other findings (eg, increased breath sounds) suggest these conditions.

Ask the patient to say "ninety-nine" as you auscultate the chest wall with a stethoscope, comparing sides. *Sounds are muffled and difficult to distinguish.*

Ask the patient to say "ee" while listening to the chest, comparing sides. *This sound is also muffled and difficult to hear.*

Ask the patient to whisper "one-two-three" while listening to the chest, comparing sides. *Expected sounds are faint, muffled, and difficult to hear.*

Bronchophony, egophony, and whispered pectoriloquy (described next) are all found with increased consolidation or compression, as with *lobar pneumonia, atelectasis, or tumour.*

The word "ninety-nine" is easily understood and louder over dense areas. It sounds as if the patient were directly talking into the stethoscope. This is called **bronchophony.**

In **egophony,** the "ee" sounds like a loud "A."

Sounds are louder and clearer than the whispered sounds, as if the patient is directly whispering into the stethoscope. This is called **whispered pectoriloquy.**

Documentation of Expected Findings

Symmetrical chest shape and expansion. Lungs clear, no crackles or wheezes heard over bilateral lung fields. Reports no chest pain or tenderness.

Anterior Chest
Inspection. Inspect the anterior chest using the same techniques as for the posterior chest. Look for any deformities or asymmetry, retraction of the supraclavicular or intercostal spaces (ICSs), or impaired respiratory movement. *Usually findings are similar as for the posterior chest.*

Palpation. Palpate the anterior chest for tenderness, masses, or lesions. Begin at the lung apices (above the clavicles) and move from side to side, ending below the costal angle and moving laterally to the midaxillary line. *Usually there is no tenderness.*

Assess anterior chest expansion by palpating with the thumbs along each costal margin near the sternum and with the palmar surface laterally on the rib cage (Fig. 18-16). Slide the thumbs medially so that they raise a small skin fold between them. Ask the patient to inhale deeply; observe the thumb movement. Feel for the extent of symmetrical chest expansion. *Anterior chest expansion is greater than posterior chest expansion because the rib cage has more anterior mobility.*

Unexpected findings are similar to those for the posterior chest. The costal margin is widened in hyperinflation of the lungs. The chest may be barrel shaped in diseases that obstruct air outflow such as *COPD* and *asthma.* See Tables 18-8 and 18-9 at the end of the chapter.

(text continues on page 478)

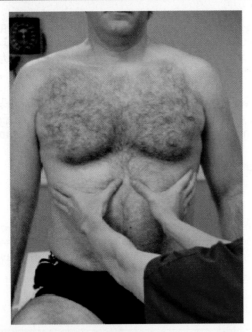

Figure 18-16 Assessing anterior chest expansion.

Assess for tactile fremitus, beginning at the lung apices and continuing to the bases and laterally, comparing bilateral symmetry. It may be necessary to ask female patients to lift or to displace their breasts to the side because fremitus is decreased over this soft tissue. *Fremitus is decreased or absent over the precordium because of the heart. Fremitus is greatest over large airways in the 2nd and 3rd ICSs near the sternum.*

Percussion. Percuss the anterior and lateral chest in the ICSs and laterally, comparing bilateral findings. Women may need to displace the breast to avoid percussion over breast tissue, which produces a dull sound. Avoid percussing over bone, which produces a flat tone. *The heart produces dullness from the 3rd to 5th ICS to the left of the sternum. The upper border of liver dullness is percussed in the 5th ICS in the right midclavicular line (MCL). Tympany is percussed over the stomach in the 5th ICS in the left MCL.*

Auscultation. Auscultate the trachea and anterior and lateral lung fields, beginning at the trachea. Listen to the lung apices, moving the stethoscope from side to side to evaluate symmetry. Place the stethoscope above or under the breasts in female patients. Listen down to the 6th ICS bilaterally or when breath sounds become absent, signaling the end of the lung fields. *Breath sounds are usually louder in the upper chest, where the larger airways are closer to the chest wall. Bronchial breath sounds are audible over the trachea; bronchovesicular sounds are heard over the 2nd to 3rd ICSs to the right and left of the sternum over the bronchi. Vesicular sounds are heard over the lung fields bilaterally. No adventitious sounds are heard (see Table 18-1).*

If indicated, auscultate for transmitted voice sounds using the same pattern and technique as for the posterior chest.

Documentation of Expected Findings

Symmetrical chest shape without kyphosis or scoliosis. Vesicular breath sounds heard bilaterally over symmetrical lung fields. Reports no chest pain or tenderness. No crackles or wheezes.

Examples of Documentation for Thorax and Lung

Area of Assessment	Expected Findings	Unexpected Findings
Inspection of thorax	Respiratory rate regular and nonlaboured at 16 per minute. Pink skin over chest wall; scattered macules over upper posterior chest wall bilaterally. Thorax symmetrical; no retractions or use of accessory muscles. Anteroposterior (AP) diameter < transverse diameter.	Respirations shallow and irregular at 20 per minute. Audible wheeze on expiration. Retractions noted at right posterior triangle of neck. AP diameter = transverse diameter.
Palpation of thorax	Chest expansion is upward, outward, and symmetrical. No tenderness with palpation of chest wall, anteriorly and posteriorly. Tactile fremitus equal over all lung fields and more intense in upper fields.	Decreased chest expansion of right thorax. No tenderness. Decreased tactile fremitus of left lung fields compared to right.
Percussion of lung fields	Resonant percussion note over all lung fields, including apices bilaterally. Diaphragm descends 5 cm bilaterally.	Hyperresonant note over left lung fields, with dull percussion note noted between the right 3rd and 5th intercostal spaces (ICS) at the midclavicular line (MCL). Diaphragm descends 2 cm on right and 4 cm on left.
Auscultation of lung fields	Vesicular breath sounds heard over lung periphery, anteriorly and posteriorly bilaterally. No crackles or wheezes bilaterally.	Breath sounds distant with delayed expiratory phase and scattered expiratory wheezes over left lung fields. Inspiratory crackles heard over right lower base. "E" to "A" changes heard at right lower-lung field.

Adapted from Edge, D. S., & Bickley, L. S. (2010). The thorax and lungs. In T. C. Stephen, D. L. Skillen, R. A. Day, & L. S. Bickley (Eds.). *Canadian Bates' guide to health assessment for nurses* (1st ed., p. 406). Philadelphia, PA: Wolters Kluwer Health/Lippincott Williams & Wilkins.

Documenting Unexpected Findings

The nurse has just finished conducting a physical examination of Mr. Jin. Review the following important findings revealed in each step of objective data collection for this patient. Compare these results with the expected findings presented in the samples of documentation.

Inspection: Temperature 38°C oral, pulse 102 beats/min and regular, respirations 24 breaths/min, blood pressure 156/78 mm Hg (left arm, sitting), oxygen saturation (SaO_2) 90%. Alert and oriented. Patient sitting in chair, having increased respiratory effort. Nasal flaring and pursed lip breathing. Needs to pause to breathe in the middle of sentences. Skin colour pale, using neck muscles to breathe, no retractions. Clubbing present in fingers, bilaterally. Coughing up moderate amounts of thick yellow sputum. Reports no chest pain. Increased dyspnea and respirations 32 breaths/min when ambulating in hall.

Palpation: Tactile fremitus increased in right base.

Percussion: Right base dull to percussion.

Auscultation: Few wheezes scattered through lung fields bilaterally. Decreased breath sounds noted in right base. Bronchophony, egophony, and whispered pectoriloquy over right base.

Table 18-3 Apgar Scoring System

	0	1	2
Heart rate	Absent	Slow below 100 beats/min	>100 beats/min
Respiratory effort	Absent	Slow or irregular	Good crying
Muscle tone	Limp	Some flexion of extremities	Active motion
Reflex irritability (response to catheter in nostril)	No response	Grimace, frown	Cough or sneeze
Colour	Blue or pale	Body pink, extremities blue	Completely pink

Lifespan Considerations

Women Who Are Pregnant

The woman's chest may appear wider and the costal angle larger in late pregnancy as the uterus pushes up on the diaphragm. Women who are pregnant may have strained or fractured ribs because of expansion of the thoracic cage.

Newborns, Infants, and Children

In newborns, Apgar scores are taken at 1 and 5 minutes after birth to determine health status and need for interventions (Table 18-3). In the respiratory component of the Apgar, the nurse evaluates respirations, using a sliding scale from absent to accompanied by strong crying.

The first breaths take great effort as the airways and alveoli are inflated. Sedatives given to the mother during labour, a compromised newborn blood supply, or airways obstructed by mucus may depress the baby's ventilation. All of these require interventions to correct the underlying cause. Premature infants are especially at risk for pulmonary concerns, because their lungs may not produce enough surfactant, causing the alveoli to collapse.

Add the scores of the five observations to get the full Apgar score. The lower the score, the more likely that there is an issue. A score of 7 to 10 is desirable. A score of 0 to 2 is a severely depressed newborn in need of emergency resuscitation.

Respiratory patterns in infants vary based on feeding, sleep state, and body temperature. Because of this irregularity, respirations in infants should be counted for 1 minute. Respiratory rates are fastest in newborns; they decrease with age (Table 18-4). The more premature the newborn, the more irregular may be the respirations because of the lack of a well-developed nervous system (Bader, Riskin, et al., 2004).

⚠ SAFETY ALERT 18-8

Apnea that lasts 10 to 15 seconds is common; longer apneic periods or cyanosis in the baby are causes for concern.

Another criterion of the Apgar score is skin colour (see Table 18-5). The lowest rating is blue or pale; the highest rating is completely pink. **Acrocyanosis** (cyanosis of the hands and feet) is expected immediately after birth or if newborns are exposed to a cool environment. If poor peripheral circulation causes the acrocyanosis, the sole of the foot turns pink when it is vigorously rubbed; if it is true cyanosis, the foot stays blue.

Newborns are nose breathers, and nasal flaring is common because their noses are often congested. Suctioning immediately after birth is usual practice. Respiratory grunting indicates increased effort to expel air or fluid. Coughing in newborns raises concern over lung involvement. Newborns use the diaphragm and abdominal muscles for respiratory effort, movements that are noticeable in this age group. Crepitus around the clavicle requires assessment; a positive finding may indicate a pneumothorax, especially following forceps delivery. Newborns delivered by cesarean section have more apnea, especially during sleep (Bader, Riskin, et al., 2004).

Table 18-4 Expected Range of Resting Values for Respiration

Age	Respirations (breaths/min)
Newborn	30–60
6 mo	24–38
1 y	22–30
3 y	22–30
5 y	20–24
10 y	16–22
12 y	16–22
14 y	14–20

From National Institutes of Health. (n.d.). *Age appropriate vital signs.* Retrieved from http://clinicalcenter.nih.gov/ccc/pedweb/pedsstaff/age.html

Table 18-5 Nursing Diagnoses for the Respiratory System

Diagnosis and Related Factors	Point of Differentiation	Assessment Characteristics	Nursing Interventions
Impaired gas exchange related to alveolar–capillary membrane changes	Describes changes at the capillary level	Low pO_2, confusion, cyanosis, fatigue, tachycardia, use of accessory muscles	Administer oxygen,* deep breathing, incentive spirometer, inhalers*
Ineffective airway clearance related to thick tracheobronchial secretions	Describes issues related to expectorating sputum	Cough, thick secretions, adventitious sounds, cyanosis, nasal flaring	Cough and deep breathe, increase fluids, expectorants,* postural drainage*
Ineffective breathing pattern related to fatigue	Describes changes in respiratory rate, rhythm, or depth	Decreased chest excursion, dyspnea, nasal flaring, increased rate, decreased depth, accessory muscles	Position to decrease workload of breathing, pace activity, provide rest, reduce fever
Excess fluid volume related to congestive heart failure (CHF)	Describes peripheral edema and fluid accumulation in the lung	Low pO_2, frothy sputum, decreased breath sounds, pleural effusion, shortness of breath, orthopnea, paroxysmal nocturnal dyspnea	Elevate head of bed, administer diuretics,* intake and output, daily weights

*Collaborative interventions.

Percussion is not useful in newborns because an adult's hands are too large for the small chest. When auscultating the lungs, make sure to use the pediatric diaphragm on the stethoscope appropriate for the newborn's size. If the baby is crying, wait for a quiet moment to auscultate. Also, take advantage of sleep in newborns to listen to breath sounds. If the baby is quiet, breath sounds are easier to hear in newborns than in adults because of their thinner and smaller chest wall. Breath sounds are also transmitted more easily, so they may be referred to areas where there are absent breath sounds; listen to fine differences in quality. Expect to auscultate crackles or gurgles because of small amounts of fluid that remain in the lungs.

If adventitious lung sounds are asymmetrical, meconium aspiration may have occurred in one section of the lung. If gastrointestinal gurgling sounds are heard in the chest, communicate these findings to a primary health practitioner, because the newborn may have a diaphragmatic hernia.

⚠ SAFETY ALERT 18-9

Stridor results from laryngeal or tracheal obstruction and is a serious sign of difficulty breathing. Cough, hoarseness, or use of accessory muscles may indicate a serious obstruction in the trachea or larynx. If signs remain, obtain assistance immediately.

Parents may hold a hesitant child or a child may want to sit in a parent's lap. Children are curious about stethoscopes; gain trust by having them listen to their own breath sounds first.

Detecting expiratory sounds in children with rapid respirations is difficult. Asking them to blow out the penlight will prolong expiratory sounds and wheezing may be detected. A child may also like to breathe like a hot or tired dog during auscultation. A child's breath sounds are louder and harsher; therefore, bronchovesicular breath sounds may often be heard through the chest.

Children begin using their intercostal muscles to breathe by the age of 6 to 7 years. A round-shaped chest that persists past 5 to 6 years may indicate pulmonary disease. If the child is crying, auscultate the chest during the deep breath that follows a sob.

Older Adults

Immobility creates a risk for airway collapse (atelectasis), reduced air exchange, hypoxia, hypercapnia, and acidosis. Reduced gag and cough reflexes can place older people at risk for aspiration of secretions and, potentially, aspiration pneumonia. Postoperative pulmonary complications are another possibility because of impaired cough reflex, weaker muscles, and decreased inspiratory capacity.

Older adults are at increased risk for pulmonary complications during stress. Attention must be paid to maintaining effective ventilation, keeping lung volumes high, clearing secretions, and positioning to prevent aspiration. Respiratory assessment may be tiring for people of this age group, so allow frequent rest periods. Postpone those activities that can wait until strength has returned so that these patients can use energy for breathing.

Remember Mr. Jin, whose health concerns have been outlined throughout this chapter. The initial subjective and objective data collection is complete, and the nurse has spent time reviewing the findings and other results. The following nursing note illustrates how subjective and objective data are analyzed and nursing interventions are developed as part of the nursing process described above. The subjective and objective data provide evidence for the analysis (the nursing diagnosis or concern). The plan includes interventions related to the diagnosis, previously described.

Subjective: "I'm still not feeling very well. When I came in last time, they said that I had bronchitis, but it feels like it's getting worse. Last time I felt wheezy; this time, I'm coughing more. Now I'm coughing up about ½ cup (125 mL) of thick yellow sputum every day. I think the coughing is making me feel so tired—more tired each day."

Objective: Alert and oriented × 3. Sitting in chair with increased respiratory effort. Temperature 38°C oral, pulse 102 beats/min and regular, respirations 24 breaths/min, blood pressure 156/78 mm Hg (left arm, sitting), oxygen saturation (SaO_2) 90%. Skin colour pale, using neck muscles to breathe, no retractions. Few wheezes scattered through bilateral lung fields. Decreased breath sounds noted in right base. No chest pain noted. Dyspnea and respirations 32 breaths/min when ambulating in hall.

Analysis: Increasing dyspnea, cough, sputum, and fatigue. Impaired gas exchange with reduced oxygen saturation. Risk for ineffective airway clearance with increasing sputum. Potential for infection in the lungs.

Plan: Contact primary health practitioner about findings. Further assess effect of health concerns on patient's sleep pattern and activities of daily living (ADLs). Teach to drink 2 L of fluid daily to liquefy secretions. Teach patient about coughing and deep breathing techniques. Teach to pace activity and rest when dyspneic. Have patient take temperature three times daily and call if >38.0°C. Contact respiratory therapy about administration of inhalers and interventions to reduce dyspnea. Contact primary health practitioner to discuss possibility of obtaining sputum culture and sensitivity, chest x-ray, and medical treatments. Discuss concerns with the patient's wife.

Critical Thinking Challenge

- Critique the objective data that were documented. How will the nursing data collection differ from that of the primary health care provider?
- What other data might be collected to identify issues affecting other body systems or functional status?
- How will the nurse work collaboratively with the primary health care provider to evaluate interventions?

Evidence-Informed Critical Thinking

Organizing and Prioritizing

It is essential for nurses to continuously think critically about the patient's condition to organize and prioritize assessments and patient care. Laboratory and diagnostic tests related to the respiratory system can add to the database of findings created after the health history and physical examination. The analysis of history, physical examination, and laboratory data helps to identify the underlying cause of signs and symptoms. Nurses use these data to identify the underlying functional condition, label the condition (sometimes in a nursing diagnosis format), and plan interventions based on patient outcomes. At times nurses make referrals for a complex health issue. They clearly communicate assessment findings and reasons for referrals to other health care providers. Nurses also work with primary health practitioners to gather information to make a diagnosis and to prescribe appropriate collaborative care. They reassess patients to evaluate the effectiveness of both nursing and collaborative care measures.

Laboratory and Diagnostic Testing

Laboratory data taken from samples of blood or other body fluids give indirect measures of disease. For example, an elevated white blood cell count may indicate infection (eg, pneumonia). Analysis of a sputum sample may help pinpoint the type of causative bacteria. Arterial blood gas sampling is a direct measure of blood levels of oxygen, carbon dioxide, and pH. Other diagnostic tests can help visualize the thorax and lungs in different ways to identify structures and densities.

Chest x-rays are commonly performed in patients with respiratory disorders. Radiography can identify areas of consolidation, which accompanies pneumonia, TB, and cancer. When more accurate testing is needed to identify the size and shape of lesions, a computed tomography scan or magnetic resonance imaging may be indicated. A ventilation/perfusion scan identifies differences in ventilation and perfusion and is commonly ordered in cases of suspected pulmonary embolism. If findings are unexpected, the patient's oxygen saturation level should be closely monitored; deep vein thrombosis prophylaxis may be indicated.

Pulmonary function tests provide information about the patient's ability to move air into and out of the lungs. Total vital capacity, inspiratory volume, and expiratory reserve are measured for patients at risk for disease or dyspneic symp-

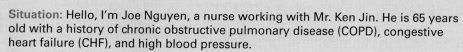

Collaborating with the Interprofessional Team

In many facilities, nurses initiate referrals for respiratory care based on assessment findings. Results that might trigger a respiratory therapy consult include an unexpected change in respiratory status, increased wheezing, absent breath sounds, gurgles, sudden decrease in oxygen saturation, accessory muscle use, respiratory rate >30 breaths/min, change in pattern and rate of breathing, cyanosis, dyspnea, or an acute change in oxygen saturation or arterial blood gasses.

Mr. Jin has been experiencing many of the symptoms/signs outlined above; therefore, a respiratory therapy consult might be indicated. In this case, the situation and background are the assessment information. The analysis is the nursing diagnosis or concern and the recommendations are the interventions. The following conversation illustrates how the nurse might organize data and make recommendations about the patient's care to the respiratory therapy department.

Situation: Hello, I'm Joe Nguyen, a nurse working with Mr. Ken Jin. He is 65 years old with a history of chronic obstructive pulmonary disease (COPD), congestive heart failure (CHF), and high blood pressure.

Background: He came in 2 weeks ago for bronchitis and returned to the clinic today with increasing cough, thick yellow sputum production, and fatigue. His temperature is 38°C, respirations are 24 breaths/min and regular, and pulse is 112 beats/min. His SaO_2 usually is 92% to 94% but now is 90%. He is short of breath with even walking in the hall. He usually has scattered wheezes but now has new decreased breath sounds in the right base.

Analysis: I'm concerned about his low oxygen saturation and ability to handle his increased sputum.

Recommendations: He is continuing to use his inhalers, and he says that they help. I was wondering if you could come to assess his need to increase the number of puffs per day of his inhalers and make sure that he is using them properly. Could you also listen to his lungs and see if you think that he might benefit from some chest physiotherapy to assist with mobilizing his secretions?

Critical Thinking Challenge

- How did the nurse prioritize which subjective information to share?
- Critique the objective data. Is the organization logical? Would it be clearer to add to or take out any of the information?
- Critique the analysis and recommendations. What is the nurse's role in coordinating collaborative care with respiratory therapy?

toms. These tests may show a need to alter medications whether the patient requires home oxygen therapy or assistance with activities of daily living (ADLs) at home.

Refer to Tables 18-8 and 18-9 at the end of the chapter that compare assessment findings for common medical diagnoses related to the thorax, lung, and respiratory functioning.

Clinical Reasoning

Assessment findings are used as a basis for nursing care. An accurate and complete assessment provides a firm foundation for setting outcomes, providing individualized interventions, and evaluating progress.

Nursing Diagnoses, Outcomes, and Interventions

Difficulty breathing could be a manifestation of many different underlying conditions. Alveolar exchange of oxygen and carbon dioxide might be impaired. The airway may have too many secretions. Breathing could be too shallow or slow. Interventions for each of these situations are very different.

If the issue is with airway clearance, fluids are given to help liquefy secretions. If the concern is shallow breathing,

deep breathing exercises are indicated. When formulating a nursing diagnosis, it is important to use critical thinking and to ensure the accuracy of assessment findings to increase the chances for arriving at a correct diagnosis. Note that the diagnosis is supported by the unexpected assessment findings. The point of differentiation summarizes the major issue related to the diagnosis. See Table 18-5 for nursing diagnoses commonly related to thorax, lung, and respiratory assessment (Bulechek, Butcher, et al., 2008).

Nurses use assessment information to identify patient outcomes. Some outcomes related to respiratory concerns include the following:

- Demonstrate improved ventilation and adequate oxygenation.
- Maintain clear lung fields and remain free of signs of respiratory distress.
- Demonstrate effective coughing.
- Maintain a patent airway at all times (Moorhead, Johnson, et al., 2007).

Once outcomes are established, nursing care can be implemented to improve the patient's status. Nurses use critical thinking and evidence-informed practice to develop

---

Pulling It All Together: An Example of Reflection and Critical Thinking

The nurse uses assessment data to formulate a nursing care plan for Mr. Jin. He or she may independently perform teaching on appropriate inhaler use, teach cough and deep breathing techniques, and teach the need for increased fluids to liquefy secretions. The nurse also may initiate a referral to respiratory therapy about inhaler use and possible chest physiotherapy and consult with the primary health practitioner about Mr. Jin's potential infection. The assessment data is included as the "as evidenced by" section of the care planning. Outcomes and interventions are established collaboratively with the patient. After the interventions are completed, the nurse will reevaluate (or reassess) Mr. Jin and document the findings in the patient health record to show the progress toward the patient outcomes. This is often in the form of a care plan or case note similar to the one below.

Nursing Diagnosis	Patient Outcomes	Nursing Interventions	Rationale	Evaluation
Ineffective airway clearance related to fatigue and inability to cough effectively as evidenced by respiration rate, dyspnea	Breath sounds return to baseline wheezing with no gurgles in right base within 1 week	Teach patient cough and deep breathing techniques to perform every 2 hours. Identify fluids that patient likes to reach goal of 2 L/d. Teach patient to call clinic for temperature higher than 38.0°C, increased dyspnea, increasing sputum.	Increases force and depth of breath to clear secretions. Fluids liquefy secretions to make them easier to expel. Signs and symptoms of worsening status should be reevaluated.	Demonstrated accurate cough and deep breathing techniques. Drank 1 L/d. Stated when to call clinic. Lungs sounds with wheezing and gurgles in right base. Encourage fluids every 2 hours. Encourage cough and deep breathing every hour. Reassess in 4 hours.

Thus, subjective and objective assessment data are used in developing a diagnosis, planning care, and evaluating progress toward established outcomes. Using this nursing process and critical thinking, consider all the case study findings woven throughout this chapter. When answering the following questions, begin drawing conclusions and see how the pieces of assessment must work together to create an environment for personalized, appropriate, and accurate care.

- Why is the sternal angle (angle of Louis) so important as a landmark for assessment of the thorax? (Knowledge)
- What collection of history (subjective) findings is concerning? (Comprehension)
- What health promotion and teaching needs are identified for Mr. Jin? (Application)
- Is Mr. Jin's condition stable, urgent, or an emergency? (Analysis)
- How will the nurse individualize assessment to Mr. Jin's specific needs, considering his condition, age, and culture? (Synthesis)
- How will the nurse evaluate the success of patient teaching for Mr. Jin? (Evaluation)

the interventions. Some examples of nursing interventions for respiratory care are as follows:

- Monitory respiratory rate, depth, accessory muscle use, and breath sounds every 1 to 4 hours.
- Monitor oxygen saturation using pulse oximetry.
- Position the patient with the head of the bed at 45°; reposition every 2 hours.
- Obtain incentive spirometer and teach the patient to use it to prevent atelectasis and retained bronchial secretions (Bulechek, Butcher, et al., 2008).

Nurses then evaluate care according to the patient outcomes that were developed, thereafter reassessing the patient and continuing or modifying interventions as appropriate.

An accurate and complete nursing assessment is an essential foundation for holistic nursing care. Even beginning nursing students can use the patient assessment to implement new interventions, evaluate the effectiveness of those interventions, and make a difference in the quality of patient care.

Key Points

- Anterior and posterior landmarks are used to identify the location of lung fields.
- Reference lines include the midsternal and midclavicular lines (anterior chest), mid-vertebral and mid-scapular lines (posterior chest), and anterior axillary, midaxillary, and posterior axillary lines (axillae)
- Anteriorly, the apex of the lung extends approximately 2 to 4 cm above the inner third of the clavicle and posteriorly, the base is near T10.
- With aging, the lungs lose elasticity, respiratory strength decreases, cartilage loses flexibility, and bones lose density.
- Dyspnea, decreased level of consciousness, respirations >30 breaths/min, oxygen saturation <90%, retractions, and

accessory muscle use may indicate an acute or emergency situation.

- Health promotion includes avoidance of smoking, occupational exposure to irritants, recreational drugs, and high-risk travel and recommendations for influenza and pneumococcal vaccines.
- Common respiratory symptoms include chest pain, dyspnea, orthopnea, paroxysmal nocturnal dyspnea, cough, mucus, wheezing, and change in functional ability.
- The initial survey includes body position, pursed lips, nasal flaring, level of consciousness, skin colour, respiratory movement and rate, oxygen saturation, accessory muscle use, and retractions.
- Unexpected respiratory patterns include tachypnea, hyperventilation, bradypnea, hypoventilation, Cheyne-Stokes, Biot, agonal, and apnea.
- Objective assessment includes inspection, palpation, chest expansion, tactile fremitus, percussion, diaphragmatic excursion, and auscultation.
- Breath sounds are auscultated and labelled as vesicular, bronchial, or bronchovesicular.
- Adventitious lung sounds include fine and coarse crackles, wheezes, rhonchi, pleural friction rub, and stridor.
- Auscultate voice sounds for bronchophony, egophony, and whispered pectoriloquy.
- The Apgar scoring system is used to assess the newborn, including respiratory effort and skin colour.
- Common nursing diagnoses include impaired gas exchange, ineffective airway clearance, ineffective breathing pattern, and excess fluid volume.
- A respiratory therapy consultation may be indicated with an unexpected change in respiratory status, increased wheezing, gurgles, sudden decrease in oxygen saturation, accessory muscle use, respiratory rate >30 breaths/min, change in pattern and rate of breathing, cyanosis, dyspnea, or an acute change in oxygen saturation or arterial blood gases.

Review Questions

1. When the nurse assesses a 78-year-old patient with pneumonia, which finding should be evaluated first?
   A. Breath sounds
   B. Airway patency
   C. Respiratory rate
   D. Percussion sounds

2. A 45-year-old man has been admitted to the hospital with pulmonary embolism. Which of the following symptoms should the nurse report to the primary health practitioner immediately?
   A. Chest pain
   B. Shortness of breath
   C. Respirations 20 breaths/min
   D. Productive cough

3. A 62-year-old woman comes to the clinic with an exacerbation of asthma. Which of the following findings indicate worsening status of her asthma?
   A. Increased wheezing
   B. Bloody sputum
   C. Increased tympany
   D. Flushed red skin

4. A 3-year-old boy is in the emergency department with stridor, intercostal and supraclavicular retractions, and respiratory rate of 40 breaths/min. What type of situation is this?
   A. Stable
   B. Acute
   C. Urgent
   D. Emergency

5. A 92-year-old woman with a history of chronic obstructive pulmonary disease (COPD) presents with increasing shortness of breath, decreased lung sounds in the bases, increased edema, and weight gain. What is the most likely health issue?
   A. Impaired gas exchange
   B. Ineffective airway clearance
   C. Activity intolerance
   D. Excess fluid volume

6. Which of the following factors is most likely to increase the risk of a patient developing COPD?
   A. Increased age
   B. Immune suppression
   C. Smoking
   D. Occupational exposure

7. When the nurse assesses the patient with respiratory symptoms, which of the following concerns should be evaluated first?
   A. Chest pain
   B. Shortness of breath
   C. Cough
   D. Sputum

8. When assessing the patient with atelectasis, what assessment findings are expected? Choose all that apply.
   A. Shortness of breath
   B. Decreased breath sounds
   C. Decreased oxygen saturation
   D. Increased tactile fremitus
   E. Hyperresonance

9. Which assessments would indicate that the inhaled bronchodilators have their desired effect?
   A. Wheezing, oxygen saturation 94%, pallor
   B. Vesicular breath sounds, oxygen saturation 96%, pink
   C. Bronchial breath sounds, oxygen saturation 100%, erythema
   D. Crackles, oxygen saturation 90%, cyanosis

10. The nurse auscultates bronchovesicular breath sounds in the 2nd intercostal space (ICS) near the sternum. The nurse interprets this as
    A. an expected finding over the trachea
    B. an expected finding over the bronchi
    C. an unexpected finding over the lung
    D. an unexpected finding over the trachea

Canadian Nursing Research

Bailey, P. H. (2004). The dyspnea-anxiety-dyspnea cycle-COPD clients' stories of breathliness: "It's scary when you can't breathe." *Qualitative Health Research, 14*, 760–778.

Bergerson, S. M., Cameron, S., et al. (2006). Diverse implications of a national health crisis: A qualitative exploration of community nurses' SARS experiences. *Canadian Journal of Nursing Research, 38*(2), 42–54.

Cicutto, L., Conti, E., et al. (2006). Creating asthma-friendly schools: A public health approach. *Journal of School Health, 76*(6), 255–258.

Klomp H., Lawson J. A., et al. (2008). Examining asthma quality of care using a population-based approach. *Canadian Medical Association Journal, 178*(8), 1013–1021.

Ratner, P. A., Johnson, J. L., et al. (2004). Efficacy of a smoking-cessation intervention for elective-surgical clients. *Research in Nursing & Health, 27*, 148–161.

Ross, C. J. M., Davis, T. M. A., et al. (2007). Screening and assessing adolescent asthmatics for anxiety disorders. *Clinical Nursing Research, 16*(1), 5–28.

Schultz, A. S. H., Johnson, J. L., et al. (2006). Registered nurses' perceptions on tobacco reduction: Views from Western Canada. *Canadian Journal of Nursing Research, 38*(4), 193–211.

References

Agency for Healthcare Research and Quality. (2005). *Helping smokers to quit: A guide for nurses*. Rockville, MD: Author.

American Lung Association. (2004). *American Lung Association offers tips to improve indoor air quality during high pollution season*. Retrieved from http://www.lungusa.org/site/apps/s/content.asp?c=dvLUK9O0E&b=34706&ct= 66959

Asthma Society of Canada. (2011). *About asthma: Who gets asthma?* Retrieved from http://www.asthma.ca/adults/about/whoGetsAsthma.php

Bader, D., Riskin, A., et al. (2004). Breathing patterns in term infants delivered by caesarean section. *Acta Paediatrica, 93*(9), 1216–1220.

Benditt, J. O. (2006). The neuromuscular respiratory system: Physiology, pathophysiology, and a respiratory care approach to patients. *Respiratory Care, 51*(8), 829–837.

Berman, S., Tanasijevic, M. J., et al. (1996). Racial differences in the predictive value of the TDx fetal lung maturity assay. *American Journal of Obstetrics and Gynecology, 175*(1), 73–77.

Bulechek, G. M., Butcher, H. K., et al. (2008). *Nursing Interventions Classification (NIC)* (5th ed.). St. Louis, MO: Mosby.

Canadian Cancer Society's Steering Committee for Cancer Statistics. (2011). *Canadian cancer statistics 2011.* Toronto, ON: Canadian Cancer Society.

Canadian Council for Tobacco Control. (2011). *Advice to health professionals: Nurses.* Retrieved from http://www.cctc.ca/cctc/EN/advicehealthprofessionals/nurses

Canadian Cystic Fibrosis Foundation. (2010). *Canadian cystic fibrosis patient data registry report 2008.* Retrieved from http://www.cysticfibrosis.ca/assets/files/pdf/CPDR_ReportE.pdf

Canadian Lung Association. (2008). *COPD.* Retrieved from http://www.lung.ca/diseases-maladies/copd-mpoc_e.php

Canadian Lung Association. (2010). *Smoking & tobacco: Second-hand smoke.* Retrieved from http://www.lung.ca/protect-protegez/tobacco-tabagisme/second-secondaire/index_e.php

Canadian Lung Association. (2011a). *Statistics: Lung diseases.* Retrieved from http://www.lung.ca/lung/o/-renseignez/statistics-statistiques/lungdiseases-maladiespoumon/index_e.php

Canadian Lung Association. (2011b). *Tuberculosis.* Retrieved from http://www.lung.ca/diseases-maladies/tuberculosis-tuberculose/world-monde/index_e.php

Caroci, A. S., & Lareau, S. C. (2004). Descriptors of dyspnea by patients with chronic obstructive pulmonary disease versus congestive heart failure. *Heart & Lung, 33*(2), 102–110.

Centers for Disease Control and Prevention. (2008). *Smoking and tobacco use. Fact Sheet: Cessation.* Retrieved from http://www.cdc.gov/tobacco/data_statistics/fact_sheet/cessation/cessation2.htm

Cohen, L., Doyle, W. J., et al. (2004). Childhood socioeconomic status and host resistance to infectious illness in adulthood. *Psychosomatic Medicine, 66*(4), 553–558.

Crapo, J., Glassroth, J., et al. (2004). *Baum's textbook of pulmonary disease* (7th ed.). Philadelphia, PA: Lippincott Williams & Wilkins.

Cystic Fibrosis Canada. (2011). *Cystic fibrosis in Canada.* Retrieved from http://www.cysticfibrosis.ca/assets/files/pdf/Cystic_fibrosis_in_canadaE.pdf

Davis, A. M., Kreutzer, R., et al. (2006). Asthma prevalence in Hispanic and Asian American ethnic subgroups: Results from the California healthy kids survey. *Pediatrics, 118*(2), e363–e370.

Duff, B., Gardiner, G., et al. (2007). The impact of surgical ward nurses practicing respiratory assessment on positive client outcomes. *Australian Journal of Advanced Nursing, 24*(4), 52–56.

Edge, D. S., & Bickley, L. S. (2010). The thorax and lungs. In T. C. Stephen, D. L. Skillen, R. A. Day, & L. S. Bickley (Eds.). *Canadian Bates' guide to health assessment for nurses* (1st ed., pp. 381–421). Philadelphia, PA: Wolters Kluwer Health/Lippincott Williams & Wilkins.

Greco, F. A. (2004). Interpretation of breath sounds. *American Journal of Respiratory and Critical Care Medicine, 169*, 1260.

Haiman, C. A., Stram, D. O., et al. (2006). Ethnic and racial differences in the smoking-related risk of lung cancer. *New England Journal of Medicine, 354*(4), 333–342.

Hancox, R. J., Poulto, R., et al. (2006). Associations between respiratory symptoms, lung function and gastro-oesophageal reflux symptoms in a population-based birth cohort. *Respiratory Research, 5*(7), 142.

Hankinson, J. L., Crapo, R. O., et al. (2003). Spirometric reference values for the 6-s FVC maneuver. *Chest, 124*, 1805–1811.

Henschke, C. I., Yip, R., et al. (2006). Women's susceptibility to tobacco carcinogens and survival after diagnosis of lung cancer. *Journal of the American Medical Association, 296*, 180–184.

Hong, S. J., Lee, M. S., et al. (2006). High body mass index and dietary pattern associated with childhood asthma. *Pediatric Pulmonology, 41*(12), 1118–1124.

Ip, M. S., Ko, F. W., et al. (2006). Updated spirometric reference values for adult Chinese in Hong Kong and implications on clinical utilization. *Chest, 129*(2), 384–392.

Jones, R. L., & Nzekwu, M. M. (2006). The effects of body mass index on lung volumes. *Chest, 130*(3), 827–833.

Kleinman, B. S., Frey, K., et al. (2002). Motion of the diaphragm in patients with chronic obstructive pulmonary disease while spontaneously breathing versus during positive pressure breathing after anesthesia and neuromuscular blockade. *Anesthesiology, 97*(2), 298–305.

Lee, T., Brugge, D., et al. (2003). Asthma prevalence among inner-city Asian-American schoolchildren. *Public Health Report, 118*(3), 215–220.

Marinella, M. A., Pierson, C., et al. (1997). The stethoscope: A potential source of nosocomial infection? *Archives of Internal Medicine, 157*(7), 786–790.

McPhee, S. J., Papadakis, M. A., et al. (2007). *Current medical diagnosis and treatment* (46th ed.). New York, NY: McGraw Hill.

Moore, K. L., & Agur, A. M., et al. (2011). *Essential clinical anatomy* (4th ed.). Philadelphia, PA: Lippincott Williams & Wilkins.

Moorhead, S., Johnson, M., et al. (2007). *Nursing outcomes classification (NOC)* (4th ed.). Philadelphia, PA: Mosby.

National Advisory Committee on Immunization. (2006). *Canadian immunization guide* (7th ed.). Ottawa, ON: Minister of Public Works and Government Services Canada.

National Institutes of Health. (n.d.). *Age appropriate vital signs.* Retrieved from http://clinicalcenter.nih.gov/ccc/pedweb/pedsstaff/age.html

Pooler, C. (2010). Structure and function of the respiratory system. In R. A. Hannon, C. Pooler, et al. (Eds.). *Porth pathophysiology: Concepts of altered health states* (1st Canadian ed., pp. 614–642). Philadelphia, PA: Wolters Kluwer Health/Lippincott Williams & Wilkins.

Public Health Agency of Canada. (2007). *Life and breath: Respiratory disease in Canada.* Retrieved from http://www.phac-aspc.gc.ca/publicat/2007/lbrdc-vsmrc/index-eng.php

Public Health Agency of Canada. (2011a). *On the move against tuberculosis.* Retrieved from http://phac-aspc.gc.ca/tbpc-latb/tb_2011-eng.php

Public Health Agency of Canada. (2011b). *FluWatch: March 6–12, 2011 (week 10)*. Retrieved from http://phac-aspc.gc.ca/fluwatch10-11/w10_11/index-eng.php

Ross, C. J. M. (2010). Management of patients with chronic obstructive pulmonary disease. In R. A. Day, P. Paul, et al. (Eds.). *Brunner & Suddarth's textbook of Canadian medical-surgical nursing* (2nd ed., pp. 646–679). Philadelphia, PA: Wolters Kluwer Health/Lippincott Williams & Wilkins.

Singh, S. K., Chowdhary, G. R., et al. (2006). Assessment of impact of high particulate concentration on peak expiratory flow rate of lungs of sand stone quarry workers. *International Journal of Environmental Research in Public Health, 3*(4), 355–359.

Smoking Cessation Leadership Center. (n.d.). *30 seconds to save a life*. Retrieved from http://smokingcessationleadership.ucsf.edu/30seconds.html

Stick, S. (2000). Paediatric origins of adult lung disease: The contribution of airway development to paediatric and adult lung disease. *Thorax, 55*, 587–594.

Tashkin, D. P. (2001). Airway effects of marijuana, cocaine and other inhaled illicit agents. *Current Opinion in Pulmonary Medicine, 7*(2), 43–61.

Taylor, Z., Nolan, C. M., et al.; Centers for Disease Control and Prevention, & Infectious Diseases Society of America. (2005). Controlling tuberculosis in the United States. Recommendations from the American Thoracic Society, CDC, and the Infectious Diseases Society of America. *Morbidity and Mortality Weekly Report, 54*(RR–12), 1–81.

Tessier, J. F., Nejjari, C., et al. (2000). Smoking and eight-year mortality in an elderly cohort. *International Journal Tuberculosis Lung Disease, 4*(8), 698–704.

U.S. Public Health Service. (2009). *Treating tobacco use and dependence: Quick reference guide for clinicians*. Retrieved from http://www.surgeongeneral.gov/tobacco/tobaqrg.htm

Woods, S. L., Sivarajan Froelicher, E., et al. (2005). *Cardiac nursing* (5th ed.). Philadelphia, PA: Lippincott Williams & Wilkins.

Wolff, A. J., & O'Donnell, A. E. (2004). Pulmonary effects of illicit drug use. *Clinical Chest Medicine, 25*(1), 203–216.

World Health Organization. (2006a). *Avian influenza (bird flu) fact sheet*. Retrieved from http://www.who.int/mediacentre/factsheets/avian_influenza/en/index.html

World Health Organization. (2006b). *Tuberculosis fact sheet*. Retrieved from http://www.who.int/mediacentre/factsheets/fs104/en/#global

World Health Organization. (2010). *Pandemic (H1N1) 2009—Update 07*. Retrieved from http://www. who.int/esr/don/2010_04_23a/en/index.html

The Canadian Jensen's Nursing Health Assessment suite offers these additional resources to enhance learning and facilitate understanding of this chapter:

* thePoint online resource, http//thepoint.lww.com/Stephen1E
* *Laboratory Manual for Canadian Jensens's Nursing Health Assessment: A Best Practice Approach*

Tables of Unexpected Findings

Visual Pattern	Description	Associated Conditions
Expected	Rate of 10–20 breaths/min Ratio of respiration to pulse is approximately 4:1 500–800 mL per breath Regular rhythm	Expected findings
Tachypnea	Rate >24 breaths/min <500 mL/breath, shallow Regular rhythm	Anxiety, fear, elevated metabolic rate, fever, exercise, respiratory diseases in which rate must be increased to maintain oxygenation
Hyperventilation	Rate >24 breaths/min >800 mL/breath, deep Regular rhythm	Extreme anxiety or fear, exercise, increased intracranial pressure Kussmaul respirations are seen with diabetic ketoacidosis, because the body is attempting to remove carbon dioxide to correct the pH.
Bradypnea	Rate <10 breaths/min 500–800 mL/breath, shallow Regular rhythm	Conditions in which the breathing center in the medulla is depressed, such as narcotic overdose, diabetic coma, and increased intracranial pressure
Hypoventilation	Rate <10 breaths/min <500 mL/breath, shallow Irregular rhythm	Narcotic or anesthetic overdose, increased intracranial pressure
Cheyne-Stokes respiration Hyperpnea Apnea	Rate variable Depth variable Regular irregular rhythm that cycles from deep and fast to shallow and slow, with some periods of apnea	Expected in children and the elderly; also, terminal illness, renal failure, drug overdose, increased intracranial pressure, and heart failure. Count the rate for 1 full minute and record the length of apnea
Biot respiration	Rate variable Depth variable Irregular rhythm	Severe brain damage, commonly at the level of the medulla. Count the rate for 1 full minute and record the length of apnea.
Agonal	Rate intermittent Depth variable Irregular rhythm	Finding in patients at the end of life. Count the rate for 1 full minute and record the length of apnea.
Apnea	No breaths	Cardiac arrest and brain death

Table 18-7 **Unexpected Thoracic Configurations**

Adult (No Thoracic Concerns)

Anteroposterior (AP)/lateral ratio is 1:2, wider than it is deep, oval shaped. Cone shaped from head to toe.

Kyphoscoliosis

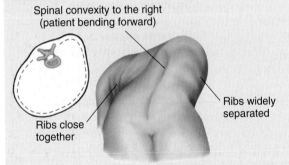

Spinal convexity to the right (patient bending forward)

Ribs widely separated

Ribs close together

With kyphosis, the thoracic spine curves forward, compressing the anterior chest and reducing inspiratory lung volumes. With scoliosis, a lateral S-shaped curvature of the spine causes unequal shoulders, scapulae, and hips. In severe cases, asymmetry may impede breathing.

Pectus Carinatum (Pigeon Chest)

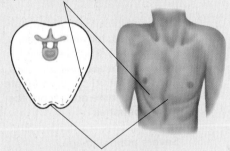

Depressed costal cartilages

Anteriorly displaced sternum

Sternum is displaced anteriorly, depressing the adjacent costal cartilages. Congenital condition with increased AP diameter.

Pectus Excavatum (Funnel Chest)

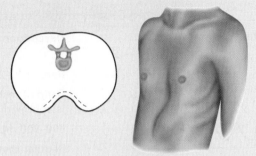

Depression in lower part of and adjacent to sternum. Congenital condition may compress the heart or great vessels and cause murmurs.

Barrel Chest

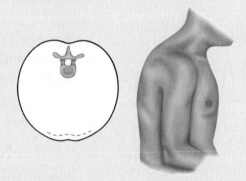

AP/lateral ratio is near 1:1, round shaped. Ribs are more horizontal, and costal margin is widened. Associated with chronic obstructive pulmonary disease (COPD), chronic asthma, and aging.

Flail Chest

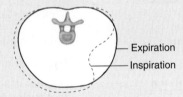

Expiration

Inspiration

When multiple ribs are fractured, paradoxical movements of the chest may occur. As the diaphragm pulls down during inspiration, negative pressure causes the injured area to cave inward; during expiration it moves out.

Table 18-8 Common Respiratory Conditions

Condition	Risk Factors	History and Subjective Data	Objective Data	Diagnostic Tests
Asthma: Allergic hypersensitivity to allergens that produces bronchospasm	Hyperresponsive airways Bronchospastic triggers	Cough worse at night and early morning	Wheezing, especially during exhalation Diminished lung sounds Clear sputum	Pulmonary function with short-acting bronchodilator
Atelectasis: Collapsed section of alveoli from immobility, obstruction, compression, or decreased surfactant	Immobility	Dyspnea Fever possible No sputum	Decreased or absent breath sounds over the atelectatic area, reduced inspiratory capacity	Chest x-ray
Emphysema: Destruction of pulmonary capillary bed and alveoli creating large air sacs and bullae	Smoking Occupational exposure	Shortness of breath Chronic cough	Cough, shortness of breath, decreased breath sounds, barrel chest	Pulmonary function tests
Bronchitis: Inflammation of bronchi that stimulate mucous glands. Secretions may partially obstruct the airways	Recent infection Chronic obstructive pulmonary disease (COPD) presents with both bronchitis and emphysema	Chest tight or wheezy Clear sputum	Occasional wheezing or fine crackles	Chest x-ray
Lobar pneumonia: Alveoli become congested with bacteria and white blood cells causing consolidation	Older adults, immune-compromised	Productive cough with yellow or green sputum	Rhonchi or gurgles from secretions Fever	Sputum culture
Pleural effusion: Collection of fluid in the intrapleural space that compresses the lung tissue	Congestive heart failure (CHF), fluid overload	Frothy white sputum	Decreased, bronchial or absent breath sounds over effusion	Chest x-ray
Pneumothorax or hemothorax: Collapsed or blood-filled lung	Trauma, central line placement	Dyspnea	Absent breath sounds over area of collapse or bleeding	Chest x-ray
Congestive heart failure: Fluid overload and pulmonary congestion	High blood pressure, renal disease	Dyspnea, edema, weight gain	Decreased breath sounds, fine late inspiratory crackles	Chest x-ray
Tuberculosis: Slow-growing mycobacterium that may form lesions or cavities in the lung	Exposure to infected person	Night sweats	Cough productive of reddish sputum, decreased breath sounds or crackles	Acid-fast bacilli sputum culture Chest x-ray
Pulmonary embolism: Blood clot in the lungs that causes shunting of blood to atelectatic area	Risk for deep vein thrombosis	Severe dyspnea, no sputum	Clear or if large may be decreased Severe hypoxemia	D-dimer assay blood test, ventilation/perfusion scan, or computed tomography of lung
Pneumocystis carinii **pneumonia:** Protozoal infection that is common in the immune suppressed	HIV/AIDS	Dry nonproductive cough	Decreased breath sounds	Chest x-ray Sputum culture

Table 18-9   Common Respiratory Diagnoses

Condition	Auscultation	Sputum	Percussion
Asthma	Wheezes Diminished lung sounds	Clear	Occasional hyperresonance
Atelectasis	Diminished lung sounds in lower lobe	None	Dullness over affected lung
Bronchitis	Occasional wheezing or fine crackles	Clear	Resonance
Chronic obstructive pulmonary disease (COPD)	Wheezes	Clear	Hyperresonance
Pneumothorax	Absent sounds	Absent	Hyperresonance over affected area
Hemothorax	Absent sounds	Bloody	Dull over affected area
Pneumonia	Wheezes, crackles, or gurgles	Purulent	Dull over affected area
Congestive heart failure	Absent over bases	Frothy	Dull over bases
Pleural effusion	Absent over affected lung	None	Dull over affected lung
Pulmonary embolism	Clear or mild wheezes	None	Tympanic

Cardiovascular Assessment

Learning Objectives

1   Demonstrate knowledge of anatomy and physiology of the cardiovascular system.

2   Identify the location of the heart and common auscultatory areas on the precordium.

3   Identify important topics for health promotion and risk reduction related to the cardiovascular system.

4   Consider age, condition, gender, and culture of the patient to individualize the cardiovascular assessment.

5   Collect subjective data related to the cardiovascular system.

6   Collect objective data related to the cardiovascular system using physical examination techniques.

7   Identify expected and unexpected findings related to the assessment of the cardiovascular system.

8   Analyze subjective and objective data from assessment of the cardiovascular system and consider initial interventions.

9   Document and communicate data from the assessment of the cardiovascular system using appropriate terminology and principles of recording.

*M*rs. Anne Lewis, a 77-year-old Caucasian woman, arrived at the emergency room of the hospital with chest pain. She has been in the cardiac care unit for 4 hours. Nurses from the previous shift documented their admitting assessment data. The patient's vital signs are oral temperature 37°C, pulse 112 beats/min regular, respirations 20 breaths/min, and blood pressure right arm (semi-Fowler's) 148/78 mm Hg. Current medications include a thiazide diuretic, chlorothiazide (Diuril) 0.5 g, a beta-blocker, atenolol (Apo-Atenolol) 50 mg for high blood pressure, and a cholesterol-lowering drug, atorvastatin calcium (Lipitor) 10 mg. She has nitroglycerin tablets (NitroQuick) 0.3 mg ordered as needed for chest pain.

You will gain more information about Mrs. Lewis as you progress through this chapter. As you study the content and features, consider Mrs. Lewis's case and its relationship to what you are learning. Begin thinking about the following points:

- Is Mrs. Lewis's condition stable, urgent, or an emergency?
- What immediate health promotion and teaching needs are evident?
- How will the nurse focus, organize, and prioritize subjective data collection?
- How will the nurse focus, organize, and prioritize objective data collection?
- How will the nurse individualize assessment to Mrs. Lewis's specific needs, considering her condition, age, and culture?

The complex cardiovascular system affects the entire body. It is important to understand the many factors that contribute to performing an accurate and complete assessment of this region for each patient. Thorough knowledge of pertinent anatomy and physiology, especially the cardiac cycle, is essential to conduct an accurate assessment and understand expected and unexpected findings. Nurses and other health care providers assess cardiovascular risk factors and common symptoms as part of subjective data collection. During the interview and health history, they gather knowledge about risks such as a diet high in fat, sodium, and cholesterol, high blood pressure, physical inactivity, stress, and smoking. During physical examination, auscultation of the heart helps examiners to check for the sounds heard upon closure of healthy heart valves and also for unexpected and extra sounds, including murmurs and gallops. Nurses document and communicate assessment information to appropriate health care providers. They plan care to promote healthy heart habits, prevent cardiovascular disease, and treat identified conditions.

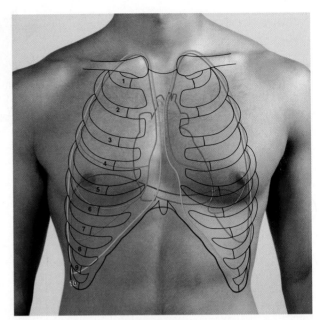

Figure 19-1 Surface anatomy of the thoracic contents. Note the outline of the heart's placement in relation to the thoracic cage.

Anatomy and Physiology Overview

The cardiovascular system includes the heart and great vessels. The peripheral vascular system includes blood vessels, capillary beds, and lymphatic system with the lymph nodes. The systems deliver oxygen and nutrients to the cells and tissues return waste products to the central circulation for excretion, maintaining perfusion of tissues and organs. This section concentrates on the heart and great vessels (see Chapter 20 for detailed discussion of the peripheral vascular system).

Anatomy

The heart and great vessels are located in the mediastinal space between the lungs and above the diaphragm from the center to the left of the thorax (Fig. 19-1). The total size of the heart is slightly larger than a clenched adult fist. The female heart is usually smaller and weighs less than the male heart across all age groups (Woods, Sivarajan Froelicher, et al., 2010).

The precordium on the anterior chest overlies the heart and great vessels, between the 2nd and 5th intercostal spaces (ICSs) at the right sternal border to approximately the 2nd and 5th ICSs at the left midclavicular line (MCL) (see Fig. 19-2). Landmarks on the anterior thoracic wall are used for inspecting, palpating, and auscultating during the cardiovascular assessment. The ICSs, midsternal line, and left MCL are used to describe the location of heart sounds and impulses (see Chapter 18). The superior border of the heart is referred to as the *base* because it is broad; the inferior border of the heart is referred to as the *apex*. This is the opposite of the lungs, where the apex is superior to the base. The base of the heart is at the right and left 2nd ICSs at the sternal border, while the apex is in the 5th left ICS 7 to 9 cm

lateral to the midsternal line. The beating inferior tip of the heart may cause a pulsation in this area, referred to as the *apical impulse*. The great vessels include the carotid arteries, aorta, pulmonary arteries, jugular veins, superior vena cava, inferior vena cava, and pulmonary veins. The great vessels are superior to the heart and then turn in the direction of the body part that they supply (Fig. 19-3).

Neck Vessels

The neck vessels include the carotid arteries and internal and external jugular veins (Fig. 19-4). The *carotid arteries* are located in the depression between the trachea and sternomastoid muscle in the anterior neck. They follow bilaterally along the trachea from clavicle to jaw. Palpation of

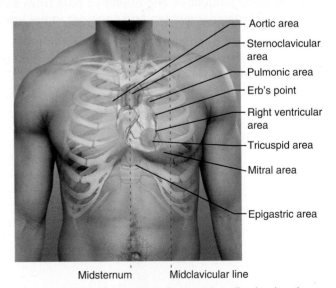

Figure 19-2 The anterior chest and cardiac landmarks.

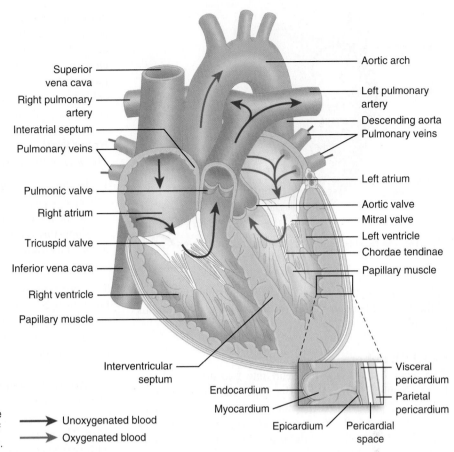

Figure 19-3 Interior anatomy of the heart. The arrows show the direction of blood flow through the heart chambers.

→ Unoxygenated blood
→ Oxygenated blood

the carotid arteries usually reveals a strong pulsation. The internal and external jugular veins are named for their position in the neck. The *internal jugular vein* is deeper and near the carotid artery. Because of its location, it usually is not visible; because it is a vein, it is not palpable. The more superficial *external jugular vein* is visible in the depression above the middle of the clavicle. Pressure in the jugular veins reflects the pressure in the right atrium. Anatomically, the

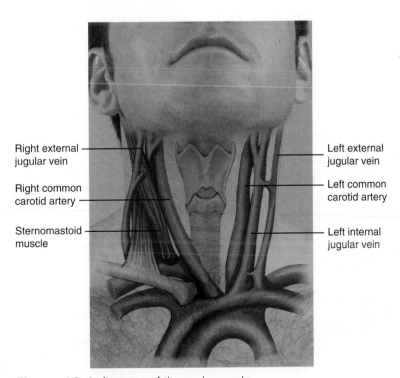

Figure 19-4 Anatomy of the neck vessels.

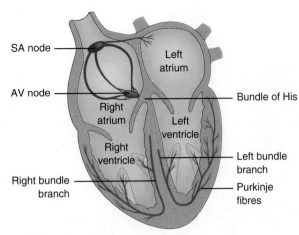

Figure 19-5 The heart wall, chambers, and valves.

right internal jugular vein is closest to the right atrium and is the preferred blood vessel for assessing jugular venous pressure.

Heart Chambers

Two main walls divide the heart into two upper and two lower chambers (Fig. 19-5). The upper chambers, or *atria*, collect and pump blood into the ventricles. The *ventricles* pump blood out to the lungs and body. The *septum* separates the left and right sides of the heart. The left side is larger and more muscular, because it circulates blood further and against a higher pressure (similar to the blood pressure). The right side circulates blood in the lower pressure pulmonary system, so it is thinner walled and smaller.

Valves

Two types of valves are located in the heart (see Fig. 19-3). They open and close to permit blood to flow forward in one direction instead of going backward during contraction. The two atrioventricular (AV) valves separate the atria from the ventricles: the *tricuspid valve* separates the right atrium and ventricle, while the *mitral valve* separates the left atrium and ventricle. The two semilunar valves separate the ventricles from the great vessels. The *pulmonic valve* lies between the right ventricle and pulmonary artery, while the *aortic valve* lies between the left ventricle and aorta. These valves are named after the vessel that they fill.

Heart Wall

The wall of the heart consists of three layers:

1 The thin *endocardium* lines the inside of the heart chambers and valves.
2 The thick muscular *myocardium* is the middle layer responsible for the pumping action of the heart.
3 The thin *epicardium* is a muscle layer on the outside of the heart.

The tough fibrous *pericardium* encloses and protects the heart. Its two layers contain a small amount of fluid for lubrication during pumping. The pericardium adheres to the great vessels, esophagus, sternum, and pleurae and is anchored to the diaphragm.

Coronary Arteries and Veins

The muscular heart needs its own blood supply. The coronary arteries arise from the base and branch out to the apex of the heart. The more muscular left side has a greater blood supply with two main arteries instead of one (Fig. 19-6). The left coronary and circumflex arteries supply the left side, and the right coronary artery supplies the right. The arteries fill when the heart relaxes. Cardiac veins empty deoxygenated blood into the coronary sinus at the base.

> **Clinical Significance 19-1**
>
> The coronary arteries may develop atherosclerotic plaques that narrow them, leading to a myocardial infarction (MI) or angina.

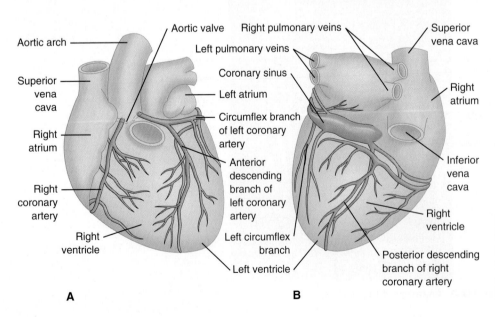

A **B**

Figure 19-6 The coronary arteries adjust the flow of oxygenated blood to the heart muscle according to metabolic needs. **A.** Anterior view. **B.** Posterior view.

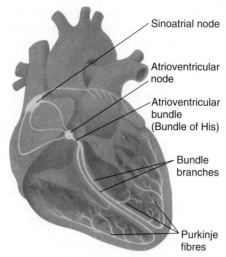

Figure 19-7 Outline of the path and involved structures of the cardiac conduction system.

Conduction System

A small electrical impulse that fires in the sinoatrial (SA) node in the right atrium generates the heartbeat. The SA node functions as the "pacemaker" of the heart (Fig. 19-7). The cells in the SA node are unique because they possess **automaticity** (a property that enables the heart to generate its own impulses). After it has been generated, the impulse moves through an electrical "wiring" pathway through the left and right atria (via intra-atrial pathways). The electrical impulse causes the atrial muscle cells to contract. Then the impulse pauses briefly at the AV junction, travels through the electrical pathways in the bundle of His and bundle branches in the left and right ventricles, and finally moves to the Purkinje fibres (see Fig. 19-7). This impulse causes the ventricular

muscle cells to contract. In healthy people, the rate of firing in the SA node determines ventricular contraction and pulse rate.

Physiology

Pulmonary and Systemic Circulation

The cardiovascular system is really a double-pump system with two major divisions: the pulmonary and systemic circulation. Blood that enters the right side circulates to the lungs; blood that enters the left side circulates to the body (see Fig. 19-6).

The *pulmonary artery* carries deoxygenated blood to the lungs. At the lungs, the blood picks up oxygen and releases carbon dioxide. The *pulmonary vein* delivers oxygenated blood to the left atrium, which circulates the blood to the left ventricle and then out to the systemic circulation. Note that this process is the opposite of other body areas, where arteries carry oxygenated blood and veins carry deoxygenated blood.

The systemic circulation supplies the tissues with oxygen and nutrients and returns waste to the central circulation for excretion. This is perfusion. The jugular veins and carotid arteries perfuse the brain and the superior vena cava, the subclavian arteries perfuse the upper limbs, and the inferior vena cava and thoracic aorta perfuse the lower limbs.

Cardiac Cycle

The continuous rhythmic movement of blood during contraction and relaxation of the heart is the *cardiac cycle*. Contraction of the ventricles is referred to as **systole**; relaxation of the ventricles is called **diastole** (Fig. 19-8).

Deoxygenated blood enters the right atrium from the superior and inferior vena cava. The right and left atria fill

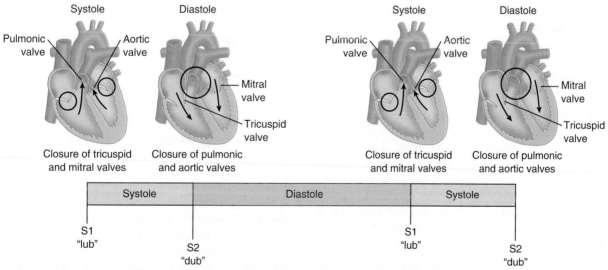

Figure 19-8 The cardiac cycle and heart sounds. Arrows represent the direction of blood flow. Closure of the mitral and tricuspid valves produces the first heart sound (S1, "lub"). Closure of the aortic and pulmonic valves produces the second heart sound (S2, "dub"). *Systole* is the phase between S1 and S2. *Diastole* is the phase between S2 and the next S1.

with blood until the SA node initiates atrial contraction by firing its pacemaker cells. When atrial contraction begins, the mitral and tricuspid valves open in response to the increased pressure. Blood moves from the atria into the ventricles.

As the impulse begins travelling down the bundle branches, it initiates ventricular contraction, leading to increased ventricular pressure. This increased pressure causes the mitral and tricuspid valves (between the atria and ventricles) to close. The closure of the valves is the *first heart sound* (S1).

The pulmonic and aortic valves open to allow blood to flow to the lungs and to the body, producing the pulse. Opening of these valves is usually silent (ie, no sounds are heard). As the ventricles finish contracting and start relaxing, pressure in the ventricles drops, and the aortic and pulmonic valves close (between the ventricles and great vessels). This causes the *second heart sound* (S2).

To summarize, S1, or "lub," results from closure of the mitral and tricuspid valves. S2, or "dub," results from closure of the aortic and pulmonic valves. Comprehension of this basic physiology is essential to understanding expected and unexpected heart sounds. If the nurse hears an unusual sound, he or she uses knowledge of physiology to determine where the pathophysiology may be.

Systole. During systole, the ventricles contract and eject blood to the lungs and body. The beginning of systole correlates with the pulse as blood is being circulated. During systole, the closed mitral and tricuspid valves prevent regurgitation (backflow) of blood into the atria. The aortic and pulmonic valves are open as blood moves forward.

Diastole. Diastole is twice as long as systole to allow time for the ventricles to fill. As the heart rate increases, however, length of diastole shortens and becomes approximately equal to systole.

During diastole the aortic and pulmonic valves are closed to prevent regurgitation of blood from the aorta and pulmonary artery into the ventricles. The open mitral and tricuspid valves allow filling from the atria to the ventricles. The three phases of ventricular filling are early filling, slow passive filling, and finally, during atrial systole, the "atrial kick." An additional 30% of blood is squeezed into the ventricles during the atrial kick.

Relation to Heart Sounds (S1 and S2). As mentioned, closure of the heart valves during the cardiac cycle causes healthy sounds. The "lub" sound of S1 signals the beginning of ventricular systole, while the "dub" sound of S2 signals the end of systole and beginning of diastole. Systole occurs between S1 and S2, while diastole occurs between S2 and the next S1. When the heart rate is faster than 100 beats/min, it may be necessary to identify S1 by palpating the pulse; the carotid upstroke occurs just prior to S2.

Cardiac Output. Volume in the right atrium at the end of diastole is called **preload**, an indicator of how much blood will be forwarded to and ejected from the ventricles. With increased blood in the right ventricle, force of contraction will be stronger, called **contractility**. The heart has to pump

against the high blood pressures in the arteries and arterioles. This pressure in the great vessels is termed **afterload**, similar to the pressure auscultated during blood pressure.

To review, preload is the amount of blood in the right atrium to be squeezed out at the beginning of the heart cycle. Contractility is the strength of the contraction in the actual heart muscle during systole, similar to having a strong muscle. Afterload is the resistance (amount of pressure) following ejection of blood from the ventricle, similar to the resistance in the arterioles with the blood pressure. These three factors influence how much blood is ejected with each beat or stroke, called **stroke volume**.

Cardiac output is the amount of blood ejected from the left ventricle each minute. In addition to stroke volume, the other factor that influences how much blood is circulated is heart rate. The formula is

$$\text{Cardiac output} = \text{Heart rate} \times \text{Stroke volume.}$$

The usual cardiac output is 6 to 8 L/min, or approximately 80 beats/min with 80 mL in each beat. Ways to increase circulating blood (cardiac output) are by increasing heart rate, stroke volume, or both. The stress hormones epinephrine and norepinephrine increase both heart rate and stroke volume during exercise, trauma, or anxiety. The heart is continually adjusting heart rate and stroke volume during daily activities to supply needed oxygen and nutrients to active tissues.

Clinical Significance 19-2

Reduced cardiac output is associated with the medical diagnosis of congestive heart failure. In this condition, reduced contractility causes preload to increase. Blood backs up, causing congestion. Congestion on the left backs blood into the lungs, while congestion on the right backs blood into the body, especially the legs and feet. Signs and symptoms of heart failure are shortness of breath, weight gain, and swollen ankles with decreased cardiac output.

Control of Heart Rate. The sympathetic and parasympathetic divisions of the nervous system control heart rate in response to stress and other variables (see Chapter 24). Overstimulation of the sympathetic division can cause heart rates that are too fast, while overstimulation of the parasympathetic division can cause rates that are too slow.

Stimulation of the sympathetic nervous system, or "fight versus flight" reactions, triggers the release of epinephrine (adrenalin) and norepinephrine. These neurotransmitters increase heart rate, contractility (to increase cardiac output), and blood pressure. The sympathetic division acts indirectly through baroreceptors and chemoreceptors. Baroreceptors in the aortic arch and carotid sinus regulate heart rate. Reduced baroreceptor stimulation (as with dehydration) increases sympathetic stimulation and subsequently heart rate. Chemoreceptors in the aortic arch and carotid body sense the body's pH, carbon dioxide, and oxygen levels. Accumulated acid or depleted oxygen levels stimulate the chemoreceptors, increasing heart rate.

The parasympathetic division, or "rest and repose" reaction, triggers a decreased heart rate by stimulating the vagus nerve that innervates the SA node to slow the natural pacemaker. The vagus nerve also slows conduction through the AV junction, which in turn slows the heart rate.

Relation to Electrocardiogram. Recall that the heart has a pacemaker (SA node) and electrical conduction system that transmits signals for the cardiac muscle cells to contract at 60 to 100 beats/min. This specialized "wiring" is a pathway similar to an electrical cord, by which signals travel quickly and efficiently to muscle cells. Once the signal is delivered, the muscle cells depolarize, causing filaments within to slide over one another and contract. Depolarization occurs when there is an exchange of electrolytes, including sodium and calcium. This shift in electrolytes causes electrical changes that can be detected by the **electrocardiogram** (ECG).

The ECG is measured through special patches placed in specific areas on the chest, arms, and legs. It records cellular depolarization primarily when sodium is released from the inside to the outside of cells. It also records when sodium shifts back into cells at the end of contraction. It records the electrical changes of contraction (depolarization) and relaxation (repolarization) as specific waves and intervals (Fig. 19-9):

- *P wave (atrial depolarization):* The spread of depolarization in the atria to cause atrial contraction (note that atrial repolarization is not seen because it is hidden when the ventricles contract in the QRS complex)
- *PR interval:* The time from firing of the SA node to the beginning of depolarization in the ventricle (includes a slight pause at the AV junction)
- *QRS complex (ventricular depolarization):* The spread of depolarization and sodium release in the ventricles to cause ventricular contraction
- *T wave (ventricular repolarization):* Relaxation of the ventricles and repolarization of the cells, with a return of sodium and restoration or recovery of the resting state.

Reading the ECG is an advanced skill used by nurses on cardiac and intensive care units. It takes practice and repetition to learn the usual variations and unexpected findings. Health care providers use information from the ECG to analyze assessment data and plan care (see later discussion).

Heart Rhythm. The heart rhythm is an important element to assess in addition to the heart rate. **Arrhythmias** are unexpected heart rhythms with early (premature), delayed, or irregular beats. They can arise from the atria, AV junction, or ventricles. The type of arrhythmia cannot be diagnosed from auscultation alone. Analysis of the ECG or rhythm strip that shows the electrical changes is necessary.

A type of rhythm common in older adults is called *atrial fibrillation.* In this situation, many sites in the atria send signals to the ventricles. The ventricles contract very irregularly, causing an irregular heart rhythm.

Many other types of heart arrhythmias can be diagnosed depending on where the impulse originates, how fast it is, and if it is continuous or intermittent. An irregular pulse indicates a need to test with an ECG or rhythm strip to diagnose the type of arrhythmia.

Jugular Pulsations

The venous neck vessels reflect the pressure in the right atrium because no valve exists between the right atrium and jugular veins. The jugular pulse has five pulsations resulting from the backward effects of activity in the heart. The waves reflect atrial contraction and relaxation, ventricular contraction, and passive atrial and ventricular filling (refer to Fig. 19-10).

🔺 Lifespan Considerations

Women Who Are Pregnant
Maternal blood volume increases throughout pregnancy, beginning in the first trimester and peaking at 40% to 45% (approximately 1,500 mL above the nonpregnant volume

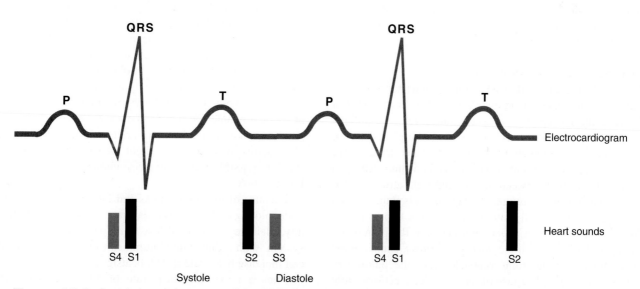

Figure 19-9 Correlation of the waves of the ECG with the cardiac cycle.

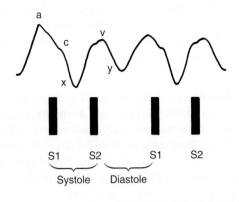

Jugular venous pulsations

S1   S2   S1   S2

Systole   Diastole

Jugular venous pressure curves

a = atrial contraction
c = carotid transmission not visible clinically
x = descent in right atrium following *a*
v = passive venous filling of atria from the vena cavae
y = descent during atrial resting phase before contraction

Figure 19-10 Jugular venous pressure curves.

close to term (London, Ladewig, et al., 2007). Volume may increase as much as 70% with a multiple pregnancy (Malone & D'Alton, 2004). Increased stroke volume and heart rate elevate cardiac output by 30% to 40% to keep up with the increased demands of supplying nutrients and oxygen to the developing fetus.

Cardiac output peaks at 30% to 50% greater than the nonpregnant state by approximately gestational week 32; it returns to prepregnancy levels about 2 weeks postpartum (Monga & Sanborn, 2004). Cardiac output is reduced when the mother is supine, because the uterus impedes venous return (Lowdermilk & Perry, 2007). This positioning may be significant enough to reduce blood pressure; it is recommended that women who are pregnant use a side-lying position. The left ventricle increases both the wall thickness and muscle mass. Also the uterus enlarges and pushes the diaphragm upward, and the position of the heart shifts more horizontally. Many of the changes in pregnancy are related to the large increase in blood volume.

Newborns and Infants

Before birth, the fetus depends on the mother for blood circulation. The placenta supplies both nutrients and oxygen because the fetus is not using the lungs yet. The umbilical vein and artery connect the fetus to the placenta. The umbilical vein connects to the inferior vena cava, which empties nutrient-rich blood into the right atrium. An open flap in the septum between the left and right atria is called the *foramen ovale*. Through this flap, blood is shunted from the right atrium directly into the left atrium, bypassing the lungs. Additionally, a connection between the pulmonary artery and aorta, called the *ductus arteriosis*, shunts blood that remains in the right ventricle from the pulmonary artery to the aorta. Because of these two connections, little blood circulates to the uninflated lungs. Blood then returns to the mother through the descending aorta to the umbilical arteries.

At birth, the newborn's lungs inflate with air, causing pulmonary vascular resistance to increase markedly. Along with clamping of the umbilical cord, this forces the pulmonary and systemic circuits to function separately. Within minutes to hours after birth, the atrial septum is pushed closed and right to left blood flow is established. Blood flow decreases in the ductus arteriosis, causing it to constrict and close within a few days, separating the pulmonary artery and aorta. In some congenital heart defects, the patent ductus arteriosis and foramen ovale remain open. If the openings are significant, they may need surgical repair.

The infant's blood pressure and arterial resistance increase when the umbilical cord is cut. Because of this increased work, the left ventricle hypertrophies and becomes more muscular than the right. By 1 year of age, the left ventricle is twice the size of the right, which is similar to adult size. The heart rate of the newborn is increased because the muscle has not yet developed and stroke volumes are lower. At birth the rate may be as high as 180 beats/min in response to stress or crying and decreases to approximately 120 beats/min at rest. The heart is positioned more horizontally in infants than in adults, which causes the apex to be in the 4th left ICS slightly lateral to the MCL (see Fig. 19-11).

Children and Adolescents

The heart grows and moves lower as the child's body changes. By 7 years of age, the child's heart is similar to an adult's. Both the left ventricular cavity size and wall thickness increase linearly with age. By 7 years, the apex is palpable in the 5th left ICS at the MCL.

Older Adults

With aging, the left ventricular wall thickens, most likely from the increased stress of pumping blood into stiffer vessels. The left atrium increases, and the mitral valve closes more slowly. The heart fills more slowly in early diastole but compensates by filling more quickly in late diastole during atrial contraction. In young hearts, approximately twice as much blood enters the ventricle during early diastolic filling compared to late diastole; in older hearts, blood flow is approximately equal during early and late diastole. Consequently, the volumes in the heart remain about the same as in younger people. During stress or exercise, younger people pump out more blood in the ventricle (ejection fraction); in older adults, there are only slight increases in the ejection fraction, possibly causing exercise intolerance (Bernhard & Laufer, 2008).

Because of fibrotic changes and fat deposits on the SA node, older adults have less heart rate variability. Additionally, their hearts respond less to the sympathetic nervous system, with reduced maximum heart rates. A 20-year-old can increase heart rate to 180 beats/min, while an 80-year-old has a maximum heart rate of 140 beats/min. The

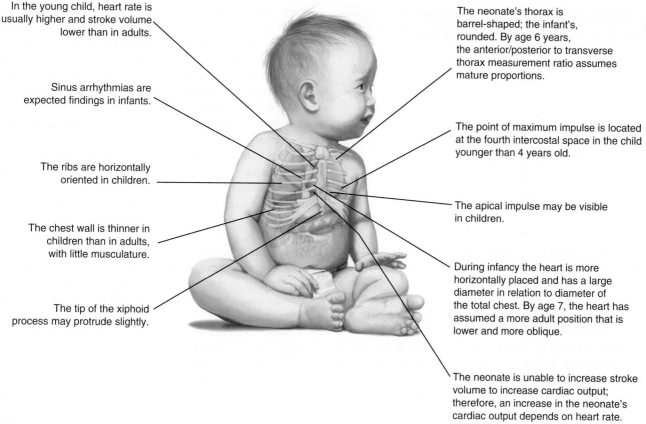

In the young child, heart rate is usually higher and stroke volume lower than in adults.

Sinus arrhythmias are expected findings in infants.

The ribs are horizontally oriented in children.

The chest wall is thinner in children than in adults, with little musculature.

The tip of the xiphoid process may protrude slightly.

The neonate's thorax is barrel-shaped; the infant's, rounded. By age 6 years, the anterior/posterior to transverse thorax measurement ratio assumes mature proportions.

The point of maximum impulse is located at the fourth intercostal space in the child younger than 4 years old.

The apical impulse may be visible in children.

During infancy the heart is more horizontally placed and has a large diameter in relation to diameter of the total chest. By age 7, the heart has assumed a more adult position that is lower and more oblique.

The neonate is unable to increase stroke volume to increase cardiac output; therefore, an increase in the neonate's cardiac output depends on heart rate.

Figure 19-11 Expected variations in cardiac anatomy and physiology in children.

formula for the expected maximum heart rate for age is 220 minus age in years (Dupuis-Blanchard, 2010). Receptors for stress hormones also may become less sensitive (Lakatta, 2002), making older adults less able to respond to stressors.

🌐 Cultural Considerations

Heart disease is the leading cause of death in high-income countries, and coronary heart disease contributes to approximately 50% of deaths from heart disease (National Heart, Lung, and Blood Institute, 2007). In Canada, Aboriginal peoples (First Nations, Inuit, and Métis) are at a greater risk of developing heart disease because of their likelihood of having high blood pressure and type 2 diabetes. Individuals of African and South Asian genetic background are also at greater risk for the same reasons (Heart and Stroke Foundation of Canada, 2010, 2011a,b).

According to the Heart and Stroke Foundation of Canada (2007), gender-related differences in symptoms of myocardial infarction (MI) may not be as pronounced as some of the literature suggests. What might be occurring is that there are differences in how men and women *report* symptoms. It is vital for nurses to be alert to the similarities and differences raised by the research. According to Pilote, Dasgupta, et al. (2007), women and men do

present with heart disease differently. Prodromal symptoms in women commonly include indigestion, anxiety, shortness of breath, disturbances in sleep, fatigue, back pain, or headache (McSweeney, Cody, et al., 2003; Norris, Dasgupta, et al., 2007). Individuals who may present with atypical symptoms are those with heart failure, diabetes, female gender, and age over 65 years (Barkmann & Porth, 2010). Women with diabetes have a significantly higher cardiovascular mortality rate than men with diabetes. Also women with atrial fibrillation are at greater risk for stroke than their male counterparts. Clinically significant heart failure is increasing in women. In older populations, much greater numbers of women develop heart failure (Dupuis-Blanchard, 2010). Women are also more likely to live with more cardiovascular disabilities and have a lower health-related quality of life than are men (Norris, Ghali, et al., 2004). Historically, women have been underrepresented in randomized clinical trials. The lack of complete evidence concerning gender-specific outcomes has led to assumptions about treatment in women, which may have resulted in inadequate diagnoses, suboptimal treatment, and less favourable outcomes. Mortality rates in men have steadily declined, while mortality rates in women have remained stable over the past decade (Pilote, Dasgupta, et al., 2007). The incidence of cardiovascular disease increases with age for both men and women.

Acute Assessment

△ *SAFETY ALERT 19-1*

If the patient is experiencing chest pain, dyspnea, cyanosis, diaphoresis, or dizziness, the nurse focuses assessment on collecting data so that the interprofessional team can resolve the underlying condition. The nurse gathers information while treatments are performed, including administration of oxygen and nitroglycerin tablets sublingually as ordered. If chest pain continues, the nurse requests help, because more than one person may be necessary to collect data and intervene appropriately.

Cardiac emergencies necessitate rapid assessment and intervention. They include *acute coronary syndrome, acute severe heart failure, hypertensive crisis, cardiac tamponade, unstable cardiac arrhythmias, cardiogenic shock, systemic or pulmonary embolism*, and *dissecting aortic aneurysm*. Patients with these conditions may have chest pain, shortness of breath, too high or too low blood pressure, or inadequate tissue perfusion. Initial assessment includes an analysis of the presenting symptom/sign (location, radiation, quality or nature, intensity, timing, associated symptoms, alleviating and aggravating factors, environmental factors, significance to the patient, and patient perspective on what is happening); a focused physical examination of the cardiovascular and respiratory systems; an ECG; and a chest x-ray. Selected laboratory tests are done emergently to evaluate for cardiac muscle damage, embolism, or electrolyte imbalance. Interprofessional team members perform interventions while gathering assessment data because prompt treatment is essential.

Accurate assessment of patients with cardiovascular conditions is critical, because nurses are often the health care providers who first identify unexpected findings. Nurses play a key role in assessment of chest pain and assist in gathering data so that the source is quickly identified and treated. Differential diagnosis of chest pain is important, because ischemic cardiac pain involves loss of muscle cells that can cause further damage if left untreated. An accurate description of the pain and alleviating or aggravating factors is often pivotal to identifying the source.

The Public Health Agency of Canada reports that Canadians postpone seeking medical care for their symptoms related to MI by about 5 hours. This has relevance for health promotion and for primary care nurses. Approximately 50% of deaths from MI will occur in the first 2 hours of experiencing symptoms. Among the recommendations of the Heart and Stroke Foundation of Canada are to

- call 911 or the local emergency number
- not drive
- suspend all physical activity
- rest comfortably in a sitting position
- take the usual dosage of nitroglycerin if on this drug
- chew, followed by swallowing, one 325 mg aspirin tablet (Roach, Roddick, et al., 2010).

Other assessments that assume priority are related to arrhythmias. Nurses quickly determine the effects of the arrhythmia by evaluating level of consciousness and obtaining the blood pressure as an indicator of peripheral perfusion. If level of consciousness, blood pressure, or both are decreased, nurses page the rapid-response team. Nurses who work frequently with patients who have cardiac conditions must think quickly, because the status of such individuals often changes rapidly.

Fluid volume overload and severe heart failure that leads to pulmonary edema also are priorities. Nurses evaluate the significance of volume overload by auscultating lung sounds, measuring respiratory rate, and obtaining an oxygen saturation level. Infectious or inflammatory disorders (eg, endocarditis, pericarditis) are evaluated by assessing related findings, such as fever, heart sounds, and pain. Patients with cardiac disease are frequently aware of subtle symptoms that indicate improving or worsening status; they can often provide valuable data that assist in accurate diagnosis and treatment.

Nurses organize data according to the clustering of signs and symptoms related to a specific condition (see Table 19-1). For example, if a nurse identifies a new murmur, he or she completes assessments that relate to fluid volume overload. Examples include weighing the patient, evaluating intake and output, auscultating lung sounds for fluid, and inspecting and palpating the extremities for edema. The nurse then analyzes findings to determine the effects of the murmur on the patient's physical and functional status.

Subjective Data Collection

Assessment of Risk Factors

Health promotion activities related to the cardiovascular system focus on preventing heart disease, identifying any conditions related to the heart and blood vessels early, and reducing complications of existing or newly established diagnoses. Important health habits to emphasize include following a low-fat, low-sodium, high-fibre diet; exercising regularly; regular screening for diabetes and cholesterol; management of stress; and not smoking (Dupuis-Blanchard, 2010). When questioning patients about risk factors, the nurse's goal is to identify how likely they are to develop or to already be experiencing the consequences of cardiovascular diseases. Such investigation creates an environment in which health care providers can implement necessary interventions to control symptoms, direct education to prevent complications or new health issues, and establish in the patient health record the areas needing ongoing follow-up and emphasis. For example, smoking, high blood pressure, physical inactivity, and diabetes mellitus are major contributors to heart disease (EPIC-Potsdam, 2007). Nurses address these risks in the health history interview. After assessment, nurses identify focused teaching areas and evaluate the patient's ongoing progress in controlling modifiable risks.

Table 19-1   **Differential Diagnosis of Chest Pain**

Condition	Significant Findings in the History	Symptoms	Aggravating Factors	Alleviating Factors
Myocardial infarction (MI)	Cardiac risk factors	Chest pain or discomfort in men; fatigue and shortness of breath in women lasting >20 min Accompanied by nausea and diaphoresis	Anxiety, physical exertion	Nitroglycerin; thrombolytic medication or angioplasty are necessary to prevent damage
Stable angina	Cardiac risk factors	Discomfort lasting <20 min	Cold, fatigue, physical exertion	Nitroglycerin and rest
Unstable angina	Cardiac risk factors	Discomfort lasting >20 min	Occurs at rest	Nitroglycerin; no relation to activity
Gastrointestinal disease: esophageal, gastritis, biliary	History of ulcer, reflux, or gallbladder disease	Described as indigestion, difficulty swallowing, burning, acid stomach; biliary pain may be colicky or cramping	Food intolerances, large or fatty meals	Antacids
Pulmonary disease/pleural chest pain	History of lung disease, pneumonia	Stabbing or grating pain, typically at the bases of the lungs	Worse with deep inhalation or coughing	Splinting chest, nonsteroidal anti-inflammatory medications
Musculoskeletal	History of trauma, such as CPR, musculoskeletal history	Muscle tenderness with palpation, located near joints or costochondral cartilages, chronic	Increased movement	Rest
Aortic dissection	Cardiovascular disease	Middle or upper abdominal pain, ischemic pain in legs	Not relieved until treated	Measures to increase perfusion
Pericardial pain	History of cardiac inflammation, such as with MI	Described as stabbing	Position changes, such as leaning forward	Nonsteroidal anti-inflammatory medications

Questions to Assess History and Risk Factors	Rationale
Obtain the following information from the patient health record: • Age • Heredity (genetic background) • Gender • Date and result of last blood pressure measurement • Date and result of last cholesterol level • Date and result of last C-reactive protein level • Date and result of B-type natriuretic peptides (BNPs) • Thyroid levels • Height and weight (needed to calculate the body mass index [BMI]) • Abdominal circumference (see Chapter 8)	Increased age, male gender, hypertension, and genetic background (Aboriginal, South Asian, African) are risk factors for *cardiovascular disease*. Risk of cardiovascular events more than doubles with elevated cholesterol and C-reactive protein levels (Ridker, Rifai, et al., 2002). BNPs are both sensitive and specific to *heart failure* (Chen & Burett, 2007). Hyperthyroidism has been linked to *atrial fibrillation,* but not to cardiovascular disease or mortality (Cappola, Fried, et al., 2006). Obesity creates a major risk for cardiovascular disease. A high-fat, high-sodium diet and physical inactivity contribute to obesity.
Past Medical History Have you ever been diagnosed with a heart condition such as chest pain? Heart attack? Heart failure? Or irregular rhythm?	A history of past concerns provides information that can assist with anticipating future needs.
Has anyone ever told you that you have high blood pressure? • What is the usual range for your blood pressure? • Do you take anything for it?	In untreated hypertension, the risk of dying from cardiac disease is approximately twice as high as if the systolic pressure were within expected range (Benetos, Thomas, et al., 2002).

(text continues on page 504)

Questions to Assess History and Risk Factors	Rationale

Has anyone ever told you that you have high blood cholesterol?
- What are your usual levels?
- Do you take anything for it?

Patients with an elevated low-density lipoprotein ("bad") cholesterol level are twice as likely to develop cardiovascular disease (Taubert, Winkelmann, et al., 2003).

Do you have a history of diabetes mellitus?
- What is your usual blood glucose level?
- Do you take anything for it?

Patients with diabetes mellitus are approximately twice as likely to develop cardiovascular disease (Taubert, Winkelmann, et al., 2003).

Medications

Are you taking any medications for heart conditions?
- What are they?
- How often are you taking them?
- How well are you able to follow your prescribed medication regimen?

Note the drug, dose, and frequency. Obtaining the reason for the medication is important, because some drugs have several purposes. Ability to take medications as prescribed is essential to review, because many cardiac medications have side effects that cause patients to stop taking them.

Are you taking any natural supplements? Or over-the-counter medications?
- What are they?
- How often do you take them?

Some supplements, such as ephedrine, may have cardiac side effects. Also note any potential drug interactions between prescribed and over-the-counter or herbal remedies.

Family History

Do you have any family history of heart concerns?
- What was the illness?
- When did the person have it?
- How was the illness treated?
- What were the outcomes?

Premature coronary artery disease in a first- or second-degree relative increases the patient's risk for the same disorder. *First degree* refers to sibling, parent, or child—ie, someone who shares 50% of the genes of the patient; *second degree* refers to grandparent, aunt, uncle, grandchild, or half sibling—ie, someone who shares 25% of the genes with the patient. Premature onset is before 55 years in men and before 65 years in women. Evidence suggests that premature coronary artery disease in siblings is a stronger risk than in parents or grandparents (Murabito, Pencina, et al., 2005; Nasir, Michos, et al., 2004). Also assess family history for risk factors such as high blood pressure, high cholesterol, diabetes, heart disease, and obesity.

Lifestyle and Behavioural Issues

Do you smoke cigarettes? Or use other tobacco products?
- How long?
- How many packs per day?

Smokers are two to four times more likely to develop *coronary heart disease* and are twice as likely to have sudden cardiac arrest (American Heart Association, 2005).

What is your usual weight? How do you feel about your weight?

Being overweight is not independently associated with an increased risk of dying from cardiovascular disease; associated variables such as diabetes, high blood pressure, and high cholesterol also may contribute (Romero-Corral, Montori, et al., 2006).

What is your usual level of physical activity?
- Do you exercise?
- What type?
- How long and how often?

A low level of activity is associated with an increased risk for cardiovascular disease (Barkmann & Porth, 2010). Physical activity can help control blood cholesterol, diabetes, and obesity, as well as help lower blood pressure. Assess occupational activities, commuting patterns, and recreational exercise to determine how much these factors contribute to overall physical activity.

What is your typical diet?

A diet low in fruits and vegetables and high in fat, salt, and cholesterol is associated with an increased risk of cardiovascular disease (Barkmann & Porth, 2010).

How much alcohol do you usually drink per day? Week? Month?
Do you use any recreational drugs such as cocaine?

Drinking more than two drinks of alcohol per day for men or one drink of alcohol per day for women can raise blood pressure and contribute to *heart failure.* It also can elevate triglyceride levels, contribute to obesity, and produce irregular heartbeats. Cocaine increases the risk of *myocardial infarction (MI) and coronary vasospasm* (Barkmann & Porth, 2010).

Risk Assessment and Health Promotion

Topics for Health Promotion

- Smoking cessation
- Control of blood pressure and cholesterol
- Dietary intake (fat, sodium, alcohol)
- Weight control
- Physical activity
- Metabolic syndrome
- Stress management
- Hormone therapy

Risk assessment helps health care providers give patients information that can positively influence their behavioural choices. Priorities for public health are both primary prevention (with individuals who have no evidence of cardiovascular disease) and secondary prevention (early detection using blood pressure, cholesterol screening, and ECGs). The most important cardiovascular focus areas are the modifiable risk factors of smoking, high blood pressure, high cholesterol levels, high-fat and high-salt diet, overweight or obesity, stress levels, and physical inactivity.

Smoking Cessation

Nurses ask patients who smoke about their willingness to quit at every visit. Individuals who quit reduce their risk of cardiac events by 50% after the first year (American Heart Association, 2005). Nurses can give patients choices about tools to help them quit, such as referrals to behavioural therapy, information about support groups, or medication. Resources to stop smoking are available from the Canadian Cancer Society and the Canadian Council for Tobacco Control.

Control of Blood Pressure and Cholesterol Level

High blood pressure should be controlled with medication if diet, exercise, and weight reduction are unsuccessful. Patients may not continue to use prescribed medications because of side effects, for example, erectile dysfunction or difficulty following the schedule. Nurses might suggest a simplified dosing regimen to improve acceptance (Schroeder, Fahey, et al., 2004). With Aboriginal populations, they can recommend *Eating Well With Canada's Food Guide —First Nations, Inuit, and Métis*, which is informed by scientific evidence.

High cholesterol can also be modified by eating a low-cholesterol diet, with reduced animal fat intake and increased intake of protein from beans, fish, and lentils. Lean cuts of grilled or roasted meat are better than deep-fried, fatty cuts. Dietary changes can usually lower cholesterol by only 5% to 10% (Pasternak, Sidney, et al., 2002). If diet alone is unsuccessful, the physician may prescribe a statin drug, which reduces the risk of cardiovascular events by approximately 30% (Pasternak, Sidney, et al.).

Control of Weight and Stress

To assess weight-related health issues, nurses include measurement of waist circumference and body mass index (BMI). Waist circumference should be <102 cm in men and <88 cm in women. The BMI calculations are constrained when nurses are assessing women who are pregnant, adults over 65 years of age, very muscular individuals, and breast-feeding women (Roach, Roddick, et al., 2010). A sedentary lifestyle contributes to weight issues. Research is demonstrating that 30 to 60 minutes of physical activity most days reduces cardiovascular risks (Roach, Roddick, et al.). A heart healthy diet supports control of weight and is rich in vegetables and fruits, nonanimal protein, whole grains, low-fat dairy products, and low in sodium <1,500 mg per day (see Chapter 8) and alcohol (no more than 1 drink/day for women, 2 drinks/day for men) (Roach, Roddick, et al.).

Stress causes a variety of physiologic responses (neurologic and hormonal) and has a strong link to cardiovascular events. Nurses discuss the sources of stress with their patients and identify their negative and positive emotions (Norris & Clark, 2010). Any emotional situation, including a stressful situation, brings about the release of catecholamines and cortisol and causes an increase in the heart rate, blood pressure, and workload of the myocardium (Clark & Norris, 2010). Nurses assist patients to identify trigger situations, for example, marital discord, work deadlines, and to select more appropriate coping mechanisms such as improving communication skills or making personal schedules that reduce procrastination. Nurses work with their patients to help them identify both psychologic and physiologic stressors in their life (Williams, 2010).

Focused Health History Related to Common Symptoms/Signs

Nurses assess some common symptoms in all patients to screen for early signs of cardiac disease. If individuals are concerned about cardiac conditions, nurses can use these concerns to identify focused areas of assessment. A thorough history of cardiovascular symptoms assists with identifying the current issue or situation.

Common Cardiovascular Symptoms/Signs

- Pain (chest, jaw, left shoulder, left arm)
- Shortness of breath (dyspnea, orthopnea, paroxysmal nocturnal dyspnea [PND])
- Cough
- Heavy sweating (diaphoresis)
- Fatigue or weakness
- Light-headedness
- Nausea and/or vomiting
- Swelling (edema)
- Urinating during night (nocturia)
- Racing heart (tachycardia, palpitations, skipped beats)
- Indigestion or heartburn (pyrosis)

Example of Questions for Symptom/Sign Analysis—Chest Pain

- "Point to where the pain is." "Does it radiate?" "Where does it radiate?" (Location, radiating)
- "Describe your chest pain." "Is it crushing?" "Does it feel like there is something heavy on your chest?" (Quality)
- "Rate your chest pain on a scale of 0–10, with 0 being no pain and 10 being the worst pain you can imagine." "Does chest pain ever wake you up at night?" (Severity)
- "When did you start having chest pain?" "What kinds of activities bring on the pain?" (Onset)
- "Has the chest pain been present since it first started?" "How long does your chest pain last?" (Duration)
- "Have there been times that the pain seemed less?" (Constancy)
- "Is there a time of day that the pain seems worse? Or better?" (Time of day/month/year)

- "What makes the pain worse?" "Does it happen when you exert yourself?" (Aggravating factors)
- "What makes it better?" (Alleviating factors)
- "Do you have any other symptoms with your chest pain?" "Shortness of breath?" "Sweating?" "Palpitations?" "Nausea?" (Associated symptoms)
- "Have you had any recent changes in your life?" "Describe the amount of stress in your life right now." "Have you been exposed to any chemicals or other substances?" (Environmental factors)
- "How is this chest pain affecting your life?" (Significance to patient)
- "What do you think may be causing your chest pain?" (Patient perspective)

Adapted from Roach, S., Roddick, P., et al. (2010). The cardiovascular system. In T. C. Stephen, D. L. Skillen, R. A. Day, & L. S. Bickley (Eds.). *Canadian Bates' guide to health assessment for nurses* (1st ed., p. 436). Philadelphia, PA: Wolters Kluwer Health/Lippincott Williams & Wilkins.

Examples of Questions to Assess Symptoms/Signs	Rationale/Unexpected Findings
△ *SAFETY ALERT 19-2* *All health care providers should assume that the patient's chest pain is heart pain until another cause can be found. If chest pain is ischemic, rapid treatment is necessary to prevent the death of cardiac cells. If medication or angioplasty can open the artery, the size of the myocardial infarction (MI) can be reduced.*	Heart pain indicates ischemic heart tissue and, if unrelieved after 20 minutes, can cause cell death and MI.
Chest Pain • Have you tried any treatments for the pain? Did they help? Have you taken any nitroglycerin? How many tablets and how far apart? • What were you doing when you noticed the pain? • What would you like to be able to do that you are unable to do because of the pain?	The pain of *MI* typically is on the left side of the chest, radiates to the jaw, left shoulder, or down the left arm, and is diffused rather than localized. Onset can be sudden or gradual. Patients often describe the pain as crushing or vise-like. Others may not identify ischemia as pain but rather as pressure or discomfort, such as "having an elephant on the chest." Some patients become nauseous and vomit; others describe indigestion resulting from cardiac ischemia. Associated symptoms include diaphoresis, pallor, anxiety, and fatigue. Palpitations, tachycardia, and dyspnea may also be present. Only one third of women with acute MI report having this typical chest pain (McSweeney, Cody, et al., 2003). *Angina* is temporary heart pain, resolving in <20 minutes. It can be aggravated by physical activity and stress, or there may be no triggers (unstable angina). Chest pain may also be from pulmonary, musculoskeletal, or gastrointestinal origin. Factors that aggravate or alleviate the pain may help identify the cause. Nitroglycerin often relieves angina (and esophageal spasm that mimics heart pain), while an antacid may relieve pain from reflux. Patients exhibit gestures such as a closed fist or palm on the chest in only approximately 50% of cases, so these signs are not particularly useful in diagnosing angina or MI (Marcus, Cohen, et al., 2007). (Refer to Table 19-1 for the differential diagnosis of chest pain.)
Dyspnea • Do any other symptoms accompany the shortness of breath? • Have you tried any treatments for the shortness of breath? Did they help? • Is it better or worse when compared to 6 months ago?	Patients with *heart failure* may be short of breath from fluid accumulation in the pulmonary bed. Onset may be sudden with *acute* or *chronic pulmonary edema*.

It is important to assess how much activity brings on dyspnea, such as rest, walking on a flat surface, or climbing. **Dyspnea on exertion** is common with physical activity. Note the amount of activity that elicits dyspnea, such as four stairs or one block. Fatigue, chest pain, or diaphoresis may accompany dyspnea. Typically, resting alleviates it; if not, there may be another cause such as worsening *heart failure, pulmonary embolism,* or *MI*. Women are more likely to have dyspnea than chest pain as an acute symptom of MI (McSweeney, Cody, et al., 2003).

Orthopnea and Paroxysmal Nocturnal Dyspnea
• How many pillows do you sleep on at night?
• Do you wake in the night short of breath?
• Have you had difficulty sleeping?

Patients with *heart failure* may have fluid in their lungs, making it difficult to breathe when lying flat (orthopnea). Fluid "backs up" into the pulmonary veins, the heart cannot keep up with the volume, and fluid leaks into the lungs. Patients also may wake up suddenly as the fluid is redistributed from edematous legs into the lungs (paroxysmal nocturnal dyspnea or PND), typically after a few hours of sleep. They may waken feeling tired, anxious, or restless.

Approximately 50% of women report difficulty sleeping 1 month prior to an acute *MI* (McSweeney, Cody, et al., 2003).

Cough
• Is it better or worse when compared to 1 month ago?
• Do you cough anything up?
• What colour is it?

Coughing occurs for the same reason as dyspnea. The cough may produce white or pink blood-tinged mucus. Mild wheezing also may occur. Treatment with an angiotensin-converting enzyme inhibitor also can cause the side effect of a dry, hacking cough.

Diaphoresis
Have you noticed any excessive sweating?
• When? Is it during any particular activities?
• Are there any associated symptoms such as heart pounding? Or chest pain?

Night-time diaphoresis is associated with other diseases, such as *tuberculosis*. Diaphoresis in response to exercise or activity may be related to cardiac stress. Diaphoresis associated with chest pain or palpitations is an autonomic response of the body to stress.

Fatigue
• When did the feeling start?
• What is going on in your life that might cause it?
• Do you wake up feeling fatigued?
• How much salt (sodium) is in your diet?

Fatigue occurs because the heart cannot pump enough blood to meet the needs of tissues. The body diverts blood away from less vital organs, particularly limb muscles, and distributes it to the heart and brain. Common activities that might cause fatigue include shopping, climbing stairs, carrying groceries, and walking. Seventy percent of women report unusual fatigue 1 month before *acute MI* (McSweeney, Cody, et al., 2003). It is the most common symptom of MI in women.

Edema
Are your shoes fitting tight?
• Does the swelling change with the time of day? Or night?
• What have you done to try to relieve the swelling?

When blood flow out of the heart is reduced, blood returning to the heart through the veins "backs up," causing fluid to accumulate in the organs and dependent areas of the body. Blood flow to the kidneys is also reduced, decreasing excretion of sodium and water and causing further fluid retention in the tissues. Usually, standing exacerbates leg edema, while elevating the legs above heart level reduces it. Patients who retain fluid may also notice weight gain.

Nocturia
Do you need to get up at night to use the bathroom?
• How often?
• Have you altered what you do because of this?

Nocturia is a common symptom associated with redistribution of fluid from the legs to the core when lying. As the fluid shifts, the kidneys are better perfused, increasing urine production. Patients may avoid drinking water after dinner because of this or they may skip their diuretic when going out for dinner.

(text continues on page 508)

Additional Questions	**Rationale/Unexpected Findings**

Palpitations

Are you having skipped or extra beats? Faster heartbeats?

- What are you doing when they start? How long do they last?
- What do you do to try and stop them?

Patients with *cardiovascular disease* may have tachycardia from decreased contractile strength of the heart muscle. With reduced stroke volume, the pulse increases to maintain cardiac output. Palpitations experienced as a rapid throbbing or fluttering of the heart may be associated with *arrhythmias. Patients* tolerate these arrhythmias differently, ranging from a mild awareness of the sensation to more severe dizziness or loss of consciousness.

> ⚠ *SAFETY ALERT 19-3*
>
> *Patients with a history of loss of consciousness should have a complete workup to diagnose the cause. They are at risk for falling and require fall precautions.*

Documentation of Expected Findings

Reports no chest pain or discomfort. Denies dyspnea, orthopnea, PND, cough, fatigue, edema, nocturia, and palpitations.

 ## Lifespan Considerations

Additional Questions	**Rationale/Unexpected Findings**

Women Who Are Pregnant

- Have you noticed your pulse or blood pressure changing during pregnancy?
- Have you had any swelling in your face or hands?
- What medications are you taking?
- Are you taking any alcohol or drugs during this pregnancy?

Typically, heart rate rises in pregnancy from increased blood volumes and demands. Swelling may indicate the beginning of *pregnancy-induced hypertension* (eclampsia) and should be monitored. Risk for *congenital anomalies* increases when the mother takes lithium, dilantin, thalidomide, or excessive alcohol during pregnancy. Additional risks include maternal rubella, lupus, or diabetes mellitus in pregnancy (Lowdermilk & Perry, 2007).

Newborns and Infants

- Did you have any complications during your pregnancy or labour?
- Do you notice any shortness of breath? Fast breathing? Unusual skin colour? Or fatigue in your baby?
- How is your baby feeding?

The baby may have signs of cyanosis or pallor, dyspnea, fatigue, and difficulty feeding or growing related to heart defects.

Children and Adolescents

- Do you or does anyone in your family have a congenital heart condition?
- Do you notice any shortness of breath, unusual skin colour, or fatigue in your child?
- Do you notice that your child squats or sits down to rest?
- Can your child keep up with friends when active?
- Is your child gaining weight and growing as you would expect for your child's age?

If one parent has a congenital anomaly, the risk of a child also having one may be as high as 10% (Lowdermilk & Perry, 2007).

Children with cardiac disorders that reduce blood flow may sit down to increase cardiac output. Defects that allow a left to right shunt result in increased pulmonary volumes and heart failure. Obstructive defects prevent blood from being pumped from the ventricles. Obstruction on the left results in backup into the lungs and periphery with symptoms of heart failure; obstruction on the right causes cyanosis and hypoxemia because blood does not move forward for oxygenation. Defects that reduce pulmonary blood flow also produce cyanosis.

Additional Questions	Rationale/Unexpected Findings
Older Adults • Have you noticed any changes in your ability to tolerate activity? • Have you had any periods where you felt dizzy or faint? Or actually passed out? • Have you been short of breath? Or had trouble breathing at night?	Age-related changes may cause decreased activity tolerance. *Arrhythmias and heart failure* are common conditions for nurses to assess with people of this age group.
Cultural Considerations • What do you do to keep your heart healthy? • How would you describe your general health? • Do you ever worry about heart disease?	Asking general questions may identify areas in which people of various cultural groups have different perceptions of heart health and risk for disease. Such questions may also provide an opportunity to educate patients and clarify misperceptions. For example, although heart disease is the number one cause of mortality in women with African heritage, studies have shown that they generally do not perceive this as a threat and are less likely to modify risk factors (Jones, Weaver, et al., 2006).

An Example of a Therapeutic Dialogue

Remember Mrs. Anne Lewis, introduced at the beginning of this chapter. She arrived at the emergency room with chest pain and was admitted to the hospital 4 hours ago. She is experiencing some anxiety about a diagnosis of myocardial infarction (MI). The nurse is meeting Mrs. Lewis for the first time at the start of the shift. In addition to obtaining an assessment, the nurse provides support and listens to the patient's responses to reduce anxiety.

Nurse: Tell me a little about what brought you to the hospital today.

Mrs. Lewis: I was taking a walk in my neighbourhood and all of a sudden it felt like there was an elephant sitting on my chest. I couldn't breathe and had to stop. I was close to home, and when I got there my husband knew that something was wrong and called 911.

Nurse: Tell me more about what you were feeling.

Mrs. Lewis: I've never felt anything like it before. It was right in the middle of my chest, and it didn't go away until the paramedics gave me a nitroglycerin tablet and aspirin. It must have lasted about 20 minutes. I was so glad that they came fast. It was the worst pain that I've ever had. I felt all clammy and kind of dizzy.

Nurse: That must have been very scary for you.

Mrs. Lewis: I'm still scared. Do you think that I had a heart attack?

Critical Thinking Challenge

• Is this an appropriate time to perform a complete health history and review of systems? Provide rationale.
• What therapeutic communication techniques did the nurse use?
• Why is the nurse more focused on Mrs. Lewis's experience than on assessment of her symptoms?
• How might the nurse respond to Mrs. Lewis's question about the diagnosis of heart attack? Provide rationale.

Objective Data Collection

Equipment

- Stethoscope with bell and diaphragm, and equipment wipes
- Sphygmomanometer
- Watch with second hand
- Two metric rulers
- Penlight or examination light for visualizing neck veins
- Scale (weight and height)
- Doppler

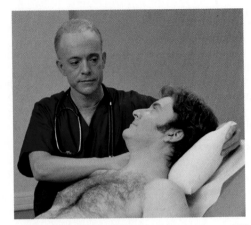

Figure 19-12 Lower the head of the bed to a 45° angle to better visualize the soft jugular venous pulses.

Promoting Patient Comfort, Dignity, and Safety

Evaluation of the neck vessels and heart requires contact with and exposure of the thorax. If possible, patients should wear a gown. Provide a drape to cover the patient when exposure of the chest is necessary. Ensure that the room is a comfortable temperature and take measures to facilitate a private and quiet setting. Wash and warm your hands to avoid spreading infection and to facilitate patient comfort.

For inspection, expose only the area of the chest that needs examination, especially for women. When visualization is required, gather the gown from the bottom to the shoulders so that the patient feels less exposed anteriorly. Cover the anterior chest when inspecting posteriorly. Explain the rationale for the need to expose the chest to ease the patient's anxiety.

If a heart condition is suspected, it may be necessary to listen to the heart in several different positions. Alert the patient that he or she will need to turn to the left or sit up to improve the volume and quality of the sounds. Also alert the patient that you will be listening for a longer period than usual and that doing so does not mean you have found something unexpected. Provide reassurance by saying, "I'm going to listen to your heart sounds carefully, but it doesn't mean that anything is wrong. I will let you know what I hear when I am finished."

Patient positioning is important for the cardiac examination. The patient may be sitting during auscultation of the carotid arteries. To evaluate the jugular pulses, lower the head of the bed to a 30° or 45° angle to allow for visualization of the softer impulses (Fig. 19-12). Most beds and examination tables have an indicator of the degree of elevation underneath to identify 30° and 45°. The jugular pulse on the right side is usually easier to identify, so it is most efficient and accurate for the examiner to stand on the patient's right. When auscultating the heart sounds, the patient may be sitting or lying (supine). Additionally, if there are concerns about cardiac conditions, the heart can be auscultated with the patient supine, in the left lateral position, or leaning forward.

Studies have shown that a stethoscope can transmit bacteria among patients (Marinella, Pierson, et al., 1997). Be sure to clean the diaphragm of the stethoscope with the equipment wipe before bringing the diaphragm into contact with the patient. Also, warm the diaphragm of the stethoscope with your clean hands prior to placing it on the chest.

Comprehensive Physical Examination: Cardiovascular System

Techniques and Expected Findings	Rationale/Unexpected Findings
Jugular Venous Pulses **Inspection** The jugular venous pulses are subtle, making their inspection challenging to learn. Accurate inspection requires practice and visualization with several patients, because chest size and shape and appearance of the jugular veins vary greatly. The jugular venous pulses have a waveform previously described. Rather than identify all the waves, nurses in clinical settings more commonly observe the pattern and rhythm.	If severe *heart failure* is suspected, invasive hemodynamic monitoring may be used. This waveform is often analyzed to identify the waves, pressures, and characteristics. These advanced techniques are used primarily in the intensive care setting.

Position the patient with the head of the bed at 30° or 45° to promote visibility of the pulsation (see Fig. 19-12). Raising the head slightly on a pillow relaxes the sternomastoid muscles for your inspection. Move any long hair in patients away to enhance visibility. The right side of the patient is easiest to see; it may help to have the patient turn the head away slightly from the side being examined. Use oblique (indirect) lighting from a 45° angle to emphasize the shadows of the pulsations. The external veins cross diagonally over the sternomastoid muscles and the pulsations are best observed in the groove near the middle of the clavicle. Do not confuse the undulating quality of the internal jugular pulsations (usually with two elevations and two descents) with the strong thrust of the carotid pulsations. The internal vein is not visible, but the pulsations are transmitted to the soft tissue and are usually most prominent in the suprasternal notch, the supraclavicular fossa, or just below the earlobe. If the pulsation is not visible, it may be necessary to lower the head of the bed. When learning to distinguish between the more subtle pulsations of the jugular veins, it may help to use a hand to shield the more prominent carotid pulsations and isolate the fluttery venous pulsations. *There are usually two pulsations with two descents, compared to the carotid pulse, which has one pulsation—a prominent ascent with systole.*

If the patient is unusually dehydrated (hypovolemic), it may be necessary to lower the head of the bed to visualize the vein, while the patient with fluid overload (hypervolemia) may need to have the head of the bed elevated. At times the neck veins are so distended that they extend all the way to the ear; in this case, raise the head of the bed until the pulsation is visible. Alternatively, patients with *dehydration* or *volume depletion* have barely visible neck veins, even when lying flat. These are described as flat neck veins.

Jugular Venous Pressures

Inspection

After locating the internal jugular vein in the sternal notch, identify the top height of the pulsation. If the internal vein is difficult to visualize, use the more prominent external vein. Locate the sternal angle, a bony ridge where the manubrium joins the body of the sternum (see Chapter 18 for technique). Using a line parallel to the horizon, from the sternal angle estimate the difference between the parallel line and the top of the pulsation in the external jugular vein (Fig. 19-13). Because of wide differences in chest shape and location of the sternal angle, exact measurement varies widely among patients (Van't Laar, 2002).

Jugular venous distention (JVD) is associated with *fluid volume overload, right-sided congestive heart failure, constrictive pericarditis, tricuspid stenosis, and superior vena cava obstruction.* The neck veins appear full, and the level of pulsation is >3 cm above the sternal angle. If the jugular venous pressure (JVP) is not measured, nurses note whether neck veins appear distended, flat, or slightly visible.

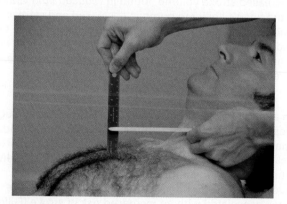

Figure 19-13 Estimate the jugular venous pressure.

(text continues on page 512)

Expected findings are up to 3 cm above the sternal angle, which is equivalent to a central venous pressure of 8 mm Hg. If exact levels are not measured, document findings as "JVP not elevated," "neck veins not distended," or "no JVD."

Hepatojugular Reflux
Inspection and palpation

Pressing gently on the liver increases venous return (Fig. 19-14). Apply gentle pressure for 30 to 60 seconds over the right upper quadrant; look for a rise of 1 cm or more in the JVP (Norris & Clark, 2010). *The pulsation increases for a few beats and then returns to <3 cm above the sternal angle.*

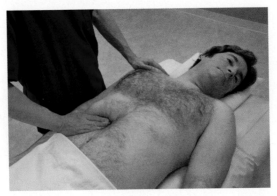

Figure 19-14 To assess hepatojugular reflux, press gently on the liver.

Carotid Arteries Inspection

Inspect the carotid artery for a double stroke seen with S1 and S2. *The contour is smooth with a rapid upstroke and slower downstroke.*

Auscultation

To detect carotid narrowing from atherosclerosis, auscultate the carotid arteries before palpation. Place the bell chestpiece lightly over each carotid artery in turn while the patient holds the breath (eliminating breath sounds). *No sounds or bruits are heard.*

If the neck vein distends >1 cm, it is a positive result (Clark & Norris, 2010). A positive result is when the highest level of pulsation stays >3 cm for >15 seconds (Wiese, 2000). The pulsation remains elevated in disorders that cause a dilated and poorly compliant right ventricle or in obstruction of the right ventricular filling by tricuspid stenosis (Woods, Sivarajan Froelicher, et al., 2010). *Heart failure* is a common cause of hepatojugular reflux.

The pulse may be bounding and prominent with hypertension, hypermetabolic states, and disorders with a rapid rise and fall of pressure (eg, patent ductus arteriosus) (Woods, Sivarajan Froelicher, et al., 2010). It may be low in amplitude and volume and have a delayed peak in aortic stenosis (from decreased cardiac output). If it is diminished unilaterally or bilaterally (often associated with a systolic bruit), the cause may be carotid stenosis from atherosclerosis (Woods, Sivarajan Froelicher, et al.).

A diminished or thready pulse may accompany decreased stroke volume, found in *reduced fluid volume.* If the heart's ability to pump is decreased and cardiac output is low, as in *heart failure,* pulse strength may be reduced. Another cause of decreased pulse strength is a narrowed carotid artery from *atherosclerosis.* Pulse strength may increase during exercise or stress.

In a middle-aged or elderly patient, a carotid bruit suggests arterial narrowing. **Bruits** are swooshing sounds that result from turbulent blood flow related to atherosclerosis. A bruit is audible when the artery is partially obstructed. With complete obstruction, no bruit is audible, because no blood gets through. Bruits have been associated with an increased risk of stroke (Gillett, Davis, et al., 2003).

Palpation

⚠ *SAFETY ALERT 19-4*

Palpate the carotid arteries one at a time. Palpating them together poses a risk for obstructing both arteries, reducing blood flow to the brain and potentially causing dizziness or loss of consciousness.

If no bruit is auscultated, palpate the carotid artery below the carotid sinus and medial to the sternomastoid muscle in the neck between the jaw and the clavicle (Fig. 19-15).

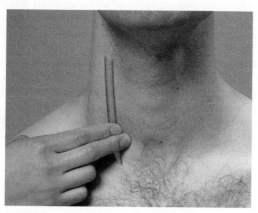

Figure 19-15 Palpate each carotid artery medial to the sternomastoid muscle in the neck.

⚠ *SAFETY ALERT 19-5*

Avoid compressing over the carotid sinus. It lies at the level of the superior border of the thyroid cartilage. Stimulation of the sinus also causes parasympathetic stimulation, which may lead to a reduced pulse rate or drop in blood pressure. Older adults and patients sensitive to this stimulation may develop periods of life-threatening asystole.

Palpate the strength (amplitude) of the pulse and grade it as with peripheral pulses (see Chapter 20). *Strength is 2+ or moderate on a scale of 0 to 4. Pulses are equal bilaterally.*

Distinguishing a murmur from a bruit can be challenging. Murmurs originate in the heart or great vessels and are usually louder over the upper precordium and quieter near the neck. Bruits are higher pitched, more superficial, and heard only over the arteries (Woods, Savarajan Froelicher, et al., 2010).

Documentation of Expected Findings

Without Jugular venous distention (JVD), hepatojugular reflux negative. Carotid pulses 2+ bilaterally/4 without bruits.

Inspection of the Precordium

Inspect the anterior chest for any lesions, masses, heaves, or lifts that appear as a forceful thrusting on the chest. Observe for the point of maximal impulse (PMI) in the apex at the 5th intercostal space (ICS) medial to the left midclavicular line (MCL). It is easier to observe in children, men, and adults with a thin chest wall. *Impulses are absent or located in the 5th left ICS medial to the MCL with no lifts or heaves.*

The enlarged heart of *cardiomegaly* displaces the PMI laterally and inferiorly. A heave or lift on the chest results from an enlarged left ventricle. A right ventricular heave is observed at the lower left sternal border; a left ventricular heave is observed at the apex.

Palpation of the Precordium

Palpate the anterior chest for any lesions, masses, or tender areas (see Chapter 18). When palpating for sensations related to the heart, use the palmar surface of the hand. Beginning at the apex of the heart, feel for the pulse in the location in which you observed it during inspection. To localize the impulse, it may help to use the finger pads and depress in the left 5th ICS medial to the MCL (Fig. 19-16). If present, the PMI is usually felt as a light tap that lasts from S1 to halfway through systole and is <1 to 2 cm. It may or may not be palpable in adults. Also palpate with finger pads in the right and left 2nd ICSs, left 3rd ICS, left 4th ICS, and left 5th ICS. Ask the patient to exhale and hold his or her breath each time. In the epigastric area, point your index finger up under the costal margin and ask the patient to inhale and hold the breath. *The PMI is in the 5th left ICS medial to the MCL when present. No pulsations are palpated in other areas.*

An unexpected PMI is one that is displaced laterally or inferiorly, is >2 cm, and sustained throughout systole. It may result from *heart failure, myocardial infarction (MI), left ventricular hypertrophy,* or *valvular heart disease.* Unexpected sensations palpated on the chest include lifts and heaves. Thrills are vibrations detected on palpation. They can feel like a cat's purr. A palpable, rushing vibration (thrill) is caused from turbulent blood flow with *incompetent valves, pulmonary hypertension,* or *septal defects.* This vibration is usually in the location of the valve in which it is associated. With chest pain that increases with movement, palpation of the costochondral junction is performed to determine if the pain is of musculoskeletal origin.

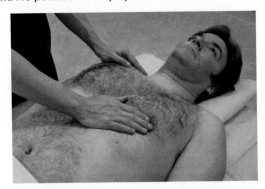

Figure 19-16 Location of the apical impulse.

Percussion of the Precordium

Chest x-ray has largely replaced chest percussion. Detecting percussion sounds over an obese or muscular chest or female breast tissue can be difficult. Without radiographic technology, percussion may be useful in identifying the left border if the heart is enlarged (as in cases of suspected heart failure). Identification of the right border is rarely useful. If heart failure or cardiomegaly is suspected, cardiac dullness may be percussed in the ICSs. Beginning at the anterior axillary line in the 4th ICS, percuss medially toward the sternum. Note the point at which the note changes from resonant (lung tissue) to dull (cardiac tissue). Repeat the procedure in the 5th and 6th ICSs. *The left border of the heart is percussed from the apex in the 4th to 5th left ICS medial to the MCL.*

When the heart is enlarged, the left lateral border of the heart is percussed laterally and inferiorly to the expected location.

Documentation of Expected Findings

PMI observed and palpated in 5th left intercostal space (ICS) medial to the midclavicular line (MCL). No thrills, heaves, or lifts.

Auscultation of the Precordium

Auscultation is the most important technique of cardiovascular examination. It is essential for the room to be quiet and for the stethoscope to be free of distracting noise. Chest hair, bumping of the stethoscope, or shivering may cause sounds that interfere with accuracy. Make sure that the patient is calm, warm, and draped as previously described.

Identify the locations for auscultation by accurately identifying the ICSs and landmarks (Fig. 19-17).

The most important landmark is the sternal angle at the junction of the manubrium with the body of the sternum. First locate the sternal angle (angle of Louis) on the sternum by sliding the index finger downward from the suprasternal notch. A vertical motion is usually best for feeling this elevation. Palpate directly across to the adjoining 2nd rib and slip the index finger into the 2nd ICS at the right sternal border; this is the first location for auscultation (*aortic*). Palpate across to the left 2nd rib and locate the 2nd ICS at the left sternal border. This is the second location (*pulmonic*) for auscultation. Walk the fingers one rib space at the left sternal border (approximately 2.5 cm apart) to locate the 3rd left ICS; this is the third site for auscultation (*Erb's point*). Walk the fingers to the 4th left ICS and 5th left ICS, these are the fourth and fifth sites for auscultation (*tricuspid area*). Move the finger from the 5th ICS at the left sternal border and follow the rib laterally 7 to 9 cm from the sternal border. This will be the sixth location for auscultation (*mitral area*) that will be just medial to the left MCL.

These auscultatory areas are near but not directly over the locations of the valves, because the sounds radiate in the direction in which blood flows. Note that although the pulmonic valve is on the right side of the heart, the valve is heard on the left sternal border. Not only does the sound radiate in this direction, but also the right side is more forward in the chest, so the pulmonic valve is turned more anteriorly

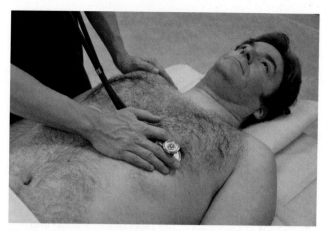

Figure 19-18 Auscultating the heart.

and laterally. Also note that the aortic valve on the left side of the heart is heard best on the right side. It is more posterior in the chest, and the vessel branches to the right side before descending inferiorly. This flow of blood causes the aortic valve sound to radiate to the right. The tricuspid valve sound radiates to the left and is heard at the sternal border; the mitral sound is heard medial to the MCL. *Erb's point* is where the valves usually are equally audible.

When listening to heart sounds, begin by hearing the rhythm of the beat and the characteristic "lub-dub." Usually the first heart sound is followed by the second with a pause before the next lub-dub. The lub, which correlates with the beginning of systole, is called S1 (see Fig. 19-7). The dub correlates with the end of systole and beginning of diastole (see Fig. 19-7). Each lub-dub is one pulse; when learning the heart sounds it may help to palpate and feel how the pulse (ventricular systole) occurs at the same time as S1.

Auscultate the heart rate and rhythm in each area, starting either in the right 2nd ICS (aortic) or the apical area (Fig. 19-18). Listen for a regular versus irregular rhythm. Count the heart rate for 60 seconds at the apical area. Listen to each of the six auscultatory areas, proceeding systematically, usually beginning at the aortic area and proceeding along the left sternal border at the sites indicated. Listen first with the diaphragm and then with the bell to hear both high- and low-pitched sounds.

In all auscultatory areas:

1. Isolate the lub-dub rhythm, listening for a regular rhythmic cadence.
2. Listen first to S1 and then to S2 for a single sound or split sound. Identify if S1 or S2 is louder or softer, depending on the area being auscultated.
3. Listen for extra heart sounds (then identify if heard before or after S1 or S2).
4. Listen for murmurs (then identify if in systole or diastole).

Some expected variations in heart sounds include a split heart sound. When the valves close at the same time, one S2 is heard for both valves. If the valves close at slightly different times, however, two discernible components of the same sound are heard, a situation referred to as a **split heart**

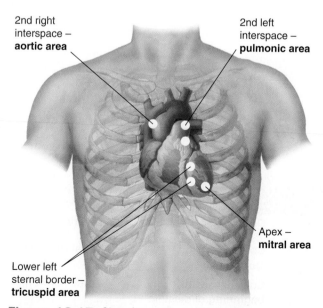

2nd right interspace – **aortic area**

2nd left interspace – **pulmonic area**

Apex – **mitral area**

Lower left sternal border – **tricuspid area**

Figure 19-17 Sites for cardiac auscultation.

sound. The right-sided pressures are lower than the left, and with inspiration the intrathoracic pressures are even lower. The right heart can fill with more blood, which takes longer, and the closure of the pulmonic valve (on the right) is delayed. The split S2 is more commonly heard during inspiration and disappears during expiration. S1 can also be split because the tricuspid valve closes slightly after the mitral valve during systole. Splitting of S1 is usually constant and does not vary with respiration, because the AV valves are less sensitive to changes in intrathoracic pressures than are the semilunar valves (see Table 19-4 at the end of this chapter).

Techniques and Expected Findings	Rationale/Unexpected Findings
Identify rate and rhythm. Using the diaphragm, listen to the apical area to identify S1, S2, heart rhythm, and heart rate as described. Rhythm may vary with respiration in some patients, especially children and young adults. Rate increases at the peak of inspiration and slows at the peak of expiration. This expected variation is referred to as a **sinus arrhythmia**. *Heart rate is 60 to 100 beats/min and regular in adults.*	If the rhythm is irregular, identify if the irregularity has a pattern or is totally irregular. For example, every third beat missed would be described as a *regular irregular rhythm*. No detectable pattern is characteristic of atrial fibrillation, common in older adults. If the rhythm is irregular, take the radial pulse while listening to the apical pulse. Count the apical and radial heart rate at the same time. The easiest way to do so is to count the apical pulse while counting the number of missed beats; the difference is referred to as the **pulse deficit**. (Refer to Chapter 6 for rate variations.)
Identify S1 and S2. After identifying S1 as lub and S2 as dub, listen to each sound separately (Table 19-2). Usually they are each heard as one sound. S1 signals the beginning of systole as the mitral and tricuspid valves close. Because the right side of the heart may contract slightly slower than the left, the triscupid valve may close slightly after the mitral, causing a split S1, as previously described. A split S1 is heard in the tricuspid area.	The rare split S1 is constant, does not vary with respiration and thus is referred to as a *fixed split*. Wide splitting occurs when bundle branch block delays activation of the right ventricle or when *stenosis of the pulmonic valve* or *pulmonary hypertension* delays emptying of the right ventricle. A paradoxical split is the opposite of expected. When closure of the aortic valve is delayed (as in *left bundle branch block, right ventricular pacing, aortic stenosis,* or *left ventricular failure*), the pulmonic valve closes before the aortic. The split is heard during expiration and disappears with inspiration (*Paradoxical split of the second sound,* 2007) (see also Table 19-4 at the end of this chapter).
S2 signals the end of systole and beginning of diastole as the aortic and pulmonic valves close. A split S2 may occur from the pulmonic valve closing slightly after the aortic; it may be heard in the pulmonic valve area during inspiration in children (see Table 19-4). Split sounds are very close together and difficult to auscultate.	
S1 is louder than S2 in the mitral and tricuspid areas because those valves close at the beginning of systole (signaled by S1). S2 is louder than S1 in the aortic and pulmonic areas because those valves close at the beginning of diastole (signaled by S2). *S1 is a single sound, louder than S2 in the mitral and tricuspid areas; S2 is a single sound, louder than S1 in the aortic and pulmonic areas; apical rate is 60 to 100 beats/min and regular.*	

Table 19-2 Characteristics of Heart Sounds

Visual Representation	Intensity and Pitch	Quality	Duration	Locations
S1	Louder at apex	Lub	Correlates with carotid pulse	Mitral tricuspid
S2	Louder at base	Dub	Correlates with beginning of diastole	Aortic pulmonic

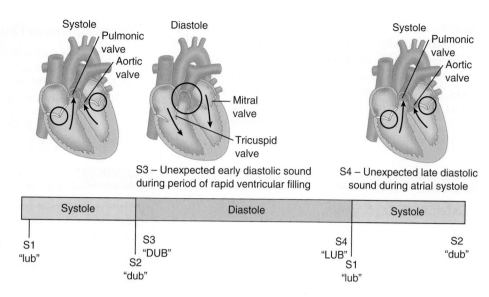

Figure 19-19 Extra heart sounds. Arrows represent the direction of blood flow. An S3 ("DUB") is an unexpected sound heard immediately following S2 (closure of the semilunar valves). S3 is generated very early in diastole as blood flowing into the right or left ventricle is met with resistance. S4 ("LUB") is an unexpected sound created during atrial systole as blood flowing into the right or left ventricle is met with resistance.

S3 – Unexpected early diastolic sound during period of rapid ventricular filling

S4 – Unexpected late diastolic sound during atrial systole

Extra Sounds. Extra heart sounds occur from vibrations during rapid ventricular filling. They include **S3** and **S4** (Fig. 19-19). The third heart sound (S3) occurs during the early rapid diastolic filling phase immediately after S2. Blood rushes into ventricles resistant to filling, distending the ventricular walls and causing vibration. S3 is quiet, low pitched, and often difficult to hear. It usually is audible in patients with heart failure (Wang, Fitzgerald, et al., 2005). At the end of ventricular diastole, the atria contract and push an additional 25% to 30% of blood into the heart, called the "atrial kick." Resistance to filling during this phase also causes vibrations. S4 is heard late in diastole immediately before S1. Both S3 and S4 sound similar to S1 or S2. They are commonly referred to as ventricular "gallops." Presence of both S3 and S4 is referred to as a "summation gallop." S3 may be expected in children, young adults, or women in the third trimester of pregnancy. S3 is immediately after S2 early in diastole, and S4 is immediately before S1 late in diastole.

Systolic ejection **clicks** may occur early or in the middle of systole (see Table 19-5 at the end of this chapter). The early systolic sound occurs quickly after S1. Causes are either a sudden bulging of an aortic or pulmonic valve or the sudden distention of the associated great artery. *Aortic stenosis, pulmonic stenosis,* and a *bicuspid aortic valve* can all produce this sound, with or without a murmur. Pulmonic ejection sounds often decrease in intensity with inspiration and are best heard at the left sternal border. Aortic ejection sounds are best heard at the apex.

The midsystolic click is associated with *mitral valve prolapse* (see Table 19-5). There may or may not be an associated late systolic murmur, which is caused by mitral regurgitation. The click is produced by systolic prolapse of the mitral valve leaflets into the left atrium. If present, the Valsalva's or squatting-to-standing manoeuvre should be performed to assess for increases in the click or murmur (*Techniques: Heart sounds and murmurs,* 2007).

The opening **snap** is an early diastolic sound associated with *mitral stenosis* (see Table 19-5). It is audible shortly after S2 and may or may not be associated with a late diastolic murmur. It results from rapid opening of the anterior mitral valve leaflet during diastole with high left atrial pressures. The opening snap is challenging to differentiate from either S3 or split S2 (*Techniques: Heart sounds and murmurs,* 2007).

The pericardial friction **rub** is the most important physical sign of *acute pericarditis.* It may have up to three components during the cardiac cycle and is high pitched, scratching, and grating (see Table 19-5). It can best be heard with the diaphragm of the stethoscope at the left lower sternal border. The pericardial friction rub is heard most frequently during expiration and increases when the patient is upright and leaning forward (Strimel, Assadi, et al., 2006).

Murmurs

Murmurs may result from intrinsic cardiovascular disease or circulatory disturbances (eg, anemia, pregnancy). Some murmurs have no underlying pathology (referred to as *innocent murmurs*). Fitting the clinical situation with the murmur is necessary to better determine if the murmur is insignificant or not.

An innocent flow murmur may originate from higher blood flow velocities in the left ventricular outflow tract and aortic valve. The increased flow velocity results from a larger stroke volume passing through the relatively narrow left ventricle and aortic valve in children (Celebi & Onat, 2006). Innocent murmurs are usually systolic. Functional murmurs in pregnancy usually result from increased circulating fluid volumes.

Murmurs in adults usually indicate disease. If the heart valve fails to totally close, during systole the blood leaks back through the valve and causes a whooshing sound (similar to the Korotkoff sounds heard during assessment of blood pressure). Similarly, a valve may fail to totally open, causing turbulence during diastole as the blood rushes against a partially closed valve to fill the heart. Therefore, these murmurs may occur during either systole or diastole. Murmurs also may result from vibration of tissue or excessive flow as in pregnancy. Additionally they may occur in any of the four valves.

Murmurs usually are heard best over the precordial area where the affected valve is loudest. To identify murmurs accurately, listen for the timing in systole or diastole, loudness versus softness, and location on the chest wall. Follow-up studies, such as an echocardiogram, will identify unexpected structural findings when a new murmur is detected.

> **Clinical Significance 19-3**
>
> Systolic murmurs occur during contraction between S1 and S2 when the mitral and tricuspid valves are closed and the aortic and pulmonic valves are open. Diastolic murmurs occur during filling from the end of S2 to the beginning of the next S1, when the mitral and tricuspid valves are open and the aortic and pulmonic valves are closed.

Techniques and Expected Findings	Rationale/Unexpected Findings
Listen for Extra Sounds ⚠ *SAFETY ALERT 19-6* *Auscultation of a new extra sound may indicate a change in the patient's condition or worsening heart failure. A new S3 or S4 requires investigation and may be the reason to consult with a physician for further diagnostic testing.* S3 and S4 are commonly called "gallops." When S3 exists, it follows S2 and sounds like "lub-dub-dub." It usually is heard best in the apex with the patient lying on the left side. It may be expected in young patients. S4 in late diastole, right before S1, sounds like "lub-lub-dub." It is usually unexpected.	S3 is unexpected in patients older than 40 years and results from increased atrial pressure related to *systolic heart failure* or *valvular regurgitation*. Using the bell of the stethoscope, listen for a left ventricular S3 over the apex of the heart. Listen for a right ventricular S3 over the lower left sternal border. Have the patient move to the left lateral position to bring the cardiac apex closer to the chest wall, making the left ventricular S3 easier to hear. S4 results from a noncompliant ventricle (a stiff wall) as a consequence of *hypertension, hypertrophy,* or *fibrosis* (*Techniques: Heart sounds and murmurs,* 2007). A left ventricular S4 is heard best at the apex with the patient lying in the left lateral position; a right ventricular S4 is loudest over the left sternal border in the 5th intercostal space (ICS).
Also listen for the short scratching sound of the pericardial friction rub, high-pitched opening snaps, and ejection clicks, as previously described. These sounds are difficult to differentiate between S3 and S4; referral to a cardiologist may be helpful in labelling them. *Usually no extra sounds are heard.*	Pericardial friction rubs can be differentiated from pleural friction rubs by having the patient hold the breath. If present without breathing, the rub is pericardial. An opening snap is associated with mitral stenosis. It is high pitched, snapping, and best heard with the diaphragm of the stethoscope in the mitral area. In patients who have undergone cardiac surgery, related trauma may produce extra sounds. An audible respirophasic squeak may be related to mediastinal or pleural tubes. Air in the mediastinum produces a crunching sound (Hamman's sign) during auscultation of the precordium (see Table 19-5 at the end of this chapter for identifying extra sounds).
Listen to Murmurs In clinical practice, nurses are more concerned with recognizing changes in murmurs rather than in diagnosing and labelling them. Describe murmurs according to timing in the cardiac cycle, loudness, pitch, pattern, quality, location, radiation, and position. When learning murmurs it is helpful to identify how other health care professionals have labelled them and attempt to hear how they have been described (see Table 19-6 at the end of this chapter). *Usually no murmurs are heard.*	The most common systolic murmurs in adults are produced by aortic stenosis, mitral insufficiency, and ventricular septal defect. In older adults, the murmur of aortic sclerosis (thickening of aortic valve leaflets with age) is common. The most common diastolic murmurs are aortic insufficiency and mitral stenosis. Nurses are often the first to identify the onset of murmurs related to papillary muscle dysfunction associated with MI. This high-pitched, crescendo–decrescendo shaped, systolic murmur must be recognized immediately so that interventions can be instituted to prevent rupture, which poses a high mortality rate (see Table 19-7 at the end of this chapter).

Documentation of Expected Findings

Heart rate and rhythm regular. Without gallops, murmurs, opening snaps, clicks, or rubs. S1 and S2 single sounds.

Area of Assessment	Expected Findings	Unexpected Findings
Blood pressure (see Chapter 6)	116/70 mm Hg right arm (sitting)	140/96 mm Hg right arm (sitting)
Radial pulses (see Chapter 18)	Rate 68 beats/min, rhythm regular	Rate 120 beats/min, thready and irregular
Skin and nails (see Chapter 10)	Pink, warm, and dry; capillary refill 1 to 2 s	Facial pallor, cyanosis in nail beds
Jugular venous pressure (JVP)	JVP 3 cm above sternal angle with head of bed elevated 30°	JVP 8 cm above sternal angle with head of bed elevated 30°
Carotid pulse	Strong and equal bilaterally, no bruits heard	Bruit heard over left carotid artery
Brachial arteries (see Chapter 18)	Strong and equal bilaterally	Left diminished, right strong
The heart	No visible pulsations, heaves, or lifts	Pulsations observed in epigastric region
Apical (mitral) heart rate	Rate 64, regular, S1 and S2 heard	Rate 120, irregular, murmur following S2
Left ventricular area—apical	PMI palpated at 5th intercostal space (ICS)	PMI palpated 3 cm lateral to left midclavicular line (MCL),
impulse or PMI	Slightly medial to left MCL as light taps, no thrills	pounding and irregular
First heart sound (S1 or lub)	Single sound, loudest at the apex	Split S1 sound
Second heart sound (S2 or dub)	Single sound, loudest at the base of heart	Diminished S2
Third and fourth heart sounds (S3 and S4)	No S3 or S4 sounds auscultated	S3 heard at apex in left lateral position, atrial gallop on left side of precordium
Right ventricular area—left sternal border, 3rd, 4th, 5th ICSs	Nonpalpable impulses	Increased amplitude 3rd ICS Nonpalpable 4th and 5th ICSs
Pulmonic area—left 2nd ICS	Impulses nonpalpable, not visualized	S2 palpable
Aortic area—right 2nd ICS	Impulses nonpalpable, not visualized	Palpable S2

Adapted from Roach, S., Roddick, P., et al. (2010). In T. C. Stephen, D. L. Skillen, R. A. Day, & L. S. Bickley (Eds.). *Canadian Bates' guide to health assessment for nurses* (1st ed., pp. 423–478). Philadelphia, PA: Wolters Kluwer Health/Lippincott Williams & Wilkins.

Lifespan Considerations

Women Who are Pregnant

Many changes in pregnancy relate to increased blood volume that accompanies gestation. Resting pulse rate increases, and blood pressure may rise slightly. Heart rate increases by 10 to 15 beats/min between 14 and 20 weeks of pregnancy. In multiple gestation, heart rate increases significantly in the third trimester (Malone & D'Alton, 2004).

The woman's skin may be slightly redder than expected because of the increased volume and metabolic state. In late pregnancy, the uterus pushes up on the diaphragm. The PMI moves upward and laterally approximately 1 to 1.5 cm, depending on uterine size and position (Lowdermilk & Perry, 2007). Heart sounds may change because of the increased blood volume. S1 and S2 may be split after 20 weeks. Systolic and diastolic murmurs may be heard over the precordium, although systolic murmurs are more common.

A unique murmur in lactating women is referred to as a *mammary souffle*. It results from increased blood flow through the internal mammary artery and is best heard in the 2nd to 4th ICS. Pressing on the artery can obliterate the mammary souffle, unlike a murmur that originates in the heart.

Newborns and Infants

If possible, place the infant on the parent's lap during examination. Do not undress the baby until necessary, because exposure may be uncomfortable and cold, and assessing a restless baby with high respiratory and cardiac rates is difficult. If the baby is crying, a bottle or pacifier might help to calm him or her. During inspection, observe for associated chromosomal characteristics, such as found with Down's or Turner's syndrome. Up to 20% of infants with Down's syndrome may have an associated cardiac anomaly (Braunwald, Zipes, et al., 2004).

Observe for cyanosis, especially with crying. Note that the infant's skin may be mottled if the examining environment

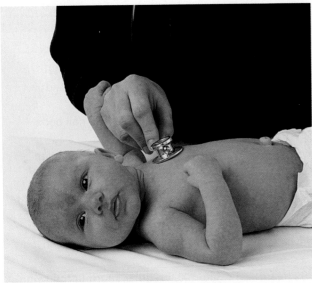

Figure 19-20 Using the small pediatric-sized diaphragm and bell.

Figure 19-21 Palpate in the 4th interspace to the right of the MCL in children aged 7 years or younger.

Aortic area

Pulmonic area

Erb's point

Apical impulse

Tricuspid area

Mitral or apical area

is cool. Inspect for subcostal retractions, left-sided chest prominence, unusual chest movement, and increased respiratory rates found with congenital heart disease (see Table 19-8 at the end of this chapter). Because infants have short necks, the jugular veins are not examined. Palpate the faint apical impulse to the left of the xyphoid, at the apex, and in the 2nd ICS left sternal border; a prominent pulse is unexpected. Percussion in infants and children is not performed, because related findings do not accurately reflect cardiac size or function. Use a pediatric stethoscope to auscultate the heart (Fig. 19-20). Innocent murmurs are less common in neonates than in children.

Children and Adolescents

If the child appears likely to cry, auscultate heart sounds before inspecting the precordium. By the time a child is 3 to 5 years old, complications from heart anomalies may manifest as cyanosis or heart failure. Angina is rare. Anomalies create diminished oxygenation, low cardiac output, or increased pulmonary pressure. Associated symptoms include fatigue, diaphoresis, and poor weight gain. Question older children about exercise, activities, edema, respiratory difficulties, chest pain, palpitations, fainting, and headaches.

If cardiac disease is suspected, auscultate the heart with the child in different positions, beginning with lying and standing (Fig. 19-21). During auscultation in the pulmonic area, S2 may be closely split in inspiration and single in expiration. Be aware that fixed splitting is an important finding that may indicate an atrial septal defect from a patent foramen ovale. In the tricuspid area, S1 may be closely split and S2 will be single; this does not vary with respiration.

At the apex, there is a single S1, single S2, and possibly an S3. S3 will be heard best with the bell; it is expected in

children because of hyperdynamic circulation and a thin chest wall. If a murmur is heard, it may be innocent, functional, or pathologic. Listen carefully to determine the characteristics, and refer any patients with suspected disorders to a physician if previously undiagnosed. Up to 50% of children have an innocent systolic murmur (Menasche, 2007) (see Chapter 28 for more information).

Older Adults

Older adults develop changes in their hearts and blood pressures primarily from age-related stiffening of the vasculature and decreased responsiveness to stress hormones. Blood and pulse pressures increase from the stiff vessels. Additionally, BMI increases, causing the heart to work harder. Elevated late diastolic filling increases the volume of atrial contraction, which may be associated with the S4 gallop of late diastolic filling.

The ventricles hypertrophy, increasing the risk for heart failure and resultant atrial fibrillation. Approximately 17% of men and 6% of women live with this chronic condition, which causes an irregular heartbeat and increases the patient's risk for stroke (Lakatta & Levy, 2003). Assess older adults for symptoms of heart failure including weight gain, shortness of breath, and edema. Symptoms of atrial fibrillation include fatigue, palpitations, and heart failure with loss of the "atrial kick" that supports ventricular filling.

Older adults are also more likely to develop atherosclerosis and cardiovascular disease. The vasculature is undergoing constant remodelling, forming new capillaries and collateral circulation (Yang, 2007). Older adults, however, are more prone to atherosclerosis because they are more sensitive to the effects of lifestyle choices, such as smoking and high-fat diets (Lakatta, 2002). Assess these patients carefully for chest pain, fatigue, and dyspnea associated with symptoms. Ideally, counselling is effective in reducing risk factors and interventions are targeted toward primary prevention of disease.

Evidence-Informed Critical Thinking

Common Laboratory and Diagnostic Testing

Laboratory and diagnostic testing helps confirm and expand information obtained through subjective and objective data collection. Some tests require explanation to the patient, some require special preparation (eg, a period of fasting), and some require special monitoring by nurses during and after the test (eg, exercise tolerance testing). Cardiac testing ranges from low-risk ECG to more invasive cardiac catheterization. Results from such tests help identify patterns of data that indicate areas for care planning and interventions.

Elevated levels of blood lipids are a risk factor for cardiovascular disease. A lipid profile includes total cholesterol, high-density lipoprotein, low-density lipoprotein, and triglyceride levels (see Chapter 8).

The myocardium releases cardiac enzymes and proteins in response to cell damage. These enzymes and proteins are measured in blood samples to diagnose or rule out MI. Creatine kinase MB (CK-MB) and troponin I are intracellular proteins specific to the myocardium; their values are elevated with MI.

The ECG, as discussed earlier, assists with diagnoses of myocardial ischemia, chamber hypertrophy, pericarditis, electrolyte imbalances, cardiac arrhythmias, and heart block. Electrodes are attached to the limbs and anterior chest wall using adhesive pads; the electrical changes in the heart are transferred onto a paper graph. Nurses with additional training may perform ECG testing. Home ECG monitoring can be conducted using an ambulatory ECG monitor or an event recorder.

A chest x-ray film helps determine the size, contour, and position of the heart; alterations in the pulmonary circulation; and acute or chronic lung disease. An echocardiogram uses high-frequency sound waves and the Doppler effect to evaluate the size, shape, and motion of cardiac structures and the direction and velocity of blood flow through the heart. A gel (often cold) is placed on the patient's chest wall and the transducer is moved around the anterior chest wall. The echocardiogram may also be done with the transducer inserted through the mouth into the esophagus (transesophageal echocardiogram). Compared to the simple echocardiogram, this invasive procedure requires fasting and sedation, with potential complications such as a perforated esophagus or impaired swallowing.

Bedside hemodynamic monitoring includes measurement of central venous pressure, pulmonary artery pressures, and systemic interarterial pressures using a catheter placed in the heart. Systemic intra-arterial pressure monitoring provides access to direct and continuous blood pressures in critically ill patients; this catheter is usually placed in the radial artery. Hemodynamic monitoring requires advanced training and skill of nurses in critical care areas.

Documenting Unexpected Findings

The nurse has just finished a physical examination of Mrs. Anne Lewis, the 77-year-old woman admitted with chest pain. Unlike the examples of expected findings previously noted, Mrs. Lewis has unexpected findings. Review the following important findings that the steps of objective data collection for this patient revealed. Consider how these results compare with the expected findings presented in the earlier examples. Begin to think about how the data cluster together and what additional data might be needed. Think critically about her conditions, and anticipate appropriate nursing interventions.

Inspection: Sitting with head of bed at 45° angle appears comfortable but somewhat anxious. Blood pressure 122/62 mm Hg right arm (semi-Fowler's), pulse 112 beats/min, irregular, respirations 16 breaths/min, temperature 37°C, oxygen saturation 94%. Skin colour pale, some diaphoresis. Chest shape symmetrical without visible apical impulse. Respirations without dyspnea. No neck vein distention.

Palpation: Apical impulse not present. Peripheral pulses 2+/4 without edema.

Percussion: Not performed.

Auscultation: Heart rate 112 with 3 to 5 premature beats/min. Pulse deficit of 5. S1 > S2 at apex and S2 > S1 at base. No murmurs, rubs, or gallops.

Stress testing compares cardiac function and perfusion at rest versus during stress. A simple exercise stress test consists of ECG monitoring for signs of ischemia or arrhythmia while the patient walks on a treadmill or rides a stationary bicycle. A radionuclide ventriculogram, also known as a multiple-gated acquisition scan, is a test in which a small amount of the patient's blood is withdrawn, mixed with a radionuclide, and reinjected. This study is most commonly used to monitor the effects of potentially cardiotoxic chemotherapeutic agents. Both of these tests are performed in specialized settings.

Cardiac catheterization and coronary angiography are invasive diagnostic procedures that delineate coronary anatomy and coronary heart disease using fluoroscopy, usually in the radiology department. Right-sided heart catheterization is performed to measure right-heart pressures and structures. Left-sided heart catheterization involves placing a catheter through the femoral artery to the coronary arteries where dye is used for visualization. Following the procedure, the patient is on bed rest and the puncture site and distal circulation must be monitored frequently. Nursing staff also monitor blood pressure and cardiac rhythm.

Cardiac electrophysiology studies are used in the diagnostic investigation of arrhythmias and syncope. Flexible catheters with multiple electrodes are placed within the heart to stimulate arrhythmias. The patient fasts for several hours before the study; usually, he or she is sedated during the procedure. Complications include the inability to induce arrhythmias, cardiac perforation and pericardial effusion, venous thrombosis or infection from the catheter site, and intractable ventricular fibrillation and death (Blancher, 2005). Patients are monitored closely following this procedure.

Clinical Reasoning

Nursing Diagnoses, Outcomes, and Interventions

Table 19-3 compares nursing diagnoses commonly related to cardiovascular assessment (North American Nursing Diagnosis Association, 2009). From the assessment information and established nursing diagnoses, nurses then work to identify patient outcomes. Some outcomes related to cardiovascular conditions include the following:

- The patient demonstrates adequate circulation status with strong peripheral pulses, blood pressure within expected parameters, and adequate urinary output.
- The patient demonstrates cardiac pump effectiveness with expected heart rate, negative JVD, no S3 or S4, and no arrhythmias.
- The patient maintains fluid balance with no edema, clear lung sounds, stable body weight, and balanced intake and output (Moorhead, Johnson, et al., 2007).

Once outcomes are established, nurses can implement care to improve the patient's status. Critical thinking and evidence-informed practice are essential to develop effective interventions. Examples of nursing interventions for cardiovascular care are as follows:

- Teach the patient the signs of cardiac ischemia and when to call 911.
- Assess for chest pain, shortness of breath, and edema and document cardiac arrhythmias.
- Weigh the patient daily; monitor trends. Maintain accurate intake and output (Bulechek, Butcher, et al., 2008).

Table 19-3	Common Nursing Diagnoses for Cardiovascular Conditions		
Diagnosis and Related Factors	**Point of Differentiation**	**Assessment Characteristics**	**Nursing Interventions**
Impaired tissue perfusion, cardiac related to chest pain, shock, or dysrhythmia	Decreased oxygen results in failure to nourish tissues at the capillary level.	Chest pain, electrocardiogram (ECG) changes, elevated creatine kinase MB or troponin-I, diaphoresis, dyspnea, low oxygen saturation	Place the patient on cardiac monitor. Administer nitroglycerin with physician order.* Start oxygen. Ensure the IV is in place for emergency use.* Notify physician.
Excess fluid volume related to heart failure, excess fluid intake, excess sodium intake	Increased fluid retention and edema	Jugular vein distention, weight gain, dyspnea, orthopnea, paroxysmal nocturnal dyspnea (PND), S3 or S4, edema	Monitor edema, intake and output. Weigh the patient daily. Auscultate lung and heart sounds. Administer diuretic with order.* Elevate head of bed for dyspnea.

*Collaborative interventions.

Nurses then evaluate care according to the developed outcomes, thereafter reassessing the patient and continuing or modifying the interventions as appropriate. An accurate and complete nursing assessment is an essential foundation for holistic nursing care. Even beginning nursing students can use assessment data to implement new interventions, evaluate the effectiveness of those interventions, and make a difference in the quality of patient care.

Nurses also collect assessment data to assist physicians to identify medical diagnoses so that appropriate treatment may be ordered. Nurses understand the association of assessment findings to underlying pathophysiology to gather data to support or discount medical diagnoses. For example, chest pain may result from MI, pulmonary embolism, or musculoskeletal tenderness. Nurses assess the patient's history to determine if the pain is acute (ie, MI, pulmomary embolism) or chronic (ie, chest wall tenderness). They assess heart sounds for S3, S4, or murmurs, which may accompany MI. Oxygen desaturation may be associated with pulmonary embolism, while tenderness to palpation is associated with chest wall tenderness. An ECG helps with diagnosis of MI. Therefore, nurses need to use critical thinking to know which data to collect and then organize findings to assist physicians to arrive at a medical diagnosis.

The health challenges of Mrs. Lewis have been outlined throughout this chapter. The initial collection of subjective and objective data is complete. Mrs. Lewis expressed concerns about her new diagnosis of myocardial infarction (MI); additionally, she developed an irregular rhythm with some pallor and diaphoresis.

Unfortunately, Mrs. Lewis also develops a new onset of chest pain, so the nurse must reassess her and document findings. The following nursing note illustrates how the nurse collects and analyzes subjective and objective data and begins to develop nursing interventions.

Subjective: "I'm having chest pain again." Describes pain as a heavy weight in the center of her chest that radiates down her left arm. Rates chest pain as 8/10. Started approximately 5 minutes ago and has been increasing. Is similar to the pain that she had earlier in the day, although this pain began at rest. Reports nausea and clamminess.

Objective: Blood pressure 100/66 mm Hg right arm (semi-Fowler's), pulse 122 with 3 to 5 premature beats/min, respirations 28 breaths/min, and O_2 saturation 94%. Increased diaphoresis, dizziness, and nausea. Skin pale, appears anxious. Peripheral pulses 1+/4 and thready.

Analysis: Impaired cardiac tissue perfusion related to possible myocardial ischemia.

Plan: Stay with patient and continue to monitor vital signs. Give nitroglycerin tablets as ordered by physician. Page rapid-response team for assistance. Obtain 12-lead ECG and bedside monitor. Place oxygen as ordered and assess lung sounds. Elevate head of bed. Ensure that intravenous (IV) site is patent and suction is at bedside if needed. Provide calm reassurance that the patient will not be left alone and that treatment will be given for the chest pain. Use touch as appropriate. Inform family of new onset of chest pain.

Critical Thinking Challenge

- What type of assessment is this? Would you further investigate any subjective data?
- Critique the documented objective data. Is the organization logical? Would you add any data?
- Why did the nurse prioritize impaired cardiac tissue perfusion as the diagnosis to document?
- How is the nurse using assessment information to organize and plan nursing interventions?

The Institute for Healthcare Improvement (Simmonds, 2005) has recommended the formation of rapid-response teams to provide prompt assistance to patients with early warning signs of deterioration. Intervening before the patient's condition further declines has been proven to improve patient outcomes. The role of the team is to assess, stabilize, assist with communication, support, and assist with transfer if needed. Results that might trigger a page to the rapid-response team are as follows:

- Any staff member is worried about the patient.
- The patient has an acute change in heart rate of <40 or >130 beats/min.
- Systolic blood pressure changes acutely to <90 mm Hg.
- Respiratory rate changes acutely to <8 or >28 breaths/min.
- Saturation falls below 90% despite oxygen administration.
- Conscious state changes acutely.
- Urinary output falls below 50 mL in 4 hours (Grimes, Thornell, et al., 2007).

Mrs. Lewis was admitted 6 hours ago with chest pain and now is having new chest pain. Rapid response is indicated because the nurse is worried about the patient's new chest pain. The following conversation illustrates how to organize data and make recommendations about the patient's situation to team members when they arrive. Usually several people on the team come to assist with care at the bedside. Assessments and interventions occur simultaneously to resolve chest pain, which indicates cardiac ischemia and is an urgent issue.

Situation: I'm Galen Indigo and I'm the nurse for Mrs. Lewis. She was admitted with chest pain 6 hours ago and a diagnosis of myocardial infarction (MI). She has a new onset of chest pain that she rates as 8 out of 10.

Background: Her medical history includes hypertension. She is taking a beta-blocker and a thiazide diuretic and also a statin to lower her cholesterol. Her blood pressure is 100/66 mm Hg, which is down from 148/78 mm Hg. Her pulse is 122 beats/min, respirations 28 breaths/min, and O_2 saturation is 94%. She's having 3 to 5 premature beats/min and had a pulse deficit earlier. Her peripheral pulses are 1+/4 and thready. I have given her one nitroglycerin tablet, and she's still rating her pain as a 7 on a scale of 0 to 10.

Assessment: I called for you because I'm worried that she might be having some cardiac ischemia and can use some help in getting her treated.

Recommendations: (To a member of rapid response) It's time for her to have another nitroglycerin, so I can do that if you can get the ECG and then set up the bedside monitor. If someone else could hook up the oxygen, that would be great. She has an IV in place already. (To the charge nurse) Could you page the physician and let her know the situation? (To Mrs. Lewis) I'll stay with you, because I know you're a little anxious. (To an assisting nurse) Her husband is in the waiting room—could you let him know that she's having chest pain? If he would like to come in that's OK. Let him know that we're working closely with her. (To the patient) "Mrs. Lewis, let me know if your pain is any better after this second nitroglycerin. How are you doing?"

Critical Thinking Challenge

- How will the nurse conduct assessments and nursing care while considering Mrs. Lewis's anxious state?
- Which part of the nursing process is highest priority during this time?
- What is the nurse's role in coordinating collaborative care with the rapid-response team?
- What will be the frequency of assessment for Mrs. Lewis after this event? What items will be assessed?

Nurses use assessment data to formulate a nursing care plan for Mrs. Lewis. After completing the outlined interventions, they reevaluate and document findings in the chart. This is often in the form of a care plan or case note similar to the one below.

Nursing Diagnosis	Patient Outcomes	Nursing Interventions	Rationale	Evaluation
Impaired cardiac tissue perfusion related to possible cardiac ischemia	Blood pressure is stable within 30 min. Chest pain resolves within 5 min.	Monitor vital signs every 5 min until stable. Ensure intravenous (IV) access. Encourage the patient to rest and reduce anxiety. Monitor for cardiac arrhythmias. Administer nitroglycerin and oxygen PRN according to orders. Elevate head of bed.	IV access is essential in case the patient's condition deteriorates and IV medications are needed. Rest reduces the demand for oxygen. Arrhythmias may accompany ischemia. Nitroglycerin causes coronary arteries to dilate, relieving chest pain. Oxygen improves supply to the heart tissue.	Blood pressure has improved to 132/78 mm Hg. Chest pain has resolved with the third nitroglycerin. Patient is resting comfortably with head of bed elevated. Heart rate 102 and rhythm with no premature beats. Transfer to coronary intensive care for unstable chest pain.

Using the previous steps of clinical reasoning, organizing, and prioritizing, consider all the case study findings woven throughout this chapter. When answering the following questions, begin drawing conclusions and see how the pieces of assessment must work together to create an environment for personalized, appropriate, and accurate care.

- What might be causing the change in Mrs. Lewis's condition? (Knowledge)
- Is Mrs. Lewis's condition stable, urgent, or an emergency? (Comprehension)
- What immediate health promotion and teaching needs are evident? (Application)
- What lifestyle factors might be contributing to Mrs. Lewis's situation? (Analysis)
- How will the nurse focus, organize, and prioritize objective data collection? (Synthesis)
- How will the nurse evaluate the effectiveness of patient teaching? (Evaluation)

Key Points

- Knowledge of cardiac anatomy and physiology is essential to understanding cardiac assessment.
- The cardiovascular system is a double pump with pulmonary and systemic circulation.
- The cardiac cycle consists of rhythmic movements of systole (ventricular contraction) and diastole (relaxation).
- The S1 or first heart sound results from closure of the mitral and tricuspid valves; this sound signals the beginning of systole.
- The S2 or second heart sound results from closure of the aortic and pulmonic valves; this sound signals the beginning of diastole and end of systole.
- A newborn's cardiac function shifts dramatically at birth as the foramen ovale and ductus arteriosus close and the right heart pumps blood to the lungs.

- A female who is pregnant has increased blood volume, heart rate, stroke volume, and cardiac output by 30% to 40% above nonpregnant values.
- Health care providers assume that chest pain is heart pain until another diagnosis is established. Chest pain is an acute situation that requires intervention in addition to assessment.
- Risk factors for cardiovascular disease include increasing age, family history, male gender, high blood pressure, high blood cholesterol level, smoking, diabetes mellitus, overweight and obesity, decreased activity, high-fat diet, excessive alcohol intake, elevated C-reactive protein, and elevated B-type natriuretic peptide.
- Common symptoms of cardiovascular disease are chest pain, dyspnea, orthopnea, cough, diaphoresis, fatigue, edema, and nocturia.
- Inspection and palpation of the PMI should be in the 5th left ICS medial to the MCL.
- The nurse auscultates heart sounds in specific areas on the precordium: aortic, pulmonic, tricuspid, and mitral.
- A split heart sound is audible when the valves close at slightly different times: the S1 is split from the mitral and tricuspid, and the S2 is split from the aortic and pulmonic.
- Murmurs are identified by their location, intensity, quality, timing in the cardiac cycle, and radiation.
- S3 and S4 are extra sounds that result from ventricular filling; the S3 follows the S2 and the S4 precedes the S1.
- Cardiac anomalies in children cause signs of decreased oxygenation, low cardiac output, or increased pulmonary pressure.
- The nursing diagnoses most commonly associated with cardiac conditions are decreased cardiac output, ineffective cardiac tissue perfusion, and excess fluid volume.

Review Questions

1. Which of the following statements describes the cardiovascular system most accurately? The cardiovascular system
   A. is a double pump with pulmonary and systemic elements
   B. has a heart with six chambers and valves
   C. includes concepts of precontractility, postcontractility, and load
   D. functions with a conduction system that starts in the ventricles

2. In a healthy patient, the myocardial cells in the ventricle depolarize and contract during
   A. prediastole
   B. diastole
   C. systole
   D. postsystole

3. When the nurse listens to S1 in the mitral and tricuspid areas, the expected finding is
   A. S1 > S2
   B. S1 = S2
   C. S2 > S1
   D. no S1 is heard

4. The nurse assesses the neck vessels in the patient with heart failure to determine which of the following?
   A. The strength of the carotid pulse
   B. The presence of bruits
   C. The highest level of jugular venous pulsation
   D. The strength of the jugular veins

5. The nurse is caring for a patient with a sudden onset of chest pain. Which assessment is of highest priority?
   A. Auscultate heart sounds
   B. Inspect the precordium
   C. Percuss the left border
   D. Obtain a blood pressure

6. The patient visits the clinic with the controllable risk factors of smoking, high-fat diet, overweight, decreased activity, and high blood pressure. What concept should the nurse use when performing patient teaching?
   A. Teach the patient the most serious information.
   B. Give the patient brochures to review before the next visit.
   C. Discuss risk factors that the patient is interested in modifying.
   D. Describe consequences of risk factors to motivate the patient.

7. Which of the following clusters of symptoms are common in women preceding a myocardial infarction (MI)?
   A. Chest pain, nausea, diaphoresis
   B. Weight gain, edema, nocturia
   C. Dizziness, palpitations, low pulse
   D. Fatigue, difficulty sleeping, dyspnea

8. The nurse auscultates a medium-loud whooshing sound that softens between S1 and S2. The nurse documents this finding as which of the following?
   A. Grade III decrescendo systolic murmur
   B. Grade IV crescendo systolic murmur
   C. Grade II crescendo diastolic murmur
   D. Grade I decrescendo diastolic murmur

9. The nurse auscultates an extra sound on the patient 1 week following an MI. It is immediately after S2 and is heard best at the apex. Which of the following does the nurse suspect?
   A. S3 gallop
   B. S4 gallop
   C. Systolic ejection click
   D. Split S2

10. The patient has dyspnea, edema, weight gain, and intake greater than output. These symptoms are consistent with which nursing diagnosis?
    A. Ineffective cardiac tissue perfusion
    B. Decreased cardiac output
    C. Impaired gas exchange
    D. Excess fluid volume

Canadian Nursing Research

Chailler, M., Ellis, J., et al. (2010). Cold therapy for the management of pain associated with deep breathing and coughing post-cardiac surgery. *Canadian Journal of Cardiovascular Nursing, 20*(2), 18–24.

Girard, B., & Murray, T. (2010). Perceived control: A construct to guide patient education. *Canadian Journal of Cardiovascular Nursing, 20*(3), 18–26.

Pfaff, K. A., El-Masri, M. M., et al. (2009). Comparing the psychological stress between non-smoking patients and smoking patients who experience abrupt smoking cessation during hospitalization for acute myocardial infarction: A pilot study. *Canadian Journal of Cardiovascular Nursing, 19*(4), 26–32.

Sherrard, H., Struthers, C., et al. (2009). Using technology to create a medication safety net for cardiac surgery patients: A nurse-led randomized control trial. *Canadian Journal of Cardiovascular Nursing, 19*(3), 9–15.

Spyropoulos, V., Ampleman, S., et al. (2011). Cardiac surgery discharge questionnaires: Meeting information needs of patients and families. *Canadian Journal of Cardiovascular Nursing, 21*(1), 13–19.

References

American Heart Association. (2005). *Coronary heart disease, acute coronary syndrome, and angina pectoris.* Retrieved from http://www.americanheart.org/presenter.jhtml?identifier=3000090

Barkmann, A., & Porth, C. M. (2010). Disorders of blood pressure regulation. In R. A. Hannon, C. Pooler, et al. (Eds.). *Porth pathophysiology: Concepts of altered health states* (1st Canadian ed., pp. 485–510). Philadelphia, PA: Wolters Kluwer Health/Lippincott Williams & Wilkins.

Benetos, A., Thomas, F., et al. (2002). Prognostic value of systolic and diastolic blood pressure in treated hypertensive men. *Archives of Internal Medicine, 162*, 577–581.

Bernhard, D., & Laufer, G. (2008). The aging cardiomyocyte: A mini-review. *Gerontology, 54*(1), 24–31.

Blancher, S. (2005). Cardiac electrophysiology procedures. In S. L. Woods, E. S. Sivarajan Froelicher, et al. (Eds.). *Cardiac nursing* (5th ed., pp. 425–438). Philadelphia, PA: Wolters Kluwer Health/Lippincott Williams & Wilkins.

Braunwald, E., Zipes, D. P., et al. (2004). *Heart disease: A textbook of cardiovascular medicine* (7th ed.). Philadelphia, PA: Saunders.

Bulechek, G. M., Butcher, H. K., et al. (2008). *Nursing interventions classification (NIC)* (5th ed.). St. Louis, MO: Mosby.

Cappola, A. R., Fried, L. P., et al. (2006). Thyroid status, cardiovascular risk, and mortality in older adults. *Journal of American Medical Association, 295*, 1033–1041.

Celebi, A., & Onat, T. (2006). Echocardiographic study on the origin of the innocent flow murmurs. *Pediatric Cardiology, 27*(1), 19–24.

Chen, H. H., & Burett, J. C. (2007). Natriuretic peptides in the pathophysiology of congestive heart failure. *Current Cardiology Reports, 2*(3), 198–205.

Clark, A. M., & Norris, C. (2010). Management of patients with coronary vascular disorders. In R. A. Day, P. Paul, et al. (Eds.). *Brunner & Suddarth's textbook of Canadian medical-surgical nursing* (2nd ed., pp. 803–853). Philadelphia, PA: Wolters Kluwer Health/Lippincott Williams & Wilkins.

Dupuis-Blanchard, S. (2010). Health care of the older adult. In R. A. Day, P. Paul, et al. (Eds.). *Brunner & Suddarth's textbook of Canadian medical-surgical nursing* (2nd ed., pp. 218–251). Philadelphia, PA: Wolters Kluwer Health/Lippincott Williams & Wilkins.

EPIC-Potsdam. (2007). Potentially modifiable classic risk factors and their impact on incident myocardial infarction: Results from the EPIC-Potsdam study. *European Journal of Cardiovascular Prevention and Rehabilitation, 14*(1), 65–71.

Gillett, M., Davis, W. A., et al. (2003). Prospective evaluation of carotid bruit as a predictor of first stroke in type 2 diabetes: The Fremantle diabetes study. *Stroke, 34*, 2145–2151.

Grimes, C., Thornell, B., et al. (2007). Developing rapid response teams: Best practices through collaboration. *Clinical Nurse Specialist, 21*(2), 85–92.

Heart and Stroke Foundation of Canada. (2007). *Heart attack warning signals:are the warning signals of heart attack the same for women?* Retrieved from http://www.heartandstroke.ab.ca/site/c.IqIRLIPJJtH/b.3650837/#womenha signals

Heart and Stroke Foundation of Canada. (2010). *South Asian resources.* Retrieved from http://www.heartandstroke.com/site/c.ikIQLcMWJtE/b.3479045/k.6516/South_Asian_Re

Heart and Stroke Foundation of Canada. (2011a). *Want to improve your heart health? First Nations, Inuit & Métis resources.* Retrieved from http://www.heartandstroke.com/site/c.ikIQLcMWJtE/b.3479041/k.FFD0/First_Nations_I

Heart and Stroke Foundation of Canada. (2011b). *People of African descent resources.* Retrieved from http://www.heartandstroke.com/site/c.ikIQLcMWJtE/b.3479039/k.3DD6/People_African

Jones, D. E., Weaver, M. T., et al. (2006). Health belief model perceptions, knowledge of heart disease, and its risk factors in educated African-American women: An exploration of the relationships of socioeconomic status and age. *Journal of National Black Nurses Association, 17*(2), 13–23.

Lakatta, E. G. (2002). Age-associated cardiovascular changes in health: Impact on cardiovascular disease in older persons. *Heart Failure Review, 7*(1), 29–49.

Lakatta, E. G., & Levy, D. (2003). Arterial and cardiac aging: Major shareholders in cardiovascular disease enterprises. Part II: The aging heart in health: Links to heart disease. *Circulation, 107*(2), 346–354.

London, M. L., Ladewig, P. A. W., et al. (2007). *Maternal & child nursing care* (2nd ed.). Upper Saddle River, NJ: Pearson Prentice Hall.

Lowdermilk, D., & Perry, S. (2007). *Maternity & women's health care* (9th ed.). St. Louis, MO: Mosby.

Malone, F., & D'Alton, M. (2004). Multiple gestation: Clinical characteristics and management. In R. Creasy, R. Resnik, et al. (Eds.). *Maternal-fetal medicine: Principles and practice* (5th ed.). Philadelphia, PA: W.B. Saunders.

Marcus, G. M., Cohen, J., et al. (2007). The utility of gestures in patients with chest discomfort. *American Journal of Medicine, 120*, 83–89.

Marinella, M. A., Pierson, C., et al. (1997). The stethoscope: A potential source of nosocomial infection? *Archives of Internal Medicine, 157*(7), 786–790.

McSweeney, J. C., Cody, M., et al. (2003). Women's early warning symptoms of acute myocardial infarction. *Circulation, 108,* 2619–2623.

Menasche, V. (2007). Heart murmurs. *Pediatrics in Review, 28,* 19–22.

Monga, M., & Sanborn, M. (2004). Biology and physiology of the reproductive tract and control of myometrial contraction. In R. Creasy, R. Resnik, et al. (Eds.). *Maternal-fetal medicine: Principles and practice* (5th ed.). Philadelphia, PA: W.B. Saunders.

Moorhead, S., Johnson, M., et al. (2007). *Nursing outcomes classification (NOC)* (4th ed.). Philadelphia, PA: Mosby.

Murabito, J. M., Pencina, M. J., et al. (2005). Sibling cardiovascular disease as a risk factor for cardiovascular disease in middle-aged adults. *Journal of the American Medical Association, 294,* 3117–3123.

Nasir, K., Michos, E. D., et al. (2004). Coronary artery calcification and family history of premature coronary heart disease: Sibling history is more strongly associated than parental history. *Circulation, 110*(15), 2074–2076.

National Heart, Lung, and Blood Institute. (2007). *Disease Statistics.* Retrieved from http://www.nhlbi.nih.gov/about/factbook/chapter4.htm

Norris, C., & Clark, A. M. (2010). Assessment of cardiovascular function. In R. A. Day, P. Paul, et al. (Eds.). *Brunner & Suddarth's textbook of Canadian medical-surgical nursing* (2nd ed., pp. 732–770). Philadelphia, PA: Wolters Kluwer Health/Lippincott Williams & Wilkins.

Norris, C., Dasgupta, K., et al. (2007). Differences in cardiovascular presentation in women and men. *CMAJ Theme Issue, 176*(6), 522–523.

Norris, C. M., Ghali, W. A., et al. (2004). Systematic review of statistical methods used to analyze Seattle Angina Questionnaire scores. *Canadian Journal of Cardiology, 20*(2), 187–193.

North American Nursing Diagnosis Association. (2009). *Nursing diagnoses, 2009–2011 Edition: Definitions and classifications (NANDA NURSING DIAGNOSIS).* West Sussex, UK: John Wiley & Sons.

Paradoxical Split of the Second Sound (2007). Retrieved from http://sprojects.mmi.mcgill.ca/mvs/GLOSSARY/P.HTM

Pasternak, R. C., Sidney, C. S., et al. (2002). ACC/AHA/NHLBI clinical advisory on statins. *Journal of the American College of Cardiology, 40*(3), 567–572.

Pilote, L., Dasgupta, K., et al. (2007). A comprehensive view of sex-specific issues related to cardiovascular disease. *Canadian Medical Association Journal, 176*(6), S1–S44.

Ridker, P., Rifai, N., et al. (2002). Comparison of C-reactive protein and low-density lipoprotein cholesterol levels in the prediction of first cardiovascular events. *New England Journal of Medicine, 347,* 1557–1565.

Roach, S., Roddick, P., et al. (2010). The cardiovascular system. In T. C. Stephen, D. L. Skillen, R. A. Day, & L. S. Bickley (Eds.). *Canadian Bates' guide to health assessment for nurses* (1st ed., pp. 423–478). Philadelphia, PA: Wolters Kluwer Health/Lippincott Williams & Wilkins.

Romero-Corral, A., Montori, V. M., et al. (2006). Association of bodyweight with total mortality and with cardiovascular events in coronary artery disease: A systematic review of cohort studies. *Lancet, 368,* 666–678.

Schroeder, K., Fahey, T., et al. (2004). How can we improve adherence to blood pressure-lowering medication in ambulatory care? Systematic review of randomized controlled trials. *Archives of Internal Medicine, 164,* 722–732.

Simmonds, T. (2005). Best-practice protocols: Implementing a rapid response system of care. *Nursing Management, 36*(7), 41–42, 58–59.

Strimel, W. J., Assadi, R., et al. (2006). *Pericardial effusion.* Retrieved from http://www.emedicine.com/MED/topic1786.htm

Taubert, G., Winkelmann, B. R., et al. (2003). Prevalence, predictors, and consequences of unrecognized diabetes mellitus in 3266 patients scheduled for coronary angiography. *American Heart Journal, 145,* 285–291.

Techniques: Heart Sounds and Murmurs (2007). Retrieved from http://depts.washington.edu/physdx/heart/tech3.html

Van't Laar, A. L. (2002). Why is the measurement of jugular venous pressure discredited? *Netherland Journal of Medicine, 61*(7), 268–272.

Wang, C. S., Fitzgerald, J. M., et al. (2005). Does this dyspneic patient in the emergency department have congestive heart failure? *Journal of American Medical Association, 294,* 1944–1956.

Wiese, J. (2000). The abdominojugular reflux sign. *American Journal of Medicine, 109*(1), 59–61.

Williams, B. (2010). Health education and health promotion. In R. A. Day, P. Paul, et al. (Eds.). *Brunner & Suddarth's textbook of Canadian medical-surgical nursing* (2nd ed., pp. 45–60). Philadelphia, PA: Wolters Kluwer Health/Lippincott Williams & Wilkins.

Woods, S. L., Sivarajan Froelicher, E. S., et al. (2010). *Cardiac nursing* (6th ed.). Philadelphia, PA: Wolters Kluwer Health/Lippincott Williams & Wilkins.

Yang, H. T. (2007). Effect of aging on angiogenesis and arteriogenesis. *Current Cardiology Reviews, 3*(1), 65–74.

The Canadian Jensen's Nursing Health Assessment suite offers these additional resources to enhance learning and facilitate understanding of this chapter:

- thePoint on line resource, http//thepoint.lww.com/Stephen1E
- *Laboratory Manual for Canadian Jensen's Nursing Health Assessment: A Best Practice Approach*

Tables of Unexpected Findings

Table 19-4   Variations in S1 and S2

Heart Sound	Description
Accentuated S1	S1 is louder when mitral valve leaflets are recessed into the ventricle, as with rapid heart rate, hyperkinetic states, short PR interval, atrial fibrillation, or mitral stenosis.
Diminished S1	S1 is softer with long PR interval, depressed contractility, left bundle branch block, obesity, or a muscular chest.
Varying Intensity of S1	S1 varies in atrial fibrillation and complete heart block when the valve is in varying positions before closing.
Split S1	The first component is heard at the base; the second component is heard at the lower left sternal border. Split S1 accompanies right bundle branch block.
Accentuated S2	S2 is increased in systemic hypertension or when the aorta is close to the chest wall. Another cause is pulmonary hypertension.
Diminished S2	S2 may be decreased from aortic calcification, pulmonic stenosis, and aging, with reduced mobility of the valves.

(table continues on page 530)

Table 19-4   Variations in S1 and S2 (continued)

Heart Sound	Description
Fixed Split  	The two components are heard during both inspiration and expiration. The split is wide and results from right bundle branch block or early opening of the aortic valve.
Paradoxical Split 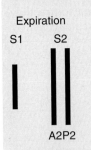 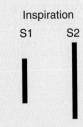	The pulmonic valve closes before the aortic from left bundle branch block, right ventricular pacemaker. The sounds usually fuse during inspiration.
Wide Split 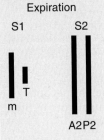 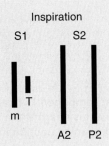	A wide split is found with right bundle branch block from delayed depolarization of the right ventricle.

Table 19-5   Identifying Extra Sounds

Heart Sound	Description
Ejection Click 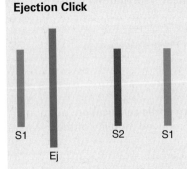	This sound results from an open valve that moves during the beginning of systole. It is heard best with the diaphragm of the stethoscope, and may be audible over aortic or pulmonic areas.

Table 19-5 **Identifying Extra Sounds** (*continued*)

Heart Sound	Description
Opening Snap 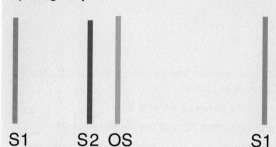	It indicates that the mitral valve is mobile and "snaps" during early diastole from high atrial pressure, such as with mitral stenosis.
Summation Gallop 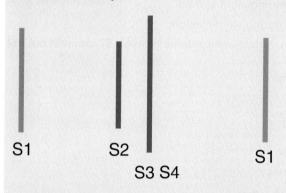	This is the same as the quadruple rhythm but with a faster rate. S3 and S4 merge to create one sound.
Pericardial Friction Rub 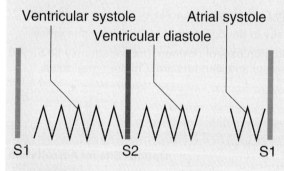	It is triple phased during midsystole, middiastole, and presystole. The scratchy, leathery quality results from the parietal and visceral pleura rubbing together. The sound increases on leaning forward and during exhalation. It is heard best in the 3rd left intercostal space (ICS) at the sternal border.
Venous Hum 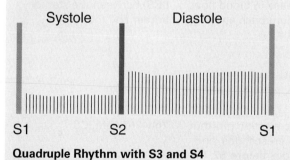	This continuous sound is expected in children and during pregnancy. It is rough, noisy, and occasionally accompanied by a high-pitched whine. It may be louder during diastole. It is low pitched and heard best with the bell above the medial third of the clavicles.
Quadruple Rhythm with S3 and S4	S3 is generated during early diastolic filling; S4 is generated during atrial contraction late in diastole. Both are present. It is heard best with the bell of the stethoscope over the apex of the heart.

Intensity: Loudness	I. Faint; heard only with special effort
	II. Soft but readily detected
	III. Prominent but not loud
	IV. Loud; accompanied by thrill
	V. Very loud
	VI. Loud enough to be heard with stethoscope just removed from contact with the chest wall (Braunwald, Zipes, et al., 2004)
Timing: Point in the cardiac cycle	Systolic: Sounds like "swish-dub"; falls between S1 and S2
	Diastolic: Sounds like "dub-swish," falls after S2 and before the next S1
	More specifically murmurs may be labelled as early, mid, or late systolic and early, mid, or late diastolic.
	Holosystolic murmurs: Occur during all of systole
	Holodiastolic murmurs: Occur during all of diastole
	Continuous murmurs: Begin in systole and continue through S2 into part but not necessarily all of diastole
Pitch: High or low tone	High: Heard best with diaphragm
	Medium
Pattern: Increasing or decreasing in volume	Low pitch: Heard best with bell
	Crescendo: Increasing intensity
	Decrescendo: Decreasing intensity
	Plateau: Remain constant
Quality: Type of sounds	Harsh, blowing, raspy, musical, rumbling
Location: Site on the precordium	Area of maximum intensity using either valvular areas or thoracic landmarks
Radiation: Direction it travels	Where the sound radiates, usually in the direction of blood flow in the vessel
Position: Changes with patient position	If the murmur changes depending on patient position. The patient may be turned to the left and right, lie down, sit up, and lean forward. Children may squat.

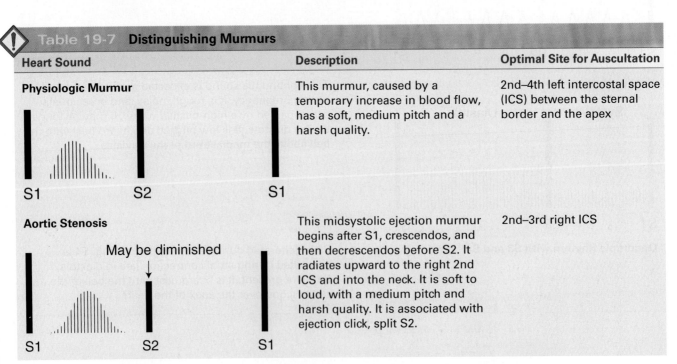

Heart Sound	Description	Optimal Site for Auscultation
Physiologic Murmur	This murmur, caused by a temporary increase in blood flow, has a soft, medium pitch and a harsh quality.	2nd–4th left intercostal space (ICS) between the sternal border and the apex
Aortic Stenosis	This midsystolic ejection murmur begins after S1, crescendos, and then decrescendos before S2. It radiates upward to the right 2nd ICS and into the neck. It is soft to loud, with a medium pitch and harsh quality. It is associated with ejection click, split S2.	2nd–3rd right ICS

Heart Sound	Description	Optimal Site for Auscultation
Pulmonic Stenosis	This midsystolic ejection murmur may radiate toward the left shoulder and neck. It is soft-loud, medium pitch, harsh quality, and associated with ejection click, split S2	2nd–3rd left ICS
Mitral Stenosis	This middiastolic murmur is associated with an opening snap and has a low-pitched, rumbling quality	Heard best with the bell over the apex with the patient turned to the left
Mitral Regurgitation	This midsystolic ejection murmur is soft to loud, medium to high pitch, with a blowing quality. It radiates to the left axilla and is associated with a thrill and lift at the apex.	Apex
Tricuspid Regurgitation	This midsystolic ejection murmur can be holosystolic with elevated right ventricular pressure. It increases with inspiration, with a medium pitch and blowing quality.	Lower left sternal border
Aortic Regurgitation	This early diastolic murmur is decrescendo, soft, high pitched, and blowing.	2nd–4th left ICS; heard best with the diaphragm of the stethoscope when the patient leans forward during exhalation
Pulmonic Regurgitation	This early diastolic murmur may begin with a loud S2. It is a high-frequency blowing murmur with a crescendo–decrescendo pattern.	
Tricuspid Stenosis	The loudness of this middiastolic murmur increases with inspiration. It has a rumbling quality and is louder during inspiration.	Heard at the lower left sternal border

Pulmonic Stenosis diagram: S1 E$_j$ S2   A$_2$ P$_2$ S1

Mitral Stenosis diagram: S1   S2   OS   Accentuated → S1

Mitral Regurgitation diagram: Diminished ↓   S1   S2   S3   S1

Tricuspid Regurgitation diagram: Diminished ↓   S$_1$ S$_2$ S$_3$ S$_1$

Aortic Regurgitation diagram: S1   S2   S1

Table 19-8   Congenital Heart Disease

Heart Sound	Description	Optimal Site for Auscultation
Patent Ductus Arteriosus 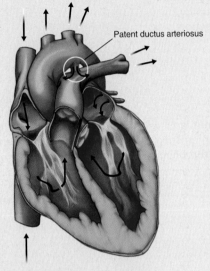 Patent ductus arteriosus	The continuous murmur peaks just before and after S2. It has a rough, harsh, mechanical quality with a palpable thrill.	2nd left intercostal space (ICS)
Atrial Septal Defect 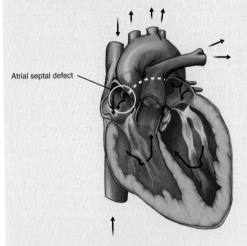 Atrial septal defect	This continuous murmur is altered by Valsalva's manoeuvre. It is a systolic ejection murmur with medium pitch.	Base in the 2nd left ICS
Ventricular Septal Defect 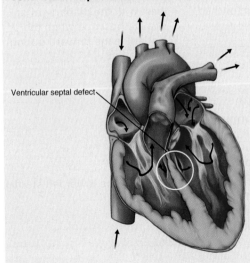 Ventricular septal defect	This murmur is holosystolic because left ventricular pressures exceed right ventricular pressures. It radiates, often loudly, with a thrill. The quality is high pitched and harsh.	3rd–5th left ICS

Table 19-8   **Congenital Heart Disease** *(continued)*

Heart Sound	Description	Optimal Site for Auscultation
Tetralogy of Fallot 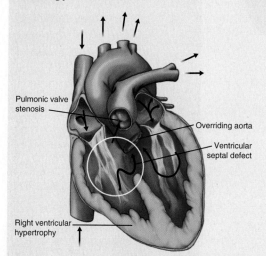 Pulmonic valve stenosis Overriding aorta Ventricular septal defect Right ventricular hypertrophy	This early diastolic murmur has a thrill. It is loud, with a crescendo–descrescendo pattern	Lower left sternal border
Coarctation of the Aorta 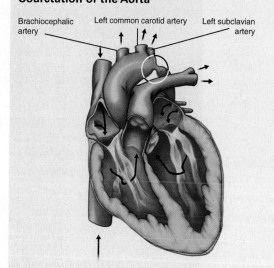 Brachiocephalic artery Left common carotid artery Left subclavian artery	This systolic murmur radiates to the back.	Left sternal border

Peripheral Vascular and Lymphatic Assessment

Learning Objectives

1 Demonstrate knowledge of the anatomy and physiology of the arterial, venous, and lymphatic systems and fascia compartments.

2 Identify important topics for health promotion and risk reduction related to the arterial, venous, and lymphatic systems and fascia compartments.

3 Collect subjective data related to peripheral vascular, lymphatic, and fascia compartment symptoms.

4 Collect objective data related to the peripheral vascular and lymphatic systems and fascia compartments, using physical examination techniques.

5 Identify expected and unexpected findings related to the peripheral vascular and lymphatic systems and fascia compartments.

6 Analyze subjective and objective data from the assessment of the peripheral vascular and lymphatic systems and fascia compartments, and consider initial interventions.

7 Document and communicate data from the peripheral vascular, lymphatic, and fascia compartment assessments, using appropriate terminology and principles of recording.

8 Consider the age, gender, and culture of the patient to individualize the peripheral vascular, lymphatic, and fascia compartment assessments.

9 Based on findings from the peripheral vascular, lymphatic, and fascia compartment assessments, identify nursing diagnoses and initiate a plan of care.

*M*r. Roman Tretski, an 88-year-old Caucasian man, lives in a long-term care facility. His medical diagnoses include a myocardial infarction 15 years ago, high blood pressure, high cholesterol level, chronic renal failure, and peripheral arterial disease (PAD). He is taking a statin drug, simvastatin (Corgard) 30 mg daily for his cholesterol, and an antiplatelet medication, ASA (aspirin) 81 mg daily for the PAD. He also is slightly confused, with impaired recent memory.

You will gain more information about Mr. Tretski as you progress through this chapter. As you study the content and features, consider Mr. Tretski's case and its relationship to what you are learning. Begin thinking about the following points:

- How does Mr. Tretski's health history relate to his current health status?
- What assessment findings might the nurse note if Mr. Tretski's PAD worsens?
- What assessment data will the nurse want to collect related to other body systems?
- How might the nurse modify history taking and physical examination based on Mr. Tretski's age and health concerns?

The focus of this chapter is a comprehensive assessment of the circulation in the periphery, primarily the arms and legs. Included are the arteries, veins, interconnecting capillary beds, the lymphatic system and its lymph nodes, and the fascia compartments. It is critical that nurses understand the independent roles of the arterial, venous, and lymphatic systems and fascia compartments, as well as their integrated functioning as the circulatory system. Doing so enables them to develop holistic plans for circulatory well-being in their patients. A review of pertinent anatomy and physiology provides the basis for the collection of subjective and objective information. The section on subjective data collection gives details to help nurses evaluate symptoms, history, and risk factors associated with peripheral vascular health. The content on objective assessment outlines a detailed approach to assessing skin condition, extremity temperature, peripheral pulses, perfusion, and fluid status and describes alterations in structure or function. This chapter also includes advanced assessment techniques.

Anatomy and Physiology Overview

The organs and tissues of the body depend on a healthy, intact peripheral vascular system, which consists of a complex network of arteries, veins, and lymphatic vessels. The vascular network transports oxygenated blood throughout the body and returns deoxygenated blood to the heart and lungs for reoxygenation. The lymphatic system supports the vascular system by returning excess fluid from the tissues to the vascular network. Disruption of the peripheral vascular or lymphatic system or increased pressure in fascia compartments of the arms and legs can have debilitating and, in some cases, fatal consequences. Thus, comprehensive and accurate assessment of the arterial, venous, and lymphatic systems and the fascia compartments provides an essential foundation for holistic and thorough nursing care. Such assessment depends on a solid understanding of the anatomy and physiology of these systems.

Arterial System

The arterial system consists of arteries, arterioles, and capillaries that deliver oxygenated blood from the heart to the rest of the body. The walls of the arteries and arterioles have three layers: the *tunica intima* or inner layer; the *tunica media*, which is the middle layer; and the *tunica externa (adventitia)* or outer layer (Fig. 20-1). Arteries have many elastic fibres, which allow them to constrict and recoil with systole and diastole.

> **Clinical Significance 20-1**
>
> Arterioles have more smooth muscle, and it is here that blood pressure is controlled (Barkman, Pooler, et al., 2010).

The largest vessel of the arterial system is the *aorta*. The subclavian arteries come off the aorta to feed the vessels of the upper extremities. The largest arteries of the upper

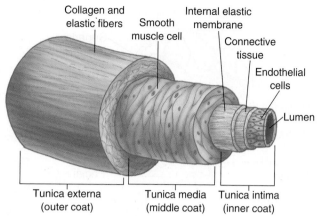

Figure 20-1 Structure of an artery.

extremities are the *brachial arteries*. They bifurcate into the *radial* and *ulnar arteries*, which further divide into two arterial arches that supply the hand (Barkman, Pooler, et al., 2010).

The aorta bifurcates 1.5–2.0 cm below the umbilicus into the *iliac arteries*. The iliac arteries continue into the femoral arteries, which go to the lower extremities. At the *popliteal fossa*, the femoral artery becomes the popliteal artery, which bifurcates into the *dorsalis pedis* and *posterior tibial arteries*. These arteries form a connecting arch at the foot (Barkman, Pooler, et al., 2010) (see Fig. 20-2).

Smooth endothelial cells line the inner layer of all blood vessels and play a critical role in the prevention of platelet adhesion and thrombus formation. Injury to the endothelial layer thus contributes significantly to the pathogenesis of atherosclerosis (Barkman, Pooler, et al., 2010). Interruption of arterial flow results from narrowing of the arteries, rupture or dissection of the layers of an artery, or thrombus formation.

Venous System

The venous system consists of veins, venules, and connecting veins called perforators, which collect unoxygenated blood from the body and return it to the heart (Fig. 20-3). In contrast to arteries, veins are thin walled. The venous system is a low-pressure system. Veins often are referred to as capacitance vessels because they can stretch and accommodate large volumes of fluid (Barkman, Pooler, et al., 2010).

The veins of the upper extremities, upper torso, head, and neck drain into the superior vena cava and then the right atrium. Those of the lower extremities and lower torso drain into the inferior vena cava and the right atrium. In the upper and lower extremities, veins are part of the superficial or deep systems. The superficial system includes the greater and lesser saphenous veins. The deep system includes the common femoral, femoral, profunda femoris, popliteal, and anterior, posterior, and peroneal tibial vessels (Barkman, Pooler, et al., 2010).

A pressure gradient created by respiration, skeletal muscle contraction, and intraluminal valves regulates blood flow

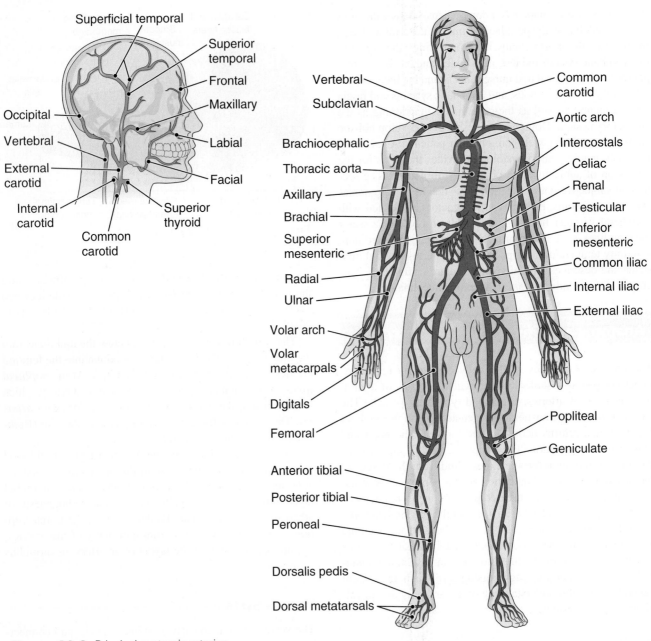

Figure 20-2 Principal systemic arteries.

in the venous system (Barkman, Pooler, et al., 2010). During inspiration, the diaphragm drops and abdominal pressure increases. During expiration, abdominal pressure decreases, creating a suction effect that promotes venous return. Because veins do not have the same muscular walls that arteries do, they also rely on the calf muscle pump to combat the pull of gravity and promote venous return. For example, as a person walks, the contraction of the calf muscles promotes venous flow. Additionally, veins contain bicuspid valves that prevent the retrograde flow of venous blood, thus maintaining unidirectional flow.

The more distal a vein is, the greater the number of valves, because the pull of gravity is stronger (Barkman, Pooler, et al., 2010). Interruption of venous flow results from obstruction, valve incompetence, or trauma.

Clinical Significance 20-2

Because the veins are the capacitance vessels and are less muscular than arteries, blood tends to collect in them. When moving from lying to standing or when standing suddenly, dizziness may result until the calf and leg muscles contract to increase the venous return to the central part of the body and brain.

Capillaries

The exchange of nutrients, gases, and metabolites between blood vessels and tissues occurs in the capillary beds (Fig. 20-4). Oxygen-rich blood delivers nutrients from the arterioles to the capillaries. Venules then return metabolites from the capillary beds to the venous system.

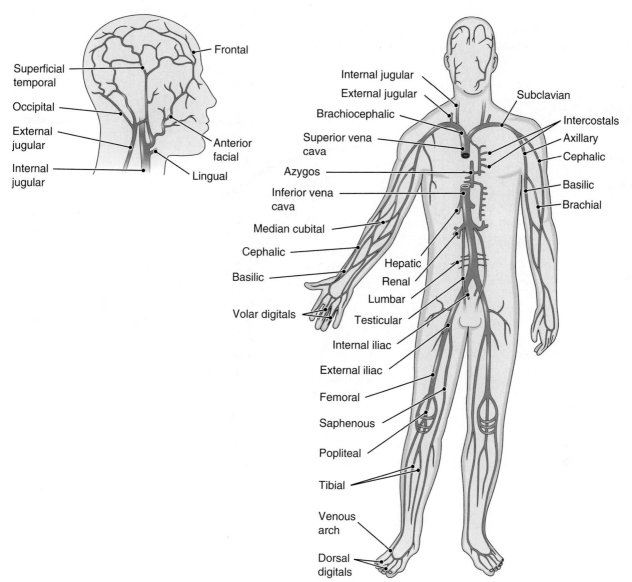

Figure 20-3 Principal systemic veins.

Lymphatic System

The lymphatic system consists of the lymph nodes and lymphatic vessels (Fig. 20-4) as well as the spleen, tonsils, and thymus (Fig. 20-5). It maintains fluid and protein balance and functions with the immune system to fight infection. The lymphatic vessels carry lymph in the tissues back to the bloodstream. The pathways of these vessels often run parallel to the arteries and veins (Barkman, Pooler, et al., 2010). The thoracic ducts at the junctions of the subclavian and internal jugular veins return the lymph fluid to the circulation (Barkman, Pooler, et al.). The lymphatic vessels contain valves to maintain unidirectional flow. Skeletal muscle contraction, passive movement, and increases in heart rate all support lymph flow.

Only the superficial lymph nodes are accessible for palpation. Lymphatic flow in the arms drains into the epitrochlear, axillary, and infraclavicular nodes. In the lower extremities, the lymph drains primarily into the inguinal nodes (Barkman, Pooler, et al., 2010).

When the amount of lymph in interstitial tissue exceeds the capacity of the lymphatic vessels, *lymphedema* occurs. Fluid high in protein fills the tissue and is ultimately replaced by fibrous tissue and collagen. If untreated, the fibrosis may progress and result in irreversible tissue enlargement. Lymphedema may be congenital or result from scarring injury, removal of lymph nodes, radiation therapy, or chronic infection (Barkman, Pooler, et al., 2010).

Fascia Compartment of Limbs

Fascia refers to the fibrous, band-like membranes covering and separating muscles. In the human body there are 46 anatomical compartments or areas where fascia enclose blood vessels, nerves, and muscles (Altizer, 2006) (Fig. 20-6). Of note is the fact that 36 of the 46 are found in the upper and lower limbs. "Any increase in pressure within a compartment can compromise vascular perfusion and lymphatic flow, resulting in *compartment syndrome*" (Edge, Day, et al., 2010, p. 569).

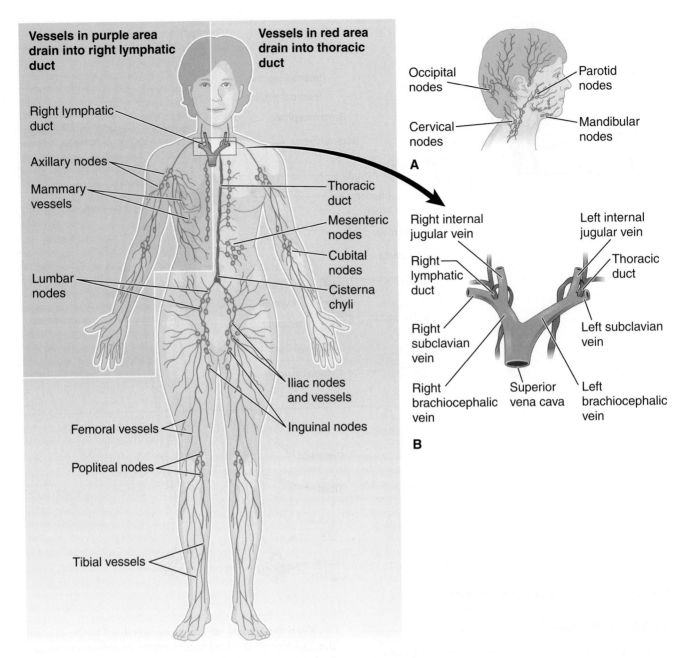

Figure 20-4 The lymphatic vessels and nodes. **A.** Lymph nodes and vessels in the head. **B.** The right lymphatic duct and thoracic duct drain into the subclavian veins.

⚠ Lifespan Considerations

Women Who Are Pregnant

Maternal blood volume nearly doubles during pregnancy. This volume, combined with obstruction of the iliac veins and inferior vena cava as a result of fetal growth, leads to increased venous pressure. The result may be dependent edema, varicosities in the legs and vulva, and hemorrhoids (Barkman, Pooler, et al., 2010). These findings are especially common in the last trimester.

Newborns, Children, and Adolescents

Intimal changes begin at birth. Atherosclerosis has been found in the arteries of children and adolescents, highly correlated with known familial hypercholesterolemia (Noto, Okada, et al., 2006), hypertension, elevated cholesterol level, obesity, physical inactivity, and high-fat diet are all risk factors that must be evaluated in children and adolescents (Kavey, Daniels, et al., 2003). Obesity in children and adolescents increased two- to fourfold from 1980 to 2000; rates were highest among those of African and Hispanic genetic descent (Brunt, Lester, et al., 2008; Williams, Haymen, et al., 2002). The association of obesity with other cardiovascular risk factors as well as other diseases makes its growing prevalence a great public-health concern (Williams, Haymen, et al.). Many cigarette smokers begin smoking in their preteen or teen years. Early education and intervention are key in this age group. Prevention of atherosclerosis begins in childhood (Barkman, Pooler, et al., 2010).

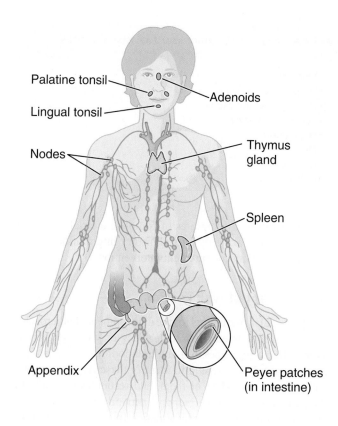

Figure 20-5 Lymphoid tissues.

Labels: Palatine tonsil, Lingual tonsil, Nodes, Appendix, Adenoids, Thymus gland, Spleen, Peyer patches (in intestine)

Older Adults

Calcification of the arteries, or *arteriosclerosis*, causes them to become more rigid in older adults. Less arterial compliance results in increased systolic blood pressure (Barkman, Pooler, et al., 2010). This is often compounded by the coexistence of atherosclerotic disease in the arteries supplying the brain, heart, and other vital organs. The incidence of peripheral arterial disease (PAD) increases dramatically in the seventh and eight decades of life (Barkman, Pooler,

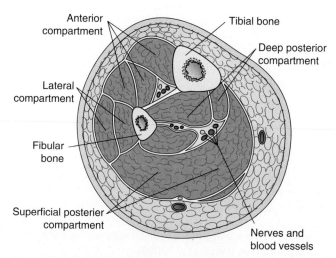

Figure 20-6 Cross section of the middle lower third of the left leg, illustrating the four compartments with their associated peripheral nerves.

Labels: Anterior compartment, Lateral compartment, Fibular bone, Superficial posterier compartment, Tibial bone, Deep posterior compartment, Nerves and blood vessels

et al.). Prevalence of PAD in men and women is equal at this stage (Ostchega, Paulose-Ram, et al., 2007).

🌐 Cultural Considerations

Incidence of PAD, the most prevalent vascular disease, is highest in men and women of African genetic background and women with Mexican heritage (Ostchega, Paulose-Ram, et al., 2007). Hypertension, a significant risk factor for PAD, is increased in African Canadians. Smoking, another primary risk factor, also may have environmental effects, such as in the case of secondary smoke inhalation (Canadian Lung Association, 2010). Genetics play a prominent role in atherosclerosis in addition to many of the cardiovascular risk factors. Hypertension, diabetes, and hyperlipidemia are cardiovascular risk factors with strong genetic components (Barkman, Pooler, et al., 2010; Ostechega, Paulose-Ram, et al.). Primary varicose veins are seen more often in people older than 50 years and in those with obesity. Varicose veins are more common in women, which may be related to the increased venous stasis that accompanies pregnancy. Varicose veins and lymphedema may be familial (Barkman, Pooler, et al.).

Acute Assessment

Nurses frequently encounter patient situations of serious vascular compromise such as arterial occlusion, deep venous thrombosis (DVT), pulmonary emboli, and compartment syndrome (Edge, Day, et al., 2010). If the patient is experiencing acute pain in an extremity, immediately assess for the six Ps (*pain* [acute and severe]; *pallor* [mottled looking skin]; *pulselessness*; *poikilothermia*, or *polar* sensation [cold to touch]; *paresthesia* [a burning, tingling, or numbness]; and *paralysis* [lack of movement]). Of these six Ps, pain and paresthesia are the most reliable (Rankin & Then, 2010a). To check for pulses in the leg, if a pulse is not palpable in the foot (dorsalis pedis, posterior tibial, or peroneal), continue proximally (toward the body) to the popliteal and then the femoral. In the arm, the progression is from radial and ulnar and then to the brachial pulse. If symptoms of complete arterial occlusion occur, such as no palpable pulses in left foot, having acute pain of left lower leg, numbness, coolness, and pallor (colour change) of left foot and lower leg, stop and get assistance immediately. This is a limb-threatening situation. Continue to monitor the patient. A Doppler ultrasound device is helpful when pulses are not palpable.

If the patient is experiencing symptoms of deep vein thrombosis (DVT) such as pain, edema, and warmth of an extremity, stop the assessment and get help. Immediate intervention to start anticoagulants is necessary. A pulmonary embolism may result from a DVT. Be alert for any signs of a pulmonary embolism including acute dyspnea, chest pain, tachycardia, diaphoresis, and anxiety (see Chapter 15). This life-threatening emergency requires immediate intervention.

The final emergency is compartment syndrome which usually involves a leg muscle. This syndrome can be characterized by "deep, throbbing, unrelenting pain" that is not relieved by analgesics, or raising or lowering the leg (Rankin & Then, 2010b, p. 2314), and the critical fact that *paresthesia* (burning, tingling, or numbness) **precedes** *paralysis*. Pain occurs because the muscle compartment becomes smaller due to external pressure (from the outside) or internal pressure. Examples of external pressure are casts or dressings that are too tight. Internal pressure is from increased muscle compartment contents that occur from edema, hemorrhage caused by fractures, crush injuries, or both. This increased pressure in the compartment leads to anoxia and necrosis of nerves and then muscle. Permanent damage to the leg occurs if the anoxia to the tissues continues >6 hours (Edge, Day, et al., 2010) (see Table 20-3 at the end of this chapter).

Subjective Data Collection

The subjective portion of the health assessment includes analysis of symptoms/signs, identification of history, and cardiovascular risk factors related to those symptoms that are frequently associated with arterial, venous, and lymphatic disorders. Evaluation of the subjective portion of the assessment includes analysis of the information for the development of health promotion measures. If the patient is

---

BOX 20-1   CARDIOVASCULAR RISK FACTORS

- Smoking
- Hypercholesterolemia
- Diet high in saturated fats
- Sedentary lifestyle
- Hypertension
- Diabetes
- Obesity
- Genetics

having any critical symptoms of complete arterial occlusion or DVT, nurses take only critical history information as they prepare the patient for emergent intervention.

Assessment of Risk Factors

Cardiovascular risk factors for the development of atherosclerosis are well defined (Box 20-1). They may be categorized as modifiable (eg, smoking) and nonmodifiable (eg, hereditary factors). It is essential to identify these risk factors, the patient's understanding of them, and resources available to the patient and his or her support network. Exploring these areas yields the necessary information from which to formulate with the patient a comprehensive plan to improve his or her cardiovascular risk profile.

Questions to Assess History and Risk Factors	Rationale
Personal History Do you have a history of heart/blood vessel concerns? • Is the illness related to arteries? Veins? Or lymph? • How was it treated? • What was the outcome? Do you have an elevated cholesterol level? • How is it treated? • How well-controlled is it? Do you have a history of high blood pressure? • How is it treated? • How well is it controlled? • Have there been any complications related to high blood pressure? Do you have diabetes? • How is it treated? • How well is it controlled? Have there been any complications related to diabetes? **Medications** What medications are you taking? What is each medication for? To what extent are you able to take them as directed? **Family History** Do you have a family history of heart/blood vessel concerns? • Who had the illness? • Was the illness related to arteries? Veins? Or lymph? • How was it treated? • What was the outcome?	*Thromboembolism* should be monitored for as a possible side effect of trauma. Arterial damage can also result from trauma such as penetrating or blunt-force injuries (Barkman, Pooler, et al., 2010). *Cardiovascular disease* has a well-established hereditary component (Pei, Wang, et al., 2006).

Questions to Assess History and Risk Factors	Rationale
Do you have a family history of diabetes? • Who had/has the illness? • How is it treated? • How well is it controlled? • Have there been any complications related to diabetes?	Family history of *diabetes* increases a person's risk of developing the same condition. Diabetes increases up to four times the patient's risk of lower-extremity peripheral arterial disease (PAD). Severity and duration of diabetes correlate with the likelihood of developing lower-extremity PAD (Chorzempa, 2006).
Do you have a family history of high blood pressure? • Who had/has the illness? • How is it treated? • How well is it controlled? • Have there been any complications related to high blood pressure?	Patients with *hypertension* are at increased risk for cardiovascular disease, especially cerebrovascular and lower-extremity PAD and abdominal aneurysms (Barkman, Pooler, et al., 2010)
Does anyone in your family have an elevated cholesterol level? • Who had/has the elevated cholesterol level? • How is it treated? • How well-controlled is it?	Increased levels of cholesterol are associated with the development of atherosclerosis and therefore with lower-extremity PAD and abdominal aneurysms (Barkman, Pooler, et al., 2010).
Do you have a family history of swelling due to lymph fluid? Who in your family had/has a type of swelling? How was it treated? What was the outcome?	*Lymphedema* may be familial but also may result from trauma or the excision of lymph nodes (Clark, 2010a).

Risk Assessment and Health Promotion

Topics for Health Promotion

> • Alterations in arterial circulation
> • Use of the ankle-brachial index (ABI) for peripheral arterial disease screening
> • Alterations in venous circulation

Adapted from Edge, D. S., Day, R. A., et al. (2010). The peripheral vascular system. In T. C. Stephen, D. S. Skillen, R. A. Day, & L. S. Bickley (Eds.). *Canadian Bates' guide to health assessment for nurses* (1st ed., p. 570). Philadelphia, PA: Wolters Kluwer Health/Lippincott Williams & Wilkins.

Risk assessment is essential for the health care professional to determine areas for health promotion and illness and disease prevention. Key areas in the prevention of atherosclerosis include exercise, a diet low in saturated fats and sodium, not smoking, an appropriate body mass index, control of blood glucose levels for those with diabetes, and control of blood pressure (McDermott, Lui, et al., 2006; White, 2007). Education provides the patient with the necessary information to make behavioural choices that may prevent future health concerns or improve the outcome of current health issues (Veazie, Galoway, et al., 2005).

Atherosclerosis is a progressive, systemic disease. Initially it manifests in one area of the body, but it is also likely to be found in other vessels. The severity of peripheral vascular disease closely parallels the risk for ischemic stroke, myocardial infarction, and death from vascular causes (Clark, 2010a).

Patients With Peripheral Arterial Disease

Identifying options for the modification of risk factors can significantly improve the outcome for patients with PAD. The most modifiable risk factors are smoking, high-fat diet, and limited activity level. Of these, smoking has been found one of the most devastating. Cessation of smoking can significantly delay the progression of atherosclerosis (Collins, Peterson, et al., 2005). Nurses ask patients about their readiness to quit smoking at every opportunity. They offer various resources to assist patients with smoking cessation, including individual and group counselling, support groups, medical treatment, and nicotine-replacement therapy (see the five "As" that nurses can use at each visit in Chapter 18).

Diet modification includes weight management and decreasing the consumption of foods high in saturated fats. Monitoring of cholesterol and triglyceride levels is important for patients with PAD. They should have a thorough understanding of the relationship that diet, activity, and genetic background factors have to cholesterol levels and the development of atherosclerosis (Aronow, 2007). Nurses also discuss with patients the preventative role of exercising at least 2.5 hours of moderate to vigourous aerobic activity each week for adults (ages 18–65 years and older) (Public Health Agency of Canada, 2011a, 2011b).

Daily assessment of the feet is critical for these patients. With decreased arterial blood supply, minor cuts or areas with excessive pressure may quickly develop into arterial ulcers. Because of the decreased blood supply, these ulcers may be difficult to heal, leading to gangrene and limb amputation (Aronow, 2007).

Hypertension, diabetes, and heredity are also risk factors for PAD. Although they may not be eliminated, hypertension and diabetes are modifiable in terms of close monitoring and tight control (Aronow, 2007). Patients with diabetes are twice as likely to develop PAD as the general population (Senthuran, 2010). Maintaining glycemic control and blood pressure within the guidelines of the Canadian Diabetes Association (2008) is critical to slowing the progression of PAD (Senthuran). Evidence that even asymptomatic or sub-clinical PAD predicts coronary artery disease and cerebro-vascular disease has resulted in the need for more intensive screening of asymptomatic at-risk patients, especially those older than 50 years (Goff, Brass, et al., 2007; White, 2007).

Patients With Venous Disease

Patients with venous disease should receive education on methods of decreasing venous pressure. Avoiding standing and sitting for long periods in addition to elevating the legs peri-odically help to combat the chronic edema that may accom-pany venous disease (Clark, 2010a). Graduated compression stockings are recommended for some patients. Patients at risk for or with a history of DVT need thorough education on the signs and symptoms of DVT and, in some cases, anticoagulant therapy (American Operating Room Nurses [AORN], 2007).

Patients With Lymphatic Disorders

Patients with lymphatic disorders have several issues that health care professionals need to address. Similar to venous disease, edema in the extremities is the primary symptom of lymphedema. Management suggestions may include avoid-ing sitting or standing for long periods, periodically elevat-ing the affected extremity, and applying compression wraps or graduated compression stockings (Clark, 2010a). Patients with chronic lymphedema may experience disfigurement that affects their body image and self-esteem (Clark). It is essential for nurses to address these areas that affect quality of life.

Focused Health History Related to Common Symptoms/Signs

Common symptoms of vascular disease should be part of the assessment of all adults. As discussed previously, the underdiagnosis of vascular conditions and lack of aggressive treatment of risk factors have been identified as major areas of concern in primary care (Oka, 2006). Consistent evalua-tion of vascular and lymphatic wellness is necessary to better serve the adult population. Common symptoms and signs are associated with various medical diagnoses (Box 20-2).

Common Peripheral Vascular and Lymphatic Symptoms/Signs

- Pain in arms, hands, legs, or feet
- Numbness or tingling sensation in hands, legs, feet, or toes
- Change in temperature of hands or feet
- Colour changes in fingertips or toes, especially in cold weather
- Pale hands or feet
- Edema of arms, hands, calves, legs, or feet
- Edema with redness and/or tenderness
- Hair loss from feet, legs

BOX 20-2 COMMON SYMPTOMS/SIGNS OF VASCULAR DISORDERS

Peripheral Arterial Disease

- Claudication
- Rest pain

Acute Arterial Occlusion

The six Ps:
- Pain
- Poikilothermia or Polar sensation (cold)
- Paresthesia
- Paralysis
- Pallor
- Pulselessness

Abdominal Aortic Aneurysm

- Bruit
- Laterally pulsating abdominal mass

Abdominal Aortic Aneurysm Dissection or Rupture

- Chest pain
- Abdominal pain
- Back pain
- Shortness of breath

Raynaud's Phenomenon and Disease

Assess the extremities for:
- Numbness (*continued in 2nd column of box*)

- Tingling
- Pain
- Coolness
- Extreme pallor

Chronic Venous Insufficiency

- Edema of the extremity

Deep Vein Thrombosis

- Unilateral edema
- Pain or achiness
- Erythema
- Warmth

Thrombophlebitis

- As with deep vein thrombosis
- Palpable mass or cord along the vein

Neuropathy

- Burning pain
- Numbness
- Paresthesias

Lymphedema

- Unilateral edema

Examples of Questions for Symptom Analysis—Lower Leg Swelling (Edema)

- "Tell me where you notice the swelling." "Are both legs swollen?" (Location)
- "Describe how your leg(s) feel(s)." (Quality)
- "How has the swelling affected your activities?" "Can you wear shoes?" "Any issues with clothing fitting too tight?" (Quantity/severity)
- "When did you first notice the swelling?" "Did the swelling start suddenly?" "Or gradually?" "Is there a time of day when the swelling seems worse?" (Timing)
- "What were you doing when you first noticed the swelling?" (Setting)
- "Describe to me what makes the swelling worse." "Do you take medicine for high blood pressure?" "Which drugs?" (Aggravating factors)
- "What makes the swelling better?" "What have you tried to reduce the swelling?" (Alleviating factors)
- "What other symptoms or signs have you noticed?" "Have you had any shortness of breath?" "Have you had any redness with the swelling?" "Or pain with the swelling?" (Associated symptoms)
- "What type of work do you do?" "How much of your day are you standing?" "How much of your day are you sitting?" "Do you have rest periods when you could put your feet up higher than your heart?" "How often do you travel by air?" "Or by car?" "Tell me about the exercise you get in a typical day." "How many flights of stairs do you climb each day (counting work and home)?" "What do you do for leisure activities?" (Environmental factors)
- "How is the swelling affecting your life?" "And the things you enjoy doing?" (Significance to the patient)
- "What do you think might be happening with your legs?" (Patient's perspective)

Adapted from Edge, D. S., Day, R. A., et al. (2010). The peripheral vascular system. In T. C. Stephen, D. S. Skillen, R. A. Day, & L. S. Bickley (Eds.). *Canadian Bates' guide to health assessment for nurses* (1st ed., p. 570). Philadelphia, PA: Wolters Kluwer Health/Lippincott Williams & Wilkins.

Examples of Questions to Assess Symptoms/Signs	Rationale/Unexpected Findings
Pain Do you have any pain in your arms? Or legs?	△ *SAFETY ALERT 20-1* *It is critical to determine if pain is acute or chronic before proceeding with the interview.*
• Where is the pain? • Can you point to where it hurts? • Does it go anywhere else?	The location of pain in PAD usually closely approximates the affected vessel.
• Describe it. • What does it feel like? • How bad is it on a scale from 0 to 10 scale, with 0 being no pain and 10 being the worst possible pain that you can imagine?	Chronic pain is described as dull or aching. Acute pain is often described as sharp and stabbing. Pain brought on by exertion and relieved by rest is called *intermittent claudication.* It is important to quantify the claudication time as much as possible. An example would be "One block claudication."
• When did you first notice the pain? • What were you doing when you first noticed the pain? • What brings on the pain? How long does it last?	
• Does anything make the pain better? • Do other symptoms accompany it? • Does the pain wake you up at night?	The patient with PAD often describes feeling the need to hang the foot of the affected extremity over the side of the bed. Pain that awakens patients from sleep is termed *rest pain* (Clark, 2010a).
Is anything going on in your environment that could be contributing to this? • What would you like to be able to do that you can't do because of the pain? • What do you think the cause is?	

(text continues on page 546)

Numbness or Tingling

Have you experienced any changes in sensation in your arms? Or legs?

- Do you experience any numbness or tingling in your hands? Or feet?
- What makes it worse?
- What makes it better?

Peripheral neuropathies often develop as a complication of diabetes. They may be very painful and also result in a loss of sensation, increasing the patient's risk for injuries. Subsequent damage to skin further increases risk for wounds that are difficult to heal. Patients with *diabetes* often experience *peripheral neuropathy*, which may manifest as numbness and tingling or pain (Senthuran, 2010).

Cramping

Do you have any cramping in your legs?

- Do cramps come on suddenly? Or gradually?
- Are cramps associated with walking? Or other activity?
- How many blocks can you walk without cramping?
- What makes the cramps better?

The area of cramping in arterial disease, termed *intermittent claudication*, closely approximates the level of arterial occlusion (Clark, 2010a).

Skin Changes

Have you had any changes in your skin? Hair? Or nails?

- Do you have hair loss on your hands? Or feet?
- Have your arms become pale? Or cool? Are your legs pale? Or cool?
- Have your nails changed? Have they become thicker?
- Have you had any colour changes in your fingers or toes related to cold weather?

Decreased arterial blood supply may lead to changes in the lower extremities, such as loss of hair, pallor, or cool temperature. Another potential consequence is hypertrophic nail changes (Edge, Day, et al., 2010). *Raynaud's disease* is characterized by colour changes especially in the extremities when exposed to cold temperature (Clark, 2010a).

Edema

Have you experienced any swelling in your arms? Or legs?

- Does it go away when you put your legs up?
- Is it worse at night? Or in the morning?
- Have you experienced any swelling in your arms that is accompanied by redness or tenderness? Or in your legs?

Vascular causes of swelling in the arms or legs may result from venous occlusion or incompetence of the valves of the venous system (Barkman, Pooler, et al., 2010).

Functional Ability

Have difficulties with your arms or legs affected your daily life in any way? Can you continue activities without fatigue? Or pain in your arms or legs?

Decreased functional ability may result from arterial insufficiency (Barkman, Pooler, et al., 2010). It is a symptom that may be overlooked.

Documentation of Expected Findings

Patient reports no upper- or lower-extremity pain; no claudication, coldness, numbness, pallor, hair loss, or nail changes in the extremity; no colour changes related to cold temperatures, swelling, or redness in fingers or toes.

▲ Lifespan Considerations

Additional Questions

Rationale/Unexpected Findings

Women Who Are Pregnant

Are you pregnant?

- If so, how many weeks' along is the pregnancy?
- Have you had prior pregnancies?
- Have you had any vascular changes related to them?

Have you experienced any swelling in your ankles? Or feet? Is it worse after long periods of standing? Have you noticed any enlarged veins in your legs? Have you developed any hemorrhoids?

Venous valvular incompetence and varicosities may develop during pregnancy as a result of hormonal factors and increased venous pressure (Barkman, Pooler, et al., 2010).

These symptoms are common in pregnancy.

Newborns, Children, and Adolescents

Is your child frequently exposed to second-hand smoke? What measures are taken to avoid such exposure?

Second-hand smoke is a cardiovascular risk factor.

Additional Questions	Rationale/Unexpected Findings
Have you noticed any unusual swelling in your child's legs?	*Primary lymphedema* is congenital and may be seen as early as the first year of life (Barkman, Pooler, et al., 2010).
Older Adults	
Have you experienced any fatigue in your legs? Any cramping? Or aching? How have these symptoms affected your activities of daily living?	Many older adults have general, sometimes vague, symptoms of arterial disease that health care professionals frequently overlook (Oka, 2006).
Have you noticed any swelling in your legs? Is it on one side? Or both sides?	Because older adults often have multisystem issues, it is important for health care professionals to clearly differentiate vascular disease from other conditions.

🌐 Cultural Considerations

Additional Questions	Rationale/Unexpected Findings
Note the patient's self-identified genetic background and gender.	People of African descent are approximately three times more likely than Caucasians to have *PAD* (Edge, Day, et al., 2010).

An Example of a Therapeutic Dialogue

The nurse's role relative to subjective data collection is to gather information to help determine the cause of the patient's current symptoms and to improve the patient's health status. Remember Mr. Roman Tretski, introduced at the beginning of this chapter. His issues include peripheral arterial disease (PAD) and confusion. His risk factors include 50 years of smoking a pack of cigarettes a day, high cholesterol level, and hypertension.

The long-term care nurse is working with Mr. Tretski today. Because the patient is confused, simple questioning is essential. Thus, the nurse arranges questions with the simplest first, leading to more complex questions as the interview progresses. Cueing Mr. Tretski during the interview is another technique that can help keep him focused on the topic of the conversation.

Nurse: Mr. Tretski, I'm your nurse today. My name is Ronald I want to ask some questions about the blood flow in your legs. I want to talk about the circulation in your legs (pauses).

Mr. Tretski: You want to ask me some questions about my circulation? It's pretty bad.

Nurse: The circulation in your legs isn't very good. Do you have any pain in your legs? Or feet?

Mr. Tretski: Just when I walk. But I don't walk very much, because the nurses make me stay in this wheelchair. I fall sometimes.

Nurse: You fall because of your bad circulation in your legs. Sometimes people with bad circulation have tingling in their legs. Do you ever have tingling?

Mr. Tretski: No. You sure are asking me a lot of questions about my legs.

Nurse: I want to know how the circulation is, and I think that you've helped me understand that. How's the feeling in your legs? (pauses 10 seconds) (touches him) How's the feeling in your legs?

Mr. Tretski: Sometimes I can't feel my feet and then I fall.

Critical Thinking Challenge

• What helpful therapeutic communication techniques did the nurse use?
• What additional data about other body systems did the nurse gather during this interview?
• Is this an appropriate time to discuss risk for falling and safety issues? Provide rationale.

Objective Data Collection

Equipment

- Examination gown
- Half-sheet or bath blanket
- Nonstretchable measuring tape
- Ultrasonic Doppler stethoscope
- Ultrasonic gel
- Sphygmomanometer
- Tourniquet

Promoting Patient Comfort, Dignity, and Safety

Objective assessment of the peripheral vascular and lymphatic systems should take place in a quiet and private setting. Vasoconstriction accompanies cool temperatures, which may affect the peripheral vascular examination. The room should be at a comfortable temperature before the assessment begins.

Wash and warm your hands as an infection-control measure and for the patient's comfort. The patient will need to wear a gown for the examination. He or she may leave on undergarments. The arms and then legs need to be accessible for inspection and palpation because side-to-side visualization for comparison is essential. Drape appropriately throughout the examination to protect the patient and to help keep the patient warm.

The examination requires the patient to be sitting, supine, and standing. Take safety precautions while helping the patient to change positions. Pay attention to mobility constraints as well as the effects of position changes on respiratory effort as they apply to the patient. Having an assistant present when examining the femoral pulses and superficial inguinal lymph nodes may be advisable if the patient is the opposite sex to the nurse.

Cleanse the ultrasonic Doppler stethoscope before and after use to prevent the spread of infection. Use soap and water, because alcohol is damaging to the transducer.

Comprehensive Physical Examination: Peripheral Vascular and Lymphatic Systems

Techniques and Expected Findings	Rationale/Unexpected Findings
Arms ***Inspection.*** Note the size and symmetry of the arms and hands as well as muscle atrophy or hypertrophy. *Arms and hands are symmetrical with full joint movement bilaterally.*	PAD may result in muscle atrophy. Hypertrophy may result from activity in which the patient uses one arm more than the other, such as with tennis.
Assess the colour of the arms and hands; evaluate for venous pattern. *Colour is pink, symmetrical, and consistent without prominent venous pattern.*	Pallor indicates arterial insufficiency. Erythema may accompany thrombophlebitis or DVT.
Evaluate the nail beds for colour and angle. *Nail beds are pink. Nail-base angle is 180° without clubbing.*	Capillary refill may be decreased with arterial disease.
Note any edema of the arms and hands. Evaluate for pitting by pressing the tissue for 5 seconds with your fingers. *No indentation remains when you remove your fingers.*	Lymphedema results in unilateral edema. Use the scale in Table 20-1 to document degree of pitting edema.
Evaluate for any ecchymoses or lesions of the upper extremities. *Ecchymoses and lesions are absent.*	Be alert for signs of abuse (see Chapter 12) or falls. Delayed wound healing occurs with arterial disease.
Palpation. Palpate the arms and hands for temperature. Use the dorsal aspect of the hands and assess the extremities simultaneously, moving from the distal (fingers) to the proximal (shoulders). *Arms and hands are warm and equal in temperature.*	⚠ *SAFETY ALERT 20-2* *Coolness of an extremity may indicate arterial occlusion. Assess quickly for the other five Ps (see Box 20-2) and determine emergent nature.*
Assess skin texture and turgor by making a fold of skin on the back of the hand to evaluate elasticity and hydration. With aging, elasticity decreases. *Skin texture is firm, even, and elastic. Turgor is intact, as shown by rapid return of skin fold, to original position bilaterally.*	Rough or dry texture and poor turgor may be noted with dehydration (see Chapter 13).

Table 20-1	Description of Edema Characteristics and Grading			
Description		Depression Depth	Time for Pitting to Disappear	Grade
Slight pitting		2 mm	Disappears rapidly	1+
Deeper pitting		4 mm	10–15 s	2+
Visible swelling of extremity		6 mm	>1 min	3+
Grossly swollen extremity		8 mm	Up to 2–3 min	4+

Adapted from Dillon, P. M. (2007). *Nursing health assessment: Clinical pocket guide* (2nd ed., p. 180). Philadelphia, PA: F.A. Davis.

Techniques and Expected Findings (continued)

Assess capillary refill by depressing and blanching the nail bed, then releasing and noting the time it takes for the colour to return (Fig. 20-7). *Capillary refill is <3 seconds bilaterally.*

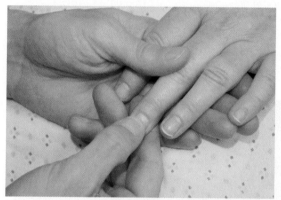

Figure 20-7 Testing capillary refill.

Palpate the brachial and radial pulses. Grade the pulses based on the scale given in Box 20-3. The radial pulse site is often used when assessing the pulse for vital signs (Fig. 20-8). The brachial pulses are located at approximately the inner third of the antecubital fossa when the palm is facing up (supination) (Fig. 20-9). It is not usually necessary to palpate the ulnar pulse, which is difficult to locate. *An expected pulse is graded as +2/4 on the scale shown. The denominator indicates the scale being used and should be indicated when documenting pulses.*

BOX 20-3   GRADING OF PULSES

0: Absent, unable to palpate
+1: Diminished, weaker than expected, thready; may be expected in pedal pulses
+2: Brisk, expected
+3: Increased
+4: Bounding (full and bounding)
Document an expected pulse as +2/4

Rationale/Unexpected Findings (continued)

Capillary refill taking 3 seconds or longer may indicate vasoconstriction, decreased cardiac output, impaired circulation, significant edema, or anemia.

⚠ *SAFETY ALERT 20-3*
Evaluate any pulse that cannot be palpated with the Doppler stethoscope for an arterial signal. If pulselessness persists, quickly evaluate the remaining "Ps" to determine emergent nature (see Box 20-2).

See Table 20-4 at the end of the chapter for variations in arterial pulses.

(text continues on page 550)

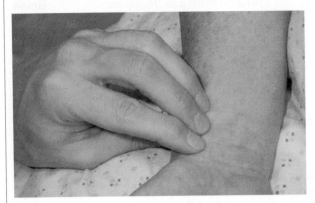

Figure 20-8 Assessing the radial pulse.

When indicated, perform the Allen test to assess the patency of the collateral circulation of the hands (Fig. 20-10). Ask the patient to make a fist. Occlude the radial and ulnar arteries of one hand. Have the patient open the hand; release pressure on the ulnar artery. *Colour returns within 2 to 5 seconds, indicating adequate circulation.*

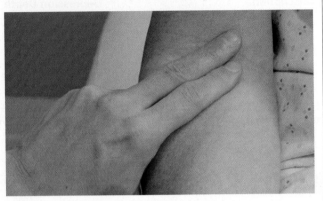

Figure 20-9 Assessing the brachial pulse.

⚠ *SAFETY ALERT 20-4*

The Allen test is done prior to radial cannulation, such as for the drawing of arterial blood gases (ABGs) or the insertion of an arterial line. Lack of colour return indicates inadequate collateral circulation. Do not draw ABGs or insert an arterial line in this hand—doing so will impede blood flow and ischemia may result.

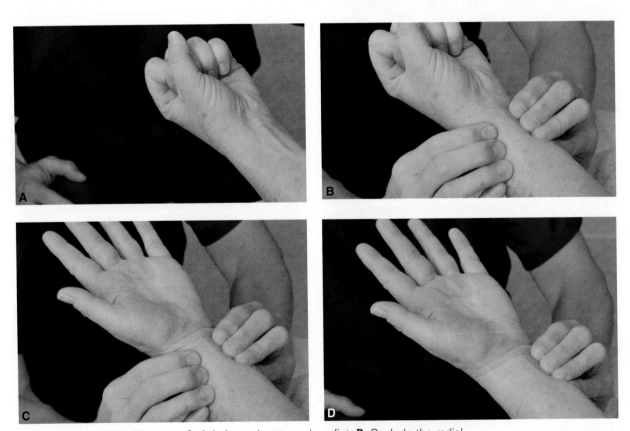

Figure 20-10 The Allen test. **A.** Ask the patient to make a fist. **B.** Occlude the radial and ulnar arteries. **C.** Ask the patient to open the hand. **D.** Release pressure on the ulnar artery.

Palpate for the epitrochlear nodes. Flex the patient's arm and palpate in the groove between the biceps and triceps muscles (medial surface of the arm), about 3 cm above the medial epicondyle. *Usually the epitrochlear nodes are not palpable.* If palpable, note size, consistency, mobility, and tenderness. *Palpable nodes are expected to be 2 cm or smaller.*

Enlarged nodes may be noted with regional inflammation, generalized lymphadenopathy, and some types of cancers such as *lymphomas.*

Auscultation. Evaluate the blood pressure in both arms. Document the arm with the higher pressure and take subsequent blood pressures in that arm. *An expected adult blood pressure is <120 mm Hg systolic and <80 mm Hg diastolic* (Clark, 2010b).

A difference >10 mm Hg between arms may indicate arterial disease. A palpatory pressure should be taken first to avoid missing an auscultatory gap (see Chapter 6).

Legs

Inspection. Note the size and symmetry of the legs as well as muscle atrophy or hypertrophy. *Legs are symmetrical with full joint movement.*

Atrophy may occur with arterial disease (see Table 20-5 at the end of the chapter).

Assess the colour of the legs; evaluate for venous pattern. *Colour is symmetrical and consistent without predominant venous pattern.*

△ SAFETY ALERT 20-5
Pallor may indicate arterial insufficiency. Evaluate the other five "Ps" to determine emergent nature. Erythema, edema, and tenderness may indicate DVT, also of an emergent nature.

Colour change to white in the toes may indicate one of the Raynaud's syndromes. Venous insufficiency may result in dilated and tortuous veins (see Table 20-6 at the end of this chapter).

Evaluate the nail beds for colour and capillary refill. Blanch the nail bed, release, and observe the time it takes for colour to return. *Nail beds are pink, with capillary refill <3 seconds.*

Delayed capillary refill may be the result of arterial disease.

Note any edema of the legs. Evaluate for pitting by pressing the tissue with your fingers. Press firmly with thumb for at least 5 seconds over dorsum of each foot, over each medial malleolus, and over shins. No indentation should remain when you remove your thumbs (Fig. 20-11). See Table 20-1 for the grading scale for pitting edema. *No edema is found bilaterally.*

Chronic venous insufficiency, DVT, and lymphedema result in edema. Asymmetry between the legs should be further investigated. Calf or leg swelling and unilateral pitting edema are associated with a DVT in 88% of patients. Localized pain or tenderness is noted in 56% of patients (Minichiello & Fogarty, 2008).

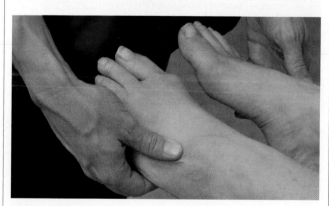

Figure 20-11 Assessing for pitting edema.

(text continues on page 552)

Evaluate for any ecchymosis or lesions of the lower extremities. *Ecchymosis and lesions are absent bilaterally.*

Palpation. Palpate the legs for temperature. Use the dorsal aspect of the hands and assess the extremities from distal to proximal separately, and then simultaneously. *Legs and feet are warm and equal in temperature.*

Differentiate ulcers as arterial or venous in cause (see Table 20-7 at the end of this chapter). Assess for gangrene.

△ *SAFETY ALERT 20-6*
One extremity cooler than the other indicates arterial occlusion. Evaluate for the emergent nature of the condition. A warm, edematous, and tender extremity indicates DVT in 30% to 40% of patients (Minichiello & Fogarty, 2008). This also is emergent.

Assess the texture and turgor of the skin by making a fold of skin on the top of the feet. *Texture is firm, even, and elastic. Turgor is intact when skin fold rapidly returns to position (indicating elasticity and hydration).*

Rough or dry texture and decreased turgor are found in *dehydration.*

Palpate the femoral, popliteal, dorsalis pedis, and posterior tibial pulses. The femoral pulse is about halfway between the symphysis pubis and anterior iliac spine, just below the inguinal ligament (Fig. 20-12). The popliteal pulse is often difficult to locate. With your thumbs braced on the knee, curl your hands around the back and press against the lower edge of the femur (Fig. 20-13). It may be felt immediately lateral to the medial tendon. The posterior tibial pulse is located in the groove between the medial malleolus and Achilles tendon (Fig. 20-14). A light touch is important to avoid obliterating the dorsalis pedis pulse. It is usually about halfway up the foot immediately lateral to the extensor tendon of the great toe (Fig. 20-15). Grade the pulses based on the scale given in Box 20-3. *An expected pulse is +2/4 on the scale shown. The denominator indicates the scale being used and should be indicated when documenting pulses. Evaluate any pulse that cannot be palpated with the Doppler stethoscope for an arterial signal.*

△ *SAFETY ALERT 20-7*
If pulselessness and no Doppler signal are present, quickly assess other five "Ps" to determine the emergent nature of the condition.

Figure 20-12 Assessing the femoral pulse.

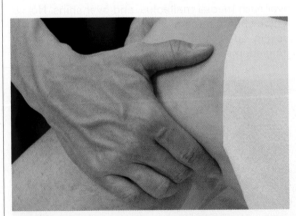

Figure 20-13 Assessing the popliteal pulse.

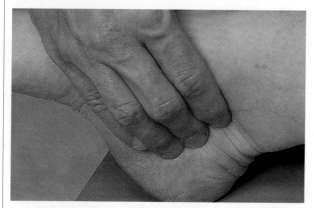

Figure 20-14 Assessing the posterior tibial pulse.

Palpate the upper and medial thigh for the superficial inguinal lymph nodes. *They may be palpable and up to 1to 2 cm, movable, and nontender.*

The Homans sign test is **not** recommended to test for DVT, because it not sensitive or specific. Additionally, palpating the calf may dislodge an existing DVT.

Auscultation. The Doppler ultrasonic stethoscope can assess weak peripheral pulses (Fig. 20-16). It magnifies pulsatile sounds from the heart and blood vessels as an arterial signal. The arterial signal is a rhythmic whooshing sound. To use the Doppler, apply a drop of ultrasonic gel to the transducer, and then place the transducer slightly angled over the artery and turn on the volume.

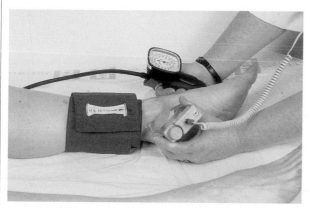

Figure 20-16 Doppler ultrasonic stethoscope.

To assess the ankle-brachial index (ABI), assist the patient to a supine position. Take the systolic pressure of the right and left brachial arteries. Then apply a blood pressure cuff to each ankle and obtain both a dorsalis pedis and posterior tibial artery systolic blood pressure.

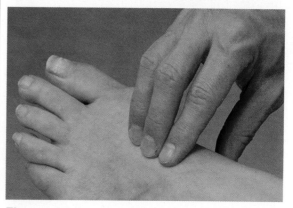

Figure 20-15 Assessing the dorsalis pedis pulse.

Nodes >2 cm may be caused by either local or generalized conditions (Edge, Day, et al., 2010). Local causes include inflammation from trauma or wounds. Generalized lymphadenopathy is noted if there are enlarged nodes in two or more noncontinuous lymph node regions.

False-positive results are commonly related to muscle tenderness and the Homans sign test is only present in 15% of patients with DVT (Minichiello & Fogarty, 2008).

Arterial sounds should not be confused with the venous sound known as a "venous windstorm." Venous sounds are not rhythmic and should not be mistaken for an arterial signal. If arterial sounds cannot be heard over the posterior tibial or the dorsalis pedis, try over the peroneal pulse site (see Fig. 20-17). An ABI of ≤0.95 is

(text continues on page 554)

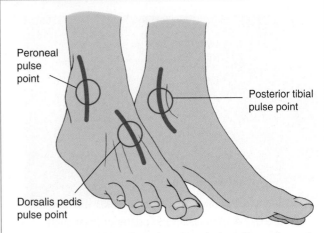

Figure 20-17 Location of peroneal, dorsalis pedis, and posterior tibial pulses

Determine the higher value of the right and left systolic brachial artery pressures to use in calculating the ABI. Determine the higher value of the posterior tibial and dorsalis pedis systolic values on the right ankle. Then determine the higher value of the posterior tibial and dorsalis pedis systolic values on the left ankle. Divide the highest right ankle pressure by the highest right brachial pressure:

$$\frac{134 \text{ systolic ankle pressure}}{128 \text{ systolic brachial pressure}} = 1.04 \text{ or } 104\%$$

The right ankle pressure is slightly higher or equal to the right brachial pressure.

Repeat for the left ankle.

The result is 1.0 (100%) or greater bilaterally (refer to Box 20-4 for a reference scale).

BOX 20-4 INTERPRETATION OF ANKLE-BRACHIAL INDEX VALUES

0.95–1.29: Expected values
0.50–0.95: Mild to moderate peripheral arterial disease (PAD), usually with symptoms of claudication
0.25–<0.50: Ischemic rest pain
0.00–0.25: Severe PAD with critical leg ischemia, tissue loss

Adapted from Clark, A. M. (2010a). Assessment and management of patients with vascular disorders and problems of peripheral circulation. In R. A. Day, P. Paul, et al. (Eds.). *Brunner & Suddarth's textbook of Canadian medical-surgical nursing* (2nd ed., p. 920). Philadelphia, PA: Wolters Kluwer Health/Lippincott Williams & Wilkins.

Advanced Techniques

Colour Change. This test is to check for arterial insufficiency. With the patient supine, elevate the legs 30 cm above the level of the heart and have the patient pump his or her feet to drain off the venous blood (Fig. 20-18A). Have the patient then sit up and dangle the legs over the side of the table (Fig. 20-18B). *Colour returns to the feet and toes within 10 seconds. The superficial veins of the feet fill within 15 seconds.*

considered to indicate arterial insufficiency (see Box 20-4 for delineation of approximate degree of occlusion based on ABI). Because of calcification of the arterial wall and subsequent arteries that are not compressible, patients with *diabetes, renal failure*, or both may have false high results. The same may be true for patients with prosthetic bypass grafts. The ABI is considered an essential assessment tool in evaluating for arterial insufficiency (Oka, 2006).

Return of colour taking longer or persistent-dependent rubor indicates arterial insufficiency.

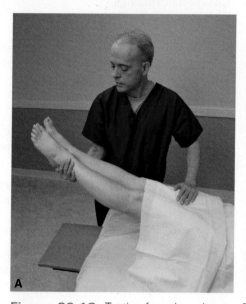 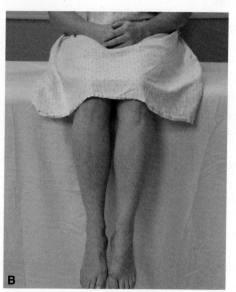

Figure 20-18 Testing for colour change. **A.** Elevating the legs. **B.** Dangling the legs.

Manual Compression Test. This test evaluates the competence of the valves in the patient with varicose veins. Have the patient stand. Compress the lower portion of the vein with one hand and place your other hand 15 to 19 cm higher (Fig. 20-19). If the valves are competent, a wave transmission is not palpable. This is considered a negative–negative result.

A transmission wave indicates that the valves are incompetent.

Trendelenburg Test. For the patient with varicose veins, this test evaluates the saphenous vein valves and retrograde filling of the superficial veins. With the patient supine, elevate the leg 90° for 15 seconds. Apply a tourniquet to the upper thigh. Assist the patient to stand and inspect for venous filling. After 30 seconds, release the tourniquet. *The saphenous veins fill from the bottom up while the tourniquet is on.*

Filling from above while the tourniquet is on or rapid retrograde filling when the tourniquet is removed indicates that the valves are incompetent.

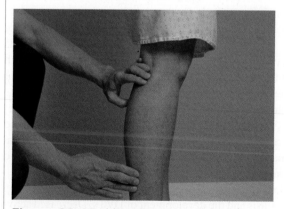

Figure 20-19 Manual compression test.

Expected Findings	Unexpected Findings
Inspection of arms	
Skin over upper extremities pink with fine macular lesions over forearms bilaterally. Arms symmetrical in size, without edema.	Skin erythemateous over right ring finger, extending 15 cm into right forearm. Lower and upper right arm edematous compared to left.
Inspection of legs	
Pink lower extremities bilaterally, without lesions, varicosities, or stasis. Equal hair distribution bilaterally.	Lower left leg pale, below the knee, with noticeable hair loss compared to right leg. Rubor when left leg dependent. No edema or ulceration bilaterally.
Palpation of arms	
Arms warm and dry to touch. Skinfold on both hands returns to original position in <1 s. No lymphadenopathy noted at epitrochlear fossa bilaterally.	Right hand and forearm hot to touch; palpable edema at wrist (2+). Two mobile, tender, 1 cm nodes palpable at right epitrochlear fossa.
Palpation of legs	
Legs warm and dry to touch bilaterally. Calves supple and nontender bilaterally. Several 1 cm nontender, superficial inguinal nodes (horizontal group) palpated bilaterally.	Left leg cool to touch below the knee compared to right leg. Skin appears thin and dry over left lower leg. No palpable edema bilaterally.
Peripheral pulses	
Brachial, radial, and femoral pulses are +2/4. Posterior tibial and dorsalis pedis pulses are +1 to +2/4 and symmetric. Popliteal pulses are +2/4 bilaterally.	Brachial, radial, femoral pulses symmetric and are +2/4. Right popliteal, posterior tibial, dorsalis pedis pulses are +2/4. Left popliteal is +1/4, with absent left posterior tibial and dorsalis pedis pulses.
Auscultation for bruits	
No aortic or renal bruits bilaterally.	Bruit over left renal artery but not over right. Bruit heard over the aorta, above the umbilicus.

Adapted from Edge, D. S., Day, R. A., et al. (2010). In T. C. Stephen, D. L. Skillen, R. A. Day, & L. S. Bickley (Eds.). *Canadian Bates' guide to health assessment for nurses* (1st ed., p. 589). Philadelphia, PA: Wolters Kluwer Health/Lippincott Williams & Wilkins.

▲ Lifespan Considerations

Women Who Are Pregnant

With the increased blood volume of pregnancy and the pressure of the growing fetus on vessels, some women may develop venous changes. An increased venous pattern over the breasts is common. Varicose veins and peripheral edema may develop, especially in the third trimester.

Newborns, Children, and Adolescents

Changes to the intimal layer of the arteries begin at birth. Significant atherosclerotic streaking that correlates with cardiovascular risk factors has been found on autopsy in children and adolescents. Cardiovascular disease does not typically manifest until later decades, but it may start histologically in childhood and adolescence (Williams, Hayman, et al., 2002).

Venous disease is also uncommon in these developmental stages. With the increased use of venous access devices in children, however, it is becoming more common. Congenital lymphedema may be diagnosed in the first year of life (Barkman, Pooler, et al., 2010).

Older Adults

Arterial disease is common in older adults as a result of arteriosclerotic changes often coupled with atherosclerosis. The literature suggests that PAD is frequently underdiagnosed in the older population (Oka, 2006). Intimal changes in the arteries begin at birth and progress throughout life. The thickening of the arterial walls decreases nourishment of the tissue, often resulting in classic findings of trophic nail changes, thin shiny skin, and hair loss of the lower extremities. Decreased functional ability such as fatigue with walking may be an indication of PAD that providers often overlook or attribute to other factors (Oka). Evidence-informed parameters suggest the integration of the ankle-brachial index (ABI), a very simple and noninvasive tool, in the assessment of patients who have exertional leg pain, are older than 50 years with cardiovascular risk factors, have diabetes for >20 years, or are older than 70 years (Clark, 2010a).

Systolic hypertension often increases with age as the arterial vessels become less compliant. Taking a palpatory blood pressure before taking the brachial blood pressure is essential to avoid missing an auscultatory gap caused by decreased compliance.

Older adults often become less active over time, increasing venous stasis and the development of DVTs. Decreased activity is also not beneficial to PAD and may be an overlooked symptom in patients with undiagnosed PAD. Venous insufficiency and chronic lymphedema may eventually decrease joint mobility (Barkman, Pooler, et al., 2010). Inclusion of the evaluation of joint mobility is therefore important to the peripheral vascular assessment.

Research has shown that risk assessment and intervention have significant effects on outcomes for patients with cardiovascular disease. Modification of risk factors significantly slows disease progression (Aronow, 2007). Because of the systemic nature of cardiovascular diseases, nurses critically investigate far beyond the initial reason for which the patient seeks care. Once the nurse has analyzed the history, physical assessment, laboratory data, and diagnostic study results, he or she can develop a plan of care. Determining and prioritizing nursing diagnoses are the basis for the plan in collaboration with the patient and family. Patient education to facilitate modification of risk factors is paramount in this patient population. The nurse educates the patient and family and coordinates support resources for effective care. A collaborative plan with the interprofessional team is the most effective way to manage patient care.

Organizing and Prioritizing

Prioritizing assessment and interventions based on emergent rather than chronic situations is essential. The patient with PAD and symptoms of acute occlusion needs immediate intervention to avoid the threat of limb loss (Clark, 2010a). Focused assessment on the six Ps (pain, pallor, poikilothermia/polar sensation [cold], paresthesias, pulselessness, and paralysis) is critical. Nurses collect past cardiovascular history as physical assessment proceeds. They may then prepare the patient for interventional radiology, surgery, or both in emergent situations. The physical area may need to be shaved and cleansed, an intravenous access established, and consent forms signed. Patient education is done simultaneously with preparation.

In the patient with a DVT, the focus is initiation of intravenous anticoagulant therapy (AORN, 2007). Nurses document baseline assessment of calf size at the widest point in addition to any findings of pain, warmth, or tenderness. Past history

of DVTs or other thrombus formation, pregnancy, recent surgery, recent travel, as well as family history are important to risk stratification (Ross, 2010). The possibility of pulmonary embolus (PE) is always a concern in the patient with a DVT. Ongoing assessments should include consideration of the signs and symptoms of a PE (see Chapter 18).

Common Laboratory and Diagnostic Testing

Accurate data collection is essential for the patient to receive the appropriate care. The physician or nurse practitioner relies on the accurate assessment of the nurse to determine the appropriate medical interventions. An example is the differentiation between issues that are arterial rather than venous. For example, an arterial ulcer has a deep necrotic base, whereas a venous ulcer is superficial and pale. The treatment for these ulcers is quite different (Sieggreen, 2006). An acute arterial occlusion will be painful with accompanying symptoms of pallor, pulselessness, poikilothermia/polar sensation (cold), paresthesias, or paralysis (six Ps). A venous occlusion will result in pain, edema, erythema, and warmth of the affected extremities (Barkman, Pooler, et al., 2010). The primary health care professional will order that the patient be prepared for an arteriogram for the arterial occlusion but venous duplex and anticoagulation for the venous occlusion.

Compartment syndrome is another serious situation requiring expert assessment. Nurses are aware that patients with casts or tight dressings who report "severe, deep, throbbing, unrelenting pain" (Rankin & Then, 2010b, p. 2314) beyond what might be expected, and unrelieved by raising or lowering the limb, or opiods, may have compartment syndrome. In this situation, the six Ps are checked. The critical fact is that *paresthesia* (burning, tingling, or numbness) **precedes paralysis** (anoxia and necrosis of nerves and then muscle). Permanent damage can occur unless treatment occurs in <6 hours (Edge, Day, et al., 2010). The nurse's critical thinking skills in assessment, prioritization, and organization will facilitate the arrival at a medical diagnosis and treatment.

Documenting Unexpected Findings

The nurse has just finished conducting a physical examination of Mr. Roman Tretski. Review the following important findings that each of the steps of objective data collection revealed for this patient. Consider how these results compare with the expected findings presented in the examples of appropriate documentation.

Inspection: Skin thin, shiny, and taut over lower legs. Hair growth absent bilaterally. Toenails hard and thickened. Rubor on lower legs when limbs are dependent. Feet become pale when elevated. Able to wiggle toes slowly. Integument intact, no lesions bilaterally.

Palpation: Dorsalis pedis and posterior tibial pulses not palpable bilaterally. Feet cool. Capillary refill 7 seconds. No pedal edema. Unable to identify sharp or light touch sensations on feet and lower legs bilaterally.

Laboratory testing related to the peripheral vascular and lymphatic systems includes serum evaluation for known risk factors as well as cholesterol and triglyceride levels. Patients with diabetes require monitoring of blood glucose level and hemoglobin A1C (Senthuran, 2010). Recently, research has led to the evaluation of C-reactive protein and homocysteine levels (Aronow, 2007). Plasma d-dimer assessment is indicated in the patient with a DVT and possible PE (Ross, 2010).

Diagnostic ultrasonography is noninvasive and can evaluate anatomic and hemodynamic functions. At the bedside, the continuous wave Doppler is a common tool to evaluate arm and ankle pressures. In the vascular laboratory, an ultrasonic duplex imaging and plethysmography provide detailed anatomic and flow information. These diagnostics are used to evaluate the degree of venous obstruction and location and degree of arterial disease as well as to provide follow-up postoperatively. In the patient with arterial disease or aneurysm, the arteriogram remains the test for definitive diagnosis (Clark, 2010a).

Diagnosis of lymphedema may include magnetic resonance imaging and computerized tomography to identify features of lymphedema or obstruction. Lymphangiography has the drawback of possibly causing acute lymphangitis. Lymphoscintigraphy is a safe alternative (Clark, 2010a).

Clinical Reasoning

The different vascular systems have some separate and some shared nursing diagnoses. Tissue perfusion is altered in arterial disease, and interventions are specific to increasing arterial blood flow and preventing further progression of atherosclerosis through modification of risk factors and use of antiplatelet medications such as clopidogrel and aspirin (Oka, 2006). In patients with venous disorders, the focus is promotion of venous flow. With DVT, interventions seek to prevent increased thrombus size and PE with the use of anticoagulants (AORN, 2007). In chronic venous and lymphatic disease, interventions are similar. To promote venous and lymphatic return, use of compression devices, avoiding long periods of sitting or standing, increasing exercise and elevating the affected extremity are recommended (Clark, 2010a).

Nursing Diagnoses, Outcomes, and Interventions

When formulating a nursing diagnosis, it is important to use critical thinking to cluster data together and identify patterns that fit together. Table 20-2 provides a comparison of nursing diagnoses, unexpected findings, and interventions commonly related to the peripheral vascular system assessment (North American Nursing Diagnosis Association-International, 2009). Additionally, pain, fatigue, impaired skin integrity, risk for infection, knowledge deficit, and a disturbance in body image may affect all patients with vascular disease.

Critical assessment of the data gathered leads to a plan with the goal of achieving specific patient outcomes. Some outcomes that are related to vascular issues include the following:

- Peripheral pulses are strong and symmetrical.
- Capillary refill is <3 seconds.
- The patient states treatment regimen including exercise, medications, and healthy behaviours.
- The patient senses sharp and light touch accurately.
- Peripheral edema is decreased.
- The patient verbalizes an understanding of risk factors.
- The patient verbalizes a decrease in pain (Moorhead, Johnson, et al., 2007).

To achieve desired outcomes, evidence-informed interventions are applied. Examples include the following:

- Monitor peripheral pulses every 2 hours.
- Assess and document degree of edema using scale every 4 hours.
- Evaluate pain on 0- to 10-point scale.
- Provide patient education on risk factors.
- Keep limbs warm and have patient wear skid-free slippers
- Perform meticulous foot care once a day (Bulechek, Butcher, et al., 2008).

Evaluation of the effectiveness of interventions is ongoing. The nurse modifies interventions as appropriate. The continual process of reevaluation and modification to achieve desired outcomes requires a thorough knowledge of assessment and accurate application.

Table 20-2	Common Nursing Diagnoses Associated With the Peripheral Vascular System		
Diagnosis and Related Factors	**Point of Differentiation**	**Assessment Characteristics**	**Nursing Interventions**
Altered tissue perfusion, arterial related to reduced blood flow	Decrease in oxygen resulting in failure to nourish tissues at the capillary level	Reduced hair, thick nails, dry skin, weak or absent pulses, pale skin, cool, reduced sensation, long capillary refill	Assess dorsalis pedis and posterior tibial pulse bilaterally. If reduced or unable to find them, assess with a Doppler and notify physician.
Risk for peripheral neurovascular dysfunction	Potential for one or more extremities to experience negative changes in circulation, sensation, or motion	Trauma, fractures, surgery, mechanical compression, burns, immobilization, obstruction	Perform assessment: pain, pulses, pallor, paresthesia, paralysis, poikilothermia. Contact physician if present.

Analyzing Findings From Health History and Physical Examination

Remember Mr. Tretski, whose health concerns have been outlined throughout this chapter. The initial subjective and objective data collection is complete, and the nurse has spent time reviewing the findings and other results. The following nursing note illustrates how subjective and objective data are analyzed and nursing interventions are developed.

Subjective: "Sometimes I can't feel my feet and then I fall."

Objective: Dorsalis pedis and posterior tibial pulses are not palpable bilaterally but are present with the Doppler. Rubor present on lower legs when limbs are dependent. Feet become pale when elevated. Feet cool. Capillary refill 7 seconds bilaterally. Able to wiggle toes slowly. Cannot differentiate sharp versus light touch sensations on feet and lower legs. Skin thin, shiny, and taut over lower legs bilaterally. Hair absent bilaterally. No pedal edema. Toenails hard and thickened. Integument intact, no lesions.

Analysis: Altered peripheral tissue perfusion related to peripheral arterial disease.

Plan: Keep lower extremities in a dependent position. Keep socks and shoes or slippers on feet during the day and loose socks at night. Remind patient to change positions frequently and provide range of motion exercises twice daily. Assist with walking twice daily and stop when pain develops. Apply skin moisturizer to legs every morning. Inspect feet daily for injuries and pressure points. Consult with physical therapy to develop a daily walking program.

Critical Thinking Challenge

- What might be included when writing another SOAP (subjective, objective, analysis, plan) note focusing on Mr. Tretski's confusion?
- What overlap is present between the peripheral vascular assessment and other body systems?
- What assessments are highest priority based upon his health history and current issues?

Collaborating With the Interprofessional Team

In many facilities, nurses initiate referrals for physical therapy based on assessment findings. Results that might trigger a consultation with physical therapy include musculoskeletal injury, reduced functional status, impaired balance, mobility issues, sensorimotor loss, assistance with techniques for seating or transfers, low endurance, impaired safety awareness, impaired strength or flexibility, use of adaptive equipment, and training for body mechanics.

Mr. Tretski has been experiencing many of the issues outlined above; therefore, a physical therapy consult is indicated. The following conversation illustrates how the nurse might organize data and make recommendations about the patient's care to the physical therapy department.

Situation: I'm Ronald, the nurse who is taking care of Mr. Tretski, an 88-year-old man with multiple diagnoses, including arterial vascular disease in his legs.

Background: Mr. Tretski has been falling because of reduced sensation in his feet and legs. He reports pain in lower legs with walking. He's also a bit confused.

Assessment: His peripheral pulses are not palpable bilaterally but are present with the Doppler. His feet are cool, and his capillary refill is prolonged. Mr. Tretski has slower and reduced range of motion in his feet and legs also.

Recommendations: I think that a more structured walking program might help him improve his circulation and reduce his risk of falling. We are ambulating him twice daily, but it doesn't seem to be helping much. Could you come to evaluate if a program like this might be helpful for him? If you have other ideas about things that the nursing staff could do to reduce his pain and increase his circulation, that would be helpful, too.

Critical Thinking Challenge

- How will the nurse organize information before initiating the call for the consult?
- Comment on the reliability of the historian. How will the nurse collect assessment data based upon the patient's reliability?
- How will Mr. Tretski be reassessed to evaluate the effectiveness of therapy? How frequently?

Pulling It All Together: An Example of Reflection and Critical Thinking

The nurse uses assessment data to formulate a nursing care plan for Mr. Tretski. He or she may independently perform teaching, give reminders to get assistance for transfers, and set up environmental cues for the patient to remember to call. Because Mr. Tretski is confused and his memory is poor, the nurse will need to take more initiative to remind him to keep his legs dependent and change position. The nurse also may initiate a referral to physical therapy about a daily walking program. After completing such interventions, the nurse will reevaluate Mr. Tretski and document the findings in the chart to show the nursing critical thinking. This is often in the form of a care plan or case note similar to the one below.

Nursing Diagnosis	Patient Outcomes	Nursing Interventions	Rationale	Evaluation
Altered peripheral tissue perfusion related to peripheral arterial disease	Patient will state that pain, numbness, and reduced sensation are improved 1 month after starting walking program.	Keep lower extremities in a dependent position. Provide range of motion exercises twice daily. Assist with walking twice daily and stop when pain develops. Consult with physical therapy to develop a daily walking program.	Keeping legs in a dependent position uses gravity to increase blood flow to the feet. Range of motion prevents loss of mobility. Walking programs stimulate improved oxygen extraction and prevent further loss of function.	Patient states that pain, numbness, and sensation remain about the same. He reports keeping his legs dependent except when in bed. Continue plan and reevaluate in another 2 weeks.

Applying Your Knowledge

Using the previous steps of clinical reasoning, organizing, and prioritizing, consider all the case study findings woven throughout this chapter. When answering the following questions about Mr. Tretski, begin drawing conclusions and see how the pieces of assessment must work together to create an environment for personalized, appropriate, and accurate care.

- List the six "Ps" used to assess for arterial occlusion. (Knowledge)
- How does Mr. Tretski's health history relate to his current health status? (Comprehension)
- What assessment findings might the nurse note if Mr. Tretski's peripheral arterial disease worsens? (Application)
- What assessment data will the nurse want to collect related to other body systems? (Analysis)
- How might the nurse modify history taking and physical examination based on Mr. Tretski's age and present state of confusion? (Synthesis)
- How will the nurse evaluate the effectiveness of health teaching with Mr. Tretski? (Evaluation)

Key Points

- Arterioles have smooth muscle and are primarily responsible for blood pressure.
- Veins are thin-walled capacitance vessels that stretch and accommodate large volumes of fluid.
- The lymphatic system maintains fluid and protein balance and fights infection.
- The six Ps to assess arterial obstruction are pain, pallor, poikilothermia/polar sensation, paresthesia, pulselessness, and paralysis.
- Pain, edema, and erythema may be signs of a DVT.
- Risk factors for peripheral vascular disease include family history, diabetes mellitus, hypertension, elevated cholesterol level, smoking, lack of exercise, and oral contraceptives.
- Common symptoms and signs of peripheral vascular disease include pain, numbness or tingling, cramping, skin changes, edema, and reduced functional ability.
- Edema is graded on a scale from 0 or absent to 4+ grossly swollen extremity, with depression depth of 8 mm, and up to 2 to 3 minutes for pitting to disappear.
- A pulse is expected to be +2 on a 4-point scale.
- The Allen test is performed prior to radial cannulation.
- A difference of >10 mm Hg in limbs may indicate arterial disease.
- Venous insufficiency may result in dilated and tortuous veins.
- Lymph nodes >2 cm may be caused by local or generalized conditions.
- The Homans sign is not sensitive or specific for DVT and is **not** to be used.
- The Doppler ultrasound is used to locate pulses that are not palpable.
- An ABI of ≤0.90 indicates arterial insufficiency.

Review Questions

1. Which of the following is an expected ankle-brachial index (ABI)?
   A. 56
   B. 87
   C. 1.0
   D. 24

2. Which of the following peripheral vascular diseases is not known to have a hereditary component?
   A. Lymphadenopathy
   B. Raynaud's disease
   C. Abdominal aortic aneurysm
   D. Peripheral arterial disease

3. When assessing the lower extremities, it is critical that the examiner
   A. start at the feet
   B. compare side to side
   C. evaluate the venous system and then the arterial system
   D. start at the femoral area

4. The six Ps of an acute arterial occlusion include
   A. polythermia
   B. popliteal edema
   C. pain
   D. polycythemia

5. A history of smoking has an extremely significant role in the development of which of the following?
   A. Venous insufficiency
   B. Deep vein thrombosis
   C. Peripheral arterial disease
   D. Raynaud's disease

6. A dorsalis pedis of 0/4 may indicate
   A. deep vein thrombosis
   B. peripheral arterial disease
   C. Raynaud's disease
   D. lymphadenopathy

7. During history taking, the patient reports cramping in his calf when walking a few blocks. He states that it goes away when he sits down for a few minutes. How would the nurse document this symptom?
   A. Intermittent claudication
   B. Rest pain
   C. Poikilothermia/polar sensation
   D. Venous stasis

8. The patient reports swelling in her ankles. How would the nurse proceed with physical examination?
   A. Have the patient elevate her feet to better visualize her ankles.
   B. Measure her ankles at their widest point.
   C. Evaluate further for the brown hyperpigmentation associated with venous insufficiency.
   D. Press the fingers in the edematous area evaluating for a remaining indentation after the nurse removes the fingers.

9. While evaluating the inguinal lymph nodes of the patient, the nurse palpates a 1 cm soft and freely movable node. What action should the nurse take next?
   A. Nothing—this finding is expected.
   B. Refer this patient to a specialist.
   C. Immediately check the patient's dorsalis pedis pulse.
   D. Refer the patient for immediate management of a life-threatening condition.

10. The patient with diabetes who closely monitors and controls her blood glucose level is very interested in preventing complications of her illness. The nurse would emphasize which of the following considerations in patient teaching?
    A. How to count calories
    B. How to assess her feet daily
    C. What are good carbohydrates
    D. The signs of venous insufficiency

Canadian Nursing Research

Girard, B. R., & Murray, T. (2010). Perceived control: A construct to guide patient education. *Canadian Journal of Cardiovascular Nursing, 20*(3), 18–26.

Le Sage, S., McGee, M., et al. (2008). Knowledge of venous thromboembolism (VTE) prevention among hospitalized patients. *Journal of Vascular Nursing, 26,* 109–117.

McLean, D. L., McAllister, F. A., et al. (2008). A randomized trial of the effect of community pharmacist and nurse care on improving blood pressure management in patients with diabetes mellitus. *Archives of Internal Medicine, 168*(21), 2355–2361.

Noon, J. P., Trischuk, T. C., et al. (2008). The effect of age and gender on arterial stiffness in healthy Caucasian Canadians. *Journal of Clinical Nursing, 17*(17), 2311–2317.

Prentice, D., Kilty, H. L., et al. (2008). Prevalence of cardiovascular risk factors in grade nine students. *Canadian Journal of Cardiovascular Nursing, 18*(3), 12–16.

References

Altizer, L. (2006). Compartment syndrome. *Orthopedic Nursing, 23*(6), 391–396.

American Operating Room Nurses. (2007). AORN guideline for prevention of venous stasis. *American Operating Room Nurses, 85*(3), 607–624.

Aronow, W. S. (2007). Management of peripheral arterial disease in the elderly. *Geriatrics, 62*(1), 19–25.

Barkman, A., Pooler, C., et al. (2010). Disorders in blood flow in the systemic system. In R. A. Hannon, C. Pooler, et al. (Eds). *Porth pathophysiology: Concepts of altered health states* (1st Canadian ed., pp. 458–484). Philadelphia, PA: Wolters Kluwer Health/Lippincott Williams & Wilkins.

Brunt, H., Lester, N., et al. (2008). Childhood overweight and obesity: Is the gap closing the wrong way? *Journal of Public Health (Oxford), 30*(2), 145–152.

Bulechek, G. M., Butcher, H. K., et al. (2008). *Nursing interventions classification (NIC)* (5th ed.). St. Louis, MO: Mosby.

Canadian Diabetes Association. Clinical Practice Guidelines Expert Committee. (2008). Clinical practice guidelines for the prevention and management of diabetes in Canada [Special Issue]. *Canadian Journal of Diabetes, 32*(Suppl. 1), S1–S201.

Canadian Lung Association. (2010). *Smoking & tobacco: Second-hand smoke.* Retrieved from http://www.lung,ca/protect-protegez/tobacco-tabagisme/second-secondaire/index_e/php

Chorzempa, A. (2006). Type 2 diabetes mellitus and its effect on vascular disease. *Journal of Cardiovascular Nursing, 21*(6), 485–492.

Clark, A. M. (2010a). Assessment and management of patients with vascular disorders and health concerns of peripheral circulation. In R. A. Day, P. Paul, et al. (Eds.). *Brunner & Suddarth's textbook of Canadian medical-surgical nursing* (2nd ed., pp. 912–955). Philadelphia, PA: Wolters Kluwer Health/ Lippincott Williams & Wilkins.

Clark, A. M. (2010b). Assessment and management of patients with hypertension. In R. A. Day, P. Paul, et al. (Eds.). *Brunner & Suddarth's textbook of Canadian medical-surgical nursing* (2nd ed., pp. 956–968). Philadelphia, PA: Wolters Kluwer Health/Lippincott Williams & Wilkins.

Collins, T. C., Peterson, N. J., et al. (2005). Ethnicity and peripheral arterial disease. *Mayo Foundation for Medical Education and Research, 80*(1), 48–54.

Dillon, P. M. (2007). *Nursing health assessment: Clinical pocket guide* (2nd ed., p. 180). Philadelphia, PA: F.A. Davis

Edge, D. S., Day, R. A., et al. (2010). The peripheral vascular system. In T. C. Stephen, D. L. Skillen, R. A. Day, & L. S. Bickley (Eds.). *Canadian Bates' guide to health assessment for nurses* (1st ed., pp. 563–593). Philadelphia, PA: Wolters Kluwer Health/Lippincott Williams & Wilkins.

Goff, D. C., Jr., Brass, L., et al. (2007). Essential features of a surveillance system to support the prevention and management of heart disease and stroke: A scientific statement from the American Heart Association Councils on Epidemiology and Prevention, Stroke, and Cardiovascular Nursing and the Interdisciplinary Working Groups on Quality of Care and Outcomes Research and Atherosclerotic Peripheral Vascular Disease. *Circulation, 115*(1), 127–155.

Kavey, R., Daniels, S., et al. (2003). American Heart Association guidelines for primary prevention of atherosclerotic cardiovascular disease beginning in childhood. *Circulation, 107,* 1562.

McDermott, M. M., Lui, K., et al. (2006). Physical performance in peripheral arterial disease: A slower rate of decline in clients who walk more. *Annals of Internal Medicine, 144*(1), 10–21.

Minichiello, T., & Fogarty, P. F. (2008). Diagnosis and management of venous thromboembolism. *Medical Clinics of North America, 92*(2), 443–465.

Moorhead, S., Johnson, M., et al. (2007). *Nursing outcomes classification (NOC)* (4th ed.). Philadelphia, PA: Mosby.

Mubarak, S. J., & Owen, C. A. (1997). Double-incision fasciotomy of the leg for decompression in compartment syndromes. *Journal of Bone and Joint Surgery, 59A,* 184

North American Nursing Diagnosis Association-International. (2009). *Nursing diagnoses: Definitions and classification.* West Sussex, UK: Wiley-Blackwell.

Noto, N., Okada, T., et al. (2006). B-flow sonographic demonstration for assessing carotid atherosclerosis in young patients with heterozygous familial hypercholesterolemia. *Journal of Clinical Ultrasound, 34*(2), 43–49.

Oka, R. H. (2006). Peripheral arterial disease in older adults: Management of cardiovascular disease risk factors. *The Journal of Cardiovascular Nursing, 21*(5), S15–S20.

Ostchega, Y., Paulose-Ram, R., et al. (2007). Prevalence of peripheral arterial disease and risk factors in persons aged 60 and older: Data from the national health and nutrition examination survey 1999–2004. *Journal of the American Geriatric Society, 55*(4), 583–589.

Pei, H., Wang, Y., et al. (2006). Direct evidence for a crucial role of the arterial wall in control of atherosclerosis susceptibility. *Circulation, 114,* 2382–2389.

Public Health Agency of Canada. (2011a). *Physical activity: Tips to get active—Information and tips for adults ages 18–65.* Retrieved from http://www.phac-aspc.gc.ca/hp-ps/hl-mvs/pa-ap/07paap-eng.php

Public Health Agency of Canada. (2011b). *Physical activity: Tips to get active—Physical activity tips for older adults (65 years and older).* Retrieved from http://www.phac-aspc.gc.ca/hp-ps/hl-mvs/pa-ap/08paap-eng.php

Rankin, J. A., & Then, K. L. (2010a). Musculoskeletal care modalities. In R. A. Day, P. Paul, et al. (Eds.). *Brunner & Suddarth's textbook of Canadian medical-surgical nursing*

(2nd ed., pp. 2238–2267). Philadelphia, PA: Wolters Kluwer Health/Lippincott Williams & Wilkins.

Rankin, J. A., & Then, K. L. (2010b). Management of patients with musculoskeletal trauma. In R. A. Day, P. Paul, et al. (Eds.). *Brunner & Suddarth's textbook of Canadian medical-surgical nursing* (2nd ed., pp. 2304–2345). Philadelphia, PA: Wolters Kluwer Health/Lippincott Williams & Wilkins.

Ross, C. J. M. (2010). Management of patients with chest and lower respiratory tract disorders. In R. A. Day, P. Paul, et al. (Eds.). *Brunner & Suddarth's textbook of Canadian medical-surgical nursing* (2nd ed., pp. 586–645). Philadelphia, PA: Wolters Kluwer Health/Lippincott Williams & Wilkins.

Senthuran, R. A. (2010). Assessment and management of patients with diabetes mellitus. In R. A. Day, P. Paul, et al. (Eds.). *Brunner & Suddarth's textbook of Canadian medical-surgical nursing* (2nd ed., pp. 1295–1353). Philadelphia, PA: Wolters Kluwer Health/Lippincott Williams & Wilkins.

Sieggreen, M. (2006). A contemporary approach to peripheral arterial disease. *The Nurse Practitioner, 31*(7), 23–27.

Veazie, M., Galoway, J., et al. (2005). Taking the initiative: iImplementing the American Heart Association Guide for Improving Cardiovascular Health at the Community Level: Healthy People 2010 Heart Disease and Stroke Partnership Community Guidelines Implementation and Best Practices Workgroup. *Circulation, 12*(16), 2538–2554.

Williams, C., Hayman, L., et al. (2002). Cardiovascular health in childhood. *Circulation, 106*, 143–160.

White, C. (2007). Intermittent claudication. *New England Journal of Medicine, 356*, 1241–1250.

The Canadian Jensen's Nursing Health Assessment suite offers these additional resources to enhance learning and facilitate understanding of this chapter:

- thePoint on line resource, http//thepoint.lww.com/Stephen1E
- *Laboratory Manual for Canadian Jensen's Nursing Health Assessment: A Best Practice Approach*

Tables of Unexpected Findings

Table 20-3 **Internal and External Causes of Compartment Syndrome**

	Acute Compartment Syndrome	Chronic Compartment Syndrome	Crush Syndrome
Internal source	• Edema • Bleeding • Contusions • Fractures • Burns • Inactivity after surgery • Infiltrated IV sites	• Exercise • Increased muscle volume • History of previous fracture, casting, or extremity surgery	
External source	• Tight dressing or cast • Braces • Traction • Surgical positioning • Pneumatic antishock garments • Automatic blood pressure devices • Burn eschar		• Crush injury with muscle infarction. Examples: • Trapped under heavy equipment or fallen objects • Overdose, with extremity under body • Wringer-type injury
Symptoms and signs	• Increasing pain out of proportion to etiology • Deep, unrelenting, throbbing, and localized pain • Pain with passive stretch • Paresthesias (burning, tingling) • Taut skin • Muscle feels edematous and hard • Sensation deficit (hypoesthesia) • Motor weakness • Usual occurrence 6–8 h after injury	• Positive history of exercise • Limb tightness, aching • Point tenderness over muscle • Rare to have neurological deficits • Usually resolved with rest	• Deep pain • Severe edema • Taut skin • Vesicles, bulla with erythema • Hypovolemia • Hyperkalemia

Adapted from Altizer, L. (2006). Compartment syndrome. *Orthopedic Nursing, 23*(6), 391–396; Rankin, J. A., & Then, K. L. (2010a). Management of patients with musculoskeletal trauma. In R. A. Day, P. Paul, et al. (Eds.). *Brunner & Suddarth's textbook of medical-surgical nursing* (2nd Canadian ed., pp. 2304–2345). Philadelphia, PA: Wolters Kluwer Health/Lippincott Williams & Wilkins.

	Characteristics	Causes
Weak pulse	Decreased pulse pressure, weak on palpation and easily obliterated, slow upstroke with prolonged systolic peak	Decreased cardiac output as with congestive heart failure, hypovolemia, and severe aortic stenosis; peripheral arterial disease
Bounding pulse	Increased pulse pressure, strong and bounding, rapid rise and fall, brief systolic peak	Increased stroke volume such as with exercise and fever, hyperthyroidism, decreased aortic compliance as with atherosclerosis or aging
Pulsus alternans	Alternating small and large amplitude, regular rate	Left ventricular failure may be accompanied by S3
Pulsus bigeminus *Premature contractions*	Alternating irregular beats; one usual beat and then one premature beat with alternating strong and weak amplitude	Premature ventricular or atrial contractions
Pulsus bisferiens	Double systolic peak	Aortic regurgitation, combined aortic regurgitation and stenosis, less often hypertrophic cardiomyopathy
Pulsus paradoxus *Expiration* *Inspiration*	Palpable decrease in amplitude on quiet inspiration; with blood pressure cuff, systolic decreases of >10 mm Hg during inspiration	Pericardial tamponade, constrictive pericarditis, and obstructive lung disease

Table 20-5   Unexpected Arterial Findings

Peripheral Arterial Disease

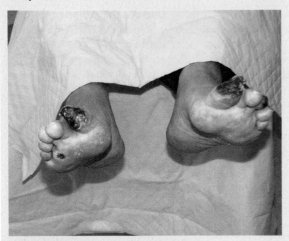

Acute Arterial Occlusion

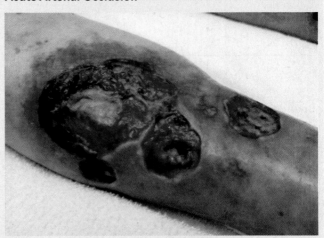

Chronic atherosclerotic occlusion may develop anywhere in the arterial system. As with coronary artery disease (CAD), peripheral arteries narrow from plaque, which limits oxygenated blood from reaching the tissues. Resulting ischemia causes cramping pain, which in the lower extremities is called *claudication*. It is usually exertional and occurs in relation to arterial blockage. Lower arterial blockage may lead to calf claudication. Blockage at the sacroiliac bifurcation may cause hip claudication. As the disease progresses, rest pain may occur. Patients report being awakened by pain. At this point, dorsalis pedis and posterior tibial are decreased significantly compared to the opposite leg. Also, the diseased leg has a cool temperature and pale or blue colour. Ankle-brachial index (ABI) is decreased. Severe occlusion is chronically painful and may cause ulcers, which in turn may lead to gangrene and amputation. Total occlusion, often from thrombus, is limb threatening. Any combination of the six Ps (see Box 20-2) constitutes a clinical emergency requiring immediate intervention. Rest generally relieves claudication. Well-refined assessment skills are paramount. Modification of risk factors is critical. Smoking cessation is of utmost importance. Stringent control of unmodifiable risk factors (eg, blood glucose level in patients with diabetes) is essential. Pain assessment and management are other issues.

Acute arterial occlusion may result from progression of peripheral arterial disease (PAD) (as discussed) or thrombus from another source (eg, cardiac catheterization puncture site). In the latter case, a thrombus may break-off and travel through the arterial system to a smaller vessel that is then occluded. The six Ps would again be assessment findings. As with PAD, this is a clinical emergency.

Table 20-5   **Unexpected Arterial Findings** *(continued)*

Abdominal Aortic Aneurysm

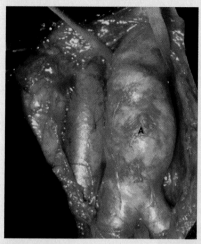

Raynaud's Phenomenon and Raynaud's Disease

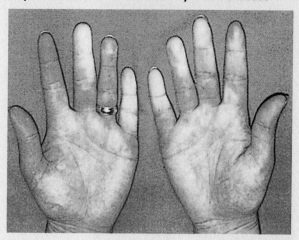

An aneurysm is an outpouching of an arterial wall which results from a weakened or damaged medial arterial layer. Aneurysms may occur in any artery but are most common in the aorta. Aortic aneurysms may be thoracic, below the renal arteries, or abdominal. The predominant cause of aortic aneurysm is atherosclerosis. Hypertension may accelerate aneurysm development in an already damaged aortic wall. Aortic aneurysms are also seen with Marfan's syndrome, a congenital disorder. In addition to smoking and hypertension, family history of aortic aneurysm is a risk factor. Aortic aneurysms affect men nearly five times more than women. Aortic aneurysms may rupture or dissect, in which the layers of the artery separate and fill with blood. Either situation results in compromised blood supply to major arteries and therefore to organs and tissues. These critical emergencies are often fatal. Assessment findings include chest pain, abdominal pain, back pain, shortness of breath, laterally pulsatile mass on palpation, and a bruit. Patients with an abdominal aortic aneurysm are usually asymptomatic.

These vasospastic disorders primarily affect women. *Raynaud's Phenomenon* is the term used when the cause is attributed to a connective tissue disorder (eg, lupus erythematosus, rheumatoid arthritis, scleroderma). When the etiology is unknown (most cases), it is called *Raynaud's Disease*. Symptoms include numbness, tingling, sometimes pain, extreme pallor progressing to cyanosis, and coolness of the hands. They usually begin in the fingers and are symmetrical. When the ischemic episode is over, hyperemia, erythema, and burning pain may follow. Smoking, emotional stress, and exposure to cold often precipitate vasospasm. Management includes smoking cessation, avoiding cold temperatures, wearing thermal socks and gloves in cool temperatures, and stress management. In patients with Raynaud's phenomenon, treatment of the underlying cause may offer relief. Tissue injury is rare but with repeated ischemic episodes skin over the fingertips breaks down and small ulcers may develop. The nails may become brittle. In rare cases, gangrene of the fingers may occur.

Arterial diseases involve narrowing of the vessels, weakening of the vessel walls, and thrombus formation. Risk factors are the same as for CAD: smoking, diabetes, hypertension, hypercholesterolemia, and family history of arterial disorders. Atherosclerosis is the most common cause.

Table 20-6   Unexpected Venous Findings

Chronic Venous Insufficiency

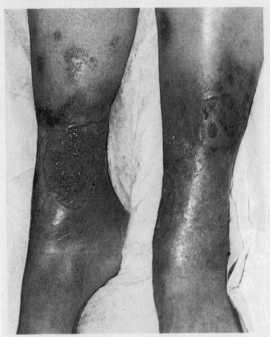

Deep Vein Thrombosis

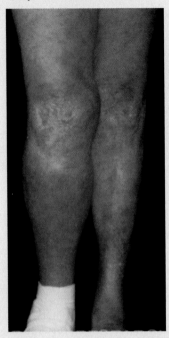

Malfunctioning of the unidirectional valves impairs venous blood return to the affected extremity. Causes are primary valvular incompetence (which may be from a congenital absence of valves), sequelae of DVT, or both. DVT permanently damages the valve leaflets, which cannot close. The veins then cannot empty, leading to edema. Venous insufficiency from dysfunctional valves causes tissue congestion, which eventually impairs nutrition to the tissue. Brown hyperpigmentation may develop from hemosiderin deposits remaining after the breakdown of red blood cells. Lymphatic insufficiency follows venous insufficiency, compounding tissue congestion. Patients report edema and aching pain. As venous insufficiency progresses, stasis dermatitis (characterized by dry, scaling skin) may lead to superficial and relatively painless venous ulcers. Chronic pressure from edema makes these ulcers difficult to heal (see Table 20-5). Long periods of standing promote edema. Elevating the legs above the heart promotes venous return, providing some relief. Graduated compression stockings are recommended to prevent increasing edema (Clark, 2010a).

DVT results from thrombus formation in the deep veins. They are more common in the lower extremities, but increasing use of venous access catheters is contributing to more upper-extremity DVTs. Virchow's triad identifies risk factors for venous thrombosis: blood stasis, vessel wall injury, and increased blood coagulability. Immobility and decreased mobility, both more common in older adults, pose risks for stasis. Trauma or surgery may damage vessel walls. Increased blood coagulability may stem from the prolonged sitting and dehydration associated with airplane travel, cancer, use of oral contraceptives, and inherited or acquired coagulation disorder. Treatment is anticoagulation; for some patients with chronic issues, anticoagulation may be long-term prophylaxis. Presenting symptoms of DVT are unilateral edema of the extremity, redness, pain or achiness, and warmth. The leg is measured daily at the same place throughout treatment. Unrecognized DVTs are responsible for most deaths from pulmonary emboli (PE). Acute-care patients often have at least one risk factor for venous thrombosis, so knowledge of the features of DVT and PE is critical.

Table 20-6 **Unexpected Venous Findings** *(continued)*

Thrombophlebitis

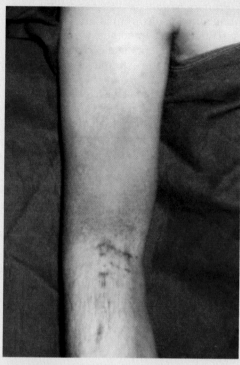

Neuropathy

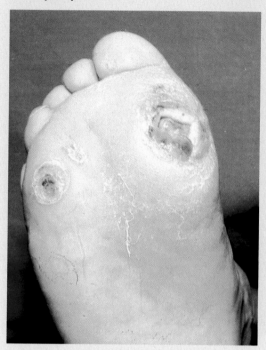

Superficial thrombophlebitis results from thrombus formation in the superficial veins. The same risk factors apply as with DVT. Assessment findings are unilateral localized pain or achiness, edema, warmth, and redness. In superficial veins, a palpable mass or cord may also be present along the vein.

Peripheral neuropathies, most common in patients with diabetes and chronic hyperglycemia, are classified as somatic or autonomic. *Somatic neuropathies* typically affect lower extremities. Paresthesias, burning sensations, and numbness may occur, along with decreased senses of vibration, pain, temperature, and proprioception. These symptoms increase risks for tissue injury and falls. Daily foot assessment is critical because these patients may not feel a break in the skin or burn and develop subsequent foot lesions, which are challenging to heal. For some patients, peripheral neuropathies cause chronic lower-extremity pain. Pain assessment and management are crucial to their quality of life. A pharmacologic approach to management is often employed.

(table continues on page 570)

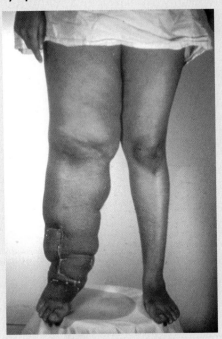

Table 20-6 Unexpected Venous Findings (continued)

Lymphedema

Lymphedema occurs when lymph channels or nodes are obstructed. *Primary lymphedema* is congenital. *Secondary lymphedema* results from injury, scarring, excision of lymph nodes, or, sometimes, trauma or chronic infection. Assessment initially reveals nonpainful pitting edema of the extremity. As lymphedema progresses, the skin may thicken, redden, and show nonpitting edema. Small vesicles with lymphatic fluid may develop in more advanced stages. Cellulitis is a frequent complication. Management begins with treating the cause. Bed rest with the leg elevated 45° at night and frequently during the day for several days is usually very effective in reducing edema. Compression pumps and manual lymphatic drainage may also be used. Patients should wear elastic compression wraps or stockings when the extremity is dependent to combat gravity-related pooling. They apply these devices in the morning when edema is lowest. Exercise enhances treatment, as do weight control and decreased salt intake. Ongoing skin assessment is essential, because breaks in the skin occur more easily in edematous extremities and are difficult to treat. Diuretics may also promote fluid elimination. Chronic lymphedema can be disfiguring and limit joint mobility. Psychosocial support for body image and self-esteem is very important in care.

The structure of veins and their reliance on a unidirectional valve, the skeletal muscle pump, and changes in abdominal and intrathoracic pressures lend them to issues of stasis and insufficiency.

Table 20-7 Arterial Versus Venous Ulcers

	Arterial	Venous
Location	Toes, metatarsals, malleoli, heel	Ankle, medial malleolus, distal third of leg
Borders	Regular,	Irregular
Ulcer base	Pale, yellow	Red, pink
Drainage	Minimal	Moderate to large amount
Gangrene	May develop	Does not develop
Pain	Intermittent claudication, progressing to pain at rest. Pain is decreased with dependency of limb	Aching pain, feeling of heaviness with dependency; decreased with elevation
Skin	Surrounding skin is thin, shiny; loss of hair over feet and toes. Nails are thickened and ridged. Temperature is cool.	Stasis dermatitis, brown pigmentation around the ankle; possible thickening of the skin. Temperature is as expected for environment
Pulses	Decreased or absent	Present, but may be difficult to palpate because of edema

Breasts and Axillae Assessment

Learning Objectives

1 Demonstrate knowledge of anatomy and physiology of the breasts and axillae.

2 Identify important topics for health promotion and risk reduction related to the breasts and axillae.

3 Collect subjective data related to the breasts and axillae.

4 Collect objective data related to the breasts and axillae.

5 Identify expected and unexpected findings related to the breast and axillae during the general survey and when performing inspection and palpation.

6 Analyze subjective and objective data from assessment of the breasts and axillae and consider initial interventions.

7 Document and communicate data from the assessment of the breasts and axillae using appropriate terminology and principles of recording.

8 Individualize health assessment of the breasts and axillae considering the age, condition, gender, and culture of the patient.

9 Identify nursing diagnoses and initiate a plan of care based on findings from the assessment of the breasts and axillae.

Mrs. Prudence Randall, a 61-year-old African Canadian elementary school teacher, meets with the nurse at the clinic. "I found another lump in my left breast. With my bad family history, I am worried it is cancer this time." She has had two previous negative breast biopsies at ages 40 and 48 years. Mrs. Randall's mother was diagnosed with breast cancer at 62 years and died at 64 years. Mrs. Randall's older sister died from breast cancer last year at age 64 years. Mrs. Randall has two daughters (40 and 38 years).

Physical examination findings include the following: height 1.6 m; weight 67 kg; body mass index 26; blood pressure 160/90 mm Hg (right arm, sitting); pulse 102 beats/min and regular; respirations 20 breaths/min. A round, firm, nontender mass is noted in the upper outer quadrant of the left breast, 4 cm from the nipple. The borders of the mass are not well delineated, but the mass is not fixed to underlying structures. Axillary, infraclavicular, and supraclavicular nodes are nontender and are not enlarged, bilaterally.

You will gain more information about Mrs. Randall as you progress through this chapter. As you study the content and features, consider Mrs. Randall's case and its relationship to what you are learning. Begin thinking about the following points:

- Are Mrs. Randall's psychosocial or physical needs in this case more important? Provide rationale.
- How should the nurse organize and prioritize data collection, considering Mrs. Randall's concerns?
- How should the nurse individualize assessment to Mrs. Randall's specific needs, considering her condition, age, culture, and profession?

This chapter includes the assessment of the breasts and regional lymphatics. Pertinent anatomy and physiology, as well as key variations based on pregnancy, lifespan, sex, and culture are included. The chapter contains methods for collecting subjective data related to the risk of breast disease (cancerous and benign). Specific unexpected findings, such as colour changes, nipple discharge, retraction, heat, warmth or redness, and lumps are described.

Anatomy and Physiology Overview

Breasts are paired mammary glands found in both sexes. Male breasts, which remain rudimentary, have a thin layer of breast tissue with a centrally located small **nipple** and surrounding **areola**. Mature female breasts are accessory reproductive organs that respond to cyclical changes in sex hormones and provide nourishment for infants through milk production. Many cultures associate the breasts with female sexuality.

Landmarks

Female breasts are located on the anterior chest wall between the 3rd and 7th ribs. They extend from the sternal margin to the midaxillary line, with the tail of each breast extending into its respective axilla. The pectoral muscles and superficial fascia provide support.

To describe clinical findings, it is best to divide each breast into four quadrants by imagining horizontal and vertical lines that intersect at the nipple. The **tail of Spence**, which extends from the upper outer breast quadrant into the axilla, can be described separately (Fig. 21-1). An alternative method is to compare the breast to the face of a clock and describe findings based on their distance from the nipple (eg, right breast at 8:00, 3 cm from nipple). Since most breast cancers occur in the upper outer quadrant, nurses pay close attention to this area (Sohn, Aurthurs, et al., 2008).

> **Clinical Significance 21-1**
>
> Breast cancer is the leading cause of cancer in females, but males also can develop the disease (approximately 1% of all cases). In 2011, the Canadian Cancer Society's Steering Committee on Cancer Statistics predicted that 190 men would be diagnosed with breast cancer and that 55 men would die from it.

Breast Structures

On the surface, the breasts lie anterior to the serratus anterior and pectoralis major muscles (Fig. 21-2A). Each breast has a nipple with a surrounding areola, as well as Montgomery glands, fibrous tissue, glandular tissue, and lymph nodes (Fig. 21-2B). The **nipple** is in the center of the breast. It is

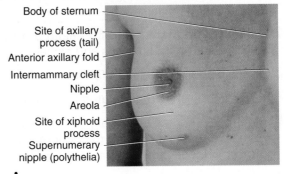

Body of sternum
Site of axillary process (tail)
Anterior axillary fold
Intermammary cleft
Nipple
Areola
Site of xiphoid process
Supernumerary nipple (polythelia)

A

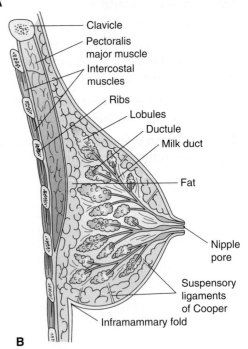

Clavicle
Pectoralis major muscle
Intercostal muscles
Ribs
Lobules
Ductule
Milk duct
Fat
Nipple pore
Suspensory ligaments of Cooper
Inframammary fold

B

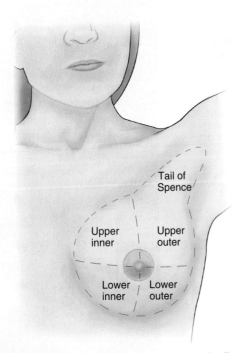

Tail of Spence
Upper inner
Upper outer
Lower inner
Lower outer

Figure 21-1 Breast with four quadrants and tail of Spence delineated.

Figure 21-2 A. Surface anatomy of the breast. **B.** Internal structures of the breast.

darkly pigmented, round, rough, and usually protuberant; it is composed of smooth muscle fibres. Autonomic, sensory, or tactile stimulation produces nipple erection and emptying of lactiferous ducts during breast-feeding. Surrounding the nipple is a 1 to 2 cm **areola**, which is also darkly pigmented. Within the areola are small sebaceous glands called **Montgomery glands**. During lactation, these glands secrete a protective lubricant.

Breasts consist of two types of tissue, fibrous and glandular, and two types of fat, subcutaneous and retromammary. The fibrous tissue is supportive. **Cooper ligaments** (fibrous bands) extend from the connective tissue to the muscle fascia, providing additional support. The glandular tissue consists of 15 to 20 glandular lobes in each breast that extends from the nipple in a radial fashion. Within each lobe, 20 to 40 lobules contain milk-producing **acini** cells. When milk is produced, it drains into the **lactiferous ducts**; the milk from each lobe empties into one sinus that terminates at the nipple. Milk is stored in these sinuses until it is released. This ductal system may be noticeable in women who are pregnant or lactating.

Most of the breast consists of subcutaneous and retromammary fat surrounding the glandular tissue. Actual breast size and the proportions of each tissue component vary with age, genetic predisposition, pregnancy, lactation, and nutritional status.

Branches of the internal mammary and lateral thoracic arteries provide most of the blood supply to the deep breast tissues and nipple. The superficial tissues receive blood from the intercostal arteries.

Axillae and Lymph Nodes

Each breast has an extensive lymphatic network for drainage. Most lymph drains into the axillary lymph nodes on the same side (ipsilateral lymph nodes; Fig. 21-3). Axillary nodes are relatively superficial, so they are more accessible than deep lymph nodes and fairly easy to palpate when enlarged.

- The *lateral (humeral) nodes* are located inside the upper arm along the humerus and drain most of the arm.
- The *central nodes* may be palpable along the chest wall from high up in the axilla between the anterior and posterior axillary folds. These nodes receive lymph from the lateral, subscapular, and pectoral lymph nodes.
- The *subscapular (posterior) nodes* lie inside the posterior axillary fold along the lateral border of the scapulae. These nodes drain the posterior chest wall and part of the arm.
- The *pectoral (anterior) nodes* are located inside the anterior axillary fold along the pectoralis major muscle. These nodes drain the anterior chest wall and most of the breast.

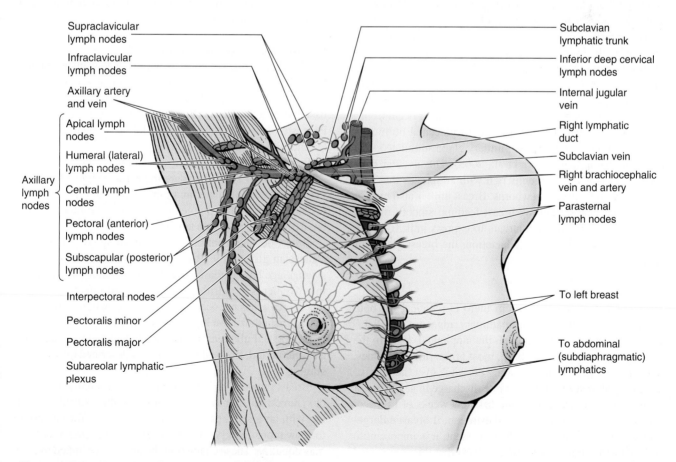

Figure 21-3 Location of lymph nodes in relation to breasts.

Lymph collected in the central nodes drains into the infraclavicular and supraclavicular nodes. However, not all lymph drainage of the breasts is into the axillae. It is possible for malignant cells from breast cancer to spread directly to infraclavicular nodes (below the clavicle), to deep channels toward the opposite breast, or into the abdomen (Day & Bickley, 2010).

Clinical Significance 21-2

Lymphatic spread of breast carcinoma cells may lead to enlargement of the axillary lymph nodes, which may be noted during the physical assessment. Tenderness or enlargement of any of these nodes also may be related to infection; this warrants further evaluation.

 Lifespan Considerations

Women Who Are Pregnant

Women experience breast changes as early as the first 2 months of pregnancy. The ductal system expands, secretory alveoli develop, and breasts enlarge, often feeling nodular as the mammary alveoli hypertrophy. Placental hormones stimulate this growth. Breasts enlarge, often feeling tender and nodular. Nipples darken, enlarge, and become more erect. As pregnancy progresses, areolae also become larger, darker, and more prominent. Small, scattered Montgomery glands develop within the areolae. Because of increased blood flow, a bluish venous pattern is often evident on the breast tissue.

The breasts may begin to express *colostrum* (milk precursor) during the fourth month of pregnancy. Colostrum is rich in protein, carbohydrates, and antibodies and low in fat, which makes it easier for newborns to digest. For the first few days after they give birth, women continue to produce colostrum. Actual milk replaces colostrum if breast-feeding occurs.

After childbirth, decreased levels of placental hormones and prolactin secretion by the pituitary gland stimulate lactation (Singleton, Sandowski, et al., 2008). The alveolar cells produce breast milk, which is rich with antibodies that protect against infection in newborns. Breast milk is also high in protein and lactose. During breast-feeding, smooth muscle in the nipple and areola contracts to express milk from the sinuses. After completion of lactation, the breast glandular tissue shrinks.

Newborns and Infants

Development of breast tissue in utero is identical for both genders. During this time, the mammary ridge, or "milk line," extends from the axillae through the nipple and down to the inguinal ligament. Prior to birth, most of the ridge atrophies, leaving two bilateral breasts along the ridge over the thorax.

Enlarged breast tissue and white discharge in newborns of either gender may occur for the first few weeks of life, secondary to the effects of maternal estrogen. If breast enlargement, white discharge, or both are present, it is important to inform the newborn's parents/caregivers that this is expected and the conditions will resolve spontaneously. At birth, the

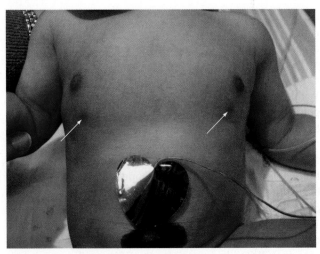

Figure 21-4 Supernumerary nipples in a newborn.

lactiferous ducts are present in females within the nipples, but alveoli do not develop in females until puberty.

In a small percentage of males and females, a **supernumerary (accessory) nipple** persists. It often looks like a mole, but when inspected closely a tiny nipple and areola are evident. If an examiner finds a supernumerary nipple, he or she should also begin evaluation of the kidneys, because of the association between extra nipples and renal anomalies (Fig. 21-4; Laufer & Goldstein, 2005). Accessory breast tissue (polymastia) is most often seen in the axillae and also along the mammary ridge.

Children and Adolescents

Until puberty, breasts consist of only a few ducts without acini. During adolescence, breasts in females develop secondary to increased production of several hormones. Adipose tissue and the lactiferous ducts grow in response to estrogen. Progesterone stimulation results in lobular growth and alveolar budding (McCowen Meahring, 2010a).

In most girls, changes in the nipples and areolae and development of breast buds are the earliest signs of puberty. Fat deposits accumulate, and nipples and areolae grow and become more darkly pigmented and more protuberant. The breasts also may become tender.

Breast development begins at a mean age of 10 years for Caucasian girls and 9 years for African Canadian girls. The average age has decreased over the past century as a result of improvements in nutrition, sanitation, and infection control; this decrease has not occurred in countries where children are malnourished or have high rates of disease (de Onis, Garza, et al., 2004). Full breast development occurs on average over a 3-year period. Breast development is described by **Tanner's staging** (Fig. 21-5).

Breast growth over this 3-year period is usually not steady or symmetrical. It may occur rapidly and then subside, changing with an uneven pace. It is not uncommon for one breast to grow more quickly than the other, but with time breast size may equalize. These changes in the breasts are linked to body image and self-esteem, especially during a developmental

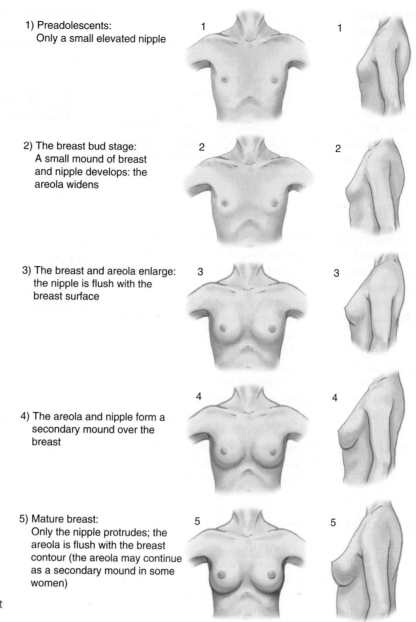

1) Preadolescents:
   Only a small elevated nipple

2) The breast bud stage:
   A small mound of breast
   and nipple develops: the
   areola widens

3) The breast and areola enlarge:
   the nipple is flush with the
   breast surface

4) The areola and nipple form a
   secondary mound over the
   breast

5) Mature breast:
   Only the nipple protrudes; the
   areola is flush with the breast
   contour (the areola may continue
   as a secondary mound in some
   women)

Figure 21-5 Tanner's staging of breast development.

stage in which the peer group assumes increasing importance. Additionally, the breasts often symbolize the development of sexuality and reproductive capacity. The adolescent girl often will compare her growth to that of others. Early-maturing girls may experience more dissatisfaction with their physical appearance, because most of their peers have the slim body shape that cultural norms perpetuate. Late-maturing girls may worry that they will be "flat." Timing of breast development in girls has a social stigma; girls who mature either too early or too late may be concerned. The nurse explains to the adolescent that the rate of breast growth is uniquely individual, as are the size and shape of the mature breast.

Menarche (the beginning of menstruation) occurs during late puberty or Tanner's stage 3 or 4, which coincides with the peak of the adolescent growth spurt (Kronenberg, Melmed, et al., 2008). During menstruation, the glandular tissues of the breasts change in response to cyclical hormonal fluctuations. At the start of the cycle, the ductal cells grow, interstitial fluid increases, and the tissue may become slightly inflamed. These conditions peak just before menses and may lead to dilatation or hyperplasia of the ducts, hypertrophy of the surrounding connective tissue, and benign conditions referred to as *fibrocystic changes* (Singleton, Sandowski, et al., 2008).

Clinical Significance 21-3

In adult women, unilateral or bilateral breast tenderness and changes in size and nodularity (lumpiness) may accompany menses. Breasts often feel full, sore, or heavy just prior to menstruation and are smallest and least tender in the days following menstruation.

Older Adults

As women age, glandular, alveolar, and lobular tissues in the breasts decrease. After menopause, fat deposits replace glandular tissue that continues to atrophy as a result of decreased ovarian hormone, estrogen, and progesterone secretion. These changes make it easier to palpate the breasts. The suspensory ligaments relax, causing breasts to sag and droop. Breasts also decrease in size and lose elasticity. Nipples become smaller, flatter, and less erectile. Axillary hair may stop growing at this time. These changes are more apparent in the 8th and 9th decades of life.

Male Breasts

Male breasts are immature structures with well-developed areolae and small nipples. During midpuberty, one or both male breasts commonly and temporarily enlarge as a result of changing hormone levels, a condition referred to as **gynecomastia**. Pubescent males also may develop breast buds or tenderness, which also is usually temporary. Almost one third of adolescent males have these conditions, which usually resolve in 1 to 2 years (Rakel, 2007). The breasts may also enlarge in adolescent males from adipose tissue related to obesity. It is important to investigate feelings related to body image and sexual identity in adolescent males with enlarged breasts. Gynecomastia is physically benign but can cause emotional distress. Information that this is temporary and expected may help alleviate the distress. As males age, gynecomastia (enlarged breasts) may recur from decreases in testosterone levels, causing the female hormones to predominate.

Cultural Considerations

Worldwide, breast cancer is the leading cause of cancer deaths for women (Anderson, 2006). Over 1.1 million women are diagnosed with breast cancer each year (Anderson). In 2000, over half of all cases of breast cancer occurred in high-income countries, with the exception of Japan, which has a low incidence rate (International Agency for Research on Cancer, World Health Organization, 2002).

Women coming to Canada from countries where the rate of breast cancer is low are often unaware that their rate of breast cancer will increase to match Canadian women. For example, incidence rates for cancer in Indo-Canadian women were different from those from India and were closer to the general population of British Columbia where they lived (Hislop, Bajdik, et al., 2007). In some cultural groups, husbands control access to health care and may also not realize the need for screening for breast cancer. The other challenge is that when an immigrant woman develops breast cancer, her community may reject the diagnosis, leaving the woman without support.

Nurses are aware of variations in breast development related to genetic background. For example, African Canadian females mature earlier than Caucasians. Variations in the colour of the skin and nipple relate to genetic background. Differences exist in the incidence and outcomes of breast cancer. Latino, Asian, and Canadian First Nations women have a lower risk for developing breast cancer. Issues of easy access to breast health services vary across Canada, particularly in rural areas. This may lead to a more advanced stage of breast cancer at the time of diagnosis.

Acute Assessment

Two breast infections, mastitis and lactational abscess, can become emergencies. *Mastitis*, an infection of breast tissue, is most common in women who are breast-feeding and often occurs 2 to 3 weeks following childbirth. The cause of the infection can be the transfer of microorganisms from the woman's hands to the breast; oral, eye, or skin infection from the breast-feeding infant; or blood-borne organisms (Day & Bickely, 2010). Infection in the breast ducts progresses and results in milk being trapped in several lobules. The patient often reports a dull pain over the affected area, with purulent, serous, or bloody nipple discharge, which should be cultured. Treatment includes 7 to 10 days of a broad-spectrum antibiotic, hot compresses and a snug bra to reduce pain and provide support, rest, hydration, and careful personal hygiene (Chow, 2010).

If untreated, mastitis can progress to a *lactational abscess* as the body tries to wall off the infection. The breast is red and painful, with purulent nipple drainage. Fever, chills, delirium, and tachycardia can occur (Day & Bickley, 2010). Treatment is incision and drainage of the abscess. Severe infection can destroy the duct structure of the breast, which can result in no milk being produced from the duct even after a subsequent pregnancy (Chow, 2010).

⚠ *SAFETY ALERT 21-1*

Conditions requiring further investigation to determine a need for tests to rule out cancer include the following:

- *A new breast lump*
- *A lump that has changed in size, shape, texture, or tenderness*
- *A lump in the axilla*
- *Bloody nipple discharge*

Nipple discharge alone is not a reliable sign of cancer; this symptom should be considered with other symptoms and the clinical presentation (Richards, Hunt, et al., 2007). Ductal ectasia (expansion) may cause green, brown, or other coloured discharge.

Subjective Data Collection

Subjective data collection begins with the current health history related to the breast (such as breast discomfort, masses or lumps, or nipple discharge) and continues with questions related to past history (previous breast disease; surgeries; menstrual, pregnancy, and lactation history; and past hormone therapy), family history (of breast cancer or other breast disease), and personal history (breast trauma, surgery, and self-care behaviours). It is important to ask questions sensitively when obtaining data, because conditions related to the breast may be difficult or embarrassing for some women to discuss.

Gathering health history information related to the breast and lymphatic system identifies specific areas of patient needs or concerns. This aids nurses in providing education regarding health-promotion activities that focus on disease prevention, early identification of concerns, and reduction of complications if health issues exist. Health promotion also reinforces existing healthy habits. Nurses are often primary patient educators, and the promotion of healthy behaviours and risk reduction are very important nursing roles.

A group needing more attention is men. Nurse researchers in Alberta reported that men with breast cancer were concerned about the lack of information and knowledge about male breast cancer among the general population but also among health professionals (Pituskin, Williams, et al., 2007). The men in the study reported body image issues, role strain, and stress about their diagnosis.

Assessment of Risk Factors

The most common cancer in Canadian women is breast cancer, accounting for an estimated 28% of cancer cases and 15% of cancer deaths in 2011 (Canadian Cancer Society's Steering Committee for Cancer Statistics, 2011). The probability of developing breast cancer increases with age, but breast cancer also occurs in young women and (rarely) in men. Canadian Cancer Society's Steering Committee for Cancer Statistics estimates that 23,400 women and 190 men will be diagnosed with breast cancer in 2011 and that 5,100 women and 55 men will die from their disease. The number of women expected to be diagnosed with breast cancer in 2011 increased by 200 from 2010.

Age Distribution of Breast Cancer Cases and Deaths in Canadian Women

Age (Years)	New Breast Cancer Cases	Breast Cancer Deaths
<29	<1%	0%
30–39	3.6%	2%
40–49	15%	7.6%
50–59	27%	18%
60–69	26.5%	22%
70–79	17%	22%
80+	11%	28.4%

Adapted from Canadian Cancer Society's Steering Committee on Cancer Statistics. (2011). *Canadian cancer statistics 2011*, Toronto, ON: Canadian Cancer Society.

The purposes of assessing risk factors are to identify the patient's likelihood of developing breast cancer and to work with her or him to modify controllable factors. Breast cancer risk factors that nurses would review with patients are included in Table 21-1. These include increased age, prior history of breast cancer, family history, genes, reproductive history, having children, and genetic background.

If patients already have a breast condition, it is important to gather more information about its effects and how it is being treated (Bowen, Alfano, et al., 2007). This information provides nurses with needed information to implement appropriate interventions that will control or improve symptoms and prevent complications. Additionally, these discussions illuminate areas in which patients need further follow-up or education. Questioning and education can occur simultaneously.

Table 21-1 Risk Factors for Breast Cancer		
Modifiable	**Nonmodifiable**	**Controversial Possibilities**
History of childbirth: Nulliparity or having first child after age 30 y slightly increases risk.	**Gender:** Women are at a much greater risk of developing breast cancer than are men.	High-fat diets
Oral contraceptive use: Controversial; findings suggest that women currently using oral contraceptives have a slightly increased risk, which declines when they stop use.	**Aging:** Approximately 2 out of 3 diagnoses of invasive breast cancer occur in women older than 55 y, while 1 out of 8 occurs in those younger than 45 y.	Antiperspirants Bras Induced abortion Oral contraceptives
Combined and estrogen-alone postmenopausal hormone therapy (HT): Long-term combined (estrogen and progesterone) HT increases risks of breast cancer and death from it; risks return to that of the general population within 5 y of stopping use of combined HT. Long-term estrogen alone (estrogen therapy) increases risk of ovarian and breast cancer.	**Genetic risk factors:** Women with *BRCA1* or *BRCA2* genes have up to an 80% chance of developing breast cancer at some point in their lives. These mutations are most common in Jewish women of Ashkenazi origin, but they also occur in African Canadian and Latino women. Other less common	Breast implants Environmental pollution Tobacco Night work

(table continues on page 578)

Table 21-1   Risk Factors for Breast Cancer (continued)

Modifiable	Nonmodifiable	Controversial Possibilities
Breast-feeding: Nursing children for 1.5–2 y may decrease risk.	genes such as ATM, CHEK2, p53, and PTEN may also increase the risk of breast cancer.	
Alcohol: Risk is slightly higher for those who consume 1 alcoholic drink/d; risk increases to 1½ times that of nondrinkers in those who consume 2–5 drinks/d.	**Family history:** Having one or more first-degree relatives (ie, mother, sister, daughter) with breast cancer doubles risk. Having two first-degree relatives with breast cancer increases risk fivefold.	
Overweight or obesity, especially after menopause: Prior to menopause, the ovaries produce most of a woman's estrogen, and fat produces a small amount. After menopause, fat produces estrogen because the ovaries stop doing so. Estrogen levels can increase postmenopause with increased fat (which increases breast cancer risk).	**Personal history of breast cancer:** Those with previous incidence have a three-fourfold increased risk of developing breast cancer in another part of the same breast or in the other breast.	
Physical inactivity: The Public Health Agency of Canada (2011) recommends 2.5 h of moderate to vigorous aerobic exercise per week.	**Genetic background:** Caucasian women are slightly more likely to develop breast cancer. Risk is the lowest in Asian, First Nations, and Latino women.	
	Unexpected breast biopsy results: Proliferative lesions (overgrowth of breast tissue) without atypia (unexpected cells) increase risk 1.5–2 times that of usual; proliferative lesions with atypia increase risk four to five times that of usual.	
	Menstrual periods: Women who begin menstruating before 12 y or stop after 55 y have a slightly increased risk due to longer exposure to estrogen.	
	Previous chest radiation: Those who underwent such treatment for another cancer are at a significantly increased risk.	
	Diethylstilbestrol (DES) exposure: Patients exposed to DES have a slightly increased risk of developing breast cancer.	

Adapted from Day, R. A., & Bickley, L. S. (2010). The breasts and axillae. In T. C. Stephen, D. L. Skillen, R. A. Day, & L. S. Bickley (Eds.). *Canadian Bates' guide to health assessment for nurses* (1st ed., pp. 488–491). Philadelphia, PA: Wolters Kluwer Health/Lippincott Willilams & Wilkins.

Questions to Assess History and Risk Factors	Rationale
Past Medical History Have you ever been diagnosed with breast cancer? • If yes, what kind of breast cancer? • When was it diagnosed? • At what age were you diagnosed? • How were you treated? And when?	It is important to evaluate the patient's previous breast conditions, especially those that may increase risk for breast cancer (ie, personal history of previous breast cancer or cancer in situ; previous atypical epithelial hyperplasia found on biopsy; personal history of endometrial, colon, ovarian, or thyroid cancer; or family history of breast cancer) to encourage diligent breast examinations and medical follow-up. Previous history of breast cancer increases risk for a new mass being cancerous by three to four times (Chow, 2010).

Questions to Assess History and Risk Factors	Rationale
Have you ever been diagnosed with any breast conditions such as cysts? Benign breast disease (BBD)? Fibroadenoma? Or breast abscess?	*Cysts (BBD)* are common lumps that are usually elliptical or round, soft, and mobile. Size may vary, and they often occur in multiple numbers, usually in both breasts, and frequently in the upper outer quadrants (Katz, Lentz, et al., 2007). They occur during the childbearing years and are most tender just before menses. BBD with a positive biopsy for atypical hyperplasia (increased unusual cells) or lobular carcinoma in situ carries an increased risk for breast cancer later in life (Katz, Lentz, et al.).
	Fibroadenoma is a well-defined, usually single (can be multiple), nontender, firm or rubbery, round or lobular mass that is freely movable. It does not change in size with menses as BBD does and occurs most commonly in patients in their 20s to 40s (Katz, Lentz, et al., 2007).
	Breast abscess (infection) may occur after *mastitis* (inflammation from a blocked duct that may develop with lactation), traumatic injury, or chest/breast surgery.
Have you ever had any breast surgery? • If yes, what kind (eg, Breast biopsy? Reduction? Augmentation? Mammoplasty? Mastectomy?) • What was the result of the surgery?	Surgery of the breast is very personal; patients may have difficulty talking openly about it. A relaxed but professional demeanor is especially important when obtaining this information. The patient who has had breast augmentation (enlargement) could have the complication of a ruptured implant.
Have you been treated for a breast infection recently?	Recent breast infection may block ducts, causing a change in breast tissue.
When was your last menstrual period?	Breast tissue may be tender in the days before the onset of menses.
Medications Are you taking any medications? • Medication/dose/schedule?	Some medications that can affect breasts include the following: • Androgens—female: decreased breast size; male: gynecomastia • Antidepressants—female: engorgement; male: gynecomastia • Antipsychotics—female: engorgement, mastalgia, galactorrhea; male: gynecomastia • Cardiac glycosides—male: gynecomastia • Oral contraceptives—female: breast secretions, enlargement, tenderness • Progestins—female: galactorrhea, breast tenderness
Are you taking any natural supplements? Or over-the-counter medications? • Which ones? How often?	Although over-the-counter supplements are not known to affect breast lumps or pain, they may interfere with concurrent medications and contribute to side effects.
Family History Do you have a family history of breast cancer? • If so, who had it? • What type of breast cancer was it? • How old was she or he when it was diagnosed? • How was it treated?	The patient's risk for breast cancer increases if one or more first-degree blood relatives (eg, mother, sister, daughter) had breast cancer (especially if it was diagnosed before the affected person was 40 years old). Breast cancer in second-degree relatives (eg, grandmother, aunt) also may increase the patient's risk.
Lifestyle and Personal Habits Do you jog or run? If so, do you wear a sports bra?	Jogging or running increases breast movement, which may put strain on the shoulders or back. Sports bras can reduce movement by about 50% (Bryner, 2007).

(text continues on page 580)

Questions to Assess History and Risk Factors	Rationale

Breast Examination

Have you ever been taught how to perform the Know Your Breasts (KYB) approach?

- If yes: How often do you perform it? Can you show me how you perform your KYB approach?
- If no: Would you like me to show you how to perform a KYB approach?

Monthly KYB coupled with yearly clinical breast examinations (CBE) by a health care professional increase the chances of detecting cancer in early stages. To optimize health maintenance, women should familiarize themselves at a young age with how their breasts usually feel to detect even slight changes. Women who perform the KYB approach are more likely to discover cancer at an earlier stage. For this reason, it is important to guide patients through the KYB approach that emphasizes timing, inspection, and palpation.

Have you ever had a mammogram? Or ultrasound? If yes, when was it done and what were the results?

Women between ages 50–69 years should have a mammogram every 2 years.

Risk Assessment and Health Promotion

Topics for Health Promotion

- Breast size
- Breast support
- Benign breast disorders
- Risk factors for breast cancer
- Breast cancer screening
- Know Your Breasts (KYB) approach
- Clinical breast examination (CBE)
- Mammography
- Magnetic resonance imaging (MRI)

Adapted from Day, R. A., & Bickley, L. S. (2010). The breasts and axillae. In T. C. Stephen, D. L. Skillen, R. A. Day, & L. S. Bickley (Eds.). *Canadian Bates' guide to health assessment for nurses* (1st ed., p. 485). Philadelphia, PA: Wolters Kluwer Health/Lippincott Williams & Wilkins.

As mentioned previously, risk assessment helps to identify potential issues so that health care professionals can educate patients to influence their behavioural choices. It is important for men to be aware of their specific risk factors for breast cancer: an affected mother and sister, increasing age (often diagnosed between ages 60 and 70 years), excess estrogen from gynecomastia and obesity, decreased testosterone from infection or injury to the testicles, cirrhosis of the liver, being Jewish with a European background, or being of African descent (Day & Bickley, 2010). Men at risk for breast cancer should be offered teaching about the KYB approach.

It is important for women to be aware of their specific risk factors for breast cancer: previous breast cancer, an affected mother or sister, biopsy showing atypical hyperplasia, density of breast tissue, increasing age, early menarche, late menopause, late or no pregnancies, and previous radiation to the chest wall (Day & Bickley, 2010). Although many factors are not modifiable, some are. When the patient is aware of her own specific risk factors, she may be more interested in practicing healthy habits (KYB approach, yearly CBEs, and mammograms if indicated) and adjust other personal behaviours (especially physical inactivity and obesity; see Table 21-1).

Nurses teach patients who are interested in how to perform the KYB approach and encourage them to get to know their breasts beginning in their 20s. Although breast cancer is more common in older women, recognizing what usual breast tissue feels like alerts young women to changes if they develop.

The KYB approach is a method designed to increase breast health awareness and was developed by the Canadian Cancer Society (2009b) in light of the discussion below. Many breast cancers are found by women themselves, though often by accident (eg, when bathing). In Canada, there has been debate about the value of regular breast self-examinations (BSEs). One side of the argument is that monthly BSE leads to more biopsies but not necessarily to finding more cancers. As well, there has been concern raised about pressuring all women to perform the previous BSE approach every month and making those who don't to feel guilty. Nurses recognize that not all women will be interested in the KYB approach. Some women have been raised to avoid looking at or touching their breasts. Others are afraid to even think about breast cancer. All patient views are to be respected.

Between 20 and 39 years, women should also have CBEs performed by a health professional every 3 years; from 40 years onward, patients should have CBEs yearly. Women over 69 years need to consult with a health care provider regarding future mammograms. Refer to the KYB approach instructions later in the chapter.

Focused Health History Related to Common Symptoms/Signs

Common Breast and Axillary Symptoms/Signs

• Breast pain or discomfort	• Swelling—changes in breast shape
• Rash/ulcerations	• Nipple discharge
• Lumps	• Trauma

Example of Questions for Symptom/Sign Analysis—Breast Lump

- "Which breast has the lump?" "Is there more than one lump?" "Show me where the lump is in your breast." (Location, radiation)
- "Describe what the lump is like." "Is the lump painful?" (Quality)
- "Describe the size of the breast lump." (Severity)
- "When did you first notice the lump?" "How did you first notice the lump?" (Onset)
- "Has the lump been present since you first noticed it?" (Duration)
- "Has the lump changed in any way since you first noticed it?" (Constancy)
- "Is there a time of the month (eg, before your menstrual period) when the lump feels different in size?" "Or different in terms of pain/discomfort?" (Time of day/month/year)
- "Has anything made the lump larger?" "Or more painful?" (Aggravating factors)
- "Does anything make the lump smaller?" "Or less painful? (Alleviating factors)
- "What other symptoms have you noticed?" "Any nipple discharge?" "Is the nipple pulled inward (retraction)?" "Any enlargement of the breast?" "Are the lymph nodes in your axillae (armpit) tender?" (Associated symptoms)
- "Have you recently changed anything in your home?" "Or in your work environment?" "Have you recently been eating different foods?" "Any change in amount of food?" "How much red meat (beef, pork, lamb) have you eaten weekly over the past 3 years?" "Have you recently changed the types of beverages you drink?" "Or the amounts you drink?" "Have you taken any new medication (including over-the-counter drugs)?" "Have you taken any hormones?" "Have you been exposed to pesticides?" "Have you had any injury to your breast/chest?" (Environmental factors)
- "Tell me how this lump is affecting your life." (Significance to patient)
- "What do you think is happening?" (Patient perspective)

Adapted from Day, R. A., & Bickley, L. S. The breasts and axillae. In T. C. Stephen, D. L. Skillen, R. A. Day, & L. S. Bickley (Eds.). *Canadian Bates' guide to health assessment for nurses* (1st ed., pp. 483–484). Philadelphia, PA: Wolters Kluwer Health/Lippincott Williams & Wilkins.

Examples of Questions to Assess Symptoms/Signs

Pain

Do you have any pain or discomfort in either breasts? Or both breasts?

- *Location:* Where is the pain? Can you point to where it hurts? Does it stay in the one spot or move around?

- *Intensity:* Can you rate the pain using a 0 to 10 scale?

- *Duration:* How long have you had the pain? When did the pain start? How long has it lasted? Does it fluctuate (or is it worse at certain times of the month)? Have you ever had this pain before? If so, when? Does the pain occur at the same time every month?

- *Quality/description:* Can you describe the pain (eg, sharp, dull, throbbing, shooting, burning, tingling)?

- Do you have any other symptoms along with the pain (eg, Warmth or redness? Fever? Muscle aches? Nausea? Vomiting?)

- *Aggravating factors:* Does anything make the pain worse?

- *Alleviating factors:* Have you tried anything to make it feel better (eg, heat, ice, Tylenol or other medications)? If so, did it work?

Rationale/Unexpected Findings

When asking questions about the symptom (pain in this case), it is important to gather all the relevant information.

Severe pain (**mastalgia**) is more likely to result from trauma or infection.

Breast pain is common at some point during a woman's life, especially during menstrual years. Pain may occur in one or both breasts and may be cyclical (same time each month). Cyclical pain is very common in women who take oral contraceptives or have benign breast disease (BBD) (Katz, Lentz, et al., 2007). Typically, cyclical pain is worst in the days preceding menstruation and spontaneously disappears during or immediately after a period. It is often generalized, whereas pain from trauma is usually localized to one spot.

Patients may describe noncyclic pain as sharp or burning; they tend to describe cyclic pain as heaviness.

Pain associated with warmth or redness at the site may indicate a localized infection; fever, muscle aches, nausea, and vomiting may indicate a systemic infection or inflammatory carcinoma.

Determining what treatments or remedies the patient has tried will help determine future treatments.

(text continues on page 582)

Examples of Questions to Assess Symptoms/Signs	Rationale/Unexpected Findings

Rash/Ulceration

Do you have a rash? If so, when did it start? Where did it start? Has it changed?

Rashes from *contact dermatitis* or *eczema* usually start on the breast tissue and move toward the nipple. *Paget's disease* produces scaly lesions that begin at the nipple and progress to a lump behind the nipple well. Axillary rashes may result from allergy to deodorant or soaps.

Lumps

Have you noticed any lumps in your breasts? Or axillae?
- Where is the lump?
- When did you notice it?
- Has it changed at all (in size, is it more painful)?
- If you have had previous lumps, does this feel the same or different?
- Do you have a history of cystic breast changes or "lumpy" breasts?

Lumps can have many causes (eg, BBD, *fibroadenoma, cancer*). It is important to investigate any lump, especially if it is new or if patients have noticed changes. Nurses must also include information about the axillae, because breast tissue and many lymph nodes extend to this area.

Single breast masses can indicate benign conditions (eg, *cysts, fibroadenoma*, fat necrosis, *lipoma*), or more serious conditions (eg, *cancer*).

Swelling—Change in Breast Shape

Do you notice any swelling of the breasts?
- Is it related to your menstrual cycle? Are you breast-feeding?
- Is it in one area? Or does it involve your entire breast?
- Has your bra size increased because of the swelling?

Cyclical swelling and tenderness on a continuum corresponding with the menstrual cycle are common and benign. Patients experiencing them often report a "full" feeling in their breasts during menstruation, most often affecting both breasts.

Discharge—Nipples

Do you have any discharge from your nipples?
- What is the colour?
- Could you be pregnant?
- What medications are you taking?

Nurses evaluate spontaneous nipple discharge. Milky discharge in the absence of pregnancy or lactation *(nonpuerpera/galactorrhea)* may be from *hyperprolactinemia* (caused by a prolactin-secreting tumour) or adrenergic medications (methyldopa).

> ⚠ *SAFETY ALERT 21-2*
>
> *Nipple discharge can be associated with a benign papilloma, ductal ectasia, and less commonly, cancer. Early diagnosis and treatment are needed (Hussain, Policarpio, et al., 2006).*

Clear discharge may rarely occur from ingestion of steroids, calcium channel blockers, or oral contraceptives (Hussain, Policarpio, et al., 2006). Tranquilizers may also cause nipple discharge. When the medication is discontinued, the discharge will cease.

Trauma

Have you had any injuries/trauma to your breasts?
- When did it occur? How did it occur?
- Did it cause any break in the skin? (Or any residual lumps? Swelling? Or discolouration)?

Injuries to the breast may cause the patient to feel a previously undetected lump or mass. A break in the skin could lead to an infection.

Documentation of Expected Findings

Patient states she has no breast pain, lumps, nipple discharge, rashes, swelling, or trauma. Negative history of breast disease or breast surgery. Reports performing monthly Know Your Breasts (KYB) approach; routine mammogram 09APR2011, which was "unremarkable."

Lifespan Considerations

Additional Questions	Rationale/Unexpected Findings
Women Who Are Pregnant	
Do you feel that your breasts are getting larger? Or feel "full?" Are you planning to breast-feed your baby? Or bottle-feed?	Breast changes are expected during pregnancy. Providing support and answering questions is beneficial.
	Breast-feeding provides antibodies that protect infants against illnesses and allergies and promotes bonding between the mother and the child.
Are your nipples inverted (go inward)? Or everted (go outward)?	Inform the woman who is pregnant that breast-feeding is possible with inverted nipples.
Adolescent Females	
Have you noticed any changes in your breasts (eg, are they getting larger? Or are they tender)? If yes, when did you first notice any changes?	It is important to assess the adolescent girl's perception of her own development and to provide appropriate teaching and support.
	Girls who develop "early" and those who develop "late" particularly need support.
Many changes occur as you grow up. Have you noticed any other changes? If yes, how do you feel about them?	This is a time when girls often compare themselves to other girls their age, and body image is important to address.

An Example of a Therapeutic Dialogue

The nurse's role relative to subjective data collection is to gather information to improve the patient's health status and to help determine the cause of the patient's current symptoms. Remember Mrs. Randall, who was introduced at the beginning of this chapter. She has a lump in her left breast. Some risk factors that the nurse assessed during subjective data collection were a family history of breast cancer in first-degree relatives (patient's mother and sister), early onset of menstruation (age 11 years), bottle-feeding of her children, a high-fat diet, and lack of exercise. In addition to obtaining a health history and physical assessment, the nurse also assesses the patient's coping skills.

Nurse: Good morning, Mrs. Randall. How are you doing today?

Mrs. Randall: I am worried that this new breast lump is cancer. I haven't had a breast lump for 13 years. I hoped I wouldn't have any more. And, I am getting close to the age my mother was when she was diagnosed with breast cancer and then passed away.

Nurse: You sound worried.

Mrs. Randall: (Begins to cry.)

Nurse: (Silent. Gives Mrs. Randall a tissue.) Is it all right if I hold your hand?

Mrs. Randall: (Nods, and continues to cry.)

Nurse: (Waits until Mrs. Randall stops crying.) It is scary not knowing what is going on in your body. Would it be okay for you to show me where the lump is?

Critical Thinking Challenge

• Why is the dialogue effective when the nurse's question and response prompted Mrs. Randall to cry?
• How did the nurse respond to Mrs. Randall's crying? Provide rationale.
• In addition to assessing Mrs. Randall's breast lump, what other areas will the nurse assess?

Equipment

- Ruler marked in centimetres
- Examination gown
- Small pillow
- Sheet for draping patient
- Disposable, nonlatex gloves (if drainage is expected)
- Adequate lighting
- Pamphlet or handout for the Know Your Breasts (KYB) approach

Promoting Patient Comfort, Dignity, and Safety

The breast examination is an important part of a woman's health care. It provides an opportunity to identify breast disease, initiate early treatment, and demonstrate techniques for the KYB approach. Variations in clinician technique and experience affect actual findings. As with any examination, the more breast examinations a nurse performs, the more likely he or she will be to identify unexpected findings or variations. Additionally, using a standardized and systematic approach to palpate the breasts increases the likelihood of detecting breast changes. The following sections review examination techniques.

Begin with a warm examination room. Keep in mind that hands-on palpation of the breasts may cause patients to feel apprehensive and embarrassed. Adopting a professional, gentle, and reassuring approach is important. Before beginning, inform patients that you will be examining the breasts. Provide as much privacy as possible and answer any questions that patients may have. This is an opportune time to ask female patients about the KYB approach. Instructing interested patients in the approach and watching return demonstrations can provide an opportunity to verify technique and provide helpful suggestions as indicated. Nurses accept that some women, for whatever reason, are not interested in the KYB approach.

The breast examination involves inspection and palpation. It is important to expose both breasts fully initially during inspection to assess for symmetry, but then to cover or drape one breast while palpating the other. Patients should begin seated with the arms in different positions (first at the sides, then over the head, then against the hips while leaning forward). For palpation, patients should be supine. The best time to examine the breasts is when they are least congested and smallest (in adult women, days 5 to 7 after the onset of menstruation and up to day 13) (Day & Bickley, 2010).

The comprehensive head-to-toe assessment includes the most important and common assessment techniques. Nurses may add focused or advanced techniques if concerns exist over a specific finding.

Comprehensive Physical Assessment

Techniques and Expected Findings

Inspection

Begin with the patient sitting with arms at the sides (Fig. 21-6). Inspect skin appearance for:

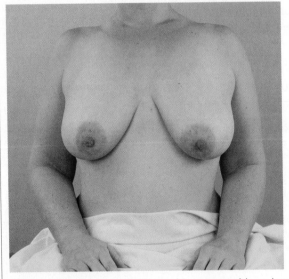

Figure 21-6 Patient sitting with arms at side as breast examination begins.

Unexpected Findings

- **Colour and texture:** Skin tone determines actual colour. Pale, linear stretch marks (striae) may be evident after pregnancy or if a woman has gained and then lost significant weight

- **Size and shape:** Wide variation exists, from small to very large (pendulous)

- **Symmetry:** The left breast is often slightly larger than the right breast (Losken, Fishman, et al., 2007)

- **Contour:** Should be uninterrupted

- **Nipple and areola characteristics:** Areola should be round or oval, and pink to dark brown or black. Most nipples are everted, but it may be usual for one or both nipples to be inverted.

Redness (erythema) and heat can indicate infection or inflammation. Hyperpigmentation can signify *cancer*. A unilateral vascular appearance could indicate increased blood flow to a malignancy (produced by dilated superficial veins). *Peau d'orange* appearance is caused by breast edema from blocked lymph drainage and indicates advanced cancer (Fig. 21-7). Rash or ulceration may occur in *Paget's disease of the breast* (see also Table 21-4 at the end of this chapter).

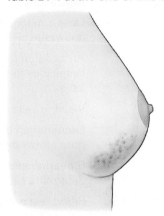

Figure 21-7 *Peau d'orange.*

If the patient has pendulous breasts, it is easier to visualize irregularities if she leans forward with her arms on her hips.

Approximately 3% of women have one breast that is underdeveloped compared to the other (Losken, Fishman, et al., 2007).

Retractions or dimpling may occur with breast cancer (Fig. 21-8).

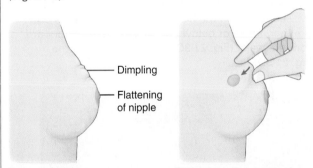

Retraction signs   Retraction with compression

Figure 21-8 *Retraction signs*

Recent nipple changes from everted to inverted or in the angle the nipple points may indicate malignancy (caused from pulling of the malignant tissue; see Table 21-2 for common diagnostic tests). Discharge (other than breast milk) can indicate cancer or infection and needs further evaluation; cracking or crusting can occur with breast-feeding.

(text continues on page 586)

Table 21-2	Common Diagnostic Testing for Breasts
Technique	**Purpose**
Mammography	Low-dose x-ray of the breasts to aid in the diagnosis of breast disease; should be performed as a screening tool biannually or ages 50–69 y
Ultrasound	Noninvasive test using high-frequency sound waves; differentiates between a solid and cystic mass; is used as a guide in needle aspirations
Magnetic resonance imaging (MRI)	Uses a magnetic field (not x-ray), radio waves, and a computer to detect and stage breast cancer and other breast changes
Excisional biopsy	An excision (cut) made into the breast to remove a portion of a suspicious lump and the surrounding tissue to examine for cancerous cells
Microscopy	Viewing cells under a microscope to enhance cellular features
Ductogram	Examination of the breast ducts to determine cause of unilateral, single-pore nipple discharge
Cytological smear	Smearing and staining a cell sample (obtained from breast discharge) to determine cause
Thyroid-stimulating hormone (TSH)	Blood test drawn (TSH) to determine if nipple discharge is secondary to a thyroid condition

An extra nipple (**supernumerary nipple**) along the embryonic nipple line (from axilla to groin bilaterally) is a common variation. If present, it is most often found 5 to 6 cm below the breast. On initial inspection it looks like a mole, but on careful inspection a tiny nipple and areola are present.

After inspecting with the arms at the side, reinspect with the patient lifting the arms over her head (Fig. 21-9A), pressed firmly on the hips (Fig. 21-9B), or hands pressed together above or below the breasts; leaning forward from the waist (Fig. 21-9C) and then lying supine (Fig. 21-9D).

Any change in colour, size (especially if unilateral), symmetry, or contour of the breast, or change in nipple characteristics requires further investigation. Lifting the arms over the head adds tension to the suspensory ligaments and accentuates any dimpling or retraction. Pressing hands on hips contracts the pectoral muscles. Leaning forward may reveal breast or nipple asymmetry.

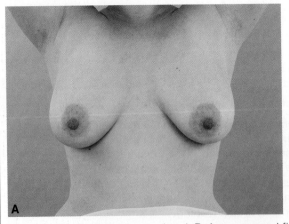

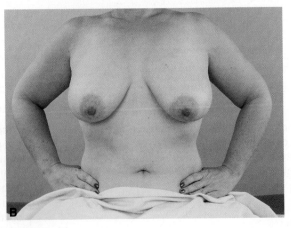

Figure 21-9 A. Arms over head. **B.** Arms pressed firmly on her hips.

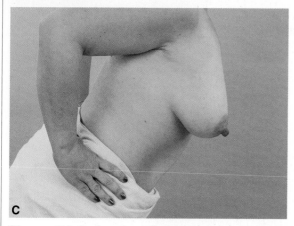

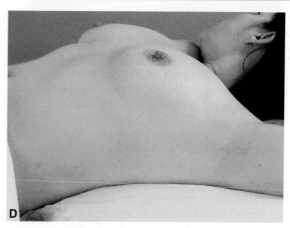

Figure 21-9 *(continued)* **C.** Leaning forward from the waist. **D.** Lying supine.

Also inspect the axillae while the patient is sitting, noting any rashes, signs of infection, texture changes, or unusual pigmentation.

Breasts are symmetrical; skin is smooth and even without redness, bulging, or dimpling. There is no rash, edema, or lesions. Nipples are symmetrical and protuberant. Nipples and areolae are the same colour and smooth or wrinkled in appearance. There is no discharge (unless the woman is pregnant or lactating), cracking, or crusting.

Palpation

Palpating the axillae is best performed while the patient is sitting. Instruct the patient to gently abduct the arm. Support the arm and wrist to aid in muscle relaxation. Use the right hand to palpate the left axilla and the left hand to palpate the right axilla (Fig. 21-10). Point your fingers toward the midclavicle, directly behind the pectoral muscles.

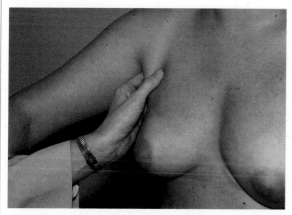

Figure 21-10 Palpation of the axilla.

These signs suggest underlying cancer but may also be from benign lesions (eg, fat necrosis, mammary duct ectasia). Rashes or infection may occur from laundry detergent or deodorant. Velvety axillary skin or deep pigmentation is associated with malignancy.

(text continues on page 588)

Feel for the central nodes (3–4 nodes). Reach as high as you can toward the apex of the axilla. Cup fingers and palpate down the chest wall. These are the most easily palpable. *One or more small, soft, nontender nodes are common findings.* Also assess the other axillary lymph nodes, but these are more difficult to palpate. For the pectoral nodes (4–5 nodes) grasp the anterior axillary fold between thumb and fingers; with finger pads palpate inside the border of the pectoral muscle. For the lateral nodes (4–5 nodes) begin high in the axilla and then palpate along the upper humerus.

Subscapular or posterior nodes (6–7 nodes) are best felt with the nurse standing behind the patient, feeling with the finger pads, inside the posterior axillary fold. Adjusting the patient's arm in various positions increases the surface area that can be assessed.

Feel for the infraclavicular nodes (6–12 nodes) below the clavicles and the supraclavicular nodes (6–12 nodes) all above the clavicles.

Palpating the breast tissue is best accomplished with the patient supine with her arm slightly to the side, no pillow under the head, and a small pillow or towel rolled under the shoulder of the side being examined **only if the breasts are large**. This will flatten the breast tissue. A thorough examination of each breast takes at least 3 minutes. Palpate a rectangular area from the clavicle to the inframammary fold (bra line) (3 cm below the breast) and from midsternum to the posterior axillary line, making sure to examine the axillae for the tail of Spence.

The American Cancer Society recommends using the **vertical pattern** (Fig. 21-11A), because some evidence supports that this is the most effective means of examining the entire breast (Steiner, Austin, et al., 2008). The Canadian Cancer Society recommends using a **horizontal pattern** (Fig. 21-11B). Both the horizontal and vertical approaches are systematic approaches that ensure that all breast tissue is examined.

The horizontal technique is described in detail.

Firm, hard, enlarged nodes (>1 cm) that are fixed to underlying tissues or skin suggest malignancy.

Tender, warm, enlarged nodes suggest infection of the breast, arm, or hand.

Enlarged axillary lymph nodes are sometimes mistaken for nodules in the tail of Spence and vice versa.

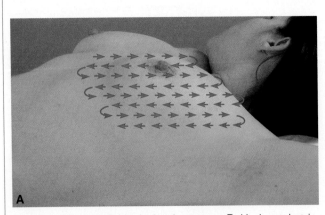

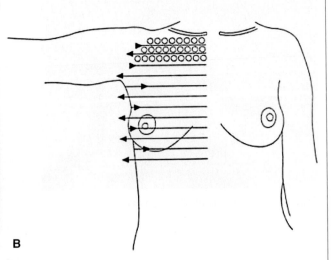

Figure 21-11 A. Vertical strip pattern. **B.** Horizontal strip pattern

Horizontal Pattern. Using the finger pads of the first three fingers (and keeping the fingers flat), palpate in small, concentric circles beginning at the sternum and moving in a straight line across to the posterior axillary line. Apply light, medium, and then deeper pressure at each examining point to reach the entire breast tissue. Continue in horizontal overlapping lines until the infra-mammary fold is met. Being systematic with the examination is important to always assess the entire breast for consistency, tenderness, and nodules.

Consistency. Breast tissue shows wide variations. Nodular masses may be present prior to menses, disappearing after menses has occurred. *The breast of a nulliparous woman feels smooth, elastic, and firm. Prior to menstruation, breasts are often engorged secondary to increased progesterone. The patient may notice nodules, a slight enlargement, and tenderness during this time. Upon examination, the lobes may be more prominent with distinct margins. After pregnancy, breasts feel softer and have less tone.*

When assessing a pendulous breast, the examiner may feel the **inframammary ridge**, which is a firm transverse ridge of breast tissue. This finding is expected.

Tenderness. Breasts are often tender during the premenstrual period.

Nodules. If a lump is palpated, document the location, size, shape, consistency, mobility, tenderness, distinctness, and delimitation. Additionally, note the skin over the lump, the nipple, and any lymphadenopathy.

- **Location:** Document by stating the quadrant, and use clock measurements or use measurements in centimetres from the nipple (eg, right upper outer quadrant or right breast, 10:00; 4 cm from nipple).

- **Size:** Measure or judge length × width × depth in centimetres by using a ruler as a guide.

- **Shape:** Oval, round, lobular, nodular, or indistinct?

- **Consistency:** Smooth, soft, firm, or hard?

- **Mobility:** Movable or immobile?

- **Tenderness:** Tender or not?

- **Distinctness:** One lump or multiple nodules?

- **Delimitation:** Are the borders of the lump well circumscribed?

- **Skin:** Dimpled, retracted, erythematous?

- **Nipple:** Retracted or displaced?

Keeping the finger pads in contact with the skin, and flexing only at the wrist, circle and slide the fingers back and forth across the chest to increase the likelihood of palpating the entire breast.

Mammary duct ectasia (dilated, painful mammary ducts) should be suspected when a lump or thickening is palpable. This benign condition may result from hormonal changes, smoking, or lack of vitamin A. Additionally, an inverted nipple may block the mammary ducts, which can cause inflammation and mammary duct ectasia.

Do not rush through the examination of a pendulous breast, because lumps are harder to identify here from the increased size.

Tenderness or pain in the breast at other times may be from infection or trauma.

All breast masses require further evaluation and may require a mammogram, ultrasound, aspiration, or biopsy (discussed later).

The most common site for breast masses is in the upper outer quadrant, because this is where the most glandular tissue lies (McCowen Meahring, 2010b).

Indistinct lumps are more suspicious for breast cancer. Poorly circumscribed, fixed, hard, and irregular nodules strongly suggest cancer.

Tenderness indicates infection or inflammation. Some cancers may also be tender.

Cancer tends to be single; fibroadenoma or cysts may be single or multiple (see Table 21-5 at the end of the chapter).

Borders of a cancerous mass are unclear or "matted."

Dimpling, retraction, or a retracted or displaced nipple can be signs of cancer. Erythema indicates inflammation.

(text continues on page 590)

- **Lymphadenopathy:** palpable lymph nodes (axillary, infraclavicular, and supraclavicular chains?

Lymphadenopathy means swelling of the lymph nodes, which may occur postmastectomy, from blocked lymph nodes or from infection.

Breast tissue is soft and homogeneous. No masses or tenderness bilaterally. No lymphadenopathy in axillary, infraclavicular, or supraclavicular nodes bilaterally.

Nipple Discharge. *Note:* Compressing the nipple to check for discharge is not part of a regular screening examination and is not a useful sign of cancer (Gulay, Bora, et al., 1994). *Nipples without discharge.*

If discharge is evident, note the colour, consistency, and amount. It is important to obtain a cytological smear for examination.

Bimanual Technique. If the patient has pendulous breasts, the bimanual technique may be more efficient in palpating lumps. With this technique, the patient should sit upright, leaning slightly forward. Place one hand underneath the breast (on the inferior surface) while palpating the breast tissue with the other hand (Fig. 21-12).

This technique could be used earlier in the examination, before having the patient supine.

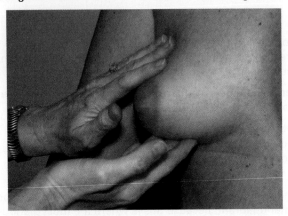

Figure 21-12 Palpating the breasts using bimanual technique.

Transillumination

Transillumination of a breast mass may be performed in a darkened room to differentiate between a solid and fluid-filled mass. When a strong light is pressed up against a mass filled with fluid, the rays will pass through, but when pressed up against a solid mass, they will not. This technique is rarely used, being largely replaced by mammography.

A solid mass is likely to be malignant, while a fluid-filled mass is more frequently a benign cyst (Katz, Lentz, et al., 2007).

Examining the Patient Postmastectomy

A woman who has had a mastectomy may be more self-conscious about her scar and anxious about a recurrence of cancer than one who has not undergone this procedure. The nurse is empathetic and sensitive to the patient's feelings. Malignancy can occur at the scar site or in other areas of the breast.

Masses, inflammation, colour changes, and thickening may signify a recurrence of breast cancer.

Always begin with inspection and palpation of the unaffected breast and axilla. Then inspect the scar and axilla for signs of inflammation, rash, colour changes, thickening, and irritation. Lymphedema may be evident in the axilla and arm secondary to impaired lymph drainage postmastectomy. **Palpate** the surgical scar and chest wall very gently with the pads of three fingers in a circular motion (as previously described) to assess for breast changes (lumps, tenderness, thickening, or swelling). Palpate the axillary nodes and supraclavicular and infraclavicular lymph nodes to assess for swelling and irritation.

Encourage the patient to consider the Know Your Breasts (KYB) approach. If the patient is willing, demonstrate the KYB approach and reiterate the importance of performing these checks.

Male Breasts

Men have less fatty tissue in their breasts, making it easier to note unexpected changes (Canadian Cancer Society, 2009a). Ask about nipple discharge and chest wall pain. Examining the male breast involves inspecting the nipple and areola for swelling, ulceration, or drainage. Additionally, palpate the areola and breast tissue for nodules or masses. Palpate the axillary lymph nodes and the infraclavicular and supraclavicular nodes.

Documentation of Objective Findings

Expected Findings
Breasts: Pendulous bilaterally. Left breast is slightly larger than right. Colour similar to body. Firm, smooth, no tenderness bilaterally. No masses or lesions; no signs of dimpling, retraction, or *peau d'orange* skin bilaterally.

Nipples: Everted bilaterally, point upward and laterally. No cracks, rashes, or discharge noted bilaterally.

Areolae: Darker in colour than breasts. No rashes noted bilaterally.

Axillae: Skin clear, intact bilaterally. No palpable axillary, infraclavicular, or supraclavicular nodes bilaterally. No tenderness bilaterally.

If the patient has undergone breast reconstruction, lumpectomy, augmentation, or reduction, perform the breast examination as described, paying close attention to the breast tissue and to the incision line.

Pay extra attention to the upper outer quadrant of the breast and the axilla.

Firm, glandular tissue (**gynecomastia**) may occur when there is an imbalance of estrogen and androgen. An ulcer or hard, irregular mass suggests cancer. Men who are obese may have gynecomastia with increased fatty tissue. Gynecomastia also occurs with the use of anabolic steroids, due to diseases, and as a side effect of some medications (see Table 21-4). "Redness, heat and swelling may indicate inflammatory cancer" (Day & Bickley, 2010, p. 498). The most common type of breast cancer in men is infiltrating ductal cancer (Day & Bickley).

Unexpected Findings
Venous pattern is asymmetrical, more prominent on right breast. A 2.0-cm mass palpated in upper outer quadrant of right breast, 3.0 cm from nipple. Mass is firm, irregular shape with no definite border, nontender, fixed to adjacent structures. No lesions or signs of dimpling, retraction, or *peau d'orange* skin visible bilaterally. No masses palpable in left breast.

Right nipple inverted for 1 month. Left is everted. Nipples are reddened but not cracked. No discharge bilaterally.

Redness, scaly appearance on right areola. No change in colour, no rashes noted on left areola.

Red rash over both axillae, with slight itchiness reported (used new deodorant yesterday). A 2.0-cm, firm, mobile central node palpable over left chest wall. No tenderness over the node or elsewhere in the axillae. No other axillary nodes or infraclavicular or supraclavicular nodes were palpable bilaterally.

Adapted from Day, R. A., & Bickley, L. S. The breasts and axillae. In T. C. Stephen, D. L. Skillen, R. A. Day, & L. S. Bickley (Eds.). *Canadian Bates' guide to health assessment for nurses* (1st ed., p. 502). Philadelphia, PA: Wolters Kluwer Health/Lippincott Williams & Wilkins.

Teaching the Know Your Breasts Approach

After completion of CBE, it is appropriate to offer to teach the patient how to perform the KYB approach. This practice is better than attempting to teach while performing the examination, because it allows nurses to concentrate on the examination separately from concentrating on teaching (see Box 21-1).

Lifespan Considerations

Women Who Are Pregnant/Lactating

During pregnancy, breasts and nipples increase in size, which may cause mild discomfort. Linear stretch marks (**striae**) may be evident. Striae may disappear completely when breasts return to the prepregnant size. A blue, vascular pattern may also be visible from increased blood flow. Nipples and areolae darken and widen. Montgomery glands become more prominent. Breasts may feel nodular, and nipples may expel yellow colostrum (milk precursor) after the first trimester.

If the woman is breast-feeding, milk production occurs most often by the third postpartum day. Breasts may become larger, reddened, warm, and engorged, especially at this time. Frequent breast-feeding will stimulate milk production, drain the sinuses, and resolve the symptoms. If these symptoms occur at other times during lactation, they could indicate **mastitis**, which usually requires antibiotic therapy, as well as more frequent nursing to resolve. Nipples often become sore, but generally this resolves spontaneously. If they become cracked and irritated, bleeding may occur.

After pregnancy and lactation, breasts return to their prepregnant state but often are less firm. The nipples and areolae usually remain darker than in the prepregnant state.

Newborns and Infants

As discussed previously, newborns may have enlarged breast tissue for the first few weeks of life from maternal estrogen. They also may secrete a clear white fluid from the nipples during this period. Should these findings occur, nurses reassure parents or other caregivers that they are expected and will resolve spontaneously.

Children and Adolescents

On inspection, the symmetrical nipples of prepubescent children lie between the 4th and 5th ribs just lateral to the midclavicular line. The nipples and areolae are flat and darker than the rest of the breast tissue.

During puberty, females begin to develop breasts (usually between 8½ and 10 years). As previously mentioned, breast tissue may be asymmetric during growth. This temporary asymmetry may upset adolescents, who may need information that this is expected and will resolve on its own. Breast tenderness may also occur. It is important to educate the adolescent female about expected body changes that will occur during this time period.

See Figure 21-5 for a review of Tanner's staging. Breast development before 7 years in Caucasian girls or 6 years in African

Canadian girls is termed **precocious puberty** and may be secondary to either dysfunction of the thyroid gland or a tumour of the ovaries or adrenal gland. Isolated breast development in the absence of other hormone-dependent changes (eg, menses, pubic hair) in girls younger than 8 years is termed **premature thelarche** (Diamantopoulos, 2007). Delayed development may occur with anorexia nervosa, malnutrition, or hormonal imbalance. Girls may be considered to have a developmental delay if breast development has not occurred by 13 years. Further evaluation is warranted if any of these conditions occur.

The breasts of an adolescent girl are uniform and firm. A mass at this age is most often benign (a cyst or fibroadenoma; see Table 21-5). Adolescence is a good time to introduce patients to what their breasts usually feel like, so that they may be more likely to perform the KYB approach as they get older.

Older Adults

As a result of the relaxation of the suspensory ligaments and atrophy of the glandular tissue, the breasts of postmenopausal women sag, flatten, and look more pendulous. On palpation, they may feel more granular. Nipples become flatter and smaller, and the inframammary ridge is more prominent from thickening. As women age, care providers should remind them to continue KYBs and yearly CBEs, because mature women are at increased risk for breast cancer. With the cessation of menses, hormonal changes will no longer affect their breasts. For this reason, patients can choose a convenient day of the month to perform the KYB approach (eg, 1st day of month).

Evidence-Informed Critical Thinking

Organizing and Prioritizing

Nurses continuously think critically about the patient's condition to organize and prioritize assessments and patient care. Laboratory and diagnostic tests related to the breasts and axillae can expand on findings from the health history and physical examination. Analysis of assessment and laboratory data help clinicians identify the underlying cause of signs and symptoms. Nurses use findings to identify the underlying functional issue, label it (sometimes in a nursing diagnosis format), and plan interventions based on patient outcomes. At times nurses need to communicate findings and reasons for referrals to other members of the interprofessional health care team. Nurses also work with primary health care professionals to gather information to make a diagnosis and to prescribe appropriate collaborative care. They reassess patients to evaluate the effectiveness of both nursing and collaborative care measures.

Laboratory and Diagnostic Testing

The clinical situation may indicate a need for additional tests (see Table 21-2).

Mammography, ultrasound, magnetic resonance imaging (MRI), and aspiration biopsy (fine-needle aspiration [FNA], core needle aspiration biopsy [CNB], or excisional biopsy)

BOX 21-1   THE KNOW YOUR BREASTS (KYB) APPROACH

*T*ake charge of your breast health. This starts with knowing your breasts so that you are more likely to notice changes that could lead to health issues.

About the KYB Approach

KYB is different from mammography and clinical breast examination (CBE). KYB is done by you, standing in front of a mirror and lying down, looking at and feeling your breasts, under your arms, and chest. The best time for KYB is 5 to 13 days after your period starts. If you no longer menstruate, select any day.

Changes to Look for

KYB will help you see and feel changes in your breasts. First you need to learn what is usual for your breasts. They may usually feel a bit lumpy. Check for any new place they feel thicker or harder than the rest of your breast. If your breasts are large, they may fold over on your chest and feel like a firm ridge. Lift them up to check the skin underneath.

The KYB Approach

Stand in front of a mirror:

- With your arms at your sides, look in the mirror at your breasts.
  - Slowly turn from side to side.
  - Check for changes in size and shape from last time you looked.
  - Check for rashes or puckers in the skin.
  - Look for any discharge from your nipples.
- Raise your arms above your head. Keep looking in the mirror.
- Put your hands behind your ears.
  - Look at your breasts and under your arms.
  - Lean forward and look at your breasts.
  - Check for any changes from last KYB check.
- Place hands on hips, pressing firmly.
  - Check for any changes from last KYB check.
- Feel your breasts with your fingers. Some women do this in the shower because soap makes it easier to move their hand over the breast. Do this step for each breast. Using a horizontal pattern to guide you, make small circles.

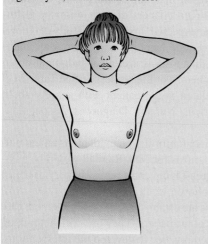

Stay standing. Using the opposite hand to each breast.

- Hold the fingers of your hand together.
- Keep your fingers stiff and your hand flat.
- Do not cup your hand.
- Use the pads of your fingers, not the tips.
- Make small circles in straight lines starting just below the collarbone.

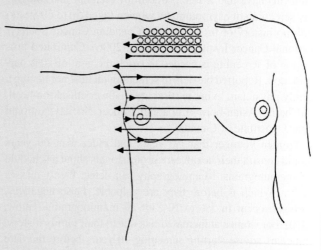

- Go slowly all the way across the breast area.
- Maintain constant contact with and pressure on your skin.
- Move your fingers down one finger width.
- Repeat the small circles back and forth across your breast.
- Bend your wrist to go over the curve of your breast.
- Make sure you feel over the nipple.
- Keep moving down until you are below your breast. You may need to make many circles to check your whole breast.
- Check under your arm.
  - Relax your arm by your side.
  - Slide your other hand under that arm and make small circles like you did over your breasts.
  - Repeat for other arm.

Lying down:

- Lie on your back, on a firm surface.
- Put one hand behind your head.
- Keep the fingers of your other hand together.
- Check both breasts again, using the pads of your fingers and bending your wrist to cover the curves of your breasts.
- Switch hands and do the other breast.

What to Do if You Feel a Change

Most of the time, changes women find in their breasts are not cancer. The only way to know that a lump or any other change is not cancer is to have your doctor check it as soon as possible.

Adapted from Canadian Cancer Society. (2009a). *Know your breasts.* Retrieved from http://www.cancer.ca/canada-wide/prevention/get%20screened/know%20your%20breasts.aspx?sc_lang=en

aid in accurately diagnosing breast cancer in 70% to 80% of cases (Dains, Baumann, et al., 2007).

Mammography consists of two x-rays (digital or conventional film). If a palpable mass has been detected or if the woman has nipple discharge, magnification and additional views are necessary. A screening mammogram is suggested for patients at 40 years of age to detect nonpalpable breast masses and as a baseline for future tests.

Since 2003, all Canadian provinces and territories (except Nunavut) have had a free program of biennial mammography screening of asymptomatic women (aged 50 to 69 years) with no history of breast cancer (Canadian Cancer Society/ National Cancer Institute of Canada, 2006). Continued promotion of screening is needed to reach the goal of 70% participation. Reported barriers to screening include not having a family physician, living in rural areas, lower education level, and being Asian-born (Canadian Cancer Society/National Cancer Institute of Canada).

Women younger than 50 years and older than 69 years should consult their health care professionals about a schedule for mammograms. Mammography can detect breast masses <1 cm, which is before they are palpable. False negatives, however, occur in 5% to 10% of all mammograms (Chow, 2010). For women at increased risk due to their family history, clinicians advise starting screening 10 years before the date of onset of cancer in the patient's relative. For example, if the patient's mother was diagnosed with breast cancer at 48 years, then the patient should begin screening at 38 years (Hartmann, Shaid, et al., 1999). For women at increased risk, many clinicians advise initiating screening mammograms between 30 and 40 years, then every 2 to 3 years until 50 years.

After 70 years, the benefits of mammography are less well defined but may continue to be important, particularly with patients who have risk factors and long-term exposure to hormone therapy. In older patients, it is easier to detect cancer using CBE (the breasts have more fatty tissue but fewer duct and lobular structures). Older women may not see themselves at risk for cancer and may be resistant to the idea of mammograms (White, Urban, et al., 1993). For men, mammograms are only used to diagnose breast cancer.

Women choosing to do KYB are encouraged to report any new breast symptoms. Intervals for mammography between the ages 40 and 50 years, however, are subject to controversy. Mammography is less accurate in glandular and dense breasts, especially when stimulated by higher estrogen levels before menopause, contributing to varying estimates of benefit. Breast density decreases approximately 1% per year (Boyd, Guo, et al., 2007). Men at risk for breast cancer are also encouraged to do the KYB approach on a regular basis.

Ultrasound is used with women younger than 40 years, who tend to have denser breast tissue, those with silicone breast implants, women who are pregnant (so they are not exposed to x-ray), and as a guide when performing a CNB (Katz, Lentz, et al., 2007). This noninvasive test produces a picture through high-frequency sound waves of the internal breast structures to help practitioners differentiate between a solid and cystic mass.

FNA and CNB are types of biopsies in which a needle is inserted into the breast mass to collect a sample of cells for analysis to determine if cancer exists. An excisional biopsy is similar to a lumpectomy, in which the lump or suspicious area and a portion of the surrounding tissue are removed and examined. It is the standard procedure for lumps that are smaller than 2.5 cm in diameter and is usually performed on an outpatient basis.

MRI is a supplemental tool to mammography. This noninvasive, painless test uses a magnetic field (not x-ray), radio waves, and a computer to detect and stage breast cancer and other breast irregularities. It may be used for women with dense breast tissue (as in those younger than 40 y), with breast implants, or with scar tissue from previous breast surgery. It also may provide more detailed information to help determine treatment choices for a woman. Pediconi, Catalano, et al. (2007) recommend that all women with newly diagnosed breast cancer in one breast should undergo MRI to pick up potential cancer missed by mammograms of the other breast (mammograms may miss these cancers in 3% of cases). MRI is also recommended for women aged 30 years or older with a mutation of *BRCA1* or *BRCA2* genes, treated for Hodgkin's disease, or with a strong family history (two or more close relatives with breast or ovarian cancer or a close relative with breast cancer before 50 y) (Saslow, Boetes, et al., 2007). MRIs show increased or unusual blood flow in breast tissue, an early sign of breast cancer not picked up by mammography, and are better at identifying cancer in women with dense breasts.

Clinical Reasoning

Nurses use assessment findings as the basis for ongoing care. An accurate and complete assessment provides a firm foundation for setting outcomes, providing individualized interventions, and evaluating progress.

Nursing Diagnoses, Outcomes, and Interventions

When formulating nursing diagnoses, it is important to use critical thinking to cluster data and identify patterns that fit together. Nurses compare clusters of data with the defining characteristics (unexpected findings) for the diagnosis to ensure the most accurate labelling and appropriate interventions. A nursing diagnosis is a clinical judgment about responses to health concerns or life processes. See Table 21-3 nursing diagnoses related to the patient with anxiety about cancer (North American Nursing Diagnoses Association-International, 2009).

Nurses use assessment information to identify patient outcomes. A nursing diagnosis for Mrs. Randall would be anxiety related to a new breast lump and a family history of breast cancer (Moorhead, Johnson, et al., 2007).

Once the outcomes are established, nurses implement care to improve the status of the patient. They use critical thinking and evidence-informed practice to develop the interventions. An example of a nursing intervention related to breast health is as follows (Bulechek, Butcher, et al., 2008): Encourage patient to verbalize concerns and anxiety related to her situation (see Table 21-3).

Table 21-3   Common Nursing Diagnoses Associated With Breast Lump

Diagnosis and Related Factors	Point of Differentiation	Assessment Characteristics	Nursing Interventions
Anxiety related to finding a new breast lump	Viewpoint or perspective of one's physical self that is different than before she found the lump	Came to clinic today about the breast lump	Acknowledge feelings as expected when coping with a new breast lump. Explore strengths. Identify support people.
Ineffective coping related to changes in function	Failure to address the presence of breast lump; using methods to handle stressors that worsen or fail to solve the concern	Substance abuse, complaining without acting, lack of resolution of the issue, overeating, sleeping too much, isolating oneself	Observe causes of ineffective coping. Help identify resources. Discuss changes and previous successful coping strategies.
Grieving related to the potential cancer diagnosis	Sadness related to potential loss of health	Sadness, crying, anger, depression, altered eating, and sleep patterns	Encourage patient to express feelings and affirm that they are part of the process. Refer to spiritual counselling if indicated.*

*Collaborative interventions.

Analyzing Findings

The initial subjective and objective data collection is complete, and the nurse has spent time reviewing the findings and other results. The following nursing note illustrates how subjective and objective data are collected and analyzed and nursing interventions are developed.

Subjective: "I'm tired, real tired. And I'm worried that this lump is cancer."

Objective: Appears stressed, crying intermittently.

Analysis: Anxiety related to finding a new breast lump in her left breast. Has first degree relatives (mother and sister) who have died from breast cancer.

Plan: Allow time to talk and express thoughts. Validate her concerns and appropriateness of her feelings. Assess support systems and who might be available to assist her as she goes through the diagnostic process.

Critical Thinking Challenge

- How would the nurse transition from collecting data about Mrs. Randall's concerns to collecting physical assessment data?
- What additional assessment data might be needed?

Collaborating With the Interprofessional Team

The following conversation illustrates how the nurse might organize data from Mrs. Randall and make a referral to the physician to evaluate Mrs. Randall's breast lump.

Situation: Mrs. Randall is a 61-year-old elementary school teacher who found a lump in her left breast yesterday.

Background: She has had two previous negative breast biopsies and has first-degree relatives (mother and sister) who have died from breast cancer.

Assessment: Mrs. Randall stated that "I am so worried that this lump is cancer. Plus, I am getting closer to the age when my mother died." She cried and appeared anxious while trying to tell me about her concerns. On examination I found a round, firm, nontender mass in the upper outer quadrant of Mrs. Randall's left breast. It is 4 cm from the nipple. The borders of the mass are not well delineated but the mass is not fixed to underlying structures. Axillary, infraclavicular, and supraclavicular nodes are nontender and are not enlarged bilaterally.

Recommendations: How soon can you see her to evaluate the breast lump?

Critical Thinking Challenge

- What is the nurse's role in coordinating collaborative care for Mrs. Randall?
- What family supports does she have?
- What other consultations might you recommend for Mrs. Randall?
- What information will the nurse gather when evaluating the effectiveness of the recommendations?

Pulling It All Together: An Example of Reflection and Critical Thinking

The nurse uses assessment data to formulate the patient care plan for Mrs. Randall based on a complete and accurate assessment. After completing these interventions, the nurse will reassess Mrs. Randall and document the findings in the patient health record to show critical thinking. The plan of care integrates separate parts of the nursing process. This thinking is illustrated in a care plan or case note similar to the one below.

Nursing Diagnosis	Patient Outcomes	Nursing Interventions	Rationale	Evaluation
Anxiety related to finding a new lump in her left breast	Patient will verbalize understanding of diagnostic process and upcoming tests. Additionally, she will verbalize feelings related to her emotional state (anxiety related to possible diagnosis of cancer). Also, she will identify personal strengths and accept support through the assessment and treatment process	Educate the patient about upcoming diagnostic tests and preparation. Allow her time to ask questions. Offer emotional support. Allow time to talk and express her thoughts. Validate her concerns and appropriateness of her feelings (Pedersen, Sawatzky, et al., 2010). Help her to assess support systems and who might be available to assist.	It is expected that the patient will experience anxiety while undergoing diagnostic tests. Confirming her feelings will assist her through the process. Effectiveness of coping is determined by the number, duration, and intensity of stressors. Her feelings are appropriate for the situation. Talking about her concerns will help support her personal strengths during this difficult period.	Mrs. Randall is feeling anxious. She has identified family members and a close friend as potential support for her. Continue to follow her through the diagnostic process and treatment.

Using the previous steps of clinical reasoning, organizing, and prioritizing, consider all the case study findings woven throughout this chapter. When answering the following questions, begin drawing conclusions and see how the pieces of assessment must work together to create an environment for personalized, appropriate, and accurate care. Consider Mrs. Randall's case with her recent discovery of a breast lump.

- What age group of women have the highest risk for breast cancer? (Knowledge)
- Why is cancer in the upper outer quadrant of the breast so high risk? (Comprehension)
- Are Mrs. Randall's psychosocial or physical needs in this case more important? (Application)
- What lifestyle factors might be contributing to Mrs. Randall's risk for breast cancer? (Analysis)
- What recommendations for screening and follow-up would you suggest for Mrs. Randall and her daughters? (Synthesis)
- How would you evaluate the success of teaching for Mrs. Randall? (Evaluation)

Key Points

- To describe clinical findings, nurses divide the breast into four quadrants by imagining lines that intersect at the nipple.
- The lymphatic spread of breast cancer may cause enlarged lymph nodes, most commonly in the tail of Spence.
- Women who are pregnant experience breast changes and enlargement beginning in the first 2 months of pregnancy.
- Breast enlargement may occur in newborns as a result of the influence of maternal hormones.
- Breast development in adolescent females occurs over a 3-year period; the stage is identified by Tanner's scale.
- Gynecomastia is common in approximately one third of adolescent boys; it usually resolves in 1 to 2 years.
- A new breast lump, change in existing lump, or bloody discharge from the nipple needs further investigation to rule out breast cancer.
- The nurse offers to teach female patients how to perform the KYB approach as part of health promotion/risk reduction.
- Risks for breast cancer include no history of childbirth, gender, oral contraceptive use, aging, combined and estrogen-alone postmenopausal hormone therapy, genetic risk factors, no breast-feeding, family history, alcohol, personal history of breast cancer, overweight or obesity (especially after menopause), genetic background, physical inactivity, unexpected breast biopsy results, early onset of menstruation and late menopause, previous chest radiation, and diethylstilbestrol exposure.
- Common signs and symptoms related to the breasts and axillae include breast pain, lumps, discharge, rash, swelling, and trauma.
- Palpation of the breasts may cause apprehension or embarrassment in patients; nurses provide support and privacy.
- The best time to palpate the breasts is 5 to 7 days after the menstrual period begins and up until day 13.

- Size and shape of the breasts show wide variation.
- A supernumerary nipple is an expected variation.
- The sequence for inspecting the breasts is with the patient sitting with arms at the side, arms overhead, arms pressed on the hips, leaning forward at the waist, and lying supine.
- A horizontal pattern of palpation is recommended.
- With pendulous breasts, a bimanual palpation technique is used.

Review Questions

1. When teaching the Know Your Breasts (KYB) approach, which of the following times should nurses inform women that it is best to perform it? Select all that apply.
   A. Just before the menstrual period
   B. Just after the menstrual period
   C. On the fifth to seventh days after the menstrual period begins
   D. On the 20th day of the menstrual cycle

2. A male patient presents to the clinic with a concern about a hard, irregular, nontender mass on his chest under the areola. Upon examination, the nurse notes that the mass is immobile and suspects
   A. gynecomastia
   B. benign lesion
   C. Paget's disease
   D. carcinoma

3. Gynecomastia may occur in an older male secondary to
   A. testosterone deficiency
   B. lymphatic engorgement
   C. trauma
   D. decreased activity level

4. When examining the breast of a 75-year-old woman, the nurse would expect to find which of the following?
   A. Enlarged axillary lymph nodes
   B. Multiple large, firm lumps
   C. A granular feel to the breast tissue
   D. Pale areola

5. It is important to examine the upper outer quadrant of the breast because it is
   A. more prone to injury and calcifications
   B. where most breast tumours develop
   C. where most of the suspensory ligaments attach
   D. the largest quadrant of the breast

6. A 23-year-old nulliparous woman is concerned that her breasts seem to change in size all month long and they are very tender around the time she has her period. The nurse can explain to her that
   A. women who are not pregnant usually do not have these breast changes and this is cause for concern
   B. breasts often change in response to stress so it is important to assess her life stressors
   C. cyclic breast changes are expected
   D. breast changes usually occur during pregnancy and she should have a pregnancy test

7. The patient with benign breast disease (BBD) is likely to
   A. develop breast cancer later in life
   B. require hormone therapy
   C. be a teenager
   D. resolve after menopause

8. The nurse palpates a fine, round, mobile, nontender nodule and suspects that it is (a)
   A. fibroadenoma
   B. cyst
   C. fibrocystic breast change
   D. breast cancer

9. *Peau d'orange* appearance is highly suggestive of which of the following?
   A. Breast cancer
   B. Gynecomastia
   C. Papillomas
   D. Colostrum

10. The correct position to place the patient to palpate the breasts is
   A. left lateral position with arm over head
   B. sitting forward with hands on hips
   C. supine with arms at side
   D. supine with arm over head

Canadian Nursing Research

Donnelly, T. T. (2008). Challenges in providing breast and cervical cancer screening services to Vietnamese Canadian women: The healthcare providers' perspective. *Nursing Inquiry, 15*(2), 158–168.

Hack, T. F., Kwan, W. B., et al. (2010). Predictors of arm morbidity following breast cancer surgery. *Psychooncology, 9*(11), 1205–1212.

Loiselle, C. G., Edgar, L., et al. (2010). The impact of a multimedia informational intervention on psychosocial adjustment among individuals with newly diagnosed breast or prostate cancer: A feasibility study. *Patient Education Counseling, 80*(11), 48–55.

Pedersen, A. E., Sawatzky, J. A., et al. (2010). The sequelae of anxiety in breast cancer: A human response to illness model. *Oncology Nursing Forum, 37*(4), 469–475.

Pituskin, E., Williams, B., et al. (2007). Experiences of men with breast cancer: A qualitative study. *The Journal of Men's Health & Gender, 4*(1), 44–51.

References

Anderson, B. O. (2006). Breast healthcare and cancer control in limited-resource countries: A framework for change. *Nature Clinical Practice Oncology, 3*(1), 4–5.

Bowen, D. J., Alfano, C. M., et al. (2007). Possible socioeconomic and ethnic disparities in quality of life in a cohort of breast cancer survivors. *Breast Cancer Research and Treatment, 106*(1), 85–95.

Boyd, N. F., Guo, H., et al. (2007). Mammographic density and the risk and detection of breast cancer. *New England Journal of Medicine, 356*(3), 227–236.

Bryner, J. (2007). *Bras don't support bouncing breasts.* Retrieved from http://www.livescience.com/health/070911_bounce_support.html

Bulechek, G. M., Butcher, J. K., et al. (2008). *Nursing interventions classification (NIC)* (5th ed.). St. Louis, MO: Mosby.

Canadian Cancer Society. (2009a). *Know your breasts.* Retrieved from http://www.cancer.ca/canada-wide/prevention/get%20screened/know%20your%20breasts.aspx?sc_lang=en

Canadian Cancer Society. (2009b). *Breast cancer in men.* Retrieved from http://www.cancer.ca/Canada-wide/About%20cancer/Types%20of%20cancer/Breast%20cancer%20in%20men.aspx?sc_lang=nn

Canadian Cancer Society/National Cancer Institute of Canada. (2006). *Canadian cancer statistics 2006.* Toronto, ON: Author.

Canadian Cancer Society's Steering Committee on Cancer Statistics. (2011). *Canadian cancer statistics 2011.* Toronto, ON: Canadian Cancer Society.

Chow, J. (2010). Assessment and management of patients with breast disorders. In R. A. Day, P. Paul, et al. (Eds.). *Brunner & Suddarth's textbook of Canadian medical-surgical nursing* (2nd ed., pp. 1609–1646). Philadelphia, PA: Wolters Kluwer Health/Lippincott Williams & Wilkins.

Dains, J., Baumann, L., et al. (2007). *Advanced health assessment and clinical diagnosis in primary care* (3rd ed.). St. Louis, MO: Mosby.

Day, R. A., & Bickley, L. S. (2010). The breasts and axillae. In T. C. Stephen, D. L. Skillen, R. A. Day, & L. S. Bickley (Eds.). *Canadian Bates' guide to health assessment for nurses* (1st ed., pp. 479–508). Philadelphia, PA: Wolters Kluwer Health/Lippincott Williams & Wilkins.

de Onis, M., Garza, C., et al. (Guest Eds.). (2004). The WHO Multicentre Growth Reference Study (MGRS): Rationale, planning and implementation. *Food and Nutrition Bulletin, 25*(1, Suppl. 1), 1–89.

Diamantopoulos, S. (2007). Gynecomastia and premature thelarche: A guide for practitioners. *Pediatrics in Review, 28*, e57–e67.

Gulay, H., Bora, S., et al. (1994). Management of nipple discharge. *Journal of the American College of Surgeons, 178*(5), 471–474.

Hartmann, L. C., Schaid, D. J., et al. (1999). Efficacy of bilateral prophylactic mastectomy in women with a family history of breast cancer. *New England Journal of Medicine, 340*(2), 77–84.

Hislop, T. G., Bajdik, C. D., et al. (2007). Cancer incidence in Indians from three areas: Delhi and Mumbai, India, and British Columbia, Canada. *Journal of Immigrant & Minority Health, 9*(3), 221–227.

Hussain, A. N., Policarpio, C., et al. (2006). Evaluating nipple discharge. *Obstetrical and Gynecological Survey, 61*(4), 278–283.

International Agency for Research on Cancer, World Health Organization. (2002). Breast cancer and screening. In *IARC handbooks of cancer prevention, Volume 7: Breast cancer screening*. Geneva, Switzerland: IARC Press.

Katz, V. L., Lentz, G. M., et al. (2007). Benign breast disease. In A. Katz (Ed.). *Comprehensive gynecology* (5th ed.). Philadelphia, PA: Mosby Elsevier.

Kronenberg, H. M., Melmed, S., et al. (2008). *Williams textbook of endocrinology* (11th ed.). Philadelphia, PA: Saunders.

Laufer, M. R., & Goldstein, D. P. (2005). The breast: Examination and lesions. In A. Sydor (Ed.). *Pediatric & adolescent gynecology* (5th ed., pp. 729–759). Philadelphia, PA: Lippincott Williams & Wilkins.

Losken, A., Fishman, I., et al. (2007). *An objective evaluation of breast symmetry and shape differences using 3-dimensional images.* Retrieved from http://cat.inist.fr/?aModele=afficheN&cpsidt=17314303

McCowen Meahring, P. (2010a). Structure and function of the female reproductive system. In R. A. Hannon, C. Pooler, et al. (Eds.). *Porth physiology: Concepts of altered health state* (1st Canadian ed., pp. 1068–1083). Philadelphia, PA: Wolters Kluwer Health/Lippincott Williams & Wilkins.

McCowen Meahring, P. (2010b). Disorders of the female reproductive system. In R. A. Hannon, C. Pooler, et al. (Eds.). *Porth physiology: Concepts of altered health state* (1st Canadian ed., pp. 1084–1118). Philadelphia, PA: Wolters Kluwer Health/Lippincott Williams & Wilkins.

Moorhead, S., Johnson, M., et al. (2007). *Nursing outcomes classification (NOC)* (4th ed.). Philadelphia, PA: Mosby.

North American Nursing Diagnosis Association-International. (2009). *Nursing diagnoses: Definitions and classification (NANDA-I NURSING DIAGNOSIS)*. West Sussex, UK: Wiley-Blackwell.

Pedersen, A. E., Sawatzky, J. A., et al. (2010). The sequelae of anxiety in breast cancer: A human response to illness model. *Oncology Nursing Forum, 37*(4), 469–475.

Pediconi, F., Catalano, C., et al. (2007). Contrast-enhanced MR mammography for evaluation of the contralateral breast in clients with diagnosed contralateral breast cancer or high-risk lesions. *Radiology, 243*(3), 670–680.

Pituskin, E., Williams, B., et al. (2007). Experiences of men with breast cancer: A qualitative study. *The Journal of Men's Health & Gender, 4*(1), 44–51.

Public Health Agency of Canada. (2011). *Physical activity, tips to get active: Information and tips for adults (ages 18–64 years)*. Retrieved from http://phac-aspc.gc.ca/hl-mvs/pa-ap/07paap-eng.php

Rakel, R. E. (2007). *Textbook of family medicine* (7th ed.). Philadelphia, PA: Elsevier.

Richards, T., Hunt, A., et al. (2007). Nipple discharge: A sign of breast cancer? *Annals of College Surgery England, 89*(2), 124–126.

Saslow, D., Boetes, C., et al. (2007). American Cancer Society guidelines for breast screening with MRI as an adjunct of mammography. *CA: A Cancer Journal for Clinicians, 57*(2), 75–89.

Singleton, J. K., Sandowski, S. A., et al. (2008). *Primary care.* Philadelphia, PA: Lippincott Williams & Wilkins.

Steiner, E., Austin, D. F., et al. (2008). Detection and description of small breast masses by residents trained using a standardized clinical breast exam curriculum. *Journal of General Internal Medicine, 23*(2), 129–134.

Sohn, V. Y., Arthurs, Z. M., et al. (2008). Primary tumor location impacts breast cancer survival. *American Journal of Surgery, 195*(5), 102–105.

White, E., Urban, N., et al. (1993). Mammography utilization, public health impact, and cost-effectiveness in the United States. *Annual Review of Public Health, 14*, 605–633.

The Canadian Jensen's Nursing Health Assessment suite offers these additional resources to enhance learning and facilitate understanding of this chapter:

- thePoint online resource, http//thepoint.lww.com/Stephen1E
- *Laboratory Manual for Canadian Jensen's Nursing Health Assessment: A Best Practice Approach*

Table 21-4   Breast Alterations

Carcinoma (skin, areola, and nipple retraction)

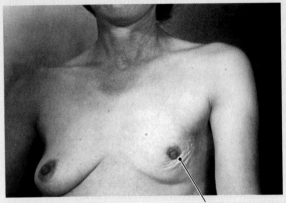

Skin, areola, and
nipple retraction

Carcinoma (bulging of breast and skin changes)

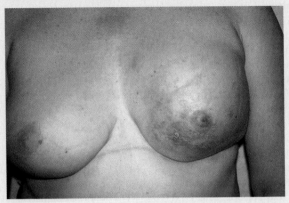

Paget Disease

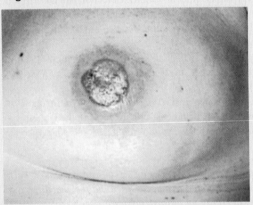

Mastitis

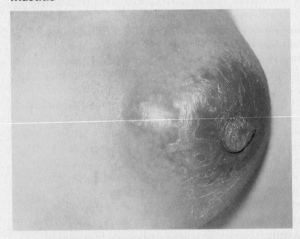

Mastectomy

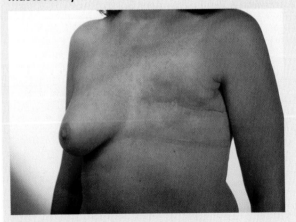

Gynecomastia

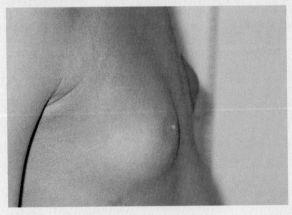

Table 21-5   **Breast Lumps**

Characteristics	Fibroadenoma	Benign Breast Disease	Cancer
	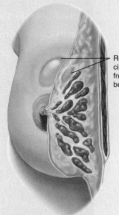Rubbery, circumscribed, freely movable benign tumor	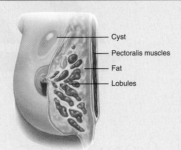Cyst / Pectoralis muscles / Fat / Lobules	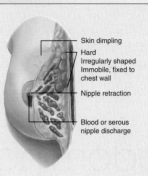Skin dimpling / Hard Irregularly shaped Immobile, fixed to chest wall / Nipple retraction / Blood or serous nipple discharge
Likely age	Appears most often before 30 y (15–39 y; some up to 55 y)	30–50 y; incidence decreases after menopause	30–80 y; risk increases after 50 y
Shape/size	Oval, round, lobular, 1–5 cm	Round, lobular, variable size	Irregular, star-shaped, variable size
Consistency	Firm or rubbery	Firm to soft, rubbery	Firm to hard
Demarcation	Well demarcated, clear margins	Well demarcated	Poorly defined
Number	Most often single; may be multiple	Most often multiple; may be single	Single
Mobility	Freely movable	Movable	Fixed
Tenderness	Painless	Painful; breast tenderness, which usually increases before menses, may be noncyclic; breasts often swollen, usually bilateral	Nontender, but can be tender
Suspicious signs	None	None	Dimpling, nipple inversion, spontaneous single-nipple bloody discharge, orange peel texture (*peau d'orange*), axillary lymphadenopathy
Pattern of growth	Rapid growing during pregnancy, with HT, or if immunosuppressed; approximately 10% disappear spontaneously	Size may increase or decrease rapidly	Continually increases in size (at varying rates)
Risk to health	None; they are benign—must diagnose by biopsy	Benign, although general lumpiness may mask other cancerous lumps	Serious, needs early treatment

HT: Hormone therapy.

Abdominal Assessment

Learning Objectives

1 Identify anatomical landmarks that guide assessment of the abdomen and documentation of findings.

2 Demonstrate knowledge of the anatomy and physiology of the body systems in the abdominal assessment.

3 Identify important topics for health promotion and risk reduction related to the systems found within the abdomen.

4 Collect subjective data related to the abdominal assessment.

5 Collect objective data related to the abdominal assessment using physical examination techniques.

6 Consider age, condition, gender, and culture of the patient to individualize the abdominal assessment.

7 Identify expected and unexpected findings related to the systems in the abdominal assessment.

8 Analyze subjective and objective data from the abdominal assessment and consider initial interventions.

9 Document and communicate data from the abdominal assessment using appropriate terminology and principles of recording.

10 Identify nursing diagnoses and initiate a plan of care based on findings from the abdominal assessment.

Mr. Barry Renaud, a 41-year-old French Canadian, was admitted to the hospital surgical unit presenting with coffee grounds vomitus. He has been on the unit for 5 days following a 3-day stay in the intensive care unit (ICU). His temperature is 36.5°C tympanic, pulse 102 beats/min and regular, respirations 20 breaths/min, and blood pressure (BP) right arm (semi-Fowler's) 148/92 mm Hg. Current medications include omeprazole (Losec) 20 mg by mouth daily, aluminum hydroxide (Amphogel), and magnesium hydroxide (milk of magnesia) 10 mL by mouth four times daily. He has had an assessment documented every shift.

You will gain more information about Mr. Renaud as you progress through this chapter. As you study the content and features, consider Mr. Renaud's case and its relationship to what you are learning. Begin thinking about the following points:

- How will the nurse prioritize health promotion and teaching needs?
- How does the nurse incorporate the different phases of the nursing process when performing the assessments?
- What information about Mr. Renaud's body systems might be useful to assess?
- How will the nurse organize the assessment during the shift?

It is not possible to perform an assessment of the abdomen without recognizing that many systems are found within the abdominal cavity. Awareness of this fact allows nurses to obtain valuable information about the functioning of the gastrointestinal (GI), cardiovascular, reproductive, neuromuscular, and genitourinary (GU) systems. Also, the integumentary system is part of every assessment.

The focus of this chapter is abdominal assessment, and it primarily addresses issues within the GI system. The GI system is responsible for the ingestion and digestion of food, absorption of nutrients, and elimination of solid waste products from the body. Parts of the GI system also reside in the head, neck, and thoracic regions (see Chapters 14 and 18). Findings need to be evaluated based on the organ systems found in those regions as well.

GI symptoms are common and send people of all ages in search of relief. Diagnosis of abdominal diseases depends heavily on accurate and thorough history taking. During the health history, it is essential to delineate the sequence of the patient's symptoms. Additionally, it is important to master the abdominal assessment to provide quality health care.

Anatomy and Physiology Overview

Understanding the anatomy and physiology of GI structures is essential before beginning an assessment. The nurse recognizes GI structures and their functions before identifying unexpected findings. Understanding the physiology associated with each system and their interactions assists the nurse to accurately interpret findings from the assessment (Fig. 22-1; Tables 22-1 and 22-2).

Anatomical Landmarks

The abdomen is a large cavity extending from the xiphoid process of the sternum to the superior margin of the pubic bone. It is bordered in the back by the vertebral column and paravertebral muscles and at the sides and front by the lower rib cage and abdominal muscles. Four layers of large, flat muscles form the ventral abdominal wall and are joined at the midline by a tendinous seam, the linea alba.

Reference Lines

For convenience in description, two methods are used to map the location of findings. The most common is the *quadrant method*, which divides the abdominal wall into four quadrants by imaginary vertical and horizontal lines bisecting the umbilicus. The quadrants are the right upper quadrant (RUQ), left upper quadrant (LUQ), right lower quadrant (RLQ), and left lower quadrant (LLQ) (Fig. 22-2). For most assessments and findings, this method is sufficient. A more specific method is to divide the abdomen into nine regions by drawing two vertical lines at the midclavicular lines (MCLs) and two horizontal lines, one beginning at the lower edge of the costal margin and the other beginning at the anterior–superior iliac spine of the iliac bones. The regions are named from right to left

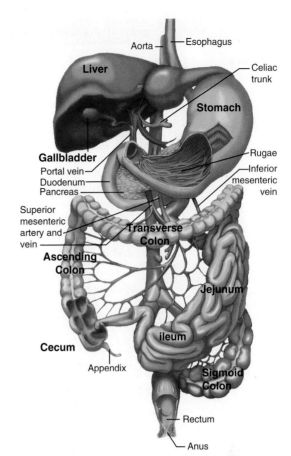

Figure 22-1 Overview of the GI system.

and top to bottom: right hypochondriac, epigastric, left hypochondriac, right lumbar, umbilical, left lumbar, right inguinal, hypogastric, and left inguinal. Findings that require a more specific location can be mapped to these regions (Fig. 22-3).

Abdominal Organs

Gastrointestinal Organs

The major GI organs found within the abdominal cavity include the stomach, small intestines, and colon (see Table 22-1). **Accessory organs** of the GI system within the

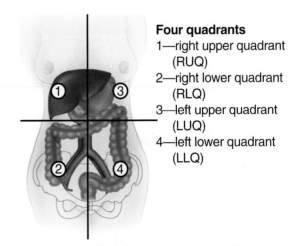

Four quadrants
1—right upper quadrant (RUQ)
2—right lower quadrant (RLQ)
3—left upper quadrant (LUQ)
4—left lower quadrant (LLQ)

Figure 22-2 Division of the abdomen into four quadrants.

Table 22-1   Major Organs of the Gastrointestinal/Genitourinary System

GI Organs

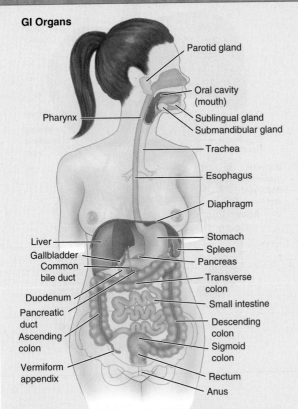

GU Organs

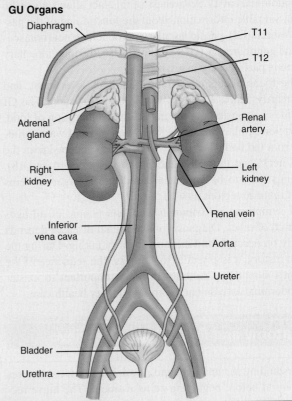

Organ	Function
Esophagus	Propels food into the stomach, controlled by the cardiac sphincter—a one-way valve at the distal end
Stomach	Site for both mechanical and chemical digestion:
	Churns food into small particles that become liquid when mixed with gastric juices
	Stores food and slowly releases it into the small intestine
	Secretes hydrochloric acid to aid in digestion; mucous cells secrete substances to coat the stomach lining; chief cells secrete pepsinogen, which is converted to pepsin to aid in digestion of protein; secretes gastrin which stimulates secretion of acid and pepsinogen and increases gastric motility
	Secretes intrinsic factor that protects vitamin B_{12} from stomach acid and facilitates its absorption by the parietal cells in the small intestine
	Absorbs water, alcohol, and some medications
	Destroys some food-borne bacteria
	Allows emptying of stomach contents based on pressure gradient, a little at a time; gravity assists with emptying
Small intestine (5.5–6 m in adults)	Propels contents by wormlike movements known as peristalsis
	Primarily responsible for absorption of nutrients
Duodenum (25 cm)	Primary site for chemical digestion
	Enzymes, hormones, and bile from pancreas and liver enter and aid in absorption of nutrients: Peptidases help break down proteins.

Organ	Function
	Enterokinase converts trypsinogen to active trypsin.
	Maltase, lactase, and sucrase break down carbohydrates.
	Cholecystokinin, secreted from duodenal wall, stimulates gall bladder to secrete bile.
	Gastric inhibitory peptide inhibits gastric motility.
	Secretin, secreted by duodenal wall, stimulates pancreatic secretions to neutralize gastric acid.
Jejunum (2.5 m) and ileum (3.5 m)	Absorb water, nutrients, and electrolytes for use in body
Large intestine (ascending, transverse, and descending colon) (1.5–1.8 m)	Absorbs salt and water and excretes waste products of digestive process from the rectum (defecation)
	Aids in synthesis of vitamin B_{12} and K
Kidneys	Control blood pressure (BP) through the production of rennin
	Stimulate red blood cell production by secreting erythropoietin
	Remove waste products filtered by the kidneys from the body
Bladder	Aids in the removal of waste products from the body in the form of urine
Aorta	Supplies oxygenated blood to the cells and organs of the lower half of the body

abdomen include the liver, pancreas, and gall bladder (see Table 22-2).

Genitourinary Organs

The organs of the GU system found within the abdominal cavity include the kidneys, ureters, and bladder; the spermatic cord in males; and the uterus and ovaries in females. Disease processes in these organs can produce abdominal symptoms.

The kidneys control blood pressure (BP) through the production of renin, stimulate red blood cell production by secreting erythropoietin, and filter and remove waste products from the blood. The ureters and bladder aid with removal of waste products in the form of urine. The spermatic cord protects the vas deferens, blood vessels, lymphatics, and nerves that run from scrotum to penis (see Chapter 25). The ovaries produce ova and secrete estrogen and progesterone. The uterus allows fertilization of the ova with sperm and, if conception occurs, provides an environment for fetal development (see Chapters 26 and 27).

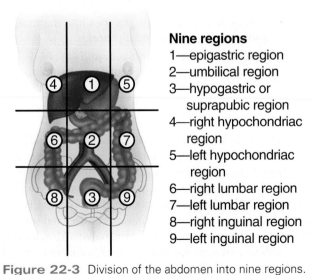

Nine regions
1—epigastric region
2—umbilical region
3—hypogastric or suprapubic region
4—right hypochondriac region
5—left hypochondriac region
6—right lumbar region
7—left lumbar region
8—right inguinal region
9—left inguinal region

Figure 22-3 Division of the abdomen into nine regions.

Figure 22-4 The aorta and branching arteries and veins within the abdominal cavity.

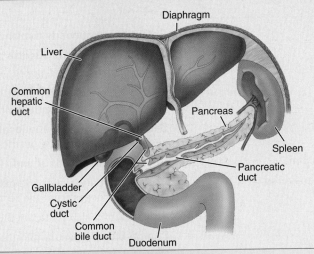

Accessory Organ	Function
Liver (located in right upper quadrant [RUQ])	Produces and secretes bile to emulsify fat
	Metabolizes protein, carbohydrates, and fats
	Converts glucose to glycogen and stores it
	Produces clotting factors, fibrinogen, and plasma proteins such as albumin
	Detoxifies drugs and alcohol
	Stores fat-soluble vitamins A, D, E, and K; vitamin B_{12}; and copper and iron
	Converts conjugated bilirubin from blood to unconjugated bilirubin
Gall bladder (located posterior to the liver in RUQ)	Stores and concentrates bile
Pancreas (located in the left upper quadrant [LUQ])	Endocrine functions:
	Secretes insulin and regulates blood glucose levels
	Secretes glucagons that store carbohydrates
	Inhibits insulin and glucagon secretion
	Secretes pancreatic polypeptide that regulates release of pancreatic enzymes
	Exocrine functions:
	Secretes digestive enzymes. Amylase digests starches into maltose. Lipase breaks down lipids into fatty acids and glycerol.
	Trypsinogen, chymotrypsinogen, and procarboxypeptidase are activated in the small intestine to break down proteins into amino acids.

Blood Vessels, Peritoneum, and Muscles

The aorta and branching arteries and veins are found within the abdominal cavity (Fig. 22-4). They supply oxygenated blood to the cells and organs of the lower half of the body. The spleen also resides in the abdominal cavity and stores red blood cells and platelets, produces new red blood cells and macrophages, and activates B and T lymphocytes.

The **peritoneum,** mesentery, and muscles also make up the abdominal cavity. The peritoneum is a serous membrane that covers and holds the organs in place. It contains a parietal layer that lines the walls of the abdomen and a visceral layer that coats the outer surface of the organs. A small amount of fluid between these layers allows them to move smoothly within the cavity. The fanlike *mesentery* supplies blood vessels and nerves to the intestinal tract. The muscles protect and support the digestive system within the abdominal cavity. Muscles also assist with ingestion, mastication, and swallowing of food and with the voluntary defecation of its by-products.

Ingestion and Digestion

The digestive process consists of mechanical and chemical digestion. *Mechanical digestion* means the breakdown of food through chewing, peristalsis, and churning. *Chemical digestion* means the breakdown of food through a series of metabolic reactions with hydrochloric acid, enzymes, and hormones.

The digestive process begins in the mouth where food is ingested and mastication (chewing) begins. During this process, saliva mixes with the food and a bolus of food forms. The bolus passes into the oropharynx and esophagus, which propel the bolus via slow peristaltic movements into the stomach. In the stomach, the bolus is churned into a liquid and mixed with digestive juices and hydrochloric acid produced there. The liquid form is called chyme.

Absorption of Nutrients

Absorption of nutrients takes place almost exclusively in the small intestine. In the first portion of the small intestine, the *duodenum*, pancreatic juices, and bile are secreted into the chyme, making it ready for absorption of nutrients by the many villi that line the walls of the *jejunum* and *ileum*. Each villus contains a blood vessel and a lymphatic vessel, which are responsible for nutrient absorption.

Elimination

Any food particles not absorbed by the small intestine pass into the large intestine, where a few electrolytes and water are further absorbed. Eventually, the remaining waste products are excreted as feces. On average, waste products of food ingested today are eliminated 48 hours later.

Lifespan Considerations

Women Who are Pregnant

The abdomen changes dramatically in pregnancy. The abdominal muscles relax, allowing the uterus to protrude into the abdominal cavity to accommodate the growing fetus. The rectus abdominis muscles, which are located medially, become separated. As the fetus grows and takes up more room in the abdominal cavity, the stomach rises and may impinge on the diaphragm. Compression of the bowels by the uterus results in diminished bowel sounds. Bowel activity decreases, which may contribute to **constipation** in women who are pregnant.

Venous pressure in the lower abdomen increases, which may lead to hemorrhoids and further difficulties with elimination. During pregnancy, the appendix is displaced upward and laterally to the right, which can complicate the diagnosis of appendicitis in women who are pregnant. A darkly pigmented line, the linea nigra, appears in the midline of the anterior abdomen from pubis to umbilicus in many women who are pregnant. Near the end of pregnancy, the umbilicus may become everted, and **striae** (stretch marks) may develop on the skin of the abdomen (see also Chapter 27).

Newborns, Infants, and Children

Because of their small size, several anatomic differences related to the abdomen are found in infants. The newborn's bladder is located above the symphysis pubis. The liver takes up more space in the abdominal cavity and may extend 2 cm below the rib cage. The infant's abdominal muscles are not developed, so the abdomen of the infant usually protrudes. As the child grows, the abdominal protuberance becomes more obvious in toddlers and preschoolers because of the curvature of the back. It diminishes to adult proportions during adolescence. Because the abdominal muscles are underdeveloped, the organs are more easily palpated in children.

Older Adults

In older adults, production of saliva and stomach acid is reduced, and gastric motility and peristalsis slow. All these changes can lead to difficulty swallowing, malabsorption, and other digestive issues. Elderly people also have changes in dentition that may affect their ability to chew. Chewing difficulties, accompanied by limited financial resources, can dramatically alter dietary choices (less protein, more carbohydrates) and may result in painful mastication. All these factors along with generally reduced muscle mass and tone may also contribute to constipation.

Fat accumulates in the lower abdomen in women and around the waist in men, making physical assessment more challenging. The liver decreases in size and liver function declines, making it harder for older adults to process medications.

Acute Assessment

If the patient has an acute abdominal injury or illness, the history and physical examination will be focused on that issue and much of the history taking discussed in the following sections will be eliminated. Direct trauma to the abdomen may cause organ rupture and peritonitis (severe, generalized inflammation of the serous membrane) and requires immediate attention. Abdominal pain, in combination with other signs and symptoms, may indicate life-threatening intra-abdominal emergencies related to the GI, GU, or hematologic systems (Harder, Skillen, et al., 2010). Severe dehydration from nausea and vomiting, black, tarry stools or frank blood in the stool, emesis with fecal odour, yellowing of the skin, inability to void, pruritis, fever, and acute abdominal pain are potentially life-threatening symptoms that require prompt attention.

Extra-abdominal emergencies related to the cardiovascular and respiratory systems may also be detected because of referred pain to the upper abdomen. These include myocardial infarction and pneumothorax (Harder, Skillen, et al., 2010).

Subjective Data Collection

A comprehensive history usually precedes the physical assessment and involves asking the patient about his or her health status. It involves a broad range of questions to discern possible concerns associated with each organ and system within the abdomen. Approach the history using a head-to-toe direction and avoid skipping around with questioning. In many conditions of the GI tract, a well-developed health history can point to a diagnosis 80% to 90% of the time. If time is an issue, a focused history on the abdomen will be sufficient.

Assessment of Risk Factors

Food-borne illnesses affect the very young, elderly, and immunocompromised patients most seriously. Risk of food-borne illness increases with emerging pathogenic organisms, improper food storage or preparation, an increasing global supply of foods, and inadequate training of food handlers. Food allergies, particularly to peanuts, are on the rise. Estimates are that food allergies affect almost 4% of children younger than 6 years and 1% to 2% of adults (Eigenmann, Scott, et al., 2009). The goal for this risk factor is to reduce infections by food-borne pathogens and anaphylactic deaths

from food allergies. Education about food handling in retail areas and at home as well as food labelling and proper preparation are the methods identified to achieve these goals.

Reducing the incidence of hepatitis A, B, and C is another goal of nurses through screening, education, and immunization programs. Hepatitis C is the most common blood-borne viral infection worldwide. To date, no vaccine is available to prevent it. Perinatal infection is the common mode of transmission of hepatitis B in infants. The infection rate among infants born to hepatitis B-positive mothers is 90% (Teo, Lok, et al., 2009). Identifying at-risk mothers and vaccinating them and their infants would reduce this transmission. In comparison, unprotected sexual intercourse and intravenous (IV) drug use are the major routes of hepatitis B spread in adults. The nurse assesses current concerns first, using symptom/sign analysis. Then the nurse inquires about personal and family history to assess genetic risk factors. After this initial history, the nurse assesses other risk factors and performs teaching about those that may be modified so that assessment is linked to health promotion and teaching.

Questions to Assess History and Risk Factors	Rationale
Current Concerns Do you have any abdominal concerns now? How is your appetite?	These questions open discussion with a general approach.
Have you had any unplanned changes in weight? Weight loss? Weight gain?	Unexplained weight changes may indicate undiagnosed *cancer, anorexia, bulimia, thyroid disorder,* psychosocial issues, or socioeconomic concerns.
Do you have any special dietary needs? Any dietary concerns? Are there cultural beliefs that affect your diet? Religious beliefs?	Special needs may indicate a nutrient imbalance or cause of symptoms. A 24-hour diet recall is helpful to determine what may be typical for the patient (see Chapter 8). If the patient has been sick for a prolonged period, ask what he or she usually eats at each meal rather than what was eaten in the previous 24 hours.
Have you had a fever or chills?	Fever may indicate an infection that could affect food or fluid intake.
Have you had any dizziness?	Dizziness may result from possible dehydration linked to inadequate fluid or caloric intake.
Medications Have you been taking any over-the-counter or prescribed medications?	Patients will frequently take antacids that may interact with other medications.
Personal History I see from your patient care record that you are 50 years of age.	Risk of colorectal cancer increases with age (Ahnen, Finlay, et al., 2009). Colorectal cancer is the second leading cause of Canadian cancer deaths (Colon Cancer Canada, 2010). It is often asymptomatic, but if caught early it is very curable.
Did you have a blood transfusion before the mid-1980s? Have you been vaccinated against hepatitis B?	Those who received blood transfusions prior to the mid-1980s (before the blood supply was tested for hepatitis B) may be at higher risk for the illness. Hepatitis B vaccine has been available to at-risk patients since the mid-1980s; in the early- to mid-1990s, school-aged vaccination programs were implemented in most Canadian provinces (Canadian Liver Foundation, 2009). Question patients about whether they received all three doses.

Questions to Assess History and Risk Factors	Rationale
Do have a history of endometrial cancer? Ovarian cancer? Breast cancer?	Personal history of endometrial, ovarian, or breast cancer also increases risk.
Have you ever had chicken pox (varicella)?	Varicella, which always precedes herpes zoster (shingles), may start along a dermatome on one side of the abdomen and back.
General Gastrointestinal Questions. Have you had any previous treatments or hospitalizations for gastroesophageal reflux disease (GERD)? Peptic ulcer disease? Inflammatory bowel disease (IBD) (Crohn's disease or ulcerative collitis)? Anemia? Thalassemia? Celiac disease? Other gastrointestinal (GI) concerns?	The patient history may reveal an exacerbation of a previously diagnosed condition or a genetic predisposition or familial propensity for a particular disorder. Long-standing ulcerative colitis (>10 years) without remission increases the patient's risk for colorectal cancer. Crohn's disease may contribute to malnutrition or multiple surgical resections of the bowel, resulting in short gut syndrome.
Have you had any previous GI diagnostic tests such as stool for occult blood? Colonoscopy? Upper GI series? Barium enema? Computerized tomography scan? Magnetic resonance imaging (MRI)?	
Do you have a history of previous abdominal surgery? Pelvic surgeries?	Previous surgeries increase risk for adhesions, infections, obstructions, and malabsorption. Appendicitis must be ruled out as the cause of the current concern.
Have you had any recent insertions of GI tubes?	GI tubes can be a source of infection.
Have you had any recent injuries from trauma, such as a motor vehicle accident? Work-related injury? Sports injury?	A history of trauma can provide insight into a previous surgery or injury, which may cause current symptoms.
Have you had any recent infection with mononucleosis?	Mononucleosis can cause hepatosplenomegaly.
Do you have a history of malabsorption disease?	This condition in the patient or family members may indicate lactose intolerance, food allergies, or celiac disease.
Do you have sickle-cell anemia?	Abdominal pain is associated with *sickle-cell crisis*.
Do you have a history of eating disorders?	Eating disorders often begin in adolescence, with tendencies continuing into adulthood.
Have you ever had intestinal polyps?	History of intestinal polyps increases risk for colorectal cancer.
Chewing and Swallowing. Have you had any history of thyroid disease? Neck masses? Recent infections? Vision changes? Any trouble swallowing? Sore throat?	Hypothyrodism or hyperthyroidism affects metabolism, weight, and elimination. Neck masses may indicate cancer or infection. Infections increase the caloric requirements. Visual changes may occur with nutritional imbalances. Difficulty swallowing may indicate an undiagnosed cancer or infection. Throat pain may impede swallowing (see also Chapter 14).
When was your last dental assessment?	Poor dentition affects the intake of major food groups and nutritional status.
Breathing. Do you have a history of breathing difficulties? Shortness of breath? Chronic obstructive pulmonary disease (COPD)?	Respiratory illnesses diminish energy level and can decrease food intake. Some foods increase mucus in the throat (see also Chapter 18).
Weight Gain. Do you have a history of cardiovascular disease? High blood pressure (BP)? Congestive heart failure?	Weight gain and increased sodium in the diet can exacerbate these illnesses.
Genitourinary Issues. What is the colour of your urine? Do you have any burning when you void? Urinary frequency? Urgency to urinate?	Dark urine can indicate inadequate fluid intake or blockage in the biliary system.
Do you have a history of sexually transmitted infections?	They may cause lower abdominal pain.

(text continues on page 610)

Questions to Assess History and Risk Factors	Rationale
Females: What is the date of your last menstrual period?	Unplanned pregnancy is often a cause of nausea and vomiting.
Do you have any vaginal discharge?	Discharge may indicate an infection.
Males: Do you have a history of prostate conditions?	An enlarged prostate may be a source of urinary difficulty and result in decreased intake of fluids.
Do you have any penile discharge?	Penile discharge may indicate a sexually transmitted infection.
Joint Pain. Do you have a history of fractures? Joint pain? Weakness?	Joint pain may result in long-term use of nonsteroidal anti-inflammatory medications, which can cause GI bleeding. Joint issues may make food preparation difficult. Decreased mobility may result in constipation.
Neurological. How many alcoholic drinks do you have each day?	Excessive alcohol intake is the number one cause of liver disease. Excessive drinking may lead to decreased caloric intake.
Have you had any numbness? Back pain? Loss of bowel/ bladder control?	Numbness and changes in the bowel or bladder are symptoms of significant spinal injury.
Metabolism. Do you have a history of diabetes? Thyroid conditions?	Diabetes may cause polyphagia, polydipsia prior to diagnosis, improper carbohydrate metabolism, insulin resistance, and obesity.
	These are associated with an altered metabolism and weight changes.
Skin. Have you had any changes in your skin? Hair? Nails?	Inadequate nutrition or imbalances in electrolytes or hormones may be exhibited in the skin, hair, or nails.
Have you had any rashes? Itching? Lesions?	Rashes and itching suggest *liver disease* or malnutrition.
Lymphatic/Hematologic. Do you have any food allergies? Have you had recent infections? Do you have sickle-cell anemia?	Food allergies may cause belching, bloating, flatulence, diarrhea, or constipation. Sickle-cell anemia may cause significant pain and anemia.
Family History Is there a family history of colorectal cancer in a first-degree relative?	Such a family history increases the patient's risk for this disease.
Do you have any family history of GERD, peptic ulcer disease, IBD, irritable bowel syndrome, anemia, thalassemia, or celiac disease?	Many of these conditions run in families.
Risk Factors **Alcohol or Substance Abuse.** Use the CAGE questionnaire if the patient has a significant history of either alcohol or substance use (or signs and symptoms lead you to suspect he or she has) (Gold, Aronson, et al., 2009) (see Chapter 10).	Alcohol use is associated with development of liver cirrhosis. Fourteen percent of Canadians are considered high-risk drinkers (National Alcohol Strategy Working Group, 2007).
Occupation • What is your profession? • Where do you work? • How careful are you about using personal protective equipment at work?	Health care workers are at high risk for hepatitis C, for which there is no vaccine.
Foreign Travel • Have you travelled to, or lived in, parts of the world where sanitation is less than optimal? • Have you eaten food prepared in places that are not sanitary? • Have you received the hepatitis A vaccine?	Hepatitis A is transmitted by the fecal–oral route, usually presenting within 30 days of exposure. The disease is vaccine preventable (Guerrant, Van Gilder, et al., 2001).

Questions to Assess History and Risk Factors	Rationale

Lifestyle

- Do you use intravenous (IV) drugs? Have you used IV drugs in the past?
- How many sexual partners have you had?
- Have you ever had sex with sex workers?

Hepatitis B is transmitted through contact with bodily secretions (ie, blood, semen, saliva, and vaginal fluids) of infected people. Patients may not be aware of previous infection with it because symptoms may have felt like flu. Transmission time for hepatitis B is 6 weeks to 6 months. Hepatitis C is the most commonly diagnosed form of hepatitis worldwide (Harder, Skillen, et al., 2010). It is transmitted through contact with the blood of infected people. IV drug users are at high risk for hepatitis C; 70% of patients with it develop serious liver complications of cirrhosis or hepatoma.

Risk Assessment and Health Promotion

Topics for Health Promotion

- Digestive health (fibre, fluid, and nutrient intake)
- Constipation and diarrhea
- Screening for alcohol and substance abuse
- Risk factors for hepatitis A, B, and C
- Vaccination for hepatitis A and B
- Risk factors and screening for colorectal cancer
- Risk factors and teaching for bowel disorders
- Risk factors for pancreatic cancer
- Risk factors and teaching for bladder disorders, kidney disease, and renal calculi

Adapted from Harder, N., Skillen, D. L., et al. (2010). The abdomen. In T. C. Stephen, D. L. Skillen, R. A. Day, & L. S. Bickley (Eds.). *Canadian Bates' guide to health assessment for nurses* (1st ed., p. 521). Philadelphia, PA: Wolters Kluwer Health/Lippincott Williams & Wilkins.

Digestive health is an essential element in health promotion because in Canada, digestive diseases create the greatest costs for the health care system (Beck, 2001). It is important to provide nutritional counselling to patients with food allergies, inadequate nutrition, and obesity at least annually, if not at every visit.

Nurses can help patients avoid constipation and diarrhea by understanding the risk factors for these conditions and promoting healthy options for prevention. Risk factors for constipation include medications such as opioids, antihypertensives, and antidepressants; patient history of GI concerns such as hemorrhoids, irritable bowel syndrome, and cancer of the bowel; patient history of conditions related to the endocrine, neurologic, metabolic, and muscular systems; inactivity; and stress (Harder, Skillen, et al., 2010). Prevention includes adequate fluid intake, physical activity, and dietary measures such as eating a diet rich in fruits and vegetables and increasing daily fibre intake to 25 mg for women and 38 mg for men (Dietitians of Canada, 2010).

Risk factors for diarrhea include medications such as laxatives, antibiotics, antacids, and thyroid hormone; endocrine

or metabolic conditions; malabsorption disorders or intestinal conditions; and travel (Harder, Skillen, et al., 2010). The nursing focus on prevention includes identifying potential causes, maintaining hydration and electrolyte stability, and counselling patients about staying healthy while travelling (Harder, Skillen, et al.).

Along with tobacco use and hypertension, alcohol use is one of the top three factors affecting the burden of disease in Canada (Harder, Skillen, et al., 2010). Patient teaching concerning alcohol and substance abuse, and the possible effects on the organs in the abdomen, should be covered with all patients, especially those at high risk for abuse (see Chapter 10).

Hepatitis A and B can be prevented through immunizations, which are recommended for all infants; people whose work may expose them to blood, body fluids, or unsanitary conditions (ie, health care, food services, sex workers); and those traveling to parts of the world where these illnesses are prevalent. Hepatitis A is transmitted through the fecal–oral route and can also be prevented through personal hygiene and sanitation. Hepatitis B is transmitted through contact with blood and body fluids of an infected person, including unprotected sexual contact, sharing needles or needle stick injuries, and transmission from mother to child (Harder, Skillen, et al., 2010).

Hepatitis C is an important threat to public health because 75% to 85% of people who are infected with the virus develop a chronic infection (Public Health Agency of Canada, 2009). Hepatitis C is spread through blood-to-blood contact, and risk factors include unprotected sex, injection drug use, tattooing, body piercing, hemodialysis, maternal infection with hepatitis C, and receiving a blood transfusion prior to 1990 when blood donations were not screened for hepatitis C (Harder, Skillen, et al., 2010).

Colorectal cancer is the fourth most common cancer in Canada and the second most common cause of cancer death (Canadian Cancer Society's Steering Committee for Cancer Statistics, 2011). Risk increases with age. Initial screening for all people is recommended at 50 years, with serial fecal occult blood and colonoscopy for anyone whose results are positive. Follow-up screening is based on findings and risks, with colonoscopy repeated every 3 to 10 years. Other factors that may increase the risk of colorectal cancer include a diet high in red meat and low in fruits and vegetables; obesity; lack of exercise; smoking; alcohol consumption, especially beer; and family history of colorectal cancer, especially in immediate family members (Health Canada, 2007).

Focused Health History Related to Common Symptoms/Signs

The focused health history should address common symptoms of the abdomen: indigestion, anorexia, nausea, vomiting, hematemesis, abdominal pain, **dysphagia, odynophagia,** changes in bowel function, constipation, **diarrhea,** and jaundice. It should also include questions about the possibility of GU disorders. Additional questions can include suprapubic pain, dysuria, urgency, frequency of urination, hesitancy, decreased urine stream in males, polyuria, nocturia, urinary incontinence, kidney or flank pain, ureteral colic, pelvic pain, and vaginal discharge in females. Some common symptoms are assessed in all patients to screen for the presence of GI disease. Nurses can use any special concerns from patients related to GI functioning to identify focal areas. A thorough history of symptoms assists with identifying a current issue or diagnosis.

Common Abdominal Symptoms/Signs

- Gastrointestinal (GI) disorders
- Indigestion
- Lack or loss of appetite (anorexia)
- Nausea, vomiting, bloody vomit (hematemesis)
- Abdominal pain
- Difficulty swallowing (dysphagia), pain with swallowing (odynophagia)
- Change in bowel movements, bloating, excessive gas
- Constipation or diarrhea
- Yellowing of skin and eyes (jaundice/icterus)
- Urinary/renal disorders
- Pain in lower abdomen (suprapubic)
- Pain with urination (dysuria), urgency or frequency of urination
- Decreased urine stream in males, hesitancy in starting urine stream
- Increased amount of urine with voiding (polyuria)
- Urination at night (nocturia)
- Loss of control of urine (urinary incontinence)
- Change in colour of urine, blood in urine (hematuria)
- Flank or back (kidney) pain
- Severe flank, back, and/or lower abdominal pain (ureteral colic)

Examples of Questions for Symptom Analysis: Right Upper Quadrant (RUQ) Pain

- "Where do you feel the pain?" "How big is the area of pain?" "Is it limited to a small area?" "Show me." (Location)
- "Does the RUQ pain go anywhere else?" "Do you feel pain in your right shoulder?" (Radiation)
- "What is the pain like?" For example, "Is it gripping?" "Colicky?" "Crampy?" (Quality/nature)
- "On a scale of 0 (no pain) to 10 (worst pain), how would you rate your pain?" "How would you compare your pain to other pain that you have had?" (Quantity/intensity)
- "When did the pain start?" (Onset)
- "Did it start suddenly or did it come on gradually?" "Is it related to eating? Drinking? Activity?" (Timing)
- "How long does the pain last?" (Duration)
- "Does it come and go?" "Or is it constant?" (Frequency)
- "What makes the pain better?" "What helps to ease the pain?" (Alleviating factors)

- "What makes the pain worse?" "Did you eat anything recently that you do not usually consume?" "Drink anything different?" "Does alcohol aggravate the pain?" "Does lying down aggravate the pain?" "Bending over?" (Aggravating factors)
- "What other symptoms have you noticed?" "Do you have a cough?" "Heartburn?" "Any bowel changes?" "Do you have loose or watery stools?" "Is the stool bloody?" "Have you noticed floating stools?" "Fever?" "Lightheadedness?" (Associated symptoms)
- "What is happening at home?" "Work?" "School?" "Or leisure?" "How much stress do you have in your life right now?" (Environmental factors)
- "Tell me how the pain is affecting your life." (Significance to patient)
- "What do you think is causing your pain?" (Patient perspective)

Adapted from Harder, N., Skillen, D. L., et al. (2010). The abdomen. In T. C. Stephen, D. L. Skillen, R. A. Day, & L. S. Bickley (Eds.). *Canadian Bates' guide to health assessment for nurses* (1st ed., p. 520). Philadelphia, PA: Wolters Kluwer Health/Lippincott Williams & Wilkins.

Examples of Questions to Assess Symptoms/Signs	Rationale/Unexpected Findings
Indigestion	
Have you had heartburn?	Heartburn suggests gastric acid reflux.
Do you have excessive gas? Belching? Abdominal bloating? Or distention?	Increased intake of gas-forming foods, chewing gum, carbonated beverages, and changes in motility can cause gas.
Have you noticed an unpleasant fullness after meals?	Decreased gastric emptying, outlet obstruction, and cancer can cause fullness.

Examples of Questions to Assess Symptoms/Signs	Rationale/Unexpected Findings

Anorexia

How is your appetite?

Loss of appetite can be related to stress, difficulty with ingestion, socioeconomic issues, age-related issues, or dementia.

Do you deliberately eat small meals? Have you ever vomited after eating?

With **anorexia nervosa,** food intake is intentionally limited.

Nausea, Vomiting, Hematemesis

Do you have nausea? Or vomiting?

Bulimia is a disease in which the patient deliberately vomits after eating.

Have you ever vomited blood?

Nausea and vomiting may result from infections, food poisoning, or stress. Hematemesis may indicate gastric ulcer, gastritis, or esophageal varices from alcoholic cirrhosis.

Abdominal Pain

Do you have any pain or discomfort? See detailed analysis of RUQ pain above for questions about location, quality, intensity, timing, associated symptoms, alleviating and aggravating factors, environmental factors, significance to patient, and patient's perspective.

Discerning pain characteristics can greatly assist in diagnosis by pinpointing the type of assessment and diagnostic procedures required:

- **Visceral pain** occurs when hollow organs are distended, stretched, or contracted forcefully. It may be difficult to localize. The patient may describe it as gnawing, burning, cramping, or aching. If severe, it may be associated with sweating, pallor, nausea, vomiting, or restlessness.
- **Parietal pain** results from inflammation of the peritoneum. It is usually severe and localized over the involved structure. Patients describe it as steady, aching, or sharp, especially with movement.
- **Referred pain** occurs in more distant sites innervated at approximately the same spinal level as the disordered structure (see Chapter 7).

Dysphagia/Odynophagia

- Do you have any difficulty swallowing or pain with swallowing?

Dysphagia may result from stress, esophageal stricture, gastroesophageal reflux disease (GERD), or tumour.

Change in Bowel Function

What was your usual bowel pattern before symptoms developed?

The nurse establishes the patient's usual pattern, which may range from several times a day to once a week. This sets a basis for determining any current constipation or diarrhea.

Constipation. What is the change from your regular pattern? Are there any changes in your diet? Medications? Or physical activity?

Usually functional constipation results from inadequate fibre and fluids in the diet. It also can result from medications such as anticholinergics or narcotics.

Diarrhea

- What is the change from your usual pattern?
- Is diarrhea associated with nausea/vomiting?

Diarrhea can result from an infection such as with *Clostridium difficile*. It also can be associated with food intolerances.

Jaundice/Icterus

Have you noticed a change in
- The colour of your skin? Or whites of your eyes (sclera)?
- The colour of your urine or stool?

Jaundice can result from obstruction of the common bile duct by *gallstones* or *pancreatic cancer*. Dark urine is from impaired excretion of bilirubin into the gastrointestinal (GI) tract. Grey or light stool is common in obstructive jaundice.

(text continues on page 614)

Examples of Questions to Assess Symptoms/Signs	Rationale/Unexpected Findings

Have you recently travelled to areas with poor sanitation?

Recent travel may indicate exposure to hepatitis A.

Have you had any recent exposure to blood or body fluids of an infected partner? Use of shared needles? Blood transfusion?

Exposure to blood or body fluids may indicate infection with hepatitis B or C.

Urinary/Renal Symptoms

Do you have

Many patients perceive these symptoms as abdominal in nature.

• Pain on urination or difficulty voiding (dysuria)?

Pain may be from infection or irritation of either the bladder or urethra. Women often report internal urethral discomfort; men typically feel a burning proximal to the glans penis.

• Urgency or frequency of urination?

Urgency may be from urinary tract or sexually transmitted infection.

• Lower abdominal (suprapubic) pain?

Suprapubic pain is usually from *cystitis*.

• In males, hesitancy or decreased urine stream?

Hesitancy may be from *benign prostatic hypertrophy (BPH)*.

• Increased production and passage of urine (polyuria)? (How frequent?)

Polyuria is a common symptom of *diabetes*.

• Frequent need to urinate at night (nocturia)? (How frequent?)

Nocturia may be from *BPH*.

• Blood in your urine (hematuria)? Painful or not painful?

Painful hematuria is usually the result of bladder infection in younger patients or renal calculi. Painless hematuria is common in older adults with urinary tract infections (UTIs) and patients with *bladder cancer*.

Urinary Incontinence

• Do you ever leak urine, especially with coughing or sneezing?
• Have you had times where you could not make it to the bathroom fast enough?

Patients need careful questioning on this topic, because they often do not volunteer this information due to embarrassment. It may be the result of urinary sepsis, pelvic floor disorders, or multiparity.

Types of urinary incontinence are as follows:

• Stress: occurs with coughing, sneezing, or increasing intra-abdominal pressure
• Urge: sudden urge and loss of continence with little warning
• Overflow: continuous dribbling or dripping and weaker urinary stream
• Functional: cannot get to toilet in time due to environmental factors or impaired health
• Total: inability to retain urine; ask also about bowel incontinence

Back (kidney) or Flank Pain. Do you have pain? Could you describe it? Prior to its development, did you have any burning? Urgency? Or bladder pain?

Renal calculi and *pyelonephritis* can be causes of flank pain described as dull, achy, and steady.

Ureteral Colic. Do you have severe cramps or pain in your flank? Is it associated with nausea or vomiting?

Obstruction of the ureters by blood clots or stones will cause a colicky, cramping type of pain.

Documentation of Expected Findings

Patient reports no change in appetite, no food intolerance, no excessive belching, no trouble swallowing, no heartburn, no nausea. Bowel movements are daily, brown in colour, soft; denies changes in bowel habits, no pain with defecation, no rectal bleeding or black tarry stools. Denies hemorrhoids, passing of gas, constipation, or diarrhea. Denies abdominal pain. No jaundice, liver or gall bladder concerns, no history of hepatitis.

Additional Questions	Rationale/Unexpected Findings
Women Who Are Pregnant Do you have heartburn? Constipation? Loss of urine? Or hemorrhoids?	Heartburn occurs in 30% to 50% of women who are pregnant. Bowel concerns such as constipation, incontinence, and hemorrhoids are common during pregnancy and postpartum. Women who are pregnant commonly have abdominal bloating and constipation. Approximately 30% to 40% have hemorrhoids. Symptoms to assess include pruritus, discomfort, and bleeding (Bianco, Lockwood, et al., 2009).
Newborns, Infants, and Children Is your baby breast or bottle fed?	Consider possible allergens in the formula or new foods. Encourage parents to add only one new food at a time to help identify allergens.
If bottle feeding, how does your baby tolerate the formula? What table foods have you introduced? How does your baby tolerate the food?	
How many wet diapers and bowel movements does your baby have in a day?	Early in life, feedings and diaper changes occur every 2 to 4 hours. As children grow and begin to eat solid foods, bowel movements decrease. Infants should have at least one bowel movement a day, more if breast fed.
How often does your toddler/child eat? Does he or she eat regular meals? How do you feel about your child's eating? Describe yesterday's eating, including meals and snacks.	Irregular eating patterns are common in young children and a source of great parental anxiety. As long as growth and development are as expected for age and nutritious foods are offered, reassure parents.
Does your child ever eat nonfoods (eg, grass, dirt, paint chips)?	*Pica* is the excessive ingestion of nonfoods. Most children attempt nonfoods at some time, but by 2 years, they should distinguish foods from nonfoods. Pica can be a source of *lead poisoning*.
Does your child have constipation? • If so, for how long? • What is the number of stools per day and week? • How much water and juice are in the child's diet? • Is constipation associated with attempts to toilet train? • What have you tried to treat the constipation?	Each child has his or her own typical bowel habits. Toilet training before a child is ready may result in the child withholding stool. Helping parents understand this may reassure them (van den Berg, Benninga, et al., 2006).
Does your child have abdominal pain? Describe what you have noticed and when it started.	This symptom is difficult to assess in young children. Vague abdominal pain may be associated with concerns in unrelated organ systems, such as *otitis media* (see Chapter 16). It may also accompany inflammation of the bowel, constipation, urinary tract infection (UTI), and anxiety.
For the child who is overweight • How long has your child been overweight? • At what age, did it first appear? • Were there any changes in diet patterns at that time? • Describe your child's current diet pattern. • Are other family members overweight? • How does your child feel about his or her own weight?	Reduced physical activity and food marketing practices contribute to the current obesity epidemic, as does intake of high-fructose corn syrup in drinks. Family history may contribute as well. Assess the child's body image.

(text continues on page 616)

Adolescents

What do you eat at regular meals? Do you eat breakfast?

What do you eat for snacks? What do you like to drink? How many soft drinks/juice servings do you have per day?

Adolescents assume control of their eating and may reject family values. The only control parents may have is over what food is in the house, although they should still supply nutritional information to their children. Fast food is high in fat, calories, and salt and has little fibre.

What is your exercise pattern?

Boys need to eat an average of 3,000 cal/d to maintain weight and continue growth. Girls require 2,200 cal/d. The number of calories may be higher if adolescents participate in sports or regular exercise.

If weight is less than body requirements

How much weight have you lost? Did you lose it by diet, exercise? How do you feel? Tired, hungry? How do you think your body looks? What is your activity pattern? Is the weight loss associated with any other body change (eg, menstrual irregularity)? What do your parents say about your eating? Your friends?

Screen any extremely thin adolescent (male or female) for *anorexia nervosa.* This serious psychosocial disorder involves loss of appetite, voluntary starvation, and excessive weight loss. People with anorexia may augment weight loss with purging (self-induced vomiting) and use of laxatives and diuretics. Denial of these feelings is common. Though these patients are thin, their distorted body image makes them think they are fat or disgusting. Patients with anorexia may have healthy activity patterns or exercise to the extreme. Absence of menstrual periods (amenorrhea) is common in young women with anorexia. Eating disorders in teens constitute a family concern and warrant referral to a psychologist or an eating-disorder specialist.

Older Adults

How do you acquire your groceries? Prepare meals?

Assess for risks for nutritional deficits: limited access to a grocery store, reduced income, compromised cooking facilities, physical disability (impaired vision, decreased mobility, decreased strength, neurological deficit).

Do you eat alone or with others?

Risks for nutritional deficit include living alone, not bothering or remembering to prepare meals, social isolation, and depression.

Describe your meals and snacks yesterday, starting with breakfast (see Chapter 8).
• Do you have any trouble swallowing these foods?
• What do you do right after eating—walk, take a nap?

A 24-hour recall may not provide sufficient information, because daily patterns may vary. Attempt to get a weeklong diary of food intake. Food pattern may vary based on income.

How often do you move your bowels? Describe what constipation means to you.
• How much liquid do you drink daily? What types of drinks?
• How much fibre is in your diet? How many fresh fruits and vegetables?
• Do you take anything for constipation? How often do you use it?

Many older adults have concerns about their bowel function. As the gastrointestinal (GI) system changes with age, appetite may decrease, and constipation may result.

What medications do you take daily?

Consider GI side effects (eg, nausea, vomiting, anorexia, dry mouth) of all prescribed and OTC medications that the patient may take.

🌐 Cultural Considerations

Additional Questions	Rationale/Unexpected Findings
African Canadians Do you or your parents have sickle-cell disease or trait?	Sickle-cell anemia has an autosomal recessive inheritance pattern. Signs begin to emerge in the second 6 months of life and include jaundice and splenomegaly.
Do you or does anyone in your family have glucose-6-phosphate dehydrogenase (G6PD) deficiency?	G6PD is a drug-induced anemia caused by a genetic lack of the G6PD enzyme in red blood cells. It is an X-linked recessive trait. Aspirin-containing medications, sulfonamides, antimalarials, and fava beans can trigger hemolysis.
Asian Canadians Do you have heartburn? Indigestion? Anorexia? Or unplanned weight loss? Any family history of gastric cancer?	Incidence of gastric and primary liver cancers is increased in Asians. Because heartburn and indigestion are often treated with OTC preparations, patients may not report that they use them. Such medications may cover symptoms, leading to a delay in diagnosis until metastasis has occurred (Madanick, Shaheen, et al., 2009).
Canadians of Jewish Descent Do you have any personal or family history of ulcerative colitis or Crohn's disease?	Inflammatory bowel diseases (IBDs) have a familial predisposition (Snapper, Podolsky, et al., 2009).
Do you have any personal or family history of lactose intolerance?	Lactose intolerance may accompany the IBDs and cloud the history. Some degree of lactose intolerance is found in approximately two thirds of the world's population.
Canadians of Mediterranean Descent Do you or does anyone in your family have lactose intolerance?	There is a familial predisposition.
Do you or does anyone in your family have chronic anemia or thalassemia?	The thalassemias are a group of hereditary, hypochromic anemias and are most prevalent in people of Mediterranean descent. They are often confused with iron-deficiency anemia and lead poisoning but do not respond to iron supplementation. Minor pallor and splenomegaly may be present.
Aboriginal Canadians • Do you have diabetes?	Type 2 diabetes is more prevalent in the Aboriginal populations.

The nurse's role in subjective data collection is to gather information to improve the patient's health status and to help determine the cause of the patient's current symptoms. Remember Mr. Barry Renaud, introduced at the beginning of this chapter. This 41-year-old man was admitted to the hospital with coffee grounds vomitus related to his ongoing alcohol intake. In addition to obtaining an abdominal assessment, the nurse will assess Mr. Renaud's needs to begin establishing a discharge plan.

Nurse: Hi, Mr. Renaud. We need to start thinking about where you're going after discharge. What are your thoughts?

Mr. Renaud: I don't want to go back to that dirty mission. I would rather be on the streets than in there.

Nurse: Tell me more about that (pause).

Mr. Renaud: The people are too rough, and I always get bedbugs there.

Nurse: It sounds like you don't like the mission, but we want you to have a safe place to go (pause).

Mr. Renaud: I don't want to go there, but I've lost everything to alcohol—my wife, my kids, my house.

Nurse: Your drinking has created some difficulties for you. How are you feeling about quitting?

Mr. Renaud: I've tried before, but it doesn't work.

Nurse: It's hard making a change. If you think that you're ready to try again, I could talk with a social worker about finding a rehab placement for you.

Critical Thinking Challenge

- Consider the questioning regarding alcohol use. What therapeutic communication skills did the nurse use?
- How might your life experiences influence your attitude toward Mr. Renaud?
- How does a nurse address the issue of homelessness?
- How might your values influence the patient assessment?

Objective Data Collection

Equipment

- Stethoscope
- Measuring tape or ruler
- Pen or marker
- Alcohol wipes
- Disposable nonlatex gloves (in case of lesions or exudates)
- Reflex hammer or tongue blade to ascertain abdominal reflexes
- Pillow placed under the knees to relax the abdominal musculature

Promoting Patient Comfort, Dignity, and Safety

Make sure the environment is warm and private. Adequate lighting is essential. Have the patient empty the bladder before the assessment. He or she should lie supine with the arms at the sides. Using a sheet for draping, cover the breasts and genitalia, exposing the entire abdomen from above the xiphoid process to the symphysis pubis. Be sure to explain what you are doing and to perform the assessment systematically, slowly, and without quick movements. Throughout, observe the patient's face for signs of discomfort. Distract the patient with questions or conversation to avoid tensing of the abdominal musculature, which will make the assessment more difficult and the findings obscure. Examine any areas of pain or discomfort last.

Clinical Significance 22-1

The order of assessment of the abdomen is different from previous systems. Inspection is followed by auscultation for bowel sounds *before* percussion and palpation. Failure to adhere to this order may result in the alteration of bowel sounds from either percussion or palpation, leading to inaccurate findings.

Techniques and Expected Findings	Rationale/Unexpected Findings

Inspection

Inspect the abdomen. Look at the condition of the skin and umbilicus. Look at the abdomen for contour, peristaltic waves, and pulsations (Fig. 22-5). Bend down or sit to look at the abdomen tangentially and horizontally. Tangential lighting may help with visualization. Inspect for size, shape, and symmetry. Are there visible organs or masses? Note whether the umbilicus is inverted or everted and its position. Observe for inflammation or bulges suggesting a hernia. Inspect from different angles to evaluate colour, surface characteristics, contour, and surface movements. Note visible veins on the abdomen. Have the patient take a deep breath and bear down to determine any hernias or organomegaly.

Unexpected skin findings include scars, striae, and veins. The umbilicus may have a hernia or inflammation.

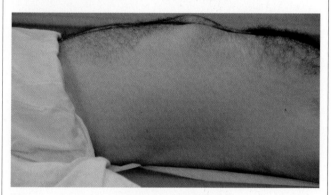

Figure 22-5 Inspecting the abdomen.

Assess for distention. If present, determine if it is generalized or only in one area. Ask the patient if the abdomen looks or feels different than usual. Inspect for any visible aortic pulsations, peristalsis, and respiratory pattern. Evaluate for ascites (fluid in peritoneal cavity).

Several simultaneous conditions can cause distention (see Table 22-4 at end of chapter for unexpected findings). Consider all possible contributory factors. Unexpected contours include bulging flanks, suprapubic bulge of full bladder, enlarged liver or spleen, or a tumour. A peristaltic wave may indicate gastrointestinal (GI) obstruction. It may be an expected finding in thin patients. Pulsation of the aorta may be increased and lateralized in an abdominal aortic aneurysm (AAA).

Urine. *Usual appearance of urine is clear and light yellow.*

Cloudy urine may indicate a urinary tract infection (UTI). Sediment may indicate kidney disease. Blood can be caused from renal injury, renal disease, or trauma to a catheter. Dark urine may be from dehydration.

Emesis. *There is no emesis.*

Medications or diseases may cause emesis. Green emesis usually results from reduced peristalsis with irritation. Coffee ground emesis is digested blood; bloody emesis is an active bleed with undigested blood.

Stool. *Stool is soft and light brown.*

Foul-smelling stool may be from Clostridium difficile. This bacterial infection leads to very liquid and light brown stool. Dark stool can be from iron supplements or digested blood. Currant-jelly stool is noted with partially digested blood from GI bleeding.

(text continues on page 620)

Auscultation

Bowel Sounds. Auscultate all four quadrants for bowel sounds. Begin by placing the warmed diaphragm of the stethoscope gently in one quadrant (Fig. 22-6). It is recommended to start at the point of the ileocecal valve, slightly right and below the umbilicus, and proceed clockwise. This is a very active area of bowel sounds. Bowel sounds are high-pitched gurgles or clicks that last from one to several seconds. *There are 5 to 30 sounds/min or one sound every 5 to 15 seconds in the average adult. Sounds indicate bowel motility and peristalsis. If no sounds are audible, listen for up to 5 minutes.* After timing the sounds in the right lower quadrant (RLQ), listen to the other quadrants. Occasionally you may hear the prolonged gurgles of borborygmi or "stomach growling."

Bowel sounds increase and decrease and indicate GI motility. They may be hyperactive at a point above a partial bowel obstruction and decreased or nonexistent below the point of obstruction. Increased bowel sounds occur with diarrhea and early intestinal obstruction. Decreased bowel sounds occur with *a dynamic ileus* and *peritonitis.* High-pitched, tinkling bowel sounds indicate intestinal fluid, air under tension in a dilated bowel, and inadequate bowel sounds. High-pitched, rushing sounds indicate partial intestinal obstruction. See Table 22-4 at end of chapter.

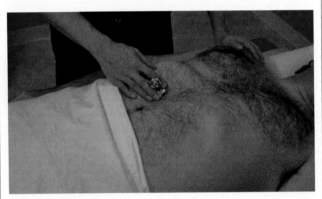

Figure 22-6 Auscultating the abdomen.

Vascular Sounds. Auscultate all four quadrants for vascular sounds. They are best heard with the bell of the stethoscope and include **bruits,** venous hums, and **friction rubs.**

Listen over the aorta in the epigastric region and over the renal and iliac arteries for bruits (Fig. 22-7). This is especially important if the patient has high blood pressure (BP). Bruits confined to systole are relatively common and may not signify an occluded vessel.

Bruits sound like a swishing sound, which indicates turbulent blood flow from constriction or dilation of a tortuous vessel. Bruits in the hepatic area suggest *liver cancer* or alcoholic *hepatitis.* Bruits over the aorta or renal arteries suggest partial obstruction of the aorta or renal artery.

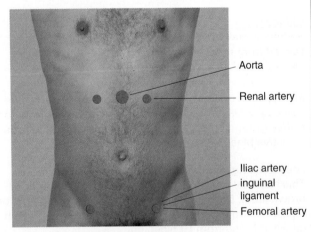

Figure 22-7 Site for auscultating for bruits.

In the epigastric region, near the liver and over the umbilicus, venous hums are heard best (Fig. 22-8).

Venous hums are a soft-pitched humming noise with a systolic and diastolic component. They indicate partial obstruction of an artery and reduced blood flow to the organ.

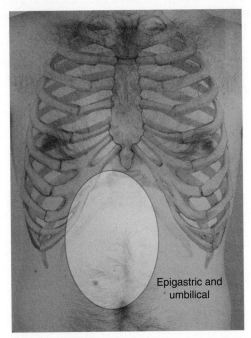

Epigastric and umbilical

Figure 22-8 Site for auscultating for venous hums.

Clinical Significance 22-2

Venous hums are an expected finding in children and women who are pregnant.

Lastly, auscultate over the liver and spleen for friction rubs (Fig. 22-9).

Friction rubs are grating sounds (like two pieces of leather rubbing together) that increase with inspiration. They may indicate a *liver tumour, splenic infarction,* or *peritoneal inflammation.*

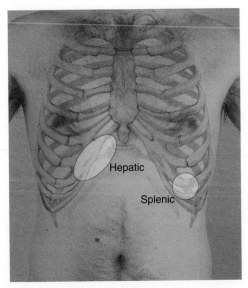

Hepatic

Splenic

Figure 22-9 Site for auscultating for friction rubs.

(text continues on page 622)

Percussion

Percussion is used to determine organ size and tenderness. It also detects any fluid, air, or masses in the abdominal cavity.

Pain when coughing or with light percussion suggests peritoneal inflammation and can indicate a ruptured viscous in the area of the pain, *appendicitis* in the RLQ, diverticulitis in the left lower quadrant (LLQ), *cholecystitis* in the RUQ, or *cystitis* over the symphysis pubis.

Dullness may be heard over organs, masses, or fluid, such as ascites, GI obstruction, pregnant uterus, and an ovarian tumour (see Table 22-4 at end of chapter).

Percuss all four quadrants, listening carefully for tympany or dullness. Watch the patient's face for nonverbal reactions of discomfort. Ask the patient if there is abdominal pain or tenderness. If an area is painful, ask the patient to point to the area and cough and determine where the cough produces pain, and then lightly percuss that area last. Try to localize the pain as accurately as possible.

Expected percussion findings include dullness over the liver in the RUQ and hollow tympanic notes in the left upper quadrant (LUQ) over the gastric bubble. Over most of the abdomen, tympanic sounds should be heard, indicating the presence of gas; however, scattered areas of dullness because of fluid or feces are typical.

Kidneys. Fingertip pressure may be enough to elicit kidney tenderness. If not, kidney tenderness is assessed by fist or blunt percussion at the costovertebral angle (CVA) posteriorly. (The CVA is where the rib cage meets the spine.) With the patient sitting, place the ball of your nondominant hand over the CVA and hit that hand with the ulnar surface of the fist of your dominant hand (Fig. 22-10). Use enough force that the patient feels a percep-tible but painless thud. Repeat on the other side. *There is slight or no pain with fist percussion.*

Significant pain upon blunt percussion at the CVA is a positive sign and can be indicative of a kidney infection (pyelonephritis) or kidney stones, which cause stretching or inflammation of capsules surrounding these organs.

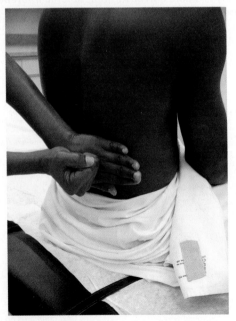

Figure 22-10 Percussing for kidney tenderness at the CVA.

Liver. A liver span test gives you an estimate of the size of the liver in the right midclavicular line (MCL). To assess the upper edge of the liver, start at the right MCL at the 3rd intercostal space (ICS) over lung tissue. Gently displace a woman's breast tissue as necessary. Percuss down until you hear resonance change to dullness over the liver between the 5th and the 7th ICS (Fig. 22-11). Place a mark where the dullness begins. To determine the lower border of the liver, start at the right MCL at the level of the umbilicus and percuss upward until tympany turns to dullness, usually at the sternal border, and mark this area with a pen. Measure the distance between the two marks.

Unexpected findings include enlarged liver (hepatomegaly) and the firm edge of *cirrhosis.* Span of liver is decreased when the liver is small or when free air is present below the diaphragm.

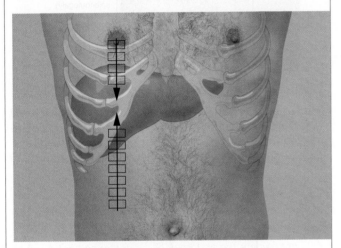

Figure 22-11 Percussing the liver.

Liver span is 6 to 12 cm. If the liver span in the MCL is >12 cm, measure it in the midsternal line. Expected midsternal liver span is 4 to 8 cm (Fig. 22-12).

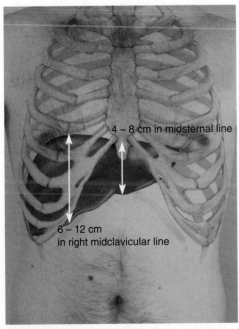

4 – 8 cm in midsternal line

6 – 12 cm
in right midclavicular line

Figure 22-12 Expected liver span.

(text continues on page 624)

Spleen. Three methods are used to assess the approximate size of the spleen:

1. Percuss from the left MCL along the costal margin to the left MAL. *If the nurse hears tympany, splenomegaly is unlikely.*

2. Percuss in the lowest ICS on the left anterior axillary line. Ask the patient to take a deep breath and hold it; percuss again. Tympany is expected, but with splenomegaly, tympany turns to dullness on inspiration.

3. Percuss from the third to fourth ICS slightly posterior to the left MAL, and percuss downward until dullness is heard. Dullness of the healthy spleen is noted around the 9th to 11th rib.

Bladder. Generally, the bladder cannot be assessed unless it is distended superior to the symphysis pubis. Percuss from umbilicus to symphysis pubis to detect dullness and determine how high the bladder rises above the symphysis pubis. *An empty bladder does not rise above the symphysis pubis.*

Palpation

Light Palpation. Both light and deep palpation are used to assess the abdomen. Begin with light palpation in all four quadrants for a general survey of surface characteristics and to put the patient at ease. Keep your hand and forearm in a horizontal plane and hold your fingers together and flat on the surface of the abdomen, press down 1 to 2 cm in a gentle rotating motion; then lift your fingers and move to the next location (Fig. 22-14). Identify superficial organs and masses and any areas of tenderness of increased resistance. Observe for nonverbal signs of pain, such as grimacing and guarding. *No tenderness should be noted.* If guarding is present, place a pillow under the patient's knees and have him or her take a few deep breaths. While the patient is concentrating on breathing, lightly palpate the rectus abdominus muscles on expiration. The patient cannot voluntarily guard this muscle during expiration.

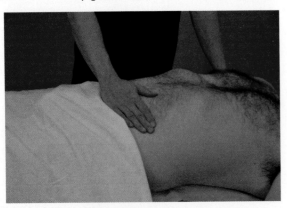

Figure 22-14 Lightly palpating the abdomen.

Dullness at the midaxillary line (MAL) is suggestive of splenomegaly (see Fig. 22-13 for indicators of the way a spleen enlarges).

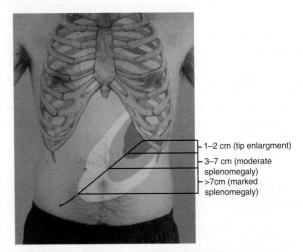

1–2 cm (tip enlargment)

3–7 cm (moderate splenomegaly)

>7cm (marked splenomegaly)

Figure 22-13 Indicators of splenomegaly.

Tenderness over the symphysis pubis may indicate a *UTI. Bladder distention may result from* an obstruction due to urethral stricture, prostate hyperpl*asia in men, medication, or neurologic disorders such as multiple sclerosis or stroke.*

⚠ *SAFETY ALERT 22-1*

Do not palpate the abdomen of patients who have had an organ transplant or of a child with suspected Wilms' tumour. Transplanted organs are often located in the anterior portion of the abdomen and not as well protected as the original placed organ. Palpating may cause the tumour to seed into the abdomen.

Involuntary guarding is a sign of possible peritoneal inflammation and should be carefully evaluated.

Deep Palpation. Deep palpation is used to assess organs, masses, and tenderness. To perform single-handed deep palpation, use the pads of your fingers and depress 4 to 6 cm in a dipping motion in all four quadrants (Fig. 22-15). *Tenderness may be noted in an adult near the xiphoid process, over the cecum, or over the sigmoid colon.* Bimanual deep palpation is necessary when palpating a large abdomen. Place your nondominant hand on your dominant hand and depress your hands 3 to 4 cm (Fig. 22-16).

If you find a mass, note its location, size, shape, consistency, tenderness, pulsation, mobility, and movement with respiration. Refer to Figure 22-1 for the location of abdominal and accessory organs. Size and changes over time offer insight into pathology and the extent of involvement (see Table 22-6 at end of chapter for gastrointestinal diseases).

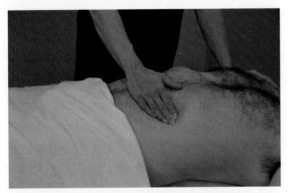

Figure 22-15 Single-handed deep palpation.

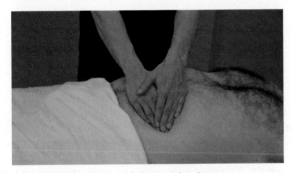

Figure 22-16 Bimanual deep palpation.

Liver. In preparation for palpation, instruct the patient to take a deep breath and percuss upward from the umbilicus to determine the lowest point of liver descent (the edge of an enlarged liver may be missed by starting palpation too high in the abdomen). To palpate the liver, place your right hand at the patient's right MCL below the border of liver dullness determined on deep inspiration. Place your left hand on the patient's back at the 11th and 12th ribs; press upward to elevate the liver toward the abdominal wall (Fig. 22-17). Have the patient take a deep breath.

An enlarged liver is palpable below the costal margin. Assess its size as described under "Percussion." An enlarged liver may indicate a *tumour* or *cirrhosis.*

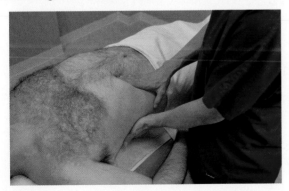

Figure 22-17 Pressing upward to elevate the liver.

(text continues on page 626)

Press your right hand gently but deeply in and up during inspiration. *The liver edge is palpable against your right hand during inspiration.* The edge of a healthy liver is usually soft, consistent, and regular with a smooth surface, and may be slightly tender.

The hooking technique is another method to palpate the liver. Stand at the patient's right shoulder, place your hands over the right costal margin, and hook your fingers over the edge. Have the patient take a deep breath and feel for the liver's edge as it drops down on inspiration (Fig. 22-18).

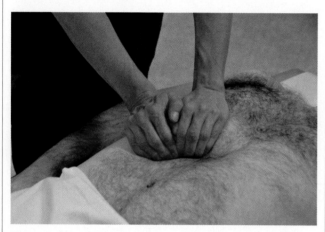

Figure 22-18 Using the hooking technique to assess the liver.

Spleen. To palpate the spleen, stand on the patient's right side. Place your left hand under the patient's left CVA and pull upward to move the spleen anteriorly (Fig. 22-19). Place your right hand under the left costal margin. Have the patient take a deep breath; during inhalation, press inward along the left costal margin and try to palpate the spleen as it comes down to meet your fingertips. An alternative approach is to have the patient turn onto the right side to move the spleen more forward (Fig. 22-20). *The spleen is not palpable.*

A palpable spleen is an unexpected finding. Note any tenderness, assess the contours of the spleen, and measure the distance between the spleen's lowest point and the costal margin. In an enlarged spleen, you can palpate the spleen tip. Enlarged spleen occurs with *mononucleosis, HIV, cancers* of the blood and lymph, infectious *hepatitis,* and red blood cell disorders of *spherocytosis, sickle-cell anemia,* and thalassemia.

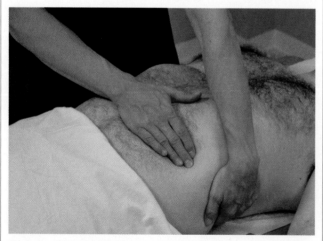

Figure 22-19 Placing the hand under the patient's left CVA to move the spleen.

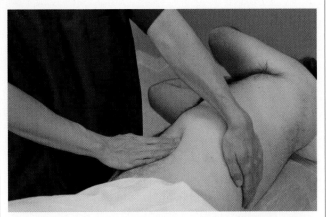

Figure 22-20 Palpating the spleen with the patient on the right side.

Kidneys. To assess the left kidney, stand on the patient's right side and reach across the patient, placing your left hand behind the patient in the left CVA. Place your right hand at the left anterior costal margin. Have the patient take a deep breath; then press your hands together to "capture" the kidney. As the patient exhales, lift your left hand and palpate the kidney with your right hand (Fig. 22-21). The left kidney is rarely palpable. If palpated, describe any tenderness, as well as its size and contour.

Kidneys enlarged from *hydronephrosis* or *tumours* may be palpable.

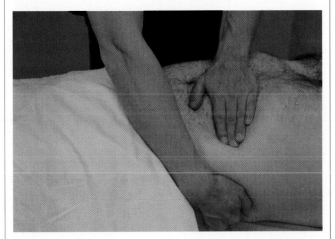

Figure 22-21 Palpating the left kidney (left-handed examiner).

To assess the right kidney (usually only if enlarged), remain on the patient's right side, and place your left hand on the right CVA and your right hand on the right costal margin. When the patient exhales, palpate the right kidney (Fig. 22-22). *It is common to be unable to palpate the kidneys except in slender patients.* The right kidney is lower than the left and might be palpated briefly.

(text continues on page 628)

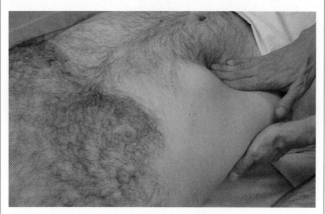

Figure 22-22 Palpating the right kidney.

Abdominal Aorta. To palpate the abdominal aorta, place your fingers in the epigastric region and slightly left of the midline. Press firmly and deeply. Palpate for aortic pulsations on either side of the aorta (Fig. 22-23). You can assess the width of the aorta by placing one hand on either side of the aorta. *Pulsations of the aorta are palpable; the aorta should measure approximately 2 cm.*

An enlarged aorta (>3 cm) or one with lateral pulsations that are palpable can indicate an *AAA (see Table 22-5 at end of chapter).*

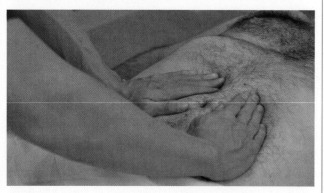

Figure 22-23 Palpating for aortic pulsations.

Bladder. If the bladder is distended, percussion is usually more comfortable for the patient than palpation. If palpation is performed, the dome of the distended bladder will feel smooth and round. *The empty bladder is neither tender nor palpable.*

A palpable bladder is either full or enlarged from an underlying mass arising in the bladder or pelvis. A tender bladder usually indicates a *UTI.*

Lymph Nodes. Inguinal lymph nodes lie deep in the lower abdomen and can be palpated using the pads of your fingers just below the inguinal ligament for the superficial horizontal nodes and along the inner aspect of the upper thigh for the superficial vertical nodes. They drain the exterior iliac, pelvic, and para-aortic areas. *Inguinal lymph nodes are nontender and slightly palpable.*

If nodes are palpable, note size, shape, mobility, consistency, and tenderness. Enlarged nodes suggest an infection in the regions drained, such as *orchitis* in males, an infection of the lower extremities, or metastatic disease from the anus or vulva.

Assessing for Ascites
A protuberant abdomen and bulging flanks suggest an accumulation of fluid in the peritoneal cavity. Assessing for ascites, which is detectable only after 500 mL of fluid has accumulated, is done in two ways: shifting dullness or fluid wave.

Ascites is found in patients with *cirrhosis* or primary or metastatic tumours of the liver.

Shifting Dullness. Shifting dullness can be detected by percussing dullness in the umbilical area when the patient is supine (Fig. 22-24), and then having the patient lie on the right side and percussing again (Fig. 22-25). You can repeat this manoeuvre by having the patient turn to the left side. In a person without ascites, the borders between tympany and dullness will stay relatively constant.

Dullness will move to the most dependent area and tympany will shift to the top.

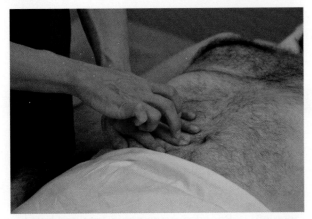

Figure 22-24 Percussing for dullness in the umbilical area with the patient supine.

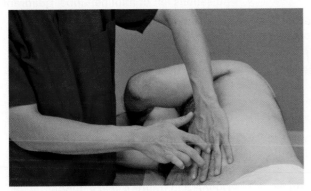

Figure 22-25 Percussing for dullness in the umbilical area with the patient turned to the side.

Fluid Wave. Have the patient or an assistant place his or her hand firmly down the midline of the abdomen. This pressure will help to stop the transmission of a wave through fat. Place your hands on both sides of the patient's abdomen and tap one side while palpating the other (Fig. 22-26). This sign may be negative in the early stages of ascites and may occasionally be positive in patients without ascites.

If ascites is present, the tap will cause a fluid wave through the abdomen and you will feel the fluid with the other hand.

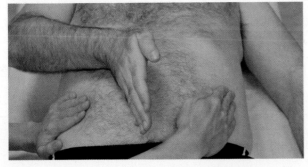

Figure 22-26 Assessing for a fluid wave to determine presence of ascites.

(text continues on page 630)

Eliciting the Abdominal Reflex

The abdominal reflex is a superficial cutaneous reflex measured by stroking the abdomen lightly with a tongue blade or the handle of a reflex hammer. The abdomen is stroked in all four quadrants toward the umbilicus. *The abdominal muscles contract and the umbilicus moves toward the stimulus. This reflex may be masked in the obese.* In this situation, use your finger to retract the umbilicus away from the side to be stimulated and feel for the muscular contraction.

The abdominal reflex is absent in patients with upper and lower motor neuron diseases (see Chapter 24).

Examples of Documentation for Abdomen Assessment

Area of Assessment	Expected Findings	Unexpected Findings
Abdomen		
Skin	No scars, old silver striae bilaterally	Pink-purple striae, purpura lower quadrants, purplish blue echymosis left upper quadrant (LUQ)
Contour	Flat, symmetric, faint aortic pulsations upper left quadrant	Rounded, asymmetric, localized bulge right lower quadrant (RLQ), marked aortic pulsations left of midline, upper quadrant
Auscultation—four quadrants	Approximately 20 clicks and gurgles per minute in RLQ, borborygmi upper quadrants, occasional clicks in left lower quadrant (LLQ)	Bruit left of midline in upper quadrant, absent bowel sounds, friction rub over liver
Percussion—four quadrants	Predominantly tympany, some dullness, all quadrants	Dullness over RUQ and LUQ
Palpation—four quadrants	Relaxed, nontender, soft all quadrants	Firm, boardlike, involuntary rigidity, rebound tenderness right midquadrant
Liver	Liver span 8 cm right midclavicular line (MCL), nontender, soft smooth edge 1 cm inferior to right costal margin	Liver span 14 cm right MCL, hard, rounded, irregular liver contour palpated 7 cm inferior to costal margin
Spleen	Tympany over Traube's space, tympany on inspiration in lowest left anterior axillary interspace, nonpalpable	Dullness in Traube's space, tender, palpable tip 1 cm inferior to left costal margin
Kidneys	Right and left nonpalpable, nontender bilaterally to fist percussion	Left CVA tenderness to finger pressure, palpable left kidney
Bladder	Percussed at level of symphysis pubis, nonpalpable	Percussed 3 cm superior to symphysis pubis, suprapubic tenderness
Aorta	2.5 to 3 cm wide, anterior pulsation	Over 3 cm wide, lateral pulsation
Appendix	Not identifiable	Localized pain right lower midquadrant, muscle rigidity, rebound tenderness, positive psoas sign, positive obturator sign
Gall bladder	Nonpalpable, nontender right upper quadrant (RUQ)	Positive Murphy's sign

Adapted from Harder, N., Skillen, D. L., et al. (2010). The abdomen. In T. C. Stephen, D. L. Skillen, R. A. Day, & L. S. Bickley (Eds.). *Canadian Bates' guide to health assessment for nurses* (1st ed., p. 541). Philadelphia, PA: Wolters Kluwer Health/Lippincott Williams & Wilkins.

Documentation of Expected Findings

Abdomen is flat with active bowel sounds, soft, and nontender; no masses or hepatosplenomegaly. Liver span is 6 cm in the right midclavicular line (MCL); liver edge is smooth and palpable 1 cm below the right costal margin. Spleen and kidneys not palpable. No CVA tenderness

Lifespan Considerations

Age-related changes that may be revealed during the physical assessment were discussed in the earlier sections on lifespan and cultural considerations. A brief review is presented here.

Women Who Are Pregnant

Assessing the abdomen of a woman who is pregnant can be very challenging. During pregnancy, abdominal muscles relax and the uterus protrudes into the abdominal cavity. The rectus muscles, which are aligned medially, separate, increasing the tendency for hernias later. The stomach rises from the increasing size of the uterus and may impinge on the diaphragm. Many women experience increasing heartburn and indigestion as the pregnancy progresses. The uterus compresses the bowels, which may diminish bowel sounds. The enlarged uterus leads to increased venous pressure in the abdomen. The appendix is displaced upward and laterally to the right, making it more difficult for practitioners to diagnose appendicitis. A dark line, the linea nigra, may appear midline from the symphysis pubis to umbilicus. The umbilicus may evert. Stretch marks (striae) may appear as the abdominal wall and skin stretch to accommodate the enlarging uterus (see also Chapter 27).

Infants and Children

The abdominal musculature is less developed in infants and children who also have a much larger liver proportionately. The liver may protrude >2 cm below the rib cage. The less developed abdominal musculature makes the contents of the abdomen more palpable and results in the expected presentation of a protuberant abdomen. The bladder is found above the symphysis pubis. This situation resolves in adolescence, when abdominal assessment findings become similar to those for adults.

Older Adults

Many elders are plagued with poor dentition, which may result in pain when chewing, dramatic changes in diet and weight, and long-term complications. Decreased production of saliva and stomach acid leads to changes in the digestive process. Motility and peristalsis decrease with age, which may result in more bloating, distention, and constipation. Also contributing is decreased muscle mass and tone. Fat accumulates in the lower abdomen of women and around the waist of men, making inspection more challenging and inaccurate. Liver size is smaller and the liver becomes less functional, resulting in decreased absorption of medications metabolized by the liver.

Cultural Considerations

Some health issues are more common in people of certain genetic backgrounds and ethnic groups. African Canadians more commonly present with sickle-cell anemia, glucose-6-phosphate dehydrogenase deficiency, and lactose intolerance. Those with sickle-cell disease may have splenomegaly and jaundice on examination. In sickle-cell crisis, patients may present with acute abdominal pain and vomiting. Lactose intolerance may cause abdominal cramping and diarrhea. A majority of the world's population has some degree of lactose intolerance. **Obesity,** defined as weight >20% of ideal weight, or >30 body mass index, is generally higher in visible minorities than in Caucasians. It is highest in non-Hispanic black women (see also Chapter 8).

GI cancers, especially stomach cancer, are more often seen in Asian Canadians. Patients with these illnesses present with long-standing heartburn, indigestion, anorexia, and weight loss. Asian Canadians have a higher incidence of infection with *Helicobacter pylori*.

Documenting Unexpected Findings

You have just finished conducting a physical assessment of Mr. Barry Renaud, the 41-year-old Caucasian man admitted to the hospital with coffee ground emesis. Review the following important findings revealed in each step of objective data collection for this patient. Consider how these results compare with the expected findings presented in the examples of expected documentation.

Inspection: Abdomen distended symmetrically. Umbilicus everted with significant ascites. Skin jaundiced with prominent venous network. Abdominal girth is 85 cm. Weight has decreased from 65 to 55 kg. Height 178 cm. Arms and legs lack muscle mass and tone.

Auscultation: Bowel sounds hyperactive in all four quadrants. No bruits present.

Percussion: Lower border of the liver percussed 4 cm below the sternal border at the right midclavicular line (MCL). Abdomen tympanic at the dome of the abdomen, flanks slightly dull.

Palpation: Abdomen firm and slightly tender with muscle guarding. Lower border of the liver palpated 4 cm below the sternal border at the right MCL. Fluid wave and shifting dullness are present. No masses present, liver smooth.

Lactose intolerance and IBD are more prevalent in Canadians of Jewish ancestry. The most common presenting symptoms are abdominal cramping, diarrhea, and rectal bleeding. Ashkenazi Jews have a greater incidence of colon cancer than other groups and are believed to carry a gene linked to the development of familial colorectal cancer.

Canadians of Greek and Italian descent more commonly present with lactose intolerance, thalassemia, and anemia. These illnesses cause abdominal cramping, **diarrhea,** jaundice, and splenomegaly.

Lactose intolerance is common among all cultural groups. The Canadian Digestive Health Foundation (2011) estimates that 7 million Canadians are affected by lactose intolerance. Research shows that people with particular genetic backgrounds are more biologically predisposed to lactose intolerance, including people of African descent, Hispanics, Asians, and members of First Nations groups (Montgomery, Grand, et al., 2009).

Alcoholism, liver and gall bladder disease, pancreatitis, and type 2 diabetes are more common in Aboriginal Canadians. GI symptoms in this group include jaundice, anorexia, ascites, abdominal pain, steatorrhea, weight loss, polyuria, polydipsia, polyphagia, and weakness.

Evidence-Informed Critical Thinking

The world of clinical decision making is uncertain. It is rare that the decision is absolutely positive or negative. Most situations involve a level of uncertainty for both health care professionals and patients. The health care team will seek out additional clinical information such as laboratory studies or radiologic procedures only if these methods can change what is done for the patient. This form of decision making is called "wait and see" or "watchful waiting."

The nurse explains clearly to the patient what constitutes a change that requires further inquiry. Symptoms may evolve and a clearer clinical picture may emerge, or symptoms may resolve without intervention.

Nurse practitioners and other advanced health care providers construct a differential diagnosis by grouping symptoms that are present or absent and weighing the probability that a condition exists against the penalty for being wrong. Each provider compiles his or her own data and then constructs an argument for a particular disease based on the facts. The strength of the case depends on how information is gathered and analyzed.

Clinical decision making initially involves a search for the simplest possible explanation. The next step involves asking what other explanation exists. Differential diagnoses should be logical and listed from most to least likely. The list should highlight conditions that cannot afford to be missed—those that would result in significant morbidity and mortality. Strange symptoms and findings more likely represent an uncommon presentation of a common health issue. The last step is asking what, if anything, can be done to rule out the "worst case scenarios" and how quickly.

Common Laboratory and Diagnostic Testing

Few specific laboratory tests focus on the abdomen and GI system. A complete blood count should be done to determine signs of anemia and infection. Iron-deficiency anemia in men, postmenopausal women, and elderly patients always warrants an endoscopy and colonoscopy to rule out GI cancer.

A basic metabolic panel (BMP) gives a good overview of various changes that can result from the malfunction of abdominal organs. Glucose level gives an indication of pancreatic endocrine function. The electrolytes Na, K, Cl, and CO_2 point to the state of the patient's hydration, which may be affected by vomiting or dehydration. The blood urea nitrogen and creatinine are indicators of basic kidney function. Liver function tests (including alanine transaminase [ALT] and aspartate transaminase [AST]) indicate the health of the liver. These levels do not change until there is significant liver compromise. To determine the exocrine function of the pancreas, amylase and lipase levels indicate the status of these enzymes, which are necessary for digestion and absorption of nutrients. These studies would need to be added to the BMP.

If ulcer disease is suspected, a breath test for *H. pylori* is indicated. It is imperative that this test be done before any acid reducers (especially the proton pump inhibitors) are ordered to assist with pain relief (Malfertheiner, Megraud, et al., 2007). If the patient has been taking OTC proton pump inhibitors, he or she must stop the medication for 2 weeks before the breath test will be accurate.

Several specialized tests are performed to identify specific concerns along the alimentary canal and its accessory organs. These tests are briefly discussed below.

Esophagogastroduodenoscopy

Esophagogastroduodenoscopy (EGD), also called endoscopy, determines the condition of the mucosa of the esophagus, stomach, and duodenum. The patient is usually given conscious sedation, and the back of the throat is numbed with a spray anesthetic. The scope is passed, and the entire upper GI tract is assessed through pictures taken and biopsies of any unexpected findings. EGD is usually ordered and performed for patients with suspected ulcer disease or cancer of the esophagus or stomach.

Barium Enema

Barium enema is a radiologic procedure in which the patient receives an enema of barium sulfate to outline the large intestine. This test helps determine if the patient has IBD or cancer of the colon. It can be done as single contrast with only the barium, or double contrast in which the barium is removed after the initial part of the assessment, air is inserted, and a closer look at the walls of the colon is possible.

Colonoscopy

Colonoscopy is done to determine the general condition of the colon and rectum and is used to determine polyps, ulcerations, and tumours of those entities. It is recommended as standard practice for patients older than 50 years as screening for colorectal cancer. The patient is given conscious sedation, the colonoscope is passed, and the entire length of the colon is visualized. Pictures of the walls of the colon are taken, and small polyps and tumours can be removed and biopsied as part of this test. This test requires preprocedure preparation of the bowel to remove all feces to enable the most accurate results.

Endoscopic Retrograde Cholangiopancreatography

Endoscopic retrograde cholangiopancreatography (ERCP) is performed to assess the ducts draining the liver and pancreas, to identify and remove gall stones in the common bile duct, and to diagnose pancreatic cancer. Similar but more extensive than the EGD, the patient receives conscious sedation, and the scope is passed through the mouth into the stomach and duodenum to the area of the ducts.

Computerized Tomography Scan

Computerized tomography (CT) scan is a radiologic procedure performed with and without contrast to identify soft tissue changes that may arise in the abdominal cavity. Cysts, abscesses, infections, tumours, aneurysms, and enlarged organs such as the liver and gall bladder may be identified in this manner.

Magnetic Resonance Imaging

MRI is a radiologic procedure performed in a large magnetic tube. It is used to evaluate the condition of organs, ducts, and blood vessels. Patients with pacemakers, ventricular assist devices, and joint replacements cannot undergo MRI, because the magnetic force can cause problems with the metal components of their embedded life-sustaining equipment.

Clinical Reasoning

Table 22-3 provides a comparison of nursing diagnoses, unexpected findings, and interventions commonly related to the abdominal assessment (North American Nursing Diagnosis Association-International, 2009).

Nurses use assessment information to identify patient outcomes. Some outcomes that are related to unexpected system functioning include the following:

- Diarrhea: Patient will defecate a formed soft stool every day to every third day.
- Constipation: Patient will maintain the passage of soft, formed stool every 1 to 2 days without straining.
- Incontinence: Patient will report relief from or decrease in the incidence and severity of incontinent episodes (Moorhead, Johnson, et al., 2007).

Once the outcomes are established, patient care is implemented to improve the health status. The nurse uses critical thinking and evidence-informed practice to develop the interventions. Some examples of nursing interventions for the GI system are as follows:

- Diarrhea: Consider inserting a tube into the rectum to drain stool and prevent skin breakdown.
- Constipation: Make sure to monitor last bowel movement and administer bulk, stool softeners, and laxatives as ordered.
- Incontinence: Teach patient to pace fluids and avoid fluids before bedtime (Bulechek, Butcher, et al., 2008).

The nurse then evaluates care according to the patient outcomes that were developed, therefore reassessing the patient and continuing or modifying interventions as appropriate. An accurate and complete nursing assessment is an essential foundation for holistic patient care. Even as a beginner, the nursing student can use the patient assessment to implement new interventions, evaluate the effectiveness of those interventions, and make a difference in the quality of patient care.

Table 22-3	Common Nursing Diagnoses Associated With the Abdomen		
Diagnosis and Related Factors	**Point of Differentiation**	**Assessment Characteristics**	**Potential Interventions**
Imbalanced nutrition, less than body requirement related to nausea and vomiting	Dietary intake that is inadequate in quantity, quality, or both for metabolic needs	Body weight decreased, body mass index less than expected	Provide nutritional supplements, for example, shakes. Administer antiemetics as ordered*
Incontinence related to disease processes	Involuntary passage of urine occurring with sudden desire to urinate (urge)	Voiding more than every 2 h while awake, awakening at night to urinate, voiding more than eight times in a 24-h period	Review medications that may contribute to incontinence, perform bladder scan to evaluate if residual is present, teach principles of bladder training

*Collaborative interventions.

Remember Mr. Barry Renaud, whose health status has been outlined throughout this chapter. The initial subjective and objective data collection is complete, and the nurse has spent time reviewing the findings and other results. Unfortunately, Mr. Renaud vomits bright red blood, so it is necessary to reassess him and document the findings. The following nursing note illustrates how subjective and objective data are collected and analyzed and nursing interventions are developed.

Subjective: "I just felt it coming on fast. I knew I shouldn't have eaten that food. Am I going to have to go back to the intensive care unit (ICU)?"

Objective: Vomited 250 mL of emesis with partially digested food and about 20% with bright red blood. Gastroccult tested positive for blood. Temperature is 37°C tympanic, pulse 124 beats/min and regular, respirations 24 breaths/min, blood pressure (BP) right arm (semi-Fowler's) 100/62 mm Hg, oxygen saturation 93%. Sitting in bed with head of bed elevated. Abdomen slightly tender, firm, and distended with hyperactive bowel sounds. Tympany present over most of abdomen. Patient states feeling nauseous, fatigued, and anxious.

Analysis: Fluid volume deficit due to gastrointestinal (GI) blood loss.

Plan: Saline lock intact. Notify the primary provider about emesis. Inform the patient about plans and assure that the nurse will be readily available if needed. Provide oral hygiene and hold food or fluids until discussed with the provider. Administer medication for nausea according to physician orders. Monitor vital signs.

Critical Thinking Challenge

- Why is information on the vital signs included as part of the nursing note?
- How has the nurse altered the assessment focus from the earlier conversation about discharge planning?
- What additional information might be documented on patient flow sheets?

Mr. Renaud, admitted 5 days ago with a gastrointestinal (GI) bleed, is having a new onset of bleeding. The new bleeding, drop in blood pressure (BP), and increase in pulse need collaborative interventions, so the physician needs to be contacted. The following conversation illustrates how the nurse might organize the data and make recommendations about the patient's situation to the physician.

Situation: Hello Dr. Plete. This is Kathy on 3 East. I'm taking care of Mr. Renaud, a 41-year-old patient on your team.

Background: He was admitted 5 days ago with GI bleed and has been stable for the past few days.

Assessment: He just vomited 250 mL of emesis with partially digested food and about 50 mL of blood; the gastroccult was positive. His pulse is 124 beats/min, respirations 24 breaths/min, BP 100/62 mm Hg (semi-Fowler's position), and oxygen saturation is 93%. Usually, his pulse is around 100, and the BP is about 150/90 mm Hg. He has a saline lock in but no intravenous (IV) fluids, and I just gave him the as-needed antinausea medication.

Recommendations: I'll see if that works in a half hour. For now I've asked him to have nothing by mouth and was wondering if you wanted me to start IV fluids. I can also call the lab to have them order a stat hemoglobin and hematocrit. He has three units of packed red blood cells on hold if they are needed. What would you like to do?

Critical Thinking Challenge

- Consider all the objective data that were collected. Why did the nurse omit some of the physical assessment findings previously documented in the SOAP (subjective, objective, analysis, plan) note?
- Which of the assessments are within the nursing domain and which are within collaborative practice with the physician?
- What further assessments will you perform, and how frequently?

Pulling It All Together: An Example of Reflection and Critical Thinking

The nurse uses assessment data to formulate the patient care plan for Mr. Renaud. After completing interventions, the nurse will reevaluate Mr. Renaud and document findings in the chart to show critical thinking. This is often in the form of a care plan or case note similar to the one below.

Nursing Diagnosis	Patient Outcomes	Nursing Interventions	Rationale	Evaluation
Fluid volume deficit	Maintain blood pressure (BP) and pulse within expected limits.	Monitor pulse and BP every 15 minutes until stable. Assess for signs of hypovolemia including postural hypotension, poor skin turgor, thirst, sunken eyeballs, and weakness. Also monitor intake and output and daily weights. Assess intravenous (IV) site for infection, inflammation, and infiltration.	Decreased intravascular volume results in decreased tissue oxygenation. Signs of hypovolemia may be noted with continued bleeding or insufficient replacement. The IV site may be a source of infection because the skin is not intact.	IV fluids started with normal saline at 100 mL/h.* IV site without redness, tenderness, or swelling. Patient placed on nothing by mouth. No further episodes of vomiting, no stools. BP 122/66 mm Hg, pulse 110 beats/min, skin turgor poor, eyeballs sunken, states feeling better.

*Collaborative interventions.

Applying Your Knowledge

Using the previous steps of clinical reasoning, organizing, and prioritizing, consider all of the case study findings woven throughout this chapter. When answering the following questions, begin drawing conclusions and see how the pieces of assessment must work together to create an environment for personalized, appropriate, and accurate care.

- What information from other body systems might be useful to assess? (Knowledge)
- How will the nurse prioritize health promotion and teaching needs? (Comprehension)
- How will the nurse organize the assessment during the shift? (Application)
- How does the nurse incorporate the different phases of the nursing process when performing the assessments? (Analysis)
- When Mr. Renaud's new gastrointestinal (GI) bleed is resolved, what recommendations do you expect the nurse, physician, and other members of the health care team to make as they continue to care for him? (Synthesis)
- How would you evaluate the success of health promotion and teaching for Mr. Renaud? (Evaluation)

Key Points

- Auscultation of the abdomen is always performed before percussion and palpation, which can alter bowel motility and diminish the nurse's ability to hear bowel sounds.
- The nurse assesses tender areas last to avoid referred pain.
- The elderly may be less likely to feel pain with abdominal conditions and do not always present with classic symptoms and laboratory findings. They are more likely to have vague, diffuse pain and tend to have a less acute presentation.
- Patients who present with fever, chills, leukocytosis, and rebound tenderness warrant a rapid assessment and referral to an acute care facility.
- Abdominal pain lasting >6 hours or pain that wakes the patient from sleep requires evaluation and possible referral.
- Hypoactive bowel sounds are common in patients with constipation and paralytic ileus.
- Hyperactive bowel sounds are common in patients with gastroenteritis and diarrhea.
- The location of the bruit sound can determine the cause of the bruit.
- Venous hums are continuous sounds found in the epigastric region and around the umbilicus and caused by portal hypertension.
- Eighty to ninety percent of GI diseases can be diagnosed by obtaining a thorough history.
- The liver takes up more space in the abdominal cavity of an infant and may extend 2 cm below the rib cage.
- As the fetus grows and the uterus enlarges into the abdominal cavity of a woman who is pregnant, the stomach rises up and may impinge on the diaphragm.
- Colorectal cancer is the fourth most common cancer in Canada.
- Food-borne illnesses affect the very young, the elderly, and immunocompromised patients more seriously.
- Seventy five to eighty percent of people who contract hepatitis C develop a chronic infection.

Review Questions

1. When performing an abdominal assessment, what is the correct sequence?
   A. Inspection, palpation, percussion, auscultation
   B. Palpation, percussion, inspection, auscultation
   C. Inspection, auscultation, percussion, palpation
   D. Auscultation, inspection, palpation, percussion

2. The patient reports a long history of changes in bowel pattern. Which is the best question to assess the change in bowel habit?
   A. How often do you have a bowel movement?
   B. What was your bowel pattern before you noticed the change?
   C. Is there a family history of inflammatory bowel disease (IBD)?
   D. Have any of your parents or siblings had cancer of the colon?

3. When palpating the abdomen, the nurse notices a mass in the left upper quadrant (LUQ), lateral to the mid-clavicular line (MCL). Which organ is involved?
   A. Liver
   B. Spleen
   C. Sigmoid colon
   D. Left kidney

4. What percussion sound is heard over most of the abdomen?
   A. Resonance
   B. Hyperresonance
   C. Dullness
   D. Tympany

5. The patient with a history of kidney stones presents with pain, hematuria, and nausea with vomiting. What assessment technique will elicit kidney pain?
   A. Rovsing's sign
   B. Psoas sign
   C. Fist percussion for costovertebral angle (CVA) tenderness
   D. Blumberg's sign

6. When auscultating the abdomen, the nurse hears a bruit to the right of the midline above the umbilicus. The nurse documents this finding as a bruit of which of the following?
   A. Right renal artery
   B. Right femoral artery
   C. Right iliac artery
   D. Abdominal aorta

7. The patient with a history of cirrhosis tells the nurse that his or her abdomen seems to be getting larger and that he or she has gained 20 lb in the last 6 months. How will the nurse determine whether accumulation of fluid (ascites) has contributed to the abdominal enlargement and weight gain?
   A. Listen for a fluid wave.
   B. Percuss the abdomen with the patient in different positions.
   C. Palpate lightly and note the movement on the surface.
   D. Inspect the abdomen with the patient in different positions.

8. The patient with a protuberant abdomen describes pain in the right upper quadrant (RUQ). Which sign would the nurse expect to be positive?
   A. Murphy's sign
   B. Psoas sign
   C. Rovsing's sign
   D. Obturator sign

9. Which assessment technique would best confirm splenic enlargement?
   A. Deep palpation under the left costal margin
   B. Fist percussion of the spleen with the patient in a sitting position
   C. Deep palpation over the RUQ with the patient lying on the right side
   D. Percussion to estimate the size of the spleen and gentle palpation

10. When documenting a finding in the region over the stomach and above the umbilicus, the nurse would identify the region as
A. epigastric
B. hypogastric
C. RUQ
D. LUQ

Canadian Nursing Research

Anderson, K. D., Baxter-Jones, A. D., et al. (2010). Assessment of total and central adiposity in Canadian Aboriginal children and their Caucasian peers. *International Journal of Pediatric Obesity, 5*(4), 342–350.

Bryant, H., & McGregor, S. E. (2008). Perception versus reality: Overcoming barriers to colorectal cancer screening. *Canadian Family Physician, 54*(4), 495–497.

Foran, A., Wuerth-Sarvis, B., et al. (2010). Bounce-back visits in a rural emergency department. *Canadian Journal of Rural Medicine, 15*(3), 108–112.

Mery, L., Desmeules, M., et al. (2007). Diet and vitamin or mineral supplementation and risk of rectal cancer in Canada. *Acta Oncologica, 46*(3), 342–354.

Montreuil, B., & Brophy, J. (2008). Screening for abdominal aortic aneurysms in men: A Canadian perspective using Monte Carolo-based estimates. *Canadian Journal of Surgery, 51*(1), 23–34.

References

Ahnen, D. J., Finlay, A., et al. (2009). *Epidemiology and risk factors for colorectal cancer.* Retrieved from http://www.uptodateonline.com.proxy.seattleu.edu/online/content/topic.do?topicKey=gi_dis/

Beck, I. T. (2001). Disproportion of economic impact, research achievements, and research support in digestive diseases in Canada. *Clinical and Investigative Medicine, 24*(1), 12–36.

Bianco, A., Lockwood, C. J., et al. (2009). *Maternal gastrointestinal tract adaptation to pregnancy.* Retrieved from http://www.uptodateonline.com.proxy.seattleu.edu/online/content/topic.do?topicKey=antenatl/10888 &selectedTitle=2~150&source=search_result

Bulechek, G. M., Butcher, H. K., et al. (2008). *Nursing interventions classification (NIC)* (5th ed.). St. Louis, MO: Mosby.

Canadian Cancer Society's Steering Committee for Cancer Statistics. (2011). *Canadian cancer statistics 2011.* Toronto, ON: Canadian Cancer Society.

Canadian Digestive Health Foundation. (2011). *Lactose intolerance.* Retrieved from http://www.cdhf.ca/digestive-disorders/lactose-intolerance.shtml

Canadian Liver Foundation. (2009). *Immunizing infants against hepatitis B is the most effective way of preventing long-term health complications and costs.* Retrieved from http://www.liver.ca/Media_Room/Press_Releases?Hepatitis_B_immunization_for_infants

Dietitians of Canada. (2010). *Increasing your fibre intake: Why this diet is important.* Retrieved from http://www.dietitians.ca/Nutrition-Resources-A-Z/Fact-Sheet-Pages(HTML)/Fibre/Increa

Eigenmann, P. A., Scott, H., et al. (2009). *Pathogenesis of food allergy.* Retrieved from http://www.uptodateonline.com.

proxy.seattleu.edu/online/content/topic.do?topicKey=food_al/7762&selectedTitle=2~100 &source=search_result

Gold, M. S., Aronson, M. D., et al. (2009). *Screening for and diagnosis of alcohol problems.* Retrieved from http://www.uptodateonline.com.proxy.seattleu.edu/online/content/topic.do?topicKey=subabuse/8392 &selectedTitle=17~112&source=search_result

Guerrant, R. L., Van Gilder, T., et al. (2001). Practice guidelines for the management of infectious diarrhea. *Clinics in Infectious Disease, 32,* 331–351.

Harder, N., Skillen, D. L., et al. (2010). The abdomen. In T. C. Stephen, D. L. Skillen, R. A. Day, & L. S. Bickley (Eds.). *Canadian Bates' guide to health assessment for nurses* (1st ed., pp. 509–561). Philadelphia, PA: Wolters Kluwer Health/Lippincott Williams & Wilkins.

Health Canada. (2007). *Diseases and health conditions.* Retrieved from http://www.hc.sc.gc.ca/fnih-spni/diseases-maladies/index_e.html

Madanick, R. D., Shaheen, N. J., et al. (2009). *Early gastric cancer.* Retrieved from http://www.uptodateonline.com.proxy.seattleu.edu/online/content/topic.do? topicKey=gicancer/6577 &selectedTitle=2~150&source= search_result

Malfertheiner, P., Megraud, F., et al. (2007). Current concepts in the management of *Helicobacter pylori* infection: The Maastricht III Consensus Report. *Gut, 56,* 772–781.

Montgomery, R. K., Grand, R. K., et al. (2009). *Lactose intolerance.* Retrieved from http://www.uptodateonline.com.proxy.seattleu.edu/online/content/topic.do?topicKey=gi_dis/13325&selectedTitle=1~77&source= search_result

Moorhead, S., Johnson, M., et al. (2007). *Nursing outcomes classification (NOC)* (4th ed.). Philadelphia, PA: Mosby.

National Alcohol Strategy Working Group. (2007). *Reducing alcohol related harm in Canada: Toward a culture of moderation.* Ottawa, ON: Canadian Centre on Substance Abuse.

North American Nursing Diagnosis Association-International. (2009). *Nursing diagnoses, 2009–2011 edition: Definitions and classifications (NANDA-I NURSING DIAGNOSIS).* West Sussex, UK: John Wiley & Sons.

Public Health Agency of Canada. (2009). *Healthy living: Hepatitis C.* Retrieved from http://www.hc-sc-gc-ca/hl-vs/iyh-vsv/diseases-maladies/hepc-eng.php

Snapper, S. B., Podolsky, D. K., et al. (2009). *Epidemiology and genetic and environmental factors in inflammatory bowel disease.* Retrieved from http://www.uptodateonline.com.proxy.seattleu.edu/online/content/topic.do?topicKey=inflambd/8588&selectedTitle=1~150 &source=search_result

Teo, E. K., Lok, A. S. F., et al. (2009). *Epidemiology, transmission and prevention of hepatitis B virus infection.* Retrieved from http://www.uptodateonline.com.proxy.seattleu.edu/online/content/topic.do?topicKey=heptitis/11026&selected Title=2~150&source=search_result

van den Berg, M. M., Benninga, M. A., et al. (2006). Epidemiology of childhood constipation: A systematic review. *American Journal of Gastroenterology, 101,* 2401–2409.

The Canadian Jensen's Nursing Health Assessment suite offers these additional resources to enhance learning and facilitate understanding of this chapter:

• thePoint on line resource, http//thepoint.lww.com/Stephen1E
• *Laboratory Manual for Canadian Jensen's Nursing Health Assessment: A Best Practice Approach*

Table 22-4   Unexpected Abdominal Findings

Common sites of referred pain. Abdominal pain may present with pain directly over the organ involved or the pain may be referred to a site where the organ was located in fetal development because the human brain has no felt image for internal organs. During fetal development, the organs migrate to their final location, but the nerves persist in the former location, and the patient feels the referring sensation. Pain in referred areas without representative history or other physical findings may not have an abdominal origin.

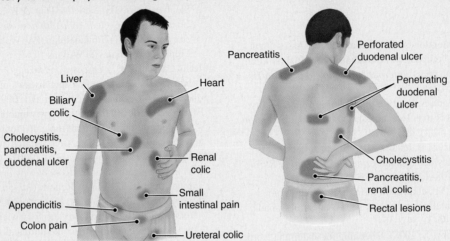

Abdominal distention. Abdominal distention occurs for a variety of reasons including obesity, gaseous distention, tumours, and ascites.

Finding	Description
Obesity 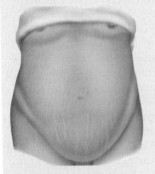	Obesity causes protuberance of the abdomen resulting in a thickened abdominal wall and fat deposits in the mesentery and omentum. Percussion sounds over an obese abdomen typically present as tympanic sounds.
Gaseous Distention 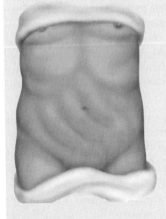	Gaseous distention is a result of increased production of gas in the intestines from the breakdown of certain foods and fluids. The average adult passes 500 mL of gas per rectum per day. It is also associated with altered peristalsis in which gas cannot move through the intestine. The altered peristalsis is seen in paralytic ileus and intestinal obstruction. Gaseous distention can be found in one area or generalized over the entire abdomen. Percussion sounds will be tympanic over the area of distention.

Finding	Description
Abdominal Tumour 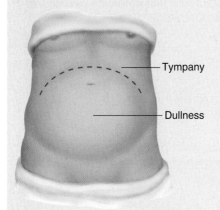 Tympany Dullness	A large abdominal tumour also produces abdominal distention. The abdomen over a tumour is firm to palpation and dull to percussion. Ovarian and uterine tumours are common types of palpable tumours in the abdominal cavity, despite their pelvic origin. As the organs enlarge from the tumour, their mass protrudes into the abdominal cavity.
Ascites Tympany Dullness Umbilicus may be protuberant Bulging flank	**Ascites** is the accumulation of fluid in the peritoneal cavity. The fluid descends with gravity resulting in dullness to percussion in the lowest point of the abdomen based on patient position. Changing the patient's position should move the fluid shift to the most dependent point. Ascites occurs in cirrhosis of the liver, heart failure, nephrosis, peritonitis, and metastatic neoplasms.

Unexpected Bowel Sounds. Auscultation of the abdomen results in bowel, vascular, and rubbing sounds. Bowel sounds may be hyperactive or hypoactive and occur in any quadrant of the abdomen. Hyperactive sounds are common in gastroenteritis and diarrhea. Hypoactive sounds are common in constipation and paralytic ileus. High-pitched bowel sounds with cramping are commonly heard in intestinal obstruction.

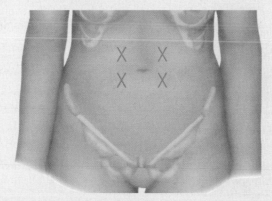

Unexpected Vascular Sounds. The most common unexpected vascular sound is a bruit. Its sound is blowing. Depending on location of the sound, the cause of the bruit can be determined. Bruits located in the midline below the xiphoid process are caused by aortic obstruction. Bruits located at the left and right costal borders at the midclavicular line (MCL) are caused by stenosis of the renal arteries. Other vascular sounds include venous hums and friction rubs.

(table continues on page 640)

Finding	Description
Bruits 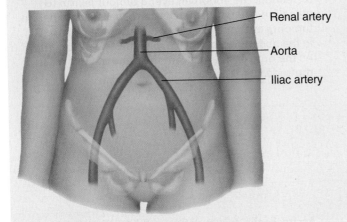	Bruits located at the left and right MCL between the umbilicus and the anterior iliac spine are caused by stenosis of the iliac arteries.
Venous Hums 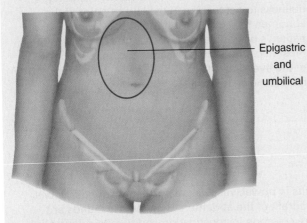	Venous hums are continuous sounds found in the epigastric region and around the umbilicus. They are caused by portal hypertension.
Friction Rubs 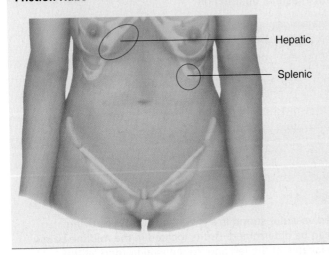	Friction rubs are harsh, grating sounds found in the right upper quadrant (RUQ) and the left upper quadrant (LUQ), over the liver and spleen. They are caused by tumours or inflammation of the underlying organs.

Abdominal Condition	Special Techniques/Rationale

Acute Abdomen

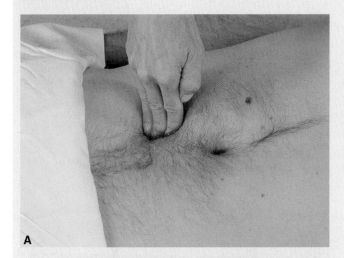

A

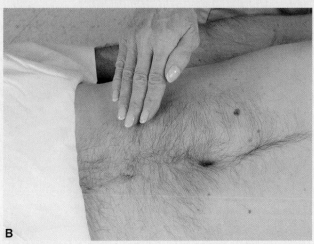

B

Apply light and deep palpation. A firm, boardlike abdominal wall suggests *peritoneal inflammation.* Guarding occurs when the patient flinches, grimaces, or reports pain during palpation.

Check for **rebound tenderness**. Press slowly and firmly with your fingers on the tender area (A) and then withdraw them quickly (B). If pain is induced or becomes greater when you withdraw your hand, this rebound tenderness suggests *peritoneal inflammation.*

Appendicitis

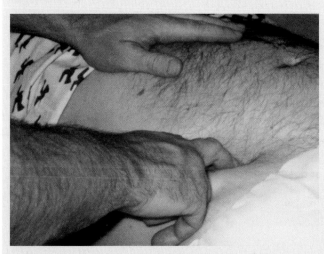

In classic appendicitis, the patient reports pain beginning at the umbilicus and moving to the right lower quadrant (RLQ). If you ask the patient to cough, he or she reports pain in the RLQ. The patient has local tenderness on palpation in the RLQ, at McBurney's point. A rectal examination, or in women, a pelvic examination, will reveal local tenderness, up into the right, especially if the appendix is retrocecal.

Other peritoneal findings include the following:

Rovsing's sign (shown left): Press deeply and evenly in the left lower quadrant (LLQ) and quickly withdraw your fingers. The patient reports pain in RLQ during LLQ pressure, suggesting appendicitis.

Psoas sign: Place your hand just above the patient's right knee. Ask the patient to raise that thigh against your hand and turn to the left side. Extend the right leg at the hip to stretch to **iliopsoas** muscle. A positive sign is pain in the RLQ with this manoeuvre, suggesting appendicitis or peritoneal inflammation.

(table continues on page 642)

Abdominal Condition	Special Techniques/Rationale

Appendicitis

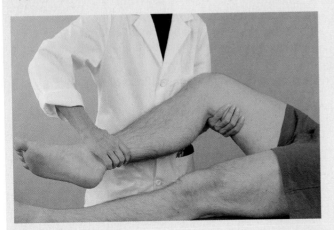

Obturator sign (shown left): Flex the patient's right thigh at the hip with the knee bent and rotate the leg internally at the hip, which stretches the internal obturator muscle. RLQ pain constitutes a positive obturator signs, suggesting an inflamed appendix or peritoneal inflammation.

Abdominal Aortic Aneurysm

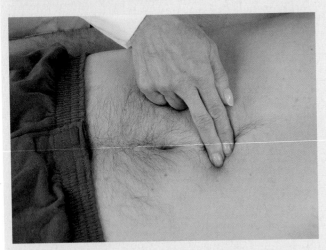

Patients describe boring, tearing pain, and referred pain. Auscultation reveals bruits or exaggerated pulsations. A mass may be palpable over the aorta. Femoral pulses may be diminished or diffuse. Patients may seem in shock: hypotensive; tachycardic; tachypneic; pale, cool, clammy skin; cool extremities.

Acute Cholecystitis

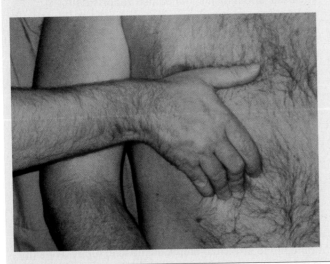

Auscultate, percuss, and palpate the abdomen for tenderness. Bowel sounds may be active or decreased. Tympany may increase with an ileus. There may be RUQ tenderness.

Assess for Murphy's sign by hooking your thumb under the right costal margin at the edge of the rectus muscle (as shown to the left); ask the patient to take a deep breath. Sharp tenderness and a sudden stop in inspiratory effort constitute a positive Murphy's sign, suggesting cholecystitis.

Disease	Signs and Symptoms
Cancer of the stomach	This form of cancer, difficult to detect on physical examination, is associated with epigastric distress, abdominal fullness, anorexia, and weight loss. In late stages, patients may have ascites, a palpable liver mass, and lymph node enlargement.
Cancer of the colon	Colon cancer occurs most frequently in the descending and sigmoid colon and rectal areas. Patients report changes in bowel habits, blood in stool, and smaller diameter of bowel movement. Pain may accompany late stages of rectal cancer. A palpable mass may be found on rectal examination or on deep palpation of the left lower quadrant (LLQ).
Constipation	Results from slow, delayed movement of feces through the intestine. Bowel sounds may be diminished on auscultation. You may be able to palpate feces in the LLQ with deep palpation. Palpation in general may be uncomfortable depending on the amount of feces and the length of time it has been present.
Diverticulitis	Diverticula are common outpouchings of the walls of the intestine in which feces may get trapped, causing inflammation, possible infection, abscess, and perforation. Patients present with severe pain (usually LLQ), diminished bowel sounds on auscultation, nausea, vomiting, and a long history of constipation. Peritoneal signs (see "Appendicitis") may be present if the bowel perforates. The patient may report that he or she had "left-sided appendicitis."
Hernias	Hernias may be found in the inguinal area, umbilical area, or along an old incision. Inguinal hernias are more uncomfortable with long periods of standing and diminish with rest. Patients may describe feeling full when straining to defecate.
	Umbilical hernias usually resolve in early life. Their protrusion worsens with crying. Incisional hernias become incarcerated or strangulated more frequently than other types. Incarceration involves the loop of intestine becoming "stuck" in the scar tissue of the incision. Strangulation is compromise of the blood supply to the loop of bowel, resulting in death of the tissue involved. It constitutes a surgical emergency.
	A hiatal hernia causes the stomach to move through the esophageal opening and rise above the diaphragm. Symptoms include acid reflux, esophageal constriction, and subsequent esophageal damage.
Inflammatory bowel disease (IBD)	This inflammatory condition involves all layers of the gastrointestinal (GI) tract and can occur anywhere from mouth to anus. Malnutrition and vitamin malabsorption are common. Abdominal pain is not relieved with defecation. Diarrhea and steatorrhea are common.
Crohn's disease	Crohn's involves the mucosal and submucosal layers of the colon. It increases the risk for colon cancer if not in remission after 10 years; it can also cause bowel perforation and toxic megacolon.
Ulcerative colitis	Colitis presents with cramping pain in the lower abdomen, relieved with defecation. Watery diarrhea with mucus in the stool and rectal bleeding are common. Surgery that removes the colon can cure colitis.
Irritable bowel syndrome	Also known as spastic colon, this condition has symptoms of diarrhea, constipation, or both. It usually presents as intermittent constipation, with hard compacted stools, and abdominal pain relieved by defecation. Many patients have a range of stools from pebbles to liquid over several days.
Liver failure	Liver failure can develop within 2–8 wk of onset of jaundice. It results from the acute onset of massive necrosis of liver cells, leading to sudden and severe impairment of liver function. Causes include acetaminophen toxicity, *viral hepatitis,* drug reaction, toxins (mushroom poisoning), *ischemic hepatitis, autoimmune hepatitis,* and the fatty liver of pregnancy.
Pancreatitis	This inflammation of the pancreas alters the flow of digestive enzymes to the small intestine. Symptoms include nausea, vomiting, weight loss, severe boring pain in left upper quadrant (LUQ), and referred pain to the back or shoulder.
Paralytic ileus	Lack of peristalsis, usually in the small intestine, may follow surgery, peritonitis, or spinal cord injury. The presentation is intermittent, colicky pain, with visible peristaltic waves on inspection and vomiting. Bowel sounds are absent. The abdomen is distended. Prompt attention is necessary to prevent bowel necrosis or perforation.

(table continues on page 644)

Disease	Signs and Symptoms
Peritonitis	This inflammation of the lining of the abdominal cavity presents with fever, nausea, and vomiting. Findings include abdominal pain of varying character, cutaneous hypersensitivity, abdominal rigidity, and guarding. Bowel sounds are diminished. Positive signs include psoas, obturator, Rovsing's, and Murphy's.
Pyelonephritis	Auscultate, percuss, and palpate the abdomen for tenderness. Bowel sounds may be active or decreased. Tympany may increase with an ileus (intestinal obstruction) there may be tenderness anteriorly over the affected kidney on deep palpation. Check for costovertebral angle (CVA) tenderness on the posterior thorax to be positive over the inflamed kidney.
Splenic rupture	This serious abdominal condition resulting in hemorrhage usually follows abdominal trauma, but can accompany mononucleosis from an enlarged spleen, which is subsequently traumatized. Presentation is severe LUQ pain, radiating to the left shoulder. Hemorrhagic shock can develop.
Ulcer	Ulcers form when gastric mucosa becomes permeable, protective mucus is reduced as a result of inflammation, or exposure to bile or other irritating substances (eg, medications, alcohol) is prolonged. *Gastric ulcers* present with gnawing pain, heartburn, anorexia, vomiting (possible hematemesis), eructations, and weight loss. *Duodenal ulcers* present with intermittent right upper quadrant (RUQ) pain 2–3 h after eating. Stools may be positive for occult blood.

Musculoskeletal Assessment

Learning Objectives

1 Demonstrate knowledge of anatomy and physiology of the musculoskeletal system.

2 Identify important topics for health promotion and risk reduction related to the musculoskeletal system.

3 Collect subjective data related to the musculoskeletal system.

4 Collect objective data related to the musculoskeletal system using physical examination techniques.

5 Identify expected and unexpected findings related to the musculoskeletal system.

6 Analyze subjective and objective data from assessment of the musculoskeletal system and consider initial interventions.

7 Document and communicate data from the musculoskeletal assessment using appropriate terminology and principles of recording.

8 Consider age, condition, gender, and culture of the patient to individualize the musculoskeletal assessment.

9 Identify nursing diagnoses and initiate a plan of care based on findings from the musculoskeletal assessment.

*M*rs. Gladys Crowfoot is an 82-year-old First Nations elder who recently fell, requiring hospitalization. Twelve days ago, she was transferred from the hospital to an extended care facility. Today, her temperature is 36.6°C orally, pulse 82 beats/min and regular, respirations 18 breaths/min, and blood pressure right arm (supine) 122/64 mm Hg. Current medications include alendronate sodium (Fosamax) 10 mg for osteoporosis. Supplements are a multivitamin, vitamin D 1,000 mg, calcium carbonate 500 mg, and magnesium 320 mg.

You will gain more information about Mrs. Crowfoot as you progress through this chapter. As you study the content and features, consider Mrs. Crowfoot's case and its relationship to what you are learning. Begin thinking about the following points:

- How are physiological and psychological data connected?
- What are some potential nursing diagnoses based on this patient's condition? Provide rationale.
- What will the nurse assess as part of a comprehensive musculoskeletal assessment? What other assessments should the nurse add?
- What are expected findings for Mrs. Crowfoot based on her age? What findings would be associated with osteoporosis?

This chapter includes an overview of the anatomy and physiology of the musculoskeletal system. It provides strategies and techniques for a comprehensive musculoskeletal assessment, including health history, physical examination (with specific procedures for joint conditions), and related laboratory and diagnostic tests. Physical assessment focuses primarily on the structure, support, and movement this system provides. A patient would undergo a complete musculoskeletal examination during the first visit to a health care professional or when a condition that involves all the joints is suspected. More commonly, patients undergo focused assessments on a specific area with injury or pain, such as a shoulder, knee, or elbow. Musculoskeletal disorders or injury are common throughout the lifespan, and an assessment of this system allows nurses to identify risk factors, unexpected findings, or dysfunction to plan appropriate health promotion, teaching, and intervention.

Anatomy and Physiology Overview

The musculoskeletal system is composed of the body's 206 bones, 600 skeletal muscles, and 360 joints. Types of connective tissues are **cartilage, ligaments, tendons**, and **fascia**. Muscles and bones facilitate movement through the joints (**articulations**). Connective tissues are located all around the muscles, bones, and joints and serve protective functions. The more elastic the connective tissue found around a joint, the greater the range of motion (ROM) in that joint. The specialized forms of connective tissue in the musculoskeletal system are described in Table 23-1.

Bones

The skeletal system is often understood as two skeletons: the **axial skeleton** (skull, vertebrae, ribs, hyoid bone, and sternum) and the **appendicular skeleton** (clavicle, scapula, upper and lower extremities, and pelvis). Bone is a living structure made up of a tough organic matrix strengthened primarily by deposits of calcium phosphate. There are two types of tissues: **compact bone** tissue (forms the shaft and outer layer of skeleton and the majority of bone mass) and spongy or **cancellous bone** tissue (makes up the bone volume in the ends and center). Compact bone tissues are stronger; cancellous bone tissues are lightweight and porous and create a circulatory-type environment for bone marrow, blood, and other fluids. Bones are classified according to shape as short, flat, long, or irregular. Short bones are space-saving bones located in areas requiring strength (eg, carpals). Flat bones have a broad surface to protect underlying organs (eg, skull bones) or provide a large surface for muscular attachments (eg, scapula). Long bones are basically hollow tubes of compact bone with widened ends containing cancellous bone. They have a shaft, body, and two extremities (eg, femur). Irregular bones often serve a specific function (eg, vertebrae). Long bones lengthen from the ends at areas called *epiphyses*. Other bones grow by endochondral or interosseous ossification centers.

Bones provide the framework for the body. They also protect internal organs, and are the primary site for storage and regulation of minerals, such as calcium and phosphate. Their marrow cavities serve as sites of **hematopoiesis** (the manufacturing of blood cells).

Muscles

The 600 skeletal muscles make up 40% to 50% of the body's weight. Muscles are classified as cardiac, smooth, or skeletal. This chapter includes only skeletal muscles, the largest of the muscle types. Skeletal muscles consist of fibres bound together in bundles and attached to bone by tendons. They contract and relax to move joints. Muscles give the body shape.

Table 23-1	Connective Tissues	
Type	**Functions**	**Example**
Cartilage	Allows bones to slide over one another, reduces friction, prevents damage, absorbs shock	Articular cartilage found on the ends of bones
Tendons	Connect muscles to bones	Biceps brachii tendon in the shoulder, which connects the biceps muscle over the head of the humerus to the glenoid fossa
Ligaments	Connect bone to bone to stabilize joints and limit movement	Anterior cruciate ligament (ACL) in the knee, which prevents lateral movement of the knee
Bursae	Fluid-filled sacs in areas of friction to cushion bones or ligaments that might rub against each other	Acromion bursa in shoulder to reduce friction during adduction
Meniscus	Cartilage disc between bones to absorb shock and cushion joints	The medial and lateral menisci in the knee, which cushion the tibia and femur
Fascia	Flat sheets that line and protect muscle fibres, attach muscle to bone, and provide structure for nerves, blood vessels, and lymphatics	The outer layer of fascia, which tapers at each end to form tendons

Joints

A joint (articulation) is the area where two bones come together. The function of joints is to provide mobility to the skeleton. Structures of joints are separated into two broad groups: **articular structures** (located *inside* a joint) and **nonarticular structures** (located *outside* a joint). Articular structures include synovium and synovial fluid, articular cartilage, intra-articular ligaments, juxta-articular bone, and joint capsule. Nonarticular structures include bursae, tendons, muscles, ligaments, fasciae, nerves, bones, periarticular ligaments, and overlying skin (see Table 23-1). Knowing the difference between articular and nonarticular structures assists the nurse to determine if a symptom/sign is arising from within a joint or from structures proximal to the joint. Joints may be classified by the type of cartilage involved:

- **Fibrous (synarthrotic) joints** are immovable, such as in the sutures in the skull.
- **Cartilaginous (amphiarthrotic) joints** are slightly movable, such as the costal cartilage between the sternum and ribs and the symphysis pubis.
- **Synovial (diarthrotic) joints** are freely movable, the most common type, and named for their major type of movement: ball and socket (hip and shoulder), hinge (elbow and knee), pivot (atlas and axis), condyloid (wrist), saddle (thumb), and gliding (intervertebral).

Usually one of the bone ends is stable and serves as an axis for the motion of the other. The joint shape and ligaments determine the movement the joint can make (Fig. 23-1).

Temporomandibular Joint

The **temporomandibular joint** (TMJ) is where the mandible and temporal bone articulate (Fig. 23-2). The TMJ is palpable below and slightly anterior to the tragus of each ear. It permits three movements of the jaw for chewing and speaking: opening and closing, **protrusion** and **retraction**, and gliding from side to side. The muscles for chewing (mastication) are the pterygoids (internal), temporal (external), and masseters (external).

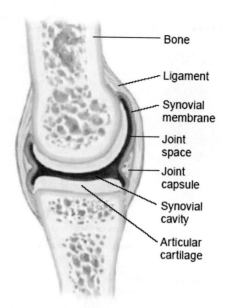

Figure 23-1 Example of a synovial joint.

Shoulder

The movement of the shoulder is complex and involves the articulation of the glenohumeral, sternoclavicular, and acromioclavicular joints (see Fig. 23-3). Because it is a ball-and-socket joint, the shoulder permits many types of movement: flexion, extension, abduction, adduction, rotation, and circumduction (see Tables 23-2 and 23-3). Four strong muscles (supraspinatus, infraspinatus, teres minor, and subscapularis) and their tendons, collectively known as the *rotator cuff*, control the strength and movement of the glenohumeral joint and surround the shoulder to support and stabilize it. Axioscapular muscles (connecting the trunk to the scapula) control movement of the scapula and include the trapezius, rhomboids, serratus anterior, and levator scapulae. The pectoralis major and minor and the latissimus dorsi form the axiohumeral muscle group and have a role in adduction and internal rotation. The large subacromial bursa protects the bones and ligaments

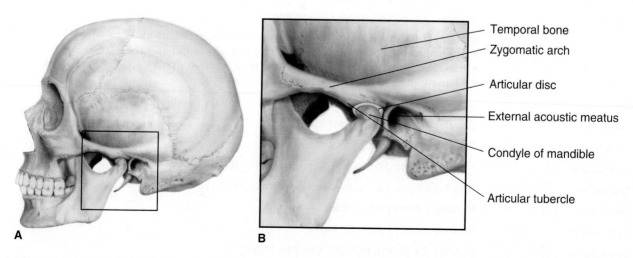

Figure 23-2 The TMJ. **A.** Location of the TMJ within the skull. **B.** Close-up view of the TMJ.

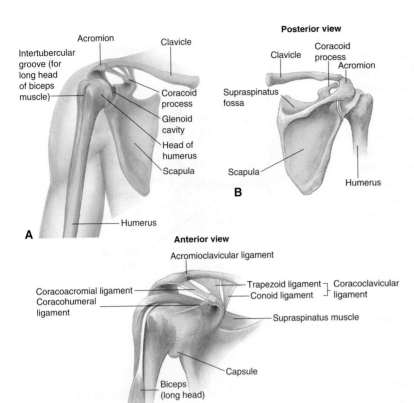

Figure 23-3 Shoulder. **A.** Anterior view. **B.** Posterior view. **C.** Ligaments.

Table 23-2	Terms for Joint Movement
Movement	**Description**
Flexion	Decreases the angle between bones or brings bones together • **Dorsiflexion:** Bending the ankle so that the toes move toward the head • **Plantar flexion:** Moving the foot so that the toes move away from the head
Extension	Increases the angle to a straight line or 0°
Hyperextension	Extension beyond the neutral position
Abduction	Movement of a part away from the center of the body
Adduction	Movement of a part toward the center of the body
Rotation	Turning of the joint around a longitudinal axis • **Internal rotation:** Rotating an extremity medially along its axis • **External rotation:** Rotating an extremity laterally along its axis • **Pronation:** Turning the forearm so the palm is down • **Supination:** Turning the forearm so the palm is up
Circumduction	A circular motion that combines flexion, extension, abduction, and adduction
Inversion	Turning the sole of the foot inward
Eversion	Turning the sole of the foot outward
Protraction	Moving a body part forward and parallel to the ground
Retraction	Moving a body part backward and parallel to the ground
Elevation	Moving a body part upward
Depression	Moving a body part downward
Opposition	Moving the thumb to touch the little finger

Table 23-3	Joints and Their Movements									
Movements	**Neck**	**Shoulder**	**Elbow**	**Wrist**	**Fingers**	**Spine**	**Hip**	**Knee**	**Ankle**	**Toes**
Flexion	X	X	X	X	X	X	X	X	Dorsiflexion	X
Extension	X	X	X	X	X	X	X	X	Plantar flexion	X
Hyperextension	X	X		X	X	X	X			X
Rotation	X					X	X			
Circumduction		X					X			
Abduction	X	X			X	X	X			X
Adduction		X					X			
Internal rotation		X					X			
External rotation		X					X			
Other				Supination–pronation of forearm	Finger–thumb-opposition				Inversion–eversion of foot	

of the shoulder during movement. The scapula and clavicle connect to form the shoulder girdle. The **acromion process** of the scapula is located on the lateral end of the bony spine of the scapula and articulates with the distal end of the clavicle. The greater tubercle of the humerus is the bony prominence lateral to the acromion; the coracoid process of the scapula is a few centimetres medial and slightly inferior.

Elbow

The **elbow** is the articulation of the humerus, radius, and ulna (Fig. 23-4). Its hinge action permits flexion and extension. The large olecranon bursa lies between the **olecranon process** and the skin. The olecranon process is centered between the medial and lateral **epicondyles** of the humerus. The sensitive ulnar nerve runs in the ulnar groove posteriorly between the olecranon process and the medial epicondyle. The median nerve is just medial to the brachial artery anteriorly. The radiohumeral and humeroulnar joints permit flexion and extension at the elbow. The **radioulnar joint** permits **pronation** and **supination** of the forearm.

Wrist and Hand

The wrist, or **radiocarpal**, joint is the articulation of the radius (on the thumb side) and a row of the eight carpal bones (ie, the proximal carpal bones). Its condyloid action permits flexion, extension, and ulnar and radial deviation of the wrist. The ulna has no direct articulation with carpal bones. The **intercarpal joints** are the articulation between the two parallel rows of carpal bones, and they allow flexion, extension, and some rotation. The bones of the hand (metacarpals and phalanges) are arranged linearly to form the smallest hinge joints of the body. The **metacarpophalangeal** and **interphalangeal** (proximal and distal) joints permit finger movement (see Table 23-2 and Fig. 23-5). The thumb lacks a middle phalanx; the joint between its phalanges is simply

the interphalangeal (IP) joint. Wrist flexion and extension occur because of two carpal, two radial, and one ulnar muscles. Muscles in the forearm permit supination and pronation. Extensor and flexor tendons insert on the fingers after crossing the wrist in tunnel-like tendon sheaths. The carpal

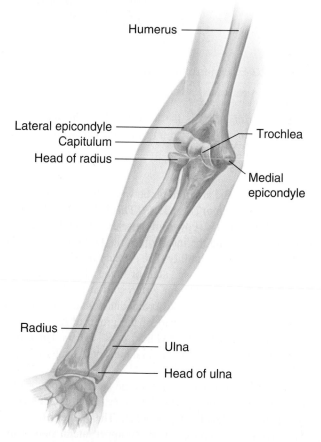

Figure 23-4 Bones of the left elbow.

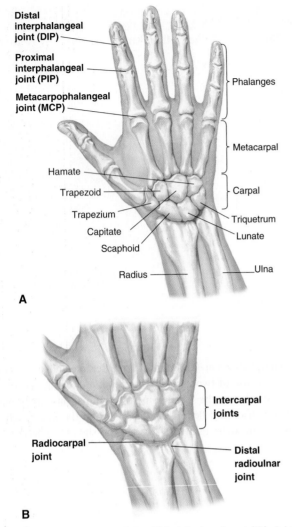

A

B

Figure 23-5 Bones of the **(A)** right hand and **(B)** right wrist.

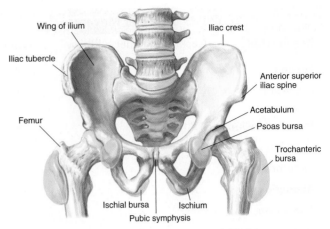

Figure 23-6 Anterior view of the hip joint.

Knee

The knee is the articulation of the femur, tibia, and patella (Fig. 23-7). It is the most complex and largest joint in the body (Tortora & Nielsen, 2012). Articulation occurs at the patellofemoral joint and two tibiofemoral joints. The medial and lateral **menisci** cushion the tibia and femur. The anterior and posterior **cruciate ligaments** cross within the knee to provide anterior and posterior stability and to control rotation. The medial and lateral **collateral ligaments** palpated in the depressions on both sides of the patella connect the joint at both sides to give medial and lateral stability and to prevent dislocation. Without ligaments, the knee has no built-in stability; without muscle or fat padding and because of the femur's lever action on the tibia, this joint is very vulnerable to being injured (Roach, Roddick, et al., 2010). Several

tunnel (anterior wrist) is the location of the flexor tendons for muscles of the forearm and the median nerve (Roach, Roddick, et al., 2010).

Hip

The hip joint is the articulation between the acetabulum and the head of the femur (Fig. 23-6). This ball-and-socket joint permits a wide ROM. Powerful muscles, strong ligaments, a fibrous capsule, and the insertion of the femur head into the acetabulum provide stability. The primary flexor of the hip is the iliopsoas; the primary extensor is the gluteus maximus. The muscles of the adductor group start at the ischium and pubis, and insert on the posteromedial femur. The gluteus medius and minimus are part of the group of muscles that abduct the thigh (Roach, Roddick, et al., 2010). Three bursae facilitate movement: the ischial bursa, trochanteric bursa, and psoas bursa.

The iliac crest is palpable from the anterior superior iliac spine to the posterior superior iliac spine. The ischial tuberosity is palpable when the hip is flexed. The greater trochanter of the femur is a depression on the upper lateral side of the thigh and is best palpated with the person standing.

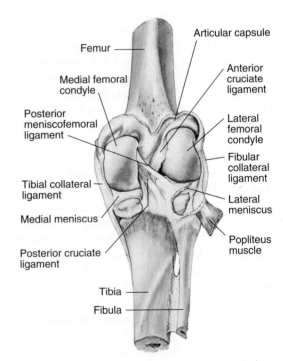

Figure 23-7 The left knee, posterior extended view.

bursae prevent friction; the most important are the prepatellar bursa, infrapatellar bursa, and suprapatellar bursa (Tortora & Nielsen). The tibial tuberosity is palpable on the midline of the anterior tibia. The lateral and medial condyles of the tibia are to the sides and slightly superior to the tuberosity. The patella (kneecap) is superior to the condyles and anterior to the articulating surface of the femur. The medial and lateral condyles of the femur can be palpated superior to the patella. Strong muscles permit extension at the knee (quadriceps femoris) and flexion (hamstrings).

Ankle and Foot

The ankle (**tibiotalar joint**) is the articulation of the tibia, fibula, and talus (Fig. 23-8). It is a hinge joint limited to **dorsiflexion** and **plantar flexion**. The medial malleolus (at the distal end of the tibia) and lateral malleolus (at the distal end of the fibula) are palpable prominences on either side of the ankle. Four strong ligaments extend from each malleolus onto the foot to provide lateral stability of the ankle: the posterior and anterior talofibulars, calcaneofibular, and deltoid. The Achilles tendon inserts on the posterior heel (**calcaneus**); plantar fascia inserts on the medial calcaneus.

The **subtalar joint** in the foot permits **inversion** and **eversion**. Weight bearing is distributed between the heads of the metatarsals and the calcaneus as a result of the longitudinal arch (an imaginary structure). The **metatarsophalangeal** and IP joints permit flexion, extension, abduction, and adduction of the toes. The gastrocnemius, posterior to the tibia, along with toe flexors permits plantar flexion. Dorsiflexion occurs because of the toe extensors and anterior tibial muscle.

Spine

The spine is a column of 33 vertebrae: 7 cervical, 12 thoracic, 5 lumbar, 5 sacral, and 3 to 4 coccygeal (Fig. 23-9). Intervertebral discs separate and cushion the vertebrae. The vertebral spinous processes are palpable in the midline of the posterior torso, with paravertebral muscles on either side. The spinous processes of C7 and T1 are more prominent. The inferior border of the scapula usually is between T7 and T8, and a line drawn between the iliac crests crosses L4. Skin dimples help identify the posterior superior iliac spines.

The vertebral column has four curves, best seen from the lateral view. The cervical and lumbar curves are concave

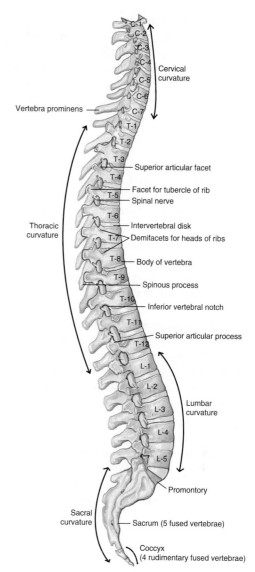

Figure 23-9 Sagittal view of the vertebral column (spine).

(inward), while the thoracic and sacrococcygeal curves are convex. These curves and the intervertebral discs allow the spine to absorb a great deal of concussive impact from running or walking and to flex and curve. At the lumbosacral junction, the spine becomes immobile. The anterior vertebral body is important for weight bearing; the posterior vertebral body encases the spinal cord.

Two large muscles, the latissimus dorsi and the trapezius, are attached to the spine and lie over small muscles between vertebrae and two deeper muscle layers. Many ligaments are part of an interconnecting system between vertebrae, spinous processes and vertebral lamina.

▲ Lifespan Considerations

While the human body is basically the same in all people, some changes occur with growth and development across the lifespan.

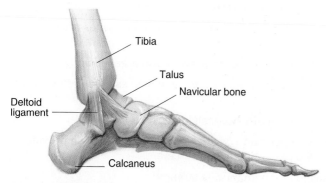

Figure 23-8 Bones of the ankle and foot.

Women Who Are Pregnant

Women who are pregnant have increased joint mobility as a result of the hormones progesterone and relaxin. Increased mobility in the sacroiliac, sacrococcygeal, and symphysis pubis joints of the pelvis contributes to changes in maternal posture. **Lordosis**, increased lumbar curvature, compensates for the enlarging uterus.

Infants and Children

The fetus forms a cartilaginous skeleton by 3 months, which calcifies and continues to grow into bone. Ninety percent of skeletal growth occurs by age 17 years, and peak bone mass occurs by age 16 years in females and 20 years in males (Osteoporosis Canada, 2011a). Bones elongate by increasing the cartilage at epiphyses (growth plates) at the ends of long bones. The cartilage later calcifies. This lengthening continues until the epiphyses close. Any injury to the epiphyses before closure may result in disrupted development and subsequent bone deformity.

All muscle fibres are present at birth, but lengthen throughout childhood. During the adolescent growth spurt, muscle fibres grow following increased secretion of growth hormone, adrenal androgens, and in boys, testosterone. Muscles vary in size and strength because of genetic factors, nutrition, and exercise. Throughout life, muscles **strengthen** with use and **atrophy** with disuse. Weight lifting can cause enlarged muscles, called **hypertrophy**.

Juvenile arthritis (JA) of uncertain etiology is estimated to affect 10% to 23% per 100,000 young people. A recent study in Québec revealed that the incidence of JA among youth younger than 16 years to be 17.8 per 100,000 (Feldman, Bernatsky, et al., 2009).

Older Adults

Aging affects all components of the musculoskeletal system (Table 23-4). Weakening of the skeletal structures, changes occurring in the joint cartilages, and weakened musculature contribute to increased immobility, pain, and fractures that can reduce independence at performing activities of daily living (ADLs).

Bone resorption occurs more rapidly than deposition, leading to porous and weakened bones. This loss of bone density is termed **osteoporosis** and leads to posture and height changes and fractures. An exaggerated curvature of the thoracic spine (kyphosis), decreased height from loss of water content in the intervertebral discs, and small compression fractures in the vertebrae occur. Some osteoporosis occurs in all people, but it is most evident in women with small bone frames. Women experience rapid loss of bone density for the first 5 to 7 years after menopause. After the initial rapid phase, bone loss continues, but slows. Men also experience bone loss but at later ages and much slower rates than women. Bone mass is related to genetic background, hormonal factors, physical activity, and calcium intake. Smoking, calcium deficiency, high sodium intake, alcohol intake, and physical inactivity increase bone loss. Resistance exercise and soy isoflavones decrease bone resorption (Valachovicova, Slivova, et al., 2004).

With aging and prolonged use, joints become less flexible because of changes in cartilage. The incidence of arthritis has grown significantly. It is projected that by 2031, one in five Canadians may be diagnosed with it (Public Health Agency of Canada [PHAC], 2010a). Although the incidence of age-related degenerative joint changes (osteoarthritis) increases with advancing years, about 58% of all types of arthritis occur in individuals younger than 65 years. Arthritis is the third most reported chronic illness among Canadians (PHAC).

Tendons and ligaments shrink and harden, decreasing ROM. Muscle mass also decreases as a result of atrophy and loss in size. Muscle mass decreases 3% to 8% per decade after age 30 years, with even greater muscle loss after 60 years (Volpi, Nazemi, et al., 2004). This involuntary loss of muscle function increases the risk of falls and disability in older adults. Exercise, strength or resistance training, and adequate nutrition are successful in improving muscle mass and strength.

Subcutaneous fat distribution changes with aging. Men and women usually gain weight after 40 years, predominantly in the abdomen and hips. After 80 years, subcutaneous fat

Table 23-4	Musculoskeletal Changes With Aging
Physiological Change	**Nursing Implications**
Decreased bone density	Encourage weight-bearing exercise to decrease bone loss.
	Teach patients about hazards to prevent falls because fragile bones break easily.
Increased bony prominences	Decrease pressure on bony prominences to prevent skin breakdown.
Cartilage degeneration	Encourage warm baths or showers prior to activity to increase blood flow and decrease joint stiffness.
Joint stiffness and laxity	Encourage active range of motion (ROM) in all joints.
	Assess the patient's ability to perform activities of daily living (ADLs); provide assistive devices to help the patient perform self-care.
Muscle atrophy	Teach isometric exercises to maintain muscle strength

continues to decrease, causing bony prominences to be more obvious and more at risk for pressure ulcers.

Cultural Considerations

Many changes related to genetic background are visible in the musculoskeletal system, although bone density is most likely related to body weight rather than a particular genetic background (Finkelstein, Brockwell, et al., 2008). The curvature of long bones results from both genes and body weight. African Canadians have straight femurs, while Aboriginal Canadians have anteriorly curved femurs. The femoral curve in Caucasians is intermediate. Although these features are useful for postmortem examination of human remains, they do not influence physical examination of the musculoskeletal system. Thin people of all cultures have less curvature than obese people. Caucasians, Latinos, and African Canadians have no difference in metabolism of vitamin D, but conversion of active metabolites by sunlight is less efficient in people of African genetic background (Tylavsky, Ryder, et al., 2005).

The increased melanin among individuals with darker skin colour may limit vitamin D synthesis; it is uncertain if other factors play a role. Nonetheless, people with darker skin colour living in more northern geographical areas such as Canada often lack sufficient levels of vitamin D.

Gender affects the skeletal system. Men have larger and stronger bones than women; therefore, men are less prone to conditions related to osteoporosis. Caucasian women have the highest risk of developing health issues from loss of bone density. Table 23-10 at the end of this chapter describes the relationship of age, genetic, and gender details to certain musculoskeletal conditions.

Acute Assessment

Assessment of patients reporting musculoskeletal concerns focuses on identifying the specific condition, alleviating pain, and preventing complications. Depending on the setting, nurses' priority assessments will vary. Nurses assess patients in emergency/urgent care centres, postoperative orthopedic care units, community health centres, and sports health centres. They look for alignment of limbs, joints, and the spine. They also observe for symmetry of size, shape, position, and movement of extremities. If a joint is swollen and tender following an injury, a strain or sprain is likely. If a bone is not aligned, it may be fractured, whereas if a joint is not aligned, it may be dislocated.

Urgent attention is required if a fracture is suspected. Fractures that are minimally displaced, do not penetrate through the skin, and do not threaten any neurovascular structures may do well with immobilization such as casting or splinting. Surgery may be indicated for fractures causing instability within the skeletal structures, obstructing blood flow, or causing nerve impingement. Fragility fractures that are associated with osteoporosis account for 80% of fractures in menopausal women over age 50 (Papaioannou, Morin, et al., 2010). Unlike fragility fractures, osteoporotic spinal fractures are not easily diagnosed. Individuals involved in motor vehicle collisions or who have fallen on their head have an increased likelihood of trauma to the spine. The nurse advises patients to seek immediate evaluation if they have sudden, severe, back pain after bending or twisting (Osteoporosis Canada, 2007). Movement of the spine is contraindicated if trauma is suspected because irreversible neurological damage can occur if it is not stabilized. Although the risk of infection does not increase dramatically if surgical repair occurs within 48 hours of injury, patients still risk pain and disability (McGregor & Atwood, 2007).

△ *SAFETY ALERT 23-1*

Nurses should not attempt to correct misalignment following an injury, because doing so can compound injury to muscle, nerves, or blood vessels. Fractures require prompt care to prevent further injury or deformity. Efforts should focus on keeping the patient calm, quiet, still, and comfortable. Nurses assess if the nerves and blood vessels distal to the injury site are compromised. If so, they seek immediate attention from the primary care provider. If not compromised, they immobilize the injury, manage pain, and perform ongoing assessment.

Damage to soft tissue often occurs at the same time as bone fracture. If there is soft tissue injury and bleeding, nurses apply pressure to stop the bleeding and assess for swelling, pain, numbness, and guarding. Muscle contractions contribute to discomfort, so helping the patient to relax is essential. Nursing actions include taking vital signs, monitoring pulses, and assessing colour, temperature, and capillary refill distal to the injury to evaluate tissue perfusion.

Subjective Data Collection

Assessment of Risk Factors

Numerous factors affect the musculoskeletal system. The nurse asks the patient about personal history, medications and supplements, family history, sports and hobbies, and working conditions. In addition the nurse notes the patient's age, gender, ethnicity, and genetic background. Knowledge of risk factors gained during the health history interview helps the nurse identify topics for health-promotion teaching.

Questions to Assess History and Risk Factors	Rationale

Demographic Data

What is your age?

Table 23-10 at the end of the chapter reviews age-related musculoskeletal diseases.

Osteoporosis causes 80% of all fractures in females over 50 years of age and a minimum of 80% of fractures in Canadians over 60 years of age (Osteoporosis Canada, 2011a). Twenty-three percent of individuals with a hip fracture die younger than 1 year (Osteoporosis Canada, 2011a). Failing eyesight and musculoskeletal changes increase older adults' risk for falls. Longer life expectancy has contributed to a growing number of people with disabilities. Young children are at risk for injury from impulsive actions, like running into the street after a ball. Adolescents are also at risk from impulsive actions, involvement in sports, and driving.

Note the patient's gender.

Incidence of many musculoskeletal diseases differs by gender (Table 23-10). A woman who is 50 years of age has a 40% risk of suffering hip, vertebral, or wrist fractures in her lifetime (Osteoporposis Canada, 2011a). Female athletes have a four to six times higher incidence of anterior cruciate ligament (ACL) tears than males (Hewett, Ford, et al., 2006).

What is your ethnic community or genetic background?

Prevalence of some disorders varies by genetic background (see Table 23-10).

Past Medical History

Have you ever had any musculoskeletal trauma or injury? Or been diagnosed with a musculoskeletal condition? Ask specifically about fractures, stroke, polio, infections of the bone or muscles, diabetes, and parathyroid disorders.
• When did it occur?
• How was it treated?
• What was the outcome?

Following hip replacement, hip dislocation can occur with hip flexion >90° or adduction of the joint past the midline. A person who has had a stroke is at increased risk of **subluxation**, or partial dislocation, of the shoulder from the weight of the arm and the lack of muscle tone to hold the joint together.

Nutrition and Medications

How many servings of dairy products do you have per day?

Do you take any calcium supplements? Vitamin D supplements?

Ask the patient if he or she is taking steroids.

Calcium is essential for bone growth and remodelling. Vitamin D is essential for calcium absorption and has been linked to osteoporosis (van Schoor, Visser, et al., 2008). Steroids can affect calcium absorption (PHAC, 2010b).

What medications do you take? Ask women about current and past birth control methods. Ask postmenopausal women about hormone therapy (HT).
• Do you take calcium and vitamin D supplements?
• Do you take any pain or anti-inflammatory medications? Muscle relaxants?
• Do you use complementary or alternative therapies (eg, chondroitin, glucosamine)?

Oral contraceptive use in young adults may contribute to risk of *osteoporosis,* while HT may help prevent it (Almstedt Shoepe & Snow, 2005; Dane, Dane, et al., 2007; MacLean, Newberry, et al., 2008). Pain or anti-inflammatory medications and muscle relaxants can mask symptoms. Glucosamine and chondroitin have been found to improve joint pain resulting from *osteoarthritis* (Towheed, Maxwell, et al., 2005).

Family History

Do your parents or siblings have any muscle conditions? Joint conditions? Or bone health concerns?
• Who had the condition?
• When did it occur?

Some musculoskeletal conditions have a familial tendency. Examples include *osteoporosis, bone cancer, and rheumatoid arthritis.*

Occupation, Lifestyle, and Behaviours

What type of work do you do?
• Does your work involve any repetitive motion? Lifting or twisting?
• How do you protect yourself from injury while working?

Some occupations increase risk of musculoskeletal injury through repetitive movements, twisting, frequent or heavy lifting, vibration, exposure to cold temperatures, and pushing or pulling heavy objects. Ergonomics and safety equipment can protect workers against injury.

Questions to Assess History and Risk Factors	Rationale
What hobbies and sports do you enjoy? • How do you protect yourself from injury while exercising or participating in sports? • Do you consistently use car seats, helmets, and protective gear?	Sports such as basketball, baseball, football, and soccer contribute to knee injuries (Hewett, Ford, et al., 2006). Skiing increases risks for lower extremity injuries, while skateboarding can lead to upper extremity injuries. Stretching and warming up prior to strenuous exercise decrease injury. Car seats, helmets, and protective gear decrease the severity of injury caused by motor vehicle collisions, sports injuries, and hobby exposures.
How well does your weekly or monthly income meet your needs?	Women of lower socioeconomic status are more likely to report limitations in activity and *arthritis, obesity,* and *osteoporosis* (Agency for Healthcare Research and Quality, 2005).
Have you ever smoked cigarettes or cigars? • If yes, how many packs per day? • For how many years?	Smoking is associated with low bone density and risk of fracture in women in the general population; it is strongly associated with fracture in those who report diabetes (Jorgensen, Joakimsen, et al., 2011). Smoking in elderly men is associated with vertebral and hip fractures and low bone mineral density (Jutberger, Lorentzon, et al., 2010). It is part of the history in individuals with an autoimmune-related arthritis, for example, rheumatoid arthritis and lupus erythematosus (Harel-Meir, Sherer, et al., 2007). Smoking is an independent, dose-related risk factor. Smoking cessation may partially reverse the risk.
Have you ever consumed alcohol? • If yes, how many drinks per week? • What do you drink?	Alcohol use is associated with increased risk of *osteoporosis*. Alcohol raises parathyroid hormone levels, which causes calcium loss from bones. Regular consumption of 2 to 3 oz. of alcohol every day interferes with absorption and use of calcium and vitamin D (National Osteoporosis Foundation [NOF], 2008).

Psychosocial History

Psychosocial assessment related to the musculoskeletal system is important, because conditions that limit or compromise movement and mobility can have wide-ranging effects and consequences. For example, if the patient has a musculoskeletal injury, how will it affect his or her ability to work, participate in hobbies, or perform routine ADLs independently? If the patient does not have sick-leave benefits and cannot work, the financial strain may be immense. If the patient lives alone, can he or she perform self-care safely? Does the patient have pain that interferes with every aspect of living? Will immobility add stress or contribute to isolation and sensory deprivation? Are deformities altering sense of self or body image?

Scoliosis Screening

Scoliosis is the lateral curvature of the spine, usually affecting both the thoracic and lumbar parts, with a deviation in one direction in the thoracic and in the other direction in the lumbar spine. Scoliosis may be structural, caused by a defect in the spine, or functional, caused by habits (eg, consistently carrying a heavy backpack on one shoulder).

If not corrected early, scoliosis can progressively worsen. Severe forms can interfere with breathing. The condition often develops in early adolescence, especially in girls. That is why school screening for scoliosis is done, although there may be false positives.

To screen for scoliosis, inspect the patient's back. While the patient stands, look for symmetry of the hips, scapulae, shoulders, and any skin folds or creases (Fig. 23-10A,B). The patient then needs to bend forward with the arms hanging toward the floor. Look for any lateral curves or prominences on one side. Then, the patient should slowly stand up while inspection of the spine continues. A **scoliometer** may be used to obtain a measurement of the number of degrees that the spine is deviated. A deviation in the thoracic area usually has a corresponding deviation on the other side in the lumbar area. During palpation of the spine, unexpected prominences or malformations.

Today scoliosis screening is regularly done in schools, but older people likely did not undergo such screening. Nurses may discover cases in the older population. Severe cases can interfere with functioning of the organs within the chest.

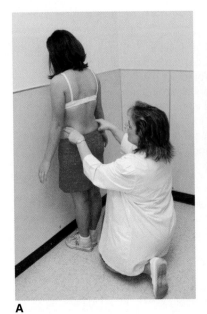
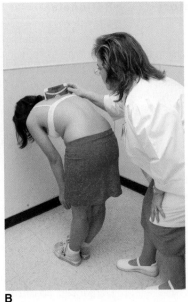

A **B**

Figure 23-10 Screening for scoliosis. **A.** Standing behind the patient to assess symmetry of the hips, scapulae, shoulders, and any skin folds or creases. **B.** While the patient bends forward, looking for any curves or prominences on one side.

Risk Assessment and Health Promotion

Topics for Health Promotion

- Prevention of back injury
- Prevention of osteoporosis
- Health promotion related to osteoarthritis
- Prevention of falls
- Risk factor assessment
- Screening

Adapted from Roach, S., Roddick, P., et al. (2010). The musculoskeletal system. In T. C. Stephen, D. L. Skillen, R. A. Day, & L. S. Bickley (Eds.). *Canadian Bates' guide to health assessment for nurses* (1st ed., p. 608). Philadelphia, PA: Wolters Kluwer Health/Lippincott Williams & Wilkins.

Ask if the patient has any congenital bone, muscle, or joint conditions. If responses are positive, ask if there are any current effects. Knowledge of congenital conditions can guide you to alter assessment and to anticipate findings during the physical examination. Assess how the patient is adapting to any deformity or malformation.

Ask about previous injuries or illnesses of muscles, joints, or bones. They can have long-lasting effects such as muscle weakness, decreased ROM, and impaired mobility. Specifically ask about fractures, sprains, strains, and dislocations, and also about childhood polio or **scoliosis**. If the patient reports previous injuries, ask about continuing effects.

Ask about surgery to the musculoskeletal system. Have the patient describe the procedure, when it occurred, and the results. Knowledge of previous surgeries provides additional information, allows the nurse to anticipate findings during the physical assessment, and enables the nurse to alter assessment procedures as needed to protect the patient.

A comprehensive method to determine the effects of previous or current conditions of the musculoskeletal system is to perform a functional assessment. An example is the Short Musculoskeletal Function Assessment developed by Swiontkowski, Engelberg, et al. (1999).

People of all ages need to learn to maintain a healthy weight and perform weight-bearing exercise most days (Roach, Roddick, et al., 2010). Children should carry backpacks on both shoulders to help prevent functional scoliosis. Encourage all patients to use recommended body mechanics with lifting and pushing, to use protective equipment for sports and work, and to wear seat belts. Exercises to increase strength and flexibility and improve posture decrease the risk of falls. Exercise training and adequate nutrition are successful in improving muscle mass and strength in older adults (Volpi, Nazemi, et al., 2004).

Bone Density

Loss of bone density and muscle strength are major concerns of aging that lifestyle modification can help control. Calcium and vitamin D are important for people of all ages, as are weight-bearing exercises. Although there is treatment for osteoporosis, there is no cure. Prevention is very important, especially for women. Current treatment includes bisphosphonates, calcitonin, estrogen and/or hormone therapy (HT), raloxifene, and parathyroid hormone (NOF, 2008). HT with estrogen may prevent bone loss, but carries an increased risk of breast cancer and heart attacks.

The PHAC (2009) recommends a comprehensive approach to prevent osteoporosis:

1. Take 1,000 to 1,500 mg of calcium daily if older than 50 years.
2. Take 400 to 800 units of vitamin D especially during the winter months in Canada.
3. Perform weight-bearing exercises such as hiking, walking, tennis, and dancing.

4. Explore activities that improve coordination and balance, such as swimming and tai chi.
5. Avoid smoking.
6. Discuss HT with your doctor.
7. Obtain an accurate diagnosis if suffering from chronic pain.
8. Keep an open mind to treatment options.

Clinical Significance 23-1

Because bone deposition begins to decrease after 30 years of age, women especially need to consume adequate calcium and perform weight-bearing exercises in the preceding decades. Weight-bearing exercise is required for older adults to prevent bone loss and muscle wasting. Walking, the most helpful form of exercise, is less detrimental to joints than other forms.

Focused Health History Related to Common Symptoms/Signs

Some common symptoms should be assessed in all patients to screen for the early presence of musculoskeletal disease. Nurses can use any special concerns from patients about joint health to identify focal areas. A thorough history of symptoms assists with identifying a current health condition or diagnosis.

Common Musculoskeletal Symptoms/Signs

- Pain or discomfort (back, neck, joint, muscle)
- Weakness
- Stiffness or limited movement
- Deformity
- Swelling and warmth of joints
- Joint pain accompanied by fever, chills, weight loss, anorexia, rash
- Lack of balance and coordination
- Bruising

Examples of Questions for Symptom/Sign Analysis—Decreased Joint Mobility

- "Which joint(s) are you having difficulty moving?" "Please point to the area(s)." (Location, radiation)
- "What movements are difficult for you?" "Describe what the movement feels like." (Quality)
- "Please tell me how much movement you have with the joint(s)." "On a scale of 0 to 10 with 0 being no movement and 10 being easy, free movement, how would you rate your mobility of this joint?" (Quantity/severity)
- "Did it start suddenly? Gradually?" "Did a particular event cause the decrease in mobility?" (Onset) "How long has it been difficult moving this joint?" (Duration) "Is there a time of day that it (joint mobility) is worse? Better?" (Time of day/month/year)
- "What makes the movement worse?" (Aggravating factors)
- "What makes it (joint mobility) better?" (Alleviating factors)
- "How does exercise affect your ability to move the joint(s)?" (Aggravating/alleviating factors)
- "Have you noticed any other symptoms? Swelling? Chills? Fever?" "Do you have pain associated with your difficulty moving the joint(s)?" "Describe the pain to me." (Associated symptoms)
- "How would you describe your work in terms of being physically demanding?" "Are there particular motions you perform several times a day?" "Do you play any sports?" "What kind of stress is in your life right now?" (Environmental factors)
- "How is this affecting your daily life?" (Significance to patient)
- "What do you think is happening?" (Patient perspective)

Adapted from Roach, S., Roddick, P., et al. (2010). The musculoskeletal system. In T. C. Stephen, D. L. Skillen, R. A. Day, & L. S. Bickley (Eds.). *Canadian Bates' guide to health assessment for nurses* (1st ed., p. 608). Philadelphia, PA: Wolters Kluwer Health/Lippincott Williams & Wilkins.

Examples of Questions to Assess Symptoms/Signs	Rationale/Unexpected Findings
Pain or Discomfort Do you have any pain or discomfort in your muscles? Bones? Or joints?	Pain is a subjective experience.
Inquire about the location, radiation, nature or quality, intensity or severity, timing, aggravating factors, alleviating factors, associated symptoms, environmental factors, significance to patient, and patient perspective.	The location and timing of pain may help differentiate if it originates in muscle (**myalgia**), bone, or joint (**arthralgia**). Pain limited to one joint is described as **monoarticular**; pain in several joints is **polyarticular**. Patients may describe it in many different terms. Burning pain may have a neurological cause. Bone pain may be aching, deep, and dull. Muscle pain is often cramping or sore. Patients often describe chronic pain as aching.
	Arthritic pain may be worse during cold, damp weather. The joint pain of *rheumatoid arthritis* is often worse in the morning, while pain from *osteoarthritis* is usually worse after rest and at the end of the day (see Table 23-12 at end of chapter).

(text continues on page 658)

Examples of Questions to Assess Symptoms/Signs	Rationale/Unexpected Findings
	Weakness, tingling, and numbness indicate pressure on nerves.
	Bone pain does not increase with movement, unless there is a fracture. Muscle and joint pain increases with movement.
	Patients with chronic pain may never experience its absence. The nurse and patient together need to determine what an acceptable level of pain is.
	Pain can limit ability to perform usual activities (ambulating, bathing, dressing, preparing food, working, sitting, changing positions, climbing stairs, lifting, pushing, or pulling).
Weakness Do you have any muscle weakness?	Muscle weakness is associated with certain diseases.
Do all or just certain muscles feel weak?	Weakness may migrate from muscle to muscle or to groups of muscles. Knowing which muscles are involved helps with determining the disease process. Distal weakness is usually a neurological condition, whereas proximal weakness is usually a muscle issue.
When does the weakness occur? How long does it last? What makes it worse? What helps the weakness? How bad is weakness on a scale of 0 to 10, with 10 being the worst? To what extent does the weakness limit your activities?	Muscle weakness after prolonged activity may result from *dehydration* or electrolyte imbalances. Grading the degree of weakness can help patients see improvement or determine the time of day when they can perform better.
Stiffness or Limited Movement Do you have stiffness or limited movement in any part of your body?	Stiffness is one type of limited movement. It may result from pain in muscles or joints, swelling, or a disease process.
Is the stiffness in one joint? Or more joints?	Generalized body swelling from *renal failure* affects the entire body, while injury may involve one joint only.
Can you grade the stiffness on a scale of 0 to 10, with 10 being the inability to move?	
Is the stiffness constant or intermittent?	Early stages of *rheumatoid arthritis* may cause stiffness that is worse in the morning, while stiffness from *osteoarthritis* is usually worse at the end of the day.
Did the stiffness start after an injury or was onset gradual?	**Contracture**—shortening of tendons, fascia, or muscles—may result from injury or prolonged positioning. Once a contracture develops, it is difficult to stretch and may require surgery.
What makes the stiffness worse? What helps the stiffness? Does the stiffness limit your activities?	
Deformity Do you have any malformation in your body? Was it present at birth or did it develop later?	Disuse, including wearing a cast, leads to some wasting or shrinking of the muscle (atrophy).
Does it affect the entire body or is it localized?	Deformities may be general (decreased overall body size) or localized (disruption in limb length and alignment from a fracture).
Does it affect your ability to perform ADLs?	
Lack of Balance and Coordination Do you have any difficulty maintaining balance?	Unusual gait or inability to perform ADLs may result from a balance or coordination issue, which may indicate a neurological disorder.

Examples of Questions to Assess Symptoms/Signs	Rationale/Unexpected Findings
Have you tripped or fallen recently?	The word "tripped" may elicit more information and less resistance than words such as "fall" or "fallen."
Have you noticed any of your movements are uncoordinated?	**Ataxia** (irregular, uncoordinated movements) or losing balance may be from cerebellar disorders, *Parkinson's disease, multiple sclerosis,* strokes, brain tumours, inner ear conditions, or medications.

Documentation of Expected Findings

The patient denies any discomfort, weakness, or stiffness in spine, bones, or joints. Reports no musculoskeletal difficulties with work, hobbies, or ADLs.

Lifespan Considerations

Additional Questions	Rationale/Unexpected Findings
Women Who Are Pregnant	
Have you noticed a change in your gait?	Hormones released during pregnancy cause ligaments to relax, which may contribute to a waddling gait in the last trimester.
Do you have back pain?	Lordosis frequently causes back pain during the last trimester of pregnancy.
Have you noticed numbness or tingling in your arms or hands?	Relaxation of the shoulder girdle and changes in neck curvature to counteract lordosis may cause pressure on nerves.
Newborns, Infants, and Children	
Were you told about any trauma to your baby during labour and birth? Was your baby born head first? Was there a need for forceps?	Traumatic birth increases the risk for fractures of the clavicle or humerus (Pressler, 2008).
How much did your baby weigh at birth?	Large babies also have an increased risk for fractures of the clavicle or humerus (Pressler, 2008).
Did your baby require resuscitation?	Prolonged hypoxia can cause muscular hypotonia or hypertonia (spasticity).
Did your baby achieve motor milestones (eg, raising head, turning over) at about the same age as age-mates or siblings?	Failure to achieve motor milestones may be from muscular or neurological causes.
Have you noticed any bone deformity? Spinal curvature?	Scoliosis, lateral curvature of the spine, develops during growth spurts. Early stages may be treated with exercise and physical therapy. Advanced scoliosis may require braces or surgery.
Unusual shape of toes or feet? At what age? How were these treated?	Common foot deformities include **polydactyly** (extra toes), **syndactyly** (fused toes), and **talipes equinovarus** (clubfoot).
Has your child broken any bones? Had any dislocations? How were these treated?	Fractures of the arms or legs during childhood may injure the epiphyseal plate and prevent bone growth, resulting in a permanent deformity.

(text continues on page 660)

Additional Questions	Rationale/Unexpected Findings
Did you breast-feed your baby? Did you take vitamin D supplements while breast-feeding?	Mothers who breast-feed require vitamin D supplementation to prevent the development of *rickets*. This is especially important in lower socioeconomic areas (Gartner & Greer, 2003).
Ask if the 6- to 12-month-old child eats a variety of vegetables and fruits (Health Canada, 2005).	Vitamin C deficiency is present in 14% of males and 10% of females (Goebel, 2007). Incidence of *scurvy* peaks in children 6 to 12 months whose diet is deficient in citrus fruits or vegetables. Incidence also peaks in elderly populations, who sometimes have diets deficient in vitamin C (Hampl, Taylor, et al., 2004).
Is your child involved in any sports? How many times per week? How was your child trained for the sport? How does your child warm up for the sport?	Children involved in sports need good training and must warm up before every session to prevent injury.
What does your child do if injured?	Children may be reluctant to report injuries for fear of not being able to participate in the sport.
What safety equipment does your child use during sports?	Properly fitted safety equipment is needed to minimize injuries.

Older Adults

Have you noticed any decrease in strength in the last year?	Decreased muscle strength is common as people age, especially in those with sedentary lifestyles.
Have you noticed an increase in tripping, stumbling, or falling in the last year?	Older adults have an increased rate of falls because of postural changes. "Tripping" may be a more acceptable term to older adults and might engage them in more forthright discussion of their risk. Loss of balance may also result from sensory or motor disorders, ear infections, side effects of certain medicines, and other factors.
Do you use any aids to help you get around? Were you taught how to use the device?	Assistive aids help older adults ambulate, but can cause falls if they do not use such devices correctly.
Postmenopausal women: Do you take bisphosphonates? Calcitonin? Estrogens and/or HT? Raloxifene? Or parathyroid hormone?	Calcium supplementation, HT, and weight-bearing exercise decrease the development of osteoporosis (Dane, Dane, et al., 2007). Of the 1.5 million Canadians 40 years or older who reported a diagnosis of osteoporosis on the 2009 Canadian Community Health Survey, <50% reported undertaking a regular program of physical activity and <50% reported an intake of vitamin D and calcium supplements (PHAC, 2010b).

Cultural Considerations

Examples of Questions to Assess Symptoms/Signs	Rationale/Unexpected Findings
How would you describe your ethnicity? What is your genetic background?	Table 23-10 describes common musculoskeletal conditions based on genetic background. A large proportion of Aboriginal people (Métis, First Nations, and Inuit) live in remote areas such as the Canadian North. Health care is limited in remote regions and rates of musculoskeletal disorders are possibly underestimated. Arthritis is the most prevalent chronic illness among each of the Aboriginal groups, affecting 19% of First Nations, 13% of Inuit, and 21% of Métis

populations (PHAC, 2009). Vitamin D deficiency is widespread across Canada due to its geographical latitude. A recent study demonstrated that 70% of the population had insufficient levels of vitamin D. The highest at-risk groups are non-Caucasians, First Nations, institutionalized Canadians (prisons, hospitals), individuals who are obese, children, and women who are pregnant (Schwalfenberg, Genuis, et al., 2010).

People of Asian heritage have lower fracture rates than Caucasians (Finkelstein, Brockwell, et al., 2008). Patients from countries with severe droughts or recent wars require assessment for signs of scurvy, including splinter hemorrhages in nails, ecchymosis, purpura, and hyperkeratotic papules on skin (Hampl, Taylor, et al., 2004). These patients are also at risk for malnutrition, which increases the risk of osteoporosis.

An Example of a Therapeutic Dialogue

The nurse's role relative to subjective data collection is to gather information to improve the patient's health status and to help determine the cause of the patient's current symptoms. Remember Mrs. Gladys Crowfoot, who was introduced at the beginning of this chapter. She is an 82-year-old First Nations elder who has been in the extended care facility for 12 days for rehabilitation. The nurse uses professional communication techniques to gather subjective data from Mrs. Crowfoot.

Nurse: Good morning, Mrs. Crowfoot. I'm Puneet. How are you doing today? (pauses)

Mrs. Crowfoot: Not so good.

Nurse: In what way are you "not so good"?

Mrs. Crowfoot: My hands and legs don't work the way they used to. My joints feel kind of stiff today and I'm cold. I'm afraid they will take me away from my home.

Nurse: Tell me a little about that.

Mrs. Crowfoot: My children tell me that I can't look after my house any more, that I'm too old. I feel useless.

Nurse: That must be difficult for you. I'm glad that you're here so that we can help you get better.

Mrs. Crowfoot: Yes, I'm really hoping that I can go home. I'll do whatever I can to get better.

Critical Thinking Challenge

- What culturally appropriate behaviours did the nurse use?
- What other assessments might the nurse make regarding Mrs. Crowfoot's coldness, stiffness, and loss of function?
- How might the nurse respond to Mrs. Crowfoot? Support your response by drawing on what you understand about culturally competent care.
- What therapeutic communication techniques might be helpful to assess how Mrs. Crowfoot is coping?

Objective Data Collection

Equipment

- **Goniometer** (Fig. 23-11) for measuring the angle at which a joint can flex or extend
- Tape measure to measure circumference of extremities or length of bones
- Felt marker

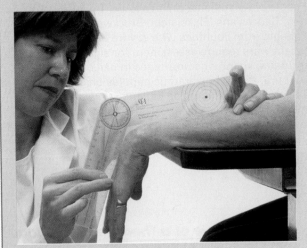

Figure 23-11 A goniometer is used to measure the angle at which a joint can extend or flex.

Promoting Patient Comfort, Dignity, and Safety

Assemble needed supplies. Make sure the room is warm and private. Perform hand hygiene and warm your hands.

Help the patient to remove clothing so that the limbs and spine are visible. Drape the patient so that only the areas being currently observed are visible. Explain that the examination will require position changes and movement. Avoid repetitive position changes by performing a systematic examination by region. Assist the patient as required; ensure that he or she is comfortable. Patients with painful joints may prefer to move by themselves; patients with extensive musculoskeletal health issues will require more time.

Weighing the patient is an important part of a comprehensive musculoskeletal examination. Obesity puts extra stress and strain on joints, increases the risk of degenerative joint disease, and decreases mobility (see Chapter 6).

> **Clinical Significance 23-2**
>
> Although nurses compare each extremity to the other, they examine the areas that patients have identified as tender or painful last.

Comprehensive Physical Examination: The Musculoskeletal System

Inspection begins with the initial contact with the patient. Whether patients are walking into an examination room, down hallways, or being taken into a bathroom, nurses continually assess for any alterations in the patient's gait, coordination, and posture. Assessment involves inspection and palpation.

Initial Survey

Techniques and Expected Findings	Unexpected Findings
Inspection **Posture** Observe the patient's posture while he or she stands with feet together. Observe the relation of the head, trunk, pelvis, and extremities. Assess for symmetry in shoulder height, scapulae, iliac crests, posterior superior iliac spines, and gluteal folds. Also observe the patient's posture while sitting. *Posture is erect with the head midline above the spine. Symmetrical height of shoulders, scapulae, iliac crests, posterior superior iliac spines, and gluteal folds.*	*Scoliosis* or low back pain may cause the patient to lean forward or to the side when standing or sitting. *Acromegaly* may result in an enlarged skull and increased length to the hands, feet, and long bones. Elevation of a shoulder may be seen in scoliosis. Asymmetry of iliac crests may indicate unequal leg length. Stiffness of the neck may result from muscle strain or arthritis. ⚠ *SAFETY ALERT 23-2* *When assessing the musculoskeletal system, ensure the patient does not fall. Ask about the person's ability to transfer and to walk or stand. Encourage the patient to steady self by holding the examination table or wall when standing.*

Gait and Mobility

Watch the patient walk across the room while observing from the side and from behind. Gait can predict a person's risk of falling. Gait is assessed for swing (non–weight-bearing stage) and stance (weight-bearing stage). The Gait Assessment Rating Scale is a useful tool for determining risk (www.ohcponline.com/tools/gars.html). Note the base width. *Walking is smooth, balanced, continuous, and rhythmic with the arms swinging in opposition to the legs. The base is 5 to 10 cm. The patient rises from sitting with ease.*

⚠ *SAFETY ALERT 23-3*

Before assessing gait, ask if the patient uses an assistive device, such as a cane or walker. Ensure that the patient has the equipment with him or her at the examination and knows how to correctly use it.

Gait conditions include hesitancy, unsteadiness, staggering, reaching for external support, high stepping, foot scraping, inability to raise the foot completely off the floor, persistent toe or heel walking, excessive pointing of toes inward or outward, asymmetry of step height or length, limping, stooping, wavering, shuffling, waddling, excessive swinging of shoulders or pelvis, and slow or rapid speed. Table 23-11 at the end of this chapter describes some unexpected gait patterns; other gait patterns are in Table 24-10. Gait conditions may result from muscle weakness, joint deterioration, misalignment of lower extremities, paralysis, impaired coordination, impaired balance, fatigue, or pain.

Balance

If the patient has a gait condition, you will not be able to assess balance. Ask the patient to walk on tiptoes, heels, heel-to-toe fashion (tandem walking), and backward. Ask the patient to step to each side and to sit down and stand. Assessment of balance includes the Romberg test, standing, and hopping on one foot.

To perform the Romberg test, ask the patient to stand with feet together, arms at sides, and eyes open; then have him or her close the eyes. If cerebral function is intact, the patient can do this without swaying (negative Romberg test). *The patient is balanced when standing and has a negative Romberg test.*

Balance is a function of the cerebellum; however, inner ear conditions can also affect balance. Balance may be assessed with the musculoskeletal system, but also involves the neurological system.

The nurse stands close to the patient with arms outstretched to protect him or her if swaying or a loss of balance occurs which is an unexpected finding.

Coordination

Ask the patient to rapidly pat the table or his or her thigh, alternating between the palm and dorsum of the hand, one hand at a time. To assess fine motor coordination of the hand, ask the patient to perform finger to thumb opposition. Assess gross motor coordination in the legs by having the patient run the heel of one foot down the opposite leg from knee to great toe and off the toe. *The patient performs rapid alternating movements of the arms and finger–thumb opposition and runs the heel of one foot down the opposite shin and off great toe smoothly.*

The dominant side usually has slightly better coordination. Uncoordinated movements may be from pain, injury, deformity, or cerebellar disorders. Coordination is often tested during assessment of the musculoskeletal system, but it is actually an assessment of the neurological system.

Inspection of Extremities

Look for any swelling, lacerations, lesions, deformity, length of long bones, size of muscles, and symmetry.

Asymmetry in bone length may be from injury. Asymmetry in muscle size may be from neurological damage (eg, *polio*). Disuse, including while wearing a cast, leads to some wasting or shrinking of the muscle (atrophy).

Swelling or edema may be the result of trauma, inflammation, or lymph node resection.

Size and Shape of Extremities. Assess both extremities at the same time to evaluate for symmetry. Bilateral assessment for muscle tone and strength is necessary for comparison. Note the size and shape of extremities and muscles, as well as alignment and any deformity or asymmetry. Are the limbs of equal length?

(text continues on page 664)

Limb Measurements. Compare the circumference of the arms and legs. Compare the length of the radius by having the patient place the arms together from elbow to wrist. Observe the knee height with the patient sitting. Limb circumference may be measured on the forearms, upper arms, thighs, and calves. Measure circumference at the midpoint, so measure the length first. The dominant side may be 1 cm larger in circumference. Measure arm length from the acromion process to the tip of the middle finger. Measure true leg length from the anterior superior iliac spine to the medial malleolus (Fig. 23-12). Measure apparent leg length from the umbilicus to the medial malleolus.

Discrepancy in leg length >1 cm may cause gait aberrations, hip and back pain, and apparent scoliosis. Limb length may appear unequal in the presence of hip and pelvic displacement. Unequal apparent leg length, but equal true leg length, is seen with hip and pelvic alterations. Unequal arm length does not cause as many difficulties as unequal leg length. Unequal circumference may be from disuse or neurological disorders.

Figure 23-12 True leg length is measured from the anterior superior iliac spine to the medial malleolus.

Palpation

Joints are palpated for contour and size; muscles are palpated for tone. Feel for any bumps, nodules, or deformity. Ask if there is any tenderness during touch.

Asymmetry in muscle size and tone may be from disuse or neurological disease. Muscle discomfort when touched may be because of inflammation, spasm, or infection. Joint tenderness may be from arthritis, infection, trauma, or inflammation.

Joint Range of Motion. Assess both extremities at the same time to evaluate symmetry. Simultaneously observe each joint while the patient performs active range of motion (ROM). If the patient cannot perform active ROM, carefully support the limb on either side of the joint and perform passive ROM. Ask the patient if there is any tenderness or discomfort with movement. If there is limited ROM, use a goniometer to measure the angle of the joint at its maximum flexion and extension (see Fig. 23-11).

Listen to and palpate the shoulder and knee joints while the patient moves through ROM. *A healthy joint moves smoothly and quietly.*

Limitation of movement, **crepitus** (cracking or popping), and nonverbal and verbal expressions of discomfort, tenderness, or pain are noted. Limitation of ROM is observed with bursitis, rotator cuff injuries, tendonitis, arthritis, tenosynovitis, and dislocations. Crepitus during movement is suggestive of degenerative changes such as osteoarthritis. Crepitus may be felt as grating in the joint as it moves.

⚠ *SAFETY ALERT 23-4*

When performing passive ROM, do not force the joint. Stop if there is resistance or reports of discomfort.

Muscle Tone and Strength. Assess muscle tone before muscle strength. Move the patient's relaxed arm in a snaking motion, ensuring that shoulder, elbow, wrist, and finger joints are put through motion. Compare sides. Repeat with legs.

Table 23-5 provides terms used when describing alterations in muscle tone.

Slight residual tension is present bilaterally.

When assessing muscle strength, it is again necessary to compare one side to the other.

Table 23-6 describes the rating scale for muscle strength, and Table 23-7 provides instructions to give the patient when assessing muscle strength.

Upper and lower extremity muscle strength is 5/5 bilaterally.

Asymmetry of muscle strength is observed with central and peripheral nervous system disorders. Symmetrical weakness suggests a muscle disorder or disorder of peripheral nerves. Tenderness over a tendon suggests a partial or complete tear.

Table 23-5 Terms for Describing Alterations in Muscle Tone

Atony	Lack of residual tension
Hypotonicity	Diminished tone of skeletal muscles
Spasticity	Hypertonic, so the muscles are stiff and movements awkward
Spasm	Sudden violent involuntary contraction of a muscle
Fasciculation	Involuntary twitching of muscle fibres
Tremors	Involuntary contraction of muscles

Table 23-6 Rating Scale for Muscle Strength

5/5 (100%)	Complete range of motion (ROM) against gravity and full resistance
4/5 (75%)	Complete ROM against gravity and moderate resistance
3/5 (50%)	Complete ROM against gravity
2/5 (25%)	Complete ROM with the joint supported; cannot perform ROM against gravity
1/5 (10%)	Muscle contraction detectable, but no movement of the joint
0/5 (0%)	No visible muscle contraction

Muscle strength can be described on a 0–5 scale, with 5 being the strongest, as percentage or by words.

Table 23-7 Instructions for Testing Muscle Strength

Muscle	Examiner Activity After Testing Muscle Tone	Patient Instructions
Neck	Place hand on side of the patient's face. Observe opposite sternomastoid contraction and force against your hand.	"Turn your head toward my hand against resistance."
Deltoid	Put hand on the patient's upper arm and try to push arm down to side.	"Hold your arm straight out to the side. Try to prevent me from pushing your arm down."
Biceps	With the patient's elbow bent, place hand on flexor surface of the patient's forearm and try to straighten the arm.	"Bend your arm. Try to resist me from straightening your arm."
Triceps	With the patient's elbow bent, place hand on extensor surface of the patient's forearm and try to further flex the elbow.	"Bend your arm. Try to resist me from bending your arm even more."
Wrist	With the patient's fist flexed downward, place hand on palmar surface of the patient's hand and try to pull the patient's fist up against resistance (flexor strength) With the patient's fist extended, try to pull the patient's fist down against resistance (extensor strength).	"Bend your arm and hold it against your side. Make a fist and flex your wrist downward. Prevent me from pushing your hand upward. Now make a fist and bring it up towards your body. Prevent me from pulling your hand downward."
Fingers	Cross your first and second fingers. Place in the hand of the patient to test grip strength.	"Squeeze my fingers firmly."
	Use your two index fingers to try to force the patient's outspread fingers together against resistance (abductor strength).	"Spread your fingers apart. Prevent me from bringing them together."
	Use your thumb to pull the patient's thumb against resistance (opposition strength).	"Touch your thumb to your little finger tip. Try to stop me from pulling them apart."
Hip	With the patient supine, try to push thigh downward as the patient raises leg against your hand (flexor strength). Then place your hand underneath the patient's thigh to assess extensor strength. Next place your two fists between the patient's thighs to assess adductor strength. Now place your fists at lateral aspects of knees to assess abductor strength of the patient.	"Keeping your leg straight, raise your leg against my resistance. Now push your thigh down against my hand. Next, bring your legs together against my fists. Now try to spread your legs against the resistance of my fists."

(table continues on page 666)

| Table 23-7 | Instructions for Testing Muscle Strength *(continued)* | |

Muscle	Examiner Activity After Testing Muscle Tone	Patient Instructions
Quadriceps	With the patient supine and knee bent, place your hand on shin of lower leg and try to further flex the patient's leg (extensor strength).	"Bend your knee and prevent me from bending your leg even more against resistance."
Hamstring	With the patient supine and knee bent, place your hand on calf of lower leg and try to straighten the patient's leg (flexor strength).	"Bend your knee and keep your foot on table. Prevent me from straightening your leg against resistance."
Ankle	With the patient's ankle neutral, push against sole of the patient's foot (plantar flexion strength).	"Lie naturally and resist my push to make your foot go towards you."
	With the patient's ankle neutral, pull against dorsum of the patient's foot (dorsiflexion strength).	"Lie naturally and resist my pull to make your foot go away from you."

Adapted from Stephen, T. C., Day, R. A., & Skillen, D. L. (Eds.). (2011–2012). *A syllabus for adult health assessment.* Edmonton, AB: Faculty of Nursing, University of Alberta.

Documentation of Expected Findings

When standing, the trunk and head are erect, with weight distributed equally on both feet. The head is midline and aligned with the spine. The shoulders, hips, scapulae, iliac crests, iliac spines, and gluteal folds are level. The feet are under the hips and knees. The toes and knees point forward. The extremities are symmetrical and in proportion to the body. The arm span is equal to the height (full growth has been reached). When sitting, both feet are flat on the floor, with toes pointed forward. The head and trunk are perpendicular to the floor. Walking is smooth, balanced, and rhythmic with the patient erect. The arms swing freely at the sides and in the opposite direction to the leg that is moving. The patient transfers from standing to sitting and sitting to standing with ease. The muscles are well formed, firm to touch, and symmetrical. Joints have full active range of motion (ROM). The patient denies any discomfort.

Clinical Significance 23-3

Handle the extremities of patients with fragile bones gently to prevent fractures.

Techniques and Expected Findings	Rationale/Unexpected Findings

Temporomandibular joint

Inspection. Inspect the temporomandibular joint (TMJ) for symmetry, swelling, and redness. *The jaw is symmetrical bilaterally.*

Palpation. Place your fingerpads in front of the tragus of each ear (Fig. 23-13).

Asymmetrical facial or joint musculature may indicate previous or current facial fractures or surgery.

Discomfort, swelling, limited movement, and grating or cracking sounds are unexpected and require further evaluation for dental or neurological issues or *TMJ syndrome.* TMJ dysfunction may present as ear pain or headache. Swelling or tenderness suggests *arthritis* or *myofascial pain syndrome* (inflammation of the fascia surrounding the muscle).

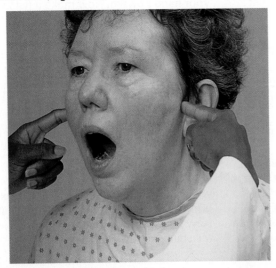

Figure 23-13 Palpating the TMJ.

Ask the patient to open and close the jaw while you palpate the joints. You should feel a shallow depression, and the mandible motion should be smooth and painless. *The jaw movement is symmetrical, smooth, quiet, and nontender.*

Range of Motion. Ask the patient to open the jaw as wide as possible, jut the lower jaw forward (protrusion), return the jaw to neutral position (retraction), and move the jaw from side to side 1 to 2 cm. *The joint may have an audible or palpable click when opened. The mouth opens with 3 to 6 cm between the upper and lower teeth. The jaw moves with ease.*

Muscle Strength. Ask the patient to repeat the above movements while you provide opposing force. This tests cranial nerve V. *The strength of the muscles is equal on both sides of the jaw; the patient can perform the movements against resistance. Muscle strength is 5/5, with no pain, spasms, or contractions.*

Difficulty opening the mouth may be because of injury or arthritic changes. Pain in the TMJ may indicate misalignment of the teeth or arthritic changes.

Decreased muscle strength may be because of muscle or joint disease.

Documentation of Expected Findings

The temporomandibular joint (TMJ) is symmetrical bilaterally. The muscles are smooth with strength of 5/5. The joint moves smoothly through all range of motion (ROM) without pain. A slight popping sound is heard when the jaw is opened widely. The teeth align correctly.

Cervical Spine

Inspection. With the patient standing, inspect the cervical spine from all sides. It should position the head above the trunk (Fig. 23-14). Observing from the side, check for the concave curve of the cervical spine. *As viewed from behind, the patient holds the head erect, and the cervical spine is in straight alignment. From the side, the neck has a concave curve.*

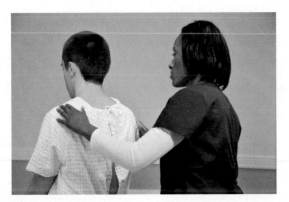

Figure 23-14 Inspecting the cervical spine from behind the patient.

Palpation. Stand behind the patient to palpate the cervical spine and neck from C1 to C7. C7 and T1 spinous processes are more prominent. *The paravertebral, sternocleidomastoid, and trapezius muscles are fully developed, symmetrical, and nontender.*

Degenerative joint disease of the cervical vertebrae may cause lateral tilting of the head and neck. Lateral deviation of the neck (**torticollis**) may be because of acute muscle spasms, congenital conditions, or incorrect head posture to correct vision changes. Weight lifting will cause hypertrophy of the neck muscles, resulting in a thickened appearance of the neck.

Osteoarthritis, neck injury, disc degeneration because of aging or occupational stress, and spondylosis can cause decreased range of motion (ROM), pain, and tenderness on palpation. Pain on palpation may indicate inflammation of the muscles (**myositis**). Neck spasm may indicate nerve compression or psychological stress.

(text continues on page 668)

Range of Motion. Ask the patient to touch the chin to the chest (flexion), look up toward the ceiling (hyperextension), attempt to touch each ear to the shoulder without elevating the shoulder (lateral flexion or bending), and turn the chin to the shoulder as far as possible (rotation) (Fig. 23-15). *Neck ROM is flexion 45°, hyperextension 55°, lateral flexion 40°, and rotation 70° to each side.*

Pain or muscle spasms may impair ROM. Hyperextension and flexion may be limited because of cervical disc degeneration, spinal cord tumour, or osteoarthritic changes. Pain may radiate to the back, shoulder, or arms. Pain, numbness, or tingling may indicate compression of spinal root nerves .

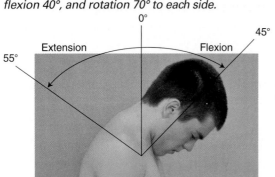

A

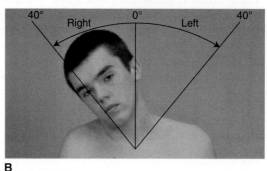

B

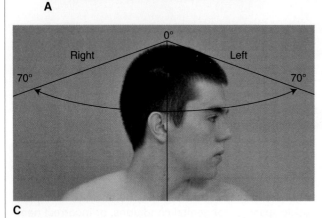

C

Figure 23-15 Assessing neck ROM. **A.** Flexion. **B.** Testing lateral flexion or bending by moving the ear to shoulder left and right. **C.** Assessing rotation by moving the chin to shoulder left and right.

Muscle Strength. Ask the patient to rotate the neck to the right and left, against the resistance of your hand on the side of the face. This tests cranial nerve XI. *Muscle strength is sufficient to overcome resistance and equal.*

Weakness or loss of sensation in arms or hands may result from cervical cord compression.

Clinical Significance 23-4
Following any trauma, do not move patients with neck pain until the neck is stabilized and cleared by x-ray. Moving the patient could cause subluxation or dislocation of the cervical vertebrae and permanent injury to the spinal cord.

Documentation of Expected Findings

Viewed from behind, the neck is straight and holds the head in alignment with the spine. Viewed from the side, the neck is slightly concave. Muscle size is symmetrical bilaterally. The neck has full range of motion (ROM) and moves smoothly and painlessly. Muscle strength is 5/5. The patient denies tenderness during palpation. C7, T1 spinous processes are prominent and palpable. The muscles are fully developed. No nodules, swelling, crepitus, or muscle spasms are noted.

Shoulder

Inspection. Compare both shoulders anteriorly and posteriorly for size and contour. Observe the anterior aspect of the joint capsule for swelling.

Shoulder joints may have some deformity because of arthritis, trauma, or scoliosis. Redness and swelling may indicate injury or inflammation. Unequal shoulder height may indicate scoliosis.

No redness, swelling, deformity, or muscular atrophy is present. Shoulders are smooth and bilaterally symmetrical. Right and left shoulders are level. Each shoulder is at an equal distance from the vertebral column.

Palpation. Stand in front of the patient and palpate both shoulders, noting any muscular spasm, atrophy, swelling, heat, or tenderness. Start at the clavicle and methodically explore the acromioclavicular joint, scapula, greater tubercle of the humerus, area of the subacromial bursa, biceps groove, and anterior aspect of the glenohumeral joint. *Muscles are fully developed and smooth. Joints and biceps groove are nontender bilaterally.*

Range of Motion. Ask the person to perform forward flexion, extension, abduction, adduction, and internal and external rotation (Fig. 23-16). Cup one hand over the patient's shoulder during range of motion (ROM) to detect any crepitus. *Movement is fluid. ROM is forward flexion 180°, hyperextension 50°, abduction 180°, adduction 50°, internal rotation 90°, and external rotation 90°.*

Tenderness may be because of inflammation of the muscles, overuse of unconditioned muscles, or sports injuries.

⚠ *SAFETY ALERT 23-5*

Suspect a cardiac origin for reports of shoulder pain without tenderness or inflammation. Assess for shortness of breath, nausea, and diaphoresis. If these symptoms are present, the patient needs to be sent to an emergency department for assessment of cardiac ischemia.

Limited ROM, pain, crepitation, and asymmetry may be from *arthritis*, muscle or joint inflammation, trauma, or sports injury. Inability to externally rotate the shoulder suggests a rotator cuff injury.

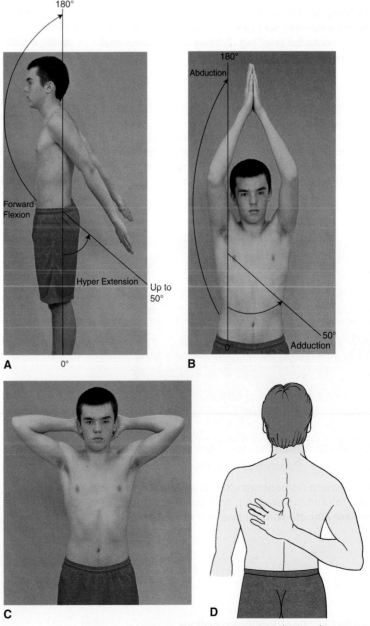

Figure 23-16 Assessing shoulder ROM.
A. Extension. **B.** Abduction/adduction.
C. External rotation. **D.** Internal rotation.

(text continues on page 670)

Techniques and Expected Findings (continued)	Rationale/Unexpected Findings (continued)
Muscle Strength. Ask the patient to shrug both shoulders, flex arms forward, extend backward, adduct, and abduct against resistance. Shrugging the shoulders tests cranial nerve XI (spinal accessory). *The patient can perform full flexion, extension, adduction, and abduction against resistance.*	Decreased ability to shrug the shoulders against resistance may indicate compressed spinal cord root nerve or spinal accessory cranial nerve (CN XI).

Documentation of Expected Findings

Shoulders are equal height and equidistant from the spinal column. Muscle size is symmetrical bilaterally. Both shoulders have full range of motion (ROM) and move smoothly and painlessly. Muscle strength is 5/5. The patient denies tenderness during palpation. No nodules, swelling, crepitus, or muscle spasms are noted.

Techniques and Expected Findings	Rationale/Unexpected Findings
Elbow	
Inspection. Inspect the size and contour of the elbow in both the extended and flexed positions. Check the olecranon bursa for swelling. *Elbows are symmetrical with no swelling.*	Subluxation of the elbow shows the forearm dislocated posteriorly. This may occur when an adult tugs on a small child's forearm or swings the child holding onto the child's forearms. Swelling and redness of the olecranon bursa are easily observed because of the proximity to the skin. Effusion or synovial thickening is observed as a bulge on either side of the olecranon process and indicates *gouty arthritis*.
Palpation. Support the patient's forearm and passively flex the elbow to 70°. Palpate the olecranon process, grooves, and medial and lateral epicondyles of the humerus (Fig. 23-17). 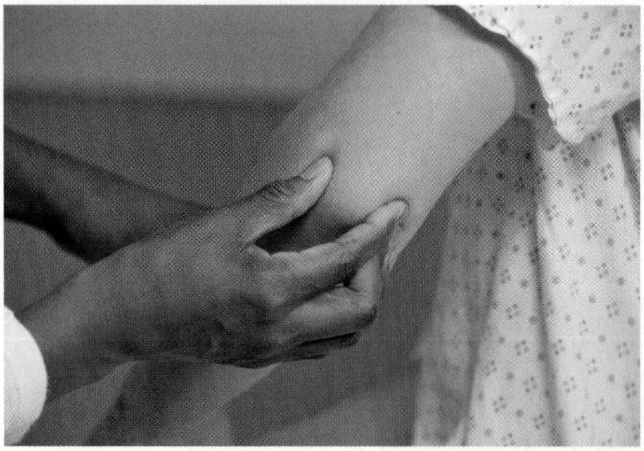 **Figure 23-17** Palpation of the elbow. The tissues and fat pads should feel solid. Check for any synovial thickening, swelling, nodules, or tenderness. *Elbows are smooth with no swelling or tenderness.*	Epicondyles and tendons are common sites for inflammation and tenderness. Soft, boggy swelling occurs with synovial thickening or effusion. Local heat or redness may indicate synovial inflammation. Subcutaneous nodules at pressure points on the olecranon process or ulnar surface may indicate rheumatoid arthritis.

| Techniques and Expected Findings (continued) | Rationale/Unexpected Findings (continued) |

Range of Motion. Ask the patient to flex and extend the elbow. Then have the person pronate and supinate the forearm by holding elbows close to sides and then turning palms downward and upward (Fig. 23-18). *Range of motion (ROM) is flexion 150° to 160° and extension 0°; however, some people cannot extend the elbow fully (only to 5–10 degrees). Some people can hyperextend the elbow –5° to –10°. Pronation and supination of 90° is expected.*

Decreased ROM, pain, or crepitation may be from *arthritis*, muscle or joint inflammation, trauma, or sports injury. Redness, swelling, and tenderness of the olecranon process may be because of *bursitis. Lateral epicondylitis* (tennis elbow) is inflammation of the forearm extensor and supinator muscles and tendons, causing disabling pain at the lateral epicondyle of the humerus that radiates down the lateral side of the forearm. *Medial epicondylitis* (golf elbow) is the same as tennis elbow, except it affects the flexor and pronator muscles and tendons.

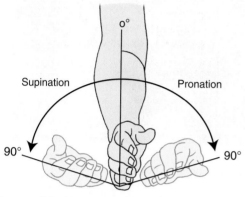

Figure 23-18 Supination and pronation of the elbow.

Muscle Strength. While supporting the patient's arm, apply resistance just proximal to the patient's wrist, and ask the patient to flex and then extend both elbows (Fig. 23-19). *The patient can perform full ROM against resistance.*

Decreased strength may be from pain, nerve root compression, or arthritic deformity. People may compensate for weakened biceps or triceps muscles by using the shoulder muscles.

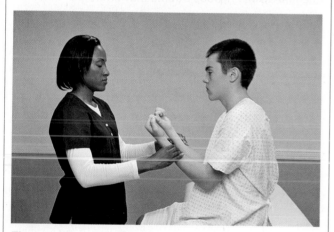

Figure 23-19 Assessing elbow muscle strength.

Documentation of Expected Findings

Elbows are equal in size and shape. Muscle size is symmetrical bilaterally. Both elbows have full range of motion (ROM) and move smoothly and painlessly. Muscle strength is 5/5. The patient denies tenderness during palpation. No nodules, swelling, crepitus, or muscle spasms are noted.

CHAPTER 23   Musculoskeletal Assessment   671

Wrist and Hand

Palpation. Hold the patient's hand in your hands. Use your thumbs to palpate each joint of the wrist and the metacarpophalangeal joints for tenderness (Fig. 23-20). *Joint surfaces are smooth without nodules, edema, or tenderness.*

Painful joints in the fingers are common in *osteoarthritis*. A firm mass over the dorsum of the wrist may be a *ganglion*. *Rheumatoid arthritis* may cause edema, redness, and tenderness of the finger and wrist joints the (see Table 23-12 at end of chapter).

A

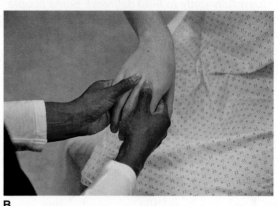
B

Figure 23-20 Palpating the joints of the **(A)** wrists and **(B)** the metacarpophalangeals (MCPs).

Palpate medial and lateral surfaces of each distal interphalangeal (DIP) joint and proximal interphalangeal (PIP) joint of the fingers, and the interphalangeal (IP) joint of the thumb for tenderness. *Joints are nontender bilaterally.*

Range of Motion. Observe the wrist and hand range of motion (ROM) (Fig. 23-21). *The wrist motions are flexion (90°), extension (return to 0°), hyperextension (70°), and ulnar (55°) and radial (20°) deviation. The metacarpophalangeal joints motion are flexion (90°), extension (0°), and hyperextension (up to 30°). Proximal and distal intraphalangeal joints perform flexion (making a fist), extension, and abduction. The thumb performs* **opposition** *with each fingertip and the base of the little finger.*

Joint or muscle inflammation may cause decreased or unequal ROM. Previous trauma may limit ROM.

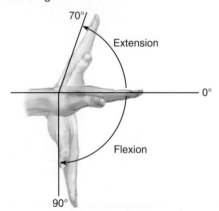

Figure 23-21 Wrist and hand flexion and extension.

Muscle Strength. Perform each motion above against resistance. Ask the patient to grasp your first and second crossed fingers tightly while you pull to remove your fingers. *Muscle strength is equal bilaterally and sufficient to overcome resistance.*

Weak muscle strength may be because of arthritic changes or fractures of the metatarsals or phalanges. By crossing your fingers, the patient's strong grip will not be uncomfortable for you.

Hip

Inspection. While standing, assess the skin, iliac crest, size and symmetry of the buttocks, and number of gluteal folds. Assist the patient to the supine position with legs straight. Look for any swelling, lacerations, lesions, deformity, size of the muscles, and symmetry. Look at the hips from the anterior and posterior views. *Hips are rounded, even, and symmetrical.*

When standing, muscle atrophy or bruising may be apparent. When lying supine, external rotation of the lower leg and foot indicates a fractured femur. Unequal gluteal folds or unequal height of iliac crests may indicate uneven leg length or *scoliosis*.

Palpation. While the patient is supine, palpate the hip joints, iliac crests, and muscle tone. Feel for any bumps, nodules, and deformity. Ask if there is any tenderness with touch. Feel for crepitus when moving the joint. *Buttocks are symmetrical in size. Iliac crests are at the same height on both sides.*

Asymmetry, discomfort when touched, or crepitus during movement may occur with hip inflammation or *degenerative joint disease*. Focal tenderness may indicate bursitis.

Range of Motion. Observe for full active ROM of each hip (Fig. 23-22): flexion (lift straight leg to 90° or draw knee to chest to 120° while observing opposite thigh), extension (standing position or lying on the examination table with the leg straight), abduction (stabilize the opposite anterior superior iliac spine and lift, if standing, or slide, if lying, foot and straight leg to the side, away from body to 45°), adduction (stabilize the anterior superior iliac spine and swing foot and straight leg in front and past the other leg to 30°), internal and external ROM (with the hip and knee flexed, move the leg medially 40° and then laterally 45°). Have the patient stand or positioned prone to test hyperextension. Ask the patient to move the straight leg backward, away from the body (15°).

Straight-leg flexion that produces back and leg pain radiating down the leg may indicate a *herniated disc*. If the opposite thigh flexes, investigate a flexion deformity of the hip being tested. When lying down, one leg longer than the other or limited internal rotation may indicate a hip fracture or dislocation. By stabilizing the opposite iliac spine, you can tell the limit of hip abduction and adduction because the spine will move at that point. Osteoarthritis of the hip may restrict abduction, adduction, and rotation.

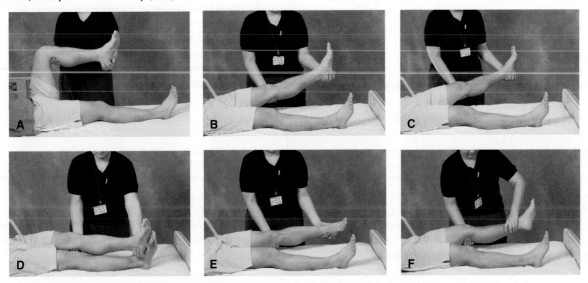

Figure 23-22 Hip ROM. **A.** Flexion. **B.** Extension. **C.** Abduction. **D.** Adduction. **E.** Internal rotation. **F.** External rotation.

(text continues on page 674)

Circumduction while standing or lying on one side moves the foot and leg in a circle beside the body in all movements. *The patient can perform full ROM without discomfort or crepitus.*

Muscle Tone and Strength. Instruct the patient to relax each leg in turn on your supporting hand. Put the leg through movement at all joints to assess for tone. *Slight residual tone bilaterally.* With the patient lying down, apply pressure to the anterior thigh while the patient flexes the hip. Place your hand underneath the thigh while the patient extends the hip. Place two fists between the patient's thighs while he or she squeezes against them (adductor strength). Apply fist pressure to the lateral thighs while the patient abducts the hips. *The patient can perform full ROM against resistance bilaterally.*

Asymmetry of strength may be from pain, or a muscle or nerve disease.

⚠ *SAFETY ALERT 23-6*
Do not test adduction or flexion >90° in anyone with a hip replacement. Doing so may cause dislocation.

Documentation of Expected Findings

The muscles are well formed, firm to touch, and symmetrical. Hip joints have full active range of motion (ROM) through flexion, extension, hyperextension, abduction, adduction, circumduction, and internal and external rotation. Muscle strength is 5/5. The patient denies any discomfort while still or moving.

Knee

Inspection. Inspect the knee both standing and sitting. Inspect contour and shape. Observe for the concavities medially, laterally, and superiorly to the patella. Look for any swelling, lacerations, lesions, deformity, size of the muscle, and symmetry. Inspect alignment. Look for symmetry in the length of long bones: when the patient is standing, is one hip higher than the other? When seated, is one knee higher than the other? When seated, does one knee protrude further than the other? *Hollows are on each side of the patella. Knees are symmetrical and aligned with thighs and ankles.*

Palpation. With the patient standing, palpate the popliteal fossa for a swelling. *No palpable swelling in popliteal space bilaterally.* While the patient is seated or supine and with the knee flexed, palpate the quadriceps muscle for muscle tone. Palpate downward from approximately 10 cm above the patella and along each side of the patella; assess the patella, both tibiofemoral joints, and the patellar tendon (Fig. 23-23).

Swelling of the knee indicates inflammation, trauma, or *arthritis.* Muscle atrophy may accompany disuse or chronic disorders. A part of a limb twisted toward or out from the midline is labelled **varus** and **valgus**, respectively. For example, *genu valgus* is knock-knee, while *genu varus* is bowlegged. Asymmetry in leg muscle size may be from disuse or nerve or muscle injury. Absence of concavities suggests bursitis or swelling from trauma.

A palpable swelling in popliteal space *while standing* may be a Baker's cyst. Pain, swelling (bogginess), thickening, or heat may indicate synovial inflammation, *arthritis,* or meniscus tear. Painless swelling may occur with *osteoarthritis. Bursitis* causes swelling, heat, and redness. Tenderness may accompany a partial or complete tear of a ligament or tendon or injury to the medial meniscus.

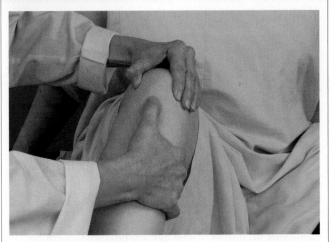

Figure 23-23 Palpating the knee.

Palpate the tibiofemoral joints with the leg flexed 90°. Assess the tibial margins and the lateral collateral ligament. Feel for any bumps, nodules, or deformity. Ask if there is any tenderness during touch. Feel for crepitus when moving the joint. *The quadriceps muscle and surrounding tissue are firm and nontender. The suprapatellar bursa is not palpable. The joint is firm and nontender.*

An advanced practice nurse may perform further examination for fluid in the knee joint using the drawer test, bulge test, and **ballottement** (see Table 23-8).

Range of Motion. Observe for full active range of motion (ROM) of each knee with the patient seated. The patient flexes the knee to 130° and returns to extended position. *The knee can perform flexion and extension without discomfort or crepitus.*

Inability to perform flexion and extension may be from contractures, osteoarthritis, pain associated with trauma or inflammation, or neuromuscular disorders.

⚠ *SAFETY ALERT 23-7*
Do not encourage the patient to hyperextend or rotate the knee medially or laterally. Attempting to do so may cause injury.

Injury or deconditioning may lead to asymmetry of strength.

Muscle Strength. With the patient seated, apply pressure to the anterior lower leg while the patient extends the leg. Also, with the leg flexed, ask the patient to maintain that position while you pull the lower leg as if to straighten it.

Muscle strength is equal bilaterally and able to overcome resistance.

Documentation of Expected Findings

The knees are aligned with the long axis of the leg. The muscles are well formed, firm to touch, and symmetrical. Knee joints have full active range of motion (ROM) through flexion and extension. No bulging or swelling is noted. Muscle strength is 5/5. The patient denies any discomfort while still or moving.

Table 23-8   Advanced Musculoskeletal Assessment Techniques

Phalen's Test

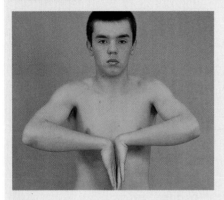

Evaluates for carpal tunnel syndrome. The patient flexes the wrists 90° and holds the backs of the hands to each other for 60 s. Expected response is denial of any discomfort. Positive signs include numbness, burning, or pain.

Bulge Test

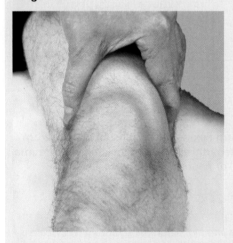

Differentiates soft tissue swelling from accumulation of excess fluid behind the patella. With the patient supine, milk upward along the medial aspect of the knee two, three, or four times. Then press on the lateral side of the knee and check for any bulging on the medial side. A bulge indicates mild joint effusion or liquid accumulation in the area, which is not an expected finding.

McMurray's Test

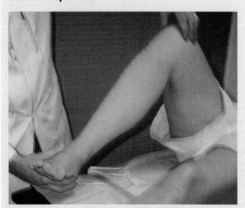

Tinel's Test

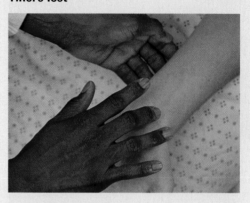

Evaluates for carpal tunnel syndrome. Percuss lightly over the median nerve located on the inner aspect of the wrist. Pain, numbness, or tingling is a positive (unexpected) finding.

Ballottement

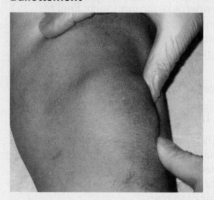

Evaluates presence of large accumulation of fluid behind the knee. With the patient supine and the knee extended, press on the quadriceps muscle just above the knee with one hand and keep that pressure there. This compresses the suprapatellar pouch. Palpate the patella with the other hand. If fluid is present, the patella will rebound or ballot against the fingers.

Checks for meniscus injury. The patient lies supine and flexes the hip and knee. The examiner supports the knee with one hand and holds the foot with the other, rotating the foot laterally. The examiner slowly extends the patient's knee, while assessing for the positive findings of pain or clicking. The examiner repeats the procedure, rotating the lower leg medially.

Table 23-8 **Advanced Musculoskeletal Assessment Techniques** (*continued*)

Thomas' Test

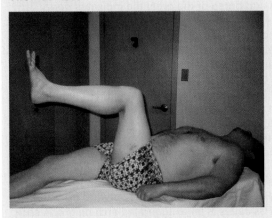

Assesses presence of a flexion contracture of the hip. Again, the patient is supine. Ask the patient to extend one leg and flex the hip and knee of the other leg, bringing the knee to the chest. A flexion contracture of the hip will cause the extended (opposite) leg to rise up off the examination table.

LeSegue's Test: Straight Leg Raising

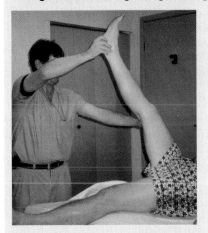

Checks for herniation of the lumbar disc and nerve irritation or pressure. With the patient supine and both legs extended, support and raise one leg. A positive response is the report of pain in the leg. Record the degree of elevation when pain occurs.

Drawer Sign

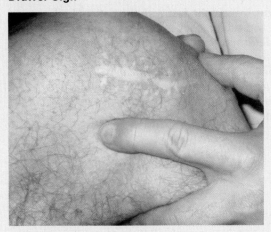

Checks for knee injury. The supine patient flexes the knee to a right angle. While standing at the patient's feet, grasp the leg just below the knee and see if you can move it toward and away from self. An expected finding is that the examiner cannot move the leg that way. A positive sign is the head of the tibia moves more than half an inch from the joint. May also be used for ankle injuries.

Trendelenburg's Test

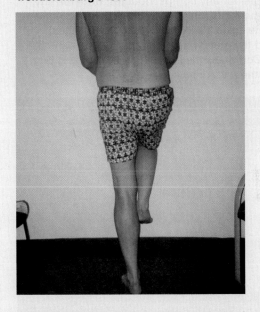

Assesses for hip disease with muscle weakness. Observe from behind the patient. Ask the patient to stand first on one foot and then the other. The pelvis remains level horizontally, which is a negative Trendelenburg's sign. An unexpected or positive finding is that the other hip drops when the patient stands on the weak side.

Drop Arm Test

Assesses for rotator cuff injury. Ask the patient to abduct the arm to shoulder level or 90°. If the patient cannot fully abduct and remain there, the drop arm test is positive as the arm drops rapidly to the patient's side or the patient reports severe shoulder pain.

Ankle and Foot

Inspection. Inspect the feet with the patient both standing and sitting. Look for any swelling, lacerations, lesions, deformity, size of the muscle, and symmetry. Look for toe alignment. *Feet are the same colour as the rest of the leg. They are symmetrical, with toes aligned with the long axis of the leg. No swelling is present. When the patient stands, the weight falls on the middle of the feet.*

An enlarged, swollen, hot, reddened metatarsophalangeal joint and bursa of the great toe indicates *gouty arthritis*. An ankle sprain or strain may cause pain on palpation and range of motion (ROM). Crepitus may indicate a fracture. Often a sprain cannot be differentiated from a fracture without an x-ray. With *hallux valgus* (*bunion*), the great toe is angled away from the midline, crowding the other toes. Flexion of the proximal interphalangeal (PIP) joint with hyperextension of the distal joint indicates *hammertoe*. A callus or corn forms on the flexed joint from external pressure. With *flatfoot* (*pes planus*), the arch of the foot is flattened and touches the floor. This may only be visible when the person is standing. *Pes varus* describes a foot that is turned inward toward the midline. *Pes valgus* is a foot turned outward from the midline. *Pes cavus* is an exaggerated arch height. A *corn* is a conical area of thickened skin from pressure. Corns may be painful and can occur between toes. *Callus* is thickened skin from pressure and usually occurs on the sole of the foot. Calluses are usually not painful.

Pain in the heel that occurs early in the morning or with prolonged sitting, standing, or walking may be *plantar fasciitis*, an inflammation of the plantar fascia where it attaches to the calcaneus.

An inward turning foot is *talipes equinovarus* (*clubfoot*).

Palpation. Feel for any bumps, nodules, or deformity. Holding the heel, palpate the anterior and posterior aspects of the ankle, the Achilles tendon (calcaneal tendon), and the metatarsophalangeal joints in the ball of the foot. Compress the forefoot for tenderness just proximal to the metatarsals (Fig. 23-24).

Pain or discomfort in the ankle or foot during palpation may indicate arthritis or inflammation. Pain and tenderness along the Achilles tendon may be from bursitis or tendonitis. Small nodules on the tendon may occur with rheumatoid arthritis. Tenderness to compression suggests early rheumatoid arthritis and also may indicate a hairline fracture.

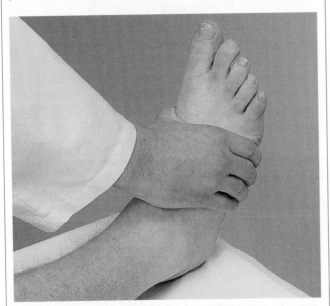

Figure 23-24 Compressing the forefoot.

Palpate each IP joint, medially and laterally, noting temperature, tenderness, and contour. Ask if there is any tenderness during touch. Feel for crepitus when moving the joint. *Ankle and foot joints are firm, stable, and nontender.*

Cooler temperature in the ankles and feet than in the rest of the body may be from vascular insufficiency, which will lead to musculoskeletal dysfunction (see Chapter 20).

Range of Motion. Observe for full active ROM of the ankle. Flexion and extension occur at the tibiotalar joint. Assess dorsiflexion by asking the patient to raise the toes toward the knee. Plantar flexion requires the patient to point toes downward toward the ground. Inversion and eversion occur when the sole of the foot is turned toward the opposite leg and away from the other leg, respectively (subtalar joint, transverse tarsal joint) (Fig. 23-25).

Limited ankle or foot ROM without swelling indicates arthritis. Inflammation and swelling with limited ROM indicates trauma. Commonly, strain of a ligament will intensify pain if the ligament is stretched during plantar flexion and inversion.

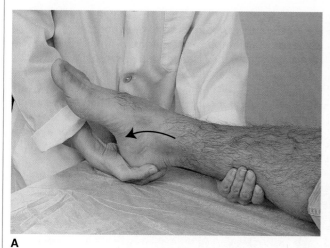

A

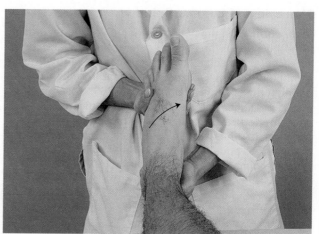

B

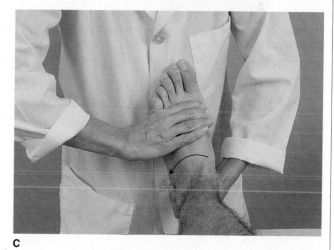

C

Figure 23-25 **A.** Plantar flexion. **B.** Foot inversion. **C.** Foot eversion.

Ask the patient to curl the toes and return them to straight position (flexion and extension). To assess hyperextension, ask the patient to keep the soles on the ground and raise the toes upward. For abduction, ask the patient to spread the toes wide open, as far apart from each other as possible. Adduction occurs when the toes return to their original position. *Expected ankle ROM is dorsiflexion 20°, plantar flexion 45°, inversion 30°, and eversion 20°. The toes can flex, extend, hyperextend, and abduct.*

Muscle Strength. Ask the patient to perform dorsiflexion and plantar flexion against the resistance of your hand. Then ask the patient to flex and extend the toes against your resistance.

Muscle strength is equal bilaterally. Able to overcome resistance.

Asymmetry of strength may be from pain, inflammation, deconditioning, or chronic disease.

The ankles and feet are symmetrical and the same colour as the legs. The muscles are well formed, firm to touch, and symmetrical. The ankles have full active range of motion (ROM) through dorsiflexion and plantar flexion; the feet have full active ROM through inversion and eversion. The toes abduct, flex, and extend. Muscle strength is 5/5. The patient denies any discomfort while sitting, standing, or walking.

Techniques and Expected Findings

Thoracic and Lumbar Spine

Inspection. With the patient standing, look at the patient from the side for the pattern (convex thoracic and sacrococcygeal spine and concave cervical and lumbar spine) (Fig. 23-26). Observe the patient from behind, noting if the spine is straight (Fig. 23-27). Observe if the scapulae, iliac crests, and gluteal folds are level and symmetrical. Ask the patient to bend forward and reassess that the vertebrae are in a straight line and the scapulae are equal in height. *The spine is in alignment both standing and sitting.*

Rationale/Unexpected Findings

Kyphosis, a forward bending of the upper thoracic spine, may accompany *osteoporosis, ankylosing spondylosis,* and *Paget's disease* (Osteoporosis Canada, 2011c). Exaggerated curvature in the lumbar spine is lordosis, which is common in late pregnancy and obesity. A flattened lumbar curve may occur with lumbar muscle spasms. A list is a leaning of the spine to one side. This may occur with paravertebral muscle spasms or a herniated disc. Scoliosis is a lateral thoracic curvature with a compensatory lumbar curve in the opposite direction.

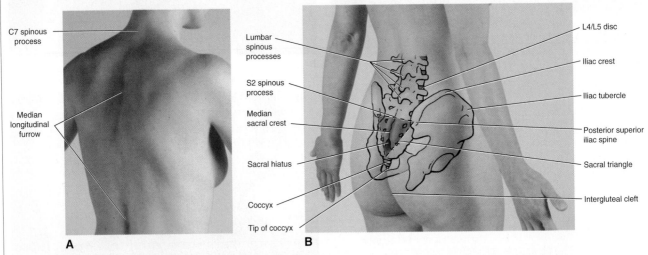

Figure 23-26 Assessing the spine and upper back. **A.** Upper portion. **B.** Lower portion.

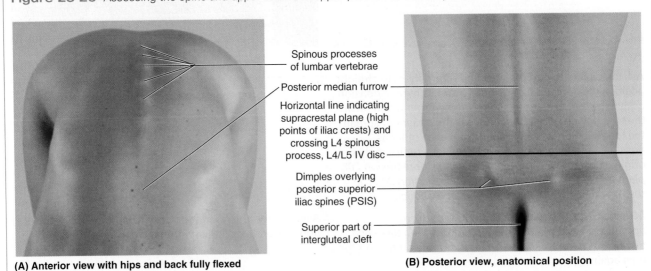

(A) Anterior view with hips and back fully flexed

(B) Posterior view, anatomical position

Figure 23-27 Lower back. **A.** Anterior view with hips and back fully flexed. **B.** Posterior view, anatomical position.

Palpation. Palpate the spinous processes from T1 to L5 using circular motion with fingerpads. Feel for any bumps, nodules, or deformities. Ask if there is any tenderness during touch. Feel for crepitus when the spine bends. *The spinous processes are in a straight line. The patient denies tenderness. The paravertebral muscles are firm. There is no crepitus.*

Range of Motion. Observe for full active range of motion (ROM) of the spine. Ask the patient to stand and bend forward to 75° to 90°. Ask the patient to lean backward (hyperextend) to 30° (Fig. 23-28). The spine assessment also includes lateral flexion (or abduction) to 35° on either side. Ask the patient to slide a hand on one side down that thigh and bend away from the midline toward the side. Do this on both sides. To perform rotation of the spine, ask the patient to keep legs and hips forward facing while the shoulders turn to the side (30°). Repeat to the other side. *The patient can perform full ROM without crepitus or discomfort.*

Pain on palpation may indicate inflammation, disc disease, or *arthritis*. Unequal spinous processes may indicate subluxation.

Pain, back injury, *osteoarthritis*, and *ankylosing spondylitis* may result in limited ROM.

⚠ *SAFETY ALERT 23-8*

Stand beside the patient and be ready to provide support while the patient performs spine ROM. The patient may lose balance and fall.

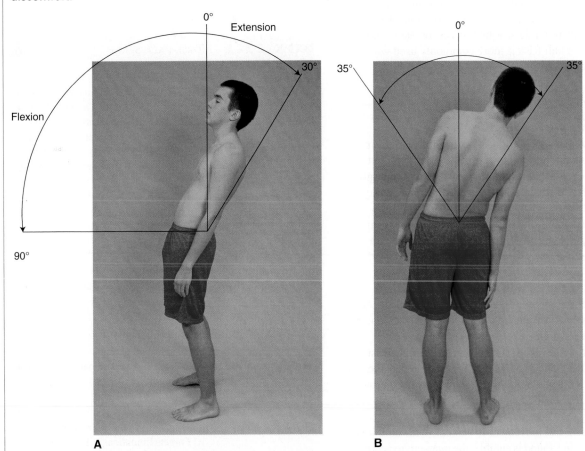

A

B

Figure 23-28 Spine ROM. **A.** Hyperextension. **B.** Lateral flexion.

Examples of Documentation for Musculoskeletal System

Area of Assessment	Expected Findings
Spine	Intact curvature of cervical, thoracic, and lumbar spine noted; full, smooth range of motion (ROM) in cervical and lumbar spine; upper and lower extremities symmetrical
Posture	Head erect and midline; patient sits upright in chair
Gait	Smooth, even gait, with arms swinging in opposition
Joints	Full ROM in all joints; no swelling or deformity
Joints	Full ROM in all joints; no swelling or deformity
Muscle strength	Strength rated 5/5; active motion against resistance for all muscle groups

Adapted from Roach, S., Roddick, P., et al. (2010). The musculoskeletal system. In T. C. Stephen, D. L. Skillen, R. A. Day, & L. S. Bickley (Eds.). *Canadian Bates' guide to health assessment for nurses* (1st ed., p. 665). Philadelphia, PA: Wolters Kluwer Health/Lippincott Williams & Wilkins.

Fall Risk

To assess if the patient is at risk for falling, nurses can use several tools. Most common are the Morse Fall Risk and Hendrich Π Fall Risk model. A high score indicates a risk for falling and a need for preventive interventions. Examples include frequent reminders, a bed alarm, or environmental cues. The Morse Fall Risk is more commonly used with hospitalized patients (see Box 23-1).

Lifespan Considerations

Women Who Are Pregnant

Lordosis shifts the weight back on the lower extremities and causes strain on the lower back muscles. Anterior flexion of the neck and slumping of the shoulder girdle compensate for lordosis. The upper back changes may put pressure on the ulnar and median nerves during the third trimester. Pressure on the nerves may cause aching, numbness, and upper extremity weakness in some women who are pregnant.

Newborns, Infants, and Children

At birth, newborns are assessed for congenital hip dislocation. The examiner performs either a Barlow-Ortolani manoeuvre or a test for Allis' sign.

In the Barlow-Ortolani manoeuvre, the infant is supine with flexed knees and hips so that the heels touch the buttocks. The examiner places his or her fingers on the baby's greater trochanter of the humerus and abducts the legs separately, moving the knees down and laterally. This manoeuvre is negative when the movement is smooth, with no clicking sound. If a clicking sound is audible, the manoeuvre is considered a positive indication of hip dislocation (Fig. 23-29).

The examiner tests for Allis' sign by placing the infant's supine with flexed hips and knees and both feet flat on the table. A negative Allis' sign is when the knees are at equal heights. A positive Allis' sign is when one knee is lower than the other, indicating hip dysplasia.

The spinal column undergoes changes in contour as the child becomes more active. At birth, the spine has a C-shaped curve. The cervical curve develops by age 3 to 4 months as the child begins raising its head. The lumbar curve develops when the child stands, usually between 12 and 18 months (see Fig. 23-30).

BOX 23-1 MORSE FALL SCALE

*N*ursing fall risk assessment, diagnoses, and interventions are based on use of the Morse Fall Scale (MFS). The MFS is used widely in acute care settings, both in hospital and long-term care inpatient settings. The MFS requires systematic, reliable assessment of the patient's fall risk factors upon admission, a fall, a change in status, and discharge or transfer to a new setting. MFS subscales include assessment of

1. History of falling; immediate or within 3 months	No = 0 Yes = 25
2. Secondary diagnosis	No = 0 Yes = 15
3. Ambulatory aid	None, bed rest, wheelchair, nurse = 0 Crutches, cane, walker = 15 Furniture = 30
4. IV/heparin lock	No = 0 Yes = 20
5. Gait/transferring	Balanced and coordinated or bed rest or immobile = 0 Weak = 10 Impaired = 20
6. Mental status	Oriented to own ability = 0 Forgets limitations = 15

Risk Level	MFS Score	Action
No Risk	0–24	None
Low Risk	25–50	See standard fall prevention Interventions
High Risk	= 51	See high risk fall prevention interventions

Adapted from Morse, J. M. (2009). *Preventing patient falls.* (2nd ed.). New York: Springer.

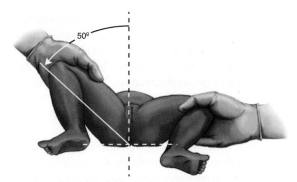

Figure 23-29 Testing for Barlow-Ortolani sign.

Examiners assess muscle tone in the newborn by observing flexion of the arms and legs and by holding the infant under the arms. With intact muscle strength, the shoulders support the weight of the infant. Infants with diminished muscle tone slide through the examiner's hands.

Older Adults

Examiners allow extra time for older adults to complete each activity. They may divide the assessment into portions if an older patient appears fatigued.

Lifestyle affects the musculoskeletal system. Hardy, Perera, et al. (2007) found that improved gait speed indicated better and longer survival and recommended assessment of gait speed as a vital sign for older adults.

Lifestyle and Work-Related Considerations

Some working conditions present potential risks to the musculoskeletal system. Workers required to lift heavy objects may strain and injure their backs. Jobs requiring substantial physical activity, such as construction work and firefighting, increase the likelihood of sprains, strains, and fractures. Frequent repetitive movements may lead to misuse disorders

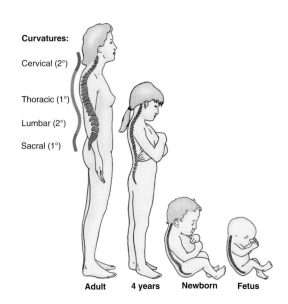

Figure 23-30 Changes in spinal curvature from infancy through adulthood.

such as carpal tunnel syndrome, pitcher's elbow, or vertebral degeneration. Musculoskeletal injuries may also occur when people sit for long periods at desks or computers with incorrect ergonomic design.

Risk-taking activities, extreme sports, mainstream sports, and recreational activities also present risks for the musculoskeletal system. Nurses inquire about the use of personal protective equipment during these activities.

Advanced Techniques

Advanced techniques may be used to assess for joint injuries, scoliosis, a herniated disc, carpal tunnel syndrome, fluid behind the patella, meniscus injury, flexion contracture of the

---

Documenting Unexpected Findings

The nurse has just finished conducting a physical examination of Mrs. Gladys Crowfoot, an 82-year-old woman in the extended care facility for rehabilitation following a fall at home. Unlike the examples of documentation previously charted, Mrs. Crowfoot has unexpected findings. Review the following important findings that were revealed in each step of objective data collection for Mrs. Crowfoot. Consider how these results compare with the expected findings presented in the documentation. Begin to think about how the data cluster together and what additional data the nurse might want to collect as he or she thinks critically about the issues and anticipates nursing interventions.

Inspection: Skin warm and sallow. Mild kyphosis present. Heberden's nodes present at the distal interphalangeal (DIP) joint; Bouchard's nodes present in the proximal interphalangeal (PIP) joints in the hands. Diffuse swelling noted in all joints, most prominent in the hands. Range of motion (ROM) approximately 50% of expected. Hip abduction and internal rotation are limited. Joints in knee and ankles are also swollen. Scattered subcutaneous nodules are present. Gait slow but stable.

Palpation: Tenderness noted over joints in hands. Muscle strength 2/5 bilaterally. Pulses 1+/4. Capillary refill 2 seconds. Identifies sharp and light touch accurately. Muscle strength in feet and legs is 2+/4.

hip, rotator cuff injury, ankle sprains, ruptured Achilles tendon, and tears of the ACL (see Table 23-8, pp. 676–677 for advanced techniques).

Evidence-Informed Critical Thinking

Organizing and Prioritizing

As with other systems, assessment of the musculoskeletal system usually proceeds from general to specific and from head to toe. Focused assessments may be more appropriate when the patient reports an injury to a specific area or joint.

Students need structure as they learn assessment skills. Medical students improved their skills in assessment of the musculoskeletal system when they were taught the GALS (gait, arms, legs, spine) locomotor screen (Doherty, Dacre, et al., 1992; Fox, Dacre, et al., 2000). The GALS is a method of quickly inspecting gait, arms, legs, and spine. The patient performs 11 tasks, and the examiner asks two questions: "Do you have any pain or stiffness anywhere?" and "Do you have any difficulty washing, dressing, or climbing stairs/steps?" Some educators and researchers have modified the first question to be more specific; that is, "Do you have any pain or stiffness in your muscles, joints, back, or neck?"

Laboratory and Diagnostic Testing

Laboratory tests can help identify specific musculoskeletal conditions. Health care professionals evaluate all test results within the context of other signs and symptoms. Common laboratory tests of muscle injury include evaluations of lactate dehydrogenase, creatinine kinase, alanine aminotransferase, and aspartate aminotransferase. Other tests can reveal responses to bone damage, such as alkaline phosphatase. Uric acid is elevated in gouty arthritis. Inflammatory markers such as erythrocyte sedimentation rate, C-reactive protein, and rheumatoid factor are elevated with all inflammatory conditions, including rheumatoid arthritis and lupus erythematosus.

Imaging tests are especially valuable in identifying musculoskeletal injuries and deformities. X-rays show bone fractures. Computerized tomography and magnetic resonance imaging can reveal soft tissue damage, including ligament and tendon injuries. Bone density scans can help identify patients with osteoporosis and at risk for injury from falls.

Clinical Reasoning

When formulating a nursing diagnosis, it is important to use critical thinking to cluster data together and identify patterns that fit together. The nurse compares these clusters of data with the defining characteristics (unexpected findings) for the diagnosis to ensure the most accurate labelling and appropriate interventions. (See Table 23-13 at end of chapter for findings in common conditions).

Nursing Diagnoses, Outcomes, and Interventions

A nursing diagnosis is a clinical judgment about responses to health challenges or life processes. Table 23-9 compares nursing diagnoses, unexpected findings, and interventions commonly related to the musculoskeletal system assessment (Bulechek, Butcher, et al., 2008).

Nurses use assessment information to identify patient outcomes. Some outcomes that are related to musculoskeletal

Table 23-9	Common Nursing Diagnoses Associated With the Musculoskeletal System			
---	---	---	---	
Diagnosis and Related Factors	Point of Differentiation	Assessment Characteristics	Nursing Interventions
Self-care deficit: specify bathing/ hygiene, dressing/ grooming, feeding, toileting	Inability to perform activities of daily living (ADLs) for oneself	Grade ability to perform activity using a scale that includes being completely independent, requires use of equipment, requires help from another person, or completely dependent	Observe the patient's ability to perform skill. Ask for input on habits and preferences. Encourage the patient to do as much independently as possible. Use adaptive devices such as Velcro or elastic versus buttons or ties.
Impaired walking	Limitation of independent movement within the environment on foot	Cannot walk on even surfaces or uneven surfaces, climb stairs, or go required distances	Follow weight-bearing restrictions.* Use assistive devices such as a cane or walker. Obtain appropriate number of people to assist with walking the patient. Limit distractions during ambulation.

*Collaborative interventions.

system conditions include the following (Moorhead, Johnson, et al., 2008):

- Patient does not fall.
- Patient dresses, grooms, and eats independently.
- Patient ambulates in hall three times daily.

Once the outcomes are established, patient care is implemented to improve the status of the patient. The nurse uses critical thinking and evidence-informed practice to develop the interventions. Some examples of nursing interventions for the musculoskeletal system are as follows (Dochterman & Bulechek, 2004):

- Teach the patient to call for help before ambulating to bathroom.
- Open packages and arrange tray prior to encouraging the patient to eat independently.
- Communicate through documentation about the type of assistance needed.

The nurse then evaluates the care according to the patient outcomes that were developed, therefore reassessing the patient and continuing or modifying the interventions as appropriate. An accurate and complete nursing assessment is an essential foundation for holistic nursing care.

Analyzing Findings

Remember Mrs. Gladys Crowfoot, whose health challenges have been outlined throughout this chapter. The initial subjective and objective data collection is complete, and the nurse has spent time reviewing the findings and other results. The following nursing note illustrates how subjective and objective data are collected and analyzed and nursing interventions are developed.

Subjective: "I feel stiff and cold. My legs and hands don't work the way that they used to."

Objective: Skin warm and sallow. Diffuse swelling noted in all joints, most prominent in the hands. Subcutaneous (rheumatoid) nodules are present. Range of motion (ROM) 50% in hands. Tenderness noted over joints in hands. Muscle strength 2/5 in hands and 3/5 in legs. CMS+ all four extremities. Identifies sharp and light touch accurately. Hip abduction and internal rotation are limited. Gait slow but stable. Needs one person assist and walker for ambulation to bathroom. Needs setup on fine motor skills for hygiene, dressing, and eating.

Analysis: Impaired physical mobility related to reduced strength and ROM.

Plan: Allow the patient to perform as much independently as possible. Provide encouragement for participation in physical and occupational therapies and positive reinforcement for small increments in improvement. Remind her to use walker and call for help before ambulating to bathroom.

Critical Thinking Challenge

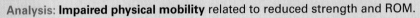

- What other assessments are important in addition to the musculoskeletal system?
- How will the nurse collect complete assessment information but avoid fatiguing Mrs. Crowfoot?
- What functional patterns might the limited ROM and joint tenderness affect?
- Which is more of a concern for this patient—physiological or psychosocial assessment? Provide rationale.

Collaborating With the Interprofessional Team

Both occupational and physical therapists work with patients to increase mobility and functional abilities for rehabilitation. Generally physical therapists focus on larger motor groups, while occupational therapists focus on fine motor skills and the upper body. Nurses may consult occupational therapists for patients with difficulties involving bathing, dressing, grooming, home and money management, assistive technology, or increasing range of motion (ROM), tone, sensation, or coordination.

Mrs. Crowfoot has been working with occupational therapy (OT) to increase function and attain adaptive devices for her in the home. The following conversation illustrates how the nurse might communicate progress when OT comes.

(case study continues on page 686)

Situation: Hi Cheryl. I'm taking care of Mrs. Crowfoot today. She said that you were going to work with her in the kitchen today. (Cheryl confirms)

Background: She's a little discouraged because she doesn't feel like she's making progress.

Assessment: I had a discussion with her about how she's coping with her decline in function. She feels frustrated that she's not making faster progress because she really wants to go home.

Recommendations: I encouraged her and talked about how much improvement I've seen and she seemed encouraged by that. I think that if you also provided her with feedback on things that she is doing well, it will be motivating for her. We talked some about working with you today and seeing how she does in the kitchen because that's her biggest concern. She wants to be able to prepare her own meals but also is aware that a service that delivers meals might be an option. I told her how you would show her some tricks for cooking and also some ergonomic and lightweight cooking tools. Can you also work with her on opening jars? She's been having difficulty for a while and thinks that you might be able to help her.

Critical Thinking Challenge

- Why didn't the nurse provide all of the physical assessment data to the OT?
- What is the role of the nurse in providing the psychosocial information to the OT?
- What types of assessments will need to be completed prior to discharging the patient to home?

Pulling It All Together: An Example of Reflection and Critical Thinking

The nurse uses assessment data to formulate a patient care plan with patient outcomes and interventions for Mrs. Crowfoot. Outcomes are specific to the patient, realistic to achieve, and measurable; they also have a time frame for completion. The interventions are actions that the nurse performs, based on evidence and practice guidelines. After implementation of these interventions, the nurse reevaluates Mrs. Crowfoot and documents the findings in the patient health record to show progress toward the patient outcome. The nurse uses critical thinking and judgment to continue or revise the diagnosis, outcomes, or interventions. This is often in the form of a care plan or case note similar to the one below.

Nursing Diagnosis	Patient Outcomes	Nursing Interventions	Rationale	Evaluation
Impaired physical mobility related to joint swelling and tenderness as evidenced by limited range of motion (ROM) and reduced strength in hands.	Demonstrates independent dressing, grooming, and toileting with assistive devices.	Allow the patient to do as much as possible. Provide positive feedback for progress each shift. Consult with occupational therapy (OT) on assistive devices. Collaborate on a plan for discharge and needed resources.	Independence provides increased control, functional ability, and a sense of accomplishment. OT can identify devices that might be helpful for discharge. A home care nurse may initially visit the patient to identify necessary resources.	Bathing and dressing with minimal assistance using elastic waist pants and Velcro shoes. Dressed the bottom half first and then the top. OT worked with the patient today and identified assistive devices for the kitchen. Recommend home OT consult for at least one visit.

Using the previous steps of clinical reasoning, organizing, and prioritizing, consider all the case study findings woven throughout this chapter. When answering the following questions, begin drawing conclusions and see how the pieces of assessment must work together to create an environment for personalized, appropriate, and accurate care:

- How are physiological and psychological data connected? (Knowledge)
- What nursing diagnoses might be activated on this patient's health conditions list? Provide rationale. (Comprehension)
- What areas will the nurse assess as part of a comprehensive musculoskeletal assessment? (Application)
- What additional assessments should the nurse add? (Analysis)
- What are expected findings for Mrs. Crowfoot based on her age compared with findings based on her osteoporosis? (Synthesis)
- How will the nurse evaluate the effectiveness of teaching for Mrs. Crowfoot to manage living in her own home? (Evaluation)

Key Points

- Functions of the musculoskeletal system include providing shape to the body and permitting movement.
- Identification of musculoskeletal risk factors is important for focused patient teaching aimed toward decreasing deformity or injury.
- Subjective data from the history and current condition guides performance of the physical assessment of the musculoskeletal system.
- The nurse compares one side of the body to the other and determines if symmetry is present.
- The nurse assesses each joint for ROM, and assesses muscle tone and strength.
- Gait, coordination, and balance involve both the musculoskeletal and neurological systems.
- Nurses use inspection and palpation to assess the musculoskeletal system.
- During passive ROM, examiners do not force joints beyond the development of resistance or the development of discomfort.
- Patients with fragile bones require gentle handling to prevent fracture.
- Nurses consider unexpected findings in ROM and muscle strength when developing nursing diagnoses and planning interventions.
- Nurses individualize assessment of the musculoskeletal system according to the patient's condition, age, gender, and ethnicity.

Review Questions

1. Mr. Brown was playing soccer and hurt his right knee. It appears swollen. What is the first assessment the nurse should make?
   A. Palpate for crepitus in the knee.
   B. Compare the swollen knee to the other knee.
   C. Assess active range of motion (ROM) in the knee.
   D. Feel the knee for warmth.

2. Mrs. Johnson, a transcriptionist, reports pain and burning in her right hand. What assessment procedures should the nurse perform next?
   A. Trendelenburg's and drawer signs
   B. McMurray's and Thomas' tests
   C. Bulge test and ballottement
   D. Phalen's and Tinel's tests

3. Which of the following assessment tasks can you appropriately delegate to an unlicensed care provider?
   A. Height, weight, temperature, and pulse
   B. Active and passive ROM
   C. History of current concern
   D. Muscle strength

4. When doing an assessment of the spine of an older adult, the nurse can expect to see which variation?
   A. Lordosis
   B. Torticollis
   C. Kyphosis
   D. Scoliosis

5. When assessing the spine of a woman in her ninth month of pregnancy, the nurse would expect to see which variation?
   A. Lordosis
   B. Torticollis
   C. Kyphosis
   D. Scoliosis

6. To correctly document that ROM in the fingers is full and active, the nurse writes that the patient can
   A. perform rotation, lateral flexion, and hyperextension
   B. make a fist, spread and close fingers, and do finger–thumb opposition
   C. touch finger to own nose and to examiner's finger back and forth
   D. perform supination, pronation, and lateral deviation

7. When assessing a newborn, the nurse notes that one knee is lower than the other when the legs are flexed and the heels are together on the bed. The nurse should correctly document this finding as positive
A. ballottement
B. Thomas' test
C. Allis' sign
D. genu varus

8. The nurse is assessing the patient who has been diagnosed with a neuromuscular disorder. The nurse notes the patient cannot lift the right leg off of the bed when the nurse is applying resistance. The nurse would document the muscle strength in the right leg as
A. fair
B. 2/5
C. 50%
D. within expected limits

9. The nurse notes an adolescent has uneven shoulder height. To differentiate functional from structural scoliosis, the nurse will ask the patient to
A. stand up straight while the nurse checks the height of the iliac crests
B. flex the elbow and pull against the nurse's resistance
C. shrug both shoulders while the nurse provides resistance
D. bend forward at the waist while the nurse inspects the spine

10. The patient reports that a previous right hip replacement is suddenly painful. Which hip assessment technique should the nurse omit?
A. Adduction
B. Hyperextension
C. Extension
D. Circumduction

11. A female patient reports that her mother has osteoporosis and wants to know what she can do to prevent developing the disease. Which of the following responses is best for the nurse to provide?
A. Engage in aerobic exercise most days of the week.
B. Eat at least one serving of dark green leafy vegetables daily.
C. Consume three servings of dairy products per day.
D. Perform muscle-strengthening exercises every other day.

Canadian Nursing Research

Cloutier, E., David, H., et al. (2008). Effects of government policies on the work of home care personnel and their occupational health and safety. *Work: A Journal of Prevention, Assessment and Rehabilitation, 30*(4), 389–402.

Mason, D., Brien S. E., et al. (2007). Musculoskeletal fitness and weight gain in Canada. *Medicine & Science in Sports & Exercise, 39*(1), 38–43.

Naylor, P. J., Macdonald, H. M., et al. (2006). Action schools! BC: A socioecological approach to modifying chronic disease risk factors in elementary school children. *Preventing Chronic Disease, 3*(2), A60.

Petit, M., Macdonald, H. M., et al. (2006). Growing bones: How important is exercise? *Current Opinion in Orthopaedics, 17,* 431–437.

Wells, R., Laing, A., et al. (2009). Characterizing the intensity of changes made to reduce mechanical exposure. *Work: A Journal of Prevention, Assessment and Rehabilitation, 34*(2), 179–193.

References

Agency for Healthcare Research and Quality. (2005). *Women's health care in the United States: Selected findings from the 2004 national healthcare quality and disparities reports.* Fact Sheet. AHRQ Publication No. 05-P021. Rockville, MD: Author. Retrieved from http://www.ahrq.gov/qual/nhqrwomen/nhqrwome

Almstedt Shoepe, H., & Snow, C. M. (2005). Oral contraceptive use in young women is associated with lower bone mineral density than that of controls. *Osteoporosis International, 16*(12), 1538–1544.

ALS Society of Canada. (2009). *A guide to ALS care for primary care physicians.* Retrieved from http://www.als.ca/system/guide/AGuidetoALSPatientCareForPrimaryCarePhysicians-English.pdf

Bulechek, G. M., Butcher, H. K., et al. (2008). *Nursing interventions classification (NIC)* (5th ed.). St. Louis, MO: Mosby Elsevier.

Canale, S. T. (2003). *Campbell's operative orthopaedics* (10th ed.). Philadelphia, PA: Elsevier.

Dane, C., Dane, B., et al. (2007). Comparison of the effects of raloxifene and low-dose hormone replacement therapy on bone mineral density and bone turnover in the treatment of postmenopausal osteoporosis. *Gynecological Endocrinology, 23*(7), 398–403.

Dochterman, J. M., & Bulechek, G. M. (2004). *Nursing interventions classification (NIC)* (4th ed.). St. Louise, MO: Mosby.

Doherty, M., Dacre, J., et al. (1992). The "GALS" locomotor screen. *Annals of the Rheumatic Diseases, 51*(10), 1165–1169.

Feldman, D. E., Bernatsky, S., et al. (2009). The incidence of juvenile rheumatoid arthritis in Québec: A population data-based study. *Pediatric Rheumatology, 7*(20), 1–4.

Finkelstein, J. S., Brockwell, S. E., et al. (2008). Bone mineral density changes during the menopause transition in a multiethnic cohort of women. *Journal of Clinical Endocrinology and Metabolism, 93*(3), 861–868.

Firestein, G. S., Budd, R. C., et al. (2008). *Kelley's textbook of rheumatology* (8th ed.). Philadelphia, PA: Elsevier.

Fox, R. A., Dacre, J. E., et al. (2000). Impact on medical students on incorporating GALS screen teaching into the medical school curriculum. *Annals of the Rheumatic Diseases, 59*(9), 668–671.

Gartner, L. M., & Greer, F. R. (2003). Prevention of rickets and vitamin D deficiency: New guidelines for vitamin D intake. *Pediatrics, 111*(4), 908–910.

Goebel, L. (2007). *Scurvy.* Retrieved from http://www.emedicine.com/med/topic2086.htm

Hampl, J. S., Taylor, C. A., et al. (2004). Vitamin C deficiency and depletion in the United States: The Third National Health and Nutrition Examination Survey, 1988 to 1994. *American Journal of Public Health, 94*(5), 870–875.

Hardy, S. E., Perera, S., et al. (2007). Improvement in usual gait seed predicts better survival in older adults. *Journal of the American Geriatric Society, 55*(11), 1727–1734.

Harel-Meir, M., Sherer, Y., et al. (2007). Tobacco smoking and autoimmune rheumatic diseases. *Nature Clinical Practice Rheumatology, 3*(12), 707–715.

Health Canada. (2005). *Food and nutrition: Transition to solid foods.* Retrieved from http://www.hc-sc.gc.ca/fn-an/pubs/infant-nourrisson/nut_infant_nourrisson_term_6-eng.p

Hewett T. E., Ford, K. R., et al. (2006). Anterior cruciate ligament injuries in female athletes. Part 2: A meta-analysis of neuromuscular interventions aimed at injury prevention. *American Journal of Sports Medicine, 34,* 490.

Jorgensen, L., Joakimsen, R., et al. (2011). Smoking is a strong risk factor for non-vertebral fractures in women with diabetes: The Tromso study. *Osteoporosis International, 22*(4), 1247–1253.

Jutberger, H., Lorentzon, M., et al. (2010). Smoking predicts incident fractures in elderly men: Mr OS Sweden. *Journal of Bone and Mineral Research, 25*(5), 1010–1016.

MacLean, C., Newberry, S., et al. (2008). Systematic review: Comparative effectiveness of treatments to prevent fractures in men and women with low bone density or osteoporosis. *Annals of Internal Medicine, 148*(3), 197–213.

McGregor, M., & Atwood, C. V. (2007). *Wait times at the MUHC, No. 3 Fracture management. Montreal,* QC: Technology Assessment Unit, McGill University Health Centre. Report number 31.

Moorhead, S., Johnson, M., et al. (2008). *Nursing outcomes classification (NOC)* (4th ed.). St. Louis, MO: Mosby.

Morse, J. M. (2009). *Preventing patient falls* (2nd ed.). New York: Springer.

MS Society of Canada. (2011). *About MS.* Retrieved from http://mssociety.ca/en/information/default.htm

Myeloma Canada. (2009). *Multiple myeloma patient handbook.* Retrieved from http://www.myelomacanada.ca/docs/patienthandbook2009_en_version2.pdf

National Osteoporosis Foundation. (2008). *Osteoporosis facts.* Retrieved from http://www.nof.org/osteoporosis/diseasefacts.htm

Osteoporosis Canada. (2007). *If you fracture.* Retrieved from http://www.osteoporosis.ca/english/About%20osteoporosis/Living-well/if-you-fracture/default.asp?s=I

Osteoporosis Canada. (2011a). *Facts and statistics.* Retrieved from http://www.http://www.osteoporosis.ca/index.php/ci_id/8867/la_id/I.htm

Osteoporosis Canada. (2011b). *Focus on fractures: Osteoporosis Canada launches new clinical practice guidelines.* Retrieved from http://www.osteoporosis.ca/index.php/ci_id/10159/la_id/I.htm

Osteoporosis Canada. (2011c). *Paget's disease.* Retrieved from http://www.arthritis.ca/types%20of%20arthritis/paget/default.asp?=I&province=bc

Papaioannou, A., Morin, S., et al. (2010). Practice guidelines for the diagnosis and management of osteoporosis in Canada: Summary. *Canadian Medical Association Journal, 182*(17), 1864–1873.

Pressler, J. L. (2008). Classification of major newborn birth injuries. *Journal of Perinatal & Neonatal Nursing, 22*(1), 60–67.

Public Health Agency of Canada. (2009). *Osteoporosis info-sheet for seniors.* Retrieved from http://www.phac-aspc.gc.ca/seniors-aines/publications/puboic/age/info/osteoporosis/osteo

Public Health Agency of Canada. (2010a). *Living with arthritis: A personal and public health challenge.* Retrieved from http://dsp-psd.pwgsc.gc.ca/collections/collection_2010/aspc-phac/HP35-17-2010-eng.pdf

Public Health Agency of Canada. (2010b). *What is the impact of osteoporosis in Canada and what are Canadians doing to maintain healthy bones?* Retrieved from http://www.phac-aspc.gc.ca/cd-mc/osteoporosis-sosteoporose/index-eng.php

Roach, S., Roddick, P., et al. (2010). The musculoskeletal system. In T. C. Stephen, D. L. Skillen, R. A. Day, & L. S. Bickley (Eds.). *Canadian Bates' guide to health assessment for nurses* (1st ed., pp. 601–681). Philadelphia, PA: Wolters Kluwer Health/Lippincott Williams & Wilkins.

Schwalfenberg, G. K., Genuis, S. J., et al. (2010). Addressing vitamin D deficiency in Canada: A public health innovation whose time has come. *Public Health, 124,* 350–359. Retrieved from http://intraspec.ca/Addressing_Vitamin_D_Deficiency_In_Canada-April2010%5BI%5D.pdf

Statistics Canada. (2006). *Health state descriptions for Canadians: Musculoskeletal diseases.* No.82-619-MWE2006003. Retrieved from http://www.statcan.gc.ca/bsolc/olc-cel/olc-cel?catno=82-619-MWE2006003&lang=eng

Stephen, T. C., Day, R. A., et al. (Eds.) (2011–2012). *A syllabus for adult health assessment.* Edmonton, AB: Faculty of Nursing, University of Alberta.

Swiontkowski, M. F., Engelberg, R., et al. (1999). Short musculoskeletal function assessment. *The Journal of Bone and Joint Surgery, 81A*(9), 1245–1260.

Tortora, G. J., & Nielsen, M. T. (2012). *Principles of human anatomy* (12th ed.). Hoboken, NJ: John Wiley & Sons.

Towheed, T. E., Maxwell, L., et al. (2005). Glucosamine therapy for treating osteoarthritis. *Cochrane Database Systematic Review, 2,* CD002946.

Tylavsky, F. A., Ryder, K. A., et al. (2005). The influence of Vitamin D on bone health across the life cycle: Vitamin D, parathyroid hormone, and bone mass in adolescents. *American Society for Journal of Nutrition, 135,* 2735S–2738S.

Valachovicova, T., Slivova, V., et al. (2004). Soy isoflavones suppress invasiveness of breast cancer cells by the inhibition of NF-kappaB/AP-1-dependent and -independent pathways. *International Journal of Oncology, 25,* 1389–1395.

van Schoor, N. M., Visser, M., et al. (2008). Vitamin D deficiency as a risk factor for osteoporotic fractures. *Bone, 42*(2), 260–266.

Volpi, E., Nazemi, R., et al. (2004). Muscle tissue changes with aging. *Current Opinion in Clinical Nutrition & Metabolic Care, 7*(4), 405–410.

The Canadian Jensen's Nursing Health Assessment suite offers these additional resources to enhance learning and facilitate understanding of this chapter:

• thePoint on line resource, http//thepoint.lww.com/Stephen1E
• *Laboratory Manual for Canadian Jensen's Nursing Health Assessment: A Best Practice Approach*

Tables of Unexpected Findings

Table 23-10 **Selected Musculoskeletal Conditions: Onset, Gender, and Genetic Background**

Condition	Age at Onset	Gender	Genetic Background
Amyotrophic lateral sclerosis (ALS)	Median age 55 y (ALS Society of Canada, 2009)	Slightly more common in men	>90% of cases have no genetic linkages.
Ankylosing spondylitis	Onset typically between 15 and 30 y	Three times more common in men	Most common in First Nations people
Bursitis	Older than 40 y	Occurs in men and women equally, related to chronic stress or acute injury	Occurs in all genetic backgrounds
Carpal tunnel syndrome	25–50 y	Three times more common in women; especially prevalent in women who are pregnant and menopausal women	Most common in Caucasians
Dupuytren's contracture	After 40 y	More common in men	Most common in Caucasians of north European ancestry
Gout	2% of the population older than 30 y (males) and 50 y (females)	Three times more common in men; earlier onset among men	Affects all genetic backgrounds
Low back pain	Average age 30–50 y	Equally in men and women (Statistics Canada, 2006)	Affects all genetic backgrounds
Multiple sclerosis	Average age 15–40 y	Three times more common in women	Canadians have one of the highest rates in the world (MS Society of Canada, 2011)
Multiple myeloma	Older than 60 y	Slightly more common in men	Affects all genetic backgrounds (Myeloma Canada, 2009)
Myasthenia gravis	Women 20–30 y; men 40–60 y	Twice as common in women	Affects all ethnicities
Osteoarthritis	>50 y in women; 40–50 y in men	Equal rates among men and women older than 60 y	Increased incidence in First Nations populations (Public Health Agency of Canada [PHAC], 2010a)
Osteoporosis	Postmenopausal women; older than 50 y in men	Twice as common in women (Osteoporosis Canada, 2011a)	Slightly more common in Caucasians
Paget's disease	Older than 40 y	More common in men	More prevalent in Europe and Australia (Osteoporosis Canada, 2011c)
Polymyalgia rheumatica	Older than 50 y	More common in women	Most common in Caucasians
Rheumatoid arthritis	35–50 y	Two to three times more common in women	Most common in First Nations people
Scleroderma	30–50 y	Four to five times more prevalent in women than men	Found in all genetic backgrounds
Scoliosis	10–15 y	Eight times more common in girls	Found in all genetic backgrounds

Adapted from Firestein, G. S., Budd, R. C., et al. (2008). *Kelley's textbook of rheumatology* (8th ed.). Philadelphia, PA: Elsevier; Canale, S. T. (2003). *Campbell's operative orthopaedics* (10th ed.). Philadelphia, PA: Elsevier.

Table 23-11   **Altered Gait Patterns***

Gait	Pathological Condition	Description
Antalgic	Degenerative knee or hip disease	Patient walks with a limp to avoid pain. The gait is characterized by a very short stance phase.
Ataxic	Cerebellar lesion	Patient shows unsteady, uncoordinated walking with a wide base, feet thrown out, and a tendency to fall to one side.
Short leg	Discrepancy in length of one leg, flexion contracture of hip or knee, congenital hip dislocation	Patient limps with walking unless he or she wears adaptive shoes.
Footdrop or steppage	Peroneal or anterior tibial nerve Injury, paralysis of dorsiflexor muscles, lower motor neuron damage, damage to spinal nerve roots L5 and S1	Patient lifts the advancing leg high so that the toes may clear the ground. He or she places the sole of the foot on the floor at one time, instead of placing the heel first. This condition may be unilateral or bilateral.
Apraxic	Frontal lobe tumours, Alzheimer's disease	Patient has difficulty initiating walking. After starting to walk, the gait is slow and shuffling. Motor and sensory systems are intact.
Trendelenburg's (compensated gluteus medius gait)	Developmental hip dysplasia, muscular dystrophy	The trunk lists toward the affected side when weight bearing is on that side. A waddling gait may develop if both hips are affected.

*Other gait alterations are described in Chapter 24, Table 24-10.

Table 23-12   **Comparison of Musculoskeletal Conditions Affecting Multiple Joints**

Assessment	Rheumatoid Arthritis	Osteoarthritis	Gouty Arthritis	Fibromyalgia
Risk factors	Physical and emotional stress	Obesity, aging	Family history, diet high in purine-rich foods, alcohol, stress	Family history Emotional stress
Pain	Upper extremities	Lower extremities	Base of big toe; may also affect feet, ankles, knees, elbows	Any joints, especially neck, back, shoulders, knees, hands
Onset	Young adulthood	50s–60s	Middle-age men	Adult women, 22–55 y
Stiffness	Significant in mornings and after inactivity	Worse later in the day and after inactivity	None in acute cases, develops with chronic cases	Some stiffness, especially in the morning
Generalized symptoms	Weakness, fatigue, low fever	None	Painful, monoarticular, nocturnal joints, later more joints, great toe most often	Sleep disturbance and morning fatigue
Physical examination—joints	Tender, swollen, may be warm	May be tender	Swollen, warm, tender, shiny, red	No swelling, tender to touch
Diagnostic tests	Elevated serum proteins in blood and synovial fluid—rheumatoid factor	X-ray, computerized tomography, magnetic resonance imaging	Elevated uric acid in blood and urine Synovial fluid aspiration	Not definitive, rule out other diagnoses

Atrophy

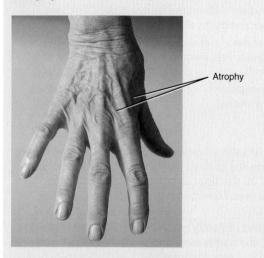

Atrophy

Hand of an 84-year-old woman

Decreased size can occur in any muscle. Causes include nerve damage, disuse, and nerve or muscle damage.

Joint Effusions

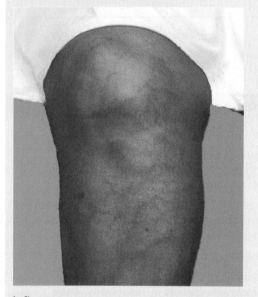

Inflammatory processes commonly resulting from trauma, joint overuse, and rheumatoid arthritis can cause synovial fluid to accumulate in a joint. When considerable fluid builds up, the joint appears swollen. The fluid is compressible, also called fluctuant. Treatment may involve rest, anti-inflammatory agents, or surgical removal.

Joint Dislocation

The ends of bones slip out of the usual position, usually from a sports-related injury, trauma, or a fall. Severe dislocation can cause tearing of the muscles, ligaments, and tendons that support the joint. Manifestations include swelling, pain, and immobility of the affected joint. Hand joints are most frequently dislocated, followed by shoulders. Hips, knees, and elbows are less commonly dislocated. Dislocations require medical intervention to prevent nerve damage.

Longstanding Rheumatoid Arthritis

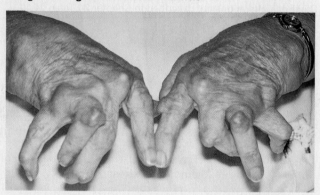

In this chronic, systemic, inflammatory disease of joints and connective tissue, inflammation causes thickening of synovial membrane. Fibrosis follows, with eventual bony ankylosis. The disorder is bilateral and symmetrical. Characteristics include heat, redness, swelling, and painful motion of affected joints. Associated symptoms include fatigue, weakness, anorexia, weight loss, low-grade fever, and lymphadenopathy.

Rotator Cuff Tear

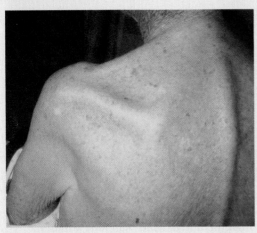

Manifestations include a hunched shoulder and limited arm abduction. A positive drop arm test (arm is passively abducted, person cannot maintain position, and arm falls to side) is diagnostic. This condition may result from trauma while arm is abducted, falling on shoulder, throwing, or heavy lifting.

Osteoporosis

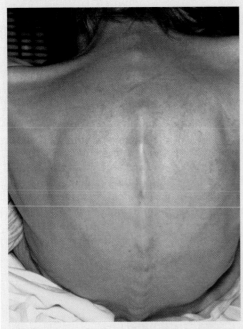

Osteoporosis occurs when bone resorption is faster than deposition. The weakened bone increases risk for fractures, especially in vertebrae, wrist, and hip. This occurs predominantly in postmenopausal Caucasian women. Risk factors include small bone frame, younger age at menopause, sedentary lifestyle, tobacco use, alcohol intake, and inadequate diet.

Osteoarthritis

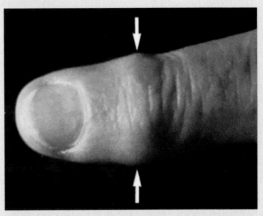

This localized, progressive, noninflammatory disease results in deterioration of articular cartilage and bone, and deposition of new bone at joint surfaces. Incidence increases with age. Commonly affected joints include hands, knees, hips, and lumbar and cervical vertebrae. Manifestations include stiffness, swelling, hard bony protuberances, pain with motion, and limited motion.

Genu Valgum ("Knock Knee")

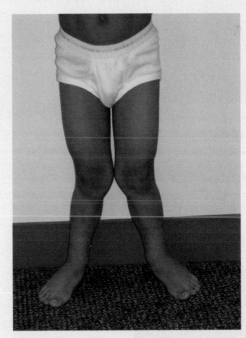

Many children have a temporary period of this condition, but persistent knock-knee may be genetic or the result of metabolic bone disease. The patient may need to swing each leg outward while walking to prevent striking the planted limb with the moving limb. The strain on the knee frequently causes anterior and medial knee pain. Physical therapy and surgical intervention may be required.

(table continues on page 694)

Ganglion Cysts

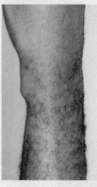

A soft, nontender, round nodule on the dorsum of the wrist that becomes more prominent during flexion. It is a benign tumour.

Epicondylitis

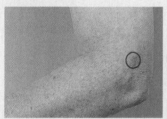

Epicondylitis

With this inflammation of the lateral epicondyle of the elbow (tennis elbow), pain radiates down the extensor surface and increases with resisting extension of the hand. It results from activities combining excessive supination of forearm with an extended wrist. Inflammation of the medial epicondyle (golf elbow) is rarer and results from excessive wrist flexion and pronation.

Congenital Hip Dislocation

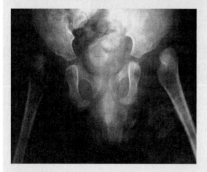

The head of the femur is displaced from the acetabulum. This condition is seven times more common in females. Signs include asymmetrical gluteal creases, uneven limb length, and limited abduction when the thighs are flexed. Diagnosis for newborns is a positive Barlow–Ortolani sign. Older children will have a positive Trendelenburg's sign.

Bursitis (eg, Olecranon Bursitis)

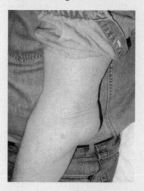

More than 150 bursae in the body cushion and lubricate joints, tendons, and ligaments. Bursitis is an inflammation of the bursa, which can follow injury, infection, or a rheumatic condition. Shoulders, elbows, and hip are common sites of bursitis; however, bursitis can occur in any joint, including knees, heels, and bases of big toes. Characteristics include swelling, tenderness, and pain that increases with movement.

Swan Neck and Boutonnière Deformity

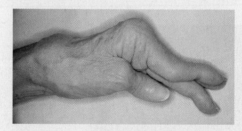

The fingers have a "swan-neck" appearance resulting from flexion contracture of the metacarpophalangeal joint with hyperextension of the distal joint. Boutonnière deformity causes flexion of the proximal interphalangeal (PIP) joint with hyperextension of the distal joint. Both conditions occur with chronic rheumatoid arthritis and are often accompanied by ulnar deviation of the fingers.

Polydactyly

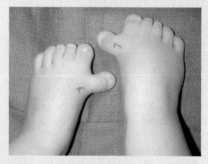

This congenital deformity results in extra fingers, usually at the thumb or fifth finger. Cosmetic removal is frequent, unless extra digit has full range of motion (ROM) and sensation.

Syndactyly

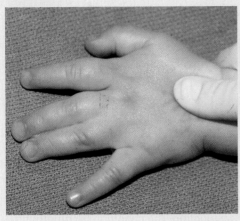

In this congenital deformity of webbed fingers, the metacarpals and phalanges of the webbed fingers are unequal in length and the joints do not align, which limits flexion and extension. Surgical separation is usual. Toes may also be webbed.

Dupuytren's Contracture

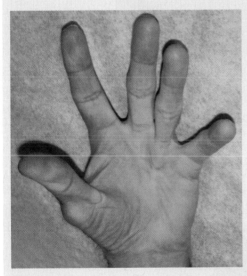

Hyperplasia of the palmar fascia causes painless flexion contracture of the digits, which impairs function. It usually starts in the fourth digit and then extends to the fifth and third. Dupuytren's contracture commonly occurs in men older than 40 y and develops bilaterally. Incidence increases with diabetes, epilepsy, family history of Dupuytren's contracture, and alcoholic liver disease.

Herniated Nucleus Pulposus

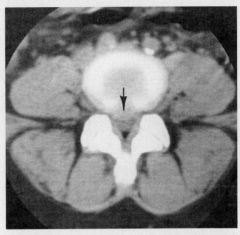

The intervertebral discs may slip out of position following trauma or strain. Rupture of the nucleus pulposus (soft inner core) may put pressure on the spinal nerve root. Symptoms include sciatic pain radiating down the leg, numbness, parasthesia, listing from the affected side, decreased mobility, low back tenderness, and decreased motor and sensory function in the affected leg. Straight leg raises produce sciatic pain.

Talipes Equinovarus ("Club Foot")

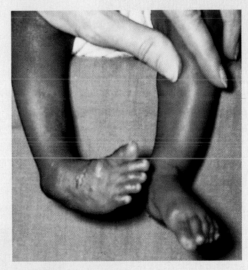

The foot is turned to the side, and the involved foot, calf, and leg are smaller and shorter than the unaffected side. One or both feet may be affected. This condition is not painful; however, if left untreated, significant discomfort and disability will develop. Treatment ranges from braces or casts to surgery.

(table continues on page 696)

Ulnar Deviation

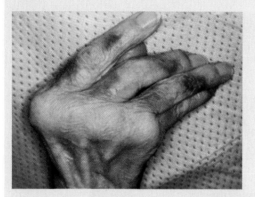

Stretching of the articular capsule and muscle imbalance in rheumatoid arthritis cause fingers to point in the ulnar direction.

Ankylosing Spondylitis

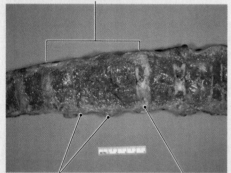

Three vertebrae fused into one

Approximate sites of destroyed intervertebral discs | Intervertebral disc

This chronic, progressive inflammation of the spine and sacroiliac and large joints in the extremities affects men 10 times more than women. It is characterized by bony growths. Muscle spasms pull the spine forward and eliminate the cervical and lumbar curves. Flexion deformities can also occur in knees and hips.

Acute Rheumatoid Arthritis

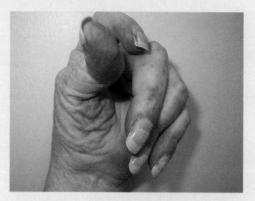

Inflammation results in painful, reddened, swollen joints and limited function. The condition is common in proximal intraphalangeal joints.

Heberden's and Bouchard's Nodes

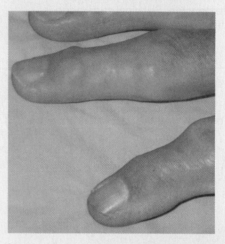

Hard, nontender bony growths on the distal (Heberden's) and proximal (Bouchard's) interphalangeal joints. Frequently occurs with deviation of the fingers.

Carpal Tunnel Syndrome

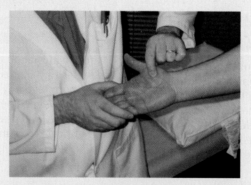

Carpal tunnel syndrome occurs from repetitive motion and develops in people 30–60 y. It occurs in women five times more frequently than men. Symptoms include burning, pain, and numbness from compression of the median nerve inside the carpal tunnel of the wrist. Atrophy of the thenar eminence at the base of the thumb is common. Diagnosis is made from a positive Phalen's test or Tinel's sign

Neurological Assessment

Learning Objectives

1 Demonstrate knowledge of anatomy and physiology of the central and peripheral nervous systems.

2 Identify important topics for health promotion and risk reduction related to the central and peripheral nervous systems.

3 Consider age, condition, gender, and culture of the patient to individualize the neurological assessment.

4 Collect subjective data related to assessment of the 12 cranial nerves, motor system, sensory system, and reflexes using elements of a complete health history.

5 Collect objective data related to cranial nerve function, motor system, sensory system, and reflexes using physical examination techniques.

6 Demonstrate knowledge of the Glasgow Coma Scale.

7 Identify expected and unexpected findings related to cranial nerve function, motor system, sensory system, and reflexes.

8 Analyze subjective and objective data from assessment of the neurological system and consider initial interventions.

9 Document and communicate data from the neurological assessment using appropriate terminology and principles of recording.

10 Identify nursing diagnoses and initiate a plan of care based on findings from the neurological assessment.

*M*r. Matthew Nderitu, a 56-year-old Nigerian-Canadian, has a history of hypertension, smoking, and mild baseline dementia. He was admitted to an intensive care unit via the emergency department (ED) following a stroke. He lives alone, has compromised hygiene, and is wearing multiple layers of mismatched clothing. He does not remember the last time he took his blood pressure medication. Vital signs are temperature 36.8°C orally, pulse 88 beats/min and regular, respiration 22 breaths/min, and blood pressure (BP) right arm (supine) 168/92 mm Hg. Mr. Nderitu is alert, but appears somewhat fearful and agitated. He asks for cigarettes and is oriented to name only. Speech is comprehensible but slurred.

You will gain more information about Mr. Nderitu throughout the chapter. As you study the content and features, consider the case and its relationship to what you are learning. Begin thinking about the following points:

- Is Mr. Nderitu's condition stable, urgent, or an emergency?
- What immediate health promotion and teaching needs are evident?
- How will the nurse focus, organize, and prioritize subjective data collection?
- How will the nurse focus, organize, and prioritize objective data collection?
- How will the nurse individualize assessment to Mr. Nderitu's specific needs, considering his condition, age, and culture?

An intact, appropriately functioning nervous system is critical for all human endeavours. It exerts unconscious control over basic body functions, such as respiration, temperature regulation, and movement coordination. The nervous system also enables very complex interactions with people and the environment. Assessment of neurological functioning serves multiple purposes. All those who perform neurological assessments use some of the same methods and, at times, share the same goals (eg, detection of change in neurological status, particularly acute and life-threatening alterations). Generally, physicians assess neurological function primarily to localize pathology and to make a medical diagnosis. Nurses perform neurological assessment mainly to identify actual or potential health concerns related to neurological dysfunction, and the patient's response to those conditions.

Common to all settings and types of neurological assessment is the use of an organized approach to maximize the value of information derived from collected data. This approach consists of general patient observation, data gathering from the health history (often performed simultaneously), and a systematic neurological examination.

Anatomy and Physiology Overview

The nervous system is divided into the **central nervous system (CNS),** consisting of the brain and spinal cord, and **peripheral nervous system,** which includes the cranial, spinal, and peripheral nerves. The nervous system also can be classified according to function as either voluntary or involuntary (autonomic). In the **voluntary** division, fibres that connect the CNS to muscles and skin facilitate deliberate motor actions in response to stimuli. In the primarily unconscious **autonomic** division, fibres connect the CNS with organs (including the heart and kidneys), smooth muscles, and glands.

Central Nervous System

Brain

The brain is a network of interconnecting **neurons** that control and integrate the body's activities. Each neuron contains a *cell body,* which serves as the control centre; smaller receiving fibres called *dendrites;* and a connecting long fibre called an *axon.* Axons are white because they are covered with a *myelin sheath* that speeds impulse conduction. Cell bodies are on the outer layer of the brain (grey matter or cerebral cortex), while axons that connect to other parts of the nervous system (white matter or bundles of myelinated fibres) are directed toward the center of the brain. Neurons communicate with one another at *synapses,* small spaces between two neurons. Important parts of the brain include the cerebrum, diencephalon, brainstem, and cerebellum (Fig. 24-1).

Cerebrum. The cerebrum has two hemispheres, left and right, and contains 80% of the brain tissue. The left hemisphere is primarily analytical, while the right is more creative (Frishkoff, 2007). The cerebral cortex, which forms the cortical layer of the cerebrum, contributes significantly to motor and sensory function, intellect, and language.

Each hemisphere of the cerebrum has four lobes: frontal, temporal, parietal, and occipital (Fig. 24-2). The *precentral gyrus* in the frontal lobe controls *motor function* on the opposite side of the body; the left side of the brain controls the

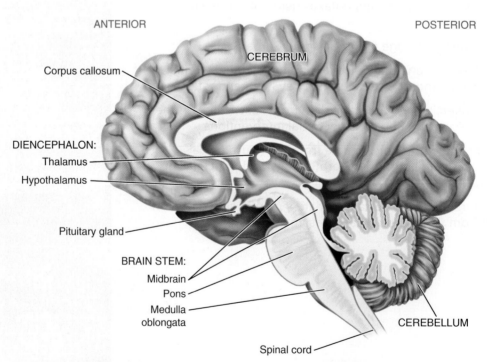

Figure 24-1 The right half of the brain and its important divisions.

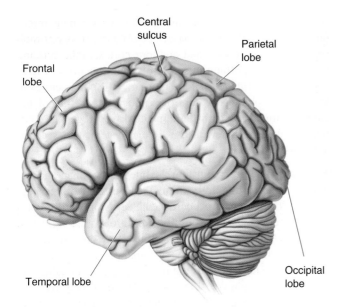

Figure 24-2 Lobes of the cerebrum.

right side of the body, and the right side of the brain controls the left side of the body. The *postcentral gyrus* in the parietal lobe receives input on *sensory function* including temperature, touch, pressure, and pain, also from the opposite side of the body. Motor and sensory function is organized from head to toe on both the left and right sides of the cerebrum, similar to a person hanging upside down, also named the *homunculus* (Fig. 24-3).

The cerebrum is also responsible for visual imaging, auditory processing, and language comprehension and expression. Each of the four lobes contributes to different functions. The **frontal lobe** is responsible for complex cognition (orientation, memory, insight, judgment, arithmetic, and abstraction), language (verbal and written), and voluntary motor function. It integrates this cognitive function with emotional responses, personality, impulse control, and social behaviour. The motor function area, discussed earlier, is located in the frontal lobe, anterior to the central gyrus. The **parietal lobe** recognizes the size, shape, and texture of objects and interprets pain, touch, pressure, vibrations, temperature, and taste. The sensory areas discussed earlier are located in the parietal lobe, posterior to the central gyrus. Language is processed in the general interpretive area (gnostic area) located at the posterior end of the lateral sulcus in the parietal and temporal lobes and the speech centre or Broca's area located anterior to the premotor cortex in the frontal lobe, usually of the left hemisphere. The **general interpretive area** integrates understanding of spoken and written words, while **Broca's area** regulates verbal expression (Martini, Timmons, et al., 2009). The visual

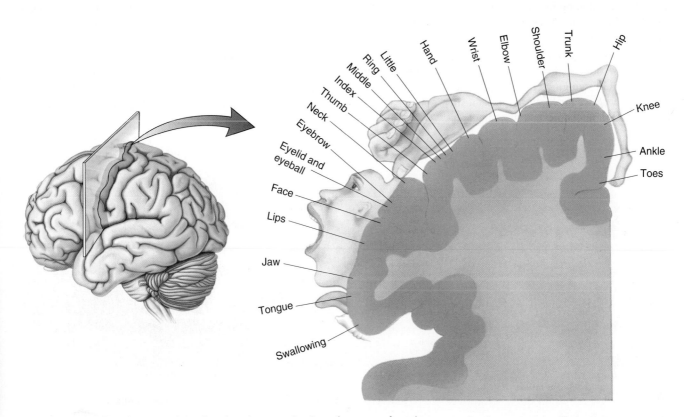

Figure 24-3 The homunculus, showing the organization of sensory function.

cortex is in the **occipital lobe** in the back of the brain, with visual associative areas that interpret and integrate stimuli. The **temporal lobe** registers auditory and olfactory input and is responsible for hearing, speech, and smell. Additionally, deep within the cerebrum is the **limbic lobe**, which consists of the hippocampus and several gyri, for example, cingulated gyrus, adjacent to the diencephalon and part of the limbic system (Martini, Timmons, et al.). The limbic system also includes the amygdaloid body, thalamus, and hypothalamus, and is primarily concerned with self-preservation, including recall of pleasurable, unpleasant, or potentially dangerous events. It also recalls mood and emotional responses in relation to events, including aggression, interpretation of smell, feeding and sexual behaviour, and autonomic responses associated with emotion. The hippocampus is particularly essential for learning and the storage and retrieval of long-term memories (Fig. 24-4B).

Clinical Significance 24-2

Because the areas that involve speech are in the brain's left hemisphere, patients who have sustained a stroke there are more likely to have language deficits. Damage to the general interpretive area may lead to difficulty understanding verbal communication, called receptive aphasia. Damage to Broca's area causes difficulties with speaking or finding words. This is called *expressive aphasia*.

Deep structures within the cerebrum also include the thalamus and hypothalamus (mentioned above) and the basal ganglia. The **basal ganglia** are four paired tracts of grey matter on both sides of the thalamus (Fig. 24-4A). They modulate automatic movements, receiving input from the cerebral cortex and sending output to the brainstem and thalamus to facilitate smooth skeletal motor function including muscle tone (eg, fluid swinging of the arms while walking).

Directly above the brainstem lies the diencephalon, which contains the thalamus and hypothalamus. The **thalamus** is the major relay station and gatekeeper for both motor (eg, from cerebellum and basal nuclei) and sensory stimuli (eg, from visual cortex and auditory cortex to the cerebral cortex). The **hypothalamus** controls vital functions of temperature, heart rate, and blood pressure (BP) with centres in the medulla oblongata; controls endocrine function of the anterior pituitary; establishes appetite drives; regulates emotions in conjunction with the limbic system; and secretes antidiuretic hormone.

Brainstem. The brainstem is integral to intact neurological functioning. Both afferent and efferent fibres pass through it from the spinal cord to the cerebrum and cerebellum. Afferent (sensory) stimuli travel through the brainstem to the cerebrum; efferent (motor) fibres leave the cerebrum to pass through the brainstem to the spinal cord.

The brainstem includes the midbrain, pons, medulla, and reticular formation (see Fig. 24-1). The **midbrain** (mesencephalon) contains nuclei that integrate auditory and visual information (cranial nerves [CNs] III and IV nuclei), ascending nerve tracts that carry sensory information to the thalamus, and descending tracts that relay information from the motor cortex to other areas of the brain and spinal cord. The **pons** contains nuclei for CNs V, VI, and VII and many ascending and descending neuron tracts relay information to and from the medulla, cerebellum, and cerebral cortex. It contains two respiratory centres: one that controls the length of inspiration and expiration, and the other that controls respiratory rate (Martini, Timmons, et al., 2009). The nuclei for CNs VIII to XII are in the **medulla**, which also contain the vital autonomic centres for respiratory, cardiac, and vasomotor function (Table 24-1). The medulla works with the pons to regulate smooth breathing rhythm. The medulla also controls involuntary functions such as sneezing, swallowing, vomiting, hiccoughing, and coughing. In addition, the medulla contains sensory and motor nerve tracts that connect the cerebrum and cerebellum with the spinal cord. The **reticular formation,** which lies deep within the length of the brainstem, contains the reticular activating system and its control centre in the

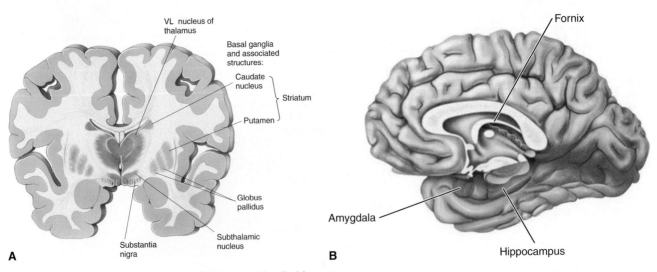

Figure 24-4 A. The basal ganglia. **B.** The primitive limbic system.

Table 24-1	Cranial Nerves	
Cranial Nerve (CN)	**Anatomy**	**Physiology**
I. Olfactory (sensory)	Originates in the nasal mucosa; ends in the olfactory lobes. Axons of the postsynaptic neurons terminate in the olfactory cortex of the cerebrum, the hypothalamus, and limbic system	Smell and smell interpretation, including peristalsis, salivation, and emotional and behavioural responses
II. Optic (sensory)	Originates in the retinal cells, axon from these photoreceptors form the optic nerve, which exits through the optic disc; travels over the optic tract to end in the visual cortex of the occipital lobe	Vision, including visual acuity and peripheral vision
III. Oculomotor (motor)	Originates in the midbrain and supplies motor fibres to the superior, inferior, and medial rectus muscles and inferior oblique muscles of the eye; levator palpebrae muscle of the eyelid; and the autonomic motor fibres to the ciliary muscles and iris	Extraocular movements (EOMs): • Upward • Medial • Downward • Up and in Eyelid raising and pupil constriction
IV. Trochlear (motor)	Originates in the midbrain and supplies motor fibres to the superior oblique muscle of the eye	EOMs: Down and in
V. Trigeminal (sensory and motor)	The motor fibres of the mandibular branch originate in the pons. The three sensory branches *ophthalmic*, *maxillary*, and *mandibular* originate in areas of the face suggested by their names and functions. The sensory branches terminate in sensory nuclei in the pons	*Ophthalmic branch:* Sensation to the cornea, conjunctiva, upper eyelid and eyebrows, nasal mucosa, forehead, and nose *Maxillary branch:* Sensation to the skin of the cheek and nose, lower eyelid, upper jaw, teeth, palate, mouth mucosa, and part of the pharynx *Mandibular branch:* Sensation to the lower jaw, including the gums, teeth, lips, palate, and part of the tongue and motor function to muscles of mastication
VI. Abducens (motor)	Originates in the pons and supplies motor fibres to the lateral rectus muscle	EOMs: lateral
VII. Facial (sensory and motor)	Originates in the pons and supplies sensory fibres to the anterior two thirds of the tongue and soft palate. The motor and autonomic fibres originate in the pons and the upper and lower branches that terminate in the muscles of the face	Taste and sensation for the anterior two thirds of the tongue and soft palate; serves as the primary motor nerve for facial expression
VIII. Acoustic (sensory)	Cochlear sensory fibres originate in the cochlea and transmit auditory sensations to nuclei in the pons and medulla oblongata and auditory cortex in the temporal lobe. Vestibular sensory fibres originate in the semicircular canals of the inner ear and are carried to vestibular nuclei in the pons and medulla oblongata	Hearing Equilibrium

(table continues on page 702)

Table 24-1   **Cranial Nerves** *(continued)*

Cranial Nerve (CN)	Anatomy	Physiology
IX. Glossopharyngeal (sensory and motor)	Sensory divisions arise from the carotid arteries of the neck, upper pharynx, palate, and posterior one third of the tongue and end in the medulla oblongata; motor divisions arise in the medulla and supply the pharyngeal muscle (somatic) and parotid gland (autonomic)	Pharyngeal muscle for swallowing and speech; parotid salivary gland secretion; general sensory (pain, touch, temperature) function; monitoring blood pressure (BP)
X. Vagus (sensory and motor)	Major parasympathetic nerve of the body; originates in the medulla oblongata and supplies respiratory, cardiovascular, and digestive organs of the thoracic and abdominal viscera. Sensory fibres receive stimuli from larynx, esophagus, trachea, carotid bodies, thoracic and abdominal viscera, and stretch and chemoreceptors from the aorta to terminate in the sensory and autonomic centres in the medulla. Voluntary motor fibres arise in the medulla and innervate the pharynx and larynx	Provides most parasympathetic innervation to a large region; effects include digestion (increase secretions of salivary glands, intestinal glands, pancreas, and liver), stimulation of defecation, slowed heart rate and reduced contraction strength, and constriction of bronchioles
XI. Spinal accessory (motor)	Originates in medulla with two branches: cranial root innervates muscles of the larynx and pharynx; spinal root innervates trapezius and sternocleidomastoid muscles	Swallowing and speaking; innervates the muscles that turn the head and elevate the shoulders (shoulder shrug)
XII. Hypoglossal (motor)	Originates in the nuclei in the medulla and ends at the muscles of tongue	Provides voluntary tongue movements

Adapted from Kandel, E. R., Schwartz, J. H., et al. (2008). *Principles of neural science* (5th ed.). Philadelphia, PA: Elsevier; Martini, F. H., Timmons, M. J., et al. (2009). *Human anatomy* (6th ed.). New York, NY: Pearson Benjamin Cummings; Standring, S. (2008). *Gray's anatomy: The anatomical basis for clinical practice* (40th ed.). London, UK: Elsevier Churchill Livingstone.

midbrain. The reticular activating system is responsible for increasing wakefulness, attention, and responsiveness of cortical neurons to sensory stimulation.

Cerebellum.   The two hemispheres of the cerebellum lie inferior to the occipital lobe in the posterior part of the brain. It coordinates and adjusts voluntary and involuntary movements, to ensure learned movements are recalled and rapid movements, posture, balance, equilibrium, and muscle tone are maintained. These actions are made possible through connections to the motor cortex, basal nuclei, and motor centres in the brainstem. Alcohol intake can affect the cerebellum, causing the characteristic loss of balance and coordination.

Protective Structures of the CNS

The *cranial meninges, cerebrospinal fluid (CSF)*, and *skull* cover and protect the brain. The meninges consist of three layers: the dura mater adherent to the skull; the arachnoid mater, which lies beneath the dura; and the pia mater, which tightly adheres to the surface of the brain. CSF is secreted by the choroid plexus located in the walls of the four *ventricles* of the brain, CSF-filled cavities that connect with the central canal of the spinal cord. Through apertures in the fourth ventricle, most of the CSF produced flows into the subarachnoid space to circulate within this space surrounding the brain, brainstem, and spinal cord. A small amount enters the central canal of the cord. In addition to cushioning the brain and cord, CSF carries nutrients, including glucose and oxygen, to nerve tissues and carries away waste products. CSF is absorbed through arachnoid granulations in the superior sagittal sinuses.

Clinical Significance 24-3

Increases in cerebrospinal fluid (CSF) pressure can lead to herniation of the brain and compression of the brainstem on the foramen magnum. Such compression may alter respiratory function and reduce consciousness.

Spinal Cord

The spinal cord continues from the brainstem, exiting from the base of the skull through the foramen magnum and extending to the level of the vertebrae L1 to L2 (Martini, Timmons, et al., 2009). The spinal pathways are often named according to point of origin and destination (eg, spinothalamic, corticospinal). Similar to the brain, the neurons of the spinal cord are aligned so that there is grey (cell bodies) and white (axons) matter. The H-shaped grey matter is in the center, surrounded by white matter. The grey matter contains the cell bodies of voluntary motor neurons, autonomic motor neurons (parasympathetic neurons from S2 to S4 and sympathetic neurons from T1 to L2), and sensory neurons (Martini, Timmons, et al.). The white matter contains the myelinated and unmyelinated axons of the ascending sensory and descending motor fibres. The axons are clustered into specific tracts for either ascending or descending fibres.

The **ascending tracts** generally carry specific sensory information from the periphery to higher levels of the CNS (Fig. 24-5). Input from sensory receptors in the skin, organs, and muscles travels through the peripheral nerves to the dorsal root ganglion of the spinal nerve and into the spinal cord. These **dorsal (posterior) columns** carry information about fine touch (stereognosis), pressure, vibration, and position sense (proprioception and kinesthetic sense) (Martini, Timmons, et al., 2009). They travel up the same side of the spinal cord to the brainstem. At the medulla, they synapse, cross to the opposite side of the body, and travel to the sensory cortex. Because of the crossing of the fibres in the medulla,

right-sided sensations are perceived on the left side of the brain, and left-sided sensations are perceived on the right side of the brain. Additionally, two specialized ascending tracts—the spinothalamic for pain, temperature, and crude touch and the spinocerebellar for proprioception and coordination of body movements—enter the dorsal ganglia, synapse with another neuron, and cross the spinal column here (instead of in the medulla as with the dorsal columns). The information is carried to the sensory cortex and cerebellum on the opposite site of the brain. Thus, all sensory information is perceived on one side of the brain for the opposite side of the body.

> **Clinical Significance 24-4**
>
> When half of the spinal cord is severed (eg, with a gunshot wound), the patient may experience *Brown–Séquard syndrome sensory loss*. Manifestations include loss of pain and temperature on the opposite side of the injury, because these fibres cross in the spinal cord. Fine touch, pressure, vibration, and position sense remain intact on the same side of the body because these fibres cross in the medulla.

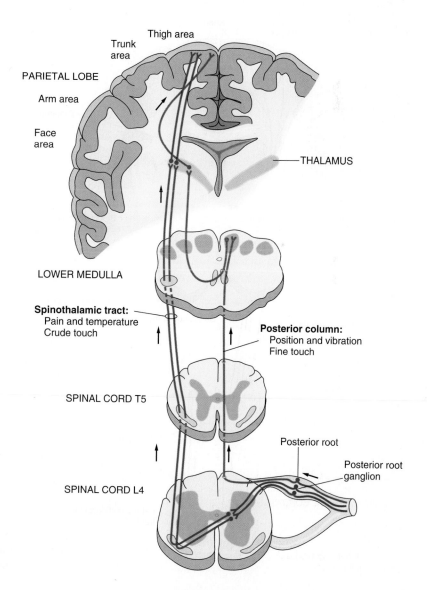

Figure 24-5 Ascending tracts of the brain carry sensory information from peripheral nerves to the CNS.

The **descending tracts** carry information related to motor function and muscle movement (Fig. 24-6). They control voluntary movement, carrying impulses from the motor cortex to the cranial (corticobulbar tract) and spinal (corticospinal tract) nerves (Martini, Timmons, et al., 2009). The corticobulbar and corticospinal tracts are referred to as the **pyramidal tract**. Axons originate in the motor cortex, travel to the brainstem, and cross at the medulla. Similar to the sensory tracts, the motor tracts on the left side of the brain control the right side; those on the right side of the brain control the left. The corticobulbar nerve tracts exit the brainstem to innervate skeletal muscles of the eye, jaw, face, neck, and pharynx. The corticospinal neurons exit the spinal cord at the ventral root of the spinal nerve, and impulses are carried to the peripheral motor nerves.

Another group of descending motor tracts, the medial and lateral pathways, originate in brainstem nuclei including the reticular formation. These nuclei also receive input from the basal ganglia. The medial and lateral nerve tracts, some of which remain uncrossed, provide subconscious control of muscle tone, balance, gross movement, and reflexes in the upper and lower extremities, and responses of the eyes and head to auditory and visual stimuli.

Peripheral Nervous System

The peripheral nervous system includes all the neurons outside the CNS. The CNs, spinal nerves, and autonomic nervous system all belong to the peripheral motor system.

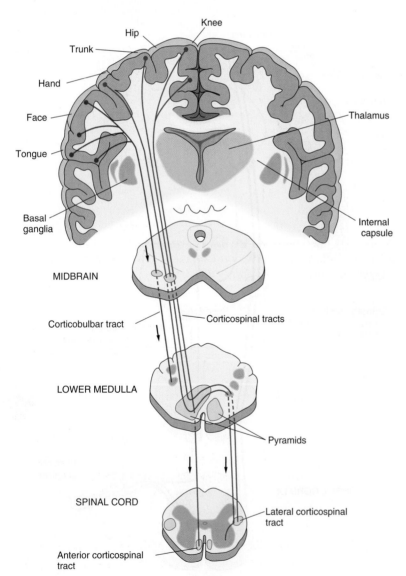

Figure 24-6 Descending tracts carry motor and muscle information from the cortex to the cranial and peripheral nerves.

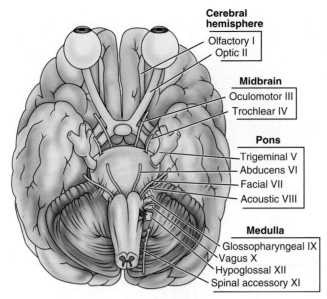

Figure 24-7 The 12 paired CNs.

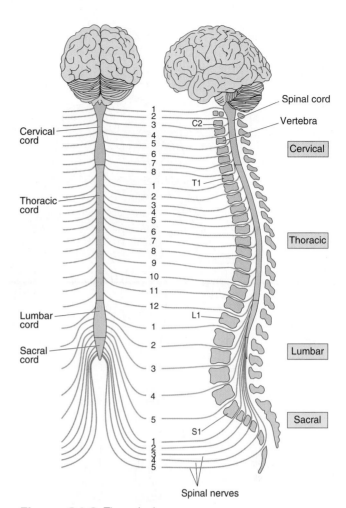

Figure 24-8 The spinal nerves.

Cranial Nerves

The 12 paired CNs exit from the brain, not the spinal cord (Fig. 24-7). Some CNs have only a sensory component, some have only a motor component, and others have both. Most CNs originate in the midbrain, pons, or medulla and innervate the eyes, ears, nose, mouth, and throat. An exception is the vagus nerve, which provides motor and sensory innervation to the heart and abdomen (see Table 24-1 for a complete description of the CNs).

Spinal Nerves

The **spinal nerves** arise from the spinal cord and innervate the rest of the body. They are described by their location in relation to the vertebrae from which the nerve exits, such as the sixth cervical (C6) or fourth thoracic (T4). Unlike the CNs, the spinal nerves each have afferent sensory fibres (located in the dorsal root) and efferent motor fibres (located in the ventral root). Where the motor and sensory fibres come together, the fibre is referred to as the spinal nerve. The 31 pairs of spinal nerves include 8 cervical, 12 thoracic, 5 lumbar, 5 sacral, and 1 coccygeal nerves (Fig. 24-8). Each pair innervates a specific region of the body from head to toe on the right and left sides. Innervation to these regions, known as **dermatomes**, may be evaluated by testing skin innervations provided by the afferent sensory fibres carried in the dorsal root of the spinal nerves (Fig. 24-9).

Although the dermatomes provide a general idea of the innervation by each nerve, some overlap exists. In addition, the integrity of motor (efferent) branches of spinal nerves is reflected in movement as described below. Again, there is overlap but greater accuracy than that offered by dermatomes.

- C1 to C3 innervate movement in and above the neck including the larynx.
- C4 to C6 innervate the neck and shoulder and diaphragm (C3–C5) for breathing independently.

- C7 to T1 innervate the arms and fingers and hand grasp to perform self-care and transfers with arms.
- T1 to T6 provide trunk stability for balance when sitting and innervate intercostal muscles for respirations.
- T6 to T12 innervate intercostal and abdominal muscles for respirations and transfer strength.
- T12 to L4 innervate muscles of the abdomen and upper leg (quadriceps and hip adductors).
- L4 to S4 innervate hip abductors and extensors (hamstrings) and muscles of the knee, ankles, and feet and the perineum for leg strength and bowel and bladder control (Martini, Timmons, et al., 2009).

Level of injury to the spinal cord affects function at and below the site of trauma. Thus, the patient with an injury at T6 would have arm movement and sensation but no leg movement or sensation. The patient with a lesion or spinal cord injury at L1 to L2 has varying control of the legs and pelvis. One with damage at L3 to L4 has weakened hamstrings and ankles, which may permit ambulation with braces and a cane.

Autonomic Nervous System

The autonomic nervous system maintains involuntary functions of cardiac and smooth muscle of the viscera and glands.

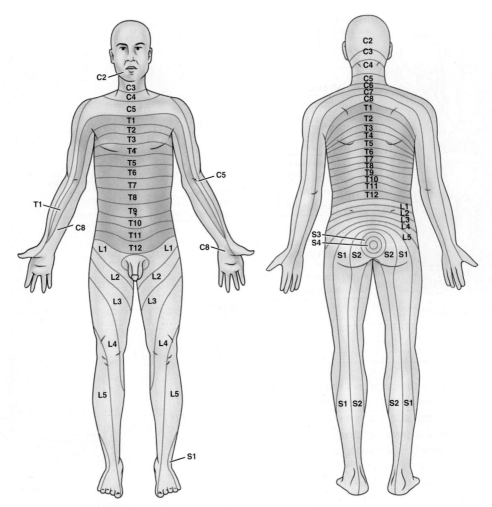

Figure 24-9 Dermatomes.

It has two components: sympathetic (fight or flight) and parasympathetic (rest and repose or rest and digest). The sympathetic ganglia are located near the spinal cord from T1 to L2. The major neurotransmitter is epinephrine (also known as adrenaline). The cell bodies of the parasympathetic nervous system are located in the brainstem (CNs III, VII, IX, and X) and spinal segments S2 to S4. The ganglia are located near the structures that they innervate; the neurotransmitter is acetylcholine (Martini, Timmons, et al., 2009).

The autonomic system can both sense and make changes based on input. To regulate heart rate and BP, it receives input from chemoreceptors and baroreceptors (see Chapter 19). Based on such input, the sympathetic system secretes epinephrine to increase BP, heart rate, and contractility; the parasympathetic system secretes acetylcholine to reduce heart rate and force of contraction. Many times, the two systems work in opposite ways to provide balance to the body's overall function.

Reflexes are involuntary responses to stimuli. They maintain balance and tone, such as the sucking reflex of a baby when the cheek is stroked. Reflexes also provide quick responses in potentially harmful situations, such as withdrawing of the foot when stepping on a sharp object. The

simplest type of **reflex arc** involves a receptor-sensing organ, afferent sensory neuron, efferent motor neuron, and effector motor organ (Fig. 24-10). The deep tendon reflexes (DTRs) are monosynaptic. One example is the patellar reflex. When the tendon of a partially stretched quadriceps muscle is percussed with a reflex hammer, the response is extension at the knee. The patellar tendon is the sensing organ, which travels through the sensory neuron to the dorsal root ganglion. It synapses in the spinal cord and travels out through the motor neuron to the quadriceps muscle, where this motor organ contracts, causing extension at the knee. The muscle must also be strong enough to cause the reflex. DTRs can also be elicited at the ankle (Achilles), wrist (brachioradialis), and elbow (biceps and triceps). Other reflexes include the superficial (eg, corneal, plantar, abdominal), visceral (pupillary response to light), and neonatal (rooting, grasp, Babinski).

Lifespan Considerations

Women Who Are Pregnant

Little is known about neurological changes in pregnancy (Lowdermilk & Perry, 2007). Notably, changes in the hypothalamic–pituitary axis lead to elevated levels of estrogen,

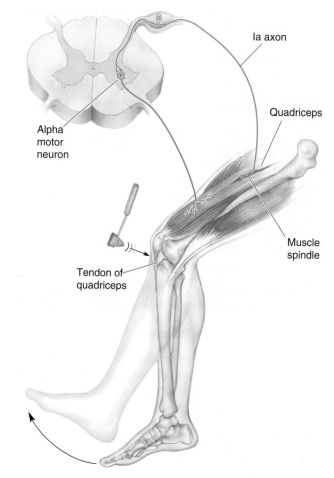

Ia axon

Quadriceps

Alpha motor neuron

Muscle spindle

Tendon of quadriceps

Figure 24-10 A commonly cited **reflex arc** is the "knee-jerk" reaction, which is a DTR that results with stimulation of the patellar tendon.

progesterone, prolactin, and oxytocin. Other changes are related to pressure on the peripheral nerves from the weight of the fetus and postural changes; these usually resolve after birth.

Newborns and Infants

The fetal nervous system grows rapidly. At birth, the incompletely integrated nervous system is developed enough to sustain life, primarily through reflexes. The autonomic nervous system is critical during this period because it stimulates the first respiration, assists in maintaining acid–base balance, and regulates temperature control (Hockenberry & Wilson, 2007).

Myelin is necessary for quick and efficient transmission of nerve impulses. Myelination is incomplete at birth; it develops from head to toe and centrally to peripherally. The earliest tracts are sensory (pain, taste, smell, and hearing), cerebellar (balance and coordination), and medial and lateral pathways (muscle tone and gross motor movement). All CNs are myelinated except the optic and olfactory (see Table 24-1).

Myelination of the spinal cord is nearly complete by 2 years, as manifested by children's ability to walk unassisted

and to move purposefully in space. Until age 4, the spinal cord continues to elongate. After that, the spinal column continues to grow to keep pace with increasing height, but the cord does not. Instead, the spinal nerves elongate below L1 to L2 to form the cauda equina (Martini, Timmons, et al., 2009). At birth, all brain cells are present; however, they continue to increase in size. Brain growth is completed by the age of about 4 years (London, Ladewig, et al., 2007). Various brain areas develop as children gain intellectual capacity. Milestones have an orderly and predictable sequence in healthy children. As toddlers begin talking, Broca's centre and the general interpretive areas develop. Cortical areas for motor control of the legs, hand, feet, and sphincters grow as toddlers learn to walk and train the bladder and bowels. Initially, their ability to attend to locomotion and elimination is limited; by 3 years of age, development and coordination of these functions allow toddlers to listen better and behave longer. Postural control continues to develop as the functions are integrated.

Children and Adolescents

School-age children are steadier on their feet than preschoolers. They are more coordinated with better posture that enables them to climb, ride bikes, and play games. Head circumference is decreased in relation to height. The skull and brain grow very slowly during this period; most of the growth has been completed (London, Ladewig, et al., 2007).

Although the number of neurons does not increase in adolescents, nourishing support cells for neurons continue to grow. Development of the myelin sheath "fine tunes" the neural system, coinciding with the adolescent's more advanced cognitive development.

Older Adults

Neurons of the CNS, brain size, weight, and neurotransmitters decrease with aging. Results include slower thought processing; sensory perception of light, taste, smell, and sound becomes less acute; reaction time is slowed; and reflexes become weaker (Martini, Timmons, et al., 2009; Miller, 2009). Ability to respond to multiple stimuli and manage multiple tasks concurrently is reduced. Peripheral nerve function and impulse conduction decrease, with resultant decreased proprioception and potential for a Parkinson-like gait. These changes put older adults at risk for altered balance, postural hypotension, falls, and injury. Light touch and pain sensation are somewhat reduced, with ischemic paresthesia common in the extremities. Overall cognitive function with aging varies with physical activity (Atkinson, Rosano, et al., 2007) and genetics (Russell, 2010).

Acute Assessment

Once baseline information has been gathered, it is often not practical or necessary to perform a complete neurological examination. Choice of elements to assess in a given setting depends on many variables. Recognition of situations requiring acute assessment and rapid communication of findings is critical to preventing or limiting negative outcomes for patients (Box 24-1).

When situations such as those in Box 24-1 are identified, rapidly assessing key areas of the neurological examination is the first step in determining the nature of the condition and possible acute interventions. This abbreviated acute assessment (details of each element are described more completely later) includes the following:

- Rapid assessment of **level of consciousness** (LOC) by using the **Glasgow Coma Scale** (GCS), scoring verbal response, eye opening, and motor function. If the patient can respond verbally, basic orientation is assessed. This also allows a basic speech/language assessment (comprehension and production of spoken language and speech quality, such as garbled or slurred).
- **Pupillary reaction:** Assess size (before and after light stimulus), shape, speed of response to light, equality, and accommodation. PERRLA (pupils equal, round, reactive to light and accommodation) is a reminder acronym.
- Gross assessment of **extremity strength**. If the patient can follow commands, ask him or her to lift each extremity off the bed, noting whether he or she can maintain limb elevation against gravity, and then against resistance from the examiner. Also note any facial asymmetry (either at rest or during facial movement).
- Gross assessment of **sensation** (only possible if the patient can communicate) by examining ability to identify presence and location of light (fine) touch on all extremities and both sides of the face.
- If consciousness is impaired, assessing selected other CNs may help differentiate neurological from metabolic causes,

particularly **extraocular movements** (EOMs), **gag reflex,** and **corneal reflex**.

Vital signs are part of this acute assessment, because they may be either a cause or a result of the acute change (see Box 24-1). As soon as is practical, obtaining health history information helps identify potential sources of the change in condition.

An individual receives immediate emergency intervention when symptoms and signs of stroke occur, even if transient. To facilitate quick transfer to a stroke unit for determination of the type of stroke and early intervention, transportation is by ambulance (Agyeman, Nedeltchev, et al., 2006). The outcome of ischemic stroke may be improved by the administration of tissue-plasminogen activator within 3 hours of onset (Heart and Stroke Foundation of Canada, 2011a).

Subjective Data Collection

Assessment of Risk Factors

An important purpose of the health history is to gather information to promote health and provide health teaching. Health promotion activities for the nervous system focus on preventing disease, identifying health issues early, and reducing complications of existing or established diagnoses.

Nurses obtain a history of past medical diagnoses, particularly head or spinal trauma, and known risk factors for common neurological conditions (eg, stroke). They note chronic or recent exposures to toxins; any recent viruses; vaccinations; and insect, spider, tick, snake, or scorpion bites or stings. While taking a health history, nurses might elicit

---

BOX 24-1 SIGNIFICANT CHANGES IN NEUROLOGICAL STATUS

- Acute change in mental status: increasing restlessness, agitation, or confusion
- Changes in consciousness not explained by known causes (eg, sedatives). This ranges from patterns of increasing difficulty in arousing the patient to complete lack of responsiveness to any stimulus.
- Seizure activity
- Onset of flexor or extensor posturing, either spontaneously or in response to noxious stimuli
  - Flexor posturing = adduction of arm with flexion at elbow and wrist, extension and internal rotation of leg with plantar flexion of foot
  - Extensor posturing = adduction, internal rotation, and extension of arm; extension and internal rotation of leg with plantar flexion of foot
- Change in size and decreased reactivity to light in one or both pupils
- Onset of conjugate or dysconjugate eye deviation
- Progressing weakness (paresis) or paralysis of an extremity or one side of the body; observe for facial weakness on the same side
- Changes in ability to identify sensation

- Significant changes in vital signs (beyond parameters established by physician)
  - Changes in blood pressure (BP) may threaten tissue oxygenation or result in direct injury from hemorrhage. For example, the patient with cerebral vascular insufficiency who is usually hypertensive may suffer a cerebral infarction if BP drops too low. In the patient with an untreated ruptured cerebral aneurysm or intracerebral hemorrhage, hypertension may trigger additional hemorrhage.
  - Change in heart rate or rhythm may threaten adequate perfusion or indicate potential etiology (eg, atrial fibrillation with emboli, causing stroke).
  - Fever may indicate infection or dysfunction of the autonomic nervous system and is associated with worsened outcome after traumatic brain injury and acute stroke.
  - Significant or progressively rising BP may lead to widening pulse pressure, decreasing pulse, and decreasing respirations, the classic signs of increased intracranial pressure (ICP) (Cushing response); these are late signs of lower brainstem compression.
- Irregular breathing patterns may indicate progressing brainstem compression.

information that suggests a seizure disorder, stroke, or traumatic injury.

When questioning patients about risk factors, the goal is to identify how likely they are to develop or to already be experiencing consequences of neurological and neurovascular diseases. Such investigation creates an environment in which health care professionals can implement necessary interventions to control symptoms, direct education to prevent new issues or complications, and establish in the patient health record the areas needing ongoing follow-up and emphasis. Smoking, stress, amount of alcohol consumed, overweight, physical inactivity, high BP, high cholesterol, and diabetes mellitus are modifiable risk factors for stroke (Heart and Stroke Foundation of Canada, 2011a). After assessment, nurses identify focused teaching areas and evaluate the patient's progress toward change in ongoing visits.

The following screening questions are important to establishing the patient's risk for neurological disease.

Questions to Assess History and Risk Factors	Rationale
From the chart obtain the following: • Age • Heredity • Gender • Height and weight • Date and result of last blood pressure (BP) reading • Date and result of last cholesterol level	Increased age and male gender increase risk for *stroke*. Another risk is stroke in a parent, grandparent, or sibling. Individuals with an African genetic background have a higher risk of death from stroke than Caucasians, partly because blacks have higher risks of BP and type 2 diabetes (Heart and Stroke Foundation of Canada, 2011b).
Have you ever been diagnosed with a neurological condition, such as seizure? • When did you have it? How often? • Seizure history: associated warning signs (aura), precipitating factors, motor activity, loss of consciousness, incontinence, sleepiness after the seizure (postictal phase) • How was the seizure treated? • How effective was the treatment?	Various scales have been developed to identify *seizure* severity; criteria include seizure frequency, seizure type, seizure duration, postictal events, postictal duration, automatisms (eg, lip smacking), seizure clusters, known patterns, warnings, tongue biting, incontinence, injuries, and functional impairment (Pierazzo & Book, 2010; Singh & Kahn, 2010).
Have you ever had a head injury? • When? • How was it treated? • What were the outcomes?	A *head injury* is suspected if there is a: • Witnessed loss of consciousness of >5 minutes • History of amnesia of >5 minutes • Unexplained drowsiness • More than three episodes of vomiting • Suspicion of nonaccidental injury • Seizure in the patient with no history of epilepsy (Thiessen, 2006)
Have you ever had a stroke? • When did you have it? • How was it treated? • What were the outcomes?	An exact time of onset, definite focal symptoms, neurological signs, and ability to lateralize the signs to the left or right side of the brain suggest a *stroke* (Hand, Kwan, et al., 2006).
Have you ever had any infectious or degenerative diseases, such as meningitis? Or muscular sclerosis?	Symptoms of *meningitis* include high fever, stiff neck (nuchal rigidity), drowsiness, and photosensitivity. Symptoms of *degenerative disease* include weakness, tingling or numbness, difficulty seeing, and elimination-control issues.
Have you had any changes in your emotional state or coping strategies related to your health? • Personality change • Alterations in level of independence • Loss of role function related to altered ability to carry out responsibilities, interact with others • Depression, apathy, or irritability • Change in ability to tolerate stress • Issues related to chronic conditions, progressive deterioration in function or hospitalization	Information regarding past and current emotional state and coping strategies is obtained through attention to functional health patterns (see Chapters 6 and 30). Family relationships and socioeconomic background provide valuable clues to the patient's support system and capacity to manage the social and financial effects of disabilities frequently associated with neurological conditions.

(text continues on page 710)

Questions to Assess History and Risk Factors	Rationale
Do you have a history of high BP? • When was it diagnosed? • How is it being treated?	Systolic BP >140 mm Hg, diastolic BP ≥90 mm Hg, or both is a risk factor for *stroke* (Canadian Hypertension Education Program, 2010).
Which of the following conditions place you at risk for neurovascular disease? • Diabetes mellitus • Carotid artery disease • Atrial fibrillation • Sickle cell disease	*Atrial fibrillation* increases risk for stroke, because quivering atria can lead blood to stagnate and form small clots. A clot that breaks off can circulate to the brain and block an artery, causing an *embolic stroke*. In *sickle cell disease*, blood cells tend to be stickier, causing clots to form more easily in narrowed arteries.
What lifestyle choices place you at risk for neurovascular disease? • Smoking • High-fat and/or high-sodium diet • Obesity • Physical inactivity • Lack of stress management	Many risk factors for stroke are the same as for cardiovascular disease (see Chapter 19).
What environmental or occupational hazards increase risks of neurological trauma? • Lack of seat belt use • No helmet when biking, skiing, snowboarding, engaging in high-risk sports • Incorrect use of car seats for children • Use of drugs or alcohol while driving • Falls (lack of window guards, pull bars, safety gates) • Ignorance of firearm safety	In Canada, males are three times as likely as females to sustain traumatic brain or spinal cord injuries, partly because they engage in riskier activities (Couris, Guilcher, et al., 2010) Approximately 50% of spinal cord injuries in Canada are the result of traumatic causes. The majority occur under the age of 60 years and the greatest number occur in the age range of 20 to 39 years (Rick Hansen Institute & Urban Futures, 2010).

Risk Assessment and Health Promotion

Topics for Health Promotion

- Risk factors for cerebrovascular disease—transient ischemic attacks and stroke (brain attack)
- Risk factors for head injury (brain trauma)
- Risk factors for spinal cord injuries
- Prevention of exposure to neurotoxins (eg, lead, mercury, pesticides)
- Risk factors for infections (eg, meningitis, encephalitis)
- Risk factors for peripheral neuropathies
- Risk factors for seizure activity
- Maintenance of brain health throughout life

Adapted from Anderson, M. C., & Bickley, L. S. (2010). The nervous system. In T. C. Stephen, D. L. Skillen, R. A. Day, & L. S. Bickley (Eds.). *Canadian Bates' guide to health assessment for nurses* (1st ed., p. 698). Philadelphia, PA: Wolters Kluwer Health/Lippincott Williams & Wilkins.

Risk assessment helps to identify potential conditions so that health care providers give patients information that can influence behavioural choices. Important focus areas for the neurological system involve prevention of stroke, unintentional injury, neurotoxin exposure, infections of meningeal layers, and seizures. The concept of *brain health* is also important for nurses to address. Factors that promote and maintain the health of the brain include aerobic exercise on a regular basis; a diet with fruits, vegetables, omega-3 fatty acids, and whole grains; and mental activity (Gillette Guyonnet, Abellan Van Kan, et al., 2007; Jedrziewski, Lee, et al., 2007; Willis, Tennstedt, et al., 2006).

Stroke Prevention

Risk factors for stroke are similar to those for cardiovascular disease; prevention involves modification of unhealthy lifestyle choices. Patients are encouraged to control BP through weight reduction, physical activity, stress management, healthy diet, and use of antihypertensive medications as prescribed. At every visit, nurses ask patients who smoke about their desire to stop. Nurses provide all patients with information about a diet low in saturated fat and sodium and high in fruits and vegetables. They ask patients who are overweight and obese about their willingness to reduce calories. Additionally, nurses advise patients to exercise moderately 30 to 60 minutes most days (Roach, Roddick, et al., 2010).

Injury Prevention

When investigating risk for traumatic injury, nurses also provide information about prevention. Nurses recommend use of protective helmets and gear to patients who engage in sports involving physical contact. During assessment of driving habits, nurses advise patients about the importance of seat belts and discourage the use of alcohol, drugs, and cell phones while driving. They provide teaching materials to reinforce concepts, especially for adolescents and adults under 40 years of age who are at highest risk of brain and spinal cord injury (see also Chapter 14). They focus on falls prevention in the older adult population and assess for risk factors that could lead to Parkinson's disease, which usually begins after the age of 60 years. Some evidence suggests that family history combined with exposure to environmental neurotoxins (eg, pesticides, herbicides, lead) at work, home, or recreation contribute to development of the disease (Guttman, Kish, et al., 2003; Kumar, Calne, et al., 2004). Nurses discuss the use of personal protective equipment in any environment where patients are exposed to neurotoxins, including chemotherapeutic drugs administered by health care providers in hospitals. They advise about avoiding frequent ingestion of foods known to be higher in mercury (eg, canned light tuna) and inquire about potential exposure to lead sources for children and for workers.

Prevention of Meningeal Infections

Nurses recommend vaccination against bacterial meningitis for infants, children, and adults at increased risk. The Public Health Agency of Canada (PHAC, 2009) provides detailed guidelines. Individuals are at risk if they acquire pneumococcal pneumonia, otitis media (acute or chronic), or basilar skull fracture or if they are immunocompromised. The majority of viral meningitis cases are caused by an arbovirus or enterovirus. Mosquitos and infected ticks are vectors. A smaller percentage of viral meningitis infections is caused by type 1 and type 2 herpes simplex viruses. Nurses advise patients about handwashing, protective clothing, insect repellants, and safer sexual practice with condoms. They encourage individuals aged 60 and over who report chicken pox (varicella zoster virus) in their past medical history to seek the vaccine ZostaVax that prevents development of shingles and its complications by about 60% (National Advisory Committee on Immunization, 2010). Also, to seek treatment immediately with an antiviral medication if they do develop shingles, which presents as an extremely painful eruption of vesicles in a dermatome.

Reduction of Risk for Seizure Activity

Seizures may be full body convulsion, localized to a body part or region, or a short-lived loss of consciousness without falling. Causes include brain tumours, fever, infection, head trauma, age over 65 years, withdrawal from drugs or alcohol, and metabolic conditions (Epilepsy Canada, 2005). About 0.6% of Canadians suffer from epilepsy, the disorder that produces seizures, and about 60% are older adults or young children (Epilepsy Canada). Nurses encourage individuals to use protective head gear for work and sports, seat belts when driving, and caution with alcohol intake (one drink per day for women, two drinks per day for men). They teach patients about seizure triggers, including stress, inadequate nutrition, sleep deprivation, strong negative emotions, flickering lights, missed medications, and skipped meals (Epilepsy Canada).

Focused Health History Related to Common Symptoms/Signs

The history of the present illness or concern requires that a detailed account be taken of each symptom (location, nature or quality, intensity or severity, timing [date of onset, frequency, duration], associated symptoms, aggravating or precipitating factors, alleviating factors, environmental factors, significance to patient, and patient's perspective on the cause). Nurses note what has been the general pattern of progression (eg, rapid, static, progressively worse, remitting, exacerbating).

During assessment of the neurological system, nurses inquire about common symptoms in all patients to screen for the early presence of disease. If the patient has specific neurological concerns, nurses focus their assessment on these areas with follow-up questions. A thorough history of symptoms assists with identifying the current condition. Nurses direct questioning toward a history of headaches, tremors, dizziness, tingling, blackouts, weakness or paralysis, loss of sensation, and involuntary movements or sensations. They inquire about changes in speech, attention, mood, orientation, memory, or judgment.

Common Neurological Symptoms and Signs

- Headache (see Chapter 14)
- Weakness (generalized, one side of body, or one extremity)
- Involuntary movements or tremors
- Difficulty with balance, coordination, or gait
- Dizziness or vertigo
- Difficulty swallowing (dysphagia)
- Changes in intellectual abilities
- Difficulties with expression or comprehension of speech/language
- Alterations in touch, taste, or smell
- Sudden vision or hearing changes (see Chapters 15 and 16)
- Numbness or loss of sensation (paresthesia)
- Pins and needles or tingling
- Loss of consciousness or syncope (fainting)
- Convulsions (seizures)

Examples of Questions for Symptom Analysis—Numbness and Tingling in Legs

- "Where do you have this sensation of numbness?" "One or both legs?" (Location)
- "Can you point to where the numbness ends in each leg?" (Location/radiation)
- "You describe this area as being 'numb.' Could other words also describe the sensation?" "Cold?" "Gone to sleep?" "Would you describe the sensation as tingling?" "Pins and needles?" "Prickling? Stinging? Crawling?" (Quality/nature)
- "Has the area of numbness extended, or become larger over time?" "Can you feel pressure?" "Cold, hot, or pain over the area?" (Severity/quantity/intensity)
- "When did you first notice the numbness?" "The tingling?" "Did the tingling occur before or after the numbness started?" "Did they occur at the same time?" (Timing—onset)
- "Has the sensation ever gone away?" "If so, how long ago?" "When did the numbness come back?" "How long has the numbness persisted?" (Timing—duration)
- "How often in the past year has the numbness gone away and returned?" (Timing—frequency)
- "Does the intensity of the numbness change throughout the day?" "Is the tingling more noticeable at night?" (Timing—time of day)
- "Does any action or position increase the intensity of the numbness or tingling?" (Aggravating factors)
- "What helps to lessen the numbness, the tingling, or both?" "A warm bath?" "Elevating the legs?" (Alleviating factors)
- "Have you noticed any other symptoms?" "Besides the numbness and tingling, have you noticed any pain with the tingling?" "Do you feel unusually cool at times?" "Do you have any back pain or pain down the leg at any time?" (Associated symptoms)
- "Can you think of anything that could contribute to these sensations?" "Anything at home?" "In your work environment?" "Leisure activities?" "For example, do you work with solvents or other chemicals? Do heavy lifting?" (Environmental factors)
- "Tell me how this numbness in your legs has affected your lifestyle at work, at home, during leisure pursuits." (Significance to the patient)
- "What do you think might be causing the numbness and tingling you are experiencing?" *(Patient perspective)*

Adapted from Anderson, M. C., & Bickley, L. S. (2010). The nervous system. In T. C. Stephen, D. L. Skillen, R. A. Day, & L. S. Bickley (Eds.). *Canadian Bates' guide to health assessment for nurses* (1st ed., p. 698). Philadelphia, PA: Wolters Kluwer Health/Lippincott Williams & Wilkins.

Examples of Questions to Assess Symptoms/Signs	Rationale/Unexpected Findings
Headache or Other Pain Do you have a headache or other pain? (see Chapter 14).	
Limb or Unilateral Weakness Do you have weakness on one side? Or in an arm or leg? • Can you smile for me? Raise both arms above your head? Speak a simple sentence to me?	Unilateral weakness, disturbed speech, and symptoms for >10 minutes increase risk of *stroke* (Rothwell, Giles, et al., 2005). Report patients with positive findings to a physician for diagnosis and treatment.
Generalized Weakness Do you have generalized weakness? • Does it occur mostly in the hands? The feet? Or core muscles? • Do any repetitive actions lead to such weakness? • Are there any associated symptoms such as rash? Or joint inflammation?	Causes may be infectious, neurological, endocrine, inflammatory, rheumatic, genetic, metabolic, electrolyte-induced, or drug-induced. *Neuropathy* primarily occurs in distal muscles. A rash may be a sign of *lupus*. Repetitive actions exacerbate *myasthenia gravis*. Common neurological causes include *demyelinating disorders, amyotrophic lateral sclerosis, Guillain–Barré syndrome, multiple sclerosis, myasthenia gravis*, and *degenerative disc disease* (Saguil, 2005).
Involuntary Movements or Tremors Have you noted any shaking or tremors? • When does it happen? At rest? With movement? While maintaining a fixed position?	Resting tremors worsen at rest and decrease with activity; they are usually a symptom of *Parkinson's disease*. Gradual onset of positional tremors suggests *essential tremor; sudden* onset suggests a *toxic* or *metabolic disorder*. Intention tremors are worse with movement toward an object; they may result from *multiple sclerosis* (Bennett, Piquet, et al., 2006).
Balance/Coordination Difficulties Do you have any difficulty with balance? Coordination? Walking?	*Multiple sclerosis, Parkinson's disease, stroke,* and *cerebral palsy* are neurological causes of impaired gait. Refer to Chapter 23 for further information.

Examples of Questions to Assess Symptoms/Signs	Rationale/Unexpected Findings
Dizziness or Vertigo Have you had any periods of dizziness? • Describe what it feels like without using the word dizziness. • Is it associated with nausea? Vomiting? • Does changing positions make it better? Worse?	Common causes include *multiple sclerosis, Parkinson's disease, cerebellar ischemia or infarction, benign or malignant neoplasms,* and *arterial–venous malformation of blood vessels in the brain*. Position changes usually worsen dizziness associated with the inner ear.
Difficulty Swallowing Have you had any difficulty swallowing? • Are any foods or liquids particularly difficult?	**Dysphagia**, associated with CN dysfunction, is a common symptom of *stroke* or *neuromuscular disease*. Generally soft foods are more easily tolerated than chewy foods or liquids.
Intellectual Changes Have you noticed intellectual changes? Or difficulty with concentration? Memory? Or attention? (Nurse may also ask family members or friends of patients about this.)	Common causes of memory loss include *Alzheimer's disease, dementia, depression, stroke, some medications,* and *metabolic imbalances*. Refer to Chapter 30 for more information.
Speech/Language Difficulties Do you notice any difficulties with expression or comprehension of speech/language? • Any difficulty understanding speech? • Any difficulty forming words? • Any difficulty finding words? Putting sentences together?	**Aphasia** is a common sign of *stroke*, especially when it affects the speech centres in the left hemisphere (Hand, Kwan, et al., 2006). Neuromuscular disease also affects the speech centre, such as with *Alzheimer's disease* or other forms of *dementia*.
Changes in Taste, Touch, Smell, or Sensation Have you noticed alterations in touch? Taste? Smell? Sensation? • Any numbness, tingling, or hypersensitivity? • Where do you feel it?	**Paresthesia**, unexpected prickly or tingly sensations, is most common in the hands, arms, legs, and feet but can occur over other body parts. Causes include *neurological disease* or traumatic nerve damage such as *carpal tunnel syndrome* or *cervical stenosis*.
Lost or Blurred Vision Have you had a loss or blurring of vision? In one or both eyes? Any double vision? • When do you notice it? • Are there associated symptoms such as weakness? Or impaired speech? • Does this create any safety issues? Can you drive?	Central causes of **diplopia** (double vision) include *stroke, vascular malformation, tumour, mass, trauma, meningitis, hemorrhage,* and *muscular sclerosis*.
Hearing Loss or Tinnitus Have you noticed any hearing loss or ringing in the ears (tinnitus)? • Was it a sudden onset? Or slow? • Is it in one ear? Or both ears?	Common causes of sensorineural hearing loss include noise (residential, recreational, occupational), *autoimmune disorders, Meniere's disease, ototoxic medications,* and *head trauma* (Isaacson & Vora, 2003). Refer to Chapter 16 for more information.

Documentation of Expected Findings

Patient without headache, weakness, tremors; denies difficulty with balance, coordination, or gait. Denies dizziness or vertigo, dysphagia, change in intellectual abilities, difficulty with concentration, memory, attention span, expression, or comprehension of speech/language; reports no alteration in sense of touch, taste, smell, or sensation. Denies loss or blurring vision or diplopia; reports no hearing loss, tinnitus, numbness, or paresthesia.

Additional Questions	Rationale/Unexpected Findings

Women Who Are Pregnant

Do you have a history of seizures?
- Have you noticed weight gain or edema? Have you had high blood pressure (BP)? Tested positive for protein in your urine?
- How are you taking any prescribed medications?

Some women who are pregnant and with epilepsy stop taking anticonvulsants because of their potentially harmful fetal effects, such as *neural tube deficits* (including *spina bifida), cleft lip or palate, congenital heart disease, developmental delay,* and *cognitive impairment* (Koren, Nava-Ocampo, et al., 2006). These patients must weigh the risk of having seizures while not taking anticonvulsants against the potentially teratogenic effects. Seizures from epilepsy must be differentiated from those of eclampsia.

Do you have a headache? Any sensory changes? Changes in your movements? Or visual changes?

Do you have a history of migraines? Epilepsy? Or multiple sclerosis?

Migraines are more common during pregnancy, possibly from increased hormone levels.

Hormones influence the course of *multiple sclerosis;* relapse rate is lower during pregnancy, especially in the third trimester, with a marked increase in the first 3 months postpartum (Vukusic, Hutchinson, et al., 2004).

Newborns and Infants

- Is there any family history of genetic neurological disorders?
- Were there any birth difficulties?
- Was your baby premature?
- Are there any congenital anomalies? Developmental delays?

Neuroblastomas are associated with chromosomal aberrations. Additionally, *Down's syndrome, muscular dystrophy, phenylketonuria,* and *Tay–Sachs disease* are genetic neurological disorders. Also pay attention to the developmental history, including perinatal history (eg, difficult labour, prematurity). Risk of *cerebral palsy* increases with a history of maternal infection in pregnancy, preterm birth, and multiple pregnancies (Bax, Tydeman, et al., 2006).

Children and Adolescents

Is there any history of head injury?
- Does your child maintain eye contact? Respond with appropriate facial expressions and gestures?
- How is he or she meeting developmental milestones?
- How well does your child interact and play with other children?
- How would you describe your child? Flexible? Focused on routines?

The age groups at highest risk for *traumatic brain injury* are 0- to 19-year-olds (Canadian Institute for Health Information [CIHI], 2006). Falls, motor vehicle injuries, and bicycle injuries are common causes of brain injury in children (Dunning, Daly, et al., 2006). Children with *autism, attention deficit disorder, attention deficit hyperactive disorder,* and other psychiatric challenges are two to three times more likely to experience injuries needing medical attention (Lee, Harrington, et al., 2008). Risk for autism increases with advanced maternal or paternal age, low birth weight, shortened gestation, and intrapartal hypoxia (Kolevzon, Gross, et al., 2007). Autism also is associated with breech presentation, low 5-minute Apgar score, birth before 35 weeks' gestation, and parental psychiatric illness (Laarson, Eaton, et al., 2005).

Does your child have fever? Chills? Headache? Vomiting? Has he or she received the meningococcal vaccine?

Infants (starting at 2 months) and children should receive meningococcal vaccine (PHAC, 2009).

Older Adults

Do you have a history of epilepsy? Stroke? Parkinson's disease? Dementia? Alzheimer's disease?

These conditions are increased in the elderly. *Hypertension; atrial fibrillation; diabetes; heart failure, chronic renal disease;* female gender; *previous cerebrovascular disease;* and *ischemic stroke* increase risk of neurovascular disease (Arboix, Miguel, et al., 2006).

Have you fallen? Had a head injury?

To the patient or caregiver: Have you noticed any cognitive impairment? Language changes (slow, slurred, and difficult or impossible to understand speech)? Hearing loss? Taste changes? Loss of smell? Vision losses? Any balance difficulties? Emotional changes?

Adults older than 60 years have a high rate of traumatic brain injury–related hospitalization, but the rate is showing a decline (CIHI, 2006). Falls are the most common cause, followed by car accidents.

Additional Questions	Rationale/Unexpected Findings
From the patient health record, note ethnicity, genetic background, gender, and area of residence.	These variables are relevant in some disorders (eg, incidence of *multiple sclerosis* is higher in temperate climates; *stroke* occurs more often in African Canadians than in Caucasian Canadians).
Is there any history of head injury?	Hospitalization rates for *traumatic brain injury* are highest among Aboriginals and individuals of African heritage. This latter population has the highest death rate from traumatic brain injury (National Center for Injury Prevention and Control, 2007). Certain military duties (eg, paratrooper) increase risk for brain injury.
Are you exposed to pesticides at work? At home?	Maternal exposure to pesticides is linked to increased incidence of *anencephaly* and *neural tube defects*. Living in areas of pesticide use also increases risks. Implications for farm workers, especially migrant workers, are particularly concerning (Rull, Ritz, et al., 2006). Folic acid deficiency also is linked to neural tube defects. Incidence of spina bifida is highest among Hispanic women, partially as a result of exposure to pesticides (Williams, Rasmussen, et al., 2005).
How old is your home? Does the paint have lead in it?	Dust and chips from deteriorating paint include lead (before 1978). Lead can cause reproductive difficulties and harm children. Severe lead exposure can cause *encephalopathy*.

An Example of a Therapeutic Dialogue

Remember Mr. Matthew Nderitu, introduced at the beginning of this chapter. He was seen in the emergency department (ED) and diagnosed with a stroke. He is confused and the health care team is finding it challenging to communicate with him. The nurse needs to accurately assess his neurological status; later, the nurse will interview Mr. Nderitu to gather details about his history and the lifestyle practices that have led to him having a stroke at a young age.

Nurse: Mr. Nderitu, I would like to ask you a few questions to find out more about your stroke. Is that alright?

Mr. Nderitu: (Nods head yes). (Speaks slowly) Can I have a cigarette?

Nurse: Your cigarettes are put away for your safety right now. I would like to ask you a few questions. Tell me where you are now.

Mr. Nderitu: I'm at home. Who are you?

Nurse: I'm your nurse. My name is Boyd. You're in the hospital because you had a stroke. You're at Mountain View Hospital. Tell me what day it is today.

Mr. Nderitu: Is it Wednesday? (correct answer is Friday)

Nurse: Today is Friday, February 11, 2011. Tell me what your name is.

Mr. Nderitu: Matthew Nderitu (smiles).

Critical Thinking Challenge

- Why did the nurse provide information on the correct day, date, and place? Provide rationale.
- Considering this patient's speech deficits, should the nurse ask open- or closed-ended questions for orientation? Provide rationale.
- How would you respond to his request for a cigarette? Provide rationale.

Objective Data Collection

Equipment

- Penlight
- Splintered tongue blade
- Intact cotton swabs
- Reflex hammer
- 128-Hz tuning fork
- Cotton ball made into fine wisp
- Familiar objects (eg, safety pin closed, coin, paper clip)
- Familiar pungent odours (eg, cinnamon, cloves, lemon extract)
- Test tube with hot water and test tube with ice water

Promoting Patient Comfort, Dignity, and Safety

Nurses anticipate that patients may attempt to minimize or to hide neurological deficits. For example, when a nurse asks, "What year were you born?" the patient might say, "Well, if I told you that, then you'd know how old I was" (and laughs). The nurse can return to this question later to evaluate long-term memory or change the question slightly to get a different response.

In healthy people, nurses can integrate the neurological examination with history taking. For example, they can evaluate function of the CNs during conversation and while observing the patient's facial expressions. Neurological screening is performed on patients at high risk for changes in health status such as following a motor vehicle collision or for patients with a documented history of previous neurological illness. Nurses add techniques according to the specific injury or disease process as part of a focused neurological examination.

Comprehensive Physical Examination: Neurological System

Physical examination of the nervous system provides information about its functional integrity. Because of how the nervous system is organized, a deficit or group of deficits often provides the information needed to localize the area of pathology. This information, combined with the history and diagnostic testing, allows determination of the nature (eg, traumatic, neoplastic, vascular, infectious, degenerative) of the pathological process.

Nurses use the general survey with vital signs, inspection, palpation, and percussion in the neurological examination. Comprehensive neurological assessment begins with general observation of how the patient relates to the environment. Such observation may occur during initial contact, before the formal process of history taking begins. Often, observation occurs during the entire encounter with the patient. Observation of level of alertness and responsiveness necessitates a focus on attention span, mood, and affect. Assessment of general appearance includes grooming, cleanliness and arrangement of clothing, use of prosthetics (eg, eyeglasses, hearing aids), and any visible evidence of trauma or unexpected finding on an exposed surface (eg, birthmarks; skin tumours; asymmetry of face, gaze, or extremities). Frequently, this initial interaction allows nurses to assess speech and language, general movement, and gait and balance. It also provides data that direct further focused assessment of individual functions during the physical examination.

Techniques and Expected Findings	Rationale/Unexpected Findings
Level of Consciousness ***Inspection and Palpation.*** Begin by assessing LOC. The initial outcome determines the extent and method of the rest of the examination. People visibly express LOC through degree of response to stimulus, with the highest level being spontaneous alertness. Be sure to apply stimulus in the correct order (Table 24-2), moving to a more intense stimulus only when the previous attempt is unsuccessful. First arouse the patient by speech, then by touch, and then by pressure to the nail beds (Fig. 24-11) or by pinching a large muscle mass on an extremity. **(Note: Do not pinch a small fold of skin, which may cause soft tissue trauma.)** Pressure to the nailbeds also can be useful in determining gross motor function when the patient's LOC makes formal strength testing impossible.	The GCS (Box 24-2) has facilitated the assessment of patients with impaired consciousness. Primarily, the GCS determines the degree of conscious impairment by evaluating behavioural responses in three areas: eye opening, best motor responses, and best verbal responses. The examiner lists, for each category, the patient's best response. The GCS weighs each response numerically to quantify overall response. The minimum score is 3; the maximum is 15. - Eye opening is in response to activity in the environment, verbal cues, non-noxious stimuli, or noxious stimuli pressure as an indicator of LOC. - Verbal response includes orientation, conversation, speech, sounds, and no response as an indicator of cognitive function. - Motor response is scored according to the most functional response from either upper extremity (eg, if the patient follows commands with the right hand but not the left, the motor score indicates ability to follow commands).

Table 24-2 Assessment of Consciousness: Applying Stimulation	
Order of Stimulation	**Example**
Spontaneous	Enter room and observe arousal.
Usual voice	State patient's name; ask him or her to open eyes.
Loud voice	Use loud voice if no response to usual voice.
Tactile (touch)	Touch patient's shoulder or arm lightly.
Noxious stimulation (pain)	Apply nailbed pressure to elicit pain response, telling patient that you will be applying pressure.

Techniques and Expected Findings (continued)

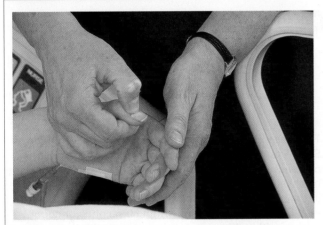

Figure 24-11 The nurse is applying pressure to the nailbeds to arouse the patient who has not responded to speech or touch.

Objective description of the patient's response is critical to evaluating changes in LOC over time. A wide range of terms has been used to describe LOC (Table 24-3). Despite careful definition within a particular institution, these terms are by nature subjective and must be used carefully to allow accurate comparisons of serial assessments by different practitioners. Description of specific response to stimulus provides the best chance of identifying change that may initially be subtle. *Expected findings are "patient alert, opens eyes spontaneously."*

Rationale/Unexpected Findings (continued)

BOX 24-2 GLASGOW COMA SCALE

The Glasgow Coma Scale (GCS) is a tool for assessing the patient's response to stimuli. Scores range from 3 (deep coma) to 15 (expected).

Eye opening response	Spontaneous	4
	To voice	3
	To pain	2
	None	1
Best verbal response	Oriented	5
	Confused	4
	Inappropriate words	3
	Incomprehensible sounds	2
	None	1
Best motor response	Obeys command	6
	Localizes pain	5
	Withdraws	4
	Flexion	3
	Extension	2
	None	1
Total		3–15

Adapted from Teasdale, G., & Jennett, B. (1974). Assessment of coma and impaired consciousness: A practical scale. *Lancet, 304*, 81–84.

Although accepted as a relatively objective assessment of consciousness, the GCS itself is also vulnerable to differences in scoring of the same patient situation, especially in the motor area (Gill, Reiley, et al., 2004; Heron, Heron, et al., 2001). Consistency in training staff to use the GCS, with periodic review, is needed to enhance result reliability. GCS is predictive of outcome from a traumatic brain injury when combined with the patient's age and pupillary response (McNett, 2007).

(text continues on page 718)

Table 24-3 Levels of Consciousness

Term	Definition
Alert wakefulness	Patient appreciates the environment and responds quickly to stimuli.
Confusion	Patient is disoriented to time, place, or person; has shortened attention span; shows poor memory; or has difficulty following commands.
Drowsiness	Patient responds to stimuli appropriately but with delay and slowness and may respond to some but not all (also described as **lethargy** or **obtunded** state).
Stupor	Patient is unresponsive and can be aroused only briefly by vigorous, repeated stimulation.
Coma	Patient is unresponsive and generally cannot be aroused.

Adapted from Hickey, J. V. (2002). The neurological physical examination and neurological assessment. In J. V. Hickey (Ed.). *The clinical practice of neurological and neurosurgical nursing* (5th ed., pp. 117–184). Philadelphia, PA: Lippincott Williams & Wilkins.

Techniques and Expected Findings (continued)	**Rationale/Unexpected Findings** (continued)

Cognitive Function

If results of LOC assessment show that the patient can interact, evaluate cognitive function (many components of which may have been done during history taking). Remember to conduct specific cognitive tests so that patients do not feel their intelligence is being challenged.

Cognitive function includes basic orientation, attention, and memory, and more complex functions, such as information and vocabulary, calculation ability, abstract thinking, constructional ability, reasoning, and judgment. Complex cognitive function can be tested informally whenever you interact with the patient, especially when teaching, establishing goals and priorities, and planning for home care. Doing so provides information about the patient's ability to learn, to reason, and to make judgments. See Chapter 10 for discussions of assessment of attention, concentration, memory, calculation, and abstract thinking.

The Blessed Dementia Rating Scale and the Mini-Mental State Examination are tools used to assess possible presence of dementia (see Chapter 10). Patients can also be asked about items related to functional ability: telling the time by using a clock face and counting change. Inability to name the time within 60 seconds or count change within 90 seconds is correlated with dementia (Inouye, Robison, et al., 1998).

Orientation. Assess orientation by directly questioning the patient about person, place, and time. Display sensitivity to the patient's environment and communication ability. Asking "What month (year, season) is it?" may be more reasonable than "What day is it?" Asking about place through yes or no questions rather than "Where are you?" may be necessary for patients with *aphasia*. Regarding person, as well as identifying himself or herself, ask the patient to identify visitors or family pictures. Also, ask the patient about his or her age (National Institutes of Health, 2003). *The patient is oriented to person, place, and time.*

If the patient has been hospitalized for several days with few cues about day of the week, loss of this specific piece of information may be expected.

The patient with aphasia has impaired ability to interpret language and/or to form or express words.

Communication (Speech/Language)

Communication is another function to assess continuously throughout the interaction. Observe clarity and fluency of speech through basic conversation. Ask the patient to repeat words or phrases with multiple combinations of consonants and vowels (eg, "aggravating conversation") to test speech articulation. Formal testing includes assessment of word comprehension, repetition, naming, reading comprehension, and writing (see Chapter 10). *Speech is clear and articulate.*

Deficits in articulation are referred to as **dysarthria**. In some cases, distinguishing speech/language deficits from confusion is difficult. Typically those with speech/language deficits behave appropriately to situation and environment, especially to visual cues. These findings are less likely in confused patients, but consultation with a speech pathologist for formal assessment of communication and cognitive function will clarify the type of deficit. Patients with a language deficit might be unable to express needs, but usually can follow simple commands (eg, "Open and close your eyes" and "Squeeze my hand"). Confused states can be described as acute (delirium) or chronic (dementia, with multiple etiologies).

Pupillary Response

Inspection. Basic assessment of pupils includes size, shape, and reactivity to light (see Chapter 15). Darken the room and instruct the patient to gaze into the distance to dilate the pupils. Ask him or her to keep looking ahead. Hold a light on the side (avoid pointing it into the eye). Observe for nystagmus in one or both eyes. Bringing the light in quickly from the side, observe the reaction of the same and then the other pupil for the direct and consensual response.

Also assess the gaze for eye contact and drifting.

If the eyes deviate, assess whether it is conjugate (move together) or dysconjugate (move separately).

Unexpected reflex posturing include flexion and extension, hemiplegia, quadriplegia, and paralysis (see Table 24-7 at the end of this chapter). Unexpected movements include tic, myoclonus, fasciculation, dystonia, tremor, chorea, and athetosis (see Table 24-8 at the end of this chapter).

Cranial Nerve Testing

Unless a thorough screening assessment is suggested by the presenting concern, it is rarely necessary to assess complete cranial nerve (CN) function (see Table 24-4 for this testing).

Inspection and Palpation.

There are 12 pairs of CNs. Each member of the pair innervates structures on the same side from which it arises (the ipsilateral side). A lesion of the CN or its nucleus results in an ipsilateral peripheral nerve deficit. A lesion in the cerebral cortex in the area that supplies the CN nucleus, or the tracts travelling from the cerebral cortex to the CN nucleus, results in a contralateral CNS deficit. For example, facial weakness caused by a lesion in the right frontal motor control centre occurs on the left side of the face. A lesion affecting the right facial nerve itself produces weakness on the entire right side of the face.

Use of the gag reflex as part of assessment varies widely (Mathers-Schmidt & Kurlinski, 2003). Many practitioners continue to use absence of gag reflex as an indicator for risk of aspiration; but they may overestimate risk when absence of gag reflex is the only deficit found. Conversely, they may miss other risks if gag reflex is the only function tested and found intact (Leder, 1997). Refer to Table 24-4 for a description of unexpected findings.

CN I—Olfactory. The sense of smell is tested bilaterally (see Table 24-4 for technique).

Sense of smell intact bilaterally.

CN II—Optic. The integrity of the optic nerve is tested by assessing visual acuity, visual fields by confrontation, and the optic fundi (see Chapter 15 and Table 24-4 for technique).

CNs II and III—Optic and Oculomotor. The integrity of these nerves acting together is assessed by inspecting the pupils for symmetry in size, shape, reaction to light, and near reactions (accommodation) (see Chapter 15 and Table 24-4 for technique).

Pupils are round, equal, and constrict briskly (within 1 second) in response to light, R6→4, L6→4, both directly and consensually. These data are also recorded as PERRL (pupils equal, round, reactive to light). When near reaction is documented with the pupils, it is charted as PERRLA (A is for accommodation). Accommodation includes constriction of the pupils and convergence of the eyes bilaterally.

Following a stroke, the patient may present with deficit in visual fields detected during screening.

Consensual reaction: When one pupil constricts to light, the other does, too.

See Table 24-9 at the end of this chapter for pupils in comatose patients.

(text continues on page 722)

Table 24-4 Summary of Cranial Nerve Assessment

Cranial Nerve (CN)	Technique	Unexpected Findings
I. Olfactory (sensory)	First, assess patency of the nose by closing off one nostril and asking the patient to inhale; perform the same technique on the opposite side. Occlude one naris. Tell the patient to close the eyes, place a familiar scent near the open naris, and ask the patient to inhale gently and identify the scent. Repeat with a different scent on the opposite side. Commonly used fragrances include orange, peppermint, cinnamon, and coffee.	Only a few neurological conditions are linked with deficits. It is important to test for patency of the naris, which can influence ability to smell. Other influences include allergies, mucosal inflammation, age-related impairment, and excessive tobacco smoking. An olfactory tract lesion may compromise ability to discriminate odours (anosmia). Some individuals do not have a sense of smell. A gentle sniff is recommended to avoid inhalation of a powdery stimulus such as cinnamon.
II. Optic (sensory)	Evaluate far vision by using the Snellen chart. Expect visual acuity of 20/20. Use a Jaeger test to evaluate near vision. Test visual fields by using confrontation (see Chapter 15 for tests of visual acuity and visual fields).	Inability to read small print is common in older adults, as a result of age-related loss of accommodation.
III. Oculomotor (motor)	Assess pupils for size, shape, equality, response to light, and accommodation. Assess the six cardinal directions of gaze. Observe for nystagmus in one or both eyes (see Chapter 15).	**Nsytagmus** may manifest as quick and jerky movements or slow pendulous movements, where the eye moves back and forth in the socket. Note whether the movement is fine or coarse and constant or intermittent. Check whether the plane of movement is either up and down or back and forth. Nystagmus is associated with disease of the vestibular system, cerebellum, or brainstem.
IV. Trochlear (motor)		
VI. Abducens (motor)		
V. Trigeminal (sensory and motor), includes corneal reflex	Evaluate sensory function by touch and motor function with movement. To evaluate the sensory component, ask the patient to close the eyes. Using a broken tongue blade, ask the patient to identify sharp or dull sensations when he or she feels them. Test once with dull end for patient reliability. Be sure to evaluate all three divisions of the nerve on the forehead (ophthalmic), cheek (maxillary), and chin (mandibular) areas on each side. Using a cotton wisp, assess light touch sensation over the same areas. See testing of light touch and pain sensations later in this chapter. Evaluate motor function by observing the face for muscle atrophy, lack of symmetry with movement, and fasciculations. Ask the patient to tightly clench the teeth; palpate over the jaw for masseter muscle and temporal muscles for symmetry.	Decreased or dulled sensation, weakness, or asymmetric movements are unexpected findings associated with CN V. A weak blink from facial weakness may result from paralysis of CN V or VII. A depressed or absent corneal response is common in contact lens wearers.

| Table 24-4 | Summary of Cranial Nerve Assessment (continued) |

Cranial Nerve (CN)	Technique	Unexpected Findings
	The corneal reflex may not be tested unless motor or sensory deficits in CNs VII and V function are noted. If worn, ask the patient to remove contact lenses. Instruct him or her to look up. Inform the patient that you will touch the eye with a cotton wisp. Bring the wisp in from the side and lightly touch the cornea, not the conjunctiva. Expect an immediate and rapid blink bilaterally as stimulus is applied.	
VII. Facial (sensory and motor)	Assess by evaluating taste. Place sweet, sour, salty, and bitter solutions on the anterior two thirds of the tongue on both sides; also test the posterior one third of the tongue for CN IX. The patient should properly identify the taste. Evaluate motor function by observing facial movements during conversation. Additionally, the patient completes the following facial movements and symmetry is observed. To evaluate the upper branch, ask the patient to raise the eyebrows, squeeze the eyes shut, wrinkle the forehead, and frown. For the lower branch, ask the patient to smile, show the teeth, purse the lips, and puff out the cheeks. Expected movements are strong and symmetric. Refer to Chapter 14 for additional information.	Fasciculations or tremors are unexpected. Asymmetric movements may be noted with the lower eyelid sagging, loss of the nasolabial fold, or mouth drooping. These findings are common following a stroke or with Bell's palsy (see Table 24-9).
VIII. Acoustic (sensory)	Evaluate hearing during the initial interaction. For screening, use the simple whisper test; Rinne and Weber tests, and an audiometer for more formalized testing. Refer to Chapter 16 for more information.	Inability to hear conversation is unexpected; note the presence of a hearing aid.
IX. Glossopharyngeal (sensory and motor)	Evaluate sensory function (taste) with CN VII (see above). Evaluate motor function with CN X upon swallowing.	Impaired taste or swallowing is common following a stroke.
X. Vagus (sensory and motor), includes gag reflex	Evaluate the motor component by placing a tongue blade on the middle of the tongue and asking the patient to say "ah"; observe the uvula and soft palate. The soft palate moves symmetrically upward and the uvula remains midline. Evaluate the sensory component by stimulating the gag reflex, which is tested only when a condition is suspected. Inform the patient that you will be touching the posterior pharyngeal wall on both sides, and it may cause gagging. Observe for upward movement of the palate and contraction of the pharyngeal muscles with the gag reflex.	Injury to the vagus or glossopharyngeal nerve causes the uvula to deviate from midline. Asymmetry of the soft palate or tonsillar pillars is also unexpected. An impaired gag reflex, coughing during oral feeding, and changes in voice after swallowing are all associated with aspiration. Closely evaluate patients with any of these symptoms (Terré & Mearin, 2006). When the patient says "ah" in the presence of a vagus nerve lesion, the uvula will deviate toward the unaffected side.

(table continues on page 722)

Table 24-4   **Summary of Cranial Nerve Assessment** (*continued*)

Cranial Nerve (CN)	Technique	Unexpected Findings
XI. Spinal accessory (motor)	Evaluate the sternomastoid and trapezius muscles for bulk, tone, strength, and symmetry. Ask the patient to press against your resistance on the opposite side of the chin. Also ask the patient to shrug the shoulders against resistance. The movements should be strong and symmetric.	Weakness or asymmetry in movement accompanies neurological and musculoskeletal conditions in the sternomastoid and trapezius muscles.
XII. Hypoglossal (motor)	Evaluate this function with CN X. First inspect the tongue as it lies on the floor of the mouth. Ask the patient to stick out the tongue and observe for symmetry and to press the tongue against the inside of the each cheek against resistance. Ask the patient to say, "light, tight, dynamite" and note that the letters l, t, d, and n are clear and distinct.	Fasciculations, asymmetry, atrophy, or deviation from midline may occur with general neuromuscular conditions or lesions of the hypoglossal nerve. In the presence of a cerebral lesion, the protruded tongue will deviate towards the weak side, indicating the lesion is on the opposite side.

Techniques and Expected Findings (continued)

CNs III, IV, and VI—Oculomotor, Trochlear, and Abducens. The integrity of these nerves is tested by observing extraocular movements (EOMs) and convergence of the eyes. If nystagmus is observed in one or both eyes, note the direction of the quick and/or slow oscillations (see Chapter 15 and Table 24-4 for technique).

Gaze is purposeful and conjugate without nystagmus, eyes converge within 5 cm of nose.

CN V—Trigeminal. To assess motor function of CN V palpate the masseter and temporal muscles as the patient clenches his or her teeth.

To assess sensory function of CN V, test pain and light touch sensation over the forehead, cheeks, and chin bilaterally (see Chapter 14 and Table 24-4 for technique).

Masseter and temporal muscle strength is 4+ bilaterally, sensations of pain and light touch over forehead, cheeks, and chin intact bilaterally.

CN VII—Facial. The integrity of this motor nerve is assessed by observing symmetry of facial expressions at rest and with movement. Further separate testing of the upper and lower nerve tracts follows. In addition, the corneal reflex may be tested (see Chapter 14 and Table 24-4 for technique).

Facial movements symmetrical at rest and with expression. Corneal reflex intact bilaterally.

Rationale/Unexpected Findings (continued)

Nystagmus is a jerking movement of the eye that can be quick and fluttering or slow and rolling, similar to a tremor. Causes include *medications* (eg, antiseizure medications), *cerebellar disease, weakness in the extraocular muscles,* and *damage to CN III* (see also Chapter 15).

If findings for pain and light touch are unexpected, assess temperature sensation as well. Nerve fibres for pain and temperature sensation run in the same track.

During conversation, observe for ptosis or facial palsy.

The corneal reflex tests the ophthalmic branch of CN V (sensory) and the upper tract of CN VII (motor). If LOC is impaired, assessment of corneal reflexes is important as, in the absence of reflexes, protection of the cornea from injury is needed.

CN VIII—Acoustic. Assess the integrity of the acoustic nerve by testing auditory acuity and presence of equal lateralization and air and bone conduction (see Chapter 16 and Table 24-4 for technique).

Hearing intact to whisper test bilaterally, lateralization equal, AC > BC bilaterally (air conduction > bone conduction).

CNs IX and X—Glossopharyngeal and Vagus. Assess the motor function of these nerves by asking the patient to say "ah" as movement of the soft palate and uvula are observed and test the gag reflex both sides. In addition, note the quality of the patient's voice and ease of swallowing (see Chapter 17 and Table 24-4 for technique).

Vocalization articulate, soft palate rises symmetrically, uvula remains midline, gag reflex and swallowing intact.

Dysphagia is difficulty swallowing.

CN XI—Spinal Accessory. Assess the integrity of this CN testing the strength of the trapezii and sternomastoid muscles (see Chapter 14 and Table 24-4 for technique).

Shoulder shrug strong 5/5 bilaterally.

CN XII—Hypoglossal. Inspect the tongue as it lies on the floor of the mouth, then assess motor function by observing symmetrical movement and strength of the tongue (see Chapter 14 and Table 24-4 for technique).

Tongue is without fasciculations, strength strong 5/5 and movement equal bilaterally.

Fasciculations are tiny irregular muscle movements.

Motor Function

Inspection and Palpation. Examination of the motor system focuses on assessment of body position; symmetry of muscle bulk, tone, and strength; coordination; and involuntary movements.

Distinct patterns of neuromotor deficits are found with CNS motor pathway (**upper motor neuron [UMN]) lesions** compared with peripheral motor nerve pathway (**lower motor neuron [LMN] lesions** (see Table 24-10 at the end of this chapter for a description of UMN and LMN deficits).

Muscle Bulk and Tone. Ensure adequate exposure of the extremity. Test muscle tone prior to muscle strength.

Inspect muscle bulk by observing and palpating muscle groups to check for any wasting (atrophy). Note any involuntary movements (eg, fasciculations). To assess tone, determine degree of resistance of muscle groups to passive stretch. Instruct the patient to relax each limb in turn. Move the limb through a modified range of motion assessing resistance. The relaxed muscle shows some muscular tension. Commonly tested muscle groups include deltoids, biceps, and triceps for the arms, hamstrings, and quadriceps for the legs. *Muscle bulk without atrophy bilaterally, slight residual tension felt during passive stretch bilaterally.*

If there is absolutely no resistance to movement, the muscles are said to be **flaccid** or **atonic.** If the tone seems to be only decreased or "flabby," note the finding as **hypotonia.** Increased resistance of the muscles to passive stretch is called **hypertonia. Spasticity** can occur with UMN disorders. It is characterized by increased resistance to rapid passive stretch, especially in flexor muscle groups in the upper extremities, resulting from hyperexcitability of the stretch reflex. In certain conditions, this resistance is strongest on initiation of the movement and "gives way" as the examiner slowly continues the movement. This characteristic has prompted the use of the term **clasp-knife spasticity** and describes the type of hypertonicity noted in patients following a chronic or late-stage stroke.

Rigidity is characterized by a steady, persistent resistance to passive stretch in both flexor and extensor muscle groups. This phenomenon has led to the descriptive phrases **"lead-pipe" rigidity** or "plastic" rigidity. **Cogwheel rigidity** is manifested by a ratchet-like jerking noted in the extremity on passive movement. Both types of rigidity are seen in Parkinson's disease.

Strength of muscle group in arms and legs is 4 to 5+.

Motor strength of 0 to 3+ indicates weakness.

(text continues on page 724)

Test for Pronator Drift. Ask the patient to close the eyes and outstretch the arms straight ahead with palms upward (supinated) for 20 seconds (Fig. 24-12). *The patient extends the hands for 20 seconds without drifting.*

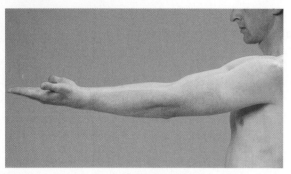

Figure 24-12 Assessing for pronator drift.

Gait, Posture, and Balance. If possible, ask the patient to walk down a corridor, turn and walk towards the examiner. Points to observe include smoothness of gait, position of feet (narrow versus wide base), height and length of step, and symmetry of arm and leg movement and position of the head on the turn. Also, ask the patient to walk on heels and toes, then tandem-walk (ie, heel-to-toe in a straight line) (Fig. 24-13). Instruct the patient to stand on each foot in turn and perform a shallow knee bend.

The patient walks smoothly without swaying.

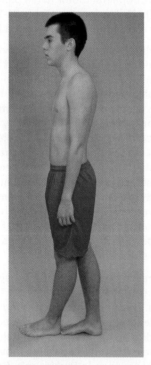

Figure 24-13 Assessing the tandem walk to evaluate gait and posture.

Pronation of the hand and downward drift of the arm on one side indicate weakness and possibly a lesion in the contralateral corticospinal tract.

Unexpected gaits include spastic hemiparesis, scissors, parkinsonian, cerebellar ataxia, sensory ataxia, waddling, dystonia, and athetoid movements (see Table 24-11 at the end of this chapter).

⚠ *SAFETY ALERT 24-1*
Be prepared to support the patient if falling is possible. This test also assesses strength of the quadriceps muscle.

In the **Romberg test**, ask the patient to stand with feet together and arms at sides (Fig. 24-14) for 20 seconds. Note any swaying (stand close enough to prevent falling). Ask the patient to close the eyes during the Romberg for additional testing. Slight swaying may be expected, because visual cues help humans maintain balance.

Maintains posture with eyes open and closed.

Moderate swaying with eyes open and closed indicates *vestibulocerebellar dysfunction*. Pronounced increase in swaying (sometimes with falling) with the eyes closed usually indicates a lesion in the posterior column of the spinal cord with loss of position sense.

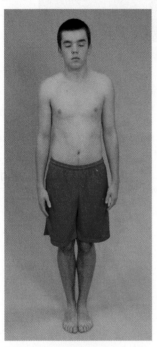

Figure 24-14 Positioning for the Romberg test.

Coordination (Cerebellar Function)

Coordination of muscle movements requires interaction among the following systems: motor, cerebellar, vestibular, and sensory.

Inspection.

Point-to-Point Movements. (Test each extremity separately.)

Assessment of finger-to-nose coordination tests upper extremity cerebellar function. Ask the patient to touch the tip of the examiner's finger with the tip of his or her forefinger (test each hand separately) and then to touch his or her own nose and to repeat this manoeuvre several times while the examiner's finger is moved each time (Fig. 24-15). With eyes closed, ask the patient to repeat this action. Do not move your finger. When the patient's eyes are closed, position sense is also tested.

Assess lower extremities coordination by the shin-to-heel test. With the patient supine, ask him or her to take the heel of one foot and move it steadily along the shin from knee to great toe of other leg. Repeat with the other leg and also with eyes closed.

Point-to-point testing of arms and legs performed smoothly and accurately bilaterally.

Testing each extremity separately ensures movement of one extremity is not influenced by the other.

Ataxia is unsteady, wavering movement with inability to touch the target. During rapid alternating movements, lack of coordination is **adiadochokinesia**. Deficits in any of these manoeuvres indicate an **ipsilateral cerebellar lesion**. Note any tremor. Other signs of cerebellar dysfunction can include hypotonia, nystagmus, and dysarthric speech. Dysarthric speech noted with cerebellar lesions may exhibit a peculiar quality called scanning speech, which is characterized by alternating patterns of slowness and explosiveness as each syllable is spoken. Refer to Table 24-11 at the end of the chapter.

(text continues on page 726)

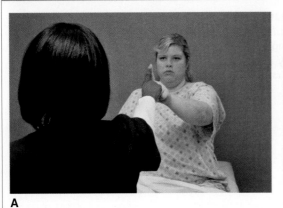 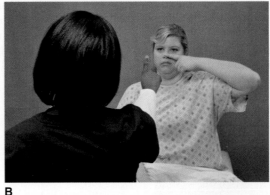

A   **B**

Figure 24-15 Assessing cerebellar function. **A.** The patient touches the examiner's finger with her forefinger. **B.** The patient touches her own nose.

Rapid Alternating Movements. (Test each extremity separately.) To assess upper extremities, instruct the patient with eyes open to slap his or her thigh with first the palm of the hand and then the back as fast as possible (Fig. 24-16). To assess lower extremities instruct the supine or sitting patient, with eyes open, to tap each foot in turn against the examiners hand as rapidly as possible.

Rapid alternating movement of hands performed smoothly and rapidly bilaterally.

It is not uncommon for people to perform better with their dominant hand.

Expect the patient to perform rapid alternating movements of the feet with less speed and smoothness than with the hands.

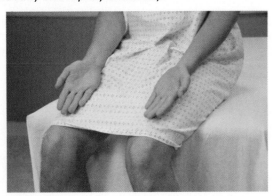

Figure 24-16 Assessing rapid alternating movements.

Sensory Function

Palpation. When assessing sensation, it is important that the patient's eyes be closed to avoid visual cues from influencing responses. Have the patient identify where or when he or she feels the sensation, but avoid cueing the patient by asking, "Do you feel this?" Allow 2 seconds between each stimulus to avoid summation, in which the patient perceives frequent, small stimulations as one long stimulation. Vary the pace of stimuli application, that is, when testing light touch. Begin with light stimulation and proceed with increased pressure until the patient reports a sensation. Observe for areas of sensory decrease or loss. Compare findings between sides. Screening is performed by testing the most distal areas and proceeding proximally if deficits are noted. Testing involves the arms, hands, legs, trunk, and face (Anderson & Bickley, 2010). Complete testing of all nerves is rare. Clinically, patterns of sensory loss are assessed depending on the condition or area of injury.

Interpret sensory deficits considering that this testing includes the peripheral nerves, sensory tracts, and cortical perception. Consider the patient's clinical situation and whether the deficit is generalized or specific, such as trauma to a nerve. *Spinal cord injury* generally follows the pattern of the dermatome, while sensory loss in *diabetic neuropathy* is distal (See also Table 24-12 at the end of this chapter).

Varying the pace ensures the patient is not just responding to a repetitive rhythm.

Light Touch. Pull the end of a cotton swab so that it is wispy. Ask the patient to close the eyes, and apply light touch to the skin with the swab (Fig. 24-17). Comparing sides, test most dermatomes over upper and lower extremities. (Focus on dermatomes highlighted in Fig. 24-9.) Ask the patient to state when he or she feels the sensation. *Light touch intact over lower extremities.*

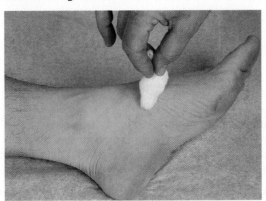

Figure 24-17 Applying a cotton swab to assess light touch sensation.

Superficial Pain Sensation. Break a tongue blade or cotton applicator so that the end is sharp. Demonstrate sharp versus dull sensation. Ask the patient to close the eyes; lightly touch the skin with the sharp end. Stimulate similar dermatomes as for light touch. Occasionally substitute the dull end of the stimulus to check the patient's reliability. Ask the patient to state when he or she feels the sharp or dull sensation. *Pain sensation intact over lower extremities.*

Temperature Sensation. Test temperature sense only if pain sensations are not intact.

Use one prong of a tuning fork that has been warmed with the hands or test tubes containing warm and cold water. Ask the patient to close the eyes. Touch the skin with warm or cold objects. Ask the patient to identify when he or she feel the warm or cold stimulus. Again, cover most dermatomes.

Temperature sensation is intact over upper extremities.

Motion and Position Sense. Demonstrate up and down positions in toes and fingers. Ask the patient to close the eyes. Grasp either side of one of the patient's fingers or toes and move it up or down, avoiding contact with adjacent digits. If the patient cannot identify the direction of the movement, test the next most proximal joints (eg, wrist if finger movement is not sensed). Test both sides. *Motion and position sense of the upper extremities is intact.*

Hyperesthesia refers to increased touch sensation. **Anesthesia** refers to absent touch sensation. Reduced touch sensation is **hypoesthesia**.

Hyperalgesia refers to increased pain sensation. **Analgesia** refers to absent pain sensation. Reduced pain sensation is **hypalgesia**.

Occasional substitution of the sharp stimulus with the dull stimulus ensures the patient feels the pain sensation and not touch.

⚠ *SAFETY ALERT 24-2*
Patients with neuropathy need to be taught to visually inspect their feet, because they may have injuries that go unnoticed.

Altered temperature sensation is common in *neuropathies*.

As the spinothalamic tract (Fig. 24-5) carries sensory nerve tracts for pain and temperature, if pain sensations are intact, temperature sensations will also be intact.

⚠ *SAFETY ALERT 24-3*
Patients with neuropathy need to learn to use a body part with good sensation to determine the temperature of hot surfaces. Getting into a too-hot bath can cause inadvertent burns to the feet. Similarly, the patient with neuropathy can be easily burned with too hot of a heating pad.

(text continues on page 728)

Discriminative Sensations. The following tests require intact touch and position sense and intact sensory cortex as the sensations require analysis and interpretation.

Point Localization. Ask the patient to close the eyes. Using a finger, gently touch the patient on the hands, lower arms, abdomen, lower legs, and feet. Ask the patient to identify where the sensation is felt, but avoid cueing the patient by asking, "Do you feel this?" Observe areas of sensory loss. Compare side to side. *Point localization is intact.*

Vibration Sensation. Strike a low-pitched tuning fork (128 Hz) on the side or heel of the hand to produce vibrations. Ask the patient to close the eyes. Holding the fork at the base, place it firmly over bony prominences, beginning at the most distal location. The toes, ankle, shin, anterior superior iliac spine, finger joints, wrist, elbow, shoulder, and sternum can all be tested (Fig. 24-18). If the sensation is felt at the most distal point, no further testing is necessary. Ask the patient to state what sensation is felt, where, and when it disappears. To stop the sensation, dampen the tuning fork by pressing on the tongs. *Vibration sense is intact in the great toe bilaterally.*

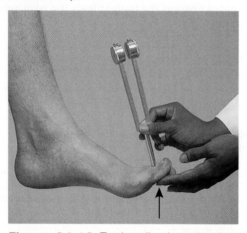

Figure 24-18 Testing vibration sensation.

Stereognosis. This test evaluates cortical sensory function. Ask the patient to close the eyes and identify a familiar object (eg, coin and key) placed in each palm in turn (*stereognosis;* Fig. 24-19). The patient must manipulate the object only with hand in which it was placed.

Stereognosis intact bilaterally.

Observe the pattern of sensory loss by mapping it out during testing. "Stocking-glove" distribution suggests peripheral nerves; dermatomal distribution suggests isolated nerves or nerve roots; reduced sensation below a certain level is associated with spinal cord injury. A crossed face-body pattern suggests the brainstem, and hemisensory loss suggests a stroke (Hickey, 2002).

Peripheral neuropathy is more severe distally and improves centrally. It is a common consequence of *peripheral vascular disease* and *diabetic neuropathy.* Often vibration sense is the first lost.

With damage to a specific dermatome, the line of sensory loss is usually marked and specific.

Inability to identify objects correctly **(astereognosis)** may result from damage to the sensory cortex caused by *stroke.*

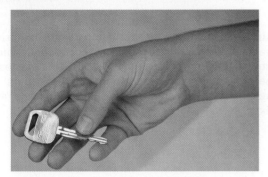

Figure 24-19 Testing stereognosis.

Graphesthesia. This test also evaluates cortical sensory function. Ask the patient to close the eyes. Use a blunt object to trace a number on each of the patient's palms in turn. Change the number. Ask the patient to identify which number has been traced *(graphesthesia)* (Fig. 24-20). *Graphesthesia intact bilaterally.*

Cortical sensory function may be compromised following a *stroke*.

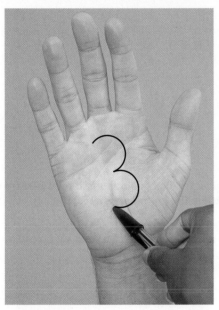

Figure 24-20 Assessing graphesthesia.

Two-Point Discrimination. Ask the patient to close the eyes. Hold the blunt end of two cotton swabs approximately 2-in. apart and move them together until the patient feels them as one point (the ends of an opened paperclip may also be used). The fingertips are most sensitive, with a minimal distance of 3 to 8 mm, while the upper arms and thighs are least sensitive, with a minimal distance of 75 mm. *Generally there is more discrimination distally than centrally.*

Cortical sensory function may be lost with a stroke.

Extinction. Ask the patient to close the eyes. At the same time, touch the same (corresponding) body area on both sides. Ask the patient to state where he or she perceives the touch. *Sensations are felt on both sides.*

Cortical sensory function may be lost with a *stroke*. Perception of the stimulus on the opposite side of the damaged cortex may be lost or reduced.

(text continues on page 730)

Reflex Testing

Percussion. Reflex testing includes DTRs, superficial (cutaneous) reflexes, and other pathological reflexes that may or may not be tested along with the others.

DTRs. DTRs tested include biceps, triceps, brachioradialis, patellar, and Achilles (see Table 24-5 for technique). Tested bilaterally, these reflexes are observed for symmetry and for briskness of reflex movement. DTRs are graded on a scale of 0 to 4, with 0 representing absent reflexes and 4 corresponding to significantly hyperactive responses.

- 4+—Very brisk, hyperactive with clonus
- 3+— Brisker than average
- 2+—Average, expected
- 1+—Diminished, sluggish
- 0—No response, absent

The reflex response depends on the force of the stimulus, accurate location of the striking area over the tendon, and patient's relaxation level. Refer to Chapter 4 for use of the reflex hammer and technique. To ensure accurate location, have the patient flex the muscle to find the tendon and then relax it for testing. Pathologic reflexes are primitive responses and indicate loss of cortical inhibition (see Table 24-13 at the end of this chapter).

Patellar and Achilles DTRs are 2+ bilaterally.

Superficial Reflexes. Superficial reflexes are elicited by stimulation of the skin. Record the response to stimulation as present, absent, or equivocal (difficult to determine).

Plantar Response. Test by stroking the sole of the foot with a blunt instrument such as the edge of a tongue blade or the handle of a reflex hammer. Apply the stimulus firmly but gently to the lateral aspect, beginning at the heel and stopping short of the base of the toes. The toes flex (a flexor–plantar response).

Clonus is characterized by alternating flexion/extension movements (jerking) in response to a continuous muscle stretch. In unconscious patients, DTRs may be tested in the usual manner; however, depth of coma alters the response. Deep coma is associated with loss of all reflexes, as well as loss of muscle stretch and tone.

Pathological reflexes include the toe-up **plantar reflex** and the **triple flexion response** (Fig. 24-21).

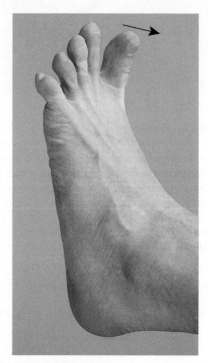

Figure 24-21 Babinski sign.

Table 24-5 **Deep Tendon Reflexes**

Deep Tendon reflex: Level Tested	Technique
Biceps: C5 and C6 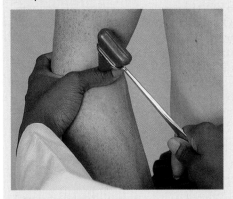	Ask the patient to partially flex the elbow and place the palm down. To assist with relaxation, the patient may rest the arm against the nurse's. Place one finger or thumb on the biceps tendon. Strike the finger or thumb with the reflex hammer briskly so that the impact is delivered through the digit to the biceps tendon. Observe for flexion at the elbow and contraction of the biceps muscle. If the patient's reflexes are symmetrically diminished or absent, ask the patient to clench the teeth or squeeze one hand tight with the opposite hand as the tendon is struck (reinforcement). This action may enhance the resulting reflex. In recording, note that reinforcement was used.
Triceps: C6 and C7 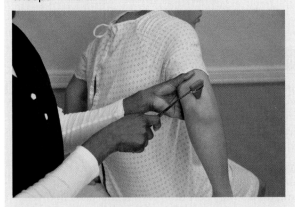	Have the patient flex the arm at the elbow and the palm toward the body if sitting or supine. If the patient is seated, it may be easiest for the nurse to hold the patient's arm in a relaxed dangling position. Palpate the triceps muscle and strike it directly just above the elbow. Observe for extension of the elbow and contraction of the triceps muscle.
Brachioradialis: C5 and C6 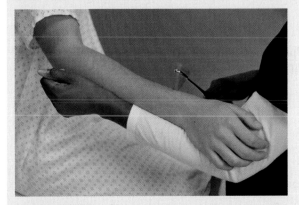	Have the patient flex the arm (up to 45°) and rest the forearm on the nurse's arm with the hand slightly pronated. Palpate the brachioradial tendon approximately 2.5–5.0 cm. above the wrist and strike it directly with the reflex hammer. Observe for supination of the forearm, flexion of the elbow, and contraction of the muscle.
Patellar: L2–L4 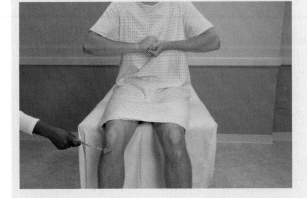	If supine, have the patient flex the knee at 90° and support the upper leg with the hand. If sitting, allow the lower leg to dangle over the edge of the examining table. Palpate the patellar tendon directly below the patella and then strike it directly. Observe for extension of the lower leg and contraction of the quadriceps muscle. If the patient's reflexes are symmetrically diminished or absent, ask the patient to lock the fingers in front of the chest and pull one hand against the other (reinforcement).

(table continues on page 732)

Table 24-5　Deep Tendon Reflexes (*continued*)

Deep Tendon reflex: Level Tested	Technique
Achilles: S1 and S2 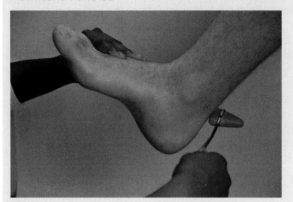	With the patient sitting and legs dangling, support the patient's foot. (The patient may also kneel on a stool with the feet dangling.) Palpate the Achilles tendon; strike the tendon directly near the ankle maleolus. Observe for plantar flexion of the foot and contraction of the gastrocnemius muscle.

Techniques and Expected Findings (continued)	Rationale/Unexpected Findings (continued)
	With unexpected plantar reflexes, the great toe extends upward and the other toes fan out (an extensor–plantar response or Babinski sign). Triple flexion describes reflex withdrawal of the lower extremity to plantar stimulus through flexion of ankle, knee, and hip.
Palpation.	Depression or absence of this reflex may result from a *central lesion, obesity,* or lax skeletal muscles (eg, post-partum). It also may be noted with *spinal cord injury.*
Upper Abdominal. This test identifies the integrity of T8 to T10. Stroke the upper quadrants of the abdomen with a tongue blade or reflex hammer diagonally toward the umbilicus. *The umbilicus moves toward each area of stimulation symmetrically.*	
Lower Abdominal. This test assesses the integrity of T10 to T12. Stroke the upper quadrants of the abdomen with a tongue blade or reflex hammer diagonally toward the umbilicus. *The umbilicus moves toward each area of stimulation symmetrically.*	Unexpected findings are the same as for the upper abdominal region.
Cremasteric (male). This test helps identify the integrity of L1 to L2 in males. Stroke the inner thigh. *The testicle and scrotum rise on the stroked side.*	Response is diminished or absent.
Bulbocavernous (male). This test helps identify the integrity of S3 to S4 in male patients. Apply direct pressure over the bulbocavernous muscle behind the scrotum. *The muscle should contract and elevate the scrotum.*	Response is diminished or absent.
Perianal. This test helps identify the integrity of S3 to S5. Scratch the tissue at the side of the anus with a blunt instrument. *The anus should pucker.* **Note: The anal reflex also can be tested when administering rectal medications.**	Response is diminished or absent.

Area of Assessment	Expected Findings	Unexpected Findings
Cranial nerves		
Olfactory, CN I	Sensation of smell intact bilaterally	Detects pungent odour on right side, not on left side
Optic, oculomotor, trochlear, abducens, CNS II, III, IV, & VI	See Chapter 17	See Chapter 17
Trigeminal, CN V	Sensations of pain and light touch intact over ophthalmic, maxillary, and mandibular branches bilaterally	Sensations of pain and light touch intact over ophthalmic branch bilaterally and maxillary and mandibular branches on right side, absent on left side
Sensory	Brisk bilateral blink	Sluggish bilateral blink (wears contact lenses)
Motor	Temporal and masseter muscle strength 5/5 on palpation bilaterally	Temporal and masseter muscle strength 3/5 on left, 5/5 on right
Facial nerve, CN VII	Raises both eyebrows, frowns, shows teeth, smiles and puffs out cheeks symmetrically. Strongly resists eyelid opening bilaterally 5/5	Unable ro raise eyebrow, frown, resist eye opening, or show teeth, smile, puff out cheek on right side. Intact on left side.
Acoustic nerve, CN VIII	See Chapter 16	See Chapter 16
Glossopharyngeal and vagus, CNs IX and X	Gag reflex intact bilaterally	Gag reflex depressed on right side, absent on left
Spinal accessory, CN XI	Shoulder shrug and sternomastoid muscle strength 5/5 bilaterally	Shoulder shrug on right = 3/5, on left side = 5/5
Hypoglossal, CN XII	Protrudes tongue midline, tongue movements to both sides equally strong. Words articulated clearly	Tongue deviates to right side when protruded. Words often slurred
Upper extremities		
Muscle tone	Slight tension felt during passive stretch bilaterally	Muscle strength 2/5 in left wrist, elbow, and shoulder; 5/5 on right side
Muscle strength	Muscle strength 5/5 in hands, wrists, elbows, and shoulders bilaterally	Muscle strength 2/5 in left wrist, elbow, and shoulder; 5/5 on right side
Coordination	Bilaterally performs rapid alternating movements smoothly. Point-to-point testing smooth and accurate with eyes open and closed bilaterally	Rapid alternating movements with right hand slow, awkward; rapid and smooth on left side. Point-to-point testing on right side slow but accurate, eyes open; inaccurate eyes closed
Sensation	Sensation of pain and light touch intact bilaterally over dermatomes C4–T1. Vibration and position sense intact bilaterally at fingers. Extinction, stereognosis, and graphesthesis intact bilaterally	Pain and light touch absent over C5–C8 to 1 cm above the wrist bilaterally. Intact proximally. Vibration sense absent in finger joints and wrist, intact at elbows bilaterally. Stereognosis and graphethesia absent on right, intact on left. Extinction absent on right at forearms.
Reflexes	Biceps 2+, triceps and brachioradialis reflexes 1+ bilaterally. Abdominal reflexes brisk bilaterally	Bicep, tricep, and brachioradialis reflexes 3+ on right, 1+ on left. Abdominal reflexes sluggish bilaterally.

(table continues on page 734)

Area of Assessment	Expected Findings	Unexpected Findings
Lower extremities		
Muscle tone	Slight muscle tension noted during passive stretch bilaterally	Left leg becomes spastic when passive movement attempted; slight muscle tension on right
Muscle strength	Muscle strength 5/5 over feet, ankles, knees, and hips bilaterally	Muscle strength 2/5 over entire left leg (gravity eliminated); 5/5 on right side
Coordination	Rapid alternating movements at toes and moderately smooth bilaterally. Point-to-point testing smooth, accurate with eyes open, eyes closed bilaterally	Rapid alternating movements on right side slow and erratic, moderately smooth on left. Point-to-point slow and awkward on right side with eyes open, inaccurate with eyes closed, smooth and accurate on left
Sensation	Pain and light touch intact over dermatomes L2 to S1 bilaterally Vibration sense at great toes and position sense at toes intact bilaterally	Pain and light touch absent over dermatomes L4-S1 to 2 cm superior to malleoli, intact proximally bilaterally. Vibration sense absent at toes and ankle on right leg, intact on left side. Position sense absent on right, intact on left
Reflexes	Patellar and ankle reflexes 2+ without reinforcement bilaterally. Plantar reflex down-going bilaterally.	Patellar reflex 4+ on right, ankle reflex triggers clonus on right. Plantar reflex- dorsiflexion of right great toe. Patellar reflex in left leg 2+, plantar reflex down-going
Posture, gait, balance	Posture upright, gait coordinated with arm swing opposite to leg, heel strike with push-off at toe, head leads when turning	Gait assisted with cane held in right hand, drags left toe slightly, left arm in sling
Cerebellar/muscle strength	Romberg: steady posture with eyes open, slight sway with eyes closed. Tandem walking smooth and coordinated; coordinated walking on heels and toes, strength and coordinated movement with shallow knee bend, and hop on one foot bilaterally	Romberg: steady stance with eyes open, moderate sway with eyes closed. Lost balance when tandem walking attempted. Unable to walk on toes or heels. Required assistance with slight knee bend, unable to hop on one foot bilaterally

Adapted from Anderson, M. C., & Bickley, L. S. (2010). The nervous system. In T. C. Stephen, D. L. Skillen, R. A. Day, & L. S. Bickley (Eds.). *Canadian Bates' guide to health assessment for nurses* (1st ed., pp. 735–736). Philadelphia, PA: Wolters Kluwer Health/Lippincott Williams & Wilkins.

🔺 Lifespan Considerations

Newborns, Infants, and Children

The neurological system develops dramatically during the first 2 to 3 years as children lose their primitive reflexes and gain control of bowel, bladder, locomotion, and speech (Fig. 24-22). At birth, newborns have protective reflexes including sucking and swallowing. Depressed or hyperactive reflexes may indicate a disorder of the CNS. Refer to Chapter 28 for more information and a complete description of neonatal reflexes. Spontaneous motor activity is noticeable, especially during crying. Transient tremors are expected and should disappear by 1 month of age. Muscle tone and strength are usually related. Depressed LOC may result from maternal sedation; this should be differentiated from hypoglycemia or CNS disorders.

Variations in state of consciousness for infants are called *sleep–wake states*. They range from deep sleep to extreme irritability. Infants use purposeful behaviour to maintain the optimal arousal state by withdrawing, fussing, and crying. A weak or high-pitched cry may indicate unexpected CNS findings. Refer to Chapter 28 for additional unexpected findings.

Persistent tremors, increased tonicity or spasticity, or twitching of the facial muscles may indicate seizures and should be evaluated. Tremors of hypoglycemia or CNS disorders should also be evaluated. Birth trauma may cause nerve damage that results in asymmetry or paralysis. CN testing is modified for newborns and infants (refer to Chapter 28).

Cognitive abilities and speech articulation develop during preschool and early childhood. Fine and coarse motor skills follow developmental milestones. Expected motor function by 2 to

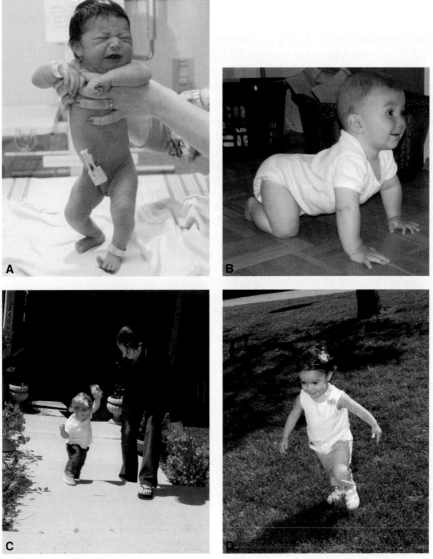

Figure 24-22 As children grow, their neurological system develops to enable more complex behaviours and movements. **A.** The newborn must be held by someone at all times. **B.** The 8-month-old child is capable of crawling. **C.** After the first birthday, the child begins to walk, at first with assistance and then independently. **D.** By 2 years of age, the child achieves independent ambulation.

3 years includes grasping, sitting, crawling, standing, and walking. Further investigation is warranted with reduced amount of rotation during crawling, delayed balance, and delayed onset and poor quality of early walking behaviour (Fallang & Hadders-Algra, 2005) (see Chapter 28 for more information).

Adolescence is also a period of cognitive growth and completion of myelinization of the nerve fibres. From preschool through adolescence, learning disabilities, hyperactivity, and tic disorders may develop (see Chapters 28 and 29). Motor delay and disorders of gait may also occur.

Older Adults

Expected changes in neurological function accompany aging. Examples include lost nerve cell mass, atrophy in the CNS, decreased brain weight, and fewer nerve cells and dendrites. Such changes lead to slower thought, memory, and thinking; plasticity enables the lengthening and production of dendrites to accommodate for this loss. Demyelinization of nerve fibres leads to delayed impulse transmission. An increased latency period (period before next stimulation) causes slowed reflexes, which may produce mobility and safety issues. Fewer cells are in the spinal cord, although this does not appear to reduce function. Peripheral nerve conduction slows. Newer research suggests that cardiovascular fitness spares the loss of brain volume in older adults (Colcombe, Erickson, et al., 2006). Assessment techniques, interpretation of findings, and linked interventions may require adjustments as appropriate (see Chapter 30 for more information).

The examples of documentation for Mr. Matthew Nderitu, the 56-year-old man admitted with a stroke, reflect unexpected findings. Review the following important findings revealed during each step of objective data collection for this patient. Begin to think about how the data cluster together and what additional data might be needed to anticipate appropriate nursing interventions.

Inspection: A 56-year-old Nigerian-Canadian man with a history of hypertension, smoking, and mild baseline dementia. Lives alone, compromised hygiene, and multiple layers of mismatched clothes. Does not remember the last time he took "high pressure pills." Is alert, appears somewhat fearful and agitated, asking for cigarettes, oriented to name only. Speech is comprehensible but slurred. Patient can follow one-step commands only—is easily distractible. Impaired short-term memory—remembers zero of three objects after 1 minute. Pupils equal, round, briskly reactive to light, and accommodate for near reaction. Appears to have left visual field loss, extraocular movements (EOMs) intact. Left lower facial weakness, tongue deviation to left.

Palpation: Muscle bulk symmetrical, tone slightly increased on left arm/leg. Strength 5/5 right arm/leg, 2/5 left arm, 3/5 left leg, left Babinski +. Right arm/leg coordination grossly intact, left arm/leg not tested because of weakness, gait not tested (on bedrest). Diminished attention to objects/people on left side of bed, difficult to assess sensation because of varying patient attention. Remains hypertensive—see flow sheet for vital signs.

Neurological Assessment in Selected Situations

Screening Examination of a Healthy Patient

Experienced nurses may complete a thorough screening neurological assessment of a healthy patient in 10 to 15 minutes or less. Issues related to perfusion and autonomic dysfunction are evident in several neurological conditions. Following a history and general observations, the nurse notes vital signs, including right and left radial pulses; right and left brachial BPs; and lying and standing BP (immediate, and after 3 minutes) (see Box 24-3 for the components of a screening examination in a healthy patient).

Serial Neurological Assessment and Documentation

Although some neurological changes are evident instantaneously, most progress over time. Consistent, accurate serial assessment is critical for timely identification and intervention. When orders for "neuro checks" are written, these usually comprise signs that, if deterioration were to occur, would signify a critical or potentially life-threatening event. These signs typically include the patient's LOC (GCS score), pupillary size, shape, equality, light responses, and accommodation for near reaction, motor ability, and, when appropriate, additional elements linked to location of pathology or existing deficits (eg, other selected CNs or sensory function). When intracranial pathology is not present (eg, postoperative laminectomy), it is sufficient to observe for motor and sensory changes only and not use the GCS.

The patient's specific risk for acute neurological deterioration dictates the frequency of assessment. Even mild neurological decline should trigger increased frequency of assessment to observe for development of a pattern of deficits that may indicate urgent or emergent intervention.

Communication of findings is critical. Documentation of the neurological examination may be handwritten or entered electronically. Nurses typically use a flow sheet to track assessment changes over time, supported by a narrative note to detail assessments not addressed by the limitations of a flow sheet. A written note should be succinct but clearly describe relevant findings. Repetition of information recorded on a flow sheet is unnecessary.

Assessment of Meningeal Signs

A stiff neck (nuchal rigidity) is associated with *meningitis* and *intracranial hemorrhage* from irritation of the meninges. Ask the patient to relax and lie down. With the patient supine, slide your hand under and raise the patient's head gently, flexing the neck. Pain and resistance to movement are considered to be nuchal rigidity. If neck stiffness is present, Brudzinski's

---

BOX 24-3 NEUROLOGICAL SCREENING
EXAMINATION IN A HEALTHY PATIENT

- Vital signs (temperature, pulse, respiration, blood pressure (BP), pulse oximetry)
- Level of consciousness (LOC)
- Communication/speech
- Orientation
- Motor (strength, pronator drift, balance, and coordination)
- Sensory (gross assessment of limbs and face)
- Pupillary reaction

Adapted from National Clearinghouse Guidelines. (2007). *Stroke assessment across the continuum of care*. Retrieved from http://www.guideline.gov/summary/summary.aspx?doc_id=7426

sign may be present. The sign is positive if there is resistance or pain in the neck and flexion in the hips or knees. Evaluate for Kernig's sign by flexing the leg at the hip. With the patient supine, raise the leg straight up (or flex the thigh on the abdomen) and extend the knee. The sign is present if there is resistance to straightening or pain radiating down the posterior leg.

Assessing the Unconscious Patient

Assessment of unconscious patients deserves special consideration for the following reasons:

- Patients who present with sudden unconsciousness require urgent evaluation to determine the cause of the impairment and, when appropriate, to implement prompt intervention.
- Unconscious patients are at risk for life-threatening complications secondary to loss of protective reflexes; these deficits may be noted during examination.
- They require special assessment techniques because they cannot participate in the examination.

The nurse should quickly review the patient's history for possible causes of impaired consciousness. Review of recent medications and laboratory values may reveal potential causes. The nurse rapidly evaluates the patient's general cardiovascular and respiratory status so that any existing compromise can be treated promptly. The patient requires thorough inspection for any visible clues, such as trauma, that might be the cause of the loss of consciousness. Physical examination includes the following:

- LOC assessment by using the GCS
- Pupillary assessment
- Brainstem assessment—gaze, facial symmetry, corneal reflex, gag reflex, cough, oculocephalic reflex (doll's eye manoeuvre, Fig. 24-23) if cervical spine injury has been ruled out
- Motor function in addition to motor component of GCS (although formal strength testing cannot be done with an unresponsive patient, observe for hemiparesis/hemiplegia by comparing right and left extremity response to pain or noting frequency and location of any spontaneous movement)
- Close observation for patterns of dysfunction associated with progressing herniation

If LOC assessment progresses to application of painful stimulus (see under eye opening), the nurse must employ a method to elicit the desired response without causing harm. Noxious stimulus can be categorized as peripheral or central. Peripheral stimulation is performed first by using nail-bed pressure. Central stimulus is more reliable in evaluating patients with impaired LOC. Application of a "sternal rub" (knuckles applied to the skin over the sternum) works but can easily bruise the skin if use is prolonged.

The oculocephalic reflex (doll's eyes) assesses brainstem function in comatose patients. Ensure that the spinal cord is intact before performing this test. Hold the patient's eyes

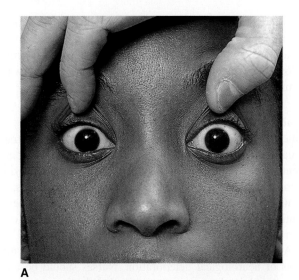

A

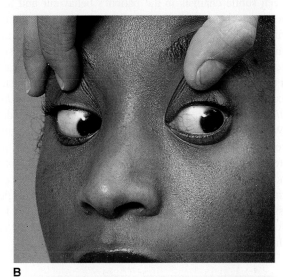

B

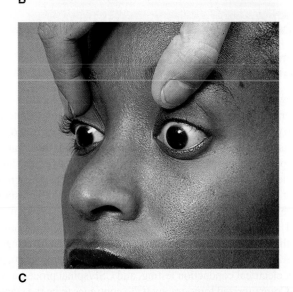

C

Figure 24-23 The oculocephalix reflex involves the doll's eye manoeuvre. **A.** The nurse holds the patient's upper eyelids open. The nurse then quickly turns the patient's head. **B.** If the eyes can move in the opposite direction of the head, this indicates that the brainstem is intact. **C.** In a comatose patient, the ability to move both eyes to one side is lost.

open and turn the head first to one side quickly and then to the other. In the patient with an intact brainstem, the eyes move toward the opposite side. If brainstem or midbrain function is lost, the eyes move with the head, still pointing forward (similar to a doll with the eyes painted on).

Brain Herniation Syndromes

Patterns of neurological change occur when increasing intracranial pressure (ICP) causes tissue shifts between compartments within the brain. Mass effect from space-occupying lesions such as brain edema, hematoma, hydrocephalus, or tumour may occur bilaterally or unilaterally. If either process continues unchecked, the cerebellum down through the foramen magnum can herniate.

Altered mentation and decreasing LOC are usually the first signs of neurological deterioration. Nurses should be alert to even subtle changes in the patient's behaviour and level of responsiveness. With *unilateral herniation*, an ipsilateral (same-sided) dilating pupil at first sluggishly reactive may signify neurological worsening. As herniation progresses, which it may do rapidly, response only to pain, contralateral (opposite-sided) posturing of extremities, and brainstem unexpected findings may be noticeable. With *bilateral herniation*, pupil change and reflex posturing are on both sides.

With *cerebellar herniation*, the patient has fixed pupils (size depends on site of original lesion), flaccid muscles, and no response to pain stimulus. The patient may rapidly experience brain death, as well as respiratory and cardiovascular changes. Certain respiratory patterns may be seen with progressive neurological deterioration related to increased ICP or focal lesions of the brainstem (see Table 24-14 at the end of the chapter).

Evidence-Informed Critical Thinking

Common Laboratory and Diagnostic Testing

Diagnostic tests serve to further define the precise location and often the nature and extent of a lesion. Many diagnostic tests also provide information regarding the integrity of surrounding areas. A wide variety of diagnostic tests can aid in the diagnosis of nervous system disease. Technological advances have made new equipment and techniques possible; such progress continues rapidly. Significant developments in genetic testing have allowed molecular diagnosis of infectious, congenital, and inherited neurological diseases, among multiple other applications. Although neurodiagnostic testing can be categorized in many ways, this review sorts tests as anatomic imaging, electrical conduction testing, and CSF/spinal procedures.

Computerized tomography (CT) continues to be the staple of neurodiagnostic imaging. It consists of passage of multiple x-ray beams through tissue in sequential planes, displayed in shades of grey. Intravenous injection of a radiopaque medium ("contrast") provides bright enhancement of vascular structures and areas of blood–brain barrier breakdown. CT detects potential causes of increased ICP and multiple other intracranial pathologies.

The magnetic resonance imaging (MRI) is a noninvasive, nonradiological test that delivers highly detailed images of neuroanatomy and associated pathology. Duration is usually significantly longer than CT. This, plus the effects of the strong magnetic field on most critical care monitors and equipment such as infusion pumps, makes MRI more problematic for critically ill patients. The procedure is noninvasive (barring intravenous infusion of contrast material for certain sequences), but patients may experience discomfort from the duration of the procedure, loud scanner sounds, possible feelings of claustrophobia, and having to lie absolutely still. Patient movement disrupts the adequacy of images (as with CT), so sedation may also be indicated.

⚠ SAFETY ALERT 24-4

Preprocedure considerations include removal of metallic objects from hair, wrists, fingers, and piercings. Professionals also screen the patient regarding previous eye injury with metal; they screen the environment for metal that could possibly become a missile if exposed to the strong magnetic field in the immediate area of the magnetic resonance imaging (MRI) scanner. Objects such as oxygen tanks, scissors, forceps, and stethoscopes have been implicated in potential or actual patient injury.

Angiography, an invasive procedure, involves intra-arterial injection of contrast material to visualize the lumen of intracranial and extracranial vessels. It is the gold standard for identification of aneurysms, arteriovenous malformations, and vasospasm following subarachnoid hemorrhage (Perry, Stiell, et al., 2006). Disadvantages of cerebral angiography are risk for complications after arterial access of vessels that typically already contain pathology.

⚠ SAFETY ALERT 24-5

Preprocedure nursing considerations include screening for allergy to shellfish or iodine or presence of renal disease (premedication to lower risk of anaphylaxis will be considered; an alternative contrast material can reduce risk of renal failure). The postprocedure focus is on observation and prevention of complications. Frequent serial assessment of the arterial puncture site, distal pulses, and limb colour and temperature targets risk for bleeding, hematoma, or occlusion of the cannulated vessel.

The largely noninvasive electroencephalogram (EEG) records spontaneous electrical impulses from scalp electrodes positioned over the brain surface area. EEG detects unexpected electrical activity such as seizures or alterations caused by neuronal damage from trauma, stroke, encephalopathies, or other cerebral pathology (Shiraishi, Ahlfors, et al., 2005). Electromyography records electrical activity in muscles at rest, during voluntary contraction, and with electrical stimulation via inserted small needle electrodes. Nerve conduction studies record speed of conduction in motor and sensory fibres of peripheral nerves by using surface electrodes. They are used to evaluate for neuromuscular disorders such as myasthenia gravis, neuropathy, or other peripheral nerve dysfunction.

Lumbar puncture involves insertion of a hollow needle into the spinal subarachnoid space to examine and measure the pressure of CSF. Placement is between L4 and L5 or L3 and L4 vertebrae to avoid the spinal cord, which typically ends at L1. Lumbar puncture is usually performed at the bedside (or in a clinic if done as an outpatient procedure), under strict asepsis.

△ SAFETY ALERT 24-6

After lumbar puncture, patients typically must remain flat in bed for 6 to 8 hours. If headache develops or becomes severe when the patient first gets up, bed rest may continue for up to 24 hours. Headache usually results from loss of the cushioning effect of cerebrospinal fluid (CSF) or from leakage of CSF from the puncture site into surrounding tissue. If the intracranial pressure (ICP) is significantly elevated, lumbar drainage of CSF could potentially precipitate downward herniation of the brain into the foramen magnum. Patients need frequent assessment for headache and level of consciousness (LOC) following a lumbar puncture.

Clinical Reasoning

When formulating a nursing diagnosis, nurses use critical thinking to cluster data and identify related patterns. They compare clusters with defining characteristics (unexpected findings) for the diagnosis to ensure the most accurate labelling and appropriate interventions (see Table 24-6) (North American Nursing Diagnosis Association-International, 2009). Note how the potential interventions often include assessments. This illustrates how the nursing process is interwoven and assessment is a continuous part of nursing practice.

Nurses use assessment information to identify patient outcomes. Some outcomes related to neurological conditions include the following (Moorhead, Johnson, et al., 2007):

- Patient cares for both sides of the body and keeps affected side safe.
- Patient does not aspirate or fall and maintains a safe environment.
- Patient improves motor function and becomes independent with activities of daily living.

After outcomes are established, patient care can be implemented. Nurse uses critical thinking and evidence-informed practice to develop interventions. Some examples of nursing

(text continues on page 742)

Table 24-6 Common Nursing Diagnoses Associated with the Neurological System

Diagnosis and Related Factors	Point of Differentiation	Assessment Characteristics	Nursing Interventions
Impaired verbal communication related to aphasia	Compromised ability to use speech (whether receiving, transmitting, or both)	Difficulty forming words or sentences, difficulty expressing thoughts verbally, inappropriate verbalization	Observe behavioural cues for needs. Maintain eye contact. Ask yes and no questions. Anticipate patient's needs. Use touch as appropriate
Acute confusion related to stroke	Abrupt onset of global, transient changes and disturbances in attention, cognition, and consciousness	Fluctuation in cognition, increased agitation or restlessness, lack of follow-through in behaviour	Perform mental status examination. Provide environmental cues (eg, large clock and calendar). Orient to time, place, and person frequently
Unilateral neglect related to left-sided muscle weakness	Lack of awareness and attention to one side of the body	Inattention to one side, inadequate positioning, leaves food on plate on affected side	Provide safe, well-lit, and clutter-free environment. Set up environment so that most activity is on unaffected side. Encourage patient to compensate for neglect
Risk for aspiration related to muscle weakness and impaired swallowing	Risk for oropharyngeal secretions, food, or fluid entering into the tracheobronchial passages	Reduced level of consciousness (LOC), facial droop, depressed cough and gag reflexes, drooling, choking, and coughing on food	Auscultate lungs before and after feeding. Request swallowing evaluation by speech therapy. Elevate head of bed when eating

The health challenges of Mr. Matthew Nderitu have been outlined throughout this chapter. Initial subjective and objective data collection is complete. The nurse is reviewing the findings and other results.

Mr. Nderitu is reassessed on the acute care unit following his admission from the emergency department (ED). The following nursing note illustrates the collection and analysis of subjective and objective data and the development of preliminary nursing interventions.

Subjective: A 56-year-old Nigerian-Canadian man with a history of hypertension, smoking, and mild baseline dementia. Lives alone, compromised hygiene, wearing multiple layers of mismatched clothes. Does not remember last time he took "high pressure pills." Is alert, appears somewhat fearful and agitated, asking for cigarettes, oriented to name only. Speech is comprehensible but slurred.

Objective: The patient can follow one-step commands only—is easily distractible. Impaired short-term memory—remembers zero of three objects after 1 minute. PERRLA (pupils equal, round, reactive to light and accommodation) @ 3 mm. Appears to have left visual field loss, extraocular movements (EOMs) intact. Left lower facial weakness, left tongue deviation. Muscle bulk symmetrical, tone slightly increased in left arm/leg. Strength 5/5 right arm/leg, 2/5 left arm, 3/5 left leg, left Babinski +. Right arm/leg coordination grossly intact, left arm/leg not tested because of weakness, gait not tested (on bed rest). Diminished attention to objects and people on left side of bed, difficult to assess sensation because of varying patient attention. Remains hypertensive—see flow sheet for vital signs.

Analysis: Findings consistent with right hemisphere stroke, complicated by baseline impaired cognitive function. Potential for further impaired cerebral perfusion. Probable left unilateral neglect, high fall risk, dysphagia, and aspiration risk.

Plan: Frequent neurological assessment to monitor for stroke progression. Monitor blood pressure (BP)—currently not treated per stroke guidelines. Consult social work for support system and financial assessment—patient may be unable to return to independent living. Evaluate safe activity of daily living performance with physical and occupational therapists. Implement fall prevention plan; discuss speech pathology consult for swallowing evaluation prior to starting diet.

Mr. Nderitu may be at risk for aspiration because of his facial droop and tongue deviation. The nurse contacts speech therapy to evaluate the patient's ability to swallow without choking or aspirating. Nurses consult speech therapy when patient needs are associated with:

- Swallowing evaluation/management and diet recommendations
- Cognitive communication and language evaluations
- Difficulty with communication
- Oral or facial trauma
- Aphasia

The nurse is contacting speech therapy at this time for the risk of aspiration, a safety issue. Speech therapy also may be involved during this patient's rehabilitation for issues related to communication. The following conversation illustrates how the nurse might organize data and make recommendations to speech therapy.

Situation: "Hello, I'm Boyd Bolt-Hasen, Mr. Matthew Nderitu's nurse on 5 East."

Background: "Mr. Nderitu was admitted yesterday with a right-sided stroke. He hasn't started a diet yet. He has some left lower facial weakness and left tongue deviation that might interfere with ability to chew and swallow. He wants to eat, but he still has an order for nothing by mouth."

Assessment: "I'm worried that he's at risk for aspiration. I would like you to evaluate his swallowing before we start feeding him."

Recommendations: "For now I'm going to keep him on nothing by mouth. After you see him, let me know what your assessment is. We may have the physician change his diet order if he's safe to eat."

Critical Thinking Challenge

- Consider all the collected subjective data. Review the above report. Should the nurse communicate any other data to speech therapy?
- Critique the objective data. Is the organization logical? Would it be clearer to add to or take out any of the information?
- Critique the analysis and recommendations. What is the nurse's role in coordinating collaborative care with speech therapy?

Pulling It All Together: An Example of Reflection and Critical Thinking

The nurse uses assessment data to formulate the patient care plan with patient outcomes and interventions for Mr. Nderitu. Outcomes are specific to the patient, realistic to achieve, measurable, and have a time frame. After interventions are completed, the nurse will reevaluate Mr. Nderitu and document the findings to show progress toward outcomes. The nurse uses critical thinking and judgment to continue or revise the diagnosis, outcomes, or interventions. This is often in the form of a care plan or case note similar to the one below.

Nursing Diagnosis	Patient Outcomes	Nursing Interventions	Rationale	Evaluation
Unilateral neglect related to hemianopsia, left-sided weakness.	Demonstrates measures to care for left side of body and keep it free from injury within 1 week.	Assess neurological function every shift including muscle strength. Assist with dressing and grooming until strength returns. Place call bell on right side of bed.	The initial priority is patient safety and injury prevention. Assess function to determine improvements or decline. Assist the patient with activities of daily living until he can care for himself.	Motor strength 2+ on left arm and leg; 4+ on right. Facial droop and tongue deviation persist. Needs assistance in two-handed tasks, such as bathing. Needs one-person assist with transfers. Continue to monitor; obtain physiotherapy consult to assess for readiness for rehabilitation.

Applying Your Knowledge

Using the previous steps of clinical reasoning, organizing, and prioritizing, consider all the case study findings woven throughout this chapter. When answering the following questions, begin drawing conclusions and see how the pieces of assessment must work together to create an environment for personalized, appropriate, and accurate care. Note how assessment forms the foundation for accurate, individualized, and holistic nursing care.

- What signs will the nurse assess to detect if Mr. Nderitu's situation is deteriorating? (Knowledge)
- Is Mr. Nderitu's condition at the end stable, urgent, or an emergency? (Comprehension)
- What ongoing health promotion and teaching needs are evident? (Application)
- How will the nurse individualize assessment to Mr. Nderitu's specific needs, considering his condition, age, and culture? (Analysis)
- How will the nurse focus, organize, and prioritize ongoing objective data collection? (Synthesis)
- How will the nurse evaluate the selection of the priority nursing diagnosis? (Evaluation)

interventions for neurological care are as follows (Bulechek, Butcher, et al., 2008):

- Use cues and anchors to promote attention to the affected side.
- Assess neurological and mental status frequently; inform physician of changes.
- Orient patient to time, place, and person frequently.

Key Points

- Nurses use experience, knowledge of anatomy and physiology, and the patient's acuity, current deficits, and risk for deterioration to select elements of the neurological examination most appropriate for the situation.
- Although some neurological changes are evident instantaneously, most progress over time. Consistent, accurate, and clearly communicated serial assessments are critical for timely identification and intervention.
- Early recognition of events requiring urgent intervention maximizes the patient's chance of optimal outcome.
- Common areas of health promotion include reducing the risk of neurovascular disease and injury prevention.
- Common symptoms and signs associated with the neurological system include headache, weakness, blurry vision, impaired motor function, and impaired speech.
- When collecting a headache history, characteristics such as pain worse in the morning on awakening and pain precipitated or made worse by straining or sneezing may indicate potentially elevated ICP.
- Clinical situations that require urgent communication of neurological assessment findings include a change in LOC, pupillary reaction, and verbal or motor response.
- Consciousness and cognition are assessed early in the neurological examination because these functions direct the method used to elicit further information.
- Use of the GCS helps to provide relatively objective information about LOC but is most reliable with staff training.
- Assessment of the function of CNs is performed at the bedside through observation of vision, pupils, EOMs, facial expression and strength, and uvula and tongue movement.
- Spinal and peripheral nerve function may be assessed by testing for motor strength and sensation at different levels of the spinal cord according to the dermatomes.
- Unexpected reflex responses include hyperactive or diminished DTR, decreased superficial reflexes, and a positive Babinski.
- Posturing occurs in late stages of injury, including unexpected flexion and extension responses.
- Unexpected motor function includes disorders of movement such as tremor and unusual gait.
- Common nursing diagnoses are impaired verbal communication, acute confusion, impaired memory, unilateral neglect, risk for aspiration, risk for intracranial adaptive capacity, and ineffective brain tissue perfusion.
- While neurological assessment findings can highlight location and acuity of neuropathology, diagnostic testing

provides the critical next step in assessing type and etiology of the condition. Knowledgeable pre- and postprocedure care aids in maximizing information obtained and reducing patient stress and complications.

Review Questions

1. Use of the Glasgow Coma Scale (GCS) provides relatively objective assessment of the level of consciousness (LOC). The three functions assessed are
   A. pupil reaction, orientation, and sensation
   B. eye opening, verbal response, and motor response
   C. eye opening, motor response, and sensation
   D. verbal response, pupil reaction, and motor response

2. The patient with a head injury and increasing intracranial pressure (ICP) is likely to have which assessment findings?
   A. Decreased LOC and sluggish pupil
   B. Left-sided weakness and facial droop
   C. Right ptosis and right-sided loss of vision
   D. Dilated left pupil and receptive aphasia

3. The patient health record states that a 62-year-old woman has a stroke in the right parietal area of the brain. The nurse expects to note which of the following?
   A. Tremors on the left side of the face
   B. Tremors on the right side of the face
   C. Weakness in the right arm
   D. Weakness in the left arm

4. The nurse performs blood pressure (BP) screening at the local community centre. As part of the health promotion intervention, the nurse also discusses the following risk factors for stroke.
   A. Low BP, lack of exercise, and diet high in fat
   B. High BP, diet high in fat, and smoking
   C. Diet high in fat, smoking, and walking five times weekly
   D. Obesity, swimming five times weekly, high BP

5. If the great toe extends upward and the other toes fan out in response to stroking the lateral aspect of the sole of the foot, this is documented as which of the following?
   A. Hyporeflexia
   B. Expected plantar reflex
   C. Cushing response
   D. Positive Babinski sign

6. A 26-year-old man was in a motor vehicle accident and suffered a complete spinal cord injury to L3. The nurse assesses the patient for loss of motor function in the
   A. legs
   B. abdomen
   C. chest
   D. arms

7. The patient from an assisted living facility was admitted with a diagnosis of dementia. He started a fire because he was cooking in his unit and forgot that there was a pan on the stove. The nursing diagnosis that is the highest priority is

A. ineffective brain tissue perfusion

B. risk for injury

C. acute confusion

D. impaired memory

8. While the nurse performs formal patient assessment, assistive personnel often observe changes when obtaining vital signs or assisting patients with activities of daily living (ADLs). When discussing care for the patient with back pain, the nurse should particularly alert the assistant to watch for

A. dizziness

B. bowel/bladder incontinence

C. difficulty swallowing

D. arm weakness

9. When collecting a health history for the patient presenting with headache, the patient reports having as many as four episodes/day of severe right orbital pain lasting about 30 minutes with tearing and nasal congestion on the right. This is most consistent with

A. cluster headache

B. migraine with aura

C. tension headache

D. migraine without aura

10. Of the following changes, which is the earliest sign of progressing brain herniation that originates in the cerebral hemispheres?

A. An enlarging pupil that is sluggishly reactive to light

B. Altered mentation

C. Widening pulse pressure with bradycardia

D. Reflex posturing of extremities

Canadian Nursing Research

Green, T., Haley, R., et al. (2007). Education in stroke prevention: Efficacy of an educational counseling intervention to increase knowledge in stroke survivors. *Canadian Journal of Neuroscience Nursing, 29*(2), 13–20.

Green, T. L., & King, K. M. (2009). Experiences of male patients and wife-caregivers in the first year post-discharge following minor stroke: A descriptive qualitative study. *International Journal of Nursing Studies, 46*(9), 1194–1200.

Krause-Bachand, J., & Koopman, W. (2008). Living with oculopharyngeal muscular dystrophy: A phenomenological study. *Canadian Journal of Neuroscience Nursing, 30*(1), 35–39.

MacKenzie, G., Gould, L., et al. (2011). Detecting cognitive impairment in clients with mild stroke or transient ischemic attack attending a stroke prevention clinic. *Canadian Journal of Neuroscience Nursing, 33*(1), 47–50.

Neufeld, S. M., & Newburn-Cook, C. (2009). The efficacy of 5-HT3 receptor antagonists for the prevention of postoperative vomiting following craniotomy: Two studies in children and young adults. *Canadian Journal of Neuroscience Nursing, 31*(1), 30–34.

References

Agyeman, O., Nedeltchev, K., et al. (2006). Time to admission in acute ischemic stroke and transient ischemic attack. *Stroke, 37*(4), 963–966.

Anderson, M. C., & Bickley, L. S. (2010). The nervous system. In T. C. Stephen, D. L. Skillen, R. A. Day, & L. S. Bickley (Eds.). *Canadian Bates' guide to health assessment for nurses* (1st ed., pp. 683–758). Philadelphia, PA: Wolters Kluwer Health/Lippincott Williams & Wilkins.

Arboix, A., Miguel, M., et al. (2006). Cardiovascular risk factors in patients aged 85 or older with ischemic stroke. *Clinical Neurology and Neurosurgery, 108*(7), 638–643.

Atkinson, H. H., Rosano, C. et al. (2007). Cognitive function, gait speed decline, and comorbidities: The health, aging and body composition study. *Journals of Gerontology: Series A, Biological Sciences and Medical Sciences, 62*(8), 844–850.

Bax, M., Tydeman, C., et al. (2006). Clinical and MRI correlates of cerebral palsy: The European cerebral palsy study. *Journal of the American Medical Association, 296*(13), 1602–1608.

Bennett, H. P., Piquet, O., et al. (2006). Cognitive, extrapyramidal, and magnetic resonance imaging predictors of functional impairment in nondemented older community dwellers: The Sydney Older Person Study. *Journal of the American Geriatrics Society, 54*(1), 3–10.

Bulechek, G. M., Butcher, H. K., et al. (2008). *Nursing interventions classification (NIC)* (5th ed.). St. Louis, MO: Mosby.

Canadian Hypertension Education Program. (2010). *2010 Canadian hypertension education program recommendations: The short clinical summary—An annual update*. Retrieved from http://hypertension.ca/chep/recommendations/-2010

Canadian Institute for Health Information. (2006). *Head injuries in Canada: A decade of change (1994–1995 to 2003–2004)*. Retrieved from http:/secure.cihi.ca/cihiweb/en/downloads/analysis_ntr_2006_c.pdf

Colcombe, S. J., Erickson, K. I., et al. (2006). Aerobic exercise training increases brain volume in aging humans. *Journal of Gerontology, 61A*(11), 1166–1170.

Couris, C. M., Guilcher, S. J. T., et al. (2010). Characteristics of adults with incident traumatic spinal cord injury in Ontario, Canada. *Spinal Cord, 48*, 39–44.

Dunning, J., Daly, J. P., et al. (2006). Derivation of the children's head injury algorithm for the prediction of important clinical events decision rule for head injury in children. *Archives of Diseases in Childhood, 91*, 885–891.

Epilepsy Canada. (2005). *Epidemiology and basic information*. Retrieved from http://www.epilepsy.ca/eng/mainSet.html

Fallang, B., & Hadders-Algra, M. (2005). Postural behavior in children born preterm. *Neural Plasticity, 12*(2–3), 175–182.

Frishkoff, G. A. (2007). Hemispheric differences in strong versus weak semantic priming: Evidence from event-related brain potentials. *Brain & Language, 100*(1), 23–43.

Gill, M. R., Reiley, D. G., et al. (2004). Interrater reliability of Glasgow Coma Scale scores in the emergency department. *Annals of Emergency Medicine, 43*(2), 215–223.

Gillette Guyonnet, S., Abellan Van Kan, G., et al. (2007). IANA task force on nutrition and cognitive decline with aging. *Journal of Nutrition, Health & Aging, 11*(2), 132–152.

Guttman, M., Kish, S., et al. (2003). Current concepts in the diagnosis and management of Parkinson's disease. *Canadian Medical Association Journal, 168*(3), 293–301, 303.

Hand, P. J., Kwan, J., et al. (2006). Distinguishing between stroke and mimic at the bedside: The brain attack study. *Stroke, 37,* 769–775.

Heart and Stroke Foundation of Canada. (2011a). *Stroke.* Retrieved from http://www.heartandstroke.com/site/c.ikIQLcMWJtE/b.3483933/k.CD67/Stroke.htm?src

Heart and Stroke Foundation of Canada. (2011b). *People of African descent resources.* Retrieved from http://www.heartandstroke.com/site/c.ikIQLcMWHtE/b.3479039/k.3DD6/People African

Heron, R., Heron, R., et al. (2001). Interrater reliability of the Glasgow Coma Scale score among nurses in sub-specialties of critical care. *Australian Critical Care, 14*(3), 100–105.

Hickey, J. V. (2002). The neurological physical examination and neurological assessment. In J. V. Hickey (Ed.). *The clinical practice of neurological and neurosurgical nursing* (5th ed., pp. 117–184). Philadelphia, PA: Lippincott Williams & Wilkins.

Hockenberry, M. J., & Wilson, D. (2007). *Wong's nursing care of infants and children.* Philadelphia, PA: Elsevier.

Inouye, S. K., Robison, J. T., et al. (1998). The time and change test: A simple screening test for dementia. *Journal of Gerontology, 53,* M281–M286.

Isaacson, J. E., & Vora, N. M. (2003). Differential diagnosis and treatment of hearing loss. *American Family Physician, 68*(6), 1125–1132.

Jedrziewski, M. K., Lee, V. M., et al. (2007). Physical activity and cognitive health. *Alzheimer's & Dementia, 3,* 98–108.

Kandel, E. R., & Schwartz, J. H. (2008). *Principles of neural science* (5th ed.). Philadelphia, PA: Elsevier.

Kolevzon, A., Gross, R., et al. (2007). Prenatal and perinatal risk factors for autism: A review and integration of findings. *Archives of Pediatric Adolescent Medicine, 161*(4), 326–333.

Koren, G., Nava-Ocampo, A., et al. (2006). Major malformations with valproic acid. *Canadian Family Physician, 52,* 441–442, 444, 447.

Kumar, A., Calne, S. M., et al. (2004). Clustering of Parkinson's disease: Shared cause or coincidence? *Archives of Neurology, 61*(7), 1057–1060.

Laarson, H. J., Eaton, W. W., et al. (2005). Risk factors for autism: Perinatal factors, parental psychiatric history, and socioeconomic status. *American Journal of Epidemiology, 767*(10), 916–925.

Leder, S. B. (1997). Videofluoroscopic evaluation of aspiration with visual examination of the gag reflex and velar movement. *Dysphagia, 72*(1), 21–23.

Lee, L. C., Harrington, R. A., et al. (2008). Increased risk of injury in children with developmental disabilities. *Research in Developmental Disabilities, 29*(3), 247–255.

London, M. L., Ladewig, P. A. W., et al. (2007). *Maternal & child nursing care* (2nd ed.). Upper Saddle River, NJ: Pearson Prentice Hall.

Lowdermilk, D. L., & Perry, S. E. (2007). *Maternity & women's health care* (9th ed.). St. Louis, MO: Mosby.

Martini, F. H., Timmons, M. J., et al. (2009). *Human anatomy* (6th ed.). New York, NY: Pearson Benjamin Cummings.

Mathers-Schmidt, B. A., & Kurlinski, M. (2003). Dysphagia evaluation practices: Inconsistencies in clinical assessment and instrumental examination decision-making. *Dysphagia, 78*(2), 114–125.

McNett, M. (2007). A review of the predictive ability of Glasgow Coma Scale scores in head-injured clients. *Neuroscience Nursing, 39*(2), 68–75.

Miller, C. A. (2009). *Nursing for wellness in older adults: Theory and practice* (5th ed.). Philadelphia, PA: Lippincott Williams & Wilkins.

Moorhead, S., Johnson, M., et al. (2007). *Nursing outcomes classification (NOC)* (4th ed.). St. Louis, MO: Mosby.

National Advisory Committee on Immunization. (2010). *Statement on the recommended use of herpes zoster vaccine.* Retrieved from http://www.phac-aspc.gc.ca/publicat/ccdr-rmtc/10vol36/acs-1/index-eng.php

National Center for Injury Prevention and Control. (2007). *Fact sheet: Spinal cord injury.* Retrieved from http://www.cdc.gov/ncipc/factsheets/scifacts.htm

National Clearinghouse Guidelines. (2007). Stroke *assessment across the continuum of care.* Retrieved from http://www.guideline.gov/summary/summary.aspx?doc_id=7426

National Institutes of Health. (2003). *NIH stroke scales and clinical assessment tools.* Retrieved from http://64.37.123.165/trials/scales/nihss.html

Neural Control of Breathing. (2007). Retrieved from http://www.meddean.luc.edu/lumen/meded/medicine/pulmonar/physio/pf11.htm

North American Nursing Diagnosis Association-International. (2009). *Nursing diagnoses, 2009–2077 edition: Definitions and classifications (NANDA-I NURSING DIAGNOSIS).* West Sussex, UK: John Wiley & Sons.

Perry, J. J., Stiell, I. G., et al. (2006). Interobserver agreement in the assessment of headache clients with possible subarachnoid hemorrhage. *Academic Emergency Medicine, 73,* S138.

Pierazzo, J., & Book, D. S. (2010). Disorders of brain function. In R. A. Hannon, C. Pooler, et al. (Eds.). *Porth pathophysiology: Concepts of altered health states* (1st Canadian ed., pp. 1246–1280). Philadelphia, PA: Wolters Kluwer Health/Lippincott Williams & Wilkins.

Public Health Agency of Canada. (2009). *Statement on meningococcal vaccination for travellers.* Retrieved from http://www.phac-aspc.gc.ca/publicat/ccdr-rmtc/09vol35/acs-dcc-4/index-eng.php

Pupillary Abnormalities: Their recognition and diagnosis. (2007). Retrieved from http://www.opt.indiana.edu/riley/HomePage/Pupil_Abnormal/1_Saint_Pupil_Abnormal.html

Rick Hansen Institute & Urban Futures. (2010). *The incidence and prevalence of spinal cord injury in Canada: Overview and estimates based on current evidence.* Vancouver, BC: Author.

Roach, S., Roddick, P., R. A. Day, & L. S. Bickley (2010). The cardiovascular system. In T. C. Stephen, D. L. Skillen, R. A. Day, & L. S. Bickley (Eds.). *Canadian Bates' guide to health assessment for nurses* (1st ed., pp. 423–478). Philadelphia, PA: Wolters Kluwer Health/Lippincott Williams & Wilkins.

Rothwell, P. M., Giles, M. F., et al. (2005). A simple score (ABCD) to identify individuals at high early risk of stroke after transient ischaemic attack. *Lancet, 366,* 29–36.

Rull, R. P., Ritz, B., et al. (2006). Neural tube defects and maternal residential proximity to agricultural pesticide applications. *American Journal of Epidemiology, 763*(8), 743–753.

Russell, M. B. (2010). Genetics of dementia. *Acta Neurologica Scandinavica, 122*(Suppl. 190), 58–61.

Saguil, A. (2005). Evaluation of the patient with muscle weakness. *American Family Physician, 77*(7), 1327–1336.

Shiraishi, H. M., Ahlfors, S. P., et al. (2005). Application of magnetoencephalography in epilepsy patients with widespread spike or slow-wave activity. *Epilepsia, 46*(8), 1264–1272.

Singh, M. D., & Kahn, S. (2010). Management of patients with neurologic dysfunction. In R. A. Day, P. Paul, et al. (Eds.). *Brunner & Suddarth's textbook of Canadian medical-surgical nursing* (2nd ed., pp. 2053–2094). Philadelphia, PA: Wolters Kluwer Health/Lippincott Williams & Wilkins.

Standring, S. (2008). *Gray's anatomy: The anatomical basis for clinical practice* (40th ed.). London: Elsevier Churchill Livingstone.

Teasdale, G., & Jennett, B. (1974). Assessment of coma and impaired consciousness. A practical scale. *Lancet, 304,* 81–84.

Terré, R., & Mearin, F. (2006). Oropharyngeal dysphagia after the acute phase of stroke: Predictors of aspiration. *Neurogastroenterology Motility, 3,* 200–205.

Thiessen, M. (2006). Pediatric minor closed head injury. *Pediatric Clinics of North America, 53*(1), 1–26.

Vukusic, S., Hutchinson, M., et al.; The Pregnancy in Multiple Sclerosis Group. (2004). Pregnancy and multiple sclerosis (the PRIMS study): Clinical predictors of post-partum relapse. *Brain, 727*(6), 1353–1360.

Williams, L. J., Rasmussen, S. A., et al. (2005). Spina bifida and anencephaly by race/ethnicity: 1995–2002. *Pediatrics, 776*(3), 580–586.

Willis, S. L., Tennstedt, S. L., et al. (2006). Long-term effects of cognitive training on everyday functional outcomes in older adults. *Journal of the American Medical Association, 296*(23), 2805–2814.

The Canadian Jensen's Nursing Health Assessment suite offers these additional resources to enhance learning and facilitate understanding of this chapter:

- thePoint online resource, http//thepoint.lww.com/Stephen1E
- *Laboratory Manual for Canadian Jensen's Nursing Health Assessment: A Best Practice Approach*

Tables of Unexpected Findings

! **Table 24-7   Unexpected Postures**

Picture	Pathological Indication	Description
Unexpected extension Plantar flexed Flexed Pronated Extended Adducted	Damage to the midbrain or upper pons; more serious than unexpected flexion, because the patient is posturing toward rather than away from a noxious stimulus	Very stiff, spastic movements may persist after noxious stimulation. Upper extremities are extended, adducted, and internally rotated; palms are pronated. Lower extremities are extended, back is hyperextended, and there is plantar flexion
Unexpected flexion Flexed Plantar flexed Internally rotated Flexed Adducted	Damage to the cerebral cortex	Very stiff, spastic movements may persist after noxious stimulation. Upper extremities are flexed and arms are adducted. Lower extremities are extended, internally rotated with plantar flexion
Hemiplegia Externally rotated Flaccid	Stroke	Sensation and motor strength are lost unilaterally
Flexion withdrawal	Central nervous system (CNS) depression or injury	Gross movements of all body parts are away from the noxious stimulus. Rather than localizing pain to one side, the patient may withdraw both arms when nailbed pressure is applied
Flaccid quadriplegia	Nonfunctional brainstem	Sensation and muscle tone are completely lost

Table 24-8   **Aberrations of Movements**

	Common Associations	Description
Paralysis 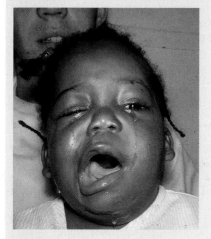	Stroke, spinal cord injury, chronic neuromuscular diseases, Bell palsy	Loss of motor function resulting in flaccidity over the area of damage; may be total, one-sided (hemiplegia), in all four extremities (quadriplegia), or in only the legs (paraplegia)
Resting tremor 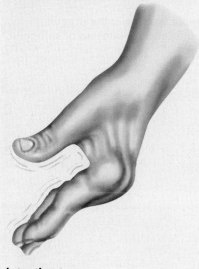	Parkinson's disease	Prominent at rest, may decrease or disappear with voluntary movement
Intention tremor 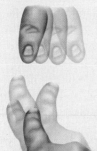	Multiple sclerosis with damage to the cerebellar pathways, or essential tremor	Absent at rest, increases with movement; may worsen as movement progresses

(table continues on page 748)

Table 24-8   **Aberrations of Movements** (*continued*)

	Common Associations	Description
Fasciculations 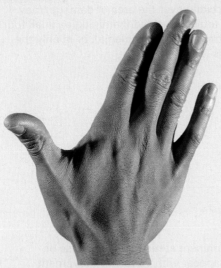	Deterioration of the anterior horn cells	Fine, flickering, irregular movements in small muscle groups seen under the skin; may not cause movement at the joint. Because fasciculations occur under the skin, it is difficult to see them clearly
Tic 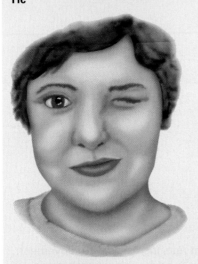	Tourette's syndrome, use of psychiatric medications, and use of amphetamines (eg, methamphetamine)	Brief, repetitive, similar but irregular movements, such as blinking or shrugging shoulders
Clonus/myoclonus 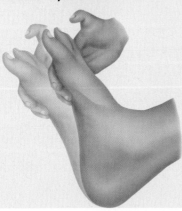	Seizures, hiccups, or just prior to falling asleep	Rapid, sudden clonic spasm of a muscle that may occur regularly or intermittently

Table 24-8 **Aberrations of Movements** (*continued*)

	Common Associations	Description
Dystonia 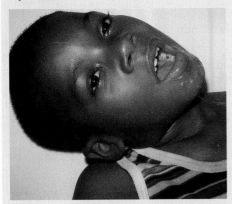	Use of psychiatric medications	Slow involuntary twisting movements that often involve the trunk and larger muscles; may be accompanied by twisted postures
Choreiform movements 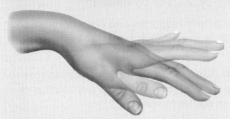	Huntington's disease	Brief, rapid, jerky movements that are irregular and unpredictable; commonly affect the face, head, lower arms, and hands
Athetoid movements 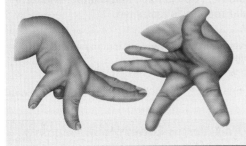	Cerebral palsy	Slow involuntary worm-like twisting movements that involve the extremities, neck, facial muscles, and tongue; may be associated with drooling and dysarthria

Table 24-9 **Pupils in Comatose Patients**

Picture	Pathological Indication	Description
Unequal pupil size, physiological	Physiological anisocoria, not associated with any disease	May be congenital in 20% of the population
Unequal pupils size—unexpected	Anisocoria related to compression of the optic nerve	One pupil is 0.1 mm different from the other
Constricted and fixed (pinpoint)	Miosis related to hemorrhage in the pons or opiate narcotics	Pinpoint pupils (<0.1 mm) or small pupils (1–2.5 mm) suggest damage to the sympathetic pathways or metabolic encephalopathy.
Dilated and fixed	Anoxia, sympathetic effects, atropine, tricyclics, amphetamines, or pilocarpine drops for glaucoma treatment; when associated with a head injury, prognosis is poor	Pupils are >6 mm bilaterally
Horner syndrome	Preganglionic, central, or postganglionic lesion	Miosis (small pupil), ptosis (lid droop), anhydrosis (lack of sweat), and apparent enophthalmos (affected eye appears to be sunken)
Adie's pupil	Denervation of the nerve supply from diabetic neuropathy or alcoholism	Both the pupillary response and accommodation are sluggish or impaired in one eye
Argyll Robertson	Neurosyphilis, meningitis	Virtually no response to light but brisk response to accommodation bilaterally. Pupils are small and frequently irregular in shape
Third nerve palsy	Third nerve palsy	Sudden ptosis, diplopia, and pain are some of the symptoms. Pupil is fixed and dilated, and extraocular motility is restricted

Adapted from *Pupillary abnormalities: Their recognition and diagnosis.* (2007). Retrieved from http://www.opt.indiana.edu/riley/HomePage/Pupil_Abnormal/1_Saint_Pupil_Abnormal.html; For details on altered pupils, see Chapter 15.

Table 24-10 **Differential Diagnosis of Upper Motor Neuron (UMN) Versus Lower Motor Neuron (LMN) Lesions**

Signs	UMN lesions (involve motor areas of cerebral cortex and white matter tracts connecting to motor nerve nuclei in brain or spinal cord)	LMN lesions (involve brainstem or spinal cord motor nuclei, nerve roots, or nerves)
Strength	Spastic paresis or paralysis (may be flaccid in acute phase)	Flaccid paresis or paralysis
Muscle tone	Increased (spasticity)	Decreased or absent (flaccidity)
Muscle stretch reflexes	Increased; presence of Babinski sign	Decreased or absent
Muscle atrophy	Absent (although disuse atrophy may occur with prolonged deficit)	Present
Muscle fasciculations	Absent	Present

Table 24-11   **Unexpected Gaits**

Picture	Pathologic Indication	Description
Spastic hemiparesis 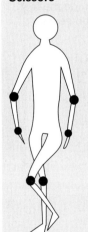	Stroke	One side functions as expected. The other side is flexed from spasticity. The elbow, wrist, and fingers are flexed; the arm is close to the side. The affected leg is extended with plantar flexion of the foot. When ambulating, the foot is dragged, scraping the toe, or it is circled stiffly outward and forward
Scissors	Spastic diplegia associated with bilateral spasticity of the legs	Moves the trunk to accommodate for the leg movements. Legs are extended and knees are flexed. Leg cross over each other at each step, similar to walking in water
Parkinsonian 	Parkinson's disease	Stooped posture, head and neck forward, and hips and knees flexed. Arms are also flexed and held at waist. There is difficulty in initiating gait, often rocking to start. Once ambulating, steps are quick and shuffling; has difficulty stopping once started

(table continues on page 752)

Table 24-11 Unexpected Gaits (continued)

Picture	Pathologic Indication	Description
Cerebellar ataxia 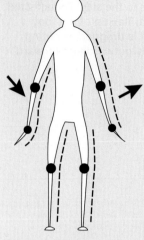	Cerebral palsy and alcohol intake	Wide-based gait. Staggers and lurches from side to side. Cannot perform Romberg with eyes open because of swaying of the trunk and wide stance
Sensory ataxia 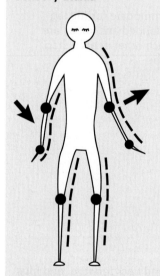	Cerebral palsy	Wide-based gait. Feet are loosely thrown forward, landing first on the heels and then on the toes. Patient watches the ground to help guide the feet. Positive Romberg from loss of position sense
Dystrophic (waddling)	Weak hip abductors	Wide gait. Weight is shifted from side to side with stiff trunk movement. Abdomen protrudes and lordosis is common

Table 24-12 **Variations of Sensory Function**

Picture	Pathological Indication	Description
Peripheral neuropathy	Diabetes mellitus or peripheral vascular disease	Sensory loss is distributed peripherally in a characteristic "glove" or "stocking" pattern. More diffuse and less specific than injury associated with an individual nerve
Individual nerves	Trauma or injury	Follows the pattern expected in the nerve, with the cutaneous distribution that follows the dermatome
Spinal cord hemisection	Brown–Séquard syndrome from spinal cord injury, tumour, or mass	Because of how the nerves cross in the spinal cord, pain and temperature are lost below the level of the lesion on the opposite side. Position sense, vibration, and motor function are affected on the same side of the body
Complete transection of the spinal cord	Spinal cord injury, tumour, or mass	All sensation and motor function is lost below the level of the lesion

Table 24-13 **Pathological (Primitive) Reflexes**

Procedure	Unexpected Findings in Adults
Grasp reflex: Apply palmar stimulation.	A grasping response is associated with dementia and diffuse brain impairment.
Snout reflex: Elicit by tapping a tongue blade across the lips.	The snout reflex is present if tapping causes the lips to purse.
Sucking reflex: Touch or stroke the lips, tongue, or palate.	Observe sucking movement of the lips; this reflex also may be noted during oral care or oral suctioning.
Rooting reflex: Stroke the lateral upper lip.	The rooting reflex is present if the patient moves the mouth toward the stimulus.
Palmomental reflex: Stroke the palm of the hand.	It is present if stroking of the palm causes contraction of the same sided muscle of the lower lip.
Hoffman's sign: Tap the nail on the third or fourth finger.	A positive Hoffman's sign is if tapping elicits involuntary flexion of the distal joint of the thumb and index finger.
Glabellar's sign: Tap the forehead to cause the patient to blink.	Usually, in healthy patients, the first five taps cause a single blink, and then the reflex diminishes.
	Blinking continues in patients with diffuse cerebral dysfunction.

Adapted from Hickey, J. V. (2002). The neurological physical examination and neurological assessment. In J. V. Hickey (Ed.). *The clinical practice of neurological and neurosurgical nursing* (5th ed., pp. 117–184). Philadelphia, PA: Lippincott Williams & Wilkins.

Table 24-14   Altered Respiratory Patterns Associated with Intracranial Conditions

	Area of the Brain Affected
Cheyne–Stokes respiration (spindle pattern)	
Breathing pattern with period of apnea (10–60 s) followed by gradually increasing depth and frequency of respiration, gradually decreasing in depth and frequency until period of apnea	Poor brainstem perfusion
Central neurogenic hyperventilation	
Rapid and deep respirations, sometimes >40/min	Medulla or pons malfunction
Apneustic breathing	
Sustained inspiratory effort, usually <12/min	Medulla or pons damage
Gasping	
Rapid and quick, difficult breaths; irregular respirations with varying rate and tidal volume	Extensive pons damage, severe hypoxia
Biot breathing (cluster pattern)	
Several short breaths followed by long irregular periods of apnea	Pons malfunction, increased intracranial pressure (ICP)
Apnea	
Absence of breathing	High cervical cord or extensive medulla damage, brain death

Adapted from *Neural Control of Breathing*. (2007). Retrieved from http://www.meddean.luc.edu/lumen/meded/medicine/pulmonar/physio/pf11.htm; For details on altered breathing patterns, see Chapter 18.

Male Genitalia and Rectal Assessment

Learning Objectives

1 Demonstrate knowledge of the anatomy and physiology of the male genitalia and rectum.

2 Identify important topics for health promotion and risk reduction related to the male genitalia and rectal assessment.

3 Consider age, condition, gender, and culture of the patient to individualize the assessment of the male genitalia and rectum.

4 Collect subjective and objective data related to the male genitalia and rectum.

5 Identify expected and unexpected findings related to the male genitalia and rectum.

6 Analyze subjective and objective findings from the assessment of the male genitalia and rectum and consider initial interventions.

7 Document and communicate data from the male genitalia assessment using appropriate terminology and principles of recording.

8 Identify nursing diagnoses and initiate a plan of care based on findings from the male genitalia and rectal assessment.

*M*r. Alex Gardner, a 50-year-old Caucasian man, was diagnosed with benign prostatic hyperplasia 3 years ago. He is visiting the outpatient urology clinic today because he is having increased difficulty with urination. Mr. Gardner has been married for 3 months. This is his second marriage. He has two children from his first marriage and two stepchildren. Mr. Gardner's temperature is 37.0°C, pulse 84 beats/min and regular, respirations 16 breaths/min, and blood pressure 122/68 mm Hg right arm (sitting). Current medications include tamsulosin hydrochloride (Flomax) 0.4 mg for the prostatic hyperplasia and lovastatin (Apo-Lovastatin) 20 mg for his elevated lipid levels. Additional supplements include a multivitamin and fish oil capsules that he takes to prevent cardiovascular disease.

You will gain more information about Mr. Gardner as you progress through this chapter. As you study the content and features, consider Mr. Gardner's case and its relationship to what you are learning. Begin thinking about the following points:

- Is Mr. Gardner's condition stable, urgent, or an emergency?
- How will the nurse work with Mr. Gardner to promote health and reduce risk for illness?
- Which nursing diagnosis is the highest priority? What is the rationale?

This chapter provides an overview of anatomy and physiology and a focused physical assessment of the male genitalia and accessory structures; these include the seminal vesicles, scrotum, penis, testicles, prostate gland, and epididymis (Fig. 25-1). While the rectum and anus are terminal structures of the gastrointestinal tract (see Chapter 22), nurses frequently integrate a holistic nursing assessment of these organs into the physical examination of the male genitalia. A basic understanding of pertinent anatomy and physiology assists nurses to perform assessments with confidence and knowledge.

During such very intimate assessment, it is important to provide patients with privacy. If desired, the patient has the right for a chaperone to be present during the examination. In language the patient will understand, remember to explain each step of the assessment. During assessment, education opportunities arise, and nurses can teach health promotion and risk reduction while collecting subjective and objective data. All findings should be documented as per protocol.

The design of this chapter is to provide the foundation for the nurse to conduct individualized health assessments, in which the nurse fully considers each patient's age, sexual orientation, and culture. Incorporated throughout are examples of evidence-informed critical thinking, points of clinical significance, and key unexpected findings. A sensitive, tactful approach to examination of this area paves the way to providing excellent health care.

Anatomy and Physiology Overview

External Genitalia

The *penis* has two functions: (1) it is the final excretory organ of urination and (2) with sexual excitement, it becomes firm or erect to allow penetration for sexual intercourse. It can be subdivided into the root, shaft (or body), and glans (Fig. 25-2).

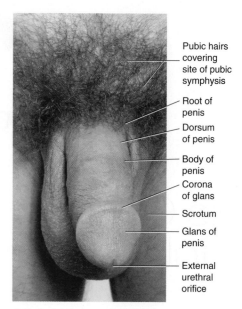

Figure 25-2 Surface anatomy of the penis.

Pubic hairs covering site of pubic symphysis

Root of penis

Dorsum of penis

Body of penis

Corona of glans

Scrotum

Glans of penis

External urethral orifice

The root of the penis lies deep within the perineum. The shaft has hairless, thin skin that adheres loosely, allowing for expansion of the erect penis. The glans (head of the penis) is lighter in pigmentation than the rest of the organ.

The penis contains three distensible structures: two *corpora cavernosa,* which form the dorsum and sides of the penis, and a single *corpus spongiosum,* which forms the bulb. The *urethra* is located in the middle of the corpus spongiosum, which ends in the cone-shaped glans with its expanded base, or *corona.* A small slit in the distal tip of the glans is the *urethra meatus.* The ridge of the corona separates the glans from the shaft.

When engorged with blood, the smooth, spongy tissue of the penis becomes erect. An erection is a complex neurovascular reflex that ensues when a decreased venous outflow and an increased arterial dilation cause the two corpora cavernosa

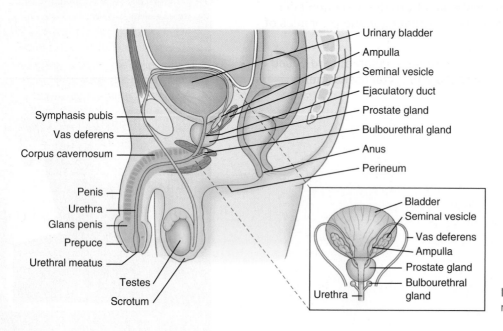

Symphasis pubis

Vas deferens

Corpus cavernosum

Penis

Urethra

Glans penis

Prepuce

Urethral meatus

Testes

Scrotum

Urinary bladder

Ampulla

Seminal vesicle

Ejaculatory duct

Prostate gland

Bulbourethral gland

Anus

Perineum

Bladder

Seminal vesicle

Vas deferens

Ampulla

Prostate gland

Bulbourethral gland

Urethra

Figure 25-1 Overview of the male genitalia.

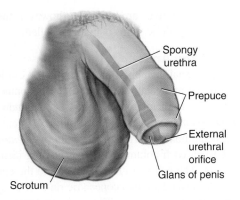

Figure 25-3 Depiction of an uncircumcised penis; note how the prepuce or foreskin covers the glans.

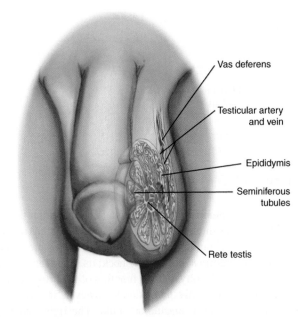

Figure 25-4 Anatomy of the testis.

to fill with blood. This reflex is under the control of the autonomic nervous system and depends on local synthesis of nitric oxide. Psychogenic and local mechanisms can induce an erection. Any type of sensory input, including auditory, tactile, visual, or imaginative can cause a psychogenic erection. Tactile stimuli initiate the local reflex mechanisms.

Ejaculation occurs with emission of semen from the epididymides, vas deferens, prostate, and seminal vesicles. Ejaculation follows constriction of the arterial vessels supplying blood to the corpora cavernosa. After ejaculation, the penis returns to its flaccid condition.

In uncircumcised males, loose, hood-like skin called the *prepuce* or *foreskin* covers the glans (Fig. 25-3). Pulling back the foreskin or prepuce exposes the glans. Sloughed epithelial cells and mucus collect between the glans and foreskin, forming a white, cheese-like substance called *smegma*. Circumcision is removal of the prepuce or foreskin.

The *scrotum* is a pouch covered with darkly pigmented, loose, rugous (wrinkled) skin. A septum divides the scrotum into two sacs, each of which contains a testis, epididymis, spermatic cord, and muscle layer known as the *cremasteric muscle*. The cremasteric muscle allows the scrotum to relax or contract.

Spermatogenesis requires a temperature below 37°C (approximately 2°C lower than core temperature). When the temperature rises, the scrotal sac relaxes; when temperature decreases, the scrotal sac rises closer to the body. The cremaster and dartos muscles control the response.

Internal Genitalia

Testes

The *testes (testicles)* are smooth, ovoid, and approximately 3.5 to 5 cm long. Commonly, the left testicle lies lower than the right. The spermatic cords suspend the testes in the scrotum (Fig. 25-4). The function of the testicles is to produce spermatozoa (sperm) and testosterone. Testosterone stimulates pubertal growth of the male genitalia, prostate, and seminal vesicles.

Inside each testicle is a series of coiled ducts known as *seminiferous tubules*, which is where spermatogenesis occurs. Mature sperm are generated approximately every 90 days. As sperm are produced, they move toward the center of the testicle, travelling into the efferent tubules adjacent to the ductus epididymis. The rete testis is a network of channels fed by the seminiferous tubules and connected to the epididymis (Diehl-Jones & Bickley, 2010).

Ducts

Ducts are responsible for moving sperm. The journey begins in the epididymides and continues to the *vas deferens*, ejaculatory duct, and urethra. The soft, comma-shaped *epididymis* is on the posterolateral and upper aspect of the testicles. This structure provides for storage, maturation, and transit of sperm. The *vas deferens (ductus deferens)* transports sperm from the epididymis to the ejaculatory duct. The vas deferens, arteries, veins, and nerves make up the *spermatic cord*, which ascends through the external inguinal ring and into the inguinal canal. Inside the canal and just before the entrance into the prostate gland, the vas deferens unites with the seminal vesicle to form the ejaculatory duct.

Once sperm enter the ejaculatory duct, they are transported downward through the prostate gland and into the posterior portion of the urethra. The urethra is approximately 18 to 20 cm long, extending from urinary bladder to meatus. The urethra can be separated into three sections: (1) posterior, (2) membranous, and (3) cavernous or anterior. It extends from the base of the bladder, travelling through the prostate gland down the shaft of the penis. The urethral opening is a small slit at the tip of the penis; it is the exit for both sperm and urine.

Secretory Structures

The seminal vesicles, prostate gland, and bulbourethral glands produce and secrete ejaculation fluid known as *semen*. The semen provides an alkaline medium needed for motility and survival of the sperm. The seminal vesicles are small pouches located between the rectum and posterior bladder wall; the vesicles join the ejaculatory duct at the base of the prostate.

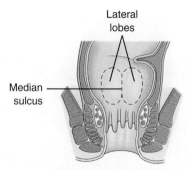

Lateral
lobes

Median
sulcus

Figure 25-5 The prostate gland.

The *prostate gland* contains muscular and glandular tissue (Fig. 25-5). It has three lobes (two lateral, one median) and is approximately 3.5 cm long × 4.0 cm wide. The prostate gland surrounds the urethra at the bladder neck; its shape resembles a large chestnut. The physiologic function of the prostate and its secretion is not fully understood; however, it produces the greatest volume of ejaculatory fluid. The right and left lobes of the prostate are divided by a slight groove known as the *median sulcus*. These two lobes are in close contact with the anterior rectal wall and are palpable during digital rectal examination (DRE). The median lobe is anterior to the urethra and cannot be palpated on a rectal examination.

Clinical Significance 25-1

Usually, the middle and lateral lobes are above the ejaculatory ducts and typically involved in benign prostatic hyperplasia (BPH). The exact cause of BPH is unknown, but the condition is believed to be associated with age-related hormonal changes. As men age, the fibromuscular structures of the prostate gland atrophy, and collagen gradually replaces the muscular element of the prostate.

The *bulbourethral glands* are located on either side of the urethra immediately below the prostate gland (Swartz, 2006).

Rectum and Anus

The rectum and anus constitute the terminal sections of the gastrointestinal tract and are included in the posterior portion of the male perineum examination.

Rectum

The rectum is approximately 12 cm long and is superior to the anus. The proximal end of the rectum is continuous with the sigmoid colon. The distal end, commonly referred to as the *anorectal junction*, is identifiable during a colonoscopy as having a sawtooth-like edge. Located above the anorectal junction, the rectum dilates and turns posteriorly into the hollow area of the coccyx and sacrum; this forms the *rectal ampulla*, which stores flatus and feces. Three semilunar transverse folds, known as *rectal valves,* are located in the rectum. The valves extend across half the diameter of the rectum with the inferior valve palpable on digital examination. The exact

functions of these valves are unknown; however, the valves may support feces while flatus is being expelled.

Anal Canal and Anus

The male anal canal is approximately 2.5 to 4.0 cm long and extends from the anorectal junction to the anal sphincter. It is lined with mucous membrane arranged in longitudinal folds called *rectal columns*, which contain a complex system of veins and arteries commonly referred to as the *internal hemorrhoidal plexus*. Between each column is a recessed area identified as the anal crypt. The perineal glands empty into the anal crypt. Around the anal canal are two concentric rings of muscles, the internal and external sphincters. The internal sphincter contains smooth muscle and is under involuntary control. The sensation to defecate comes when the rectum fills with stool, which causes reflexive stimulation that relaxes the internal sphincter. The striated external sphincter consists of skeletal muscles and is under voluntary control; this allows for control of defecation.

The anal canal perceives pain differently; the autonomic nervous system controls the upper portion, which is relatively insensitive to stimuli. Conversely, the lower portion, which is controlled by somatic sensory nerves, is sensitive to stimulation. The anal canal direction is on an imaginary line between the anus and the umbilicus.

The anus is the terminal portion of the rectum. The moist mucosal tissue is pink and surrounded by hyperpigmented perianal skin; hair may be present in the adult. The anus is closed except during defecation.

▲ Lifespan Considerations

Infants and Children

Newborns usually pass the first meconium stool within 24 to 48 hours of birth. At this time, both the internal and external sphincters are under involuntary reflexive control because the myelination of the spinal cord is incomplete. It is common for infants to have a stool after each feeding because of the gastrocolic reflex. Commonly between 12 and 18 months of age, infants gradually achieve control of the external anal sphincter (Seidel, Ball, et al., 2003).

There is much debate over whether circumcision should be performed routinely. Recent evidence suggests fewer urinary tract infections in males who have been circumcised. A 2009 Cochrane review of observational studies presented strong evidence that male circumcision was associated with a reduced risk of acquiring HIV through vaginal intercourse (Siegfried, Muller, et al., 2009). Nonetheless, these benefits are not significant enough to recommend that all males be circumcised.

Because circumcision has potential benefits and risks, parents should determine what is in the best interest of the child. Often the decision is based on family tradition, culture, religion, and ethnic traditions. If parents decide to circumcise their son, the nurse needs to obtain informed consent before the procedure. The Canadian Paediatric Society (CPS, 1996) reviewed its position statement on circumcision and recognized that evidence for analgesia during circumcision is strong, but could not recommend the most effective mode of analgesia without further research. A review of that position statement

Figure 25-6 A health care professional is injecting a local anesthetic while preparing an infant boy for circumcision.

commenced in 2009, but currently the CPS does not recommend that circumcision be performed routinely. Pain-relieving interventions that are used include local anesthetics, dorsal penile nerve blocks, and subcutaneous ring blocks (Fig. 25-6).

Adolescents

With the onset of puberty, testicular growth begins and the scrotal skin thins and becomes pendulous. During puberty, the testes become active and begin to secrete testosterone, which promotes bone maturation and epiphyseal closure. Genital hair begins to appear at the base of the penis. As physical development continues, genital hair darkens and extends over the entire pubic area; it is at this time that the prostate gland enlarges. When maturation is complete, genital hair is curly, dense, and coarse, with a diamond shape from umbilicus to anus. Growth and development of the scrotum and testes are complete, and the length and width of the penis are increased.

> ### Clinical Significance 25-2
>
> Each adolescent has his own unique growth timetable and final growth results. The nurse considers the patient's external environment and genetic predispositions. Nevertheless, chronological patterns are consistent for all (see Table 25-1 for the Tanner stages).

Table 25-1	Tanner Stages: Male Development	
Stage*	**Male Development**	**Age Range (y)**
1	There is no pubic hair. Testes and penis are small (prepubertal).	<10
2	Sparse thin hair is at base of the penis. Testes enlarge. Scrotal skin becomes coarser and redder.	10–13
3	Scrotum and testes continue to grow. Penis lengthens, with diameter increasing slowly. Pubic hair increases, becoming darker, coarse, curly, and extending laterally.	12–14
4	Penis and testes continue to grow. Pubic hair extends across pubis but spares the medial thighs.	13–15
5	Penis is at its full size. Pubic hair is diamond shaped in appearance with adult colour; texture extends to surface of medial thighs.	14–17

*The Tanner stages present a scale of physical development for children, adolescents, and adults. The maturation process is based on external primary and secondary sex characteristics. Each person passes through each stage at different rates. See also Chapters 21 and 26. From Tanner, J. (1962). *Growth at adolescence*. Oxford, UK: Blackwell.

Older Adult

Older men may experience distention of the rectum from degeneration of afferent neurons in the rectal wall, which interferes with relaxation of the internal sphincter. The distention can cause an elevated pressure threshold for the feeling of rectal distention, causing retention of stool. At the same time, the autonomically controlled internal sphincter loses tone, the external sphincter cannot, by itself, control the bowels; this may result in incontinence (Seidel, Ball, et al., 2003).

With aging, pubic hair becomes finer, gray, and less plentiful. Pubic alopecia may also occur. Testosterone levels decline with aging, which may affect both libido and sexual function. Erection becomes more dependent on tactile stimulation and less responsive to erotic cues. The penis may decrease in size and testes drop lower in the scrotum. As the male ages, the fibromuscular structures of the prostate gland atrophy. Ironically, benign hyperplasia of the glandular tissue often obscures the atrophy of aging.

Cultural Considerations

When the patient becomes ill, his or her recognition and reaction are rooted in cultural beliefs, values, social, and family structures. Illness is more than physical symptoms and pain. The concept of illness includes perceived alterations in emotional, physical, and spiritual states (Leininger & McFarland, 2002). Appreciating the patient's perception of manhood, cultural beliefs, and sexual orientation helps the nurse understand how the patient perceives health, illness, and disease. Establishing an open and trusting relationship with the patient requires a nonjudgmental attitude. A dedicated nurse can develop an awareness of cultural beliefs and values through genuine interest, active listening, and self-awareness.

In societies for thousands of years, piercings have occurred in various forms and fashions. In the last 10 years, genital piercing has increased in popularity (see Table 25-4 at the end of this chapter). Nevertheless, it can be an unexpected finding for the nurse during assessment of the male genitalia. In a professional nonjudgmental manner, it is important to talk to the patient about the care of the piercing. Because this site is very prone to infection, discussion involves how the patient cleans the piercing and ways to avoid infection. The nurse inquires how the site feels to the patient—it is possible for him to lose sensation in the area of the piercing. It may also damage strategic nerves, thus leading to an inability to achieve an orgasm.

Investigate where the piercing was done; health risks such as hepatitis, tetanus, and tuberculosis among other diseases are possible when procedures are performed in an unsterile environment. Health Canada offers guidelines for the purpose of preventing and controlling infection from establishments in the body piercing and tattooing industry. No national legislation exists to govern the industry; most businesses are regulated by municipal licensing bodies and local health units.

Acute Assessment

⚠ SAFETY ALERT 25-1

Six conditions can result in an acute scrotum: ischemia, trauma, infectious conditions, inflammatory conditions, hernia, and acute situations accompanying a chronic condition (eg, testicular tumour with rupture). Although differential diagnosis is broad, an accurate history and physical examination can often accurately define the condition. Imaging studies can correlate with the clinical assessment and expedite therapeutic decisions.

The signs and symptoms of the acutely ill genitourinary patient can range from subtle to obvious. An example of subtle signs is the patient reporting fatigue or shortness of breath upon exertion (eg, anemia from rectal bleeding). An example of more obvious behaviours is the patient reporting sudden and severe testicle pain (eg, possible testicle torsion). Patients presenting with an acute condition are anxious and tense; staying calm will help the patient relax and promote clear thinking.

Anorectal conditions can cause significant discomfort and concern. Because of the sensitive nature of this subject, patients often delay treatment. Colorectal cancer is common in adults and may be present with a benign condition. All reports need thorough investigation. Early detection has been clearly shown to lower the mortality rate for colorectal cancer.

All acute situations need immediate evaluation. It is important to compare two acute scrotal conditions: testicular torsion and epididymitis. Because torsion is a surgical emergency, it is imperative for health care providers to understand the difference (Cole & Vogler, 2004). Both diagnoses may present with the same chief concern of scrotal pain (see Table 25-3 at the end of this chapter for a discussion of the two disorders).

The patient with rectal bleeding needs rapid assessment. Bleeding associated with anorectal conditions can resolve spontaneously or with local pressure. The patient undergoing anticoagulation therapy, however, may need hospitalization. Inquire about bleeding disorders.

Newborns who have dark tarry stools or who are vomiting blood may have a vitamin K deficiency. Infants presenting with rectal bleeding could have necrotizing enterocolitis. This life-threatening disease needs immediate action.

Acute infection (eg, perirectal abscess) may require immediate hospitalization, especially for immunocompromised patients. Infection usually is associated with purulent discharge from the penis. Patients with HIV/AIDS or receiving chemotherapy are especially at risk (Dains, Baumann, et al., 2003).

Subjective Data Collection

Subjective data collection includes a focused health history related to common symptoms, assessment of risk factors, health promotion, and health-related patient education. This includes assessments for prostate and testicular cancer. Additionally, it is important to assess risk for sexually transmitted infections (STIs).

Assessment of Risk Factors

Numerous factors affect the male genitalia, rectum, and anus. The nurse asks the patient about current concerns, personal history (including age, gender, and ethnicity), medications and supplements, family history, and risk factors for infections or cancer. Knowledge of risk factors helps identify topics for health promotion.

Questions to Assess History and Risk Factors	Rationale
Personal History Do you have any current or chronic illnesses such as diabetes? Hypertension? Neurologic impairment? Respiratory conditions (asthma, chronic obstructive pulmonary disease, chronic bronchitis)? Or cardiovascular disease?	Men with these illnesses are at increased risk for erectile dysfunction (Lewis, Rosen, et al., 2003).
Medical and Surgical History • Was surgery ever performed on your penis, scrotum, or rectum? • What type of procedure was performed (please include year and date)? • How has this procedure affected you?	Surgery is used to treat an enlarged prostate, testicular cancer, hydrocele, varicocele, and undescended testicle. Some men choose permanent sterilization through vasectomy. Rectal or anal conditions requiring surgery include hemorrhoids, anorectal fissures, and carcinoma of the rectum and anus.
• Have you ever been treated for a sexually transmitted infection (STI)? • Where and when did you receive this treatment? • What type of STI was diagnosed? • How was it treated? • Did you have a test of cure following the procedure?	There are more than 50 different STIs, which are sensitive but important subjects. Tactful direct questioning is an essential part of the assessment (see Box 25-1).

> **BOX 25-1   RISK FACTORS FOR SEXUALLY TRANSMITTED INFECTIONS**
>
> • Engaging in sexual relations with a new or multiple partners*
> • Personal history of sexually transmitted infections (STIs) or engaging in sexual activity with a partner with a history of STIs*
> • Engaging in a relationship with a partner who has several partners*
> • Failure to practise safer sex*
>
> STIs can be transmitted through vaginal, rectal, or oral sex between homosexual or heterosexual partners.
>
> *The risk factor is modifiable.

• Have you ever had an injury to or other concerns with your scrotum? Penis? Or testes? If yes, please explain.	Examples include *testicular torsion, hydrocele, spermatocele,* and *varicocele.*
• Have you had a condition affecting the prostate gland such as benign prostatic hyperplasia (BPH) or prostatitis?	Identification of previous problems may help when documenting current health concerns.
• Do you have a history of cancer? • When was the diagnosis? • What treatment did you have?	See Box 25-2 for risk factors for testicular, prostate, and penile cancers (common cancers found in men). Even with removal of a cancerous testicle, cancer can recur in the other testicle.

(text continues on page 762)

BOX 25-2 RISK FACTORS FOR TESTICULAR, PROSTATE, AND PENILE CANCER

Testicular Cancer

- Age 15 to 49 years (higher incidence in males 15–29 years)
- Genetic background (highest incidence among Caucasian men)
- Cryptorchidism (undescended testicle at birth)
- History of testicular cancer in other testicle
- Family history (increased risk if brother or father has had testicular cancer)

Prostate Cancer

- Third leading cause of cancer death in men
- Family history of prostate cancer
- Age: Highest incidence is in older men; 75% of new cases occur in men older than 65 years

- Heritage: Men of African genetic background have the highest incidence of prostate cancer—two times higher than white men. Worldwide, the highest prevalence is in North America and northwestern Europe

Penile Cancer

- Phimosis (the foreskin of the penis cannot be pulled back over the glans)*
- Age ≥60 years
- Compromised personal hygiene*
- Sexual promiscuity*
- Use of tobacco products*
- Possible link with human papillomavirus*

*This risk factor is modifiable.
Data from American Cancer Society. (2008). *What are the risk factors for testicular cancer?* Atlanta, GA: Author; www.nci.nih.gov and http:www.cancer.org American Urology Association (www.urologyhealth.org); National Cancer Institute's Factsheets http://www.nci.nih.gov/cancertopics; Canadian Cancer Society's Steering Committee for Cancer Statistics. (2011). *Canadian cancer statistics 2011*. Toronto, ON: Canadian Cancer Society.

Questions to Assess History and Risk Factors	Rationale
Medications	
What medications do you currently take? Herbal supplements? Recreational drugs? And over-the-counter drugs?	Many medications and supplements can affect the genitourinary tract and its function.
Family History	
Is there a family history of testicular cancer?	Risk for testicular cancer is greater in men whose brother or father had the disease (Canadian Cancer Society [CCS], 2010a) (see Box 25-2).
Is there a family history of prostate cancer?	Prostate cancer in a first-degree relative increases the patient's risk. Men of African heritage have the highest incidence of prostate cancer—two to three times higher than Caucasian men. Prevalence is highest in North America and Europe (American Cancer Society, 2008) (see Box 25-2).
Is there a history of penile cancer in your family?	Although rare, some studies suggest an association between penile cancer and human papillomavirus (Palefsky, 2007) (see Box 25-2).
Is there infertility in siblings?	Encourage the patient to review his family tree for signs of infertility, especially if he is unable to impregnate.
Is there a history of hernia in your family?	Congenital weakness may predispose the patient to develop a hernia.
Additional Risk Factors	
What protective gear do you wear during contact sports?	Lack of protection can lead to injury of sensitive genitalia. This question can provide a good teaching opportunity to encourage the use of protective equipment.
Have you received the hepatitis A or B vaccine?	△ SAFETY ALERT 25-2 *The Centers for Disease Control and Prevention (CDCP, 2006) recommend the hepatitis A vaccine for unimmunized men who have sex with other men. The CDC recommends the hepatitis B vaccine for all unimmunized people at risk for STIs.*
Do you perform genital self-examination?	This question serves as an excellent teaching opportunity while stressing to the patient the importance of the self-examination.
How often do you have clinical examinations by a health professional?	Primary prevention helps patients maintain health. Age-appropriate health screenings should be discussed during the appointment.

Risk Assessment and Health Promotion

It is important for men to screen themselves for testicular cancer by performing self-examination. Screening for prostate cancer is through laboratory blood testing (prostate-specific antigen [PSA] level) and physical examination (DRE). Diagnosis is made using needle biopsy.

Testicular Self-Examination

The purpose of performing self-examination is not to find something currently wrong. By performing monthly self-examinations, men older than 14 years become familiar with what is usual for them. Once this baseline is established, changes are easier to identify. Testicular cancer can be detected at an early (and most often curable) stage. Steps for testicular self-examination (TSE) are as follows:

1. TSE is best performed after a warm shower or bath. Heat relaxes the scrotum, which makes the TSE easier.
2. Examine each testicle one at a time with both hands. Place the index and middle fingers under the testicle with the thumbs placed on top. Roll the testicle gently from side to side. You should not feel pain. Remember that one testicle may be larger; this finding is expected (Fig. 25-7).
3. Cancerous lumps usually are on the sides of the testicle but can show up on the front. Become familiar with the location of the epididymis; this soft, tube-like structure behind the testes collects and carries sperm. If you become familiar with this structure you won't mistake it for a lump.
4. Make an appointment with a physician, preferably a urologist, as soon as possible if you find a lump or any of the following warning signs: enlargement of the testes, pain or discomfort, heaviness in the scrotum, a dull ache in the groin, significant loss of size of one testicle, or a sudden collection of fluid in the scrotum (CCS, 2010a, 2011).

Screening for Prostate Cancer

After nonmelanoma skin cancer, prostate cancer is the most common cancer in Canadian men. One in 7 will develop prostate cancer, and 1 in 28 will die from it in Canada (CCS, 2011). The screening PSA test has benefits and risks. Earlier detection improves chances of survival, but the risks include false-positive and false-negative results, as well as identification of tumours that would not need treatment (CCS, 2010b). Several factors are considered in the debate over PSA testing. The PSA test does not diagnose cancer, PSA levels naturally increase with age, and many prostate cancers are slow-growing. Nonetheless, in combination with DRE, PSA can put men's concerns at ease or lead to further testing (biopsy) and early diagnosis before the cancer leads to symptoms or spreads beyond the prostate (CCS, 2010b).

Focused Health History Related to Common Symptoms/Signs

Common Symptoms/Signs Related to the Male Genitalia and Rectum

- Pain
- Difficulty with urination (weak stream, frequent urination)
- Erectile dysfunction
- Change in sexual desire (libido)
- Penile lesions, discharge
- Scrotal swelling, heaviness, pain, or aching
- Bulge in the groin (hernia)
- Rectal bleeding, itching, or burning
- Anal pain
- Passing gas (flatulence)
- Dribbling (urinary or fecal incontinence)

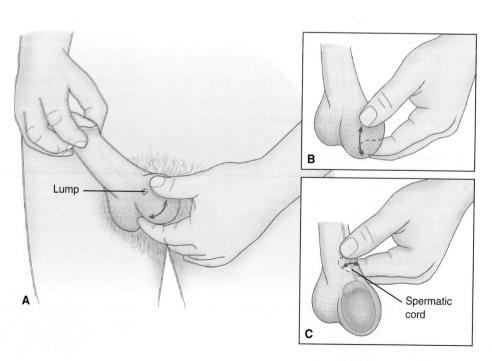

Figure 25-7 The testicular self-examination. **A.** The patient holds the penis in one hand away from the testicles while using the other hand to palpate one testicle at a time. The patient should roll the area side to side to feel for any lumps. **B.** He also should manoeuvre his fingers up and down. **C.** The patient should also run his fingers along the surface length of the spermatic cord to become familiar with how it feels, so that he does not mistake this for a lump.

Lump

B

Spermatic cord

A

C

Adapted from Diehl-Jones, W., & Bickley, L. S. (2010). Male genitalia and hernias. In T. C. Stephen, D. L. Skillen, R. A. Day, & L. S. Bickley (Eds.). *Canadian Bates' guide to health assessment for nurses* (1st ed., p. 765). Philadelphia, PA: Wolters Kluwer Health/Lippincott Williams & Wilkins.

Examples of Questions to Assess Symptoms/Signs	Rationale/Unexpected Findings
Pain Please point to the painful area. • Do you feel the pain anywhere else? • What does the pain feel like? • Can you rate your pain on a scale of 0 to 10, with 10 being the worst pain you ever had? • When did it begin? How long have you had this pain? Have you ever experienced this pain before? • Is the pain associated with nausea? Vomiting? Fever? Abdominal distention? Or, burning on urination? Is your urine a different colour? • What makes the pain worse or better? What have you done to help alleviate the pain, if anything? How well did this intervention help? • Is anything going on in your environment that could have contributed to this? • What is your pain goal? • What do you think is causing your pain?	Several conditions can lead to pain in the lower abdominal, pelvic, or rectal areas. Sudden distention of the ureter, renal pelvis, or bladder may cause flank pain. Pain around the costovertebral angle may be from distention of the renal capsule. *Kidney stone* pain may radiate down the spermatic cord and present as testicular pain. Pain in the groin or scrotum may result from a *hernia* or conditions of the spermatic cord, testicles, or prostate. Testicular pain can occur secondary to any disorder of the testes such as *epididymitis, orchitis, hydrocele, spermatic cord torsion,* and *tumour.* Understanding what interventions the patient does to relieve the pain assists with developing a treatment plan. Always ask about use of over-the-counter medications, current prescriptions, and complementary substances.
Have you ever had a prolonged painful erection?	A long-lasting and painful erection is called *priapism.* It can be seen in patients with *leukemia* or *hemoglobinopathies* (eg, sickle cell anemia). This is not from sexual excitation—the prolonged erection results from vein thrombosis in the corpora cavernosa (Swartz, 2006) or medications (eg, Cialis).
Are you experiencing rectal or anal pain?	*Perianal abscess, rectal fissure,* and *hemorrhoids* are among the most painful conditions of the anus and rectum.
Difficulty With Urination • Do you have trouble starting a stream of urine? • Is there a change in the flow of urine? • Do you have sudden urges to urinate? • Can you estimate how much urine is passed with each void or urination? • Do you need to urinate at night? • Are you straining to urinate? • Have you been drinking more fluids than usual?	Urgency and frequency may be from *UTI, prostatitis, sexually transmitted infection (STI),* or low-grade *bladder cancer.* Prostate enlargement is common in older men. Because of the location of the gland, it can affect urine flow. The following are signs of partial prostate obstruction: recurrent acute UTIs, the sensation of residual urine, decreased calibre of the urine stream, hesitancy, straining, and terminal dribbling.
• Do you involuntarily lose small amounts of urine? • What colour is your urine? Do you ever notice red urine?	Blood in the urine can be associated with a benign disease, a clinically insignificant issue (eg, eating red-coloured food such as beets), or life-threatening malignancy. It is, therefore, one of the most common and important signs for the nurse to investigate (Turner, 2008).

Examples of Questions to Assess Symptoms/Signs	Rationale/Unexpected Findings

Male Sexual Dysfunction

- Do you have persistent erections unrelated to sexual stimulation?
- With an erection, do you have a curvature of the penis in any direction?
- Do you have difficulty achieving erection; is there pain associated with the erection?
- When you have sexual stimulation or intercourse, how often do you ejaculate (colour, consistency, and amount)?
- How strong is your sex drive? Over the last month how would you rate your confidence to keep and maintain an erection?
- If you were to spend the rest of your life with your sexual function just the way it is now, how would you feel about that?

The main types of sexual dysfunction include premature ejaculation, erectile dysfunction (difficulty achieving or maintaining erection), low libido (sexual interest), delayed orgasm, and physical abnormalities of the penis (Albaugh, Amargo, et al., 2002). Erectile dysfunction cannot be seen or felt during an assessment; this issue is important to discuss with the patient. Many men welcome the opportunity to discuss erectile dysfunction, but often, nurses are reluctant to bring up the subject. Presenting the topic in a nonthreatening, nonjudgmental manner encourages the patient to talk about matters of concern. An example of an opening statement for the patient whose hypertension is controlled with medication is "High blood pressure medications often cause erectile dysfunction. Have you experienced any difficulties?" (Lewis, Rosen, et al., 2003)

Penile Lesions, Discharge, or Rash

- When did you first note the lesion? Is there more than one?
- Does the lesion itch? Burn? Sting? Or is it painful?
- Is there discharge? When did discharge begin? Is there an odour or colour associated with it?
- If you are sexually active, does your partner have the same symptoms? Has there been a change in sexual partners?

Direct, tactful questions about history of exposure to STIs are important. A lesion should alert the nurse to the possibility of STI. Ask if the patient has had *genital warts, syphilis, gonorrhea, trichomoniasis,* or other STIs. Assess if any discharge is continuous or intermittent. Bloody penile discharge is associated with *urethritis* and *neoplasm.* Tactfully explore if the patient has been with a new partner recently or if there has been a change in sexual habits.

Scrotal Enlargement

- When did you first notice the enlargement?
- Is there pain associated with it? Is pain intermittent or constant? Associated with lifting or straining?
- Has there been any recent trauma to the groin?
- Have you ever had a hernia? Do you use a truss or any treatment?
- Have you had any concerns about fertility?

Although rarely fatal, scrotal enlargement and pain carry a risk of morbidity from testicular atrophy, infarction, or necrosis. Any patient with scrotum pain should be presumed to have testicular torsion until this diagnosis can be proven otherwise. Accurate history and assessing skills contribute to an accurate diagnosis. Assess the patient for *varicoceles,* which are often linked with infertility.

Documentation of Expected Findings

Patient denies pain or discomfort. Reports no difficulty with urination. States that he has no premature ejaculation, erectile dysfunction, low libido, delayed orgasm, or physical changes of the penis. No lesions, discharge, or scrotal enlargement.

 Lifespan Considerations

Additional Questions	Rationale/Unexpected Findings

Newborns, Infants, and Children

Has your baby ever had any genital defects (such as phimosis, hydrocele, failure of the testes to descend, hypospadias, epispadias, or ambiguous genitalia)?

External genital defects are usually obvious at birth. Surgical correction may be necessary.

For toddlers: Is your child toilet trained? Is there any difficulty with wetting the bed at night?

Toilet training usually begins at around 2 years.

For adolescents: At around your age, boys often experience body changes, "wet dreams," and other issues related to sexuality. Do you have any concerns related to these issues?

Allow adolescents permission to discuss these sensitive issues. A boy may feel guilty about these things if he is not told that they are common.

For adolescents: Have you ever had oral sex or sexual intercourse?

The American Academy of Pediatrics (1999) recommends asking adolescents about sexual activity at each annual clinic visit and offering sexually transmitted infection (STI) screening to all sexually active teens. Adolescents are at higher risk for STIs than adults.

(text continues on page 766)

Additional Questions	Rationale/Unexpected Findings
Older Adults	
Are you noticing urinary dribbling? Urgency? Or frequency? Do you feel that your bladder does not completely empty?	Disorders of the prostate, including hyperplasia and cancer, are more common in older adults.
Often older adults may notice a change in their sexual function as they age. Have you noticed any such changes?	Older adults may notice that it may take longer to obtain an erection or ejaculate. Also consider coexisting illnesses and medications that may affect sexual function. A trend to increasing incidence of STIs among older adults is being seen. Menopause and drugs for erectile dysfunction are increasing the risk of chlamydia infections when safer sex is not practised.

Cultural Considerations

Additional Questions	Rationale/Unexpected Findings
Based on your age, ethnicity, and sexual preference, what do you perceive as your risk for developing HIV or STIs?	In young men who have sex with men, new HIV infections in blacks are 1.6 times the number in whites and 2.3 times the number in Hispanics (Quinn, Bartlett, et al., 2011). Men who have sex with men are also at higher risk for genital herpes. They should be offered STI screening at the annual visit.

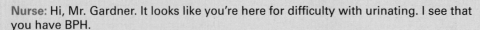

An Example of a Therapeutic Dialogue

Remember Mr. Alex Gardner, who was introduced at the beginning of this chapter. He is a 50-year-old man with a history of benign prostatic hyperplasia (BPH) and increasing symptoms. The nurse uses professional communication techniques to gather subjective data from Mr. Gardner.

Nurse: Hi, Mr. Gardner. It looks like you're here for difficulty with urinating. I see that you have BPH.

Mr. Gardner: Yes, I've had it for 3 years.

Nurse: Tell me more about your symptoms.

Mr. Gardner: Well, I am having more trouble with urination.

Nurse: So is that difficulty with starting your urine stream?

Mr. Gardner: Yes, and when I go, it seems like it starts and stops.

Nurse: And sometimes men also have some dribbling ...

Mr. Gardner: Yes, I've had that too, and it's embarrassing. It also seems like my bladder never completely empties. I go and then I have to go back an hour or two later.

Nurse: That must be very uncomfortable.

Mr. Gardner: Yes, it is. I am newly married and I'm worried that this might affect my relationship if I have to have surgery.

Critical Thinking Challenge

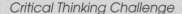

- How might the nurse prepare for the interview?
- How will the nurse discuss his concerns regarding these intimate issues?
- What concerns might Mr. Gardner have that could be further assessed?

Objective Data Collection

Equipment

- Clean nonlatex gloves
- Water-soluble lubricant
- Flashlight or penlight (for transillumination)
- Stethoscope (to listen for bowel sounds if hernia is suspected)
- Sterile swab
- Sterile saline
- Glass slide and tissue fixative
- Biohazard disposal container
- Measurements of the nurse's index finger, which can be used as a ruler to measure the patient's penis, testes, and prostate gland

Preparation: Promoting Patient Comfort, Dignity, and Safety

As a nurse, it is important to maintain a confident, professional, matter-of-fact attitude throughout the examination. Upon entering the examination room, introduce yourself and include your title. Greet the patient by his full name and ask what he prefers to be called. Before beginning the genital examination, ask permission to perform it. This step is especially important if the nurse is female. Asking permission allows the patient to gracefully ask for a male clinician for this part of the examination.

If performing a complete history and physical assessment, conduct the genital examination last. Doing so allows the patient to become more comfortable with the overall interaction. A parent should always be present for a child's genital examination. An adolescent should have a choice whether he prefers a parent or guardian present. When accompanied by a companion, an adult man should be given the same option.

The patient is examined supine, on his side, and then standing. While the patient is standing, the nurse is seated in front of him.

Clinical Significance 25-3

If the patient has an erection during the physical examination, reassure him that this is a common physiologic response to touch that he could not have prevented. Do not stop the examination—doing so could cause further embarrassment.

Comprehensive Physical Assessment: Male Genitalia and Rectum Assessment

Techniques and Expected Findings	Rationale/Unexpected Findings
Groin and Pubic Area With the patient supine, inspect the groin and pubic area. Observe genital hair distribution. *Skin is clear, intact, and smooth. Hair is diamond shaped or in an escutcheon pattern. Hair appears coarser than on the scalp and has no parasites.*	Unexpected genital hair findings are no hair, patchy growth, or distribution in a female or triangular pattern with the base over the pubis. Observe for any infestations such as *pediculosis, scabies,* or any parasites. Look for inflammation, lesions, or dermatitis. *Candidiasis* infections cause crusty, multiple, red, round erosions and pustules; this infection is associated with immunological deficiencies (Albaugh & Kellogg-Spadt, 2003). *Tinea cruris* (commonly referred to as "jock itch") is a fungal infection on the patient's groin and upper thighs. It appears with large red, scaly patches that are extremely itchy. Tinea cruris rarely involves the scrotum.
Penis Observe the penis for surface characteristics, colour, lesions, and discharge. Be sure to inspect the posterior surface. *The dorsal vein is apparent on the dorsal surface of the penis. The penis has no edema, lesions, discharge, or nodules.* In the patient with an uncircumcised penis, the prepuce covers the glans. Ask him to retract the prepuce. *The prepuce retracts easily. Smegma (a thin, white, cheesy substance) may be present around the corona.* In the patient with a circumcised penis, the glans and corona are visible, lighter in colour than the shaft, and free of smegma. *Circumcised penises have varying lengths of foreskin: some have folds of skin, while others have no extra foreskin* (see Fig. 25-1).	Unexpected conditions include piercings, *phimosis* (foreskin cannot retract), *paraphimosis* (foreskin is retracted and fixed), and *balanitis* (related to diabetes) (see Table 25-4 at the end of this chapter).

(text continues on page 768)

Glans. Inspect the glans. *It is glistening pink, smooth in texture, and bulbous.*

Shaft. Inspect and palpate the shaft. *It feels smooth without lesions or pain. Variations include ectopic sebaceous glands on the shaft that appear as tiny, whitish-yellow papules.*

External urethral meatus. Inspect and palpate the external urethral meatus (Fig. 25-8). *It is located centrally on the glans. The orifice is slit-like and millimetres from the tip of the penis. The external urethral meatus has no discharge, stenosis, or warts.* The glans can be opened by pressing it between the thumb and forefinger. The patient can be instructed to do this. Next, strip or milk the penis from the base toward the glans or head. Note colour, consistency, or odour of any discharge. *The glans is smooth and pink with no discharge.*

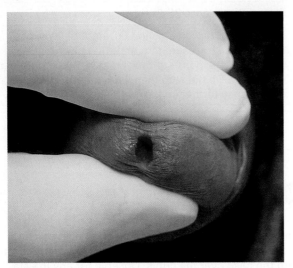

Figure 25-8 Inspecting and palpating the external urinary meatus.

Scrotum

Ask the patient to hold the penis out of the way, and inspect the scrotal septum. Inspect the anterior and posterior scrotum for any sores or rashes. *It is divided into two sacks. The scrotum hangs asymmetrically, with the left side lower than the right usually. Sebaceous cysts or sebaceous glands may be noted on the scrotal sac. The anterior and posterior scrotal skin appears darker in pigmentation with a rugous or wrinkled surface.*

Sacrococcygeal Areas

Inspect the sacrococcygeal areas for surface characteristics and tenderness. *Skin is clear and smooth with no palpable masses or dimpling.*

Perineal Area

With the patient on his side, spread the buttocks and inspect the perineal area. *Skin surrounding the anus is coarse with darker pigmentation. The anal sphincter is closed.*

Aberrations of the glans include *hypospadias* (urethral meatus on underside) and *epispadias* (meatus on upper side) (see Table 25-4 at the end of this chapter).

Discharge may be yellow, milky-white, or greenish and may have a foul odour. It needs immediate attention (see Table 25-5 at the end of this chapter).

Scrotal lesions, edema, and redness are unexpected. When examining the scrotum, certain diseases (eg, diabetic neuropathy, syphilis) may render the testes totally insensitive to pain. Renal, cardiac, and hepatic illness may result in scrotal edema. If there are inconsistencies in size or texture, be alert for possible infection, tumour, or cyst. Unexpected scrotal conditions include *testicular torsion, epididymitis, varicocele, hydrocele,* and *spermatocele* (see Tables 25-4 and 25-6 at the end of this chapter).

A dimple with an inflamed tuft of hair or a tender palpable cyst in the sacrococcygeal area suggests a *pilonidal cyst* or *sinus*. Generally, the patient is asymptomatic unless the area becomes infected. Once infected, redness, tenderness, and a cyst can be palpated. When ruptured, the cyst drains purulent, mucoid secretions. Often, the patient is febrile.

A penlight assists in inspecting for *warts,* loose sphincter, lesions, *hemorrhoids,* fissures, fistulas, or polyps. Infestations from pinworms or fungal infections make this area appear irritated and erythemic (see Table 25-7 at the end of this chapter).

Techniques and Expected Findings (continued)

Inguinal Region and Femoral Areas

Instruct the patient to stand. Ask him to bear down. While he does so, inspect the inguinal canal area and femoral area for bulges or masses.

Rationale/Unexpected Findings (continued)

Bulges or masses suggest a **hernia**. If a bulge is noted, the inguinal canal needs to be palpated (see Table 25-8 at the end of this chapter).

Documentation of Expected Findings

Skin is clear, intact, and smooth. No masses or lesions noted. Foreskin intact. No phimosis or paraphimosis. Penis size is appropriate to age and smooth without lesions or pain. No discharge, edema, or redness.

Special Circumstances or Advanced Techniques

Technique and Expected Findings

Rationale/Unexpected Findings

Testicles

After inspection of the scrotal sac, palpate each testicle separately. *Note the smooth, rubbery consistency of each testicle; no nodules are felt.*

The epididymis is located discretely on the posterolateral surface of each testicle. *It feels smooth and nontender.*

Vas Deferens

Next, palpate the vas deferens, which is located in the spermatic cord and has accompanying arteries and veins (Fig. 25-9). It may be difficult to palpate; however, it feels like a smooth, cord-like structure. *As the nurse palpates from the testicle to the inguinal ring, no nodules or lesions are palpable.*

Irregularities in texture or size may indicate an infection, tumour, or cyst.

Note the place of any concerns with the epididymis and if the condition resolves itself when the patient is supine.

An unexpected finding is tenderness, tortuosity, thickening, or a mass-like structure (see Table 25-6 at the end of this chapter).

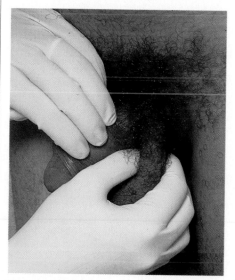

Figure 25-9 Palpating the vas deferens.

Transillumination of the Scrotum

Transillumination of the scrotum is done to assess for evidence of a mass or fluid.

The testes and epididymides do not transilluminate.

Note any masses proximal or distal to the testes. Assess for any pain or tenderness. *Hydroceles* and *spermatoceles* contain fluid and transilluminate. Tumours, epididymitis, and hernias do not (Swartz, 2006) (see Table 25-6 at the end of this chapter).

(text continues on page 770)

After palpating the scrotum for a mass or fluid, transilluminate each pouch. Use a bright penlight or transilluminator and press the light against the scrotal sac. *The sac does not contain additional fluids or contents.*

Hernias

The nurse is seated; the patient is standing. Palpate the inguinal canal for hernia. With the patient relaxed, insert your finger into the loose folds of the scrotal sac and follow it upward along the vas deferens into the inguinal canal. Which finger the nurse uses depends on the age of the patient; for a child, the little finger is appropriate, but for an adult, the index finger is used. Use the right finger for the right scrotum; left finger for the left scrotum. Palpate the oval external ring and ask the patient to bear down. If a hernia is present, you feel the sudden presence of a viscus against your finger (Fig. 25-10).

Hernias are common, but not expected. There is no bulging or pain.

Hernia occurs when a loop of intestine prolapses through the inguinal wall or canal or abdominal musculature. The patient reports pain on exertion or lifting. On examination, pain increases when manoeuvres or positioning increases intra-abdominal pressure. The only way to stop a hernia from worsening is to repair the defect surgically. Three of the more common hernias are direct/indirect inguinal and femoral (see Table 25-8 at the end of this chapter).

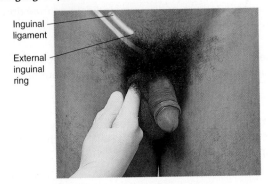

Inguinal ligament

External inguinal ring

Figure 25-10 Palpating for a hernia.

Perianal and Rectal Examination

A standing position is preferred for rectal examination, because it allows for visualization of the anus and palpation of the rectum. If the patient cannot stand, the rectal examination can be performed with the patient on his left side with the right leg flexed and the left leg semiextended. This is also known as the Sims position. A female nurse is encouraged to use the Sims position for the rectal examination, and careful draping.

Have the standing patient place both feet together, slightly flex both knees, and bend forward over the examination table (Fig. 25-11).

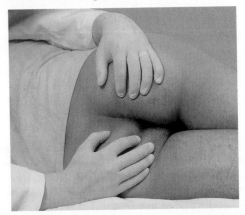

Figure 25-11 Sims positioning for rectal examination.

Anus. Spread the buttocks apart and inspect the anus. A penlight helps with visualization. Next, have the patient bear down. Observe the anus for lesions, warts, tags, hemorrhoids, fissures, and fistulas. It is helpful to use a clock for reference, 12 o'clock being ventral midline and 6 o'clock being dorsal midline.

Apply a lubricant to the index finger of the gloved hand. Explain to the patient the lubricant is used for his comfort and might feel cool. Further explain that initially he may feel like he is going to have a bowel movement; however, this will not happen. Have the patient take a deep breath while you insert the finger into the rectum, pointing towards the umbilicus along its natural direction. Rectal tone can be assessed at this time. *Full closure around the finger is palpable.* Rotate your index finger around the anal ring. *It feels smooth without nodules, masses, or irregularities.*

Continue to advance your index finger into the anal canal. *The lateral and posterior rectal walls feel smooth and uninterrupted. Internal hemorrhoids are usually not felt.*

Note any nodules, masses, irregularities, or polyps. Pay attention to any discomfort felt by the patient. Rotate your index finger to palpate the anterior rectal wall, repeating the above process. *There are no nodules, masses, irregularities, or polyps.*

Prostate. At this point of the examination, the posterior surface of the prostate gland can be felt (Fig. 25-12). Take time to explain to the patient that it may feel like he is going to urinate, but he will not. Note the prostate gland for its size, contour, consistency, and mobility. *The prostate gland has the consistency of a rubber ball. It is nontender, firm, smooth, and slightly movable. The diameter is approximately 4 cm; <1 cm protrudes into the rectum.* The lateral lobes should feel symmetric and divided by the median sulcus. The sulcus may be obliterated when the lobes are neoplastic or hypertrophied. The digital rectal examination of the prostate allows palpation of the posterior surface, which is the area where cancer often starts.

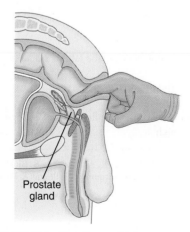

Prostate gland

Figure 25-12 Palpating the prostate.

Look for thrombosed hemorrhoids, rectal fissures, or hard stool. Hemorrhoids can be classified as external or internal. Hemorrhoids are usually caused by constant or excessive straining upon defecation. Stellate fissures may be associated with anal sex. Hard stool may be caused by diet low in fruits and vegetables, inadequate hydration, medications, or inattention to signals to defecate.

A hypotonic or lax sphincter could be from rectal surgery, neurological deficit, or trauma (often associated with anal sex). Hypertonic or tight sphincter may be associated with inflammation, scarring, or anxiety about the examination.

Patients report pain when *anal fissures* or *fistulas* are present. Local anesthesia may be necessary to complete the examination. Extreme rectal pain is associated with local disease. Because the anterior rectal wall is in contact with the peritoneum, you may be able to detect the tenderness of peritoneal inflammation and nodularity of peritoneal metastases. Unexpected findings may be related to *benign prostatic hyperplasia (BPH), prostatitis,* and *prostate cancer* (see Table 25-9 at the end of this chapter).

Prostate enlargement is classified by the amount of projection into the rectum (see Table 25-9). If the prostate feels hard, this may indicate *carcinoma, prostatic calculi,* or chronic fibrosis.

A rubbery or boggy glandular consistency may suggest BPH, a common finding in men older than 60 years. The gland may feel soft, tender, and boggy from infection. BPH is a condition of older men and may be associated with obesity and physical inactivity (Parson, Sarma, et al., 2009) It is one of the most common concerns in men older than 50 years of age. Signs and symptoms of BPH are urine retention, hesitancy, urgency, dribbling, nocturia, and straining to void. If the problem becomes chronic, the patient can develop overflow incontinence from increased intra-abdominal pressure.

⚠ *SAFETY ALERT 25-3*

Acute urine retention needs immediate intervention (Dains, Baumann, et al., 2003).

The seminal vesicles are not palpable unless they are inflamed (Uphold & Graham, 2003). Prostatitis is an inflammation or infection of the prostate gland.

(text continues on page 772)

Upon completion of the examination of the rectum, explain to the patient that you are going to remove your finger. Offer the patient a cleansing wipe and a private few minutes to redress.

Stool. Upon removing your finger from examining the rectum, inspect the gloved finger for consistency and colour of the stool.

The stool is brown and soft.

Under provincial and territorial health insurance in Canada, patients are insured for regular fecal occult blood testing (FOBT) through laboratories, using self-administered stool collection over a period of 3 days. Vitamin C supplements are to be avoided 3 days prior and during the testing period.

⚠ SAFETY ALERT 25-4

Do not massage the prostate if acute prostatitis is suspected because of the possibility of releasing bacteria and producing septicemia.

Unexpected findings include stools with an unusual colour, blood, purulent drainage, or mucus. Black tarry stool raises suspicion of upper gastrointestinal bleeding. Very light tan or grey stool could indicate obstructive jaundice. A subtle loss of blood may not change the colour of the stool but may yield a positive FOBT result, which is used to evaluate occult blood in the stool. Twelve percent of all cancer deaths in Canada are due to colorectal cancer (Canadian Cancer Society's Steering Committee for Cancer Statistics, 2011).

Examples of Documentation for Male Genitalia and Inguinal Regions

Area of Assessment	Expected Findings	Unexpected Findings
Penis	Free of skin lesions and indurations	Oval, dark red, nontender erosion with indurated base, dorsal surface of glans penis
	Prepuce retracts easily	Prepuce not retractable
	White, cheesy material present (smegma)	Foul-smelling smegma
	Glans smooth	Inflamed skin on glans penis dorsally
	Urethral meatus at distal end of glans	Meatus displaced to ventral surface of glans
	Urethral meatus opens readily and is free of discharge	Meatus does not open
	Free of tenderness	Yellow discharge at meatus
	No lateral curvature or flexion	Tenderness on palpation of shaft
Scrotum	Wrinkled, loose, free of lesions	Swelling right scrotum
	Spermatic cord palpable, smooth bilaterally	Spermatic cord thicker on left side with thickenings along cord length
		Multiple, tortuous veins in left scrotal sac
Testes	Left testis lower than right	Right testicle unyielding
	Testes firm, smooth, slightly rubbery on palpation	Firm, fixed nontender nodule 1 cm × 1 cm on right lateral testis
		Right epididymis enlarged, tender
	Free of nodules, tenderness	
	Epididymis palpable and nontender on posterior surface bilaterally	
Inguinal	Nonpalpable lymph nodes bilaterally	Tender lymph nodes in the left horizontal region >1 cm in size
	Bilaterally symmetrical and no inguinal or femoral bulges	Bulged right femoral canal
	Spermatic cord palpable into inguinal canal bilaterally	Mass touches palpating fingertip in left inguinal canal upon cough

Adapted from Diehl-Jones, W., & Bickley, L. S. (2010). Male genitalia and hernias. In T. C. Stephen, D. L. Skillen, R. A. Day, & L. S. Bickley (Eds.). *Canadian Bates' guide to health assessment for nurses* (1st ed., p. 774). Philadelphia, PA: Wolters Kluwer Health/Lippincott Williams & Wilkins.

Examples of Documentation for the Anus, Rectum, and Prostate		
Area of Assessment	**Expected Findings**	**Unexpected Findings**
Sacrococcygeal and perianal areas	Skin intact, coarse, colour of surrounding skin	Red, tender, ulcerated skin perianal area
Anus	Anal opening darkly pigmented, hairless, moist, closed; external sphincter tone intact	Tender swollen bluish mass 0.5 cm × 0.5 cm protruding from anal margin at 7 o'clock position
Rectum	Smooth, nontender rectal walls	Nonintact mucous membrane and tenderness posterior rectal wall
Prostate gland	Smooth, rubbery, heart-shaped gland; slightly moveable and nontender; defined median sulcus	1.0 cm × 1.0 cm firm hard nodule, left lateral prostate lobe; obscured median sulcus

Adapted from Bornais, J. A., & Bickley, L. S. (2010). The anus, rectum, and prostate. In T. C. Stephen, D. L. Skillen, R. A. Day, & L. S. Bickley (Eds.). *Canadian Bates' guide to health assessment for nurses* (1st ed., p. 839). Philadelphia, PA: Wolters Kluwer Health/Lippincott Williams & Wilkins.

Lifespan Considerations

Infants and Children

Rectal examination is not performed routinely on infants or children. Symptoms/signs that indicate a need for such examination include bowel alterations, abdominal distention, pelvic pain, a mass or tenderness, bleeding, bladder discomfort, pain, or distention.

If an examination is necessary, prepare the patient and caregiver before it begins. The nurse must explain every step. Use your little finger when performing rectal examinations on infants or small children. Explain to the caregiver that it is not unusual for the child or infant to have a small amount of bleeding directly following the examination. It is easier for the nurse to perform the rectal examination with the infant or child in a lithotomy position. Hold the feet together and flex the knees and hips on the abdomen. Routinely inspect the perineum, anal and surrounding areas for masses, redness, or ecchymosis. Inspect the anal area for abscess, perirectal tears, or fistulae.

When assessing an infant for rectal patency, assess whether the infant has passed meconium. If the infant has not passed any stool in the first 48 hours after birth, suspect rectal atresia.

If perirectal redness and/or excoriation are noted, remember to check for enterobiasis. Candida and other irritants can produce perineum excoriation. Rectal prolapse may be present from constipation, diarrhea, or sometimes from severe coughing. Hemorrhoids are rare in children; if they are present, it may suggest portal hypertension. Inspect the rectum for small flat flaps of skin that may be condylomas, which are syphilitic in origin. Finally, inspect the coccyx area for dimpling, sinuses, and tufts of hair in the pilonidal area, which would indicate lower spinal deformities. Lightly touching the anal area should produce an anal contraction. If no contraction is noted, assess for lower spinal cord lesion (Seidel, Ball, et al., 2003).

Next, assess for rectal tone. It should feel tight but not loose. A lax sphincter could indicate lesions in the peripheral spinal nerves or spinal cord. Bruises, scars, anal tears, and anal dilation could indicate sexual abuse and must be investigated. Lastly, feel for stool in the rectum; note whether the stool is hard or soft. Look for indications of bleeding in the fecal material on the glove.

Older Adults

In older adults, pubic hair may be thin and gray. The testes may be smaller and feel softer. The scrotal sac has less ruggae and appears to droop more. Rectal tone is intact, but strength of the rectal reflex may be reduced slightly.

Cultural Considerations

Patients with darkly pigmented skin may have darker pigmentation in the scrotal and anal area. The pubic hair may also be darker and coarser.

Evidence-Informed Critical Thinking

Nurses use assessment findings as the basis for ongoing care. An accurate and complete assessment provides a firm foundation for setting outcomes, providing individualized interventions, and evaluating progress.

Common Laboratory and Diagnostic Testing

The PSA test is a blood test that measures a protein produced by the prostate gland in men. Levels of PSA increase with infections, prostatitis, hyperplasia, age, and cancer. The test is used in combination with the DRE. It can also be used as a marker for men with a previous history of cancer to see if the cancer recurs. Because prostate cancer is more common in older men, PSA is recommended for men older than 50 years. The test is controversial because it has many false positives (positive but there is no disease) and false negatives (negative but prostate cancer is present). The

The nurse practitioner is assessing Mr. Gardner, the 50-year-old man with benign prostatic hyperplasia. Unlike the previous examples of documenting expected findings, Mr. Gardner has unexpected findings. Consider how Mr. Gardner's symptoms are increasing. Consider what other data the nurse will collect while thinking critically and anticipating nursing interventions.

Inspection: Genital hair intact and appropriate to age. No odour. Glans and corona are visible, darker in colour than the shaft of the penis, and free of smegma. Glans is slightly reddened around the meatus. The shaft of the penis is smooth without lesions or pain. Scrotum without swelling or inflammation. No masses or lesions in the inguinal or femoral area. Anal, sacrococcygeal area, perianal area, and anus are without redness, lesions, or masses. Skin is smooth and pink.

Palpation: The prostate is enlarged, symmetrical, firm, smooth, and nontender. Median sulcus is obscured.

test for fecal occult blood is done through laboratories that provide self-administered packages for testing. The FOBT is a screening strategy, and results are used to determine further investigations that would lead to diagnosis. The number of new cases of colorectal cancer and mortality from colorectal cancer has been reduced by regular screening (CCS/National Cancer Institute of Canada, 2006).

Clinical Reasoning

Nursing Diagnosis, Outcomes, and Interventions

When formulating a nursing diagnosis, it is important to use critical thinking to cluster data and identify patterns that fit together. The nurse compares these clusters with the defining characteristics (unexpected findings) for the diagnosis to ensure the most accurate labelling and appropriate interventions. Table 25-2 compares nursing diagnoses, unexpected findings, and interventions commonly related to the male assessment (North American Nursing Diagnosis Association-International, 2009).

Nurses use assessment information to identify patient outcomes. Some outcomes that are related to male genital issues or concerns include the following:

- The patient will describe alternative safe sexual practices.
- The patient will remain free of infection.
- The patient will be continent of urine (Moorhead, Johnson, et al., 2007).

Once the outcomes are established, nursing care is implemented to improve the status of the patient. The nurse uses critical thinking and evidence-informed practice to develop the interventions. Some examples of nursing interventions for the male genital system care are as follows:

- Assess the patient's knowledge and understanding of safer sexual practices.
- Teach care for the infection-prone site.
- Teach the patient exercises to strengthen the pelvic floor (Bulechek, Butcher, et al., 2008).

The nurse evaluates the care according to the patient outcomes that were developed, therefore, reassessing the patient and continuing or modifying the interventions as appropriate. Even as a beginner, the nursing student can use the patient assessment to implement new interventions, evaluate the effectiveness of those interventions, and make a difference in the quality of patient care.

Table 25-2	Common Nursing Diagnoses Associated With the Male Genital System		
Diagnosis and Related Factors	**Point of Differentiation**	**Assessment Characteristics**	**Nursing Interventions**
Ineffective sexuality pattern related to erectile dysfunction	Concern, dissatisfaction, or verbalized concerns about sex life	Alteration in relationship with significant other, changes or limitations in sexual activities and behaviours	After establishing a relationship, give the patient permission to discuss issues by asking, "Are you concerned about sexual function because of changes in your health?"
Urinary retention related to obstruction	Inability to completely empty the bladder	Increased urinary residual volume, slow stream, hesitant urination, dribbling	Obtain a postvoid bladder ultrasound. Teach double voiding and to avoid over-the-counter cold medications with decongestant

Remember Mr. Alex Gardner, whose health concerns have been outlined throughout this chapter. Initial subjective and objective data collection is complete, and the nurse has spent time reviewing the findings and other results. Unfortunately, Mr. Gardner has urinary retention, so it is necessary to reassess him and document the findings. The following nursing note illustrates how subjective and objective data are collected and analyzed and nursing interventions are developed.

Subjective: "I can't urinate and it feels like my bladder is full."

Objective: Urinary residual volume 250 mL, slow stream, hesitant urinary voiding, dribbling.

Analysis: Urinary retention related to partial obstruction

Plan: Inform urologist about residual volume. Teach the patient to avoid caffeine and alcohol, because of the diuretic effects. Teach the patient to avoid pseudoephedrine and phenylephrine found in over-the-counter cold medications. Teach double voiding. Teach to urinate every 2 to 3 hours and when first feeling the urge. Avoid rapid intake of fluids that may overdistend the bladder. Repeat bladder scan to ensure that residual volume is not increasing.

Critical Thinking Challenge

- What can Mr. Gardner do to improve his health?
- How can Mr. Gardner talk with his wife about his symptoms?
- At what point will the nurse contact the urologist regarding an acute assessment?

In this case, Mr. Gardner will need insertion of a urinary catheter if he cannot void. The nurse will need to talk with the urologist to obtain an order for a urinary catheter. Results that might trigger a consult with a urologist include urinary retention, incontinence, blood in the urine, prostate disease, kidney stones, infection of the urinary tract, infertility, and sexual dysfunction.

Mr. Gardner has been experiencing urinary retention; therefore, a urology consult is indicated. The following conversation illustrates how the nurse might organize the data and make recommendations about the patient's situation.

Situation: Hello, I'm Denise, a nurse in the outpatient urology clinic. Mr. Gardner is a 50-year-old man who has had benign prostatic hyperplasia for the past 3 years.

Background: He came in today with symptoms of incomplete bladder emptying and he had a bladder scan that showed a residual volume of 250 mL. He is also having a slow stream, hesitant urinary voiding, and dribbling.

Assessment: I am concerned that Mr. Gardner is experiencing urinary retention and will be at risk for reflux and an infection.

Recommendations: He might be developing severe enough symptoms that he needs to have a urinary catheter inserted. When would you be able to assess him?

Critical Thinking Challenge

- When will the nurse intervene with health promotion activities?
- At what point will the nurse talk with the wife about the patient's symptoms?
- What symptoms will prompt the nurse to call the urologist?

The nurse uses assessment data to formulate the patient care plan with patient outcomes and interventions for Mr. Gardner. Outcomes are specific to the patient, realistic to achieve, measurable, and have a time frame for meeting the outcome. The interventions are actions that the nurse performs based on evidence and practice guidelines. After these interventions are completed, the nurse reassesses Mr. Gardner and documents the findings in the chart to show progress toward the patient outcome. The nurse uses critical thinking and judgment to continue or revise the diagnosis, outcomes, or interventions. This is often in the form of a care plan or case note similar to the one below.

Nursing Diagnosis	Patient Outcomes	Nursing Interventions	Rationale	Evaluation
Urinary retention related to obstruction	Patient will be free from urinary tract distress.	Teach the patient to double void by urinating, resting for 3–5 min and then trying again to urinate.	Double voiding promotes more efficient bladder emptying by allowing the muscles to contract, rest, and then contract again.	Patient states that he has tried double voiding but he has discomfort and dribbling. Urologist contacted for evaluation of symptoms and possible surgery for retention.

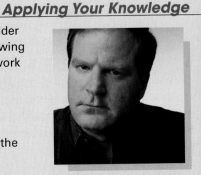

Using the previous steps of clinical reasoning, organizing, and prioritizing, consider all the case study findings woven throughout this chapter. When answering the following questions, begin drawing conclusions and see how the pieces of assessment must work together to create an environment for personalized, appropriate, and accurate care.

- Is Mr. Gardner's condition stable, urgent, or an emergency? (Knowledge)
- What are potential causes for difficulties with urination? (Comprehension)
- How will the nurse assist Mr Gardiner to relax during inspection and palpation of the male genitalia and rectum? (Application)
- What factors contribute to the patient's concerns? (Analysis)
- How will the nurse work with Mr. Gardner to promote health and reduce risk for illness? (Synthesis)
- How will the nurse evaluate the effectiveness of patient teaching? (Evaluation)

Key Points

- The anatomy of the male genitalia includes external and internal structures.
- Tanner staging is used to determine the level of male sexual development for children and adolescents.
- Health promotion topics include TSE, family planning, prevention of STIs, and screening for prostate and colorectal cancers.
- Common symptoms/signs related to male genitalia include pain, difficulty with urination, erectile dysfunction, penile lesions or discharge, and scrotal enlargement.
- During the intimate male genital assessment, it is important to provide the patient with privacy.
- The acute scrotum may be caused by ischemia, trauma, infections, inflammation, hernia, and chronic conditions with an acute exacerbation.
- Advanced practice nurses perform perianal, rectal, and prostate examinations.
- The stool is assessed for the appearance and presence of blood.
- Nursing diagnoses common following male genital assessment include ineffective sexuality patterns, risk for infection, urinary retention, and urge incontinence.

Review Questions

1. Where does spermatogenesis occur?
   A. Ductus epididymis
   B. Seminiferous tubules
   C. Ampulla of the spermatic cords
   D. Vas deferens
2. During a physical assessment, the nurse, using the handle of the reflex hammer, gently strokes the inner left thigh of the patient, which causes the ipsilateral testicle to rise. What superficial reflex is demonstrated?
   A. Abdominal reflex
   B. Babinski's reflex
   C. Brachioradialis reflex
   D. Cremasteric reflex
3. A 20-year-old Caucasian man reports a mass in his left testicle. In addition to his age and genetic background, what else is a risk factor for testicular cancer?
   A. Colon cancer in his mother
   B. Personal history of cryptorchidism
   C. Urinary tract infection last month
   D. Congenital hydrocele
4. Which of the following does the nurse recognize as an unexpected finding while performing the male genitalia examination?
   A. Smegma is present on the uncircumcised patient.
   B. Testes are palpable and firm within the scrotal sac.
   C. Impulse noted at the tip of nurse's finger during hernia examination.
   D. The urethral meatus has a slit-like opening central to the distal tip of the glans.
5. Which Tanner stage finds the base of the penis having sparse thin hair, testes beginning to enlarge, and the scrotal skin becoming coarser and redder?
   A. Stage 1
   B. Stage 2
   C. Stage 3
   D. Stage 4
   E. Stage 5
6. A 15-year-old boy presents with severe testicular pain. Which of the following is not consistent with testicular torsion?
   A. Elevation of affected testicle usually lessens pain.
   B. Testicular torsion pain is acute.
   C. There is no urethral discharge.
   D. The patient does not have a fever.
7. Upon ambulation, the patient reports a soft, irregular mass on the left side of the scrotum. The nurse palpates a mass that feels distinctly like "a bag of worms." These findings are consistent with which condition?
   A. Hydrocele
   B. Varicocele
   C. Spermatocele
   D. Epididymitis
8. A 70-year-old man presents with the following symptoms: straining to void, nocturia, dribbling, and hesitancy when voiding. These signs are consistent with what condition?
   A. Benign prostatic hyperplasia
   B. Prostatitis
   C. Testicular cancer
   D. Phimosis
9. The nurse is inspecting the genital area of an older adult man in a long-term care facility. Which of the following is an expected finding that the nurse documents?
   A. Pediculosis in hair distribution
   B. Hypospadias on glans
   C. Yellow discharge from meatus
   D. Smegma under foreskin
10. Which sexually transmitted infection presents with painful red superficial vesicles along the penis or on the glans?
    A. Gonorrhea
    B. Chlamydia
    C. Syphilis
    D. Herpes II

Canadian Nursing Research

Hunter, K. F., Moore, K. N., et al. (2007). Pelvic floor muscle training to improve urinary incontinence after radical prostatectomy: A systematic review of effectiveness. *BJU International, 100*(5), 1191–1192.

Milne, J. L., Spiers, J. A., et al. (2008). Men's experiences following laparoscopic radical prostatectomy: A qualitative descriptive study. *EMBASE International Journal of Nursing Studies, 45*(5), 765–774.

Moore, K. N., Truong, V., et al. (2007). Urinary incontinence after radical prostatectomy: Can men at risk be identified preoperatively? *EMBASE Journal of Wound, Ostomy and Continence Nursing, 34*(3), 270–279.

References

Albaugh, J., Amargo, I., et al. (2002). Health care clinicians in sexual health medicine: Focus on erectile dysfunction. *Urologic Nursing, 22*(4), 217–231.

Albaugh, J. A., & Kellogg-Spadt, S. (2003). Genital and dermatologic examination. Part II: The male patient. *Urologic Nursing, 23*(5), 366–367.

American Academy of Pediatrics. (1999). Circumcision policy statement. *Pediatrics, 103*(3), 686–693.

American Cancer Society. (2008). *What are the risk factors for testicular cancer?* Atlanta, GA: Author.

American Gastroenterology Association. (2009). *Prostate specific antigen best practice statement: 2009 update.* Retrieved from http://www.auanet.org/content/guidelines-and-quality-care/clinical-guidelines/main-reports/psa09.pdf

Bornais, J. A., & Bickley, L. S. (2010). The anus, rectum, and prostate. In T. C. Stephen, D. L. Skillen, R. A. Day, & L. S. Bickley (Eds.). *Canadian Bates' guide to health assessment for nurses* (1st ed., pp. 829–845). Philadelphia, PA: Wolters Kluwer Health/Lippincott Williams & Wilkins.

Bulechek, G. M., Butcher, H. K., et al. (2008). *Nursing interventions classification (NIC)* (5th ed.). St. Louis, MO: Mosby.

Canadian Cancer Society. (2010a). *Causes of testicular cancer.* Retrieved from http://www.cancer.ca/canada-wide/about%20cancer/types%20of%20cancer/causes%20of%20testicular%20cancer.aspx?sc_lang=en

Canadian Cancer Society. (2010b). *What you should know about PSA testing.* Retrieved from http://www.cancer.ca/Canada-wide/Prevention/Getting%20checked/What%20you%20should%20know%20about%20PSA%20testing.aspx?sc_lang=en

Canadian Cancer Society. (2011). *Risk factors for testicular cancer.* Retrieved from http://info.cancer.ca/cce-ecc./default.aspx?cceid+2024&Lang=E&toc=50

Canadian Cancer Society/National Cancer Institute of Canada. (2006). *Canadian cancer statistics 2006* (Special Topic). Toronto, ON: Authors.

Canadian Cancer Society's Steering Committee for Cancer Statistics. (2011). *Canadian cancer statistics 2011,* Toronto, ON: Canadian Cancer Society.

Canadian Paediatric Society. (1996). Neonatal circumcision revisited. Fetus and Newborn Committee, Canadian Paediatric Society. *N Engl J Med, 360,* 1320–1328.

Centers for Disease Control and Prevention. (2006). *Sexually transmitted disease treatment guidelines, 2006.* Retrieved from http://www.cdc.gov/STD?treatment/2006/clinical.htm database

Cole, F. L., & Vogler, R. (2004). The acute, nontraumatic scrotum: Assessment and management. *Journal of the American Academy of Nurse Practitioners, 16*(2), 50–56.

Dains, J. E., Baumann, L. C., et al. (2003). *Advanced health assessment & clinical diagnosis in primary care* (2nd ed.). Philadelphia, PA: Elsevier.

Diehl-Jones, W., & Bickley, L. S. (2010). Male genitalia and hernias. In T. C. Stephen, D. L. Skillen, R. A. Day, & L. S. Bickley (Eds.). *Canadian Bates' guide to health assessment for nurses* (1st ed., pp. 759–783). Philadelphia, PA: Wolters Kluwer Health/Lippincott Williams & Wilkins.

Leininger, M., & McFarland, M. (2002). *Transcultural nursing: Concepts, theories, research, and practice* (3rd ed.). New York, NY: McGraw Hill.

Lewis, J. H., Rosen, R., et al. (2003). Erectile dysfunction in primary care. *American Journal of Nursing, 10*(103), 48–57.

Moorhead, S., Johnson, M., et al. (2007). *Nursing outcomes classification (NOC)* (4th ed.). Philadelphia, PA: Mosby.

North American Nursing Diagnosis Association International. (2009). *Nursing diagnoses, 2009–2011 edition: Definitions and classifications (NANDA I NURSING DIAGNOSIS).* West Sussex, UK: John Wiley & Sons.

Palefsky, J. (2007). HPV infection in men. *Disease Markers, 23,* 261–272.

Parson, J. K., Sarma, A. V., et al. (2009). Obesity and benign prostatic hyperplasia: Clinical connections, emerging etiological paradigms and future directions. *Journal of Urology, 182,* S27–S31.

Quinn, T. C., Bartlett, J. A., et al. (2011). The global human immunodeficiency virus pandemic. Retrieved from uptodate.com/contents/the-global-human-immunodeficiency-virus-pandemic.

Seidel, H. M., Ball, J. W., et al. (2003). *Mosby' guide to physical examination* (5th ed.). St. Louis, MO: Elsevier.

Siegfried, N., Muller, M., et al. (2009). Male circumcision for prevention of heterosexual acquisition of HIV men. Cochrane Database of Systemic Review, Issue 2, Art. No. CD003362.

Swartz, M. H. (2006). *Textbook of physical diagnosis* (5th ed.). Philadelphia, PA: Saunders Elsevier.

Tanner, J. (1962). *Growth at adolescence.* Oxford, UK: Blackwell.

Turner, B. (2008). Haematuria: Causes and management. *Nursing Standard, 23*(1), 50–56.

Uphold, C. R., & Graham, V. (2003). *Clinical guidelines in family practice* (4th ed.). Gainesville, FL: Barmarrae Books.

The Canadian Jensen's Nursing Assessment suite offers these additional resources to enhance learning and facilitate understanding of this chapter:

- thePoint online resource, http//thepoint.lww.com/Stephen1E
- *Laboratory Manual for Canadian Jensen's Nursing Health Assessment: A Best Practice Approach*

Tables of Unexpected Findings

 Table 25-3 **Testicular Torsion Versus Epididymitis**

Testicular Torsion	Epididymitis
Pain is acute.	Pain is gradual.
Nausea and vomiting occur in 50% of patients.	Nausea and vomiting are rare.
Fever is rare.	Fever occurs in 50% of patients.
Voiding symptoms, urethral irritation, and urethral discharge are rare.	Voiding symptoms, urethral irritation, and urethral discharge occur in 50% of patients.
0%–30% of patients have altered urinalysis results.	Urinalysis will be diagnostic in 20%–95% of those with epididymitis.
Elevation of affected testicle does not lessen pain.	Elevation of affected testicle usually lessens pain.
Surgical intervention is immediately required.	Antibiotic therapy is indicated.

Table 25-4 **Unexpected Conditions of the Penis**

Genital Piercing

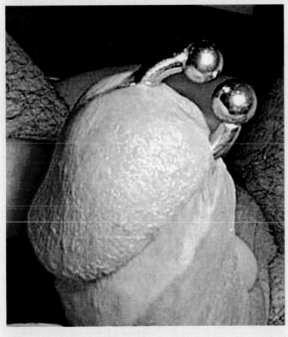

The Prince Albert is a common type of male genital piercing in which a ring is inserted through the urethra and out the bottom of the glans. The most common issue associated with piercing is infection. Other complications include bleeding and difficulty urinating.

Phimosis

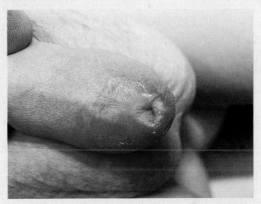

The prepuce cannot be retracted over the glans. It can occur during the first 6 y of life. It may be congenital or follow recurrent infections or *balanoposthitis* (inflammation of the prepuce and glans). Occasionally, the narrowed foreskin obstructs urinary flow, resulting in a dribbling stream or ballooning of the foreskin. Severe phimosis is treated by circumcision.

(table continues on page 780)

Table 25-4 **Unexpected Conditions of the Penis** (*continued*)

Paraphimosis

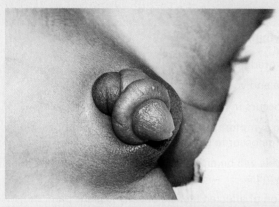

The retracted prepuce cannot be placed back over the glans. Paraphimosis may be severe enough to restrict circulation to the glans. An uncircumcised male would always have the foreskin pulled toward the urethral opening.

Hypospadias

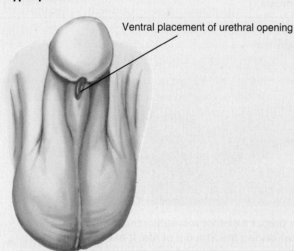

Ventral placement of urethral opening

The urethral meatus opens on the ventral side of the penis. The deviation of the meatus makes it difficult to urinate when standing. The physical appearance of the penis is altered, sometimes causing body image disturbances.

Balanitis or Balanoposthitis

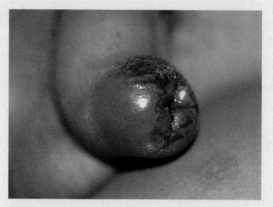

Inflammation of the glans and prepuce occurs in uncircumcised men. Many of these men have poorly controlled diabetes. Scars and narrowing of the urethral opening may cause inflammation, infections, and foul discharge. The scarring may make it difficult to clean under the foreskin.

Epispadias

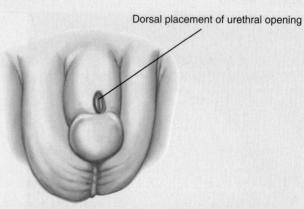

Dorsal placement of urethral opening

The urethral meatus opens on the dorsal surface of the penis. Epispadias may be associated with underlying congenital anomalies in genital urinary development. The lower urinary tract may be exposed in severe cases.

STI	Findings and Clinical Implications

Scabies Infection

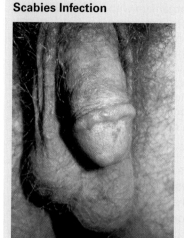

Scabies is a highly communicable skin condition caused by an arachnid, commonly known as the itch mite. It is transmitted by direct skin contact. The females live in burrows that appear as slightly darkened lines. There are associated papules, vesicles, pustules, and intense itching

Chlamydia

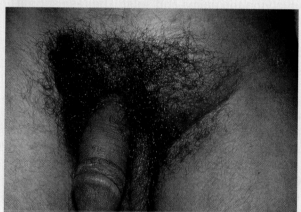

Chlamydia trachomatis is a bacterium with a variable incubation period, usually 1 wk of exposure. In men, the urethra has a mucopurulent discharge. There is burning on urination. Commonly, chlamydia can present asymptomatically. A chlamydia infection can cause nongonococcal urethritis and acute epididymitis. If urethral discharge is present, obtain specimen for diagnostic testing.

Gonorrhea

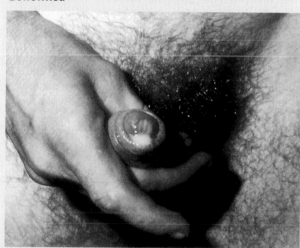

Gonorrhoeae organisms are gram-negative diplococci present in exudates and secretions of infected mucous surfaces. Transmission results from intimate contact; incubation period is 2–7 d. Men may present with dysuria, urethral discharge, rectal pain, or discharge. Common sites include the urethra, epididymis, prostate, rectum, and pharynx. If urethral discharge is present, obtain specimen for diagnostic testing.

(table continues on page 782)

STI	Findings and Clinical Implications

Syphilis

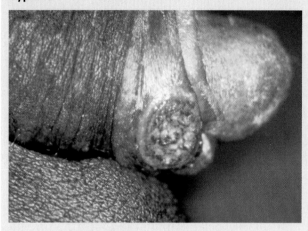

Syphilis is a thin, fragile organism with humans as the only host. The organism penetrates intact skin or mucous membrane during sexual contact, multiplies, and rapidly spreads to regional lymph nodes. Primary incubation period for acquired syphilis is about 3 wk but can occur 10–90 d after exposure. Secondary syphilis develops 6–8 wk later. Latent and tertiary syphilis can occur years later. **Report all cases of syphilis to appropriate public health department.**

The five stages of syphilis are as follows:

1. With primary syphilis, genital lesions are usually indurated and painless. Regional lymphadenopathy is usually present. Chancre persists for 1–5 wk and heals spontaneously.
2. Secondary syphilis occurs 6–8 wk later and is characterized by flu symptoms. A macular, papular, annular, or follicular rash is present, often involving the palms and soles. The rash spontaneously heals in 2–6 wk. Secondary syphilis is the most contagious.
3. A latent stage occurs after the second stage. It can last from 2 to 20 y.
4. Tertiary syphilis has the most devastating effects on the cardiovascular, neurological, musculoskeletal, and ophthalmic systems of the body.
5. Congenital syphilis occurs from mother to child, usually when the mother has primary or secondary syphilis. Signs and symptoms in the infant include retinal inflammation, glaucoma, destructive bone and skin lesions, and central nervous system disorders.

Human Papillomavirus (HPV)

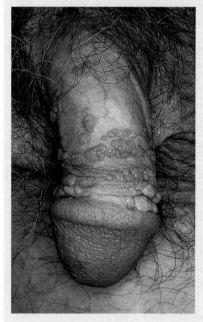

A virus that produces epithelial tumours of the skin and mucous membranes. More than 40 types of sexually transmitted HPV can infect the genital tract. Incubation period is unknown but can range from 3 mo to several years. Most men with HPV never develop genital warts. Some strains of the virus can progress to genital warts. Although rare, a complication is penile or anal cancer. Visible genital warts usually result from HPV types 6 or 11. They can appear on the scrotum, perineum, perianal skin, and penis. Individual warts may become confluent and appear as a single, large fleshy lesion.

STI	Findings and Clinical Implications
Herpes Simplex Virus (HSV) Types 1 and 2 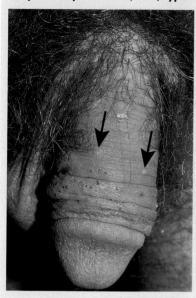	• HSV-1 and HSV-2 are epidermotropic viruses. Transmission is only by direct contact with active lesions or virus-containing fluid such as saliva. Incubation period is 2–14 d. HSV-1 is associated with infection of the lips, face, buccal mucosa, and throat. HSV-2 is associated with genitalia. There may be an overlap in site of infection; type 1 strains can be recovered from the genital tract, and type 2 strains could be recovered from the pharynx following orogenital activity. The usual sequence is painful papules followed by vesicles, ulceration, crusting, and healing.

Note: There are >50 different STIs. Six common STIs are presented in the table.
Information obtained from http://www3.niaid.nih.gov/topics/sti/; http://www.cdc.gov /std/stats07/toc.htm

⚠ Table 25-6   **Unexpected Findings in Scrotum and Testes**

Unexpected Finding	Description
Testicular Torsion 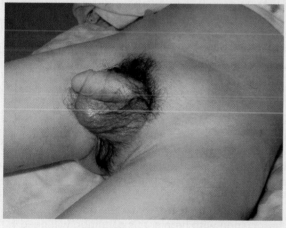 This sudden twisting of the spermatic cord typically occurs on the left side because the left cord is longer. Most common in late childhood or early adolescence, it is rare after 20 y and results from faulty anchoring of the testis on the scrotal wall, which enables rotation. The anterior part of the testis rotates medially toward the other testis. Blood supply is impaired, resulting in ischemia and venous engorgement. Because the testis can become gangrenous within a few hours, this *is considered a surgical emergency.*	**Epididymitis** 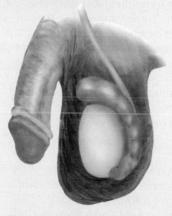 This acute infection of the epididymis is commonly caused by chlamydia, gonorrhea, or other bacterial infection (eg, *Escherichia coli*). In men younger than 35 y, the most common cause is a sexually transmitted infection. Epididymitis is often linked to prostatitis, especially after surgical intervention/ urethral instrumentation. Uncommon causes include tuberculosis, trauma, systemic fungal infections, and use of the drug amiodarone. Pain in the scrotum is severe, accompanied by swelling and fever. The scrotum can become very enlarged, inflamed, and painful to touch. Treatment with antibiotics is often needed.

(table continues on page 784)

Unexpected Finding	Description

Varicocele

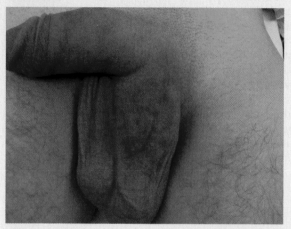

Dilated, tortuous varicose veins most often affect the left spermatic cord, which is longer and inserts at a right angle into the left renal vein. These are common in young males (5% of teens and 15% of adults) but rare before 10 y. In boys younger than 10 y, varicocele may correlate with malignancy. It is important for nurses to screen for varicocele in early adolescence, because this condition *is the most common cause of infertility*. Correction of testicular atrophy in early adolescence results in improved sperm count. Increased fertility has been noted in 80%–90% of those who undergo surgical correction. No visual change may appear on the scrotum, but a bluish tinge may be seen in light-skinned patients. When the patient is upright, the nurse can palpate a soft, irregular mass that feels distinctly like a "bag of worms" posterior and superior to the testis. The varicocele collapses when the patient is supine but enlarges when the patient bears down or does the Valsalva manoeuvre. Testes on the affected side may be smaller because of impaired circulation, so the nurse needs to compare both testes (length, width, and depth). In advanced practice, orchidometers are often used to measure testicular volume in millilitres:

- Grade 3: "bag of worms" >2 cm in diameter and easily visualized
- Grade 2: 1–2 cm in diameter and easily palpable
- Grade 1: (most common) very small, difficult to palpate; Valsalva manoeuvre may help
- Asymptomatic: patient has no symptoms from the varicocele
- Grade 1 varicocele with usual testicular volumes usually do not require intervention in adolescents, but ultrasound is recommended every 6 mo to evaluate size (American Urological Association, 2009).

Hydrocele

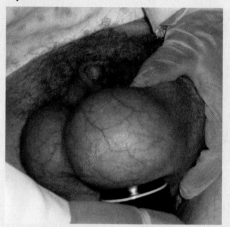

This circumscribed collection of serous fluid develops in the tunica vaginalis surrounding the testis. There are two types of hydroceles: noncommunicating and communicating. In *noncommunicating hydrocele*, fluid collects only in the scrotum but is persistent. A *communicating hydrocele* has a patent process vaginalis, so fluid can move from the abdomen to scrotum. Edema is intermittent, usually flat in morning, swollen during the day, or when the patient cries or performs the Valsalva manoeuvre. A communicating hydrocele is associated with a hernia. Incidence is 0.5%–2% of males, It primarily appears before 1 y of age; if it persists beyond 1 y, the nurse should assume it to be in conjunction with a hernia. In older children and adults, hydrocele may follow epididymitis, trauma, hernia, and tumour of testis. The patient will present with unilateral edema but no pain. He may report sensation of weight or bulk to the scrotum, which does not cause any apparent distress. On palpation of the scrotum, a large mass is noted, which can be transilluminated with a pink or red glow. If a hernia is involved, the hydrocele will not transilluminate. The nurse's fingers should be able to get around the mass; however, this is not possible if a hernia is present. If a noncommunicating hydrocele is present, no treatment is indicated unless the hydrocele is so large that it causes discomfort or persists for more than 1 y, because by then, there should be spontaneous absorption. A communicating hydrocele can resolve, but because of its association with hernia, this condition will need surgical repair. The nurse may order a scrotal ultrasound to help confirm the diagnoses (American Urological Association, 2009).

Table 25-6   Unexpected Findings in Scrotum and Testes (continued)

Unexpected Finding	Description
Spermatocele 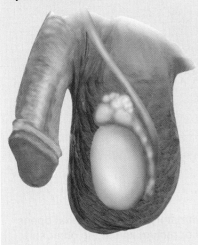	This benign scrotal mass or cyst develops on the head of the epididymis or testicular adnexa, which contains sperm. This uncommon finding occurs in <1% of all males from the neonatal period to a peak at 14 y. For the nurse, it is virtually impossible to differentiate from a simple epididymal cyst that does not contain sperm. Patients may report a lump in the scrotal sac or edema. Upon palpation, the nurse will find a mobile, cystic nodule usually <1 cm superior and posterior to the testis. The mass will transilluminate with a pink or red glow. The spermatocele will not change in size when the patient performs the Valsalva manoeuvre. The advanced practice nurse orders a scrotal ultrasound for diagnostic purposes.

Table 25-7   Conditions of the Anus, Rectum, and Prostate

External Hemorrhoids	**Internal Hemorrhoids**
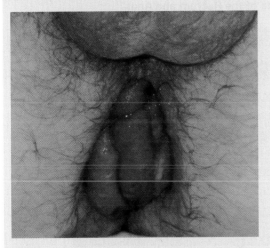	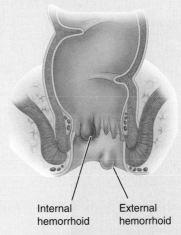 Internal hemorrhoid External hemorrhoid
External hemorrhoids are varicose veins that originate below the pectinate line and are covered by anal skin. Patients report rectal itching, pain, or burning. External hemorrhoids are usually not visible at rest but become visible upon standing or on defecation. If conventional hemorrhoid treatment proves ineffective or the hemorrhoids become edematous and thrombosed, surgery may be indicated. A thrombosed hemorrhoid presents as a blue, shiny, edematous mass on the anus. The patient is very uncomfortable and requires immediate attention.	Internal hemorrhoids can be painless unless they are thrombosed, infected, or prolapsed. They occur above the pectinate line and are covered by the mucosa of the anal canal. Internal hemorrhoids create soft swelling and are difficult to palpate on a digital examination unless they are prolapsed through the rectum. They can bleed daily with or without defecation. This can cause the patient to be anemic. This condition requires a referral for further treatment (American Gastroenterology Association, 2009).

(table continues on page 786)

Anorectal Fissure

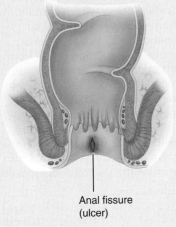

Anal fissure
(ulcer)

Anorectal fissure is a tear in the anal mucosa and can occur midline or posterior or anterior to it. Usually, a fissure is caused by the passage of large, hard stool. On observation, a sentinel skin tag may be seen at the lower end of the fissure. Ulcerations may appear at the site. The patient has bleeding, pain, and itching. As the internal sphincter is spastic, anesthesia of the site is necessary for examination.

Rectal Polyp

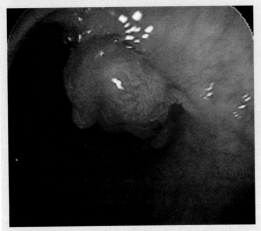

Polyps, common findings, can occur anywhere in the intestinal tract. They can be adenomas or inflammatory in origin, occurring singly or in clusters. They can cause rectal bleeding and be seen protruding through the rectum on examination. On digital rectal examination, polyps can felt as soft nodules and be either pedunculated or sessile. Many times, the nurse cannot palpate polyps. Colonoscopy is needed to differentiate between a polyp and carcinoma. Older adults are more prone to rectal polyps and are at higher risk for carcinoma, making the rectal portion a significant part of the examination for them.

Anal Fistula

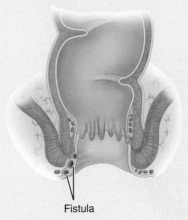

Fistula

Anal fistula is an inflammatory tract or tube that opens at one end in the anus or rectum and at the other end onto the skin surface. It originates in the anal crypts. The fissure can occur spontaneously or from perirectal abscess. On compression, serosanguinous or purulent drainage may appear. Externally, the area appears raised, red, and granular. This condition requires referral for further treatment (American Gastroenterology Association, 2009).

Carcinoma of the Rectum and Anus

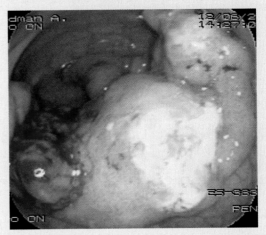

Although rare, cancers of the rectum and anus are becoming more common. The most common cause is anal intercourse, especially if associated with chronic irritation, such as with human papillomavirus. Symptoms of rectal or anal cancer include constant discharge, change in bowel habits, blood in the stool, and weight loss. On examination, a stony, irregular, sessile polypoid mass is felt. It is nodular with areas of ulceration. The cancer initially is asymptomatic, so routine clinical rectal examination and regular screening are key to early detection.

Table 25-7   **Conditions of the Anus, Rectum, and Prostate** (*continued*)

Rectal Prolapse

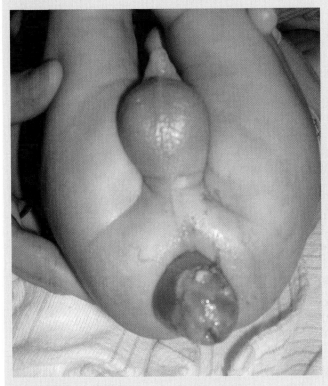

Rectal prolapse usually occurs with defecation; the rectal mucosa, with or without muscular wall, prolapses through the anal ring. On examination, a prolapse may present like a doughnut. A complete prolapse includes the muscular wall and is larger with circular folds. Cystic fibrosis is associated with children who present with rectal prolapse (Seidel, Ball, et al., 2003).

Prostatitis

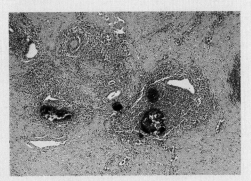

Inflammation or infection of the prostate gland can be acute or chronic. Acute **bacterial prostatitis** may result from ascending urethral infection, reflux of infected urine, extension of a rectal infection, or hematogenous spread. **Chronic prostatitis** results from autoimmune, allergic, neuromuscular, or psychological disorders of the bladder, detrusor hyperreflexia, or pelvic floor tension myalgia. Signs and symptoms for acute and chronic prostatitis are similar. Acute prostatitis usually presents with severe symptoms. Signs and symptoms include fever, chills, malaise, dysuria, frequency, inhibited urinary voiding, low back pain, suprapubic discomfort, and perineal pain. Many also report painful sexual intercourse, pain when defecating, and hematuria. On examination, the prostate is tender, warm, swollen, and boggy. Carefully and gently palpate because vigorous massage can disseminate bacteria into the bloodstream, resulting in bacteriemia. The patient with prostatitis is acutely ill and needs immediate intervention (Uphold & Graham, 2003).

Prostate Cancer

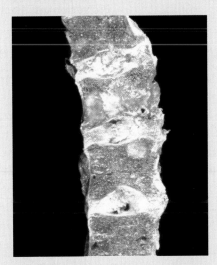

This second most common cancer among men (nonmelanoma skin cancer is first) is also the third leading cause of death among men (exceeded by and colorectal cancers). It is usually very slow growing and asymptomatic in the early stages. As the prostate enlarges, patients may develop hesitancy, dribbling, frequency, urgency, nocturia, retention, slow stream, or feeling of bladder fullness. Screening is done with a prostate-specific antigen test and rectal examination; diagnosis is made with needle biopsy.

Table 25-8   **Types of Hernias**

Feature	Direct Inguinal	Indirect Inguinal	Femoral
Affected population	Middle-aged and elderly men	All ages	Least common, found more frequently in women
Bilaterality	55%	30%	Rare
Origin of swelling	Above inguinal ligament. Directly behind and through external ring	Above inguinal ligament. Hernial sac enters inguinal canal at internal ring and exits at external ring	Below inguinal ligament
Scrotal involvement	Rare	Common	Never
Impulse location	At side of finger in inguinal canal	At tip of finger in inguinal canal	Not felt by finger in inguinal canal; mass; below canal

Table 25-9   **Classifications of Prostate Enlargement**

Grade	Protrusion Into Rectum
I	1–2 cm
II	2–3 cm
III	3–4 cm
IV	>4 cm

26

Female Genitalia and Rectal Assessment

Learning Objectives

1 Demonstrate knowledge of anatomy and physiology of the female genitalia and rectum.

2 Identify important topics for health promotion and risk reduction of the female genitalia and rectum.

3 Collect subjective data related to the female genitalia and rectum.

4 Collect objective data related to the female genitalia and rectum using physical examination techniques.

5 Identify expected and unexpected findings related to the female genitalia and rectum.

6 Analyze subjective and objective data from assessment of the female genitalia and rectum and consider initial interventions.

7 Document and communicate data from the assessment of the female genitalia and rectum using appropriate terminology and principles of recording.

8 Individualize health assessment of the female genitalia and rectum considering age, gender, condition, and culture of the patient.

9 Identify nursing diagnoses and initiate a plan of care based on findings from the assessment of the female genitalia and rectum.

*T*eresa Nguyen, a 28-year-old Vietnamese Canadian woman, is being seen in the clinic for the first time with clear vaginal secretions and pelvic pain. Her temperature is 38.8°C orally, pulse 82 beats/min and regular, respirations 16 breaths/min, and blood pressure 102/66 mm Hg (left arm, sitting). She is taking no medications.

You will gain more information about Ms. Nguyen as you progress through this chapter. As you study the content and features, consider Teresa Nguyen's case and its relationship to what you are learning. Begin thinking about the following points:

- What is the role of the nurse in assessing physiological symptoms versus psychosocial issues?
- What are some questions that the nurse should ask? What language or words might the nurse use?
- What cultural considerations should the nurse incorporate into the care provided?

The focus of this chapter is genital and rectal assessment of the female patient across the lifespan. By identifying key factors in the process of this assessment, the nurse can explore opportunities for positive communication and accurate information regarding women's health. Nurses can guide female patients in risk reduction and health promotion from the onset of puberty to the menopausal years and into healthy aging.

Anatomy and Physiology Overview

The female genitalia can be subdivided as external and internal. External genitalia include the mons pubis, labia majora, labia minora, prepuce, and clitoris. The internal genitalia are the vagina, fornix, uterus, cervix, fundus, fallopian tubes, ovaries, and supporting tissues.

External Genitalia

The external genitalia are also called the *vulva* (Fig. 26-1). The **mons pubis** is the most anterior structure and is comprised of subcutaneous fatty tissue covered by pubic hair. The mons pubis lies directly over the pubic bone and creates a cushion that protects the bone during sexual intercourse. The **labia majora** consist of two folds that extend from the mons pubis downward to the perineum. The **clitoris**, an embryologic homologue of the penis, responds in an erectile fashion when stimulated. It consists of the glans that lies posterior to two crura. Nerve fibres in the clitoris respond to touch and produce pleasurable feelings for the female. The ventral surface of the **glans** is known as the **frenulum** and is where the **labia minora**, two small folds that extend from clitoral hood to the **posterior fourchette** of the vagina, fuse. The **vestibule** lies between the labia minora and is bound anteriorly by the clitoris and posteriorly by the perineum. Within the vestibule lie the urethra at the upper middle area, with bilateral **paraurethral Skene's glands** at the 7 and 5 o'clock positions, respectively. The Skene's glands produce clear fluid that aids in lubrication during intercourse. The **vaginal introitus** lies posterior to the

urethra. The **Bartholin's glands**, located at the base of the vestibule, secrete clear mucus into the vaginal introitus during intercourse. They are positioned at 7 and 5 o'clock positions of the posterior vestibule. The **perineum** is the area between the vaginal introitus and rectum. This is the location where an episiotomy is occasionally done to facilitate difficult childbirth.

Internal Genitalia

Vagina

The **vagina** is a tube of muscular tissue that extends from vaginal introitus to the uterus. The three-layer vaginal muscle wall is extremely expandable especially during childbirth. It is lined by glandular mucous membrane, within which are folds called **rugae**. These rugae become less prominent in advanced years. The vagina is approximately parallel to the lower portion of the sacrum. This position is the reason the anterior wall of the vagina measures 7 cm while the posterior wall is about 9 cm. The **vesicovaginal septum** separates the anterior wall of the vagina from the urethra and bladder. The **rectovaginal septum** separates the posterior wall of the vagina from the rectum.

Uterus

The hollow **uterus**, often referred to as the "womb," is the organ that holds the endometrial lining and is prepared to accept an implanted ovum (Fig. 26-2). It lies between the bladder and rectum and is approximately 7 to 8 cm long and 4 to 5 cm at its widest part. The uterine walls consist of an outer layer called the **peritoneum**, a muscle layer called the **myometrium**, and an inner layer called the **endometrium**.

The uterus has two parts separated by a narrow isthmus: the corpus (body) and the cervix. If implantation occurs, the uterus accommodates the growing fetus for the remaining 9 months. If no fertilization occurs, the endometrial lining sheds and the woman will have a menstrual period. The freely mobile uterus is supported bilaterally by the **round**, **cardinal**, **uterosacral**, and **broad ligaments**.

Cervix

The **cervix** is the posterior portion of the uterus that protrudes into the vagina. The cervix is smooth, rounded, and has a midline opening called the **os**. In a nonpregnant female, the os resembles a donut with a small hole in the middle. Once a pregnancy has occurred and thereafter, the opening resembles a horizontal slit.

Fallopian Tubes

The **fallopian tubes** transport ova from the ovary to the uterus. They are approximately 12 cm long and 1 mm in diameter. The tubes are composed of four layers of tissues: **peritoneal** (serous), **subserous** (adventitial), **muscular**, and **mucous**. These layers are responsible for the blood and nerve supply as well as providing the peristaltic condition necessary to move the ovum toward the uterus. The fallopian tubes are divided into three parts: **isthmus**, **ampulla**, and the **fimbria**. Fertilization most often occurs in the ampulla portion of the fallopian tubes.

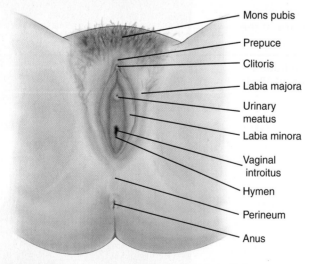

Mons pubis

Prepuce

Clitoris

Labia majora

Urinary meatus

Labia minora

Vaginal introitus

Hymen

Perineum

Anus

Figure 26-1 Anatomy of the external genitalia.

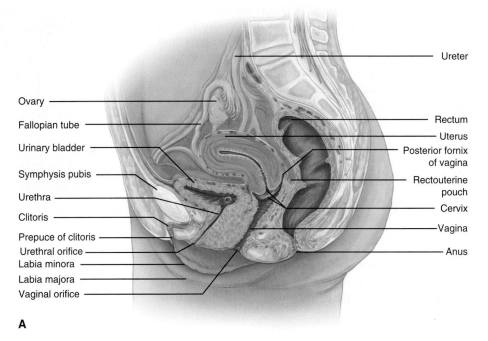

Labels (side view, A):
- Ureter
- Ovary
- Fallopian tube
- Rectum
- Uterus
- Urinary bladder
- Posterior fornix of vagina
- Symphysis pubis
- Rectouterine pouch
- Urethra
- Cervix
- Clitoris
- Vagina
- Prepuce of clitoris
- Anus
- Urethral orifice
- Labia minora
- Labia majora
- Vaginal orifice

A

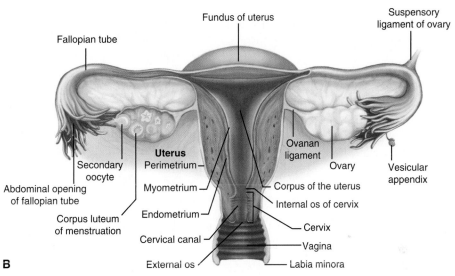

Labels (frontal view, B):
- Fundus of uterus
- Suspensory ligament of ovary
- Fallopian tube
- Secondary oocyte
- Abdominal opening of fallopian tube
- Corpus luteum of menstruation
- **Uterus** Perimetrium
- Myometrium
- Endometrium
- Cervical canal
- External os
- Ovanan ligament
- Ovary
- Vesicular appendix
- Corpus of the uterus
- Internal os of cervix
- Cervix
- Vagina
- Labia minora

B

Figure 26-2 Internal female genitalia. **A.** Side view. **B.** Frontal view.

Ovaries

The **ovaries** are two almond-shaped structures measuring approximately 3 × 2 cm. They develop after puberty and reduce in size (atrophy) after menopause. The ovaries are held in place by ligaments called the **infundibulopelvic** and **ovarian ligaments**. The ovaries provide ova to be fertilized by sperm and secrete the hormones estrogen and progesterone (discussed later).

Rectum, Anal Canal, and Anus

Anatomy and physiology of the rectum, anal canal, and anus are covered in detail in Chapter 25.

Hormone Regulation

Many hormones regulate the female reproductive system. The main sources of these hormones are (1) the **anterior pituitary**, (2) the **hypothalamus**, and (3) the **ovaries**.

The anterior pituitary secretes **follicle-stimulating hormone** (FSH) and **luteinizing hormone** (LH). The function of FSH is to stimulate the growth and maturation of the ovarian follicle and the production of testosterone, which maintains spermatogenesis in the male. LH functions to luteinize the follicle, which increases production of progesterone by the granulose cells (McCowen Meahring, 2010a). The luteinizing process ultimately produces the corpus luteum.

The hypothalamus is responsible for the release of FSH and LH by way of the **gonadotropin-releasing hormones (GnRH)** and luteinizing-releasing hormones (LnRH). The hypothalamus acts as an inhibitor of prolactin release. This is referred to as the **prolactin inhibiting factor** as well. These cyclic hormones drive the function of menstruation, reproduction, sexuality, and physical as well as emotional health (McCowen Meahring, 2010a). The pelvic organs are the recipients of the hormones.

The ovaries are the source of two hormones—estrogen and progesterone. Estrogen regulates the development of secondary sex characteristics; contributes to the growth of the vagina, fallopian tubes, and uterus; contributes to the proliferation of the endometrial lining; and plays a role in maturation of ovarian follicles. Progesterone develops the corpus luteum and is necessary for the successful implantation of the embryo. If no implantation happens, a menstrual cycle occurs (see also Fig. 26-3).

▲ Lifespan Considerations

Women Who Are Pregnant
Assessment of women who are pregnant is discussed in detail in Chapter 27.

Infants, Children, and Adolescents
On assessment of the newborn, it is not uncommon to see some pink discharge at the opening of the vagina. This is most

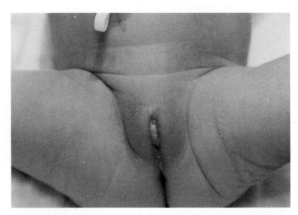

Figure 26-4 Surface anatomy of the female infant genitalia.

often a result of maternal estrogen. In the female child, the genitalia continue growing, except for the clitoris (Fig. 26-4).

Age of onset of puberty in girls has continued to decline. Girls in Canada usually begin menstruation between ages 9

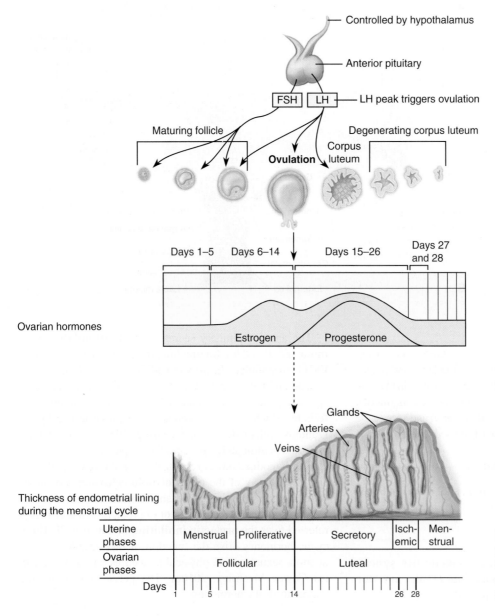

Figure 26-3 Diagram of the relationship between hormonal levels and **(top)** follicular development and **(bottom)** the menstrual cycle.

and 16 years (Estes & Buck, 2009). African Canadian girls may begin puberty before 8 years. Onset of menses correlates with estrogen release by the **hypothalamic–pituitary–ovarian axis** (McCowen Meahring, 2010a). Budding of the breast occurs first, followed by development of pubic hair (see Chapter 21). Onset of menses follows breast budding by approximately 2 to 3 years. Tanner's stages of maturation are used in the assessment of preadolescent and adolescent females (Marshall & Tanner, 1969). Female pubic hair stages are reviewed in Table 26-1.

Genital assessment of the adolescent is not required unless there has been initiation of sexual activity or there are genital tract concerns. The opportunity to provide education is greatest at this time, however. The adolescent is experiencing body changes, self-identity exploration, and relationship questions. The nurse is direct and honest with the teen. Establishment of a trusting and confidential nurse–patient relationship is vital. Sexually active adolescent females should have an annual examination.

Table 26-1	Tanner's Staging: Female Pubic Hair
Stage	**Description**
Stage 1: Preadolescent 	The vellus over the pubes is not further developed than that over the anterior abdominal wall (ie, no pubic hair).
Stage 2 	Long, slightly pigmented, downy hair that is straight or only slightly curled appears chiefly along the labia.
Stage 3 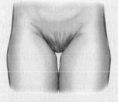	Hair is considerably darker, coarser, and more curled. It spreads sparsely over the junction of the mons pubis.
Stage 4 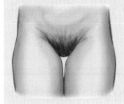	Hair is now adult in type, but the area covered by it is still considerably smaller than in most adults. There is no spread to the medial surface of the thighs.
Stage 5 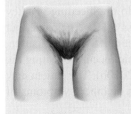	Hair is adult in quantity and type, distributed as an inverse triangle of the classically feminine pattern. Spread is to the medial surface of the thighs, but not up the linea alba or elsewhere above the base of the inverse triangle.

Older Adults

The number of women older than 50 years continues to increase in Canada. As women age, they experience many changes in the genitourinary tract. Most of these are related to limited or absent estrogen in the system.

Menopause is defined as 12 consecutive months without menses (McCowen Meahring, 2010a). As estrogen levels decrease, the uterus becomes smaller, the ovaries shrink, the vaginal rugae flatten, and the epithelium atrophies. These expected changes may lead to concerns such as vaginal infections, urinary tract infections (UTIs), **dyspareunia**, and lowered libido (Chow, 2010a). Older women are at increased risk for endometrial cancers and need education regarding unexpected signs and symptoms. The nurse has an opportunity to provide counselling and education regarding intimacy issues and physiologic changes, and to answer the patient's questions. Sexuality continues to be important for many older women, and the nurse raises the subject in a matter-of-fact manner.

Acute Assessment

If the patient is experiencing severe pain or excessive bleeding, the assessment needs to be truncated to involve only questions pertinent to the immediate condition and necessary for current care. It is highly important to obtain a focused health history and to conduct a physical examination germane to the presenting health concern to reach an accurate diagnosis before intervening.

Excessive Vaginal Bleeding

Unexpected bleeding is not uncommon during the childbearing years and at menopause. During the childbearing years, causes of bleeding are associated with clinical types of abortion (threatened, missed, inevitable, incomplete, and septic).

While excessive vaginal bleeding does not always accompany most gynecologic conditions, nurses are aware that there is always a possibility of concealed excessive bleeding. Excess bleeding is associated with interstitial tumours and subendometrial fibromyomata. Bleeding after menopause (even a small amount) is highly significant, and malignancy of the endometrium must be ruled out (McCowen Meahring, 2010b). Canadian Cancer Society's Steering Committee for Cancer Statistics (CCSSCCS) (2011) expected 4,700 cases of cancer of the endometrium (body of the uterus) and 750 deaths in 2011.

Abdominal Pain

Abdominal pain, acute or chronic, can be of gynecologic origin. Causes include infection related to acute salpingo-oophoritis, septic abortion, or ruptured abscess; irritation from blood in the peritoneal cavity following a ruptured ectopic pregnancy, retrograde menstruation, an intrauterine device, dilatation and curettage (D&C), or uterine perforation; vascular complications from torsion of an adnexal or a paraovarian cyst; and carcinoma of the body of the uterus or cervix (McCowen Meahring, 2010b).

Bartholin's Gland Infection

Bartholin's glands keep the internal labial surfaces continuously lubricated (McCowen Meahring, 2010a). Inflammation usually results from infection with streptococci, staphylococci, *Chlamydia*, or *Escherichia coli* (McCowen Meahring, 2010c). Affected glands are typically inflamed and painful, and the patient may be febrile. In addition, the ducts leading to the glands are susceptible to obstruction, which may result in Bartholin's cysts. Route of entry of these organisms is through infection of the lower part of the female external genitalia. Teaching patients to follow appropriate hygiene practices (including wiping from front to back after toileting), having protected sex, and engaging in a monogamous sexual relationship will reduce the incidence of Bartholin's gland infection.

Pelvic Inflammatory Disease

Pelvic inflammatory disease (PID) is most often the result of a sexually transmitted infection (STI) of the fallopian tubes (salpingitis) or tubes plus ovaries (salpingo-oophoritis). It is caused by *Neisseria gonorrhoeae*, *Chlamydia trachomatis*, and other organisms. Patients with PID experience lower abdominal pain. *Acute* disease is associated with very tender, bilateral adnexal masses, although pain and muscle spasm usually make it impossible to identify them. Movement of the cervix produces pain. If not treated, a tubo-ovarian abscess or infertility may ensue (McCowen Meahring, 2010c). Patients with multiple sexual partners have a greater occurrence of PID than those who are monogamous.

Ruptured Tubal Pregnancy

Ruptured tubal pregnancy spills blood into the peritoneal cavity, causing severe abdominal pain, shoulder pain, and tenderness. Bleeding also may occur with an ectopic pregnancy. In this case, pain prior to the bleeding is a key symptom. A unilateral adnexal mass may be palpable, but tenderness often prevents its detection. Syncope, nausea, vomiting, tachycardia, and shock may occur, reflecting the hemorrhage (McCowen Meahring, 2010b). The patient may have a prior history of amenorrhea or other symptoms of pregnancy.

Subjective Data Collection

Subjective data collection begins with the health history, continues with questions about specific genital and rectal conditions, and ends with detailed collection of information about areas of concern. Each assessment of the female genitalia is unique to the individual patient. When beginning the history portion of the assessment, it is important to establish a trusting relationship with the patient. The assessment of the female is very invasive and can be uncomfortable to both patient and nurse. In initiation of the health history, you allow the patient to become comfortable with you; at the same time, the acquisition of important data instills confidence in the nurse. The establishment of a respectful, nonjudgmental demeanour is imperative.

When obtaining the history, the room should be private and comfortable, and the nurse should be seated at eye level or lower to the patient. Assure the patient that all information is kept confidential. It is best to obtain the history while the patient is still dressed. This reduces embarrassment and vulnerability of the patient. If this is not possible, make sure the patient is completely covered, warm, and comfortable. Make eye contact but be careful with nonverbal communication. It is important to listen to the patient without thinking of your next question. Often minor cues give the greatest amount of information. Begin the interview with basic biographical data. The age of the patient plays an important role in the direction of examination and counselling.

Specific to the female population, an integral part of the assessment is sexual behaviour. STIs are the most common infectious diseases in Canada and the United States and are considered an epidemic in many parts of the world (Groenveld, 2010). Three reportable STIs in Canada are chlamydia, gonorrhea, and infectious syphilis. Although human papillomavirus (HPV) infection is the most commonly occurring STI, it is not a reportable disease in Canada (Public Health Agency of Canada, 2010a, 2011a). Complications of STIs include cervical cancer, pelvic infections, infertility, and pelvic pain. Education is the most powerful tool the nurse can offer regarding prevention. Maintaining confidentiality and offering the most current evidence-informed information encourages greater patient understanding.

Assessment of Risk Factors

Questions to Assess History and Risk Factors	Rationale
Personal History ***Menstrual History.*** Ask about menstrual history first. • How old were you when you got your first menstrual period? • What was the first day of your last menstrual period? • What is the character or consistency of your flow? • Do you use tampons? • How many days do you experience flow during your cycle? How many pads or tampons do you use per day? How many days is there "heavy" flow? "moderate" flow? or "light" spotting?	Menarche usually begins around 12 years of age. If the patient has not had menarche by 16 years, an endocrine evaluation is recommended. The menstrual cycle is calculated from the first day of the last menstrual period to the first day of the next menstrual period. Usual cycle is 28 to 32 days, but cycles can be as short as 20 days or as long as 40 days without requiring intervention. Flow is approximately 25 to 60 mL per menstrual period. Expected length is 2 to 8 days.
Obstetrical History. • Have you ever been pregnant? • If so, how many times? • How many living children do you have? • Did you give birth vaginally? Or by cesarean section? • Were there any complications before your pregnancy? During? Or after your pregnancy? • Have you ever had a miscarriage? • Have you ever had an abortion? If yes, was it an elective termination? Spontaneous miscarriage? Or incomplete miscarriage?	**Gravida:** The number of pregnancies a woman has had, including if she is presently pregnant. **Para:** The number of births a woman has had after 20 weeks even if the fetus died at birth. **Term:** Infant born after 37 weeks' gestation. **Preterm:** Infant born after 20 weeks but before 37 weeks. **Abortion:** Number of pregnancies that ended spontaneously or for therapeutic reasons. **Living:** Number of living children either delivered or adopted. A woman could be a **Gravida 1** (one pregnancy), and have two children. How? Twins!
Menopause. • Have you stopped having menstrual periods? • Are your menstrual cycles irregular? • Do you experience any symptoms of irregularity or absence of menses?	**Menopause** is the cessation of menstrual periods for 12 months or more. **Perimenopause** includes irregularity of menstrual cycles and accompanying symptoms (hot flashes, night sweating, mood swings, vaginal dryness, decreased sexual drive (**libido**) between 40 and 55 years and before actual cessation of menses) (McCowen Meahring, 2010a).

(text continues on page 796)

Questions to Assess History and Risk Factors	Rationale

Gynecologic History.

- Have you ever had a Papanicolaou smear (Pap smear)? If so, when was it done?
- Have your Pap smear results always been unremarkable?
- If not, did you receive any treatment for it and when?
- Have you had any previous procedures or surgeries?

Pap smear is a cytologic evaluation of the cells of the cervix to screen for precancerous cervical lesions. It does NOT screen for sexually transmitted infections (STIs) or any cancers other than cervical cancer. In 2011, the CCSSCCS estimated 1,300 new cases of cervical cancer and approximately 350 deaths from it in Canada. The nurse needs to provide the most up-to-date evidence-informed information. By educating the patient regarding the importance of follow-up and collaborating with health care professionals to encourage compliance, the nurse plays a part in the reduction of cervical cancers (Martin, 2008).

- Have you ever been treated for any vaginal infections?
- Do you have frequent vaginal infections?

The patient with recurring yeast infections should be evaluated for diabetes and human immunodeficiency virus (HIV) infection (Chow, 2010a).

- Do you use over-the-counter (OTC) vaginal medication?
- Have you ever had any pelvic infections?

Frequent use of OTC vaginal creams or suppositories can possibly mask other more serious infections.

- Do you use scented vaginal products such as sprays? Or scented tampons? Or scented pads?

Use of scented products may result in a **contact dermatitis** of the vulva or vagina.

- Do you douche? How often do you douche? What solution do you use?

Nurses educate the patient that the vagina is self-cleansing, and that issues can arise from douching, such as vaginal infections, imbalance of usual vaginal flora (pH), allergic reactions, and the possibility of transferring a vaginal infection into the uterus. The consequence can be pelvic inflammatory disease (PID).

Immunizations.

- Have you received the vaccine against the **human papillomavirus (HPV)**?
- When did you receive it?
- Did you receive all three doses?

Quadrivalent HPV vaccine (types 6, 11, 16, and 18) (Gardasil) is available for females aged 9 to 26 years. The vaccine is given in three doses: the second dose 2 months after the first and the third dose 6 months after the first (Society of Obstetricians and Gynaecologists of Canada, 2007).

Sexual History.

- Have you ever had sex?
- What type (vaginal? Oral? Or anal?)

Frank discussion opens opportunities for inquiry otherwise not brought up by the patient. Current statistics show that adolescents may not engage in vaginal intercourse but may have anal or oral sex (Centers for Disease Control and Prevention [CDCP], 2008).

- Approximately how many sexual partners have you had? Male? Female? Or both?
- Are you currently in a sexual relationship? Is it monogamous?

Ascertaining the patient's experience is important to determine risks. It is important to provide accurate and health-promoting information to homosexual, bisexual, and heterosexual females (Clark & Marrazzo, 2006).

- Have you ever experienced any type of sexual abuse?

Obtaining history of sexual abuse not only opens discussion about it and the patient's current feelings but also allows the nurse to proceed to the examination giving the emotional support that is necessary (Laumbach, 2004).

- Do you experience any pain with intercourse? Or after intercourse? Do you experience bleeding with intercourse? Or after intercourse?

Bleeding during intercourse may indicate an infection or possibly a cervical polyp.

- Do you experience urinary burning or infections related to intercourse?

Dysuria (burning with urination) or frequent urinary tract infections (UTIs) may be related to bladder trauma from intercourse. Educate the patient to empty her bladder before and after intercourse to reduce trauma and introduction of bacteria into the urethra.

Questions to Assess History and Risk Factors	Rationale

Contraception.

* Do you use condoms during sexual intercourse? Sometimes? Or always? Do you use other barrier methods such as a female condom? Or a dental dam for oral sex? Sometimes? Or always?
* Do you use any contraception?
* If so, what is currently used? FemCap (which has replaced the diaphragm)?
* Have you used anything different in the past?
* Have you had any concerns with any contraceptive types?

Condoms provide some but not complete protection against STIs. They provide protection only if used consistently. An innovative program "Take Care Down There" in Brandon, Manitoba uses taxi cabs to provide free condoms and information about getting tested for STIs. The free condoms are available Thursdays through Saturdays. (Perspectives, 2010). It is just as important for females who are homosexual to use barrier methods to prevent transmission of certain infections. Contraceptive use is different than practising "safer-sex." The only 100% safe sex practice is abstinence. Contraceptives protect ONLY against pregnancies, not STIs.

Medications and Supplements

* Are you currently taking any prescribed medications?
* Are you taking any over the counter (OTC) medications?
* Have you recently been on any antibiotics?
* Do you use any herbal products?
* Do you currently take any vitamins?

Certain medications including oral contraceptives, antidepressants, and antihypertensive agents can cause changes in menstrual cycles, appetite, and libido. Certain antibiotics can strip the vagina of its usual flora and create an environment that promotes yeast infections. Antibiotics can interfere with the absorption of oral contraceptives. A backup method of contraception or abstinence is advised during the treatment period. Use of herbal therapy requires caution. Although there have been some reported positive effects with herbal preparations, there are also reported herb–drug interactions. Often herbal products affect other medications being taken. Patients taking anticoagulants, digoxin, oral contraceptives, statins, and HIV medications should exercise caution. All herbal products should be avoided during pregnancy

Family History

Tell me about your family history of the following, including two generations:

* Diabetes
* Heart disease
* Cancer
* Thyroid conditions
* Gynecologic conditions
* Hypertension
* Asthma
* Allergies
* Diethylstilbestrol (DES) use in mother
* Multiple pregnancies
* Congenital anomalies

Current studies show that the major factors in breast and ovarian cancer are the *BRCA1* and *BRCA2* genes. These genes may be transmitted from the father's side as well as the mother's side (Kolesar, 2004). DES was a hormone given to pregnant women to prevent miscarriages from 1940 to 1970. Maternal DES use is associated with higher risks of clear cell cancers as well as breast cancers in older women. Ongoing studies continue regarding DES exposure (CDCP, 2008).

Risk Factors
Sexually Transmitted Infections.

* Do you engage in unprotected sex?
* Do you have multiple sexual partners?
* How many sexual partners have you had in your lifetime?
* Are you between 15 and 24 years?

Are you experiencing any pain within the pelvic region? Or discharge from the pelvic region?

Using condoms consistently reduces the risk of HPV by 70% but does not ensure total protection (Winer, Lee, et al., 2006).

Having 10 or more lifetime partners increases the risk for HPV to 69%, compared to 21% with one partner (Ley, Bauer, et al., 1991). "Each partner brings to a sexual encounter possible exposure to HPV from all previous partners" (Sethi & Bickley, 2010, p. 796).

(text continues on page 798)

Questions to Assess History and Risk Factors	Rationale

Systematic interviews of individuals with STIs are recommended, and should include the 5 Ps; partners, prevention of pregnancy, protection from STIs, practices, and past history of STIs (CDCP, 2006).

Screening, treating, and counselling of and about chlamydia, and gonorrhea, are currently recommended for all sexually active adolescents (Burns, Briggs, et al., 2007; Langille, Proudfoot, et al., 2008), as well as infectious syphilis (Public Health Agency of Canada [PHAC], 2010a). *Chlamydia trachomatis* is currently the most common and frequently reported bacterial **STI** in Canada. The rate for 2009 was 258.5 cases/100,000 Canadians, and the rates continue to increase (PHAC, 2010a). Because of the asymptomatic nature of this infection, risk for infection is high. Long-term infection can cause **PID** and subsequent potential infertility. The 2009 Canadian rate for gonorrhea was 33.1 cases/100,000, a drop from the previous year. Rate for infectious syphilis in 2009 was 5/100,000, with increases noted in Alberta, Québec, and Ontario (PHAC, 2010a). The incidence of HIV increased 14% since 2005, with total cases of 65,000 in 2008 (PHAC, 2010b). First Nations people are overrepresented, with a rate that is 3.6 times higher than that for non-Aboriginal people (PHAC, 2010b). About 14,300 Canadian women were living with HIV and AIDS in 2008. In 2008, 66% of new cases were from intravenous drug use, followed by 23% of cases by heterosexual spread (PHAC, 2010b).

Obesity. Obesity is considered an independent risk factor for coronary heart disease. **Central obesity** (apple shape) increases this risk. Women with pear-shaped bodies are thought to be at less risk.

A **body mass index (BMI)** of 18.5 to 24.9 is considered usual, a BMI of 25 to 29 is overweight, and >30 is considered obese (see Chapter 8). PHAC (2011b) currently recommends 2.5 hours of moderate to vigorous activity each week for adults aged 19 to 64 years.

Osteoporosis. Osteoporosis is a bone disorder characterized by decreased bone mass, which leads to fragility and potential fracture especially in females. This condition contributes to approximately 138,600 fractures annually and costs the Canadian health care system $1.9 billion annually (Osteoporosis Canada, 2011)

Bone mineral density screening is a simple and cost-efficient test recommended for all women 65 years or older. Those at risk for osteoporosis (Caucasian or Asian women with a family history of osteoporosis, thin frame, tobacco use, glucocorticoid use, or any fracture after the age of 45 years) should be screened earlier (Osteoporosis Canada, 2011).

Hormonal Contraceptive and Tobacco Use.
- Do you smoke?
- Are you using hormonal contraceptives?
- How old are you?

Tobacco is contraindicated for any patient 40 years or older who uses hormonal contraceptives. The combination of tobacco and hormonal contraceptives increases risk for vascular conditions (eg, deep vein thrombosis, pulmonary emboli) as well as risk for a cardiovascular incident. About 19% of all Canadians aged 15 years and older smoke cigarettes on a daily or nondaily basis (PHAC, 2007a). First-time myocardial infarction in women who smoke precedes that for nonsmokers by 19 to 20 years. Even light or "social" smoking doubles a female patient's risk of cardiovascular mortality (Mosca, Banka, et al., 2007).

⚠ SAFETY ALERT 26-1

Any patient taking isotretinoin (Accutane) for treatment of acne MUST have two negative pregnancy tests before starting therapy and continue them monthly until treatment is discontinued. Because of the severe teratogenic effects of this medication, any woman of childbearing age must either abstain or use at least two forms of birth control 1 month before, after, and during treatment.

Risk Assessment and Health Promotion

Topics for Health Promotion

- Menopause changes
- Risk factors and prevention of human papillomavirus (HPV) and cancer
- Risk factors and prevention of other sexually transmitted infections (STIs), including human immunodeficiency virus (HIV) (see Box 26-1)
- Genital self-examination and health practices (see Box 26-2)
- Female genital mutilation (FGM)

Adapted from Sethi, S., & Bickley, L. S. (2010). Female genitalia. In T. C. Stephen, D. L. Skillen, R. A. Day, & L. S. Bickley (Eds.). *Canadian Bates' guide to health assessment for nurses* (1st ed., p. 794). Philadelphia, PA: Wolters Kluwer Health/Lippincott Williams & Wilkins.

Reducing risk factors can occur through the provision of accurate, evidence-informed information. Giving women throughout the lifespan an opportunity to ask questions and allowing open and nonjudgmental discussion about sexuality are important.

Any woman with a history of multiple partners has the highest risk of developing HPV and cervical cancer.

Discussing this factor and recommending monogamy, abstinence, or consistent use of condoms with each act of intercourse is important.

Women currently using oral contraceptives are less likely to use any barrier methods such as condoms or FemCaps. When counselling women on oral contraceptive use, it is important to stress that the pills do not protect against STIs.

Incidence of cervical cancer has decreased in the past decades because of widespread use of Pap screening (Canadian Cancer Society, 2010). The greatest risk factor for cervical cancer is infection with HPV. More than 100 types of HPV cause genital warts, anal cancer, cancer of the vagina and vulva, oropharyngeal cancer, and cancer of the cervix (Sethi & Bickley, 2010). Having unprotected sex increases the chance of contracting HPV. While genital HPV is common in young women, about 70% to 90% of cases clear spontaneously over a 2-year period (Pinto & Crum, 2000). HPV lies dormant but can be reactivated at some later time (Provencher & Murphy, 2007). Other risk factors for cervical cancer are tobacco use, infection with *Chlamydia* or HIV, inadequate diet, low income, and family history of cancer. HPV-DNA testing is a simple swabbing of the external and

---

BOX 26-1 SELF-CARE PRACTICES

Review these self-care practices with female patients.

Ways to Prevent Sexually Transmitted Infections (STIs)

- Delay first sexual intercourse.
- Restrict the number of sexual partners.
- Avoid sex with people who have multiple partners.
- Use condoms regardless of whether you use other birth control methods (eg, oral contraceptives).
- Obtain the human papillomavirus (HPV) vaccine. Ideally you should have the vaccine before you are sexually active. It protects against cancer of the cervix; some skin cancers; cancer of the vulva, vagina, and anus; and genital warts.

Use of Oral Contraceptives (Chow, 2010b)

- Use a condom.
- Take birth control pill at same time each day.
- Stop smoking, or cut down.
- Report the following symptoms immediately: ACHES
  A—abdominal pain
  C—chest pain
  H—headaches
  E—eye symptoms (blurred vision, seeing spots)
  S—severe leg pain.

Plan B to Prevent Pregnancy

- If you have intercourse without birth control or the birth control method fails (eg, the condom breaks), see a pharmacist right

away about Plan B (emergency contraceptive pills) to prevent pregnancy. The drug is available without a prescription and is safe to use (Beaulieu, Kools, et al., 2011).

Know the Warning Signs/Symptoms of STIs

- Pain in pelvic area
- Itchy rash around the vagina
- Changes in vaginal discharge (colour, amount, appearance)
- Bleeding between menstrual periods
- Pain or burning on urination (passing urine)

Practise Genital Hygiene

- Wash external genitals with water and a very mild (nonperfumed) soap.
- The vagina is self-cleaning, so there is no need to put solutions into it (eg, douching). Douching solutions may cause irritation or an allergic reaction in the vagina and nearby tissue.
- Reduce a moist genital environment by wearing cotton panties (or at least ones with a cotton crotch) and not wearing jeans in hot weather.

Reduce Risk of Bladder Infections

- Increase intake of fluids (avoid fluids containing caffeine).
- Pass urine every 2 to 3 hours during the day and evening.
- Pass urine before and after sexual intercourse.
- Avoid bubble baths.

Adapted from Potter, P. A., Perry, A. G., et al. (Eds.). (2006). *Canadian fundamentals of nursing* (3rd ed.). Toronto, ON: Elsevier Canada.

BOX 26-2 FEMALE GENITAL SELF-EXAMINATION

A self-genital examination is a systematic approach for detecting changes such as lesions, warts, and discharge. The instructions are as follows:

- Do the examination *sitting* on the edge of a chair or *standing*.
- Have a good light source and use a hand mirror to see the structures.
- Check pubic hair for nits (pubic lice) and at base of hairs for skin rashes.
- Gently spread apart the outer folds (labia majora), one side at a time. Look for swelling, redness, bumps, sores, blisters, lacerations, or warts (cauliflower-like sores).

- Gently spread apart the inner folds (labia minora), one side at a time. Look for swelling, redness, bumps, sores, blisters, lacerations, or warts.
- Look near the top of the inner folds for the clitoris—check colour and look for any sores.
- Look at the vaginal opening. (It appears as a slit if you have not had sexual intercourse. It is larger if you have had sexual intercourse and more so if you had a baby by vaginal birth.) Look for vaginal discharge, if you find any note its amount, colour, and appearance.
- Examine the anal area for rashes, sores, or warts

Adapted from Sethi, S., & Bickley, L. S. (2010). Female genitalia. In T. C. Stephen, D. L. Skillen, R. A. Day, & L. S. Bickley (Eds.). *Canadian Bates' guide to health assessment for nurses* (1st ed., pp. 802–803). Philadelphia, PA: Wolters Kluwer Health/Lippincott Williams & Wilkins.

---

endocervical areas. This testing captures the nine types of HPV (16, 18, 31, 33, 35, 45, 51, 52, and 56) that cause high-grade cervical lesions that lead to cancer.

⚠ SAFETY ALERT 26-2

Human papillomavirus (HPV) vaccines target HPV types 16 and 18, which cause 70% of cervical cancer cases. The only cervical cancer symptoms are precancerous changes in the cervix, which can be detected during regular pelvic examinations with a Pap smear. Current literature suggests that HPV-DNA testing along with cytology testing is significantly more sensitive than cytology testing alone (American College of Obstetricians and Gynecologists, 2008).

Since 2008, the HPV vaccine has been provided free of charge by the government of Canada for girls aged 9 to 10 years in all provinces and territories (PHAC, 2007a). Ideally, the vaccine is given before girls become sexually active. The vaccine is recommended for females 9 through 26 years. Annual Pap screening is still recommended until 2 negative tests are obtained, even if the patient has received the vaccine (Sethi & Bickley, 2010).

Female genital mutilation (FGM) consists of all procedures that involve partial or total removal of the external female genitalia for nonmedical reasons. It is usually carried out on minors and as such is a violation of the rights of children. "The practice also violates a person's rights to health, security and physical integrity, the right to be free from torture and cruel, inhuman or degrading treatment …" (World Health Organization, 2010, p. 1). There are four types of FGM:

Clitoridectomy: is partial or complete removal of the clitoris.
Excision: partial or complete removal of the clitoris and labia minora and may or may not include excision of the labia majora.
Infibulation: narrowing of the vaginal opening by creating a covering seal by cutting and repositioning the inner or outer labia.

Other: all other dangerous procedures to the female genitalia for nonmedical purposes, for example, pricking, piercing, incising, and cauterizing the genital area.

There are no health benefits to FGM. Immediate complications include severe pain, shock, hemorrhage, tetanus, sepsis, and urine retention. Long-term concerns are recurrent bladder and UTIs, infertility, increased risk of complications with childbirth, and death of newborns. If infibulation was carried out, the vaginal opening has to be cut open for sexual intercourse and childbirth. In some situations the opening is sutured closed and then reopened, further increasing risks.

Causes of FGM are a mix of cultural, religious, and social factors within families and communities, and it occurs in western, eastern, and northeastern regions of Africa, some countries in Asia and the Middle East, and in some immigrant communities in Europe and North America. It is estimated that between 100 and 140 million girls and women worldwide are living with the consequences of FGM. WHO is advocating for international, regional, and local efforts to end FGM within a generation.

Focused Health History Related to Common Symptoms/Signs

When assessing the patient who presents with a specific concern, the nurse performs a focused assessment. He or she asks questions relating to the reason for seeking care. Begin with asking about the onset of the symptom. It is best to get specifics such as the number of hours, days, or weeks that the patient has been experiencing the symptom(s). If bleeding is the issue, inquire about the number of pads or tampons used per hour or day. Ask about the location of the bleeding. Many patients are not comfortable with anatomical descriptions and just say "down there." Use appropriate terminology in a matter-of-fact manner. Ask if pain involves the abdomen, bladder, vagina, urethra, uterus, or rectum. If possible, have the patient point to the area of concern. Inquire about the duration of the concern. Again, specifics help: How long does the symptom last? Is it ongoing? Ask about the character of the pain, bleeding, itching, discharge, or lesion.

If necessary, the nurse can provide the patient with descriptions such as dull, sharp, burning, stinging, colour and consistency of blood, presence of clots, thick or thin discharge, odour, or not. Find out if there are any associated symptoms or signs such as nausea, vomiting, fever, malaise, fainting, or change in urinary or bowel habits. Inquire about things that might aggravate symptoms such as intercourse, menses, physical activity, hygiene products, or self-treatment. If the patient has experienced any relief, ask what has made it better. Has the symptom been experienced before and when? What was done for it? Ask about the severity of the symptom. How bad is

the pain, itching, or bleeding on a scale of 0 to 10, with 0 being no concern and 10 being the worst ever?

Find out if anything has changed in the patient's environment that could affect the symptom. Ask how daily life is affected by the symptom. Finally, ask what the patient thinks is causing it.

Common Female Genital or Rectal Symptoms/Signs

- Pelvic pain
- Vaginal burning, discharge, or itching
- Menstrual disorders
- Structural concerns
- Hemorrhoids

Examples of Questions for Symptom/Signs Analysis—Vaginal Bleeding

- "Where is the bleeding coming from?" (Location)
- "Describe the bleeding—colour, odour, consistency, any clots?" (Quality)
- "Describe the amount of bleeding in 24 hours, as to number and size of pads/tampons used." "How often do you have to change?" "Are pads and tampons soaked when you change?" "Do you need to use more than one pad or tampon at a time?" "Is there a reason for seeking help today regarding your condition?" (Severity)
- "When did you first notice the bleeding?" "Did it start suddenly? Or gradually?" (Onset)
- "How long have you had the bleeding?" "Have you had it like this before?" (Duration)
- "When did the bleeding start?" "How long does it last?" "What is the interval between bleedings?" "When is it at its worst?" "Daytime? Or nighttime?" (Time of day/month/year)
- "What do you do to make the bleeding better?" Explore: "Medications?" "Dietary practices (eating or restricting certain foods)?" "Mental activities?" "Physical activities?" "Applying heat or cold to abdomen?" "What has worked in the past?" (Alleviating factors)
- "What makes the bleeding worse?" "Any activity?" "Sexual intercourse?" (Aggravating factors)
- "What other symptoms have you noticed with the bleeding?" Explore with the patient: "Cramping?" "Bloating?" "Heavy feeling below?" "Abdominal pain?" "Constipation?" "Diarrhea?" "Fatigue?" (Associated symptoms)
- "How is this condition affecting your life?" (Significance to patient)
- "What do you think is causing the bleeding?" (Patient's perspective)

Adapted from Sethi, S., & Bickley, L. S. (2010). Female genitalia. In T. C. Stephen, D. L. Skillen, R. A. Day, & L. S. Bickley (Eds.). *Canadian Bates' guide to health assessment for nurses* (1st ed., p. 794). Philadelphia, PA: Wolters Kluwer Health/Lippincott Williams & Wilkins.

Examples of Questions to Assess Symptoms/Signs	Rationale/Unexpected Findings
Pelvic Pain Do you have any pain or discomfort? • Location • Intensity • Duration • Description • Aggravating factors • Alleviating factors • Associated symptoms • Environmental factors • Functional impairment • Pain goal • Patient perspective on cause	Measurable pain identification allows the nurse to address symptoms individually. Ask the patient to rate the pain or discomfort from 0 to 10, with 0 (no pain) to 10 (worst pain ever). Differences between acute and chronic pain may alter the course of intervention and goals set. Always ask the patient to point to the area of pain or discomfort to gather more accurate and reliable data. Many gynecological issues differ in the pain characteristics. The description of burning versus dull and gnawing can help the nurse and practitioner identify the concern sooner. Conditions involving the pelvic region increase in pain and intensity with activities such as exercise, intercourse, or prolonged standing. Relief may be in the form of over-the-counter (OTC) medications or remedies such as warm baths or a heating pad. If the current concern is impairing functional ability, the nurse addresses this as a priority as much as if he or she had the pain or discomfort. The goal is to assist in expediting the relief of the presenting symptom/sign and to contribute to the return of functionality in the patient.

(text continues on page 802)

Vaginal Burning, Discharge, Itching

- Have you ever been treated for a sexually transmitted infection (STI)?
- If you were treated, were your partner(s) treated?
- Did you have a follow-up examination to confirm treatment?
- Are you aware of the different types of STIs?
- Do you currently have any vaginal discharge? If so, is there a colour? Odour? Or consistency to it?
- Do you have any itching or burning of your pubic hair? Vulva? Or vagina?

An STI survey allows the nurse to educate the patient on all the possible infections. Differentiate itching between external and internal location. Vaginal discharge is a common symptom of STIs; however, a patient with an STI may have few or no symptoms. External itching can be caused from any number of sources: **pediculosis pubis** (commonly called "crabs"), **contact dermatitis**, **herpes simplex virus**, **condyloma acuminatum (external genital warts)**, or **atrophic vulvitis**.

Menstrual Disorders

- Have you ever experienced irregular menstrual cycles? Or skipped a cycle?
- Do you experience cramps during your menses?
- Do you take any medication for menstrual cramps? If so how much? And how often? Does it help?
- Do you experience preflow bloating? Mood swings? Headaches? Or breast tenderness? Does it go away once your flow begins?
- Are there any times other than your menstrual period that you experience bleeding? Or spotting?
- Do you experience any bleeding or spotting following intercourse?
- Do any menstrual conditions cause you to miss work? School? Or social functions?

Amenorrhea is the absence of menstrual periods. The most common causes of secondary amenorrhea are pregnancy and anovulation. **Dysmenorrhea** is pain with menses. *Premenstrual syndrome* is the emotional and physical symptoms that occur at the same time before menses each month (Chow, 2010a). Nonsteroidal anti-inflammatory drugs have been shown effective for dysmenorrhea. Intermenstrual bleeding or spotting or bleeding could be expected or could indicate an ongoing infection. Postintercourse bleeding or spotting could indicate an STI or possibly a cervical polyp.

Structural Conditions

- Have you ever been treated for any cancer of the reproductive organs?
- Have you ever been treated for any gynecological conditions such as endometriosis? Uterine fibroids? Ovarian cyst? Or unexpected bleeding?
- Have you noticed any change in the amount of hair you have on the vulva? Abdomen? Or around the nipples?
- Have you gained weight especially in the midabdomen in the past 6 months?
- Have you noticed changes in your skin?

Patients with a history of **endometriosis** have increased risk of infertility (Curtis, Overholt, et al., 2005). Frequent ovarian cysts along with menstrual irregularities warrant evaluation for **polycystic ovarian syndrome**. In this condition, the patient presents with obesity, acne, **hirsutism** (increased hair along the abdomen and around the nipples), and **acanthosis nigricans** (areas of hyperpigmentation around the back of the neck and under arms). Vaginal ultrasound reveals multicystic ovaries. The patient may have variations in hormone levels, including increased free testosterone (Barron & Falsetti, 2008).

Hemorrhoids

- Do you have hemorrhoids?
- Do you drip bright red blood into the toilet bowl with bowel movements?

They are very common during pregnancy and following childbirth. Hemorrhoids may be either external or internal.

▲ Lifespan Considerations

| Additional Questions | Rationale/Unexpected Findings |

Women Who Are Pregnant

Have you had any bleeding since you became pregnant? Or cramping?

Any bleeding or spotting following confirmation of pregnancy must be investigated further by a specialist.

Have you had any unusual Pap smears in the past?

Patients who have had unexpected results may have a recurrence during pregnancy. Those who have had surgery to remove suspicious cells may have scar tissue, which needs to be released during labour in order to permit a vaginal delivery.

Additional Questions	Rationale/Unexpected Findings
Have you had any sexually transmitted infections (STIs) in the past?	Verify that any STIs were treated per protocol. Assess risk of reexposure (many STIs, especially syphilis, can harm the fetus).
What type of contraception have you used? When was the last time you used it?	If the patient was using hormonal contraceptives within three cycles prior to conception, it is difficult to assess when ovulation occurred. The patient taking such contraceptives does not have true menses but rather has "withdrawal bleeds" when she is not taking progesterone for 7 days. Even if pregnant, if she continues her birth control pills, she may have withdrawal bleeds at the usual time. If her conception date is not clear, ultrasound dating in the first trimester can be offered.
Have you had any concerns about infertility?	If the response is positive, fully document the patient's history, including any medication taken and type of assisted reproduction. In vitro pregnancies have a somewhat increased risk of multiple gestation and fetal loss.
Do you have any symptoms of pregnancy? (see also Chapter 27)	Morning sickness, growing pains, increased vaginal discharge or urination, breast tenderness/discharge, periumbilical pain, fetal hiccups, or Braxton Hicks contractions may be uncomfortable.

Newborns, Infants, and Children

Additional Questions	Rationale/Unexpected Findings
Do you use bubble baths for your child?	Just as for any females, contact with perfumed bath products or lotions may cause a contact dermatitis. For young girls, it is best to avoid bubble bath and fragrance products.
Does your child have frequent pain with urination?	Challenges with bladder control may require a specialist. Sudden regression in bladder or bowel control may signal sexual abuse.
Does your child (older than 2.5 years) have control over the bladder?	
Do you notice your child scratching his or her genitals?	Itching or scratching in the genitals could be infection, pinworm, abuse, or hygiene related.
Have you noticed any vaginal discharge on the underwear? Do you notice any odour in the genital area?	Young children, especially toddlers, may insert foreign objects in orifices including the vagina.

Older Adults

Additional Questions	Rationale/Unexpected Findings
Have you noticed any bleeding since your menses stopped?	Any bleeding of any amount that occurs after the patient has had 1 year without menses must be investigated (Chow, 2010b).
Have you noticed any vaginal concerns such as dryness? Itching? Or vaginal secretions?	Loss of estrogen in the vagina along with loss of usual rugae can lead to irritation and possible spotting from the vagina.
Are you currently having sexual relations? Have you experienced any pain with intercourse? Do you have a satisfactory sexual relationship with your partner?	Regular sexual activity is expected in older women and encouraged unless it causes pain. Recommendation of vaginal lubricants will help provide relief from vaginal dryness. The nurse practitioner may prescribe local estrogen to help with dryness.

(text continues on page 804)

Additional Questions	Rationale/Unexpected Findings
Have you noticed any vaginal pressure or loss of urine if you cough or sneeze? Have you noticed any rectal pressure? Or experienced difficulty with bowel movements? Or incontinence of feces?	Vaginal pressure may indicate *uterine prolapse*. With accompanying bladder symptoms, there may be bladder support *(cystocele)* issues. Rectal pressure may indicate a *rectocele*, *prolapsed rectum*, or mass and should be evaluated.

 Cultural Considerations

Have you ever had a pelvic examination? Would you prefer a female practitioner? Are you from a community that practises female genital mutilation (FGM)? Have you undergone any type of FGM?	Some cultures and religions have rules about who can see women unclothed and when pelvic examinations are allowed (Hahm, Lee, et al., 2007). FGM is a tradition practised in many countries, many of them African (World Health Organization, 2010). FGM has implications for women in their sexual life and for pregnancy and labour. See the Point for links to additional women's health information.

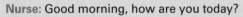

An Example of a Therapeutic Dialogue

Teresa Nguyen, introduced at the beginning of this chapter, is a 28-year-old woman with vaginal discharge, pelvic pain, and fever. The following is an example of an interview style used by the nurse.

Nurse: Good morning, how are you today?

Teresa: Good, thank you.

Nurse: What name would you like me to call you?

Teresa: You can call me Teresa.

Nurse: And you can call me Shelly. Let me look over your patient health record (looks at chart). It looks like you've been having some pelvic pain and vaginal discharge.

Teresa: Yes.

Nurse: Tell me a little more about those symptoms.

Teresa: Well, I really notice that the pain is bad when my boyfriend has sex with me.

Nurse: (Listens)

Teresa: I'm really afraid that I have a sexually transmitted infection (STI). My friends really don't like my boyfriend and they said that he cheated on me.

Nurse: You sound very concerned.

Teresa: I just don't want my parents to know. They are very traditional.

Nurse: You are protected by privacy laws, but we may need to notify the health department if there is an illness that needs to be reported.

Critical Thinking Challenge

• How should the nurse proceed with questioning about privacy?
• What questions should the nurse ask regarding sexual activity and sexual practices? Give specific examples.
• What are your thoughts about Teresa's relationships with her parents? How might they affect the care?

Objective Data Collection

Equipment

- Examination gown
- Sheet or drape
- Nonsterile examination gloves (both latex and nonlatex)
- Water-soluble vaginal lubricant
- Light unit either goose neck or speculum attachment
- Wooden/plastic spatula
- Cervical brush (broom)
- Endocervical brush
- Glass slide
- Slide fixative
- Liquid pap base
- Culture tubes (DNA) for chlamydia and gonorrhea
- Sterile cotton swabs

- Large cotton balls
- Small bottles with tops, one containing saline solution, one containing potassium hydroxide (KOH), and one containing acetic acid solution (white vinegar)
- Vaginal specula (either metal or plastic) (several sizes and types, preferably warmed via heat source in examination drawer)
- Pederson: narrow blades
- Graves: wider blades
- Pediatric: smaller Pederson with narrow blades and shorter length
- Mirror

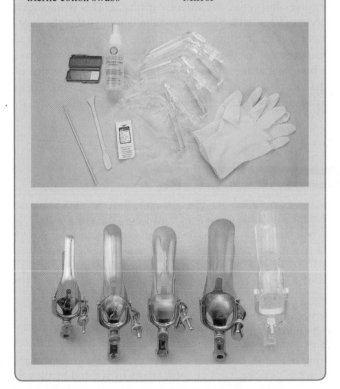

Promoting Patient Comfort, Dignity, and Safety

It is important to provide a warm, comfortable, and private environment. The nurse displays confidence while staying in tune with the patient's feelings of fear or embarrassment. A room containing information pamphlets and three-dimensional models encourages inquiry and lessens anxiety. Ensure privacy throughout the interview and examination. The examination table should be facing away from the door and instructions given not to disturb during the examination.

The patient remains dressed for the interview. Try to not have the patient wait too long as this may increase her anxiety.

Offer a step-by-step description of what will occur during the examination. Allow the patient to see all the instruments to be used and explain what they are for. The nurse takes time, especially if this is the first examination for the patient, to answer all the questions and concerns verbalized. Assure the patient that if she is uncomfortable at any time to let you know, as the examination will stop or be altered. Empowering the patient and allowing patient control will enhance the examination experience and will ensure that the patient returns in the future. Ask the patient to empty her bladder before the examination. Make sure all equipment is set up and within reach.

It is important to make sure the patient is not menstruating or has not had intercourse or douched before the Pap test. These conditions interfere with the cytology reading. Unless otherwise indicated, allow the patient to keep her socks on during the examination. Covers should be provided for table stirrups.

The nurse assists the patient into a semilithotomy position, helps her to move down just before the examination

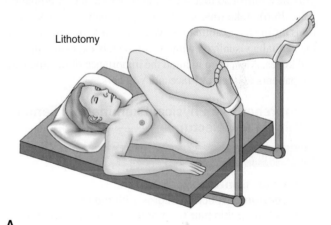

A

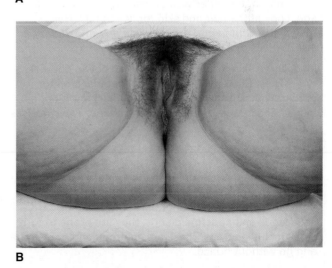

B

Figure 26-5 Lithotomy positioning for the examination of the female genitalia. **A.** Illustration showing the positioning of the lower extremities and buttocks. **B.** Frontal view of surface anatomy.

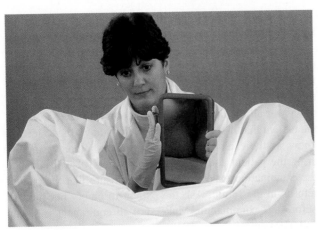

Figure 26-6 The nurse or nurse practitioner may want to offer the patient a mirror during the examination, so she can watch what is happening.

(Fig. 26-5), and assists the patient in placing her feet into the stirrups and ensures she is comfortable after the feet are placed. Elevating the patient's head and shoulders allows visualization of the examination by the patient. It is helpful to provide a mirror so that she might better see the examination (Fig. 26-6). Take time to encourage the patient to ask questions during the examination. When draping the patient, keep the genitalia visualized without completely exposing the legs and knees. Also, keep in mind the importance of making sure the patient can see your face and you hers.

The nurse washes hands and puts gloves on both hands. At this point, the examination chair can be positioned in front of the examination table. Slowly have the patient move toward the end of the table. Reassure her that you will not let her fall. Holding the gloved hands out to the side of each knee, instruct the patient to allow her knees to drop into your hands, or allow her legs to go limp. If the patient is having difficulty abducting her legs, consider physical limitations or previous sexual abuse. It is possible to conduct an examination with the patient in the side-lying position, if necessary. It is important never to force the legs apart with your hands or arms. Also, the nurse talks through each step and lets the patient know what is going to happen next.

Advanced Techniques

The routine head-to-toe assessment includes the most important and common assessment techniques. Nurse practitioners may add specialty or advanced steps if concerns exist over a specific finding. In clinical practice, the assessment includes inspecting the external genitalia. This is important because yeast infections are common during antibiotic treatment or with incontinence where there may be skin irritation. Inspection of the internal vagina, obtaining a Pap smear, and a bimanual examination are within the scope of practice of the nurse practitioner and specially prepared nurses. These examinations require additional education and skills.

Comprehensive Physical Examination: Female Genitalia and Rectum

Technique and Expected Findings

External Genitalia
Inspection. Inspection begins with the mons pubis. Inspect the pubic hair for amount and distribution. The pubic hair of the older woman becomes thinner with age. Look at the hair and skin for lice or nits. *Hair is evenly distributed and growing in a downward direction. No lice or nits are seen.*

Inspect the skin for any redness, breakdown, papules, or vesicles. Bilaterally observe the inguinal area for erythema, fissures, or enlarged inguinal lymph nodes. Inspect the clitoris, noting size, and shape. *The clitoris is 1 to 1.5 cm long.*

Inspect the labia majora for size, symmetry, and for piercings. Look for any swelling or redness. Because both labia majora and minora are composed of sebaceous and apocrine glands, they are prone to form small inclusion cysts. These are common and may come and go without notice.

Inspect the vaginal opening for swelling or redness (Fig. 26-7). *No protrusions are seen from the vagina.*

Unexpected Findings

Pediculosis pubis (crab lice) commonly presents with itching (see Table 26-4 at the end of the chapter).

Symptoms of herpes simplex virus 2 include vulvar or vaginal pain, flu-like symptoms such as chills or fever, sores on the vulva or genital region, scattered vesicles along the labia, matching vesicles on the labia reflecting "kissing" lesions, surface ulcerations or crusted healing lesions, and inguinal lymphadenopathy (see Table 26-3 at the end of the chapter).

Piercings of the labia require careful hygiene measures. Symptoms of condyloma acuminatum (warts) include vulvar or vaginal itching, vaginal secretions, and growths along the vagina or rectum. Examination may reveal fleshy pink or gray papilloma or wart-like projections at the vulva, vagina, or anus (see Table 26-3).

Cancer of the vulva is usually asymptomatic until the lesion becomes large enough that there may be itching, burning, pain, and bleeding or watery discharge from the lesion. Any discharge or mucus is considered unexpected and requires a culture (Chow, 2010b).

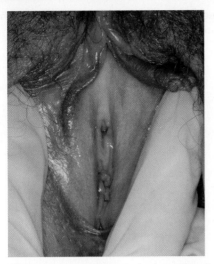

Figure 26-7 Inspecting the vaginal opening (introitus).

Inspect the vestibule for colour, redness, swelling, odour, or discharge. Inspect the urethra for position and patency. *There is no discharge or redness.* Observe the Skene's glands at the 1 and 11 o'clock positions lateral to the urethra. *They are small, noninflamed, and occasionally not seen.*

Inspection is completed with the perineum. *The area between the introitus and anus is smooth with no lesions or tears. Scars from any episiotomies are healed. The anus is intact with no swelling, lacerations, or protrusions.*

Internal Genitalia

Palpation. Using the thumb and middle finger of the gloved hand separate the inner portion of the labia minora, insert the index finger approximately 1 cm, and rotate the finger so that it is facing upward. Gently press the index finger forward to assess the urethra and Skene's glands (Fig. 26-8). Do not do this for a lengthy period because it will irritate the urethra and cause the patient discomfort.

Candidiasis is associated with vulvovaginal and possibly rectal pruritus and dyspareunia. Examination may reveal vulvovaginal edema, erythema, excoriation, and thick white secretions, sometimes only along the inner vaginal walls (see Table 26-3).

Look for unexpected findings such as contact dermatitis and chancres of syphilis (Chow, 2010a). (See Table 26-4).

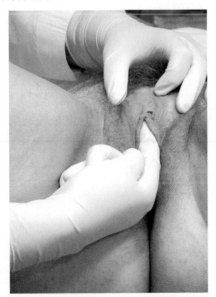

Figure 26-8 Palpating the Skene's glands and urethra.

(text continues on page 808)

With the index finger still inserted approximately 1 cm into the vagina, rotate the finger downward again and palpate with the index finger and the thumb the Bartholin's glands on each side (Fig. 26-9). The Bartholin's glands are located bilaterally in the lower labial areas at approximately 8 and 4 o'clock positions. *No swelling or tenderness is noted on either side.*

Unexpected findings include an abscess of Bartholin's gland or urethral caruncle (see Table 26-4).

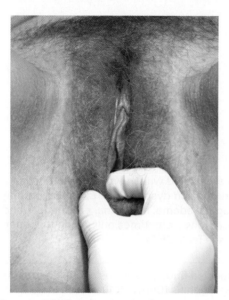

Figure 26-9 Palpating the Bartholin's glands.

While the finger is inserted, it is a good idea to advance it to locate the cervix. Explain to the patient what you are doing. This will help avoid inaccurate placement of the speculum around the cervix. While the index finger is still in place ask the patient to squeeze the vaginal muscles around your finger to check vaginal tone. Ask the patient to then bear down slightly to assess for pelvic organ prolapse.

Assessment of vaginal tone is important, especially if the patient has concerns about pelvic relaxation or urinary incontinence. Pelvic organ prolapse is not limited to older women; many times, obesity and gravity are factors (Smith, 2007).

Speculum Examination

Inspection. The speculum is chosen based on the patient's history, not weight or outward appearance. The speculum should be warmed in the examination table drawer if possible; if not, run the speculum under warm water. Hold the speculum between the index and middle finger of the dominant hand. Make sure that the blades are pushed together and stay together during insertion to ensure comfort and to avoid pinching any part of the labia or vaginal walls between them. Place the thumb under the thumbscrew on the metal or the lever on the plastic type of speculum. The opposite hand will insert the index finger as done in the initial vaginal examination and place slight pressure downward.

⚠ *SAFETY ALERT 26-3*

Do not use lubricants on the speculum because it can interfere with the cytology and culture readings.

The speculum is then inserted in an oblique position along the top of the finger (Fig. 26-10). A constant downward insertion prevents the anterior blade of the speculum from hitting the urethra or bladder and causing discomfort or pain. As the speculum moves in and downward, slowly remove the index finger. Have the patient exhale slowly as the speculum is inserted. This helps in relaxing the pubococcygeal muscles. Slowly rotate the speculum so that it is in a horizontal position with the bottom blade continuing to be pressed in a downward position at 45°. Once the blade is completely inserted, slowly open the speculum blades while continually keeping a posterior pressure on the lower blade.

△ *SAFETY ALERT 26-4*
Do not try to force the complete blade in if it causes the patient discomfort or pain.

ENTRY ANGLE **ANGLE AT FULL INSERTION**

Figure 26-10 The speculum. **A.** Angle at entry. **B.** Angle at full insertion.

For many women the speculum most often used is the Pederson. The length of this speculum is approximately 6 cm, which is the usual length of the vagina. Once the speculum is inserted fully, the blades are opened slowly by pressing on the thumb piece until the cervix comes into view at the end of the blades. As the cervix comes into view, the speculum is locked into place by tightening the screw on the thumb piece. Check with the patient at all steps to make sure that she is comfortable (Fig. 26-11).

If the cervix is not visualized, the speculum may be too high. Repositioning with the blades pressed posterior may be necessary.

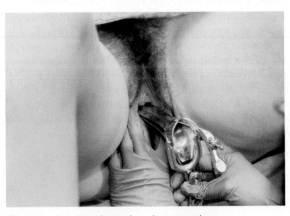

Figure 26-11 Inserting the speculum.

(text continues on page 810)

Cervix and OS. Inspect the cervix and vaginal walls (Fig. 26-12). *The cervix is smooth and pink and positioned midline in the vagina.* The position is based on the angle of the uterus and may tilt anteriorly or posteriorly as well. The cervix of a nulliparous woman has a small round os, while the parous woman has a horizontal or fish-mouth-looking slit. Inspect the cervix and surrounding area for increased discharge. Clear secretions are usually present and may be more or less productive based on the woman's cycle or menstrual history. It is best not to remove too much of this secretion because doing so may compromise cervical cells needed for the Pap smear. If the woman has an intrauterine device, this is the time to check for the strings (two strings clear in colour).

If there have been any birth traumas, there may be a tear of the cervix resulting in an irregular slit. It is common in women who have had vaginal births to have one or several **nabothian cysts**. These small benign nodules resemble yellow pustules. These are not treated but documented as findings. There may be a small polyp at the opening of the os. It may be removed in the office and sent to pathology for testing (Fig. 26-13). Additional unexpected findings include *cervical polyps, Diethylstilbestrol (DES) syndrome, cervical dysplasia, carcinoma in situ,* and *cervical cancer* (see Table 26-6 at the end of this chapter).

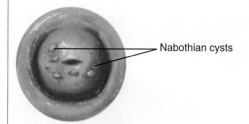

Figure 26-13 Nabothian cysts.

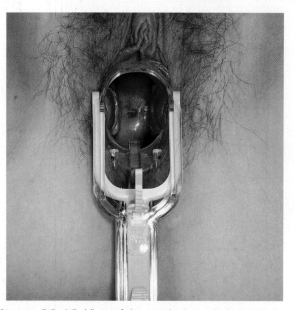

Figure 26-12 View of the cervix through the speculum.

Pap Smear and Cultures. The Papanicolaou (named after Dr Nicholas Papanicolaou) or Pap smear is a screening tool for cervical neoplasia. An Ayers spatula (either wood or plastic) is used in conjunction with an endocervical brush for glass slide examinations. The longer portion of the spatula is inserted into the cervical os and rotated 360° as it is pressed against the cervix to gently scrape the cells from the **squamocolumnar junction** of the cervix (Fig. 26-14). This is also called the *transformation zone* and includes the outer and inner areas of the endocervix. It is the area of highest neoplastic involvement. Secretions obtained from the spatula are then spread gently on a clear glass slide and a fixative spray is applied. The endocervical brush is then inserted into the endocervix and rotated 720° to ensure an adequate cell sample (Fig. 26-15). The endocervical brush is then gently rolled out on a clean glass slide, avoiding cell destruction. A spray fixative is applied and the slide labelled for cytology. For the liquid-based cytology (LBC) test, a plastic cytology broom is used to obtain both exocervical and endocervical cells.

The Pap smear is used to evaluate cells from the cervix for precancerous or cancerous status. Newer technologies and techniques for obtaining the cervical cells have helped to improve screening and early detection. Currently several types of cytological testing exist. The conventional Pap test (smear to slide method) has a 20% false negative rate (ACOG, 2008). Liquid-based cytology (LBC) uses a similar technique except the practitioner uses a plastic broom and the cells and tip of the broom are placed into a preserving liquid solution. The LBC has more accurate results than the Pap smear, possibly because of the better preservation of the cells (Murphy, 2007). In addition, a portion of the LBC fluid can be sent for HPV-DNA testing (two tests can be done from one sample) (McCowen Meahring, 2010). At the present time, LBC and HPV-DNA tests are not available in all Canadian provinces/territories.

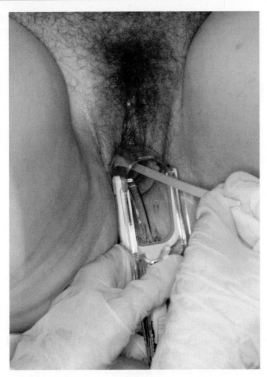

Figure 26-14 Using the spatula to retrieve ectocervical cells.

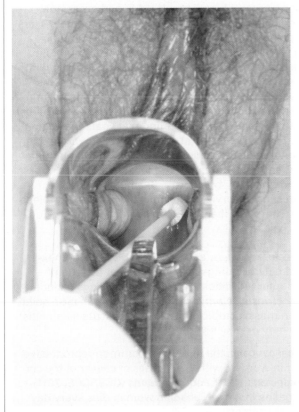

Figure 26-15 Using the endocervical brush.

(text continues on page 812)

The tip of the broom is inserted into the endocervix and rotated 720°. The tip of the broom is removed and placed into a preserving liquid solution (Fig. 26-16).

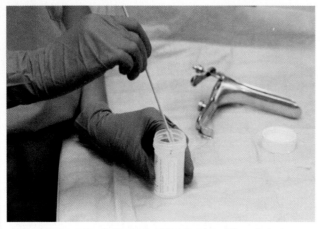

Figure 26-16 Collected cells are placed in a solution during liquid-based cytology (LBC) testing.

Vaginal Wall. The vaginal wall is inspected during insertion and removal of the speculum. The lateral and anteroposterior walls are inspected for lesions, bleeding, erythema, or edema. In the older patient, it is not *uncommon to see atrophic changes to the lining of the vagina from lack of estrogen.* The examiner will notice a lack or thinning of the vaginal rugae. This is very tender and uncomfortable and so should be examined gently. The speculum should be removed in the reverse order of insertion, with careful attention given to keeping the blades open until the cervix has slid away from the blades. The thumb stays on the lever and is slowly released. As the speculum is rotated to an oblique position, the blades are slowly closed avoiding pinching the vaginal walls or labia, or pulling the pubic hair.

Bimanual Examination

Inform the patient that this part of the examination is to assess the organs by manually palpating from the inside and outside the size, shape, and position of the uterus and ovaries as well as assessing general support of the organs. At this time, the examiner removes the gloves and places a new glove on the hand doing the internal examination. The index and second fingers are inserted in a downward fashion and slowly turned upward once the fingers reach the cervix. The thumb is kept upward or tucked in during this time to keep it from pressing on the clitoris. The fingers rest internally at the posterior area of the cervix. The cervix is palpated for size, shape, and

Collection of cells from the endocervix or cervix may cause some spotting or bleeding; this can occur with a Pap smear or with a sexually transmitted infection (STI) screening.

> ⚠ *SAFETY ALERT 26-5*
> *It is important to do the Pap smear or LBC test first so that bleeding is minimal on the cytology specimen. The cultures for chlamydia trachomatis (CT) and Gonococcus (GC) which causes gonorrhea are done after the Pap smear.*

Most commonly, a DNA-based probe is used. This cultures both CT and GC at the same time. The Dacron probe is inserted into the endocervical canal and kept there for 30 seconds to 1 minute. Remove the probe, avoiding contact with vaginal secretions, and place the specimen into the culture tube.

Any secretion, unexpected in amount, colour, or odour is sampled for infection (see Table 26-3 at the end of this chapter). *Trichomoniasis* often presents with vaginal pruritus (itching), thin or thick secretions, a foul vaginal odour, purulent yellow to green frothy discharge, pain on pelvic examination, cervical redness (strawberry looking), contact bleeding, pH > 4.5, and occasional dysuria. *Gonorrhea* is indicated by yellow vaginal secretion, pain with urination (dysuria), and dyspareunia (pain with intercourse). In addition, there is purulent discharge from the cervix and tenderness or pain with the pelvic examination. *Bacterial vaginosis* presents with vaginal secretions that have a strong "fishy" odour and vaginal itching or burning. Examination may reveal a creamy white to gray secretion that coats the vaginal walls (Elkins, Mayeaux, et al., 2006). *Chlamydia* is often asymptomatic. Occasional clear or white secretion may be evident, and there may be bleeding after intercourse. Dyspareunia may be present. Examination shows changes in the cervix, which may be reddened or bleed easily. There may be pain with the pelvic examination.

Cystocele, rectocele, and *uterine prolapse* are unexpected pelvic findings (see Table 26-5 at the end of this chapter). Additional unexpected findings include *endometriosis, leiomyoma* (fibroid), *ovarian cyst,* solid ovarian mass, ectopic pregnancy, and acute salpingitis. These may or may not cause pain.

Cervical cancer is the third most common reproductive cancer in women, with 1,300 cases of cancer of the cervix expected in 2011 and 350 deaths (CCSSCCS, 2011). This means that one Canadian woman dies every day from a treatable

movement. The nonexamining hand is placed midway between the symphysis pubis and umbilicus (Fig. 26-17).

cancer! (Sethi & Bickley, 2010). Preinvasive cancer of the cervix is often asymptomatic. In later stages, unexpected bleeding, especially after intercourse, is the first sign.

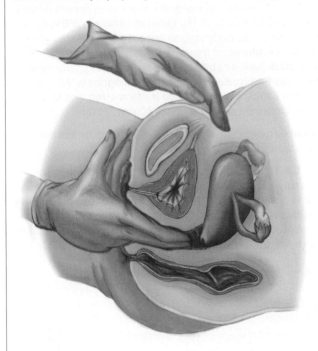

Figure 26-17 Positioning of the hands in bimanual palpation of the cervix.

The uterus is now palpated between the pads of the fingers. The uterus is moved upward so that the examining fingers can palpate between the top and back of the uterus (Fig. 26-18). This position allows for evaluation of the size and shape of the uterus as well as its ability to move without tenderness or resistance. *Expected size is approximately 7 × 4 cm (size is occasionally larger in mulitgravid women). The uterus feels pear shaped and smooth and is freely mobile.*

Leiomyomas (fibroid tumours) can cause unexpected uterine bleeding and backache, abdominal pressure, constipation, incontinence, and dysmenorrhea if large.

Endometrial cancer (body of the uterus) is the most common malignancy of the reproductive system in Canada and is associated with unexpected uterine bleeding, uterine enlargement, or mass. A total of 4,700 cases and 750 deaths were expected in 2011 (CCSSCCS, 2011).

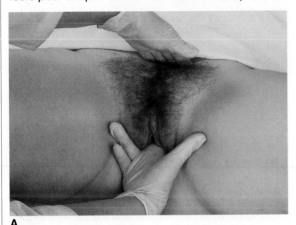

A **B**

Figure 26-18 Bimanual palpation of the uterus. **A.** External view. **B.** Internal position of the hands.

Once the uterus has been assessed, let the patient know that you are now going to check her ovaries. With the two fingers still deep in the vagina and facing upward,

With an *ovarian cyst*, there may be pain, tenderness over the ovary, irregular menses, and intraperitoneal bleeding if it ruptures. A solid ovarian mass raises the

(text continues on page 814)

move to the lateral side of the uterus. If the right hand is examining, the fingers move first to the patient's right and the hand on the abdomen is placed medial to the anterior superior iliac spine. The two hands are brought together as close as possible. With a slow sweeping motion, the fingers are moved down toward the introitus while allowing the adnexae to be palpated between them (Fig. 26-19). This is repeated on the patient's left side. The palpation is done quickly and gently. *The ovary is often not felt, especially in older menopausal women. If palpated, it feels like a small almond.* As stated above, this part of the examination should be brief because the ovaries are similar to gonads in their sensitivity.

possibility of ovarian cancer, which is the second most frequent reproductive cancer, with 2,600 expected cases in 2011 in Canada, and with the highest expected deaths of 1,750 (CCSSCCS, 2011). Ovarian cancer is difficult to diagnose in the early stages because it presents with vague symptoms of increase in waist size, pelvic pressure, back pain or abdominal pain, bloating, constipation, and flatulence. By the time of diagnosis, 75% of ovarian cancers have already metastasized and 60% have spread beyond the pelvis (Chow, 2010b)

Palpable ovaries in an older woman must be further investigated.

The CA-125 blood test is currently used in Canada to measure response to treatment for ovarian cancer. The test is not useful for screening because of too many false positive results. Research is in progress to determine if combining CA-125 with other cancer markers will lead to more accurate results (Ovarian Cancer Update, 2010).

⚠ *SAFETY ALERT 26-6*

In an ectopic pregnancy, the most common symptoms are lower quadrant pain, nausea, and referred pain in the neck or shoulder from blood beneath the diaphragm. If severe hemorrhage occurs, the patient is at risk for life-threatening shock and death (Chow, 2010a)

Salpingitis is also referred to as *pelvic inflammatory disease or PID.* Infection spreads throughout the uterus and up into the tubes (see Table 26-7 at the end of this chapter).

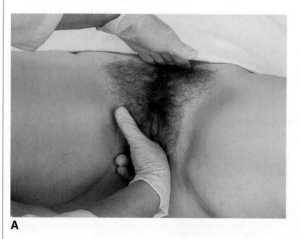
A

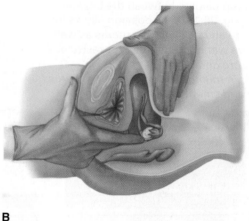
B

Figure 26-19 Bimanual palpation of the ovaries. **A.** External view. **B.** Internal position of the hands.

Rectovaginal Examination

After completing the vaginal examination, circumstances may warrant a rectovaginal examination (see Chapter 25 for a complete rectal examination). The nurse practitioner changes gloves and lubricates the index and middle fingers with the water-based gel. He or she tells the patient that the examination will be slightly uncomfortable and may create pressure, but should not be painful. Ask the patient to bear down slightly as the fingers are inserted. The index finger is inserted into the vagina and the middle finger is placed

This examination is used to evaluate any *rectocele* (bulging of rectum into the vagina) or *rectovaginal fistula* (opening between the vagina and the rectum allowing feces to enter the vagina). A *retroverted uterus* can also be detected with this examination.

into the rectum (Fig. 26-20). *The septum is palpated with the two fingers and feels smooth and intact. The posterior portion of the uterus may be felt and is smooth.* Withdraw the gloved fingers and keep the hand lower while removing the glove and disposing of it. Have tissues available for the patient to clean with after the examination. Assist the patient by placing your hands on her knees and pushing them back on the table. At the same time, extend your hand to help her sit up.

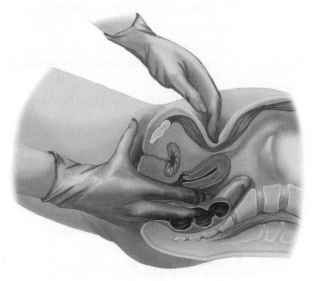

Figure 26-20 Rectovaginal examination.

Examples of Documentation: Female Genitalia

Areas of Assessment	Expected Findings	Unexpected Findings
External genitalia	• Mons pubis: Skin colour consistent; labia majora and minora symmetrical. No ecchymosis, excoriation, rashes, swelling, or inflammation. Even hair distribution in shape of inverted triangle. No nits or lice. No tenderness elicited on light and deep palpation. • Clitoris: Not enlarged • Urethral opening slit-like, midline, and not prolapsed • No discharge or odour • No evidence of female circumcision • Vaginal opening: no lesions or discharge noted • Anal area pigmented and clear	• Mons pubis: Pubic hair sparse. Asymmetry of labia majora and minora. • Rash over mons pubis • External genitalia tender to touch • Hypertrophy of clitoris • Urethral opening slightly reddish and indurated • Vaginal opening ulcerated, and a large amount of thick yellow, foul-smelling discharge noted • Evidence of female circumcision • Evidence of trauma to vaginal region
Internal genitalia	Inspection and palpation • Cervix midline, smooth, evenly pink. Projects 3 cm into the vagina	Inspection and palpation • Cervical surface asymmetrical, reddened; ulceration and lacerations noted.

Areas of Assessment	Expected Findings	Unexpected Findings
	• No lacerations or ulceration noticed • Vaginal wall pink, moist, smooth, and totally rugated • Vaginal discharge clear and odourless • Vaginal walls strong without bulging of anterior or posterior walls • Vaginal muscle strong; tone intact	• During Pap smear, cervical area bleeding noted • Tenderness on palpation of cervix • Lacerations all over vaginal mucosa • Thick, copious, green, foul-smelling discharge • Vaginal area tender to touch • Weak vaginal muscle strength/tone
	Bimanual examination • Cervix smooth and firm • No pain while cervix moved from side to side • No tenderness elicited • Uterus not enlarged • Fundus round and firm • Uterus moves freely • No tenderness elicited on palpation	**Bimanual examination** • Cervix firm but not smooth, contour irregular, mobility intact, tenderness to palpation • Uterus enlarged, irregular in shape • Does not move freely • Tenderness elicited during palpation
	Rectovaginal examination • On palpation posterior wall of uterus firm, smooth, moves freely • No tenderness elicited • No nodules felt	**Rectovaginal examination** • On palpation tenderness elicited • A mass and/or small nodules felt

Adapted from Sethi, S., & Bickley, L. S. (2010). Female genitalia. In T. C. Stephen, D. L. Skillen, R. A. Day, & L. S. Bickley (Eds.). *Canadian Bates' guide to health assessment for nurses* (1st ed., pp. 815–816). Philadelphia, PA: Wolters Kluwer Health/Lippincott Williams & Wilkins.

Documenting Unexpected Findings

The nurse has just finished a physical examination of Teresa Nguyen, the 28-year-old being seen with vaginal drainage and pelvic pain. Unlike the examples of expected documentation charted in the box above, Ms. Nguyen has unexpected findings. Review the following important findings revealed in each of the steps of objective data collection for her. Consider how these results compare with the expected findings presented in the samples of expected documentation. Begin to think about how the data cluster together and what additional data the nurse practitioner might want to collect as she or he thinks critically about Teresa's health issues and anticipates nursing interventions. This note is documented by the nurse practitioner who will work collaboratively with the registered nurse.

Inspection: External genitalia has even hair distribution, no lesions present. Bartholin's glands, urethra, and Skene's glands with no erythema, edema, or discharge. Vaginal introitus and walls pink, moist with expected rugae, strong anterior and posterior wall support, moderate clear discharge present.

Palpation: Cervix smooth round and red, some tenderness upon movement. Clear drainage present. Uterus expected size, shape, mid position, and freely mobile. Adnexae with no palpable masses, but positive tenderness to examination. Perineum smooth. Anal area pink, with no hemorrhoids, fissures, genital warts, or bleeding present. Nonspecific tenderness present over lower half of abdomen during bimanual examination.

Lifespan Considerations

Women Who Are Pregnant

The physical examination of the female who is pregnant is discussed in Chapter 27. To review quickly, the first assessment the nurse makes is whether the membranes are ruptured or not. This can be done by inspection, in the case of gross rupture; using nitrazine (either paper or swab) to test the pH of the discharge; or through a sterile speculum examination by the nurse practitioner. Vaginal examinations by the nurse are deferred if the membranes are ruptured, especially if the patient does not appear to be in active labour.

Even with ruptured membranes, the nurse would perform a vaginal examination if requested to do so by the nurse practitioner or physician, or if he or she suspected that birth might be imminent. The nurse documents cervical dilation (in centimetres), effacement (in centimetres), station (degree of descent into the pelvis of the presenting part), consistency of the cervix (firm, medium, soft) and position (posterior, mid position, anterior). Together, these values can be used to calculate a Bishop's score. A Bishop's score of >9 suggests that vaginal birth is very likely, even if induction or augmentation is necessary.

Child

Allow the parent to hold the child and have the child place her feet together positioned like a frog. Allow the child to take part in the examination. Have the parent let the child know it is OK to allow this examination by the nurse practitioner, especially if she has been taught not to allow anyone to touch her genitals.

Adolescent

Ask the patient if she would like her mother or a friend to be present during the examination. Provide a mirror so that she may observe the examination and have opportunities to ask questions. By placing the examining finger just at the posterior fourchette and gently pressing downward, the pubococcygeal muscle will gradually relax allowing the insertion of the finger. The patient can identify the muscles to relax when the practitioner is inserting the speculum. Do a one-finger vaginal examination before inserting the speculum. This allows the practitioner the ability to estimate the vaginal capacity as well as the position of the cervix and ensures a more comfortable examination. Inform her that the speculum you will use will be no larger than your index finger, which she just felt. Avoid using words such as "pain"; instead use words such as "mild pressure" (Hewitt, 2006).

Older Adult

Menopause usually occurs between 48 and 51 years, although variability is wide. The ovaries stop producing estrogen and progesterone, causing the uterus to droop and the cervix to shrink. There is a thinning of the genital hair, thinning and loss of elasticity of vaginal mucosa, and diminished vaginal secretions as a result of lower estrogen levels. The fat pads atrophy and the labia, clitoris, cervix, uterus, fallopian tubes, and ovaries decrease in size.

Evidence-Informed Critical Thinking

The registered nurse and nurse practitioner work collaboratively to provide care for the patient with issues related to the female reproductive system. After collecting data, unexpected findings and health promotion areas will be identified. The data will be clustered to reveal significant patterns and make clinical judgments about outcomes and potential interventions.

Common Laboratory and Diagnostic Testing

Because the annual gynecological visit by the female patient is commonly the only physical examination she has, complete laboratory work is often done, including tests for anemia, cholesterol, thyroid, and diabetes, and to rule out elevated white blood cell count in the case of infections. A urinalysis is commonly done at each visit. If the patient has signs or symptoms of a UTI, a mid stream urine specimen for urinalysis and culture and sensitivity are done. If the patient is having any bleeding, or lack of menses, a serum human chorionic gonadotropin is drawn to rule out pregnancy. The wet mount analysis of vaginal secretions is done to identify what, if any, vaginal infections are present. A slide is made with the vaginal secretions and a single drop of either or both KOH and saline. The examination findings are then matched with the signs and symptoms and the wet mount findings. Infection with one STI means that serology tests for HIV and syphilis should also be conducted (Groenveld, 2010). Blood tests, such as LH, FSH, and GnRH, are drawn if there are any endocrine irregularities. The vaginal and abdominal ultrasounds are the gold standard diagnostic tests for unexpected findings of the fallopian tubes, ovaries, uterus, and the endometrial lining. More in-depth testing is done if the woman has infertility concerns.

The Canadian Cancer Society's current Pap smear screening recommendations follow. For initial screening, women should undergo a Pap test within 3 years of onset of sexual activity or at age 21 (whichever comes first). Women who have no sexual activity should still be screened. Women younger than 30 years should have a Pap annually. Women older than 30 years who have three acceptable Pap tests in a row have two options. They may receive a LBC test every 2 to 3 years; but if the patient has any history of DES exposure, HIV, or any previous cervical cancer diagnosis, she should continue annual Pap testing. The second option is to be screened with a LBC test and an HPV-DNA hybrid capture (HC2) (a culture specifically for HPV) tests a culture specifically for the HPV. If both test results are as expected, the patient can go 3 years without screening. Unfortunately, the LBC and the HPV-DNA tests are not currently available in all Canadian provinces/territories. Generally, Pap testing may be discontinued after the age of 70 years. Women older than 70 years who have had cancer in earlier years involving HPV are still at risk for further infection in the vagina by HPV and require ongoing follow-up. Women who have had a total hysterectomy (for noncancerous reason) do not require Pap testing (Canadian Cancer Society, 2010).

Diagnosis and Related Factors	Point of Differentiation	Assessment Characteristics	Nursing Interventions
Ineffective sexuality patterns related to illness and altered body function	Limitations from disease or therapy, alteration in sex role, change in interest of self or others	Altered body function, recent childbirth, reproductive surgery, medications, abuse	Gather sexual history. Determine patient and partner's knowledge. Observe for stress, loss, or depression. Explore physical causes with chronic disease.
Risk for infection	Potential for invasion by pathogens	Chronic illness, unsafe practices, rupture of amniotic membranes, recent surgery	Consider risk for methicillin-resistant *Staphylococcus aureus*. Observe and report signs of infection. Use appropriate hand hygiene and follow routine practices. Avoid use of indwelling catheters when possible.

Nursing Diagnosis, Outcomes, and Interventions

The formation of the nursing diagnosis is based on all the information given. Many times, it is considered a presumptive diagnosis, especially if the patient has multiple conditions. Validation of the data is needed in order to analyze the findings and the subsequent management of the patient's symptoms. The nurse sees not only the condition of the patient but also the possibilities for education and long-term benefits to the patient. Table 26-2 provides a comparison of nursing diagnoses, unexpected findings, and interventions commonly related to assessment of the female genitalia (North American Nursing Diagnosis Association-International, 2009).

Analyzing Findings

Remember Teresa Nguyen, whose concerns have been outlined throughout this chapter. The initial subjective and objective data collection is complete, and the nurse practitioner has spent time reviewing the findings and other results. Ms. Nguyen has pelvic inflammatory disease (PID) caused by *Chlamydia*, so it is necessary for the nurse practitioner to treat her with antibiotics. The following nursing note illustrates how data are collected and treatment is prescribed by the nurse practitioner.

Subjective: States has pelvic pain and vaginal discharge. Increased during intercourse. Is present in the lower half of the abdomen, increases with palpation. States is 3/10 at rest, 8/10 with intercourse. Has had pain for 2 weeks, increasing in intensity. Pain has limited intercourse over the past 1.5 weeks. Taking acetaminophen for pain with minimal effect. States that discharge is clear and increasing in amount.

Objective: Temperature 38.8°C orally, appears flushed. Culture is positive for *Chlamydia trachomatis*. White blood cell count and erythrocyte sedimentation rate elevated.

Analysis: Knowledge deficit related to *Chlamydia trachomatis* infection.

Plan: Obtain prescription for broad-spectrum antibiotic. Teach to take acetaminophen for pain and fever, drink 2 L of fluid and get additional rest. Teach to abstain from intercourse until she and her boyfriend's treatment is complete. Assess knowledge level of safer sexual practices and provide accurate information. Report results to public health department and initiate partner notification process. Allow time for her to express her feelings and role play the words she will use when talking with her boyfriend.

Critical Thinking Challenge

- What are the differences between the nurse practitioner and registered nurse roles?
- What nursing diagnoses might be appropriate given the *Chlamydia* infection?
- How will the effects on Teresa, her family, and her partner be assessed? What specific questions would the nurse ask?

Teresa Nguyen will need to have further teaching and support based on her new diagnosis. The following conversation illustrates how the clinic nurse might communicate with a nurse at the local sexually transmitted infections (STI) clinic.

Situation: Hello, I'm Linda in the family medicine clinic and we have a patient, Teresa Nguyen, a 28-year-old Vietnamese Canadian, who has not been to our clinic before. She has just been diagnosed with pelvic inflammatory disease (PID), caused by *Chlamydia*. The nurse practitioner has prescribed an antibiotic and acetaminophen (Tylenol) for symptoms.

Background: Teresa reports that her boyfriend, Joe Tran, is her first and only sexual partner. Her parents do not know about the boyfriend. Teresa's friends don't like the boyfriend and told her that he is cheating on her with other women.

Assessment: Teresa is angry and upset with her boyfriend for giving her *Chlamydia*. She is upset with herself for not listening to her friends. When I tried to talk with her about what she might say to her boyfriend, she became distraught and cried.

Recommendations: Is there any way that you or one of the other nurses could see her today or tomorrow?

Critical Thinking Challenge

- What additional issues should be assessed when considering Teresa's future care?
- What questions will the nurse use to assess Teresa's knowledge of PID and *Chlamydia*?
- What will be the top three priorities for assessment and teaching?

The nurse uses assessment data to formulate a nursing care plan with patient outcomes and interventions. Outcomes are specific to the patient, realistic to achieve, measurable, and have a time frame for completion. After interventions are completed, the nurse reevaluates and documents the findings in the chart to show progress toward the patient outcome. The nurse uses critical thinking and judgment to continue or revise the diagnosis, outcomes, or interventions. This is often in the form of a care plan or case note similar to the one below.

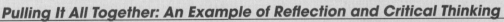

Nursing Diagnosis	Patient Outcomes	Nursing Interventions	Rationale	Evaluation
Anxiety related to effects on sexual relationships and family processes	Patient states that she feels prepared to discuss situation with partner. Patient identifies one person with whom she feels comfortable sharing her concerns.	Rehearse words to use when telling partner about infection. Discuss which family or friends she would feel comfortable talking with. Offer assistance and time for processing the issues.	Practising in advance can reduce anxiety. Talking about her concerns is therapeutic. During the initial crisis, the nurse can provide therapeutic communication.	Expressing anger at boyfriend and feeling betrayed. Able to state she feels prepared to notify partner. Has a sister who is very supportive that she can talk with. Given phone number to clinic if she has questions or needs to talk more.

Using the previous steps of clinical reasoning, organizing, and prioritizing, consider all the case study findings woven throughout this chapter for Teresa Nguyen. When answering the following questions, begin drawing conclusions and see how the pieces of assessment must work together to create an environment for personalized, appropriate, and accurate care.

- What are some causes of vaginal discharge? (Knowledge)
- What are the implications of Teresa's presenting condition for her boyfriend? (Comprehension)
- What cultural considerations should the nurse incorporate into the care provided for Teresa? (Application)
- What lifestyle factors might be contributing to Teresa's present condition? (Analysis)
- What recommendations for screening and follow-up would the nurse suggest for Teresa? (Synthesis)
- How would the nurse evaluate the effectiveness of patient teaching for Teresa? (Evaluation)

Nurses use assessment information to identify patient outcomes. Some outcomes that are related to female genitalia concerns include the following:

- Expresses ability to perform sexually despite physical imperfections
- States the risk factors for, causes of, and ways to prevent STIs
- States disease process, treatment effects, and side effects (Moorhead, Johnson, et al., 2007).

Once the outcomes are established, nursing care is implemented to improve the status of the patient. Some examples of nursing interventions for the female genitalia are as follows:

- Normalize the experience of situations related to sensitive sexual topics and allow time for patient to express concerns.
- Offer a variety of options for safer sex practices to provide choices and promote respect for differences.
- Teach about disease process, treatment effects, side effects, and expected outcomes (Bulechek, Butcher, et al., 2008).

The nurse evaluates the care according to the patient outcomes that were developed, therefore reassessing the patient and continuing or modifying the interventions as appropriate. This is a sensitive and embarrassing topic for many patients and their nurses. It is important to include the psychosocial dimensions and become comfortable talking about the topic. The process can be modified to the individual so that outcomes can be positive for all those involved.

Key Points

- Examination of the female genitalia provides opportunity for open communication, exchange of information, and education between patient and nurse.
- Women have ongoing needs and concerns throughout the lifespan.

- Evidence-informed research and protocols are the driving forces for health promotion and disease prevention.
- A genital examination does not need to cause anxiety or pain; through empathetic exchange and respect, the nurse can make it a positive experience.
- Adolescents' struggle with issues of self-esteem can lead to early experimentation with drugs, sex, and risk-taking behaviours. Nurses can attend to the physiologic and psychological needs of the adolescent female during this annual visit.
- The older female represents a great portion of the female population. As the average lifespan becomes longer, nurses need to be current with newer screening, therapeutics, and interventions that allow the greatest quality of life.

Review Questions

1. The nurse is taking a menstrual history. What would be an appropriate question to ask?
   A. Do you have any history of cancer in your family?
   B. Do you ever skip periods?
   C. Do you use condoms during intercourse?
   D. How many sexual partners have you had?

2. The nurse is inspecting the urethra and the Skene's glands. She knows these are a part of what area?
   A. Mons pubis
   B. Vulva
   C. Posterior fourchette
   D. Vestibule

3. A Pap smear is recommended to screen for what condition?
   A. Cervical cancer
   B. Ovarian cancer
   C. Endometrial cancer
   D. Vaginal cancer

4. After completing a history on a 45-year-old patient, the nurse suspects she may have uterine fibroids. What information might have led her to this?
A. History of sexually transmitted infections (STIs)
B. History of multiple births
C. Vaginal discharge
D. Heavier than usual menstrual periods

5. The nurse practitioner has decided to place a patient on isotretinoin (Accutane) for her acne. What is the most important information she needs to tell the patient?
A. She needs to take the medication daily and avoid missing a dose.
B. She should not take this medication with antibiotics.
C. She needs to be on two forms of birth control or abstain from sexual intercourse 1 month before, during, and 1 month after taking this medication.
D. She needs to take a weekly pregnancy test to make sure she hasn't gotten pregnant while on this medication.

6. What is the organism that contributes to salpingitis?
A. *Trichinosis*
B. *Chlamydia trachomatis*
C. *Candida albicans*
D. *Condyloma acuminatum*

7. The nurse is preparing the patient for her examination. What position will the nurse assist the patient into for a comfortable genital examination?
A. Semi-Fowler's
B. Prone with her knees bent
C. Supine with her knees bent
D. Semilithotomy

8. The nurse is a part of a health promotion fair. One of the participants asks her what the greatest killer of women is. The nurse knows by current evidence that it is
A. cardiovascular disease
B. lung cancer
C. breast cancer
D. osteoporosis

9. What other test would the nurse know is important in a woman with frequent candidiasis?
A. Cultures for chlamydia
B. Blood test for glucose
C. Blood test for syphilis
D. Vaginal ultrasound

10. Upon inspection, the nurse sees flesh-coloured lesions surrounding the anal area. What are these most likely indicative of?
A. Hemorrhoids
B. *Herpes simplex II*
C. *AIDS*
D. *Condyloma acuminatum*

Canadian Nursing Research

Donnelly, T. T. (2008). Challenges in providing breast and cervical cancer screening services to Vietnamese Canadian women: The healthcare providers' perspective. *Nursing Inquiry, 15*(2), 158–168.

Mill, J. E., Edwards, N., et al. (2010). Stigmatization as a social control mechanism for persons living with HIV and AIDS. *Qualitative Health Research, 20*(11), 1469–1489.

Mill, J. E., Jackson, R. C., et al. (2008). HIV testing and care in Canadian Aboriginal youth: A community based mixed methods study. *BMC Infectious Diseases, 8,* 132.

Steele, R., & Fitch, M. I. (2008). Supportive care needs of women with gynecologic cancer. *Cancer Nursing, 31*(4), 284–291.

Strohschein, F. J., Thomas, J., et al. (2010). Strengthening data quality in studies of migrants not fluent in host languages: A Canadian example with reproductive health questionnaires. *Research in Nursing & Health, 33*(4), 369–379.

References

American Cancer Society. (2008). *Cancer facts and figures 2008*. Atlanta, GA: Author.

American College of Obstetricians and Gynecologists (ACOG). (2008). *Revised cervical cancer screening guidelines require reeducation of women and physicians*. Retrieved from http://acog.org

Barron, A., & Falsetti, D. (2008). Polycystic ovary syndrome in adolescents: A hormonal barrage and metabolic upheaval. *Advance for Nurse Practitioners, 16*(3), 49–53.

Beaulieu, R., Kools, S. M., et al. (2011). Young adult couples' decision making regarding emergency contraceptive pills. *Journal of Nursing Scholarship, 43*(1), 41–48.

Bulechek, G. M., Butcher, H. K., et al. (2008). *Nursing interventions classification (NIC)* (5th ed.). St Louis, MO: Mosby.

Burns, N., Briggs, P., et al. (2007). Chlamydia screening in teenage girls. *The Nurse Practitioner, 32*(6), 41–43.

Canadian Cancer Society. (2010). *Cervical cancer*. Retrieved from http://www.cancer.ca/Canada-wide/Prevention/Gettingchecked/CervicalcancerNEW.aspx?sc_lang=en

Canadian Cancer Society's Steering Committee for Cancer Statistics. (2011). *Canadian Cancer Statistics 2011*. Toronto, ON: Canadian Cancer Society.

Centers for Disease Control and Prevention. (2008). *The history of DES*. Retrieved from http://www.cdc.gov/DES/hcp/nurse/history

Chow, J. (2010a). Assessment and management of female physiologic processes. In R. A. Day, P. Paul, et al. (Eds.). *Brunner & Suddarth's textbook of Canadian medical-surgical nursing* (2nd ed., pp. 1522–1567). Philadelphia, PA: Wolters Kluwer Health/Lippincott Williams & Wilkins.

Chow, J. (2010b). Management of patients with female reproductive disorders. In R. A. Day, P. Paul, et al. (Eds.). *Brunner & Suddarth's textbook of Canadian medical-surgical nursing* (2nd ed., pp. 1568–1608). Philadelphia, PA: Wolters Kluwer Health/Lippincott Williams & Wilkins.

Clark, B., & Marrazzo, J. (2006). Reproductive health and sexually transmitted infections in lesbian women. *The Female Patient, 31*(8), 38–40.

Curtis, M., Overholt, S., et al. (2005). *Glass' office gynecology* (6th ed.). Philadelphia, PA: Lippincott Williams & Wilkins.

Elkins, B., Mayeaux, E. J., et al. (2006). Bacterial vaginosis: Diagnosis and therapy. *The Female Patient, 31*(8), 41–46.

Estes, M. E. Z., & Buck, M. (2009). *Health assessment and physical examination* (1st Canadian ed.). Toronto, ON: Nelson Education.

Groenveld, A. (2010). Management of patients with infectious diseases. In R. A. Day, P. Paul, et al. (Eds.). *Brunner & Suddarth's textbook of medical-surgical nursing* (2nd ed., pp. 2346–2381). Philadelphia, PA: Wolters Kluwer Health/ Lippincott Williams & Wilkins.

Hahm, H. C., Lee, J., et al. (2007). Predictors of STDs among Asian and Pacific Islander young adults. *Perspectives on Sexual and Reproductive Health, 39*(4), 231–239.

Hewitt, G. (2006). The young woman's initial gynecologic visit. *The Female Patient, 31*(9), 25–29.

Kolesar, J. (2004). Clinical implications of BRCA1 and BRCA2 genes in hereditary breast and ovarian cancer. *The Female Patient, 29*(6), 39–45.

Langille, D. B., Proudfoot, K., et al. (2008). A pilot project for chlamydia screening in adolescent females using self-testing: Characteristics of participants and non-participants. *Canadian Journal of Public Health, 99*(2), 117–120.

Laumbach, S. (2004). Detecting domestic violence: To screen or not to screen? *The Female Patient, 29*(6), 30–34.

Ley, C., Bauer, H. M., et al. (1991). Determinants of genital human papillomavirus infection in young women. *Journal of the National Cancer Institute, 83*(14), 997–1003.

Marshall, W. A., & Tanner, J. M. (1969). Variations in pattern of pubertal changes in girls. *Archives of Diseases in Childhood, 44*(235), 291–303.

Martin, J. (2008). Do women comply with recommendations for Papanicolaou smears following colposcopy? *Journal of Midwifery & Women's Health, 53*(2), 138–142.

McCowen Meahring, P. (2010a). Structure and function of the female reproductive system. In R. A. Hannon, C. Pooler, et al. (Eds.). *Porth pathophysiology: Concepts of altered health states* (1st Canadian ed., pp. 1068–1083). Philadelphia, PA: Wolters Kluwer Health/Lippincott Williams & Wilkins.

McCowen Meahring, P. (2010b). Disorders of the female reproductive system. In R. A. Hannon, C. Pooler, et al. (Eds.), *Porth pathophysiology: Concepts of altered health states* (1st Canadian ed., pp. 1084–1118). Philadelphia, PA: Wolters Kluwer Health/Lippincott Williams & Wilkins.

McCowen Meahring, P. (2010c). Sexually transmitted infections. In R. A. Hannon, C. Pooler, et al. (Eds.). *Porth pathophysiology: Concepts of altered health states* (1st Canadian ed., pp. 1119–1133). Philadelphia, PA: Wolters Kluwer Health/Lippincott Williams & Wilkins.

Moorhead, S., Johnson, M., et al. (2007). *Nursing outcomes classification (NOC)* (4th ed.). Philadelphia, PA: Mosby.

Mosca, C., Banka, et al. (2007). Evidence-based guidelines for cardiovascular disease prevention in women. 2007 Update. *Circulation Journal of the American Heart Association, 115,* 1481–1501.

Murphy, K. J. (2007). Screening for cervical cancer. *Journal of the Society of Obstetrics and Gynaecology Canada, 29*(8, Suppl.3). S27–S36.

North American Nursing Diagnosis Association-International. (2009). *Nursing diagnoses, 2009–2011 edition: Definitions and classifications (NANDA I NURSING DIAGNOSIS)*. West Sussex, UK: John Wiley & Sons.

Osteoporosis Canada. (2011). *Osteoporosis: Towards a fracture-free future*. Retrieved from www.osteoporosis.ca

Ovarian Cancer Update. (2010). *Best Health,* September, p. 15.

Perspectives. (2010). Where the rubber hits the road. *Canadian Nurse, 106*(3), 10.

Pinto, A. P., & Crum, C. P. (2000). Natural history of cervical neoplasia: Defining progression and its consequence. *Clinical Obstetrics & Gynecology, 43*(2), 352–362.

Provencher, D. M., & Murphy, K. J. (2007). The role of HPV testing. *Journal of the Society of Obstetrics and Gynaecology Canada, 29*(8, Suppl. 3), S15–S21.

Public Health Agency of Canada. (2007a). *Recommendations on a human papillomavirus immunization program.* Retrieved from http://www.phac-aspc.gc.ca/publicat/2008/papillomavirus-papillome/papillomavirus-papillome-index-eng.php

Public Health Agency of Canada. (2010a). *Reported cases of notifiable STI from January 1 to June 30, 2009 and January 1 to June 30, 2010 and corresponding annual rates for the years 2009 and 2010.* Retrieved from http://www.phac-aspc.gc.ca/std-mts/stdcases-casmts/

Public Health Agency of Canada. (2010b). *Summary: Estimates of HIV prevalence and incidence in Canada, 2008.* Retrieved from http://www.phac-aspc.gc.ca/aids-sida/publication/survreport/estimat08-eng.php

Public Health Agency of Canada. (2011a). *Canadian guidelines on sexually transmitted infections.* Retrieved from http://www. phac-aspc.gc.ca/std-mts/sti-its/guide-lignesdir-eng.php

Public Health Agency of Canada. (2011b). *Physical activity. Information and tips for adults (ages 18–64 years).* Retrieved from http://www.phac-aspc.gc.ca/hp-ps/hl-mvs/pa-ap/07 paap-eng.php

Sethi, S., & Bickley, L. S. (2010). Female genitalia. In T. C. Stephen, D. L. Skillen, R. A. Day, & L. S. Bickley (Eds.). *Canadian Bates' guide to health assessment for nurses* (1st ed., pp. 785–828). Philadelphia, PA: Wolters Kluwer Health/ Lippincott Williams & Wilkins.

Smith, D. A. (2007). Pelvic organ prolapse. *Advance for Nurse Practitioners, 15*(8), 39–42.

Society of Obstetricians and Gynaecologists of Canada. (2007). *Canadian consensus guidelines on human papillomavirus.* Retrieved from http://www.sogc.org/guidelines/documents/gui196CPG0708revised.pdf

Speroff, L. & Fritz, M. A. (2005). *The clinical gynecology and infertility* (7th ed.). Philadelphia, PA: Lippincott Williams and Wilkins.

Winer, R. L., Lee, S. K., et al. (2006). Condom use and the risk of genital human papillomavirus infection in young women. *New England Journal of Medicine, 354*(25), 2645–2654.

World Health Organization. (2010). *Media centre: Female genital mutilation.* Retrieved from http://who.int/mediacentre/factsheets/fs241/en/

> *The Canadian Jensen's Nursing Health Assessment suite offers these additional resources to enhance learning and facilitate understanding of this chapter:*
>
> • thePoint online resource, http//thepoint.lww.com/Stephen1E
> • *Laboratory Manual for Canadian Jensen's Nursing Health Assessment: A Best Practice Approach*

Tables of Unexpected Findings

 Table 26-3 **Common Infections**

Condition and Presentation	Physical Examination and Wet Mount Findings	Diagnostic Follow-Up
Candidiasis 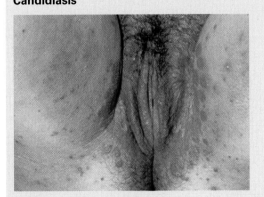 The patient reports vulvovaginal and possibly rectal pruritus and dyspareunia. Vaginal secretions can be thick or thin.	*Examination:* Vulvovaginal edema, erythemia, and excoriation; thick white secretions, sometimes only along inner vaginal walls *Wet Mount:* Pseudohyphae, occasional budding yeast	If chronic infection needs serum glucose to rule out diabetes and possibly human immunodeficiency virus (HIV) testing (seen often in immunocompromised patients)
Bacterial Vaginosis 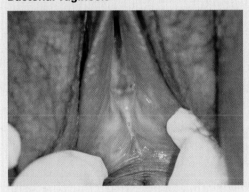 Signs and symptoms include vaginal secretions with a strong "fishy" odour and vaginal itching or burning.	*Examination:* Creamy white to gray secretions that coats the vaginal walls *Wet Mount:* Positive findings of clue cells on microscopy; possibly white blood cells (WBC s) present as well	Positive amine (fishy odour) when secretion is mixed with KOH pH > 4.5 Gram stain
Chlamydia 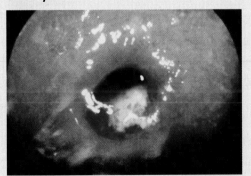 Many times, this is asymptomatic, although there are occasionally clear or white secretions. The patient reports dyspareunia, bleeding after intercourse, or both.	*Examination:* Changes in the cervical condition—reddened, mucopurulent discharge from os; may bleed easily; possibly pain with pelvic examination *Wet Mount:* Increased WBCs and red blood cells (RBCs) on slide	DNA probe for chlamydia (CT) and gonorrhea (GC) Serology for syphilis HIV testing Hepatitis B and C testing

(table continues on page 824)

Table 26-3 **Common Infections** (*continued*)

Condition and Presentation	Physical Examination and Wet Mount Findings	Diagnostic Follow-Up
Gonorrhea 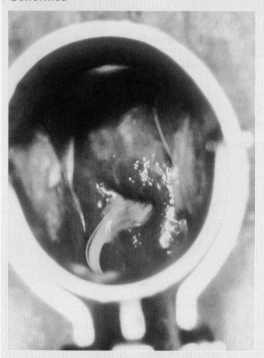 Vaginal secretions are yellow. The patient reports pain with urination (dysuria) and dyspareunia.	*Examination:* Purulent discharge from the cervix; tenderness or pain with the pelvic examination *Wet Mount:* Gram stain shows intracellular diplococci	Same testing as *Chlamydia*
Trichomoniasis 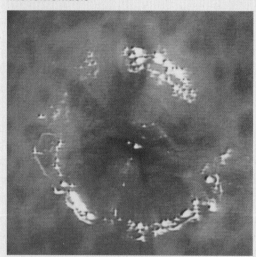 The patient has vaginal pruritis, thin or thick vaginal secretions, a foul vaginal odour, and occasionally dysuria.	*Examination:* Purulent yellow to green frothy discharge with foul odour; pain on pelvic examination; cervical redness (strawberry looking) and contact bleeding *Wet Mount:* Motile organisms >10 WBCs per high powered microscopy	Cultures for CT, GC, Serology for syphilis. HIV testing UA

Table 26-3 **Common Infections** (*continued*)

Condition and Presentation	Physical Examination and Wet Mount Findings	Diagnostic Follow-Up
Herpes Simplex Type 2 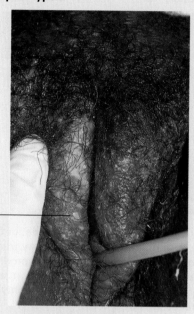 Shallow ulcers on red bases The patient reports vulvar or vaginal pain, flu-like symptoms (eg, chills, fever), and sores on the vulva or in the genital region.	*Examination:* Scattered vesicles along labia or matching vesicles on labia reflecting "kissing" lesions; surface ulcerations or crusted healing lesions; inguinal lymphadenopathy *Wet Mount:* > 10 WBCs per high-powered microscopy	Viral culture from freshly incised vesicle Serology for syphilis HIV testing
Condyloma Acuminatum 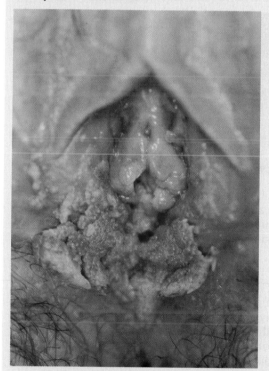 Common reports include vulvar or vaginal itching, vaginal secretions, and growths along the vagina or rectum.	*Examination:* Fleshy pink or gray papilloma or wart-like projections at vulva, vagina, or anus *Wet Mount:* Direct visualization	Application of 5% acetic acid (white vinegar) enhances visibility

Conditions with the external genitalia can be isolated or part of another infectious process involving the internal genitalia as well. Listed are some examples of external findings.

Pediculosis Pubis (crab lice)

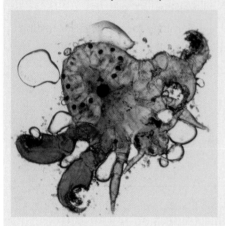

The patient presents with mild to severe itching, especially in the mons pubis and perineum. The external genitalia are excoriated based on the amount of itching. Tiny spots of blood may be seen on the underwear and possible lice not only on the underwear but around the pubis. Nits, which are the eggs, usually adhere to the pubic hair and can appear as small yellow specks or may be translucent. The photograph is an enlarged view of a single louse.

Chancre

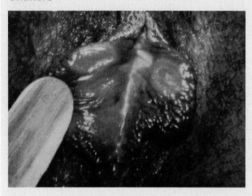

Seen in primary syphilis, this 1-cm button-like papule forms at the area of inoculation. This painless lesion with raised borders has a center of serous exudate. Present for 10–90 d.

Contact Dermatitis

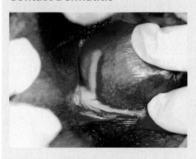

Urethral Caruncle

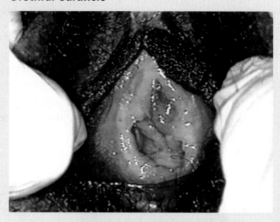

The patient usually has dysuria, **hematuria,** or frequently no response to antibiotics given for urinary tract infection (UTI). This condition is seen primarily in women who are postmenopausal. The caruncle develops from **ectropion** of the posterior urethral wall, which commonly develops as the vaginal tissue atrophies.

Abscess of the Bartholin's Gland

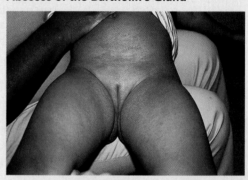

The patient has pain or tenderness in the Bartholin's area. Some abscesses develop gradually but usually very quickly within 2–3 d. They may rupture spontaneously or may need to be incised and drained.

The patient has acute symptoms of external itching or burning, which may extend to the inner thigh. The perineum may be erythematous and possibly excoriated. Occasionally, the perineum has localized wheals or vesicles with possible drainage where the source of the inflammation came in contact with it. Scented sanitary pads can cause this type of inflammatory response, which will appear in the shape of the pad. Douche products can cause allergic reactions.

Table 26-5 **Pelvic Organ Prolapse Conditions**

Cystocele

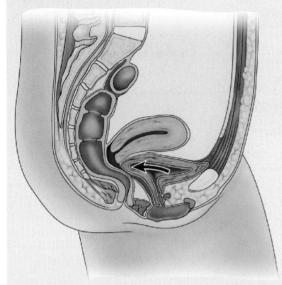

Protrusion of the bladder into the anterior vaginal canal and beyond is most common in women aged 40 years and older. It usually results from weakening of the supporting pelvic tissues (Chow, 2010a). To evaluate this condition, the patient needs to be examined while standing as well as while lying down. The patient may have such symptoms as stress incontinence, urge incontinence, and discomfort with intercourse.

Rectocele

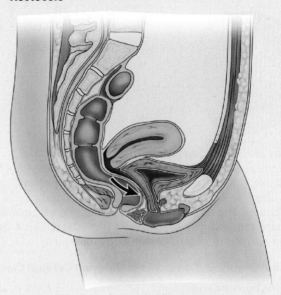

Prolapse of the rectum into the posterior vaginal wall can result from a lack of pelvic tissue support, which commonly follows lengthy vaginal labours and births. The patient has difficulty with bowel movements, pain with intercourse, and rectal pressure.

Uterine Prolapse

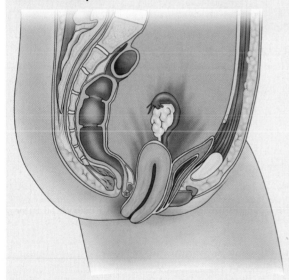

Descent of the uterus into the vagina and beyond results from pelvic relaxation and gradual weakening of uterine ligaments supporting the uterus. It may be a consequence of multiple vaginal births or an enlarging uterus. The patient presents with low pressure, fecal impaction, and vaginal and uterine irritation.

Cervical Polyps

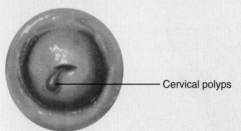

Cervical polyps

Polyps are 2–5 cm red lesions that sit at or protrude from the cervical os. Some polyps are pedunculated (stalk like). Most are benign. The patient may present with bleeding between menses or bleeding after intercourse. The polyp can be removed in the office and the base touched with silver nitrate (AgNO3) to cauterize it. The polyp is then sent to pathology for testing.

Diethylstilbestrol (DES) Syndrome

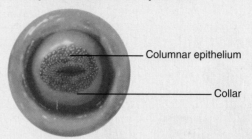

Columnar epithelium

Collar

DES as described earlier causes changes in the cervix in some women who were exposed to it in utero.

Cervical Dysplasia, Carcinoma in Situ, and Cervical Cancer

Carcinoma in situ

Squamous cell carcinoma

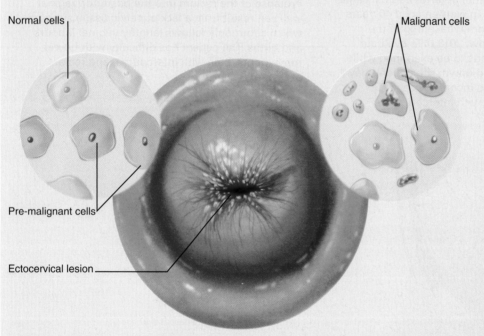

Normal cells

Malignant cells

Pre-malignant cells

Ectocervical lesion

- Cervical dysplasia is a neoplastic process that does not involve the basement membrane cells of the cervix. It may also be referred to as cervical intraepithelial neoplasia.
- Carcinoma in situ involves the full thickness of the epithelium.
- Cervical cancer is the diagnosis when carcinoma in situ invades the basement membrane.

Endometriosis

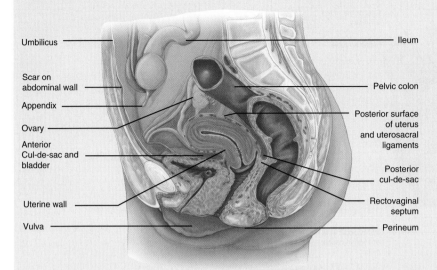

Umbilicus

Scar on abdominal wall

Appendix

Ovary

Anterior Cul-de-sac and bladder

Uterine wall

Vulva

Ileum

Pelvic colon

Posterior surface of uterus and uterosacral ligaments

Posterior cul-de-sac

Rectovaginal septum

Perineum

Endometrial tissue is found outside the uterus because of a retrograde flow of menstruation into the peritoneal cavity. This tissue adheres to other organs and causes pelvic pain, dyspareunia, dysmenorrhea, and often infertility. Treatments range from drug therapy to surgical removal.

Leiomyoma: Uterine Fibroids

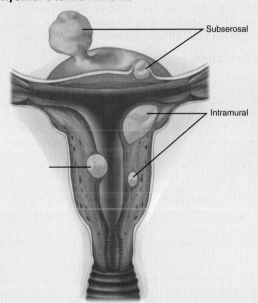

Subserosal

Intramural

This benign (99%) condition of the uterus appears as single or multiple tumours within the wall of the uterus, often extending from it on stalks Heavy flows, irregular bleeding, or pelvic pressure suggest fibroids, or there may be no symptoms. Many women with fibroids are asymptomatic. Symptoms guide intervention, which usually involves surgery. If a woman is considering pregnancy and has fibroids >8 cm, surgical removal prepregnancy is often advised. Uterine fibroids often enlarge with exposure to estrogen. Fibroids occur in one of 4–5 women (35+ years) and occurs with increased frequency and growth rate in African-Canadian women (McCowen Meahring, 2010b).

Fluctuant Ovarian Cyst

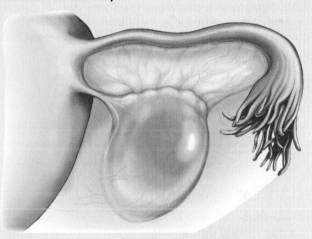

The ovarian follicle fails to rupture during the maturation phase. A fluid-filled cyst develops and either stays the same size or grows to be greater than the ovaries. The patient does not ovulate and has secondary amenorrhea (no menses). The cysts usually resolve spontaneously within two cycles. If the cyst enlarges, the patient presents with amenorrhea and low pelvic tenderness. Once pregnancy is ruled out and an ultrasound is done to confirm the presence and size of the cyst, treatment is implemented. Most commonly, the patient is put on two or more cycles of a low-dose hormone contraceptive to suppress the gonadotropin stimulation of the cyst.

(table continues on page 830)

Solid Ovarian Mass

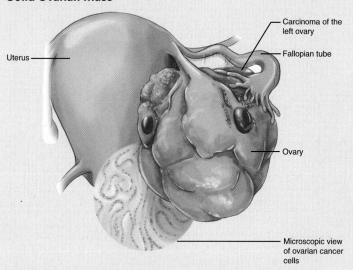

There are many types of solid masses but the two most common will be discussed. The first is a **benign cystic teratoma**. This tumour forms in the ovaries and contains structures such as bone, cartilage, or teeth. Many of the tissues come from dermoid derivatives such as skin, hair follicles, and sebum. This is why it is also known as a **dermoid** cyst. The second mass is a malignant ovarian neoplasm. Approximately 2,600 cases of ovarian cancer are expected in Canada and 1,750 deaths in 2011 (Canadian Cancer Society's Steering Committee for Cancer Statistics, 2011). Symptoms are so vague that many ovarian cancers are not found until advanced stages. Most ovarian cancers are diagnosed after menopause (80%), with the median age of diagnosis being 62 years (Chow, 2010b). The greatest risk factor is a family history of the disease. To date, there are no cost-effective screenings available.

Ectopic Pregnancy

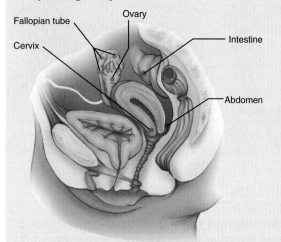

A fertilized ovum implants in a site other than the uterine endometrium. Risk factors include previous ectopic pregnancy, past pelvic infection, endometriosis, or unexpected findings of the tube. The patient presents with symptoms of a usual pregnancy initially. As the ectopic pregnancy grows larger, there are internal hemorrhage and subsequent lower quadrant pain. The most common symptoms are lower quadrant pain, nausea, and referred pain in the neck or shoulder from blood beneath the diaphragm (Chow, 2010a). If hemorrhage is severe, the patient is at risk for shock.

Acute Salpingitis

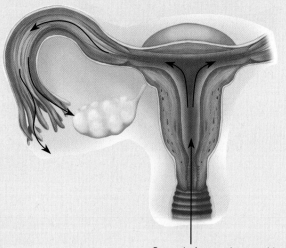

Spread of gonorrhea or chlamydia

The most common cause of fallopian tube disease, salpingitis is also referred to as pelvic inflammatory disease (PID). Infection spreads throughout the uterus and up into the tubes. The tubes become swollen and rupture. Scarring can occur even with treatment; potential for infertility is high. *Chlamydia trachomatis* and *Neisseria gonorrhoeae* are the most common organisms that cause salpingitis. Chronic infections with either of these organisms can lead to tubal occlusion or obstruction. The patient presents with pain in the lower quadrant, chills, fever, dysuria, pyuria, and often vaginal discharge (Chow, 2010b).

Special Populations and Foci

Women Who Are Pregnant

Learning Objectives

1 Demonstrate knowledge of anatomy and physiology related to pregnancy.

2 Describe how preexisting conditions are affected by and affect pregnancy.

3 Identify important topics for health promotion and risk reduction related to pregnancy.

4 Collect subjective data related to the woman who is pregnant.

5 Collect objective data related to the woman who is pregnant using physical examination techniques.

6 Identify expected and unexpected findings related to the woman who is pregnant.

7 Analyze subjective and objective data from the assessment of the woman who is pregnant and consider initial interventions.

8 Document and communicate data from the woman who is pregnant using appropriate terminology and principles of recording.

9 Consider age, condition, and culture of the woman who is pregnant to individualize the assessment.

10 Identify nursing diagnoses and initiate a nursing care plan based on findings from the assessment of the woman who is pregnant.

*M*ichelle Sherman is seeing the nurse at her family physician/midwife's office following a positive home pregnancy test. She is a 21-year-old First Nations Canadian, accompanied by her male partner and their 22-month-old son. Ms. Sherman is 163 cm and currently weighs 93 kg. She is concerned because she has not yet lost all the weight she gained during her first pregnancy and is starting this pregnancy at 93 kg. She reports that she quit smoking during her last pregnancy but resumed smoking a half pack each day after the baby was born to manage the high stress of being a new mother. She thinks her last menstrual period (LMP) was 6 weeks ago and reports that it was lighter than usual.

- What additional history does the nurse need to gather from Michelle today?
- What physical assessment data are the nurse's responsibilities to gather and assess?
- What health promotion needs does Michelle have today?
- What findings would indicate that Michelle's condition is stable, urgent, or emergent?
- What factors does the nurse consider to individualize the patient care plan that meets Michelle's needs?

This chapter is based on the premise that, for most women, pregnancy is not an illness. Usually, pregnancy, labour, childbirth, and postpartum recovery are uncomplicated and need only health-promotion and risk-reduction interventions. Overall, the experience of being pregnant is a journey that includes substantial physical and emotional changes for a woman. Her body will change to provide nourishment to her growing fetus, to deliver her baby, and to provide nourishment (breast-feed) for the baby in the postpartum phase. The pregnancy and child birthing process can include a myriad of emotions: apprehension, anticipation, and joy. For some patients, however, serious and even life-threatening issues can occur. Therefore, it is important for nurses to be able to distinguish expected findings from variations and from conditions that require further attention.

This chapter includes an overview of the anatomical and physiological changes of pregnancy, as well as expected variations based on age, risk factors, and environment. It considers how cultural variations can affect care during pregnancy. Specific symptoms common to pregnancy and the nurse's role in their identification and management are discussed.

Anatomy and Physiology Overview

Preconception

Preconception "refers to the 3 months immediately before a pregnancy; however, because 50% of pregnancies are unplanned (Society of Obstetricians and Gyaecologists of Canada [SOGC], 2007), sexually active women of childbearing age are potentially in the preconception phase at all times unless they have been sterilized or are in menopause" (Bowen & Bickley, 2010, p. 849).

During preconception, the left and right ovaries typically ovulate in alternate cycles. Either ovary releases one egg into the fallopian tube approximately 14 days before the next menstrual period is expected (Fig. 27-1). After the release of the egg, the corpus luteum forms on the ovarian surface and produces progesterone, which supports the uterine lining until the placenta is formed. Without sufficient progesterone, the woman menstruates and there will not be a successful pregnancy.

Sperm meet the egg in the fallopian tube, where fertilization occurs. Cilia in the fallopian tube assist the egg toward the uterus. Factors that can delay progression of egg to uterus include endometriosis, smoking, and inflammation of the fallopian tube, most commonly caused by chlamydia or gonorrhea. Women with histories of smoking or these sexually transmitted infections (STIs) are at increased risk for ectopic (tubal) pregnancy (see Chapter 26).

△ SAFETY ALERT 27-1
Ectopic pregnancy occurs when the egg implants in the fallopian tube or the abdominal cavity. Symptoms/signs of this potentially life-threatening condition include lower abdominal pain on one side, referred pain in neck and shoulder from blood beneath the diaphragm, nausea, and spotting of blood. Confirmation of ectopic pregnancy is considered an obstetric emergency requiring hospitalization and termination of the pregnancy to save the mother's life (Chow, 2010).

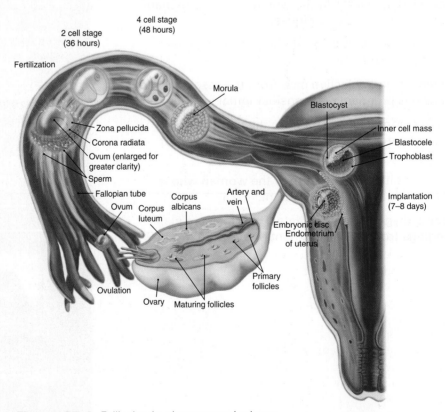

Figure 27-1 Follicular development and release.

First Trimester

The embryo travels from the fallopian tube and implants in the uterine lining, often with a resulting small bleed. Typically, the process from ovulation to implantation takes approximately 2 weeks, so implantation bleeding can occur at the same time the woman expects her period. Implantation bleeds are usually lighter and shorter than a typical period. Bleeding after implantation is a potential concern that requires investigation.

> ### Clinical Significance 27-1
> It is important to ask about the date and characteristics of the last menstrual period. If a woman confuses implantation bleeding with her period, the pregnancy is 1 month more advanced than she thinks.

The outer layer of the developing embryo produces human chorionic gonadotropin (hCG). Pregnancy tests (both urine and blood) measure levels of this hormone, whose presence validates the existence of a pregnancy and initiates a feedback loop that preserves the corpus luteum for longer than the usual 14 days.

At implantation, the embryo is far too small to be seen on ultrasound. One way to evaluate the progression of early pregnancy is by checking levels of hCG and progesterone. Serum hCG levels should double every 48 hours, and progesterone levels slowly increase.

> ### Clinical Significance 27-2
> Women who bleed in early pregnancy worry that they are miscarrying. Levels of human chorionic gonadotropin (hCG) that double in 48 hours are reassuring. Even hCG levels that increase more slowly may indicate a stable pregnancy. If hCG levels are falling, progesterone level is not increasing, or both, miscarriage is likely.

From weeks 2 to 8 after conception, all major fetal organs form. Therefore, it is very important for women to avoid teratogens during this period (which can be difficult because many are not even aware that they are pregnant this early). **Teratogens** are substances or infections that can cause malformations in the embryo. Examples of teratogens include tetracycline drugs, thalidomide, DES (Diethylstilbestrol), alcohol, x-rays and other radiation, rubella vaccine, isotretinoin (Accutane), lithium, and some anticonvulsants.

Between 25% and 50% of conceptions do not result in a viable pregnancy. Eighty percent of miscarriages (spontaneous abortions) occur during the first trimester, and more than half of these miscarriages are the result of chromosomal aberrations. Another 40% have altered development of the egg just after fertilization, sometimes characterized as a "blighted ovum" or "chemical pregnancy." Nearly all first-trimester miscarriages cannot be prevented by either mother or clinician. Nevertheless, women commonly wonder if they could have done something to prevent the tragedy and blame themselves. The ready availability of home pregnancy tests does not help. In the past, most women did not even know for sure that they were pregnant before they miscarried. Now, women bond before it is clear that the pregnancy is viable. Given these facts, reassurance from nurses that early miscarriages are not preventable can help women grieve and heal from their losses.

The rate of miscarriage drops dramatically after the first trimester. At 10 weeks, the placenta weighs only on average 20 g, yet this may be sufficient for it to produce enough progesterone to maintain a pregnancy. By 12 weeks' gestation, the placenta has grown sufficiently to take over production of progesterone and the corpus luteum is reabsorbed. Most women who have had morning sickness start feeling better once the placenta takes over progesterone production.

Second Trimester

During the second trimester, fetal growth is significant. The fetus begins this trimester about 8 cm long and weighing < 0.8 g. By the end of the second trimester, the fetus is about 38 cm long and weighs more than 1,000 g. Major organs develop to the point that the fetus may survive (with help) outside the womb.

At the beginning of the second trimester, the maternal uterus is large enough to extend beyond the pelvic bone into the abdomen. Many health care professionals perform a fetal survey by ultrasound at 20 weeks' gestation or halfway through the pregnancy. By this time, the fetus is large and developed enough that all major organs are visible on ultrasound, including the sex organs that indicate gender. In some cases, functionality of organs (eg, cardiac output) can also be assessed (Fig. 27-2). In addition, if ultrasound identifies certain unexpected findings, such as gastroschisis (intestines

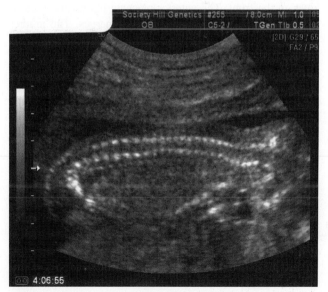

Figure 27-2 Ultrasound fetal scanning, focusing on spinal development, which in this case is progressing as expected.

formed outside the abdomen) or spina bifida (defect of the spinal canal), preparations can be made to improve fetal chances for survival at birth.

The fetal survey also indicates placement, functional grade, and size of the placenta. At week 20, it is not uncommon for the placenta to be close to the cervical os, or "low lying." Usually, as the uterus continues to expand, the placenta moves away from the os. When the placenta actually covers the os (**placenta previa**) at the end of the pregnancy, safe vaginal birth is not possible, and a cesarean delivery is planned. The placenta is grade 1 early in pregnancy and grade 3 at birth. If the placenta is "old" or small early in pregnancy, the fetus may need to be delivered early, because the placenta may not be able to support the required third-trimester growth.

Two milestones for the healthy first-time mother (primipara) occur at about 20 weeks. Her uterus reaches the umbilicus, and she begins to "show." She also clearly feels fetal movements. In the 2 weeks leading up to the 20-week mark, she may feel "flutters" that she confuses with gas. By 20 weeks, however, most women feel definite kicks or "**quickening.**"

Clinical Significance 27-3

Women who compare notes with friends or search the Internet may worry if they do not feel distinct kicks by 20 weeks. The most common reason a woman does not sense kicking by 20 weeks is that her dates are incorrect. The second most common reason is that the placenta has randomly implanted on the anterior aspect (belly side) of the uterus.

Unless a cesarean is required, it makes no difference where the placenta implants as long as it does not cover the **cervical opening** (os). The anterior abdomen has many more sensory nerves than the posterior, so it is much easier to feel kicks in the front. The anterior placenta blunts the force of the fetal kicks on the anterior sensory nerves. The mother with an anterior placenta feels the kicks when the fetus grows big enough to kick the anterior abdomen around the edges of the placenta, usually at about 22 weeks. As the fetus continues to grow and gain strength, the mother can feel the kicks through the "padding" of the placenta.

Third Trimester

During the third trimester, the fetus gains weight at a rapid pace, but proportionally not as rapidly as during the second trimester. It begins the trimester weighing about 1,000 g and at birth averages about 2,500 to 4,000 g. In the first two trimesters, most fetal growth is in the head and skeleton, but during the third trimester, fetal organs grow and mature, muscles increase in size and strength, and a protective fat layer forms to assist with temperature control after birth. Fetal skin thickens and forms a more protective barrier than during the second trimester. During the last 4 weeks of pregnancy,

the mother transfers IgG antibodies to the fetus to assist in the formation of the fetal immune system. Integration of the nervous and muscular functions proceeds rapidly during the third trimester. The average length of newborns is between 48 and 53 cm.

Near term, the fetus swallows nearly half the amniotic fluid volume each 24 hours, and insoluble debris in the fluid is removed and stored as the baby's stool (meconium) before the fluid is returned to the amniotic sac via fetal urine.

Clinical Significance 27-4

If the fetus does not swallow the expected amount of amniotic fluid (as can occur with maternal diabetes), then excess fluid collects in the amniotic sac (polyhydramnios). If the renal system is not fully formed and fetal urination is decreased, a deficiency of amniotic fluid results (oligohydramnios). Oligohydramnios is a risk factor for poor lung development.

A key task of the third trimester is maturation of the fetal lungs. Growth factors in amniotic fluid promote growth and differentiation of lung tissue. With expected amniotic fluid volume, functionality of the lungs depends on their ability to form surfactant, which prevents collapse of the alveoli upon expiration. If a fetus must be delivered between 28 and 34 weeks, a glucocorticosteroid injection is given to the mother to promote formation of surfactant.

Determining Weeks of Gestation

Human pregnancies last an *average* of 266 days after fertilization. By convention, pregnancies are dated from the first day of menstruation in a 28-day cycle, so 14 days are added (for a total of 280 days from the last menstrual period [LMP]) to calculate the "due date" or estimated date of birth (EDB). Thus, a woman who says that she is 6 weeks pregnant conceived 4 weeks ago.

Due date may be estimated by using **Naegele's rule**, which says to subtract 3 months from the first day of the LMP and add 7 days to the result. Thus, a woman whose LMP began 17APR2010 would have an EDB of 24JAN2011. Another way to calculate EDB is with a pregnancy wheel (Fig. 27-3), which is turned to line up the LMP on the inner wheel with the corresponding EDB on the outer wheel. The marker on the inner wheel then aligns with the probable date of delivery, which corresponds to a 40-week pregnancy (38 week since conception).

If a woman is known to have a longer or shorter menstrual cycle than 28 days, adjustments should be made to her EDB. For instance, if her cycle averages 32 days, her EDB will be 4 days later than the date calculated using the LMP on the pregnancy wheel. Because women usually do not know exactly how long their cycles are or when they ovulated, and there are variations in how each woman carries her pregnancy, "due date" is only an approximation. The nurse plays an important

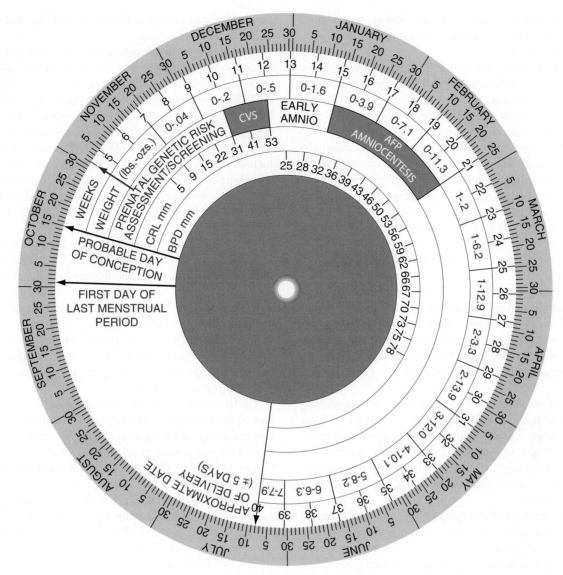

Figure 27-3 A pregnancy wheel can be used to find the EDB on the outer wheel by lining up the date of the LMP on the inner wheel.

role by asking detailed questions to ensure that all pertinent facts are considered to establish a probable due date.

Ultrasounds are used to determine accurate dates for gestation. Accurate dating helps prevent early induction or postterm complications.

Clinical Significance 27-5

Inducing labour too soon can result in premature birth, difficult labour, and complications such as cesarean surgery. Failing to induce a postterm fetus can result in postmaturity syndrome or even stillbirth. The nurse can help prevent difficulties by explaining at the first visit that a baby is not premature after 37 weeks and is not "late" before 42 weeks. Babies born anytime during this 5-week window are considered "on time"

Role of the Nurse in the Outpatient Setting

Health care for most women who are pregnant occurs in outpatient settings, in which nurses may be responsible for conducting intake interviews. Associated tasks include dating the pregnancy, taking a very detailed history, obtaining consents for prenatal testing, arranging for referrals if needed, and educating the patient about the practice. An intake visit typically lasts 60 to 90 minutes and gives the patient an idea of how the physician/midwife will care for her. A caring, nonjudgmental, open attitude from the nurse can not only reassure the patient but also increase the chances that she will reveal personal information that will improve her prenatal care. Development of a trusting relationship requires that the nurse use his or her best communication skills at a time when the patient usually has many questions, and sometimes fears.

Another outpatient role for nurses is triage. Patients who are pregnant are understandably worried about events they think might be unexpected. It is impossible for busy physicians/midwives to see the patient each time she has a concern; therefore, the nurse handles many questions from women who are pregnant over the telephone or, increasingly, via secure e-mail. The nurse knows which concerns can be handled by phone or computer; which require a visit to identify or confirm a diagnosis, and if so, the urgency; and which require that the patient proceed immediately to a hospital or birth centre. Consequently, the nurse is familiar with the symptoms of common diagnoses in pregnancy and is able to ask questions necessary to make safe recommendations to the patient.

A third outpatient role is to gather preliminary data before a physician/midwife sees the patient for her prenatal visit. Typically, the nurse weighs the patient, records her blood pressure, assesses her urine for protein and glucose, and identifies any concerns. The nurse notes any variations from expected findings and reports them to the physician/midwife.

A fourth outpatient role is conducting and interpreting **nonstress tests** (NSTs). During the third trimester, patients with risk factors for early delivery may be tested as often as twice weekly to assess whether the fetal heart rate (FHR) is reassuring. Typically, the nurse conducts NSTs and reports findings verbally to the physician/midwife, who will view the monitoring strip later.

A fifth outpatient role is education regarding unexpected test results and options for treating issues, including medication teaching. In many offices, the nurse, under the supervision of the physician/midwife, sends the prescription to the pharmacy.

Acute Assessment

Some conditions in pregnancy require immediate attention from a physician/midwife, immediate hospitalization, or both. In an ectopic pregnancy, the pregnancy is implanted in the fallopian tubes or the abdominal cavity. This can occur in 2% of pregnancies (Bowen & Bickley, 2010). Ectopic pregnancy is an obstetrical emergency, because if it ruptures, the woman may die from internal bleeding before surgery can be performed (Chow, 2010).

Another example is pyelonephritis, which occurs when a urinary tract infection (UTI) is not treated promptly. Because the immune system does not fight infections as well during pregnancy, a bladder infection can quickly become a kidney infection, characterized by severe flank pain and a fever above 38°C. While pyelonephritis is often treated on an outpatient basis for nonpregnant patients, during pregnancy pyelonephritis requires intravenous (IV) antibiotics immediately to prevent generalized sepsis, which is potentially fatal (Bowen & Bickley, 2010).

Any nonhospitalized patient with *hemorrhage*, defined as soaking a menstrual pad in <30 minutes, should be referred immediately to the nearest emergency department (ED) for evaluation and treatment. Also, any woman who has lost enough blood to be symptomatic (light-headed, dizzy, cold, confused, diaphoretic, anxious) should be referred immediately to the ED. Possible causes of bleeding include placenta previa (placenta near or over the cervical os), abruptio placenta (placenta separates from the uterine wall), and disseminated intravascular coagulation (painful bright red bleeding with excessive clotting) (Bowen & Bickley, 2010).

Pain in the calf with redness and edema of the leg may indicate a deep vein thrombosis (DVT). This requires immediate treatment to prevent a pulmonary embolus (Edge, Day, et al., 2010) (see Chapter 20). Dyspnea or chest pain could indicate a pulmonary embolus or a cardiac emergency.

Abdominal conditions requiring emergency attention include appendicitis, cholecystitis/cholelithiasis, pancreatitis, bowel obstruction (especially during the third trimester), and ovarian tumours. The safest time for surgery is the second trimester (Varner, 1994).

Gestational hypertension, preeclampsia, is a blood pressure >140/90, with or without edema and with or without proteinuria (Magee, Helewa, et al., 2008). Treatment is required to prevent progression to eclampsia (convulsions and coma occur). Delivery of the infant results in rapid recovery from eclampsia.

Sudden absence of fetal movements is also an emergency. Lastly, if a woman is having regular, painful contractions before 37 weeks, she should be seen immediately for evaluation, preferably in an acute care setting with appropriate postpartum facilities.

Subjective Data Collection

Cultural Considerations

Many racial disparities in fact are related to socioeconomic status (Headley & Harrigan, 2009) and lack of access to appropriate services. First Nations women and other high-risk women who are pregnant can access prenatal and postpartum information and support through the Canada Prenatal Nutrition Program (Public Health Agency of Canada [PHAC], 2008a). In many practices, nurses play key roles in providing the education essential to reducing such disparities.

In Africa, in some cultures in Asia and the Middle East, and in some immigrant communities in Europe and North America, woman may undergo female genital mutilation (FGM) (see Chapter 26). FGM can contribute to chronic pelvic inflammatory disease, infertility, fear of intimacy, and challenges with labour and birth (World Health Organization,

2010). Of particular concern is the type of FGM called "infibulation" in which the vaginal opening is narrowed by cutting and repositioning the inner or outer labia. The vaginal opening has to be cut open to allow for a vaginal birth. In some women, the vaginal opening is sutured after delivery, leaving a small opening for menstruation. The vagina then has to be reopened for sexual intercourse. Closing and reopening the vagina further increases risks of infection and scarring (World Health Organization).

Assessment of Risk Factors

As discussed earlier, the nurse gathers basic information during the intake interview, such as medical and obstetric

Questions to Assess History and Risk Factors	Rationale
Personal History **Age.** What is your date of birth? What is your age?	Teens who are pregnant have increased nutritional requirements because they, too, are still growing. In addition, their pelvises may not be fully developed. These teens are at increased risk for complications, especially preeclampsia, probably from inadequate nutrient intake. On the other hand, mothers of increased maternal age are those who will be 35 years or older at the estimated date of birth (EDB). They may have decreased fertility, are at increased risk for miscarriage and genetic anomalies, and may have increased preexisting health issues (eg, fibroids, advanced endometriosis, hypertension).
Culture. What is your cultural background? Do you have a religious preference? **Clinical Significance 27-6** Examples of beliefs that can affect the care of women who are pregnant include that Jehovah's Witnesses accept no blood products, even to save the life of mother or baby; women from some parts of Africa, Asia, and the Middle East have experienced Female Genital Mutilation (FGM); and Russian patients may refuse cesarean surgery for a breech presentation.	Some cultures or religions have important childbirth rituals, which may influence the role of the baby's father during labour, preferred anesthesia for surgery, handling of the newborn, or required or prohibited foods during the postpartum period. Some cultures may consider the violation of such norms as potentially harmful for mother or fetus. Some genetic diseases or pregnancy complications (eg, gestational diabetes, hypertension) are more prevalent in certain ethnic groups. For example, individuals of South Asian, Chinese, African, and Latin genetic backgrounds have higher rates of impaired glucose tolerance, abdominal (central) obesity, and gestational diabetes. For First Nations, Inuit and Métis women, 8% to 18% will have gestational diabetes compared to 3.7% for the rest of the multiethnic female population in Canada (Canadian Diabetes Association Clinical Practice Guidelines Expert Committee [CDACPGEC], 2008).
Pregnancy History. Have you had any previous pregnancies? Any miscarriages? Termination of a pregnancy?	Document each pregnancy (including miscarriages and terminations) by date, length of gestation, length of labour, type of delivery (vaginal, forceps/vacuum, or cesarean), type of anesthesia and any adverse reaction, sex and weight of the infant, and any complications. Past patterns can suggest possible current issues.
Pap Smears. Have you had any unexpected Pap smear results in the past?	Patients with past alterations may have a recurrence with pregnancy. Those who have had surgery to remove unusual cells may have scar tissue that needs to be released during labour to permit vaginal birth.
Sexually Transmitted Infections (STIs). Have you had any STIs in the past? Do you currently have an STI?	Verify that prior STIs were treated according to protocol. Assess risk of reexposure, because many STIs are potentially harmful to the fetus.

(text continues on page 840)

Questions to Assess History and Risk Factors	Rationale

Breast History. Have you ever had a mammogram? Any unexpected mammogram results? Have you had a breast reduction? Or breast implants? Have you had discharge from your breasts? Have you had a breast infection (abscess)? Have you breast-fed in the past? Were there any challenges with breast-feeding?

Document augmentation or reduction surgeries, and whether an attempt was made to preserve ability to breast-feed. Document any other breast health issues (discharge, abscesses). Document any past challenges with breast-feeding.

Infertility. Have you had any concerns with infertility?

If it was difficult for the woman to conceive or maintain the pregnancy, fully document her history, including any medication that she took and what, if any, type of assisted reproduction was used. In vitro pregnancies have a somewhat higher risk than spontaneous pregnancies of multiple gestation and fetal loss.

Psychological Issues. Have you ever experienced depression? Anxiety? Or eating disorders? Other mental health conditions?

Patients with a history of these psychiatric conditions are at risk for exacerbations during pregnancy and postpartum. For women considered at high risk during pregnancy (low socioeconomic level, First Nations, and younger age), as many as 29% have depression and anxiety (Bowen & Muhajarine, 2006).

Headaches. Have you had headaches during your pregnancy? Or migraines?

Only acetaminophen is recommended during pregnancy, so patients with frequent headaches may need to change their medication, especially in the third trimester. Those with frequent migraines are at somewhat increased risk for postpartum stroke. Severe headaches may be a sign of preeclampsia.

Allergies. Do you have any allergies to medications? What is your reaction? Do you have other allergies? What are your reactions?

Note both the allergen and reaction to it. Although physicians/midwives try to minimize medications prescribed during pregnancy and labour, some conditions common in pregnancy (ie, urinary tract infections [UTIs], positive Group B streptococcus status) are treated with antibiotics, to which the patient may be allergic.

Violence. Begin this discussion by reassuring the patient that their health history is confidential; it is only accessible to health care professionals providing specific care to them. "Because violence is common for so many people, I routinely ask all patients about violent experiences—in the past and currently. I wonder if you have experienced in the past any type of violent act (eg, verbal abuse? Physical abuse? Rape? Or are currently experiencing violence?" (see Chapter 12).

In the initial interview, it is common for patients to minimize their experience with violence and abuse. Nevertheless, pregnancy and labour can elicit painful memories or cause overprotective behaviour. In severe cases, the patient may experience flashbacks or psychotic episodes during labour. Also, pregnancy is a time when intimate partner violence increases. It is estimated as occurring in 6% to 8% of pregnancies (Bowen & Bickley, 2010).

Medications and Supplements
Contraception. What type of contraception have you used? When did you last use it?

If the patient was using hormonal contraceptives within three cycles of conception, it is difficult to assess when she ovulated. Patients using hormonal contraceptives do not have true menses, but have "withdrawal bleeds" when they do not take progesterone for 7 days. Even if a woman is pregnant, she may have withdrawal bleeds at the usual time if she continues her birth control pills. If her conception date is unclear, ultrasound dating in the first trimester can be offered.

At the present time, are you taking any prescribed medications? Any over-the-counter (OTC) medications? Any vitamins? Minerals such as calcium? Folic acid?

It is important to know what prescribed medications and OTC medications the patient is taking. Some may not be safe during pregnancy. Taking vitamins, calcium, and folic acid should begin in the preconception phase and continue throughout the pregnancy (Health Canada, 2007a,b; Wilson, Désilets, et al., 2007).

Questions to Assess History and Risk Factors	Rationale
Family History Do you have a family history of diabetes? High blood pressure? Twins? Or genetic illnesses?	Positive family history of these findings may increase the patient's risk for them.
Additional Risk Factors ***Support System.*** Do you have a support system that has been assisting you during your pregnancy? After you deliver, will the same support system be available to assist you at that time?	Patients without a stable support system are at risk for poor nutrition, domestic violence, poor housing, and increased stress. Some patients achieve stability in marriage, others with a supportive family and friends.
Personal Habits. Do you smoke? If yes, how long have you smoked? Amount smoked? Do you drink alcohol? If yes, how much do you drink per day? Or week? Do you take other drugs? If yes, what drugs do you take? How often?	Pregnancy is a time when patients are more likely to discontinue habits known to be harmful for their baby. The nurse provides support and cessation resources to patients who want them.
How often do you exercise? For how long? Intensity of the exercise?	Exercise before and during pregnancy promotes overall maternal and fetal health (PHAC, 2008b). Guidelines for exercise during pregnancy are available at http://www.phac-aspc.gc.ca/hp-gs/pdf/hpguide-eng.pdf
Recent Immigration. How long have you lived in this country?	Immigrants may have been exposed to infections that can harm them or the fetus. A refugee may have had inadequate nutrition when the bony pelvis was forming, resulting in a small or misshapen pelvis. With better nutrition in this country, she may be at increased risk for cephalopelvic disproportion, which would require cesarean surgery for a safe delivery. Immigrants from certain areas may have had female circumcision (FGM), which reduces the size of the introitus.
Access to Care. Do you have any financial concerns related to your pregnancy? Are you able to come to appointments?	Everyone in Canada has access to health care (Joseph, Liston, et al., 2007). However, in some areas it may be difficult to find a family physician or a maternity physician or midwife. Provincial/territorial and federal programs are available, particularly to offer prenatal care to women who might otherwise not have easy access to care. If the pregnancy was unplanned, patients will not have had a preconception visit to address any issues that might affect the pregnancy. On average, they begin care later and receive less prenatal care in pregnancy (Stewart, Dean, et al., 2007).

history and personal history that might affect the pregnancy. The nurse asks about current concerns, family history, age, gender, genetic background, medications and supplements, and additional risk factors. Knowledge of the patient's risk factors helps identify topics for health promotion and disease and injury prevention.

Risk Assessment and Health Promotion

Since pregnancy involves increased contact with health care professionals, it is an excellent time to introduce and support lifestyle changes that will promote health throughout the lifespan.

Topics for Health Promotion

- Prevention of gestational diabetes
- Promotion of good nutrition and oral health
- Promotion of healthy lifestyle habits
- Promotion of mental health and safety
- Prenatal and breast-feeding classes
- Follow-up visits and prenatal monitoring

Adapted from Bowen, A., & Bickley, L. S. (2010). Assessing the woman who is pregnant. In T. C. Stephen, D. L. Skillen, R. A. Day, & L. S. Bickley (Eds.). *Canadian Bates' guide to health assessment for nurses* (1st ed., p. 862). Philadelphia, PA: Wolters Kluwer Health/Lippincott Williams & Wilkins.

Prevention of Gestational Diabetes

Women who are pregnant and who exercise and eat a well-balanced diet will be less likely to gain extensive weight or develop gestational diabetes. Gestational diabetes places women at increased risk for gestational hypertension, infection, cesarean delivery, larger infant, and an infant with anomalies. If the gestational diabetes is well managed, the risk for type 1 or 2 diabetes later in life is decreased. Universal screening for diabetes should ideally begin in the preconception phase, and then test for gestational diabetes mellitus (GDM) in the first trimester, and between 24 and 28 weeks, and as necessary.

GDM is defined as "glucose intolerance with first onset or recognition occurring during pregnancy" (Senthuran, 2010, p. 1297). Gestational diabetes occurs in 3.5% to 3.8% of all pregnancies, usually in the second and third trimesters (Senturan). Risk factors for gestational diabetes include diagnosis of gestational diabetes with a previous pregnancy; delivery of an infant with a high birth weight; genetic background (Aboriginal, Latino, South Asian, Asian, or African descent), age of >35 years, obesity present at beginning of pregnancy; history of polycystic ovary syndrome, and use of corticosteroids (CDACPGEC, 2008).

Promotion of Nutrition and Oral Health

Preconception Phase. Three months before planning to try to conceive is the ideal time for a woman to meet with a health care professional to review her current health (eg, hypertension, diabetes, obesity, anemia, or bowel disorders).

Any dental work that includes x-rays or an anesthetic should be done prior to conception.
All of these conditions can affect maternal and fetal health. Be sure that all current medications and over-the-counter (OTC) medications and supplements will be safe for the fetus. Switch medications as needed.

Improve diet as needed—include more foods with folate or fortified with folate (eg, breads and cereals). Begin prenatal vitamins with 0.4 mg of folic acid and 27 g of iron. For women with type 1 or 2 diabetes, increase folic acid to 0.5 mg for 3 months preconception and increase to 0.6 mg for the pregnancy (Wilson, Désilets, et al., 2007). Lose weight if needed. Begin exercising.

Folate from foods and fortified foods and folic acid as a supplement are needed to reduce risk of neural tube disorder in the fetus (Wilson, Désilets, et al., 2007).

Pregnancy. Women who are underweight need to increase intake during pregnancy. Women who are obese and gain more than the recommended weight during the pregnancy are at risk.

Low weight gain during pregnancy increases the risk for a low-birth-weight infant and preterm birth.
High weight gain and obesity are risks for a larger infant and a late birth.

Recommended daily servings for women who are pregnant:

Vegetables and fruit: 5 to 11

Grain products: 8 to 10

Milk and alternatives: 4 to 5

Meat and alternatives: 4 to 5

(Health Canada, 2007a,b,c)

In the second trimester, increase intake by 350 calories/d, which is 2 or 3 food guide servings. Emphasis is on protein sources such as dairy and meat or meat alternatives. In the third trimester, increase calories by 450/d (Health Canada, 2007b).

Increase folic acid to 0.6 mg.

Calcium: 1,000 mg

Magnesium: 350–400 mg

Vitamin A: No more than 10,000 IU daily

Iron: 27 or 48 mg/d if vegetarian

Increase folic acid to 1.0 mg if at increased risk for neural tube defect—taking an anticonvulsant—or had a baby with a neural tube defect (Wilson, Désilets, et al., 2007).

Promotion of Healthy Lifestyle Habits
Smoking: Quit Smoking

Smoking is linked to increased numbers of spontaneous abortions and perinatal mortality (Health Canada, 2005); complications during and related to labour: placenta previa, abruption placenta, and preterm delivery; low-birth-weight infants; babies with cleft lip or palate; and an increase in sudden infant death syndrome (London, Ladewig, et al., 2007).

Health Promotion	Rationale/Unexpected Findings
Stop Drinking Alcohol	Alcohol increases the risk for mental retardation, heart anomalies, intrauterine growth restriction, and fetal alcohol spectrum disorder (London, Ladewig, et al., 2007).
Decrease Caffeine intake.	Drug use can cause a variety of congenital anomalies and the newborn is challenged by withdrawal symptoms (London, Ladewig, et al., 2007).
Stop all "Street Drugs" such as heroin; barbiturates; stimulants such as amphetamines and cocaine; psychotropic drugs such as PCP (phencyclidine hydrochloride), LSD (lysergic acid diethylamide), and marijuana.	
Avoid Unprotected or Risky Sex	Unprotected sex can lead to sexually transmitted infections (STIs). Syphilis can be transferred to the fetus during pregnancy. Between 2005 and 2007 in Alberta, 14 babies were born with congenital syphilis and 5 died (Simons, 2008). HIV can also be transmitted to the infant during pregnancy, during childbirth, and during breast-feeding (Bowen & Bickley, 2010).
Promotion of Mental Health and Safety Pregnancy is a time of many changes and increased stress that can result in anxiety and depression.	Bowen and Muhajarine (2006) reported that 29% of women who were identified as high risk during pregnancy had depression and anxiety. In a study comparing women in Taiwan who were not pregnant and women who were pregnant, 27.3% to 36% of the women who were pregnant were depressed (Ko, Chang, et al., 2010).
Intimate partner violence is of concern. This is dangerous for the woman who is pregnant and for the fetus (SOGC, 2005).	Nurses are encouraged to look for signs of violence (eg, bruising on the abdomen) (SOGC, 2005).
Prenatal and Breast-feeding Classes ***Prenatal Classes.*** Classes help to prepare the woman who is pregnant and her partner (or support person) for the birthing process.	Classes include information on how labour progresses and coping techniques to use to decrease the pain sensations during labour. Some classes include content on the postpartum period and parenting strategies.
Breast-feeding Classes. The Breastfeeding Committee for Canada (2007) promotes exclusive breast-feeding to 6 months of age, and addition of safe and appropriate foods from 6 months to 2 years.	Breast-feeding classes and/or individual counselling with a lactation specialist can increase success (Bowen & Bickley, 2010).
Follow-Up Visits and Prenatal Monitoring The frequency of follow-up visits depends on risk factors.	Urinary protein and glucose are checked at each visit.

Focused Health History Related to Common Symptoms/Signs in Pregnancy

The nurse responsible for triaging pregnancy-related calls can make an enormous difference in how the patient views her competence as a mother, in how much trust she has in her heath care team and the staff where she plans to give birth (home, hospital, or birth centre), and in how well she will labour. Use of sound therapeutic communication is especially important during pregnancy, because a woman who is pregnant is understandably concerned not only about her own health but also about the health of the fetus. What may seem like a "common concern" of pregnancy to an experienced nurse may seem much more ominous to the patient who is pregnant. So-called "common concerns" of pregnancy are annoying, but not dangerous for either mother or fetus. Supportive care is usually all that is required.

Focused Health History Related to Common Symptoms/Signs in Pregnancy

- Fatigue
- Morning sickness
- Growing pains
- Increased vaginal discharge
- Increased urination
- Breast tenderness or discharge
- Periumbilical pain in the second trimester
- Fetal hiccups
- Braxton Hicks contractions

Examples of Questions for Symptom/Sign Analysis—Fatigue

- "Where in your body are you most aware of your fatigue?" (Location)
- "Describe your fatigue." (Quality)
- "To what degree does the fatigue affect your ability to perform your usual daily activities?" (Severity)
- "When did you notice your energy levels change?" (Onset)
- "Have your energy levels stayed low? Or do they change?" (Constancy)
- "Is there a time of day that you feel more fatigued?" (Timing)
- "What makes the fatigue worse?" (Aggravating factors)
- "What helps reduce the fatigue?" "Can you put your feet up during the day?" "Can you take a nap?" "Do you get any help with household chores?" "Or help with other children?" (Alleviating factors)
- "Are you noticing any other symptoms?" "Are you feeling sad?" "Depressed?" "How are you sleeping?" "Have you had your blood checked for anemia?" (Associated symptoms)
- "What is going on in your work/school/home/recreational environment that might be affecting your fatigue?" "How much stress is in your life right now?" (Environmental factors)
- "Tell me how the fatigue is affecting your life." (Significance to patient)
- "What do you think is contributing to the fatigue you feel?" (Patient perspective)

Adapted from Bowen, A., & Bickley, L. S. (2010). Assessing the woman who is pregnant. In T. C. Stephen, D. L. Skillen, R. A. Day, & L. S. Bickley (Eds.). *Canadian Bates' guide to health assessment for nurses* (1st ed., p. 861). Philadelphia, PA: Wolters Kluwer Health/Lippincott Williams & Wilkins.

Examples of Questions to Assess Symptoms/Signs	Rationale/Unexpected Findings
Morning Sickness Have you been experiencing any nausea with this pregnancy? Any vomiting? • Is there a particular time of day when you have nausea? Or vomiting? • Does anything help relieve the nausea? Or the vomiting? • Does anything seem to make the nausea worse? Or make the vomiting worse? ⚠ *SAFETY ALERT 27-2* *Some women have severe morning sickness (hyperemesis gravidarum). They cannot keep anything in their stomachs long enough to digest. As a result, they lose weight and their fluid and electrolyte balance is altered. These patients may require intravenous (IV) fluids or even hospitalization to restabilize. Untreated hyperemesis gravidarum can be fatal.*	It is unknown why some women who are pregnant have morning sickness. This condition is thought to be associated with high estrogen levels, but it is also influenced by diet and emotions. Tense or anxious patients seem to be at risk, as are those who do not drink enough water or get enough B vitamins in early pregnancy. Usually, morning sickness can be managed on an outpatient basis if the woman increases B vitamins and fluid intake (sips only, not large glasses at a time) and uses methods of relaxation (eg, meditation, yoga, prayer). The nurse does the necessary teaching if the woman reports her concern. Once the woman can keep down sips of water, the nurse advises her to try the BRAT diet—bananas, rice, applesauce, and toast—starting with one bite and increasing intake by an additional bite every 15 minutes so long as there is no emesis. For most patients, nausea and vomiting is a self-limiting condition that does not require medical intervention.
Growing Pains • Have you experienced any sensations in your lower abdomen? Any pain? • If so, describe how they feel and how long they last. • Does any movement/activity seem to trigger the pains? • How often do they occur? ⚠ *SAFETY ALERT 27-3* *Appendicitis, pyelonephritis, ectopic pregnancy, and miscarriage can also present with abdominal pain. With these conditions, pain is more constant, increasing in severity, or less sharp.*	In the first trimester, sharp pains in the lower abdomen are common. Stretching of the round and broad ligaments that support the growing uterus causes them, which are usually very short (<5 seconds) and have a stabbing quality. They are not repetitive, but often associated with position changes or, later, fetal movements. However, there are many other sources of abdominal pain during pregnancy, some of which are potentially fatal.

Examples of Questions to Assess Symptoms/Signs	Rationale/Unexpected Findings

Increased Vaginal Discharge
- Have you noticed any increase in vaginal discharge with this pregnancy?
- If so, describe how much? What is it like?
- Does it have a particular odour? Or colour?
- With the discharge, do you have any itching? Burning? Or discomfort?

It is usual for women who are pregnant to have increased clear vaginal discharge from increased estrogen production. Patients describe this discharge as just like their usual vaginal discharge, except that there is more of it. If the discharge is like nasal mucus or cottage cheese, is any colour other than clear, or has a foul odour, it may be a sign of a vaginal infection or sexually transmitted infection (STI) (SOGC, 2007). Infections during pregnancy should be diagnosed and treated promptly because some can affect the fetus. Patients who report such symptoms need evaluation.

Increased Urination
- Have you noticed a need to pass your urine more frequently with this pregnancy?
- How much water are you drinking every day?
- How often do you pass your urine?
- Is passing urine accompanied by any pain? Or pressure?
- Have you noticed any blood in your urine?

Increased urination in pregnancy is common as a result of the relaxation of the urinary system by increased progesterone. This is one reason why it is important for the woman to drink 2 L/d of water. If urinary frequency is accompanied by suprapubic pressure, dysuria (painful urination), hematuria (blood in the urine), or flank pain, she may have a urinary tract infection (UTI) or a kidney infection that requires prompt treatment.

> #### Clinical Significance 27-7
>
> Patients already urinating more than usual are reluctant to increase fluid intake. Nevertheless, doing so helps prevent UTIs and constipation and reduces morning sickness. Fibre intake is also important, especially in later pregnancy when the growing fetus compresses the intestines, and therefore, transit time increases.

Breast Tenderness and Discharge
- Have you noticed any changes in your breasts?
- Have you experienced any feelings of fullness? Or breast pain?
- Have you noticed any nipple discharge? If so, please describe it.

Some patients can feel breast changes even before the pregnancy test is positive. Rapid growth of alveoli, addition of a fat layer, and construction of the duct system for breast-feeding can result in feelings of fullness or even pain. The nurse teaches the patient to use a supportive, properly fitted bra and to take acetaminophen, if necessary, for pain relief. Later in pregnancy, the patient may notice nipple discharge. This is almost always colostrum leaking in preparation for birth, but the nurse instructs the patient to mention the discharge when she sees the physician/midwife. The physician/midwife should evaluate to verify that discharge is not from infection or a tumour.

Periumbilical Pain
- Have you experienced pressure around your umbilicus? Any pain?
- If so, does any movement trigger the pain? Or a specific activity?

About halfway through pregnancy, women commonly feel a stretching pain all around the umbilicus. The pain is similar to "growing pains," which usually subside by the end of the first trimester. However, these second-trimester pains are similar in origin, resulting from additional ligaments stretching as the uterus accommodates the growing fetus.

Fetal Hiccups and Other Spasms
- Do you notice any regular fetal movements?
- Do you think that the fetus might be having hiccups? Or sucking his or her thumb?

By the third trimester, the patient may be aware of fetal hiccups, which result from spasms of the fetal diaphragm triggered by an immature neurological system (Popescu, Popescu, et al., 2007). Hiccups can be thought of as "practice breathing," and they tend to resolve as the neurological system matures. Women sometimes report that it

(text continues on page 846)

Examples of Questions to Assess Symptoms/Signs	Rationale/Unexpected Findings

feels as if the fetus is having a seizure. Rarely, this is true. Usually, the rapid movement is again from the immature neurological system: the fetus has a hypersensitive startle reflex and "jumps" when stimulated. Such symptoms tend to resolve near term. Upon further questioning by the nurse, it may become obvious that what the mother feels is rhythmic thumb sucking by the fetus.

Braxton Hicks Contractions
- Have you experienced any contractions with this pregnancy?
- If so, how often do they occur? How long do they last?
- How painful are these contractions?
- Is there anything you do that stops the contractions?

Braxton Hicks contractions prepare the body for labour. They are usually irregular in frequency and duration, with fewer than five in 1 hour. They are also short (<30 seconds) but may be painful. These contractions may begin as early as the second trimester, especially for patients who have had babies before, but are more common in the third trimester. They often resolve with position changes, a hot shower, hydration, or relaxation. They are to be differentiated from preterm labour contractions, which are regular, do not resolve with comfort measures, occur more frequently than four in 1 hour, get longer and stronger over time, and result in cervical change. The triage nurse must be able to distinguish between Braxton Hicks and preterm labour contractions.

An Example of a Therapeutic Dialogue

Michelle calls the hospital on a Sunday when she is 30 weeks of gestation and says she is afraid she is in labour, but that she knows it is too early for the baby to come.

Nurse: Tell me more about what has happened so far and how you are feeling.

Michelle: Well, I am cramping.

Nurse: How long have you been cramping?

Michelle: They have been coming all day.

Nurse: Have you been timing them?

Michelle: Not really, but it seems like every few minutes, and they hurt!

Nurse: I'm sorry. Could you tell me when one is starting?

Michelle: Well, one is starting now.

Nurse: Can you tell me where you are feeling it and what it feels like?

Michelle: All over my tummy, and it feels kind of like menstrual cramps.

Nurse: Can you tell me when it's over? It's over now? Ok, then that lasted about 20 seconds. Let me know if you feel another one.

Michelle: Should I be worried? It's too early to have the baby. Will my baby be OK?

Nurse: We'd like to see you as soon as you can get a ride, just to be sure, but you are not telling me anything that makes me sure that something is wrong. So far, everything you are saying could happen in a usual pregnancy. We will do some tests so that we know everything is OK. When could you get here?

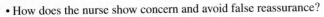

Critical Thinking Challenge

- How does the nurse show concern and avoid false reassurance?
- Why does the nurse assess social issues?'
- What knowledge base is important for a nurse to have to perform a complete assessment?

Objective Data Collection

Equipment

- Stethoscope
- Fetoscope or Doppler
- Equipment wipes
- Sphygmomanometer
- Weigh scale with height measure
- Nasal speculum
- Penlight
- Tongue blades
- Cup of water (for the thyroid examination)
- Reflex hammer
- Tape measure
- Gynecological speculum—different types and sizes
- Equipment for Pap smear, cytology, and bacteriology specimens
- Disposable nonlatex gloves
- Water-soluble lubricant

Adapted from Bowen, A., & Bickley, L. S. (2010). Assessing the woman who is pregnant. In T. C. Stephen, D. L. Skillen, R. A. Day, & L. S. Bickley (Eds.). *Canadian Bates' guide to health assessment for nurses* (1st ed., p. 873). Philadelphia, PA: Wolters Kluwer Health/Lippincott Williams & Wilkins.

Promoting Patient Comfort, Dignity, and Safety

Before performing the examination, it is important to consider the environment. A draft-free, private room with a comfortable room temperature is appropriate for the examination. If this is the patient's first assessment, the physician/midwife explains the procedures, shows the instruments that will be used, and answers any questions. It is important that the woman who is pregnant be treated with dignity; during the health history, the patient should be fully dressed. It is important to explain to the patient about the pelvic examination. Some women may not be comfortable with this examination and may refuse it, especially if they have been sexually abused. After the history is taken, a male clinician should ask to have a female nurse in the room to serve as chaperone (and the patient's advocate) during the examination. The nurse may hand instruments and specimen containers to the physician/midwife during the examination. However, her primary role is to support the patient. The nurse labels specimens, verifying the patient's name and birth date, before they are removed from the examination room.

Assessment During the Initial Visit

A maternity physician/midwife usually conducts the initial full physical assessment, with a pelvic examination (see Chapter 26), at the first or second visit. Ideally, this happens during the first trimester. For the healthy gravida (pregnant woman), examination includes the following:

- General survey and vital signs
- Nutrition
- Skin integrity, assessing for unexpected findings (including large moles, piercings, or tattoos)
- Head for unexpected bumps, lesions, or infestations
- Eyes to test pupils for PERRLA and the ocular fundus (see Chapter 15)
- Ears for a clear canal and pearly gray tympanic membrane
- Mouth for lesions, signs of infection, unusual anatomy, and oral/dental health
- Neck for size, smoothness, and placement of the thyroid
- Lung fields to make sure they are clear bilaterally
- Heart sounds (mild systolic ejection murmurs are common in pregnancy)
- Extremities to note any vascularities or edema
- Breasts and axilla for any unexpected lumps or lesions
- Abdomen for scars, adipose tissue, symmetry, striae, and fetal heart tones past 10 weeks
- Reflexes (see Chapter 24)
- External genitalia for signs of infection and details of any FGM
- Vagina and cervix with a speculum. Samples for a wet mount or cultures may be collected if infection is suspected. Samples may also be taken for Papanicolaou, human papillomavirus, chlamydia, gonorrhea, and infectious syphilis tests if these have not been done in the last year (see Chapter 26)
- Uterus and adnexa (ovaries) with a bimanual examination (see Chapter 26)
- Pelvis to assess the size and shape of the birth canal (see advanced techniques—Nonstress Test and Leopold's Manoevres)
- Rectum for hemorrhoids (see Chapter 25)

The nurse often performs assessments and teaching related to nutrition and changes in the skin, breast, abdomen, urine, and vaginal secretions.

Techniques and Expected Findings	Unexpected Findings
General Survey and Vital Signs Document weight, blood pressure, other vital signs (Fig. 27-4). Although randomized trials have not shown a benefit for obtaining a urine sample from women who are pregnant with each visit, it is the standard of care in many hospitals and clinics. Test urine for glucose and protein, and chart the findings.	

(text continues on page 848)

Figure 27-4 Assessing the patient's blood pressure during the initial pregnancy visit.

Nutrition

Most women gain very little weight (if any) in the first trimester. Typical gains are <3 kg partly because of morning sickness for those who have it. In addition, not much structural change is necessary for the woman to accommodate the fetus and uterus, which are still small enough to fit behind the pubic bone. A simple rule of thumb for a woman whose prepregnant BMI is within expected parameters is that she will gain about 4.5 kg by 20 weeks and about 0.5 kg/wk for the remaining 20 weeks, for a total of about 14.5 kg (see Table 27-1).

Call excessive (or not enough) weight gain to the attention of the physician/midwife.

Table 27-1	Weight Distribution

Weight is distributed approximately as follows:

Tissues and Fluids	Average at Term (g)
Fetus	3,400
Placenta	650
Amniotic fluid	800
Uterus enlargement	970
Breasts	405
Blood (excess volume)	1,450
Extravascular fluid volume increase	1,480
Maternal stores (fat)	3,345
Total	12,500

Nutritional requirements to produce a healthy baby and associated weight gain include increasing intake by about 350 cal/d in the second trimester and 450 cal/d in the third trimester, increasing complete protein intake to 60 g/d, increasing elemental iron intake to 27 mg/d, and increasing vitamin intake and folic acid to 0.6 mg, especially for women with multiple fetuses, who

Women who fail to meet these nutritional requirements risk *low-birth-weight* or *intrauterine growth-restricted babies* and increased difficulties with breast-feeding.

smoke, or who use alcohol or drugs. A good resource for women to check dietary adequacy is Canada's Food Guide (Health Canada, 2007a,b). Women with healthy preconception diets provide an optimal start toward healthy child development.

Skin

Increased melanization in the first trimester may lead to **linea nigra** (a hyperpigmented line between the symphysis pubis and the top of the fundus) and **chloasma** (mask of pregnancy—a blotchy hyperpigmented area on the cheeks, nose, and forehead.

Abdomen

Smooth muscles (ie, intestines and kidneys) relax and dilate as a result of increased circulating progesterone levels.

Stasis can result, causing *constipation* and *urinary tract infections (UTIs)*.

By 10 to 12 weeks, it is common to be able to hear the fetal heartbeat with a Doppler (Fig. 27-5). Ultrasonic gel is placed on the Doppler's transducer, which is then placed with some pressure on the woman's abdomen. In the first trimester, the fetal heartbeat usually is audible just above the symphysis pubis. If the uterus is palpable superior to the pubic bone, the heartbeat may be heard higher in the abdomen as well.

For women who are overweight, it may take until 14 weeks to hear the baby's heartbeat with a Doppler. Women who are morbidly obese may need serial ultrasounds to monitor fetal well-being.

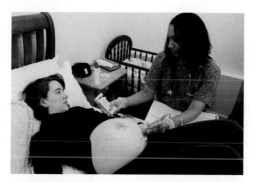

Figure 27-5 Assessing the FHR through use of Doppler ultrasound.

As pregnancy progresses, the experienced nurse can palpate the fetal back, which feels firm and smooth. Usually, it is easiest to hear the fetal heart by placing the Doppler on the fetal back, because the bony skeleton transmits sound well. For Dopplers that do not give a digital readout of fetal heart rate (FHR), the number of beats is usually counted for 15 seconds and then multiplied by 4 to obtain a rate per minute. Chart both the rate and the place on the abdomen where the heartbeat was heard.

By the end of pregnancy, the uterus will have stretched and grown from its nonpregnant 40–70 to 1,100 g, a >15-fold increase (Fig. 27-6).

Supporting ligaments also stretch, which can lead to sharp round ligament pain as soon as the first trimester. Extension of the pain to the inguinal area helps distinguish it.

(text continues on page 850)

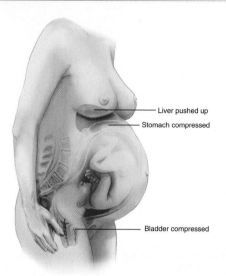

Figure 27.6 Growth of the uterus near term, with evident displacement of internal organs.

Breasts

First-trimester changes include increased breast size and more fullness and sensitivity. Areolae may darken, Montgomery glands may become more prominent, and nipples may be more erectile from increased progesterone and estrogen.

Genitalia

The woman may notice frequent urination and an increase of usual vaginal secretions.

Breast changes may result in upper backache. As pregnancy progresses, some women notice the growth of accessory breast tissue, often near the axillae. While the appearance is unusual, such tissue poses no danger.

Assessment During Routine Pregnancy Visits

Women who are pregnant typically have prenatal visits once a month for the first two trimesters, then every other week until the last month, and then every week until delivery. Scientific evidence suggests that patients may have equally good outcomes with fewer visits, especially if they have had children before (Dowswell, Carroli, et al., 2010).

General Survey and Vital Signs

While collecting data, ask the patient how she is doing. Elicit a description of and chart any concerns she may be having (Dowswell, Carroli, et al., 2010).

Assist with diagnosis by checking the urine, including specific gravity to ensure that the patient is well hydrated. Draw blood, if ordered, to check for low blood glucose level or anemia.

Counsel patients who feel dizzy, especially when changing positions rapidly, to sit down in order to avoid possible syncope, falling, or both. Check for postural hypotension (see Chapter 6). Other possible causes of dizziness include dehydration, anemia, inner ear changes, and hypoglycemia.

Proteinuria 1+ or greater may indicate *preeclampsia* and thus requires a physician/midwife's attention. Other signs of preeclampsia include significantly increased blood pressure as compared to baseline; sudden edema, especially of the face; persistent headache; and malaise.

Skin

Changes during pregnancy are primarily attributable to the increasing fetus, uterus, and amniotic fluid volume (Fig. 27-7). As the abdomen continues to grow, the woman may get **striae gravidarum** ("stretch marks"). Striae may also appear on the enlarging thighs and breasts (Ghasemi, Gorouhi, et al., 2007). Linea nigra may darken further, and terminal hairs may appear on the abdomen. Some women have **melasma** ("mask of pregnancy") as melanin production increases.

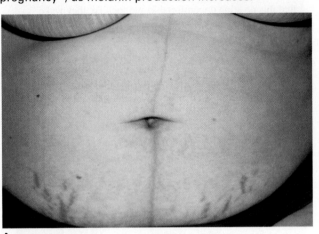
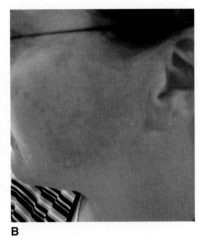

A   B

Figure 27-7 Skin changes in pregnancy. **A.** Evident linea nigra and striae. **B.** Melasma evident on the cheeks.

Nose, Mouth, and Throat

Capillaries with lax walls proliferate from increased production of progesterone by the placenta. Ask the patient if she has dental pain or if she is having any dental procedures in the near future. Assess her gums and teeth.

Epistaxis (nosebleed) is a common result. Some women have nonpathological cervical spotting when a capillary breaks.

Thorax and Lungs

Respirations increase, in response to both increased blood flow through the lungs and increased need for oxygen by the fetus and mother. The growing fetus limits the ability of the lungs to expand.

Toward the end of the second trimester, women may experience dyspnea with exertion.

Although respiratory rate changes very little during pregnancy, tidal volume and minute ventilation increase dramatically to meet the increased oxygen needs of both fetus and mother.

The woman may experience this change as shortness of breath.

Heart

Maternal circulatory system changes significantly during the second trimester. Blood volume and cardiac output increase by about 40%; however, hematocrit falls. Increased work for the heart leads to a 10- to 15-beat increase in maternal heart rate.

The woman who is pregnant may subsequently experience palpitations.

Cardiac output decreases when the woman is supine, because the weight of the fetus impedes venous return and increases when she is in lateral positions. Sitting and standing also decrease venous return from the extremities.

Dependent edema may result. In the arms, it may lead to *carpal tunnel syndrome* when edematous tissues impinge on the nerve bodies. In the legs, standing for long periods can result in *varicosities*. Help prevent these issues by teaching ways to promote venous return. Examples include avoiding constrictive clothing (especially ankle hose/socks with tight tops); elevating

(text continues on page 852)

the arms and legs whenever possible, ideally above the heart (lie on a sofa with feet elevated on the arm rest); and sleeping on the side (see Box 27-1).

BOX 27-1 PATIENT TEACHING—SLEEPING AND POSITIONING IN PREGNANCY

Women who are pregnant are advised to sleep on their sides during the third trimester. Unfortunately, many women find this position uncomfortable and feel like they wake up more tired than when they went to sleep. Help alleviate discomfort of it by teaching about strategic placement of pillows (as shown below). In addition to the pillow under her head, the woman can put a thick pillow between the legs, which raises the upper leg until it is parallel with the mattress and relieves strain on the abdominal muscles and ligaments. Wedging another pillow behind the woman's back allows her to lie at a 45° angle with her back supported, without impeding venous return. A pillow under the abdomen further supports the suspensory ligaments. When the nurse uses pillows to show the woman how this feels, most women can relax and are less anxious about getting a good night's sleep.

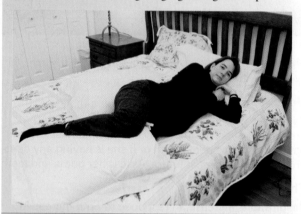

In the third trimester, the rate of iron transfer from mother to fetus increases. The amount of iron required for a healthy pregnancy is not usually available from the woman's prepregnant iron stores and a healthy diet. Prenatal vitamins provide the extra iron required to maintain health during pregnancy.

Women whose initial iron stores are low or who do not obtain sufficient iron during pregnancy become anemic. Women with anemia at the time of childbirth are at increased risk for transfusion, especially if they have a cesarean birth, because average blood loss for a cesarean is twice that for a vaginal delivery.

Clinical Significance 27-8
Mothers with a scheduled cesarean or at risk for postpartum hemorrhage (eg, multiple gestation) need teaching about eating iron-rich foods, taking prenatal vitamins daily, and using any prescribed iron supplements as directed.

Iron is better absorbed with citrus fruits or juices (including vitamin C) than with calcium (dairy).

Peripheral Vascular

Decreased peripheral vascular resistance results in a somewhat lower blood pressure during the second trimester. Optimal circulation to the placenta (and fetus) is achieved in the left lateral position, but right lateral is also acceptable for sleeping once the woman is past 20 weeks.

As blood volume increases and the growing fetus impedes venous return, pressure on valves in the lower extremities can result in their failure. *Varicose veins* form or worsen.

Spider veins may appear late in pregnancy, but disappear shortly after delivery.

Breasts

The Montgomery tubercles (sebaceous glands) on the areola may enlarge. Nipples may darken, enlarge, and begin to discharge colostrum (Fig. 27-8).

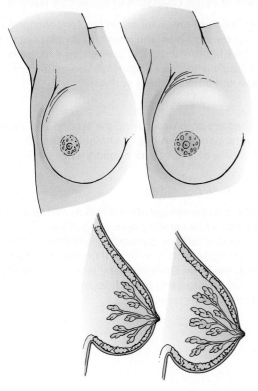

Nonpregnant   Pregnant

Figure 27-8 Comparison of the breasts in the nonpregnant versus pregnant states.

Abdomen

By 20 weeks' gestation, the uterus is level with the umbilicus; by 36 weeks, it nears the bottom of the sternum (Fig. 27-9). Muscles of the abdominal wall may separate (**diastasis recti**) and not return to previous approximation until several weeks after childbirth.

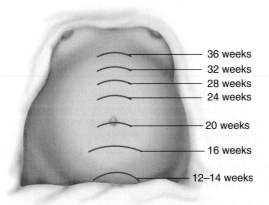

— 36 weeks
— 32 weeks
— 28 weeks
— 24 weeks

— 20 weeks

— 16 weeks

— 12–14 weeks

Figure 27-9 Growth in fundal height over the three trimesters of pregnancy.

Gastric reflux (heartburn) is common during the third trimester, as sphincter tone decreases and gastric pressures increase from displacement of the stomach. Over-the-counter (OTC) antacids can usually relieve infrequent heartburn; however, frequent use of them during pregnancy causes a rebound effect, meaning that the woman needs more over time for less relief. Use of OTC H2 blockers (eg, ranitidine [Zantac]) is both safe in pregnancy and more efficacious than antacids.

(text continues on page 854)

The gallbladder does not contract as well as usual during pregnancy.

Retained bile salts can increase risk of gallstones. Stasis of bile salts can also occur in the liver, causing **pruritus gravidarum**, which produces a rash with intense itching often along the striae of the abdomen. The itching resolves soon after delivery once circulation of bile salts is restored.

During the third trimester, the growing uterus mechanically displaces the intestines.

Women who are pregnant are at risk for constipation. Straining during bowel movements can also cause painful or itchy hemorrhoids. The primary way to prevent hemorrhoids is to prevent constipation by increasing exercise and intake of fibre and water.

Musculoskeletal System

With fetal growth, the maternal center of gravity changes, and the woman's risk for falls increases. Women who are pregnant should not lift anything weighing >9 kg (including toddlers, groceries, and laundry). They should use proper body mechanics when lifting anything.

Backaches are common during the second and third trimesters, partly from poor technique when lifting and also because of lack of back support when sleeping.

Clinical Significance 27-9

One of the psychological tasks for a mother during a second pregnancy is to disengage sufficiently from her toddler so that the first child can become more independent. The best time to do so is by 20 weeks. This gives the toddler (and the mother!) an additional 20 weeks to adjust to new roles before the baby comes. Help by noticing if a mother is lifting the toddler, teaching the mother to protect her back, and helping her to think ahead about how she will cope once she has a newborn in her arms.

Not only is it physiologically difficult to maintain good back health while carrying both a rapidly growing fetus and a growing toddler, but also carrying the toddler also sets up potential psychological difficulties for the toddler after the birth. Once the baby is born, the mother will not be able to carry both children, especially when breast-feeding the newborn.

The musculoskeletal systems change noticeably at the end of pregnancy. The modest increase in the pelvic diameter that results from the relaxation of the cartilage allows the fetus to "drop," "lighten," or "engage" in the pelvis in preparation for childbirth.

Increased weight from the fetus and breast tissue, with the accompanying change in the center of gravity, places increased strain on the abdominal muscles. The nurse teaches the woman who is pregnant exercises to strengthen her abdominal muscles ("cat stretch" and pelvic tilts against a wall), which may provide some relief. Also, hormonal changes near term, especially increased relaxin, loosen the cartilage between the pelvic bones. Women report that they are "waddling like a duck" when they walk.

Clinical Significance 27-10

Women often ask how soon the fetus will "drop." For many women, this process is gradual rather than sudden, so it is difficult to say exactly when engagement has happened. For a woman who has had children before, the fetus may not "drop" until labour has already progressed. Commonly, nulliparous mothers sense that their fetuses have dropped 2 to 3 weeks before birth.

Genitalia

As the woman's abdomen grows, couples may worry about the advisability of sexual relations. In the first trimester, before the woman was "showing" it was likely less of a psychological and practical concern. Couples benefit from being informed that sexual relations do not hurt the fetus, which is well protected, and that receptors for any oxytocin produced with orgasm are inactive until pregnancy ends. Couples may find that certain positions for intercourse are more comfortable than others, and women can be encouraged to try new positions.

Research shows that women's interest in sexual relations during pregnancy varies. For many, there is no change; for others, libido increases, while for still others it decreases, possibly from fatigue, depression, or relationship challenges that surface during pregnancy (DeJudicibus & McCabe, 2002).

The physician/midwife will advise if sexual intercourse is to be avoided because of concerns about the pregnancy.

Area of Assessment	Expected Findings	Unexpected Findings
Psychosocial	States "getting excited about meeting the baby"; discusses preparations for the upcoming birth, accompanied by husband	Crying, reports "crying all the time" and "scared." Unaccompanied.
General inspection	Upright posture, appears relaxed, smiles readily, walks with widened gait, sits and rises from chair easily	Limping favouring right leg, difficulty sitting in chair and mobilizing, looking down, teary
Vital signs	Temperature (T) 37.2, pulse (P) 76, respirations (R) 18, blood pressure (BP) right arm (sitting) 120/70	T 38.2, P 84, R 22, BP right arm (sitting) 135/85
Weight gain at 26 wk	4 kg	10 kg total weight gain, 4 kg in last 4 wk
Head and neck	Chloasma present, hair dry, sclera white, slightly reddened gums	Facial edema bilaterally, patches of hair loss distributed over scalp, swollen gums
Thorax and lungs	Thoracic breathing, vesicular sounds throughout lung fields	Use of accessory muscles, fine crackles in both lower lobes
Heart	S1, S2, systolic murmur present, heart rate 80	Heart rate 135, radial pulse, and apical beat unequal
Breasts	Venous patterns present bilaterally, darkened areola, symmetrical, Montgomery glands visible	Venous pattern more prominent on right breast. Bloody discharge from right nipple
Abdomen	Fundal height 27 cm at 26 weeks' gestation. Striae present bilaterally. Fetal heart rate (FHR) 155	Fundal height 32 cm at 26 wk. Singleton. FHR 105
Genitalia, anus, rectum	Hemorrhoids present, milky white vaginal discharge	Dark yellowish vaginal discharge, labial varicosities present bilaterally
Extremities	Pink, edema to ankles and feet 1+ bilaterally, all reflexes 1+	Edema in left ankle and foot 4+, all reflexes 3+

Adapted from Bowen, A., & Bickley, L. S. (2010). Assessing the woman who is pregnant. In T. C. Stephen, D. L. Skillen, R. A. Day, & L. S. Bickley (Eds.). *Canadian Bates' guide to health assessment for nurses* (1st ed., p. 881). Philadelphia, PA: Wolters Kluwer Health/Lippincott Williams & Wilkins.

Evidence-Informed Critical Thinking

Common Laboratory and Diagnostic Testing

The nurse should be familiar with common laboratory tests administered during pregnancy and the significance of unexpected findings. The hospital or office/clinic setting will have protocols (either written or verbal) about how unexpected findings are treated. It is common for the nurse to explain findings to the mother and also the proposed treatment. Table 27-2 includes common laboratory tests performed throughout pregnancy. Two advanced techniques are described below.

Nonstress Test (NST)

During the third trimester, the patient may be scheduled for an NST in conjunction with her prenatal visit. The purpose of the NST is to assess fetal well-being. The nurse will put the patient on the electronic fetal monitor (Fig. 27-10) after her usual data are gathered. The nurse puts the patient in a comfortable position, places the tocodyamometer on the fundus to assess uterine contractions, and places the ultrasound monitor where the fetal heart can be heard to measure its rate (FHR). The nurse checks periodically to make sure that the sensors are tracing accurately and that the mother is still comfortable. If the monitoring strip is not becoming **reactive**, the nurse may offer the mother a position change or a drink of juice in hopes of stimulating the fetus to react to these changes. The nurse reports any sign of fetal distress to the physician/midwife immediately.

Leopold's Manoeuvres

Leopold's manoeuvres are designed to estimate the position of the fetus. First, the nurse palpates the fundus of the uterus to determine whether it contains the head or the buttocks. The head moves independently of the torso, but the buttocks do not (Fig. 27-11A). Second, the fetal back is located by holding the fetus firmly on one side while the other is palpated, and then the procedure is reversed. The back feels firm and smooth; the opposite side contains

(text continues on page 858)

Table 27-2 Laboratory Tests Performed During Pregnancy

Test	Rationale	Example of Plan/Treatment
Blood type	If the mother needs an emergent blood transfusion during or after labour, the blood bank will need her blood type.	Mothers with Rh negative blood are offered RhoGam at approximately 28 weeks' gestation or if they miscarry.
Complete blood count (CBC)	Checks for anemia, thalassemias, platelets, white blood cells (WBCs).	Anemia may be treated with iron supplementation or iron-rich foods. Thalassemias may require referral to specialists, because the condition poses some risks to the fetus. Patients with low platelet levels are at risk for disseminated intravascular coagulation and may not be candidates for epidurals. WBC counts are usually elevated in pregnancy; they may be as high as $12,000/mm^3$ in the prenatal period, and during labour they may rise as high as $30,000/mm^3$. WBCs in excess of these numbers suggest a potential infection.
Serology (VDRL, RPR)	Syphilis crosses the placental barrier to the fetus.	A positive result is usually verified by additional testing, and if those results also are positive, the mother is treated with antibiotics.
HBsAg (Hepatitis B surface antigen)	Hepatitis can be transmitted from the mother to the fetus.	Newborns of positive mothers are given an HBIG (IgG antibodies) injection and are immunized for hepatitis B shortly after birth.
HIV	HIV can be transmitted from the mother to the fetus.	Administration of retroviral medications to the HIV-positive mother during pregnancy significantly reduces the risk of transmission of the virus to the baby.
DNA probe for chlamydia and gonorrhea	If either of these tests is positive, also test for HIV.	Ideally, test for chlamydia and gonorrhea during the preconception period as both these sexually transmitted infection (STIs) can cause infertility and ectopic pregnancies.
Human papillomavirus (HPV)	HPV can cause anogenital warts that increase in size during pregnancy and resolve after delivery.	HPV is rarely transmitted to the infant during delivery.
Genital herpes	A viral culture is taken from a fresh vesicle located along the labia.	Precautions are required during delivery to decrease the risk of transmission to the infant.
Rubella titre	Maternal infection with rubella during pregnancy (especially the first 2 mo) can cause congenital heart malformations, intrauterine growth restriction, cataracts, and deafness in the fetus.	Patients without sufficient titres to protect them from infection cannot be vaccinated during pregnancy, because the vaccine is a live virus. However, they can be vaccinated promptly after delivery.
Triple- or quad-screen	Maternal blood drawn between 15 and 20 wk screens for Down's syndrome and other trisomies, neural tube defects, gastroschisis, and other fetal anomalies.	This test has a high false-positive rate; further testing is required for a definitive diagnosis. Test accuracy depends on accurately dating the pregnancy. Ultrasound can usually clarify dating issues and also help with identifying any anomalies. Amniocentesis is offered if the ultrasound does not reveal any dating issues.
Gestational diabetes screen: 50-g glucose load	Maternal blood is drawn exactly 1 h after the 50-g glucose load. All women who are pregnant should be screened for gestational diabetes at 24–28 wk, when maternal glucose metabolism changes. It may be done earlier for those at high risk for diabetes (obese or extensive family history). Uncontrolled diabetes during pregnancy can result in	A 1-hour plasma glucose level $\geq$**10.3** mmol/L is considered gestational diabetes mellitus (GDM).

Table 27-2   Laboratory Tests Performed During Pregnancy *(continued)*

Test	Rationale	Example of Plan/Treatment
	macrosomia, difficult delivery, neonatal hypoglycemia, perinatal morbidity and mortality, and other complications.	
75-g oral glucose tolerance test		If the 1-h plasma glucose level is **7.8–10.2** mmol/L, follow up with a 75-g oral glucose tolerance test with expected scores of fasting plasma glucose of ≥**.3** mmol/L, 1-h plasma glucose of ≥**10.6** mmol/L, and a 2-h plasma glucose of >**8.9** mmol/L. If two of the three scores are met or exceeded, GDM is confirmed. If one score is met or exceeded, then impaired glucose tolerance of pregnancy is confirmed. Patients are referred to a dietitian/diabetes educator for diabetes counselling and education about blood glucose monitoring. With strict diet control, some patients can control their blood glucose level; however, if control is not achieved in 2 wk, insulin therapy (up to 4 injections/d) is required to protect the fetus from glucose overload (CDACPGEC, 2008).
A1C test	The A1C test is too sensitive to use to monitor blood glucose levels during pregnancy (CDACPGEC, 2008).	
Group B streptococcus (GBS)	Mothers with urine cultures positive for GBS are called "colonizers" and are at increased risk for fetal infection. Colonizers are treated with oral antibiotics immediately and offered intravenous (IV) antibiotics during labour for the current and all future pregnancies. For other mothers, a swab of the vagina and rectum is collected at 35–37 wk (or sooner if prematurity is a risk). If the mother is GBS-positive, there is a small chance that the infant will be infected during prolonged rupture of membranes or a vaginal birth. If the infant is infected, there is a small chance it would not survive.	Protection for the infant results when antibiotics are administered 4 h prior to delivery, so GBS positive women are encouraged to notify their physician/midwife early in labour.

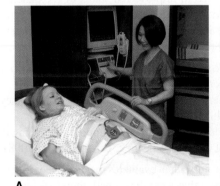
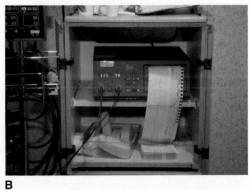

A **B**

Figure 27-10 Nonstress testing. **A.** The nurse is observing external fetal monitoring of the patient. **B.** A reactive strip.

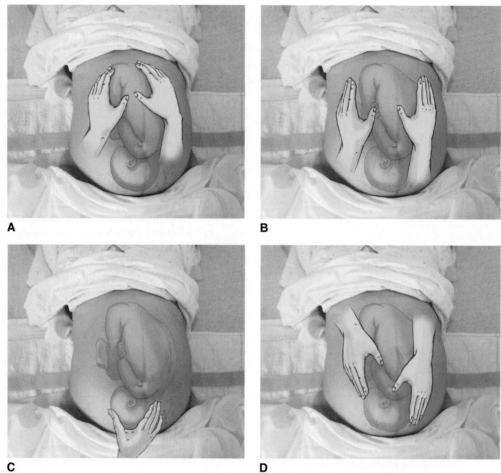

Figure 27-11 Leopold's manoeuvres. **A.** First manoeuvre. **B.** Second manoeuvre. **C.** Third manoeuvre. **D.** Fourth manoeuvre.

"small parts" (arms and legs) that feel irregular (Fig. 27-11B). Third, palpating just above the symphysis pubis identifies the presenting part. It should be the part opposite that found in the fundus (Fig. 27-11C). Fourth and finally, the fetal head is palpated to determine whether it is flexed or deflexed. If it is properly flexed, a protrusion (the brow) will be palpated on the opposite side as the fetal back. If the head is deflexed, the protrusion (the occiput) will be palpated on the same side as the back (Fig. 27-11D). Experienced nurses usually only need to use the first and second manoeuvres to locate the FHR and verify that the presenting part is the head.

Clinical Reasoning

Nursing Diagnosis, Outcomes, and Interventions

When formulating a nursing diagnosis, it is important to use critical thinking to cluster data together and identify patterns that fit together. Table 27-3 provides a comparison of nursing diagnoses, unexpected findings, and interventions commonly related to pregnancy (North American Nursing Diagnosis Association-International, 2009).

Nurses use assessment information to identify patient outcomes. Some outcomes related to pregnancy include the following:

- Family will affirm desire to improve parenting skills.
- Family will perform tasks needed for change.
- Family states positive effects of changes made (Moorhead, Johnson, et al., 2007).

Once the outcomes are is established, patient care is implemented to improve the status of the patient. The nurse uses critical thinking and evidence-informed practice to develop the interventions. Some examples of nursing interventions for pregnancy are as follows:

- Assess the influence of cultural beliefs on the patient's perception of parenting.
- Teach family about the effects of pregnancy and adding a child to the family system.
- Identify resources for support and coping during this time of change (Bulechek, Butcher, et al., 2008).

The nurse then evaluates the care according to the patient outcomes that were developed, therefore reassessing the patient and continuing or modifying the interventions as appropriate. See Table 27-3 for documentation of assessment data.

Table 27-3 Common Nursing Diagnoses Associated With Pregnancy

Diagnosis and Related Factors	Point of Differentiation	Assessment Characteristics	Nursing Interventions
Health-seeking behaviours related to pregnancy	Actively seeking ways to move toward a higher level of health.	Concern about environmental conditions on health status, desire for increased level of wellness, unfamiliarity with community resources.	Educate on nutrition and overeating, develop exercise plan, and teach stress management techniques. Instruct in smoking cessation, provide health screening.
Readiness for enhanced family coping due to new role	Effective task management with desire for enhanced growth and health.	Moves toward enriching lifestyle and moves toward health promotion and optimal wellness.	Assess the structure, resources, and coping abilities of families, encourage caregivers to become involved in support groups, acknowledge cultural influences.

Collaborating with the Interprofessional Team

Michelle is tested for plasma glucose because she is obese (body mass index [BMI] is 40.8). Further testing reveals that Michelle has gestational diabetes. The nurse also notes that recommended weight gain for Michelle is 7 kg or less for the pregnancy, but Michelle has already gained 11.8 kg (weight at last visit was 100.5 kg).

After the physician/midwife reviews laboratory values and determines the plan of care, the nurse calls Michelle to report the findings and conveys the recommendation that Michelle needs to see a diabetes educator for nutritional counselling. The educator will answer Michelle's questions about the potential effects of gestational diabetes on her and the fetus. The educator will also explain that Michelle should be retested when the baby is 6 weeks old to ensure that Michelle has not developed type 2 diabetes.

Below is the initial conversation between the nurse and the diabetes educator. The nurse uses SBAR (situation, background, assessment, recommendations) to organize information for the educator.

Situation: Hello, I'm Kathleen, and I am taking care of Michelle Sherman, a 21-year-old First Nations Canadian. She is 35 weeks pregnant by last menstrual period (LMP) dates and a 20-week ultrasound. Michelle did not pass her gestational diabetes screen (50 g glucose load followed by a plasma glucose test 1 hour later) with a score of 13 mmol/L (≤ to 10.3 mmol/L is the expected value).

Background: Michelle had a prepregnancy BMI of 35.2, so was given a gestational diabetes screen (a 50 g glucose load followed by a plasma glucose test 1 hour later at her first visit). The result was a plasma glucose of 6.8 mmol/L (<7.8 mmol/L is expected). Both her mother and her sister have type 2 diabetes. So far, Michelle has gained 11.8 kg since her initial visit.

Assessment: Michelle now has gestational diabetes and is at risk for type 2 diabetes as evidenced by unexpected plasma glucose test results. The fetus is also at risk.

Recommendation: Because she is pregnant, Michelle cannot wait for 1 to 2 months for the placement in a regularly scheduled diabetes education class. Michelle needs immediate counselling regarding her diet, a diary to record everything she eats, a blood glucose monitor and instructions on its use, testing strips and lancets for the monitor, and a schedule for testing her blood glucose levels. If her diabetes cannot be controlled with diet within 2 weeks and she needs insulin, please let us know.

Critical Thinking Challenge

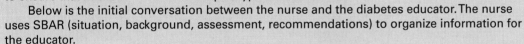

- What additional assessments should the nurse perform related to the diabetes?
- Why did the nurse choose a food diary as the assessment tool?
- How might Michelle's cultural background and age affect her perceptions of her pregnancy?

The nurse uses assessment data to formulate the patient care plan with patient outcomes and interventions for Michelle. Outcomes are specific to the patient, realistic to achieve, measurable, and have a time frame for meeting them. The interventions are actions that the nurse performs, based on evidence and practice guidelines. After these interventions are completed, the nurse reevaluates Michelle and documents the findings in the chart to show progress toward the patient outcomes. The nurse uses critical thinking and judgment to continue or revise the diagnosis, outcomes, or interventions. This is often in the form of a care plan or case note similar to the one below.

Nursing Diagnosis	Patient Outcomes	Nursing Interventions	Rationale	Evaluation
Health-seeking behaviours related to pregnancy	Patient will limit weight gain to 7 kg.	Assess the role that stress plays in overeating. Use nutritional guidelines to plan a diet high in protein, fibre, fruits, and vegetables.	People who eat under stress are more likely to gain weight and have elevated insulin and cortisol levels.	Goal has not been met. Patient has gained 11.8 kg. Discuss changes that patient is willing and able to make in her diet. Refer to diabetes educator.

Using the previous steps of clinical reasoning, organizing, and prioritizing, consider all the case study findings woven throughout this chapter. When answering the following questions, begin drawing conclusions and see how the pieces of assessment must work together to create an environment for personalized, appropriate, and accurate care.

- What physical assessment data are the nurse's responsibilities to gather and assess? (Knowledge)
- What additional history does the nurse need to gather from Michelle today? (Comprehension)
- What health-promotion needs does Michelle have today? (Application)
- What findings would indicate that Michelle's condition is stable, urgent, or emergent? (Analysis)
- What factors does the nurse need to consider to individualize Michelle's care? (Synthesis)
- How will the nurse evaluate the success of patient teaching for Michelle? (Evaluation)

Key Points

- The estimated due date is calculated using Naegele's rule. Subtract 3 months from the first day of the LMP and add 7 days, or about a 40-week pregnancy.
- Ultrasound data are used to determine expected date of delivery.
- The role of the nurse includes conducting the intake interview, performing triage, gathering preliminary data, conducting NSTs, and educating patients and families.
- Acute conditions of pregnancy include ectopic pregnancy, pyelonephritis, hemorrhage, dyspnea or chest pain, pain in the calf (possible DVT and pulmonary embolus), absence of fetal movements, and contractions before 37 weeks.
- Health-promotion issues for women who are pregnant include physical activity; recommended weight gain; avoidance of tobacco; avoidance of alcohol and street drugs; nutritious diet; prenatal vitamins, iron, and folic acid; and preparing for breast-feeding.
- Some cultures and religions have important rituals around birth.
- Common symptoms occurring during pregnancy include fatigue, morning sickness, growing pains, increased vaginal discharge, increased urination, breast tenderness, periumbilical pain, fetal hiccups, and Braxton Hicks contractions.
- An expected weight gain is 4.5 kg by 4.5 months of pregnancy and about 0.5 kg a week for the remaining 20 weeks for a total for about 14.5 kg.
- Increased skin melanization occurs during pregnancy, resulting in linea nigra or chloasma.
- By 10 to 12 weeks of gestation, the fetal heartbeat may be heard with a Doppler.

- Breast changes include more fullness, sensitivity, darkened areola, more prominent Montgomery glands, and more erect nipples.
- Signs of preeclampsia include elevated blood pressure, sudden edema, headache, and malaise. Treatment is needed to prevent eclampsia (convulsions and coma).
- As the abdomen enlarges, the woman who is pregnant may develop striae gravidarum, linea negra, and melasma.
- Women may experience dyspnea toward the end of pregnancy as the growing fetus limits the ability of the lungs to expand.
- Cardiovascular changes include lower hematocrit, elevated pulse, edema, and varicosities.
- Gastric reflux is common in pregnancy from displacement of the stomach.
- Musculoskeletal changes include relaxed cartilage, lower back pressure, and a waddling gait.
- Nursing diagnoses commonly related to pregnancy include health-seeking behaviours, readiness for enhanced parenting, and readiness for enhanced family coping.

Review Questions

1. Michelle says that her last menstrual period was 15JUN. Using Naegele's rule, her expected birth date (EBD) is
   A. 08SEP
   B. 08MAR
   C. 22MAR
   D. 22JAN

2. Michelle is halfway through her pregnancy (20 weeks). The top of her uterus should be
   A. at the symphysis pubis
   B. halfway between the symphysis pubis and the umbilicus
   C. at the umbilicus
   D. at the xyphoid process

3. A healthy electronic fetal monitoring strip shows
   A. a fetal heart rate (FHR) of 90 beats/min
   B. variability of 0 to 5 beats/min
   C. two decelerations in 20 minutes
   D. three accelerations in 20 minutes

4. Which of the following conditions would be the highest priority to contact the health care professional about?
   A. Striae gravidarum
   B. Varicosities
   C. Contractions before 37 weeks
   D. More prominent Montgomery glands

5. The patient calls the physician/midwife's office to schedule an appointment because a home pregnancy test was positive. The nurse knows that the test identified the presence of which of the following in the urine?
   A. Estrogen
   B. Progesterone
   C. Human chorionic gonadotropin (hCG)
   D. Follicle-stimulating hormone

6. Important health promotion activities include recommending
   A. physical activity
   B. weight gain of 7 kg
   C. increase in intake of vitamin A
   D. shallow breathing

7. The patient comes for a nonstress test (NST) and the nurse notes that the FHR is 100 beats/min. Which of the following nursing actions would be appropriate to do first?
   A. Document the findings
   B. Notify the physician/midwife
   C. Inform the patient that everything is as expected
   D. Instruct the patient to return to the clinic in 1 week for reevaluation of the FHR

8. The nurse is performing patient teaching about expected changes during late pregnancy. These include which of the following?
   A. Dark cloudy urine
   B. Waddling gait
   C. Vaginal bleeding
   D. Sudden edema

9. The nurse is caring for the patient who is admitted to the hospital with a possible ectopic pregnancy. Which of the following nursing actions is the priority?
   A. Monitoring daily weight
   B. Assessing for edema
   C. Monitoring the temperature
   D. Monitoring the blood pressure

10. The nurse assesses for common symptoms in pregnancy including
    A. headache
    B. high blood pressure
    C. gastric reflux
    D. hemorrhage

Canadian Nursing Research

Bowen, A. N., & Muhajarine, N. (2006). Prevalence of depressive symptoms in an antenatal outreach program in Canada. *Journal of Obstetrical, Gynecological, and Neonatal Nursing, 35*(4), 492–498.

Heaman, M. I., & Chalmers, K. (2005). Prevalence and correlates of smoking during pregnancy: A comparison of aboriginal and non-aboriginal women in Manitoba. *Birth, 32,* 299–305.

Heaman, M., Sprague, A. E., et al. (2006). Reducing the preterm birth rate: A population health strategy. *Journal of Obstetric, Gynecologic, & Neonatal Nursing, 30,* 20–29.

Strass, P., & Billay, E. (2008). A public health nursing initiative to promote antenatal health. *The Canadian Nurse, 104*(2), 29–35.

Strohschein, F. J., Merry, L., et al. (2010). Strengthening data quality in studies of migrants not fluent in host languages: A Canadian example with reproductive health questionnaires. *Research in Nursing and Health, 33*(4), 369–379.

References

Bowen, A. N., & Bickley, L. S. (2010). Assessing the woman who is pregnant. In T. S. Stephen, D. L. Skillen, R. A. Day, & L. S. Bickley (Eds.). *Canadian Bates' guide to health assessment for nurses* (1st ed., pp. 849–885). Philadelphia, PA: Wolters Kluwer Health/Lippincott Williams & Wilkins.

Bowen, A. N., & Muhajarine, N. (2006). Prevalence of depressive symptoms in an antenatal outreach program in Canada. *Journal of Obstetrical, Gynecological, and Neonatal Nursing, 35*(4), 492–498.

Breastfeeding Committee for Canada. (2007). *Breastfeeding statement for the Breastfeeding Committee for Canada.* Retrieved from http://breastfeedingcanada.ca/html/webdoc5.html

Bulechek, G. M., Butcher, H. K., et al. (2008). *Nursing interventions classification (NIC)* (5th ed.) St. Louis, MO: Mosby.

Canadian Diabetes Association Clinical Practice Guidelines Expert Committee. (2008). Clinical practice guidelines for the prevention and management of diabetes in Canada. *Canadian Journal of Diabetes, 32*(Suppl 1), S1–S201.

Chow, J. (2010). Assessment and management of female physiologic processes. In R. A. Day, P. Paul, et al. (Eds.). *Brunner & Suddarth's textbook of Canadian medical-surgical nursing* (2nd ed., pp. 1568–1608). Philadelphia, PA: Wolters Kluwer Health/Lippincott Williams & Wilkins.

DeJudicibus, M. A., & McCabe, M. P. (2002). Psychological factors and the sexuality of pregnant and postpartum patients. *Journal of Sexual Research, 39*(2), 94–103.

Dowswell, T., Carroli, G., et al. (2010). Alternative versus standard packages of antenatal care for low-risk pregnancy. *Cochrane Database of Systematic Reviews*, Issue 10, art. no. CD000934.

Edge, D. S., Day, R. A., et al. (2010). In T. C. Stephen, D. L. Skillen, R. A. Day, & L. S. Bickley (Eds.). *Canadian Bates' guide to health assessment for nurses* (1st ed., pp. 563–600). Philadelphia, PA: Wolters Kluwer Health/Lippincott Williams & Wilkins.

Ghasemi, A., Gorouhi, F., et al. (2007). Striae gravidarum: Associated factors. *Journal of the European Academy of Dermatology and Venereology, 21*(6), 743–746.

Headley, A. J., & Harrigan, J. (2009). Using the pregnancy perception of risk questionnaire to assess health care literacy gaps in maternal perception of prenatal risk. *National Medical Association, 101*(10), 1041–1045.

Health Canada. (2005). *Smoking and your body.* Retrieved from http://www.hc-sc.gc.ca/hl-vs/tobac-tabac/body-corps/index-eng.php

Health Canada. (2007a). *Eating well with Canada's food guide.* Retrieved from http://www.hc-sc.gc.ca/fn-an/food-guide-aliment/index-eng.php

Health Canada. (2007b). *Guidelines for gestational weight gain ranges.* Retrieved from http://www.hc-sc.gc.ca/fn-an/nutrition/prenatal/national_guidelines-lignes_directrices_nationales-06_e.html

Health Canada. (2007c). *Nutrition for a healthy pregnancy: National guidelines for the childbearing years.* Retrieved from http://www.hc-sc.gc.ca/fn-an/nutrition/prenatal/national_guidelines-lignes_directrices_nationales-06_e.html

Joseph, K. S., Liston, R. M., et al. (2007). Socioeconomic status and perinatal outcomes in a setting with universal access to essential health care services. *Canadian Medical Association Journal, 177*, 583–590.

Ko, S. H., Chang, S. C., et al. (2010). A comparative study of sleep quality between pregnant and nonpregnant Taiwanese women. *Journal of Nursing Scholarship, 42*(1), 23–30.

London, M. L., Ladewig, P. W., et al. (2007). *Maternal and child nursing care* (2nd ed.). Upper Saddle River, NJ: Pearson Prentice Hall.

Magee, L. A., Helewa, M., et al. (2008). Diagnosis, evaluation, and management of the hypertensive disorders of pregnancy. *Journal of Obstetrics and Gynaecology Canada, 30*(3), S9–S15.

Moorhead, S., Johnson, M., et al. (2007). *Nursing outcomes classification (NOC)* (5th ed.). St. Louis, MO: Mosby.

North American Nursing Diagnosis Association-International. (2009). *Nursing diagnoses, 2009–2011 Edition: Definitions and classifications (NANDA NURSING DIAGNOSIS).* West Sussex, UK: John Wiley & Sons.

Popescu, E. A., Popescu, M., et al. (2007). Magnetographic assessment of fetal hiccups and their effect on fetal heart rhythm. *Physiological Measurement, 28*(6), 665–676.

Public Health Agency of Canada. (2008a). *Canada prenatal nutrition program.* Retrieved from http://www.phac-aspc.gc.ca/dca-dea/programs-mes/cpnp_main_e.html

Public Health Agency of Canada. (2008b). *The Sensible Guide to a Healthy Pregnancy.* Retrieved from http://www.hac-aspc.gc.ca/hp-gs/pdf/hpguide-eng.pdf

Senthuran, R. A. (2010). Assessment of patients with diabetes mellitus. In R. A. Day, P. Paul, et al. (Eds.). *Brunner & Suddarth's textbook of Canadian medical-surgical nursing* (2nd ed., pp. 1295–1353). Philadelphia, PA: Wolters Kluwer Health/Lippincott Williams & Wilkins.

Simons, P. (2008). Province hushes up syphilis outbreak. *The Edmonton Journal*, pp. A1, A2.

Society of Obstetricians and Gynaecologists of Canada. (2005). Intimate partner violence consensus statement. *Journal of Obstetrics and Gynaecologists of Canada, 27*, 365–388.

Society of Obstetricians and Gynaecologists of Canada. (2007). *Understanding sexually transmitted infections.* Ottawa, ON: Author.

Stewart, A. L., Dean, M. L., et al. (2007). Race/ethnicity, socioeconomic status and the health of pregnant women. *Journal of Health Psychology, 12*(2), 285–300.

Varner, C. M. W. (1994). Physiologic changes in pregnancy: Surgical implications. *Clinical Obstetrics and Gynecology, 37*, 241.

Wilson, R. D., Désilets, V., et al. (2007). *Pre-conceptional vitamin/folic acid supplementation 2007: The use of folic acid in combination with a multivitamin supplement for the prevention of neural tube defects and other congenital anomalies.* Retrieved from http://www.sogc.org/guidelines/documents/guiJOGC201JCPG0712.pdf

World Health Organization. (2010). *Media centre: Female genital mutilation.* Retrieved from http://who.int/mediacentre/factsheets/fs241/en/

The Canadian Jensen's Nursing Health Assessment suite offers these additional resources to enhance learning and facilitate understanding of this chapter:

- thePoint on line resource, http//thepoint.lww.com/Stephen1E
- *Laboratory Manual for Canadian Jensen's Nursing Health Assessment: A Best Practice Approach*

Newborns and Infants

Learning Objectives

1   Demonstrate knowledge of anatomy and physiology of the newborn and infant.

2   List critical components of an acute assessment of the newborn and infant.

3   Identify important topics for health promotion and risk reduction related to the newborn and infant.

4   Collect subjective data related to the newborn and infant.

5   Collect objective data related to the newborn and infant using physical examination techniques.

6   Identify expected and unexpected findings related to the newborn/infant assessment.

7   Analyze subjective and objective data from assessment of the newborn and infant and consider initial interventions.

8   Document and communicate data from the newborn/infant assessment using appropriate terminology and principles of recording.

9   Consider age, condition, gender, and culture of the patient to individualize the newborn/infant assessment.

10 Identify nursing diagnoses and initiate a plan of care based on findings from the newborn/infant assessment.

*K*eri Dumont, a 2 month old, is visiting the clinic today for her well-child checkup and routine immunizations (DTaP-IPV-Hib, pneumococcal, and meningococcal vaccines). She was born at term and has had no health concerns. Her mother is breastfeeding her; they have adjusted well.

Keri is the first child in a two-parent family. The mother, Diane Dumont, is a nurse who plans on returning to work in 1 year; the father is an accountant. Paternal grandparents live in the area and provide child care 1 day a week.

As you consider this case study, begin thinking about the following points:

- What assessments will be the highest priorities?
- How should the nurse assess for growth?
- What physical and social developmental milestones would you expect to see in this infant?

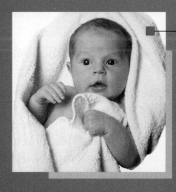

Infancy encompasses the first 12 months of life. A newborn is an infant 28 days old or younger. This chapter examines health assessment of newborns and infants. It discusses important past and present health history and pertinent findings of the physical examination. Because infants are preverbal and totally reliant on parents/guardians, the nurse must develop excellent observation skills and involve parents in the assessment and care planning. For ease of communication, the term "parents" is used throughout this chapter to indicate one or both parents or a guardian.

Anatomy and Physiology Overview

When assessing the individual infant's physical, motor, and language development, it is important to determine whether these areas are progressing as expected. Using rigid timetables to measure the infant's development is not helpful and does not provide an accurate assessment. Milestones serve only as guidelines so that developmental delays can be identified early and appropriate interventions instituted.

Chapter 9 explores physical growth, motor, and language development milestones in detail. A brief review is presented in the following paragraphs.

Physical Growth

Physical growth and development that began in utero continue rapidly after birth. In fact, during the first year of life, the growth rate is more accelerated than at any other time in childhood. Expected weight range for a full-term newborn is 2,500 to 4,000 g. Average length is 48 to 53 cm. Most infants gain approximately 450 to 1,000 g, double their birth rate by 6 months, and triple their birth rate by 1 year. By the end of the 12th month, most infants have increased their length by approximately 50% (Alberta Health Services, 2011a).

Motor Development

Motor development progresses in predictable patterns: cephalocaudally, central to distal, and gross to fine. For example, the infant develops head control before walking and can bat at a mobile before manipulating an object (Alberta Health Services, 2011b). Nurses assess newborn and infant motor development using their knowledge of development milestones, observations, and parent reporting.

Language, Psychosocial, and Cognitive Development

Speech development begins with vocalizations and babbling. The infant learns language through listening, watching, and interacting with the environment. The spectrum of language development is wide. More on language development, as well as psychosocial and cognitive development of the infant, is discussed in Chapter 9 (Santrock, 2006).

Acute Assessment

Acute assessment of the newborn is performed immediately after birth. Because the newborn must adapt rapidly to life outside the womb, the nurse must quickly make several key assessments. Nurses use the Apgar score at 1- and 5-minute intervals to determine the newborn's immediate adjustment to extrauterine life. The Apgar score consists of five components: (1) heart rate, (2) respiratory effort, (3) muscle tone, (4) reflex irritability in reaction to nasal bulb suctioning, and (5) colour. Each component is given a score of 0, 1, or 2 for a total of a possible 10 (see Table 18-5 in Chapter18). Initial Apgar scores are expected to be 8 or 9, which then improve to 8 to 10 after 5 minutes. Apgar scores of 6 or less are concerning and warrant futher assessment and possible intervention. The scoring can be used every 5 minutes if ongoing assessment is necessary.

After the initial physical assessments, nurses and/or physicians assess for gestational age using Ballard's tool (see Fig. 28-2). A more extensive physical assessment is performed by a nurse, a nurse-midwife, or a physician once the infant is stable after birth. This assessment may occur in the labour and delivery room, in a nursery environment, or in the home.

Emergent Concerns

Most emergent situations for the newborn involve respiratory or cardiac decompensation, congenital anomalies, and extremes in weight or gestational age. It can be difficult to identify emergent illnesses in the newborn or infant, especially if there are no obvious anomalies. The Apgar scoring system helps to identify those at risk. Signs indicative of serious illness include severe respiratory retractions and grunting, high pitched or moaning cry, hypotonia, change in level of consciousness and central cyanosis (Morley, Thornton, et al., 1991). Signs of newborn respiratory distress include increased respiratory and heart rates, nasal flaring, and intercostal and substernal retractions. The first sign of respiratory distress in a newborn is often tachypnea (heart rate > 160 at rest). Moderate respiratory distress includes nasal flaring, sternal tracheal and intercostal retractions, grunting heard on auscultation, cyanosis on room air, and unexpected blood gas values. Severe distress is indicated by increasing work of breathing, deep retractions, audible grunting, and central cyanosis. Central cyanosis in the absence of respiratory symptoms is unexpected and suggests a cardiac cause. Deviations from expected findings in regard to vital signs, weight, gestational age, and general appearance are assessed as emergent depending on their severity.

> △ SAFETY ALERT 28-1
> *Respiratory distress in the newborn and infant often progresses rapidly to severe distress requiring bag and mask or mechanical ventilation. Nurses intervene early at the first sign of distress to avert an emergency resuscitation, if possible.*

Assessment of Risk Factors

Health promotion for parents of newborns and infants focuses on prevention, health education, early detection of illness and developmental delays, and early intervention to optimize outcomes. The nurse can help parents understand the importance of laying a foundation of healthy living and lifestyle choices that will help the infant achieve his or her potential.

Questions to Assess History and Risk Factors	Rationale
• What brings you to the clinic today? • Do you have any questions or concerns about your baby? • Is your baby developing as you expected? Is he or she doing all the things you expected him or her to do at this age? • Has your son or daughter had any health concerns or illnesses? • If yes, what was useful in helping your baby recover/feel better?	The first two questions allow the parent to lead the appointment. They help to assert the parent in the "expert" role when discussing the infant. These questions help to flesh out the parents' concerns and their expectations regarding infant development. This question helps to establish a health history. This question identifies what action the parents took and how they comforted and soothed the baby.
Personal History (Infant) • Can you describe your pregnancy? Did you have any health concerns? If yes, did you need to take any medication to help you with it?	These questions help elicit the obstetric and birth history to identify risk factors. This broad question helps the examiner understand the socioeconomic situation, living conditions, other family members, and background and education of the parents. Follow up with questions to obtain desired information if the broader question fails to provide enough detail. Conversely, ask questions to gently refocus parents if they provide too much extra detail.
• Did you take any drugs during the pregnancy? Or ingest alcohol?	This question is important and should be shared in a non-judgmental manner.
• How would you describe your labour and birth experience? Were there any complications or need for extra treatment? Did you choose to accept pain medication for your birth experience?	These questions allow the parent to share key elements of the pregnancy without judgment or bias.
• Did your baby require any resuscitation or extra medical help at birth? • Did your baby spend any time in the neonatal intensive care unit (NICU)? • Since birth, has your baby had any infections? Illnesses? Hospitalizations? Or surgeries? • Has the baby had a checkup with a physician? Did the physician have any concerns? Who is your baby's physician? Tell me a little bit about your family and your home. • Are there any chronic/serious health problems in your family? Or the father's family? Allergies? • Does anyone in either parent's families have any learning disabilities?	These questions elicit the medical history of the baby after birth.
Medications and Supplements Do you give your baby any medications? Or supplements including vitamins?	This is to determine if baby is receiving medication and vitamins.

(text continues on page 866)

Questions to Assess History and Risk Factors	Rationale

Risk Factors

- Can you describe your baby's sleep environment?
- How does your baby fall asleep at night or at naptime? Does he or she use a bottle to fall asleep?
- Does anyone in your home smoke? How do you ensure that your baby is not exposed to second- or third-hand smoke?
- What types of changes or modifications have you made to your home to make it safe for your baby?
- What kind of car seat do you use? How and where is it secured in the car? Is it rear facing?
- Have you thought of taking a cardiopulmonary resuscitation (CPR) course?
- Has your son or daughter had any accidents or injuries?

This is to identify risk factors and topic areas for health promotion teaching (see Box 28.1).

This question helps to open a discussion about smoking around the baby.

BOX 28-1 FOUR STEPS THAT YOU CAN TAKE TO HELP CREATE A SAFE SLEEP ENVIRONMENT FOR YOUR BABY

1. Provide a **smoke-free environment**—both before and after birth
2. Always place your baby on his or her **back to sleep**—nighttime and nap time.
3. Place your baby to sleep in a **crib next to the adult's bed** for the first 6 months.
4. Provide a **safe crib environment** that has no toys or loose bedding (use only a fitted sheet).

Adapted from Public Health Agency of Canada. (2010). *Safe sleep for your baby.* Page 3 of http://www.phac-aspc.gc.ca/hp-ps/dca-dea/stages-etapes/childhood-enfance_0-2/sids/pdf/sleep-sommeil-eng.pdf

---

Risk Assessment and Health Promotion

Topics for Health Promotion

- Injury prevention
- Immunizations
- Safe sleep habits
- Oral health

Infants should have regular examinations with a pediatrician or another health care professional with specialized pediatric education. Ideally, parents schedule an initial visit before the baby is born. At this visit, the primary care provider obtains the family and prenatal history, shares anticipatory guidance, inquires about the chosen feeding method, and encourages breastfeeding. If discharged within 48 hours of birth, the Canadian Pediatric Society (1996) recommends assessment by a competent health professional (nurse, midwife, or physician) within 48 hours of discharge and follow up care with a physician initiated within a week. This position statement is currently under revision.

After birth, Health Canada recommends immunizations and well child visits at 2, 4, 6, and 12 months. This frequency gives the primary care provider or public health nurse an opportunity to identify potential developmental delays and other health issues, to continue anticipatory guidance, and to give immunizations on schedule.

The nurse performs a risk assessment to plan for care and teaching. Anticipatory guidance for parents of newborns and infants focuses on safety. Most unexpected deaths during infancy are related to injury, sudden infant death syndrome (SIDS), respiratory arrest, or near drowning. The three leading causes of injury-related death for infants and children are drowning, motor vehicle collisions, and suffocation (including choking) (Public Health Agency of Canada [PHAC], n.d.; Safe Kids Canada, 2010) Parents require anticipatory guidance to avert preventable injury and illness. Major topics include safe sleep habits, choking prevention, immunization schedules, child safety car seats, cardiopulmonary resuscitation (CPR) training for parents, poison control, breastfeeding and infant nutrition, vitamin D supplementation, and preventing baby bottle tooth decay.

Safe Sleep Habits

Incorporating safe sleep habits for infants helps prevent SIDS. Infants should always be placed on their backs to sleep. The mattress should be firm. Pillows, soft toys, excessive blankets, and bedding should not be in the crib when the infant is asleep. The infant should not sleep in the same bed in which an adult is sleeping. It is too easy for the tiny face to be covered inadvertently and for the infant to be smothered (Public Health Agency of Canada, 2010). (See Box 28-1). See the**Point** ✳ for a link to details about the safe sleep program.

Choking

To prevent choking, parents should remain vigilant about the environment and remove choking hazards. Curtain and blind cords should be secured out of the infant's reach and away from the crib. The nurse should advise parents to get down on their hands and knees and survey the environment from the infant's perspective. Any small object within the infant's reach is a possible choking hazard. Anything that can fit in the infant's mouth and be inhaled should be removed from his or her reach. Examples include balloons, toys with small parts, safety pins, small balls, broken crayons, and coins. Certain foods can increase the risk for choking. Firm or round foods, such as hot dogs, seeds, grapes, and raw carrots and apples, should be cooked or chopped into tiny pieces before serving to an infant or a very young child. See Chapter 29 for further discussion regarding safeguarding the home for young children.

Immunization Schedules

Newborns and infants need vaccines to protect them from diseases that can have serious consequences, such as seizures, brain damage, blindness, and even death. Health Canada, the Canadian Pediatric Society, and the provincial health departments collaborate and set provincial guidelines for immunizations. Canadian provinces have similar schedules but reflect their own unique demographic and health reality. See Table 28-1 for an example of a provincial immunization schedule.

Because immunizations are typically administered in conjunction with routine checkups, determine whether the parents are keeping regularly scheduled appointments. Next, check the immunization record. If the record is not up-to-date, ask if the parents are familiar with the immunization schedule and if there are any challenges for them to get immunizations for their baby. Provide a schedule, if needed, and help the parents determine where they can go to have the infant immunized.

Parents should be informed that it is important for their infant to receive vaccines at the ages and times recommended to ensure the highest level of protection against vaccine-preventable diseases. If the infant misses an immunization or gets behind schedule, there are catch-up schedules available to follow as set by provincial guidelines.

Table 28-1	Routine Immunization Schedule (Effective: 03FEB2011)
Age	**Vaccine**
2 mo	• DTaP-IPV-Hib[1] • Pneumococcal conjugate (PCV13) • Meningococcal conjugate (Men C)
4 mo	• DTaP-IPV-Hib • Pneumococcal conjugate (PCV13) • Meningococcal conjugate (Men C)
6 mo	• DTaP-IPV-Hib • Pneumococcal conjugate (PCV13) (for high-risk children only)
6 mo and older	• Influenza[2]
12 mo	• MMRV[3] • Meningococcal conjugate (Men C) • Pneumococcal conjugate (PCV13)
18 mo	• DTaP-IPV-Hib
4–6 y	• DTaP-IPV[4] • MMR • Pneumococcal conjugate (PCV13) only for children up to 71 mo (catch-up program)
Grade 5	• Hepatitis B (3 doses) • HPV[5] (3 doses for females)
Grade 9	• dTap[6] • HPV (only female students for 3 y, from SEP2009 to JUN2012—catch-up program) • MCV4[7]

Note: Each bullet represents one vaccine/injection unless otherwise noted.
[1]Diphtheria, tetanus, acellular pertussis, polio, haemophilus influenzae type b.
[2]Annually, during influenza season.
[3]Measles, mumps, rubella, and varicella.
[4]Diphtheria, tetanus, acellular pertussis, polio.
[5]Human papillomavirus.
[6]Diphtheria, tetanus, acellular pertussis.
[7]Meningococcal Conjugate Vaccine (groups A, C, W-135, and Y).
Adapted from Alberta Health Services. (2010a). *Immunization schedules.* Retrieved from www.health.alberta.ca/health-info/imm-routine-schedule.html

Child Safety Car Seat

At least 44% of car seats are not used properly in Canada; therefore, it is vital to discuss car seat safety with parents (Safe Kids Canada, 2010). Questions can include: Do you restrain your newborn or infant in a car seat? What type of seat is it? How old is it? Where is it placed in the vehicle? How is it secured into the vehicle? In Canada, each province has its own legislation regarding car seat safety. In general, infants need to be in an approved 5-point harness restraint system that is rear facing in the back seat until at least 1 year of age and approximately 9 kg (Fig. 28-1). Infants can then be restrained (5-point harness) in a forward facing car seat until at least 18 kg or 5–6 years of age. At this point, booster seats are recommended until the child turns 9 years of age or reaches the height of 145 cm. Some provinces have booster seat legislation, which requires children to be in booster seats until they reach the recommended height or age. Many safety agencies advocate for all provinces to join in this commitment (Safe Kids Canada). Many health centres, public health centres, fire stations, and hospitals in Canada offer education sessions on the topic of car seat safety for infants and children.

Cardiopulmonary Resuscitation Training for Parents

Inquire if the parents know CPR. Traditionally, health professionals in NICUs recommend parents learn infant CPR before discharge because these infants are at higher risk than are healthy infants for respiratory and cardiac arrest.

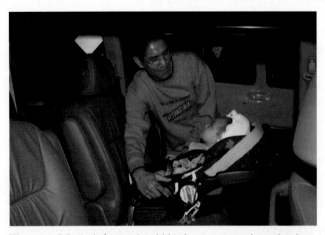

Figure 28-1 Infants should be in an appropriate sized car seat in the back seat of the vehicle.

Nevertheless, it is important for all parents and baby-sitters to know CPR. Many communities, learning institutions, and private companies offer CPR classes for nominal fees.

Poison Control

The nurse asks the parents how they have secured medications, cleaning compounds, and other chemicals in the home. It is important to explain that safety locks should be placed on cabinets located close to the floor and that it is wise to put medication and other toxic chemicals in high, locked cabinets. The nurse explains that ordering all prescription medications with childproof lids is another safety precaution. The nurse should ask if emergency numbers are posted near all phones in the home. In Canada, each province has its own poison control centre emergency telephone number. This is available online and inside the cover of phone books and can also be accessed by dialing the emergency number (usually 9-1-1 in most areas).

Breastfeeding/Iron-Rich Foods

It is helpful to ask the mother how she is feeding the baby and, if she is breastfeeding, discuss how long she plans to continue. If the mother is planning to return to work, the nurse asks if she wishes to discuss pumping, alternate milk sources, and possibly weaning.

Breast milk is the best food for the growing infant. For the first 6 months, it is the only food that the infant needs. As long as the woman has adequate iron stores, iron supplementation for exclusively breastfed infants is not necessary during the first 6 months (World Health Organization [WHO], 2011). Ideally, every baby should be breastfed for the first year of life. Iron-fortified infant formula is an acceptable alternative for mothers who cannot or choose not to breastfeed. The nurse cautions the parents that whole cow's milk is not an appropriate food for babies younger than 1 year. The nurse can also facilitate a discussion around adding solids and other fluids into the infant's diet according to the age and developmental stage of the infant. After 6 months, the parents may introduce meats or other iron-rich food sources to the infant's diet.

Baby Bottle Tooth Decay

The nurse should inquire regarding daily intake of sugar, especially the frequent consumption of sugary drinks (eg, soft drinks, punch, juice). He or should assess if the infant is ever allowed to go to sleep with a bottle of milk, formula, juice, or other sugary drink. This practice can lead to a condition known as **baby bottle tooth decay** (see Chapter 17). The problem is that the sugar sticks to the primary teeth and coats them. Bacteria in the mouth break down the sugars to use for food. As this breakdown occurs, the bacteria produce acids that attack the teeth and cause decay (Health Canada, 2009).

Some parents may not understand why the primary teeth are important. Unlike adult tooth decay, baby bottle tooth decay is most pronounced on the upper front teeth and is highly visible while the child's self-image is forming. In addition, if the primary teeth experience significant decay, they may require extraction. Because the primary teeth serve as placeholders for the secondary teeth, if they are lost too early, the secondary teeth may come in excessively crooked.

Focused Health History Related to Common Symptoms

Common Newborn/Infant Symptoms/Signs

- Respiratory concerns and/or distress
- Fever
- Skin conditions
- Gastrointestinal distress
- Crying/irritability

Examples of Questions to Assess Symptoms/Signs	Rationale/Unexpected Findings
Respiratory Concerns/Distress Has your baby had trouble breathing? Has your baby been ill with a cold? Or cough? Has the infant had a stuffy or runny nose? Have there been any episodes in which he or she stopped breathing? Or turned blue? Has your baby been coughing? Or sneezing? Is there any sputum production or secretions? Have you noticed any wheezing? Have you taken your baby's temperature? Has he or she had a fever? Are his or her immunizations up-to-date?	It is important to determine associated signs to identify severity and possible causation. This knowledge will guide the focused assessment. Detailed symptom/sign analyses are included in Chapters 12 through 27, which can be used with parents of an infant or newborn.
Fever In addition to the respiratory questions above, ask: • Has your baby been exposed to anyone with a communicable illness? • Has your family travelled recently? If so, where? • Was your baby born prematurely? Did your baby have to stay in neonatal intensive care unit (NICU)? • Has your baby had previous infections? Or hospitalizations? • Have you noticed if your baby has been pulling on one or both ears? • Have you noticed any change in your baby's eating pattern? Has he or she lost interest in eating? Has the number of wet diapers changed? • Has your baby demonstrated any unexpected behaviour such as irritability? Difficult to wake? Excessive fatigue? Difficult to soothe? • Has your baby had any periods when he or she stopped breathing momentarily (apnea)? • Is there an unusual odour to the urine? • Does there seem to be any pain associated with urination? • What treatments have you tried? Has anything helped so far?	Fever is associated frequently with infection, which can range in severity from mild to life-threatening. This line of questioning helps reveal the infant's risk factors for as well as possible causes of infection. The provider needs to determine if the fever likely has a respiratory origin (hence the respiratory questions). Could it be an *ear infection* (pulling on the ears) or *urinary tract infection?* Are there symptoms of *meningitis* (posturing), or is a blood infection likely? Although the nurse will not make a final medical diagnosis, these data will guide the nursing assessment and care planning (Wong, Scarfone, et al., 2008).
Skin Conditions • When did the rash begin? On what part of the body did it begin? Has it spread? If so, where? • Have you noticed your baby scratching? Has there been any oozing? Unusual odour? Or pus-type material associated with lesions? Has there been crusting or erosion? • Has there been a recent change in laundry detergents, soaps, or shampoos? • Has there been a change in the texture or luster of the hair or nails? • Has your baby had a fever? • Has he or she been exposed to anyone with a communicable disease? • Are your baby's immunizations up-to-date?	These questions help pinpoint possible causes. Many skin conditions have predictable patterns of spread, parts of the body affected, and associated symptoms, such as pruritis (itching). It is important to differentiate if the symptoms are localized versus systemic or if there might be an infectious versus an allergic origin.

(text continues on page 870)

Examples of Questions to Assess Symptoms/Signs	Rationale/Unexpected Findings

Gastrointestinal Distress

- Has there been vomiting? Is it projectile? What colour? And how much vomitus has there been?
- When was your baby's last bowel movement? Describe your baby's usual stool pattern and consistency. Has there been a change in the stooling? Has the stool been watery? Or unusually hard? What is the colour? And amount?
- Have you noticed a yellowish color to your baby's skin?
- Does the baby seem to be in pain? Has there been a fever?

Gastrointestinal symptoms can be associated with a wide range of conditions. In addition, infants can become dehydrated very quickly in the presence of vomiting or diarrhea.

Crying/Irritability

- What about your baby's crying is worrying you?
- Has your baby's crying changed? When did you notice the change?
- How do you usually help to soothe your baby when he or she cries? Are these strategies working now? What does help to soothe your baby now?
- Can you tell me about your baby's usual eating pattern?
- When was the last bowel movement? Has the pattern of bowel movements changed? How many wet diapers does your baby have in one day?
- Have you taken your baby's temperature? Has he or she had a fever?
- Has your baby been exposed to a communicable disease? Are any other friends or family members currently ill? If so, what is the illness?
- Are the immunizations current?
- How would you describe your baby's usual activity level? Has there been a change?

Crying and irritability are nonspecific symptoms implicated in conditions that range in severity from minor to life-threatening. It is important to identify associated symptoms, because this will guide the primary care provider's choice of diagnostic tests (Simon, 2009).

Cultural Considerations

Additional Questions	Rationale/Unexpected Findings
Many families use home remedies to treat certain conditions. Are there any home remedies your family finds helpful?	If the parent describes a harmful practice (eg, giving the infant a bottle of water with honey), then respectfully educate about possible consequences. Follow up by negotiating with the parent for a healthier way to meet the particular need that fits the family's culture.

An Example of a Therapeutic Dialogue

The nurse's role relative to subjective data collection is to gather information to improve the patient's health status and to help determine the cause of the patient's current symptoms. Remember Keri, who was introduced at the beginning of this chapter. This 2-month-old is visiting the clinic today for her well-child checkup and routine 2-month immunizations.

The nurse uses professional communication techniques to gather subjective data from the mother, Diane Dumont.

Nurse: Good morning, Mrs. Dumont. I am Shannon, Keri's nurse for today. I see you have Keri wrapped up snugly for the cold weather we're having!

Mrs. Dumont: Yes, it's cold out.

Nurse: I will be asking you a few questions as part of the assessment today, and I will be performing a physical examination of Keri. Before we get started, do you have any concerns or questions you would like to discuss today?

Mrs. Dumont: No, but I'll ask if I have any.

Nurse: Great. Now during the first few weeks of life the parents and baby are getting to know one another and establishing routines. What is Keri's routine at home?

Mrs. Dumont: She goes to bed around 8:30 pm and wakes up around 8 am, but is up once or twice during the night. During the day, she nurses every 2–3 hours. Do you think that she's getting enough milk?

Nurse: It looks like Keri is growing nicely. That usually means that she is getting plenty of milk. Later we will weigh and measure her to see how she is growing. Please tell me about your breastfeeding experience. (Waits for Mrs. Dumont to describe her experience.) Do you have any concerns about breastfeeding?

Critical Thinking Challenge

- What strategies does the nurse use to gather and share information?
- How does the nurse encourage Mrs. Dumont to describe things in her own words?
- How does the nurse convey to Mrs. Dumont that she is open to questions?

Objective Data Collection

After completing subjective data collection with the parent holding the infant, the nurse will collect equipment and prepare for the objective assessment. Well-child assessments include head-to-toe physical examinations, but the order is altered for infants, saving the least comfortable portions for last.

Equipment

- Equipment wipes
- Tape measure
- Pediatric stethoscope
- Disposable nonlatex gloves
- Thermometer
- Watch or clock with second hand
- Infant scale
- Otoscope
- Ophthalmoscope
- Pacifier (if acceptable to parent)

Promoting Patient Comfort, Dignity, and Safety

Perform the examination in a well-lit area in a comfortable, quiet environment, free of drafts. Have a place for both the parent and the nurse to sit while obtaining the history and the subjective data. Performing parts of the examination with the infant on the parent's lap can help to keep the infant feeling safe and calm.

After washing your hands, ensure that the parent and infant are comfortable. Introduce yourself and explain what the parent can expect. It may help to ease the parent if you comment on positive features of the infant. Engage the baby with friendly conversation while the parent continues to hold him or her. Sit at eye level and not towering above the family, a stance that can be viewed as threatening or authoritative. It may be helpful to have a soft clean toy to offer the infant while you obtain the health history from the parent.

Warm your hands by placing them in warm water before touching the infant. This can be accomplished in conjunction with washing the hands just before the examination. Likewise warm the stethoscope with the hands before placing it on the infant's skin. For the older infant, let him or her hold the stethoscope and demonstrate listening to the heart on the parent to prepare the infant for what to expect. These measures can decrease the infant's stress during the examination.

Comprehensive Physical Examination: Newborn and Infant

The physical examination typically is not completed in a head-to-toe fashion as for adults. Order varies depending on the baby's developmental level, temperament, and individual needs. Nevertheless, use a systematic approach to minimize the omission of parts of the examination. The most invasive techniques (ie, assessment of tonsils, uvula, ears) can be performed at the end. If the infant is asleep or quietly alert, take the temperature, count the respirations, and listen to the heart, lungs, and abdomen before performing other parts of the examination that may disturb the infant, which can cause crying that disrupts your ability to hear clearly.

Two comprehensive assessments specific to newborns are also included below: the Apgar score assessment and the initial newborn assessment (including gestational age and reflexes). A complete head-to-toe assessment of the newborn occurs sometime in the first hour or two after birth and is similar to that for older infants.

Techniques and Expected Findings	Rationale/Unexpected Findings
Newborn: Apgar Score The Apgar score is one of the first newborn assessments. It is not used to guide resuscitation efforts but gives important clues about how well the newborn is adapting to life outside the uterus. The newborn receives a score of 0 to 2 in each of 5 areas for a possible total score of 10. The score is calculated at 1 minute and again at 5 minutes of life (see Table 18-5 in Chapter 18). *A score of 7 to 10 indicates a vigorous newborn adapting well to the extrauterine environment.*	If the 5-minute score is <7, continue to score every 5 minutes until the score is >7, the newborn is intubated, or the newborn is transferred to the nursery. If the 5-minute score is 4 to 6, the newborn is having some difficulty adapting and requires closer observation than a vigorous newborn. A score <4 signifies that the newborn is having severe difficulty adapting to life outside the womb and requires observation and care in a neonatal intensive care unit (NICU).
Newborn: Gestational Age During pregnancy, gestational age is calculated from the date of the last menstrual period or by results of an early ultrasound. After birth, physical characteristics and neuromuscular assessment are used to evaluate gestational age. The Ballard Gestational Age Assessment Tool (Fig. 28-2) is commonly used in newborn nurseries. *The New Ballard score ranges from –1 to 4 or 5 for each criterion. Possible totals range from –10 to 50, or a gestational range of 20 to 44 weeks. An increase in the score by 5 increases the age by 2 weeks.*	The New Ballard Scale includes extremely premature newborns and has been refined to improve accuracy in more mature newborns.
Reflexes Evaluation of newborn reflexes gives information about neurological status. Assess rooting, suck, Moro (startle), Galant's (trunk incurvation), stepping, palmar grasp, tonic neck, and Babinski reflexes (see Table 28-2).	Diminished reflexes indicate the possibility of neurological or developmental deficits.
General Survey/Observation Begin the general survey, keeping in mind the age of the infant in months and the correlated expected development. Continue to collect data through observation during the entire visit. Observation is a crucial skill in the assessment. Always survey for symmetry, movement, colour, and tone. Continue to observe throughout the assessment. • *The healthy infant has good muscle tone, has a symmetrical appearance, and is quietly active. Respirations are quiet and unlaboured.* Notice interactions between the infant and the parent. If stranger anxiety is present, perform as much of the examination as possible with the infant on the parent's lap. • *The parent is receptive to the infant's behaviour cues. The infant appears alert and engaged in the environment, unless sleeping. An expected variant is stranger anxiety that begins around 9 months.*	The infant appears listless and uninterested in interaction. The parent pays little attention to the infant and does not pick up on cues, such as stress or readiness for interaction. Make note of any unusual odours. Certain diseases, such as *phenylketonuria, maple syrup urine disease*, and *diabetic acidosis*, have characteristic odours (see Table 18-5 in Chapter 18). Poor hygiene or inappropriate dress for the weather should alert the nurse to watch for other signs of neglect.

NEUROMUSCULAR MATURITY

NEUROMUSCULAR MATURITY SIGN	SCORE							RECORD SCORE HERE
	−1	0	1	2	3	4	5	
POSTURE								
SQUARE WINDOW (Wrist)	>90°	90°	60°	45°	30°	0°		
ARM RECOIL		180°	140°–180°	110°–140°	90°–110°	<90°		
POPLITEAL ANGLE	180°	160°	140°	120°	100°	90°	<90°	
SCARF SIGN								
HEEL TO EAR								

TOTAL NEUROMUSCULAR MATURITY SCORE

SCORE
Neuromuscular ____
Physical ____
Total ____

MATURITY RATING

Score	Weeks
−10	20
−5	22
0	24
5	26
10	28
15	30
20	32
25	34
30	36
35	38
40	40
45	42
50	44

PHYSICAL MATURITY

PHYSICAL MATURITY SIGN	SCORE							RECORD SCORE HERE
	−1	0	1	2	3	4	5	
SKIN	sticky, friable, transparent	gelatinous, red, translucent	smooth, pink, visible veins	superficial peeling and/or rash, few veins	cracking pale areas, rare veins	parchment, deep cracking, no vessels	leathery, cracked, wrinkled	
LANUGO	none	sparse	abundant	thinning	bald areas	mostly bald		
PLANTAR SURFACE	heel-toe 40–50 mm:−1 <40 mm:−2	>50 mm no crease	faint red marks	anterior transverse crease only	creases ant. 2/3	creases over entire sole		
BREAST	imperceptible	barely perceptible	flat areola no bud	stippled areola 1–2 mm bud	raised areola 3–4 mm bud	full areola 5–10 mm bud		
EYE-EAR	lids fused loosely:−1 tightly:−2	lids open pinna flat stays folded	sl. curved pinna; soft; slow recoil	well-curved pinna; soft but ready recoil	formed and firm instant recoil	thick cartilage, ear stiff		
GENITALS (Male)	scrotum flat, smooth	scrotum empty, faint rugae	testes in upper canal, rare rugae	testes descending, few rugae	testes down, good rugae	testes pendulous, deep rugae		
GENITALS (Female)	clitoris prominent and labia flat	prominent clitoris and small labia minora	prominent clitoris and enlarging minora	majora and minora equally prominent	majora large, minora small	majora cover clitoris and minora		

TOTAL PHYSICAL MATURITY SCORE

Figure 28-2 Ballard Gestational Age Assessment Tool for use in screening newborns.

Techniques and Expected Findings (continued)	Rationale/Unexpected Findings (continued)
Vital Signs Axillary temperature measurement is appropriate for the newborn and infant (Canadian Pediatric Society, 2010). Temperature is taken again after the first bath. *Range of temperature is the same as for adults: 36.3 to 37.2°C.*	Both elevated and decreased temperatures can signal infection in the newborn because the regulatory mechanisms are not fully mature. The newborn may cool during bathing and cannot shiver to raise heat.

(text continues on page 874)

Table 28-2 Newborn Reflexes

Rooting

Gently stroke the cheek. The newborn turns toward the stimulus and opens the mouth. This reflex disappears at 3–4 mo, although it may persist longer. Absence indicates a neurological disorder.

Suck

Observing the infant feeding at the breast or bottle is the best indicator of a suck reflex. If necessary, place a gloved finger in the newborn's mouth. He or she should vigorously suck. The reflex may persist during infancy. A weak or absent reflex indicates a developmental or neurological disorder.

Moro (Startle)

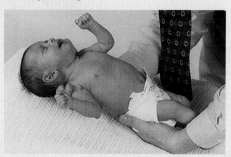

The Moro reflex occurs when the infant is startled or feels like he or she is falling. Sudden noise also can stimulate it, verifying that the infant can hear. Bring the infant to sit. Support the upper body and head with one hand; flex the chest. Suddenly let the head and shoulders drop a few inches while releasing the arms. The arms and legs extend symmetrically. The arms return toward midline with the hand open and the thumb and index finger forming a "C." Moro disappears by 4–6 mo of age. Its absence or weakness points to an *upper motor neuron lesion*. An asymmetrical Moro occurs with *brachial plexus or shoulder injury*.

Tonic Neck

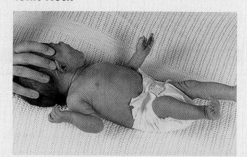

Turn the head of the supine infant to one side. The arm and leg extend on the side to which the face is pointed. The contralateral arm and leg flex, forming the classic fencer position. Repeat by turning the head to the other side—the position will reverse. This reflex is strongest at 2 mo and disappears by 6 mo. If still present at 9 mo (an indicator of neurological damage), the infant will not be able to support weight to crawl.

Galant's (Trunk Incurvation)

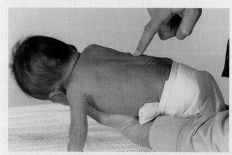

Place the newborn in ventral suspension. Stroke the skin on one side of the back. The trunk and hips should swing toward the side of the stimulus. Galant's reflex is typically present for the first 4–8 wk of life. Its absence may indicate *spinal cord lesions*.

Palmar Grasp

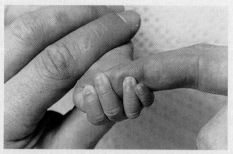

Place your finger in the newborn's palm; the infant's fingers will firmly grasp your finger. This reflex is strongest between 1 and 2 mo. Persistence after 3 mo indicates a *neurological disorder*.

Table 28-2   **Newborn Reflexes** *(continued)*

Stepping

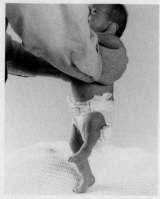

Hold the infant upright. Allow the soles to touch a flat surface. The legs flex and extend in a walking pattern. This reflex exists for the first 4–8 wk of life and persists with neurological conditions (eg, *cerebral palsy*).

Babinski

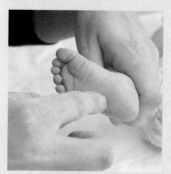

Stroke one side of the infant's foot upward from the heel and across the ball of the foot. The infant responds by hyperextending the toes: the great toe flexes toward the top of the foot and the other toes fan outward. This reflex lasts until the child is walking well. Persistence after age 2 y is associated with neurological damage (eg, *cerebral palsy*).

Techniques and Expected Findings (continued)

Apical pulse and respiratory rate should be measured for a full minute each with the infant at rest. *Expected pulse range for the newborn is 110 to 160 beats/min, decreasing slightly to 80 to 140 for infants older than 1 month. Respiratory rate is 30 to 60 beats/min for newborns and 22 to 35 for infants.*

Blood pressures are not measured routinely in the infant. If the blood pressures are taken, measure pressures in all four extremities. Make sure that the cuff fits appropriately.

• *Healthy systolic pressures are 50 to 70 for newborns and 70 to 100 for infants older than 1 month.*

Pain
Assess for pain (see Chapter 7).
The infant without pain appears comfortable and not excessively irritable.

Measurements
Weigh the infant using an infant scale that is calibrated regularly. Place a protective covering on it, zero the scale, and then position the infant with your hands just above, but not touching, to prevent a fall (Fig. 28-3). Use the tape measure and carefully measure from the crown of the head to the heel. Some nurses find it helpful to place the infant on the examination table, then using a pencil, place a mark at the crown and another mark at the infant's heel (with the hip and knee extended). Use the tape measure to measure the length between the

Rationale/Unexpected Findings (continued)

Tachycardia, bradycardia, tachypnea, and bradypnea are unexpected findings at rest. These terms are defined as falling above or below the ranges listed.

A difference between upper and lower extremity blood pressures may indicate *coarctation of the aorta*.

Because the infant is preverbal, ask the parent to help interpret pain signals. Newborns cry indiscriminately when in pain. It may help to systematically eliminate other causes of crying, such as hunger or a soiled diaper.

> **Clinical Significance 28-1**
>
> When plotting measurements for premature infants, use the corrected age for comparison instead of the chronological age for at least the first 24 months. For example, if the infant was born at 30 weeks' gestation, the birth was 10 weeks before term (40 minus 10). So at 12 weeks' (3 months) chronological or postnatal age, the infant's corrected age would be 2 weeks (12 minus 10).

(text continues on page 876)

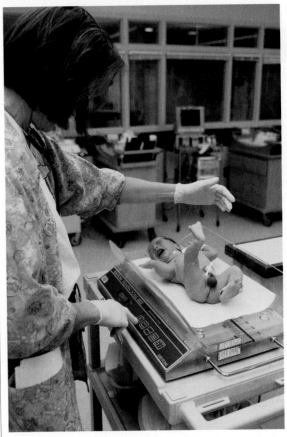

Figure 28-3 Weighing the newborn.

two markings, which, if done properly, is an accurate measurement of length (Fig. 28-4). Measure head and chest circumferences (Fig. 28-5). Plot the measurements on a standardized growth chart. *In general, the measurements are above the 10th percentile and below the 90th percentile. Compare measurements with previous visits to gain a sense of what is the growth pattern for each individual infant. Observe for the infant to gain weight and grow in height and increase head circumference at a steady pace.*

Growth patterns can vary depending upon genetic background. A small head may indicate *microcephaly*, while a large head may be from *hydrocephalus* or *increased intracranial pressure*. A small chest circumference may be from prematurity

The World Health Organization has new growth charts that are being introduced into Canada and the United States. These growth charts reflect both breastfeeding and formula-fed growth patterns (WHO, 2011).

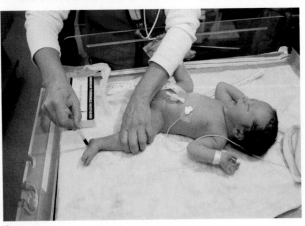

A

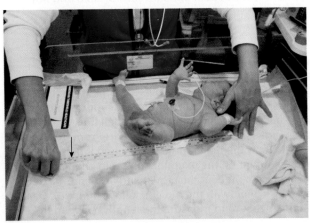

B

Figure 28-4 A. Marking the foot placement of the newborn with a pen. **B.** Using the tape measure to measure the length between the head and the foot to arrive at an accurate length measurement.

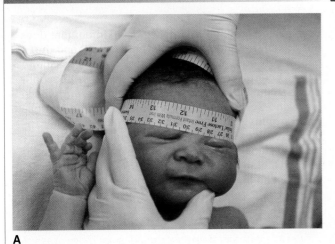

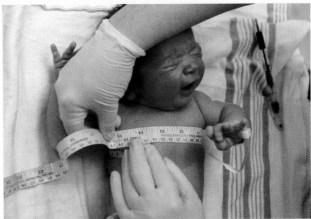

A   **B**

Figure 28-5 **A.** Measuring newborn head circumference. **B.** Measuring newborn chest circumference.

A sudden or progressive slowing of growth in height, weight, or head circumference can be a sign of concern. The nurse must also connect these measurements with the infant's behaviour, health, and eating patterns.

Clinical Significance 28-2

One measurement in time is not a basis for determining appropriate growth. Only by comparing measurements over time are growth delays documented, because each infant grows as an individual guided by genetics and environment.

Nutrition

Inspect the general condition of the skin, hair, and nails. *A well-nourished infant has soft, supple skin and shiny hair.* Ask about urination and bowel movements. *On average, the infant getting enough to eat wets a diaper four to six times per day and has regular bowel movements that are soft and not watery.*

If the infant is bottle-feeding, ask the parent how many ounces per feeding and how many feedings per day. *The infant is consuming approximately 105 to 108 kcal/ kg/d* (London, Ladewig, et al., 2007). For example, if the infant weighs 4.5 kg (10 lb), then he or she should be eating approximately 472 kcal/d. Formulas for term infants usually contain 20 kcal/30 mL. If the parent is having difficulty determining intake and there is a question as to adequacy, ask the parent to keep a diary of the infant's intake and output for the next 3 days and report back.

An indication that the infant is not eating enough is parental reports of fussing, crying, and not seeming satisfied after feeding. Other indications of inadequate nutrition include sallow skin tones with poor turgor, dry brittle hair and nails, losing weight or falling behind on growth charts compared to previous visits, and consuming <100 kcal/kg/d.

One important sign of failure to thrive is described as weight that falls below the fifth percentile for the infant's age (El-Baba, Bassali, et al., 2009). Signs to further evaluate include inadequate calorie intake, inadequate absorption, increased metabolism, or improper use of food sources. Be sure to differentiate inadequate intake from signs of acute dehydration, which include decreased skin turgor, sunken anterior fontanel, dry mucous membranes, no tears, concentrated urine, and an acutely ill appearance. Ask the parent to describe how infant formula is prepared in the home. Improperly prepared formula is an important cause of inadequate nutrition. Provincial health departments and public health centres offer information how to safely mix and store infant formula.

(text continues on page 878)

Mental Status

In infants, mental status is determined by observing sleep and alert states and behaviour throughout the examination. Observe for developmentally appropriate behaviour. *For example, an alert 2-month-old engages with the eyes and facial expressions when face to face with the parent or nurse and responds to the voice by turning toward the sound or tracking with the eyes. An older infant reaches for an object the parent or examiner offers.*

During the first month or two, crying is an expected response to handling and undressing during a physical examination. Crying should stop with gentle rocking in the arms or while holding the infant against the shoulder. As the infant matures, the infant may smile and interact with the examiner, as long as movements are not sudden or threatening and the voice maintains a calm and reassuring quality.

Violence

It is prudent to assess the parent for signs of domestic violence because children living in violent situations are much more likely to suffer abuse than children in households uncomplicated by violence (Department of Justice Canada, 2009) (see Chapter 12).

- *Healthy parental findings include a relaxed, confident demeanour with appropriate affect, good grooming, and appropriate interaction with and concern for the infant. Healthy infant findings include appropriate grooming and dress, no injuries, and willingness to engage with the parent and the nurse.*

Skin, Hair, and Nails

Inspect skin, hair, and nails.

- *Healthy infant skin is soft, not excessively dry, and supple. It quickly returns back to original shape after gentle pinching. It is free of rashes, lesions, bruising, and edema. Typical skin variants (eg, **Mongolian spot**(s), macular stains, spider nevi) are illustrated in Table 28-3. Hair is soft and shiny. Some infants shed hair in the first 2 months of life. Nails are soft, of an appropriate length, and not growing inward. They are securely attached to the nail beds, which are pink, unless the infant is dark skinned.*

Unexpected findings would include an infant that does not wake throughout a physical assessment and the parent subsequently confirms a lack of alertness in the baby. Other unexpected findings are when interactions between the infant and the parent do not seem synergistic and the older infant is excessively clingy or does not warm up to the examiner after a period of interaction. Excessive irritability and inconsolable crying may be early signs of a change in mental status. Later signs may be a high-pitched cry or lethargy and listlessness. Illness in an infant may alter his or her behaviour as well.

⚠ SAFETY ALERT 28-4

If the infant cannot be aroused or does not move evasively when prodded during an examination, he or she is showing signs of a severe change in mental status. This infant needs immediate medical attention.

Signs that should raise the index of suspicion for child abuse and neglect are listed in Table 28-6 at the end of the chapter.

Clinical Significance 28-3

Of all age groups, infants are the most likely to be abused (PHAC, 2008). Too often health care providers do not suspect or report suspected abuse. Long-term psychological and emotional sequelae from abuse are cumulative (Anda, Felitti, et al., 2005). When the nurse reports suspected abuse and thereby prevents future episodes, he or she has made a significant difference in that child's lifelong health.

Observing the skin is key to understanding the infant's overall health, hydration, nutrition, and environment. Investigate and describe any rashes, lesions, or bruising. Note if any rashes or lesions are macular, patchy, petechial, or vesicular. Is there excoriation from scratching? Does the skin seem sensitive to touch? Is there edema? Are any nails lifting off the nail bed? Are nails dry and brittle? Areas of inflammation around nails, with nails poking into the skin suggest *ingrown nails*. Poor elasticity and tenting of the skin when lightly pinched over the calf muscles and on the abdomen are associated with *dehydration*. Pallor or pale mucous membranes may indicate *anemia*. Yellow, jaundiced skin tones require further investigation because elevated bilirubin levels are toxic to the growing brain. Periorbital edema has various causes, such as crying, allergies, renal disease, or hypothyroidism. Dependent edema may occur with renal or cardiac disease. Multiple bruises in varied stages of healing, well-demarcated lesions, or bilateral burns may indicate physical abuse. See also Table 28-6 at the end of this chapter.

Table 28-3   Skin Variants in Newborns and Infants

Mongolian Spots

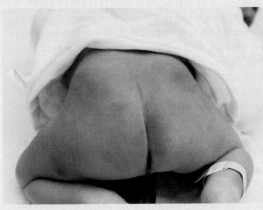

These bluish pigmented area(s) on the lower back or buttocks are common in infants of Asian, African, or Hispanic descent.

Spider Nevus

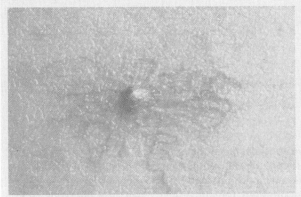

This benign lesion has a central arteriole from which thin-walled vessels radiate outward like spider legs. The lesion blanches when compressed.

Erythema/Neonatorum Toxicum (Newborn Rash)
This is a transitory newborn rash with an unknown cause. It presents as a red or pale bump or pustule, fades in a few days, and requires no treatment (London, Ladewig, et al., 2007).

Macular Stains

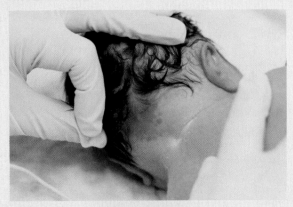

Also known as "stork bites," these capillary malformations appear on the eyelid(s), between the eyebrows, or on the nape of the neck. They tend to fade within 1–2 y.

Strawberry Hemangioma (Nevus Vasculosus)
These marks consist of enlarged capillaries and usually increase until about 6 mo of age and then involute on their own. They can be a concern if they continue to enlarge or obstruct an essential structure (eg, the eyelid).

Techniques and Expected Findings (continued)	Rationale/Unexpected Findings (continued)
Head and Neck Assess the head size and shape. Check for symmetry throughout the assessment. Palpate the anterior and posterior fontanels and sutures (Fig. 28-6). Trace along each suture line with the tips of the fingers to ensure they have not fused prematurely.	A head flattened from the back or one side may indicate positional *plagiocephaly* or *brachycephaly*, unexpected head shapes from consistent positioning on the back or one side to sleep without enough "tummy time" while awake. It is important to differentiate positional plagio

(text continues on page 880)

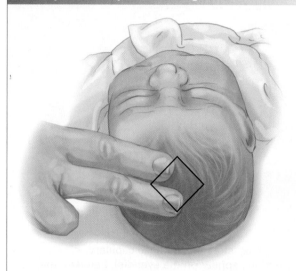

Figure 28-6 Assessing the fontanels and sutures.

- *The posterior fontanel usually is palpable until approximately 3 months of age, although it may be closed at birth. The anterior fontanel does not close until 9 to 18 months of age. The anterior fontanel is flat, not sunken or bulging, with the infant at rest and sitting. Sometimes, pulsations correlating with the infant's pulse can be felt while palpating the anterior fontanel. The fontanel may bulge slightly when the infant is crying. Suture lines are easily palpable.* **Craniotabes**, *soft areas on the skull felt along the suture line, are expected in infants, particularly those born prematurely.*

Observe the infant's face. Look for symmetry of movement during rest, smiling, and crying if possible.

Check range of motion by rotating the head toward the right shoulder and then the left, and then bending the neck so that the right ear moves toward the right shoulder and the left ear toward the left shoulder.

- *The neck has full range of motion. Head lag and head control correlate with expected development. For example, there is significant head lag in the newborn (Fig. 28-7A), whereas the 4-month-old can hold the head up without support (Fig. 28-7B).*

Inspect and palpate the trachea. *The trachea is midline and no swelling or masses are palpable.* Auscultate for any bruits. *No bruits are present.* Palpate the clavicles in the newborn. *They are smooth with no pain or crepitus.* Palpate the following lymph node chains: preauricular (in front of the ear), posterior auricular (behind the ear); occipital; submental; submandibular; tonsillar; superficial, posterior, and deep cervical; supraclavicular; infraclavicular; epitrochlear (medial surface of the arm, just above the elbow), and inguinal (horizontal group below the inguinal ligament, and vertical group near upper part of saphenous vein). *Any palpable lymph nodes are small, mobile, and nontender.*

cephaly from plagiocephaly caused by *craniosynostosis*, premature closure of the cranial sutures. This condition can lead to impaired brain development if several sutures are involved and corrective surgery is not done in a timely fashion. See also Table 28-7 at the end of this chapter. Bulging fontanels with the infant at rest are a sign of increased cranial pressure or *hydrocephalus*, enlarged head from increased cerebrospinal fluid. Sunken fontanels are associated most commonly with acute dehydration.

Asymmetrical facial movements may indicate *Bell's palsy* or a more serious heart condition. Bell's palsy sometimes results from traumatic birth or delivery assisted by instrumentation (eg, forceps). Bell's palsy typically fades over time, although occasionally it may persist.

Persistence of head lag beyond the 4th month is a sign of developmental delay. Limited range of motion of the neck is associated with torticollis and can be a sign of *meningeal irritation*. Webbing on the sides of the neck may indicate a congenital anomaly. An enlarged thyroid gland with a bruit is a sign of *thyrotoxicosis*.

A deviated trachea should be reported to the primary care provider. Crepitation over the clavicles in a newborn immediately after birth may indicate a *fracture*. By 3 weeks of age, a small lump may be felt on the bone following a clavicle fracture. Treatment usually is not indicated.

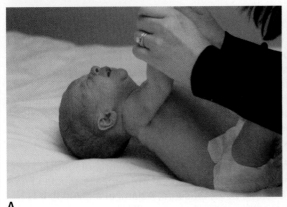
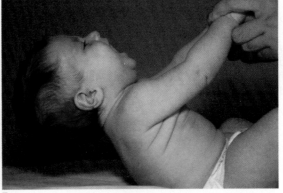

A   **B**

Figure 28-7 Head lag. **A.** The newborn has significant head lag. **B.** By 4 months of age, head lag has decreased noticeably.

Eyes

Look for symmetry. Assess spacing of the eyes. Inspect the lids for proper placement and observe the general slant of the palpebral fissures. Inspect the inside lining of lids (palpebral conjunctiva), bulbar conjunctiva, sclera, and cornea. *Eyes are parallel and centered in the face. Ptosis is absent. Sclera is clear and white.*

Upward or downward slanting or small palpebral fissures can be expected; however, these findings are associated with some congenital conditions, such as *fetal alcohol syndrome (FAS)*. Eyes too close together, too far apart, or asymmetrical can occur with chromosomal deviations or illnesses. Exophthalmos is rare during infancy; its presence may indicate *thyrotoxicosis*. An eyelid that droops (ptosis) may indicate *oculomotor nerve (cranial nerve III) impairment*. It is important to correct any misalignment before 4 to 6 years to prevent visual loss.

Assess ocular alignment to detect strabismus using the corneal light reflex test or cover test. *Some strabismus is expected in the first few months of life.* Assess pupils for shape, size, and movement. *They are round, equal, and clear.* Test their reaction to light. Quickly shine a light source toward the eye and then remove it. *The pupils are equal and reactive to light.*

Coordinated eye movements begin at approximately 2 months. Pupils that are asymmetrical, respond sluggishly, are "blown," or are pinpoint are unexpected.

Use an ophthalmoscope to obtain the red reflex. Ensure that you have a +1 or 2 D lens. With the infant lying on the examination table or sitting in the parent's lap, approach from the side while looking into the ophthalmoscope. Shine the light into the eye from approximately 40 to 70 cm away. If you do not visualize a red/orange reflection from the eye, make small adjustments with the instrument until you see the red reflex. Repeat in the opposite eye. *A red reflex is present.*

If the red reflex cannot be elicited in the newborn, the infant needs a complete eye examination by a specialist. The absence of the red reflex in newborns is associated with *congenital cataracts* and *neuroblastoma*.

Observe the infant for light perception and ability to fix on and follow a target. *Newborns are sensitive to light and often keep their eyes closed for long periods. They have a limited ability to focus, but by 3 months, they can follow objects.* An infant with any unexpected findings from the eye assessment should be referred to an advanced practitioner for further testing.

At birth, the visual system is the least mature of the sensory systems. Development progresses rapidly over the first 6 months and reaches adult level by 4 to 5 years. During infancy, it is thought that visual acuity is sharpest at the distance from the infant to the mother's face.

(text continues on page 882)

Ears

Assess ear placement. *Ears are symmetrical. The top of the pinna lies just above an imaginary line from the inner canthus of the eye through the outer canthus and continuing past the ear.* Most skin tags on the ears are a typical finding. Reassure the parent that these are easily removed if desired for cosmetic reasons.

Position the infant. Ask the parent to hold him or her with the body facing the parent. Then the parent should wrap one arm around the infant to draw the body close and pin down the arms. The other arm should hold the infant's head against the parent's chest. Gently pull the pinna down and back. Gently insert the otoscope approximately one fourth into the ear canal. Visualize the tympanic membrane and light reflex. *The tympanic membrane is convex, intact, and translucent and allows visualization of the short process of the malleus. The cone of light is visible in the anterior inferior quadrant.*

Screening for hearing acuity in infants and young children includes parental report and the evaluation of developmental milestones, such as the Moro reflex in neonates. Ask the parents how they know their baby can hear.

Nose, Mouth, and Throat

Inspect the nose. *It is in the midline of the face with symmetrical nares. The philtrum below the nose is fully formed (ie, not flat), and the nasolabial folds are symmetrical.* A newborn is an obligate nose breather and therefore patency can be assessed by closing off each naris one at a time. The best way to check patency is to hold a small mirror or specimen slide that has been chilled under the nose. Condensation on the glass is evidence of patency. *The nares are patent bilaterally.* Inspect the lips, mouth, and throat. Include a visual assessment of both the hard and the soft palate. Throat examination should be deferred to the end of the examination unless the infant cries. The uvula can easily be visualized when the infant is crying. *The lips are symmetrical and fully formed. Young infants may have a white nodule on the upper lip. Sometimes referred to as a sucking blister, this is harmless. The tongue is of expected size and does not get in the way of feeding. The mucous membranes of the mouth, nose, and throat are moist and pink.*

Ears that fall below the imaginary line are low-set and may indicate *chromosomal deviations*. It may be helpful to note if either parent has low-set ears. If so, then the low-set ears may be an inherited variant. One ear that is significantly smaller than the other or has extra ridges and pits may be associated with middle ear disorders or congenital kidney disorders. See Table 28-8 for ear shapes associated with Down's or Turner's syndrome (Ranweiler, 2009).

Otitis media is common in infants. Early diagnosis and intervention result in the best outcomes (Canadian Pediatric Society, 2009; Waseem, Aslam, et al., 2008). It is important to ensure that every ill infant has an otoscopic examination (Rennie, van Wyk, et al., 2009).

> ⚠ *SAFETY ALERT 28-5*
> *Always brace the hand holding the otoscope against the infant's face so that if the infant moves, the otoscope moves with him or her to avoid injuring the tympanic membrane.*

If there is no or diminished movement, suspect *otitis media*. Other conditions that can cause diminished movement include perforation (in one ear only) or tympanosclerosis (see also Chapter 16).

Unexpected findings include lack of Moro reflex, inability to localize sound, or lack of understandable language by 24 months.

Nasal flaring is a sign of respiratory distress. A flattened nasal bridge and macroglossia (enlarged tongue) are associated with *chromosomal deviations*. A flat philtrum and thin upper lip are associated with FAS. A tight lingual frenulum can interfere with breastfeeding and may need to be clipped by a qualified physician or nurse practitioner. A deviated uvula or a uvula with a cleft (rare) and red, inflamed tonsils should be noted. If concerned about the patency of the hard and/or soft palate, put on disposable gloves and palpate the palates.

Thorax and Lungs

Auscultate breath sounds and observe respiratory movements and effort in a newborn and infant. Breathing movements are best observed in the abdomen from pronounced diaphragmatic excursion in the infant. *The thorax is symmetrical. Chest expansion is equal bilaterally.* Observe the infant's breathing pattern. Newborns may have occasional irregularities in their respiratory pattern. *There are no signs of distress, apneic episodes, or use of accessory muscles.* Auscultate all lobes of the lungs from the front, back, and under the arms on both sides. *Breath sounds are equal bilaterally and typically louder and more bronchial than in adults. Inspiration is slightly longer than expiration.*

Assess oxygenation. *Pink nail beds with crisp, <3 seconds, capillary refill time, and pink mucous membranes and tongue are all signs of adequate oxygenation. Blueness surrounding the mouth, circumoral cyanosis, can be usual, especially when the infant is crying, as long as the lips and tongue remain pink.*

Heart and Neck Vessels

Palpate the point of maximum impulse (PMI). Auscultate the heart in the four key areas—aortic, pulmonic, tricuspid, and apex (mitral) (Fig. 28-8)—and inspect and auscultate the neck vessels. *The PMI may be difficult to palpate in the infant. The heart rhythm is regular with a single S1 and a split S2. Some murmurs are nonpathologic—typically they are soft and nonspecific in character (see Chapter 29 for discussion of innocent murmurs). The neck vessels are nondistended without bruits.*

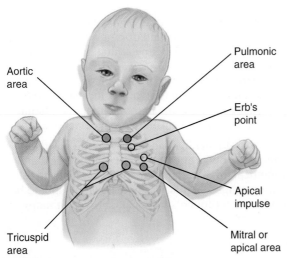

Figure 28-8 Four auscultation sites for cardiac assessment. **A.** Aortic area. **B.** Pulmonic area. **C.** Tricuspid area. **D.** Mitral area.

Labels: Aortic area; Pulmonic area; Erb's point; Apical impulse; Mitral or apical area; Tricuspid area

It is important to carefully listen to all lobes as sounds are easily transmitted in a newborn's and infant's small chest. An asymmetrical chest wall, or an expanded anterior–posterior diameter (pigeon chest) or funnel shape chest (depressed sternum) should not be present. Retractions anywhere on the chest wall are a sign of respiratory distress. Wheezes, crackles, and/or grunting are always unexpected, as are absent or diminished breath sounds.

Central cyanosis, blueness in the center portions of the torso or of the lips, tongue, or oral mucous membranes, is a sign of poor oxygenation. Congenital heart disease is one possible cause.

Clinical Significance 28-4

If the infant is very pale and anemia is suspected, it is prudent to check the oxygen saturation. This is because it takes at least 5 g of reduced hemoglobin to produce the typical blueness of cyanosis. Anemic infants often do not have enough hemoglobin to exhibit cyanosis, even though they have very low oxygen saturation levels.

Tachycardia at rest, persistent bradycardia, and clubbing should not be present. Unexpected findings suggestive of a cardiac defect include a single S2, ejection clicks, and some murmurs, particularly loud, harsh murmurs. If central cyanosis is present, evaluation of preductal and postductal oxygenation saturation is in order. Measure and compare readings in both upper extremities and one lower extremity. Oxygen saturation <90% is unexpected, as are disparate readings between the upper and lower extremities. Infants with central cyanosis need a full cardiac evaluation by a cardiologist.

(text continues on page 884)

Peripheral Vascular

Note the character and quality of the brachial and femoral pulses. Compare left to right and upper with lower. *All pulses are equal; pulse rate matches apical heart rate.*

Weak, thready pulses indicate low cardiac output. Bounding pulses are associated with conditions characterized by right to left shunts (eg, *patent ductus arteriosus*). Palpable pulses in the upper extremities in correlation with diminished pulses in the lower extremities may indicate *coarctation of the aorta* or an *interrupted aortic arch*.

Breasts

Observe the nipples. *The areolae are full and the nipple bud well formed. It is typical for both male and female newborns to have swollen breasts that may even leak a watery fluid.* The lingering effects of maternal hormones cause this.

Check for any supernumerary (extra) nipples (see Fig. 21-2). These are usually found below the nipples and may not be recognized as nipples because they are usually small and not well formed. Although the condition is fairly common and usually benign, the number and location of the extra nipples should be documented. Reassure the parent that these nipples will not develop at puberty. See Table 28-8 at the end of the chapter for deviations related to Klinefelter's disease.

Abdomen

Inspect the abdomen. *It is cylindrical, protrudes slightly, and moves in synchrony with the diaphragm. Superficial veins may be visible in fair-skinned infants. The umbilical area is clean without discharge, odour, redness, bulging areas, or scarring.* Auscultate bowel sounds. In the newborn, assessing by quadrant is ineffective because the sound from one quadrant travels to all quadrants. In the older infant, assessment by quadrant is more significant. Percuss the abdomen of the older infant. *Dullness noted in the right upper quadrant helps outline the lower edges of the liver. Tympany is expected over an air-filled stomach and bowel.*

A dull sound when percussing above the symphysis pubis may indicate a distended bladder. If abdominal distention is present, evaluate for a fluid wave. Note the size, shape, position, and mobility of any masses. Palpable kidneys indicate enlargement and should prompt further investigation by the primary care provider. Loud, grumbling sounds may indicate hunger. Bowel sounds heard in the chest can indicate a diaphragmatic hernia.

Palpate the abdomen. *It is soft, without rigidity, tenderness, or masses. The lower margins of the liver can be palpated from 1 to 2 cm below the right costal margin. The tip of the spleen may be palpable in the left upper quadrant.* Be sure to palpate for hernias in the umbilical and inguinal regions. *Usually, the kidneys cannot be palpated and no hernias are present.*

The abdomen may be distended and firm with genitourinary masses or malformation. Gastrointestinal obstruction and an imperforated anus are also the causes of a firm abdomen.

Musculoskeletal

By this point in the examination, there have been many opportunities to observe for symmetry of movement and strength and tone of the musculoskeletal system. Note shape and appearance of the hands, palms, fingers, feet, and toes. *The ankles have full range of motion, and feet return to a neutral position without assistance.*

Throughout examination, note any asymmetrical or limitations in movements and/or range of motion. Crepitus with joint movement or any limitation of movement is unexpected. In *talipes varus (club foot)*, one or both feet are plantar-flexed and turn inward. In *talipes valgus*, seen less commonly, the foot or feet turn outward (see also Chapter 23). Variations in the palmar and plantar creases can be signs of chromosomal deviations.

Assessment of the hips includes observing for symmetry, movement and some health care professionals may perform Ortolani's manoeuvre and elicit Barlow's sign and Galeazzi's sign to check for signs of hip dislocation.

Signs of congenital hip dislocation include positive Ortolani's, Barlow's, and Galeazzi's manoeuvres and asymmetrical thigh and gluteal folds. Infants with talipes varus, talipes valgus, or hip dislocation should be referred to an orthopedist for evaluation and treatment.

Galeazzi's Sign. *With the infant supine on a firm surface, bend the legs and place the feet together and flat on the surface. Observe for differences in the knee heights (see Fig. 28-9).*

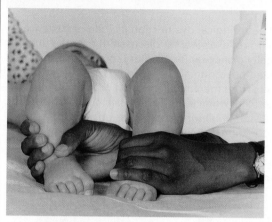

Figure 28-9 Galeazzi's sign.

Ortolani's Manoeuvre. Position the infant supine on the examining table. With the baby's legs together, flex the knees and hips 90°. Then, with your middle fingers over the greater trochanters and thumbs on the inner thighs, abduct the hips while applying upward pressure (Fig. 28-10). *No clicking or clunking sounds are heard.*

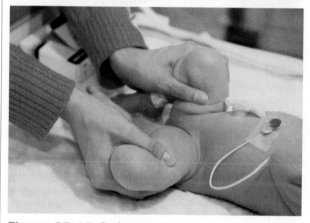

Figure 28-10 Performing Ortolani's manoeuvre.

Barlow's Manoeuvre. Maintain your hold and the 90° flexion; apply downward pressure while adducting the hips (Fig. 28-11) *The head of the femur remains in the acetabulum.*

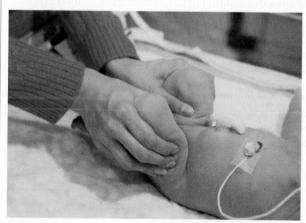

Figure 28-11 Performing Barlow's manoeuvre.

(text continues on page 886)

Neurological

Many assessments made throughout the examination give clues regarding intactness of the nervous system and cranial nerve function. These include motor function (muscle size, symmetry, strength, tone, and movement), developmental maturation, and reaction to touch. *The infant blinks when a bright light is shined in the eyes and when a loud noise, such as a clap, is produced close by.* Inspect and then palpate along the length of the spine. *There are no deep pilonidal dimples or tufts of hair. Spine is midline.*

Clinical Significance 28-5

Infants can experience cerebral palsy despite having no risk factors. When the condition is identified early and therapy initiated promptly, long-term functioning is optimized. Watch for signs of neuromuscular dysfunction, such as hand preference before 1 year old, bilateral fist clenching after 3 months old, and involuntary or unexpected movements.

Genitalia

Female. Inspect the genitalia. *The labia majora cover the vestibule. The newborn girl may have an enlarged clitoris and labia, and the parent may have noticed a few drops of blood in the diaper.* These findings result from lingering effects of maternal hormones and should not be present after the first few weeks of life. Gently part the labia and observe the structures of the vestibule. Visualize the vaginal opening. *The genital area is clean and free of foul odours.*

Male. Inspect the penis. Note cleanliness and placement of the urethral meatus. *It is at the top of the glans penis and midline.* For the uncircumcised penis, you will need to partially retract the foreskin to observe the meatus. Do not forcibly retract the foreskin. Palpate down the inguinal canal and scrotum. Evaluate the scrotum for size, color, and symmetry. *Testes are descended bilaterally; the area is free of edema, masses, and lesions.*

Anus and Rectum

Inspect the anus for presence and patency. Use the little finger of a gloved hand to palpate it. *The anus is well formed with no redness or bleeding. The muscle contracts with light pressure to the area.* Rectal examination is not done routinely unless there is evidence of irritation, bleeding, or other symptoms.

Signs of neurological dysfunction include persistence of newborn reflexes (earlier discussion) past the time they usually disappear, involuntary movements, and unexpected posturing. Opisthotonos (Fig. 28-12) usually results from meningeal irritation or severe illness. Failure to blink when a bright light is shined in the eyes may be a sign of blindness, whereas absence of a blink upon production of a loud noise may denote deafness. Further evaluation is indicated in both instances. Dimpling or tufts of hair on the spine may indicate *spina bifida occult or a tethered spinal cord.*

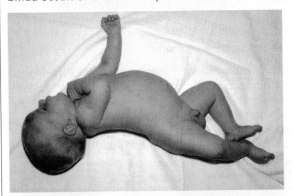

Figure 28-12 Opisthotonos, an indicator of meningitis.

Redness, swelling, bleeding (after 1 month of age), or torn tissue may indicate sexual abuse. The law mandates the reporting of signs of abuse to child protective services. When the hymen completely covers the vagina, the infant has an *imperforate hymen*, which requires minor surgery before puberty to allow exit of menstrual flow. Other unexpected findings include *labial adhesions/fusion, lesions*, and foul-smelling discharge. If there is a foul smell, you may suspect infection or a foreign body.

Meatal stenosis, an inadequate urethral opening, or a malpositioned meatus, *hypospadias*, or *epispadias*, should be referred to a pediatric urologist for evaluation. Note if the testes remain undescended. This condition requires evaluation if it persists into the toddler stage.

Enquire about initial newborn bowel movements to confirm anal patency. Investigate redness, bleeding, or other signs of irritation for the possible cause (eg, sexual abuse, fissures). Small white worms indicate a *pinworm infection.*

Documentation of Examination Findings

Any parental concerns and teaching are documented to inform the care process, help with consistency, and confirm the appropriate follow-up. The nurse also documents all unexpected findings and reports those that warrant further examination and attention. The parent is informed appropriately of all referrals, and he or she is considered a partner in the infant's care.

🌐 Cultural Considerations

The length and weight of the newborn and infant vary according to genetic background, so ranges outside of usual may be expected for some patients. For example, children of Filipino genetic background tend to be smaller and shorter than children of Caucasian background. It is useful to observe the height and weight of the infant's parents to give information about expected growth. Also, genetic background significantly influences the skin of infants including colour and variations. For example, Mongolian spotting is more common in infants of African Canadian, Asian, and First Nations origin.

Evidence-Informed Critical Thinking

Organizing and Prioritizing

The nurse gleans a wealth of data throughout the examination. With the first observations of the infant and parent, the nurse begins to understand the infant's emotional, musculoskeletal, neurological, and nutritional status as well as the developmental level. As the examination progresses, additional details add to the nurse's understanding so that by the end, the nurse is ready to prepare the care plan. An approach that cultivates rapport and respect with the infant and parent from the beginning and throughout the examination will facilitate the parent's participation in the process.

The nurse has enough data to communicate a concise yet thorough description of the infant's health status. This information assists the nurse in planning the care of the family. When necessary, the nurse reports pertinent data to other health care professionals to help inform subsequent follow-up care.

Laboratory and Diagnostic Testing

After the first 24 hours, a newborn needs a metabolic screen that tests for metabolic, hormonal deficiencies/deviations, and possibly for cystic fibrosis. Each provincial health department administers and tracks the screen and the results. Many hospitals routinely test for blood type and ABO compatibility. Those that do not routinely perform these tests can be requested by care providers if necessary for clinical decision making. For example, if a mother is blood type O, a nurse may request a Coombs test to help determine blood incompatibility in the case of newborn jaundice.

Clinical Reasoning

Nursing Diagnosis, Outcomes, and Interventions

When formulating a nursing diagnosis, it is important to use critical thinking to cluster data and identify patterns. The nurse compares these clusters of data with the defining characteristics (unexpected findings) for the diagnosis to ensure the most accurate labelling and appropriate interventions. Table 28-4 compares nursing diagnoses, unexpected findings, and interventions commonly related to newborn and infant assessment (North American Nursing Diagnosis Association-International, 2009).

Nurses use assessment information to identify patient outcomes. Some outcomes related to newborn or infant concerns include the following:

- Bilirubin is within parameters for age when plotted on a nomogram.
- Infant is gaining weight with expected pattern of growth.
- Infant is afebrile (Moorhead, Johnson, et al., 2007).

Table 28-4	Common Nursing Diagnoses Associated With Newborns and Infants		
Diagnosis and Related Factors	**Point of Differentiation**	**Assessment Characteristics**	**Nursing Interventions**
Neonatal jaundice related to destruction of fetal hemoglobin	Yellow orange tint of the skin resulting from accumulation of unconjugated bilirubin	Bilirubin high for age in hours or days (plotted on a nomogram), yellow-orange skin, yellow sclera	Prompt early and frequent feeding to stimulate stooling and removal of bilirubin. Reassessment as necessary with feeding history, bilirubinometer, serum bilirubin, and phototherapy as ordered
Effective breastfeeding as evidenced by newborn reflexive and behavioural responses and mother's efforts and knowledge	Mother and infant calm and learning about each other and breastfeeding.	Appropriate weight for age, expected outputs according to infant's age, eagerness of infant to nurse, infant content after feeding	Facilitate skin-to-skin contact. Give positive feedback and encouragement. Refer to lactation consultant for assistance, if desired

Once outcomes are established, nurses implement care to improve the status of the patient. The nurse uses critical thinking and evidence-informed practice to develop the interventions. Some examples of nursing interventions for newborn care are as follows:

- Protect the infant's eyes to prevent overexposure to phototherapy.
- Use valid and appropriate data to determine infant feeding patterns.
- Perform Apgar score after birth (Bulechek, Butcher, et al., 2008).

Analyzing Findings

Remember Keri Dumont, whose story has been outlined throughout this chapter. One month after the 2-month appointment, Keri's mother calls the office to state that Keri is fussy at the breast and she is worried Keri is not gaining enough weight. It is necessary for her to return to the clinic, so health care professionals can reassess her and document findings. The following nursing notes illustrate how subjective and objective data are collected and analyzed and nursing interventions are developed.

Subjective: Mother states that she is extremely frustrated with breastfeeding. At first, it went well, but she is worried that she isn't making enough milk. Baby Keri has been "fussy" in between feeds and she seems to want to eat "all the time."

Objective: Keri is irritable. Abdomen is soft and nondistended. Temperature 37°C, pulse 138 beats/min, and respirations 40 breaths/min. Mucous membranes are moist, and fontanels are palpable and within expected range. Mother states Keri is stooling twice per day and urinates at least 6 times per day. Weight is 5,920 g, which is an expected weight for Keri and for a 3-month-old baby girl. Using the growth charts, it was found that Keri is currently growing on the 75th percentile.

Analysis: Altered infant feeding pattern related to possible infant growth spurt at 3 months of age.

Plan: Validate and support her concerns. Encourage mother to drink 2 L/d of fluid and get proper rest and nutrition. Teach mother about growth spurts and the supply and demand principles of breastfeeding. Encourage mother to feed when Keri is hungry and assure her that her milk supply should increase over the next few days. Discuss resources and possible referral to a lactation specialist if no improvement or if infant begins to lose weight.

Critical Thinking Challenge

- How will the nurse assess the mother's knowledge and comfort level with the information provided?
- What psychosocial issues might the nurse assess for this family?

Collaborating with the Interprofessional Team

Results that might trigger a consult with a lactation specialist include pain while breastfeeding, a newborn who is wetting fewer than six diapers a day, a newborn having less than two bowel movements per day, a baby who is not gaining weight, or a baby who is not swallowing after milk is ejected. Some mothers wish to see a lactation specialist prenatally or postnatally for support and care in the absence of concerns.

Keri and her mother have been experiencing many of the concerns outlined above and a consult is indicated. The following conversation illustrates how the nurse might organize the data and make recommendations about the patient's situation.

Situation: Hi, I'm Jan, a nurse in the public health clinic, and saw Keri Dumont and her mom today.

Background: Keri is 3 months old and her mom brought her to the clinic today because she is concerned that Keri is not getting enough to eat and is irritable and wants to "eat all the time."

Assessment: Growth spurt resulting in changes in the amount of breastfeeding needed.

Recommendations: I think that a 1-hour appointment would be helpful. Mrs. Dumont has been successfully breastfeeding Keri for 3 months and just needs some help with some strategies to improve her milk supply. I've already given her some suggestions.

Critical Thinking Challenge

- What are some other things that the nurse might want to assess?
- When would a referral to a lactation specialist be most helpful for Mrs. Dumont and Keri?

Pulling It All Together: An Example of Reflection and Critical Thinking

The nurse uses assessment data to formulate a nursing care plan with patient outcomes and interventions for Keri and her mother. Outcomes are specific to the patient, realistic to achieve, measurable, and have a time frame for completion. Interventions are actions that the nurse performs, based on evidence and practice guidelines. After completion of interventions, the nurse reevaluates Keri and documents the findings in the chart to show progress toward the patient outcomes. The nurse uses critical thinking and judgment to continue or revise the diagnosis, outcomes, or interventions. This is often in the form of a care plan or case note similar to the one below.

Nursing Diagnosis	Patient Outcomes	Nursing Interventions	Rationale	Evaluation
Altered infant feeding pattern related to possible infant growth spurt at 3 month of age.	Keri feeds on demand and is content between feedings with six to eight wet diapers and at least two stools in 24 hour.	Refer to lactation specialist if no improvement or weight loss occurs. Encourage 2 L of water per day and appropriate nutrition.	An infant experiences an expected growth spurt at 3 month. The increased feeding demands can confuse and exhaust a new mother.	Patient followed by clinic nurse in 3 days. Mother reports that infant is more settled now in between feeds. Mother weighed Keri yesterday and she had gained 56 g (2 oz) since the clinic visit.

Applying Your Knowledge

Using your knowledge of the nursing process and critical thinking, consider all the case study findings woven throughout this chapter. When answering the following questions, begin drawing conclusions and see how the pieces of assessment must work together to create an environment for personalized, appropriate, and accurate care.

- What is the expected growth for an infant each week for the first 6 months? (Knowledge)
- Why is vitamin D supplementation important in a breastfeeding baby? (Comprehension)
- What would you teach Mrs. Dumont to observe in Keri to know that she is "getting enough breastmilk"? (Application)
- What factors could contribute to a slowed growth pattern in a newborn or an infant? (Analysis)
- What health promotion teaching would be important to discuss with Mrs. Dumont as Keri grows? (Synthesis)
- How would you evaluate if Mrs. Dumont is confident and comfortable in her knowledge of infant feeding and growth? (Evaluation)

Key Points

• The infant's growth and development progress in predictable ways: cephalocaudally, from central to distal, and from gross motor to fine motor control. It is important to evaluate patterns of growth and document progress.

• Emergent situations for the infant often have respiratory causes.

• Anticipatory guidance for parents of the infant includes education regarding immunization schedules, supporting breastfeeding, expected growth and development, safe sleep practices, preventing baby bottle tooth decay, car seat safety, childproofing the home, and other general safety topics.

• Infants commonly present with respiratory symptoms, fever, skin disorders, gastrointestinal distress, and crying. Interview questions for these symptoms should elicit information regarding severity and possible causation.

• Key assessments immediately after birth are vital signs including respiratory status, gestational age, and reflexes including muscle tone.

• Performing a physical examination on an infant requires the nurse to be flexible about the order and timing of specific assessments based on the developmental stage and the unique needs of the infant and the family.

• Many assessment techniques are unique to the infant or newborn, such as Apgar scoring, evaluating reflexes, performing gestational age assessment, and manoeuvres to identify congenital hip dislocation. Other techniques require adaptation to accommodate the infant's unique anatomical and developmental needs. Examples include use of the ophthalmoscope and otoscope and examination of the throat.

• The nurse can glean a wealth of information about the infant's development and the mental, psychosocial, neurological, musculoskeletal, and nutritional status by carefully observing the infant's appearance, muscle tone, behaviour, activity levels, and interaction with parents throughout the examination. Observing for symmetry is a key assessment principle.

• Because infants are the age group most likely to be abused, screening for and identifying signs of child abuse and neglect are important ways the nurse can make a difference in long-term outcomes.

• A thorough skin assessment also reveals information about the infant's nutrition and hydration status, cardiac and respiratory function, and renal and lymphatic systems.

• Positional plagiocephaly and brachycephaly must be distinguished from craniosynostosis, which can lead to impaired brain development if not caught and treated early.

• Many unexpected findings in infants result from chromosomal defects or are acquired congenital conditions resulting from environmental conditions (eg, FAS).

Review Questions

1. A mother brings her 6-month-old to the clinic for a routine evaluation. At birth, the term infant weighed 3,540 g and was 51 cm long. He now weighs 4,590 g. Which assessments are the *most* important for the nurse to do next?
A. Obtain a thorough obstetric and neonatal history and say, "I'm very worried that the baby hasn't gained more weight. What are you feeding him?"
B. Measure head and chest circumference and length and then plot current weight, length, and head and chest circumferences on standardized growth charts.
C. Review the immunization history, and ask the mother if she has noticed any unusual patterns or behaviours.
D. Screen for domestic violence and focus on the neurological, cardiac, and abdominal portions of the physical examination.

2. The nurse is evaluating the growth pattern of a 5-month-old born at 27 weeks' gestation. Which of the following actions will yield the most accurate assessment of growth for this infant?
A. Calculate how many kilocalories per day the infant is consuming, evaluate his bowel movement pattern, plot his measurements, and compare with the last two visits.
B. Determine if he has gained at least 2,200 g since birth, because infants should double their birth weight by 4–6 months of age.
C. Plot the weight and length on a standardized growth chart for a 7-week-old and compare with birth measurements and measurements on previous visits.
D. Plot the weight and length on a standardized growth chart for a 12-week-old and compare with birth measurements and measurements on previous visits.

3. The nurse is assessing a 2-month-old whose mother brought her to the emergency department because the baby wasn't eating well and she "just looks sick." Which of the following assessment findings is most worrisome?
A. Stiff neck with an arched back
B. Circumoral cyanosis noted when crying
C. Point of maximum impulse (PMI) not palpable, anterior fontanel bulges slightly when crying
D. Temperature 36.7°C, heart rate 160 beats/min, respiratory rate 38 breaths/min

4. The nurse is triaging infants who have presented to the emergency department on a Friday night. Which infant should the nurse take in for treatment *first*?
A. A 2-week-old whose mother reports, "She just won't stop crying. I'm so worried." The cry is medium pitch. Temperature 37.2°C, heart rate 160 beats/min, respirations 50 breaths/min. Abdomen moves with each breath.
B. A 6-week-old whose father reports, "He's vomited several times and he won't take his bottle." Temperature 36.0°C, heart rate 70 beats/min, respirations 20 breaths/min. His lips are white. He is limp.

C. A 5-month-old with a stuffy nose who has been unusually fussy and has had three loose stools in the last 8 hours. Temperature 37.7°C, heart rate 140 beats/min, respirations 45 breaths/min while crying.

D. An 8-month-old whose parents report he choked on a bean at dinner. The bean came out after five back pats. He turns blue around his mouth when he cries. Temperature 37.0°C, heart rate 130 beats/min, respirations 30 breaths/min.

5. The nurse is teaching a parenting class, and the parents are sharing baby pictures. Which picture indicates that the parent may need additional education?
   A. Baby is playing peekaboo in his car seat, which is installed in the middle part of the rear seat.
   B. Daddy is brushing his son's two front teeth while baby is splashing in the bathtub.
   C. Baby (10 month old) is in his high chair feeding himself a banana cut in small pieces.
   D. Baby is sleeping supine in her crib, no pillow, one blanket, bottle lying beside baby and a tiny dribble of milk at the corner of her mouth.

6. The infant has a new onset of rash, but otherwise seems well. Which interview question is *best* when trying to pinpoint a possible cause?
   A. Was there a prolonged neonatal intensive care unit (NICU) stay?
   B. What treatments have you given her for the rash?
   C. Has anything changed lately, such as shampoos, soaps, or laundry detergent?
   D. How many diapers is she wetting per day and what is the stool pattern?

7. Which of the following activities *best* facilitates anticipatory guidance?
   A. Becoming very proficient in interviewing and performing the physical examination
   B. Doing as much of the examination as possible with the infant in the parents' lap
   C. Recognizing and reporting signs of physical abuse and neglect
   D. Encouraging parents to make an appointment with the pediatrician before the baby is born

8. Which of the following infants has the most signs that point to possible abuse?
   A. History of a long NICU stay for extreme prematurity; does not respond to loud clapping
   B. Positive Ortolani's and Barlow's manoeuvres; one leg looks shorter than the other
   C. Small baby with large areas of denuded skin on his face and torso
   D. When baby cries, mother says, "Shut up already." Baby has a foul odour and looks dirty

9. Which of the following 6-month-olds has the most markers for a possible genetic disorder?
   A. Has large ears, is in the 95th percentile for weight and height, babbles
   B. Has large scaly plaques on face and torso, red reflex is absent in one eye, posterior fontanel has closed
   C. Has significant head lag, one ear is small and malformed, nipples are unusually close together
   D. Sits up alone, cranial sutures are palpable, back of the head is flat

Canadian Nursing Research

Duhn, L. (2010). The importance of touch in the development of attachment. *Advances in Neonatal Care, 10*(6), 294–300.

Letourneau, N., Young, C., et al. (2011). Supporting mothering: Service providers' perspectives of mothers and young children affected by intimate partner violence. *Research in Nursing and Health, 9*(10), 35–38.

Semenic, S., Loiselle, C., et al. (2008). Predictors of the duration of exclusive breastfeeding among first time mothers. *Research in Nursing and Health, 31*(5), 428–441.

Twells, L., & Newhook, L. A. (2010). Can exclusive breastfeeding reduce the likelihood of childhood obesity in some regions of Canada? *Canadian Journal of Public Health, 101*(1), 36–39.

References

Alberta Health Services. (2010a). *Immunization schedules.* Retrieved from www.health.alberta.ca/health-info/imm-routine-schedule.html

Alberta Health Services. (2010b). *How family violence affects young children.* Retrieved from:http://www.calgaryhealthregion.ca/pem/PublicSearch?direct=displayPdf&number=605994

Alberta Health Services. (2011a). *Growing miracles: Physical development – infants.* Retrieved from www.albertahealthservices.ca/1906.asp

Alberta Health Services. (2011b). *Growing miracles: Developmental milestones 0–3 months.* Retrieved from www.albertahealthservices.ca/1869.asp

Anda, R. F., Felitti, V. J., et al. (2005). The enduring effects of abuse and related adverse experiences in childhood. A convergence of evidence from neurobiology and epidemiology. *European Archives of Psychiatry and Clinical Neuroscience, 256*(3), 174–186.

Anderson, M. L. (2005). Atopic dermatitis—More than a simple skin disorder. *Journal of the American Academy of Nurse Practitioners, 17*(7), 249–255.

El-Baba, M. F., Bassali, R. W., et al. (2009). Failure to thrive. In M. R. Mascarenhas, M. L. Windle, et al. (Eds.). *eMedicine.* Retrieved from http://emedicine.medscape.com/article/985007

Bulechek, G. B., Butcher, H. K., et al. (2008). *Nursing interventions classification (NIC)* (5th ed.). St. Louis, MO: Mosby.

Canadian Pediatric Society. (2009). *Position statement: Management of acute otitis media.* Retrieved from http://www.calgaryhealthregion.ca/pem/PublicSearch?direct=displayPdf&number=605994

Canadian Pediatric Society. (2010). *Position statement: Temperature measurement in pediatrics*. Retrieved from http://www.cps.ca/english/statements/cp/cp00-01.htm

Canadian Pediatric Society. (1996). *Position statement: Facilitating discharge home following a normal term birth*. Retrieved from www.cps.ca/english/statements/FN/fn96-02.htm#TABLE 1- (under revision)

Department of Justice Canada. (2009). *Child abuse: A fact sheet from the department of justice Canada*. Retrieved from http://www.justice.gc.ca/eng/pi/fv-vf/facts-info/child-enf.html#widespread

Eczema Canada. (2007). *What is Eczema?* Retrieved from http://www.eczemacanada.ca/en/what/index.php

Giardino, A. P., & Giardino, E. R. (2008a). Child abuse and neglect: Physical abuse. In C. J. Johnson, M. L. Windle, et al. (Eds.). *eMedicine*. Retrieved from http://emedicine.medscape.com/article/915664

Giardino, A. P., & Giardino, E. R. (2008b). Child abuse and neglect: Sexual abuse. In C. J. Johnson, M. L. Windle, et al. (Eds.). *eMedicine*. Retrieved from http://emedicine.medscape.com/article/915841

Health Canada. (2009). *Healthy living: Cavities*. Retrieved from http://www.hc-sc.gc.ca/hl-vs/oral-bucco/disease-maladie/cavities-caries-eng.php

Hornor, G. (2005). Physical abuse: Recognition and reporting. *Journal of Pediatric Health Care, 19*(1), 4–11.

Hurme, T., Alanko, S., et al. (2008). Risk factors for physical child abuse in infants and toddlers. *European Journal of Pediatric Surgery, 18*(6), 287–291.

Kemp, A. M., Dunstan, F., et al. (2009). Patterns of skeletal fractures in child abuse: Systematic review. *Child: Care, Health & Development, 35*(1), 141–142, 1365–2214.

London, M. L., Ladewig, P. W., et al. (2007). *Maternal and child nursing care* (2nd ed.). Upper Saddle River, NJ: Pearson Education.

Moorhead, S., Johnson, M., et al. (2008). *Nursing outcomes classification (NOC)* (4th ed.). Philadelphia, PA: Mosby.

Morley, C. J., Thornton, A. J., et al. (1991). Symptoms and signs of infants younger than 6 months of age correlated with the severity of their illness. *Pediatrics, 88*(6), 1119–1124. Retrieved from www.pediatrics.org

North American Nursing Diagnosis Association-International. (2009). *Nursing diagnoses: Definitions and classification*. West Sussex, UK: Wiley-Blackwell.

Nelson, K. E., & Williams, C. M. (2006). *Infectious disease epidemiology: Theory and practice* (2nd ed.). Sudbury, MA: Jones and Bartlett Publishers.

Polonko, K. A. (2006). Exploring assumptions about child neglect in relation to the broader field of child maltreatment. *Journal of Health and Human Services Administration, 29*(3), 260–284.

Public Health Agency of Canada. (2008). *Canadian incidence study of reported child abuse and neglect*. Retrieved from http://www.justice.gc.ca/eng/pi/fv-vf/facts-info/child-enf.html#widespread

Public Health Agency of Canada. (2010). *Safe sleep for your baby*. Retrieved from http://www.phac-aspc.gc.ca/hp-ps/dca-dea/stages-etapes/childhood-enfance_0-2/sids/pdf/sleep-sommeil-eng.pdf

Public Health Agency of Canada. (n.d.). *Leading causes of death and hospitalization in infants under 1 year*. Retrieved from http://www.phac-aspc.gc.ca/publicat/lcd-pcd97/table1-eng.php

Ranweiler, R. (2009). Assessment and care of the newborn with Down syndrome. *Advances in Neonatal Care, 9*(1), 17–24.

Rennie, C. E., van Wyk, F. C., et al. (2009). Pneumatic otoscope examination. In R. G. Bachur, M. L. Windle, et al. (Eds.). *eMedicine*. Retrieved from http://emedicine.medscape.com/article/1348950

Ricci, L., & Botash, A. S. (2008). Pediatrics, child abuse. In K. A. Bechtel, M. L. Windle, et al (Eds.). *eMedicine*. Retrieved from http://emedicine.medscape.com/article/800657

Safe Kids Canada. (2010). *Safety information for professionals*. Retrieved from http://www.safekidscanada.ca/Professionals

Santrock, J. (2006). *Life-span development* (10th ed.). New York, NY: McGraw-Hill.

Shin, H. T. (2006). Diaper dermatitis that does not quit. *Dermatologic Therapy, 18*(2), 124–135.

Simon, H. K. (2009). Pediatrics, crying child. In K. A. Bechtel, M. L. Windle, et al. (Eds.). *eMedicine*. Retrieved from http://emedicine.medscape.com/article/800964

Waseem, M., Aslam, M., et al. (2008). Otitis media. In O. Brown, M. L. Windle, et al. (Eds.). *eMedicine*. Retrieved from http://emedicine.medscape.com/article/994656

Wong, S. C., Scarfone, R. J., et al. (2008). Fever in the neonate and young child. In K. A. Bechtel, M. L. Windle, et al. (Eds.). *eMedicine*. Retrieved from http://emedicine.medscape.com/article/800286

World Health Organization. (2011). *The WHO child growth standards*. Retrieved from http://www.who.int/childgrowth/standards/en/

The Canadian Jensen's Nursing Health Assessment suite offers these additional resources to enhance learning and facilitate understanding of this chapter:

- thePoint on line resource, http//thepoint.lww.com/Stephen1E
- *Laboratory Manual for Canadian Jensen's Nursing Health Assessment: A Best Practice Approach*

Tables of Unexpected Findings

⚠ Table 28-5 · Diseases With Characteristic Odours Evident in Infants

Odour	Disease or Condition
Rotten or offensive odour from the nose or vagina	Retained foreign body (eg, anything little hands can grasp and push into these body openings), poor hygiene
Mousy odour	Phenylketonuria
Maple syrup odour to the urine	Maple syrup urine disease
Foul odour of umbilical area	Omphalitis
Noxious mouth odour	Ingestion of a chemical such as kerosene, bleach, glue, and alcohol

⚠ Table 28-6 · Red Flags for Child Abuse

Category	Details
Reported history of injury	The story keeps changing or is inconsistent between partners or over time. Details of the trauma do not correlate with the type or extent of injury. No history of trauma is given.
Delay in treatment	A significant delay elapses between the time of injury and when the parent seeks treatment.
"Doctor shopping"	Parent changes physicians, health care facilities, or both frequently.
Injuries consistent with abuse	Bruises appear on infants before they walk. Bruising or other injuries are in varied stages of healing. Multiple types of injuries appear. Injuries resemble an object, such as cigarette burns, burns in the shape of an iron, or loop marks. Grab or slap marks or human bite marks are visible. Evidence exists of immersion burns—these are usually well-demarcated and bilateral (eg, both hands or feet) or occur on the buttocks and feet.
Fractured bone	Any fracture in an infant who is not walking should raise the index of suspicion for abuse, unless there is a verifiable cause (eg, motor vehicle collision, documented bone disorder predisposing to bone fragility).
Types of fractures associated with physical abuse	These include the following: • Multiple fractures • Fractured ribs ≈ 70% chance infant was abused • Fractured humerus (especially mid-shaft and spiral/oblique) ≈ 50% chance of abuse • Skull fracture ≈ 30% chance of abuse (Kemp, Dunstan, et al., 2009).
Pattern of injury consistent with shaken baby syndrome	Signs include subdural hematoma, retinal hemorrhages, rib fractures, and bilateral bruising in the rib cage.
Injuries consistent with sexual abuse	Any of the following in the genital area, anus, or both indicates sexual abuse: • Bleeding • Bruising • Redness
Signs of neglect	Examples include failure to thrive, lack of emotional bonding with parent(s), developmental delays, overly anxious behaviour, poor hygiene, clothes inappropriate for the weather, evidence of tissue wasting, signs of poor nutrition, failure to gain weight, and untreated illness.

Adapted from Alberta Health Services. (2010b). *How family violence affects young children*. Retrieved from:http://www.calgaryhealthre-gion.ca/pem/PublicSearch?direct=displayPdf&number=605994; Giardino, A. P., & Giardino, E. R. (2008a). Child abuse and neglect: Physical abuse. In C. J. Johnson, M. L. Windle, et al. (Eds.). *eMedicine*. Retrieved from http://emedicine.medscape.com/article/915664; Giardino, A. P., & Giardino, E. R. (2008b). Child abuse and neglect: Sexual abuse. In C. J. Johnson, M. L. Windle, et al. (Eds.). *eMedicine*. Retrieved from http://emedicine.medscape.com/article/915841; Hornor, G. (2005). Physical abuse: Recognition and reporting. *Journal of Pediatric Health Care, 19*(1), 4–11; Hurme, T., Alanko, S., et al. (2008). Risk factors for physical child abuse in infants and toddlers. *European Journal of Pediatric Surgery, 18*(6), 287–291; Polonko, K. A. (2006). Exploring assumptions about child neglect in relation to the broader field of child maltreatment. *Journal of Health and Human Services Administration, 29*(3), 260–284; Ricci, L., & Botash, A. S. (2008). Pediatrics, child abuse. In K. A. Bechtel, M. L. Windle, et al. (Eds.), *eMedicine*. Retrieved from http://emedicine.medscape.com/article/800657

Table 28-7   Unexpected Skin Conditions in Newborns and Infants

Infections and Infestations

Pediculosis Capitis (Head Lice)

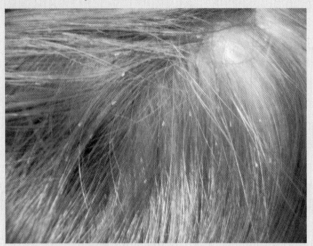

This highly contagious condition results from infestation with the human head louse, *pediculus humanus capitis*. Lice spread easily among children through close personal contact and sharing hairbrushes and other belongings.

Scabies

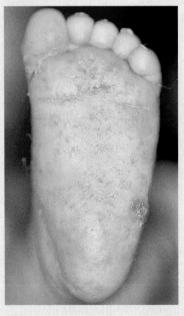

Scabies results from an allergic reaction to the *Sarcoptes scabiei* mite and her eggs. In infants, large blistering lesions and suppurative vesicles comprise the characteristic rash. The condition is highly contagious.

Tinea Corporis (Ringworm)

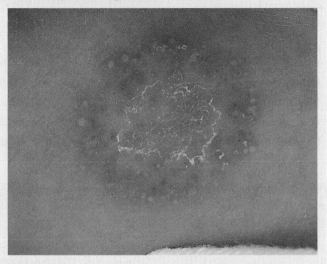

This fungal infection (dermatophytosis) is superficial. Because fungi prefer warm, moist environments, preventing ringworm involves keeping skin dry and avoiding contact with infectious material. Children are most likely to acquire the infection from an animal host, although human-to-human contact does occur as well.

Staphylococcal Scalded Skin Syndrome

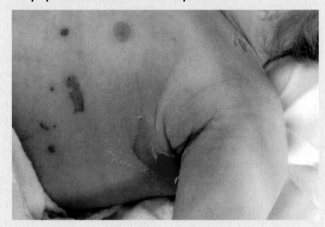

Acute exfoliation of the skin results from infection with a staphylococcal exotoxin. Pediatric populations are most susceptible to the condition, which usually heals within 2 wk.

Molluscum Contagiosum

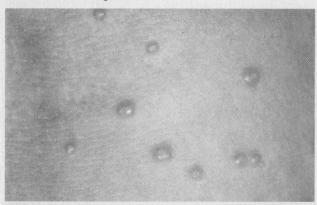

This virus spreads by direct contact; children with atopic dermatitis are especially vulnerable. The infection takes approximately 6–9 mo to resolve.

Bullous Impetigo

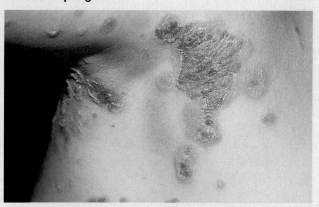

This common superficial staphylococcal infection is characterized by fluid-filled vesicles and blisters that easily rupture. It is a milder form of staphylococcal scalded skin syndrome (see previous page).

Contact Dermatitis and Inflammatory and Allergy-Related Conditions

Intertrigo

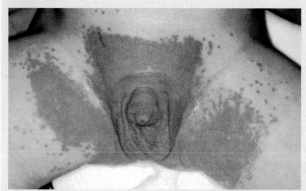

Inflammation of the skinfolds results from skin-on-skin friction. It can be a cause of diaper rash. Intertrigo frequently develops in people who are obese and are in older age groups as well.

Irritant Diaper Dermatitis

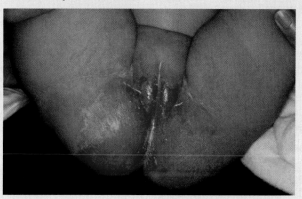

The typical "diaper rash" results from prolonged exposure of the affected areas to urine and stool. Aggravating factors include a diaper left on too long, a tight-fitting diaper, rubbing and chafing of the diaper, and diarrhea (Shin, 2006).

Candidal Diaper Dermatitis

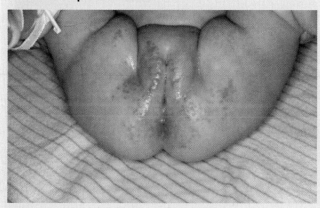

This type of diaper rash results from infection with *Candida albicans*, a fungus.

Allergic Contact Diaper Dermatitis

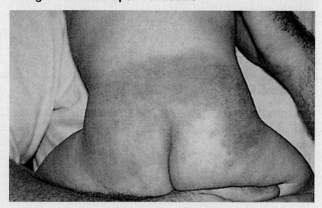

This type of diaper rash develops when the child's skin is in contact with an allergen.

(table continues on page 896)

Eczema (Atopic Dermatitis)

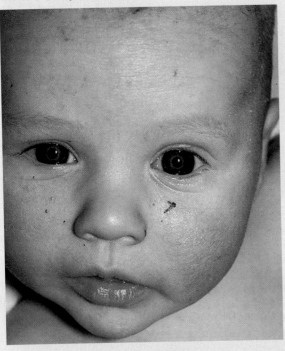

This skin condition usually appears in the first 6 mo of life and typically resolves by age 5 y. It is characterized by dry, itchy, irritated skin. The exact cause is unknown, but a familial link and allergic component exist. Treatment, generally with topical corticosteroids, aims at controlling symptoms (Anderson, 2005; Eczema Canada, 2007).

Lichen Simplex Chronicus

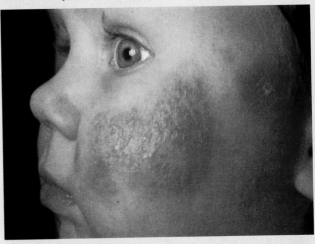

These discrete patches of eczema (thickened skin with scaling) result from irritation that follows repetitive rubbing or scratching. Secondary infections occasionally occur from breaks in the skin caused by excessive scratching.

Psoriasis

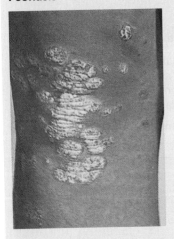

This proliferative, inflammatory, autoimmune disease is characterized by well-defined plaques covered by silvery scales.

Hives (Urticaria)

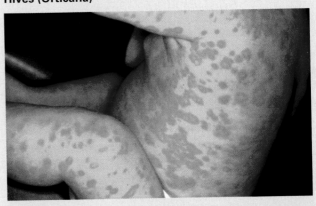

Hives are an allergic skin reaction characterized by pruritic plaques with pale centralized edematous wheals surrounded by erythematous areas, called flares. Hives are considered chronic if they last longer than 6 wk.

Skin Tumours/Hyperpigmented Lesions

Café Au Lait Spots

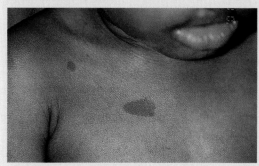

Spots start out as light brown pigmented lesions during infancy. They grow and darken as the child grows. If these spots are noted during an examination, the infant needs medical evaluation to rule out neurofibromatosis. Café au lait spots may be the only sign of this inherited disorder; however, the child needs close medical observation throughout childhood because of the devastating sequelae of neurofibromatosis.

Port Wine Stains

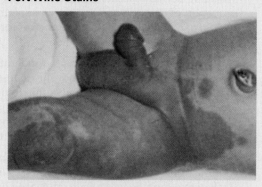

Also called *nevus flammeus*, these congenital capillary lesions are characterized by pink-to-purple or red patches anywhere on the body. The lesions can be disfiguring, particularly if they are large or on the face. Port wine stains grow proportionately with the child and often darken over time. Laser treatment is often effective.

Adapted from Nelson, K. E., & Williams, C. M. (2006). *Infectious disease epidemiology: Theory and practice* (2nd ed.). Sudbury, MA: Jones and Bartlett Publishers.

Disorder	Description
Cystic fibrosis	This autosomal-recessive disorder is most common in Caucasians. It is characterized by unexpected transport of chloride and sodium in exocrine tissues. The result is thick viscous secretions in the lungs, pancreas, liver, intestine, and reproductive tract. Pulmonary complications generally lead to early death. Average life expectancy is 30 y but is increasing due to successful lung transplantation.
Down's syndrome (Trisomy 21)	An extra chromosome 21 leads to moderate-to-severe mental retardation and affects almost every organ system. Common dysmorphic features include microcephaly, brachycephaly, up-slanting palpebral fissures, bilateral epicanthal folds, Brushfield's spots, flat nasal bridge, pronounced curve on the ear helix, protruding tongue, and unusually placed nipples. Low-set thumbs, inward curvature of the little fingers, a simian (single palmar) crease, and a wide space between the great and second toes are other characteristics. Generalized hypotonia is noted in infants.
Fragile X syndrome	This most common cause of inherited mental retardation results from extra genetic material on the X chromosome. Dysmorphic features in infants include a prominent forehead, long narrow face with a high arched palate, and large ears, jaw, and testes. Young children demonstrate delayed development, hyperactivity, and autistic behaviour.
Klinefelter's syndrome	A male inherits an extra X chromosome, with genotype XXY. The earlier the syndrome is diagnosed, the better the outcome; however, many patients are not diagnosed until adulthood when infertility becomes apparent. Characteristics include enlarged breasts, sparse hair, small testes, and no sperm production.
Triple X syndrome	A female inherits an extra X chromosome, with genotype XXX. This condition does not typically result in infertility. Some females experience learning disabilities and social difficulties; others are affected so mildly that they are never diagnosed.
Trisomy 13	The effects of an extra chromosome 13 are so devastating that only approximately 18% of infants with it live >1 y. Survivors are severely retarded. Physical characteristics include microcephaly, microphthalmia (small eyes), cleft lip/palate, spina bifida, polydactyly, deafness, and heart defects.
Trisomy 18	An extra chromosome 18 severely affects all organ systems. Characteristics include profound retardation, microcephaly, prominent occiput, microphthalmia, epicanthal folds, short palpebral fissures, micrognathia (small jaw), ear malformations, and severe cardiac defects. Only approximately 10% of infants survive beyond 1 y of age.
Turner's syndrome	Caused by a missing X chromosome, this condition affects females only. Physical characteristics vary greatly, partly depending on how much X chromosome is missing. Characteristics include micrognathia, prominent ears, short neck with webbing, short fourth and fifth fingers, and heart and kidney defects. Incomplete sexual development and infertility are characteristics in adult women.

Children and Adolescents

Learning Objectives

1 Demonstrate knowledge of anatomy and physiology of each body system in the child or adolescent that may be different than in the adult.

2 Identify important topics for health promotion and risk reduction related to children and adolescents.

3 Collect subjective data including the health history and review of systems from the child's and caregiver's perspectives.

4 Collect objective data related to the child or adolescent using physical examination techniques.

5 Identify expected and unexpected findings related to the assessment of children and adolescents.

6 Consider the condition, age, gender, and culture of the patient to individualize health assessment.

7 Analyze subjective and objective data from the assessment of children and adolescents to identify nursing diagnoses and plan initial interventions.

8 Document and communicate data from the assessment of children and adolescents using appropriate terminology and principles of recording.

9 Identify nursing diagnoses and initiate a plan of care based on findings from the assessment of children and adolescents.

*S*am Maratas, a 4-year-old Filipino boy, presents to the school-based health centre for a preschool physical examination. He lives with his parents. His 23-year-old mother stays home all day with him and his newborn sister and his 24-year-old father drives a delivery truck for a local grocery distributor; Sam's father leaves for work at 0700 and returns most evenings by 1730 when he assists with care of the children.

Sam has not been in a structured preschool or day care environment. This fall will be his first exposure to care and formalized instruction outside the home. He seems excited about his new opportunity and is willing to discuss the new school with the nurse. Sam has never been hospitalized, but he has been treated in the emergency department twice for coughing and wheezing. He also has had frequent ear infections; the last one was 3 weeks ago. He has never had surgery. He has no known allergies; his only medication is a daily multivitamin with iron.

You will acquire more information about Sam's present health status and past health history as you progress through this chapter. As you study this content and features, consider Sam's situation. Begin thinking about the following points:

* What health information and assessments are important for the toddler, preschooler, school-aged child, and adolescent?
* How do assessment findings differ between the child and adult?
* What adaptations will the nurse make when assessing a child?

The focus of this chapter is health assessment for children and adolescents. It includes information about past and present health history along with related physical examination findings most pertinent for children and adolescents. These patients live with caregivers who have legal health care decision-making capacity for them. Therefore, caring for children and adolescents requires the nurse to involve both the parent/caregiver and child/adolescent in assessment, diagnosis, planning, intervention, and evaluation.

The Child Health divisions of the Public Health Agency of Canada (2011) and Healthy Canadians (2011) are national health promotion and injury prevention agencies that address children's health needs within the context of family and community. They acknowledge that a multitude of support people and agencies are necessary to raise healthy children and to build the necessary foundation for them to develop into healthy productive adult citizens. Therefore, health assessment of the child or adolescent also includes assessing community support, environmental exposures, and potential opportunities for health promotion (see thePoint ✳ for a link to more information about national child health programs in Canada).

Anatomy and Physiology Overview

Physical Growth

Although children grow and develop at varying rates, they do both at predictable times according to previously established ranges. Health care professionals must evaluate a child's physical growth with the use of standardized growth charts. The World Health Organization (WHO) 2006 Child Growth Standards for children from birth to 5 years and the WHO 2007 Growth Reference Charts for children and adolescents from 5 to 19 years are recommended for the assessment of growth of Canadian children (Canadian Paediatric Society, 2010). These can be downloaded from the Canadian Paediatric Society (2010) or Dietitians of Canada (2011) websites.

Growth charts are separate for boys and girls. Charts for children 0 to 3 years are for heights measured while recumbent; charts for children 2 to 18 years are for children measured upright with a stadiometer. Children are weighed on a calibrated scale. For children older than 2 years, health care professionals calculate and plot body mass index (BMI) on the appropriate BMI chart. **Head circumference** is measured on children 0 to 3 years and plotted on similar growth charts (see Chapters 9 and 28).

Motor Development

Motor development of children is described as cephalocaudal (from head to toe) and proximal distal (from the center outward). For example, the infant gains head control before the ability to lift the chest off the bed. In addition, children master gross motor movements before attaining fine motor control.

Refinement of motor activity and skills continues throughout childhood and adolescence. Refer to Chapter 9 for more information. Assessment of motor development is discussed later in the "Objective Data Collection" section.

⚠ SAFETY ALERT 29-1
Safety precautions in children change according to age group because of the variation in their developing motor abilities. For instance, covering electrical outlets is important once a child begins to sit well, while protecting the child from falls down stairs begins to matter more once the child can roll, crawl, or walk.

Language

A child develops speech and speech sounds in a predictable manner. Evaluation of the child's initiation and continuance of sounds, as well as articulation, is critical throughout the early years.

At birth the child cries. He or she then learns to coo and babble, as well as how to gesture. By 10 to 15 months, the child says the first word; by 18 months, he or she has a vocabulary of approximately 50 words. Most children use two-word sentences by 2 years of age. By 3 years of age, their sentences are more complicated, and their speech is completely understandable to most people. Refer to Chapter 9 for more information.

A delay in **speech development** may signal a hearing loss or mental health concerns (eg, autism). Screening for autism is recommended at 18 months and 2 years of age with a tool such as the Modified Checklist for Autism in Toddlers (Robins, Fein, et al., 1999) and with a structured developmental tool when the child is 2½ years old.

Clinical Significance 29-1

Children who babble at 4 to 6 months of age and then stop babbling may have an acquired hearing loss. Those who never babble may have a congenital hearing loss or a hearing loss since birth.

Psychosocial and Cognitive Development

Psychosocial and cognitive development related to and influential on the health of children and adolescents is discussed in detail in Chapter 9.

Acute Assessment

Children who present in physiological distress compensate with increased respiratory and heart rates. Physiological distress often results from a respiratory disorder or significant blood loss (even children with a known congenital heart disorder rarely present in acute distress from ischemic heart

Table 29-1 Recommended Intervals for Health Assessment of Children and Adolescents

American Academy of Pediatrics
DEDICATED TO THE HEALTH OF ALL CHILDREN™

Recommendations for Preventive Pediatric Health Care

Bright Futures/American Academy of Pediatrics

Bright Futures™
Prevention and health promotion for infants, children, adolescents, and their families™

Each child and family is unique; therefore, these **Recommendations for Preventive Pediatric Health Care** are designed for the care of children who are receiving competent parenting, have no manifestations of any important health problems, and are growing and developing in satisfactory fashion. **Additional visits may become necessary** if circumstances suggest variations from normal.

Developmental, psychosocial, and chronic disease issues for children and adolescents may require frequent counseling and treatment visits separate from preventive care visits.

These guidelines represent a consensus by the American Academy of Pediatrics (AAP) and Bright Futures. The AAP continues to emphasize the great importance of **continuity of care** in comprehensive health supervision and the need to avoid **fragmentation of care.**

The recommendations in this statement do not indicate an exclusive course of treatment or standard of medical care. Variations, taking into account individual circumstances, may be appropriate.

Copyright © 2008 by the American Academy of Pediatrics.

No part of this statement may be reproduced in any form or by any means without prior written permission from the American Academy of Pediatrics except for one copy for personal use.

	INFANCY								EARLY CHILDHOOD							MIDDLE CHILDHOOD						ADOLESCENCE										
AGE[1]	PRENATAL[2]	NEWBORN[3]	3–5 d[4]	By 1 mo	2 mo	4 mo	6 mo	9 mo	12 m	15 mo	18 mo	24 mo	30 mo	3 y	4 y	5 y	6 y	7 y	8 y	9 y	10 y	11 y	12 y	13 y	14 y	15 y	16 y	17 y	18 y	19 y	20 y	21 y
HISTORY																																
Initial/Interval	●	●	●	●	●	●	●	●	●	●	●	●	●	●	●	●	●	●	●	●	●	●	●	●	●	●	●	●	●	●	●	●
MEASUREMENTS																																
Length/Height and Weight		●	●	●	●	●	●	●	●	●	●	●	●	●	●	●	●	●	●	●	●	●	●	●	●	●	●	●	●	●	●	●
Head Circumference		●	●	●	●	●	●	●	●	●	●	●																				
Weight for Length		●	●	●	●	●	●	●	●	●	●																					
Body Mass Index												●	●	●	●	●	●	●	●	●	●	●	●	●	●	●	●	●	●	●	●	●
Blood Pressure[5]		★	★	★	★	★	★	★	★	★	★	★	★	●	●	●	●	●	●	●	●	●	●	●	●	●	●	●	●	●	●	●
SENSORY SCREENING																																
Vision		★	★	★	★	★	★	★	★	★	★	★	★	●[6]	●	●	●	★	●	★	●	★	●	★	★	●	★	★	●	★	★	★
Hearing		●[7]	★	★	★	★	★	★	★	★	★	★	★	★	●	●	●	★	●	★	●	★	★	★	★	★	★	★	★	★	★	★
DEVELOPMENTAL/BEHAVIORAL ASSESSMENT																																
Developmental Screening[8]								●			●		●																			
Autism Screening[9]											●	●																				
Developmental Surveillance[8]		●	●	●	●	●	●		●	●		●		●	●	●	●	●	●	●	●	●	●	●	●	●	●	●	●	●	●	●
Psychosocial/Behavioral Assessment		●	●	●	●	●	●	●	●	●	●	●	●	●	●	●	●	●	●	●	●	●	●	●	●	●	●	●	●	●	●	●
Alcohol and Drug Use Assessment																						★	★	★	★	★	★	★	★	★	★	★
PHYSICAL EXAMINATION[10]		●	●	●	●	●	●	●	●	●	●	●	●	●	●	●	●	●	●	●	●	●	●	●	●	●	●	●	●	●	●	●
PROCEDURES[11]																																
Newborn Metabolic/Hemoglobin Screening[12]		←	●	→																												
Immunization[13]		●	●	●	●	●	●	●	●	●	●	●	●	●	●	●	●	●	●	●	●	●	●	●	●	●	●	●	●	●	●	●
Hematocrit or Hemoglobin[14]						★			●		★	★		★	★	★	★	★	★	★	★	★	★	★	★	★	★	★	★	★	★	★
Lead Screening[15]							★	★	● or ★[16]		★	● or ★[16]		★	★	★	★															
Tuberculin Test[17]				★			★		★		★	★		★	★	★	★	★	★	★	★	★	★	★	★	★	★	★	★	★	★	★
Dyslipidemia Screening[18]												★			★		★		★		★	★	★	★	★	★	★	★	←		●	→
STI Screening[19]																						★	★	★	★	★	★	★	★	★	★	★
Cervical Dysplasia Screening[20]																						★	★	★	★	★	★	★	★	★	★	★
ORAL HEALTH[21]							★	★	● or ★[21]		● or ★[21]	● or ★[21]	● or ★[21]	●[22]			●[22]															
ANTICIPATORY GUIDANCE[23]	●	●	●	●	●	●	●	●	●	●	●	●	●	●	●	●	●	●	●	●	●	●	●	●	●	●	●	●	●	●	●	●

1. If a child comes under care for the first time at any point on the schedule, or if any items are not accomplished at the suggested age, the schedule should be brought up to date at the earliest possible time.
2. A prenatal visit is recommended for parents who are at high risk, for first-time parents, and for those who request a conference. The prenatal visit should include anticipatory guidance, pertinent medical history, and a discussion of benefits of breastfeeding and planned method of feeding per AAP statement "The Prenatal Visit" (2001) [URL: http://aappolicy.aappublications.org/cgi/content/full/pediatrics;107/6/1456].
3. Every infant should have a newborn evaluation after birth, breastfeeding encouraged, and instruction and support offered.
4. Every infant should have an evaluation within 3 to 5 days of birth and within 48 to 72 hours after discharge from the hospital, to include evaluation for feeding and jaundice. Breastfeeding infants should receive formal breastfeeding evaluation, encouragement, and instruction as recommended in AAP statement "Breastfeeding and the Use of Human Milk" (2005) [URL: http://aappolicy.aappublications.org/cgi/content/full/pediatrics;115/2/496]. For newborns discharged in less than 48 hours after delivery, the infant must be examined within 48 hours of discharge per AAP statement "Hospital Stay for Healthy Term Newborns" (2004) [URL: http://aappolicy.aappublications.org/cgi/content/full/pediatrics;113/5/1434].
5. Blood pressure measurement in infants and children with specific risk conditions should be performed at visits before age 3 years.
6. If the patient is uncooperative, rescreen within 6 months per AAP statement "Eye Examination in Infants, Children, and Young Adults by Pediatricians" (2007) [URL: http://aappolicy.aappublications.org/cgi/content/full/pediatrics;111/4/902].
7. All newborns should be screened per AAP statement "Year 2000 Position Statement: Principles and Guidelines for Early Hearing Detection and Intervention Programs " (2000) [URL: http://aappolicy.aappublications.org/cgi/content/full/pediatrics;106/4/798]. Joint Committee on Infant Hearing. Year 2007 position statement: principles and guidelines for early hearing detection and intervention programs. *Pediatrics.* 2007;120:898–921.
8. AAP Council on Children With Disabilities, AAP Section on Developmental Behavioral Pediatrics, AAP Bright Futures Steering Committee, AAP Medical Home Initiatives for Children With Special Needs Project Advisory Committee. Identifying infants and young children with developmental disorders in the medical home: an algorithm for developmental surveillance and screening. *Pediatrics.* 2006;118;405–420 [URL: http://aappolicy.aappublications.org/cgi/content/full/pediatrics;118/1/405].
9. Gupta VB, Hyman SL, Johnson CP, et al. Identifying children with autism early? *Pediatrics.* 2007;119:152–153 [URL: http://pediatrics.aappublications.org/cgi/content/full/119/1/152].
10. At each visit, age-appropriate physical examination is essential, with infant totally unclothed, older child undressed and suitably draped.
11. These may be modified, depending on entry point into schedule and individual need.
12. Newborn metabolic and hemoglobinopathy screening should be done according to state law. Results should be reviewed at visits and appropriate retesting or referral done as needed.
13. Schedules per the Committee on Infectious Diseases, published annually in the January issue of *Pediatrics.* Every visit should be an opportunity to update and complete a child's immunizations.
14. See AAP *Pediatric Nutrition Handbook,* 5th Edition (2003) for a discussion of universal and selective screening options. See also Recommendations to prevent and control iron deficiency in the United States. *MMWR.* 1998;47(RR-3):1–36.
15. For children at risk of lead exposure, consult the AAP statement "Lead Exposure in Children: Prevention, Detection, and Management" (2005) [URL: http://aappolicy.aappublications.org/cgi/content/full/pediatrics;116/4/1036]. Additionally, screening should be done in accordance with state law where applicable.
16. Perform risk assessments or screens as appropriate, based on universal screening requirements for patients with Medicaid or high prevalence areas.
17. Tuberculosis testing per recommendations of the Committee on Infectious Diseases, published in the current edition of *Red Book: Report of the Committee on Infectious Diseases.* Testing should be done on recognition of high-risk factors.
18. "Third Report of the National Cholesterol Education Program (NCEP) Expert Panel on Detection, Evaluation, and Treatment of High Blood Cholesterol in Adults (Adult Treatment Panel III) Final Report" (2002) [URL: http://circ.ahajournals.org/cgi/content/full/106/25/3143] and "The Expert Committee Recommendations on the Assessment, Prevention, and Treatment of Child and Adolescent Overweight and Obesity." Supplement to *Pediatrics.* In press.
19. All sexually active patients should be screened for sexually transmitted infections (STIs).
20. All sexually active girls should have screening for cervical dysplasia as part of a pelvic examination beginning within 3 years of onset of sexual activity or age 21 (whichever comes first).
21. Referral to dental home, if available. Otherwise, administer oral health risk assessment. If the primary water source is deficient in fluoride, consider oral fluoride supplementation.
22. At the visits for 3 years and 6 years of age, it should be determined whether the patient has a dental home. If the patient does not have a dental home, a referral should be made to one. If the primary water source is deficient in fluoride, consider oral fluoride supplementation.
23. Refer to the specific guidance by age as listed in Bright Futures Guidelines. (Hagan JF, Shaw JS, Duncan PM, eds. *Bright Futures: Guidelines for Health Supervision of Infants, Children, and Adolescents.* 3rd ed. Elk Grove Village, IL: American Academy of Pediatrics; 2008.)

KEY

● = to be performed ★ = risk assessment to be performed, with appropriate action to follow, if positive ←●→ = range during which a service may be provided, with the symbol indicating the preferred age

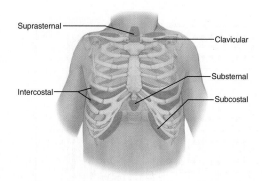

Figure 29-1 Sites of retractions.

Labels: Suprasternal, Clavicular, Substernal, Intercostal, Subcostal

disease). Therefore, administration of oxygen and support of the child's ability to breathe are the first interventions. The child should remain sitting upright with the parent or in the parents' lap to promote optimal ventilation and to prevent the child from becoming upset, because crying requires additional oxygen and respiratory effort. Supplemental oxygen can be delivered by the parent via a mask held in place or close to the child's nose and mouth. The additional work of breathing is evidenced in a distressed child by nasal flaring accompanied by supracostal, intercostal, and subcostal chest retractions (Fig. 29-1) or abdominal breathing.

Emergency assessment and care is indicated for children in distress; once they cannot compensate for oxygen requirements, they may soon require mechanical ventilation. Other acute situations include trauma, head injury, meningitis, and acute abdomen (eg, ruptured appendix).

Subjective Data Collection

Often several caregivers are involved with one child. If parents and child have agreed upon and given consent to include other family members or friends in their care, the nurse may share information with those designated people. This is especially true if the child is very young or has a chronic condition requiring adaptations to everyday life. This is less true as the child becomes an adolescent and begins to seek care for himself or herself alone.

Legal consent for health care treatment is 18 years of age. Most provinces, however, permit contraception and treatment for sexually transmitted infections (STIs) at 13 years.

⚠ **SAFETY ALERT 29-2**
Most provinces require patients to be of legal consenting age for the treatment of other infections or health conditions unless an adolescent has been deemed an emancipated minor by being married, being a parent themselves, or having the appropriate legal documentation.

Health assessment of a child or adolescent begins the moment that he or she enters the facility. Nurses can ascertain much information by observing the patient's interactions with caregivers and nurses. The nurse can assess the pediatric patient's ability to communicate along with movement capabilities when transferring from one room to the next. Children and teens demonstrate many developmental skills during the screening process. Focused observation of, and purposeful interactions with, children provide opportunities for nurses in the health care setting to assess children in a nonthreatening manner.

The nurse's assessment requires patience and skill to acquire the health information from children. The health assessment should not be traumatic for patient or nurse. It is a time to learn about staying healthy and a chance for the nurse to reinforce positive lifelong health habits. For children and adolescents, health-related patient teaching focuses on healthy lifestyle choices such as nutrition and exercise. Teaching also includes information about the avoidance of unhealthy habits frequently acquired at early ages (eg, tobacco use). Additional information includes safety and the importance of emotional health and positive interpersonal relationships. Nurses can also incorporate assessment of school performance and its compatibility with stated life goals into the well-child health assessment.

Assessment of Risk Factors

Questions to Assess History and Risk Factors	Rationale
Reason for Seeking Care Tell me why you came to the clinic today? Or why did you have to come to the hospital?	Obtain information on the reason for seeking care. Ask follow-up questions if the child has pain or discomfort.
Personal History Has your child been hospitalized? Has he or she had surgery? What were the reasons? What were the outcomes? Does your son/daughter have any health conditions?	Significant past health issues may be related to a present concern.
Prenatal History The nurse asks questions related to • Maternal health • Medications	Perinatal environment and exposures may affect the child's present health. Premature and small-for-gestational-age babies may have long-term sequelae if their transition to

- Exposure to toxic substances, alcohol, or illicit drugs
- Birth history
- Birth weight
- Birth date/due date
- Labour and birth experience

Postnatal History

- Did the baby go home with the mother from the hospital?
- Were there any difficulties once home?
- Did the baby have jaundice? If so, did he or she require treatment?

Developmental History (Depending on Current Age of Child)

- Did the child develop like other children?
- At what age did he or she sit? Stand? Walk?
- When was his or her first word? What was it?
- When was the child toilet trained? Daytime? Nighttime?

Medications and Supplements

- Is the child taking any medications now?
- Is the child taking any prescription medications? How?
- Is the child taking any over-the-counter medications? How and how often?

Family History

Does anyone in your family have diabetes? High blood pressure? Heart disease? Elevated cholesterol level? Asthma? Allergies? Cancer? Any concerns with liver? Kidney? Or gastrointestinal issues? Arthritis? Or learning challenges?

Has anyone in the family died before age 50 years?

How is the health of the mother? Father? Siblings?

Risk Factors

Lead-risk Screening

- Does your child live in or regularly visit a house or child-care facility built before 1950?
- Does your child live in or regularly visit a house or child-care facility built before 1978 that is being or has recently (within the last 6 months) been renovated or remodelled? (Centers for Disease Control and Prevention, 2009)
- Does your child have a brother, sister, or playmate who has or had lead poisoning (American Academy of Pediatrics, 2008, p. 1074)?

Infectious Disease Screening

- Is your son/daughter in close contact with people known or suspected to have tuberculosis?
- Is your son/daughter in close contact with people known to be alcohol dependent or intravenous drug users or to reside in a long-term care facility, correctional or mental institution, nursing home/facility, or other long-term residential facility?

extra-uterine life was difficult (see Chapter 28). If they experienced anoxia, long-term sequelae are possible.

The postnatal period is the time just after birth; the nurse can assume that the child's difficulties were limited if he or she went home with the mother 24 to 72 hours after birth. Extremely elevated postnatal bilirubin levels (≥ 25 µg/dL) may be associated with neurological disorders.

An accurate developmental history alerts the nurse to possible delays requiring further intervention (see Chapter 9).

All medications may affect the child's illness and also behaviour. Medications taken together may interact. Children can be given too much or too little of an over-the-counter drug (eg, Tylenol).

A positive response to any of these increases the child's risk as well and may signal a need for additional testing (eg, serum cholesterol screening).

Family history provides information about the seriousness of diseases reported above. Additionally, cardiac arrest of unknown origin may be associated with altered cardiac rhythms (eg, prolonged Q-T interval); an electrocardiogram may be indicated.

Illness in an immediate family member can affect the child/adolescent, causing changes in family functioning and dynamics and in the availability or accessibility of health care resources.

"Yes" to any of these three questions requires health care professionals to take a blood level on children 0 to 72 months old (and possibly beyond if at risk). Some toys, jewelry, and Christmas decorations may also contain lead (Public Health Agency of Canada, 2010).

(text continues on page 904)

Questions to Assess History and Risk Factors	Rationale

- Where was your child born?
- Is your child/adolescent alcoholic dependent, an intravenous drug user, or a resident of a long-term-care facility, correctional or mental institution, nursing home/facility, or other long-term residential facility (Selekman, 2007)?

"Yes" to any of these questions requires the administration of a purified protein derivative tuberculin test to the patient.

Immunizations. Are immunizations current?

Immunization schedules for children and adolescents can be found on the provincial health websites. Health Canada, the Canadian Paediatric Society, and the provincial health departments collaborate and set provincial guidelines for immunizations. Canadian provinces have similar schedules but reflect their own unique demographic and health reality (see Table 29-1 for an example of a provincial immunization schedule).

Car Safety. Does the child sit in an approved car seat? In the back seat? Does the adolescent always wear a seat belt (Fig. 29-2)?

A rear facing car seat is required by law for newborns and infants up to 10 kg. A car seat with a 5-point harness is required by law in all provinces for infants and children until they reach 18 kg in weight. A booster seat is recommended (required in some provinces) for children 18 kg and over until they reach the age of 9 years or 145 cm in height.

Figure 29-2 Adolescents need to understand the importance of the use of seat belts to optimize their protection while driving and as passengers.

Poison Control. Are hazardous substances stored safely away from the child?

The house and other environments where the child spends significant time should be childproofed by locking up cleaning supplies and keeping all medicines out of the child's reach. Each province has its own poison control centre and the phone numbers can be located on the cover of a telephone book, online, or by calling the emergency access line (9-1-1 in most areas). For a child suspected of ingesting a nonfood substance, contact the provincial poison control centre or call 9-1-1. For a listing of provincial poison control centres, see www.safekids.org/pcc.htm.

Safety in the Home. Is your child protected from falls down stairs? Falls from windows? Are guns in the home? Are they secured?

Children need to be protected from falls at windows and down stairs. Guns should not be loaded; they should be locked.

Fire Safety. Does your family have a fire escape plan?

Children need protection from burns related to open fire pits, campfires, grills, gas stoves, stovetop cooking of food, and matches.

Questions to Assess History and Risk Factors	Rationale
Water Safety. Is the pool secured by fencing? Ask the child if he or she can swim. Can he or she swim to the side of the pool if he or she falls in the deep end?	Pools should have 2 metre fences and entrance gates with high locks.
Outdoor Safety. Has your child been taught to safely cross streets?	Child pedestrians are at risk for injury and need instruction about where and when to cross frequently travelled streets, as well as where and how to walk on the street.
Does the child wear a helmet for high-risk activities such as biking, downhill skiing, toboganning, and skating?	Bike helmets are encouraged when a child begins to ride a tricycle or a bicycle. Nova Scotia, British Columbia, Prince Edward Island, and New Brunswick require all cyclists to wear protective helmets. Alberta and Ontario require cyclists under the age of 18 to wear helmets. Manitoba requires children younger than 5 years to wear helmets (Safekids Canada, 2010a).
Does the child use sunscreen when outside?	Unprotected sun exposure increases risks for melanoma, basal cell carcinoma, and squamous cell carcinoma.
Drug and Alcohol Use. For the older child or adolescent, have you or your friends used drugs? Alcohol? Or tobacco?	Alcohol consumption is linked with increased rates of injury, potential for addiction, and other health conditions (Health Canada, 2010).
Nutrition and Obesity. Describe what you would eat in a typical day.	Overweight and obesity have serious health consequences among children and adolescents including a greater risk of high cholesterol, hypertension, and diabetes.
Violence and Suicide. Ask children and teens if they feel threatened at school (see Chapter 12). Ask directly if the patient has thought about hurting self or others.	Youth violence includes bullying, slapping, or hitting. Other physical behaviours include robbery, assault, or rape.
Contraception and Sexually Transmitted Infections. Ask adolescents, are you sexually active? Do you engage in oral sex?	Adolescents are more likely than adults to have multiple sexual partners and short-term relationships, to engage in unprotected intercourse, and to have partners at high risk for STIs.

Risk Assessment and Health Promotion

In addition to taking family and individual histories, the nurse performs health-related education to prevent disease or injury. Important education areas include immunizations, car safety, poison control, home safety, fire safety, water safety, outdoor safety, prevention of substance use, nutrition and prevention of obesity, and promotion of contraception and prevention of STIs.

Immunization Schedules

For children who have not received the full roster of recommended immunizations, the nurse encourages catch-up doses. He or she documents administration and dates of the immunizations and provides this information to caregivers/parents for their own records in addition to maintaining the health record at the place of regular health care.

Car Safety

The nurse should discuss with parents and children as appropriate the use of car seats, booster seats, and seat belts according to provincial laws. Car safety includes promoting car seats and booster seats for children from birth to 9 years of age, seatbelts for older children and adolescents and teaching adolescents about the dangers of drunk driving.

Promoting Use of Car Seats and Belts. The infant car seat should be in the backseat facing backward for the first year minimally. Depending upon the car seat, it may be in the back seat facing backward until the child is 14 to 16 kg. A child may be turned facing forward after 1 year of age if in the correct car seat. At approximately 5 years of age or 18 kg, the child may graduate from a car seat to booster seat. He or she should be seated and restrained with a seat belt in such a seat, which is designed for use until children are at least 145 cm (Fig. 29-3).

Once out of the booster seat, children should ride in the back with a seat belt fastened securely. A child may move to the front seat after 12 years if he or she is of adult size. Front air bags have been known to hurt younger and smaller children as a result of the force with which they are deployed. Although car seat and booster seat laws vary among provinces, the use of restraints in vehicles (seat belts, car seats, or booster seats) is mandatory in all provinces.

Preventing Drunk Driving. The nurse discusses this topic by providing scenarios in which the adolescent has alternatives to riding with an impaired driver. He or she encourages the use of a designated driver if the teen is in a situation in which he or she anticipates drinking or drug use.

Figure 29-3 A booster seat is used to restrain a child with a seat belt in the back seat of the vehicle.

Poison Control

The poison control centres provide information needed for the home or hospital treatment of a child who has ingested toxic substances. Recommendations might include the use of ipecac syrup, activated charcoal, or both. Parents can buy these medications without a prescription; however, these should be used only if instructed to do so. Presently, these medications are not recommended for home use because they have been used inappropriately in the past. Telephone numbers for the provincial poison control centres are located on the covers of telephone books, online, or by calling the emergency access number (usually 9-1-1).

Safety in the Home

Signs of a home that has been modified to optimize child safety include the following:

• Open windows have well-maintained screens.
• Additional bars or barriers protect open low windows from which a toddler can reach and fall.
• Doors or gates block stairwells.

Fire Safety

Children have a larger skin surface area than body weight. Burns on them make up a larger percentage of their surface area than for adults; therefore, burns are much more serious for children in terms of fluid replacement and potential for infection. Children and adolescents require protection against fire and must be taught the dangers of and significant respect for fire. The family should establish and discuss a family fire plan and escape routes from the house.

Water Safety

When near a pool the young child unable to swim should always wear a life jacket. Around lake and murky water, the necessity of a life jacket may continue until the adolescent can demonstrate strong swimming skills. Children should be encouraged to learn to swim and take swimming lessons to develop the ability to at least save themselves in water over their head. The use of lifejackets while boating is recommended and some provinces are in the process of legislating the use of lifejackets for all watersports.

Outdoor Safety

Outdoor safety includes safety while crossing streets, using helmets while riding tricycles, bicycles, or all-terrain vehicles, and using sunscreen.

Safe Street Crossing. Assess if the child walks to school or other places such as parks or playgrounds. The safest route and safe street rules should be discussed with the child. Discuss walking facing traffic and crossing the street safely. Safekids Canada (2010b) outlines that children under the age of 9 years lack the ability to make judgments about traffic and safety. Children under the age of 9 should be accompanied by adults when walking to places requiring street crossings.

Helmet Use. Most provinces require helmets for riders of motorized vehicles on provincial roads. A child on an all terrain-motorized vehicle is required to always wear a helmet. Helmets should also be worn during high-risk sports, such as skating, football, hockey, baseball, skiing, and snowboarding. Head trauma secondary to accidents is a common childhood injury with long-term sequelae. Wearing a bicycle helmet reduces the incidence of brain injury in children (Thomas, Acton, et al., 1994).

Use of Sun Screen. All children, no matter what their skin type or colour, should apply sunscreen with SPF of at least 30 when exposing skin to the sun or be completely covered with clothing and a large brimmed hat to prevent skin damage and skin cancer. Sunglasses that block both UVA and UVB light are also recommended to prevent the development of cataracts.

Prevention of Drug and Alcohol Use

Nurses continue to answer questions and educate pediatric patients and their caregivers about the dangers of alcohol and drugs, emphasizing immediate over long-term risks. He or she also should assess for mental health issues, because drug-seeking behaviours are often ways in which people self-medicate for other issues (see Chapter 10). A potentially effective way to prevent young people from using substances is to explain how they interfere with the accomplishment of developmental tasks, which are difficult if the child or teen is impaired.

Nutrition and Prevention of Obesity

The nurse should discuss the child's BMI according to sex and age. Nutritional and activity information early is important if the BMI is at or above the 85th percentile. The family should receive nutritional information from Canada's Food Guide guidelines (see Chapter 8). Children 2 to 18 years should consume daily 4 to 8 servings of fruits and vegetables, with at least one third being dark green or orange; and 3 to 7 servings of grain products, with at least half being whole grains; 2 to 4 servings of milk; and 1 to 3 servings of meat and alternatives. Children 2 years and older should consume daily <10% of calories from saturated fat, no more than 30% of calories from total fat, and 1,500 mg or less of sodium; they also need to meet dietary recommendations for calcium (see thePoint ✱ for a link to more information).

Nurses can ask and educate families about multivitamins with iron and vitamin D for high-risk individuals as well as about food choices at school and how they can correlate with the guidance offered by Canada's Food Guide. Children and caregivers also need explanations about vigorous physical activity and assessment of their engagement in such activity. Young people need to engage in moderate physical activity for a total of 90 minutes each day (Health Canada, 2011).

Mental Health Issues

The nurse discusses strategies to deal with threats at school, conflict resolution, and school resources available. He or she needs to intervene immediately if a parent or child admits to concerns about hurting self or others. The patient or family member who describes a plan to complete suicide requires hospital admission for mental health concerns.

Promotion of Contraception and STI Prevention

The nurse discusses abstinence, safer-sex practices, and avoidance of high-risk behaviours with sexually active adolescents and answers questions from all patients regarding sexuality and sexual health. The nurse can encourage group activities and normalize the decision not to engage in sexual activity. For those adolescents who choose to continue sexual activity, the nurse should encourage the use of condoms.

The nurse also should educate adolescents on the signs, symptoms, and consequences of untreated STIs. He or she should urge immediate screening and treatment for symptoms and yearly examinations for sexually active adolescents even if they are asymptomatic.

Focused Health History Related to Common Symptoms

The following symptoms have been implicated as valid; however, they are also common in children attempting to avoid school. The pain goal is pain free (zero on FACES; see Chapter 7) and elimination of the contributing symptom. Also, the nurse should consider if the situation represents acute illness and requires immediate attention.

Common Symptoms in Children and Adolescents

- Abdominal pain
- Headache
- Leg pain

Example of Questions to Assess Symptoms/Signs	Rationale/Unexpected Findings
Abdominal Pain • Can you point to where it hurts? • How bad is the pain? • How long have you had this pain? • What does the pain feel like? Cues may need to be added (eg, sharp or dull). • Does anything make your pain worse? • Does anything make your pain better? • Has your pain stopped you from going to school, playing sports, or other things?	Children usually cannot isolate abdominal pain to one specific area. If the child points to the right lower quadrant or only tiptoes, *appendicitis* should be ruled out with abdominal scans. ⚠ *SAFETY ALERT 29-3* *Acute intense pain with vomiting may indicate appendicitis. A child who stops activity or play because of pain requires additional evaluation.*
Headache • Can you point to where it hurts? • How bad is the pain? • How long have you had this pain? • What does the pain feel like? Cues may need to be added (eg, sharp or dull). • Does anything make your pain worse? • Does anything make your pain better? • Has your pain stopped you from going to school, playing sports, or other things? • Have you vomited?	For headaches children usually cannot isolate to one specific area. ⚠ *SAFETY ALERT 29-4* *Acute intense pain with vomiting may indicate a migraine or brain tumour. A child who cannot walk or stops activity or play because of pain requires additional evaluation.*
Leg Pain • Can you point to where it hurts? • How bad is the pain? • How long have you had this pain? • What does the pain feel like? Cues may need to be added (eg, sharp or dull). • Does anything make the pain worse? • Does anything make the pain better? • Has your pain stopped you from going to school, playing sports, or other things?	For leg pain children usually cannot isolate to one specific area. ⚠ *SAFETY ALERT 29-5* *If the child consistently limps, then fractures, dislocations, and bone tumour should be ruled out.*

Examples of Questions to Assess Symptoms/Signs—Foot Pain

- "Point to where the pain is." "Does it move around?" "Or stay in one place?" (Location, radiation)
- "Is the pain stopping you from walking?" "Playing?" "Is this the worst pain you have ever felt?" (Severity)
- "What does the pain feel like?" "Aching?" "Stabbing?" (Quality)
- "When did it start?" "Did it start all of a sudden?" "Or did it start gradually?" (Timing)
- "Do you have any other changes in your foot?" "Tingling?" (Associated symptoms)
- "Is there anything that makes it worse?" (Aggravating factors)
- "Is there anything that makes it feel better?" (Alleviating factors)
- "Have you been doing any activities that you don't usually do?" (Environmental factors)
- "Is your foot pain stopping you from doing things you usually do?" (Significance to patient)
- "Do you know what might be causing the pain?" (Patient perspective)

An Example of a Therapeutic Dialogue

Sam, introduced at the beginning of this chapter, is 4 years old and undergoing a preschool assessment. The nurse uses professional communication techniques to gather subjective data from Sam. The following conversation is an example of an interview.

Nurse: It's nice to see you again, Sam and Mrs. Maratas. How are you today?

Mrs. Maratas: We are very well, thank you.

Nurse: Sam, how are you?

Sam: Chood.

Nurse: (Leans in closer to hear speech clearly) So, Sam, why are you visiting the clinic?

Sam: I am choing to go to shool! (speech is somewhat garbled)

Nurse: It sounds like you are excited to be going to school Sam. Mrs. Maratas, is it difficult for you to understand Sam sometimes?

Mrs. Maratas: Yes, but I thought that it might be because he speaks both Tagalog and English. His father's parents visit from The Philippines once a year. They bring him toys and candy that I don't like. I try to keep him healthy. He only watches TV 1 hour a day. He eats meat only once a day. He brushes his teeth every night and saw a dentist last year.

Nurse: Thank you Mrs. Maratas and thank you Sam

Critical Thinking Challenge

- What are some of the family's strengths?
- How will the nurse continue to assess Sam?
- What risk factors might be identified?

Cultural Considerations

Every child grows and develops in a family or care setting unique to that child regardless of genetic background. Health habits are not ethnicity related but defined culturally within the local community and family. Nevertheless, certain genetic groups are more prone than others to specific disorders or diseases. For instance, rates of obesity and type 2 diabetes are higher among Latinos, African Canadians, and First Nations peoples than among Caucasians.

The norms of each family setting deserve assessment in regards to patterns of rest, activity, nutrition, illness intervention, health habits, and member roles. This includes who eats together, what is eaten, where food is obtained, who prepares food, and how food is prepared. These norms contribute to the health of the child and are important components of a nutritional assessment. Each area of assessment listed also contributes to or discourages the development of obesity. Some families do not prepare food at home and eat out most of the time, some families do not eat together, some eat in the front of the TV, some children eat only in their rooms, and some eat with grandparents. These norms are not known unless the nurse asks about them. They are different for each family based not on genetics, but on familial cultural norms.

Another example of cultural differences in families concerns activity levels. One family would never consider walking to the grocery store even if it is just one block away. Another family would consider themselves lazy if they did not hike at least 3 miles every Saturday in the park close to their house.

Assessment of language development is difficult if the nurse is not bilingual and the child speaks another language. If a language other than English is spoken in the home, language development may be delayed if the child is attempting to develop two languages at the same time. These children will be bilingual and their language delay is not of concern as long as there are no concerns with their hearing.

Objective Data Collection

Equipment

In addition to the equipment needed for a head-to-toe assessment (see Chapter 4), the nurse needs to include selected developmental screening test equipment and a tape measure.

Preparation: Promoting Patient Comfort, Dignity, and Safety

Ensure that the room is a comfortable temperature and that chairs are available for the nurse, parent, and child. During the health interview the child can be in the parent's lap or in his or her own chair. The toddler or very anxious small child can remain in the parent's lap for most of the physical examination. Wash your hands prior to beginning the examination. By the age of 3 years, most children enjoy the independence of climbing on the examination table. Most 4-year-olds are able to climb on the examination table without difficulty if the initial screening process is without trauma. While the child is climbing, watch carefully and maintain a close hand to prevent a fall. The child is undressed at the beginning of the examination or after the assessment of the head and neck.

The examination of the child will start at the head and end at the toes. If, however, the child is predicted to become upset, listen to heart sounds first and then breath sounds. This is best done while the child is sitting on the parent's lap. Wipe the stethoscope with an equipment wipe and warm the stethoscope first with your clean hand.

Children, and most specifically young adolescents, want to be reassured that everything evaluated is "okay." They may frequently mention what seems to be a minor concern to the health professionals. To gain trust, it is important to evaluate or intervene for all stated concerns.

Developmental Assessment

Although not commonly used in Canada, the **Denver Developmental Screening Test-II** (DDST-II; Frankenburg, Dodds, et al., 1992) is one of several standardized developmental screening tests used in the examination of the child and required for Early and Periodic Screening and Developmental Testing. The DDST-II is for the developmental evaluation of children ages 1 month to 6 years. It evaluates four developmental areas of interest: personal-social, language, fine motor/adaptive, and gross motor.

During screening with the DDST-II, the examiner asks questions of the parent but the child also performs certain tasks. Toys and blocks provided with the screening tool assist in standardizing the assessment (Fig. 29-4). The DDST-II and accompanying required materials to perform it can be purchased at www.denverii.com/DenverII.html. A standardized evaluation such as the DDST-II is recommended, because behaviours or skills in a checklist are not standardized assessments. They are without validity or reliability, which makes results of the checklist difficult to interpret and intervene.

Assessment tools for development of young children vary across provinces, health care agencies, and health care professionals. The Peabody Developmental Motor Scale (PDMS-2) is a commonly used assessment tool in Canada and is composed of six areas: (1) reflexes; (2) stationary—including balance and other items to measure body control; (3) locomotion—including crawling, walking, running and other items to measure ability to move; (4) object manipulation—including items to assess ability to hold and manipulate an object; (5) grasping—including tests to assess the ability to use their hands; and (6) visual–motor integration—including items that assess eye and hand coordination (Markusic, 2009). The Ages and Stages Questionnaire is another commonly used assessment tool for child development.

Figure 29-4 The nurse will use special toys and blocks to conduct the DDST-II.

Comprehensive Physical Examination

Techniques and Expected Findings	Unexpected Findings

Vital Signs

Take the patient's height, weight, heart rate, respiratory rate, temperature, oxygen saturation, and blood pressure (Fig. 29-5). Plot height and weight on the appropriate growth charts; calculate body mass index. Routine blood pressures with a cuff and sphygmomanometer begin at 3 years of age if the newborn's blood pressure is recorded in the nursery as within expected limits in all extremities. Assessment of blood pressure includes the percentile according to height and sex. The blood pressure cuff covers 80% of the child's upper arm. *Charts for blood pressure parameters are found on the National Heart, Lung and Blood Institute's (2004) and thePoint websites.*

Any blood pressure over the 90th percentile is considered borderline hypertensive and deserves follow-up. The 90th percentile is 1.28 SD, 95th percentile is 1.645 SD, and the 99th percentile is 2.326 SD over the mean.

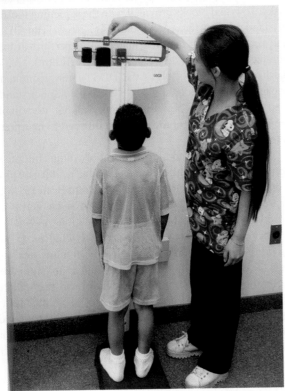

Figure 29-5 The child will typically enjoy standing on the scale and learning his progress from the last appointment.

General Survey

Observe the child's demeanour. Look for signs of distress, discomfort, or anxiety. Note attentiveness and affect. *A 4-year-old is generally talkative and engaged in the visit and can answer simple questions about self and concerns.* Listen for speech difficulties. *By 2 years, the child uses two-word sentences; by 3 years, a child should speak in more complicated sentences with speech that is understandable 75% or more of the time (Drumwright, Drexler, et al., 1973).*

There are assessments of the child's ability to understand and cognitive processing during the interview. Flat affect, no eye contact, and clinging to the caregiver may need further evaluation to assess for *autism* and other psychiatric concerns.

Observe for range of motion (ROM) and musculoskeletal symmetry and coordination. *ROM is full with 4–5+/5 strength symmetrically.*

Asymmetry of movement and lack of coordination should be further assessed.

Skin, Hair, and Nails

Inspect and palpate the skin, hair, and nails. *Skin is smooth and dry. Hair is smooth and evenly distributed. Nails are smooth and without clubbing.* Eccrine (sweat) glands begin to function by 2 to 18 days of life but become fully functional at adolescence. Apocrine (sex) glands do not become active until puberty.

Note any absence or overgrowth of nails. Dimpling, ripples, or discoloration in nails can be signs of *trauma* or *fungus.* There should be no unusual moles or hyperpigmented areas.

Note *acne* during adolescence; sebaceous glands work in utero and continue until the infant is 6 to 12 months. At this point they stop working and then begin activity again at puberty. With a gloved hand, feel any rash or skin lesions for elevation and size of papules, nodules, or cysts.

Head and Neck

Inspect the head and neck; observe ROM of the neck. *The head and neck are symmetrical with full ROM in neck.*

Palpate the head and neck. *Anterior and posterior cervical nodes may be palpable but not enlarged and also are nontender.* Palpate the head for nodules or pain due to infectious processes or trauma. *No nodule or tenderness is noted on the head.* Palpate fontanels of head on children up to 2 years old. *The anterior fontanel closes by 18 months and posterior fontanel by 6 months.*

Limited neck ROM requires further evaluation for possible meningitis or *torticolis.* Tender swollen lymph nodes of the neck and posterior head may indicate an infection. Lymph nodes are frequently palpable in children, but they should be small, shotty, moveable, and nontender. The lymphatic system grows exponentially between 6 and 12 years and reaches adult size around 12 years. Therefore, tonsils frequently look large at this time but will appear smaller as the head and neck grow throughout adolescence.

Eyes and Vision

Inspect the eyes. *The eyes are PERRL (A). Extraocular movements (EOMs) are at 180°. Corneal light reflexes (CLRs) are equal. There is no deviation during the cover and alternate cover tests. Funduscopic examination reveals a distinct disk with no vessel nicking.*

Assessment of accommodation is difficult in young children. Unequal and nonreactive pupils may signify *increased intracranial pressure.* Unequal EOMs or CLR may indicate *esotrophia* or *exotropia* (see Chapter 15). Deviation with the cover test demonstrates an *esophoria* or *exophoria*, depending on direction. All these findings require further assessment. By age 3 years, most children are cooperative enough for the nurse to obtain a quick glimpse of the retina.

Assess distance vision using a screening test based on developmental stage (Table 29-2). *Expected findings in toddlers are 20/200 bilaterally. Expected visual acuity in preschoolers is 20/40, improving to 20/30 or better by 4 years. By 5 to 6 years, visual acuity should approximate that of adults (20/20 in both eyes).*

Screen for colour blindness in patients 4 to 8 years old.

Ears and Hearing

Inspect the ears. *They have a formed pinna, the top of which touches an imaginary straight line through the outer canthus of both eyes* (Fig. 29-6).

Ear deformities are connected to kidney conditions, because organogenesis for both ears and kidneys occurs about the same time in utero. Evaluate renal function if the ears appear malformed. Low-set ears are correlated with cognitive deficits and learning challenges (Fig. 29-6B).

(text continues on page 912)

Table 29-2 **Eye-Screening Guidelines***

***From birth to 3 y of age* perform the following:**

1. Ocular history
2. Vision assessment
3. External inspection of the eyes and lids
4. Ocular motility assessment
5. Pupil examination
6. Red reflex examination

***For children 3 y and older* perform the following:**

Numbers 1 through 6 above, plus:

7. Age-appropriate visual acuity measurement
8. Attempt at ophthalmoscopy

Children ages 3–5 y			
Function	*Recommended Tests*	*Referral Criteria*	*Comments*
Distance visual acuity	Snellen letters Snellen numbers Tumbling E HOTV vision chart Picture tests • Allen figures • LEA symbols	1. Fewer than 4 of 6 correct on 6.1-m (20-ft) line with either eye tested at 3 m (10 ft) monocularly (ie, <10/20 or 20/40) or 2. Two-line difference between eyes, even within the passing range (ie, 10/12.5 and 10/20 or 20/25 and 20/40)	1. Tests are listed in decreasing order of cognitive difficulty; the highest test that the child is capable of performing should be used; in general, the tumbling E or the HOTV vision chart test should be used for children 3–5 y of age and Snellen letters or numbers for children 6 y and older. 2. Testing distance of 3 m (10 ft) is recommended for all visual acuity tests.
Ocular alignment	Cross cover test at 3 m (10 ft)		3. A line of figures is preferred over single figures.
	Random dot E stereo test at 40 cm		4. The nontested eye should be covered by an occluder held by the examiner or by an adhesive occluder patch applied to eye; the examiner must ensure that it is not possible to peek with the nontested eye.
	Simultaneous red reflex test (Bruckner test)	Any asymmetry of pupil colour, size, and brightness	Direct ophthalmoscope used to view both red reflexes simultaneously in a darkened room from 60 to 90 cm (2–3 ft) away; detects asymmetric refractive errors as well.
Ocular media clarity (cataracts, tumours, etc.)	Red reflex	White pupil, dark spots, and absent reflex	Direct ophthalmoscope, darkened room. View eyes separately at 30–40 cm (1–2 ft); white reflex indicates possible retinoblastoma.

Table 29-2   **Eye-Screening Guidelines*** *(continued)*

Children 6 y and older			
Function	*Recommended Tests*	*Referral Criteria*	*Comments*
Distance visual acuity	Snellen letters Snellen numbers Tumbling E HOTV vision chart Picture tests • Allen figures • LEA symbols	1. Fewer than 4 of 6 correct on 4.5-m (15-ft) line with either eye tested at 3 m (10 ft) monocularly (ie, <10/15 or 20/30) or 2. Two-line difference between eyes, even within the passing range (ie, 10/10 and 10/15 or 20/20 and 20/30)	1. Tests are listed in decreasing order of cognitive difficulty; the highest test that the child is capable of performing should be used; in general, the tumbling E or the HOTV vision chart test should be used for children 3–5 y of age and Snellen letters or numbers for children 6 y and older. 2. Testing distance of 3 m (10 ft) is recommended for all visual acuity tests. 3. A line of figures is preferred over single figures. 4. The nontested eye should be covered by an occluder held by the examiner or by an adhesive occluder patch applied to eye; the examiner must ensure that it is not possible to peek with the nontested eye.
Ocular alignment	Cross cover test at 3 m (10 ft) Random dot E stereo test at 40 cm Simultaneous red reflex test (Bruckner test)	Any asymmetry of pupil colour, size, and brightness	Direct ophthalmoscope used to view both red reflexes simultaneously in a darkened room from 60–90 cm (2–3 ft) away; detects asymmetric refractive errors as well.
Ocular media clarity (cataracts, tumours, etc.)	Red reflex	White pupil, dark spots, and absent reflex	Direct ophthalmoscope, darkened room. View eyes separately at 30–40 cm (1–2 ft); white reflex indicates possible retinoblastoma.

*Assessing visual acuity (vision screening) represents one of the most sensitive techniques for the detection of eye conditions in children. The American Academy of Pediatrics Section on Ophthalmology, in cooperation with the American Association for Pediatric Ophthalmology and Strabismus and the American Academy of Ophthalmology, has developed these guidelines to be used by physicians, nurses, educational institutions, public health departments, and other professionals who perform vision evaluation services.

Adapted from Committee on Practice and Ambulatory Medicine, Section on Ophthalmology, American Association of Certified Orthoptists, American Association for Pediatric Ophthalmology and Strabismus and American Academy of Ophthalmology (2003 and reaffirmed in 2007). Policy statement: Eye examination in infants, children, and young adults by pediatricians. *Pediatrics, 111*(4), 902–907. Retrieved from aappolicy.aappublications.org/cgi/content/full/pediatrics%3b 111/4/902

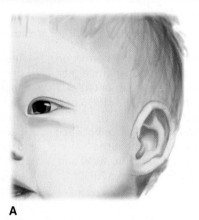 

A **B**

Figure 29-6 A. Positioning of the eyes in relation to the upper portion of the ears. **B.** Ear position that is much lower set than the outer canthus of the eye may be an indicator of genetic deviations or other health conditions.

As head shape changes, visualization of the tympanic membrane requires alterations in technique. Before the child is 1 year old, pull the pinna down and toward the face to straighten out the ear canal and promote visualization of the tympanic membrane. From 1 to 2 years, pull straight back on the pinna to straighten the ear canal for visualization of the tympanic membrane. After 2 to 3 years of age pull up and back on the top of the pinna to visualize the tympanic membrane. *The tympanic membrane is grey, nonerythematous with the light reflex and landmarks visualized.*

Infection is suspected if the tympanic membrane is erythematous or yellow, there is drainage in the canal, or there is limited mobility (see Chapter 16).

Clinical Significance 29-2

Children are prone to frequent cases of otitis media because the Eustachian tube is more horizontal than in adults (see Chapter 16). This is one reason why a child should never be put to bed with a bottle. Formula can pool in the back of the throat and ascend the Eustachian tubes, contributing to *otitis media*. As the head grows and shape changes, the Eustachian tubes become more vertical and the child is less prone to otitis media.

Palpate the pinna for tenderness and nodules. *The tympanic membrane is intact; no tenderness or nodules are on the pinna* (Cunningham & Cox, 2003).

Tenderness with manipulation of the pinna may indicate *otitis externa*. Swollen, erythematous turbinates may indicate infection. Pale swollen turbinates may indicate *allergic rhinitis* and seasonal allergies.

Screening for hearing acuity in infants and young children includes evaluation of developmental milestones, such as the Moro reflex in neonates (see Chapter 28). If there is a developmental lag or caregivers are concerned, a pediatric audiologist should perform a formal pediatric evaluation (Table 29-3).

Unexpected findings include lack of Moro reflex, inability to localize sound, or lack of understandable language by 24 months.

Nose, Mouth, and Throat

Inspect the nose, mouth, and throat. *The nose is midline, nares are patent, and turbinates are pink with unrestricted air passage.* Note the number of deciduous and permanent teeth. *No caries are present.* In the mouth, tonsils are present and between +1 and +4 (see Chapter 17). *There is no erythema or exudate.*

Dental caries are the most common infectious disease in childhood. Poor dental health is associated with poor physical health. Note any missing teeth. Erythema and exudate may be an infectious process.

Thorax and Lungs

Inspect the thorax and lungs. *There are no increased work of breathing and retractions.* Palpate the thorax. *There is no tenderness along intercostal spaces (ICSs).* Percuss the thorax and lungs. *The lungs are resonant.* Auscultate the thorax and lungs. *Breath sounds are clear in all lobes. No crackles, gurgles, or wheezes are noted.*

Pain along ribs may be indicative of injury or viral infection such as costochondritis.

⚠ *SAFETY ALERT 29-6*

Respiratory distress requires immediate intervention and oxygen.

Table 29-3	Audiologic Tests for Infants and Children				
Developmental Age of Child	**Auditory Test/ Average Time**	**Type of Measurement**	**Test Procedures**	**Advantages**	**Limitations**
All ages	Evoked otoacoustic emissions test, 10-min test	Physiologic test specifically measuring cochlear (outer hair cell) response to presentation of a stimulus	Small probe containing a sensitive microphone is placed in the ear canal for stimulus delivery and response detection	Ear-specific results; not dependent on whether patient is asleep or awake; quick test time	Infant or child must be relatively inactive during the test; not a true test of hearing, because it does not assess cortical processing of sound
Birth to 9 mo	Automated brainstem response, 15-min test	Electrophysiologic measurement of activity in auditory nerve and brainstem pathways	Placement of electrodes on child's head detects auditory stimuli presented through earphones; one ear at a time	Ear-specific results; responses not dependent on patient cooperation	Infant or child must remain quiet during the test; not a true test of hearing, because it does not assess cortical processing of sound
9 mo–2.5 y	Conditioned orienting response or visual reinforcement audiometry (VRA), 30-min test	Behavioural tests measuring responses of the child to speech and frequency-specific stimuli presented through speakers	Both techniques condition the child to associate speech or frequency-specific sound with a reinforcement stimulus (eg, lighted toy); VRA requires a sound-treated room	Assesses auditory perception of child	Only assesses hearing of the better ear; not ear-specific; cannot rule out a unilateral hearing loss
2.5–4 y	Play audiometry, 30-min test	Behavioural test measuring auditory thresholds in response to speech and frequency-specific stimuli presented through earphones, bone vibrator, or both	Child is conditioned to put a peg in a pegboard or drop a block in a box when stimulus tone is heard	Ear-specific results; assesses auditory perception of child	Attention span of child may limit the amount of information obtained
4 y to adolescence	Conventional audiometry, 30-min test	Behavioural test measuring auditory thresholds in response to speech and frequency-specific stimuli presented through earphones, bone vibrator, or both	Patient is instructed to raise his or her hand when stimulus is heard	Ear-specific results; assesses auditory perception of patient	Depends on the level of understanding and cooperation of the child

Adapted from Bachmann, K. R., & Arvedson, J. C. (1998). Early identification and intervention for children who are hearing impaired. *Pediatric Review, 19*, 155–165, with permission; and Cunningham, M. D., & Cox, E. O. (2003). Clinical report: Hearing assessment in infants and children. Recommendations beyond neonatal screening by the Committee on Practice and Ambulatory Medicine and Section on Otolaryngology and Bronchoesophagology. *Pediatrics, 111*(2), 436–440.

Percussion is not recommended for very young children since the chest wall is so small compared with the nurse's hands. For older children, percuss the lungs if pneumonia is suspected. To encourage children to take deep breaths for an adequate assessment a spinning pinwheel on which the child must blow so that the wheel spins may be helpful.

The young child has a pliable skeletal system and the lung's functional reserve can be exhaled with a gentle chest squeeze. The next breath then is deep and longer than previous and assists with a complete assessment. Lower airway diameters in children are approximately half that of adults, which contributes to increased wheezing and **pneumonia.** *The* left main stem bronchus comes off at a more acute angle than the right in children. Therefore, if a child aspirates, generally the foreign object is found in the right bronchus.

Heart and Neck Vessels

Inspect for visible pulses on the thorax. Palpate and auscultate the point of maximal intensity (PMI). *The PMI is at the midclavicular line (MCL) in infancy and moves slightly laterally with age to the fourth ICS just to the left of the MCL in children younger than 7 years and then to the fifth ICS in children older than 7 years. There is no bounding PMI.*

A visible PMI may signify increased cardiac load and increased oxygen requirements.

If heart enlargement is suspected, percussion can assist in determining size.

Auscultate the heart in all six designated areas on the chest and in the back. Assess with the child in two positions: lying and/or sitting and/or standing. *Closure of the tricuspid and mitral valves (S1) and the pulmonic and aortic (S2) valves is clear, crisp, and single. There are no murmurs, rubs, or gallops. Observe the jugular venous pulsations. The neck vessels are not distended or flat.*

If a murmur is detected, description of the murmur should include the intensity (grades 1 through 6), timing, duration, quality, pitch, PMI, and if and to where it radiates (see Chapter 19). Characteristics of **innocent heart murmurs** and pathological murmurs are noted in Box 29-1.

BOX 29-1 CHARACTERISTICS OF INNOCENT AND PATHOLOGIC HEART MURMURS

Innocent Murmurs

Innocent murmurs are associated with expected first and second heart sounds (S1 and S2). They occur in systole (except for the venous hum). They are usually very brief, well localized, and heard near the left sternal border. On a scale from 1 to 6, these usually are graded 1 or 2 without a thrill. The intensity changes with position, usually decreasing when standing. Innocent murmurs that may be auscultated in children are as follows:

- *Still's murmur:* A vibratory functional murmur, louder in the supine position
- *Pulmonary flow murmur:* Increased flow, louder in the supine position, accentuated by exercise, fever, and excitement
- *Venous hum:* Continuous, loudest when sitting

Pathological Murmurs

A murmur that sounds like a breath sound or is harsh or blowing (of any degree of intensity) signifies regurgitation of blood and pathology. Factors that increase the likelihood of an murmur include the following:

- Symptoms such as chest pain, squatting, fainting, tiring quickly, shortness of breath, or failure to thrive
- Family history of Marfan's syndrome or sudden death in young (<50 y) family members
- Other congenital anomaly or syndrome (eg, Down's syndrome)
- Increased precordial activity
- Decreased femoral pulses
- Altered S2
- Clicks
- Loud or harsh murmur (higher than grade 2)
- Increased intensity of murmur when the patient stands (McConnell, Adkins, et al., 1999)

Peripheral Vascular

Inspect the peripheral vascular system. *The skin is pink in all extremities, pink mucous membranes.* Palpate peripheral pulses (Fig. 29-7). *Pulses are equal in all extremities; there are no differences between upper extremity and lower extremity pulses.* Assess blood pressure in each extremity. *If there are slight differences, they are <10 mm Hg.*

Outside of the immediate newborn period, cyanosis requires immediate intervention. **Coarctation of the aorta** can present with unequal pulses between the upper and lower extremities (see Chapter 19). After the aorta leaves the heart, if there is a narrowing of the vessel then the lower extremities are not well oxygenated and pressure increases on the left side of the heart.

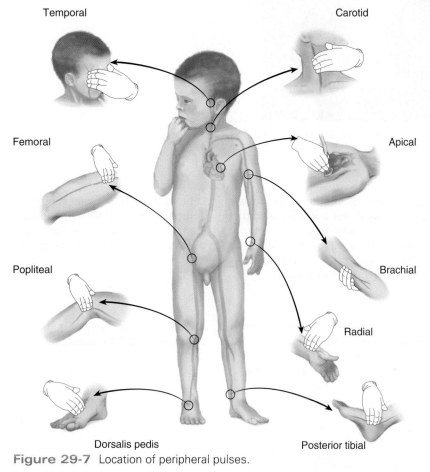

Figure 29-7 Location of peripheral pulses.

Breasts

Inspect the breasts. Refer to Chapter 26 for sexual maturity and Tanner's staging for females. *Breast development begins with a "breast bud" or enlargement of the areola followed by enlargement of breast tissue.*

Onset of pubertal changes before 8 years in girls and 9 years in boys may be too early and needs further evaluation.

Abdomen

Inspect the abdomen. *No distension is noted.* A protuberant abdomen is a common finding in toddlers (Fig. 29-8). The abdomen has a hollow or tympanic sound. Palpate the abdomen. *There are no masses or tenderness.* Percuss the abdomen. *There is no tenderness with percussion and tympany throughout.* Percussion can assist in determining the size of the liver. *The liver is at the lower right costal margin.*

If distension is present assess for tenderness and ascities; if these are present, further intervention is required. Palpation of the abdomen to assess for abdominal masses is important, because *Wilms' tumours* of the kidney occur in toddlers and early school-age children. The protuberant abdomen, however, may interfere with detection of these tumours until they are of significant size. Significant abdominal tenderness requires further evaluation for *appendicitis, Crohn's disease, ulcerative colitis, gastroenteritis,* or other illnesses. Percussion can assist in determining the size of a palpable mass.

(text continues on page 918)

Figure 29-8 Note the protuberant abdomen, common in toddlers.

Musculoskeletal

Inspect the muscles and joints. Evaluation of scoliosis begins when the child can stand, but it is a focused part of the examination just prior to, and during, puberty (see Chapter 23). Observe ROM in all joints. Palpate the muscles and joints. *The spine is straight. No joint tenderness is noted. ROM is full and symmetrical.*

Limited ROM in any joint requires further evaluation. Joint tenderness with palpation should be further evaluated for trauma and infection. Screening for scoliosis usually occurs during the school screening.

Neurological

Assess orientation. Observe for symmetry. Test deep tendon reflexes (DTRs) and evaluate for equality (Fig. 29-9). Ensure active movement and full strength in all extremities. *Older children are oriented to time and place. Movements are symmetrical; DTRs are 2+. Strength is 4 to 5+.*

Any noted asymmetry of gait, facial features, or movement needs further assessment.

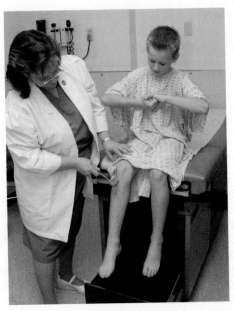

Figure 29-9 Testing DTRs in children.

Assess developmental progress for age. The Denver Developmental Screening Test-II (DDST-II) is used for children 1 month to 6 years. For children older than 6 years, academic performance is noted. *Scores are within norms for the age.*

Male and Female Genitalia

Inspect the genitalia. Refer to Chapters 25 and 26 for sexual maturity and **Tanner's staging** for males and females.

In females, the genitalia show no signs of erythema, discharge, or irritation.

Note if the male is circumcised or uncircumcised with the urethra midline at the end of the glans. Palpate the male scrotum. *The testes are in the scrotal sac and are smooth with no nodules noted.*

Inspect the anus and rectum. *Skin on the anus and rectum is without irritation, erythema, or fissures.*

Confusion, unusual behaviours, delayed development progress, and poor academic performance need further assessment.

Onset of pubertal changes before 8 years in girls and 9 years in boys may be too early and needs further assessment. Visualization of the genitalia is recommended in a complete examination to detect early infections, trauma, or developmental concerns (eg, labial adhesions for girls, undescended testicles *[cryptochoidism]* for boys) that require intervention.

The testes descend into the scrotal sac by age 6 months. If surgical repair is required, it should ideally happen before 2 years of age to prevent decreased fertility. *Hypospadias* requires intervention; it is usually diagnosed and treated in infancy (see Chapter 25). Adolescent boys should be assessed for testicular nodules; if found, they must be evaluated to rule out testicular cancer. Other testicular conditions (eg, hydrocele, varicocele, spermatocele) can be detected with testicular palpation.

Rectal irritation or fissures require further evaluation for constipation, worms, or sexual abuse.

Evidence-Informed Critical Thinking

Common Laboratory and Diagnostic Testing

No laboratory or diagnostic tests are recommended specifically for children and adolescents. Blood chemistry screening, hemoglobin (for anemia screening in patients 5 years or older), tuberculin skin screening (for children at average risk), and urinalysis are recommended when clinically indicated.

> ### Clinical Significance 29-3
>
> A general hearing evaluation is required for children with speech difficulties prior to their being evaluated by a speech pathologist or undergoing speech therapy.

In the primary care setting, vision screening is recommended for children younger than 4 years old. By age 5 years, vision screening is part of the preschool assessment. The use of safety precautions including car seat and seat belt use, helmet use, and other safety strategies is assessed. The BMI is calculated as a screen for overweight and obesity. Sexually active female adolescents are screened for chlamydia.

Clinical Reasoning

When formulating a nursing diagnosis, it is important to use critical thinking to cluster data and identify patterns that fit together. The nurse compares these clusters with the defining characteristics for the diagnosis to ensure the most accurate labelling and appropriate interventions. Table 29-4 provides a comparison of nursing diagnoses, unexpected findings, and interventions commonly related to assessment of the child.

Nurses use assessment information to identify patient outcomes. Some outcomes related to the child include the following:

- The family identifies health-promotion systems.
- The child achieves developmental tasks on schedule for age.
- The family seeks information regarding health promotion.

Once outcomes are established, patient care is implemented to improve the status of the child. The nurse uses critical thinking and evidence-informed practice to develop the interventions.

Some examples of nursing interventions for the child are as follows:

- Provide information about community support systems available to the family during times of stress.
- Identify conditions that contribute to altered growth and development.
- Provide information that contributes to an improved state of health.

Table 29-4 Common Nursing Diagnoses Associated With the Child or Adolescent

Diagnosis and Related Factors	Point of Differentiation	Assessment Characteristics	Nursing Interventions
Readiness for enhanced family processes	Pattern of family functioning that supports the well-being of family members	Activities support individual and family growth	Assess the family's coping abilities and stressors. Encourage attendance at community groups and classes. Assess cultural beliefs and norms.
Health-seeking behaviours	Actively seeking ways to change health habits to improve health level	Concern about current conditions, unfamiliarity with wellness community resources	Discuss benefits and barriers to staying healthy, environmental factors to health, and stress placed on the family.

Analyzing Findings

Subjective: Sam's mother reports that he has been very healthy. The family speaks Tagalog at home but English at church and with his maternal grandparents. His paternal grandparents live in the Philipines and visit once a year. The family lives in a large Victorian home built in the 1920s; they are renovating the house on the weekends.

Objective: Four-year-old child responds appropriately to questions and requests, generally pleasant. No reports of pain, present discomfort, or health concerns. Temperature 37°C, pulse 86 beats/min, respirations 20 breaths/min, blood pressure 94/50 mm Hg left arm, O_2 saturations 99%, height 104 cm, weight 17.5 kg, and body mass index 16.3. Alert and cooperative; answers questions appropriately although difficult to understand at times. Knows what day it is and why he has come to the clinic for evaluation. Hearing = passed at 20 dB at 500, 1,000, 2,000, 4,000 Hz. However failed at 30 dB for 1,000, 2,000, 4,000 Hz. Passed Denver Developmental Screening Test-II (DDST-II) in personal-social, fine motor, and gross motor areas. Failed language area.

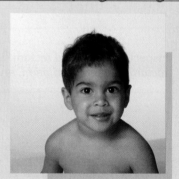

Assessment: Altered sensory perception, auditory. Hearing impairment detected. Immunizations recommended for children 4 to 6 years of age needed. At risk for elevated blood lead level. Speech difficulties.

Plan: Order blood lead level and refer for speech evaluation. Update immunizations. Provide information and handouts on nutrition, activity, limiting TV, reading, school readiness, immunizations, discipline, and safety. Refer to audiologist for further testing and treatment.

Critical Thinking Challenge

- How do the subjective and objective data fit together?
- What findings of Sam's are unexpected?
- What is the nurse's role in his care?

Hearing screening is becoming increasingly common in the newborn period. Without such testing, the average age of detection of hearing impairment is 14 months (American Speech Language Hearing Association, 2010). If impairment is not detected until late in the preschool period, speech can be affected.

Sam's hearing loss was detected when he was 4 years old, which is likely contributing to his speech difficulties. The nurse needs to refer Sam to an audiologist in addition to speech therapy. The information below illustrates the nurse's communication with the audiologist.

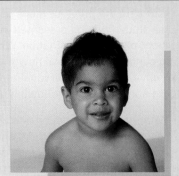

Situation: Hello, I am Paula Singala, a nurse practitioner. I saw Sam Maratas earlier this morning.

Background: He is 4 years old and has some speech difficulties and hearing loss.

Assessment: Sam passed his hearing test at 20 dB at 500; however, he failed at 30 dB for 1,000, 2,000, and 4,000 Hz.

Recommendations: I would like you to assess him further.

Critical Thinking Challenge

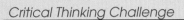

- Why might Sam be having hearing loss?
- What other things would you assess as the nurse?
- How might his ability to speak two languages affect his speech?

Pulling It All Together: An Example of Reflection and Critical Thinking

The nurse uses assessment data to formulate a patient care plan with patient outcomes and interventions for Sam. This plan includes a diagnosis, outcomes, and interventions, which the nurse uses critical thinking and judgment to continue or revise. This is often in the form of a care plan or case note similar to the one below.

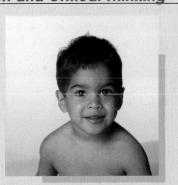

Nursing Diagnosis	Patient Outcomes	Nursing Interventions	Rationale	Evaluation
Altered sensory perception related to altered hearing	Patient uses assistive devices correctly. Speech becomes easier to understand.	Turn off TV and radio when communicating. Speak in lower tones if possible. Stand directly in front of the patient when talking.	Background noise interferes with hearing voices. The patient can use nonverbal cues, such as lip reading.	Patient obtained and is using hearing devices. Assess speech improvement at next visit.

Using the previous steps of assessment and nursing process, consider all the case study findings presented in this chapter about Sam, who is undergoing a pre-school physical examination. When answering the following questions, begin drawing conclusions and see how the pieces of assessment must work together to create an environment for personalized, appropriate, and accurate care. Consider Sam's case and answer the following questions.

- What health information and assessments are important for the toddler, pre-schooler, school-aged child, and adolescent? (Knowledge)
- How do assessment findings differ between the child and adult? (Comprehension)
- What adaptations will the nurse make when assessing a child? (Application)
- What factors could be contributing to Sam's language development? (Analysis)
- What recommendations for follow-up and future screening would you recommend for Sam? (Synthesis)
- How would you evaluate Mrs. Maratas's understanding of Sam's follow-up needs? (Evaluation)

Key Points

- Assessment of a child's physical growth is performed with standardized growth charts.
- Head circumference is measured on children from birth to 3 years old.
- Motor development progresses cephalocaudally and from proximal to distal.
- Health-related education for families with children and adolescents includes obtaining immunizations; using safety precautions such as car seats, seat belts, window/stair guards, pool fences, life jackets, and bike helmets; keeping a safe distance from firepits; crossing streets safely; following poison control measures; avoiding underage drinking and driving; contraception; use of condoms; and taking measures for adequate nutrition and sunscreen.
- Most of the physical assessment of a toddler can be performed with the child sitting in the parent's lap.
- The DDST-II, PDMS-2, and the Ages and Stages Questionnaire are assessment tools for developmental evaluation of children ages 1 month to 6 years.
- Innocent murmurs occur in systole, are brief and well localized, and are usually heard near the left sternal border.

Review Questions

1. What is the best time to assess the respiratory rate of a young child?
   A. While the child is crying
   B. While the child is playing in the playroom
   C. Immediately after taking the child's blood pressure
   D. While the child is quietly sitting on the parent's lap

2. Which factor places an infant at greater risk than an adult for developing otitis media?
   A. Introduction of solid foods
   B. Eustachian tubes that are more horizontal (flat) than vertical
   C. Immature cardiac sphincter
   D. Feeding in a semi-Fowler's position

3. During assessment of a child's visual acuity, which finding may indicate myopia or nearsightedness?
   A. Holding a book close to the face
   B. Squinting
   C. Rapid eye movements
   D. Closing one eye

4. What is an easy way to determine whether a child has strabismus?
   A. Observe the red reflex
   B. Check eyes for unequal pupil size
   C. Shine the light in his or her eyes
   D. Do a funduscopic examination

5. All the following may be symptoms of a child experiencing lead poisoning except
   A. irritability
   B. cardiomegaly
   C. headaches
   D. abdominal pain

6. As soon as the child can stand, begin to measure the height in the upright position.
  - A. True, using the scale as soon as the child can stand on it is fine.
  - B. False, measure the child standing starting between 2 and 3 years of age.
  - C. It depends on when the child can stand independently.
  - D. False, a child should always be measured in the recumbent position.

7. A child's head circumference is a measurement that should be obtained at every well-child visit until the child is 5 years old.
  - A. True, this measure is indicative of brain growth.
  - B. False, one or two measurements are the standard of care.
  - C. True, it will provide information on the child's readiness for kindergarten.
  - D. False, the charts for head circumference norms end at 36 months.

8. A blood pressure of 110/70 (left arm) was obtained in a 5-year-old boy. What would the nurse do about this blood pressure?
  - A. Call the physician immediately.
  - B. Bring the child back to the clinic two more times to ensure accuracy of the assessment.
  - C. Determine the blood pressure percentile based on age, sex, and height percentile.
  - D. Nothing needs to be done.

9. Health-promotion concepts for children that would affect their lifelong cardiovascular health include which of the following?
  - A. Information on good nutrition
  - B. Information on the prevention of illnesses
  - C. Information on exercise
  - D. All of the above

10. Children are usually brought for health care by a parent. At about what age should the interviewer begin to question the child regarding presenting symptoms?
  - A. 5 years
  - B. 7 years
  - C. 9 years
  - D. 11 years

Canadian Nursing Research

Cohen, B. E., & McKay, M. (2010). The role of public health agencies in addressing child and family poverty: Public health nurses' perspectives. *The Open Nursing Journal, 30*(4), 60–71.

Moores, P. S. (2010). Engaging community partners to promote healthy behaviours in young children. *Canadian Journal of Public Health, 101*(5), 369–373.

Olmstead, D. L., Scott, S. D., & Austin, W. J. (2010). Unresolved pain in children: A relational ethics perspective. *Nursing Ethics, 17*(6), 695–704.

Ravindran, V. P., & Rempel, G. R. (2011). Grandparents and siblings of children with congenital heart disease. *Journal of Advanced Nursing, 67*(1), 169–175.

References

American Academy of Pediatrics. (2008). *Bright futures: Guidelines for health supervision of infants, children and adolescents.* Retrieved from www.brightfutures.aap.org/3rd_Edition_Guidelines_and_Pocket_Guide.html

American Speech Language Hearing Association. (2010). *Hearing screening.* Retrieved from www.asha.org/public/hearing/testing/on

Bachmann, K. R., & Arvedson, J. C. (1998). Early identification and intervention for children who are hearing impaired. *Pediatric Review, 19*, 155–165.

Canadian Paediatric Society. (2010). *Promoting optimal monitoring of child growth in Canada: Using the new WHO growth charts.* Retrieved from www.cps.ca/english/statements/N/growth-charts-statement-FULL.pdf

Centers for Disease Control and Prevention. (2009). *Lead prevention.* Retrieved from http://www.cdc.gov.nceh/lead/tips.htm

Committee on Practice and Ambulatory Medicine, Section on Ophthalmology, American Association of Certified Orthoptists, American Association for Pediatric Ophthalmology and Strabismus and American Academy of Ophthalmology (2003 and reaffirmed in 2007). Policy statement: Eye examination in infants, children, and young adults by pediatricians. *Pediatrics, 111*(4), 902–907.

Cunningham, M. D., & Cox, E. O. (2003). Clinical report: Hearing assessment in infants and children: Recommendations beyond neonatal screening by the Committee on Practice and Ambulatory Medicine and Section on Otolaryngology and Bronchoesophagology. *Pediatrics, 111*(2), 436–440.

Dietitians of Canada. (2011). *WHO Growth charts adapted for Canada.* Retrieved from www.dietitians.ca/Secondary-Pages/Public/Who-Growth-Charts.aspx

Drumwright, M. A., Drexler, H., et al. (1973). Denver articulation screening exam. *Journal of Speech and Hearing Disorders, 38*(3), 1–42. Retrieved from www.denverii.com/DASE.html

Frankenburg, W. K., Dodds, J., et al. (1992). The Denver II: A major revision and restandardization of the Denver developmental screening test. *Pediatrics, 89*, 91–97. Retrieved from www.denverii.com/DenverII.html

Health Canada. (2010). *Drug and alcohol use statistics.* Retrieved from www.hc-sc.gc.ca/hc-ps/drugs-drogues/stat/index-eng.php

Health Canada. (2011). *Eating well with Canada's food guide.* Retrieved from www.healthcanada.gc.ca/foodguide.

Healthy Canadians. (2011). *Kids' health and safety.* Retrieved from www.healthycanadians.gc.ca/kids/

Markusic, M. (2009). *Assessing motor skills in early childhood— Using the PDMS.* Retrieved from www.brighthub.com/education/special/articles/13499.aspx#ixzz1JS4vhszi

McConnell, M. E., Adkins, S. B., et al. (1999). Heart murmurs in pediatric patients: When do you refer? *American Family Physician, 60*(2), 558–565.

National Heart, Lung and Blood Institute. (2004). *Blood pressure tables for children and adolescents from the fourth report on the diagnosis, evaluation, and treatment of high blood pressure in children and adolescents*. Retrieved from www.nhlbi.nih. gov/guidelines/hypertension/child_tbl.htm

Public Health Agency of Canada. (2010). *Poisons*. Retrieved from www.phac-aspc.gc.ca/hp-ps/dca-dea/stages-etapes/childhood-enfance/poisons-eng.php

Robins, D., Fein, D., et al. (1999). *M-CHAT tool and scoring*. Retrieved fromwww.firstsigns.org/downloads/m-chat.PDF

Safekids Canada. (2010a). *Position statement on bicylce helmet legislation*. Retrieved from www.safekidscanada.ca/Professionals/Advocacy/Documents/2738-helmet

Safekids Canada. (2010b). *Pedestrian safety*. Retrieved from www.safekidscanada.ca/Parents/Safety-Information/Pedestrian-Safety/FAQ/Pedestrian-FAQs.aspx

Selekman, J. (2007). Changes in the screening for tuberculosis in children: Screening for TB. *Pediatric Nursing, 32*(1), 73–75.

Thomas, S., Acton, C., et al. (1994). Effectiveness of bicycle helmets in preventing head injury in children: Case–control study. *British Medical Journal, 308,* 173–176.

The Canadian Jensen's Nursing Health Assessment suite offers these additional resources to enhance learning and facilitate understanding of this chapter:

- thePoint on line resource, http//thepoint.lww.com/Stephen1E
- *Laboratory Manual for Canadian Jensen's Nursing Health Assessment: A Best Practice Approach*

Older Adults

Learning Objectives

1 Identify expected changes that occur with aging.

2 Identify important topics for health promotion and risk reduction in older adults.

3 Describe common symptoms and signs reported by older adults.

4 Collect subjective data using interviewing techniques that include adaptations based upon age.

5 Collect objective data on the body systems using physical examination techniques and considering expected variations based on age.

6 Consider age, condition, gender, and culture of the patient to individualize the health assessment.

7 Identify expected and unexpected findings from inspection, palpation, percussion, and auscultation of body systems.

8 Analyze subjective and objective data from assessment of the older patient and consider initial interventions.

9 Identify nursing diagnoses and initiate a plan of care based on findings from the assessment of the older patient.

10 Document and communicate data from the health assessment using appropriate terminology and principles of recording.

Mr. Pierre Lehmann is a 76-year-old man with a history of Parkinson's disease. He has been a resident in an assisted living facility for the past 3 months because of functional limitations. He reports "terrible constipation" and asks, "What causes this?" His daily medications include carbidopa–levodopa (Sinemet) 25/250 four times before meals for Parkinson's, calcium 600 mg with vitamin D 1,000 IU for bone health, and lisinopril (Zestril), an angiotensin-converting enzyme (ACE) inhibitor, 5 mg for his blood pressure (BP).

Begin thinking about the following points:

- What are some causes of constipation that would immediately be apparent in this case?
- What health-promotion activities is Mr. Lehmann already doing to stay healthy?
- What assessments might the nurse perform in addition to the screening examination?

Conducting an accurate and complete assessment of an older adult is essential for the planning and management of care. **Geriatric** nursing experts identify the need for a comprehensive assessment of this population, because elders often have a unique presentation of illness. In addition, many aspects of the lives of older adults can affect their health and ability to cope with chronic changes (Samaras, Chevally, et al., 2010). An older adult's social situation, living situation, relationship with a caregiver, access to transportation, mobility, financial or economic situation, understanding, expectation, and cultural or religious views on disease can influence health as much as his or her health history, past medical diagnoses, understanding of medications, physical examination findings, and functional ability (Lach & Smith, 2007).

Canadian seniors are a heterogeneous population. Because of their variations in health status, cultural backgrounds, functional abilities, financial situation, and housing, seniors may be subcategorized into three groups: 65 to 74 years, 75 to 84 years, and 85 years or older. Currently, individuals 65 years or older compose 13.1% of Canada's population. By 2036, almost 9.8 million people will be over 65 years of age in Canada, accounting for about 25% of the total population. By 2021, almost 800,000 Canadians will be 85 years or older. Life expectancy for Canadians in 2003 was approximately 80 years (Turcotte & Schellenberg, 2006).

This chapter begins with a review of physiologic changes associated with aging and then moves to a discussion of best practices for conducting an interview with an older adult. It includes some common assessment tools used to identify risk for specific geriatric syndromes. The chapter then introduces such tools in the context of physical examination findings. In that section, the primary aging process is separated from findings that represent unexpected changes commonly found in older adults. Primary aging refers to physiologic changes that are not related to disease or environmental factors (Masoro, 2006). In contrast, secondary aging involves interactions of primary aging processes with environmental and disease factors (Masoro; Miller, 2009). To support healthy aging to the 80s or 90s, it is important that the nurse encourage appropriate nutrition, smoking cessation, strength training, aerobic exercise, and engagement with social and intellectual activities (Bradshaw & Klein, 2007). Previous chapters covered specific assessment considerations for older adults related to general survey, pain, nutrition/supplements/medications, developmental stages, mental status, social/spiritual/cultural concerns, and violence. Refer to Chapters 6 to 12 for more specific information on those areas.

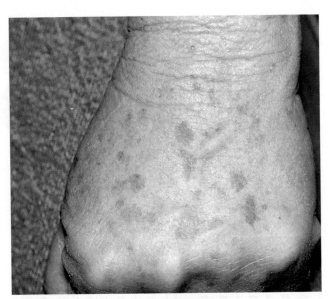

Figure 30-1 Solar lentigines, or "liver spots," are a common and expected skin finding in older adults.

degeneration of the elastic fibres providing dermal support, a loss of collagen, and a loss of subcutaneous fat. The number of sweat and sebaceous glands decreases as a result of atrophy; vascularity and capillary fragility of the skin layer are diminished. Nail beds become more rigid, thick, and brittle, with slowed growth (Makrantonaki & Zouboulis, 2007).

It is important to note the difference between expected aging processes and the lifelong cumulative exposure to sun, called **photoaging** (Helfrich, Sachs, et al., 2008). For example, fine wrinkling of the skin is an expected part of aging, but coarse wrinkling is evidence of photoaging. Sun exposure also increases **solar lentigines** (age or liver spots; Fig. 30-1), mottled **dyspigmentation** areas, and **actinic keratoses**. Long-term smoking also alters skin by reducing dermal elastic fibres, reducing blood flow to the dermal layers, and slowing healing times for wounds.

Head and Neck

With aging, facial subcutaneous fat decreases, making the skeleton more pronounced. Skin may sag and wrinkle across the forehead, surrounding the eyes, at the tip of the nose, and on the cheeks, which alters facial appearance. Skin lesions are more likely, and careful assessment for possible cancers, especially in commonly sun-exposed areas, is important (Centers for Disease Control and Prevention, 2010; see Chapter 13).

Thyroid function and thyroid hormones do not change with aging. Poor thyroid function in an older adult is related to thyroid dysfunction, not expected changes with aging.

Eyes and Vision

Older adults have less fat in the orbital area, laxity of the orbital muscles, and decreased lid elasticity. They have fewer goblet cells that provide mucin, resulting in less lubrication for the eyes. Tear production decreases, which leads to dry

Anatomy and Physiology Overview

Skin, Hair, and Nails

The epidermis thins with aging, and the epithelium renews itself every 30 days instead of every 20 days as in children and adults. This decreased mitotic activity of cells leads to a 50% reduction in rate of wound healing. In addition, there is

eyes. Corneal sensitivity may diminish. Increased lipid deposits may be found at the periphery of the cornea around the iris. The ciliary body secretes less aqueous humour, and the ciliary muscle may atrophy, compromising the ability to focus the lens. The lens becomes less elastic, larger, and denser with age and can become progressively yellowed and opaque. The iris loses some pigment, and the pupil becomes progressively smaller. Slowed pupillary responses lead to a difficulty in accommodating to changes in light, difficulty with night driving, and issues with glare (Miller, 2009).

Ears and Hearing

Physiological changes to ears and hearing include a widening and lengthening of the auricle, coarse wiry hair growth in the external ears (especially in men), narrowing of the auditory canal, and dry cerumen in the ear canal. The tympanic membrane in the middle ear becomes dull, less flexible, retracted, and grey. The organ of Corti atrophies, causing sensory hearing loss, and cochlear neurons are lost, causing neural hearing loss (Linton & Lach, 2007). Changes to the inner ear can reduce the older adult's ability to discriminate sounds, especially in noisy conditions (Bance, 2007).

Nose, Mouth, and Throat

Because of an age-related loss of olfactory receptor neurons, older adults have a decreased sense of smell, which can start as early as the fourth decade of life. The threshold for odours in older adults is 2 to 15 times greater than that for a younger person (indicating a need for a much stronger smell for testing recognition) (Boyce & Shone, 2006). In addition, chronic medical conditions can alter the sense of smell. For example, older adults with Alzheimer's or Parkinson's disease may have difficulty with odour recognition. Olfactory dysfunction can significantly reduce food intake, because smell and taste are important in the enjoyment of foods.

Teeth surfaces become worn with aging, which increases the risk of dental caries. Collagen and elasticity changes affect oral tissues, with mucosal thinning and smoothing of the tongue. Oral hygiene practices throughout the lifespan, however, greatly influence gum recession and tooth loss. Taste buds are replaced every 10 to 100 days. Many older adults experience changes in taste starting around the age of 60 years. Changes in taste detection and sensation were originally thought linked to a loss of taste buds; however, recent studies have shown that healthy older adults do not lose taste buds. Researchers now believe loss of taste sensation is more likely caused by medications, diseases, long-term smoking damage, or malnutrition. Older adults who regularly take medications or have diseases that create less saliva or xerostomia are more likely to have concerns about taste (Boyce & Shone, 2006).

Thorax and Lungs

Changes to connective tissue related to aging are evident throughout the respiratory system. The chest wall is less elastic, and rigidity or lack of compliance limits chest expansion. Decreased respiratory muscle strength creates a less effective cough for older adults. Alveoli are thicker and fewer in older adult smokers, but the number of alveoli remains relatively constant in healthy older adults.

Loss of alveolar elastic recoil produces an approximately 20% decrease in lung vital capacity. Loss of alveolar surface area creates less area available for oxygen exchange and difficulties responding to hypoxic or hypercapneic episodes. Fewer cilia lining the airways create less efficiency in clearing the lungs. Residual volume (the volume of air remaining in the lung after a maximal expiration) increases with age. The forced expiratory volume in 1 second/forced vital capacity ratio declines about 0.2% per year after 40 years (Sharma & Goodwin, 2006). Major changes in respiratory function are usually related to deconditioning and disease or damage from long-term smoking rather than the aging process itself.

Heart and Neck Vessels

Changes in connective and smooth muscle tissue affect the peripheral vessels and heart. Arterial walls are less elastic and stiffen. Subsequent decreased compliance affects blood pressure (BP) by increasing the afterload on the left ventricle. Systolic BP increases, the left ventricle wall hypertrophies or thickens, and there is an increased dependence on atrial contraction. Coronary artery blood flow decreases by about one third. The loss of atrial pacemaker cells and bundle of His fibres may result in decreased heart rate. Intrinsic cardiac contractile function diminishes, reducing cardiac output, stroke volume, and cardiac reserves (Bernhard & Laufer, 2008). Responsiveness to beta-adrenergic receptor stimulation and reactivity of baroreceptors and chemoreceptors decrease, while circulating catecholamines increase. Jugular venous pulsations increase with fluid volume excess and decrease with fluid volume deficit.

Peripheral Vascular and Lymphatics

Calcification of the arteries, or *arteriosclerosis*, causes them to become more rigid (Fig. 30-2). Less arterial compliance results in increased systolic BP (Barkman & Porth, 2010). This is often compounded by the coexistence of atherosclerotic disease in the arteries supplying the brain, heart, and other vital organs. Incidence of peripheral arterial disease (PAD) increases dramatically in the seventh and eighth decades of life (Barkman, Pooler, et al., 2010). Prevalence of PAD in men and women is equal at this stage (Ostechega, Paulose-Ram, et al., 2007). Patients with venous congestion may also develop edema from poor lymphatic drainage (see Chapter 20).

Breasts and Lymphatics

Glandular breast tissue atrophies, becomes less dense, and is replaced by fat. As women age, glandular, alveolar, and lobular breast tissues decrease. After menopause, fat deposits replace glandular tissue that continues to atrophy as a result

Healthy vessel

Arteriosclerosis

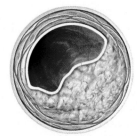
Atherosclerosis

Figure 30-2 Arteriosclerosis (hardening of the arteries) develops as people age. It can eventually progress to atherosclerosis, which can cause life-threatening complications.

of decreased secretion of the ovarian hormones, estrogen, and progesterone. The inframammary ridge thickens, making this area easier to palpate. Suspensory ligaments relax, causing the breasts to sag and droop. Additionally, breasts decrease in size and lose elasticity. Nipples become smaller, flatter, and less erectile. Axillary hair also may stop growing. These changes are more apparent in the eighth and ninth decades of life. Women who have had mastectomies may develop lymphedema in the affected arm.

Abdomen, Metabolism, and Elimination

Although it was previously thought that parietal and chief cells in the stomach decrease with aging, reducing hydrochloric acid and pepsin, some studies now show that older adults actually have increased gastric acid secretion. Slowed peristalsis creates a delayed emptying of the stomach and delayed movement of food through the gastrointestinal system. Absorption of vitamin D, calcium, and zinc in the small intestine may be reduced (Elmadfa & Meyer, 2008). The number and size of hepatocytes decrease, and hepatic blood flow is reduced. Metabolism of medications on the first pass through the liver decreases, leaving older adults at risk for higher circulating medication levels. Secretion of bicarbonate and enzymes in the pancreas decreases, and the pancreatic duct becomes more dilated. The colonic transit rate is slower.

The size and function of the kidneys' decrease with age. Nephrons in the cortex of the kidneys are fewer, while unexpected changes may occur in the glomeruli. The body responds to the sclerotic changes in the glomeruli by increasing the size of the remaining healthy glomeruli.

Older adults develop diverticular changes in the distal renal tubules. For older patients with vascular conditions, the decrease in blood flow to glomerular units leads to a decrease in glomerular filtration rate (Miller, 2009). These changes are reflected in a decrease in creatinine clearance and a loss of ability to conserve sodium. Older adults also experience a general reduction in peak bladder capacity and a weakening of the bladder muscles, which can lead to incomplete emptying of the bladder.

Musculoskeletal

Older adults often lose height. Gradual compression of the spinal column is related to narrowing of intervertebral discs. Beginning at around age 30 years, bone absorption starts to

exceed bone formation. In women, this bone loss accelerates in the decade immediately following menopause. Decreased lean body mass also occurs with aging. There is a loss of type II muscle (fast-twitch) fibres as compared with type I muscle (slow-twitch, fatigue-resistant) fibres, which leads to muscle wasting. Regeneration of muscle tissues slows with age, but studies show that exercise can increase lean muscle mass even in frail older adults (Peterson, Rhea, et al., 2010).

Neurological

With aging, the number of neurons and glial cells gradually decline, and these cells show structural changes. Nevertheless, current studies do not support the notion of extensive brain atrophy in healthy aging. Atrophy is common in people with degenerative neurological diseases. The overall number of neuronal synapses decreases, while lipofuscin granules in the nerve cells accumulate. There is increased production and accumulation of oxyradicals in all body systems (Foster, 2006).

Neurological changes are worsened in people who have changes to the vessels that supply the nervous system (eg, people with diabetes mellitus, smokers). Efficiency of the autonomic functions of the central nervous system decreases, so that recovery from stress becomes more difficult. Healthy older adults maintain cognitive function, but retrieval speed for information slows. Speed of brain processing on tests of psychomotor performance shows slowing with age. Reaction times are slower but may be affected by other changes including vision and musculoskeletal changes. Postural control, decreased vibratory sense, and decreased righting reflex ability may affect the balance of older adults (Linton & Lach, 2007).

Male and Female Genitourinary

Age-related enlargement of the prostate can contribute to urinary retention or outlet obstruction. Genital hair thins and is distributed more sparsely. The vaginal mucosa thins and loses elasticity. Vaginal secretions diminish from lower estrogen levels with age (see Chapters 25 and 26).

Endocrine

The pituitary gland decreases in size, weight, and vascularity. Secretion of growth hormone and circulating levels of insulin-like growth factor decrease. Plasma levels of the adrenal steroids (dehydroepiandrosterone and dehydroepiandrosterone sulfate) show a significant decline with aging. Prevalence of glucose intolerance and type 2 diabetes increases. Older adults are more likely to have a decreased responsiveness to immunizations. Because of changes in the immune system, older adults may have more autoantibodies and risks for autoimmune diseases (Chahal & Drake, 2007).

Acute Assessment

Older adults frequently have altered presentations of illnesses. The nurse never attributes changes in an older adult to "old age." A change in functional ability or a sudden onset of any one of the geriatric syndromes such as delirium, falls, vascular disorders, or incontinence warrants further assessment (Anderson, Hunter, et al., 2010). Falls, especially if accompanied by fracture, are the most common reason for admission of older adults to emergency departments (Hastings, Whitson, et al., 2009). Chronic conditions also may be exacerbated; for example, worsening of chronic obstructive pulmonary disease or congestive heart failure (CHF) can be an acute condition. Infection, chest pain, abdominal pain, and delirium need to be assessed and treated rapidly. Because older adults may not mount an immune response, infection may be present even in the absence of fever.

Subjective Data Collection

Interviewing the Older Adult

Before interviewing the older adult, the nurse sets up the room and creates an environment that facilitates hearing and understanding of communication. Although some acute situations do not allow for finding a quiet space, an environment that is calm and quiet is essential for conducting an interview with an older person. It is important to reduce or eliminate background noise as much as possible when carrying on conversations. This includes turning off the television or radio in the patient's room and closing the door to reduce sounds of telephones, beepers, alarms, or pagers. Cold or drafty environments are uncomfortable and can distract the older adult from tasks at hand. The older adult needs to be warm and comfortable during the interview (Ham, Sloane, et al., 2007). The nurse avoids sitting with his or her back to a window so that the patient is able to see the face of the interviewer clearly.

The interview of an older adult can take much longer than that for a younger, healthier person. It might not be completed in one encounter. Nurses need to allow additional time for an interview or health history (Lach & Smith, 2007; Fig. 30-3). Frail older adults may hesitate before answering questions. The nurse pauses, not rushing in to fill the silence. For an older adult with intact cognition, it is disrespectful to ignore him or her and address all questions to the patient's family member. The nurse respectfully addresses questions directly to the patient and allows time for his or her responses. If

Figure 30-3 History taking with older adults needs to be at a slow and deliberate pace; it may need to be conducted over several visits for a comprehensive picture of the patient's health.

the patient cannot provide information, the nurse may then address the family member with questions.

Consideration of the patient's educational level is critical, and interview questions should match the older adult's knowledge level. It is not appropriate to ask an elderly patient with limited education "Have you noticed any signs of cerebrovascular or neurological changes?" Instead, questions are phrased in a way that might be better understood and specific to what is being asked. For example, "Have you ever noticed more clumsiness in one hand compared with the other?" or "Has your speech been slurred? Or jumbled?"

When older adults are hospitalized or are more seriously ill, the nurse gathers as much information as possible from previous records so that he or she can review and clarify findings with the older adult, rather than trying to gain all the information from the patient's memory (Lach & Smith, 2007). This helps the older person to conserve energy. If the older adult is acutely ill and fatigues easily, the nurse may need to return and complete the interview later.

Some older adults are reluctant to report symptoms that past health care professionals have dismissed or that they believe might be part of the aging process. For example, an older adult may avoid reporting knee pain because she has had the same pain for several years or believes that arthritis pain is expected for older people. It is best to use specific health-screening questions to detect common concerns. Cues during the physical examination can help the nurse complete some of the health history. For example, when the nurse identifies three scars during examination of the abdomen, he or she might say, "During our interview you told me that you had your appendix removed when you were 7, but could you tell me about these other two scars?"

When interviewing older adults with limited physical or mental abilities, the interview may need to be conducted somewhat differently to gain desired information. Box 30-1 presents suggestions for conducting interviews with older adults who are hearing impaired or deaf, or visually impaired, patients with aphasia, and patients with cognitive impairments (eg, Alzheimer's disease and other dementias).

Hearing Impaired Older Adults

Before starting the interview, check that a hearing aid is in place, turned on, and has a working battery. It is helpful to have a pocket amplifier and earphones available if you cannot locate the patient's hearing aid. Seat yourself directly in front of the person at eye level so that he or she can observe your face for visual cues (Lach & Smith, 2007). Do not stand and talk down to the seated patient. If necessary, seat yourself on the bedside so that the patient can see you. Make certain that you have the patient's attention and are close enough to him or her before you begin speaking. Hearing-impaired patients benefit from seeing your lips move, so keep your hands away from your face while talking. Speak normally or in a slightly louder fashion (ie, a soft-spoken person may need to speak a bit more boldly). Use a low-pitched, calm voice without shouting. If the person has difficulty understanding something, find a different way of saying the same thing and avoid continually repeating the original words. If the person has more profound hearing impairment, be prepared to write questions or messages if necessary or use pictures, illustrations, body language, or gestures to facilitate communication. Speak close to the better ear if necessary. Do not assume that the hearing-impaired older adult is unreliable or has dementia. Try to gain as much information as possible within the limitations of his or her hearing impairment.

Visually Impaired Older Adults

If you are entering a room to speak with someone who is visually impaired, identify yourself and your intentions. Avoid shouting or speaking too loudly (visually impaired older patients are not also hearing impaired). If the patient wears corrective lenses, make sure these are clean. Repeat or reflect the patient's responses to your questions a little more frequently during the interview if he or she cannot see your face for the usual visual cues that indicate understanding. When you speak, let the person know whom you are addressing, especially if you are directing that question to an adult child or colleague and not to the patient. Ask what you can do to facilitate the interview, increasing the light, placing yourself in a different spot, and describing where things are. Be sure to say the individual's name and tell him or her what you are going to touch or do during the physical examination. Keep in mind that people categorized as legally blind may have some vision. When you complete your interview and examination, be sure to return items to their original location unless the person asks you to move them.

Older Adults With Aphasia

Patients who have experienced a stroke or another type of neurological injury or illness may have total or partial aphasia. Those with *expressive aphasia* may be able to partially or fully understand what you say but unable to respond to your questions. Be patient and allow plenty of time to communicate with a person with aphasia. You may want to seek out a picture board or communication device provided by a speech therapist to better facilitate the discussion. Let the patient know if you cannot understand what he or she is telling you. Allow the patient to try to complete thoughts, to struggle with words. Although it is recommended that you provide some words, avoid being too quick to guess what the person is trying to express. If possible, encourage the person to write the word he or she is trying to express and read it aloud. Use gestures or pointing to objects if helpful in supplying words or adding meaning.

Patients With Alzheimer's Disease or Related Disorders

As you conduct an interview with an older adult, you may find the patient has repeated the same story about three times within 20 minutes. This repetitive storytelling is often an indicator of cognitive impairment. Patients who repeat the same story as if you have not heard it before should be screened with the Mini Mental Status Examination (MMSE). If you conduct an MMSE early in the interview, you can better determine whether it is wise to continue to seek information from the patient. People in early stages of Alzheimer's may be fairly accurate in their responses, especially about issues from early adulthood or childhood (remote memory). They are more likely to omit information about more recent issues (short-term memory). People with MMSE scores of 11 or less are unlikely to be reliable reporters for your interview.

When interviewing an older adult with known dementia, make sure that you approach from the front within the patient's line of vision. Provide the same respect that you would to any older patient, introduce yourself, and greet the patient by formal name. Be sure to face the person as you interview. A quiet, calm environment is essential. Avoid a heavy-traffic area, an area with multiple conversations, or a very noisy place. A low-pitched, calm tone of voice tends to be heard well and sets the tone. Ask only one question at a time. Repeat key words if the person does not understand the first time. As much as possible maintain eye contact and provide respect for personal space (Miller, 2008).

People with mild to moderate dementia who maintain language skills can still be accurate reporters of current symptoms and concerns. As dementia progresses, the patient may overestimate abilities to carry out self-care activities, instrumental activities of daily living (IADLs), or safe and independent medication management. Be sure to clarify the accuracy of the patient's responses with a caregiver or family member. If the patient with dementia is more anxious and tends to wander or pace, you may need to walk with him or her while asking simple questions. Try to limit questions to yes or no for those with moderate to severe dementia; avoid open-ended questions or those that require abstract thinking or reasoning (Miller, 2008).

🌐 Cultural Considerations

In many cultures, an older person would never be called by his or her first name at a first meeting and especially would not be addressed as "Sam" or "Inge" by a young stranger.

The nurse sets a tone of respect for the older person at the beginning of the interview by introducing himself or herself and then calling the patient by his or her formal name (Fig. 30-4). The nurse can then clarify how the patient would like to be addressed in the interview.

Figure 30-4 A respectful and pleasant introduction with an older patient can set the tone not just for the immediate health visit, but also for the overall nurse–patient relationship.

Assessment of Risk Factors

Nurses working with older adults are familiar with instruments that have been developed to detect older adults' risk for the most common conditions or issues that accompany aging. They are often referred to as *geriatric syndromes* because of the interaction of multiple chronic diseases (Linton & Lach, 2007). As these syndromes are common, nurses can provide a key role in early detection or assessment of the condition so that interventions can be implemented (Linton & Lach). It is important to ask questions regarding personal history, family history, and risk factors to detect the possibility of one or more of the following common health issues in older adults:

- Nutritional changes
- Mobility impairments (activities of daily living [ADL] and instrumental activities of daily living [IADL] changes)
- Falls risk
- Polypharmacy
- Skin breakdown

Questions to Assess History and Risk Factors	Rationale
Current Concern The reason for seeking care is a brief statement, usually in the patient's own words, about why he or she is making the visit. Ask, "Tell me what caused you to come to the clinic today" or "What happened that brought you to the hospital?" Record this information in the subjective part of documentation or put the statement in quotes.	If the patient replies by giving a medical diagnosis such as "heart attack," encourage the patient to describe symptoms such as "shortness of breath and chest pain."
Personal History ***Nutritional Changes.*** The most commonly used instrument to identify elders at nutritional risk is the DETERMINE instrument (Table 30-1; Posner, Jette, et al., 1993). This simple 10-item checklist can be used to identify older adults who would benefit from health education about nutrition or who have other issues that may affect their nutritional health. The screening tool also identifies older adults at high nutritional risk who may require interventions to improve nutritional status. If the DETERMINE shows risk, other tools may be used to follow up (see Chapter 8).	Nutritional screening is an abbreviated assessment of risk factors that identify older adults who may require a more comprehensive nutritional assessment. The combination of physiological changes with aging, physical or mental health issues, medications, or functional losses can significantly increase risk for weight loss in older adults. Regulation of energy intake is often impaired in later life (Roberts & Rosenberg, 2006). Chapter 8 reviews components included in a comprehensive dietary and nutritional history. Poor nutritional status indicators are linked to longer hospital stays, poor wound healing, and poor health outcomes (Stratton, King, et al., 2006; Thomas, Isenring, et al., 2007).
Items in DETERMINE include such issues as "I eat fewer than two meals per day," "I eat alone most of the time," "I don't always have enough money to buy the food that I need." Higher scores correlate with increased risk.	Financial and transportation issues can limit an older adult's access to nutritional foods. Functional abilities or sensory losses can affect ability to physically prepare nutritious foods. Early cognitive losses that impair judgment, planning, foresight, or sequencing of complex tasks may reduce an older adult's ability to follow recipes or prepare complete meals. Recent weight loss can cause dentures to fit poorly and interfere with chewing. Medications can change tastes and interfere with appetite.
Family History Ask the patient about the health of close family members (ie, parents, grandparents, siblings) to help identify those diseases for which patients may be at risk and to provide counselling and health teaching.	The following familial conditions are important to note: *high blood pressure (BP), coronary artery disease, high cholesterol, stroke, cancer, diabetes mellitus, obesity, alcohol or drug addiction, and mental illness* (Kane, Ouslander, et al., 2008).

(text continues on page 932)

Table 30-1 DETERMINE Nutrition Checklist

Possible Issue	Question to Answer	Score for "Yes" Answer (Circle If "Yes")
Disease	Do you have an illness or condition that makes you change the kind and/or amount of food you eat?	2
Eating poorly	Do you eat fewer than two meals/ day?	3
	Do you eat few fruits, vegetables, or milk products?	2
	Do you have three or more drinks of beer, liquor, or wine almost every day?	2
Tooth loss/mouth pain	Do you have tooth or mouth alterations that make it hard for you to eat?	2
Economic hardship	Do you sometimes have trouble affording the food you need?	4
Reduced social contact	Do you eat alone most of the time?	1
Multiple medications	Do you take three or more prescribed or over-the-counter (OTC) drugs a day?	1
Involuntary weight Loss/gain	Have you lost or gained 10 lb in the last 6 mo without trying?	2
Needs assistance in self-care	Are you sometimes physically not able to shop, cook, or feed yourself?	1
Elder years >age 80	Are you over 80 years old?	1
	Total	

Note: *0–2*: **Good!** Recheck your nutritional score in 6 months. *3–5*: **You are at moderate nutritional risk**. See what can be done to improve your eating habits and lifestyle. Your office on aging, senior nutrition program (eg, Meals on Wheels), senior centre, or health department can help. Recheck your nutritional score in 3 months. *6 or more: You* **are at high nutritional risk**. Bring this checklist the next time you see your doctor, dietitian, or other qualified health or social service professional. Talk with them about any difficulties you may have. Ask for help to improve your nutritional health.
Adapted from the Nutrition Screening Initiative, a project of American Academy of Family Practice, American Dietetic Association, and National Council on Aging, Washington, DC, 1992.

Questions to Assess History and Risk Factors

Risk for Falls. Ask the patient, "Have you ever fallen before? Do you have any dizziness?" Several fall risk assessment instruments assist health care providers in identifying those older adults most at risk. The Morse Fall Scale developed for hospitalized elders (Morse, Tylko, et al., 1987) is widely used in hospital settings and does not require major training of staff. Even modified, however, it does not include the risks posed by medications the elder is taking or potential environmental contributors (Morse, 2006). Another assessment instrument designed for hospitals is the Hendrich II Fall Risk Model (Hendrich, Bender, et al., 2003). This assessment tool measures intrinsic risk factors and does not include environmental factors. It does include higher risks for patients taking medications that might contribute to falling, although it limits this to two drug classes: seizure medications and benzodiazepines. The scale includes points for confusion or disorientation, depression, altered elimination, dizziness or vertigo, male sex, medications, and a partial use of the Get Up and Go test.

Rationale

Falls are a significant risk for older adults. Between 1998 and 2003, almost 85,000 Canadian seniors injured the femur, pelvis, hip, or thigh from a fall. Among seniors living in their own community, home is the location of most falls. Only 7.4% of Canadian seniors live in residential facilities, but fall rates are much higher in those settings (Public Health Agency of Canada, 2005). According to Health Canada (2006), almost one half of injuries from seniors' falls occur in the home. Each year, one out of three seniors in Canada will fall a minimum of one time and hip fractures are the most common outcome. Approximately 20% of seniors' injury-related deaths can be attributed to a fall. Hip fractures can lead to increased dependence as measured by admission to assisted living facilities.

Serious injuries related to falls increase with age and are four to five times greater in people 85 years or older compared to those 65 to 74 years (Stevens, 2006).

Questions to Assess History and Risk Factors	Rationale

The Get Up and Go section of the Hendrich II Fall Risk Model is a portion of the Timed Get Up and Go test (Mathias, Nayak, et al., 1986). However, the Hendrich II version does not time the subject in this section. The patient is simply asked to rise from sitting in a chair. If the patient can stand in a single movement without using his or her hands, the test score is 0 points. If the patient uses the hands to push up from the chair in one attempt, the score is 1 point. If the patient must make several attempts to push up but succeeds in standing, he or she receives 3 points. If the patient requires assistance to stand up, he or she receives a score of 4 points. See the**Point** ✳ for a link to a demonstration of how to use this instrument.

The patient receives 4 points under the "confusion, disorientation, impulsivity" section if he or she demonstrates any of the following: impulsive or unpredictable behaviour; hallucinations; agitation; fluctuations in attention, cognition, psychomotor activity, or level of consciousness (delirium symptoms); unrealistic, inappropriate, or unusual behaviour; disorientation to time, person, or place; inability to follow directions or retain instructions about self-care or ADL care. Patients receive 2 points under "depression" if they demonstrate any of the following: prolonged feelings of helplessness, hopelessness, or being overwhelmed; tearfulness; flat affect or lack of interest; loss of interest in life events; melancholic mood; withdrawal; or statements about being depressed. The patient receives a point for altered elimination if he or she has any of the following: urgency or fecal incontinence, urgency or stress incontinence, diarrhea, frequent urination, or nocturia. Having an indwelling Foley catheter is not considered a risk unless the patient also has one of the symptoms listed above. When the patient receives a score of 5 or more, he or she is considered at risk for falling.

Medications/Polypharmacy. Ask the patient the following:
- "What medications are you taking?"
- "What is the dose of medication that you take?"
- "What is your schedule for taking your medications?"
- "What do you understand about the reason you are taking each of your medications?"

Ask the patient to bring in a bag of all medications that he or she has at home and to identify those currently being taken (Ham, Sloane, et al., 2007). If this is not possible, phrase questions about medications based on body system. For example, "Do you take any medications for your heart? For BP? Do you take any medications for pain?" This approach is also useful when asking about over-the-counter (OTC) medications. "Do you take any medicine from the drugstore to help you sleep? Do you take anything from the drugstore to help your stomach? Your bowels? Are you taking any vitamins or minerals?" Be sure to specifically ask how frequently the patient takes each OTC medication or supplements.

While examining the label of each medication, determine whether the patient is taking the drug as prescribed and if he or she has medications that should not be used together because of interactions. Older adults with cognitive impairment may not take medications as scheduled, even though they report that they do. Nurses can identify accuracy by calculating how many days are between today's date and the refill date, noting how many pills the pharmacist included and counting out the number of tablets left in the container to obtain an estimate of pills taken.

In addition to asking about herbal or nutritional supplements, ask if any alternative health care providers have recommended other kinds of treatments.

Older patients may believe that drinking Chinese herbs boiled into tea is not considered a medication or supplement.

Finally, it is wise to ask, "Do you take any medications belonging to other people, including medications prescribed to a spouse, caregiver, friend, or neighbour?"

It is not unusual for elders living in retirement communities to share medications.

In addition to finding out what particular medications the patient takes, identify how often and when he or she takes each drug:
- "Does your pattern of taking the medication follow the prescription on the bottle? If not, what caused your pattern to change?"
- "Are you experiencing side effects from the medication? If so, what kinds?"
- "Do you take medications with food? With water? Or alcohol?"

This important information allows the nurse to identify how frequently the patient is missing doses or overdosing.

(text continues on page 934)

Questions to Assess History and Risk Factors	Rationale
Older adults with limited education may not understand a question about a "history of substance abuse" but would understand direct questions such as: • "Do you take street drugs? Or drink alcohol?" • "Have you been treated in a rehabilitation facility?" "Do you need refills of prescription drugs because of withdrawal symptoms?"	
Skin Breakdown. Identify risk for skin breakdown, which is especially important in hospitalized and inactive patients. Many health care facilities use the Braden scale, with interventions based on the total score (Bergstrom, Braden, et al., 1987; see Table 13-16 in Chapter 13). Alternatively, the Norton scale includes incontinence and other variables (Defloor & Grypdonck, 2005).	The Braden scale scores patients from 1 to 4 in six subscales: sensory perception, moisture, activity, mobility, nutrition, and friction (Braden & Bergstrom, 1989). The Norton scale uses a 1 to 4 scoring system in each of five subscales: physical condition, mental condition, activity, mobility, and incontinence. A score <14 on Norton and 14 to 18 on Braden indicates a high risk for pressure ulcers.

Risk Assessment and Health Promotion

Topics for Health Promotion

- Risk factors
- Screening
- Exercise and physical activity
- Immunizations

Adapted from Anderson, M. C., Hunter, K., & Bickley, L. S. (2010). The older adult. In T. C. Stephen, D. L. Skillen, R. A. Day, & L. S. Bickley (Eds.). *Canadian Bates' guide to health assessment for nurses* (1st ed., p. 908). Philadelphia, PA: Wolters Kluwer Health/Lippincott Williams & Wilkins.

Teaching for older adults includes the use of sunscreen, adequate nutrition, management of polypharmacy, prevention of elder abuse, and falls prevention.

Skin cancers increase with age and lifelong exposure to the ultraviolet radiation from the sun. Most skin cancers are preventable (Canadian Cancer Society's Steering Committee for Cancer Statistics [CCSSCCS], 2011). Nurses especially observe for skin cancer changes in older adults with the following risk factors: fair, freckling skin; light-coloured eyes, red or blond hair, tendency to burn easily with sun exposure, male gender, and history of cigarette smoking. Patients are taught to wear sunscreen at all times. Hats and clothing that cover the skin are also recommended. Teach patients to do a skin assessment and observe for cancers.

Basal cell carcinoma is a common form of skin cancer in older Caucasians. Basal cell lesions in their early stage form a small, smooth, hemispherical translucent papule covered by a thinned epidermis most often located on the face, the nasal tip and alae or below the eye. The papule gradually enlarges into a pearly nodule and has a central ulcerated lesion. Basal cell carcinoma tends to grow slowly and metastasizes rarely (Stephen & Bickley, 2010). Squamous cell carcinoma usually starts as a hard, red, wart-like lesion with a raised or rolled grey-yellow edge located on a highly sun-exposed area. Look for these types of lesions on the auricle of the ear or face and neck areas with the most sun exposure. Malignant melanoma is a pigmented macule, papule, nodule, patch, or

tumour with the ABCDE warning signs: A for asymmetry; B for borders (look for irregular, ragged, notched, or imprecise edges); C for colour (look for change with brown, black, red, grey, blue, or white areas); D for diameter >6 mm (larger than a pencil eraser in width); and E for evolution (look for change in colour, size, shape, reports of itchiness or tenderness, surface elevation, bleeding) (Canadian Dermatology Association, 2008). This is a highly malignant form of cancer. Document any suspicious lesions and refer the patient for follow-up (Byrd, 2008). See Chapter 13 for more information.

Older adults need added vitamin D, because aging and smoking tend to impair vitamin D synthesis. Groups at risk for folate deficiency include patients with alcoholism, older adults, those who follow "fad" diets, and individuals of low socioeconomic status. Older adults also require special consideration during assessments of dietary requirements. They may compensate for diminished taste of sweet and salty foods by adding sugar and salt to their diet at a time when they are at increased risk for diabetes, hypertension, and heart disease. Their basal metabolic rate is declining concurrently with reductions in physical activity. When this occurs, caloric needs are significantly reduced. Older adults are also at increased risk for malnutrition as a result of social isolation. Eating alone is particularly problematic for people with reduced mobility, receiving social assistance, or both. They may lack the resources required to maintain a nutritious and appealing diet. Poor dentition may also be an issue. Missing teeth, gum disease, or poor-fitting dentures can all detract from enjoying meals. Community programs such as Meals on Wheels offer food services to individuals with disabilities or chronic illnesses who live in social isolation.

Older adults often have multiple chronic conditions and are prescribed multiple medications, which makes medication management and assessment of patient knowledge and adherence to medication schedules especially complex. Safety also becomes important, ranging from assessment for elder abuse to assessment of safety in the home. The older adult may have stairs that create a risk for falls, cooking surfaces that can be a fire hazard, or cords that can easily be tripped over. Teaching focuses on keeping cooking surfaces clean and having cords out of the usual path of walking. Rooms should also be well lit. For hospitalized patients, a bed alarm may be a good reminder to call for help.

Key Symptoms and Signs Reported by the Older Adult

- Falls
- Leaking (urinary or fecal incontinence)
- Inability to get around (mobility impairment)
- Pain (acute, chronic)
- Vision or hearing changes (sensory impairments, including visual, auditory, taste, tactile, olfactory)
- Skin lesions
- Symptoms of vascular disorders (cerebrovascular, peripheral vascular)
- Sleep deprivation
- Depression
- Abuse
- Cognitive changes

Adapted from Anderson, M. C., Hunter, K., et al. (2010). The older adult. In T. C. Stephen, D. L. Skillen, R. A. Day, & L. S. Bickley (Eds.). *Canadian Bates' guide to health assessment for nurses* (1st ed., p. 900). Philadelphia, PA: Wolters Kluwer Health/Lippincott Williams & Wilkins.

Detailed Analysis of Symptom/Sign: Falls

- "Where have you fallen?" (Location)
- "What does it feel like when you fall?" "Do you lose consciousness (black out)? Or feel the room spinning?" (Quality)
- "How many falls have you had in the past year?" (Quantity)
- "When did the falls start?" (Onset)
- "How often do they occur?" (Frequency)
- "What makes the falls worse/more frequent for you?" (Aggravating factors)
- "What do you do to try to avoid falling?" (Alleviating factors)
- "What else do you notice about yourself when you fall?" (Associated symptoms)
- "What are you doing at the time of your fall?" "What is going on in your life?" "What things in your home might contribute to falls?" (Environmental factors)
- "How do these falls affect your day-to-day living?" (Significance to patient)
- "What do you think is the cause of your falls?" (Patient perspective)

Adapted from Anderson, M. C., Hunter, K., et al. (2010). The older adult. In T. C. Stephen, D. L. Skillen, R. A. Day, & L. S. Bickley (Eds.). *Canadian Bates' guide to health assessment for nurses* (1st ed., p. 902). Philadelphia, PA: Wolters Kluwer Health/Lippincott Williams & Wilkins.

Focused Health History Related to Common Symptoms/Signs

Examples of Questions to Assess Symptoms/Signs	Rationale/Unexpected Findings
Incontinence • "Have you ever leaked urine?" • "Have you ever lost control of your bladder?"	There are three basic types of incontinence to assess: stress, urge, and functional. Incontinence is very common among hospitalized patients and those in long-term care. Risks include increasing age, caffeine intake, limited mobility, impaired cognition, diabetes, use of medications such as diuretics, obesity, Parkinson's disease, stroke, and prostate conditions in men or pelvic floor weakness in women.
Sleep Deprivation • "What time do you turn off the lights?" • "How many times do you wake up in a night?" • "How rested do you feel upon arising?"	Insomnia may be either acute or chronic. It may affect falling asleep, staying asleep, or early morning wakening. Risk factors include female gender, increased age, medical or psychiatric illness, and shift work.
Pain • "Do you have pain or discomfort?" (If so, inquire about location, radiation, quality, intensity, onset, frequency, duration, associated factors, alleviating or aggravating factors, environmental factors, significance to patient [eg, Affected diet? Sleep? Mood?] and patient's perspective on the cause.)	Chronic illness such as osteoarthritis or diabetic neuropathy may increase pain in the older adult. The patient may be hesitant to report pain because of fear of dependence or wanting to be a "good patient" for his or her health care providers. Pain may affect usual functions.
Cognitive Status Assessment of cognitive status helps guide nursing care in various settings and can give important information for discharge planning, patient and family education, interventions needed for safety, and general support. Some specific tips for using this examination in older adults are found in Box 30-2.	The Mini-Cog is a shorter and less stressful version while the Mini Mental Status Examination (MMSE) takes 10 to 15 minutes and is a more detailed screen of mental status. The MMSE is not a diagnostic instrument.

BOX 30-2 ASSESSMENT OF COGNITIVE STATUS

- Introduce the test. State "I am going to conduct a test of your thinking skills. This is a screening test and I want you to do your best."
- If a family member is present, it is wise to let him or her know that he or she is not allowed to answer for the older adult. Patients with mild dementia may look to a spouse or child to assist them with questions.
- If you detect that the patient is somewhat suspicious of your questions based on previous interactions, start with questions under the language section of the examination (ie, "What is this?" point to your watch, and have him or her identify watch). Usually these questions offer the patient some success in responses and allow you to complete more of the screening.

- Do not provide clues to answers. For example, when asking the orientation questions, simply say, "Can you tell me what month this is?" Do not say, "Well, we recently had our Thanksgiving break." If the patient is uncertain, simply restate the question: "Can you tell me the month?"
- Allow enough time for the patient to respond to the question that you have asked.
- Reassure the patient if he or she worries that the response might be incorrect. "It's OK if some of these are difficult for you." However, don't falsely tell patients that they are doing fine. Identify that this is simply a screening test and will help you better understand how to provide care for this patient.

Examples of Questions to Assess Symptoms/Signs

The MMSE is the most widely used instrument to screen mental status in older adults. It assesses several areas of cognition: orientation (time and place), registration (ability to immediately register information), attention and calculation (ability to subtract sequential sevens), recall (short-term memory of three objects), language, ability to follow a three-step command, and visual-perceptual abilities (Folstein, Folstein, et al., 1975;) see Chapter 10).

Expected findings are a score of 24 to 30.

Depression

Although older adults are at risk for depression, the illness is not an expected or inevitable part of aging. To assess for depression, ask the following:

- "In general, how satisfied are you with life?"
- "How often do you feel sad?"
- "Have you ever suffered from depression?"

The Geriatric Depression Scale (GDS) provides a brief screening for depressive symptoms. The longer 30-item version of the GDS asks about symptoms, self-image issues, and losses in a yes/no format. The short-form 15-item GDS, also in a yes/no format, is used for patients with mild to moderate dementia (Yesavage, Brink, et al., 1982; Sheikh & Yesavage, 1986). Either version can be asked aloud (for visually impaired patients) or offered to the patient to read and complete privately (see Chapter 10).

If the screening examination reveals risk for or actual depression, assess for potential suicide risk. Mentally healthy older adults report that thoughts about death and suicide ideation are relatively rare. Chapter 10 discusses depression and suicide screening in more depth.

Abuse

Many older adults are vulnerable to psychological, financial, or physical abuse by family members or caregivers. Often elderly patients do not report violence. In Canada, several jurisdictions have put legislation in place to protect elders who are abused (Department of Justice, 2007). If indicated, comment "Injuries like yours could have been caused by someone hurting you." Ask "Did someone hurt you?"

Rationales/Unexpected Findings

Clinical Significance 30-1

Suspicious patients with mild to moderate dementia have difficulty with time orientation questions, so asking these questions first will highlight their deficits and may make them more likely to refuse to answer the rest of the examination.

Patients with *Parkinson's disease* may have a slow retrieval time and very delayed responses (Miller, 2009).

Depression may occur in older adults for various reasons. It is more common in individuals with multiple chronic health conditions (Hybels & Blazer, 2003) or who have recently suffered the loss of a spouse, friend, family member, or pet. Decisions about moving out of a family home because of increasing care needs may also lead to depressive symptoms.

On the short-form GDS, a score >6 suggests depression and a score >9 indicates depression.

Factors that contribute to suicide in older adults include mental disorders (especially depression), physical illness, personality traits such as hostility, hopelessness, inability to verbally express psychological pain and dependency on others, and recent life events and losses (DeoLeo & Spathonis, 2003).

Many victims of abuse are isolated or may not report abuse because of shame, embarrassment, dependence on the abuser, or cognitive impairment. They may fear loss of independence and reprisal from the abuser. Others are pressured by relatives not to report.

Cultural Considerations

Additional Questions	Rationale/Unexpected Findings
• "Do you have any food preferences?" • "What is your primary language?" • "What are your favourite activities?" • "To what extent do you feel part of your community?"	Senior First Nations, Métis, Inuit, and immigrants contribute to Canada's linguistic and ethnic diversity. Only 1% of seniors are First Nations. Over 56% of Canadian seniors are immigrants aged 65 to 84 years (Turcotte & Schellenberg, 2006). Immigration patterns are changing, and a number of immigrant seniors do not speak either official language, creating a communication challenge. Many older adults prefer to experience environments similar to those they had in younger years. On the basis of assessment findings, the nurse may provide interventions such as facilitating a Korean diet for the patient, using translators effectively, finding "patient navigators" from the family or community, and using nonverbal communication styles with sensitivity (Anderson, Hunter, et al., 2010).

An Example of a Therapeutic Dialogue

Remember Mr. Lehmann, introduced at the beginning of this chapter. This 76-year-old man with a history of Parkinson's disease is concerned about constipation. The nurse uses professional communication techniques to gather subjective data from Mr. Lehmann.

Nurse: Hello, Mr. Lehmann. How are you doing?

Mr. Lehmann: Not so well. How about you?

Nurse: I'm OK. Tell me what "not so well" means for you.

Mr. Lehmann: I don't like my roommate. He snores all night. I don't like the people here.

Nurse: Sounds as if the snoring might be disturbing your sleep. We can talk about that a little bit later. What is it that you are not liking about the people here?

Mr. Lehmann: They are not friendly. They do not talk to me.

Nurse: Perhaps I can help by introducing you to a few more residents (pause).

I noticed that you have been taking the wheelchair to your meals. What has caused you to do that?

Mr. Lehmann: The aides say that it's faster. I would rather take my walker on my own.

Nurse: We can talk with them. How about your eating?

Mr. Lehmann: I drink one to two glasses of milk or juice at each meal. But I have trouble eating their food because my dentures don't fit (pause).

Nurse: (nods head, waits)

Mr. Lehmann: I also would like to move my bowels before breakfast but I can't because I need help with zipping and buttoning my pants and the aides don't have time.

Critical Thinking Challenge

• What did the nurse do to obtain more information?
• What follow-up questions would you recommend?
• What additional assessments might the nurse make?

Objective Data Collection

After completing subjective data collection, the nurse collects equipment and prepares for the objective assessment. For a well older adult assessment, a head-to-toe examination will be done. If the patient is being seen because of a concern, the highest priority assessment related to the patient's concern is performed first. The assessment may need to be broken into several sessions, because older adults tend to fatigue easily.

Equipment

- Stethoscope
- Thermometer and blood pressure (BP) cuff or electronic vital signs monitor
- Watch or clock with a second hand
- Otoscope
- Ophthalmoscope
- Reflex hammer
- Tongue blades
- Cotton balls
- Familiar objects (eg, coin, pin, key)
- Clean gloves
- Tuning forks
- Nasal speculum
- Snellen chart
- Tape measure
- Bivalve vaginal speculum and specimen supplies
- Equipment wipes

Promoting Patient Comfort, Dignity, and Safety

Ask patients how they prefer to be addressed. Perform hand hygiene. Older adults experience changes in their immune system and a declining ability to fight infection (Htwe, Mushtaq, et al., 2007).

When assessing an older adult, nurses allow extra time. It is important to rely on general observations and focus on the patient's functional abilities. Be alert to mobility issues. Assist patients on and off the examination table and avoid having them lying on a bony prominence for a long time. Pressure sores are one of the geriatric syndromes (Inouye, Studenski, et al., 2007).

Documentation of unexpected findings is very important for this population because of their frequent transitions across health care settings. Excellent documentation can assist health care providers in a new setting to evaluate and compare the patient's current examination findings.

Comprehensive Physical Examination: The Older Adult

The nurse first performs a general survey and measures the vital signs. See Chapter 6 regarding the four traditional vital signs (BP, pulse, respiration, and temperature) and pain as the fifth vital sign. In the older adult, functional status is the sixth vital sign. Assessment of functional abilities is performed universally in every hospital, assisted living facility, nursing home, and community-based assessment clinics. *Functional ability* refers to the ability to perform tasks and carry out social roles in the ADL. Researchers who study interventions for chronic diseases in older adults often use functional ability to measure efficacy of outcomes (Kane, Ouslander, et al., 2008). Assessment of functional status starts at the beginning of an interaction with the patient. A number of well-validated and efficient assessment instruments are available to the nurse for focusing his or her assessment. The goal in assessment of *functional ability* is to determine the resources required for patients to maximize independence and to compensate for any challenges to their abilities (Duthie, 2007).

Instruments

The 10-Minute Geriatric Screener incorporates some functional issues. Issue-focused instruments such as the Tinetti Gait and Balance Tool (Tinetti, 1986) or the Berg Balance scale (Berg, Wood-Dauphinee, et al., 1992) provide more in-depth assessment of function and include ADLs and IADLs. The Katz Index of ADL (Katz, Ford, et al., 1963) quantifies the degree of disability in a chronically ill patient. Other measures include the Functional Independence Measure (FIM; Wright, 2000), the Jette Functional Status Index (Jette, 1987), and the Barthel Index (Mahoney & Barthel, 1965). The FIM is a more sensitive measure and frequently used in research. Well-tested and validated versions for use include original in-person, short-form, telephone version, and proxy report (Wright, 2000). The Lawton IADL scale (Lawton & Brody, 1969; Box 30-3) measures ability to use a telephone, manage finances, shop, do laundry, prepare food, perform housekeeping, and use transportation. The Lawton IADL instrument has been designed for older adults to self-report their abilities in these important tasks. The tool relies on accurate self-report by the elder; information can be misleading with cognitively impaired elders who lack insight into their functional losses. For example, an individual with Alzheimer's disease may report that he or she can manage the telephone but in fact cannot demonstrate how to call for help if assistance is needed. Another option is to use the Direct Assessment of Functional Abilities, a 10-item observational instrument for use with individuals with dementia (Karagiozis, Gray, et al., 1998). It requires the older adult to physically demonstrate tasks of meal preparation, money management, shopping, transportation use, reading, hobbies, and safety awareness. Occupational therapists sometimes use this. Many older adults define their health by their ability to perform self-care. Some require complete assistance with care, while others are functionally independent. Ability to carry out daily activities can be affected by depression, motivation, cognitive status, medical conditions, or sensory losses (Miller, 2009).

BOX 30-3 LAWTON INSTRUMENTAL ACTIVITIES OF DAILY LIVING

INSTRUCTIONS: Ask the patient to describe his or her functioning in each category and then complement the description with specific questions as needed.

Ability to Telephone

1. Operates telephone on own initiative: looks up and dials number, etc.
2. Answers telephone and dials a few well-known numbers.
3. Answers telephone but does not dial.
4. Does not use telephone at all.

Shopping

1. Takes care of all shopping needs independently.
2. Shops independently for small purchases.
3. Needs to be accompanied on any shopping trip.
4. Completely unable to shop.

Food Preparation

1. Plans, prepares, and serves adequate meals independently.
2. Prepares adequate meals if supplied with ingredients.
3. Heats and serves prepared meals, or prepares meals but does not maintain adequate diet.
4. Needs to have meals prepared and served.

Housekeeping

1. Maintains house alone or with occasional assistance (eg, heavy work done by domestic help).
2. Performs light daily tasks such as dishwashing and bed making.
3. Performs light daily tasks but cannot maintain acceptable level of cleanliness.
4. Needs help with all home maintenance tasks.
5. Does not participate in any housekeeping tasks.

Laundry

1. Does personal laundry completely.
2. Launders small items; rinses socks, stockings, and so on.
3. All laundry must be done by others.

Mode of Transportation

1. Travels independently on public transportation or drives own car.
2. Arranges own travel via taxi, but does not otherwise use public transportation.
3. Travels on public transportation when assisted or accompanied by another.
4. Travel limited to taxi, automobile, or ambulette, with assistance.
5. Does not travel at all.

Ability to Handle Finances

1. Manages financial matters independently (budgets, writes checks, pays rent and bills, goes to bank); collects and keeps track of income.
2. Manages day-to-day purchases but needs help with banking, major purchases, controlled spending, and so on.
3. Incapable of handling money.

Scoring: Circle one number for each domain. Total the numbers circled. The lower the score, the more independent the older adult is. Scores are only good for individual patients. It is useful to see the score comparison over time.

Techniques and Expected Findings	Rationale/Unexpected Findings
General Survey ***Inspection.*** Observe expected changes that occur with aging. Assess for any decreasing abilities to function and care for self. Observe for gait, mobility, hygiene, speech, affect, and indications of thought processes. Note any changes in mental status. *By the eighth or ninth decade, physical appearance changes, with sharper body contours and more angular facial features. Posture tends to have a general flexion, and the patient's gait tends to have a wider base of support to compensate for diminished balance. Steps tend to be shorter and uneven. The patient may need to use the arms to help aid in balance.*	Compromised hygiene and inappropriate dress may indicate decreased functional ability or may result from medications, infection, dehydration, or nutritional status. Inappropriate affect, inattentiveness, impaired memory, and inability to perform ADLs may indicate *dementia* from Alzheimer's disease or another cause. Changes in mental status may be from medications, dehydration, inadequate nutrition, underlying infection, or hypoxia.
Height and Weight An essential component of assessing nutritional status is an accurate measure of height and weight. If possible, measure height with the person standing erect against a wall without shoes. Measure weight annually and height periodically.	△ *SAFETY ALERT 30-1* *Avoid having an older adult stand and balance on a weight scale when measuring height. Do not attempt to determine height when a frail older adult is standing on the weight scale. This creates a risk of falling because of the unsteadiness of the weight scale base.*

(text continues on page 940)

Height and weight are important components of the calculation for body mass index (BMI). *For adults over 65 years, a BMI of 22.0 to 26.9 is healthy (Brunet, Day, et al., 2010). This BMI is slightly higher than the recommended BMI for younger adults.*

Vital Signs

Pain Assessment. Pain, the fifth vital sign, affects the other vital signs. Assess for pain/discomfort first (see Chapter 7).

Temperature. Assess temperature. *The temperature of older adults is at the lower end of the expected range. Mean body temperature for older adults is 36°C to 36.8°C.*

Auscultation

Pulse. Assess rate at apex for 1 minute. *The apical rate may provide more information about arrhythmias in older patients. The aging adult continues to have a range of 60 to 100 beats/min.*

The pulse rate of older adults takes longer to rise to meet sudden increases in demand and longer to return to its resting state. Resting heart rate of older adults tends to be lower than for younger adults.

Inspection

Respirations. Assess respirations. *Decreased vital capacity and inspiratory volume can cause respirations to be shallower and more rapid than in younger adults, with a respiratory rate of 16 to 24 breaths/min for older adults.*

Pulse Oximetry. Assess pulse oximetry. Placement of the pulse oximetry probe can present a challenge in older adults. Sensors designed for the forehead or bridge of nose may be indicated. *Oxygen saturation is >92%.*

Functional Ability. Select the instruments according to the context in order to assess the sixth vital sign in older adults (see discussion above).

BMI >29 increases health risks for osteoarthritis of hips and knees, heart disease, diabetes, and breast and colon cancers in older adults (Douketis, Paradis, et al., 2005). A BMI <22 is associated with increased morbidity (Brunet, Day, et al., 2010). Undernutrition can alert the nurse to depression, alcoholism, malignancy, poverty, caregiver neglect, and cognitive impairment (Anderson, Hunter, et al., 2010).

Over 15% of Canadians have chronic pain with neuropathic features (ACTION, 2008).

Because of changes in the body's temperature regulatory mechanism and decreased subcutaneous fat, the aging adult is less likely to develop a fever, but more likely to succumb to hypothermia. Temperatures within expected range for a younger adult may constitute fever in an older adult.

Variation in rhythm may develop in some older adults. The radial artery may stiffen from peripheral vascular disease. A rigid artery does not indicate vascular disease elsewhere.

Heart sounds may be more difficult to assess because of increased air space in the lungs, which increases the anterior–posterior diameter of the chest.

Aging causes the costal cartilage to become more rigid, decreasing chest expansion and vital capacity. Decreased efficiency of respiratory muscles results in breathlessness at lower activity levels. Respiratory rates >24 are not expected and should be followed with further examination for cyanosis of the nail beds or the perioral area.

> ⚠ *SAFETY ALERT 30-2*
>
> *In older adults with chronic lung disease or congestive heart failure (CHF), observe for generalized distress, confusion, or an impression that the patient is working hard to breathe. These signs may indicate decompensation.*

Peripheral vascular disease, decreased carbon dioxide levels, cold-induced vasoconstriction, and anemia may complicate assessment of oxygen saturation on the fingers.

Skin, Hair, and Nails

Inspection. Inspect the skin, hair, and nails. The older adult's skin bruises and breaks down easily, exposing the patient to increased risk of infections of wounds. Nurses examine the skin carefully for breakdown, especially in the perineal area of older adults who are incontinent, and in any area that is at risk for pressure ulcers because of reduced mobility or shear forces (see Chapter 13).

Seborrheic keratoses are extremely common in older individuals. These dark brown, pigmented lesions are waxy-appearing areas seen on the trunk of the body. They may appear on sun-exposed areas of the body. They can feel warty or greasy to palpation.

Photoaging findings of the skin include coarse wrinkles over sun-exposed areas, solar lentigines (age or liver spots) on the face, hands, forearms, upper chest, or back, and actinic keratoses (Helfrich, Sachs, et al., 2008). *There is increased wrinkling, and skin is coarse in sun-exposed areas. Scalp hair is thinned. The skin will be less elastic and may be dry (although dryness of skin is more often linked to poor hydration status). It is common to note thinning of the epidermal layer, more pronounced in the eighth and ninth decades. Nail beds may have ridges. Toenails may become thickened.*

Head and Neck

Inspection. Inspect the structures of the head and neck. *The appearance is symmetrical. Facial expression is appropriate to the situation.*

Inspection and Palpation. Inspect and palpate the skull and hair. *The skull is smooth and there is no pain or mass. The hair is usually thin and grey in an older adult.* Palpate the temporomandibular joint. *The joint moves smoothly, without tenderness.* Palpate the sternocleidomastoid and trapezius muscles. *There are no masses or pain.* Inspect and palpate the thyroid. *The thyroid is not enlarged.*

Nurses are alert for **bruising** in various stages of healing that might indicate abuse.

Pressure ulcers in any of the following areas should be staged and interventions begun immediately: sacral and ischial areas, greater trochanteric area, and heels. Pressure ulcers are one of the geriatric syndromes (Anderson, Hunter, et al., 2010).

Patchy white scaly areas on the scalp are indicative of seborrhea, common in persons with Parkinson's disease and usually treated with corticosteroids. Very thick yellow overgrown toenails are usually a sign of onychomycosis (tinea unguium), a **fungal infection** of the nail beds. These infected nails are difficult to treat and may eventually fall off leaving a dry nail bed base.

Stasis dermatitis is another common finding in older adults with a history of varicosities, phlebitis, and trauma. Lower extremities have a reddish-brown ruddy appearance and are usually edematous, but are not inflamed or infected. Nurses may confuse stasis dermatitis with **cellulitis**, but the stasis changes do not respond to antibiotics. Stasis dermatitis may lead to leg ulcers on the lower shin area. These ulcers can become infected. Comprehensive assessment of the area includes the location, colour, and size of the area, size and depth of the ulcer (if present), presence of inflammation or warmth, and presence and severity of edema.

Herpes zoster (shingles) is a red painful vesicular or pustular rash that follows the distribution of a dermatome. It is a reactivation of the latent varicella-zoster virus in the dorsal root ganglia. Older adults have a less vigorous immune response and are at risk for developing this rash, especially during times of illness or hospitalization. Prompt treatment is important to reduce postherpetic neuralgia pain. Older adults are advised of the availability of a vaccine, Zostavax, which reduces the incidence of herpes zoster.

A downward gaze with little eye contact may be a sign of depression. Any swelling, masses, or tumours are unexpected. Flat affect or facial tension may signify depression or anxiety.

Degenerative changes result from osteoarthritis in the temporomandibular joint, causing crepitations and pain with movement. The patient who is extremely thin may have sunken hollows in his or her face. The patient with extremely thick structures may have thyroid disorders. A goitre in the thyroid gland is also unexpected. Clicking or crepitus in the temporomandibular joint may be associated with jaw or neck pain. Note limitations in movement in the neck.

(text continues on page 942)

Eyes and Vision

Inspection. Inspect the eyebrows and structures of the eyes. *Senile ptosis or a sagging of the upper lid down across the eye, dry eyes that appear irritated and red, and a decrease in the corneal reflex may be present.*

Ectropion, a turning of the lid outward, or entropion, a turning of the lid inward, may also be observed. **Entropion** can cause the eyelashes on the lower lid to scratch the corneal surface (Stephen & Bickley, 2010; Fig. 30-5). Reduced visual fields, especially unilaterally, can be a sign of a stroke or central neurological lesion. Refer to Chapter 15. Loss of vision can significantly affect daily functioning including dressing, grooming, and ambulating safely.

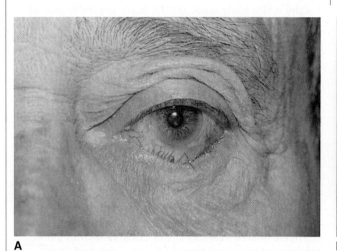

A

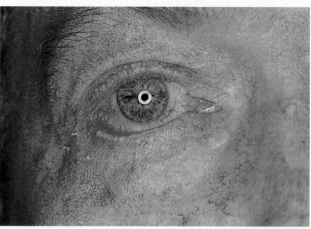

B

Figure 30-5 Eye findings in older adults. **A.** Entropion. **B.** Ectropion.

Test vision and cranial nerve functions (CN II–VII) (see Chapter 15). *Older adults may have difficulty focusing properly (presbyopia) and may have difficulty with glare and accommodating to changes in light. A smaller pupil size and a slower or sluggish pupillary accommodation to light are expected. Upward gaze is reduced because of muscle changes and laxity. Also commonly seen is a greyish-yellow ring at the edge of the cornea, called arcus senilis. This was thought to be an expected change of aging, but more recently has been linked to elevated lipid deposits. Visual fields may be slightly diminished with confrontation but should not show unilateral differences.* Perform the ophthalmoscopic examination (see Chapter 15). *Disc margins may be less distinct; drusen, yellow spots, may be on the retina* (Stephen & Bickley, 2010).

Ears and Hearing

Perform inspection and palpation of the ear (see Chapter 16).

Inspection. Inspect the auricle and mastoid surface for any lesions or changes. *No pain, masses, or lesions are present.*

Ulcerated lesions on the auricle in older men with a history of sun exposure (eg, golfers, outdoor workers, farmers) may represent *squamous cell carcinoma* and should be evaluated.

Palpation. Palpate the mastoid surface, press on the tragus, and pull up and down on the auricle to assess for tenderness. *No tenderness to palpation.*

Inspection. Perform gross hearing whisper test, Weber and Rinne tests. *Weber is heard midline or in both ears and air conduction (AC)> bone conduction.*

Perform the otoscopic examination. *There may be a pearly grey tympanic membrane or an ear canal that is narrowed or occluded with wax. The patient with wax may have conductive hearing loss and will lateralize hearing to the ear occluded with wax on the Weber test or will hear bone conduction (BC) longer than air conduction (AC) in the ear occluded with wax on the Rinne test.*

Nose, Mouth, and Throat

Inspection. Inspect the nose, mouth, and throat. Ask the patient to remove dentures. Make note of the colour and moisture of the mucosal membranes of the nose and oral cavity. *These are pink to pinkish red and moist. The tongue is pinkish red, moist, and has no fissures. A slightly dry oral mucosa is more common in older adults, but a fissured tongue is a sign of dehydration. Varicosities under the tongue are more common in older adults. The gag reflex is intact, although it may diminish mildly in frail older adults. The gums are intact and pink.*

Test nasal patency (Fig. 30-6). *Deviation of the nasal septum is common in older adults.* Test CN I. *The ability to smell declines.*

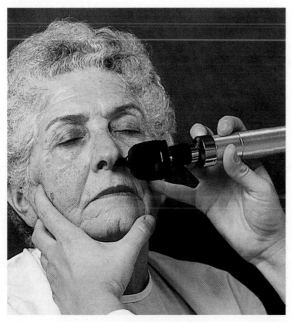

Figure 30-6 Assessing for nasal patency in the older adult.

Loss of hearing is found in 30% of people older than 65 years and in 47% of those older than 75 years (National Institute of Deafness and Communication Disorders, 2010). High-frequency sounds are lost most commonly for older adults, so they may have difficulty hearing a female examiner with a high-pitched voice. More than 50% of Canadians over 65 years are affected by this inner ear hearing impairment (Public Health Agency of Canada, 2006). Hearing loss can affect emotional health and functional abilities. Early treatment of the causes of conductive hearing loss or information on assistive devices is important.

Vasomotor rhinitis is common. Pale mucosal membranes can indicate *anemia* or *malnutrition*. Malodorous breath may indicate dental disease, poor dental hygiene, or underlying diseases. Compromised dental condition, fractured teeth, or untreated dental caries should be referred to a dentist, because these can markedly influence nutritional intake. A bright-red tongue can indicate *vitamin C* or B_1 *deficiency*. An overgrowth of white patchy plaque on the tongue may be related to poor dental hygiene or may be a **fungal** or **yeast infection** (*oral candidiasis*). Limited oral care may be indicative of forgetting to manage ADLs, a sign of cognitive impairment. An absent or markedly diminished gag reflex can be found in patients who have had a *stroke*, longstanding *alcoholism*, or *neurological disorders*. *Patients with diminished or absent gag reflexes are at risk for aspiration pneumonia* (see Chapter 17).

(text continues on page 944)

Spine, Thorax, and Lungs

Inspection. Inspect the curvatures and alignment of the spine (see Chapter 18). *The dorsal curvature of the thoracic spine may increase.*

Inspect the chest (thorax). *The older adult may have an increased anterior–posterior diameter that does not affect function.*

Palpation. Palpate the chest wall to test for tactile fremitus. *Chest wall is nontender and free of swelling or masses. Tactile fremitus is not increased.*

Percussion. Percuss the lungs. *Percussion notes are resonant throughout lung fields.*

Auscultation. Auscultate breath sounds. *Older adults who can take ample breaths should have vesicular breath sounds over anterior and posterior lung fields. Harsh rhonchi are sometimes found because of the difficulty of clearing materials from the lungs. Have the patient cough and then listen for breath sounds again. It is common for older adults to have some scattered fine crackles at the bases of their lungs.*

Heart and Neck Vessels

Inspection of the Neck. Inspect the jugular venous pressure (JVP). *Pulsations have soft, rapid, undulating quality. JVP is <3 cm at the sternal angle.*

Inspection, Auscultation, and Palpation. Inspect for carotid pulsations. Auscultate for carotid bruits from atherosclerosis before palpating each carotid separately, avoiding the carotid sinus. *Amplitude correlates fairly well with the pulse pressure.*

Inspection and Palpation. Inspect and palpate the precordium (see Chapter 19). *Pulsations may be seen in very thin or anxious patients. No heaves or thrusts are seen or palpated.*

Auscultation. Auscultate heart sounds. *Pulse rates in the 50 to 60 range are common and often related to use of beta-blocker or other cardiac medications. Heart rate and rhythm are regular with no murmurs, rubs, or gallops. As older adults reach their 80s and 90s, murmurs are common, especially grade 2 systolic murmurs.*

Increased fremitus or dullness with percussion, especially at the lung bases, can indicate fluid accumulation.

Older adults with chronic lung disease have hyperresonance on examination.

Older women may have kyphosis (curvature of the thoracic spine related to osteoporosis) that can affect the nurse's ability to hear lung sounds at the bases. The nurse may need to listen for breath sounds laterally on the posterior wall. Lung sounds may be difficult to hear with advanced lung disease or may sound diminished and tight. Note any associated purse-lipped breathing. Listening after a nebulizer treatment may give a clearer picture (see Chapter 18).

⚠ *SAFETY ALERT 30-3*

JVP >3 cm suggests right-sided congestive heart failure (CHF) or, less frequently, pericarditis, stenosis of the tricuspid valve, or obstruction of the superior vena cava.

Prevent creating a drop in blood pressure (BP) or pulse rate by avoiding pressure on the carotid sinus. A decreased stroke volume can reduce pulsations. Weak or thready pulses are palpated in cardiogenic shock. A bounding pulse indicates aortic insufficiency.

Pulses >100 are unexpected and should be taken seriously. Because of their diminished cardiac reserves, older adults do not tolerate these pulse rates well for long periods.

Comprehensive assessment of heart murmurs includes location, timing, shape, radiation, intensity, pitch, and quality (Roach, Roddick, et al., 2010a). Loud (grade 3 or greater) or harsh holosystolic murmurs suggest valvular (usually aortic) stenosis and can sometimes be heard radiating up to the neck. Loud murmurs that can be heard radiating from the apex laterally over the left chest wall are usually mitral valve in origin. Findings from the whole examination should be considered when the patient has a loud murmur. Nurses specifically look

for lower extremity edema and abdominal distension as well as conduct a thorough respiratory
examination to identify signs of *CHF*. Jugular venous
distention is a sign of CHF. Arrythmias, especially
atrial fibrillation, are common in older adults, but
warrant consideration as unexpected findings. Nurses
need to note whether this is an irregularly irregular rhythm and specifically be concerned if the rate
is >100.

Peripheral Vascular

Inspection. Inspect the abdomen for pulsations.
No pulsations are visible.

Abdominal aortic pulsations that extend over a wide
area indicate an **aortic aneurysm**.

Auscultation. Auscultate the aorta, renal, and iliac
arteries for bruits. *No bruits are heard.*

Palpation. Palpate peripheral pulses. *Pulses are 1+ to
2+/4 and symmetrical.*

Absent peripheral pulses are of great concern
and are documented. Contact the primary care
provider if this finding is new. It is more common in
a person with a long history of smoking or who has
diabetes; it can seriously interfere with wound healing. Vascular disease may be venous or arterial (see
Chapter 20).

Breasts and Axillae

Inspection: Female. Inspect the axillae for rashes.
Inspect the breasts for symmetry and for rashes in the
inframammary region. *Skin of axillae is free of rashes.
Axillary hair diminished (Miller, 2009). Breasts are symmetrical, perhaps slightly different in size. Inframammary region is free of rashes.*

Asymmetry of nipples, areolae, or breasts warrants further examination. Puckering suggests "peau d'orange"
skin associated with lymphedema and possible malignancy. Inspect mastectomy scars and the axillae for
masses or nodularity. Impaired lymph drainage following surgery may cause lymphedema (Day & Bickley,
2010).

Inspection: Male.

A hard irregular nodule in male breast tissue suggests breast cancer (Day & Bickley, 2010). It is easier
to detect deviations using inspection and palpation in
men. Nodules and increased warmth require further
examination.

Palpation. Palpate breasts and tail of Spence for
masses. Palpate for axillary lymph nodes. Because
breast tissue loses density with age, masses or nodules are easier to feel. *No masses or nodules are
present. Breasts soft, flaccid. May also be granular
or nodular.*

Mastectomy scars should be palpated gently. Describe
location, size, shape, contour, fixation or mobility, and
tenderness of lymph nodes or breast masses.

Abdomen and Elimination

Inspection, Auscultation, Percussion, Palpation.
Inspect, auscultate, percuss, and palpate the abdomen. *Take extra time to listen for bowel sounds in older
adults with a history of constipation. Finding a mass of
stool in the lower left quadrant is common. A flaccid or
soft, distended abdomen is common, but can be related
to deconditioning and loss of muscle control. Bowel
sounds may be slow, but easy to hear.*

A distended abdomen can signify excessive gas, stool,
or fluid. Asymmetry or masses are important findings
and may be signs of *severe constipation* or *cancer*.
A rectal check should be performed for anyone with a
lower abdominal mass. Patients with large amounts of
abdominal ascites usually have *liver disease* or *cancerous involvement of the liver*. Hemorrhoids, internal
or external, are common, but should not be painful,
fiery red, or inflamed. Fecal **incontinence** or involuntary passage of stool is unexpected in older adults
(see Chapter 22).

(text continues on page 946)

Inspect the anus and perform the rectal examination. *The rectal examination may show external hemorrhoids.*

Musculoskeletal System

Inspection and Palpation. Obtain height. *Loss of height of up to 15 cm can occur by 70 to 80 years of age.* Perform focused assessments of the bones, muscles, and joints. Inspection and palpation include muscle mass, range of motion (ROM), muscle tone and strength; joint swelling, tenderness, or crepitations. *Flexion and hyperextension of the neck are somewhat reduced. Likelihood of kyphosis of the spine is increased (more common in women than men). There may be a generalized decrease in strength and mildly decreased ROM. Older adults with arthritis may have enlarged joints, especially at the knees and in the hands.* When possible, nurses test the patient's ability to stand from a seated position, walk 6 m (20 feet) briskly, turn around, and return to sitting position (see *10-Minute Geriatric Screener*). *Patients should be able to do this smoothly, without loss of balance, stumbling, or assistance.*

Examination of ROM of the upper extremities is important, especially for hospitalized older adults. Limited abduction of the shoulder can be addressed immediately to prevent "frozen shoulder," a condition that commonly occurs during or after a hospital stay. Pain on palpation of the spine after a fall should raise concerns about possible *compression fracture* of the spine. Large nodules in the distal interphalangeal joints are *Heberden nodes*, while enlargements of the proximal interphalangeal joints are *Bouchard nodes*, common with *arthritis* (Roach, Roddick, et al., 2010b). Contractures of the hips and knees are common (but not expected changes with aging) in patients who spend much of their day in a wheelchair. These contractures change the structure of gait and balance and place the patient at risk for further immobility (see Chapter 23).

Neurological

Assess cranial nerves, motor system, sensory system, and reflexes. (Mental status and speech are assessed during the health history interview.)

Any asymmetrical findings require a detailed neurological examination. Older adults who appear to have a blank or blunted affect may have *depression, dementia,* or *Parkinson's disease.*

Inspection and Palpation.

Cranial Nerves. Test cranial nerves in pairs. *Common expected findings in older adults include decreased upward gaze.*

Motor System. Assess balance, involuntary movements, coordination, and the tone and strength of muscles. *There may be slowing of psychomotor finger-to-nose testing or finger-to-finger testing. Observation of gait with or without an assistive device shows smooth steps that may be wide based. Patients walk on heels and toes, rise from chairs without using the arms, and sit down without assistance. Heel-to-toe walking may be impaired related to musculoskeletal conditions.*

Muscle strength against resistance may be slightly diminished in those with musculoskeletal conditions.

Unexpected gait changes include difficulty initiating gait; a small, short, stepped gait that gradually changes to an expected gait is a sign of **Parkinson's disease**. A wide-based gait with a heel-to-toe foot slap to the floor is a sign of a cerebellar disorder; a gait in which the leg does not swing through smoothly, catches on the floor, drags, or stops next to the other foot is a sign of *cerebrovascular disease* (Miller, 2007; see Chapter 24).

⚠ *SAFETY ALERT 30-4*

The Romberg test should only be done with an older adult when a chair is directly behind the patient and the examiner is at the patient's side to assist if the patient begins to fall.

Test sensation (see Chapter 24). Include tests for pain, temperature, position, vibration, light touch, and discrimination sensation. *Peripheral sensation and proprioceptive (position) sense may diminish slightly with aging. Vibratory sensation may be absent in toes and ankles.*

> **Clinical Significance 30-2**
>
> Unilateral findings on neurological examination are always important and may be evidence of a previous cerebrovascular accident.

Techniques and Expected Findings (continued)	Rationale/Unexpected Findings (continued)
Percussion. Test reflexes. *Deep tendon reflexes usually remain intact bilaterally but slightly diminished with aging.*	A positive plantar reflex is unexpected (toes upgoing). Tremors are unexpected. Determine if the tremor occurs at rest, with motion, or with intention; if it involves only one limb, one side, or all extremities. *Parkinson's disease* has a resting tremor that usually starts unilaterally and does not include the head and neck. Tremor of the hand or neck, tremor that is heard in the voice, or tremor that occurs in the hand only when the person is initiating an action is intentional or "essential" and has a very different treatment (Miller, 2007). Diminished grip strength or unilateral loss of strength against resistance is unexpected. Severely diminished or absent sensation or proprioception indicates *peripheral neuropathy.*
Male and Female Genitourinary **Inspection.** Inspect the vulva, labia, urethra, clitoris, and vaginal walls in women. Inspect the penis and scrotum in men.	Observe for a distended lower abdomen with midline percussion going from tympany to dullness (percussion of fluid). A full bladder after recently voiding is a sign of **urinary retention**. Underwear smelling of urine, staining of urine, or leaking urine indicates incontinence, which becomes more common with age but is not expected in older adults and should be treated. Discharge, masses, swellings, erythema, and skin lesions are unexpected (see Chapters 25 and 26).
Palpation. Palpate the genitals. *Thinning of genital hair and testicular or penile atrophy is common. Skin in the vaginal area may be thinned. No nodules are palpated.*	
Endocrine, Immunologic, and Hematologic Systems Evaluate laboratory data. *Older adults are likely to demonstrate decreased lean muscle and bone mass, increased fat mass and vasomotor symptoms, fatigue, depression, anemia, erectile dysfunction, decreased libido, and decline in immune function (Chahal & Drake, 2007).*	Nurses may find that older adults do not mount a very high **febrile response** in the presence of *infection.* Total white lymphocyte count may remain low despite infection.

🌐 Cultural Considerations

Common integumentary findings in African Canadians include curly hair that tends to be coarser than in Caucasians because of an impaired ability of secreted sebum to travel along the hair shaft to the skin. Commonly, skin is excessively dry, resulting in dermatitis. Pityriasis rosea, a macular hyperpigmented viral dermatitis in Caucasians, frequently presents as papular, maroon to purplish lesions in African Canadians. Skin cancers are more common on the palms, soles, and nail beds in African Canadians (Hemenway, 2006).

Men of Southeast Asian genetic backgrounds have less body and facial hair than patients of other genetic heritage. Tattoos, body piercings, and other skin adornments are common in various Asian cultures. Skin discolourations from cupping or coining are often found. Henna tattoos or applications are seen in Arabic and Indian females to recognize or celebrate events.

Examples of Documentation—the Older Adult

Area of Assessment	Expected Findings	Unexpected Findings
General survey	Dressed in a clean, pressed pant suit; neatly groomed 70-year-old *female*. Responds articulately to questions. Walks with assurance. Hand grip firm. Skin colour light pink.	Frail-looking 70-y-old *male*. Clothes rumpled and tie soiled. Walks slowly using a cane. Requires assistance to mount examination table. Colour pale. Responds slowly and hesitantly to questions.
Vital signs	Temperature/pulse/respirations (TPR): 36.5°C; 80; regular with occasional extra beat; 24 and regular. Blood pressure (BP) 130/82 sitting, right arm; 132/84, left arm. Height: 165 cm; Weight: 60 kg; body mass index (BMI): 22.	TPR: 36.4°C; 88, irregular irregularity; 26 regular, increases with effort. BP 146/96 sitting, right arm, 148/94 left arm. Height: 180 cm; Weight: 85 kg; BMI: >27.
Skin	Face light pink. Forearm skin thin, warm, and dry; small purpura lesion on right forearm. Skin over lower legs pale and dry, states uses lotions twice daily. Few coarse hairs under chin.	Face skin pale, reddish patch on right cheek, purpura lesions on left forearm; brown, shiny skin over lower shins and malleoli bilaterally, without ulceration.
HEENT	Hair grey, full, carefully groomed. Vision 20/20 bilaterally with corrective glasses. Pupils equal (3 mm), react briskly—direct and consensual. Extraocular movements intact bilaterally. Conjunctivae clear. Disc margins soft, no foveal light reflex, arterial light reflex increased bilaterally. Tympanic membrane with intact cone of light bilaterally. Air conduction (AC) > bone conduction (BC) bilaterally. Nasal mucosa pink. No sinus tenderness bilaterally. Oral mucosa pink, moist, without lesions. Dentition—molars capped, several fillings, no obvious caries, gums moist and pink. Tongue midline, bilaterally strong. Pharynx without exudates. Uvula rises midline with phonation. Neck range of motion (ROM) intact bilaterally, slight restriction to lateral flexion, especially to right. Thyroid not palpable. No cervical lymph nodes palpable.	Marked receded hairline at temples. Vision 20/30 in right eye, 20/40 in left. Conjunctivae reddened. Ectropion bilaterally. Disc margins dull, drusen patches within macular area and frequent arterio-venous (A-V) nicking bilaterally. Tympanic membrane with intact cone of light on right, obscured with dry, dark-brown cerumen on left. Right ear—AC > BC, left ear AC = BC. Oral mucosa pink, less moist, breath slightly malodorous, no lesions. Dentition—partial dental plates upper and lower, possible caries, gums moist, dark pink, slightly edematous. Tongue deviates to right. Uvula deviates to left. Neck ROM restricted in lateral flexion and rotation, forward flexion and extension intact bilaterally. Palpable tender tonsillar lymph node, 1 cm x 1.5 cm on right.
Thorax and lungs	Chest excursion upward, outward, equal bilaterally. Slight kyphosis. Lungs resonant throughout. Vesicular breath sounds over anterior and posterior lung fields bilaterally.	Chest excursion equally decreased. Lungs resonant and breath sounds vesicular over upper lung fields, dull with late inspiratory coarse crackles in bases bilaterally.
Cardiovascular system	Carotid pulses strong and equal bilaterally, without bruits. Apical impulse in left 5th intercostal space (ICS), midclavicular line (MCL), 2 cm in diameter. No splitting of S2, no S3, S4, or murmurs	Carotid bruit on right, none on left. Apical impulse 3.5 cm in diameter, 6th ICS, left of MCL. S3 and S4 present. Harsh midsystolic murmur in second right interspace, radiates down left sternal border
Breasts and axillae	Left breast slightly larger than right breast, nipples erect without discharge, areola round, colour pinkish brown, no dimpling or retractions, soft, slightly stringy to palpation, no nodules felt. Minimal greying hair in axillae, no rashes bilaterally.	Small mobile lump, 1.5 cm x 1.5 cm in right axilla, left clear, both without hair.
Abdomen	Flat, without lateral bulges, soft, nontender, without masses. Active bowel sounds in all four quadrants. Liver span 7 cm in right midclavicular line; edges smooth.	Protuberant, lateral bulging, left > right, soft mass 3 cm x 2 cm left lower quadrant. Hyperactive bowel sounds in all four quadrants. Liver span 11 cm in right midclavicular line; edges firm

Area of Assessment	Expected Findings	Unexpected Findings
Female genitalia and pelvic examination	Pubic hair greying and thinned. Labia and clitoris small without lesions. Introitus tight, vaginal walls pink, moist, slightly rugated. No lesions or bulges noted. Cervix pink, tight, without lesions. Pap smear taken. Uterus small, ovaries nonpalpable. Anorectal area without lesions, no masses felt with rectal exam. Stool negative for occult blood.	Shiny, red vaginal mucosa. Right ovary palpable.
Male genitalia and prostate	Sparse grey pubic hair. Small noncircumcised penis. Prostate walnut sized, rubbery, with identifiable median sulcus.	Enlarged left scrotal sac. Enlarged nontender prostate; median sulcus not defined.
Peripheral vascular system	Aorta, renal, iliac, and femoral arteries without bruits. Brachial and radial pulses 2+/4 bilaterally. Popliteal, dorsalis pedis, posterior tibial pulses 1+/4 bilaterally. ROM over arms and legs intact bilaterally.	Bruits over aortic and iliac arteries. Aorta 4 cm in diameter. Brachial and radial pulses 1+/4, firm to palpation. Popliteal, posterior tibial, and dorsalis pedis pulses nonpalpable bilaterally.
Musculoskeletal system	ROM in thoracic and lumbar spine intact, decreases slightly with lateral flexion. Most joints nontender. Mild tenderness at left acromioclavicular joint.	Flexion at knees and hips very limited bilaterally. Knee joints enlarged and tender, hip joints tender bilaterally.
Nervous system	Oriented to person, place, and time. Mini Mental State score 29/30. Cranial nerves II to XII intact bilaterally. Decreased muscle mass over all extremities. Tone intact. Strength 4/5 throughout. Rapid alternating movements and point-to-point testing intact over arms and legs bilaterally with eyes open and closed. Gait slightly wide based. Sensations of pain, light touch, and position sense intact throughout. Vibration sense absent in toes, intact at ankle bilaterally. Romberg test: slight sway, increased with eyes closed. Reflexes 2+, symmetrical over arms, patella, 1+ at ankles. Plantar flexion bilaterally to stimulus.	Mini Mental State score 23/30, unable to recall three items on 10-Minute Geriatric Screener. Muscle mass markedly decreased over legs, used arms of chair to rise. Gait shuffling, leans on cane. Rapid alternating movements slow in hands. Point-to-point testing slow but intact with eyes open, inaccurate with eyes closed, upper and lower extremities. Vibration sense absent at toes and ankles. Romberg test: slight sway with eyes open, marked sway with eyes closed. Reflexes 1+ over arms and patella, nonresponsive at ankles.

Adapted from Anderson, M. C., Hunter, K., et al. (2010). The older adult. In T. C. Stephen, D. L. Skillen, R. A. Day, & L. S. Bickley (Eds.). *Canadian Bates' guide to health assessment for nurses* (1st Canadian ed., pp. 923–925). Philadelphia, PA: Wolters Kluwer Health/Lippincott Williams & Wilkins.

Evidence-Informed Critical Thinking

Organizing and Prioritizing

Assessment of the older adult usually proceeds from general to specific and from head to toe, and may need to be conducted over several visits to avoid tiring the patient. The prime goal of the nurse is to assist the older patient to maintain health, well-being, and functional ability. Various instruments have been described in this chapter to assist the nurse to assess functional status and cognitive ability. Throughout the examination, the nurse observes for restrictions to mobility, balance, and coordination.

Common Laboratory and Diagnostic Testing

Routine blood tests can reveal dyslipidemia. Screening is accomplished through a fasting lipoprotein profile that indicates levels of total and low-density lipoprotein cholesterol in the blood (Roach, Roddick, et al., 2010b). Women older than 69 years should consult their health care providers about a schedule for mammograms. In older patients, the clinical breast examination detects cancer more easily due to the breasts having fewer duct and lobular structures (Day & Bickley, 2010). Colorectal cancer is the fourth most common cancer overall in Canadian men and women (CCSSCCS, 2011). Fecal occult blood tests with follow-up screening could avoid 10,000 to 15,000 deaths over the next 10 years (CCSSCCS, 2011).

Table 30-2 Common Nursing Diagnoses Associated With the Older Adult

Diagnosis and Related Factors	Point of Differentiation	Assessment Characteristics	Nursing Interventions
Disturbed sensory perception: visual or auditory, related to aging process	Change in stimuli	Reduced vision or hearing	Provide adequate lighting. Keep background noise low, such as turning off the TV when talking. Make sure that the patient has devices such as glasses or hearing aid.
Imbalanced nutrition, less than body requirements relating to isolation	Insufficient nutrient intake for metabolic needs	Nausea, vomiting, diarrhea. Anorexia. Lack of food. Eating alone. Shopping, cooking, and cleaning functional abilities are reduced.	Note laboratory tests such as total protein, albumin, and prealbumin. Weigh the patient daily. Monitor food intake and record the percentage of meal eaten.

Diagnostic testing of bone mineral density detects osteoporosis, an insidious condition more common in older adults (Osteoporosis Canada, 2007a,b). Women >69 years should discuss their risk factors with their health care professional and draw conclusions about the regularity of Pap smears.

Clinical Reasoning

Nursing Diagnosis, Outcomes, and Interventions

When formulating a nursing diagnosis, it is important to use critical thinking to cluster data and identify patterns that fit together. The nurse compares these clusters with defining characteristics for the diagnosis to ensure the most accurate labelling and appropriate interventions. Table 30-2 provides a comparison of nursing diagnoses, unexpected findings, and interventions commonly related to the older adult assessment.

Nurses use assessment information to identify patient outcomes (Moorhead, Johnson, et al., 2007). Some outcomes related to the older adult include the following:

• Patient maintains current weight.
• Patient has appropriate conversation that flows smoothly.
• Patient eats at least 75% of ordered meals.

After outcomes are established, nursing care is implemented to improve the status of the older adult. The nurse uses critical thinking and evidence-informed practice to develop interventions (Bulecheck, Butcher, et al., 2008). Some examples for older adult care are as follows:

• Provide between-meal snacks for smaller more frequent meals.
• Locate and clean eyeglasses.
• Place hearing aid in the patient's ear.
• Assess food preferences and obtain favourite foods.

Common nursing diagnoses are provided in Table 30-2 (North American Nursing Diagnosis Association-International, 2009).

Analyzing Findings

Mr. Lehmann's concerns have been outlined throughout this chapter. Initial subjective and objective data collection is complete, and the nurse has spent time reviewing the findings and other results. The following nursing note illustrates how the nurse collects and analyzes subjective and objective data and develops nursing interventions.

Subjective: A 76-year-old man, 10-year history of Parkinson's disease, mild dementia, seen for new constipation. Has large, hard, dry, brown stool every fourth day. New admission to assisted living facility 3 months ago; "still adjusting"; does not like roommate. Ambulates with walker. Takes wheelchair to meals "because the aides says it's faster." Ambulates in room. Fluids at meals 3 to 5 glasses milk or juice total, no additional water. Denies swallowing difficulties. Documented weight loss 7.3 kg over past year, poorly fitting dentures, prefers soft foods, diet contains no fresh fruit. Prefers bowel movement (BM) before breakfast, states toileting assistance not available before breakfast, needs help with pants zipping and buttoning. Medications: carbidopa–levodopa (Sinemet) 25/250 four times daily before meals, calcium 600 mg with vitamin D 1,000 units daily, and lisinopril (Zestril) 5 mg daily.

Objective:

- Vitals: Weight 71 kg (decreased 2 kg since admission), blood pressure (BP) right arm (sitting) 104/60 mm Hg, pulse 76 beats/min and regular, respirations 12 breaths/min, afebrile
- General survey: Alert, conversant, thin man with resting tremor of hands bilaterally. Groomed. Dressed appropriately for situation. Makes eye contact
- Skin: Dry, flaky, red raised areas on posterior scalp 3 cm × 5 cm.
- HEENT: Dry oral mucosa, ill-fitting dentures, no oral sores or open areas, thyroid not palpable, diminished gag reflex bilaterally
- Respiratory: Vesicular sounds over lung fields bilaterally
- Cardiac: S1 single, S2 single, regular rate and rhythm, no murmurs, rubs, or gallops
- Breasts: Symmetrical, nontender. No masses palpated. Axillae without rashes or masses
- Abdomen: Soft, nondistended, tender left lower quadrant (LLQ), with mass palpable. Approximately 4 cm diameter, nonpliable, nonmobile, rough contour, bowel sounds (BS+) all four quadrants
- Rectal: 2 to 3 cm external hemorrhoid, no fissures, sphincter tone tight, large amount, hard stool high in rectal vault
- Neurological: Decreased blink, blunted affect, increased tone, rigidity in all extremities, short-stepped gait with walker, steady, slow, difficulty rising and sitting

Analysis: Constipation related to immobility, medications, dehydration related to disease processes, and medications as evidenced by frequent use of wheelchair, limited walking, insufficient fibre intake, inadequate liquid intake for body weight, use of carbidopa–levodopa, calcium, and lisinopril (all potentially constipating medications).

Plan: *Goal:* Mr. Lehmann will have one bowel movement within 2 to 3 days without straining. *Interventions:* Ambulate to meals with walker three times daily. Increase fluids to >1.5 L every day. Offer 250 mL of water at 1000 hours, 1400 hours, and 1600 hours and with meals. Start fibre pudding 2 oz. every day. Routinely schedule time for BM and find private bathroom near dining room. Investigate use of Velcro closures to promote independence and control over timing of BM.

Evaluate need for lisinopril with primary provider. Evaluate need for multivitamin with iron. Refer to dietitian to increase dietary fibre. Refer to denturist for denture repair and refitting.

Critical Thinking Challenge

- What effects does functional status have on body systems?
- Provide rationale for the unexpected abdominal and rectal assessment findings.
- Interpret the neurological findings in the context of the patient's Parkinson's disease.

Collaborating With the Team

An interprofessional health care team specializing in the care of older adults ensures the assessment and evaluation of all aspects of Mr. Lehmann's physical and psychosocial health, as well as the development of a plan of action. The patient would benefit from consultation with a denturist, geriatrician, geriatric nurse practitioner, dietitian, social worker, and physical and occupational therapists. Further assessment of his dislike of his roommate and residents is needed.

Results that might trigger a dental consult include chipped or loose teeth, dental caries, tooth pain, denture care, malodorous breath, snoring or sleep apnea, and dry mouth.

Mr. Lehmann has been experiencing loose dentures stemming from weight loss; an early denturist consult is indicated. The following conversation illustrates how the nurse might organize data and make recommendations about the patient's situation.

(case study continues on page 952)

Situation: Hello, I am Pat Jackson, the nurse practitioner who is caring for Mr. Pierre Lehmann, date of birth 02OCT1934.

Background: He was admitted 3 months ago to an assisted living facility with a loss of functional status related to Parkinson's. He has reported difficulty chewing, and he has lost 2 kg since admission, 7.3 kg in the past year.

Assessment: His oral mucosa is very dry. His dentures are loose and malfitting, although he has no oral sores or open areas.

Recommendations: Would you have an opening to see him for denture fitting in the next week?

Critical Thinking Challenge

- How did the nurse practitioner prioritize which information to include and delete in her report?
- What assessments might be considered related to Mr. Lehmann's nutrition?
- What nursing diagnoses are appropriate related to his mouth and dentures?

Pulling It All Together: An Example of Reflection and Critical Thinking

The nurse practitioner uses assessment data to formulate a nursing care plan with patient outcomes and interventions for Pierre Lehmann. Outcomes are specific to the patient, realistic to achieve, attainable, measurable, and have a time frame for completion. Interventions are based on evidence and practice guidelines, and after their implementation, the nurse reevaluates Mr. Lehmann and documents findings in the chart to show progress. The nurse uses critical thinking and judgment to continue or revise the diagnosis, outcomes, or interventions. This is often in the form of a care plan or case note similar to the one below.

Nursing Diagnosis	Patient Outcomes	Nursing Interventions	Rationale	Evaluation
Constipation related to multiple medications, inactivity, and low fluid/fibre intake	Patient will have one BM in next 2 to 3 days without straining. Patient eliminates moderate amount of soft brown stool every 2 days.	Ambulate with walker three times daily (TID), offer fluids every 2 hours, order fibre pudding with lunch, schedule time for BM with assistance or clothing adaptation, and initiate diet consult.	Activity stimulates peristalsis, ensure that the patient is well hydrated with fluid intake sheet, examination of integument, increase fibre in the diet.	Patient had bowel movement of moderate, hard, brown stool. Will continue to monitor for improvement and reestablishment of regular patterns.

Applying Your Knowledge

Using the previous steps of clinical reasoning, organizing, and prioritizing, consider all the case study findings about Mr. Lehman woven throughout this chapter. When answering the following questions, begin drawing conclusions and see how the pieces of assessment must work together to create an environment for personalized, appropriate, and accurate care.

- Define primary and secondary aging. (Knowledge)
- What is your rationale for selecting the Mini Mental Status Examination (MMSE) and a nutritional assessment tool with Mr. Lehmann? (Comprehension)
- What screening tests would you request for this 76-year-old male patient? (Application)
- What factors might contribute to Mr. Lehman's dislike of his roommate and other residents? (Analysis)
- What recommendations would you make about Mr. Lehmann's requirements for immunizations? (Synthesis)
- How would you evaluate your counselling regarding nutritional intake with Mr. Lehmann? (Evaluation)

Key Points

- Adults heal more slowly because of slower growth of new cells.
- Loss of vision can significantly affect daily activities including dressing, grooming, and ambulating safely.
- Older adults require extra time to answer subjective data questions.
- Special challenges to interviewing older adults include hearing, visual, language, and cognitive impairments.
- Geriatric syndromes include nutritional changes, mobility impairment, falls, polypharmacy, and pressure ulcers.
- Common symptoms/signs of older adults include urinary incontinence, sleep difficulties, pain, alterations in mobility, cognitive changes, depression, and bruising/injuries related to elder abuse.
- The skin of the older adult is wrinkled, thinner, less elastic, and drier. Pressure ulcers in any of the following areas are staged and interventions are begun immediately: sacral and ischial areas, greater trochanteric area, and heels.
- Senile ptosis, dry or red eyes, smaller and slower pupillary responses, and difficulty with glare are common ocular findings.
- Loss of hearing is common in the older adult.
- Unexpected findings in the mouth include pallor, malodorous breath, poor dentition, and candida.
- The older adult has a less elastic chest wall, decreased respiratory muscle strength, loss of alveolar recoil, and increased residual volume.
- Arterial walls are less elastic and stiffer, causing increased systolic BP, increased ventricular wall hypertrophy, decreased coronary blood flow, reduced cardiac output, and increased circulating catecholamines.
- Arrythmias, especially atrial fibrillation, are common in older adults but are unexpected findings.
- Gastrointestinal changes include slowed peristalsis, reduced hepatic flow, and decreased metabolism of drugs on the first pass.
- Common expected neurological findings include decreased upward gaze, slowed coordination, slowed gait, decreased reflexes, decreased strength, and impaired sensation.
- The older adult needs to be assessed for depression, dementia, Parkinson's, and signs of cerebrovascular accident.
- Older adults often lose height and lean body mass.
- Large nodules in the distal interphalangeal joints are Heberden nodes and enlargements of the proximal interphalangeal joints are Bouchard nodes, common with arthritis.
- Kidney function decreases with age, causing a decreased glomerular filtration rate, decreased creatinine clearance, and inability to conserve sodium.
- Endocrine changes include decreased growth hormone, decreased adrenal hormones, decreased response of the immune system, and increased glucose intolerance.
- Common nursing diagnoses for older adults include impaired mobility and risk for falls.

Review Questions

1. Which of the following findings is an age-related change in the skin?
   A. Solar lentigines (liver spots)
   B. Actinic keratoses
   C. Loss of subcutaneous fat
   D. Photoaging

2. Which of the following statements is true with aging?
   A. The lens becomes smaller and less dense.
   B. The tympanic membrane becomes more flexible and retracted.
   C. Changes in the inner ear interfere with sound discrimination.
   D. Increased pupillary responses lead to difficulty in light accommodation.

3. When working with a frail older adult, the nurse knows that it is best to
   A. fill in silences to avoid discomfort
   B. address all questions to the patient's family
   C. try to gain all information directly from the patient's memory
   D. ask the question in lay terms rather than medical terms

4. The nurse assesses for geriatric syndromes, which are
   A. the interaction of multiple diagnoses that contribute to these health concerns
   B. the exacerbation of chronic conditions such as congestive heart failure (CHF) or chronic obstructive pulmonary disease (COPD)
   C. conditions in which older adults may not mount an immune response
   D. decreases in growth hormones and steroids that reduce functional status

5. The DETERMINE nutritional screening is an abbreviated assessment of risk factors that
   A. indicate that the patient is at high nutritional risk
   B. identify older adults who may require a more comprehensive nutritional assessment
   C. calculate body mass index (BMI) and classify patients as obese versus malnourished
   D. describe food frequency and microelements that may be lacking in the diet

6. What is the best question for the nurse to assess medication use in the older adult living in the community?
   A. "What medications are you taking?"
   B. "How are you supposed to be taking your medications?"
   C. "What do you understand about the reason for taking your medications?"
   D. "What side effects are you experiencing from your medications?"

7. The nurse asks the patient to immediately repeat three words that he or she states as part of the Mini Mental Status Examination (MMSE). This is a measure of which of the following?
A. Orientation
B. Registration
C. Recall
D. Attention

8. Which of the following patients should the nurse see first? The patient with
A. unilateral changes in vision
B. ectropion of the lower lid
C. presbyopia
D. senile ptosis

9. The nurse auscultates a loud murmur. The nurse should also assess for which of the following?
A. Coarse rhonchi and purulent sputum
B. Irregular heartbeat and pulse deficit
C. Crackles in the lungs and leg edema
D. Abdominal distention and costal margin tenderness

10. The patient demonstrates evidence of cognitive decline, minimal nutritional intake, neglect of the home environment, and failure to manage finances. The nurse labels this diagnosis as
A. disturbed sensory perception
B. impaired individual coping
C. imbalanced nutrition, less than body requirements
D. adult failure to thrive

Canadian Nursing Research

Hunter, K. F., Moore, K. N., et al. (2007). Pelvic floor muscle training to improve urinary incontinence after radical prostatectomy: A systematic review of effectiveness. *BJU International, 100*(5), 1191–1192.

Low, G., & Molzahn, A. (2007). A replication study of predictors of quality of life in older age. *Research in Nursing & Health, 30*(2), 141–150.

Robinson, J. G., & Molzahn, A. E. (2007). Sexuality and quality of life. *Journal of Gerontological Nursing, 33*(3), 19–29.

Wilson, D. M., & Palha, P. (2007). A systematic review of published research articles on health promotion at retirement. *Journal of Nursing Scholarship, 39*(4), 330–337.

References

ACTION. (2008). *Chronic and neuropathic pain*. Retrieved from http://www.nepaction.ca/main.htm

Anderson, M. C., Hunter, K., et al. (2010). The older adult. In T. C. Stephen, D. L. Skillen, R. A. Day, & L. S. Bickley (Eds.). *Canadian Bates' guide to health assessment for nurses* (1st ed., pp. 887–932). Philadelphia, PA: Wolters Kluwer Health/Lippincott Williams & Wilkins.

Bance, M. (2007). Hearing and aging. *Canadian Medical Association Journal, 176*(7), 925–927.

Barkman, A., Pooler, C., et al. (2010). Disorders of blood flow in the systemic circulation. In R. A. Hannon, C. Pooler, et al. (Eds.). *Porth pathophysiology: Concepts of altered health states* (1st Canadian ed., pp.458–484). Philadelphia, PA: Wolters Kluwer Health/Lippincott Williams & Wilkins.

Barkman, A., & Porth, C. M. (2010). Disorders of blood pressure regulation. In R. A. Hannon, C. Pooler, et al. (Eds.). *Porth pathophysiology: Concepts of altered health states* (1st Canadian ed., pp. 485–510). Philadelphia, PA: Wolters Kluwer Health/Lippincott Williams & Wilkins.

Berg, K., Wood-Dauphinee, S., et al. (1992). The balance scale: Reliability assessment. *Archives of Physical Medicine and Rehabilitation, 73*, 1073–1083.

Bergstrom, N., Braden, B. J., et al., (1987). The Braden scale for preventing pressure sore risk. *Nursing Research, 36*(4), 205–210.

Bernhard, D., & Laufer, G. (2008). The aging cardiomyocyte: A mini-review. *Gerontology, 54*(1), 24–31.

Boyce, J. M., & Shone, G. R. (2006). Effects of ageing on smell and taste. *Postgraduate Medicine, 82*, 239–241.

Braden, B., & Bergstrom, M. (1989). Clinical utility of the Braden scale for predicting pressure sore risk. *Advances in Skin and Wound Care, 2*(3), 44–51.

Bradshaw, J., & Klein, W. C. (2007). Health promotion. In J. A. Blackburn & C. N. Dulmus (Eds.). *Handbook of gerontology: Evidence-based approaches to theory, practice, and policy* (pp. 171–200). Hoboken, NJ: John Wiley & Sons.

Brunet, K., Day, R. A., et al. (2010). Nutritional assessment. In T. C. Stephen, D. L. Skillen, R. A. Day, & L. S. Bickley (Eds.). *Canadian Bates' guide to health assessment for nurses* (pp. 167–201). Philadelphia, PA: Wolters Kluwer Health/Lippincott Williams & Wilkins.

Bulecheck, G. M., Butcher, H. K., et al. (2008). *Nursing interventions classification (NIC)* (5th ed.). St. Louis, MO: Mosby.

Byrd, L. (2008). Making a stand against malignant melanoma. *Geriatric Nursing, 29*(3), 174.

Canadian Cancer Society's Steering Committee for Cancer Statistics. (2011). *Cancer statistics 2011*. Toronto, ON: Canadian Cancer Society.

Canadian Dermatology Association. (2008). *Malignant melanoma*. Retrieved from www.dermatology.ca/patients_public/info_patients/skin_cancer/malignant_melanoma.html

Centers for Disease Control and Prevention. (2010). *Basic information about skin cancer*. Retrieved from http://www.cdc.gov/cancer/skin/basic_info/

Chahal, H. S., & Drake, W. M. (2007). The endocrine system and aging. *Journal of Pathology, 211*(2), 173–180.

Day, R. A., & Bickley, L. S. (2010). The breasts and axillae. In T. C. Stephen, D. L. Skillen, R. A. Day, & L. S. Bickley (Eds.). *Canadian Bates' guide to health assessment for nurses* (pp. 470–508). Philadelphia, PA: Wolters Kluwer Health/Lippincott Williams & Wilkins.

Defloor, T., & Grypdonck, M. F. H. (2005). Pressure ulcers: Validation of two risk assessment scales. *Journal of Clinical Nursing, 14*(3), 373–382.

DeoLeo, D., & Spathonis, K. (2003). Suicide and euthanasia in later life. *Aging: Clinical and Experimental Research, 15*(2), 99–110.

Department of Justice. (2007). *Abuse of older adults: A fact sheet from the Department of Justice Canada*. Ottawa, ON: Department of Justice.

Duthie, E. H. (2007). History and physical examination. In E. H. Duthie, P. R. Katz, et al. (Eds.). *Practice of geriatrics* (4th ed., pp. 3–15). Philadelphia, PA: Saunders Elsevier.

Douketis, J. D., Paradis, G., et al. (2005). Canadian guidelines for body weight classification in adults: Application in clinical practice to screen for overweight and obesity and to assess disease risk. *Canadian Medical Association Journal, 172*(8), 995–998.

Elmadfa, I., & Meyer, A. L. (2008). Body composition, changing physiological functions and nutrient requirements of the elderly. *Annals of Nutrition and Metabolism, 52*(Suppl. 1), 2–5.

Folstein, M. F., Folstein, S. E., et al. (1975). "Mini-mental state" a practical method for grading the cognitive state of patients for the clinician. *Journal of Psychiatric Research, 12*, 189–198.

Foster, T. C. (2006). Biological markers of age-related memory deficits: Treatment of senescent physiology. *CNS Drugs, 20*(2), 153–166.

Ham, R., Sloane, P., et al. (2007). *Primary care geriatrics: A case-based approach* (5th ed.). St. Louis, MO: Mosby.

Hastings, S. N., Whitson, H. E., et al. (2009). Emergency department discharge diagnosis and adverse health outcomes in older adults. *J Am Geriatr Soc, 57*(10), 1856–1861.

Health Canada. (2006). *It's your health: Seniors and aging—preventing falls in and around your home.* Retrieved from http://www.hc-sc.gc.ca/hl-vs/iyh-vsv/life-vie/fp-pc-eng.php

Helfrich, Y. R., Sachs, D. L., et al. (2008). Overview of skin aging and photoaging. *Dermatology Nursing, 20*(3), 177–183.

Hemenway, M. (2006). Skin cancer: Skin color doesn't matter. *EastWestMagazine.* Retrieved from http://www.eastwestmagazine.com/content/view/39/40

Hendrich, A. L., Bender, P. S., et al. (2003). Validation of the Hendrich II Fall Risk Model: A large concurrent case/control study of hospitalized patients. *Applied Nursing Research, 16*, 9–21.

Htwe, T. H., Mushtaq, A., et al. (2007). Infection in the elderly. *Infectious Diseases Clinics of North America, 21*, 711–743.

Hybels, C. F., & Blazer, D. G. (2003). Epidemiology of late life mental disorders. *Clinics in Geriatric Medicine, 19*(4), 663–696.

Inouye, S. K., Studenski, S., et al. (2007).Geriatric syndromes: Clinical, research, and policy implications of a core geriatric concept. *Journal of the American Geriatrics Society, 55*, 780–791.

Jette, A. M. (1987). The functional status index: Reliability and validity of a self-report functional disability measure. *Journal of Rheumatology, 15*(Suppl.), 15–21.

Kane, R. L., Ouslander, J. G., et al. (2008). *Essentials of clinical geriatrics* (6th ed.). New York, NY: McGraw-Hill.

Karagiozis, H., Gray, S., et al. (1998). The direct assessment of functional abilities (DAFA): A comparison to an indirect measure of instrumental activities of daily living. *Gerontologist, 38*(1), 113–121.

Katz, S., Ford, A. B., et al. (1963). Studies of illness in the aged: The index of ADL: A standardized measure of biological and psychosocial functioning. *JAMA, 185*, 94–101.

Lach, H., & Smith, C. (2007). Assessment: Focus on function. In A. Linton & H. Lach (Eds.). *Matteson & McConnells' gerontological nursing concepts and practice* (3rd ed.). St. Louis, MO: Saunders Elsevier.

Lawton, M. P., & Brody, E. M. (1969). Assessment of older people: Self-maintaining and instrumental activities of daily living. *Gerontologist, 9*(3), 179–186.

Linton, A., & Lach, H. (2007). *Matteson & McConnells' gerontological nursing concepts and practice* (3rd ed.). St. Louis, MO: Saunders Elsevier.

Mahoney, F. I., & Barthel, D. W. (1965). Functional evaluation: The Barthel index. *Maryland State Medical Journal, 14*, 61–65.

Makrantonaki, E., & Zouboulis, C. C. (2007). Molecular mechanisms of skin aging: State of the art. *Annals of the New York Academy of Sciences, 1119*, 40–50.

Masoro, E. J. (2006). Are age-associated diseases an integral part of aging? In E. J. Masoro & S. N. Austad (Eds). *Handbook of the biology of aging* (6th ed., pp. 43–62). Boston, MT: Elsevier.

Mathias, S., Nayak, U. S., et al. (1986). Balance in elderly patients: The Get up and Go test. *Archives of Physical Medicine in Rehabilitation, 67*(6), 387–389.

Miller, C. (2008). Communication difficulties in hospitalized older adults with dementia. *American Journal of Nursing, 108*(3), 58–66.

Miller, C. A. (2009). *Nursing for wellness in older adults* (5th ed.). Philadelphia, PA: Wolters Kluwer Health/Lippincott Williams & Wilkins.

Miller, J. (2007). Parkinson's disease. In R. Ham, P. Sloane, et al. (Eds.). *Primary care geriatrics: A case-based approach* (5th ed.). St. Louis, MO: Mosby.

Moorhead, S., Johnson, M., et al. (2007). *Nursing outcomes classification (NOC)* (4th ed.). Philadelphia, PA: Mosby.

Morse, J. M. (2006). The modified Morse Fall Scale. *International Journal of Nursing Practice, 12*(3), 174–175.

Morse, J. M., Tylko, S. J., et al. (1987). Characteristics of the fall-prone patient. *Gerontologist, 27*(4), 516–522.

National Institute of Deafness and Communication Disorders. (2010). *Quick statistics.* Retrieved from http://www.nidcd.nih.gov/health/statistics/quick.htm

North American Nursing Diagnosis Association-International. (2009). *Nursing diagnoses, 2009–2011 edition: Definitions and classifications (NANDA-I NURSING DIAGNOSIS).* West Sussex, UK: John Wiley & Sons.

Ostechega, Y., Paulose-Ram, R., et al. (2007). Prevalence of peripheral arterial disease and risk factors in persons aged 60 and older: Data from the National Health and Nutrition Examination Survey 1999–2004. *Journal of the American Geriatric Society, 55*(4), 583–589.

Osteoporosis Canada. (2007a). *What is osteoporosis?* Retrieved from http://www.osteoporosis.ca/index.php/ci_id/5526/la_id/1.htm

Osteoporosis Canada. (2007b). *Osteoporosis and osteoarthritis.* Retrieved from http://www.osteoporosis.ca/index.php/ci_id/5507/la_id/1.htm

Peterson, M. D., Rhea, M. R., et al. (2010). Resistance exercises for musculoskeletal strength in older adults: A metaanalysis. *Ageing Research Reviews, 9*(3), 226–237.

Posner, B. M., Jette, A. M., et al. (1993). Nutrition and health risks in the elderly: The nutrition screening initiative. *Journal of American Public Health, 83*(7), 927–978.

Public Health Agency of Canada. (2005). *Report on seniors' falls in Canada.* Ottawa, ON: Minister of Public Works and Government Services Canada.

Public Health Agency of Canada. (2006). *Hearing loss info-sheet for seniors.* Retrieved from http://www.phac-aspec.gc.ca/seniors-aims/pubs/info-sheets/hearing_loss/pdf/hearing_e.pdf

Roach, S., Roddick, P., et al. (2010a). The musculoskeletal system. In T. C. Stephen, D. L. Skillen, R. A. Day, & L. S. Bickley (Eds.). *Canadian Bates' guide to health assessment for nurses* (1st Canadian ed., pp. 601–681). Philadelphia, PA: Wolters Kluwer Health/Lippincott Williams & Wilkins.

Roach, S., Roddick, P., et al. (2010b). The cardiovascular system. In T. C. Stephen, D. L. Skillen, R. A. Day, & L. S. Bickley (Eds.). *Canadian Bates' guide to health assessment for nurses* (1st Canadian ed., pp. 423–478). Philadelphia, PA: Wolters Kluwer Health/Lippincott Williams & Wilkins.

Roberts, S. B., & Rosenberg, I. (2006). Nutrition and aging: Changes in the regulation of energy metabolism with aging. *Physiological Reviews, 86*(2), 651–667.

Samaras, N., Chevalley, T., et al. (2010). Older patients in the emergency department: A review. *Annals of Emergency Medicine, 56*(3), 261–269.

Sharma G., & Goodwin, J. (2006). Effect of aging on respiratory system physiology and immunology. *Clinical Interventions in Aging, 1*(3), 253–260.

Sheikh, J. A., & Yesavage, J. A. (1986). Geriatric Depression Scale (GDS): Recent findings and development of a shorter version. In T. L. Brink (Ed.). *Clinical gerontology: A guide to assessment and intervention* (pp. 165–176). New York, NY: Howarth Press.

Stephen, T. C., & Bickley, L. S. (2010). The eyes. In T. C. Stephen, D. L. Skillen, R. A. Day, & L. S. Bickley (Eds.). *Canadian Bates' guide to health assessment for nurses* (1st Canadian ed., pp. 299–339). Philadelphia, PA: Wolters Kluwer Health/Lippincott Williams & Wilkins.

Stevens, J. A. (2006). Fatalities and injuries from falls among older adults in the US 1993–2003 and 2001–2005. *Morbidity and Mortality Weekly Report, 55*(45), 1–32.

Stratton, R. J., King, C. L., et al. (2006). Malnutrition Universal Screening Tool predicts mortality and length of hospital stay in acutely ill elderly. *British Journal of Nutrition, 95*(2), 325–330.

Thomas, J. M., Isenring, E., et al. (2007). Nutritional status and length of stay in patients admitted to an Acute Assessment Unit. *Journal of Human Nutrition and Diet, 20*(4), 320–328.

Tinetti, M. E. (1986). Performance-oriented assessment of mobility problems in elderly patients. *Journal of the American Geriatrics Society, 34*, 119–125.

Turcotte, M., & Schellenberg, G. (2006). *A portrait of seniors in Canada 2006*. Ottawa, ON: Statistics Canada.

Wright, J. (2000). The FIM™. The Center for Outcome Measurement in Brain Injury. Retrieved from http://222.tbims.org/combi/FIM

Yesavage, J. A., Brink, T. L., et al. (1982). Development and validation of a geriatric depression screening scale: A preliminary report. *Journal of Psychiatric Research, 17*, 37–49.

The Canadian Jensen's Nursing Health Assessment suite offers these additional resources to enhance learning and facilitate understanding of this chapter:

• thePoint on line resource, http//thepoint.lww.com/Stephen1E
• *Laboratory Manual for Canadian Jensen's Nursing Health Assessment: A Best Practice Approach*

UNIT

5

Putting It All Together

Head-to-Toe
Assessment of the Adult

Learning Objectives

1   Identify the rationale for a comprehensive, screening, or focused health assessment depending on the patient situation and setting.

2   Collect subjective data, including history and risk assessment.

3   Identify important topics for health promotion and risk reduction.

4   Collect objective data by completing a head-to-toe physical assessment.

5   Consider the condition, age, gender, and culture of the patient to individualize health assessment.

6   Identify expected and unexpected findings from inspection, palpation, percussion, and auscultation during the head-to-toe assessment.

7   Document and communicate data from health assessment using appropriate terminology and principles of recording.

8   Analyze subjective and objective data from health assessment findings to plan initial interventions.

9   Identify nursing diagnoses and initiate a plan of care based on findings from the adult head-to-toe assessment.

Mrs. Dorothy Jane Suleri, 44 years old, is admitted with diarrhea, obesity, ulcerative colitis, abdominal pain, rosacea, fatigue, and anemia. Her current concern is bleeding related to the colitis, for which she uses prescribed medications. She has had three bloody stools today. She is married with two children, 15 and 13 years old.

As you read through the chapter, consider the following questions:

- How will the nurse individualize the admitting history to focus on Mrs. Suleri's current concerns?
- How will the nurse focus the physical assessments considering Mrs. Suleri's diagnosis?
- How will the nurse use the assessment information to develop a plan of care?

This chapter includes an outline of a comprehensive assessment of the patient. Although the chapter includes some typical assessments, it is important to keep in mind that adaptations are wide ranging, depending on the patient's status, clinical setting, and standards of practice. Beginning nurses learn the range of assessment skills, but the application of how and when to use these skills occurs in the clinical setting. The nurse combines sensitive history taking with accurate and thorough physical assessment techniques by beginning with a firm foundation of evidence and scientific knowledge. With experience and support, patient assessment becomes an art. The most important thing is to develop a consistent, logical approach organized in a way that is comfortable for the nurse and individualized and focused on the patient.

The comprehensive health assessment integrates all body systems; findings help the nurse form an overall impression of the patient and his or her condition. Complete subjective data collection includes data related to the patient's history and risk factors. The nurse typically collects these data once and then gathers focused data more frequently. Comprehensive assessment also includes collection of objective and physical examination data beginning at the head and ending at the toes. This arrangement provides a practical organizational framework, facilitating efficient movement for the nurse and energy conservation for the patient. The nurse usually also collects objective data once and then either collects focused data or, in the case of an acute or critically ill patient, may repeat the head-to-toe examination. After gathering all data, the nurse then reorganizes it according to the body system, condition, or diagnosis. He or she detects patterns and identifies findings in associated systems. The nurse analyzes assessment data by using critical thinking to identify health issues and then plan, implement, and evaluate care. Therefore, an accurate history (subjective data) and physical examination (objective data) create an essential foundation for complete and individualized care.

This chapter also includes specific assessments to use for a hospitalized patient: admitting, screening, and focused.

Acute Assessment

The nurse constantly assesses and observes the patient.

△ SAFETY ALERT 31-1

If skin is cyanotic or pale, breathing is difficult, posture is strained, facial expression is anxious, and overall appearance indicates distress, the nurse focuses on the immediate issue. Other cues that indicate an unstable condition in the patient are difficulty managing the airway; rapid or slow respirations or pulse; high or low blood pressure; acute change in mental status; seizure; new onset of chest pain; or any other concerns by the nurse (Offner, Heit, et al., 2007).

In cases like those just described, the nurse gathers pertinent subjective and objective assessment data related to the

health issue to assist with identifying the cause and intervening promptly. The patient may be treated while additional data are collected. It may be necessary to request additional nursing assistance, contact the physician, or activate a rapid response. The nurse immediately reports any concerns.

Subjective Data Collection

Subjective data collection involves assessing present concerns, taking a health history, and evaluating risk factors. The nurse gives the patient time and encouragement to tell his or her story and experience of health or illness. Doing so provides an opportunity for the patient to express concerns in his/her own words; it often forms the foundation for a therapeutic relationship. If the patient is anxious, the nurse acknowledges that it is common for patients to feel uncomfortable at times; the patient is given permission to disclose only information with which he or she is comfortable. Additionally, the nurse informs the patient that the information is confidential except in situations where there is concern about safety or harm.

If the patient is stable, the nurse may perform the history first and then complete the physical examination. Alternatively, the nurse may thread collection of subjective data throughout the physical examination (eg, asking about cough just before auscultating the lungs). After reviewing the patient health record, the nurse formulates a list of initial concerns or topics to discuss, including health promotion and risk-reduction assessment. The history is usually performed with the patient clothed because most patients are more comfortable when covered.

Areas for Health Promotion

An important purpose of the health history is to gather information to promote health and provide health teaching. Health-promotion activities focus on preventing disease, identifying issues early, and reducing complications of existing or established diagnoses. They also serve to reinforce existing healthy habits and encourage refinements to approaches the patient already is practising.

Patient education, health promotion, and risk reduction are some of the most important roles in nursing. The nurse weaves relevant topics into the conversation during health history collection and follow-up teaching sessions. Nurses promote patient education and healthy behaviours as they apply the nursing process.

Assessment of Risk Factors

Assessment of risk factors involves collecting comprehensive subjective data, including demographic information and other data from the patient health record, history of present concern, past health history, psychosocial history, functional status, activities of daily living (ADLs), growth/development, family history, and review of systems. After collecting and analyzing all these data, the nurse determines potential and actual risk factors for the patient and uses this information to plan specific screening, health promotion, and patient teaching activities.

The Canadian Task Force on Preventive Care (CTFPC, 2011) recommends that primary providers discuss priority screening services with patients and offer them (see Table 31-1). Screening and resulting teaching (see the section "Demographic Data") are primary prevention services that nurses offer as part of their professional responsibilities. The nurse assesses risk factors according to the individual's risks (eg, injury in a teenager, genetic diseases in a woman who is pregnant). Cancer screening, dental caries prevention for preschoolers, Rh incompatibility screening for women who are pregnant, and behavioural counselling for a healthy diet are included as primary prevention activities. These screenings are essential in maintaining high-level wellness. Between 2000 and 2006, the CTFPC recommendations included falls prevention; screening for depression, type 2 diabetes, and lung cancer; promotion of breastfeeding; prevention of influenza; hormone therapy for primary prevention of chronic diseases; prevention of violence against women; and more. See **thePoint** ✳ for helpful links.

Demographic Data

Initially the nurse begins with common items, such as demographic information, primary concerns, and a medication list, along with allergies. The nurse reviews the patient health record before meeting the patient to avoid repetitive questions. He or she compares the medication list with actual medications as stated by the patient. Additionally, the nurse validates the concern list and medications with the patient. If areas are inconsistent or unclear, the nurse obtains additional information, notifies the primary care provider, and notes the differences.

Figure 31-1 illustrates how the nurse implements this in the clinical setting, using information related to Mrs. Suleri as presented in the case study. The nurse completes a screening assessment. The following data are obtained from the patient health record during the preinterview phase.

History of Present Concern/Illness

The patient interview begins with a focus on the primary concern. The nurse asks about the reason for the visit and history of the present concern. He or she evaluates the reasons for the visit by asking, "What can I help you with today." At this point, the nurse obtains a history of the present illness by assessing pain or discomfort using the following parameters:

- Location: "Where does it hurt?" "Does the pain stay in one place?"
- Timing: "When did it start?" How long has it lasted?"

Table 31-1	Screening and Health Promotion Activities From Canadian Task Force on Preventive Care (CTFPC)				
		Adults		Special Populations	
Recommendation		**Men**	**Women**	**Women Who Are Pregnant**	**Children**
Alcohol misuse screening and behavioural counselling interventions, counselling to prevent tobacco use and tobacco-caused disease, screening for human violence, depression, and other mental health issues		X	X	X	X
Screening for asymptomatic streptococcus B, bacteriuria, Rh (D) incompatibility screening				X	
Breast cancer, cervical cancer, osteoporosis in postmenopausal women screening			X		
Prevention of dental caries in preschool children, screening for visual impairment in children younger than age 5 y					X
Depression screening, colorectal cancer screening, screening for type 2 diabetes mellitus in adults, behavioural counselling in primary care to promote a healthy diet, screening for high blood pressure and lipid disorders, screening for lung and skin cancer, fall risk, prevention of influenza, screening for obesity in adults		X	X		
Gonorrhea, hepatitis B virus, infectious syphilis, human papillomavirus, and chlamydia infection screening; behavioural interventions to promote breastfeeding			X	X	

Demographic Information for Mrs. Suleri

PIN: 833445632

Gender: Female

Primary Language: English

Marital status: Married

Name: Dorothy Jane Suleri

Date of birth: 25AUG1966

Ethnicity: Caucasian

Emergency Contact: James Suleri (123) 555-2619

Concern List for Mrs. Suleri

Date of Onset	Concern List	Date Resolved
17JUNE2000	Diarrhea	
17JUNE2000	Obesity	
07JULY2000	Ulcerative colitis	
20MAR2004	Abdominal pain	
12JUNE2008	Rosacea	20 MAR 2009
4MAR2010	Fatigue	
4MAR2010	Anemia	

Allergies for Mrs. Suleri

Substance	Reaction	Severity	Type	Treatment
Zofran	Rash	Severe	Allergic	Benadryl, IV dexamethasone

Latex allergy? Yes **No** Reaction

X-ray contrast dye allergy? Yes **No** Reaction

Medication List for Mrs. Suleri

Prescription Medication	Dose	Route	Frequency
Mesacal	800 mg	Oral	Three times daily for colitis
Loperamide	2 mg	Oral	As needed up to four times daily for diarrhea
Zolpidem	10 mg	Oral	As needed at bedtime for sleep

Figure 31-1 Concern list for Mrs. Suleri.

- Intensity/severity: "On a scale of 0 to 10 with 0 being no pain and 10 being the worst pain, rate your pain?"
- Quality: "Tell me what it feels like."
- Alleviating factors: "What makes it better?"
- Aggravating factors: "What makes it worse?"
- Associated symptoms: "What other symptoms have you noticed?"
- Environmental factors: "Have you been doing anything different lately?"
- Significance to patient: "Is the pain making it difficult for you to do the things you usually do?"
- Patient perspective: "What do you think might be happening?"
- Pain goal: "What level of pain is manageable for you?"
- Functional goal: "What would you like to be able to do if you were not in pain?

Past Health History

The nurse assesses past health history to provide context for how the current issue might be related. He or she assesses findings considering the information previously reviewed in the patient health record. For example, the nurse might say, "I'm going to ask you some questions about your health history. I noticed that your chart says that you have an allergy to Zofran. Tell me about that." This is a way of verifying information and obtaining further details. Some examples of categories for the past medical and family history include the following:

- **Assess for allergies.** Include iodine, shellfish, and latex. Also assess the patient's reaction including rash, hives, anaphylaxis, uticaria, pruritis, gastrointestinal upset, nausea, vomiting, or diarrhea. Validate answers with the information in the patient health record. Include reaction.
- **Obtain past history of illnesses.** Include medical, surgical, psychiatric, and obstetric history.
- **Obtain list of medications.** Include over-the-counter drugs, herbals, and supplements (medications listed in the patient health record and double checked).
- **Assess family history.** What was the condition? Who had it?
- **Assess childhood illnesses and immunizations.** Include influenza, pneumococcal, and human papillomavirus (HPV) immunization.

- **Obtain information on most recent screening assessments.** These include TB, vision or hearing screening, dental examinations, Pap smears, stools for occult blood, cardiac screening tests, and mammograms.
- **Assess mental health and psychiatric history.** Medications may provide clues to mental health issues, such as antidepressants.

Growth and Development

Assessment of developmental stage occurs over time, as the nurse works with the patient. Some things to consider when working with patients across the lifespan are the psychosocial development described by Erikson (1980). The nurse will also assess developmental milestones or stage of development in children. Refer to Chapter 9 for more information.

Review of Systems

The nurse reviews the body systems using lay language focused on the following common symptoms (or the patient may complete a form; see Chapter 3). The nurse documents findings, however, using appropriate terminology (Fig. 31-2).

- **General survey:** Fever, chills, weight loss, weight gain, fatigue, weakness, malaise, pain, usual activity.
- **Nutrition and hydration:** Nausea, loss of appetite, vomiting, indigestion, difficulty swallowing or chewing, typical daily intake, dehydration, dry skin, diet practices to promote health, conditions that increase the risk of malnutrition or obesity
- **Skin, hair, and nails:** Rash, itch, lesions, nails, hygiene practices, hair loss, disease processes, pigmentation changes, sweating, brittle or thin nails, thick or yellow nails
- **Head and neck:** Headaches, dizziness, syncope, seizures, enlarged lymph nodes, range of motion
- **Eyes:** Glasses, contacts, blurry vision, double vision, loss of vision, swelling, tearing or dry eyes, date of last vision examination, light sensitivity, burning, redness, discharge

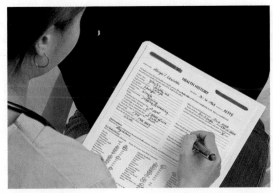

Figure 31-2 The nurse carefully documents findings from the health history in the patient health record, using appropriate terminology.

- **Ears:** Hearing loss, pressure, earache, change in hearing, tinnitus, vertigo, discharge, last hearing examination, ear protection
- **Nose, mouth, throat:** Congestion, sore throat, voice change, usual dental care, last dental visit, colds, nosebleeds, cold sores, bleeding or swollen gums, tooth pain, enlarged tonsils, dry mouth, difficulty chewing or swallowing
- **Thorax and lungs:** Shortness of breath, wheezing, cough, sputum, last chest x-ray, pain
- **Heart:** Fast or slow pulse, heart murmur, chest pain, pounding or fluttering in chest, swelling in feet, rings tighter than usual, electrocardiogram, other cardiac tests
- **Peripheral vascular:** Cramping, pain, numbness/burning/tingling in extremities, edema, ulcers, circulation, redness, pallor, coolness, warmth, tenderness, varicose veins, unable to move limbs
- **Breast:** Pain, tenderness, nipple discharge, rash, lump, date of last breast examination, last mammogram
- **Abdominal/gastrointestinal:** Frequency of bowel movements and description, bloody stool, diarrhea, constipation, soiling of clothes, hemorrhoids, appetite, last stool for occult blood, last sigmoidoscopy, colonoscopy
- **Abdominal/genitourinary:** Frequency and description of urine, difficulty or burning with urination, blood in urine, urination at night, urgency, increased frequency, wetting of clothes, feeling of incomplete emptying or dribbling, pain
- **Musculoskeletal:** Mobility, pain, stiffness, swelling, spasm, tremor, gait, impaired balance, foreign bodies or implants, weakness
- **Neurological:** Headache, one-sided weakness, memory loss, confusion, seizures, tremors, loss of sensation or coordination, change in mood or speech
- **Genitalia, female:** Vaginal discharge, pain with menstruation, excessive bleeding with menstruation, last menstrual period, pain with sexual intercourse, last Pap smear, burning, lesions, itching, pregnant
- **Genitalia, male:** Discharge, pain, swelling, lumps, trauma, erectile dysfunction, lesions, testicular self-examination
- **Anus, rectum, and prostate:** Hemorrhoids, enlarged prostate, prostate cancer, urinary incontinence, pain, burning, hesitancy, dribbling
- **Endocrine:** Excessive thirst, increased urination, hair loss, skin changes, hot flashes, intolerance to heat or cold
- **Hematology:** Anemia, excessive bruising, transfusions
- **Mental health:** Anxiety, depression, thoughts of harming self or others, alcohol use, drug use, addiction, mood, memory, concentration, dementia, difficulty sleeping
- **Summary:** How would you say that your health is in general?

Psychosocial History. The nurse assesses psychosocial, spiritual, and cultural history, language of choice, and need for interpreter. He or she may ask "Do you have any special religious, spiritual, or cultural needs? Would you like an interpreter?" "Describe your support systems." The nurse assesses use of tobacco, alcohol, and recreational drugs by asking directly "Do you use tobacco? alcohol? or other substances?"

He or she assesses for safety and domestic violence by asking "Because violence is so common in many people's lives, I ask all patients about it routinely. Are you in a relationship with a person who physically or sexually hurts or threatens you?"

Functional Health Status. As time allows and as the relationship is established, the nurse also can obtain information about the patient's functional health status. For these questions, it is best to prioritize and weave one or two questions into care (see Chapters 3 and 6).

Activities of Daily Living. In addition, nurses assess ability to perform self-care activities, or ADLs (see Chapter 3). These include behaviours such as eating, dressing, and grooming. Nurses score these items based on whether patients are totally independent, need assistance from a person or a device such as a cane, or are dependent on others (see also Chapter 3).

Risk Assessment and Health Promotion ———

Risk assessment and screening help identify potential issues so that health care professionals can give the patient information to influence behavioural choices. Potential or actual issues requiring health education are identified. The most important focus areas for health-related patient education involve ensuring adequate nutrition, increasing physical activity, maintaining weight, and reducing stress. Avoidance of behaviours that contribute to disease (eg, smoking, overuse of alcohol) is important as well. Another teaching point is immunizations and pneumococcal and influenza vaccines.

Injury prevention involves education on topics such as bicycle helmets, avoiding drinking and driving, wearing personal protective gear, hand hygiene, and using seat belts. Primary prevention of disease and promotion of health are priorities for increased quality and quantity of life. An additional specialized focus area is promotion of health during pregnancy and breastfeeding. Maintaining health during pregnancy is vital for both mother and fetus. Teaching regarding importance of prenatal appointments and screenings and promotion of breastfeeding are key topics.

Focused Health History Related to Common Symptoms ———

In addition to the overall review of systems and general health promotion, the nurse focuses questions on concerns specific to the patient. In this way, the patient is viewed as a person with multiple areas affected by the health status. These questions are related to the primary issues and concerns for the patient, included in each system-specific chapter.

An Example of a Therapeutic Dialogue

Mrs. Suleri, introduced at the beginning of this chapter, is a 44-year-old mother of two children admitted with bloody diarrhea. The nurse uses professional communication techniques to gather subjective data from her. The following conversation is an example of a therapeutic interview.

Nurse: How are you and your family coping with your illness?

Mrs. Suleri: Thanks for asking. It's been hard. Usually I take the kids to soccer practice and ballet. My husband is a backup but he works late so this has been a stress on all of us. I've been so tired lately that I haven't been able to keep up.

Nurse: Do you generally feel rested and ready for activities after sleeping?

Mrs. Suleri: Not really, I'm exhausted (pause) and I barely can make it to work.

Nurse: How is this hospital stay affecting your work?

Mrs. Suleri: I've been missing a lot of work.

Nurse: Do you have benefits or disability plans that cover you for lost work time?

Mrs. Suleri: I do have some benefits but my salary isn't completely covered when I'm not working. I'd like to talk with someone about this if I can.

Nurse: We can arrange for you to see the social worker who can help access benefits for you while you are off work.

Critical Thinking Challenge

- How would you approach the subject of referral to a social worker?
- How might you ask the question about coping, which can be a sensitive subject?
- How would you approach the subject of referral to a social worker?

Objective Data Collection

Pulling together a smooth and organized physical examination is challenging. It is important to practice and develop a pattern of assessment that eventually becomes automatic to avoid skipping or repeating items. The nurse links together sections of the assessment according to the body part being examined, even if they are related to different body systems. For example, while the patient is upright, the nurse assesses alignment of spine and landmarks, symmetry, veins, arches, popliteal fossae, cerbellar tests, position sense, muscle strength, gait, balance, and posture.

Equipment

- Cotton balls
- Equipment wipes
- Drapes, gown
- Disposable nonlatex gloves
- Nasal speculum
- Ophthalmoscope/otoscope
- Reflex hammer
- Blood-pressure cuff
- Scale with height measure
- Stethoscope
- Doppler stethoscope
- Thermometer
- Tongue blades
- Watch with second hand
- Vision charts
- Tuning forks 128 or 256 Hz and 512 or 1024 Hz
- Familiar object (key, coins, paper clip)
- Pungent odours
- Measuring tape or ruler
- Eye cover
- **If specimens are needed:**
  - Vaginal speculum (lubricated only with water)
  - Cotton swabs
  - Culture media
  - Glass slides and fixative
  - KOH, acetic acid, saline
  - Spatula, cervical brush (broom), endocervical brush
- **After specimens are taken:**
  - Water-soluble lubricant for vaginal and rectal examinations

Promoting Patient Comfort, Dignity, and Safety

Following completion of the health history previously described, the nurse explains the process for the physical examination from head to toe and including auscultation of heart and lung sounds, auscultation and palpation of the abdomen, and screening for neuromuscular conditions. Because some examinations may be uncomfortable (eg, breast, gynecological, male genitalia, and prostate), the nurse asks the patient for permission to perform them. Additionally, the nurse asks the patient if he or she prefers to have a third person in the room or, if appropriate, a same gender nurse.

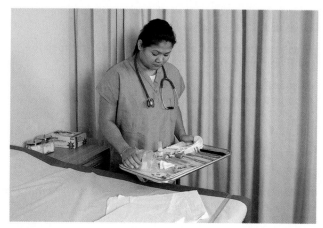

Figure 31-3 The nurse is setting up the examination room for a head-to-toe physical assessment.

The nurse explains that the patient will be draped and protecting modesty will be a priority; only the body part being examined will be exposed.

The nurse asks if the patient would like to empty the bladder because pressure during abdominal palpation may elicit the urge to void. He or she instructs the patient to change into a gown that ties in back. At this point, the nurse obtains the necessary equipment and leaves the room so that the patient can change (Fig. 31-3). He or she instructs the patient to sit on the examination table after finishing undressing. Upon return, the nurse washes and warms the hands to avoid chilling the patient and asks the patient about comfort level and room temperature. If the patient is cold, an additional blanket may be used. The nurse encourages the patient to ask questions about the assessment techniques and findings.

Patients may sense or be fearful of unexpected findings, so it is important to be honest when there are difficulties, such as "Your blood pressure is a little high. We can talk more about that after we're finished." Instead of giving false reassurances, the nurse instead provides objective data. Nevertheless, the nurse avoids sharing conclusions before collecting all data because the initial concern list may change during the interaction. The nurse assesses the response of the individual and family to actual or potential health concerns and also performs assessments related to the direct care role.

Comprehensive Physical Examination

The physical examination begins with height, weight, and vital signs if not previously obtained. Next is the head-to-toe assessment, with the nurse moving efficiently and reducing the number of changes in the position for the patient. It is important to consider how to remember each of these steps by combining items or developing cues to remember them. As a beginner, a pocket guide might be helpful so that at the end the nurse can review it for any forgotten items. The nurse can review this before leaving the patient's room, so it is not necessary to return asking for more information. Reviewing findings with the patient at the end provides closure before leaving.

Techniques and Expected Findings	Unexpected Findings
Wash hands or use hand sanitizer. Wipe stethoscope with equipment wipe.	
Vital Signs	
Obtain temperature. *36.5°C to 37.5°C.*	Hypothermia, hyperthermia.
Obtain pulse. *60 to 100 beats/min.*	Tachycardia, bradycardia, irregular rate. If irregular, take apical pulse.
Obtain respirations. *12 to 20 breaths/min.*	Bradypnea, tachypnea, hyperventilation, Cheyne-Stokes, apnea.
Obtain blood pressure (BP). *systolic 100 to <120 mm Hg; diastolic 60 to <80 mm Hg.*	Hypertension, hypotension, auscultatory gap. Perform orthostatic BP and pulse if indicated. BP that stays 120 to 139/80 to 89 is considered *prehypertension*; above this level (140/90 mm Hg or higher) is hypertension (Canadian Hypertension Education Program, 2011).
Obtain oxygen saturation level. *92% to 100%.*	<92%.
General Survey	
Inspect overall skin colour. *Pink, dark-skinned.*	Pallor, jaundice, flushing, cyanosis (central vs peripheral), erythema, ruddy, mottled.
Assess breathing effort. *Effortless.*	Dyspnea, head of bed elevated, tripod position.
Observe appearance. *Appears stated age.*	Appears older than stated age
Assess mood. *Patient is calm, pleasant, and cooperative. Affect appropriate to situation.*	Flat or inappropriate affect, depression, elation, euphoria, anxiety, irritable, labile.
Observe nutritional status. *Appears well nourished.*	Appears malnourished, overweight, or obese.
Assess personal hygiene. *Clean and groomed.*	Diminished personal hygiene.
Assess posture. *Posture erect.*	Slouching, leaning.
Observe for physical deformities. *No obvious physical deformities.*	Obvious physical deformity present.
Perform safety check. *Call bell within reach; bedside stand positioned; ID band correct; intravenous (IVs), medications, tubes, and drains intact.*	Unsafe environment, medications or IVs not verified.
Skin	
Inspect skin with each corresponding body area. Inspect colour; check for rashes and lesions. *Skin pink, no cyanosis. No telangiectasia, erythema, or papules.*	Changes in skin pigmentation. If there are lesions or rashes, identify configuration, distribution, colour, and type (primary or secondary). Note any infections (eg, cellulitis). Infestations include scabies, lice, ringworm, and fleas.
Palpate for moisture, temperature, texture, turgor, and edema. *Skin warm, slightly dry, and intact. Brisk turgor on upper extremities; no edema, lesions, or tenderness.*	Growths or tumours are unexpected. Describe any wounds or incisions, including size, depth, colour, exudate, location, and wound borders. Turgor on upper extremities is 30 seconds or longer.
Head	
Assess facial structures. *Symmetrical structures without edema, deformities, or lesions. Patent nares.*	Asymmetry, edema, deformities, ptosis, lesions. Absence of "sniff," deviated septum, polyps, drainage.
Observe facial expression. *Appropriate to situation.*	Anxious, facial grimace; facial droop, asymmetry.
Inspect hair, scalp. *Curly hair with even distribution. Hair supple and thick. Scalp dark-skinned and smooth without pests, flaking, lesions, or tenderness.*	Thinning scalp hair in adolescent male.

Palpate cranium, temporal arteries, and temporomandibular joints (TMJs). *Normocephalic, head midline. Temporal artery +1 to 2/4 bilaterally, nontender. TMJs move smoothly, without crepitus or tenderness.*

Facial asymmetry may indicate damage to the facial nerve [cranial nerve (CN) VII] or a serious condition such as a *stroke*. Enlarged bones or tissues are associated with *acromegaly*. A puffy "moon" face is associated with *Cushing's syndrome*. Increased facial hair in females may be a sign of *Cushing's syndrome* or *endocrinopathy*. Periorbital edema is seen with *congestive heart failure* and *hypothyroidism* (*myxedema*).

Assess the trigeminal (CN V), motor strength and sensation, three facial branches. *Strong contraction of temporal and masseter muscles and senses light touch and pain on ophthalmic, maxillary, and mandibular areas bilaterally.*

Decreased or dulled sensation, weakness, or asymmetrical movements are atypical findings associated with the trigeminal nerve (CN V).

Assess the trigeminal and facial nerves (CN V and VII): squeeze eyes shut, wrinkle forehead, clench teeth, smile, puff cheeks. *Facial movements are strong and symmetrical. Assess corneal reflex. Bilateral blink.*

A weak blink from facial weakness may result from paralysis of the trigeminal or facial nerves (CN V or VII).

Depressed or absent corneal response is common in contact lens wearers (CN V).

Inspect lids, lashes, and brows. *No ptosis, lid lag, discharge, or crusting. Even lash distribution, curled outward. Brows with hair loss on outer third.*

Ptosis present Right eye.

Mouth and Throat

Inspect mouth with light and tongue blade. Inspect inside lips, buccal mucosa, gums, teeth, hard/soft palates, uvula, tonsils, pharynx, tongue, and floor of mouth. *Lips, mucosa, gums, palates are pink and smooth. Floor of mouth intact, moist, smooth. Pharynx pink, intact. Tongue pink and rough. No lesions or tenderness. Teeth white, intact with good occlusion.*

Lesions, sponginess, or edema; bleeding gums; missing or discoloured teeth; malocclusion; inflammation or tenderness of ducts.

Grade tonsils. *Tonsils 0 to 2+ bilaterally. Pink with no discharge or lesions.*

Swollen glands or tonsils (grade 3+ to 4+).

Assess glossopharyngeal (CN IX and Vagus nerve (CN X). Check speech-intact.

Speech unclear.

Note mobility of uvula when patient says "ahh": *Uvula midline and rises symmetrically. Test gag reflex. Intact bilaterally.*

Uvula asymmetrical or enlarged. No gag reflex on right side.

Assess hypoglossal nerve (CN XII); look for symmetry of tongue when extended. *Tongue at midline and extends symmetrically. Tongue strength is strong.*

A tongue that deviates to one side is common with *stroke*. Decreased tongue strength on right side.

Eyes

Assess near and distant vision if appropriate. *Reads newsprint accurately. Snellen test 20/20 right eye; 20/20 left eye.*

<20/20 corrected. Vision blurred. Note use of glasses, contact lenses, or assistive devices.

Inspect conjunctiva and sclera. *Pink, moist conjunctiva; white sclera.*

Sclera yellow with *jaundice*. Conjunctiva pink with *inflammation*.

Inspect cornea, iris, and anterior chamber. *Cornea and lens are clear.*

Assess oculomotor (CN III), trochlear nerve (CN IV), abducens (CN VI), and extraocular movements (EOMs). *EOMs intact, no nystagmus or lid lag.*

Assess visual fields, peripheral vision. *Visual fields equal to the examiner's.*

A narrow angle indicates *glaucoma*. Cloudiness of the lens can indicate *cataract*, which is associated with increased age, smoking, alcohol intake, and sunlight exposure. Risk factors for cataracts are primarily environmental.

Darken room. Obtain light. Assess optic nerve (CN II). *Pupils equal, round, and reactive to light and accommodation (PERRLA left 6–4, right 6–4).*

Asymmetry, pinpoint, or "blown" pupils; describe measure of pupil and response to light.

(text continues on page 968)

Perform ophthalmoscope examination: check red reflex, disc, vessels, and macula. Move to opposite side of the patient. *Red reflexes symmetrical. Discs cream-coloured with sharp margins. Retina pink. No hemorrhages or exudates; no arteriolar narrowing. Macula yellow.*

Lack of *red reflex* may need urgent follow-up. If a white pupil reflex (leukokoria) is elicited, then an urgent ophthalmologic referral is required. Disease or trauma (eg, *retinoblastoma, hyphema, toxocariasis, retinal detachment*) often causes a white pupil reflex. Blood vessels can be directly observed in the retina. Systemic diseases are often reflected in the blood vessels and can be directly observed in the eye.

Ears

Turn on lights. Inspect ear alignment. *Ears aligned and symmetrical.* Palpate auricle, lobe, and tragus. *Ears are without lesions, crusting, masses, or tenderness.*

Microtia, macrotia, edema, cartilage pseudomonas infection, carcinoma on auricle, cyst, and frost bite are unexpected findings.

Change to otoscope head. Perform otoscope examination of canal and tympanic membrane. Move to opposite side of the patient. *Canals with small amount of moist yellow cerumen. Tympanic membranes intact, grey, and translucent; light reflex intact and bony landmarks present bilaterally.*

Redness, external swelling, and discharge indicate *external otitis.* Obstructed canal can be by foreign body, discharge, or cerumen.

Assess acoustic nerve (CN VIII) hearing. *Whispered words heard bilaterally.*

Unable to repeat whispered words.

Obtain 512 or 1024 Hz tuning fork. Perform Rinne test (on mastoid) if the patient has hearing loss. *Air conduction > bone conduction.*

Bone conduction longer or the same as air conduction is evidence of *conductive hearing loss.*

Perform Weber test (at midline of skull or midforehead) if the patient has hearing loss. *No lateralization of sound. Heard equally in both ears.*

If lateralizes to affected ear, this is a *conductive hearing loss.* If lateralizes to unaffected ear, this is a *sensorineural loss.*

Nose and Sinuses

Inspect external nose. *Midline, no flaring or crusting.*

Asymmetry, swelling, or bruising may result from trauma or occur with lesions or growths.

Assess nostril patency. *Patent bilaterally.* Assess olfactory (CN I). *Intact bilaterally.*

Unable to sniff because of *deviated septum* or *obstructed nares. Unable to test CN I.*

Perform otoscopic examination of mucosa, turbinates, and septum. *Nasal mucosa pink, intact; no polyps. No drainage. Turbinates and septum intact and symmetrical.*

Infection, inflammation of nasal mucosa may be present with *viral, bacterial, or allergic rhinitis.*

Palpate frontal and maxillary sinuses. *No frontal or maxillary sinus tenderness bilaterally.*

Redness, swelling, or tenderness over the sinuses may represent *acute infection, abscess,* or *mucocele.*

Neck

Inspect symmetry. *Neck symmetrical, moves freely without crepitus.*

Neck asymmetrical or with crepitus

Test flexion, extension, lateral bending, rotation, range of motion (ROM), and strength. *Full ROM, strength 4 to 5+ bilaterally.*

Reduced neck ROM is <4+ bilaterally.

Test spinal accessory (CN XI). Turn head against resistance to each side. Strength—strong and equal bilaterally. Provide resistance to shoulders—*no atropohy of trapezius muscles.*

Reduced strength on right side. Weakness with *atrophy and fasciculations* of trapezius muscle on right side noted.

Palpate tracheal position midline. *Trachea midline.*

Deviated trachea.

Inspect carotid arteries for pulsations.

Auscultate carotid arteries with bell of stethoscope.

Bruits over the carotid indicate *carotid artery stenosis.*

Palpate carotid pulses separately. *Carotid pulse +2/4 bilaterally.*

Carotid pulses may be reduced from *carotid stenosis.*

Inspect jugular veins. *No jugular venous distention.*

Palpate preauricular, postauricular, occipital, and posterior cervical chains. *Lymph nodes are not palpable or tender bilaterally.*

Palpate tonsillar, submandibular, submental, and anterior cervical chains. *They are not palpable or tender.*

Palpate supraclavicular nodes. *They are not palpable or tender.*

Neurological
Assess mental status and level of consciousness. *Patient is alert. Eyes open spontaneously.*

Assess orientation. *Oriented × 4.*

Assess ability to follow commands. *Follows directions.*

Evaluate short- and long-term memory. *Immediate, recent, and distant memory intact.*

Assess speech. *Speech clear and appropriate.*

Assess hearing. *Hears sounds and responds appropriately.*

Upper Extremities
Assess circulation, movement, and sensation (CMS). Assess hands and joints. Examine nails on upper extremities. *CMS intact. Nails smooth without clubbing. Capillary refill <3 seconds. Brachial and radial pulses +2/4. Joints without swelling, tenderness, or deformity.*

Test ROM. Perform finger grip for muscle strength. *4 to 5+ muscle strength symmetrical. Full ROM bilaterally.*

Musculoskeletal and Neurological. Perform finger-to-nose test if indicated. *Smooth, accurate, and intact.* Test rapid alternating movements if indicated. *Smooth and intact.*

Test stereognosis if indicated. *Patient identifies key or other object.*

Test graphesthesia if indicated. *Patient identifies the correct numbers bilaterally.*

Anterior Thorax
Assess breathing effort, rate, rhythm, and pattern; position to breathe. *Breathes easily, with symmetrical expansion and contraction.*

Inspect thorax shape and skin. *Anteroposterior (AP) to lateral ratio 1:2 symmetrical. Skin intact.*

If patient is on an examination table, move to front of the patient. Inspect costovertebral angle, configuration, and pulsations. *No pulsations visible. No dyspnea, retractions, or accessory muscle use.*

Jugular veins may be either flat or distended.

Lymph nodes are not freely movable or are tender, and larger than 2 cm.

Tonsillar nodes are enlarged and tender bilaterally *(tonsillitis).*

Agitated, asleep, lethargic, obtunded, restless, stuporous. Use coma scale if reduced (eye opening, verbal, motor). Does not respond to stimuli or pain; decorticate rigidity, decerebrate rigidity, or no response to pain.

Alert and oriented × 2 (person and place). Alert and oriented × 1 (person); disoriented × 3. Can also assess orientation to situation (alert and oriented × 4).

Unable to follow commands such as "squeeze my fingers" or "sit up."

Immediate, recent, or distant memory impaired; describe specific details.

Speech difficult to understand.

Difficulty understanding spoken words. Hard of hearing. Note hearing aids or assistive devices.

Decreased CMS, including colour, temperature; capillary refill >3 seconds, pulses, decreased movement, decreased sensation and paresthesia. Nails are breakable, cracking, inflamed, jagged, bitten, and clubbing is present.

Decreased ROM, swelling, or nodules in joints. Muscle strength asymmetrical (Right: 0; Left: 3+).

Ataxia is an unsteady, wavering movement with inability to touch the target. During rapid alternating movements, lack of coordination is *adiadochokinesia.*

Inability to identify objects correctly *(astereognosis)* may result from damage to the sensory cortex caused by *stroke.*

Cortical sensory function may be compromised following a *stroke.*

Dyspnea, orthopnea, paroxysmal nocturnal dyspnea. Rhythm regular; sitting straight upright or using tripod position to breathe.

Barrel chest, funnel chest, pigeon chest, thoracic kyphoscoliosis.

Using accessory muscles. Reports feeling "short of breath."

(text continues on page 970)

Auscultate breath sounds. *Bronchovesicular sounds over large airways, vesicular in lung fields. Lung sounds clear.*

Diminished or absent breath sounds, bronchial or bronchovesicular sounds in lung periphery. Describe adventitious sounds (crackles, gurgles, wheezes, stridor, pleural rub). Are they inspiratory or expiratory? Do they clear with coughing? Where specifically do you hear them?

Assess for cough and inspect sputum. *No cough or sputum.*

Cough (brassy, harsh, loose, productive) present. Sputum (colour, consistency, amount) present.

Inspect precordium. *Point of maximal impulse (PMI) may be visible or absent.*

PMI lateral to left midclavicular line (MCL); heaves or thrills.

Assess heart rate, rhythm, murmurs, and extra sounds. *Heart rate and rhythm regular. No gallops, murmurs, or rubs. S1, S2 single sounds.*

Tachycardia, bradycardia, irregular rhythm, murmurs (systolic vs diastolic), extra sounds (S3, S4, friction rub).

Auscultate heart with bell and diaphragm in aortic, pulmonic, left sternal border, tricuspid, and mitral areas with patient supine. *Heart rate and rhythm regular; no murmurs, gallops, or rubs.*

If rhythm is irregular, identify if the irregularity has a pattern or is totally irregular. For example, every third beat missed would be a regular irregular rhythm. No detectable pattern is characteristic of *atrial fibrillation*, common in older adults. Murmurs, rubs, or gallops are unexpected in adults.

Palpate chest for fremitus, thrill, heaves, and PMI. *Tactile fremitus symmetrical; no thrill, heave, or lift. Cardiac impulse nonpalpable.*

Asymmetrical fremitus may occur with unilateral disease (eg, lung tumour). Thrills, heaves, and lifts indicate turbulence over a valve and are concerning.

Percuss anterior chest from apex to base and sides. *Lung fields resonant with dullness over heart area.*

Dull lung percussion indicates increased consolidation as with *pneumonia*.

Female Breasts

Inspect the breasts. Have patient raise arms overhead, press hands together, and lean forward. *No retraction or dimpling; symmetrical movement and shape.*

Retraction, dimpling, or nipple discharge (other than breast milk) may indicate *breast cancer*.

Palpate breasts. *No lesions or masses; no nipple discharge. Nontender.*

Palpate axillary nodes. *Axillary nodes not palpable, nontender bilaterally.*

Positive nodes may indicate *breast cancer*, especially if hard, irregular shape, immovable, larger than 1 cm.

Abdomen

Inspect abdomen. *Abdomen symmetrical, rounded, or flat. Smooth, intact skin without lesions or rashes. Peristalsis and pulsations evident in thin patients. Inverted, round umbilicus.*

Scars, striae, ecchymosis, lesions, prominent dilated veins, rashes, marked pulsation. Red, everted, enlarged, or tender umbilicus.

Auscultate bowel sounds. *Bowel sounds present all quadrants.*

Hypoactive, hyperactive, or absent bowel sounds.

Auscultate aorta, renal, and iliac arteries with bell. *No bruit.*

Venous hum, friction rub, or bruits are unexpected arterial sounds.

Percuss abdomen in all quadrants and for gastric bubble. *Abdomen mixed tympany and dullness in all quadrants. Gastric bubble percussed 6th left intercostal space (ICS) at MCL.*

Percussion notes over abdomen are dull or flat.

Percuss liver margin at right MCL. *Liver border above costal margin at right MCL. Liver span 8 cm.*

Liver margin percussed 3 cm below right costal margin. Liver span 13 cm.

Percuss spleen. *Spleen percussed in lowest left ICS at the anterior axillary line.*

Spleen 2 cm below left costal margin, deviates downward and medially on inspiration.

Palpate for abdominal tenderness, distention in all quadrants. *Nontender, soft.*

Palpate for liver, spleen, and kidneys. *Liver lower border less than one finger below costal margin at right MCL. Spleen and kidneys nonpalpable.*

Large masses, hard, tenderness with guarding or rigidity, rebound tenderness. Liver palpable more than one finger below costal margin at right MCL.

Palpate aorta, femoral pulses, and inguinal horizontal and vertical lymph nodes and for hernias. *Aorta palpable, smooth. Femoral pulses +2/4. No inguinal nodes or hernias bilaterally.*	An enlarged aorta (>3 cm) or one with lateral pulsations that are palpable can indicate *abdominal aortic aneurysm.*
Assess swallowing, chewing, aspiration risk, special diet. *Eats >75% of meal without difficulty.*	Dysphagia, impaired chewing, impaired swallowing, medically prescribed diet, tube feedings, significant weight gain/loss.
	Describe characteristics of emesis (eg, coffee grounds, blood).
Inspect stool; record last bowel movement (BM). *Last BM typical, soft and brown. Passing flatus.*	Dark stool may indicate blood in it. If hemorrhoids are present, the stool may be light colour but have bright red blood coating it.
Inspect urine colour, character, and amount with voiding. *Urine clear, yellow, and >30 mL/h.*	Urine dark, bloody, red, with sediment, cloudy, or <30 mL/h.

Lower Extremities

Inspect skin and nails for symmetry, edema, veins, and lesions. *Toenails white and smooth. Skin intact, slightly pale, and symmetrical, without edema, varicose veins, or lesions.*	Note areas of pressure on heels and if they blanch with pressure. Lesions, ulcers, varicosities, edema. Mottled, ruddy, reddened, or flaky skin. Note indurations with infection or inflammation.
Palpate dorsalis pedis pulses bilaterally (+1 to 2/4). Palpate popliteal pulse (+2/4) and posterior tibial pulse (+1 to 2/4). *Pulses + 1 to 2/4 bilaterally.*	If diminished or absent pulses, obtain Doppler for assessment. Bounding (4+) pulses are also unexpected.
Assess capillary refill on both feet. *Brisk capillary refill <3 seconds bilaterally.*	Capillary refill >3 seconds bilaterally.
Inspect and palpate for edema over dorsum of each foot, each medial malleolus, and shins. *No edema.*	**Edema Characteristics and Grading:** 1+ slight (2 mm depth), disappears rapidly 2+ deeper (4 mm), disappears in 10 to 15 seconds 3+ visible swelling of extremity (6 mm), disappears in > 1 minute 4+ grossly swollen extremity (8 mm), disappears in 2 to 3 minutes (Dillon, 2007, p. 180).
Palpate for tenderness and temperature. *Feet warm, no tenderness.*	Tenderness to palpation, feet cool or cold.
Palpate lower extremities and joints from hips to toes. *No tenderness or swelling.*	
Observe ROM of joints. *Full joint ROM.*	Limited or reduced ROM.
Test muscle strength on feet, observe for symmetry. Test muscle strength of hips, knees, and ankles. *Strength 4 to 5+.*	Strength 0 to 3+.
Test sensation. *Appropriately identifies when touched.*	Loss of sensation (identify location).
Obtain reflex hammer. Perform deep tendon reflexes (DTR)—patellar, Achilles, and Babinski. *Patellar, Achilles DTR 2+ bilaterally; Babinski negative bilaterally.*	If reflexes are 3 to 4+, they are brisker than usual. If they are 1+ to 0, they are diminished or absent. A positive Babinski indicates a poor neurological outcome.

Posterior Thorax

Move behind patient. Palpate for thyroid. *Thyroid borders palpable, no enlargement, nodules, or masses noted. Thyroid moves upward with swallow.*	Thyroid enlargement or masses can be seen more easily when the patient swallows and while illuminating the neck with tangential lighting.
Inspect skin, symmetry, configuration, and observe respirations. *Chest symmetrical, oval, without barrel chest. AP/lateral ratio 1:2. Respirations 18 without dyspnea.*	In barrel chest, which can accompany *chronic obstructive pulmonary disease (COPD),* the AP/ lateral ratio approximates 1:1, giving the chest a round appearance.

(text continues on page 972)

Inspect spine. *Spine straight, skin intact.*

Skeletal scoliosis and kyphosis can limit respiratory excursion. Asymmetry and paradoxical respirations occur in flail chest.

Palpate spine and scapulae. *Spine straight, without scoliosis, kyphosis, or lordosis. Scapulae symmetrical.*

Assess spinal accessory (CN XI). *Strong and equal shoulder shrug.*

Right shoulder droops.

Assess tactile fremitus. *Tactile fremitus symmetrical.*

Increased tactile fremitus over an area indicates increased consolidation.

Percuss posterior chest from apex to base to sides. *Lung fields resonant throughout.*

Dullness occurs with increased consolidation; hyper-resonance occurs with hyperinflation as in *COPD.*

Test costovertebral angle tenderness (kidney). *No tenderness to indirect fist percussion bilaterally.*

Kidney tenderness is present with *urinary tract infection and kidney disease.*

Auscultate breath sounds. *Vesicular breath sounds throughout.*

Coarse breath sounds are unexpected. Crackles, gurgles (rhonchi), and wheezing are adventitious sounds.

Inspect lower back, buttocks (redness, symmetry). *No redness, breakdown.*

Any redness, especially over pressure areas, is a concern. Scoliosis, lordosis, and kyphosis are unexpected spine findings.

Gait and Balance/Fall Risk

Assess fall risk—history of falling, secondary diagnosis, ambulatory aid, IV therapy, gait, and mental status. *Scores at low risk on fall scale.*

Gait alterations include hesitancy, unsteadiness, staggering, reaching for external support, high stepping, foot scraping, inability to raise the foot completely off the floor, persistent toe or heel walking, excessive pointing of toes inward or outward, asymmetry of step height or length, limping, stooping, wavering, shuffling, waddling, excessive swinging of shoulders or pelvis, and slow or rapid speed.

Musculoskeletal and Neurological

Perform heel-to-shin test for coordination. *Smooth, coordinated movement.* Have patient stand. Note muscle strength and coordination when moving. *Moves easily in the environment. Balanced and coordinated movements.*

The dominant side usually has slightly better coordination. Lack of coordination may be from pain, injury, deformity, or *cerebellar disorders.* Coordination is often tested during assessment of the musculoskeletal system, but it is actually an assessment of the neurological system.

Observe spinal alignment, hip level, gluteal and knee folds. *Spine straight, posture erect.*

Scoliosis or low back pain may cause the patient to lean forward or to the side when standing or sitting, and have unequal gluteal folds.

Assess spine flexion, extension, lateral bending, and rotation. *Full ROM in spine.*

Ask patient to walk on heels and then toes, and then to stand on one foot and then the other. Shallow knee bend, hops on one foot. *Balance and coordination intact.*

Unsteady. Unable to do shallow knee bend or stand on one foot.

Skin Breakdown

Assess risk for skin breakdown—sensory perception, moisture, activity, mobility, nutrition, friction, and shear. *Scores at low risk for skin breakdown.*

The Braden scale scores patients from 1 to 4 in six subscales: sensory perception, moisture, activity, mobility, nutrition, and friction (Braden & Bergstrom, 1989). High scores place the patient at high risk *(skin breakdown).*

Wounds, Drains, Devices

Assess intravenous, drainage, catheter, suction. *Wound healing, drains intact, catheter draining well, suction on. IV site clean, dry intact without erythema or tenderness.*

Pressure ulcers may be deep tissue, stage I, stage II, stage III, stage IV, or unstagable (National Pressure Ulcer Advisory Panel, 2007). Stages I and II are partial thickness into the dermis. Stages III and IV are full thickness. Wound drainage is classified as serous (clear), sanguineous (bloody), serosanguineous (mixed), fibrinous (sticky yellow), or purulent (pus). Note any signs or symptoms of infection.

Male Genitalia

Obtain gloves. *No redness, discharge, skin intact.* Recommend test of stool specimens for occult blood × 3.

Atypical genital hair findings are no hair, patchy growth, or distribution in a female or triangular pattern with base over the pubis. Observe for infestations such as *pediculosis, scabies,* or parasites. Look for inflammation, lesions, or dermatitis. *Candidiasis* infections cause crusty, multiple, red, round erosions and pustules; this infection is associated with immunological deficiencies and diabetes mellitus. *Tinea curis* (commonly referred to as "jock itch") is a fungal infection on the patient's groin and upper thighs. It appears with large red, scaly patches that are extremely itchy. Tinea curis rarely involves the scrotum.

Palpate the scrotum for tenderness, lumps, and masses. *No tenderness, lumps, or masses.*

Assess for inguinal hernia. *No hernia.*

Female Genitalia

Obtain gloves, speculum, gel, and supplies for Pap and other tests. Inspect perineal and perianal areas. *No redness, discharge, odour, protrusions from vagina, tenderness, skin intact.*

Symptoms of herpes simplex virus 2 include vulvar or vaginal pain, flu-like symptoms (eg, chills, fever), sores on the vulva or genital region, scattered vesicles along the labia, matching vesicles on the labia, reflecting "kissing" lesions, surface ulcerations or crusted healing lesions, and inguinal lymphadenopathy.

Insert speculum using water as lubricant. Inspect cervix and vaginal walls. *Vaginal walls pink, no lesions. Cervix pink, slit-like, no discharge.*

Candidiasis: *Thick white secretions, perineal itching, and dyspareunia.*

Obtain Pap smear first and then other specimens. Remove speculum. *No infections, Pap test negative.*

Bacterial vaginosis: *Vaginal itching and burning, fishy odour when mixed with KOH.*

Chlamydia: *Clear or white discharge, dyspareunia, bleeding after intercourse, cervix may bleed easily, pain with examination.*

Gonorrhea: *Yellow secretions, painful urination, dyspareunia, pain with examination.*

Trichomoniasis: *Vaginal itching, purulent yellow to frothy green discharge with foul odour, cervical redness (strawberry looking), and contact bleeding.*

Primary syphilis: *A 1-cm button-like painless papule at the site of inoculation. Raised border with a center of serous exudate (present for 10 to 90 days).*

Use lubricant to perform bimanual examination of cervix, uterus, and adnexa. *No pain when moving the cervix, uterus midline and anteverted; no enlargement, masses, or tenderness. Adnexa and ovaries smooth, no masses or tenderness.*

Ovaries tender, larger than almond size, uterus retroverted, fibroids palpated.

Rectum

Inspect perianal area. *No redness or tenderness, skin intact.*

Look for gential warts, thrombosed hemorrhoids, rectal fissures, or hard stool. Hemorrhoids can be classified as external or internal. Hemorrhoids are usually caused by constant or excessive straining upon defecation. Prostate enlarged, smooth, and firm. Area of hardness palpated.

(text continues on page 974)

With lubricated finger, palpate rectal wall (and prostate in male). *No hemorrhoids, fissures, lesions, masses, or tenderness. Rectal wall smooth and intact. Male: prostate smooth and round.*	
Order three stool samples for occult blood. *Stool soft and brown.*	
Closure • Summarize and clarify findings for patient. "Does this sound accurate?" • Assess room for safety (bedside table, lights, call light, toileting). "Do you have any concerns?" • Assess for questions or further needs. "Is there anything else I can do?" • Wash hands or use hand sanitizer when leaving.	Summarizing findings provides closure and ensures accurate conclusions. Asking an open-ended question allows the patient to add any other information that might have been overlooked. Assessing for safety is of primary importance. Always assess the patient and environment for risks. Follow-up on care planning and interventions for the next visit.

Lifespan and Cultural Considerations

The complete assessment needs adaptations for the age, gender, and cultural background of the patient. A woman's body changes during pregnancy, and fetal growth needs to be assessed (see Chapter 27). A newborn requires a special assessment to evaluate breathing, circulation, and alertness (see Chapter 28). The child may need to be examined while sitting in a parent's lap. An adolescent will need privacy and a safe place to express concerns (see Chapter 29). The older adult may fatigue easily and need to have the assessment divided over several time periods (see Chapter 30). Some men or women, especially in some cultures, prefer to have a health care provider of the same gender (see Chapter 11). A translator may be used when the patient has limited English. Lifespan and cultural consideration are included when providing individualized and holistic care.

Documenting Abnormal Findings

Mrs. Suleri's primary concern is related to the bleeding caused by ulcerative colitis. Other issues that can be clustered and further assessed include diarrhea from ulcerative colitis, pain from cramping, anemia from blood loss, fatigue from anemia, and nutritional status related to obesity and dietary intake. Focusing on these issues, the nurse notes the following findings.

Inspection: Five dark brown liquid stools over 12 hours totalling 500 mL. Hemoccult positive for blood. Reports abdominal pain primarily in lower quadrants. Rates pain as 5 on a 0 to 10 scale. Describes it as a cramping, gnawing sensation that comes in waves but never completely goes away; rates it as 2/10 when best. Skin colour pale, pressure 110 beats/min, blood pressure 112/80 mm Hg (right arm, semi-Fowler's), last hemoglobin 10 g/dL (low), and hematocrit 31% (low). Intake for past 12 hours 800 mL and output 860 mL. Weight 92 kg, down 1.5 kg from yesterday. Abdomen protuberant.

Auscultation: Bowel sounds hyperactive in all four quadrants.

Palpation: Abdomen soft but tender to light palpation. Facial grimace present, guarding abdomen.

Percussion: Abdomen tympanic.

Hospital Assessment

The nurse in the hospital performs a comprehensive assessment of the patient on admission. This assessment is more detailed and complete than screening and focused assessments that assess progress toward a goal later in the hospital stay. The comprehensive admitting, screening, and focused assessments are important for establishing and maintaining documentation of current findings.

Comprehensive Admitting Assessment

The nurse performs the initial hospital assessment and documents results in the patient health record. It includes collection of both subjective and objective data. Subjective data include assessment of risk factors, symptoms, and health history as previously described; however, the nurse may need to gather history from secondary sources such as the health record or relatives to avoid fatiguing the acutely ill patient. The general survey and vital signs are also the same. Risks for falling and skin breakdown are added because of the hospital environment.

Because acuity of the hospitalized patient is often increased, the nurse prioritizes which data to collect related to the presenting issues and performs a basic screening of other body systems. He or she uses clinical judgment about which items to include and to omit. Techniques are adapted based on the individual patient's situation. The admitting assessment is usually documented in a separate area of the patient health record and may include input from other health care professionals. Refer to Chapter 5 for a common admitting assessment on the hospitalized patient in a systems format.

Initial patient history and head-to-toe physical examination may take 30 or more minutes to complete, but subsequent assessments are shorter because they focus on areas of concern rather than the entire body. It is important to make this assessment comfortable and smooth with practice. The assessment is adapted to the patient in a style that is professional yet personal and individualized. The nurse also allows some time for documentation of findings and analysis of data. In addition to positive findings, it is essential to document absence of findings because, in the legal world, "if it's not documented, it's not done." For example, if the patient develops a pressure sore, it is important for the nurse to look back in the chart and see "skin intact" to identify this change in status as significant.

Some time is also needed for patient teaching, validation of concerns, mutual goal setting, and discussion of an action plan. This way the nurse knows the patient and his or her concerns well and agrees on an action plan to establish a trusting and therapeutic relationship. Creating and maintaining a professional therapeutic relationship to make a difference in the outcomes is one of the most important and satisfying elements in the process.

Screening Hospital Assessment

Because of the complications of immobility and being in a hospital environment, the nurse performs a short screening assessment at the beginning of each shift. He or she does so for all patients. This assessment typically takes 5 to 10 minutes to provide a basis for comparison in the event of a sudden change in condition. This screening enables the nurse to identify patient acuity; need for immediate treatment, teaching, or discharge planning; and care priorities. See Table 31-2 for a typical beginning-of-shift screening assessment for the patient with expected findings. The nurse completes and documents this assessment on an assessment form.

Focused Hospital Assessment

The nurse working in a hospital also performs a focused assessment on each patient, which can take anywhere

Table 31-2	Basic Screening Assessment
System	**Expected Findings**
Pain	0 on pain scale
Respiration	On room air Breath sounds clear to auscultation Respiration unlaboured and symmetrical
Cardiovascular	Pulse regular No edema Vital signs stable
Neurological	Responds appropriately Speech clear Moves all extremities
Gastrointestinal	Bowel sounds present Tolerates prescribed diet Abdomen soft, nontender, nondistended Passing flatus Last BM _____
Genitourinary	Continent Urine output adequate Urine clear yellow
Musculoskeletal	Moves all extremities without difficulty Activity at expected level
Skin/mucosa	Skin warm, dry, and intact Mucous membranes pink and moist Skin colour uniform Sacrum and heels skin intact
Safety	Low fall risk, environmental check Double check IVs, tubes, drains
Psychological/social	Patient calm and interactive

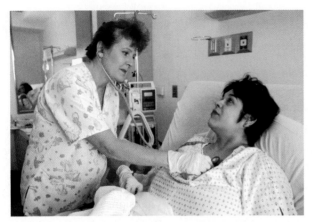

Figure 31-4 Reassessments in hospital settings focus on key areas for ongoing evaluation. One example would be assessing the lungs in a postpartum woman.

from 1 minute when assessing one or two items to 10 to 20 minutes for a more complete review of complex issues (Fig. 31-4). Therefore, the nurse must prioritize information. Usually an unexpected finding or diagnosis triggers the need for a more complete and focused assessment. The nurse also uses clinical judgment to determine which data are most important.

Initially the beginning nurse may need to consult with a more experienced nurse, but with experience typical patterns emerge. These assessments are individualized to the specific patients. Trends of improving or declining status are identified, treatment is modified, and other health care professionals are consulted for changes in the patient's orders or need for further diagnostic testing. The documenting findings example above illustrates how the assessment is focused on the individual patient's condition.

Common Laboratory and Diagnostic Testing

Many patients in primary care settings and most hospitalized patients have a standard set of screening tests done to identify common conditions. Electrolytes are measured to identify electrolyte imbalances.

> △ *SAFETY ALERT 31-2*
> *Serum potassium level may affect nerve or heart cell conduction, leading to arrhythmias and potentially cardiac arrest. A potassium level outside the expected narrow range of 3.5 to 5.5 mmol/L requires immediate correction.*

Serum sodium can be a reflection of sodium intake, but is more likely a reflection of having too much or too little water, therefore diluting or concentrating the sodium. The red blood cells, hemoglobin, and hematocrit reflect the blood's oxygen-carrying capacity. Many patients also receive a chest x-ray that can identify areas of infection, collapse, or fluid. Routine urinalysis may be ordered to identify if there is an infection, blood, or sediment. Additional tests depend on the individual patient's condition. It is important for the nurse to be able to recognize the significance of test results.

Clinical Reasoning

Nursing diagnoses must be individualized to the patient and his or her current conditions. These include both actual diagnoses and those for which the patient is at risk. Table 31-3 provides a comparison of nursing diagnoses, unexpected findings, and interventions for Mrs. Suleri (North American Nursing Diagnosis Association-International, 2009).

Table 31-3   Common Nursing Diagnoses Applied to Mrs. Suleri

Diagnosis and Related Factors	Point of Differentiation	Assessment Characteristics	Nursing Interventions
Diarrhea related to inflammatory changes of the bowel	Loose, unformed, and watery stools	Three or more loose liquid stools per day, abdominal cramps, hyperactive bowel sounds, urgency to use toilet	Observe and document stool characteristics. Provide medications as ordered.* Ensure adequate hydration and electrolyte replacements.*
Fatigue related to low hemoglobin and hematocrit and inability to sleep	Overwhelming exhaustion; decreased capacity for physical and mental work	Decreased performance, drowsiness, inability to maintain usual routine or to feel restored and energetic after usual sleep	Monitor lab results. Provide periods of rest by clustering care. Gradually increase activity as tolerated. Gather resources for home care and daily activities such as house cleaning.

*Collaborative interventions.

The nurse analyzes findings and synthesizes information to initiate a plan of care. The nurse's thinking is shown in progress notes, in this case, using the SOAP format. The subjective and objective data are from the assessment that the nurse has performed. The analysis then leads to a preliminary plan of care.

Subjective: "I've been having about 10 bloody stools a day, and I'm just exhausted. This pain and cramping have just really gotten to me."

Objective: Reports abdominal pain primarily in lower quadrants. Rates pain as 5 on a 0 to 10 scale. Describes it as a cramping, gnawing sensation that comes in waves but never completely goes away; rates it as 2/10 when best. Soaking in her bathtub and staying quiet seem to alleviate the pain. Stress, coffee, increased activity, and the end of the day make it worse. Hopes to achieve pain of 2/10 at peak and reduction in cramping. Functional goal is to return to usual activities at home, including cooking meals and transporting children, and also return to work. Concerned about financial issues. Facial grimace present, guarding abdomen.

Assessment: Pain related to ulcerative colitis exacerbation as evidenced by pain 5/10, facial grimace and guarding. Risk for ineffective coping because of illness and financial concerns.

Plan: Provide medication for pain as ordered. Teach relaxation techniques as a nonpharmacological pain measure. Limit mobility and provide rest. Allow periods of sleep at night. Assess foods that are preferred. Contact social work to evaluate need for additional resources.

Critical Thinking Challenge

- What other assessment should be gathered based upon the number of bloody stools?
- Are there other items that the nurse may want to assess based upon the pain level?
- What other body systems might be affected based upon the known assessments?

Collaborating With the Interprofessional Team

In many facilities, nurses initiate referrals based on assessment findings. Social workers help patients to cope with and solve issues related to family and personal issues. Some social workers help patients who face a disability, life-threatening disease, inadequate housing, unemployment, financial concern, or substance abuse. Social workers also assist families with domestic conflicts, such as child or spousal abuse. In the hospital setting they assist with financial issues, patient placement, and funding for placements and resources after discharge.

Mrs. Suleri has been experiencing many of the problems outlined above; therefore, a social work consult is indicated. The following conversation illustrates how the nurse might organize the data and make recommendations about the patient's situation.

Situation: Hello, Margie (the social worker for the unit). I'm Olga, the nurse taking care of Mrs. Suleri today. Do you know her? (Margie replies "No.")

Background: She is a 44-year-old woman who was admitted with bleeding related to her ulcerative colitis. She is married and has two children ages 15 and 13 years old.

Assessment: She is currently employed but has been missing a lot of work because of her colitis. She's worried about caring for her family as she has two young teenagers. She is also worried about her finances.

Recommendations: Do you think that you would be able to see her in the next day or so to talk with her about resources?

Critical Thinking Challenge

- What other assessments might the nurse make based upon Mrs. Suleri's role in the family?
- How might her additional stressors be affecting her physiological health?
- What other nursing diagnoses might be considered regarding her psychological health?

Pulling It All Together: An Example of Reflection and Critical Thinking

The nurse uses assessment data to formulate the patient care plan with patient outcomes and interventions for Mrs. Suleri. Outcomes are specific to the patient, realistic to achieve, measurable, and have a time frame for meeting the outcome. The interventions are actions that the nurse performs, based on evidence and practice guidelines. After these interventions are completed, the nurse reassesses Mrs. Suleri and documents the findings in the patient health record to show progress toward the patient outcome. The nurse uses critical thinking and judgment to continue or revise the diagnosis, outcomes, or interventions. This is often in the form of a care plan or case note similar to the one seen below.

Nursing Diagnosis	Patient Outcomes	Nursing Interventions	Rationale	Evaluation
Fatigue related to anemia as evidenced by low hematocrit and hemoglobin, pale, tired	Patient will explain an energy conservation plan to offset effects of fatigue.	Assess severity of fatigue on a 0–10 scale. Evaluate adequacy of nutrition and sleep patterns. Collaborate with health care professional to treat anemia.	Fatigue is discomfort that can be rated using a numeric scale. A commonly suggested treatment is rest. Fatigue is related to the anemia from bleeding.	Patient stated that she has not been sleeping well because of cramping, pain, and frequent stools at night. Will plan to provide medication for diarrhea and sleeping tonight. Would like to have sign on the door asking to not be woken up. Taking 50% of meals at this time.

From Bulechek, G. M., Butcher, H. K., et al. (2008). *Nursing interventions classification (NIC)* (5th ed.). St. Louis, MO: Mosby; Moorhead, S., Johnson, M., et al. (2007). *Nursing outcomes classification (NOC)* (4th ed.). Philadelphia, PA: Mosby.

Applying Your Knowledge

Using the previous steps of clinical reasoning, organizing, and prioritizing, consider all the case study findings woven throughout this chapter. When answering the following questions, begin drawing conclusions and see how the pieces of assessment must work together to create an environment for personalized, appropriate, and accurate care.

- When is a focused health assessment used? (Knowledge)
- Describe the differences among a comprehensive, focused, and screening assessment. (Comprehension)
- How will the nurse individualize the admitting history to focus it on Mrs. Suleri? (Application)
- How will the nurse focus the physical assessments considering Mrs. Suleri's diagnosis? (Analysis)
- How will the nurse use the assessment information to develop a plan of care? (Synthesis)
- How will the nurse evaluate the effectiveness of the assessment? (Evaluation)

Key Points

- Health assessment is individualized considering the condition, age, gender, and culture of the patient.
- Nurses adapt assessments depending on scope of practice, clinical setting, and patient situation.
- Indications of unstable status that necessitate intervention include cyanosis or pallor, dyspnea, strained posture, anxious facial expression, distressed appearance, difficulty managing the airway, extremely slow or rapid pulse, very high or low blood pressure, acute change in mental status, or new onset of chest pain.
- Subjective data collection includes health promotion, risk factors, history of present concern, past medical and family history, personal and social history, and assessment of common symptoms. Subjective data collection includes personal history, past history, medications, family history, lifestyle, occupational history, personal behaviour, risk assessment, and health promotion.
- Objective data collection is organized by body area, moving from head to toes for efficiency and patient comfort.
- Inspection, palpation, percussion, and auscultation are techniques used during the head-to-toe assessment.
- Nurses document and communicate assessment data using appropriate terminology and reporting principles.
- Assessment occurs during all phases of the nursing process.
- An accurate and complete health assessment is the foundation for appropriate holistic and individualized patient care.

Review Questions

1. The nurse performs the first assessment on the hospitalized patient and documents it in the patient health record as the
   A. sporadic assessment
   B. functional assessment
   C. focused assessment
   D. admitting assessment

2. The patient is anxious, dyspneic, pale, and using accessory muscles to breathe. Vital signs are temperature 37°C, pulse 126 beats/min, respirations 40 breaths/min, and blood pressure (BP) 122/74 mm Hg. The type of assessment that the nurse would perform is
   A. acute assessment
   B. general survey
   C. health history
   D. objective assessment

3. The nurse assesses the patient presenting with nausea, vomiting, and diarrhea. When the focused assessment is performed, the nurse uses the following techniques:
   A. Auscultate lungs, auscultate heart, auscultate abdomen
   B. Evaluate for dehydration, assess skin turgor, auscultate lungs
   C. Auscultate abdomen, palpate abdomen, evaluate for dehydration
   D. Palpate abdomen, percuss abdomen, auscultate heart

4. After being given report and gathering data from the patient health records, the nurse will assess a group of four patients. Which one will the nurse assess first?
   A. 32-year-old man with an open wound and receiving antibiotics
   B. 66-year-old woman 2 days postoperatively following ankle surgery
   C. 45-year-old man with HIV and *Pneumocystis pneumonia* with dyspnea
   D. 88-year-old woman with confusion and stroke 4 days ago

5. The nurse gathers subjective data related to the history of the present illness. Items that are included are
   A. onset, location, frequency, quality, aggravating/alleviating factors, quantity
   B. asymmetry, borders, colour, diameter, elevation, pain
   C. heart rate, respiratory effort, response, colour, pain
   D. eye opening, verbal response, motor response, orientation

6. The nurse usually performs a complete physical examination with elements in the following order:
   A. Face, heart, legs, arms
   B. Head, abdomen, lungs, legs
   C. Eyes, heart, abdomen, legs
   D. Ears, back, lungs, arms

7. The patient develops a sudden onset of acute chest pain. In addition to a complete description of the symptoms, what objective assessment is a priority?
   A. Pulse, BP, peripheral pulses
   B. Heart sounds, rate, and rhythm
   C. Circulation, sensation, and movement
   D. Murmurs, rubs, and gallops

8. A 50-year-old patient is seen in the clinic for an annual physical examination and screening. The patient has no known health conditions. This type of care is referred to as
   A. primary prevention
   B. promotion prevention
   C. tertiary prevention
   D. healthy prevention

9. The nurse assesses if the patient outcome, "Patient drinks 1 L every shift," has been met. This is called
   A. assessment
   B. planning
   C. implementation
   D. evaluation

10. Auscultation is one of the most important components of assessment of which body systems?

A. Reproductive, neurological, integumentary
B. Cardiovascular, pulmonary, gastrointestinal
C. Pulmonary, gastrointestinal, neurological
D. Gastrointestinal, neurological, reproductive

References

Braden, B., & Bergstrom, M. (1989). Clinical utility of the Braden scale for predicting pressure sore risk. *Advances in Skin and Wound Care, 2*(3), 44–51.

Bulechek, G. M., Butcher, H. K., et al. (2008). *Nursing interventions classification (NIC)* (5th ed.) St. Louis, MO: Mosby.

Canadian Hypertension Education Program. (2011). *Hypertension Canada.* Retrieved from www.hypertension.ca/

Canadian Task Force on Preventive Care. (2011). *Past task force recommendations.* Retrieved from www.canadiantaskforce.ca/recommendations_past_eng.html

Dillon, P. M. (2007). *Nursing health assessment: Clinical pocket guide* (2nd ed., p. 180). Philadelphia, PA: F.A. Davis.

Erikson, E. H. (1980). *Identity and the life cycle.* New York, NY: W.W. Norton.

Moorhead, S., Johnson, M., et al. (2007). *Nursing outcomes classification (NOC)* (4th ed.). Philadelphia, PA: Mosby.

National Pressure Ulcer Advisory Panel. (2007). *Pressure ulcer stages.* Retrieved from http://www.npuap.org/pr2.htm

North American Nursing Diagnosis Association-International. (2009). *Nursing diagnoses, 2009–2011 edition: Definitions and classifications (NANDA-I NURSING DIAGNOSIS).* West Sussex, UK: John Wiley & Sons.

Offner, P. J., Heit, J., et al. (2007). Implementation of a rapid response team decreases cardiac arrest outside of the intensive care unit. *Journal of Trauma, 62*(5), 1223–1227; discussion 1227–1228.

> *The Canadian Jensen's Nursing Health Assessment suite offers these additional resources to enhance learning and facilitate understanding of this chapter:*
>
> • thePoint on line resource, http//thepoint.lww.com/Stephen1E
> • *Laboratory Manual for Canadian Jensen's Nursing Health Assessment: A Best Practice Approach*

Answers to Review Questions

For full rationale for each question, visit http://thepoint.lww.com/Stephen1e. At the same site, you can find guidance for responding to the case studies as well.

Chapter 1: The Nurse's Role in Health Assessment
1. B. 2. C. 3. A. 4. A. 5. D. 6. A. 7. D. 8. C. 9. D. 10. D.

Chapter 2: The Interview and Therapeutic Dialogue
1. A. 2. C. 3. D. 4. C. 5. A. 6. C. 7. D. 8. C. 9. C. 10. D.

Chapter 3: The Health History
1. A. 2. A. 3. C. 4. C. 5. A. 6. D. 7. A. 8. C. 9. B. 10. A.

Chapter 4: Techniques of Physical Examination and Equipment
1. B. 2. A. 3. D. 4. C. 5. D. 6. B. 7. C. 8. A. 9. C. 10. A.

Chapter 5: Documentation and Interprofessional Communication
1. A. 2. A, B, C, and D. 3. C. 4. A and B. 5. D. 6. A. 7. C. 8. B. 9. D. 10. D.

Chapter 6: General Survey and Vital Signs Assessment
1. The apical pulse is close to the left nipple. 2. Rate, rhythm, force (amplitude), and elasticity. 3. C. 4. C. 5. B. 6. D. 7. A. 8. C. 9. B. 10. A, B, and C.

Chapter 7: Pain Assessment
1. A. 2. C. 3. D. 4. B. 5. A. 6. B. 7. B. 8. A. 9. C. 10. D.

Chapter 8: Nutrition Assessment
1. D. 2. D. 3. D. 4. C. 5. D. 6. A. 7. B. 8. C. 9. D. 10. C.

Chapter 9: Assessment of Developmental Stages
1. C. 2. A. 3. B. 4. D. 5. C. 6. D. 7. C. 8. B. 9. A. 10. A.

Chapter 10: Mental Health Assessment
1. A. 2. D. 3. B. 4. D. 5. C. 6. C. 7. D. 8. A. 9. C. 10. D.

Chapter 11: Assessment of Social, Cultural, and Spiritual Health
1. D. 2. A. 3. B. 4. C. 5. B. 6. C. 7. C. 8. D. 9. C. 10. D.

Chapter 12: Assessment of Human Violence
1. D. 2. A. 3. B. 4. C. 5. D. 6. B. 7. A. 8. A. 9. D. 10. A.

Chapter 13: Skin, Hair, and Nails Assessment
1. C. 2. D. 3. B. 4. A. 5. B. 6. D. 7. A. 8. A. 9. C. 10. A. 11. B.

Chapter 14: Head and Neck with Lymphatics Assessment
1. A. 2. B. 3. B. 4. C. 5. D. 6. C. 7. D. 8. B. 9. B. 10. C.

Chapter 15: Eyes Assessment
1. B. 2. A. 3. D. 4. C. 5. B. 6. D. 7. A. 8. C. 9. B. 10. B.

Chapter 16: Ears Assessment
1. A. 2. D. 3. A, B, C, and D. 4. A and C. 5. C. 6. A. 7. D. 8. B. 9. D. 10. A, B, and C.

Chapter 17: Nose, Sinuses, Mouth, and Throat Assessment
1. C. 2. C. 3. A. 4. D. 5. A. 6. B. 7. D. 8. B. 9. C. 10. A.

Chapter 18: Thorax and Lungs Assessment
1. B. 2. A. 3. A. 4. D. 5. D. 6. C. 7. B. 8. A, B, C, and D. 9. B. 10. B.

Chapter 19: Cardiovascular Assessment
1. A. 2. C. 3. A. 4. C. 5. D. 6. C. 7. D. 8. A. 9. A. 10. D.

Chapter 20: Peripheral Vascular and Lymphatic Assessment
1. C. 2. B. 3. B. 4. C. 5. C. 6. B. 7. A. 8. D. 9. A. 10. B.

Chapter 21: Breasts and Axillae Assessment
1. B, C. 2. D. 3. A. 4. C. 5. B. 6. C. 7. D. 8. A. 9. A. 10. C.

Chapter 22: Abdominal Assessment
1. C. 2. B. 3. B. 4. D. 5. C. 6. A. 7. B. 8. A. 9. D. 10. A.

Chapter 23: Musculoskeletal Assessment
1. B. 2. D. 3. A. 4. C. 5. A. 6. B. 7. C. 8. B. 9. A. 10. A. 11. C.

Chapter 24: Neurological Assessment
1. B. 2. A. 3. D. 4. B. 5. D. 6. A. 7. B. 8. B. 9. A. 10. B.

Chapter 25: Male Genitalia and Rectal Assessment
1. B. 2. D. 3. B. 4. C. 5. B. 6. A. 7. B. 8. A. 9. D. 10. D.

Chapter 26: Female Genitalia and Rectal Assessment
1. B. 2. D. 3. A. 4. D. 5. C. 6. B. 7. D. 8. A. 9. B. 10. D.

Chapter 27: Women Who Are Pregnant
1. C. 2. C. 3. D. 4. C. 5. C. 6. A. 7. B. 8. B. 9. D. 10. C.

Chapter 28: Newborns and Infants
1. B. 2. C. 3. A. 4. B. 5. D. 6. C. 7. D. 8. D. 9. C.

Chapter 29: Children and Adolescents
1. D. 2. B. 3. A. 4. C. 5. B. 6. B. 7. D. 8. C. 9. D. 10. A.

Chapter 30: Older Adults
1. C. 2. C. 3. D. 4. A. 5. B. 6. C. 7. C. 8. A. 9. C. 10. B.

Chapter 31: Head-to-Toe Assessment of the Adult
1. D. 2. A. 3. C. 4. C. 5. A. 6. C. 7. A. 8. A. 9. D. 10. B.

ILLUSTRATION CREDIT LIST

CHAPTER 1
Figure 1-4: Photo by B. Proud.

CHAPTER 2
Case Figure: Photo by A. Powdrill, Getty Images®.
Figure 2-1: Adler, R. B., & Proctor, R. F. (2007). *Looking out/looking in* (12th ed.). Belmont, CA: Thomson/Wadsworth.
Figures 2-2A and 2-4: Photo by B. Proud.

CHAPTER 4
Figure 4-1: Skillen, D. L., & Bickley, L. S. (2010). The physical examination: Objective data. In T. C. Stephen, D. L. Skillen, R. A. Day, & L. S. Bickley (Eds.). *Canadian Bates' guide to health assessment for nurses* (1st ed., pp. 91–111). Philadelphia, PA: Wolters. Kluwer Health/Lippincott Williams & Wilkins.
Figures 4-2, 4-3, 4-5, 4-7, and 4-11: Photo by B. Proud.

CHAPTER 5
Figures 5-2, 5-4, and 5-6: Photo by B. Proud.

CHAPTER 6
Figures 6-2, 6-4, 6-5, and 6-6: Photo by B. Proud.
Table 6-5: *Cardiac Output, Viscocity, Elasticity of Vessel Walls*: Asset provided by Anatomical Chart Co.; *Circulating Blood Volume*: Fleisher, G. R., Ludwig, S., & Baskin, M. N. (2004). *Atlas of pediatric emergency medicine*. Philadelphia, PA: Lippincott Williams & Wilkins.
Table 6-9: *Achondroplastic Dwarfism*: Sadler, T. (2003). *Langman's medical embryology* (9th ed. Image Bank). Baltimore: Lippincott Williams & Wilkins; *Acromegaly*: McConnell, T.H. (2007). *The nature of disease pathology for the health professions*. Philadelphia, PA: Lippincott Williams & Wilkins; *Gigantism*: Gagel R. F., & McCutcheon, I. E. (1999). Images in Clinical Medicine. *New England Journal of Medicine, 340*, 524. Copyright © 2003. Massachusetts Medical Society; *Obesity, Anorexia Nervosa*: Biophoto Associates/Photo Researchers, Inc.

CHAPTER 7
Figure 7-6: Adapted from McCaffery, M., & Pasero, C. (1999). *Pain: Clinical manual* (2nd ed., p. 37). St. Louis, MO: C. V. Mosby.
Figure 7-7: Copyright © 1991, Charles S. Cleeland, PhD.
Figure 7-8: Hockenberry, M. J., & Wilson, D. (2009). *Wong's essentials of pediatric nursing* (8th ed.). St. Louis, MO: C. V. Mosby. Used with permission. Copyright Mosby.

CHAPTER 8
Figure 8-1: Used with permission from Hark, L. & Darwin, D. Jr. (1999). Taking a nutrition history: A practical approach for family physicians. *The American Family Physician, 59*(6), 1521–1523.
Figure 8-3: From Baer, H. J., Blum, R. E., Helaine R. H., et al. (2005). Use of a food frequency questionnaire in American Indian and Caucasian pregnant women: A validation study. *BMC Public Health, 5*, 135. Retrieved from http://www.biomedcentral.com/content/pdf/1471-2458-5-135.pdf on May 12, 2009.

Figure 8-4: L. Wayne Day, BSc., MSc., Faculty of Nursing, University of Alberta.
Table 8-8: *Alopecia, Bitot's Spots, Magenta Tongue*: Ostler, H. B., Maibach, H. I., Hoke, A. W., & Schwab, I. R. (2004). *Diseases of the eye and skin: A color atlas*. Philadelphia, PA: Lippincott Williams & Wilkins; *Follicular Keratosis*: Tasman, W., & Jaeger, E. (2001). *The Wills eye hospital atlas of clinical ophthalmology* (2nd ed.). Lippincott Williams & Wilkins; *Genu Varum*: Courtesy of Shriners Hospitals for Children, Houston, TX.

CHAPTER 9
Figure 9-4: Jeffrey Greenberg/Photo Researchers, Inc.
Figure 9-5A: Bill Aron/Photo Researchers, Inc.
Figure 9-5B: Lawrence Migdale/Photo Researchers, Inc.

CHAPTER 11
Figure 11-1: Adapted from Andrews, M. M. & Boyle, J. S. (2008). *Transcultural concepts in nursing care* (5th ed.). Philadelphia: Lippincott Williams & Wilkins.
Figure 11-2: Anderson, E. T., & McFarlane, J. (2011). *Community as partner: Theory and practice in nursing* (6th ed.). Philadelphia, PA: Wolters Kluwer Health/Lippincott Williams & Wilkins.

CHAPTER 13
Figures 13-5A, B, 13-8, 13-13A, B, C: Goodheart, H. P. (2008). *Goodheart's photoguide of common skin disorders* (3rd ed.). Philadelphia, PA: Lippincott Williams & Wilkins.
Figure 13-6: Photo by B. Proud.
Figure 13-10: Courtesy of Philip Siu, MD.
Figure 13-14: From O'Doherty, N.(1979). *Atlas of the newborn*. Philadelphia, PA: JB Lippincott.
Table 13-1: *A, C, D, E*: Goodheart, H. P. (2008). *Goodheart's photoguide of common skin disorders* (3rd ed.). Philadelphia, PA: Lippincott Williams & Wilkins; *B*: Courtesy of Art Huntley, M.D., University of California at Davis.
Table 13-7: *Pallor, Café-au-lait Macules*: Fleisher, G. R., Ludwig, W., & Baskin, M. N. (2004). *Atlas of pediatric emergency medicine*. Philadelphia, PA: Lippincott Williams & Wilkins; *Pigmented Macules*: Robinson, H. B. G., & Miller A. S. (1990). *Colby, Kerr, and Robinson's color atlas of oral pathology*. Philadelphia, PA: JB Lippincott; *Hirsutism*: (2008). *Goodheart's photoguide of common skin disorders* (3rd ed.). Philadelphia, PA: Lippincott Williams & Wilkins; *Malar Rash*: McConnell, T. H. (2007). *The nature of disease pathology for the health professions*. Philadelphia, PA: Lippincott Williams & Wilkins; *Pallor of Fingers*: Effeney, D. J. & Stoney, R. J. (1993). *Wylie's atlas of vascular surgery: Disorders of the extremities*. Philadelphia, PA: Lippincott Williams & Wilkins.
Table 13-8: *Macule, Patch, Papule, Plaque, Wheal, Lipoma, Vesicle, Bulla, Pustule, Cyst*: (2008). *Goodheart's photoguide of common skin disorders* (3rd ed.). Philadelphia, PA: Lippincott Williams & Wilkins.
Table 13-9: *Atrophy, Keloid, Scale, Lichenification, Excoriation, Erosion, Fissure, Ulcer*: (2008). *Goodheart's Photoguide of Common Skin Disorders* (3rd ed.). Philadelphia, PA: Lippincott Williams & Wilkins; *Scar*: Weber, J. & Kelley, J. (2003). *Health assessment in nursing* (2nd ed.). Philadelphia, PA: Lippincott Williams & Wilkins; *Crust*: McConnell T. H. (2007). *The nature of disease pathology for the health professions*. Philadelphia, PA: Lippincott Williams & Wilkins.
Table 13-10: *Annular, Iris, Linear, Polymorphous, Serpiginous, Nummular, Umbilicated, Verrucaform*: (2008). *Goodheart's photoguide of common skin disorders* (3rd ed.). Philadelphia, PA: Lippincott Williams & Wilkins; *Filiform*: Ostler, H. B., Maibach, H. I., Hoke, A. W., & Schwab, I. R. (2004). *Diseases of the eye and skin: a color atlas*. Philadelphia, PA: Lippincott Williams & Wilkins.
Table 13-11: *Asymmetric, Diffuse, Discrete, Generalized, Grouped, Localized, Satellite, Symmetric, Zosteriform*: (2008). *Goodheart's photoguide of common skin disorders* (3rd ed.). Philadelphia, PA: Lippincott Williams & Wilkins; *Confluent*: Bickley, L. S. (2009). *Bates' guide to physical examination and history taking* (10th ed.). Philadelphia, PA: Lippincott Williams & Wilkins.
Table 13-12: *Pustular Acne, Cystic Acne, Warts, Cellulitis, Impetigo, Herpes Simplex (Cold Sores), Measles (Rubeola), Pityriasis Rosea, Roseola, Candida, Tinea Corporis, Tinea Versicolor*: (2008). *Goodheart's photoguide of common skin disorders* (3rd ed.). Philadelphia, PA: Lippincott Williams & Wilkins.
Table 13-13: *Psoriasis, Eczema, Contact Dermatitis, Urticaria, Allegic Drug Reaction, Insect Bites, Seborrhea*: (2008). *Goodheart's photoguide of common skin disorders* (3rd ed.). Philadelphia, PA: Lippincott Williams & Wilkins.
Table 13-14: *Lice (Pediculosis) A & B, Scabies, Ticks*: (2008). *Goodheart's Photoguide of Common Skin Disorders* (3rd ed.). Philadelphia, PA: Lippincott Williams & Wilkins.
Table 13-15: *Moles or Nevi, Skin Tags, Lentigo, Actinic Keratosis, Basal Cell Carcinoma, Squamous Cell Carcinoma, Malignant Melanoma, Kaposi's Sarcoma*: (2008). *Goodheart's Photoguide of Common Skin Disorders* (3rd ed.). Philadelphia, PA: Lippincott Williams & Wilkins; *Lipoma*: Image provided by Steadman's.
Table 13-16: *Hemangioma*: O'Doherty, N. (1979). *Atlas of the newborn*. Philadelphia, PA: JB Lippincott; *Nevus Flammeus*: From Sauer G. C., & Hall J. C. (1996). *Manual of skin diseases* (7th ed.). Philadelphia, PA: Lippincott-Raven; *Venous Lake*: (2008). *Goodheart's Photoguide of Common Skin Disorders* (3rd ed.). Philadelphia, PA: Lippincott Williams & Wilkins, 2008.
Table 13-17: *Petechiae*: McConnell, T. H. (2007). *The nature of disease pathology for the health professions*. Philadelphia, PA: Lippincott Williams & Wilkins; *Purpura, Ecchymosis*: (2008). *Goodheart's Photoguide of Common Skin Disorders* (3rd ed.). Philadelphia, PA: Lippincott Williams & Wilkins; *Hematoma, Laceration, Puncture Wound*: From Fleisher, G. R., Ludwig, S., Baskin, M. N. (2004). *Atlas of pediatric emergency medicine*. Philadelphia, PA: Lippincott Williams & Wilkins; *Avulsion*: Dr. P. Marazzi/Photo Researchers, Inc.

Table 13-18: *Stage I, Stage II, Stage III, Stage IV:* Nettina, S. M. (2001). *The Lippincott manual of nursing practice* (7th ed.). Philadelphia, PA: Lippincott Williams & Wilkins.

Table 13-19: *Venous Ulcer (Vascular), Arterial Ulcer (Vascular):* Nettina, S. M. (2001). *The Lippincott manual of nursing practice* (7th ed.). Philadelphia, PA: Lippincott Williams & Wilkins, 2001.

Table 13-22: *Longitudinal Ridging, Onycholysis, Pitted Nails, Yellow Nails, Half-and-half Nails, Dark Longitudinal Streaks:* (2008). *Goodheart's Photoguide of Common Skin Disorders* (3rd ed.). Philadelphia, PA: Lippincott Williams & Wilkins; *Koilonychia, Clubbing, Splinter Hemorrhages:* Image provided by Steadman's; *Beau's Lines:* Bickley, L. S. (2009). *Bates' guide to physical examination and history taking* (10th ed.). Philadelphia, PA: Lippincott Williams & Wilkins.

Table 13-23: *Alopecia Areata, Traction Alopecia, Trichotillomania:* (2008). *Goodheart's photoguide of common skin disorders* (3rd ed.). Philadelphia, PA: Lippincott Williams & Wilkins; *Hirsutism:* Image provided by Steadman's.

CHAPTER 14

Table 14-2: *Hydrocephalus, Fetal Alcohol Syndrome:* Gold, D. H., Weingeist, T. A. (2001). *Color atlas of the eye in systemic disease.* Baltimore, MD: Lippincott Williams & Wilkins; *Cretinism (Congenital Hypothyroidism):* Centers for Disease Control and Prevention Public Health Image Library.

Table 14-3: *Acromegaly:* Willis, M. C. (2002). *Medical terminology: A programmed learning approach to the language of health care.* Baltimore, MD: Lippincott Williams & Wilkins; *Bell's Palsy, Cerebral Vascular Accident (Stroke), Myxedema:* Dr. P. Marazzi/Photo Researchers, Inc.; *Cushing's Syndrome:* Ostler, H. B., Maibach, H. I., Hoke, A. W., & Schwab, I. R. (2004). *Diseases of the eye and skin: A color atlas.* Philadelphia, PA: Lippincott Williams & Wilkins; *Scleroderma:* Gold, D. H., & Weingeist, T. A. (2001). *Color atlas of the eye in systemic disease.* Baltimore, MD: Lippincott Williams & Wilkins; *Goiter:* Scott Camazine/Photo Researchers, Inc.

CHAPTER 15

Figures 15-15, 15-27, 15-28, and 15-29: Tasman, W., & Jaeger, E. (2001). *The Wills eye hospital atlas of clinical ophthalmology* (2nd ed.). Philadelphia, PA: Lippincott Williams & Wilkins.

Figures 15-17, 15-32: Gold, D. H., & Weingeist, T. A. (2001). *Color atlas of the eye in systemic disease.* Baltimore, MD: Lippincott Williams & Wilkins.

Figure 15-19: Fleisher, G. R., Ludwig, S., & Baskin, M. N. (2004). *Atlas of pediatric emergency medicine.* Philadelphia, PA: Lippincott Williams & Wilkins.

Figure 15-20: Courtesy of Terri Young, MD.

Figures 15-22, 15-23, 15-24: Bickley, L. S. (2009). *Bates' guide to physical examination and history taking* (10th ed.). Philadelphia, PA: Lippincott Williams & Wilkins.

Table 15-5: *Nystagmus:* Bickley, L. S. (2009). *Bates' guide to physical examination and history taking* (10th ed.). Philadelphia, PA: Lippincott Williams & Wilkins; *Esotropia:* Courtesy of Dean John Bonsall, MD, FACS; *Exotropia, Vertical Deviation:* Tasman, W., & Jaeger, E. (2001). *The Wills eye hospital atlas of clinical ophthalmology* (2nd ed.). Philadelphia, PA: Lippincott Williams & Wilkins.

Table 15-6: *Jaundice, Cataract:* Rubin, E., & Farber, J. L. (1999). *Pathology* (3rd ed.). Philadelphia, PA: Lippincott Williams & Wilkins; *Iris Nevus,*

Blepharitis, Bacterial Conjunctivitis, Glaucoma, Amblyopia, Hordeolum (Stye): Tasman, W., & Jaeger, E. (2001). *The Wills eye hospital atlas of clinical ophthalmology* (2nd ed.). Philadelphioa, PA: Lippincott Williams & Wilkins; *Hyphema, Allergic Conjunctivitis:* Fleisher, G. R., Ludwig, S., & Baskin, M. N.. *Atlas of pediatric emergency medicine.* Philadelphia, PA: Lippincott Williams & Wilkins; *Chalazion:* Bickley, L. S. (2009). *Bates' guide to physical examination and history taking* (10th ed.). Philadelphia, PA: Lippincott Williams & Wilkins; *Exophthalmos:* Goodheart, H. P. (2008). *Photoguide of common skin disorders* (3rd ed.). Philadelphia, PA: Lippincott Williams & Wilkins; *Osteogenesis Imperfecta:* Ostler, H. B., Maibach, H. I., Hoke, A. W., & Schwab, I. R. (2004). *Diseases of the eye and skin: A color atlas.*

Table 15-7: *Horner's Syndrome, Adie's Pupil, Mydriasis (Dilated Fixed Pupil), Oculomotor (CN III) Nerve Damage:* Tasman, W., & Jaeger, E. (2001). *The Wills eye hospital atlas of clinical ophthalmology.* (2nd ed.). Philadelphia, PA: Lippincott Williams & Wilkins; *Key Hole Pupil (Coloboma):* Courtesy of Brian Forbes, MD; *Miosis (Small Fixed Pupil):* Gold, D. H., & Weingeist, T. A. (2001). *Color atlas of the eye in systemic disease.* Baltimore, MD: Lippincott Williams & Wilkins.

Table 15-8: *AMD, Retinopathy, Retinitis Pigmentosa:* Tasman, W., & Jaeger, E. (2001). *The Wills eye hospital atlas of clinical ophthalmology* (2nd ed.). Philadelphia, PA: Lippincott Williams & Wilkins; *Copper Wiring:* McConnell, T.H. (2007). *The nature of disease pathology for the health professions.* Philadelphia, PA: Lippincott Williams & Wilkins.

CHAPTER 16

Figure 16-16: Moore, K. L., & Dalley, A. F. (1999). *Clinically oriented anatomy* (4th ed.). Baltimore, MD: Lippincott Williams & Wilkins.

Figure 16-17: Mills S. E. (2007). *Histology for pathologists* (3rd ed.). Philadelphia, PA: Lippincott Williams & Wilkins.

Figure 16-20: Bickley, L. S. (2009). *Bates' guide to physical examination and history taking* (10th ed.). Philadelphia, PA: Lippincott Williams & Wilkins.

Table 16-2: *Microtia:* Biophoto Associates/Photo Researchers, Inc.; *Macrotia:* Saturn Stills/Photo Researchers, Inc.; *Edematous Ears, Cartilage Staphyloccous or Pseudomonas Infection:* Ostler, H. B., Maibach, H. I., Hoke, A. W., & Schwab, I. R. (2004). *Diseases of the eye and skin: a color atlas; Carcinoma on Auricle:* (2008). *Goodheart's photoguide of common skin disorders* (3rd ed.). Philadelphia, PA: Lippincott Williams & Wilkins, 2008; *Cyst:* Young, E. M. Jr., Newcomer, V. D., & Kligman, A. M. (1993). *Geriatric dermatology: color atlas and practitioner's guide.* Philadelphia, PA: Lea & Febiger; *Tophi:* Weber, J. & Kelley, J. (2003). *Health assessment in nursing* (2nd ed.). Philadelphia, PA: Lippincott Williams & Wilkins.

Table 16-3: *TM Rupture:* Courtesy of Michael Hawke, MD, Toronto, Canada; *Acute Otitis Media:* Moore, K. L., & Dalley, A. F. II. (1999). *Clinically oriented anatomy* (4th ed.). Baltimore, MD: Lippincott Williams & Wilkins; *Scarred TM:* Weber, J., & Kelley, J. (2003). *Health assessment in nursing* (2nd ed.). Philadelphia, PA: Lippincott Williams & Wilkins; *Foreign Body:* Dr P. Marazzi / Photo Researchers, Inc.

CHAPTER 17

Figure 17-1: Moore, K. L., & Dalley, A. F. II. (2008). *Clinically oriented anatomy* (6th ed.). Baltimore, MD: Lippincott Williams & Wilkins.

Figures 17-6, 17-15: Bickley, L. S. (2009). *Bates' guide to physical examination and history taking* (10th ed.). Philadelphia, PA: Lippincott Williams & Wilkins.

Figures 17-19, 17-27: (2008). *Goodheart's photoguide of common skin disorders* (3rd ed.). Philadelphia, PA: Lippincott Williams & Wilkins.

Figure 7-20: Fleisher, G. R., Ludwig, W., & Baskin, M. N. (2004). *Atlas of pediatric emergency medicine.* Philadelphia, PA: Lippincott Williams & Wilkins.

Figure 17-22: Courtesy of Seth Zwillenberg.

Figure 17-23: Langlais, R. P., & Miller, C. S. (1992). *Color atlas of common oral diseases.* Philadelphia, PA: Lea & Febiger. Used with permission.

Figure 17-29: Robinson, H. B. G., & Miller, A. S. (1990). *Colby, Kerr, and Robinson's color atlas of oral pathology.* Philadelphia, PA: JB Lippincott.

Table 17-5: *Epistaxis (Nosebleed):* Ian Boddy/ Photo Researchers, Inc.; *Nasal Polyps:* Handler, S. D., & Myer, C. M. (1998). *Atlas of ear, nose and throat disorders in children* (p 59). Ontario, Canada: BC Decker; *Deviated Septum:* Moore, K. L., & Dalley, A. F. II. (2008). *Clinically oriented anatomy* (6th ed.). Baltimore, MD: Lippincott Williams & Wilkins; *Perforated Septum, Foreign Body:* Dr P. Marazzi/Photo Researchers, Inc.

Table 17-6: *Cleft Lip/Palate:* Rubin, E., & Farber, J. L. (1999). *Pathology* (3rd ed.). Philadelphia, PA: Lippincott Williams & Wilkins; *Bifid Uvula:* Courtesy of Paul S. Matz, MD; *Acute Tonsillitis or Pharyngitis:* BSIP/Photo Researchers, Inc.; *Strep Throat:* Centers for Disease Control and Prevention Public Health Image Library.

Table 17-7: *Herpes Simplex Virus, Candidasis, Leukoplakia, Black Hairy Tongue, Carcinoma:* (2008). *Goodheart's photoguide of common skin disorders* (3rd ed.). Philadelphia, PA: Lippincott Williams & Wilkins.

Table 17-8: *Baby Bottle Tooth Decay:* Fleisher, G. R., Ludwig, S., & Baskin, M. N. (2004). *Atlas of pediatric emergency medicine.* Philadelphia, PA: Lippincott Williams & Wilkins; *Dental Caries:* Langlais, R. P., & Miller, C. S. (1992). *Color atlas of common oral diseases.* Philadelphia, PA: Lea & Febiger. Used with permission; *Gingival Hyperplasia:* Courtesy of Dr. James Cottone; *Ankyloglossia (Tongue Tie):* Courtesy of Paul S. Matz, MD.

CHAPTER 18

Figure 18-1: Moore, K. L., & Dalley, A. F. II. (2008). *Clinically oriented anatomy* (6th ed.). Baltimore, MD: Lippincott Williams & Wilkins.

Figures 18-4, 18-5, 18-6, 18-7, 18-8: Bickley, L. S. (2009). *Bates' guide to physical examination and history taking* (10th ed.). Philadelphia, PA: Lippincott Williams & Wilkins.

Figures 18-11, 18-12, 18-13, 18-14, 18-15: Photos by B. Proud.

CHAPTER 19

Figure 19-4: Photo by B. Proud.

Figure 19-15: Bickley, L. S. (2009). *Bates' guide to physical examination and history taking* (10th ed.). Philadelphia, PA: Lippincott Williams & Wilkins.

Figure 19-17: T. C. Stephen, D. L. Skillen, R. A. Day, & L. S. Bickley (Eds.). (2009). *Canadian Bates' guide to health assessment for nurses.* Philadelphia, PA: Wolters. Kluwer Health/Lippincott Williams & Wilkins.

CHAPTER 20

Figure 20-6: Mubarak, S. J., & Owen, C. A. (1997). Double-incision fasciotomy of the leg for decompression in compartment syndromes. *Journal of Bone and Joint Surgery,* 59A, 184.

Table 20-5: *Acute Arterial Occlusion:* Nettina, S. M. (2001). *The Lippincott manual of nursing practice* (7th ed.). Philadelphia, PA: Lippincott Williams & Wilkins; *Abdominal Aortic Aneurysm:* Moore, K. L., & Dalley, A. F. II. (2008). *Clinically oriented anatomy* (6th ed.). Baltimore, MD: Lippincott Williams & Wilkins; *Raynaud's Phenomenon and Raynaud's Disease:* Marks, R. (1987). *Skin disease in old age.* Philadelphia, PA: JB Lippincott.

Table 20-6: *Chronic Venous Insufficiency, Neuropathy:* Marks, R. (1987). *Skin disease in old age.* Philadelphia, PA: JB Lippincott; *Deep Vein Thrombosis:* Dr. P. Marazzi/Photo Researchers, Inc.; *Thrombophlebitis:* Biophoto Associates/Photo Researchers, Inc.; *Lymphedema:* Rubin, E., & Farber, J. L. (1999). *Pathology* (3rd ed.). Philadelphia, PA: Lippincott Williams & Wilkins.

CHAPTER 21

Figures 21-2A, 21-3: Moore, K. L., & Dalley, A. F. II. (2008). *Clinically oriented anatomy* (6th ed.). Baltimore, MD: Lippincott Williams & Wilkins.

Figure 21-4: Courtesy of Esther K. Chung, MD.

Figures 21-6, 21-9A–D, 21-11A: Photo by B. Proud.

Figures 21-10, 21-12: Mulholland, M. W., & Maier, R. V. (2006). *Greenfield's surgery scientific principles and practice* (4th ed.). Philadelphia, PA: Lippincott Williams & Wilkins.

Figure 21-11B: Stephen, T. C., Day, R. A., & Skillen, D. L. (2011–2012). *A syllabus for adult health assessment.* Edmonton, AB: Faculty of Nursing, University of Alberta.

Table 21-4: *Carcinoma 1, Carcinoma 2:* Mulholland, M. W., & Maier, R. V. (2006). *Greenfield's surgery scientific principles and practice* (4th ed.). Philadelphia, PA: Lippincott Williams & Wilkins; *Paget Disease, Mastitis:* (2005). *Atlas of infectious diseases of the female genital tract.* Philadelphia, PA: Lippincott Williams & Wilkins; *Mastectomy:* Steve Percival/Photo Researchers, Inc.; *Gynecomastia:* Courtesy of Christine Finck, MD.

CHAPTER 22

Figures 22-8, 22-9, 22-12, 22-13: Photo by B. Proud.

Figures 22-7, 22-10: T. C. Stephen, D. L. Skillen, R. A. Day, & L. S. Bickley (Eds.). (2009). *Canadian Bates' guide to health assessment for nurses.* Philadelphia, PA: Wolters. Kluwer Health/Lippincott Williams & Wilkins.

Table 22-5: *Acute Abdomen 1, Acute Abdomen 2, Abdominal Aortic Aneurysm:* Photo by B. Proud; *Appendicitis (Rovsing's Sign), Acute Cholecystitis:* Berg, D. & Worzala, K. (2006). *Atlas of adult physical diagnosis.* Philadelphia, PA: Lippincott Williams & Wilkins; *Obturator Sign:* Bickley, L. S. (2009). *Bates' guide to physical examination and history taking* (10th ed.). Philadelphia, PA: Lippincott Williams & Wilkins.

CHAPTER 23

Case Figure: Joe Sohm/Photo Researchers, Inc.

Goniometer: Oatis, C. A. (2004). *Kinesiology - The mechanics and pathomechanics of human movement.* Baltimore, MD: Lippincott Williams & Wilkins.

Figures 23-12, 23-24: Bickley, L. S. (2009). *Bates' guide to physical examination and history taking* (10th ed.). Philadelphia, PA: Lippincott Williams & Wilkins.

Figures 23-23, 23-25A–C: Photo by B. Proud.

Figures 23-26A, B, 23-27 A, B, and 23-30: Moore, K. L., & Dalley, A. F. II. (2008). *Clinically oriented anatomy* (6th ed.). Baltimore, MD: Lippincott Williams & Wilkins.

Table 23-8: *Bulge Test:* Bickley, L. S. (2009). *Bates' guide to physical examination and history taking* (10th ed.). Philadelphia, PA: Lippincott Williams & Wilkins; *McMurray's Test, Thomas Test, LeSegue's Test, Drawer Sign, Trendelenburg Test:* Berg, D. & Worzala, K. (2006). *Atlas of adult physical diagnosis.* Philadelphia, PA: Lippincott Williams & Wilkins.

Table 23-13: *Atrophy, Joint Effusions, Epicondylitis:* Bickley, L. S. (2009). *Bates' guide to physical examination and history taking* (10th ed.). Philadelphia, PA: Lippincott Williams & Wilkins; *Joint Dislocation, Polydactyly, Swan Neck and Boutonniere Deformity, Syndactyly, Ulnar Deviation:* Strickland, J. W., & Graham, T. J. (2005). *Master techniques in orthopedic surgery: The hand* (2nd ed.). Philadelphia, PA: Lippincott Williams & Wilkins; *Rheumatoid Arthritis:* Gold, D. H., & Weingeist, T. A. (2001). *Color atlas of the eye in systemic disease.* Baltimore, MD: Lippincott Williams & Wilkins; *Rotator Cuff Tear, Bursitis, Ganglion Cyst, Dupuytren's Contracture, Heberden's and Bouchard's Nodes, Carpal Tunnel Syndrome:* Berg, D. & Worzala, K. (2006). *Atlas of adult physical diagnosis.* Philadelphia, PA: Lippincott Williams & Wilkins; *Genu Valgum:* Courtesy of Bettina Gyr, MD; *Congenital Hip Dislocation:* Bucholz, R. W., & Heckman, J. D. (2001). *Rockwood and Green's fractures in adults* (5th ed.). Philadelphia, PA: Lippincott Williams & Wilkins; *Herniated Nucleus Pulposus:* Daffner R. H. (2007). *Clinical radiology the essentials* (3rd ed.). Philadelphia, PA: Lippincott Williams & Wilkins; *Talipes Equinovarus:* Courtesy of J Adams; *Acute Rheumatoid Arthritis:* Image provided by Stedman's; *Ankylosing Spondylitis:* McConnell, T. H. (2007). *The nature of disease pathology for the health professions.* Philadelphia, PA: Lippincott Williams & Wilkins.

CHAPTER 24

Figures 24-12, 24-18, 24-21, 24-23A–C: Bickley, L. S. *Bates' guide to physical examination and history taking* (10th ed.). Philadelphia, PA: Lippincott Williams & Wilkins.

Figure 24-17: Photo by B. Proud.

Table 24-8: *Paralysis:* Centers for Disease Control and Prevention Public Image Library; *Dystonia:* Fleisher, G. R., Ludwig, W., Baskin, M. N. (2004). *Atlas of pediatric emergency medicine.* Philadelphia, PA: Lippincott Williams & Wilkins.

CHAPTER 25

Figure 25.2: Moore, K. L., & Dalley, A. F. II. (2008). *Clinically oriented anatomy* (6th ed.). Baltimore, MD: Lippincott Williams & Wilkins.

Figures 25.8, 25.9, 25.10, 25.11: Photos by B. Proud.

Table 25-4: *Phimosis, Paraphimosis, Hypospadias:* Courtesy of T. Ernesto Figueroa; *Balanitis:* Fleisher, G. R., Ludwig, S., & Baskin, M. N. (2004). *Atlas of pediatric emergency medicine.* Philadelphia, PA: Lippincott Williams & Wilkins; *Epispadias:* MacDonald, M. G., Seshia M. M. K., et al. (2005). *Avery's neonatology pathophysiology & management of the newborn* (6th ed.). Philadelphia, PA: Lippincott Williams & Wilkins.

Table 25-5: *Scabies Infection, Syphilis:* Goodheart, H. P. (2008). *Goodheart's photoguide of common skin disorders* (3rd ed.). Philadelphia, PA: Lippincott Williams & Wilkins; *Chlamydia:* Image from Rubin, E. & Farber, J. L. (1999). *Pathology* (3rd ed.). Philadelphia, PA: Lippincott Williams & Wilkins; *Gonorrhea:* Sanders,

C. V. & Nesbitt, L. T. (1995). *The skin and infection.* Baltimore, MD: Williams & Wilkins.

Table 25-6: *Testicular Torsion, Varicocele:* Courtesy of T. Ernesto Figueroa, MD.

Table 25-7: *Rectal Polyp, Carcinoma of the Rectum and Anus:* Mulholland, M. W., Maier, R. V., et al. (2006). *Greenfield's surgery scientific principles and practice* (4th ed.). Philadelphia, PA: Lippincott Williams & Wilkins; *Rectal Prolapse:* Courtesy of Mary L. Brandt, MD; *Prostatitis:* Image from Rubin, E. & Farber, J. L. (1999). *Pathology* (3rd ed.). Philadelphia, PA: Lippincott Williams & Wilkins.

CHAPTER 26

Equipment Box, Figures 26-5B, 26-6, 26-9, 26-12, 26-16, 26-18A, 26-19A: Photo by B. Proud.

Figures 26-7, 26-14, 26-15: Berg, D. & Worzala, K. (2006). *Atlas of adult physical diagnosis.* Philadelphia, PA: Lippincott Williams & Wilkins.

Table 26-3: *Candidiasis:* Goodheart, H. P. (2008). *Goodheart's photoguide of common skin disorders* (3rd ed.). Philadelphia, PA: Lippincott Williams & Wilkins; *Bacterial Vaginosis, Chlamydia, Gonorrhea, Trichomoniasis, Condylomata Acuminatum:* Sweet, R. L., Gibbs, R. S. (2005). *Atlas of infectious diseases of the female genital tract.* Philadelphia, PA: Lippincott Williams & Wilkins.

Table 26-4: *Pediculosis, Chancre, Abscess of the Bartholin's Gland:* Sweet, R. L., Gibbs, R. S. (2005). *Atlas of infectious diseases of the female genital tract.* Philadelphia, PA: Lippincott Williams & Wilkins; *Urethral Caruncle:* Courtesy of Allan R. De Jong, MD; *Contact Dermatitis:* Courtesy of George A. Datto, III, MD.

CHAPTER 27

Case Figure: Lawrence Migdale/Photo Researchers, Inc.

Figure 27-7A: Goodheart, H. P. (2008). *Goodheart's photoguide of common skin disorders* (3rd ed.). Philadelphia, PA: Lippincott Williams & Wilkins.

CHAPTER 28

Figure 28-2: Ballard, J. L., Khoury, J. C., Wedig, K., et al. (1991). New Ballard score, expanded to include extremely premature infants. *J Pediatr, 119,* 417–423.

Figure 28-12: MacDonald, M. G., Seshia, M. M. K., et al. (2005). *Avery's neonatology pathophysiology & management of the newborn* (6th ed.). Philadelphia, PA: Lippincott Williams & Wilkins.

Table 28-7: *Pediculosis Capitis:* Courtesy of Hans B. Kersten, MD; *Tinea Corporis, ****Scabies, Café-au-Lait Spots:* Fleisher, G. R., Ludwig, S., Baskin, M. N. (2004). *Atlas of pediatric emergency medicine.* Philadelphia, PA: Lippincott Williams & Wilkins; *Staphylococcal Scalded Skin Syndrome:* Courtesy of Gary Marshall, MD; *Molluscum Contagiosum, Bullous Impetigo, Allergic Contact Diaper Dermatitis, Eczema:* Goodheart, H. P. (2008). *Goodheart's photoguide of common skin disorders* (3rd ed.). Philadelphia, PA: Lippincott Williams & Wilkins; *Intertrigo, Lichen Simplex Chronicus:* Sauer G. C., & Hall J. C. (1996). *Manual of skin diseases* (7th ed.). Philadelphia, PA: Lippincott-Raven; *Irritant Diaper Dermatitis, Candidal Diaper Dermatitis:* Courtesy of Jan E. Drutz, MD.

CHAPTER 30

Figures 30-5 A, B, 30-6: T. C. Stephen, D. L. Skillen, R. A. Day, & L. S. Bickley (Eds.). (2009). *Canadian Bates' guide to health assessment for nurses.* Philadelphia, PA: Wolters. Kluwer Health/Lippincott Williams & Wilkins.

Note: Page numbers in *Italics* indicates figures and those followed by "b" indicates boxes and "t" indicates tables.

A

A delta fibres, 126
ABCDEs, melanoma, *274–275*
Abdominal aortic aneurysm, 567t, 642t
Abdominal assessment
  abdominal organs
    blood vessels, peritoneum, and muscles, *605, 606*
    GI organs, 603, 605
    GU organs, 605
  Aboriginal Canadians, 617
  acute assessment, 607
  adolescents, 616
  African Canadians, 617
  anatomical landmarks, 603
  anatomy and physiology, 603–607, 604t–606t
  Asian Canadians, 617
  Canadians of Jewish Descent, 617
  Canadians of Mediterranean Descent, 617
  clinical reasoning, 633, 633t
  cultural considerations, 617, 631–632
  documentation, 630, 631
  elimination, 607
  equipment, 618
  evidence-informed critical thinking, 632–635
  expected *vs.* unexpected findings
    abdominal reflex, 630
    assessing for ascites, 628–629
    auscultation, 620–621
    inspection, 619
    palpation, 624–628
    percussion, 622–624
  gastrointestinal diseases, 643t–644t
  health history and symptoms signs
    abdominal pain, 613
    anorexia, 613
    constipation, 613
    diarrhea, 613
    dysphagia/odynophagia, 613
    indigestion, 612
    jaundice/icterus, 613–614
    nausea, vomiting, hematemesis, 613
    urinary incontinence, 614
    urinary/renal, 614
  health promotion and risk factors assessment, 611–612
  ingestion and digestion, 607
  laboratory and diagnostic testing
    barium enema, 632–633
    colonoscopy, 633
    computerized tomography scan, 633
    endoscopic retrograde cholangiopancreatography, 633
    esophagogastroduodenoscopy, 632
    magnetic resonance imaging, 633
  lifespan considerations, 607, 615–616, 631
  newborns, infants, and children, 607, 615, 631
  nursing care plan, 635
  nursing diagnoses, 633t
  nursing intervention, 633t
  nutrient absorption, 607
  objective data collection, 618–632
  older adults, 607, 616, 631
  patient outcome, 633t
  personalized, appropriate, and accurate care, 635
  pregnancy, 607, 615, 631
  preparation, 618
  reference lines, 603, *603, 605*
  risk factors assessment
    alcohol or substance abuse, 610
    current concerns, 608
    family history, 610
    foreign travel, 610
    lifestyle, 611
    medications, 608
    occupation, 610
    personal history, 608–610
  Situation, background, assessment, recommendations (SBAR) 634
  Subjective, objective, analysis, plan (SOAP), 634
  subjective data collection, 607–618
  therapeutic dialogue, 618
  unexpected findings
    abdominal aortic aneurysm, 642t
    abdominal distention, 638t
    abdominal tumour, 639t
    acute abdomen, 641t
    acute cholecystitis, 642t
    appendicitis, 641t
    ascites, 639t
    bowel sounds, 639t
    bruits, 640t
    common sites of referred pain, 638t
    friction rubs, 640t
    gaseous distention, 638t
    obesity, 638t
    vascular sounds, 639t
    venous hums, 640t
Abdominal distention, 638t
Abdominal pain, female genitalia, 794
Abdominal tumour, 639t
Abdominal-gastrointestinal system, 46
Abdominal-urinary system, 46
Abscess of the Bartholin glands, 826t

Abuse Assessment Screen, 253b
Achondroplastic dwarfism, 123t
Acne
  adolescents, 282–283
  cystic, 311t
  expected *vs.* unexpected findings, 285
  papular lesions, 271, 281
  pregnancy, 282
  pustular lesions, 271, 281
  resurgence, 282
Acromegaly, 123t, 348t
Actinic keratosis, 286, 293, 316, 317
Active listening, 23
Activities of daily living (ADLs), 43, 45b, 964
Acute arterial occlusion, 557, 566
  pain, 544b
  poikilothermia/polar sensation (cold), 544b
  paresthesia, 544b
  paralysis, 544b
  pallor, 544b
  pulselessness, 544b
Acute assessment
  abdominal assessment, 607
  breasts and axillae assessment, 576
  cardiovascular assessment, 502, 503t
  children and adolescents, 900, 902, *902*
  ears assessment, 393
  eyes assessment, 355
  female genitalia, 794
  general survey and vital signs, 92
  head assessment, 330–331
  head-to-toe, 960
  male genitalia and rectal, 760
  mental health assessment, 206
  mouth assessment, 420
  musculoskeletal, 653
  neck assessment, 330–331
  neurological assessment, 707–708, 708t
  newborns and infants, 864
  nose assessment, 420
  nutrition assessment, 160
  older adults, 929
  pain assessment, 131
  peripheral vascular and lymphatic assessment, 541–542
  pregnancy, 838
  sinuses assessment, 420
  skin hair and nails assessment, 273
  thorax and lungs assessment, 459
  throat assessment, 420
Acute cholecystitis, 642t
Acute otitis media, 413t
Acute rheumatoid arthritis, 696t
Acute salpingitis, 830t
Acute tonsillitis, 447t
Adam's apple, 328
Adenoids, 417
Adequate intake (AI), 154

Adie's pupil, 384t
Adolescent. *See also* Children and adolescents
  cardiovascular assessment, 500, 508, 520
  developmental stage assessment, 186, 188
  ears assessment, 392
  eyes assessment, 355, 359
  health history, *48,* 48–49
  human violence assessment, 257–258
  intercultural communication, 31–32
  nutrition assessment, 157, 157t, 166–167, 175–176
  skin assessment, 270–271, *271,* 282–283
Advanced practice nurse roles, 5
Advocacy, 5
Age-related macular degeneration (AMD), 385t
Alcohol-based hand rubs, 55, *55*
Allergic conjunctivitis, 382t
Allergic contact diaper dermatitis, 895t
Allergic salute, 434, *435*
Allergies, 356
Alopecia, 183t
Alveoli, 457
Amblyopia, 382t
Anemia, 104
Angle of Louis, 454
Angular cheilitis, 436
Anisocoria, 384t
Ankyloglossia, 435, 451t
Ankle-brachial index (ABI), 553, 554b, 556, 566
Ankylosing spondylitis, 696t
Anorexia nervosa, 124t
Anterior chamber, 353
Anthropometric measurements
  expected *vs.* unexpected findings
    height, 95, *95*
    infants and children, 113
    weight, 95–96, *96*
  unexpected findings
    achondroplastic dwarfism, 123t
    acromegaly, 123t
    anorexia nervosa, 124t
    gigantism, 123t
    obesity, 123t
Anus, 46
Anxiety, 104
Aorta coarctation, 535t
Aortic regurgitation, 533t
Aortic stenosis, 532t
Aphthous ulcers, 448t
Apnea, 104
  infants and children, 426
  intracranial conditions, 754t
  newborns, 480
  snoring, 424
  unexpected respiratory patterns, 489t

Apocrine glands, 269
Appendicitis, 641t
Arcus senilis, 372, *373*, 942
Argyle Robertson, 384t
Arm blood pressure, 108–109, *109*
Arrhythmias, 499
Arterial *vs.* venous ulcers, 570t
Ascites, 639t
Asthenopia, 378t
Asthma, 491t
    childhood, 466
    influenza-related
            complications, 460
    non-steroidal anti-infl ammatory
            agents, 461
    nonprofessional involvement, 27
    SOAP, 47
    personalized, appropriate, and
            accurate care, 49
    prevention of, 463
    wheezing, 465
Astigmatism, 378t
Asystole, 101
Atelectasis, 491t
Atrial septal defect, 534t
Atrophy, 692t
Axillary temperature, 99

B
Babinski, 875t
Baby bottle tooth decay, 450t
Bacterial conjunctivitis, 382t
Bacterial vaginosis, 823t
Barlow's Manoeuvre, 885, *885*
Barrel chest, 490t
Bartholin gland infection, 794
Basal ganglia, 700, 704
Batch charting, 74
Bednar aphthae, 435
Behaviour, mental health
            assessment
    consciousness level, 220
    eye contact and facial
            expressions, 220
    speech, 220–221
Bell's palsy, 348t
Biased questions, 26
Bifid uvula, 420, 446t
Biomedical model, 232
Bitot's spots, 183t
Black hairy tongue, 449t
Blepharitis, 381t
Blindness, 379t
Blood pressure (BP)
    diastolic blood pressure, 105
    expected *vs.* unexpected findings
            arm blood pressure,
                108–109, *109*
            orthostatic (postural) vital
                signs, 111
            thigh blood pressure, 110, *110*
    factors contributing, 106t
    measurement and errors, 107
    systolic blood pressure, 105
    unexpected findings, 124t
Body mass index, 170
Body systems approach, 15
Boutonnière deformity, 694t
Bowel sounds, 639t
Bradycardia, 101
Bradypnea, 104, 466
Brain attack, 349t
Brawny, 285
Breastfeeding
    colostrum, 574
    control of weight and stress, 505

iron-rich foods, 868
mastitis, 576
prenatal classes, 843
Breasts and axillae assessment, 46
    acute assessment, 576
    adolescent females, 583
    anatomy and physiology, 572–576
    axillae and lymph nodes, *573*,
            573–574
    breast structures, *572*, 572–573
    children and adolescents,
            574–575, *575*, 592
    clinical reasoning, 594
    comprehensive physical assess-
            ment, 584
    cultural considerations, 576
    documentation, 582, 591
    evidence-informed critical
            thinking, 592,
            594–595, 595t
    expected *vs.* unexpected findings
            breast alterations, 600t
            breast lumps, 601t
            colour and texture, 585, *585*
            contour, 585, *585*
            male breasts, 591
            nipple and areola character-
                istics, 585,
                586–587, 586t
            objective findings, 591
            palpation, 587–590,
                587–590
            patient postmastectomy,
                590–591
            size and shape, 585
            symmetry, 585
            transillumination, 590
    health history and symptoms
            nipples discharge and rash/
                ulceration, 582
            pain, 581
            swelling and trauma, 582
    health promotion and risk
            assessment, 580
    Know Your breasts (KYB)
            approach, 592, 593b
    laboratory and diagnostic test-
            ing, 586t, 592, 594
    landmarks, *572*, 572
    lifespan considerations,
            574–575, 583, 592
    male breasts, 576
    newborns and infants, 574, 592
    nursing care plan, 596
    nursing diagnoses, 594, 595t
    nursing interventions, 594, 595t
    nursing outcomes, 594, 595t
    objective data collection,
            584–592
    older adults, 576, 592
    organizing and prioritizing, 592
    personalized, appropriate, and
            accurate care, 597
    preparation, 584
    risk factors assessment
            breast examination, 580
            family history, 579
            lifestyle and personal
                habits, 579
            medications, 579
            modify controllable factors,
                577t–578t
            past medical history, 578–579
    SBAR, 596
    subjective data collection,
            577–583

SOAP, 595
    therapeutic dialogue, 583
    women who are pregnant, 574,
            583, 592
Brochophony, 477
Bronchioles, 457
Bronchitis, 491t
Bruits, 640t
Bullous impetigo, 895t
Bullying, 251–252
Bursitis, 694t

C
C fibres, 126
Café au lait spots, 897t
Calcium, 154, 176, 329
    bone density, 656–657
    food-frequency
            questionnaires, 164
    musculoskeletal assessment,
            654, 660
    obesity prevention, 906
    older adults, 157
    slowed peristalsis, 928
    women who are pregnant,
            166, 842
Canada's Food Guide, 156, 163,
            906, 907
Canadian Nurse Association (CNA),
            4, 5, 12, 27, 232, 237
Canadian Registered Nurse
            Examination (CRNE), 9
Canadian Task Force on Preventive
            Care (CTFPC),
            961, 961t
Canal of Schlemm, 353
Candidal diaper dermatitis, 895t
Candidiasis, 448t, 823t
Carbohydrates, 153
Cancer, *See also* Carcinoma
    breast, 27, 38
            risk factors, 577t
                age distribution, 577
                therapeutic dialogue, 583
    colon, 46
    hyperpigmentation, 585
    in older adults, 130
    lung, 46
    lymphatics, 331
    pain, 128
    pharynx, 420
    prostate, 46
    ovarian, 46
    skin, 268
    suicide rates, 207
    testicular, 40
    throat, 46
Carcinoma, 449t
Carcinoma in situ, 828t
Cardiovascular assessment
    acute assessment, 502, 503t
    anatomy and physiology,
            494–497, 494–502
    cardiac cycle
            cardiac output, 498
            diastole, 498
            electrocardiogram, 499
            heart rate control, 498–499
            heart rhythm, 499
            heart sounds, 498
            systole, 498
    children and adolescents, 500,
            508, 520
    comprehensive physical exami-
            nation, 510
    conduction system, 497

coronary arteries and veins,
            496, *496*
    cultural considerations,
            501–502, 509
    documentation, 508, 513, 514,
            518, 519, 521
    evidence-informed critical
            thinking, 521–523, 522t
    expected *vs.* unexpected findings
            auscultation, 512, *514*, 515
            carotid arteries
                inspection, 512
            congenital heart disease,
                534–535t
            extra sounds, 517, 518,
                530t–531t
            hepatojugular reflux inspec-
                tion and palpation,
                512, *512*
            identify rate and
                rhythm, 516
            jugular venous pressures,
                511, 511–512
            jugular venous pulses
                inspection, 510–511
            murmurs, 517, 518, 532t–533t
            palpation, 513
            precordium, 514
            S1 and S2 identification, 516
            S1 and S2 variations, 529t
    health history and symptoms
            chest pain, 506
            cough and diaphoresis, 507
            dyspnea, 506–507
            edema and fatigue, 507
            nocturia, 507
            orthopnea and paroxysmal
                nocturnal dyspnea, 507
            palpitations, 508
    health promotion and risk
            assessment, 505
    heart chambers, 496, *496*
    heart wall, 496
    jugular pulsations, 499
    lifespan considerations, 359,
            499–501, 508–509,
            519–521
    neck vessels, 494–496, *495*
    newborns and infants, 500, 508,
            519–520
    nursing care plan, 525
    nursing diagnoses,
            522–523, 522t
    nursing interventions,
            522–523, 522t
    nursing outcomes, 522–523, 522t
    objective data collection
            510–521
    older adults, 500–501, 509,
            520–521
    personalized, appropriate, and
            accurate care, 525
    physiology, 497–499
    preparation, 510
    pulmonary and systemic circula-
            tion, *496*, 497
    risk factors assessment
            family history, 504
            medications, 504
            past medical history,
                503–504
            weight and stress
                control, 505
    SBAR, 524
    subjective data collection,
            502–509

SOAP, 523
therapeutic dialogue, 509
women who are pregnant, 499–500, 508, 519
valves, *494,* 496
Carpal tunnel syndrome, 696t
Cartilage *Staphylococcus* infection, 411t
Cataracts, 383t
Celsius (C), 97
Central nervous system, 126–127, *127*
brainstem, 700–702, 701t–702t
cerebellum, 702
cerebrum, 698–700, *699, 700*
protective structures, 702
spinal cord, 702–704, *703, 704*
Cerebral vascular accident, 349t
Cervical cancer, 828t
Cervical dysplasia, 828t
Cervical polyps, 828t
Chalazion, 381t
Chancre, 826t
Changing the subject, 26
Charting by exception (CBE), 82–83
Child maltreatment, 250
Children and adolescents
abdominal assessment, 607, 615, 616, 631
acute assessment, 900, 902, *902*
anatomy and physiology, 900
anthropometric measurements, 113
breasts and axillae assessment, 574–575, *575,* 592
cardiovascular assessment, 500, 508, 520
cultural considerations, 908–909
developmental assessment, 909, *909*
ears assessment, 391–392, *392,* 397
equipment, 909
evidence-informed critical thinking, 919, 920t
expected *vs.* unexpected findings
abdomen, 917, *918*
anthropometric measurements, 113
behaviour, 113
breasts, 917
chest circumference, 115
ears and hearing, 911, 914, *914,* 915t
eyes and vision, 911, 912t–913t
general survey, 113, 910–911
head and neck, 911
head circumference, 114, *115*
heart and neck vessels, 916
length/height, 113–114, *114*
male and female genitalia, 919
mobility, 113
musculoskeletal, 918
neurology, *918,* 918–919
nose, mouth, and throat, 914
parent–child interaction, 113
peripheral vascular, 917, *917*
physical appearance, 113
skin, hair, and nails, 911
thorax and lungs, 914, 916
vital signs, 115–117, 910, *910*
weight, 114, *114,* 196

eyes assessment, 355, 359
female genitalia assessment, *792,* 792–793, 793t, 803, 886
head assessment, 330, *331,* 335, 341
health history, *48,* 48–49, 907
health promotion and risk assessment
car safety, 905, *906*
contraception and STI prevention, 907
drug and alcohol prevention, 906
fire safety, 906
immunization schedules, 905
mental health issues, 206, 217, 223, 907
nutrition and obesity prevention, 906–907
outdoor and water safety, 906
poison control and safety in home, 199, 906
human violence assessment, 257–258
intercultural communication, 31–32
language development, 194, 900
male genitalia and rectal assessment, 758–759, *759, 759,* 759t, 765, 773, 886
mental health assessment, 216
motor development, 196–197, 900
mouth assessment, 420, 435
musculoskeletal assessment, 652, 659–660, 682–683
neurological assessment, 707, 714
newborns, infants, and children, 330, *331,* 335, 341, 868, 887, 904, 917
nose assessment, 419, 434, 435, *435*
nursing care plan, 921
nutrition assessment, 157, 157t, 166–167, 175–176
objective data, 113–117
objective data collection, 909–919
pain assessment, 130, 141–143
personalized, appropriate, and accurate care, 922
physical growth, 900
preparation, 909
psychosocial and cognitive development, 900
risk factors assessment
abuse, 249t, 893t
car safety, 904
contraception and sexually transmitted infections, 905
developmental history, 903
drug and alcohol use, 905
family history, 903
fire safety, 904
immunizations, 901t, 904
infectious disease screening, 903–904
lead-risk screening, 903
medications and supplements, 903
nutrition and obesity, 905

outdoor safety, 905
personal history, 902
poison control, 199, 904
postnatal history, 903
prenatal history, 902–903
safety in home, 199, 904
seeking care, 902
violence and suicide, 250, 893t, 905
water safety, 905
sinuses assessment, 419–420
SBAR, 921
skin assessment, 270–271, *271,* 282–283
subjective data collection, 902–909
SOAP, 920
therapeutic dialogue, 908
throat assessment, 420, 435
Chlamydia, 823t
Choana, 417
Choanal atresia, 435
Choroids, 353
Chronic obstructive pulmonary disease (COPD), 470
patterns of inheritance, 459
risk factors assessment, 459
SBAR, 483
therapeutic dialogue, 468
Chronic venous insufficiency, 568t
Ciliary body, 353
Clarification, 24
Cleft lip, 420, 446t
Cleft palate, 420, 446t
Clinical pathway, 75
Clinical reasoning, *9,* 9–10, 10t
abdominal assessment, 633, 633t
breasts and axillae assessment, 594
cardiovascular assessment, 522–523, 522t
children and adolescents, 919, 920t
developmental stage assessment, 201
ears assessment, 406, 407t
head assessment, 342, 342t
mouth assessment, 437–438, 438t
neck assessment, 342, 342t
nose assessment, 437–438, 438t
nursing process, *9,* 9–10, 10t
nutrition assessment, 177, 177t
peripheral vascular and lymphatic assessment, 558
sinuses assessment, 437–438, 438t
thorax and lungs assessment, 481t, 484–485
throat assessment, 437–438, 438t
Cognitive function, mental health
attention span, 221
judgment, 221
memory, 221
Mini-Cog, 222b
Mini-Mental status, 222
orientation, 221
Set test, 222
thought process and perception, 222
Coining, 283, *283*
Coloboma, 384t
Colour blindness, 379t
Columella, 415

Community as Partner Assessment model, 236, *236*
Compartment syndrome, 564t
Complementary and alternative medicine (CAM) model, 232
Comprehensive assessment, 11, 205
Computerized provider order entry (CPOE), 71
Concrete operational stage, 190
Condyloma acuminatum, 825t
Confidentiality, 72, *72*
Congenital heart disease, 534–535t
Congenital hip dislocation, 694t
Congenital hypothyroidism, 347t
Congestive heart failure, 491t
Conjunctiva, 352
Contact dermatitis, 826t
Cooper ligaments, 573
Coordinators, 4
Copper wiring, 386t
Cornea, 353
Cough etiquette, 57
Cranial nerves (CNs)
autonomic nervous system, 705–706
expected *vs.* unexpected findings, 719–723, 720t–722t
spinal nerves, 705, *706*
Craniocytosis, 348t
Cranium, 327, *327*
Cretinism, 347t
Crossed eye, 380t
Cultural health assessment, 12
abdominal, 617, 631–632
aims of, 237–238, *238*
beliefs and practices
food and nutrition, 239
illness and pain, 240
pregnancy and childbirth, 239–240
breasts and axillae assessment, 576
cardiovascular assessment, 501–502, 509
characteristics, 237
children and adolescents, 908–909
developmental stage assessment, 194–196, *195*
ears assessment, 393
evidence-informed critical thinking, 242, 243t
female genitalia, 804
general survey, 118
head assessment, 330
health history, 49
human violence assessment, 258
male genitalia and rectal assessment, 760
mental health assessment, 217–218
mouth assessment, 420
musculoskeletal, 653, 660–661
neurological assessment, 715
newborns and infants, 887
nose assessment, 420
nutrition assessment, 158–159, 158b
older adults, 930, 937, 947
pain assessment, 131
peripheral vascular and lymphatic assessment, 541, 547
personalized, culturally safe, and accurate care, 244

Cultural health assessment (*Continued*)
physical examination and equipment, 65
pregnancy, 838–839
sinuses assessment, 420
skin, hair and nails assessment, 272–273, 283
SOAP, 243
therapeutic dialogue, 241
thorax and lungs assessment, 459, 467
throat assessment, 420
Cupping, 273, 283
Cushing's syndrome, 349t
Cutaneous pain, 128, 129
Cutis marmorata, 292
Cyanosis, 285, 466
Cyst, 412t
Cystocele, 827t

D
Deep palpation, 61
Deep vein thrombosis (DVT), 541, 568t
Dental caries, 450t
Denver Developmental Screening Test-II (DDST-II), 919
Dermis, 269
Developmental stage assessment
clinical reasoning, 201
cognitive development
adolescent, 191
infant, 188, 189t
middle adult, 192, *192*
older adult, 192–193, 192t
school-age child, 190, *190*
toddler and preschooler, 188–190, *190*
young adult, 191–192
cultural considerations, 194–196, *195*
Erikson's psychosocial model, 186, *187*
evidence-informed critical thinking, 198–201, 199t
language development, 194, 194t
motor development, 196–197, 197t
nursing care plan, 200
nursing diagnoses, 198, 200t
nursing interventions, 198, 200t
objective data collection, 196–197, 196t–197t
patient outcomes, 198, 200t
personalized, appropriate, and accurate care, 201
physical growth, 196, 196t
psychosocial development
adolescent, 186, 188
early adult, 188
Erikson's psychosocial model, 186, *187*
infant, 186
late adult, 188
middle adult, 188
preschooler, 186
school-age child, 186
toddler, 186
subjective data collection, 186–196
Deviated Septum, 444t
Diastole, 497, 498
Dietary reference intakes (DRIs), 156
Diethylstilbestrol (DES) syndrome, 828t

Dilated fixed pupil, 385t
Direct (nonmediated) percussion, 62, *62*
Distractions, 26
Documentation, 14–15
abdominal assessment, 630, 631
cardiovascular assessment, 521
ears assessment, 397
eyes assessment, 358, 373
female genitalia assessment, 815–816
head assessment, 334, 340
head-to-toe assessment, 974
human violence assessment, 256, 257b
male genitalia and rectal assessment, 765, 772–774
mental health assessment, 215, 223
mouth assessment, 436–437
musculoskeletal assessment, 659, 666, 682
neck assessment, 334, 340
neurological assessment, 733–734, 736
newborns and infants, 887
nose assessment, 436–437
nutrition assessment, 174
objective data, 111, 112
older adults, 948–949
pain assessment, 142t
patient health record (*see* Patient health record)
peripheral vascular and lymphatic assessment, 557
physical examination and equipment, 64
pregnancy, 855
sinuses assessment, 436–437
skin, hair and nails assessment, 290–291
thorax and lungs assessment, 479
throat assessment, 436–437
verbal communication (*see* Verbal communication)
Down's syndrome, 347t, 435
Dupuytren's contracture, 695t
Dysplastic nevi, 275, *275*
Dyspnea, 104, 464

E
Ears, 46
Ears assessment
acute assessment, 393
adolescents, 392
clinical reasoning, 406, 407t
cultural considerations, 393
documention, 405
evidence-informed critical thinking, 406–408
expected findings *vs.* unexpected findings
auditory acuity, 403
equilibrium, 403
inspection, 398, *398*
otoscopic evaluation, 401–403, *401–403*
palpation, 399
Rinne Test, 399–401, *400*
Weber test, 401, *401*
Whisper test, 399, *399*
health history and symptoms, 395
documentation, 397
hearing loss, 396
otalgia, 396

tinnitus, 396
vertigo, 396
health promotion and risk assessment, 393, 395
lifespan considerations, 391–393, 397
newborns, infants, and children, 391–392, *392*, 397
nursing care plan, 407
nursing diagnoses, 406, 407t
nursing interventions, 406, 407t
objective data, 398–406
older adults, 392–393
patient outcomes, 406, 407t
personalized, appropriate, and accurate care, 408
preparation, 398–403
risk factors, 393
family history, 394
loud noises, 394–395
medications, 394
personal history, 394
SBAR, 406
SOAP, 405
subjective data, 393–397
therapeutic dialogue, 397
unexpected findings
external ear, 411t–412t
internal ear, 413t
vestibular function, 391
women who are pregnant, 391
Ecchymosis, 282
Eccrine glands, 269
Ectopic pregnancy, 830t, 838. *See also* Ruptured tubal pregnancy
Eczema, 896t
Edentulous, 435
Electrocardiogram (ECG), 499
Electrolytes, 155
Electronic thermometer, 98, *98*
Emergency assessment, 10–11
Emphysema, 491t
Encouraging elaboration, 24
Endocrine and hematological system, 46
Endometriosis, 829t
Epicondylitis, 694t
Epidermis, 268–269
Epistaxis (nosebleed), 443t
Epstein pearls, 435
Erikson's psychosocial model, 186, *187*
Erythema, 285
Erythema toxicum, 292
Esotropia, 380t
Eupnea, 104
Evidence-informed critical thinking, 9, 16–17
abdominal assessment, 632–635
breasts and axillae assessment, 592, 594–595, 595t
cardiovascular assessment, 521–523, 522t
children and adolescents, 919, 920t
cultural health assessments, 242, 243t
developmental stage assessment, 198–201, 199t
ears assessment, 406–408
eyes assessment, 373, 374t
female genitalia assessment, 817–820
general survey, 118, 119t

head assessment, 342, 342t
head-to-toe assessment, 976, 976t
human violence assessment, 258–261
male genitalia and rectal assessment, 773–776
mental health assessment, 223, 224t
mouth assessment, 437–438
musculoskeletal assessment, 684–687
neck assessment, 342, 342t
neurological assessment, 738–742
newborns and infants, 887–889
nose assessment, 437–438
nutrition assessment, 176–177
older adults, 949–952
pain assessment, 146–147
peripheral vascular and lymphatic assessment, 557–558
pregnancy, 855–860
sinuses assessment, 437–438
social assessment, 242, 243t
spiritual assessment, 242, 243t
thorax and lungs assessment, 482–485
throat assessment, 437–438
Exophthalmos, 383t
Exotropia, 380t
Expiration, 103
External ear
edematous ears, 411t
External nose, 415, *415*
External otitis, 412t
Extraocular muscle function, *352, 352–353*, 353t
Extraocular structures, 352, *352*
Eye strain, 378t
Eyelids, 352
Eyes assessment, 46
acute assessment, 355
anatomy and physiology, 352–354, *352–354*, 353t
cultural considerations, 355
documentation
expected findings, 358
unexpected findings, 373
evidence-informed critical thinking, 373, 374t
extraocular muscle function, *352, 352–353*, 353t
extraocular structures, 352, *352*
health history and symptoms, 356–357, 357b
health promotion and risk assessment, 357
internal (intraocular) structures, 353–354, *354*
lifespan considerations
children and adolescents, 355, 359
newborns and infants, 355, 359
older adults, 355, 359
women who are pregnant, 354–355, 359
nursing care plan, 375
nursing diagnoses, 373, 374t
nursing interventions, 373, 374t
objective data collection, 360–373
personalized, appropriate, and accurate care, 376

risk factors assessment, 355
  allergies, 356
  corrective prescriptions, 356
  environmental exposure, 356
  eye health, 356
  eye protection, 357
  family history, 356
  medications, 356
  nutritional status, 357
  personal history, 356
  virus exposure, 356
SBAR, 375
SOAP, 374
subjective data collection,
  355–360
therapeutic dialogue, 360
unexpected findings
  external eye conditions,
    381t–383t
  eye movement, 380t
  in pupil, 384t–385t
  refractive errors, 378t–379t
  retinal conditions, 385t–386t
vision, 354, *354*

F

Facial bones, 327, *328*
Facial muscles, 327, *328*
Facial pain, 334
Fahrenheit (F), 97
False reassurance, 24
Family violence
  child maltreatment, 250, 893t
  elder abuse, 251
  intimate partner violence,
    250–251, 250t
  sibling violence, 250
Farsightedness, 378t
Fascia, 537, 539
Fats, 153, 540, 543. *See also* Lipids
Female genital mutilation (FGM),
  799–800, 804, 838
Female genital self-
  examination, 800b
Female genitalia assessment, 46
  abdominal pain, 794
  acute assessment, 794
  adolescent, 817
  advanced techniques, 806
  anatomy and physiology,
    790–794
  Bartholin gland infection, 794
  child, 817
  comprehensive physical exami-
    nation, 806
  cultural considerations, 804
  documentation, 815–816
  equipment, 805
  evidence-informed critical
    thinking, 817–820
  excessive vaginal bleeding, 794
  expected *vs.*unexpected findings
    bimanual examination,
      812–814, *813, 814*
    external genitalia,
      806–807, *807*
    internal genitalia, *807,*
      807–808, *808*
    rectovaginal examination,
      814–815, *815*
    speculum examination,
      808–812, *809–812*
  external genitalia, 790, *790*
  health history and symptoms
    hemorrhoids, 802
    menstrual disorders, 802

pelvic pain, 801
  structural problems, 802
  vaginal burning, discharge,
    itching, 802
health promotion and risk
  factors assessment,
  799–800
hormone regulation,
  791–792, *792*
infants, children, and adolescents, *792,* 792–793,
  793t, 803
internal genitalia
  cervix, 790
  fallopian tubes, 790
  ovaries, 791
  uterus, 790
  vagina, 790, *791*
laboratory and diagnostic testing, 817
lifespan considerations, 792–
  794, 802–804, 817
nursing care plan, 820
nursing diagnosis, 818, 818t
nursing interventions, 818, 818t
nursing outcomes, 818, 818t
objective data collection,
  805–817
older adults, 794, 803–804, 817
pelvic inflammatory
  disease, 794
pregnancy, 792, 802–803, 817
preparation, *805,* 805–806, *806*
risk factors assessment
  family history, 797
  hormonal contraceptive and
    tobacco use, 798
  obesity, 798
  osteoporosis, 798
  personal history, 795–797
  sexually transmitted infec-
    tions, 797–798
  ruptured tubal pregnancy, 794
    (*see also* Ecotopic
    pregnancy)
SBAR, 819
self-care practices, 799b
SOAP, 818
subjective data collection,
  795–804
Tanner's staging, 793t
therapeutic dialogue, 804
unexpected findings
  abscess of the Bartholin
    glands, 826t
  acute salpingitis, 830t
  bacterial vaginosis, 823t
  candidiasis, 823t
  carcinoma in situ, 828t
  cervical cancer, 828t
  cervical dysplasia, 828t
  cervical polyps, 828t
  chancre, 826t
  chlamydia, 823t
  condyloma
    acuminatum, 825t
  contact dermatitis, 826t
  cystocele, 827t
  diethylstilbestrol
    syndrome, 828t
  ectopic pregnancy, 830t
  endometriosis, 829t
  fluctuant ovarian cyst, 829t
  gonorrhea, 824t
  herpes simplex Type 2, 825t
  leiomyoma, 829t

  pediculosis pubis, 826t
  rectocele, 827t
  solid ovarian mass, 830t
  trichomoniasis, 824t
  urethral caruncle, 826t
  uterine prolapse, 827t
Fetal alcohol syndrome, 347t
Fibromyalgia, 130, 691t
First Nations, 207
Fissures, 436
Flail chest, 490t
Fluctuant ovarian cyst, 829t
Flushing, 285
Focused assessment, 11, 205
Focusing, 24
Follicular keratosis, 183t
Food safety and food security, 155
Food-frequency questionnaires, 164
Foreign body, 413t, 445t
Friction rubs, 640t
Functional assessment, 15
Functional health patterns, 43, 233

G

Galant's (Trunk incurvation), 874t
Galeazzi's sign, 884, *885*
Ganglion cysts, 694t
Gaseous distention, 638t
Gate control theory, 127, *127*
General health state, 46
Genetic disorders, 898t
Genu valgum, 693t
Genu varum, 184t
Geriatric Depression Scale, 217b
Gigantism, 123t
Gingival hyperplasia, 450t
Gingivitis, 420, 451t
Glasgow Coma Scale, 717b
Glaucoma, 382t
Goiter, 350t
Gonorrhea, 795, 812, 824t, 834
Gordon's functional health model,
  45t, 233
Gustatory rhinitis, 420
Gynecomastia, 576, 591, 600t

H

Hair assessment, 46, 269, *270. See
  also* Skin, hair and nails
  assessment
Hair loss patterns, men, 272, *272*
Handoff, 83
Hate crimes, 252
Head assessment, 46
  acute assessment, 330–331
  anatomy and physiology,
    327, *328*
  clinical reasoning, 342, 342t
  comprehensive physical exami-
    nation, 337–340
  cultural considerations, 330
  documentation
    subjective findings, 334
    unexpected findings, 340
  evidence-informed critical
    thinking, 342, 342t
  health history and symptoms
    facial pain, 334
    headache, 333, 333b–334b
    lumps or masses, 334
  health promotion and risk
    assessment, 332–333
  inspection, 337, *337*
  lifespan considerations, 330,
    331, 335, 341
  lymphatics, 329–330, *330*

  newborns, infants, and children,
    330, *331,* 335, 341
  nursing care plan, 344
  nursing diagnosis, 342, 342t
  nursing interventions, 342, 342t
  objective data collection,
    335–342
  older adults, 330, 335
  patient outcomes, 342, 342t
  personalized, appropriate, and
    accurate care, 344
  preparation, 335, 336b
  risk factors assesssment,
    331–332
  SBAR, 343
  SOAP, 343
  subjective data collection,
    331–335
  therapeutic dialogue, 336
  unexpected findings
    acromegaly, 348t
    Bell's palsy, 348t
    cerebral vascular
      accident, 349t
    craniocytosis, 348t
    Parkinson's disease, 349t
    scleroderma, 349t
    torticollis, 348t
Head circumference, 900
Headache, 333, 333b–334b
Head-to-toe assessment, 15
  acute assessment, 960
  ADLs, 964
  body system review, *963,*
    963–964
  clinical reasoning, 976, 976t
  comprehensive admitting, 975
  comprehensive physical exami-
    nation, 965
  documentation, 974
  equipment, 965
  evidence-informed critical
    thinking, 976, 976t
  examination room, 965, *965*
  expected *vs.* unexpected findings
    abdomen, 970–971
    anterior thorax, 969–970
    closure, 974
    ears, 968
    eyes, 967–968
    female breasts, 970
    female genitalia, 973
    gait and balance/fall
      risk, 972
    general survey, 976
    head, 966–967
    lower extremities, 971
    male genitalia, 973
    mouth and throat, 967
    musculoskeletal and neuro-
      logical, 972
    neck, 968–969
    neurological, 969
    nose and sinuses, 968
    posterior thorax, 971–972
    rectum, 973–974
    skin, 976
    skin breakdown, 972
    upper extremities, 969
    vital signs, 966
    wounds, drains, devices, 972
  focused hospital assessment,
    975–976
  functional health status, 964
  health history and
    symptoms, 964

Head-to-toe assessment (*Continued*)
health promotion, 960
health promotion and risk assessment, 964
hospital assessment, 975–976, 975t
laboratory and diagnostic testing, 976
lifespan consideration, 973
nursing care plan, 978
objective data collection, 965, 973
personalized, appropriate and accurate care, 978
psychosocial history, 963–964
risk factor assessment
CTFPC, 961, 961t
demographic data, 961, *962*
growth and development, 963
past health history, 962–963
present history, 961–962
SBAR, 977
screening, 975
SOAP, 977
subjective data collection, 960–964, 960t, *961, 962*
terminology, 963, *963*
therapeutic dialogue, 964
Health assessment, 5–6
components, 13–14
frequency, 11–12, *12*
organizing frameworks for, 15, 15t
types, 10–11
Health history
abdominal assessment
abdominal pain, 613
anorexia, 613
constipation, 613
diarrhea, 613
dysphagia/odynophagia, 613
indigestion, 612
jaundice/icterus, 613–614
nausea, vomiting, hematemesis, 613
urinary incontinence, 614
urinary/renal, 614
abdominal pain, 613
anorexia, 613
breasts and axillae assessment
nipples discharge and rash/ulceration, 582
pain, 581
swelling and trauma, 582
cardiovascular assessment
chest pain, 506
cough and diaphoresis, 507
dyspnea, 506–507
edema and fatigue, 507
nocturia, 507
orthopnea and paroxysmal nocturnal dyspnea, 507
palpitations, 508
components, 38–39
current medications and indications, 40, 42, *43*
demographical data, *39*, 39–40
family history, 42–43, *44*
functional health assessment, 43, 45b, 45t
growth and development, 43
past health history, 40
present illness, 40, 41t
review of systems, 44, 46
seeking care reasons, 40

constipation, 613
cultural health assessments, 49
deformity, 658
diarrhea, 613
dysphagia/odynophagia, 613
ears assessment, 395
documentation, 397
hearing loss, 396
otalgia, 396
tinnitus, 396
vertigo, 396
eyes assessment, 356–357, 357b
female genitalia assessment
hemorrhoids, 802
menstrual disorders, 802
pelvic pain, 801
structural conditions, 802
vaginal burning, discharge, itching, 802
head assessment
facial pain, 334
headache, 333, 333b–334b
lumps or masses, 334
head–to–toe assessment, 964
indigestion, 612
jaundice/icterus, 613–614
lack of balance and coordination, 658–659
lifespan considerations, *48*, 48–49
male genitalia and rectal assessment
male sexual dysfunction, 765
pain, 764
penile lesions, discharge/rash, 765
scrotal enlargement, 765
urination, 764
mental health assessment
altered mental health, 213b
altered mood and affect, 213
auditory hallucinations, 215
olfactory and tactile hallucinations, 215
suicidal ideation, 214–215, 214b
visual hallucinations, 215
nausea, vomiting, hematemesis, 613
neck assessment
hyperthyroidism, 334
hypothyroidism, 334
limited neck movement, 334
lumps or masses, 334
neck pain, 333
neurological assessment
balance/coordination difficulties, 712
difficulty swallowing, 713
dizziness/vertigo, 713
generalized weakness, 712
headache/other pain, 712
hearing loss/tinnitus, 713
intellectual changes, 713
involuntary movements/tremors, 712
limb/unilateral weakness, 712
lost/blurred vision, 713
speech/language difficulties, 713
taste, touch, smell/sensation, 713
newborns and infants
crying/irritability, 870
fever, 869
gastrointestinal distress, 870

respiratory concerns/distress, 869
skin conditions, 869
newborns, children, and adolescents, *48*, 48–49
nutrition assessment, 163, 164b
body weight, 163
direct observation, 165
eating habits, 163
food records, 164–165
malnutrition, 163
objective data, 38
older adults, 49
abuse, 936
cognitive status, 935–936, 936b
depression, 936
incontinence, 935
pain, 935
sleep deprivation, 935
pain assessment, 134
pain/discomfort, 657–658
peripheral vascular and lymphatic assessment
edema and cramping, 546
functional ability, 546
pain, 545
tingling/numbness and skin changes, 546
vascular disorders, 544b
pregnancy, 48
Braxton Hicks contractions, 846
breast tenderness and discharge, 845
fetal hiccups and other spasms, 845–846
growing pains, 844
increased urination, 845
increased vaginal discharge, 845
morning sickness, 844
periumbilical pain, 845
primary and secondary data sources, 38
prioritized, appropriate, and holistic care, 49
psychosocial and lifestyle factors
human violence, 48
mental health, 47–48
sexual history and orientation, 48
social, cultural, and spiritual assessment, 47
reliability of the source, 38
routine annual physical examination, 38, *38*
skin assessment
pruritus (itching), 281
rash, 280, 280b, 281
stiffness/limited movement, 658
subjective data, 38
therapeutic dialogue, 42
thorax and lungs assessment
chest pain, 464
cough, 464–465
dyspnea, 464
functional abilities, 465
orthopnea and paroxysmal nocturnal dyspnea, 464
sputum, 465
wheezing, 465
urinary incontinence, 614
urinary/renal, 614
weakness, 658

Health promotion, 4, *4*
abdomen, cancer screening, 611–612
colorectal, 633
kidneys, 633
liver, 633
pancreas, 633
stomach, 633
breasts and axillae assessment, 580
breast and lymph nodes, cancer screening, 580
Know Your Breasts approach, 592, 593b
cardiovascular assessment, 505
cholesterol screening, 505
children and adolescents
car safety, 905, *906*
contraception and STI prevention, 907
drug and alcohol prevention, 906
fire safety, 906
immunization schedules, 905
mental health issues, 907
nutrition, 906–907
obesity prevention, 906–907
outdoor and water safety, 906
poison control and safety in home, 906
ears assessment, 393, 395
eyes assessment, 357
female genitalia assessment, 799–800
cancer screening cervix, ovaries, uterus, 580
female genital self-examination, 800b
rectal cancer screening, 961
self-care practices, 799b
head assessment, 332–333
head–to–toe assessment, 964
health history assessment, 6–7
male genitalia and rectal
prostate cancer screening, 763
rectal cancer screening, 961
testicular self-examination, 763, *763*
mental health assessment
addiction, 207–208
anxiety, 206
Canada's National Mental Health Strategy, 208
cultural background, 212
current health status, 208–209
dementia, 207
depression, 207
family history, 210
identification/biographical data, 208
medication, 210
past health history, 209
psychological trauma, 210
psychosocial, 210–212
spirituality, 212, 212b
suicide, 207
musculoskeletal assessment
bone density, 656–657
previous injuries/illnesses, 656
surgery, 656
neck assessment, 332–333

neurological assessment
  injury prevention, 710–711
  meningeal infections, 711
  seizure activity, 711
  stroke prevention, 710
newborns and infants
  baby bottle tooth decay, 868–869
  breast-feeding/iron-rich foods, 868
  cardiopulmonary resuscitation training, 868
  child safety car seat, 868, *868*
  choking, 866–867
  immunization schedules, 867, 867t
  poison control, 868
  safe sleep habits, 866
nutrition assessment, 163
objective data
  Doppler technique, 112
  vital signs monitoring device, 112, *112*
older adults, 934–935
pain assessment, 131–134
peripheral vascular and lymphatic assessment
  lymphatic disorders, 544
  peripheral arterial disease, 543–544
  venous disease, 544
pregnancy
  follow-up visits and prenatal monitoring, 843
  gestational diabetes, 842
  healthy lifestyle habits, 842–843
  mental health and safety, 843
  nutrition and oral health, 842
  prenatal and breast-feeding classes, 843
risk assessment, 7
skin assessment
  self-skin examination, 278, *279*
  sunblocks, 278
  sun-protective factor, 278
  sunscreens, 278
  tanning booths, 278
  UV index, 278, 280t
  vitamin D deficiency, 278
thorax and lungs assessment
  asthma prevention, 463
  immunizations, 463
  occupational exposure prevention, 463
  smoking cessation, 462–463
Heart and neck vessels, 46
Heberden's and Bouchard's nodes, 696t
Hemoptysis, 465
Hemothorax, 491t
Herniated nucleus pulposus, 695t
Herpes simplex virus, 448t
Hives, 896t
HOPE assessment, spiritual beliefs, 212
Hordelum (Stye), 383t
Horizontal (minor) fissure, 456
Horner's syndrome, 384t
Hospital assessment
  comprehensive admitting, 975
  focused, 975–976, *976*
  screening, 975, 975t
Human trafficking, 252

Human violence assessment, 48
  cultural considerations, 258
  documentation, 256, 257b
  evidence-informed critical thinking, 258–261
  family violence
    child maltreatment, 250
    elder abuse, 251
    intimate partner violence, 250–251, 250t
    sibling violence, 250
  hate crimes, 252
  human trafficking, 252
  infants, children, and adolescents, 257–258
  lifespan considerations, 257–258
  mandated reporting, 256–257
  medical power and control, 261
  nursing care plan, 261
  nursing diagnoses, 258, 258t
  objective data collection, 255–258
  older adults, 258
  patient interview, 253–254, 254b
  patient outcomes, 258, 260
  personalized, appropriate, and accurate care, 261
  safety plans, 260–261, 260b
  SBAR, 259
  sexual violence, 252
  significance, 252, 253b
  SOAP, 259
  subjective data collection, 253–255, 254b
  therapeutic dialogue, 255
  violence against vulnerable adults, 251
  war-related and military violence, 252, 253b
  women who are pregnant, 257
  youth and school violence, 251–252
Hydration, 46
Hydrocephalus, 347t
Hyperopia (farsightedness), 378t
Hyperpnea, 104
Hypertension, 109
  cardiovascular risk factors, 542b
  extra sounds, 518
  newborns, infants, and children, 540
  peripheral arterial disease, 541
  pregnancy-induced, 508
Hyperventilation, 104
Hyphema, 381t
Hypotension, 109
Hypoventilation, 104

I

Inaccurate historian, 38
Increased intracranial pressure, 104
Indirect (mediated) percussion, 62–63, *63*
Infants. *See also* Newborns and infants
  expected *vs.* unexpected findings
    anthropometric measurements, 113
    behaviour, 113
    chest circumference, 115
    general survey, 113
    head circumference, 114, *115*
    length/height, 113–114, *114*
    mobility, 113

    parent–child interaction, 113
    physical appearance, 113
    vital signs, 115–117
    weight, 114, *114*
  female genitalia assessment, *792*, 792–793, 793t, 803
  male genitalia and rectal assessment, 758–759, *759*, 765, 773
  mouth assessment, 420, 435
  musculoskeletal assessment, 652, 659–660, 682–683
  nose assessment, 419, 434, 435, *435*
  sinuses assessment, 419–420
  throat assessment, 420, 435
Inferior oblique, 353
Inferior rectus, 352
Innocent heart murmurs, 916b
Inspection, 59–60, *60*
Inspiration, 103
Intercostal space (ICS), 454
Intercultural communication
  children and adolescents, 31–32
  communication etiquette, 29
  family-practice and pediatric care settings, *31*
  gender and sexual orientation issues, 30
  interpreter-dependent communication, 30, 30b
  lifespan considerations, 31–32
  newborns and infants, 31
  older adults, 32
Internal (intraocular) structures, 353–354, *354*
Interprofessional Team Collaboration, 85, 244, 295
  abdominal assessment, 634
  breasts and axillae assessment, 596
  cardiovascular assessment, 524
  children and adolescents, 921
  ears assessment, 406
  eyes assessment, 375
  female genitalia assessment, 819
  head assessment, 343
  head-to-toe assessment, 977
  human violence assessment, 259
  male genitalia and rectal assessment, 775
  mouth assessment, 439
  musculoskeletal assessment, 685–686
  neck assessment, 343
  neurological assessment, 740–741
  newborns and infants, 888–889
  nose assessment, 439
  nutrition assessment, 178
  older adults, 951–952
  pain assessment, 147
  peripheral vascular and lymphatic assessment, 559
  pregnancy, 859
  sinuses assessment, 439
  skin, hair and nails assessment, 294
  thorax and lungs assessment, 483
throat assessment, 439
Interrupting, 26
Intertrigo, 895t
Interview process, phases
  beginning phase, 27–28
  closing phase, 28

  preinteraction, 27, *27*
  working phase, 28, *28*
Intimate partner violence
  definition, 250
  immigrants and refugees, 251
  power and control methods, 250t
  pregnancy, 251
Iris, 353
Iris nevus, 381t
Irritant diaper dermatitis, 895t

J

Jaundice, 285, 293, *293*, 381t
Joint effusions, 692t

K

Kaposi's sarcoma, 446t
Key hole pupil, 384t
Kiesselbach plexus, 416, *416*
Koplik spots, 435, *435*
Korotkoff sounds, 110t
Kyphoscoliosis, 490t

L

Lacrimal apparatus, 352
Lactiferous ducts, 573
Lanugo, 270
Lateral rectus, 353
Latissimus dorsi, 470
Lazy eye, 382t
Leiomyoma, 829t
Lens, 353
Leopold's manoeuvres, 855, 858, *858*
Leukoplakia, 449t
Lichen simplex chronicus, 896t
Lifespan considerations, 12
  abdominal assessment, 607, 605–616, 631
  breast/axillae assessment, 574–575, 583, 592
  ears assessment, 391–393, 397
  eyes assessment, 354–355, 359
  female genitalia assessment, 792–794, 802–804, 817
  head assessment, 330, *331*, 335, 341
  heart assessment, 499–501, 359, 508–509, 519–521
  health history, *48*, 48–49
  human violence assessment, 257–258
  intercultural communication, 31–32
  lymphatic assessment, 540–541, 546–547, 556
  male genitalia/rectal assessment, 758–760, 765–766, 773–776
  mental health assessment, 216, 217b
  mouth assessment, 419–420, 434–436
  musculoskeltal assessment, 651–653
  neck assessment, 329–330, *331*, 335, 341–342
  neurological assessment, 706–707, 714, 734–735
  nose assessment, 419, 434
  nutrition assessment, 157–158, 158b, 165–167, 175–176
  objective data, 112–118
  pain assessment, 130–131, 141–143

Lifespan considerations (*Continued*)
peripheral vascular assessment, 540–541, 546–547, 556
physical examination and equipment, 65, *65*
sinuses assessment, 419–420
skin hair and nails assessment, 269–271, 282–283, 291–292
social assessment, 233
spiritual assessment, 47
thorax/lungs assessment, 458–459, 466, 480–481
throat assessment, 419, 420, 435
Light palpation, 60–61, *61*
Limbus, 352
Linea nigra, 270, 282
Lingual frenulum, 417
Lipids, 153–154
Lips, 448t–449t
Lobar pneumonia, 491t
Local inspection, 59–60, 59t, *60*
Lymphatics, 329–330, *330*
Lymphedema, 570t

M

Macrotia, 411t
Macula, 354
Macular lesion, 281
Macular stains, 879t
Magenta tongue, 184t
Male breasts, 576
Male genitalia and rectal assessment, 46
acute assessment, 760
adolescents, 759, 759t
comprehensive physical assessment, 767
cultural considerations, 760, 766, 773
diagnostic reasoning, 774
documentation, 765, 772–774
equipment, 767
evidence-informed critical thinking, 773–776
expected *vs.* unexpected findings
groin, 767
hernias, 770, *770*
inguinal region and femoral areas, 768
penis, 767–768, *768*
perianal and rectal examination, *770*, 770–772
perineal area, 768
sacrococcygeal areas, 768
scrotum, 768
testicles, 769
transillumination of the scrotum, 769–770
vas deferens, 769
health history and symptoms
male sexual dysfunction, 765
pain, 764
penile lesions, discharge/rash, 765
scrotal enlargement, 765
urination, 764
health promotion and risk factors assessment
prostate cancer screening, 763
rectal cancer screening, 961
testicular self-examination, 763, *763*
infants and children, 758–759, *759*, 765, 773

laboratory and diagnostic testing, 773–774
lifespan considerations, 758–760, 765–766, 773–776
nursing care plan, 776
nursing diagnosis, 774, 774t
nursing intervention, 774, 774t
nursing outcomes, 774, 774t
objective data collection, 767–773
older adult, 760, 766, 773
personalized, appropriate, and accurate care, 776
preparation, 767
risk factors assessment
additional risk factors, 762
family history, 762
medical and surgical history, 761
medications, 762
personal history, 761
SBAR, 775
SOAP, 775
special circumstances/advanced techniques, 769–773
structure and function
external genitalia, *756*, 756–757, *757*
internal genitalia, *757*, 757–758, *758*
rectum and anus, 758
subjective data collection, 761–766
therapeutic dialogue, 766
unexpected findings
anus, rectum, and prostate, 785t–787t
balanitis/balanoposthitis, 780t
epispadias, 780t
genital piercing, 779t
hernias, 788t
hypospadias, 780t
paraphimosis, 780t
phimosis, 779t
scrotum and testes abnormalities, 783t–785t
sexually transmitted infections (STIs), 781t–783t
testicular torsion *vs.* epididymitis, 779t
Managers of care, 4–5
Manubriosternal angle, 454
Mastalgia, 581
Mastectomy, 600t
Mastitis, 600t
McGill model, 233
Mean arterial pressure, 109
Medial rectus, 353
Melanoma, 277
Melasma, 270, 282
Menarche, 575
Mental health assessment, 47–48
acute assessment, 206
anxiety, 206
confusion, 223, 223t
cultural considerations, 217–218
definition, 205
delirium, 223, 223t
dementia, 223, 223t
depression, 207, 223, 223t
documentation, 215, 223
evidence-informed critical thinking, 223, 224t
expected *vs.* unexpected findings
appearance, 219–220

behaviour, 220–221
cognitive function, 221–222
health history and symptoms
altered mental health, 213b
altered mood and affect, 213
auditory hallucinations, 215
olfactory and tactile hallucinations, 215
suicidal ideation, 214–215, 214b
visual hallucinations, 215
lifespan considerations, 216, 217b
nurse role, 205
nursing diagnoses, 223, 224t, 225
nursing intervention, 223, 224t, 225
objective data collection, 218–223
patient outcomes, 223, 224t, 225
personalized, appropriate, and accurate care, 225
risk factors and health promotion
addiction, 207–208
anxiety, 206
Canada's National Mental Health Strategy, 208
current health status, 208–209
dementia, 207
depression, 207
family history, 210
genetic background/spirituality, 212, 212b
identification/biographical data, 208
medication, 210
past health history, 209
psychological trauma, 210
psychosocial, 210–212
suicide, 207
SOAP, 225
subjective data collection, 206–218
therapeutic dialogue, 218
unexpected findings
mood disorders, 229t
motor movements, 229t
speech patterns, 230t
thought process, 230t
Metabolic acidosis, 104
Microtia, 411t
Mid upper arm muscle circumference (MAMC), 173, *173*
Midclavicular line (MCL), 455
Milia, 434, *435*
Military violence, 252, 253b
Mini-Mental Status, 222
Miosis, 384t
Mitral regurgitation, 533t
Mitral stenosis, 533t
Modulation, 128
Molluscum contagiosum, 895t
Mongolian Spots, 879t
Montgomery glands, 573
Moro, 874t
Morse Fall Scale, 682, 682b
Mouth assessment, 46
acute assessment, 420
anatomy and physiology
oral cavity, 417, *417*
salivary glands, *418*, 418–419
teeth and gums, 419, *419*
tongue, 417–418, *417–418*

clinical reasoning, 437–438, 438t
common and specialized techniques, 428
comprehensive physical examination, 430–432, *430–432*
cultural considerations, 420
documentation, 436–437
evidence-informed critical thinking, 437–438
infants and children, 420, 435
lifespan considerations, 419–420, 434–436
nursing care plan, 440
nursing diagnosis, 437–438, 438t
nursing interventions, 437–438, 438t
objective data collection, 428, 430–432, *430–432*
older adults, 420, 436, *436*
patient outcomes, 438
personalized, appropriate, and accurate care, 440
preparation, 428
SBAR, 439
SOAP, 439
subjective data collection, 420–427
therapeutic dialogue, 427
women who are pregnant, 419
Multidimensional pain scales
Brief Pain Impact Questionnaire, 136, 138
Brief Pain Inventory, 135–136, *137–138*
McGill Pain Questionnaire, 135
Musculoskeletal assessment, 46
acute assessment, 653
advanced technique, 683–684
anatomy and physiology, 646–653
bones, 646
clinical reasoning, 684
connective tissues, 646, 646t
cultural considerations, 653, 660–661
documentation, 659, 666, 682
equipment, 662
evidence-informed critical thinking, 684–687
expected *vs.* unexpected findings
ankle and foot, *678*, 678–679
balance, 663
cervical spine, 667–668
coordination, 663
elbow, 670–671
gait and mobility, 663
inspection of extremities, 663–664, *664*
joint range of motion, 664
knee, 674–675, *675*
muscle tone and strength, 664, 665t–666t
posture, 662
shoulder, 668–670
temporo mandibular joint, 666–667
thoracic and lumbar spine, *680*, 680–681, *681*
wrist and hand, *672*, 672–674
fall risk, 682

health history and symptoms
deformity, 658
lack of balance and coordination, 658–659
pain/discomfort, 657–658
stiffness/limited movement,
658
weakness, 658
health promotion, 653
health promotion and risk
assessment
bone density, 656–657
previous injuries/illnesses,
656
surgery, 656
infants and children, 652,
659–660, 682–683
joints, 647, *647*
ankle and foot, 651, *651*
elbow, 649, *649*
hip, 650, *650*
knee, *650*, 650–651
movement, 648t–649t
shoulder, 647, 649
spine, 651, *651*
temporomandibular joint,
647, *647*
wrist and hand, 649–650,
650
laboratory and diagnostic testing, 684
lifespan considerations, 651–653
lifestyle and work-related considerations, 683
muscles, 646
nursing care plan, 686
nursing diagnosis, 684–685, 684t
nursing interventions, 684–685,
684t
nursing outcomes, 684–685,
684t
objective data collection,
662–684
older adults, 652–653, 652t,
660, 683
organizing and prioritizing, 684
personalized, appropriate, and
accurate care, 687
pregnancy, 652, 659, 682
preparation, 662
risk factors assessment
demographic data, 654
family history, 654
nutrition and medications,
654
occupation, lifestyle, and
behaviours, 654–655
past medical history, 654
psychosocial history, 655
scoliosis screening, 655, *656*
SBAR, 685–686
SOAP, 685
subjective data collection,
653–661
techniques
Ballottement, 676t
Bulge test, 676t
Drawer sign, 677t
drop arm test, 677t
LeSegue's test, 677t
McMurray's test, 676t
Phalen's test, 676t
Thomas' test, 677t
Tinel's test, 676t
Trendelenburg's test, 677t
therapeutic dialogue, 661

unexpected findings
acute rheumatoid arthritis,
696t
ankylosing spondylitis, 696t
atrophy, 692t
bursitis, 694t
carpal tunnel syndrome, 696t
congenital hip dislocation,
694t
Dupuytren's contracture, 695t
epicondylitis, 694t
gait patterns, 691t
ganglion cysts, 694t
genu valgum, 693t
Heberden's and Bouchard's
nodes, 696t
herniated nucleus pulposus,
695t
joint dislocation, 692t
joint effusions, 692t
longstanding rheumatoid
arthritis, 692t
multiple joints, 691t
onset, gender, and genetic
background, 690t
osteoarthritis, 693t
osteoporosis, 693t
polydactyly, 694t
rotator cuff tear, 693t
swan neck and boutonnière
deformity, 694t
syndactyly, 695t
talipes equinovarus, 695t
ulnar deviation, 696t
Mydriasis, 385t
Myopia, 378t
Myxedema, 350t

N
Nails assessment, 46, 269, *270. See
also* Skin, hair and nails
assessment
Nasal polyps, 444t
Nasal septum, 415, *415*
Nearsightedness, 378t
Neck assessment, 46
acute assessment, 330–331
anatomy and physiology,
327–329, *328–329*
clinical reasoning, 342, 342t
comprehensive physical examination, 337–340
cultural considerations, 330
documentation
subjective findings, 334
unexpected findings, 340
evidence-informed critical
thinking, 342, 342t
expected *vs.* unexpected findings
auscultation, 340, *340*
inspection, 338, *338*
palpation, 338–340, *339*
health history and symptoms
hyperthyroidism, 334
hypothyroidism, 334
limited neck movement, 334
lumps or masses, 334
neck pain, 333
health promotion and risk
assessment, 332–333
lifespan considerations, 329–
330, *331*, 335, 341–342
lymphatics, 329–330, *330*
newborns, infants, and children,
330, *331*, 335, 341
nursing care plan, 344

nursing diagnosis, 342, 342t
nursing interventions, 342, 342t
objective data collection,
335–342
older adults, 330, 335, 341–342
patient outcomes, 342, 342t
personalized, appropriate, and
accurate care, 344
posterior surface anatomy, *328*
preparation, 335, 336b
risk factors assessment,
331–332
SBAR, 343
SOAP, 343
subjective data collection,
331–335
therapeutic dialogue, 336
thyroid and parathyroid glands,
329
trachea, 328, *329*
unexpected findings
Cushing's syndrome, 349t
fetal alcohol syndrome, 347t
goitre, 350t
hydrocephalus, 347t
myxedema, 350t
torticollis, 348t
women who are pregnant,
329–330, 335
Neural pathway, 354, *354*
Neurological assessment, 46
acute assessment, 707–708,
708b
anatomy and physiology,
698–707
central nervous system (*see*
Central Nervous System)
cranial nerves (*see* Cranial
nerves)
peripheral nervous system,
704
brain herniation syndromes, 738
children and adolescents, 707,
714
comprehensive physical examination, 716–734
cultural considerations, 715
diagnostic reasoning, 739, 742
documentation, 733–734, 736
equipment, 716
evidence-informed critical
thinking, 738–742
expected *vs.* unexpected findings
cognitive function, 718
communication (speech/
language), 718
coordination (cerebellar
function), 725–726, *726*
cranial nerve testing, 719–
723, 720t–722t
deep tendon reflexes, 730,
731t–732t
discriminative sensations,
728
extinction, 729
graphesthesia, 729, *729*
level of consciousness,
716–717, 717f, 717t,
718t
light touch, 727, *727*
motion and position sense,
727
motor function, 722–725,
724, 725
point localization, 728
pupillary response, 719

reflex testing, 730, *730, 732*
stereognosis, 728, *729*
superficial pain sensation,
727
temperature sensation, 727
two-point discrimination,
729
vibration sensation, 728, *728*
health history and symptoms
balance/coordination dif-
ficulties, 712
difficulty swallowing, 713
dizziness/vertigo, 713
generalized weakness, 712
headache/other pain, 712
hearing loss/tinnitus, 713
intellectual changes, 713
involuntary movements/
tremors, 712
limb/unilateral weakness,
712
lost/blurred vision, 713
speech/language difficul-
ties, 713
taste, touch, smell/sensa-
tion, 713
health promotion and risk factors assessment
injury prevention, 710–711
meningeal infections, 711
seizure activity, 711
stroke prevention, 710
laboratory and diagnostic testing, 738–739
lifespan considerations, 706–
707, 714, 734–735
meningeal signs, 736–737
newborns and infants, 707, 714,
734–735, *735*
nursing care plan, 741
nursing diagnoses, 739
objective data collection,
716–738
older adults, 707, 714, 735
personalized, appropriate and
accurate care, 741
pregnancy, 706–707, 714
preparation, 716
risk factors assessment, 708–710
SBAR, 740–741
screening examination, 736,
736b
SOAP, 740
subjective data collection,
708–715
therapeutic dialogue, 715
unconscious patient, 737–738
unexpected findings
athetoid movements, 749t
choreiform movements, 749t
clonus/myoclonus, 748t
dystonia, 749t
fasciculation, 748t
gaits, 751t–752t
intention tremor, 747t
paralysis, 747t
pathological (primitive)
reflexes, 753t
postures, 746t
pupils, comatose patients,
750t
respiratory patterns, intracranial conditions, 754t
resting tremor, 747t
sensory function, 753t
UMN *vs.* LMN, 750t

Neuronal plasticity, 128–130
Neuronal windup, 129, 130
Neuropathy, 569t
Newborns and infants
  abdominal assessment, 607, 615, 631
  acute assessment, 864
  anatomy and physiology, 864
  breasts and axillae assessment, 574, 592
  cardiovascular assessment, 500, 519–520
  clinical reasoning, 887–888
  comprehensive physical examination, 871–886
  cultural considerations, 887
  documentation, 887
  ears assessment, 391–392, 392, 397
  emergent concerns, 864
  equipment, 871
  evidence-informed critical thinking, 887–889
  expected vs. unexpected findings
    abdomen, 884
    anus and rectum, 886
    Apgar score, 872
    breasts, 884
    ears, 882
    eyes, 881
    general survey/observation, 872
    genitalia, 886
    gestational age, 872, 873
    head and neck, 879–880, 881
    heart and neck vessels, 883, 883
    measurements, 875–877, 876, 877
    mental status, 878
    musculoskeletal, 884–885, 885
    neurological, 886
    nose, mouth, and throat, 882
    nutrition, 877
    pain, 875
    peripheral vascular, 884
    reflexes, 872
    skin, hair, and nails, 878, 879t
    thorax and lungs, 883
    violence, 878
    vital signs, 873, 875
  eyes assessment, 355, 359
  head assessment, 330, 331, 335, 341
  health history and symptoms, 48, 48–49
    crying/irritability, 870
    fever, 869
    gastrointestinal distress, 870
    respiratory concerns/distress, 869
    skin conditions, 869
  health promotion and risk factors assessment
    baby bottle tooth decay, 868–869
    breast-feeding/iron-rich foods, 868
    cardiopulmonary resuscitation training, 868
    child safety car seat, 868, 868
    choking, 866–867

  immunization schedules, 867, 867t
    poison control, 868
    safe sleep habits, 866
  intercultural communication, 31
  laboratory and diagnostic testing, 887
  language, psychosocial, and cognitive development, 864
  motor development, 864
  neck assessment, 330, 331, 335, 341
  neurological assessment, 707, 714, 734–735, 735
  nursing care plan, 889
  nursing diagnosis, 887–888, 887t
  nursing interventions, 887–888, 887t
  nursing outcomes, 887–888, 887t
  objective data collection, 871–887
  organizing and prioritizing, 887
  pain assessment, 130, 141–143
  peripheral vascular and lymphatic assessment, 540, 546–547, 556
  personalized, appropriate, and accurate care, 889
  physical growth, 864
  preparation, 871
  reflexes
    Babinski, 875t
    Galant's (trunk incurvation), 874t
    Moro (startle), 874t
    palmar grasp, 874t
    rooting, 874t
    stepping, 875t
    suck, 874t
    tonic neck, 874t
  risk factors assessment
    medications and supplements, 865
    personal history, 865
    sleep environment, 866
  SBAR, 888–889
  skin assessment, 270, 282
  skin variants
    macular stains, 879t
    Mongolian Spots, 879t
    spider nevus, 879t
    strawberry hemangioma, 879t
  SOAP, 888
  subjective data collection, 865–871
  therapeutic dialogue, 870–871
  thorax and lungs assessment, 466
  unexpected findings
    allergic contact diaper dermatitis, 895t
    bullous impetigo, 895t
    café au lait spots, 897t
    candidal diaper dermatitis, 895t
    characteristic odours, 893t
    eczema (atopic dermatitis), 896t
    genetic disorders, 898t
    hives (urticaria), 896t
    intertrigo, 895t
    irritant diaper dermatitis, 895t

    lichen simplex chronicus, 896t
    molluscum contagiosum, 895t
    pediculosis capitis, 894t
    port wine stains, 897t
    psoriasis, 896t
    red flags, 893t
    scabies, 894t
    staphylococcal scalded skin syndrome, 894t
    tinea corporis, 894t
Nociception, 127–128
Nonstress test, 855, 857
North American Nursing Diagnosis Association-International (NANDA-I), 8, 9, 177, 242
Nose assessment, 46
  acute assessment, 420
  anatomy and physiology, 415–416, 415–416
  clinical reasoning, 437–438, 438t
  common and specialized techniques, 428
  comprehensive physical examination, 428–429
  cultural considerations, 420
  documentation, 436–437
  evidence-informed critical thinking, 437–438
  infants and children, 419, 434, 435, 435
  lifespan considerations, 419–420, 434–436, 435
  lymphatic drainage, 416
  nerve and blood supply, 416, 416
  nursing care plan, 440
  nursing diagnosis, 437–438, 438t
  nursing interventions, 437–438, 438t
  objective data collection, 428–429, 434–437
  older adults, 420, 435–436
  patient outcomes, 438
  personalized, appropriate, and accurate care, 440
  preparation, 428
  SBAR, 439
  SOAP, 439
  subjective data collection, 420–427
  therapeutic dialogue, 427
  unexpected findings, 443t–445t
  women who are pregnant, 419, 434
Numeric Pain Intensity (NPI) Scale, 135
Nursing care plan
  abdominal assessment, 635
  breasts and axillae assessment, 596
  cardiovascular assessment, 525
  children and adolescents, 921
  developmental stage assessment, 200
  ears assessment, 407
  eyes assessment, 375
  female genitalia assessment, 820
  head assessment, 344
  head-to-toe assessment, 978
  human violence assessment, 261
  male genitalia and rectal assessment, 776

  mental health assessment, 225
  mouth assessment, 440
  musculoskeletal assessment, 686
  neck assessment, 344
  neurological assessment, 741
  newborns and infants, 889
  nose, sinuses, throat assessment, 440
  nutrition assessment, 179
  older adults, 952
  pain assessment, 144
  peripheral vascular and lymphatic assessment, 560
  pregnancy, 860
  skin, hair, and nails assessment, 295
  social and spiritual assessment, 242, 243t
  thorax and lungs assessment, 484
Nursing diagnosis
  abdominal assessment, 633t
  breasts and axillae assessment, 594, 595t
  cardiovascular assessment, 522–523, 522t
  children and adolescents, 921
  developmental stage assessment, 198, 200t
  ears assessment, 406, 407t
  eyes assessment, 373, 374t
  female genitalia assessment, 818, 818t
  head assessment, 342, 342t
  human violence assessment, 258, 258t
  male genitalia and rectal assessment, 774, 774t
  mental health assessment, 223, 224t, 225
  mouth assessment, 437–438, 438t
  musculoskeletal assessment, 684–685, 684t
  neck assessment, 342, 342t
  neurological assessment, 739
  newborns and infants, 887–888, 887t
  nose assessment, 437–438, 438t
  nutrition assessment, 177
  older adults, 950, 950t
  pain assessment, 144, 144t
  peripheral vascular and lymphatic assessment, 558, 558t
  pregnancy, 858–859, 859t
  sinuses assessment, 437–438, 438t
  skin, hair and nails assessment, 295
  social and spiritual assessment, 242, 243t
  thorax and lungs assessment, 950, 950t
  throat assessment, 437–438, 438t
  vital signs, 118, 119t
Nursing intervention
  abdominal assessment, 633t
  breasts and axillae assessment, 594, 595t
  cardiovascular assessment, 522–523, 522t
  child and adolescent assessment, 920
  cultural assessment, 242

developmental stage assessment, 198, 200t
ears assessment, 406, 407t
eyes assessment, 373, 374t
female genitalia assessment, 818, 818t
head assessment, 342, 342t
male genitalia and rectal assessment, 774, 774t
mental health assessment, 223, 224t, 225
mouth assessment, 437–438, 438t
musculoskeletal assessment, 684–685, 684t
neck assessment, 342, 342t
newborns and infants, 887–888, 887t
nose assessment, 437–438, 438t
nutrition assessment, 177
older adults, 950, 950t
pain assessment, 144, 144t
peripheral vascular and lymphatic assessment, 558, 558t
pregnancy, 858–859, 859t
sinuses assessment, 437–438, 438t
skin, hair and nails assessment, 295
social assessment, 242, 243t
spiritual assessment, 242, 243t
thorax and lungs assessment, 950, 950t
throat assessment, 437–438, 438t
vital signs, 118, 119t
Nursing process, phases, 7, 8–9
Nutrition assessment, 46
acute assessment, 160
adults/older adults, 157–158, 158b, 167, 168b, 176
body mass index, 170
clinical reasoning, 177, 177t
common laboratory and diagnostic testing, 176–177
comprehensive nutritional history, 163–164
critical thinking, 179
cultural considerations, 158–159, 158b
documentation, 174
equipment needed, 169
evidence-informed critical thinking, 176–177
expected vs. unexpected findings
body mass index, 170
mid upper arm muscle circumference, 173, 173
physical assessment, 169–170
skinfold thickness, 172, 172–173
waist circumference, 171–172, 172
waist-to-hip ratio, 172
weight calculations, 170–171
food records, 164, 165
food safety and security, 155
health history and symptoms, 163, 164b
body weight, 163
direct observation, 165
eating habits, 163
food records, 164–165

malnutrition, 163
health promotion and risk assessment, 163
infants, children, and adolescents, 157, 157t, 166–167, 175–176
lifespan considerations, 157, 165–167, 175–176
mid upper arm muscle circumference, 173
nursing care plan, 179
nursing diagnosis, 177, 177t
nursing interventions, 177, 177t
nutritional data collection, 159, 159–160
nutritional deficiency, 183t–184t
nutritional guidelines, 156, 156b, 156t
objective data collection, 169–176
patient outcomes, 177
personalized, appropriate, and accurate care, 179
physical assessment, 169–170
pregnancy, 156, 165–166, 175
primary nutrients
carbohydrates, 153
fluid and electrolytes, 154–155
lipids, 153–154
proteins, 153
supplements, 154
vitamins and minerals, 154
risk factors assessment
family history, 163
food and fluid intake patterns, 162
medications and supplements, 161
personal history, 160–161
psychosocial profile, 162
SBAR, 178
skinfold thickness, 172–173
SOAP, 175
subjective data collection, 160–168
therapeutic dialogue, 168
waist circumference, 171–172
waist-to-hip ratio, 172
weight calculations, 170–171
Nystagmus, 380t

O
Obesity, 123t, 638t
Objective data, 13–14, 38
abdominal assessment 618–632
anthropometric measurements, 94–96
breasts and axillae assessment, 584–592
cardiovascular assessment, 510–521
children and adolescents, 909–919
cultural variations, 118
developmental stage assessment, 196–197, 196t–197t
documentation, 111, 112
ears assessment, 398–406
expected vs. unexpected findings
behaviour, 93–94
height, 95, 95
mobility, 94
physical appearance, 93
weight, 95–96, 96
eyes assessment, 360–373

female genitalia assessment, 805–817
general inspection, 92–94
general survey and vital signs, 92–118
head assessment, 335–342
head-to-toe assessment, 965, 973
health promotion and risk assessment
Doppler technique, 112
vital signs monitoring device, 112, 112
infants and children, 113–117
lifespan variations, 112–118
mental health assessment, 218–223
mouth assessment, 428, 430–432, 430–432
musculoskeletal assessment, 662–684
neck assessment, 335–342
newborns and infants, 871–887
nose assessment, 428–429, 434–437
nutrition assessment, 169–176
older adults, 113, 117–118
pain assessment, 139–145
peripheral vascular and lymphatic assessment, 548–556
pregnancy, 847–855
preparation, 92
sinuses assessment, 428–430, 434–437
skin, hair and nails assessment, 284–293
thorax and lungs assessment, 467–482
throat assessment, 428, 433–437
vital signs, 96–97
blood pressure (see Blood pressure)
frequency, 97b
oxygen saturation, 104–105
pulse, 100–103, 101t, 102, 103t
respirations, 103–104
temperature, 97–100, 98, 98t, 100
Oblique fissure, 456
Oculomotor (CN III) nerve damage, 385t
Older adults
abdomen, metabolism, and elimination, 928
abdominal assessment, 607, 616, 631
acute assessment, 929
anatomy and physiology, 926–929
breasts and axillae assessment, 576, 592
breasts and lymphatics, 927–928
cardiovascular assessment, 500–501, 509, 520–521
clinical reasoning, 950
comprehensive physical examination, 938, 939b
cultural considerations, 930, 937, 947
developmental stage assessment, 192–193, 192t
documentation, 948–949
ears and hearing, 927
ears assessment, 392–393

endocrine, 928–929
equipment, 938
evidence-informed critical thinking, 949–952
expected vs. unexpected findings
abdomen and elimination, 945–946
auscultation, 940
breasts and axillae, 945
ears and hearing, 942–943
endocrine, immunologic, and hematologic systems, 947
eyes and vision, 942, 942
general survey, 117, 939
head and neck, 941
heart and neck vessels, 944–945
height, 117
height and weight, 939–940
inspection, 940
male and female genitourinary, 947
musculoskeletal system, 946
neurological, 946–947
nose, mouth, and throat, 943, 943–944
peripheral vascular, 945
skin, hair, and nails, 941
spine, thorax, and lungs, 944
vital signs, 117–118, 940
weight, 117
eyes and vision, 926–927
eyes assessment, 355, 359
female genitalia assessment, 794, 803–804, 817
head and neck, 926
head assessment, 330, 335
health history, 49
health history and symptoms/signs
abuse, 936
cognitive status, 935–936, 936b
depression, 936
incontinence, 935
pain, 935
sleep deprivation, 935
health promotion and risk factors assessment, 934–935
heart and neck vessels, 927
human violence assessment, 258
intercultural communication, 32
interview, 929, 930b
laboratory and diagnostic testing, 949–950
male and female genitourinary, 928
male genitalia and rectal assessment, 760, 766, 773
mental health assessment, 216, 217t
mouth assessment, 420, 436, 436
musculoskeletal assessment, 652–653, 652t, 660, 683, 928
neck assessment, 330, 341–342
neurological assessment, 707, 714, 735, 928
nose assessment, 420, 435–436
nose, mouth, and throat, 927
nursing care plan, 952
nursing diagnosis, 950, 950t
nursing intervention, 950, 950t

Older adults (*Continued*)
  nursing outcomes, 950, 950t
  nutrition assessment, 157–158, 158b, 167, 168b, 176
  objective data, 113, 117–118, 938–949
  organizing and prioritizing, 949
  pain assessment, 130–131, 143
  peripheral vascular and lymphatic assessment, 541, 547, 556–557, 927, 928
  personalized, appropriate, and accurate care, 952
  preparation, 938
  risk factors assessment
    current concern, 931
    personal history, 931–934, 932t
  sinuses assessment, 420
  situation, background, assessment, recommendations, 951–952
  skin assessment, 272, 272, 283, 293
  skin, hair, and nails, 926, 926
  subjective data collection, 929–937
  subjective, objective, analysis, plan, 950–951
  therapeutic dialogue, 937
  thorax and lungs assessment, 458–459, 481, 927
  throat assessment, 420
One-dimensional pain assessment tools
  Combined Thermometer Scale, 135, 135
  Numeric Pain Intensity Scale, 135
  Verbal Descriptor Scale, 135
  Visual Analog Scale, 134
Opioid hyperalgesia, 143
Optic disc, 354
Orthopnea, 464
Orthostatic hypotension, 111
Ortolani's Manoeuvre, 885, 885
Osteoarthritis, 693t
Osteogenesis imperfecta, 383t
Osteomeatal complex, 415
Osteoporosis, 693t
Otitis media with effusion, 413t
Otosclerosis, 392

P
Paget's disease, 600t
Pain assessment
  acute assessment, 131
  acute pain, 128, 129, 541, 544, 558, 607, 613
  barriers, 146
  cancer pain, 130
  chronic pain, 128–129
  comprehensive physical examination, 140–141
  continuous/intermittent/episodic pain, 129
  cultural considerations, 131
  definition, 128b
  documentation, 142t
  duration, 128–129, 129
  etiology, 130
  evidence-informed critical thinking, 146–147
  health history and symptoms, 134
  lifespan considerations, 130–131, 141–143

location, 130
neuroanatomy of pain
  central nervous system, 126–127, 127
  gate control theory, 127, 127
  nociception, 127–128
  peripheral nervous system, 126
neuropathic pain, 129–130
newborns, infants, and children, 130, 141–143
nociceptive pain, 129
nursing diagnoses, 144, 144t
nursing interventions, 144, 144t
objective data collection, 139–145
older adults, 130–131, 143
patient outcomes, 144, 144t
patients unable to report pain, 143–144
personalized, appropriate, and accurate care, 148
physiological and behavioural pain indicators, 141t
preparation, 139–140
reassessment and documentation, 144, 145
risk assessment and health promotion, 131–134
SBAR, 147
SOAP, 146
subjective data collection, 131–138
therapeutic dialogue, 139
tools
  multidimensional pain scales, 135–138, 137–138
  one-dimensional pain assessment tools, 134–135, 135
Pallor, 92, 285, 299t, 544b
Palmar grasp, 874t
Palpation
  deep palpation, 61
  light palpation, 60–61, 61
Palpebral fissure, 352
Papular lesion, 281
Paralysis, 541, 542, 544, 558
Paranasal sinuses, 416, 416
Parathyroid gland, 329
Paresthesia, 542, 544b, 551, 557, 558
Parietal pain, 129
Parietal pleura, 458
Parkinson's disease, 349t
Parotid gland, 418
Paroxysmal nocturnal dyspnea, 464
Patent ductus arteriosus, 534t
Patient health record
  charting by exception, 82–83
  components, 71
  critical thinking and clinical judgment, 75
  discharge note, 83
  electronic patient health record, 71, 72
  flow sheets, 75
  nursing admission assessment, 75, 76–79
  plan of care/clinical pathway, 75
  progress note, 75, 80
    documentation formats, 80t–81t
    focus system, 82
    narrative notes, 80, 82

Problem Intervention and Evaluation (PIE), 82
  SOAP, 82
purposes of
  communication and care planning, 70
  education, 71
  legal document, 70, 70b
  medical research, 71
  quality assurance, 70–71
quality documentation, 71
  accurate and complete data entry, 72–73, 74, 74t
  assessment data entry duration, 73–74, 74
  clinical significance, 74
  concise, 74
  confidentiality, 72, 72
  critical thinking and nursing interventions, 75
  organized data entry, 73
written handoff, 83
Patient/nursing outcomes
  abdominal assessment, 633t
  breasts and axillae assessment, 594, 595t
  cardiovascular assessment, 522–523, 522t
  children and adolescents, 921
  developmental stage assessment, 198, 200t
  ears assessment, 406, 407t
  eyes assessment, 375
  female genitalia assessment, 818, 818t
  head assessment, 342, 342t
  human violence assessment, 258, 260
  male genitalia and rectal assessment, 776
  mental health assessment, 223, 224t, 225
  mouth assessment, 438
  musculoskeletal assessment, 684–685, 684t
  neck assessment, 342, 342t
  newborns and infants, 887–888, 887t
  nose assessment, 438
  nutrition assessment, 177
  pain assessment, 144, 144t
  peripheral vascular and lymphatic assessment, 558, 558t
  pregnancy, 858–859, 859t
  sinuses assessment, 438
  skin, hair and nails assessment, 295
  thorax and lungs assessment, 950, 950t
  throat assessment, 438
Peabody Developmental Motor Scale (PDMS-2), 909
Pectus carinatum, 470, 490t
Pectus excavatum, 470, 490t
Pediculosis capitis, 894t
Pediculosis pubis, 826t
Perception, 128
Percussion sound
  direct (nonmediated) percussion, 62, 62
  indirect (mediated) percussion, 62–63, 63
  notes and characteristics, 62t
Perforated septum, 445t
Peripheral nervous system, 126

Peripheral sensitization, 129, 130
Peripheral vascular and lymphatic assessment, 46
  acute assessment, 541–542
  anatomy and physiology, 537–541, 537–541
  arterial system, 537, 537, 538
  capillaries, 538, 540
  clinical reasoning, 558
  common laboratory and diagnostic testing, 557–558
  comprehensive physical examination, 548
  cultural considerations, 541, 547
  documentation, 546, 556, 557
  evidence-informed critical thinking, 557–558
  expected *vs.* unexpected findings
    advanced techniques, 554–555, 555
    arms, 548–551, 549, 550
    arterial pulse variations, 565t
    arterial *versus* venous ulcers, 570t
    compartment syndrome, 564t
    legs, 551–553, 551–554, 554b
    unexpected arterial findings, 566t–567t
    unexpected venous findings, 568t–569t
  health history and symptoms
    cramping, 546
    edema, 546
    functional ability, 546
    pain, 545
    skin changes, 546
    tingling/numbness, 546
    vascular disorders, 544b
  health promotion and risk assessment
    lymphatic disorders, 544
    peripheral arterial disease, 543–544
    venous disease, 544
  lifespan considerations, 540–541, 546–547, 556
  limb, fascia compartment, 539, 541
  lymphatic system, 539, 541
  newborns, infants, and children, 540, 546–547, 556
  nursing care plan, 560
  nursing diagnoses, 558, 558t
  nursing interventions, 558, 558t
  nursing outcomes, 558, 558t
  objective data collection, 548–556
  older adults, 541, 547, 556–557
  organizing and prioritizing, 557
  personalized, appropriate, and accurate care, 560
  risk factors assessment
    family history, 542–543
    medications, 542
    personal history, 542
    smoking, 541
  SBAR, 559
  subjective data collection, 542–547
  SOAP, 559
  therapeutic dialogue, 547
  venous system, 537–538, 539
  women who are pregnant, 540, 546, 556

Persistent pain, 129
Personalized, appropriate, and accurate care
  abdominal assessment, 635
  breasts and axillae assessment, 597
  cardiovascular assessment, 525
  children and adolescents, 922
  cultural health assessments, 244
  developmental stage assessment, 201
  ears assessment, 408
  eyes assessment, 376
  female genitalia and rectal assessment, 820
  general survey and vital signs, 120
  head assessment, 344
  health history, 49
  human violence assessment, 261
  male genitalia and rectal assessment, 776
  mental health assessment, 225
  mouth assessment, 440
  musculoskeletal assessment, 687
  neck assessment, 344
  neurological assessment, 741
  newborns and infants, 889
  nose assessment, 440
  nutrition assessment, 179
  older adults, 952
  pain assessment, 148
  peripheral vascular and lymphatic assessment, 560
  physical examination and equipment, 66
  pregnancy, 860
  sinuses assessment, 440
  skin, hair and nails assessment, 296
  social assessment, 244
  spiritual assessment, 244
  therapeutic dialogue, 34
  thorax and lungs assessment, 485
  throat assessment, 440
Petechiae, 282
Phantom pain, 129
Pharyngitis, 447t
Photoallergy, 277
Photoreactions, medications, 276–277, 276t
Physical examination and equipment
  anatomical terms
    anatomical position, 53, *53*
    anatomical quadrants, 53
    anatomical regions, 53–54
    anatomical surface, 53
    comparison and movement, 54t
  cultural considerations, 65
  documentation, 64
  handwashing and hand hygiene
    alcohol-based hand rubs, 55, *55*
    gloves, 55–56, *56*
    indications, 56b
    pathogen transmission, 55
    soap and warm running water, 55
  inspection, 59–60, *60*
  latex allergy, 57–58
  lifespan considerations, 65, *65*
  objective data collection, 59, 59b

palpation
  deep palpation, 61
  light palpation, 60–61, *61*
  personalized, appropriate, and accurate care, 66
  routine practices, 56–57, 56b–57b
  skin reactions, 58
  SOAP, 66
  sound and sound transmission
    auscultation, 63–66, 63t, *64*
    characteristics, 61
    percussion (*see* Percussion sound)
  subjective data collection, 59
  therapeutic dialogue, 58
Physiologic murmur, 532t
Plan of care, 75
Planners, 4
Plaque (lesion), 281
Pleural effusion, 491t
Pleural friction fremitus, 471
Pneumocystis carinii pneumonia, 491t
Pneumonia, 916
Pneumothorax, 491t
Poikilothermia, 541, 544b, 558,
Point-of-care documentation, 74, *74*
Polydactyly, 694t
Port wine stains, 897t
Posterior chamber, 353
Potassium, 155, 176
Precocious puberty, 592
Preconception, 834, *834*
Pregnancy *See* Women who are pregnant
Premature thelarche, 592
Presbyopia, 379t
Pressure ulcer, 277
Primary data, 38
Primary prevention, 7
Priority setting, 11
Prostate, 46
Proteins, 153
Pseudomonas infection, 411t
Psoriasis, 896t
Psychosocial assessment, 205
Pulmonary embolism, 491t
Pulmonic regurgitation, 533t
Pulmonic stenosis, 533t
Pulse deficit, 101–102, 516
Pulselessness, 541, 544b, 549, 552, 557
Pulse pressure, 109
Punking, 251
Pupil, 353
Pustular lesion, 281
Pyogenic granuloma, erythema nodosum, and pruritic urticarial papules and plaques of pregnancy (PUPPP), 291, 292

R
Raynaud's disease, 567t
Rectal temperature, 100, *100*
Rectocele, 827t
Red flags, 893t
Referred pain, 128, 129
Reflection, 23–24
Registered nurse (RN), 5
Reliable historian, 38
Research, 5
Respirations, 103–104
Respiratory hygiene, 57
Restatement, 23
Retina, 353

Retinitis pigmentosa, 386t
Retinopathy, 385t
Review of systems, 44, 46
Rheumatoid arthritis, 692t
Rhinitis, 443t
Rhonchal fremitus, 471
Rinne test, 399–401, *400*
Rooting, 874t
Rotator cuff tear, 693t
Roy's Adaptation model, 232–233
Rubeola measles, 435
Rubor, 285
Ruptured tubal pregnancy, *See* Ecotopic pregnancy

S
Scabies, 894t
Scalene, 470
Scarred TM, 413t
Scholarship, 5
School violence, 251–252
Sclera, 353
Scleroderma, 349t
Scrotal tongue, 436, *436*
Sebaceous glands, 269
Secondary data sources, 38
Secondary prevention, 7
Sentinel events, 70
Set test, 222
Sexual violence, 252
Sexually transmitted infections (STIs), 781t–783t
Sibling violence, 250
Silence, 24
Sinus arrhythmia, 101, 516
Sinus dysrhythmia, 101
Sinuses assessment
  acute assessment, 420
  anatomy and physiology, *416,* 416–417
  clinical reasoning, 437–438, 438t
  common and specialized techniques, 428
  comprehensive physical examination, 428–430, *430*
  cultural considerations, 420
  documentation, 436–437
  evidence-informed critical thinking, 437–438
  infants and children, 419–420
  lifespan considerations, 419–420
  nursing care plan, 440
  nursing diagnosis, 437–438, 438t
  nursing interventions, 437–438, 438t
  objective data collection, 428–430, 434–437
  older adults, 420
  patient outcomes, 438
  personalized, appropriate, and accurate care, 440
  preparation, 428
  SBAR, 439
  SOAP, 439
  subjective data collection, 420–427
  therapeutic dialogue, 427
  unexpected findings, 443t–445t
  women who are pregnant, 419
Sinusitis, 444t
Situation, background, assessment, recommendations (SBAR)
  abdominal assessment, 634

breasts and axillae assessment, 596
  cardiovascular assessment, 524
  children and adolescents, 921
  ears assessment, 406
  eyes assessment, 375
  female genitalia assessment, 819
  head assessment, 343
  head-to-toe assessment, 977
  human violence assessment, 259
  male genitalia and rectal assessment, 775
  mouth assessment, 439
  musculoskeletal assessment, 685–686
  neck assessment, 343
  neurological assessment, 740–741
  newborns and infants, 888–889
  nose assessment, 439
  nutrition assessment, 178
  older adults, 951–952
  pain assessment, 147
  peripheral vascular and lymphatic assessment, 559
  pregnancy, 859
  sinuses assessment, 439
  skin, hair and nails assessment, 294
  thorax and lungs assessment, 483
  throat assessment, 439
Skin, hair and nails assessment, 46, 267–296
  acute assessment, 273
  anatomy and physiology, *268*
    dermis, 269
    epidermis, 268–269
    subcutaneous layer, 269
  children and adolescents, 270–271, *271,* 282–283
  comprehensive skin assessment
    primary lesions, 285
    secondary lesions, 285
  cultural considerations, 272–273, 283
  documentation
    examination findings, 290–291
    unexpected findings, 291
  head-to-toe format, 285
  health history and symptoms
    pruritus (itching), 281
    rash, 280, 280b, 281
  health promotion and risk assessment
    self-skin examination, 278, *279*
    sunblocks, 278
    sun-protective factor, 278
    sunscreens, 278
    tanning booths, 278
    UV index, 278, 280t
    vitamin D deficiency, 278
  lifespan considerations, 269–271, 282–283, 291–292
  newborns and infants, 270, 282
  objective data collection, 284–293
  older adults, 272, *272,* 283, 293
  preparation, 284
  risk factors
    family history, 277
    lifestyle, 277
    occupational history, 277
    personal behaviour, 277

Skin, hair and nails
        assessment (*Continued*)
    personal history, 274–275,
        274t–275t, *275*
    photoreactions, medications,
        276–277, 276t
    subjective data collection,
        273–284
    therapeutic dialogue, 284
    women who are pregnant,
        269–270, 282, 291–292,
        292
Skinfold thickness, *172,* 172–173
Small fixed pupil, 384t
Smooth glossy tongue, 436, *436*
Social assessment
    community level, 233, *236,*
        236–237
    evidence-informed critical
        thinking, 242, 243t
    individual, 233, *234–235*
    nursing diagnoses, 242, 243t
    personalized, culturally safe,
        and accurate care, 244
    SOAP, 243
    societal level, 237
    therapeutic dialogue, 241
Solid ovarian mass, 830t
Somatic pain, 128, 129
Speech development, 900
Spider nevus, 879t
Spiritual assessment, *240,* 242b
    church and religion, 241–242
    evidence-informed critical
        thinking, 242, 243t
    Hindus, 242
    Jews, 242
    Muslim, 242
    nursing diagnoses, 242, 243t
    personalized, culturally safe,
        and accurate care, 244
    SOAP, 243
    therapeutic dialogue, 241
Split heart sound, 515–516
Staphylococcal scalded skin syn-
    drome, 894t
Stepping, 875t
Sternocleidomastoid, 470
Strabismus (cross-or wall-eyed), 380t
Strawberry hemangioma, 879t
Strep throat, 447t
Stye, 383t
Subcutaneous layer, 269
Subjective data, 13, 38
    abdominal assessment,
        607–618
    breasts and axillae assessment,
        577–583
    cardiovascular assessment,
        502–509
    children and adolescents,
        902–909
    cultural assessment 237–240
    developmental stage assessment,
        186–196
    ears assessment, 393–397
    eyes assessment, 355–360
    female genitalia assessment,
        795–804
    head assessment, 331–335
    head-to-toe assessment,
        960–964
    human violence assessment,
        253–255, 254b
    male genitalia and rectal assess-
        ment, 761–766

mental health assessment,
    206–218
mouth assessment, 420–427
musculoskeletal assessment,
    653–661
neck assessment, 331–335
neurological assessment,
    708–715
newborns and infants,
    865–871
nose assessment, 420–427
nutrition assessment, 160–165,
    160–168
older adults, 929–937
pain assessment, 131–138
peripheral vascular and lym-
    phatic assessment,
    542–547
physical examination and equip-
    ment, 59
pregnancy, 838–846
sinuses assessment, 420–427
skin hair and nails assessment,
    273–284
social assessment, 233–237
spiritual assessment, 240–242
thorax and lungs assessment,
    459–467
throat assessment, 420–427
Subjective, objective, analysis, plan
    (SOAP)
    abdominal assessment, 634
    breasts and axillae assessment,
        595
    cardiovascular assessment, 523
    children and adolescents, 920
    cultural health assessments, 243
    ears assessment, 405
    eyes assessment, 374
    female genitalia assessment, 818
    general survey and vital signs,
        119
    head assessment, 343
    head-to-toe assessment, 977
    human violence assessment, 259
    male genitalia and rectal, 775
    mental health assessment, 225
    mouth assessment, 439
    musculoskeletal assessment, 685
    neck assessment, 343
    neurological assessment, 740
    newborns and infants, 888
    nose assessment, 439
    nutrition assessment, 175
    older adults, 950–951
    pain assessment, 146
    peripheral vascular and lym-
        phatic assessment, 559
    sinuses assessment, 439
    skin, hair, and nails assessment,
        294
    social assessment, 243
    spiritual assessment, 243
    therapeutic dialogue, 28
    thorax and lungs assessment,
        482
    throat assessment, 439
    women who are pregnant,
Sublingual salivary gland, 418
Submandibular gland, 418
Sucking tubercle, 435
Summarizing, 24
Sunblocks, 278
Sunscreens, 278
Superior oblique, 353
Superior rectus, 352

Supernumerary nipple, 586
Supernumerary (accessory) nipple,
    574
Suprasternal (jugular) notch, 453
Suspicion, 282
Sutures, 327
Swan neck deformity, 694t
Sweat (cutaneous) glands, 269, *271*
Sympathy, 25
Syndactyly, 695t
Systole, 497, 498

T
Tachycardia, 101
Tachypnea, 104, 466
Tactile fremitus, 471
Talipes equinovarus, 695t
Tanner's staging, 574, *575,* 919
Technical/overwhelming language,
    26, *26*
Teeth
    anatomy and physiology, 419,
        419
    unexpected findings, 450t–451t
Temporal artery thermometers, 99
Temporal temperature, 100, *100*
Tenacious sputum, 465
Terminal hair, 269
Tertiary prevention, 7
Therapeutic dialogue
    abdominal assessment, 618
    alcohol or drugs, 33–34
    altered level of consciousness, 32
    anger, 33
    anxiety, 33
    breasts and axillae assessment,
        583
    cardiovascular assessment, 509
    caring, 21–22
    children and adolescents, 908
    cognitive impairment, 33
    crying, 33
    cultural health assessments, 241
    ears assessment, 397
    empathy, 22
    eyes assessment, 360
    head assessment, 336
    head–to-toe assessment, 964
    health history, 42
    hearing impairment, 32
    human violence assessment, 255
    limited English skills, 29
    mental health assessment, 218
    mental health illnesses, 33
    mouth assessment, 427
    neck assessment, 336
    neurological assessment, 715
    newborns and infants, 870–871
    nontherapeutic responses
        biased questions, 26
        changing the subject, 26
        distractions, 26
        false reassurance, 24
        interrupting, 26
        sympathy, 25
        technical/overwhelming
            language, 26, *26*
        unwanted advice, 25
    nonverbal communication, *22,*
        22–23
    nose assessment, 427
    nutrition assessment, 168
    older adults, 937
    pain assessment, 139
    peripheral vascular and lym-
        phatic assessment, 547

personal questions, 34
personalized, appropriate, and
    accurate care, 34
physical examination and equip-
    ment, 58
pregnancy, 846
self-concept, 22
sexual aggression, 34
sinuses assessment, 427
skin, hair, and nails assessment,
    284
social assessment, 241
spiritual assessment, 241
therapeutic communication, 21
thorax and lungs assessment,
    468b
throat assessment, 427
verbal communication
    active listening, 23
    clarification, 24
    encouraging elaboration, 24
    focusing, 24
    reflection, 23–24
    restatement, 23
    sensory impaired patient,
        23, *23*
    silence, 24
    summarizing, 24
Thigh blood pressure, 110, *110*
Thoracic cage, 453
Thoracic cavity, 453
Thorax and lungs assessment, 46
    acute assessment, 459
    anatomy and physiology
        anterior thoracic landmarks,
            453–454, *454*
        lower respiratory tract, *457,*
            457–458
        lung lobes, *456,* 456–457
        posterior thoracic land-
            marks, 454–455, *455*
        reference lines, *455,*
            455–456
        respiration mechanics, 457
        upper respiratory tract, 458
    breath sounds auscultation,
        474–477, 475t, 478
    common and specialty/advanced
        techniques, 467
    cultural considerations, 459, 467
    diaphragmatic excursion, *473,*
        473–474, *474*
    documentation, 466, 470, 477,
        479
    evidence-informed critical
        thinking, 482–485
    expected *vs.* unexpected findings
        anterior chest, 477–479
        common respiratory condi-
            tions, 491t
        common respiratory diagno-
            ses, 492t
        posterior chest, 470–477
        respiratory movement, 470
        respiratory patterns, 489t
        retractions, 470
        skin colour, 470
        thoracic configurations, 490
        tripod position, 469–470
    health history and symptoms
        chest pain, 464
        cough, 464–465
        dyspnea, 464
        functional abilities, 465
        orthopnea and paroxysmal
            nocturnal dyspnea, 464

sputum, 465
wheezing, 465
health promotion and risk
assessment
asthma prevention, 463
immunizations, 463
occupational exposure
prevention, 463
smoking cessation, 462–463
infants and children, 458
inspection, 470, 477
laboratory and diagnostic testing, 483–484
lifespan considerations, 458–
459, 466, 480–481
newborns, infants, and children,
466
nursing care plan, 484
nursing diagnosis, 950, 950t
nursing interventions, 950, 950t
nursing outcomes, 950, 950t
objective data collection,
467–482
older adults, 458–459, 466–467,
481
organizing and prioritizing, 482
palpation, *470, 470–471, 471,*
477–478, 478
percussion, 472–473, 478
personalized, appropriate, and
accurate care, 485
preparation, 467
risk factors assessment
environmental exposures, 462
family history, 461
lifestyle and personal habits,
461
medications, 460–461
occupational history, 461
past medical history, 460
SBAR, 483
subjective data collection,
459–467
SOAP, 482
tactile fremitus, 472
therapeutic dialogue, 468b
women who are pregnant, 458,
466, 480–481, 480t, 481t
Three-day food diary, 164
Throat assessment, 46
acute assessment, 420
anatomy and physiology, 419
clinical reasoning, 437–438,
438t
common and specialized techniques, 428
comprehensive physical examination, 433–437
cultural considerations, 420
documentation, 436–437
evidence-informed critical
thinking, 437–438
lifespan considerations
infants and children, 420, 435
older adults, 420
women who are pregnant, 419

nursing care plan, 440
nursing diagnosis, 437–438,
438t
nursing interventions, 437–438,
438t
objective data collection, 428,
433–437
patient outcomes, 438
personalized, appropriate, and
accurate care, 440
preparation, 428
SBAR, 439
SOAP, 439
subjective data collection,
420–427
therapeutic dialogue, 427
unexpected findings, 446t–447t
Thrombophlebitis, 569t
Thyroid gland, 329
Tinea corporis, 894t
Tongue
anatomy and physiology,
417–418, *417–418*
unexpected findings, 448t–449t
Tonsillar Grading Scale, 433b
Tonsillitis, 419
Tophi, 412t
Torticollis, 348t
Torus palatinus, 447t
Trachea, 328, *329*
Transduction, 128
Transmission, 128
Trapezius, 470
Trichomoniasis, 824t
Tricuspid regurgitation, 533t
Tricuspid stenosis, 533t
Trisomy 21, 347t, 435
Tuberculosis, 491t
Turgor, 272, *272*
Tympanic membrane (TM), 413t
Tympanic temperature, 100
Tympanostomy tube, 413t

U
Ulnar deviation, 696t
Unequal pupils, 384t
Unwanted advice, 25
Uremic frost, 285
Urethral caruncle, 826t
Uterine prolapse, 827t
UV index, 278, 280t

V
Vallate papillae, 417, *418*
Vascular sounds, 639t
Vellus hair, 269
Venous hums, 640t
Ventricular septal defect, 534t
Verbal communication
critical thinking and clinical
judgment, 86
patient rounds and conferences,
86
reporting, 83–85
telephone communication, 85
verbal handoff, 83, 83b

Verbal Descriptor Scale (VDS), 135
Vernix, 270
Vesicular lesion, 281
Vestibule, 415
Viral conjunctivitis, 381t
Visceral pain, 128, 129
Visceral pleura, 458
Vision, 354, *354*
Visual Analog Scale (VAS), 134
Vitiligo, 285
Vitreous chamber, 353

W
Waist-to-hip ratio, 172
Wall eye (exotropia), 380t
War-related violence, 252, 253b
Water, 154
Weber test, 401, *401*
Weight calculations, 170–171
Wellness, 6
Wharton's ducts, 418
Whisper test, 399, *399*
Women who are pregnant
abdominal assessment, 607,
615, 631
acute assessment, 838
anatomy and physiology,
834–836
clinical reasoning, 858–859,
859t
cultural considerations,
838–839
documentation, 855
ears assessment, 391
equipment, 847
evidence-informed critical
thinking, 855–860
expected *vs.* unexpected findings
abdomen, 849–850, *850,*
853–854
breasts, 850, 853
general survey and vital
signs, 847–848, *848,* 850
genitalia, 850, 854
heart, 851–852
musculoskeletal system, 854
nose, mouth, and throat, 851
nutrition, 848–849, 848t
peripheral vascular, 852
skin, 849, 851
thorax and lungs, 851
female genitalia assessment,
792, 802–803, 817
first trimester, 835
health history, 48
health history and symptoms
Braxton Hicks contractions,
846
breast tenderness and discharge, 845
fetal hiccups and other
spasms, 845–846
growing pains, 844
increased urination, 845
increased vaginal discharge,
845

morning sickness, 844
periumbilical pain, 845
health promotion and risk
factors assessment,
841–843
follow-up visits and prenatal
monitoring, 843
gestational diabetes, 842
healthy lifestyle habits,
842–843
mental health and safety,
843
nutrition and oral health, 842
prenatal and breast-feeding
classes, 843
initial visit assessment,
847–850
laboratory and diagnostic testing, 855–858, 856t–857t
Leopold's manoeuvres, 855,
858, *858*
mental health assessment, 216
mouth assessment, 419
neck assessment, 329–330, 335
neurological assessment,
706–707, 714
nonstress test, 855, *857*
nose assessment, 419, 434
nurse role, 837–838
nursing care plan, 860
nursing diagnosis, 858–859,
859t
nursing interventions, 858–859,
859t
nursing outcomes, 858–859,
859t
objective data collection,
847–855
personalized, appropriate, and
accurate care, 860
preconception, 834, *834*
preparation, 847
risk factors assessment
additional risk factors, 841
family history, 841
medications and supple-
ments, 840
personal history, 839–840
routine visit assessment,
850–854
SBAR, 859
second trimester, *835,* 835–836
sinuses assessment, 419
subjective data collection,
838–846
therapeutic dialogue, 846
third trimester, 836
throat assessment, 419
weeks of gestation, 836–837,
837

X
Xerostomia, 420

Y
Youth violence, 251–252